The Limits of Power

of Power

The World and United States Foreign Policy, 1945-1954

Joyce and Gabriel Kolko

THE LIMITS OF POWER

Books by Gabriel Kolko

THE ROOTS OF AMERICAN FOREIGN POLICY

THE POLITICS OF WAR:
The World and United States Foreign Policy, 1943–1945

RAILROADS AND REGULATION, 1877–1916

THE TRIUMPH OF CONSERVATISM:
A Reinterpretation of American History, 1900–1916

WEALTH AND POWER IN AMERICA:
An Analysis of Social Class and Income Distribution

Joyce and Gabriel Kolko

THE
LIMITS
OF POWER

The World and United States Foreign Policy, 1945-1954

HARPER & ROW, PUBLISHERS
New York • Evanston • San Francisco • London

FIRST EDITION

STANDARD BOOK NUMBER: 06-043753-7

LIBRARY OF CONGRESS CATALOG CARD NUMBER: 70-156530

To Wray

Contents

Abbreviations and Acronyms Used

AFL — American Federation of Labor
AK — Home Army, Poland
AMG — American Military Government, Korea
ANTIFAS — Anti-Nazi organizations in Germany, 1945
CD — Christian Democrats, Italy
CDU — Christian Democratic Union, Germany
CEEC — Committee of European Economic Cooperation
CGT — General Confederation of Labor, France
CIA — Central Intelligence Agency
CIO — Congress of Industrial Organizations
Cominform — Communist Information Bureau
CP — Communist Party
CRS — French elite police
EAM — National Liberation Front, Greece
ECA — U.S. Economic Cooperation Administration
ECE — Economic Commission for Europe
EDC — European Defense Community
EEC — Emergency Economic Commission, Europe (also EECE)
ELAS — Greek People's Liberation Army
EPU — European Payments Union
ERP — European Recovery Program
FEC — Far Eastern Commission
FO — an anti-CGT French trade union, *Force Ouvrière*
GATT — General Agreement on Tariffs and Trade
IBRD — International Bank for Reconstruction and Development
ICFTU — International Confederation of Free Trade Unions
IMF — International Monetary Fund
ITO — International Trade Organization

JCS — Joint Chiefs of Staff, U.S.
KKE — Greek Communist Party
KMT — Kuomintang, China
KPD — German Communist Party
LDP — Liberal Democratic Party, Germany
MSA — Mutual Security Act
NATO — North Atlantic Treaty Organization
NSC — National Security Council, U.S.
OEEC — Organization for European Economic Cooperation
ROK — Republic of Korea
SCAP — Supreme Commander for the Allied Powers, Japan
SFIO — French Socialist Party
SED — German Socialist Unity Party
SNOF — Slav-Macedonian National Liberation Front, Greece (later NOF)
SPD — German Social Democratic Party
SWNCC — State-War-Navy Coordinating Committee
TUC — Trades Union Congress, England
UMT — Universal Military Training
UNRRA — United Nations Relief and Rehabilitation Administration
WFTU — World Federation of Trade Unions

Introduction

World War II was a prelude to the profound and irreversible crisis in world affairs and the structure of societies which is the hallmark of our times.

The war had come to an end, but no respite allowed the wounds of the long era of violence to heal completely. Two vast epics of bloodletting within thirty years' time had inflicted seemingly irreparable damage to traditional societies everywhere. From the moment World War II ended, civil war, uprisings, and the specter of them replaced the conflict between the Axis and allies in many nations, and implacable hostility superseded tense relations between the Soviet Union and the other members of what had scarcely been more than a temporary alliance of convenience born wholly out of necessity. After global conflagration came not peace, but sustained violence in numerous areas of the world—violence that was to intensify with the inevitable, broadening process of social transformation and decolonization that became the dominant experience of the postwar epoch.

For the individual in vast regions of the world, the war's outcome left hunger, pain, and chaos. Politically, conflict and rivalry wracked nations, and civil war spread in Greece and in Asia. Outside of the Western Hemisphere, ruin and the urge toward reconstruction were the defining imperatives in all the areas that war had touched. Affecting the very fabric of world civilization, the postwar strife threatened to undermine the United States' reasons for having fought two great wars and its specific aims in the postwar world.

Surrounded by this vast upheaval, the United States found itself immeasurably enriched and, without rival, the strongest nation on the globe.

1

It emerged from the war self-conscious of its new strength and confident of its ability to direct world reconstruction along lines compatible with its goals. And these objectives, carefully formulated during the war, were deceptively simple: Essentially, the United States' aim was to restructure the world so that American business could trade, operate, and profit without restrictions everywhere. On this there was absolute unanimity among the American leaders, and it was around this core that they elaborated their policies and programs. They could not consider or foresee all the dimensions of what was essential to the attainment of their objective, but certain assumptions were implicit, and these in turn defined the boundaries of future policy options. American business could operate only in a world composed of politically reliable and stable capitalist nations, and with free access to essential raw materials. Such a universal order precluded the Left from power and necessitated conservative, and ultimately subservient, political control throughout the globe. This essential aim also required limitations on independence and development in the Third World that might conflict with the interests of American capitalism.

The United States therefore ended the war with a comprehensive and remarkably precise vision of an ideal world economic order, but with only a hazy definition of the political prerequisites for such a system. With these objectives before it, Washington confronted the major challenges to their fulfillment. Preeminent among these were the prewar system of world capitalism and its accumulation of trade and investment restrictions and autarchic economic nationalism that World War I and the subsequent depression had created. Traditional nationalism, consequently, was an obstacle to America's attainment of its goals, and this shaped the United States' relations to Britain and its huge economic alliance, the sterling bloc. Washington's dealings with Britain throughout the war had been profoundly troubled because of London's reticence in collaborating with American plans for restructuring world trade. To the English such a program looked very much like expansion in the name of an internationalism that ill concealed the more tangible advancement of American power along quite conventional lines. This rivalry among nominal allies was to become a basic theme of the postwar experience as well, because in attempting to attain the leading role for itself in the international economy the English had to consider whether the United States might also recast Britain's once-dominant role in major areas of the earth.

It was this same effort to foster a reformed world economy that compelled the United States to turn its attention, with unprecedented energy and expense, to the future of the European continent and Germany's special position in it. The failure of Germany and Japan to collaborate economically with the world throughout the interwar period was, in Washington's opinion, the source of most of the misfortunes that had befallen mankind. And however weak Europe might be at the moment, the United States had to consider how its reemergence—with or without Germany—might potentially affect the United States' contemplated role on the Continent should Europe once again assume an independent role. Allied with Russia, or even a resurgent Germany, Western Europe could become the critical, perhaps decisive, factor in international economic and political power. And it was an unshakable premise of America's policy that world capitalism become a unified system that would cease being divided into autonomous rivals.

Its desire and need for global economic reform, integration, and expansion almost immediately required the United States to confront the infinitely more complex issue of the political preconditions for establishing an ideal world order. This meant relating not only to the forces of nationalism and conservatism that had so aggressively undermined America's goals until 1945 but more especially to the ascendant movements of change we may loosely associate with the Left—forces that posed a fundamental threat to America's future in the world. The war had brought to fruition all the crises in the civil war within societies that World War I had unleashed, a conflict that interwar fascism and reaction had forcibly, but only temporarily, suppressed. The intensity of these national social and class conflicts was to increase with time, spreading to Asia and the Third World even as the United States was now compelled to consider how best to cope with the immediate threat of the radicalized European workers. The manner in which America balanced its desire for the reformation of European capitalism against its need to preserve it immediately as a system in any form, in order to later attempt to integrate it, is a key chapter in postwar history involving all of Europe and Japan. For the sake of its own future in the world, Washington had to resolve whether it wished to aid in the restoration of the traditional ruling classes of Germany and Japan—the very elements who had conducted wars against America in the past.

To American leaders, the European Left included the Communists as well as radicalized Social Democrats whose militancy the war had temporarily revived. But such a narrow definition can become a misleading literary convenience when it associates the working class too narrowly with specific political expressions, for the workers' most radical activities invariably found their expressions in spontaneous mass actions, from strikes to the formation of workers' councils, which were the truly fundamental and immediate threats to the established orders. In reality the Left was the ascendant working class, transcending and frequently opposing the Communists time and again—in the largest sense an aggressive element in European society agitating for basic change. Elsewhere, mainly in Asia, the Left was the radical anticolonial movement, the active, armed peasants and individuals in and also beyond the Communist parties. The Left was everywhere an overriding aspect of the postwar scene on which the United States had scarcely calculated during most of the war, a force that was to compel Washington time and again to address itself to the indispensable political preconditions for the ultimate attainment of its primary objectives.

In much of Asia and Europe a resurgent and formidable Left was a major effect of World War II, just as the Soviet Union was the main outcome of World War I. Each war had generated vast upheavals and a period of flux, and the United States' own goals and interests had colored its responses to them. Washington neither feared nor suspected that the world was irrevocably in transition, decentralized, unpredictable, and beyond the control of any nation—and especially its own mastery. But, in the short run, American leaders had to consider whether the Left had the will and capacity to act and take power—and how to respond in the event it did. At the same time they had to confront the question of the future of the USSR, a prospect that the deepening wartime diplomatic crisis between Russia and the West had left enshrouded in dark pessimism. The Left and Russia usually appeared as synonymous in America's litany, as Washington often assigned the Kremlin powers in the world that must have surprised the quite circumspect rulers of that war-devastated country. For the USSR's very existence was a reminder of the profound weakening of European capitalism and the traditional order after World War I, and potentially a catalyst for undermining capitalism in the future. But was Russia, given America's self-assigned destiny, *the* critical problem for the United States to confront in the postwar era? To place this question in perspective, one has only to ask, given its articulation of its larger goals, what the United States' policy would have been regarding innumerable problems and areas had the Bolshevik Revolution never occurred. As it was, during the war the Russians repeatedly showed their conservatism in their inhibiting advice to the various Communist parties and their refusal to move freely into the power vacuum capitalism's weakness had created everywhere. And what were the possibilities of negotiations and conventional diplomacy in resolving the outstanding issues with the Soviet Union, such as Eastern Europe, the future of Germany, and Russia's future role in the world, especially given America's definitions of the causes of the world's problems as well as its own interests? In light of American needs and perspectives, and the nature of the postwar upheaval and the forces of our age, were expansion and conflict inevitable? Washington never dissociated the USSR from the Left, not only because bolshevism is but one twentieth-century expression of a much larger revolutionary trend but also because it was often politically convenient for America's leaders to fix the blame for capitalism's failures on the cautious men in the Kremlin.

It was no less certain that the intricate effort to reshape and guide the nonsocialist world's destiny also threatened to bring with it much tension and conflict between anti-Soviet allies who were grouped together in a rather tenuous alliance of convenience. If, in the end, all of Washington's postwar leaders superficially attribute to one cause—Russia—the justification for everything they wish to do, it is only because such a style of explanation becomes critical to the very conduct and future of an American foreign policy for which these men have yet to find domestic legitimation and enthusiasm. To locate true motives and isolate real objectives is our task here, and it is a story in which one must separate as well as interrelate the problems of Russia, England, Western capitalism, and the revolution in much of the world in the overriding context of the United States' expansion and advancement of its national interest.

During World War II the United States had confidently planned for the future, believing that its newly created international economic organizations as well as the United Nations would form a sufficient foundation for the application of its power and the relatively quick attainment of its goals. It based this optimistic assumption on the continuation of an essentially static social order throughout the world. Only after the conflict could Washington gauge the war's trauma and dislocations and fully determine the adequacy of the world organizations it had hoped would suffice to attain the framework within which it would realize its objectives. But World War I had shown the extent to which international affairs had become integrally linked to internal social and class dynamics, with great power intervention defining and limiting movements of change, shattering pluralism and diversity in the nation-state, and linking social progress in one area to global political and economic events. That first global conflagration had partially transformed world politics from conventional wars between states into international alliances of classes as well—classes forced to act in unison to survive as national entities. This theme of internationalization of the process of national change is also crucial to the World War II experience and central to postwar history. Given America's global ends, the manner in which it developed its instruments to seek the inextricably linked reformation of world capitalism and the defeat of the Left is one of the major dimensions of postwar history—and the experiences of our lifetime.

And so the United States entered the postwar era, incomparably the most powerful nation in modern history. Its strength was economic rather than ideological, for here the inspiration and initiative rest with national revolutionaries whom the Americans could abhor and fear—and the Russians, at best, might only halfheartedly and belatedly endorse. The United States' military power and technology were no less formidable than its economic resources, but the manner in which to apply them, and the areas of the world to which they were relevant, it had to balance against larger economic priorities and domestic political constraints. How Washington was to conclude its search for a military strategy capable of substituting technology for the appeals and unsuspected decisive potency of revolutionary ideologies in the Third World is vital not only to the history of the postwar decade but to the nature of our existence and the future of mankind. It is a story integrally linked to the very character of the postwar world and the enormously ambitious destiny that America's leaders assumed in it.

We have not written a book about the "Cold War," an egregious term that burdens one's comprehension of the postwar era with oversimplifications and evokes the wrong questions. At best, that unfortunate phrase describes United States–Soviet diplomacy in the narrowest context, as if the relationship subsumes most that is crucial in the history of our times. It gives us no framework within which to understand the fact that the postwar experience, the formal cold peace between Russia and the United States notwithstanding, has been one of conflict, war, repression, and ever-mounting violence. That process has occurred despite literal peace between Russia and the West essentially because the larger, more significant context for understanding postwar history is the entire globe and the revolution, the counterrevolution, and the great, often violent, interaction between the United States, its European allies, and the vast social and economic transformation in the Third World that is the defining fact of our world. It is only in this context that Soviet-American relations should be placed, and it is here that the limits of the notion of the Cold War become most apparent. For that static concept conditions us not to probe further the real character of the forces of intervention and expansion—and therefore violence—in our times. It minimizes the nature and causes of mankind's fate today, leading us to believe that conflict and violence are accidental rather than inevitable consequences of the objectives of American foreign policy and the imperatives it has imposed on movements of social transformation throughout the world.

To approach the history of the postwar world as if Soviet-American rivalry encompasses its major theme—a notion implicit in the term "Cold War"—is to leave most of the critical dimensions of our epoch off to the side of any picture in a bewildering, disconnected profusion. Such a specialized focus leads to myopia, for the bulk of the crucial events of our time are interrelated, and one cannot truly understand anything without comprehending a great deal more than United States–Soviet diplomacy. This global context, and the goals motivating the conduct of American foreign policy, are the main subject of our book. Its length is a necessary function of the topic's scope as well as our disbelief in the premise, which has dominated American academic life for decades, that ideological correctness on contemporary foreign relations is an adequate substitute for accuracy and depth. Therefore the need for a comparative history which draws deeply on American documentary sources as well as those of foreign nations—an analysis which defines structures and purposes and the manner in which they were actually expressed in the real world of diplomacy and conflict. With necessary detail comes greater perspective, even if it demands greater patience.

This, then, is a history of United States foreign policy during the crucial postwar decade, a period that is a microcosm of the entire postwar experience and during which most of America's basic problems—and failures—emerge. We have seen enough of the subsequent documents, unpublished as well as published, to feel confident that the post-1954 events are but an extension of the principles and procedures crystallized during the first postwar decade. That policy and practice has been deliberative and quite consistent because the goals, structure, and requirements of the United States' social system have remained durable throughout the period. The notion of American leadership's errors or misperceptions is reassuring to those who believe the society can be redeemed merely by abler, superior men. But that species of liberal theory ignores the reasons for the constancy and also the justifications and explanations for action any careful student of the facts will encounter during any judiciously objective search of the historical sources. Official speeches and memoirs are, of course, frequently devoid of revelations of true motives. But articulate men, with a clear sense of purpose and objectives, invariably are at the helm; even their obfuscations often have reasons. And where the insight and articulated purposes of actors do not suffice, descriptions of the constancy and patterns in their actions will. As we shall see repeatedly, it is the expansive interests of American capitalism as an economy with specific structural needs that guide the definition of foreign economic policy and the United States' larger global role and needs. This fact, so internalized by those who rule, delineates the options of the men who decide policy just as it shapes the lives of those who pay for—and fulfill—it. America is not an abstract, classless society of men of equivalent interests and power; yet it remains now to show the manner in which this overriding social reality determines the definition and implementation of American foreign policy in the world. But of this, more follows.

BOOK I

The Global Crisis from the End of the War until Early 1947

1

The Reconstruction of the World Economy

The United States' ultimate objective at the end of World War II was both to sustain and to reform world capitalism. The tension between doing both eventually prevented America from accomplishing either in a shape fully satisfactory to itself. The task confronting Washington was to dissolve the impact not merely of World War II on the structure of the world economy but of the depression of 1929 and World War I as well—to reverse, in brief, most of the consequences of twentieth-century history. "The main prize of the victory of the United Nations," the State Department summed up the United States' vision in November 1945, "is a limited and temporary power to establish the kind of world we want to live in ."[1]* That was the prodigious task before it.

The goal was monumental, and always beyond attainment. The clarity with which the men in power perceived it, however, reflected the intensely sophisticated wartime discussions of economic peace aims that had especially preoccupied the State Department. What they could not overcome was the direct contradictions between the various instrumentalities and policies with which the United States hoped to achieve its goals, the incompatibility between reforming world capitalism and stemming the seemingly no less imminent threat of the Left and Communism, and the fact that the other non-Communist states were always to retain a very different conception of their national interest from the one that Washington advanced for them.

*Superior figures refer to Notes beginning on page 717.

In essence, during and immediately after World War II the key American leaders articulated an economic interpretation of the sources of world conflict that usefully complemented their vision of the United States' postwar global needs. With or without such a rationale, the structural problems and goals of the American economy would have persisted, but the fact remains that the conjunction between an American-sponsored internationalist ideology and objective national necessity was made, and it was to grow with time. Cordell Hull, who assumed major responsibility for the United States' wartime definition of its economic goals, was completely devoted to the premise that economic rivalry was the primary cause of world military conflict and that if one could remove barriers to freer trade and the exchange of raw materials and goods, universal harmony would follow. "International monetary and financial problems have been a source of conflict for a generation," Secretary of the Treasury Henry Morgenthau, Jr., typically explained to the Senate in June 1945. "We must see that after this war they do not become the basis for new conflicts." The danger was that as a result of wartime exchange and trade controls, all the prewar impediments to trade were emerging ". . . with greater ingenuity and with greater effectiveness than ever before ."[2]

In the name of future peace, therefore, the United States committed itself to the reconstruction of prewar world capitalism—to the elimination of trade and financial barriers, exclusive trading blocs, and restrictive policies of every sort. It more frequently advanced this solution, however, on behalf of long-term American prosperity, and it was this motive that the rest of the world—capitalist and noncapitalist alike—most fully appreciated. This purpose, too, shaped the contours of functional United States trade and financial policies and convinced the remainder of the world that in the name of universal welfare the United States was actually advancing its own self-interest. For when American leaders referred to multilateral trade or the "open door," not for a moment did they conceive of the emergence of a situation in which United States businessmen were naturally excluded from some central, even dominant role in a region because of superior competition from other countries. Virtually synonymous with multilateral trade, in Washington's definition, was greater American economic activity and expansion.

"[T]he establishment of a liberal trading system and the attainment of an expanding world economy," to cite Secretary of State James F. Byrnes's well-worn phrase taken from Hull, was one of the most frequent themes in the policy statements of key American leaders in the years following the war.[3] Unless it were attained, "American exports will face new and greater obstacles in various foreign markets . . . ," the tireless State Department trade specialist, Willard L. Thorp, warned in November 1945.[4] His superior, Assistant Secretary William L. Clayton, was always candid about the goals of this policy: "So, let us admit right off that our objective has as its background the needs and interests of the people of the United States. . . . We need markets—big markets—around the world in which to buy and sell. We ask no special privileges in any of these markets."[5] Men such as Clayton were aware of the critical weight which a relatively small increase in American exports or investments overseas might have in sharply increasing net profits of United States firms, but above all they were concerned with the nation's shifting position and dependence on foreign raw materials. "Due to the serious depletion of our natural resources during the war, we must now import many metals and minerals. . . . Indeed we are today net importers of practically all the important metals and minerals except two —coal and oil. Who knows how long we can go without importing oil?" Given this vital dependence, which extended well beyond principle but had far-reaching implications to the economic sinews of national power, " . . . what happens to American-owned reserves of such materials abroad is a matter of national concern."[6] There was a point, in brief, at which the question of nominal ideology would prove secondary to that of "national security and interest." In the area of petroleum, preeminently, this consideration was repeatedly to justify American efforts to create dominant and exclusive positions in various countries.

The necessary conclusion of this vision, as we shall see again and again, was the belief that socialism, state ownership, and Third World economic development were fundamentally inimical to American global objectives. Decision-makers articulated this assumption both privately and publicly, with sophistication or at times rather baldly. "The selective processes of society's evolution through the ages have proved that the institution of private property ranks with those of religion and the family as a bulwark of civilization," Assistant Secretary of State Spruille Braden declared in September 1946. "To tamper with private enterprise, except to apply well-conceived, legal, and essential controls, will precipitate a disintegration of life and liberty as we conceive and treasure them."[7] Key American leaders who were not, as in Braden's case, also personally major overseas investors fully shared such premises. ". . . [O]ur foreign trade, export and import, must in the long run be privately handled and privately financed if it is to serve well this country and world economy," Truman stated in June 1946;

"[o]ur common aim is the return of our foreign commerce and investments to private channels as soon as possible."[8] Even when temporarily unattainable, these values and objectives helped to reorient the goals and tools of American foreign economic policy after periods of enforced compromises.

What was clear from such premises was that the American vision of the new world economy it was seeking to recast from the materials of the old had no place in it for socialism or for the exclusion, for whatever the reason, of American investment. "We believe that the best way to get oil and develop it," Thorp phrased it in a variation of this theme in February 1948, "is through the operation of private oil companies. . . . We are trying in general and in particular to convince these other countries that it is very much in their own interest to let down the barriers and permit foreign capital to come in and help develop their reserves and their resources."[9] Certain it was that such "freedom" was deemed essential to American economic and strategic interests.

The historian will search in vain for any dissenting analyses in Washington of the causes of the world's economic malaise, alternative responses to it, and other less self-serving goals the United States might seek to attain in the ideal world system the American leaders were to articulate so clearly. Key leaders readily confronted the operational disparity between the loftier justifications for American objectives and crass self-interest. What the United States would not consider, however, was that the problem facing the world was not simply the maladjustment of the trade and financial structure, which was to prove but a reflection of much deeper ills, but the beginning of a vast, slowly evolving shift in the control of world power and the purposes and actions of the larger bulk of mankind. For the Americans based their definition of the global situation on their evaluation of European events, first and foremost, and on power-in-hand or as it had been in the past when England or Germany defined the course of world affairs. They did not estimate the potential of Asia, Latin America, or Africa as being of central importance. And they saw even the current economic problems of Europe, ultimately, as something superficial and short-lived.

Given the disparity between its articulated goals and the realities of both Europe and the world, and the fact that the political and social preconditions for the attainment of its economic ends scarcely prevailed, the basis for subsequent American interventionism was further intensified. By 1946, only the United States was strong enough to attempt to reform world capitalism and to define ambitious goals that by necessity were to lay down major obstacles to the revolutionary social, political, and economic patterns already evolving throughout the world. Washington was almost immediately to learn that to reform and integrate the remaining capitalist nations, it would first have to preserve them. Such a policy was to involve gains, and losses too. Its success was ultimately to prove partial and temporary.

In its role as a reformer of the world economy in order to achieve its own national interest and expand, the United States was able to evoke liberal rhetoric even as it sought to penetrate and assimilate Britain's former economic power. And in its function as a preserver of the vestiges of capitalism and moribund social classes and systems, it was also to call upon its power and conservative sense of order. There was no contradiction in this seeming duality; they are simply the two sides of what was ultimately to prove a remarkably consistent and clear national policy throughout the postwar era and down to this very day.

The Legacy for Reform

The trauma of the Great Depression defined Washington's wartime plans for the reconstruction of the world economy. Perhaps the most disturbing outcome of the depression had been the creation of increasingly exclusive trade blocs—of which Britain's sterling bloc was far and away the most important—that tended increasingly to reduce the United States' importance in world trade. One of the immediate effects of this tendency was that while the world manufacturing export trade fell off generally after 1929, during the recovery that occurred after 1932 the United States' absolute share of the world manufacturing exports declined dramatically until war-induced demand restored it. At the same time, the growing American raw materials and food deficits caused imports of such goods not to fall, if at all, as deeply as exports, so that, in constant dollars, the United States sustained a negative balance of trade during seven years of the post-1929 decade.

With the sterling bloc controlling one-third of all world trade, exchange restrictions in many other nations, and cartels dominating as much as one-half of world trade, the United States as an increasingly dependent raw materials importer, unable to sell as much manufactured goods as was essential to maintain its prosperity, determined to undo the consequences of the depression. Despite publicized exceptions, United States investments as a whole in Europe in the two decades after 1920 had proved immensely profitable. As buyer and seller, investor and trader, the reform of the depression and war-wracked world economy was also an absolute requisite of prosperity and profits for the United States.[10] But the motive behind this aspiration was not only self-interest, though it was primarily that, but also the awareness of Hull and others that the corollaries of economic blocs were military and political blocs not merely independent of the United States but also in competition with it. Economics was the key, therefore, to a politically integrated world system as well as economic prosperity, and England they considered to be the prime factor in such an ambitious reconstruction.

The English had with reluctance endorsed the contours of the American postwar vision in Article VII of the Lend Lease Agreement of February 1942, but not without first making it general enough to provide for the contingencies their own economic weakness might later necessitate. Yet taking Article VII as an abstract proposition, the wartime British government also hoped England might later be able to exist in a world in which Hull's few and simple premises of lower trade barriers and nondiscrimination might prevail. Only its very realistic sense of the extent to which England had mortgaged a great part of the imperial legacy of centuries to fight the war caused it to insist on reservations in all wartime advances toward the realization of the American goal.

The reform of the world financial system was the only significant structural step the United States was able to implement, and the rest would remain in the realm of articulating principles to which the United States tried to obtain allied accession. The July 1944 Bretton Woods Conference led to the formation of the International Monetary Fund (IMF), which sought to eliminate foreign exchange impediments to trade, and the International Bank for Reconstruction and Development (IBRD), both of which were constructed so that the United States could dominate their policies via the voting mechanisms. The IMF's framers designed it not merely to implement disinterested principle but to reflect the United States' control of the majority of the world's monetary gold and its ability to provide a large part of its future capital. The IBRD was tailored to give a governmentally assured framework for future private capital investment, much of which would be American. Underlying these organizations was the American belief, optimistic to the core, that one could plan for the future by overcoming the problems of the past and that the postwar world would essentially offer the same difficulties—challenges that America could master within a few years. It would be a world, as Henry Morgenthau put it, ". . . in which international trade and international investment can be carried on by businessmen on business principles."[11] The dissolution of the exceptional depression and wartime exchange and trade controls and mechanisms would, in essence, lay the foundation for a reconstructed, liberalized world capitalism which American leaders, from Wilson to Hull, had long cherished.

What the Bretton Woods Conference had been to the reconstruction of the world financial structure, Washington planners hoped a world trade conference and charter would be to exports and trade. Yet during the war itself they considered only the principles of such an organization, if only because the English, while nominally in favor of the purpose, were wary regarding its details. After the beginning of 1945 the State Department, under Clayton's supervision, preoccupied itself with translating Hull's principles into a blueprint for a formal organization—the International Trade Organization (ITO)—intended to free world commerce by lowering tariffs drastically, opening raw materials to all nations (the United States in particular), and dissolving trade restrictions of nearly every sort.

Until the British translated their own essentially favorable policy into a timetable, one that took into account their specific needs, there could be no progress on the ITO—for British and sterling bloc trade was the key to the planned reformation. The ITO principles, as we shall see, were preeminently a statement of United States goals rather than a description of its practice, if only because the Americans had yet to resolve the inevitable contradiction of their restrictionism as an agricultural nation and exporter —and this, too, the British understood. The resolution of this internal conflict, as well as America's relations with England, form a major chapter in postwar history.

The ideological underpinning for a world trade reform was essentially the same as for finance. Excluded altogether, scarcely even imagined, were colonial transformations that might deprive the industrial world of access to raw materials and markets. Most explicit was the assumption, as Clair Wilcox, one of Clayton's key assistants, phrased it, that ". . . freedom of international trade depends on the preservation of freedom in domestic economic life . . . governed by competition between independent enterprises in free markets."[12] In effect, without the continuation of world capitalism the structure could not be reformed on the terms America envisaged. The Soviet Union, Washington fully appreciated, would have no place in such a world economic order, for its economy could be integrated into world capitalism only haphazardly at best. The capitalist nations might ignore bolshevism or outflank it—but it could have no integral role as an aspect of a new, infinitely more complicated world system attempting to bring reality closer to its desires. Yet more significant was the no less logical opposition to socialism and national planned economies in Europe, an American premise which both the rise of the Left in politics and the extension of Soviet power into Eastern Europe challenged even before the end of the war. In brief, the American response to Eastern European developments, anticolonial revolutions, British Labourism, and managed Western European capitalism to a very great measure reflected the American desire to attain its own deeply rooted wartime and historical goals—and needs—for the world economy.

While some American leaders, such as Henry Morgenthau, at times called America's wartime plans essentially nonpolitical in nature, organized on "a strictly business basis," they could not help but inevitably acknowledge that such business carried with it political prerequisites regarding the Left, social change, and the USSR.[13] And this assumption of the permanency and continuation of capitalism, in something like the form in which it had existed for many preceding decades, was for many nations the crux of their dilemma, inescapably requiring them to confront the American problem along with their own internal conditions. For if the Americans were to achieve their goals, they would have to preserve the essence of the *ancien régime,* if only temporarily, as a precondition for the reformation of traditional capitalism—and the advancement and attainment of United States interests.

If, in the last analysis, one cannot divorce principle from its practice and fulfillment, and we must spell out the application of these American objectives in regard to England, Eastern Europe, and, indeed, the whole world until 1954, this economic foundation of the conduct of American diplomacy and its objective needs warrants constant attention. For the admixture of the United States' advocacy of a superficial reformism of the prewar structures of economic power, and the degree to which such goals must be profoundly counterrevolutionary in the very different postwar context, is the central theme of postwar history.

While the United States articulated and advanced principles, it also planned during World War II to apply its formidably enlarged economic power to achieve its goals, and it is only when economic pressures proved unsuccessful in the postwar era that the mobilization and, in some instances, application of military power became essential.

Since American leaders erroneously conceived England as the main barrier to the attainment of their postwar economic goals, they also thought purely economic levers to be adequate. Here, as elsewhere, Washington saw economic power in the form of Lend Lease aid, food, and relief and reconstruction assistance largely as sufficient. By the end of the war, however, the limited application of military power, in the form of the stabilizing presence of United States troops in Western Europe, was also accepted as a lesser means of creating the preconditions for the fulfillment of American aspirations.

A society's goals, in the last analysis, reflect its objective needs—economic, strategic, and political—in the light of the requirements of its very specific structure of power. Since this power structure in America has existed over many decades in a capitalist form, its demands are the common premises for the application of American power—one that theorists attribute to social consensus and sanction, but which in reality has always reflected the class structure and class needs. With time, such structural imperatives and limits appear to take on independent characteristics, so that whether academics or businessmen administer it, the state invariably responds in nearly identical ways to similar challenges. Apart from the fact that no bureaucrat, however chosen, could rise to a position of responsibility without continuous and proven conformity to norms of conduct and goals defined by the society's economic power structure which is, in the last analysis, the source of national goals, there is little intrinsic significance in the nature of the bureaucratic selection process and administrative elite. Indeed, officials may be chosen by entirely "democratic" means at any given time and still function according to criteria established for them.

Routine administrative responsibility, even at the highest level, demands reliability to established norms—standards that precedent defines for the bureaucrat, no matter what his class origins. When the state apparatus considers innovative policies more likely to have larger consequences, historically it has invariably sought the advice of, or formally involved in the bureaucratic administration, the interested elements of the economic power structure.

However, there is some curious interest in the fact that the objectives handed down to the State Department from the era of Woodrow Wilson, when the United States became the world's foremost power, were left to William L. Clayton to administer as assistant secretary and then as under secretary of state. Clayton, who took over the department's Economic Affairs division upon Hull's retirement, also held 40 percent of the stock in the world's largest cotton merchant house and constantly defined official policy on issues that directly affected his firm's activity.[14] More significant is that even before the Texas millionaire's arrival on the scene, his predecessors had legacied to him the major contours and many of the key instruments of postwar foreign economic diplomacy. For given the needs of the American social system, as other men of power defined them, there was precious little space for new initiatives.

Apart from the reform of the world financial and trade structures, even before the peace America's wartime leaders had already begun to apply their immense economic resources to help attain their economic peace aims. For the postwar needs of the American economy transcended any man or specific interest, but impinged on the issue, so central to the future of American capitalism, of whether the society would return to the conditions of the prewar depression, isolated in a world of revolution and profound change, or sustain the wartime prosperity and contain the forces of upheaval in world politics and economy.

The Specter of Depression

The deeply etched memory of the decade-long depression of 1929 hung over all American plans for the postwar era. The war had ended that crisis in American society, but the question remained whether peace would restore it. The historical analyst is perpetually challenged and confounded by the danger that the effects of a policy may only rarely reveal its true motives, and specific interests and causal elements may distort its visible roots. But at the end of World War II the leadership of the United States determined on a policy intended to prevent the return of an economic and social crisis in American society—a policy that explicitly demanded that they resolve America's dilemma in the world arena.

The official and unofficial wartime debate on the postwar economic challenge was immense in scope and alone sufficient for a book. Yet the facts —and goals—were clear in the minds of nearly all commentators: the depression had damaged profoundly the United States' position in the world economy, lowering by almost half its share of a far smaller world trade, and the problem in the postwar era was to restore and then extend this share, to maintain the high wartime profits that had followed the parched 1930's, and to utilize a labor force temporarily absorbed in the military services and war plants. By June 1945 the capital assets in American manufacturing had increased 65 percent, largely from federal sources, over the 1939 level. Stated simply, for Washington's planners the question was how to use this vast plant after the end of hostilities. In the farm sector, the return of surplus gluts, largely due to the depression's impact on the world economy, seemed probable if no action were taken to prevent it. Apart from the vague measures and assumptions that Congress wrote into the Full Employment Bill of 1945, steps focused mainly on mitigating the extent and hardships of mass unemployment which the Senate's Committee on Banking anticipated would likely produce six or seven millions out of work by the winter of 1945–1946, tangible proposals occurred mainly in foreign economic policy. "Our international policies and our domestic policies are inseparable," Secretary of State Byrnes informed the Senate on August 21, 1945.[15] In extending its power throughout the globe, the United States hoped to save itself as well from a return of the misery of prewar experience.

From the 1932 low of $1.6 billion in exports, the United States attained $12.8 billion in 1943 and $14.3 billion in 1944, most of the new peak representing a favorable balance of trade. The figure of $14 billion in postwar exports—well over four times the 1939 level—therefore became the target of most wartime planners and their calculated precondition of continued American prosperity. Assistant Secretary of State Dean Acheson, by early 1945, publicly endorsed a $10 billion minimum figure, but Commerce Department experts thought it to be too low. Even if backlogged domestic wartime savings and demand sustained business activity for two or three years after 1946, Commerce experts warned, this alone would not prevent unemployment of as great as 4.5 million men in 1948. The most optimistic estimates calculated that the United States would not import more than $6 billion a year through 1947, and probably much less, and American private business could not, at best, profitably invest more than $3 billion a year for some time—figures that later proved much too high.

At the very least, $5 billion in annual United States loans and grants would for a time be required to attain the $14 billion export target for domestic prosperity, though some estimates ran to $8 billion. For this reason, key Washington officials publicly warned before the end of the war that the United States would have to provide ". . . the necessary financing of our foriegn trade during the crucial period of reconversion at home and reconstruction abroad . . ."[16] From the outset, Washington set the entire question of postwar American foreign economic policy and aid in the context, as Clayton phrased it as late as November 1946, that ". . . let us admit right off that our objective has as its background the needs and interests of the people of the United States."[17] Such a formulation was also based on the premise, as Byrnes had put it one year earlier, that "[p]olitical peace and economic warfare cannot long exist together."[18] The failure to restore world trade would not only affect American prosperity but in addition lead to a continuation of the world trade restrictions which it was a prime American goal to eliminate as part of the reformation of world capitalism. For if the nations of Europe could not finance reconstruction via American aid, they would attempt to find the resources by tight exchange and import controls—in effect, continuing the *status quo* in the world economy inherited from the debacle of 1929. Loans would also become the key vehicle of structural change in the capitalist world. "We cannot play Santa Claus to the world but we can make loans to governments whose credit is good, provided such governments will make changes in commercial policies which will make it possible for us to increase our trade with them," Byrnes added.[19] Trade, the reformation of foreign capitalism, and American prosperity were all seen as part of one interlocked issue.

From this viewpoint, even before America's leaders could evaluate the specific political and economic conditions of Europe—indeed, even when they were relatively sanguine—they determined on a postwar economic policy compatible with American interests. Not only, therefore, did Washington have to confront both bolshevism and the social-economic consequences of the great upheaval in the war-torn world, but it had also to redefine the nature of world capitalism as it had evolved after 1918. No responsible American leader had any illusions regarding the nation's critical role in the postwar world economy or any grave doubts as to its ability to fulfill its self-appointed role.

American economic planners were continuously aware of exports, full employment, and the transformation of the world economy. No less imperative to them, so much so that it could not be compromised, was the nation's need to gain access to the world's raw material output. Nominal anticolonialism, or an open door doctrine, Washington continuously linked to this need throughout the war, tying the advancement of American interests to a very specific notion of international welfare. The heart of the matter, however, was that for two decades the United States had increasingly been a net importer of raw materials, without which a substantial and growing section of its economy could not operate, and the fulfillment of the United States' goals for the world economy were a vital aspect of guaranteeing access to future world resources output. Much discussed at the time, for the problem was very real, raw materials assumed a weight and significance far beyond the dollar value of such imports. America's economic power was dependent on them. Only coal and oil, of the important minerals, did not have to be imported in significant quantities by 1946. "Because of our dependence upon imports of strategic metals and minerals," Clayton told the National Foreign Trade Convention in November 1946 in a rather typical exposition, "what happens to American-owned reserves of such materials abroad is a matter of national concern."[20] One of the critical assets of temporary massive United States loans, noted the key National Advisory Council on International Monetary and Financial Problems, comprising the secretaries of state, treasury, and commerce and the chairmen of the Export-Import Bank and Federal Reserve System, was that it would help offset the unfavorable trade balance the nation inevitably would confront. Ultimately many factors, not the least of which was ". . . the depletion of our natural resources," would require such a shift.[21] This, too, was a critical aspect of the United States' relation to the postwar world economy, one that made isolation from the world impossible and impinged far more on its relations with Western Europe and the Third World than the Soviet Union.

The question of foreign economic policy was not the containment of Communism, but rather more directly the extension and expansion of American capitalism according to its new economic power and needs. Primarily, America was committed to inhibiting and redirecting other forces and pressures of change abroad in the world among non-, even anti-, Soviet states. Russia and Eastern Europe were an aspect of this problem, but the rest of the world was yet more important even in 1946.

There was a remarkable consensus on this question among key Washington decision-makers and big businessmen. The larger public was either uninformed or uninterested in the entire matter of the world economy. In one sense, of course, the historian should not draw too significant a dichotomy between political officials and Wall Street executives—for many of the key Washington personnel were merely businessmen-on-leave. Yet academics and long-time politicians also failed to strike a dissonant note—which in large part explains their political success—and very few, if any, could be found who rejected the spirit of Secretary of Commerce Henry A. Wallace's February 1946 definition that ". . . we conceive our primary function . . . to be to represent the United States' trade interest. . . ."[22] All agreed, in principle, as Byrnes put it in August 1945, that "in the field of international relations we have joined in a cooperative endeavor to construct an expanding world economy based on the liberal principles of private enterprise, nondiscrimination, and reduced barriers to trade."[23] To attain these goals the United States would have to preserve "private enterprise," or capitalism, in as wide an area of the world as possible. "Freedom in the domestic economy," Clair Wilcox phrased it four years later, "fits into the pattern of multilateralism and non-discrimination in world trade. Regimentation in the domestic economy makes for bilateralism and discrimination."[24] The question was how to stop it from defining foreign economic developments.

These premises, so vital to understanding the foundations and objectives of American foreign policy at both the planning and the operational levels, deserve the attention that key American leaders themselves gave to it. For the Third World it meant, as Assistant Secretary of State for Latin American Affairs Spruille Braden expressed it in September 1946, "I wish to emphasize that private enterprise is the best and in most circumstances the only really sound means to develop the known or unknown resources of a new country. . . ."[25] Policy-makers such as Braden, Willard Thorp, and others warmly endorsed initial governmental risk or development loans, but only as a means of paving the way for United States investors. They might also justify temporary government-to-government loans and grants to provide alternatives to statism. ". . . [I]f this loan should not be approved," Clayton was to warn in May 1946, "it will, in my opinion, mean a much more rapid socialization of the British economy . . . , the reason being that Britain will be compelled to regiment completely international trade."[26] Put another way at the same time by Charles S. Dewey of the Chase National Bank:

There are three business ideologies existent in the world today, the Soviet system, our own free-enterprise system, and a third which is neither one nor the other. . . . I am extremely troubled about the future of free enterprise. To put it bluntly, are we going to let this third group abandon the policy of free enterprise and open competition and become state trading nations or are we going to take a smart gamble and back our own future by advancing funds that may tide them over their difficult period and permit them to play the game under the rules we adhere to.[27]

"The world political problem today," wrote Joseph M. Dodge, the Detroit banker who was to help formulate and implement many of the most important foreign policy decisions of the period covered in this book, "is the extent to which Government controls of ownership will replace private enterprise. . . . Underlying these problems and trends is the ultimate fact that the expansion of socialism and Government control and ownership finally leads towards some form of totalitarianism."[28]

These premises and objectives meant that during the postwar era the government and key sectors of private capital adopted a common, complementary strategy that led to state aid to American capitalism not only to maintain and extend its prosperity into the postwar era, but not the least also to preserve the larger global political-economic structure within which long-term United States capitalist interests and power might function. This meant, in the end, that Washington would define a brand of internationalism which, at its core, was never to be anything less than a mechanism for advancing specific American interests. For this reason, the only largely disinterested international economic program on which the United States embarked during the war, the United Nations Relief and Rehabilitation Administration (UNRRA), it abandoned as expeditiously as possible merely because the organization did not lend itself well enough to the advancement of American objectives.[29]

Fear of socialism, preventing Communism, the hope that America could use its economic power to define the structure of postwar trade and the world economy, and the need to maintain a market for American goods and supplies for its industry—all merged into a kind of general ideology, various elements of which were continuously reiterated by the same men in the appropriate context. It is this pragmatic synthesis, which is both a counter-revolutionary ideology and doctrine capable of sustaining immediate losses in funds on behalf of a larger, more accurate theory of national and class interest, that makes too limited the description of American diplomacy as based on the open door, for it was that and much more besides. Because there was a longer-range interest in it, the use of the state to sustain American power in the world, ultimately for economic and necessarily related strategic ends, becomes a vital aspect of the larger thrust of American foreign policy. The immediate financial losses which the integrated economic and political elites could transfer to the state and, in the end, to the larger public made the undertaking look charitable and generous even as it was justified with moral rhetoric that scarcely concealed its true function.

Utilizing these merged considerations, the Truman administration embarked on its postwar career, freely citing the ". . . liberal principles of trade which must be the basis of any permanent prosperity," loans that would "increase the markets for American products," and the need to "oppose these exclusive trading blocs"—phrases that the administration repeated endlessly over coming years and blended with numerous diverse causes.[30] Truman's National Advisory Council formalized them yet once again in

February 1946, and in June the President added to it a committee of leading export-oriented bankers and industrialists to assist the council in ". . . our common aim . . . [to] return . . . our foreign commerce and investments to private channels as soon as possible," a step that both Truman and Winthrop W. Aldrich, chairman of the new committee and Chase National Bank as well, saw as a means of coordinating public and private funds for identical goals.[31]

Given the nature of the world at the end of World War II, and the temporary domestic investment opportunities, private American capital was not ready to send much capital abroad, and, indeed, in 1946 began liquidating its foreign portfolio investments. The obligation to take the risks would be on the government, it was explicitly understood, especially if the United States were to assume the monumental task of dissolving the almost intact British trading bloc. As the familiar pattern of prewar trade began to reemerge threatening the long-term American objectives and it could no longer postpone action, with the sanction of the constituency reflected in the Aldrich committee, Washington embarked on its postwar course because it was to the national interest as the government's officials and their private advisers and friends defined it. These objectives and the logical policy they implied reflected America's needs—needs based on economic and political elements that predated the war but which special circumstances that emerged from the conflict also shaped. Well before the crises of 1947, which historians erroneously mark as a distinctive change in the purpose and assumptions of American foreign policy, the United States in 1946 authorized $5.7 billion in new foreign grants and credits—almost as much as the average for the next three years and fifth highest in postwar history. During the war it had fully determined to embark on such a policy because it was a response to both the condition of the world and the needs of the American economy, a fact so self-evident at the time that Western European governments could with some measure of confidence expect to tap American resources if only because it was of great interest to the United States to make them freely available to achieve its own goals.[32]

The United States entered the postwar world circumscribed by itself, by the heritage of the depression, the limitations and logic of its domestically oriented capitalism, and the structural conditions the war created and thrust upon it. These factors would have existed regardless of the status of the Left in the world, the problem of the Soviet Union, the disintegration of the colonial systems, and the like, but they only helped to color the specific nature of America's response to a complicated world it was determined, in any event, to reform and guide in ways compatible with American requirements and interests. That the United States would have thrust outward after the war, with something like its poorly fitting synthesis of moralism, charity, calculation, and need, was certain.

The real question was less America's postwar role, destined to be active under any circumstance, than how it would respond to the prospect of failure on its own terms. Its ultimate policy would be expressed in the consistency with which it, too, practiced its standard of economic conduct for other states, and also whether the logic of its goals required domination or true internationalism in the sense of a community of interests that were compatible. But nothing in the history of the twentieth century justified the belief that a nation can attain great economic power without profoundly serious conflicts with other states. Wartime economic experience with England had shown how deeply inconsistent American ideals became in practice. Ultimately, the question of the logic of successful economic expansion and transformation raised the fateful issue, which all imperialist powers had confronted in preceding decades, of the political and military preconditions of American economic hegemony requiring physical intervention into any corner of the globe that might demand it.

If what the United States proposed as a doctrine for the rest of the world proved irrelevant, the question would reduce itself to the control of power, returning world affairs to the conflict between states within parameters and assumptions well known to the bloodied world by 1946. If England would not conform, how then to relate to it, in terms of both the future of its sphere of influence and its economic role? If Western Europe should go its way, what then? If Eastern Europe were divorced from the world economy, how might this affect relations with the responsible culprits? If change in the colonial world threatened to produce a vacuum or, even worse, new societies inimical to long-term American interests and needs, what response did the great stakes warrant? And, should the most optimistic assumptions fail, and the American fear of the Left, in both its Communist and its socialist forms, prove well founded, would the United States prefer the natural and only allies it might find in the opposition to profound social changes in the world that threatened their common interests? What role would the classic Right and forces of counterrevolution, and the entities of Germany and Japan, play in the fulfillment of America's goals? What, ultimately, would be the compromises between the abstract, often incompatible ideals of American economic postwar goals and the realities of a war-wracked world moving to heal itself in its own way? At the end of World War II, as the American leaders considered such dilemmas as they then comprehended, and went ahead without consciousness of the ultimate significance of not a few of their acts, the United States' economic goals and needs provided the foundations for their responses to the dominant problems of our era.

2

American Diplomacy and Russia, 1945–1946

World War II shattered the prewar structures of power and order in all of Europe and much of Asia, and stemming the forces of profound change became, in the largest sense, a dominant theme and purpose in United States foreign policy. The restoration of a modicum of stability and the containment of both the Soviet Union and the dynamic forces of the Left became guiding ends of American diplomacy because the triumph of the Left precluded the possibility of the United States' eventually attaining its own larger economic and political goals for the postwar world.

These objectives, even before the end of the war, shaped American diplomacy and intervention in Europe and China and Washington's responses to specific conditions and challenges, but during the first year of peace the United States' political and diplomatic strategy superficially conveyed an appearance of remaining in gestation, if only because the full consequences of the war on the prewar social systems could not immediately be plumbed. The revolutionary and human impact of World War I was seemingly telescoped in history, for after the epic upheaval in Russia and frightful but brief days for the rulers of Bavaria and Hungary, counterrevolutionary forces turned the tide and restored order in Europe on the basis of profoundly moribund and decayed prewar foundations, while outside Europe the colonial systems were scarcely touched.

The consequences of World War II for traditional power unfolded far more slowly, leading neither to apocalypse nor to stability, but the intensity of its impact was too great for many of the prewar societies to resist. The conservative forces of order were fatally weakened and compromised everywhere, even physically liquidated in such regions as Eastern Europe, especially Poland, where the ravages of Nazism had been most profound. The Left, which had gone into eclipse or had been repressed after 1921, emerged as *the* dynamic political force in Europe, Asia, and elsewhere. If seen in the perspective of the over-all social and political impact of a war that did not end with negotiations, but in the bloodiest destruction of life and material institutions in all of history—a cataclysm that ripped apart the moorings and foundations of a world already gravely wounded by the prior war—World War II was a critical event in the final transformation of the pre-1914 world, a profoundly disturbing process the end of which we have yet to see.

At the end of World War I the United States could recognize vital parties and forces in Europe with which it could associate and identify, and Wilson at Versailles spoke not only as the leader of America but also for classic liberalism everywhere. At the end of World War II no parallel situation existed, and only the United States among the great powers unswervingly stood for the kind of world system Wilson had defended. For this reason, only the United States was in a position to resist those larger forces of change, upheaval, and revolution that the war had unleashed. As in the case of the immediate post-1917 period, external intervention into the affairs of nations became a critical mode of diplomacy for both the United States and Russia—indeed, it was well advanced before the end of the war—both to revive the Right and control the Left. But unlike the case after World War I, the local forces with which the United States aligned itself were far weaker than an ascendant Left growing midst the frustration and hunger of the peoples of Europe and Asia. For the moment, at least, history appeared to have passed beyond the control of traditional European capitalism and conservatism.

The most important national expressions of this crisis—the Far East, Germany, and Greece—we deal with in later chapters; but the problem of the collapse of social and economic systems Washington translated not only into diplomatic strategies but also into a larger global assessment and estimate of Russian intentions that profoundly influenced detailed American responses and set the broader context for its diplomacy marked by the interacting themes of containment, stability, and counterrevolution.

The inevitable consequence of the upheaval in world affairs was an active and aggressive American intervention in ever-widening reaches of the globe, for, left alone, the transformation of European and Asian societies in unknown and undesirable ways—from Washington's viewpoint—was certain. This meant the seeming "internationalization"—in reality it was Americanization—of internal social conflict to prevent the imminent victories of leftist forces and provide economic and military aid and sustenance to rightist and capitalist elements wherever they might still be found to fill the breach. Only in Eastern Europe was such a strategy impossible, if only because there the security interests of the Soviet Union clashed with the restorative policies of the United States, and the breakdown of traditional societies was too profound for the casual support the Americans might, at best, be able to give to them. Elsewhere, especially in Asia, where nationalist movements with social revolutionary tendencies confronted the remnants of European colonialism, it was partially feasible in the form of selective aid; but in Indochina it was ultimately to demand massive American intervention when both the colonial power and their local compradors proved far too weak to stem the Left. If this eventual direct intervention is perhaps the most significant theme and development of the decades after the end of the war, it could not yet be predicted during 1945–1946. It was merely the inevitable logic of larger American objectives.

But Washington's concern for Russian policies and actions must not obscure the great measure to which American policy merely fitted the Soviet problem into a much larger context, a framework which would have existed apart from anything Russia might have done. Indeed, no one can understand Soviet-American relations save as one of a number of vital aspects of the larger advancement and application of heightened American power in the postwar world, a greater undertaking that time and again was never caused by Russian policy and very often in no way involved Moscow. The so-called Cold War, in brief, was far less the confrontation of the United States with Russia than America's expansion into the entire world —a world the Soviet Union neither controlled nor created. If the imperatives of narrative demand consideration of Soviet-American relations, by no means should the reader believe that this story is the essence of postwar world history.

It was both easy and rational for Washington in the months immediately after the war to focus on the intentions of the Soviet Union and the seeming threat it posed to the restoration and reformation of the prewar world which was the starting point for American wartime planning for the peace. The events in Iran, Eastern Europe, and elsewhere reinforced the exacerbating, increasingly bitter wartime diplomatic relations with Russia. Washington could not distinguish between the Left in the Greek mountains or northern French mine fields and the dictates of the Kremlin, and it was hardly prone to attribute the dynamism of local radicals to the decay of capitalism.

It did not necessitate the total collapse of the London Foreign Ministers Conference during September 1945 to create a deeply pessimistic vision in Washington of the future course of relations with Russia, for that had existed for well over a year. It certainly did not require the hypersensitive dispatches of chargé George F. Kennan from the Moscow embassy, with their ingenious discoveries of grand strategies and meanings in this or that *Pravda* article or Paris trade union resolution; these were filed away and largely ignored. The ambassador to Moscow, W. Averell Harriman, had his own cheerless opinion, which the London conference merely reinforced, and the more important Soviet experts in the State Department fully shared it. James Forrestal, the secretary of the navy, and by then a key figure in the major foreign policy discussions, might briefly complain during 1945 that Secretary of State James F. Byrnes was not sufficiently hard-nosed regarding Soviet ideology, but he was not to complain much longer on this point. Byrnes was perhaps less caustic than Forrestal, but his wartime record and first six months as secretary had shown his stern firmness toward Russia, and by the beginning of 1946 Byrnes adopted the tone as well as the substance of the American policy toward the USSR. "I'm tired of babying the Soviets," Truman admonished him on January 5, 1946. "Unless Russia is faced with an iron fist and strong language another war is in the making."[1] Such blunt, tough style made the President most comfortable, and the Russians had already been familiar with it since April 1945.

No later than the beginning of 1946, the critical American policy-makers assumed that Russia had embarked on a course that would certainly lead to sharp conflict and probably, someday, to war. Forrestal was scarcely alone in this belief, if only because Truman himself had virtually said as much. When Harriman resigned his post and returned to Washington during February 1946, he again sounded the tocsin on alleged Soviet territorial and ideological expansion, its development of a military economy, and its use of Communist agents globally to fan the flames of rebellion. His successor, General Walter Bedell Smith, was intensively briefed during early 1946, and the general interpretation of American policy communicated to him was that Russia was incapable of collaborating with the outside world, but that it would respond to firmness and power, and this realism alone might create stability. The immediate policy of neither peace nor war, neither formal *détentes* and *quid pro quo*'s nor direct American military intervention, was not merely the result of internal debates or the muscular public speeches of Senator Arthur H. Vandenberg of Michigan, the leading Republican foreign policy spokesman, but the logic of the

American policy of not abdicating American rights in areas, such as Eastern Europe, Greece, or Manchuria, in which it might have present or future interests.[2]

The question of eventual war with Russia was one of distant possibilities or, for Forrestal, probabilities, but there is no doubt whatsoever that throughout 1946 Washington considered immediate war—within, say, six months or a year—as highly unlikely, an estimate that was not to alter substantially for years. The critical factor in this assessment was a realistic picture of the condition of the Soviet economy in the wake of the holocaust. Summing up "Soviet Capabilities and Possible Intentions" at the beginning of 1946, Naval Intelligence portrayed a nation incapable of offensive warfare via sea and air power, unable to mount a sustained land operation in the Far East, and not yet able to reabsorb its army into the civilian sector. "Maintenance of large occupational forces in Europe is dictated to a certain extent by the necessity of 'farming out' millions of men for whom living accommodations and food cannot be spared in the USSR. . . . Economically, the Soviet Union is exhausted." Over the next five years, the navy's experts predicted, Russia would consolidate its power in Eastern Europe primarily to strengthen its own security. "The USSR is not expected to take any action during the next five years which might develop into hostilities with Anglo-Americans."[3] The Moscow embassy's economic expert at the end of 1945 reported much the same picture: an economy being strained to the utmost, consolidation of economic and political power along the adjacent rim lands, and the ability of the Russians ultimately to succeed in economic reconstruction and expansion. Intelligence sources later that year reassured the United States that the Russians were unprepared for war and seeking to avoid it, and Dulles reflected general opinion in Washington when in January 1947 he publicly stated that war ". . . is one thing which Soviet leadership does not want and would not consciously risk. Economically the nation is still weak in consequence of war devastation. Also, for the time being, the Soviet military establishment is completely outmatched by the mechanized weapons—particularly the atomic weapons—available to the United States."[4]

Such facts assured even Forrestal by June 1946 that the Russians were unlikely soon to do anything leading to war with the United States, and this view was commonly shared by most key American leaders. Instead, the dominant theme of America's assessment of Soviet intentions was to shift to the more subtle question of overt Soviet probings, as in Iran and Turkey, and the infinitely more intricate question of the local Communist and leftist movements in various stages of opposition to pro-Anglo-American and conservative parties. Both, in Washington's view, demanded stern resistance lest Russia exploit Western weaknesses to increase its alleged demands; but clearly the shift in American policy was from a fear of conventional conflict between states toward concern for the larger global socioeconomic-political fabric which the war had ripped apart, and which it would be infinitely more complex to mend. In this context, therefore, it was not the question of the strength of Russia, but the weakness of Western capitalism and traditional societies that was to become primary to the conduct of American diplomacy.

Given the need to reconstruct and save these areas for the West and capitalism as a necessary precondition for maximizing broader American economic goals in the world, such shifting perspectives were no less logical. And since the United States did not segregate the USSR from the world revolutionary movements and forces of decisive change, and indeed held it accountable for them, by mid-1946 the assumption was increasingly toward the themes of containment of the Left outside Russia and Eastern Europe and the stabilization of capitalism. Russia thereby became one question of a number arising out of the collapse of world capitalism, a disintegration that had begun before 1917, along with the survival, reconstruction, and advancement of America's larger economic-political goals within that mended framework. No one doubted, however, that such intransigent resistance to Russia or the Left, whichever the case might be, would require the United States to take the leadership everywhere.

The problem of the Left was preeminently, in American eyes, a question of Europe, even though it was quite obvious by the end of 1946 that leftist revolutions by arms were occurring in nonindustrialized nations, primarily in Asia. The reasons for this obliviousness, which was to be of immense historic significance, had a superficial rationale we consider later in this chapter; but essentially it reflected a short-term estimate of the nature of world power as well as the need to find a relatively limited and inexpensive area in which to apply American power. Hence a reinforcing global geopolitical theory was mustered up, one which blended a perception of political-economic dangers with a conveniently reinforcing doctrine of the nature of military power. But even in Europe the question of the relationship of the Left to Russia was elusive. Ultimately, despite the obvious signs of independence of the more aggressive Left from Russia, it was necessary to conclude, in the words of one American representative, that "[i]t is one thing to oppose Soviet penetration in central and western Europe, but quite another thing to attempt to sweep back local political forces which are determinedly on the march. Yet, in dealing with parties which represent not only domestic revolutionary forces but the foreign policy of the Soviet government it is difficult to grapple with the one without grappling with the other."[5]

The assumption was to remain that the Communist parties were both agents of Moscow and on the verge of the conquest of power, and the logic of this position demanded that the United States be ready to intervene militarily to save Western Europe from any Communist takeover in the streets or at the polls. Concomitant with this fear of the Communists was a profound anxiety over the non-Communist Left, which key policy-makers such as Joseph M. Dodge, the Detroit banker, shared. "The world political problem today," he concluded in a view that he later translated into policy, "is the extent to which Government controls or ownership will replace private enterprise and how or whether any degree of the former can be balanced with the latter so as to leave a substantially effective system of free, private enterprise."[6] To men like Dodge any form of socialism would lead toward "totalitarianism" and defeat American objectives, and in this view the enemy was decisive reform from any source. For this reason, as well as a myopia which took the Jacobin rhetoric of the Western European Communist parties at its face value and ignored their reformist functions, one had to meet head on the social dynamics and economic weaknesses of Western Europe. Containment and stability required reconstruction and military security intended to confront internal forces of change much more than the USSR, and actually precluded a diplomacy of the reconciliation of conflicting national interests. And since such a program was fully compatible, indeed essential, to the attainment of United States goals for the world economy, the larger American reading of the Russian problem merged with that of the entire Continent.

The broader issue of colonialism at the end of the war seemed to Washington, by comparison, very minor in importance. During the last months of war the United States had arranged a *quid pro quo* with England, and then France, to obtain support for a transfer of the Japanese-mandated islands to American control, or opening the economic resources of the colonial regions to American interests, in return for a tacit approval of a continuation of colonialism suitably updated with United Nations (UN) rhetoric and sanctions. Late in 1946 the American delegation to the UN successfully initiated the transfer of the Japanese-mandated islands to the United States as strategic areas under Security Council jurisdiction, where the veto applied and therefore left the United States, for practical purposes, with absolute control. It attempted, succeeding at least in the terminology employed, to modify British, Belgian, and French mandate rights in Africa to expose the economies of those colonial nations to American capital. Washington quietly supported the French return to Indochina because it feared the Communist leadership of the Vietminh, but in the Dutch East Indies it saw an opportunistic nationalist leadership ready to open the region to foreign business, and it therefore became increasingly "anticolonialist" on that controversy. The index to America's policy toward colonial independence movements was the extent to which such elements sought social and economic change as well as political freedom. There was nothing equivocal about this inconsistency, based as it was on opposition to the revolutionary Left everywhere as a primary objective, and the belief, as John Foster Dulles phrased it in June 1946, that "Soviet leaders stimulate the independence movements. . . . Soviet leaders encourage that resort to violence. . . ."[7] Within the context of what was a much lower priority, the United States immediately aligned itself with colonialism or pliable domestic forces of conservatism in the Third World.

The London and Moscow Conferences and United States Policy

Diplomacy is a complex ritual, often scarcely more than a stratagem preceding haggling and trading akin to a bazaar. Power, the conflict of objectives, and the advancement of state goals are the real world in which great nations operate. Words at formal diplomatic conferences are uttered to conceal real meanings; stances are adopted to satisfy allies, placate critics, intimidate or bluff enemies. The experiences of centuries were quite as relevant to the diplomatic maneuverings of the year and one-half after Potsdam.

There were specific crises—Germany, China, Iran, and Japan—and these we consider in detail in subsequent chapters; but subsuming them all was the larger texture and mood of American foreign policy immediately after the war—a mood that interacted with specific diplomatic conferences that are interesting mainly insofar as they reveal the true concerns of American decision-makers at the time.

The Russians' diplomatic strategy during World War II revealed their profound commitments to direct diplomacy via the three great allies and to their guiding role over the future of Eastern Europe, with Russia's right to help define the future of a Germany it had made the greatest sacrifices to defeat. Moscow's prewar isolation now fitted uncomfortably, for within their area of concern the Russians sought a role proportionate to their wartime contributions. The Council of Foreign Ministers meeting in London, which opened September 11 and lasted three weeks, was that body's first reunion since its formal creation at the Potsdam Conference the preceding July for the purpose of preparing the peace treaties. The council was to spend much time disagreeing on Germany as well as many other problems, but it was to end in total failure over a seemingly minor question of protocol—the participation of China and France in its meeting—that really reflected fundamental approaches to future global diplomacy. To Russia, China was in America's sphere of influence, the Kuomintang essentially under its control; and it was most certainly not a great power. It regarded France as a secondary dependency of England, though of more significance in European affairs. To justify a major role for these nations struck Moscow as a poor substitute for direct reconciliation of conflicts between the three great powers, if that were possible, and merely a means of outvoting and embarrassing Russia and accomplishing nothing. The Soviets had expressed similar opinions throughout the war regarding the future UN organization.

At the very first meeting between Byrnes, Bevin, and Molotov the question arose whether China and France could participate in the discussion of any question, as opposed to voting on matters involving Axis states with whom they had not signed the armistice; and after some confused quibbling Molotov agreed to what, in effect, was an important modification of the procedure determined at Potsdam. There it was agreed the council members would include only signatories to the surrenders, save for French participation on Italy alone, and discussion rights were never implied. Yet the council was also free to alter its procedures, and this it had done at the opening of the London Conference. Over the subsequent days there was a stalemate on Germany, but on the more extensively discussed matter of Italy the Russians strenuously resisted the American effort to transfer the city of Trieste to Italy. The United States, as well, proposed a UN trusteeship over the former Italian colonies of Libya, Eritrea, and Somaliland, and in effect attempted to spare Italy reparations. But the Russians insisted on a $300 million reparations burden on Italy, one-third of which they would receive, and that the Tripolitanian section of Libya become a Russian trusteeship.

Since the British and French both were opposed to the eventual independence of these colonies, for fear it would create precedents for them to imitate, there was never any chance of the American plans being accepted, and the Russians failed to make much of their colonial pretension, for at times Molotov suggested the possibility of collective trusteeships as well. The Anglo-American-French refusal to concede on any figure for Italian reparations, however, appeared vital to Molotov, and by the twenty-second he began to retract on the begrudging earlier concession on Chinese and French participation in discussions. The Russians also failed to win American diplomatic recognition of Rumania or Bulgaria, unsuccessfully tried to discuss the future of Japan, and had scarcely anything to show by way of gain. Now Byrnes saw the Sino-French issue as a Soviet pretext to close up the conference, and a wire from Truman to Stalin failed to budge the Russians. Bevin, for his part, thought ". . . we are all agreed that Molotov is strictly legally right, although morally unsound," but the Russians would concede no further.[8] Molotov by October 1 freely informed Byrnes and Bevin that the issue to the Soviet Union was equality and protection against unwanted decisions, and clearly he was unhappy about the manner in which Russia had been continuously scolded and granted nothing in return. Yet there can be slight doubt that the Russians were on firm ground regarding the Potsdam decision on conference participation, had grudgingly hoped their consent to modification of the rules on the eleventh would produce concessions, and were now ready to abandon the illusion. Unable to agree, the meeting was simply terminated with not even a semblance of unity or a final communiqué. Several days later Byrnes released a full, detailed report of the magnitude of the disagreements and breakdown, placing the entire blame on the Russians. Next, without conceding on any substantive matters, Truman wrote Stalin that he hoped Russia would approve a later peace conference to deal with Italy and the other Axis satellites, with most of his advisers agreed that American intransigence had been correct until then.

Before the Russians could make a definite response, Truman on October 27 delivered a major statement on the need to maintain a high degree of peacetime military power ". . . to support a lasting peace, by force if necessary."[9] More important was his enunciation of those "fundamental principles of righteousness and justice" which would guide American diplomacy: self-government everywhere, including the colonial regions "prepared" for it, no territorial changes without the consent of a nation, nonrecognition of governments imposed by the force of a foreign power, and freedom of navigation and equal access for all to global raw materials. Even if they could not immediately be implemented, Truman avowed, these goals would still be the basis of American policy. Such a policy was scarcely the death of diplomacy, but it did carefully delineate how far it might go and sharply circumscribed its value.

Such public definitions of the situation were warranted by the fact that the etiquette of conference protocols could no longer manufacture agreements, much less conceal the profound cleavage then fully acknowledged in Washington. As for the United States, it could only do what was functional to its objectives and character. In their press and forums the two sides spoke more frankly; but however minimal its anticipated value, at the end of November Byrnes proposed to Molotov that a three-power foreign ministers meeting convene in Moscow in mid-December, presumably as required by the Potsdam Conference, this time without Chinese or French participation. The British deeply resented this unilateral step, and for a time threatened not to attend, but Byrnes thought that direct access to Stalin at such a meeting might produce better results than with the reputedly hard-line Molotov. London's unhappiness was compounded when Truman announced to a press conference on November 29 that he saw no further point to three-power conferences, but rather that the UN might handle global diplomacy. Seemingly contradictory, in reality it revealed that the United States would downgrade diplomacy between states, but also that in the conferences in which it participated it would not compromise on essential goals.

While Washington tested diplomacy and defined its objectives yet more precisely, it continued to rely on more informal pressures available to it as the strongest power on earth. In China, as noted in Chapter 10, it aided with its own marines the Kuomintang conquest of North China. On the economic level it decided to instruct the Russians on the penalties as well as the rewards of their intransigence. For at the beginning of 1945 the Russians had requested a postwar credit of $6 billion, but Harriman and most of Truman's advisers urged the President to use the promise of credit as a means of exacting political concessions. The Russians, still naïvely hoping to obtain some measure of assistance for reconstruction, during August asked for a $1 billion loan, as well as $400 million credit to buy Lend Lease goods for Russia still in the United States but cut off as a result of Truman's abrupt termination of all Lend Lease shipments on August 18. In mid-September, Stalin complained to a group of visiting American congressmen in some detail how Washington had ignored the nine-month old request, but toward the end of October, in part not to be loaded with useless materials for which it had no need, Washington loaned the USSR $400 million to purchase what was left in the Lend Lease pipe line. At the very same time, it asked the Russians for an inventory of what remained of $11 billion in earlier Lend Lease shipments, preparatory to a final Lend Lease financial settlement certain to cost Russia a great deal. Harriman still wished to link larger credits to settlements on other political and economic questions, including the restoration of United States property in Eastern Europe and Soviet collaboration with America's economic program for Europe, and Byrnes agreed with the general strategy, preferring to leave the matter dormant for the time being. Meanwhile, the United States pressed Moscow to provide the data essential for a Lend Lease settlement, a proposal which the Russians vocally denounced as ignoring their sacrifices for a common cause. Washington fully analyzed the value of American credits to accelerating Soviet reconstruction, and there was an explicit understanding that such aid would rebuild Russian power, which could only adversely affect American interests. The Russians would be strong enough, embassy reports indicated, especially given their anticipated integration of Eastern Europe's economy into their own. The State Department was to dun the Russians for their Lend Lease data and to follow Harriman's admonition to concert ". . . our economic policy with our political policy towards the Soviet Union."[10]

During early 1946 the Russians again discussed the loan question with American officials, who persisted in the strategy of linking the matter to an omnibus agreement on an economic policy that neither a socialist nor a capitalist nation was likely to accept willingly. Still, the State Department during May held out the promise of such a credit if the Russians gave the United States satisfaction on its other demands, though by the following July the President publicly discounted the possibility. The State Department was fully aware of the contradiction between asking Congress for money to strengthen Western Europe against Russia and a loan to the alleged threat itself, and chose not to pursue the inconsistency. The Russians, perhaps because of their great need, ignored the probabilities, and as late as October, Stalin publicly expressed a desire for a loan from the United States, having not yet learned the lesson that capitalist nations do not consciously underwrite their own enemies.[11]

The Moscow Conference was very different from the disastrous London talks, but it hardly resolved the conflicts between the former allies, much less touched the structure of societies in turmoil and change. There was no form of diplomacy that could do so, for the Russians had not ripped the world apart since 1914 and they were quite powerless to put it back together. On China and Japan, as we shall see, they paid obeisance to American objectives, but on Germany and Iran they would not, and on Eastern Europe they persisted in remaining elusive. Bevin confided to Byrnes at the opening of the conference that just as the Americans were extending the Monroe Doctrine into the Pacific, the Russians were applying an equivalent spheres-of-influence policy in Eastern Europe and dangerously impinging on British interests in Iran, Greece, and Turkey. Byrnes, of course, denied such a bloc strategy on America's part, as did Stalin on his side when Bevin raised the subject with him a week later. The Russian ruler noted England's domination of the Indian Ocean and the United States' supremacy in China and Japan, but he alleged Russia had nothing. In effect, he implied, the Anglo-Americans could scarcely wax righteous.

Still, the Moscow talks resulted in several important agreements, the most significant being the convocation of a peace conference the following spring to write peace treaties with Italy and the other German satellites. The gathering even agreed on the procedure, permitting the three great powers first to define treaty terms with minimum interference. An impotent Far Eastern Commission for Japan, a nominal two-power commission on Korea, a procedure for Rumania and Bulgaria gaining United States recognition, and even the establishment of a UN commission on atomic energy and disarmament were among the incidental results of the Moscow Conference.

Bevin and English opinion, despite the failure to reach any agreement on Iran, regarded the results of the conference as highly successful, especially by contrast to the London meeting. Byrnes, however, while also very pleased with the results, committed several political blunders. In Truman's opinion, he had failed to keep him fully informed while in Moscow, and he released the final conference communiqué prior to Truman's seeing it. As Truman recalled, "I did not like what I read." Both Vandenberg and Leahy, now one of Truman's closest advisers, regarded the outcome as another "give away" or even as appeasement, though Stimson, former Secretary of War, praised it highly to the President. His ego damaged by the conduct of Byrnes as "Assistant President in full charge of foreign policy," as he later termed it, Truman's earlier apprehensions concerning the man now burst into fury, and he saw no merit whatsoever in the conference results.[12] Byrnes, for his part, went on the radio on the thirtieth to give an unusually optimistic account of the results of the conference, which he implied would usher in a peace satisfactory to the United States in many parts of the world. The President was now ready to cut Byrnes down, and on January 5 he read to his face a vitriolic denunciation of the Russians, portrayed their "outrages" and imminent invasion plans for Turkey, and demanded "I do not think we should play compromise any longer."[13] But for the moment all he attained was mastery over one of Roosevelt's legatees.

Byrnes was no compromiser, either before or after the Moscow Conference, and the larger policy conflict some read into the crisis at the time is unjustified. Byrnes had been Roosevelt's intimate, one of his favored candidates for Vice-President in 1944, and a man with an independent political backing and reputation. At Potsdam he had instinctively pursued a stern line. Truman was now more self-confident, and well before Moscow he had been cooling toward Byrnes. His abilities as a diplomat were challenged less on policy than his capacity for applying it and his experience. The following April, Byrnes's doctors told him to work less, and he informed Truman that he would see the peace treaties through and then resign. In effect, he was to remain until January 1947.[14]

The only real division between Truman and Byrnes was one of ego and tone. Confidence in Byrnes among hard-line leaders never ceased to grow, and even Forrestal was his strong admirer. Harry Truman, on the other hand, preferred to mince no words and "to lead from strength."[15] From his first weeks as President, Truman could not successfully conceal his strong antipathy toward Soviet policy, whether in private meetings or in public utterances. His vituperation, which left him open in later years to visions of diabolical Soviet plots, was nevertheless not the source of American policy, which was based essentially on the belief, as the much more agile and restrained Forrestal phrased it in November 1945, that ". . . the United States is the one beacon of hope everywhere." This global logic, this sense of world "dependence upon us," was grounded on economic and political foundations far more permanent than Truman's style.[16] Still, such manners expressed the form that destiny took from time to time, and it reinforced the natural tendency throughout Washington during the months and years following the war to base the confrontation with Russia, the Left, and unwanted change throughout the world on the physical power which sheer American economic might made possible. Truman did not originate such a global strategy, but he reinforced it.

Fulfilling a Great Power's Role, 1946

There was no fundamental change in American policy during early 1946, and the decision to press the Iran question in the UN, or utilize that organization as a "bar of world opinion," was the logic both of wartime discussions and of Truman's martial October 27, 1945, speech. Despite the substantial Soviet concessions at Moscow, the general opinion in Washington was that it was necessary publicly to harden America's diplomatic stance and to make unequivocal its hostility to Russian conduct. Truman's desire alone was sufficient to make this official policy, but during the first months of 1946 Washington often reiterated this explicitly tough diplomacy. Both Vandenberg and Byrnes prepared, independently of each other, major addresses, and on February 27 the Michigan senator, in a speech more significant for its belligerent tone than its specifics, called for plain speaking, vigor, and a refusal to compromise on principles. Over the preceding days Byrnes, too, had prepared a speech, which won Truman's hearty approval, and which he delivered the following day. It was a yet greater rebuke. Russia, he declared, had engaged in ". . . a unilateral gnawing away at the *status quo*" and aggression ". . . by coercion or pressure or by subterfuges such as political infiltration."[17] He damned Soviet actions in Germany and Eastern Europe, especially regarding reparations, and made Russia responsible not only for its own actions but for those of the world's radical labor movement as well. "To banish war, nations must refrain from doing the things that lead to war," Byrnes warned, calling for the maintenance of a military establishment "commensurate with our responsibilities."[18] Vandenberg, who had not had a hand in Byrnes's statement, was delighted and never again criticized the secretary of state.

During these same days George Kennan's February 22 dispatch from Moscow began making the rounds in Washington, and if Byrnes read the document it seems most likely it was after he had prepared his own speech. Kennan's cable was of no special importance in helping to formulate American policy, which was only the logical outcome of years of precedent, but it was simply an able articulation of a yet more ideological view of alleged Soviet belligerence, expansion, and conspiracy, directly and via the leftist parties of the globe, that was useful to policy-makers such as Forrestal who were too busy or lacking in verbal skills to draft their own quite clear ideas along the same line. What is perhaps most interesting about the success of the "sermon," as Kennan later called it, was that for the obscure chargé, especially irritable after his bouts in Moscow with sinus, colds, and toothaches, "My reputation was made. My voice now carried."[19] In reality, however, his voice was to carry primarily for Forrestal, who made this essay required reading for hundreds and was to use Kennan as a useful ideologue until his own retirement, when Kennan's opinions ceased to have any real weight. The naval attaché in Moscow and other naval officers brought the man and his ideas to Forrestal's attention as a wronged prophet whom Harriman had allegedly cruelly mocked, and who like other stern-minded State Department officers was a victim of ". . . the White House era of wooing the Kremlin at any price."[20] There was, of course, no validity in these paranoid visions, but they suited Forrestal's inclinations, and Kennan, too, indulged in them from time to time, confessing in his memoir that some of his writings during those years ". . . might suggest I was headed for a job as a staff consultant to the late Senator Joe McCarthy. . . ."[21] Instead, Forrestal installed him close by in the National War College.

Far more significant was Churchill's famous March 5 speech at Fulton, Missouri, with Truman present on the platform. Some hours before he delivered the speech, Churchill showed a copy to Truman, who expressed strong, unreserved approval. Byrnes and Leahy, too, had enthusiastically endorsed it, Byrnes having known of its contents for some weeks. Technically a private citizen—in fact, he had not consulted the British government regarding the speech—Churchill spoke partially for the United States but wholly for himself, and hence the speech is marked by his characteristic flamboyance, obscurity, and braggadocio. The statement was preeminently a plea to speak to Russia from the position of overwhelming strength, and for the United States to create and dominate a grand alliance with England that would force Russia to a "settlement" and "good understanding"—the details of which Churchill left to the imagination. And while he endorsed maintaining the Anglo-American atomic monopoly, he also wished to create a UN armed force. What was most grasped upon was Churchill's classic phrase that "[f]rom Stettin in the Baltic to Trieste in the Adriatic, an iron curtain had descended across the continent," with Communist "fifth columns" operating everywhere else save the British Commonwealth and the United States.[22] Vienna, Prague, and Berlin were virtually written off as part of the poetic imagery; yet Churchill insisted war was neither inevitable nor imminent.

Churchill's speech caused immediate consternation in the British government, which was scarcely interested in the alliance he proposed and was distressed that the former Prime Minister's opinions were considered official. Trygve Lie was quite as distraught, not merely because it damaged the UN even as it was struggling to be born but because it also undermined the "Third Force" advocates in Europe, mainly liberals and social democrats, who wished to see such a bloc emerge to balance Russian and American power. However, neither Truman nor the British government would denounce the statement, and London simply declared that Churchill spoke only for himself. Stalin, the following week, unleashed an attack against Churchill's racial notions of Anglo-Saxon destiny as reminding him of Hitler's earlier racist theories, and he denounced the speech as "a call to war." Communism, he insisted, was a political force in Western Europe because of the patriotic role of the parties in the resistance, and in double measure he answered Churchill's references to "democracy" in Greece and totalitarianism in Poland. Several weeks later Stalin informed Ambassador Smith that the speech had been an unfriendly act.[23]

The Fulton manifesto was certainly unfriendly, as was the virtual American endorsement of it, but it was also factually inaccurate and politically confused. Churchill thought in terms of power relationships between states, and such material factors defined the limits of foreign policy and the extent of concessions. It was poetic and adventurous, but by referring to settlements and understandings it hinted at a possible *détente* which neither Truman nor Byrnes grasped upon and which Churchill failed to spell out. The speech immediately became an anti-Soviet manifesto, nothing more nor less. Back in office five years later, Churchill was not so flamboyant, and he again fell into his sometime wartime role as a mediator between Russia and the United States.

Yet these were the larger moods and thoughts in Washington during early 1946, impulses that the specific crises of Germany, Iran, or China merely reinforced. It was in this context, too, that Byrnes went to Paris in April, first to attend the three-power Foreign Ministers Conference that was to write peace treaties, and then the peace conference of all the wartime allies that was called merely to ratify what the great powers had already decided.

The stern American approach toward global problems was not an exploration for alternatives in light of the failure of existing policies, but simply the inflexible application of power in the hope the Russian recalcitrance would end. In this light, even Churchill's weak appeal for a "settlement" was more than the Americans could conceptualize and apply. Yet what was a year later called a "containment" policy was in fact already the official policy in Washington and among the key Republican leaders as well. Both John Foster and Allen Dulles during May circulated an analysis of the irreconcilable, nonnegotiable differences of Soviet-American policies that demanded the "insulation" of Russia until it underwent sufficient internal changes to enter into normal diplomatic relations with the rest of the world. John Foster Dulles publicized these ideas in *Life* and immediately won Byrnes's hearty endorsement.[24]

There was nothing new in containment and insulation, for they had been explicit parts of the antirevolutionary policy of the United States and the West since 1918, and at no point since then, much less since 1943, did Washington doubt that it was a fixed policy to thwart the Left wherever it might do so. Given American aims, it could hardly do otherwise. The notion of containment embraced the threatened internal transformation of societies by forces of decisive change, and also predicated the possible movement of the Soviet army into this or that nation. As a long-term strategy, this American vision looked toward a static world or one that channeled change into formal, predictable, and stable relations. As such it failed to distinguish between various kinds of Left movements and their connections to Russia, since it was uncontrollable change more than the extension of Soviet power that threatened the larger American vision of an ideal world order. Hence a pluralist but aggressive Left was, in the long run, no more satisfactory than a Russian-dominated Communist movement. Only where the economic and military price of containment was too high, as in China, did the United States acknowledge the limits of its power— not to endorse the new movements of change, but simply to abandon the field before its own weakness. The United States' economic goals of an open door to American trade and investments, which still encompassed Eastern Europe, also assumed that there would be no closed Soviet economic sphere of influence, and that while being contained politically or militarily, the newer acquisitions to the Soviet bloc would remain accessible to expanding American business. During 1946 the leaders in Washington still believed that Russia might accept the inequality of this dual standard and not fully consolidate—economically as well as politically—along its borders. There was some valid reason, as we shall see, for this supposition, but the United States did not believe it precluded the isolation of the Communist threat in Europe at one and the same time.

The Paris Conferences

The Council of Foreign Ministers meeting convened in Paris April 25 until mid-May, adjourned, and then met again from June 15 to July 12. It was only natural that each of the three powers drag a whole spate of other political questions into the discussion with the hope of winning concessions or gains. But insofar as the formal purpose of writing peace treaties was concerned, the preparatory meetings were ultimately quite successful. The question of Germany, for example, arose repeatedly; but, as we shall see, no agreement was attained on such matters, and Washington was already determined to consolidate Anglo-American power in Germany without Soviet collaboration.

Closer to the actual treaty question was Byrnes's attempt to win Soviet adherence to American economic penetration into Eastern Europe via equality of economic opportunity in the former Axis states and free navigation on the Danube, a proposal Stalin had already rejected at Potsdam. To Molotov, however, the Danube question was one for the bordering countries to settle among themselves, and the economic proposals were an effort to impose American hegemony over weak countries. Nothing came of the American suggestion. The Russians, for their part, were essentially thwarted in their effort to get $100 million in reparations out of Italy in the form of current production, and instead were finally authorized to take stray Italian overseas assets and surplus property of very dubious value. The nations that had been major victims of Italian aggression, however, were awarded $225 million, or a tiny fraction both of what they claimed and of what they actually lost. The other matters involving Italy also posed complex problems. The conference members all sought to woo the Italian government, and the Russians were in the delicate position of wishing to satisfy Yugoslav claims on Trieste as well as not to undermine the influence of the Italian Communist Party.

The large majority of the population in the disputed region of Trieste and the surrounding Julian March, taken together, were Croats or Slovenes, but even Yugoslav maps conceded Italian majorities in the heart of the port city, in the coastal area to the south, and in the city of Fiume. The essential Yugoslav argument was that the port was integral to the economy of the region and had been won by Italy as a result of its aggression. For good measure, they advanced claims to the west of the ethnic line which was the logical basis for a settlement, but the proposed American demarcation was well to its east and gave the Italians a handsome piece of foreign property. The Russians, somewhat uncomfortably, backed the Yugoslav demand, but after several weeks dropped their lackadaisical claim to a Tripolitanian trusteeship and instead proposed that Italy itself resume its colonial role in Libya under the UN's aegis, as well as be spared post-treaty controls at home. France, too, wished the colonies to go back to Italy, but it also proposed a compromise on the Trieste region that was as close to the actual ethnic distribution and equity as was likely to be devised, and on May 13 both the United States and England approved it. But the jockeying and trading on this or that issue—too complex as well as too insignificant to summarize here—meant that each of the four powers retracted and hedged on all these questions in the hope of winning some other concessions.[25]

During the first session the American position on most questions had been essentially intractable, and in a sense Byrnes's basic objective was to communicate, with the assistance of Vandenberg and Senator Tom Connally, Democratic head of the Senate Foreign Relations Committee, the United States' determination to assert its power and achieve its ends. By May 11 the American delegates acknowledged the fact that the Russians were proving flexible on such issues as the Italian colonies, as if to say, to quote Vandenberg's paraphrase of their posture, "What are you going to trade us for what we have given up." Soon a significant group of officials and reporters became aware of Anglo-American inflexibility and Soviet pliancy and the intense American desire to make the Soviets look stubborn before world opinion—as if the only purpose of the conference was to wage a propaganda war. Henry R. Luce, publisher of *Time,* confronted Vandenberg with such a report from one of his Paris correspondents, and the senator confided that "I think we *had* to do at least *one* thing at Paris— namely (speaking loosely) to demonstrate that the 'appeasement' days are over. . . . Paris was Munich in reverse. . . . There is no doubt that Molotov was in a 'trading mood.' "[26] If Vandenberg felt the United States had nothing left to trade, the fact remains that the United States went unprepared to offer concessions or explore the possibility of any form of diplomatic settlement on any substantial issues.

At the next session of the conference, which opened June 15, the Russians were ready to make compromises in return for almost none, as if to communicate their general willingness to reach a *détente*—if that were possible. From the opening day, in Vandenberg's terms, the American delegates decided ". . . we shall seek an early show-down," and a week later he noted with satisfaction that ". . . the United States spoke with the finality which becomes its position in the world."[27] Five days after the opening of the session the Russians, in effect, accepted the American proposal to leave the *status quo* of British-French occupation in the Italian colonies for another year, and if agreement could not be reached to refer the matter to the UN General Assembly. Then on July 27 the Russians assented to French border claims against Italy and that the Dodecanese Islands go to the clamoring Greeks. During the next days, after more bitter haggling, the Russians accepted the shadow compromise on Italian reparations, in return agreeing to the American procedure for the subsequent peace conference the Soviets had been threatening to hold up. Finally, they consented to the creation of an autonomous city of Trieste with a border contiguous to Italy under UN Security Council control, quite independent of Yugoslavia.

Now the actual peace conference of twenty-one nations was convened for July 29 in Paris, and while the rules of procedure to govern it had been bitterly contested in the Council of Foreign Ministers meetings, it was eventually decided the conference could only make recommendations to the council of great powers, which would have to reach its decisions unanimously. Unfinished problems, as Byrnes was quick to point out, included several dozen matters, some of them vital, that had not been decided on by the Big Four; and now he declared that the United States would support any conference decision with a two-thirds majority in the future council meetings, even if that decision reversed a previous American stand. This play for public opinion was gratuitous, for Byrnes well knew that the large majority of participants would vote on the United States' side. Indeed, he insisted all meetings of the conference be open to the press, thereby turning the entire proceedings into a propaganda forum that many regarded as maximizing histrionics and preventing serious progress. Despite wounded American protestations, the Russians saw it as a packed conference, an interpretation which America's handling of the independent Czechs was to reinforce. For weeks the speechmakers droned on, the unreality of the boring drama being punctured during August only by Yugoslav unwillingness to release the crew of one American air transport that illegally entered their airspace and was forced to land, and their shooting down of another on the nineteenth. But Molotov intervened to scold the apparently independent Yugoslavs, who made satisfactory amends almost immediately. On October 15 the unreal, contrived meeting ended.

The Paris Conference was a forum of despair, one organized in a manner calculated to generate and compound that which was already abundant. During these months Washington further toughened its policies in every area of the world and consolidated its own ranks with the elimination of Secretary of Commerce Henry A. Wallace from the cabinet. Molotov, speaking to the final session of the conference, judged its work a failure largely because the United States had lined up small or distant states to vote against Russia as a bloc on matters vital to its interests but not at all to those of, say, India. What was still urgent for world cooperation, the Russian added, was agreement and unity among the great powers, for contrived majorities would never bring it. In effect, the Russians urged a return to a classic diplomacy.[28]

Cooperation versus Hegemony

A fundamental assumption of American policy at the end of the war was the necessity to transform Soviet policy and objectives, and that such a profound alteration would have to occur in ways compatible with American national interests. Until then, the United States would utilize a combination of pressures—economic, propagandistic, and political—to alter Russian policy or to isolate the negative consequences of the bolshevik system. Even where Washington recognized that this might be difficult, even impossible, as in Eastern Europe, it refused to condone, and thereby legitimize, an unalterable reality in return for some vital concession or recognition of American interests. Yet what was clear about Soviet conduct, since the middle of the war, was that exactly such *quid pro quo*'s were essential objectives of its foreign policy. In brief, in the name of a moralism which, if implemented, would have opened Eastern Europe to American economic and political interests, the United States had embarked even during the war on a policy of containment and insulation in the hope that it might circumscribe the epidemic of social change and expanded Russian influence and, hopefully, eventually force Communism to retreat. Not for a moment did the United States consider that the affairs of Europe or the Near East were not its own, nor accept less than parity with England or Russia in all the distant areas of the world.

The numerous expressions of this policy comprise the content of the diplomatic history of this era, but several more general aspects of it illustrate the mood quite vividly. One involved the fate of Truman's erratic but peaceful-minded cabinet member, Henry A. Wallace. Wallace himself was motivated by a hodgepodge of liberal impulses and a naïveté regarding the role of world trade in bringing global peace. Attracted to mysticism as well as an agricultural policy of restricted output that led to his conservative reputation when he was secretary of agriculture in the 1930's, Wallace since March 1946 had been urging Truman to attempt a new approach to Russia via economic and trade relations. In fact, of course, Wallace favored a variation of the free trade, open door logic that also motivated the State Department, which only drew different tactical conclusions from the same premises. What is most significant about the episode is not the policy it reveals, but how entirely monolithic was American leadership at this time, and how demanding of total conformity was the allegedly democratic, pluralist society.

By the end of July, Wallace had made fully public his doubts regarding the larger contours of United States diplomacy, but then on September 12 he openly criticized the anti-Soviet excesses of the administration and claimed that Truman had approved the speech. Truman, of course, had scant prior knowledge of the speech's contents and had only passed a few vague pleasantries with Wallace concerning the merit of giving addresses to Democratic Party rallies. The military was distraught over Wallace's criticisms of continued large-scale arms spending and bases, but Byrnes in Paris quickly offered his resignation unless the President silenced and, in effect, repudiated Wallace. Truman hedged for a few days in the hope of avoiding politically disadvantageous publicity, for the dispute was filling all headlines, but on the twentieth he asked Wallace for his resignation. In the name of unity and bipartisanship, Truman eliminated one of the few remaining nonconformists in the government. Leahy, at the time, considered "Wallace . . . an honest 'fellow traveller' with the Soviets, at least a 'pink' and completely uninformed. . . ."[29]

Wallace's elimination was simply one more aspect of a consistent foreign policy that had not altered significantly since the end of the war and was not to change for the remainder of the Truman presidency. There were no shifts, but simply various allegations of Soviet expansionism and the United States' need to contain it and the forces of internal rebellion throughout the world. Such diplomacy as took place was seen essentially as tangential to the main business of economic stabilization and American power restraining a lesser Soviet state via military might. Byrnes's October 18 public report on the Paris Peace Conference is just one of many measures of this strategy, and the containment article Kennan was to publish at the beginning of 1947 was but another. Byrnes's report was a free discussion and delineation of the magnitude of the dispute with Russia, of the ". . . real and deep differences in interest, in ideas, in experience. . . ." Russia's "false and misleading propaganda" was decried, as was its asserted arbitrary use of the veto in the UN. Attaining lasting peace, Byrnes emphasized, would be a long, slow process. Such delays did not make armed conflict inevitable, but patience was essential. Then Byrnes might "deplore" Soviet talk of being encircled, or its criticism of the American trade program, denying that the United States had created a voting bloc at Paris or elsewhere.[30] In fact, of course, the United States had made vital decisions regarding the German question, was consciously moving toward a major role in the Near

East, and was scarcely reticent about action everywhere in light of Soviet refusal to negotiate on American terms. At the November 4 Council of Foreign Ministers meeting, which met for a month to tidy up the final details on the peace treaties, efforts to consider yet unsettled disputes led nowhere along courses by then well charted since the end of the war. There had never been illusion regarding the value of diplomacy in solving Soviet-American conflict, and there was to be none in the future.[31]

The United Nations

The UN, however, remained. Despite Truman's declaration of full support for that organization in October 1945, or even the European-sponsored move to locate the UN headquarters in the United States so as to maintain America's interests, the UN as a forum for effective diplomacy got off to a bad start and quickly became worse. The choice of Trygve Lie as Secretary General had initially been accompanied by much back room maneuvering —successful for the Americans—to keep him from becoming the first President. Then Truman and Byrnes designated John B. Hutson, undersecretary of agriculture, a tobacco expert and political crony, to be Assistant Secretary General. At the very first meeting of the Security Council, as we shall see, the United States mercilessly pressed the UN into immediate political service against Russia on the Iran question. The Soviet Union, outvoted at every turn, resorted to the veto time and time again. The Russians had their first taste of the bloc line-up at San Francisco and openly criticized the procedure. By May 1946, despite homilies concerning their faith in the UN, they were freely complaining about the combinations organized against them, and the experiences at the Paris Peace Conference only strengthened their earlier commitment to the veto as a shield for their minority status in world diplomatic bodies. Cooperation would come, Molotov stressed repeatedly in 1946, when interests were reconciled, and the veto aided that goal by preventing blocs that could implement their will. Otherwise the UN would collapse.[32] The Russians never wavered from this position.

Under these circumstances, all the inordinately complex provisions in the Yalta Accords and UN Charter on "procedural" questions made the veto an infuriating weapon against effective American control over the Security Council. By the fall of 1946 Senator Tom Connally warned the UN that continued arbitrary and willful use of the veto ". . . would over a period of time cause the disintegration of the Organization. The life of the Charter depends on the lofty and unselfish discharge of their duties by the members of the Security Council."[33] Again the United States wished the Russians to forgo the veto on procedural and other issues and abstain from its use on controversies to which they were a party. As the United States well understood, there was no chance of this occurring. The realities of international affairs, therefore, took place outside the arena of organized inequality but in the world of material power and social and economic change. Indeed, the United States was again and again to use Russia to justify its efforts to attain its larger economic and political goals, objectives that would have existed even without a Communist Russia. In the end, Soviet reticence was ironically to become one more functional rationale—ultimately the most crucial —in Washington's efforts to attain its ideal world order, the contours of which Woodrow Wilson had outlined even before 1918.

Russian Perspectives and Power

Just as the United States could aspire to relate to the conditions of the world after World War II because of its economic and military power, and its overwhelmingly superior might opened new vistas and possibilities, so, too, did Russia's economic and military condition limit its actions. Quite apart from intentions, one may define the Soviet Union's capacity to act as an expansive power in terms of industrial and agricultural resources—in terms, in brief, of its abilities and capabilities to pursue one or another type of foreign policy against a far stronger nation and its allies. These realities would determine whether Russia would be passive or aggressive in global affairs, aside from its purely verbal support for the immense forces of social and political change loose in the world—forces Russia had not initiated and could not stop.

The Germans overran an area containing 45 percent of Russia's prewar population, one-third of its industrial output, and 47 percent of its agricultural land. The prewar value of the property lost in the occupied territory was $128 billion. Industrial output in all of the USSR in 1945 was 58 percent of the 1940 level, and by 1947 reached 92 percent. Yet while industry suffered much, agriculture was decimated and on the verge of catastrophe. Livestock declined between 1938 and 1945 from about one-quarter for cattle to two-thirds for pigs. But at the beginning of spring 1946 a drought began spreading through the southwest regions that was eventually to encompass an area larger than that of the great drought of 1921, when 25 million people suffered from famine. The wheat harvest was about one-half the prewar average; yet while in 1921 the avowedly anti-Communist world, led by Herbert Hoover, had provided succor, the UNRRA missions of Russia's wartime allies began folding their operations in the sorely affected Ukraine. But Russia now had its traditional reserves and rationing to fall back upon, and though its sugar crop was ruined and meat rations were comparable to defeated Germany's, the country hobbled through midst great human suffering. During 1947, however, it produced a bumper wheat crop.

The Russian leaders talked of surpassing the United States in output and per capita consumption, but such promises remained in the realm of useful fantasy. Despite the difficulty of penetrating official statistics, Western experts estimated that in 1948 Russian national income was less than 30 percent of the United States', and although Russia spent 13 to 14 percent of this income on national defense—about twice the percentage of the United States—the absolute dollar value of American military expenditures was almost twice as high. Soviet military expenditures in 1947 were at about the same level as in 1939, whereas the United States outlays were about nine times those of 1940. Despite the striking economic recovery the Russians effected by dint of intense toil and the sacrifice of consumer goods, the immense material and military lead of the United States over Russia until 1949 was never in doubt.[34]

Under such straitened conditions, for the Kremlin economic recovery at home was the precondition of internal stability and, ultimately, international security. The Russian people were war-weary and anxious to rebuild, and Stalin and the party were quite aware of the grave limits this placed on an active foreign policy. The emphasis in the Soviet press, even during the diplomatic crisis year of 1947, was overwhelmingly on domestic, essentially economic, affairs. Victory had raised the prestige of the party among the Soviet masses, but military adventures might deplete whatever good will the rulers had accumulated as nationalist leaders during the war. Awareness of the limits of reality and freedom to act had always been the keystone of bolshevism's tactical success and survival. Stalin eschewed adventure and insulated the public from global crises with lack of news; and by early 1948 critical observers noted a "semi-liberal spell" in Soviet society that was to hurt the inefficient party bureaucrats most of all.[35]

Conscious of the limits of its economy, there can be no doubt the Kremlin saw the practical necessity that, in the words of one *Pravda* writer, "The building of Communism in one country, especially in such a country as the Soviet Union, is entirely possible—so teaches Comrade Stalin."[36] Such a program for reconstruction and growth, which Stalin publicly announced in February 1946, was seen as a question of three Five Year Plans, but for the immediate future he fixed his sights on attaining prewar levels in industry and agriculture. But this long-range perspective, which would indeed give Russia a formidable industrial capacity, Forrestal and the State Department regarded as a direct threat to American power, even as what the navy secretary called "The Declaration of World War III."[37]

From this viewpoint, Russia's ability eventually to develop into a great economic power and competitor was as dangerous as its immediate political intentions. Yet there were few references to war in Soviet statements, but mainly to economic growth and the concomitant promise of individual consumption. *Izvestia's* New Year's editorial of January 1, 1947, stressing internal reconstruction and peace, was typical of the mood Russia's leaders cultivated. What the Russians needed, for any policy or eventuality, was time and high national morale, for during 1946–1947 they were too broken to do much more than mend their wartime wounds. This was their preoccupation as the United States set out on its own postwar course.

The Soviet estimate of the global scene was a rationalization of the path on which reality had forced them to embark. There were certain physical facts the Russian leaders had to acknowledge immediately—their economic and material weaknesses, or war-weariness—and these facts profoundly affected the Soviet definition of the world situation. General theories of the motives of Soviet conduct during the postwar period are still contrived, not only because of the impossibility of knowing what was discussed in the Kremlin but mainly because all existing evidence reveals a lack of coherence and consistency in Soviet statements. It is safe enough to say that Stalin wished to firm up his power at home, but Isaac Deutscher's notion of Stalin's desire for ". . . socialism in one zone, in the Russian zone," imputes an expansiveness in Eastern Europe that cannot be divorced from an exact survey of the process and causes of the consolidation of Russian power in that region.[38] During the war itself the Russians showed a flexibility regarding Eastern European internal affairs that permitted significant diversity in national social systems but also demanded an end to prewar *cordons sanitaires* and hostile regimes. Soviet diplomacy, one is safe to state, was oriented toward Europe as the central arena of future world power, and in this regard it reinforced Anglo-American strategies. But it is likely the Russians felt that the unilateral Anglo-American direction of political affairs along Soviet borders, at least in Europe and the Near East, had to come to an end. Even the "re-isolation" of Russia from the world, as Isaac Deutscher argued, can only be understood, if the concept is relevant at all, as an effect rather than as the cause of the Soviet desire to find external security and stability in order to reconstruct at home.

Such an emphasis was possible because, as Barrington Moore, Jr., has noted, the Kremlin always believed that any policy that strengthened the socialist fatherland today eventually aided the world proletariat in the future, and that flexibility is the hallmark of the relationship of Soviet ideology to practice. Going one step further, one can posit that there is too little intrinsic consistency in bolshevik theory, which since its inception has been doctrinally opportunist, to expect much more than pragmatic adjustments to power, always conditioned by the primary desire to survive in what has usually been an unfavorable internal and global situation. Rarely was this condition worse than in the three years after the war.

The Soviet perspective appears based on several parallel theories, if not inconsistent at least not quickly reconcilable, that show much Russian probing, confusion, and wishful optimism concerning the West and the future of the world. In a sense these proved merely useful rationalizations for a necessity which limited Russia to a policy that its material resources permitted it to afford. The sixty divisions of Soviet troops in Eastern Europe and Germany during 1946 can be seen as the spearhead of an invading army or as a man-power conglomeration unable to return home because of the desperate food and housing shortage there. Moreover, it is quite certain that the Soviet army was incapable of mounting and *sustaining* a land war in Western Europe, especially given the American ability—freely discussed at the time—to destroy half of Russia's remaining industry and most of its cities with atomic bombs.[39]

The dominant theme in Soviet proclamations on international affairs in the three years after the war was the possibility and likelihood of coexistence and peace between Russia and the West, and Soviet writers produced a rather elaborate ideological superstructure to give a "Marxist" justification to this notion. The leading and best-known advocate of this view, Eugene Varga, emphasized future international conflict and imperialist rivalries as being centered on the Anglo-American dispute over world capitalist hegemony, a conflict he documented in detail. The United States would, in Varga's view, defeat England in the struggle to become heir to the nineteenth-century imperialism, but the power of the USSR made war with Russia unlikely, even though it was quite possible between the two English-speaking nations. For the United States itself, Varga predicted a crisis of overproduction within three years after the war, a notion for which Varga was later criticized as being too optimistic. There was a certain superficial sophistication to such an analysis, but even Stalin, Molotov, and Andrei Zhdanov, the assistant secretary of the party, repeated it in various forms. They all stressed the economically expansive designs of the United States, not only vis-à-vis England but in Eastern Europe, where, they contended, America's immense power in that ruined area would quickly lead to economic control over it.[40]

The Russian leaders argued that although the United States was an imperialist power, and its wrath would befall England, if anyone, coexistence between Russia and the United States, Communism and capitalism, was most likely. Stalin, in his rare public interviews during 1946, naturally maintained that friendship between Russia and the West was possible and that the danger of war was unreal. Stalin, in his famous February 1946 speech that so agitated Washington, dimly implied that any future conflicts would be between only capitalist nations quarreling over raw materials and spheres of influence, as had been the case with the two world wars. Stalin stressed this theme, as did the Soviet press, even more emphatically during the spring of 1947, as he found in diplomatic failures and crises the dialectical, tortured rationalizations to prevent general pessimism from becoming a self-fulfilling prophecy. The following September, Zhdanov told the founding meeting of the Cominform that "Soviet foreign policy proceeds from the premise that the two systems—capitalism and Socialism—will exist side by side for a long time. From this it follows that cooperation between the U.S.S.R. and the countries with other systems is possible, provided that the principle of reciprocity is observed. . . ."[41] In any event, Soviet leaders suggested, even if the imperialists wanted war they could not engineer it, and variations of such themes appeared in Russian statements consistently thereafter. Indeed, the united front strategy the Russians advocated between foreign Communists and nationalist forces was just one more example of the lack of dogmatism that made coexistence theory an integral part of Soviet foreign policy.

What is most interesting about Soviet comment on the direction of world affairs at this time is the curious admixture of naïveté and realism that accompanied it. The decision of the United States to make England rather than the USSR and the world Left the primary enemy was a conjecture based purely on wish fulfillment, for which scant substantiation could be found by 1946. The Russians, in brief, ignored the evidence as they marshaled their resources and gambled for time during which to compensate for the decisively unfavorable material balance of power then prevailing. The most impressive proof for this pragmatism—which is a reflection not so much of a flexible doctrine but of a confused attempt to relate to an uncontrollable world—is the repeated Soviet statements that they would welcome loans from the United States, long after there was even the remotest possibility of the United States' aiding Russia in any way. During October 1946 Stalin told American journalists that he was still interested in getting a loan from America and, the following month, in expanding trade relations. And both at the Marshall Plan conference in Paris during July 1947, and then the following September, the Russians openly expressed their earnest desire to obtain credits from the United States on terms that did not involve political or economic subjugation.

But at the same time that the Russians entertained illusions regarding possible United States economic aid, they could not ignore the fact of American troops and military bases around the world, and they repeatedly condemned such military trends, particularly operations in the Arctic region. Stalin feigned indifference toward some of these moves, but there can be little doubt that their import and strategic significance deeply disturbed the Russians, especially in China, the Arctic, Iceland, Britain, and nations from which the United States could deliver atomic bombs.[42]

The reconciliation of analysis and reality did not occur in public Soviet discussions of the world global situation, a world to which they could relate only haphazardly, on the basis of fact, and least of all because of ideological commitment. The instinct of survival, based on caution, remained the keystone of Soviet conduct in a global context which they less and less understood or controlled and whose direction and future they, too, could only dimly perceive.

3

Great Britain and the
New World Economy

At the end of World War II the United States' main strength was its unrivaled and unscathed economic and industrial power—a power that Washington hoped would prove decisive in shaping the political and economic contours of the postwar world. What it might not win at the bargaining table America might attain via the purse, and in relating to England and the Soviet Union the United States might aspire to define for its former allies the losses inherent in noncooperation with American aims.

America's immense might was based on the existence of its intact physical plant, but its leaders appreciated that the reform of the prewar world structure was the key to sustained national prosperity and full employment. They saw the problems of reconstruction of prewar capitalism as essentially short-term and as intimately bound to its simultaneous reform. If capitalism were to recede in the industrial world before triumphant socialist forces, America's economic power and promise would be gravely restricted, for its total application was possible only through world economic integration.

As strong as it might be, America's ability to employ its economic resources to reform the world economy, and attain its own goals thereby, confronted various contingencies, many of which it could not anticipate during the war. Current political exigencies, such as the need to obtain England's full cooperation, were the critical premise in planning, as was the assumption that Britain would be neither too weak nor too strong at the war's end. Yet even before the peace, the disturbing successes of leftist parties and forces throughout the world, and the advance of Soviet power into Eastern Europe in a manner that threatened that region's economic as

59

well as political destinies, challenged the critical political premises on which America founded its wartime planning. The very weakness of European capitalism and colonialism might impose new circumstances bringing unanticipated complications and delays in the attainment of goals, and the feebleness of the nations Washington hoped to integrate into its cherished new world economy might prove debilitating to a neat American economic strategy. Not the least, as well, was the fact that European powers, though sapped by the war, might seek to extract terms of their own from the United States as a part of the process of reciprocity.

To the weakened Western European states, the proof of America's free trade doctrines, which Britain, too, had found a congenial theory during its heyday, would be in the selfless manner in which the United States relinquished its own trade restrictions and prerogatives, giving to others what it demanded for itself. In short, if the United States were bent on domination rather than equality, the wracked European powers might still be strong enough to resist its advance, and in that resistance we have much of the story of what is nominally the politics and diplomacy of the postwar decade. It is a history in which Russia's role is not especially important in defining the initial terms of the controversy. But beyond even this, and perhaps most dangerous to the Americans, was the possibility, even then in the epochal process of unfolding, that both the political and the economic forces of change in the uncontrollable world—Asia as well as Europe— might ultimately rest beyond the reach of any nation. As the war ended, the signs of this eventuality were appearing everywhere.

England: The Key to Reform

Washington's wartime economic planning was largely contingent on winning Britain to full cooperation with the United States aspirations, and both on the level of abstract theory and the more significant control of material power, whether in the form of economic resources or oil concessions, America had acted to bring England into its orbit. Since the American vision was preeminently one of a capitalist world, and England was the most important remaining element in it, the urgency attached to the problem of England made, within its premises, good sense. For England and its sphere of influence was the key to trade as well as raw materials, of which oil was by far the most important in America's eyes.

If England could not be won over to cooperation, the entire American goal for the world economy would necessarily fail. After the collapse of the world economy in 1930, the official sterling bloc, as well as the numerous small nations everywhere that banked in London and pegged their currencies to sterling, more and more excluded dollar imports and greatly helped to reduce the American share of world and especially sterling bloc trade. Britain's share of the world market for manufactured exports, amounting to 19 percent in 1937, far exceeded America's and certainly would not diminish if the sterling bloc remained intact after the war. By 1938 half of all world trade was transacted in either dollars or sterling, and the demise of the Axis states meant that Britain's postwar share would rise. Lowering the barriers between the two currencies was essential to the vast expansion of postwar exports on which Washington planned.

During World War II the United States had embarked on a strategy of controlling Lend Lease so that Britain would emerge from the conflict neither rich enough to stand aloof from American economic pressures nor so weak as to be forced to impose an autarchic program of trade and currency restrictions. The delicate balance which was to make England cooperative was not found, as even some Washington planners began realizing by 1945. For England, as Harold Macmillan was later to recall, "The battlefields of the Second War mark the end of the heroic age of the British Empire."[1] Succinctly, to fight the enterprise virtually alone for almost two years, and then in concert, England went bankrupt in everything but name. It liquidated £1.1 billion of its overseas investment and accumulated an external sterling indebtedness of £3.4 billion by 1945, piling up a deficit in its balance of payments of £1 billion in 1944 alone. Its gold and dollar reserve, which the United States had carefully tailored via Lend Lease, was less than $2 billion at the war's end.

This vast debt within sterling bloc nations tied up the largest single postwar market, amounting to almost $14 billion, for sterling. Even the dollar earnings of bloc members were not convertible to other currencies, leaving India, Argentina, and other large creditors fully integrated in the British trade system. England's indebtedness, therefore, in its wartime form represented a very great threat to America's postwar plans and to the Bretton Woods Agreement, which England had yet to ratify. The United States had to obtain freely convertible currencies, among other things, if it was not to be thwarted. Bretton Woods, in any event, permitted a five-year period after the creation of the International Monetary Fund before imposing free currency convertibility on all its members, and was scarcely sufficient to solve the really central issue of Anglo-American economic relations. British endorsement of Article VII of the Lend Lease Agreement meant everything to everybody, and the British had frustrated all American wartime efforts to confer on its specific terms and future economic collaboration. By the spring of 1945 the State Department's fear that British procrastination would undo its carefully constructed plans helped along the decision to drastically cut Lend Lease aid to England in May 1945. Despite an earlier formal understanding to reduce Lend Lease in a manner calculated to permit some planned British reconversion to civilian production, ugly and growing rumors of fierce competition for export markets were circulating in both nations—a symptom of more to come.[2]

The dangers of British autonomy to American ends Washington articulated with immense sophistication during the last months of the war. "The British financial problem is admittedly the greatest present barrier to rapid progress towards free multilateral payments and relation of barriers to trade," Clayton wrote on June 25; "it threatens not only delay but, indeed, the ultimate success of our economic foreign program." Despite "British reluctance to borrow," a fact no one disputed at the time, it would be necessary to pressure the British to take a large loan, ". . . laying down conditions that would insure a sound advance towards our post-war objectives."[3] Above all, these would include the elimination of the sterling area's dollar pool, the introduction of free currency convertibility by non-British residents on current transactions, and the substantial reduction of Empire trade preferences as part of a reciprocal trade agreement.

This loan, an issue "of the utmost importance," the United States ratified the following month as a key step in using "every possible measure . . . to take advantage of the present unique opportunity to preserve and strengthen the free-enterprise basis of world trade."[4] During those very days the British made clear their objections to most of the critical specifics of America's plans for the ITO and its interpretation of Article VII. The triumph of the Labour Party in the general elections at the end of July deepened the threat to America's postwar goals, adding the menace of noncooperative socialism to the English problem. At the beginning of August, with the admonition that he was there to reach a "business-like" agreement, Clayton visited London and outlined the contours of demands already well known to the British. The British resisted over the subsequent days in terms the American ambassador, John G. Winant, thought "extremely pessimistic," and the chief British negotiator, John Maynard Keynes, in the name of equalizing wartime sacrifices, naïvely held out for an interest-free loan or even an outright grant. By mid-August, as the war against Japan was coming to an end, the discussions linking general postwar economic policy to a loan became acrimonious, even threatening. Then, on August 21, Truman terminated all Lend Lease aid to Britain. "This devastating blow," Harold Macmillan recalls, ". . . was wholly unexpected." [5] "It was a great shock. The tap was turned off at a moment's notice," a plaintive Prime Minister, Clement Attlee, later commented in bewilderment. "It made quite an impossible situation. That's why we had to go and ask for an American loan right away."[6] With the initiative on their side, the Americans pressed for full-scale talks that were to open in Washington on September 11.

The United States approached the loan negotiations determined to fit the British into the larger commercial and financial structure so vital to its postwar goals and to make its success in doing so the price of a loan. It was the need to develop American export trade, and to penetrate nations under British sterling restrictions, that underlay American policy, and the private, internal State Department documents on this question leave no doubt that selfless, abstract questions of idealism played no role whatsoever in the matter. Equally relevant was the fact that "should a credit be extended to the United Kingdom, most of it would be utilized to make purchases in the United States."[7]

The details of the acrimonious, hard bargaining that continued for nearly three months have been reported elsewhere. The disagreements, which ranged from Keynes's naïve suggestion that the United States award a $6 billion outright grant to the far more serious issue of currency convertibility, were all predictable. More to the point than the hard bargaining that brought the compromise sum down to $3.75 billion, or the British failure to withdraw over the currency convertibility issue after considering doing so, was the very event itself, an episode reflective of the shift in world power that history had effected and that the United States was now seeking to formalize to its own advantage. For the loan discussion was only the first of many steps during the months following the war in which the United States transferred to its own jurisdiction the obligations, and privileges, of British imperial power. Raw materials and base privileges also came to the fore during the debates, to recede temporarily as the Americans got on with their main concern, but in due course they touched upon every issue of the distribution of world power between Britain and the United States.

The final agreement charged the English 2 percent interest for the $3.75 billion loan, but it could be waived under certain circumstances. Within a year after the loan went into effect the British were obligated to end their so-called "dollar pool," which had forced all sterling bloc members' dollar earnings to go to London, where only the British could release them. More significant was the free convertibility of all sterling for current transactions into any currency, also to take effect within a year. Import restrictions were sharply circumscribed, and the British were obligated to the principle of not reducing their imports from the United States by import ceilings not also applied to the Empire. And in a separate statement the two countries endorsed the ITO charter draft the United States was to release on December 6 and agreed to enter bilateral talks to take ". . . definitive measures for the relaxation of trade barriers of all kinds."[8]

Events were soon to reveal that the precariously optimistic assumptions on which the United States based the loan, especially regarding a worsening of the British balance of trade or American inflation, made the entire undertaking a dubious commitment for the British. It was possible, indeed, mainly because of Keynes's distinctive role in Anglo-American economic relations and the ambiguous Labour Party tradition of internationalism which led to further buffeting for British power over subsequent years. In effect, Britain had grown to unrivaled stature under the ideology of free trade, and many of its leaders, of all parties, at the end of 1945 failed to see how completely irrelevant it was either to the decline of British power or their own internal social goals. Keynes's own record on this score was no less ambivalent, for at times he saw the dangers of American-style world economic integration to an inflationary full-employment policy. By fall 1945, however, like many of his peers he still was attracted to the convertibility of sterling and all currencies as having a virtue in itself, a doctrine upon which he had been raised but which was about as realistic as the hope for an outright $6 billion American gift. The Labour Party, for its part, had neither a consistent theory of the relationship of the international economy to domestic socialism nor a clear vision of the larger, exclusively power, dimensions of the American loan campaign. Neutralized by the seemingly internationalist rhetoric of the American program, as they had been by Wilsonianism after World War I, Labour's penchant for vague moral responses disarmed them sufficiently to permit their obeisance to outmoded ideas applied to very different conditions from those prevailing for England when it gave birth to the theory of economic liberalism, leaving it to face Britain's future by looking toward its past.

The British reaction to the loan terms revealed how rationally many other Englishmen could still evaluate the facts of life, for they recognized that no charity or friendship was intended. Apart from the sense of abuse, as expressed by the *Economist* that "it is, of course, aggravating to find that our reward for losing a quarter of our total national wealth in the common cause is to pay tribute . . . to those who have been enriched by the war," was the realization that the terms were onerous beyond endurance.[9] Empire-oriented Conservatives made it plain they were confronting ". . . the robust buccaneering spirit of modern American economic imperialism. . . . The British Empire is the oyster which this loan is to prise open."[10] The Conservative Party was furious and profoundly divided, despite Churchill's endorsement of the loan, with the majority either abstaining or voting against it. A minority of the Labour Party opposed the loan as "Wall Street" imperialism, but on December 12, without enthusiasm, the Labour Party sustained it through Parliament.

Despite its initial profound skepticism toward the Labour Party's nominal socialism, which the loan was also intended to control, the State Department now knew that the socialists had delivered what conservative capitalists, motivated by nationalist doctrine, had denied them throughout the war. The lesson was formally acknowledged in Winant's dispatches, which spelled out the conflict between the "internationalist" aspects of socialist doctrine and the imperialist and bloc strategy of traditional conservatism.[11] Temporarily, at least, Labour had abandoned much of its autonomy over internal economic planning to accept a program scarcely consistent with doctrinaire socialism. Suffused with anti-Communism, such social democracy might indeed become a most natural, perhaps the most reliable, ally of the special brand of internationalism the United States was now offering the torn world.

The British Loan: Power and Purpose

The loan to Britain involved a panoply of considerations, but in the end it reflected the United States' desire to thrust out into the world, assume great tasks, and overcome obstacles, no matter how expensive, to the fulfillment of its peace aims. It was, both in principle and in magnitude, the first major test of American postwar policy. Aside from the fact that it represented a seeming triumph in the elimination of British obstacles to Washington's deeply cherished wartime goals, and just one more aspect of the shift of world economic power to the United States, it also involved the first great confrontation with domestic forces, especially Congress, that might hobble the efficient implementation of the Truman administration's global strategy. It was the overture to what was to follow.

American leaders always perceived the true reasons for the British loan and were quite aware that it had been forced upon the hesitant English in order to eliminate what appeared to be the major obstacle to the realization of American objectives. More important was to be the fact that they attempted to have Congress and the public accept the program in the name of these goals and that they almost failed thereby—a lesson they were not to forget. For America's first major postwar expansion was not initially justified in the name of anti-Communism, and only later was this rationale move to the fore. For with or without the existence of Russia, the circumstances would have required something akin to the loan to remove the English barrier to the implementation of the American dream.

The reasons for the loan to England were quite uncomplicated, and England was the first to obtain aid not because it was the neediest or most war-torn—it was scarcely either—but because it was so important to the American foreign economic strategy. This obvious fact immediately disturbed the more "modern" Republicans, such as John Foster Dulles, then a key foreign policy adviser, and Senator Arthur Vandenberg of Michigan, the indispensable architect of a bipartisan foreign policy and the White House's main link to a Senate majority. In effect, the two men worried, the logic of giving England a loan could also be applied to other nations if necessary, and they could not even deny Russia if they might purchase its cooperation. At this rate, they concluded, other loans would follow so long as the circumstances warranted, and for this they were not quite prepared, even though they were not willing to oppose the English loan in principle.

On January 30 Truman sent Congress a special message urging the passage of the loan as a major step in creating a world economy compatible with American interests, one that would define ". . . the course of American and British economic relations for many years to come," and nearly all subsequent official administration spokesmen, from Acheson to Secretary of Treasury Fred Vinson down, restricted themselves to variations of this theme. "It will keep open a market . . .," but ". . . its most important purpose from our point of view is to cause the removal of emergency controls exercised by the United Kingdom over its international transactions far more speedily. . . ."[12] Not once did they allude to the question of Russia. "In some ways," Acheson was to declare that month, "the joint American and British statement on commercial policy is the most important part of the agreement."[13] With increasing sophistication, the United States integrated the importance of eliminating Empire preferences or inconvertible sterling pools into a complete and accurate picture of America's effort to remake the world economy and supply itself with large foreign markets, full employment, and ample supplies of the world's raw materials.

Yet the White House initiated the campaign for the colossal sum on an abstract level, however accurate it was, and was soon to hear that congressional sentiment, aided by an overwhelmingly hostile public reaction, was reticent at best. It was not sufficient to proclaim, as Truman told a Democratic gathering on March 23, "World trade must be restored—and it must be returned to private enterprise."[14] The administration, and especially Clayton's office, then initiated an offensive to translate the question into markets for cotton, tobacco, and trucks. Senator James O. Eastland of Mississippi, certain the loan would aid his region, urged the White House to mobilize the Cotton Growers Association, and the administration soon made the suitable gestures to the region. Clayton wrote virtually hundreds of businessmen about the magnitude of the issue, urging them in turn to reach their congressmen.

Such assistance from the ranks of key businessmen with export orientations and needs was to prove critical, perhaps decisive, where the administration's rather abstract arguments failed to succeed. For the interested business community knew what was at stake. In the prewar decade, *Business Week* warned, Britain held a stronger hand than the United States in both world imports and exports, and if the sterling bloc reemerged in its unreconstructed form, and proceeded to create bilateral trade arrangements, ". . . the U.S. would be in a weak bargaining position. . . ." Not only would England cut off America's access to such potentially vast trade areas as India, Australia, or the colonies, but it would be compelled to intensify its own socialization at home, specially in export-oriented industries. Should Congress pass the loan and London's cooperation be obtained, "Britain thus would have a larger quid to offer for a quo."[15] The truth of this warning was taken to heart by knowledgeable businessmen, who generally paid little attention to hostile critics of the loan, such as Bernard Baruch, who did not agree that an American loan was the way to stop socialism.

But the Senate scarcely responded to administration pleas, and it took all of Vandenberg's ingenuity to warm it to the proposal. The question was ". . . a matter of *intelligent self-interest,*" he was to argue to the Senate in late April, ". . . *full production* under *free enterprise* and *free competition* . . ." or ". . . a dominating surge of bloc arrangements and trade alliances . . . which would force us into kindred action in reciprocal self-defense. It would be economic politics in the pattern of power politics."[16] "Washington this week threatens to precipitate a world economic crisis of the first order," *Business Week* correctly speculated in early May in describing the loan's possible defeat.[17] Hesitantly, after narrowly defeating nine major amendments, including one to force Britain to sell some of its Latin American possessions (a proposition that had House followers as well), the Senate barely passed the bill 46 to 34. The House was yet more unruly and problematical, and administration spokesmen appeared before its Committee on Banking and Currency with their traditional arguments and documented appeals to the farm bloc that had proved critical in the Senate but were now to meet a frightening hostility. Major business groups and bankers also spoke for the loan, but the combination of statistics on meat or textile exports, and pleas to rechannelize the socialist government, barely offset the efforts of the Zionists, Irish, and traditional Midwestern isolationists. Only the most intense pressures from key business and farm leaders, especially those high in the councils of the Republican Party, convinced a sufficient number of House members to pass the loan bill by 219 to 155 on July 13.

The British loan experience marked a turning point in the Truman administration's handling of foreign economic policy. That policy was based, in the first instance, on the American economy's needs, and the United States had decided on it well before a hesitant England asked for a loan on the terms it knew the Americans would attach to it. One cannot reiterate too often that whatever the policy Russia had pursued, or even had it not existed, the forward thrust of American power the loan symbolized would have occurred in any event. In presenting the matter to Congress the administration had been quite candid and honest about its purposes and goals, a fact that had only increased British anxieties. But the strategy failed with domestic public opinion, for polls during mid-1946 revealed that the large majority of the nation was hostile and indifferent to the loan and thought the United States would obtain no benefit from it. The administration's approach, seeking to justify an economic program in economic terms, had been insufficient, and it was only the fear of Russia and Communism, a weak and irrelevant argument the administration did not believe and had not exploited, that finally swung the critical number of Senate and especially House members to vote for the bill. "I have felt that the loan was soundly based on just one thing," John Taber, the critical Republican in the House Committee on Appropriations, who was to prove a linchpin to much more legislation in the future, was to argue, "i.e., the helping to build up a buffer state which would be friendly to us as against Russian aggression. . . ."[18] In reality the issue was not whether England would be strong or weak, pro- or anti-Russian, for the loan was not to alter its position in either regard, but willing to cooperate with the United States' global economic mission—a point Truman reiterated upon signing the loan on July 15. But the lesson could not be lost on the administration. If packaging the implementation of its foreign economic policy in anti-Communism would assist its enactment through a reticent Congress and past a hostile public, it was a step of less consequence than risking failure in the attainment of vital goals.

American economic expansionism, essentially from mid-1946 onward, therefore became justified very largely in the name of anti-Communism. The administration was already clearly aware that the defeat of the Left, whether socialist or bolshevik, was a vital precondition of the United States' economic goals, and to this degree the connection is quite logical.[19] But it is essential to comprehend the specific reasons for its genesis and for the subsequent submergence of all the fundamental and real causes of American actions. For moralism and a brand of internationalism, and a seeming charity in the name of anti-Communism, proved more successful than data on the export of textiles or trucks. When the next great crisis of the world economy was to arise, the American response was colored by its experience with the British loan. It would not be a transaction; it would be a crusade, under the guise of a sharp departure in the assumptions and purposes of American foreign policy.

The Middle East Cockpit

In the last analysis, the critical measure of United States intentions for the world economy was what it did rather than promised, and the extent of its selflessness would depend almost entirely on sacrifices it made and opportunities it allowed other nations to seize. Only such forbearance on the part of the most powerful nation in the world would reveal whether or not it had embarked on an expansive course, a variation of traditional imperialism, rather than a misguided but essentially moralistic and disinterested undertaking. To the British, this was the essence of the matter, and impinged on the question of real privileges and objects: oil, colonies, concessions, tin, rubber, and the like. Only the outcome in the world of material affairs would reveal to England whether America was concerned with reform or a new division of the world economy.

The wartime experience had filled the British with initial skepticism, and the question of oil had become the sharpest source of disagreement, soon spilling over to the intimately related political issues involving Middle Eastern regimes and their international allegiances.

The United States, despite its public affirmation of multilateralism and the open door, saw Middle Eastern affairs as essentially a question of Anglo-American relations and a reallocation of traditional spheres of influence. Starting in 1943, Washington pressed England to reopen the question of prewar oil divisions fixed for the area in 1928, when British predominance was acknowledged in the "Red Line" agreement, and in mid-1944 it forced the British to accept a quite abstract postwar petroleum agreement the Senate then refused to ratify. The 1944 draft treaty, which was to be followed by bilateral agreements covering other vital world raw materials, appeared so universal as to impinge on domestic United States oil output —thereby mobilizing internal opposition from Southwest interests—when in fact it was intended mainly to break further British supremacy in the Middle East. United States oil policy firmly postulated that America would not open the Western Hemisphere to outside interests and that it would attempt to increase, both absolutely and relatively, American-controlled world oil output elsewhere. This exclusion of England from new areas revealed very clearly the difference between the rhetoric of the open door, or erstwhile trade equality for all, and imperialist designs on the most vital ingredient of industrial power.

The United States' task was simplified by the desire of Iraq and Iran to welcome new and greater American involvement as a balance to British domination over their region, and to this extent moderate nationalism served to weaken British power and aid American goals at one and the same time. At the end of the war nearly one-half of the world's known reserves were located in the Middle East, a radical shift from the situation existing at the end of World War I, when the Western Hemisphere was the center of the world's output. And in 1939 Britain and its European partners had controlled nearly four-fifths of the Middle East's output. These facts, if nothing else, required a new and active American role in the Middle East.

In the months preceding the end of the war, well before there arose any crises involving Russia or the Left, America renewed its determination to greatly extend its postwar role in the area. This required not only new concessions to American firms but ". . . a cessation of British political interventionism . . .," a process that threatened to deprive United States investors of success. "The Middle East is and will remain one of the principal testing grounds of the ideals for which the war is being fought," the State Department insightfully predicted in May 1945, "and of the world security system now being constituted."[20]

The key areas in the Middle East for the United States were Saudi Arabia and Iran, and though we have confined Iran to Chapter 9, it was very much a part of the larger question of the control of oil as well as relations with the USSR. To Washington, Saudi Arabia was a place ". . . where the oil resources constitute a stupendous source of strategic power, and one of the greatest material prizes in world history. . . ."[21] The problem there was how to keep financing Ibn Saud's feudal regime so as to thwart alleged British efforts to penetrate the nation, a cabal which American diplomats exaggerated all out of proportion to fact, and maintain the American monopoly over its oil output. The United States was glad to meet Saud's needs and to reap the ultimate rewards as well. Washington justified such extensions of American power in the name of profit and strategic interests, and portrayed Britain as the villain in a regional picture not wholly confined to Arabia or Iran. American security in Saudi Arabia, the American minister to that country, William A. Eddy, warned in September, required that ". . . the mortmain of British economic strangulation . . . be relaxed from the throats of neighboring governments" and that ". . . the notorious political and diplomatic precedence of the British . . . be abolished in Egypt and Iraq." Informally, as well, during the latter months of 1945 the State Department was sorely tempted to take over the training of Syria's military forces as a means of extending America's power and presence in the region. In November the directors of both the European and the Near Eastern offices thought such a course advisable because the United States ". . . should not be content, as was so often the case prior to the war, to adopt a passive attitude and to avoid embarrassing decisions in distant parts of the world. . . ."[22] If this mood was not fulfilled via aid to Syria at the time, it immediately found other expressions that were no less important. In March 1946 the State Department reiterated its desire to expand into the Persian Gulf fields by giving ". . . all possible diplomatic support to U.S. commercial interests, both present and potential, vis-a-vis the British and local Governments," cooperating with the British but also ". . . expanding our existing business interests wherever practicable. . . ."[23]

Formally, in September 1945 Washington sent a delegation to England under Harold Ickes to renegotiate a comprehensive oil agreement less likely to meet domestic opposition, taking along for good measure some of the earlier opponents close to the domestic industry. The result was a document that was quite vague and open to conflicting interpretation, dedicating itself at one and the same time to competition and nondiscrimination in the world oil industry as well as respect for the existing divisions that effectively excluded all but the Anglo-Americans. But the British made no secret of the fact that they wished to exclude United States firms from areas that they had already concessioned, particularly Iran. Rather cleverly they suggested to the Americans that if they really favored the open door on oil, they permit Shell to participate in Latin American oil development, something Washington was quite determined to prevent.

Informally, however, the State Department and American oil interests prepared for the more serious work of inflicting a fatal blow to British power in Middle Eastern oil. Standard Oil of New Jersey had already embarked on a giant new pipe line for its Iraqi concessions that threatened the fragile output and marketing agreements reached in the 1928 Red Line Agreement, as if to warn that its termination was now merely a matter of time. In December, Standard let the embassy in London know that it was prepared to abolish the Red Line Agreement and would welcome Washington's official help in the undertaking. Washington was to prove more than willing, for it fully equated Standard's and other American concessions with the larger national interest. And in the same period the State Department announced the designation of at least thirteen petroleum officers and attachés to key posts throughout the world to further aid United States expansion into the world oil economy.

All that was now necessary was finally to destroy the 1928 agreement and to begin the combat for control of the Middle East in earnest. The first hint that this would happen came in January 1946, when Standard of New Jersey dissociated itself from it, and for the remainder of the year the American firms, formerly supporting the compact, now made clear their intent to dissolve it. By August, with full State Department encouragement to increase their share of output in the region, the destruction of the Red Line compact was far advanced as Washington urged the American companies to obtain a larger share of the area's production. No later than November the agreement was informally ruptured. Though the matter was to go into court for several years, the British could not stem their inevitable demise. Whereas in 1946 the British-Dutch firms controlled 66 percent of Middle East oil output, by 1953 they fell to 31 percent, while the American share leaped from 31 percent to 60 percent over the same period—as contrasted to 16 percent in 1939![24]

These official and private actions went hand in hand and were part of a unified American expansion into the Middle East whose original impetus was oil, or what Truman later termed ". . . the raw-material balance of the world. . . ."[25] We cannot overemphasize that the United States had embarked on this course before the end of the war and accelerated it immediately thereafter, well before the crises which are the major themes of this book and in great measure primarily a reflection of such central economic concerns and their political consequences. The first round of that sustained crisis, and the ultimate justification for the rest that followed, was oil and Anglo-American relations. The leaders in London, Washington, and Moscow saw this very clearly, and the Russians sanguinely regarded the traditional imperialist rivalry for markets and materials as a decisive weakness in the Anglo-American alliance.

The Russians based their optimism on an appreciation of the extent to which the British had stoutly resisted American designs during the war, but failed to take account of how consistent defeat and economic decline had lowered their ability and willingness to defend their prewar prerogatives. During the spring of 1946, Harriman noted the emergence of a British "inferiority complex," as Leahy recalled, and the extent of American leverage over England, as expressed in the loan discussions, was now plain to see.[26] The British were now less concerned with defending their old privileges than with being able to market the oil they had left as they saw fit. The Anglo-Americans saw themselves both as rivals and as allies, the British hoping to stress cooperation, the United States, penetration. Still, the United States did not wish to see the complete demise of traditional British power in the Middle East for fear the Russians, instability, and radical nationalism would fill the vacuum. The Americans did not care initially to assume all the political and military overhead charges that befall imperialist nations, but Britain's inability to sustain those inherited obligations meant that it would now welcome some greater measure of American assistance in this sphere—and attempt to tend its restricted area with less cost. Moderate nationalism, therefore, became a useful tool to the United States insofar as it helped ease out England, but a danger to it when it opened the door to Russia or also designated the United States as the major obstacle to autonomous economic development. In a sense, therefore, the United States hoped to enter into the Middle East at the expense of British power, but in fact it helped weaken England faster than it had anticipated or desired, and for this reason it was soon compelled to maintain a fleet as a first step in compensating for the growing vacuum. But given its objectives, the United States could only proceed in the region to follow the course it had elected even before the end of the war. America responded predictably to the stormy Middle Eastern crises of the year and one-half after the war, perhaps as important as any prior to the spring of 1947, for they were the logic of the conscious expansion of American power into the area.[27]

Anglo-American Relations: Spheres of Influence

For England the question of United States foreign economic policy was whether the Americans would give as much as they asked, and if the immediate postwar experience might be more satisfactory than the sordid intrigues that had continuously marred Anglo-American relations during the common cause itself. Otherwise, what the Americans called a recon- structed, open door world economy would merely mean an American- dominated world in which Britain would play a declining role.

After petroleum, the United States had an ever-growing interest in the numerous other mineral and agricultural raw materials and foodstuffs that had also been a source of rivalry and contention between the Americans and English after World War I. These commodities, because they were often concentrated in a few countries, impinged on nominal political questions which were really an aspect of economic control. Moreover, as we shall see in greater detail later in this chapter, the United States defined its policy in light of its peculiar role both as a deficit nation in certain materials, such as rubber, tin, and minerals, and as surplus producer and exporter in others, of which cotton was the most notable.

To the British and their imperial allies, it appeared as if the Americans were calling for freer trade and reform where it was to their interest as an importer, but pursuing a very different line regarding their exports, particu- larly cotton. There, as the Egyptians pointed out, the United States was subsidizing its exports at the ultimate expense of the interested Third World nations. But on the questions of the role of cotton, tin, rubber, and wool the United States throughout 1945–1946 adopted variable strategies de- signed, in the last analysis, to buy cheaply and sell dearly. In April 1945 it proposed the international regulation of cotton production and export prices—a far cry from Hullian trade doctrine—in order to prevent the surpluses it constantly feared. In natural rubber the United States, in con- sultation with the American rubber industry, worked with Britain, France, and the Netherlands to regulate the buying price for the United States at a level it wished to pay, an act that was as close to state trading as any Washington was to condemn on the part of others. In wool and tin, too, the United States was to attempt to bring price and demand into line via international coordination designed to aid United States interests.[28]

But the decisive element in the control over world raw materials prices and output was political, and this meant, in the last analysis, that the sterling bloc and colonial regimes, and British power in the largest sense, was the critical obstacle to the United States at the war's end. This fact remained no less true over the following years, when the United States rediscovered that its unfavorable balance of trade with the raw materials nations was endemic in the unequal relationship between industrial and Third World nations on which the United States has developed a critical, growing dependency. So long as these nations were in the sterling bloc, their earnings of United States dollars would go to aid England's dollar reserves, and not be spent to purchase American goods.

The importance of this problem, encompassing the tin- and rubber-rich nation of Thailand, arose even before the war was over, but reflects a constant Anglo-American struggle that never ceased but occurred in numerous ways beyond the sights of journalists and scholars who write about world politics in more deductive and less sordid and informed terms. The Thais had been an ally of Japan during the war, but when Bangkok declared war on the United States and England, the Americans chose to ignore it. The British, much more interested in the future of the region, took the gesture as it was intended and at the end of the war moved to discipline the chronically opportunistic Bangkok government. But having nominally been at war with its traditional regional customers, the Thais had accumulated vast reserves of scarce rice that had tripled in value over the war. To counter this inflation, Britain demanded that the Thais deliver 1.5 million tons of free rice. In the largest sense, the real issue of Thailand was the future control of the region and British predominance in it, and since the British had fought the war against Japan along the Southeast Asian rim, and the United States had immediately claimed predominance in the Pacific and East Asian region, London was ready to draft Thailand for its sphere of influence. Along with the demand for rice, the British asked for Thai consent to vague military and economic concessions sufficient to make it a protectorate. And since this explicitly involved control over Thai tin and rubber, the United States immediately balked, asking the British for assurance ". . . that its economic and commercial policies in regard to Thailand are in general harmony with the American principles. . . ." Those principles demanded not the implementation of free trade or Wilsonian liberalism, but rather equal participation in a combined Anglo-American board controlling all Thai exports. The Thais, anxious to avoid Britain's vengeance, now assured Washington of their future "unreserved collaboration," and left it to the Americans to save them.[29]

Their confidence was not misplaced, for the controversy soon became a matter for the attention of no less than Acheson, Bevin, and Attlee themselves, and London's substantial alterations of its demands on the Thais only partially mollified Washington. American insistence that the British exclude any hint of authorizing a regional military of economic bloc from the Thai surrender to the British led to new modifications. American officials covertly encouraged the grateful Thais to hold firm and delay. During November and December 1945 the United States threatened even to reestablish diplomatic relations with Bangkok, technically still at war with England, and by the end of the year forced the British to back down again and again to the point that both the Thais and the Americans were satisfied. To the Thais, a new friend and protector had arrived to replace Japan. Acheson, cabling Winant on December 19, correctly and fully perceived the implications of the episode: "US interested in whole economic development and stability Southeast Asia. Economic open door cornerstone American policy."[30]

This profound, yet still partially abstract, concern for the future of American power even in Southeast Asia encompassed India as well and was only one more phase of the deeply held American desire to dissolve and replace British privileges with their own. In India, Westmore Wilcox, special representative to the Foreign Economic Administration from August 1945 to May 1946, advised Washington of that nation's vast raw materials supplies and potential markets and urged a strategy of gaining India's independence from England's political and economic control at one and the same time. The Congress Party, he pointed out, should be offered loans if, upon independence it awarded special trade guarantees to the United States.[31]

England, not Russia, was the main object of this eager and aggressive American thrust into Asia. And in this willingness to intervene into the remoteness of even Thailand, a proposition few Americans would have thought credible at the time, we may find one of the many seeds of the greatest crisis in postwar American diplomacy.

Latin America and the Closed Door

If denied a sphere of influence in the Middle East or Asia because of the nominal American dedication to freedom of trade, what could Britain expect in return in that area—Latin America—historically assigned a special, exclusive status in Washington's international doctrine?

During the war the United States had already begun to lay obstacles in the path of England's efforts to restore its prewar Latin American markets, and gradually the issue focused on Argentina, which Washington considered pro-German but with whom the British had continued normal trade for meat and foodstuffs. Argentina was a threat, insofar as it was traditionally the leader of efforts to mobilize a bloc of neighboring states to counterbalance the Yankees, but also an attractive market that had managed by the end of the war to pile up a billion dollars in gold and dollar reserves. Until February 1946, Washington remained implacably hostile to Juan Perón, who up to October 1945 was the real power in the Farrell government. In the management of delicate relations with Perón, no man was to play a more important role in 1946 than George S. Messersmith, the ambassador to Mexico and, after March 1946, to Buenos Aires.

Messersmith saw Anglo-American rivalry as perhaps the central diplomatic issue in Latin America, the ultimate stakes being the control of the economic development of the vast, rich continent. As ambassador to Mexico he had feared, without cause, that British interests would manage to reenter the nationalized oil industry there, to the exclusion of the United States. Elsewhere, he informed Washington, they were disrupting hemispheric unity, which in his mind was tantamount to United States hegemony, and threatening to close off United States exports. But by the time Messersmith arrived in Argentina to repair the very low state of affairs with that country, Perón, who had won a stunning electoral triumph in February in large part due to open, crude State Department opposition to him, was having second thoughts about his relations with England and his own ambitions. He wished to hedge against the shift in world power toward the United States by improving relations with Washington while moving more cautiously elsewhere, but also to maintain traditional independent national goals. For one thing, England's relative importance in Latin American trade was sharply declining as its industrial and arms exports proved inadequate for Perón's desires, and it was selling off the larger part of its investments, particularly in Argentina. When Perón met Messersmith in mid-March 1946 he disparaged British plotting and began opening the way to the normalization of relations which Spruille Braden, now the assistant secretary of state for Latin America after openly warring with Perón while ambassador to Buenos Aires until August 1945, had adamantly refused to repair. Messersmith was easily convinced, and his confidence in Perón grew as the dictator added pleas for anti-Russian solidarity along with criticisms of London. Braden was realistically suspicious of the Argentine leader's professions, and his dispute with Messersmith over this question ultimately forced Truman to retire both of them the following year. But in April 1946, Washington imposed three demands on Perón as the condition of normalized relations, essentially to assert its power as the undisputed leader of the hemisphere, ranging from ratification of the Act of Chapultepec to the denazification of schools and the liquidation of Nazi-owned properties. Braden, himself one of the largest investors in Chile's copper industry, shared the United States copper firms' justifiable fear that Perón would seek to dominate the region and compete with them via state-owned investing companies for control of the Chilean economy. He inclined toward forcing his removal from power. At the same time, he could not minimize the fact that whenever possible Argentina was buying European goods in preference to American.[32]

Despite Washington's reticence, essentially the result of Braden's strategy, Messersmith's equally hard-nosed view eventually prevailed, for Perón was temporarily ready to cater a great deal more to the colossus to the north without abandoning a return to his competitive "third position." Messersmith urged Byrnes to help him ". . . endeavor to get the Argentine to turn her eyes away from Europe," to smash ". . . the strange impression in London . . . that they must counteract us in the Argentine to maintain a spearhead for Britain's trade and influence in this hemisphere."[33] Perón's ambition to lead a southern bloc, the ambassador now concluded prematurely, had given way to more realistic considerations.

The utter failure of its policy of hostility eventually caused the United States to welcome the ever independent and unpredictable Perón back into the hemispheric system. For one thing, in May 1946 representatives of United States oil companies asked Messersmith to broach the question of new concessions to Perón; the dictator had exhibited enthusiasm; and now the influential United States firms were thinking more highly of the regime. The ambassador was also convinced that Argentina was one of the few hemispheric powers ". . . prepared to collaborate in any sound measures . . . to prevent communist penetration." Though Perón recognized Russia that June, even as he was attempting to buy arms from the United States, he also moved to approve the Act of Chapultepec and on August 1 publicly avowed that Argentina would fight on the United States' side in any major war. Lastly, by late 1946 Messersmith felt that ". . . the British will play more fairly with us in the future than they have in the past . . ." and that had they done so earlier " [a] good deal of our trouble with the Argentine would not have arisen. . . ."[34]

The broader power context superficially settled, largely because of Britain's straitened economic condition, the hemisphere was to become yet more United States–dominated, as yesterday's independent unacceptable dictators became today's allies. The new policy, which the United States initiated in earnest after January 1947, reflected the decline of British power and the added weight the United States possessed in the postwar context. To a much smaller extent, it revealed a fear of the Left and the need for powerful, ideologically reliable friends. Lastly was the new market for arms that Latin America offered, and in May 1946, on behalf of the Joint Chiefs of Staff, General Dwight D. Eisenhower informed Congress that it was necessary to begin ". . . securing within the vital areas of South America a structure that is oriented toward us militarily. . . ."[35] This proposition had an "economic side" as well as a military, as Secretary of War Robert P. Patterson warned Acheson the following spring: ". . . if they cannot get the weapons from us, they will get them elsewhere, and to our disadvantage."[36] Argentina, business circles predicted at the time, would provide the largest market for arms exports.

The British could see or read all this, and much more as well. For their wartime fear that the Americans would continue to treat the Western Hemisphere as a special sphere unto themselves, and have new power to fulfill their will, was quickly realized. And from this, too, they could gauge their future relations to their ally of years past.

United States Exceptionalism

The United States' belief that the attainment of multilateralism and freer trade in the world economy would bring it both prosperity and peace was an unquestioned keystone of its faith, a few critical exceptions notwithstanding. What is most essential about this doctrine is that it revealed only what the United States would demand from others, and often act aggressively to obtain, but not what it would concede in return. Not once would the United States in the immediate postwar period abdicate its assumed right freely to invest and trade, even in Eastern Europe. Apart from the natural desire of other countries to safeguard their own economic interests and needs, what the responsible American leaders never considered was the validity of the thesis of high United States exports automatically following from the total elimination of trade discrimination, and at no time did they intend to permit opening American doors and risking losses to the eventual influx of world competitors.

In Latin America much of the United States' trade was largely the result of its investments rather than the lack of trade discriminations, but the existence of its special quotas and price agreements with Cuba was only one instance where the United States deviated from the standards to which it asked others to conform. It was not so much privileged trade arrangements as the insistent United States demand for total freedom to invest in the region, which axiomatically required a dependent, neocolonial status for the continent, that deepened Latin America's economic ties to the north. United States–owned firms accounted for fully one-third of its exports by 1967. In 1949, 51 percent of all Latin American imports were from the United States, a vast increase over prewar. By the end of the war many British traders saw that the irresistible combination of high United States investment, aggressive trade practices, and special economic treaties and quotas, as with Cuba, would cause the prewar British position to decline substantially.[37]

The starkest case of total United States control over a nation was the Philippines, which was scheduled to receive nominal independence in 1946. At war's end power in the nation rested with political and economic compradors who had extensively collaborated with the Japanese during the war in the same manner they had with the Americans over the preceding decades. Early in 1945 Washington drafted the pending Philippine independence treaty to provide for total free trade between the two countries for twenty years, save for traditional quotas—a measure the State Department immediately acknowledged would create a special and dominating economic relationship. Despite this, and a parallel effort to obtain exclusive United States base rights that seriously compromised Philippine sovereignty, on May 5, 1945, Truman publicly acknowledged that the essentially colonial "special relationship" with the Philippines would continue after independence, greatly embarrassing the trade reformers in the State Department. The following September, American officials began to press the Manila authorities to allow special United States landownership rights in the post-independence era. All this was too blatant for Acheson, who warned Truman on October 1 that the "special relationship" the United States was about to continue in the Philippines ". . . would embarrass our representatives and inevitably lessen our chances of getting satisfactory commitments with respect to trade preferences from the United Kingdom," an observation that did not prevent the State Department the following month from endorsing a twenty-eight-year preferential trade bill that became the core of future United States–Philippines relations.[38]

United States penetration of the Philippine economy was so comprehensive by 1945 that the Americans involved were able successfully, especially via their congressional friends, to preserve the neocolonial trade relationship. The Truman administration was somewhat embarrassed, but easily justified the Philippine Trade Act of April 30, 1946, as a rehabilitation gesture and a step toward ". . . encouragement of private enterprise and private initiative" in the islands. Truman could only add, "We have never entered into similar agreement with any foreign government. Preferential trade relations are alien to the policy of this administration."[39] Such willingness to modify ideology for convenience was precisely what the United States was deploring when it was practiced by others, and the British carefully noted the episode. But the reward for such inconsistency was to be the continued United States domination of the Philippine economy after 1946.

If the United States could not profit from the restrictive measures of other nations, it at least profited from its own, and therefore the United States never adopted a consistent policy and practice on foreign economic policy. Its dual-standard policy was intensified, as well, by the division between the State Department, representing importers of raw materials and exporters of industrial goods and capital, and the Agriculture Department, with its formidable congressional base in the Midwestern farm states. From one-quarter to one-third of all United States exports in the postwar era were agricultural, and this constituency could not be ignored. Farm interests, subsidized by an Agricultural Act of 1935 which stipulated that up to 30 percent of all customs income might go to subsidize farm exports, were especially vulnerable after the war had induced many to move into high-cost production. To them, protectionism was a way of life.

Over the decade after World War II Congress granted an average of about $25 million a year as direct cash payments, mainly for wheat, cotton, and fruit, to agricultural exporters composed of the richer farmers; but indirect subsidies were far larger yet. Up to $300 million were available for direct subsidies in the event prices fell below parity levels. More important, however, were the tariff walls and quotas that kept our foreign agricultural goods: cotton, wheat, sugar, corn, rice, tobacco, peanuts, or any crop under the surplus disposal program. The entire thrust of the United States' agricultural program was to dump surplus crops overseas, exclude competition, and maximize farm income by tailoring food and farm policy to avoid the gluts and depressions that had pauperized prewar agriculture. Though in principle the State Department pursued an ambiguous line, in practice it, too, supported world commodity agreements that aided American producers.[40]

Such inconsistency affected the United States' relations with other agricultural producing nations, and in the long run hurt the Third World most of all. It also revealed to the world that the United States could, in addition to demanding trade concessions from others, define for itself a doctrine of convenience. Hardly any nation could afford to ignore that fact.

It was in this context, with its pragmatic actions in the Middle East, Latin America, or the Philippines revealing the practical import of its goals, that the United States formulated its seemingly more abstract principles and structures for the reformation of the postwar world economy.

The ITO: Means and Ends

Just as Article VII was the United States' wartime theoretical statement of aims for the world economy, the International Trade Organization (ITO) soon became its organizational expression. But the ITO was a means to an end, and even as it was being discussed and structured the United States sought to fulfill its goals in the real world. Practice preceded the theory and illustrated precisely what it was the United States sought to achieve, not the least because time did not stand still for the attainment of American needs, and the experience was a significant, but not major, aspect of United States foreign policy immediately after the war. Well before the ITO proposal was formally offered the world, and during its consideration, the United States was actively cultivating numerous other means of implementing the same goals.

Washington's "Proposals for Expansion of World Trade and Employment" released November 1945 were the formal embodiment of United States peace aims, intended to do for trade what the IMF was designed to in finance. The State Department had drafted them after consultations with such export-oriented business groups as the Committee on Economic Development, National Planning Association, and National Foreign Trade Conference. They were preeminently the work of Hull's leading disciples in the State Department, Clayton and Clair Wilcox. Subsequently others elaborated and hammered them out essentially in the context of the dominating problem of Anglo-American postwar economic relations.

Washington offered the Proposals as the basis of reforming world trade, creating machinery ". . . to promote national and international action for the expansion of the production, exchange, and consumption of goods, for the reduction of tariffs and other trade barriers, and for the elimination of all forms of discriminatory treatment in international commerce. . . ." They covered quotas, embargoes, subsidies, and local taxes—whatever was essential to its general end—but also stipulated that the ITO would have as its major function "[t]o facilitate access by all members, on equal terms, to the trade and raw materials of the world. . . ."[41] Yet they were not a plan for free trade or laissez faire; rather they were structured to meet needs which, in the last analysis, were peculiarly American. They provided for commodity agreements, which would help the United States as a producer of agricultural commodities, but stipulated that consumers, too, should be involved in their drafting, which would help the United States as an importer of minerals. The Proposals appeared, indeed, almost as a doctrine of convenience.

One example of such pragmatism was the United States' own preferential tariffs with Cuba, which shortly before the Proposals were released Clayton clarified privately to mean would not lead to their immediate abrogation but only to further consultations on them, not the least because the American ambassador in Havana warned that their termination would mainly hurt United States exports to Cuba. Yet more important was that the United States scheme postulated "commercial" cooperation, which it equated with normal capitalist methods; but the existence of the Soviet Union and numerous other state trading nations, many not socialist but attempting to regulate foreign exchange, raised fundamental problems. The American Proposals asked that state trading firms ". . . be influenced solely by commercial considerations" and that nations organized wholly on this basis agree to minimum purchase contracts negotiated commercially, clearly requiring the abandonment of the premises of state trading.[42] In effect, it was also an assault on the future of socialism in the world economy.

The State Department was fully aware of the implications of this policy to relations with Russia. The Russians had refused to discuss Article VII throughout the war, and the embassy in Moscow warned Washington that the Russians regarded tariffs as an aspect of economic planning and would not join the American scheme. Since, as we shall see, nations not joining the ITO and granting tariff and trade *quid pro quo*'s were, in effect, to be excluded from the American-led trade system, Russia would become a pariah unless it cooperated. For the rest of 1945 Harriman warned against illusions on this score, but Acheson thought that in the unlikely chance they agreed, the Proposals would permit "intermeshing two economic systems," especially if the Russians would make fixed commitments for future pur-

chases, helping to ". . . contribute to the stability of world trading conditions
. . ." while respecting "commercial" principles in buying.[43] Russia's refusal
to debolshevize was to disappoint Washington's less-than-disinterested
standard for cooperation yet one more time.

Washington labeled the ITO "multilateral," but it was preeminently a
scheme for selective bilateralism, one that acknowledged the fact that once
it solved the problem of England, its bloc, and a handful of other nations,
what happened in the remainder of the world was of minor concern to the
United States. The ITO's executive was to give permanent seats only to
". . . states of chief economic importance," but more important was the way
it was to be implemented at the international conference on trade and
employment Washington hoped to convene by no later than the following
summer.[44] The United States invited only the fifteen most important trading
nations to the planned meeting, including England, France, China, Russia,
India, and the Netherlands. As envisaged from the beginning, each of these
countries was to present schedules of tariff and trade concessions and
demands to every one of the nations gathered there, granting them all equal
rights and ideally leading eventually to some eight hundred bilateral treaties. The world economic sector this alliance controlled would exclude those
who refused to comply.

In the real world, however, it was more vital for the United States to sign
bilateral agreements with the major trading nations, Britain in particular.
When the Anglo-American loan agreement was announced December 6 the
two nations also reported that England ". . . is in full agreement on all
important points in these proposals and accepts them as a basis of international discussion," a concession London gladly made because it knew that
America's deep commitment to its own trade controls, preferences, and
agricultural program would, on the basis of reciprocity, permit England
numerous means for later defending itself.[45] Indeed, America's Proposals
were so vague, and its own inconsistencies so numerous, that over the next
year Poland and Czechoslovakia joined five other nations in endorsing its
purposes.

American efforts to define the nature of the world economy were not
restricted to ITO, for the Bretton Woods Conference, the International
Monetary Fund, and World Bank (IBRD) were scheduled to begin reorgan-
izing world finance in the critical first meeting scheduled for March 1946
in Savannah, Georgia. Washington understood that many of the world's
critical monetary and exchange problems were but a defensive symptom of

the world's trade structure, and the British for this reason regarded monetary and trade problems as a unified issue. Despite its clear understanding of the limits of a one-dimensional approach, the United States was ready to invest some of its hopes as well as cash in the IMF's contribution to attaining American goals. What the experience illustrated was the increasing irrelevance of those objectives to world realities.

The British delegation, headed by Keynes, arrived in Savannah sufficiently committed to the same ultimate goals as the United States to give the new mechanism the opportunity to work, but his bitter experience there shook Keynes's last shred of confidence in working with the United States. Keynes naïvely believed that the IMF and World Bank might be truly international in their scope—aiding the world's return to an economic liberalism that he, too, deeply cherished—despite its voting mechanism allotting votes in proportion to capital, giving the United States, without Latin American help, almost one-third of its votes. He was immediately disillusioned when, over British and the majority of delegates' objections, Secretary of the Treasury Fred Vinson forced the meeting to take Washington as the IMF's and Bank's headquarters. Next the United States began "railroading," to quote a British view, its will on questions of staff and administration, including a responsive American as IBRD executive director—one who had the confidence of Wall Street, the main market for bank bonds. It was now even more apparent that Washington's definition of "internationalism" meant simply using international institutions as methods for extending the United States' economic and political interests. It was to underscore this fact that it situated the headquarters of the new economic structures in the seat of what was intended to be the new center of world power. Chastened by the experience, the British were to put aside their nostalgia for liberal ideology and never again willingly so lower their guard with the Americans.[46]

The World Bank's main deficiency, however, was not its organization, but its purpose—and irrelevance to the existing world economy. Its loans were to be for "productive purposes," and mainly to provide foreign exchange requirements for projects overwhelmingly financed by local capitalists. If it helped such elements find mainly the dollars they needed, thereby aiding American exports after the war, its insistence on high interest from profitable investments, not to mention its practice of selling its bonds through a syndicate headed by the First Boston Corporation and Morgan, Stanley & Company, immediately made it a factor of small significance to Washington's much larger and formidable aims. As American leaders were soon to perceive, both the IMF and the World Bank were pitifully inadequate for the often profitless goals of reconstruction and reformation wartime Washington had projected ahead for peacetime. The world economic and political structure had been shattered far too profoundly to be overhauled by such tepid mechanisms.

The issue of trade policy seemed inordinately more complex, not the least because the English, no sooner than they had endorsed the American proposals for an ITO, declined to meet within three months to reach a detailed accord. Their ostensible excuse was lack of staff and the need to prepare more carefully on the issue of tariffs on their colonial products, but they were probably also waiting for the outcome of the Savannah meeting. While events there confirmed the worst English fears, State Department planners translated their Proposals into a draft charter of the ITO for the London preparatory committee of nineteen nations that eventually opened October 15. Apart from the general developments in Europe we have described in Chapter 6, by the fall of 1946 the British were even more apprehensive about United States intentions and its willingness to give as much as it sought to receive. Socialist critics hit a telling point when they argued that United States multilateralism might also internationalize its depression, spreading unemployment everywhere and necessitating the defensive financial and trade regulations of the post-1929 era. Full employment became this group's justification for proceeding with caution on the ITO, a line the Keynesians also had weakly advanced during the war. Nondiscrimination among unequal economic units merely froze the weak in a position of permanent inferiority, the British Left argued. In the meantime, Britain was already signing massive bilateral, long-term agreements that revealed the course it was to chart.[47]

The United States delegation to the ITO discussion arrived in London with what it thought to be ". . . a very thoroughgoing document . . . to cover almost all types of cases . . .," including, in general, the problems of American agriculture. Here, care was given to commodity agreements that would avoid "serious consequences" to uneconomic producers, while it also demanded adequate supplies at fair prices for consumers.[48] The question of state trading, mainly from Russia but also from other government-endorsed monopolies, was carefully outlined. But the Russians did not attend, and Wilcox thought "[t]heir absence was fortunate," for then state trading could be tabled altogether and purely capitalist forms of trade considered in greater detail. The United States' major objective was to outlaw unauthorized import quotas, the main effect of which was ". . . to discriminate against

American goods." Tariff reductions, also to achieve high United States exports, were the other key goal. It was Australia, with the quiet support of the British and perhaps as its ploy, that stressed the importance of full-employment–oriented economic policies—which implicitly might require a wide range of restrictions. Quite explicitly, they pointed to the consequences of a United States slump to American imports, forcing other nations to protect their monetary reserves by cutting dollar trade. Teaming with the Indians, Australia argued for the desirability of import quotas to promote industrialization in the Third World, an illusory concession the United States made when it granted the ITO the right to permit limited quotas—fully expecting later also to control the ITO executive. Yet the central issue was not Australia or Brazil, but England, which, while "scrupulously correct in its . . . formal support," privately remained passive and "fairly independent," refusing to take a role of leadership. "One gets the impression," reported Wilcox, the head of the delegation, "that the commitments which the United Kingdom has made to us are highly unpalatable to important segments of British opinion. . . ."[49]

Confronted with the impending ITO, powerful elements of American business as well began looking askance at the charter. Despite all its loopholes and special reservations for American interests, particularly in agriculture, protected industrial interests now began seeing the ITO less as a means of exporting than as an opening to foreign competition entering their domestic market. The State Department originally intended using the first meeting, held in London, as a place also to negotiate general tariff reductions. This was delayed until the April 1947 Geneva ITO meeting in order to avoid political difficulties before the November 1946 elections. Indeed, even as Wilcox was in London trying to overcome foreign resistance, reasonable doubt arose whether the Truman administration could sell its foreign economic policy at home. Along with a Republican electoral sweep in the House that was to threaten Truman's military spending policy as well, what was at stake was the very scope and conduct of American foreign policy and the attainment of the United States' fundamental objectives in the world.

The delay in tariff negotiations scarcely mollified the Republicans and their friends in the nonexport sectors of American industry. Aware of this predicament, on November 9 Truman announced the forthcoming Geneva meeting along with its tariff negotiations, stressing that "[t]hey are not solely trade bargains," but would also ". . . pave the way for the kind of economic world . . . envisaged in the [ITO] charter." The trade agreement negotiations that were to come out of Geneva were especially important. "Their success or failure will largely determine whether the world will move towards a system of liberal international trade . . . or will pay the heavy costs of narrow economic nationalism."[50]

From November 1946 onward the existence of the first hostile Congress threatened the very thrust and feasibility of American foreign policy as it had emerged after 1942. This fact cannot be divorced from the United States' response to other world events, for the justification of new policy had to take account of domestic opposition as well as external facts. This interaction is one of the most significant developments in postwar American foreign policy.

After the November elections the Republican Party drove home the dangers the administration now confronted. Symptomatic of the new situation was the demand of the conservative but powerful American Farm Bureau's president, Edward A. O'Neil, that bipartisan advisers representing farmers, labor, and industry be sent to the Geneva and subsequent meetings. Writing O'Neil, Truman warned him there were simply too many conflicting economic groups to consult, which was correct enough, but informally forced Clayton to let the Farm Bureau know such an arrangement could probably be made. At the end of the year Vandenberg asked Clayton to submit any specific agreement on trade he might reach at Geneva to the affected industry for final consultation, a proposition so dangerous as to threaten, if the British knew of it, the very ITO system. But by the beginning of 1947 the mounting tension between Congress and the administration over trade policy was being publicly discussed. Both parties agreed that they wished to remove foreign trade controls, but that they had to consider those American farmers protected by quotas, and the Republicans were in addition supporting industries demanding high tariffs. The Republicans, *Business Week* reliably announced, wanted congressional approval of each tariff-cut package, or a veto over individual agreements. Apart from the monumental complications this new mood was to generate in 1947, "The foreigners may take it as fair warning that the whole reciprocal tariff program will fall in a heap, come 1948," when presumably a Republican White House would undo the ITO and much else besides.[51]

Though the State Department organized public hearings in various cities on the ITO over the next months, they were inadequate. Vandenberg and Senator Eugene D. Millikin of Colorado, Republican head of the critical Committee on Finance, applied powerful pressures. Clayton was forced to add to the ITO charter draft an American-sponsored escape clause to protect United States producers from future trade agreements damaging to their interests. For the British, whose reticence regarding the United States world economic system had virtually reached the point of noncooperation, the open split in Washington represented the realization of all their fears. At the beginning of 1947, as the architects of American foreign economic policy surveyed their dilemma, only danger and crises lay ahead. To find the means to overcome them was their overriding concern.

A central issue in the crisis of American foreign economic policy at the end of 1946 was the relationship of the United States to the rest of the capitalist world, particularly Britain. If the ITO appeared throughout 1946 to be the most useful means for gaining British cooperation, there were others as well. On a formal level, diplomacy might suffice; informally, a better measure of real power was America's influence among nations and control of resources, and here, too, the United States, as we have seen and shall soon perceive yet more, was active. What ultimately concerned the United States was world markets and world power.

The question of markets was really an issue of the health of the postwar American economy, and these outlets were desired long before Washington saw any decisive political justification, such as Russia or the Left, for exports. Now the United States was demanding that Europe accept a dual-standard code of conduct for future world economic relations, especially after the period of wartime reconstruction. Without such European acceptance of a privileged American status, in the long run perfect free trade in the world economy would hurt the United States far more than it helped it, for European states would again trade with each other, restore their power in the world economy and Third World, and inevitably challenge America's supremacy even in its domestic market. Since there was a limit to European toleration of American exceptionalism, at that point retaliation would define American-European economic affairs. Beyond that limit the United States' world market would come only if it could create an artificial demand, via loans and grants, and extract concessions to the United States' privileged dual standard in the process. The loan to England was to prove only the first manifestation of this strategy—a strategy based on America's definition of its long-term interest rather than a fear of Russia.

From the viewpoint of extending American power, apart from the direct intervention that might hold the Third World regions for the jurisdiction of American and world capitalism, the question of Europe's role as the decisive factor in the balance of world power was of prime import. Alone, even without Germany, a Western European economic bloc successfully able to incorporate the sterling area would inevitably become a formidable, perhaps decisive, balance to American as well as Soviet power. Such a Europe would not merely significantly close off the United States' most promising export market but might also seek to determine its own political and military fate as it had done over preceding decades. To bind it loyally into a new system of internationalism was well worth the risks and the costs. And since the first major challenge confronting the extension of American power after World War II was economic, so was the first attempt at forging a new international system. Ultimately the necessity for that system could be sold to Congress, Europe, and the American people only in the name of anti-Communism.

4

Military Power and Foreign Policy, 1945–1946

If military power is the instrument of political policy, and if material capabilities and intentions must be equal in order for a great nation to avoid diplomatic defeat, the very weakness of its possible antagonists made the United States' military force by far the most powerful for sustained, modern warfare. American policy toward its military establishment was based on a global perspective: in effect, that a powerful military arm was an essential aspect of diplomacy and the attainment of United States global objectives. But it was also complicated by intense public war-weariness and desire to demobilize, and the need to reorganize and rationalize a military structure full of intense interservice rivalries.

Throughout the war the United States failed to scale its peacetime postwar military plans to prewar standards, and the three military services were divided on everything save their common aspiration to play a world role. No one questioned the supposition, which Forrestal and the service leaders expounded, that a powerful American military establishment would, according to their definition, preserve international peace—which was tantamount to saying attaining United States global objectives. During 1943 the War Department hoped for a postwar army of 3 million men, with special emphasis on air power. The ambition was reduced to 275,000 men in late 1944, plus a much larger reserve, but the air force refused to accept their lesser role in this plan. The navy simply assumed it would be far and away the largest in the world, and deployed everywhere. Plans for global bases for the navy were extended in June 1945 to permanent air bases in France and Italy, but with the growing American fear of the Left and

Russia in Europe the War Department by summer 1945 hoped for an immediate postwar military establishment of 2.5 million men.

Explicit in such plans was the proposition that they could maintain peace through strength. And, save for the navy (which still felt Britain might be its enemy), the preeminent strategic doctrine was that air power would determine the future of modern warfare. This notion, which was not laid to rest for well over a decade, meant that despite demobilization, the elimination of the mass of the navy, or the like, so long as the United States retained a far superior air arm, equipped with atomic weapons, it could relax its efforts to maintain what it considered to be partially obsolescent land and sea forces. Indeed, this strategic controversy, which wracked the military services over the postwar years, reinforced certain unavoidable steps to reduce the military budget and man power, but it also opened the prospect of a doctrine of force compatible with a policy of fiscal caution. But it was not only the strategic doctrine that the United States could best afford, for it also struck most key American leaders as valid for a war with Russia, which was widely regarded by the summer of 1945 as the probable adversary in case of war.

Every strategy carries a price tag with it, but also a perception of political realities and likely dangers. Such definitions of the situation become reinforcing and imperceptibly color each other, and what a leadership thinks it can afford also seriously affects its judgments. Washington genuinely believed Russia in the distant future to be its likely adversary, and concentrated industrial and military installations its probable targets. This assumption was most compatible with the level of military expenditures America wished to spend in the inflationary postwar economy as well as its belief that the major stakes of world power were still in Europe. It was five years before Washington questioned the validity of this fundamental premise, and almost a decade before American leaders began unsuccessfully to grope for a new strategic and global doctrine to supplement it.[1]

The United States therefore demobilized its manpower without essentially weakening itself by the strategic criterion it defined as relevant to global realities. It reduced the army from 8,000,000 men in August 1945 to 4,229,000 at the end of the year and 1,890,000 by July 1946. The number of its effective air groups declined by half by the beginning of the year, and the navy fell by over half by March 1946, or to 1,600,000 men. Public clamor to get the boys home, and then troop protests and strikes at the end of the year, all accelerated the process. Yet Truman had no intention of permitting the demobilization to go too far, and he much regretted that public pressures accelerated it. At the end of October, he reassured the nation that even with the speedy breakup of the services, the navy would remain the most powerful on earth, with all the bases it might require, that the air force was hardly less preeminent, and that rapid national mobilization was also possible. Since June 1945 Truman had been calling for the creation of a system of universal military training to establish a vast manpower reserve, and he reiterated it in October.

There can be slight doubt that events imposed demobilization on Washington far faster than desired, and it was not in any manner an index of United States "trust" or naïveté toward the USSR. By fall 1945 there were frequent discussions of the negative impact of the demobilization on United States freedom to pursue its foreign policy, and the American ambassadors in France and Italy warned against publicizing troop withdrawals in those countries. The troop strikes at the opening of 1946 especially disturbed the administration; the State Department thought them an embarrassment to the conduct of foreign relations; and by the end of February, Byrnes publicly made the formal linkage between foreign and military policy when he made it plain that ". . . in the interest of peace we cannot allow our military establishment to be reduced below the point required to maintain a position commensurate with our responsibilities. . . ."[2] Indeed, that very month Washington decided to show the flag in a fleet visit to the Mediterranean; over the following weeks it began the first of numerous naval tests in polar regions to develop short routes to Russia; and during July the Bikini atomic bomb tests both improved the power of the bomb and reiterated the fact that America still retained overwhelming offensive air power.

At the very same time that the United States demobilized its World War II military establishment for reasons having nothing to do with America's diplomatic visions, analysis, or ambitions, it rationalized, modernized, and, in important areas, greatly expanded the postwar military machine. These were not two distinct phases reflecting the changing global environment, but rather occurred at one and the same time, for not even the strongest advocates of a firm anti-Soviet policy called for maintenance of the wartime military, if only because it was quite superfluous for the tasks at hand and could only increase inflationary pressures on the already strained economy. Ironically, speedy demobilization greatly eased this process of change, breaking up many of the vast service empires and prerogatives that were to prove the greatest impediment to modernization, and made possible the creation of a military establishment commensurate with both American material power and the protracted global diplomatic crisis which Washington saw, even in mid-1945, as the most probable future.

The main military problem for Washington in the immediate postwar era was to unify and reorganize the services, and this in turn directly involved the question of basic military strategy and the size of the budget. The movement to merge the army, navy, and army air force under a single Defense Department, as opposed to the existing War and Navy Departments, began almost immediately after Truman became President. His experience as head of the Senate investigation of the war effort particularly suited Truman for the task, and the army air force strongly supported his efforts in the hope it would become a fully independent service, even if one that was a part of a much more centrally coordinated structure. The army was ready to support unity in the hope it might sustain its existing privileges in the future. The navy, afraid of being downgraded both financially and strategically, opposed the unification, and for the next three years fought a rear-guard struggle for maximum decentralization and autonomy in the Defense Department. The details of the inordinately long, complex reorganization need not detain us, but in December, Truman formally initiated the legislation, and over the next months the various interests supporting the three services modified this or that clause as best they could—until the National Security Act of July 1947 created the Department of Defense.[3]

In a sense the struggle over unification was one of service traditions and fiefdoms, but in the last analysis it was a matter of which strategic doctrine the nation would adopt and how much it could afford to pay for its armed might. The navy feared obsolescence, and the Bikini tests exposed its easy vulnerability to destruction. For offensive war the air force seemed most economical and effective at one and the same time, and Truman saw unification and a balanced federal budget as a single issue. The reform plan allotted many traditional navy functions to land-based aircraft, and this the navy much resented. But however noisy this interservice rivalry, the basic fact that should not be obscured is that none of the alternative strategies differed on the central mission to be achieved: the defeat of Russia in war. None did anything more than reflect the larger global definitions of the world crisis as handed down by the Executive branch and civilians.

The question of the military budget was an ambiguous one for most of the men around Truman and for the President himself. None were able to extirpate a kind of mechanistic, reverential attitude toward the balanced budget, and Truman in his memoir treats his ability to produce a surplus of revenue over expenses during 1946–1952 as one of his major achievements. For one thing, the immediate pressure to spend money on defense did not come from the general business community, but from a small minority of military contractors, and most business journals and organizations until 1950 favored minimal defense and government expenditures. Fiscal stability at home, to many, was consistent with anti-Communism, perhaps its very essence, and this penurious tough-mindedness was best reflected in the Taft faction in the Republican Party.[4] Besides, inflationary pressures at home, which greater arms spending would only aggravate, and the need to export capital and goods for European reconstruction, seemed to most sophisticated big businessmen to be more pressing considerations. Truman imbibed this ideology, as did most others in Washington, but eventually opted for a strategy of a balanced, hopefully declining budget, but neither too much nor too quickly, and never at the sacrifice of clear military superiority. For one thing, the Budget Bureau's chief fiscal analyst, Arthur Smithies, had predicted in January 1946 that pent-up consumer demand and capital spending would last only a few years and that a business contraction was then likely, perhaps even one as serious as 1932. "The safe assumption to make is that history will repeat itself."[5] Under the circumstances, the larger the government spending, the less likely a depression. Prematurely heavy expenditures, conversely, would fan the inflation plaguing the economy immediately after the war. But in mid-May 1946, Truman defined the general rule that the armed services should not receive more than one-third of the federal budget. By prewar standards this was still extremely large and more than adequate for the problem of Russia. In fiscal year 1940, with American entry into war far more imminent than in 1946, the national security budget was $1.5 billion, or 1.5 percent of the gross national product, but in fiscal 1947 it was $14.4 billion and 6.2 percent of the GNP. In fiscal 1948, presumably a period of rising international tensions Washington also implied included greater risk of war, the budget fell to $11.8 billion, or 4.5 percent of the GNP, and both fiscal 1949 and 1950 were lower than 1946.

Such a decline was possible because of Truman's desire to balance the budget and massive Marshall Plan exports, but also because it sufficed to meet real needs. In purely dollar terms, it was about twice the Russian expenditures, though relative costs lowered this gap slightly. The War Department resorted to ingenious statistical calculations to try to convey pacific American intentions in these data, and it attempted to neutralize rare factual press accounts of the sharply declining Soviet military outlays.

The various services complained about cuts in their allowances, and while Forrestal and Marshall saw the need for more money, they also freely acknowledged that the budget could not permanently remain at such high levels. Congress might cut taxes in January 1947, and Truman could veto it, but even at the end of February, as the State Department plotted the Truman Doctrine and vast foreign aid expenditures, Truman was outlining his plans for massive budget cuts over the coming years.[6] In this larger context of sufficiency for real overseas objectives but also stringency for all the service demands, the army, navy, and air force quickly discovered that the best, indeed only, way of obtaining their hardware and funds was to attempt to take it at the expense of the other services. To justify such increasingly bitter infighting, which prevented any serious military challenge to civilian control over the decision-making structure, the various services were to propound various strategic doctrines compatible with a larger share of the limited budget for themselves.

A unified military strategy was to accompany a unified military structure, but none of the services would concede to the basic objectives of the other. The army hoped to create a vast mobilization base via Universal Military Training, the air force aspired to have a 70-group force, and the navy eventually settled on giant aircraft carriers capable of offensive operations anywhere in the world. Each service, however, accepted the concept of a future war as a total conflict against Russia—in brief, against industrial power for which the services' own hardware would be relevant. The deeply bitter outcome of this grand struggle we have left for Chapter 18, but suffice it to say that Truman's repeated efforts until 1950 to get Congress to pass UMT failed not merely because of its political unpopularity but also because the air force's supporters in congressional ranks thought it a diversion of money better spent on air power.

Each of the services had their own constituencies in industrial firms that tended to make products for one or another service, but these companies, being fairly diffuse geographically, had a wide influence over congressmen and senators who equated service strategies and budgets with contracts for their districts. While this pattern favored the air force most of all, the other services could partially neutralize it, and the White House never permitted the frequent air force budget victories to weaken excessively the navy and army. These firms soon acquired a dynamism and lobbying talent denied the military branches and were quick to become, at the very least, coequals in defining military tactics, possible new types of military hardware, and strategic theories appropriate to service weapons systems—justifications generally following weapons innovations. Almost from the very end of the war itself the military services passed into a state of growing dependence on various specific civilian interests seeking to grasp a share of their budgets. The key to this changing relationship, and civilian mastery, was the general awareness in Washington, well before the end of the war, that atomic energy, the jet engine, and new propulsion and electronics systems were effecting a total revolution in future wars between industrial nations. The overwhelming scientific sophistication of the new weaponry made the generals and admirals more than ever dependent on civilian researchers—in brief, on arms producers and universities. In July 1945, the Joint Chiefs of Staff decided to bring over German rocket specialists, who happily offered to switch their allegiances, and over the next seven years imported 642 of them.[7] Moreover, given the rapid obsolescence of weapons systems in a period of stringent budgets and rapid changes in knowledge, the navy and air force began spending a much larger proportion of their limited funds on research and development into promising new weapons systems.

Despite the over-all decline of military expenditures, research and development allocations increased. The navy's Bureau of Aeronautics, desperate to find appropriate weapons to counter those of the air force, spent 50 percent more in fiscal 1946 than in 1944. Before the war, industry-sponsored research had been far greater than that of the government, but the war reversed the relationship and it continued throughout the postwar period. In fiscal 1947 the military spent $563 million on research and development, and the wartime innovation of financing university-based research grew and expanded. The academics who had flourished in the new, affluent environment of sponsored science were eager for it to continue, and the relationship became mutually satisfying. But while both universities and business, as a whole, could exist without military research contracts, the officers quickly acknowledged their critical dependence on the civilian scientists.

During the spring of 1946 various civilian experts in the War Department worked out the model of a desirable relationship between civilians and military, and had General Dwight D. Eisenhower, then army chief of staff, enunciate a policy based on the premise that "[t]he future security of the nation demands that all those civilian resources which by conversion or redirection constitute our main support in time of emergency be associated closely with the activities of the Army in time of peace. . . . [t]here appears little reason for duplicating within the Army an outside organization which by its experience is better qualified than we are to carry out some of our tasks." The critical military need for a high level of scientific research meant it would ". . . find much of the talent we need for comprehensive planning in industry and universities" via research contracts and support.[8]

The United States entered the postwar era determined to maintain an overwhelming, superior military establishment fully adequate for the range of problems it expected from Russia and in Europe. It demobilized its man power without disarming in some decisive manner, and the leaders in Washington retained military power adequate for their political and diplomatic vision. That perspective, however, excluded a serious involvement in Asia, much less a protracted guerilla conflict. It is not merely that such warfare would have upset the budget calculations so carefully hammered out, but simply that American priorities still ranked Europe as the central arena of future world power, the most likely source of instability, and Russia the cause of much of the world's turmoil. Such a definition of reality proved incorrect, but we can scarcely call it peaceful, for the United States based it on the need to sustain and improve the largest peacetime military establishment it had ever known. This conviction preceded numerous diplomatic crises, later cited as justification for the maintenance of military power, and it was to determine America's response to atomic disarmament. It was, as well, the origin of the grotesque technological escalation which is one of the most terrifying aspects of the precarious condition of modern civilization.

Atomic Disarmament—The Uses of Rhetoric

The issue of the atomic bomb was a question of power, the relationship of the United States to the world, and the extent to which the atomic bomb was useful in advancing American global objectives and sustaining its might. Only one of many aspects of the world political crisis at the end of the war, there could be no solution to the bomb for the leaders in Washington short of a resolution of a whole myriad of other, yet more critical and insoluble diplomatic and economic issues which reached to the root causes of the world crisis.

In the last months of World War II various American leaders, and especially scientists around Stimson and the Manhattan Project such as Vannevar Bush and Karl T. Compton, had debated the future of atomic energy in the postwar era. They prepared memos and tentative plans, but both Byrnes and Marshall opposed raising the matter with the USSR, either because the Russians were proving uncooperative on general questions or because they felt the United States should maintain its clear military lead. This policy prevailed until the United States dropped its bombs on Japan. On August 9, reporting on the Potsdam Conference and making his first detailed statement on the bomb, Truman, pressured by Attlee, had declared that the United States and England would retain the secret of the terrible new weapon and ". . . constitute ourselves trustees of this new force—to prevent its misuse. . . ."⁹ The difficulty of this position, as the leaders in Washington well knew, is that the exclusive trust would not last in perpetuity, that the Russians had been working on the bomb for some time, and that, sooner or later, knowledge of atomic energy would become quite widespread. Bush and Conant had already drawn up an outline for international control of atomic energy with strict checks, and at the beginning of June, Stimson and Truman tentatively talked about a rigidly controlled sharing of atomic information, which they made contingent on a general political settlement on most of the outstanding controversies.

But Attlee's prods in August, and again during early September, kept the matter alive. Then, on September 11, Stimson gave some parting thoughts to Truman on the question, revising his earlier admonition that some sharing of knowledge would have to wait for internal changes in Russia and a political settlement. Now he feared that the Anglo-American monopoly over the bomb would prompt Russia to develop its own at any cost, that it would succeed in anywhere from four to twenty years, and that in the meantime the bomb would poison all aspects of relations with Moscow. It would be far better, he now suggested, immediately to try to negotiate some system of joint control. But Stimson stressed that the three major powers would have to negotiate the issue among themselves, for the Russians would be suspicious of any plan debated in a larger body, such as the UN. Tentatively, he suggested a plan whereby the three powers would stop all development in the field, perhaps even agreeing not to make more bombs—in effect leaving the United States with a monopoly over the secret of its manufacture. Both Truman and Acheson seemed to agree, as did most of the cabinet several weeks later. Forrestal and the Joint Chiefs of Staff, however, made it clear they opposed any transfer of secrets to Russia, but no one had proposed giving away data on the manufacture of the bomb or relinquishing the United States' lead without foolproof guarantees. The United States' first impulse, therefore, was to devise a system that would assure its continued monopoly over knowledge of the bomb's manufacture.¹⁰

In the long run, Washington recognized, to hope to maintain control over the bomb's secret was futile, and, on this premise, Acheson thought everything was to be gained from negotiating a system of collaboration but, in the meantime, disclosing nothing. At the same time, American leaders were quite certain that the Russians were attempting to spy on American developments, and the embassy in Moscow urged an intense effort to do the same there.

Stimson's retirement, however, left no one in Washington ready to attach urgency even to his cautious approach, and Forrestal, who did not disagree with the principle of Stimson's plans, enjoined Truman temporarily to delay commitment to any policy. The main initiatives, such as they were, came from London. The British were interested not merely in the future of world peace but in a wartime atomic partnership the United States had casually exploited to British disadvantage. England had contributed heavily of its scientific knowledge and vital resources at the earliest stages of the bomb project, and in September 1944 the two nations again agreed to share knowledge in the postwar era and to consult on the use of the bomb. But the Americans gave the English no information, but merely notified them when they were ready to use the bomb against Japan and consciously sought to retain an atomic monopoly. From this viewpoint it was not merely Russia but also the unrivaled military role of the United States in the world that was at question in the future of the bomb and atomic energy.

At the end of September, when Attlee requested further talks on the failing partnership, Truman's advisers recognized that they could not wholly deny their ally, but planned instead to give the British as little information as possible. Although Truman at the beginning of October had publicly declared that the secret of the bomb would not last forever, and that the United States would hold discussions with Britain and Canada in the future, in reality he procrastinated as long as possible. Byrnes, for his part, now urged that they indefinitely postpone talks with Russia. But they could not put off Attlee, who was under intense political pressure at home not merely to renew the limp agreement to share knowledge but to confront the larger diplomatic implications of the weapon and the impending arms race. On October 16 he volunteered to come to Washington, and now the United States could no longer avoid the question. Not taking any chances, and learning from experience, the British in the meantime took major steps toward developing their own bomb on the basis of their then limited knowledge.[11]

The essential fact of the mid-November discussions between Truman, Attlee, and Prime Minister Mackenzie King of Canada is that Washington was determined not to transfer critical data to *any* of its erstwhile allies. As for world atomic disarmament, the Bush Plan of the prior May, which Stimson had helped to draft, was quickly polished and offered to the English, who accepted it *in toto* and managed to get it leaked to the press as the "Attlee Plan." The Americans regarded the wartime agreements to share data as void, but rather than so inform the British they were prepared to consent to generalities and fail to provide information—as proved to be the case the following years. To some extent, atomic disarmament negotiations were necessary if only to put the British off with the promise of eventually outlawing all bombs. In the scale of contemporary events, disarmament was of minor consequence, but later historical treatments have made it a major myth in postwar history—one which justifies the details that follow. In the context of Washington's strategy during 1945–1946, however, disarmament was not a matter of ending the recourse to military power in solving international political or economic rivalries, or even of preventing an arms race, but overwhelmingly a question of how the United States might best preserve its monopoly on atomic power.

"We want no future war," Bush argued, but, "[i]f we cannot avoid one, we at least wish to be in our full strength and to have the rest of the world with us. We also want to have atomic bombs and to be in a clear position to use them promptly, if there is any chance that our enemy has them." Hence our program toward international understanding should involve no premature 'outlawing of the bomb,' which is a dangerous phrase. It should be realistic at every step." The first stage would demand free scientific interchange and personnel exchanges to basic research laboratories—though not atomic weapons plants—without policing or intergovernmental regulation. Since information produced in such labs was already available, "This step probably costs us nothing."[12] Its duration might be long or short, but it would be introduced gradually so as not to reveal United States secrets prematurely. Once implemented, a UN inspection system with freedom to travel and examine anything would be created. After the UN established such minimal inspection, there would follow another graduated process of control over fissionable materials, at the end of which the United States would dismantle its bombs. "Many years would be necessary to carry out all three steps . . .," Bush predicted.[13] But he attached no approximate timetable nor details on enforcement.

The advantage of this plan to the United States, the outline of which the three leaders released November 15, was that while it froze the atomic research of all other countries it failed to disturb the existing bombs and technical advantages of the United States until the very end of its indefinite process. It was, in brief, essentially a system of comprehensive, indefinite control which would only eventually lead to atomic disarmament. Until that time it would leave the United States with an atomic monopoly. Formulas of this nature were to remain the core of United States disarmament proposals for another decade.

Such an arrangement was preeminently to the interests of the United States because, despite some speculations that the Russians would not have access to sufficient uranium, experts believed that the United States atomic monopoly would end perhaps even by late 1949. Reports sent back from the embassy in Moscow stressed the obvious Soviet determination and public threats to develop the weapon, and their eventual success was hardly doubted. Both privately and publicly, American leaders acknowledged that the secret of the bomb would spread. Even so, the military and Forrestal urged the utmost caution in any moves toward disarmament.

All that remained was for the United States to initiate discussions with the Russians, and at the Moscow Conference, Byrnes proposed exploratory discussions under the aegis of a UN commission. Molotov readily agreed, but insisted that the commission operate under the jurisdiction and rules of the Security Council—where, of course, the veto applied. The Russian amendment was accepted after some debate, but in turn they approved without protest the important clause that the disarmament commission would complete a whole stage of control before going on to the implementation of the next stage. This, of course, was the principle of full control before the destruction of any atomic bombs, and upon further thought the Russians realized it. Still, at this point the Russians had substantially endorsed the American approach, and Byrnes publicly claimed they could not even block the commission via the Security Council. Even Vandenberg, at first concerned about the vagueness in the diplomatic verbiage, felt comforted that the provisions fully protected American interests.[14] But Washington's victory of the dispatches was to prove illusory.

At the beginning of January 1946 Byrnes publicly declared that the United States could use its Security Council veto, or the Senate refuse to ratify the treaty, should an international commission attempt to force information from it. He left it to Acting Secretary of State Dean Acheson to translate the broad principles of the Bush memo and official policy into a more negotiable proposal. Acheson, in turn, sought the advice of such tough-minded men as John J. McCloy, Bush, and Major General Leslie R. Groves, who had supervised the building of the bomb, and they decided to transform existing policy into a study of necessary control and inspection systems, emphasizing once more the theme of controls before disarmament. A board of consultants under David E. Lilienthal, chairman of the Tennessee Valley Authority, was created to prepare a report within this framework —and given less than two months to accomplish the task.

At first Lilienthal regarded his report not as a final negotiating position but as a foundation, but it merely amplified existing policy along the lines of the Bush Plan. It contributed the dimension, however, of asserting that international inspection, control, and policing of nations alone would not give sufficient security. As a great regional developer, Lilienthal added the theme that an international agency would have to assume responsibility for the control and ownership of all raw materials and the development of peaceful atomic energy. This International Atomic Development Authority, which was to control every phase of atomic development, suited the implementation of one man's visions, but it also added myriad complexities to the already cumbersome American scheme. As such, it made it yet less likely of acceptance, for the Russians were not prone to transfer control of a critical sector of their economy to an international body. Many of the movements and economic functions of the Authority would go well beyond that required for secure inspection and control, and a decade later the United States was to drop it from all its arms control proposals. But until the scheme was put into operation, and all raw materials brought under control, the United States would retain its monopoly on the bomb—a monopoly Lilienthal's committee freely admitted would be lost otherwise. And while it suggested that the formulation of a timetable was possible, neither Lilienthal nor Baruch was to insert one in American plans—which remained open-ended. Acheson himself, who accepted the plan as his own, thought it might take five to six years to implement.[15]

The Lilienthal Plan substituted international ownership for international inspection of nationally owned plants, but it was preeminently designed to strengthen American security. If the plan failed the United States would remain in the relatively strongest position, and it only implied the fact that it would freeze Soviet and British development of a weapon that only the United States would possess, but otherwise lose. Ultimately, the United States might conceivably forfeit its mastery of the atomic bomb, but that time always remained painfully vague in its proposals.

The appointment of Bernard Baruch as United States representative to the UN Atomic Energy Commission only superficially colored the next phase of United States arms control strategy. The darling of Senate conservatives, Baruch was inordinately vain, disliked Acheson, and was prone to antipathy toward anyone who overshadowed him. Lilienthal reciprocated the hostility. Truman announced his nomination March 18, the day after Acheson released the Lilienthal report. But the plan was conservative in every regard, and Baruch later acknowledged it guided him on most questions. Moreover, on March 26 he confessed to Harold Ickes that "I know nothing about the subject and, therefore, approach it with an open and ignorant mind."[16] He needed guidance, and while he was to swallow his pride and take some from the State Department, he preferred men such as Ferdinand Eberstadt, a fellow investment banker and close associate of Forrestal, John Hancock, a banker, and a group of assorted businessmen and generals such as Groves.

Too much should not be made of Baruch's jurisdictional struggle over the weeks following his nomination. He horrified the scientists, he was well known as an administrator rather than as a diplomat, and he often bypassed Byrnes; but ultimately he implemented the standing American policy in its broadest contours. The hasty and eccentric Acheson-Lilienthal report was transcended because it was not, as Acheson admitted, a final report, much less a negotiable treaty. The Russians were not likely to accept either. But there were so many gaps in the report that they had to fill them in, and men such as Groves and McCloy were ready to compensate for Baruch's ignorance or his desire to drag in the issue of conventional arms control. Hancock, after mining executives pressed him, convinced Baruch that international ownership of uranium or thorium mines would be harmful to the existing corporate structures. And Eberstadt could make sure that "[t]he basic guide in the formulation of our proposal is that it be in complete harmony with our own foreign policy. If this policy is one of reserve toward Russia, our proposal should reflect it."[17] In general, Baruch and his aides sought to stress control and enforcement even more than the Acheson-Lilienthal group; but Baruch, as was his wont, alternated between paying effusive compliments to Lilienthal's scheme and doing battle with the State Department over issues essentially of prestige and ego. Byrnes and Acheson differed with him only on details, for the objectives had been common to the key decision-makers since September, but they magnified personality clashes into substantive differences. Truman partially sustained Baruch in his tortured effort to be able to have his exact definition of the plan presented as the American proposal, but the President correctly recalled in later years that "Mr. Baruch's principal contribution to the atomic energy program was that he transformed the Acheson-Lilienthal Report from a working paper into a formal, systematic proposal and that he added a section that called for sanctions against any nation violating the rules."[18]

Baruch also attempted to get the advice of the Joint Chiefs of Staff and key military leaders, and they fully perceived the Acheson-Lilienthal Plan as a mechanism that extended the American atomic monopoly until the very end of its timetable. None opposed it, for they were not to so quickly lose their faith in the efficacy of force as a deterrent. Also, as General Carl Spaatz, the commander of the army air force, recognized, the bomb had to be maintained to preserve the existing American military advantage, but "On the other hand we must achieve some arrangement for the control of atomic explosives before other nations develop and perfect the bomb, or else undertake to maintain our present advantage in an all out atomic race."[19] Yet the larger question of mass war by other, no less destructive means remained, and several officers wished to link atomic disarmament to the broader question of arms control of every type. The military establishment, therefore, endorsed the premises and objectives of the existing atomic bomb proposals as fully compatible with national interests—indeed, even as the best means for advancing them.

The so-called Baruch Plan that the American spokesman read to the UN on June 14 embodied the thoughts and objectives that had preceded it, as well as more specific proposals. A UN International Atomic Development Authority was to manage or own all resources, plants, and research, with free access to all countries. After it had created an effective control system, for which it offered no timetable, all nations would cease to manufacture bombs and would destroy existing bombs. The Security Council could not veto the plan, and it would include a system of penalties for violations. Loosely inserted into Baruch's speech was the vague but critical proviso that ". . . before a country is ready to relinquish any winning weapons it must have more than words to reassure it," and this also meant the elimination of chemical-biological weapons and "war itself."[20] But the American proposal was not a plan for general disarmament and peace, and precisely what role this reference was to play in atomic arms control was left unstated —a safety-valve contingency should Russia startle everyone and accept the American plan. The State Department fully approved this vague clause.

The American plan would have had only one immediate effect if implemented: to guarantee the United States' monopoly over the bomb. In return, it would have deprived all other nations of control over free development of peaceful atomic energy. It would have modified the UN voting structure in some decisive manner, and the American-controlled majority would have held firm control over its atomic energy administration. Under the circumstances, four days later Gromyko rejected the Baruch Plan and instead proposed a resolution to renounce the use of atomic bombs, a ban on their production, and immediate destruction of existing stocks. He referred questions of the peaceful use and development of atomic energy, the outlawing of the bomb, and the creation of control systems to the UN commission for discussion, but he insisted it operate under Security Council rules, with a veto. The American plan for immediate total control, with a vague pledge of ultimate atomic disarmament, and the Russian plan for immediate atomic disarmament and indefinite controls remained the basis of the positions of the two countries for years.

The United States did not regard the Baruch Plan as negotiable or think its atomic monopoly in danger of imminent loss. Given the general political mood in Washington, and global American objectives, atomic disarmament was nothing more than a fancy, worth talking about for several reasons. The first was propaganda, and this aspect of the question remained constant over the next two decades. The other motive, as Baruch explained it, was that "[t]he greatest fear we can have is that time works against us."[21] But Washington did not consider eventual loss of the monopoly worth the risk of sacrificing it immediately in return for substantive concessions on control, and it never offered such a compromise to the Russians.

The Russians cleverly focused on the United States veto proposals rather than controls, which they also opposed, and their propaganda successes immediately disturbed Washington. Baruch and Smith in Moscow thought introducing the issue of general disarmament would brighten the American posture, but Acheson and Truman both insisted, in the President's words, ". . . we should stand pat on our program. . . . [W]e should not under any circumstances throw away our gun until we are sure the rest of the world can't arm against us."[22] In the meantime, during July the Bikini atomic tests were held to improve the existing American atomic arsenal. Wallace, the same month, urged Truman to submit a more specific plan with, above all, a timetable attached to each phase of an agreement so that Russia would not have to rely only on vague American good will. But American memos to the UN commission which discussed the matter remained obscure and inflexible, though this did not prevent the United States' allies from endorsing its position. Washington would remain intransigent.

Under the circumstances, and given the clever vagueness of the Soviet position, by early September even Baruch had to admit that "[w]e have lost the initiative to Russia, and other nations are beginning to waver more and more."[23] The problem was that the United States stood firmly by the policy defined before the opening of negotiations, and since then the Russians had implied that they would accept some form of international control—though how much remained unclear. For the military, however, there were certain windfalls from the stalemate. Eberstadt thought a showdown with Russia would, to quote Baruch's official biographer, ". . . awaken the public to the need for preparedness."[24] Baruch, for his part, felt that in anticipation of a breakdown ". . . efforts should be redoubled to accumulate stockpiles with raw materials and atomic bombs."[25] And Clark Clifford urged Truman to avoid any limits on arms until the alleged Soviet aggressive impulses disappeared. The United States was about ready to wash its hands of the issue, and it was unwilling to modify its position. During October, Baruch and his advisers determined to force the American plan to a vote in the UN during December, not the least because they learned of an imminent new Russian proposal that Molotov himself was to bring to New York.

Before the Russian foreign minister sprang his new scheme, the Russian Assistant UN Secretary General, A. A. Sobolev, informally contacted some of Baruch's key advisers concerning American policy. Continued bomb production was destabilizing, he argued, and the American control scheme was a far too ambitious project for world government. But such private diplomacy never appealed to Washington, and on October 29 Molotov delivered a major Soviet statement, attacking the United States effort to retain a monopoly on the bomb—which he predicted would not last forever —and calling for general arms reduction, with special emphasis on atomic bombs, under Security Council guidance.

Although Truman and the State Department consented to pressing the Baruch Plan to a UN vote, as a propaganda issue even Baruch freely admitted at the beginning of November that "the Soviets have taken advantage of our indecision, have moved in, and now apparently have become the advocates of disarmament."[26] They could push for a vote, or slow down the work of the UN commission ". . . to the extreme of recess or adjournment."[27] It was generally conceded in Washington that the fact that the United States position said almost nothing on nonatomic disarmament, and that the Russians were leading that cause, had left the Americans confused and ineffective. But before the UN commission could vote on the American plan—where ten of the twelve nations probably would support it—the Russians advanced their propaganda lead even further.

During the two weeks after November 20 Molotov made a half-dozen major statements on the arms race and disarmament to the UN, creating general dismay in Washington. First he pressed for a voluntary inventory of foreign troops outside their borders and their return home, alluded to general disarmament of every sort, and repeated Soviet willingness to agree to atomic disarmament based on "strict international control."[28] While the Soviet position on the inviolability of the veto remained unaltered, it had broadened sufficiently to appear to make possible new negotiations and a reconsideration of the concrete steps necessary for genuine arms control.

The State Department insisted Baruch's efforts exclude completely the larger issue of nonatomic disarmament, and Walter Lippmann warned that if public talk on the topic went too far it would stimulate antibomb sentiment at home and make it difficult to obtain adequate military appropriations. Acheson let it be known that making the United States position on the veto hazier might be good strategy to undercut Russian successes on the matter. At the end of the month Truman and his cabinet discussed general disarmament, and the group unanimously agreed that they could not consider the question seriously at the time and that the atomic bomb talks could suffice for the time being. Such a decision not only rubbed the independent Baruch's ego the wrong way; is also genuinely strapped his efforts to strike effective propaganda blows by bringing in his own ideas on the issue.

Baruch was now alternately furious at the Russians and Washington. On December 4, the day before the UN commission was to vote on the Baruch Plan, Molotov stated that the Russians would suspend the veto over routine atomic control operations, once the Security Council approved them, and even accept "effective inspections."[29] Moreover, on December 14 the General Assembly adopted a resolution for discussions on general disarmament that Washington insisted was not in Baruch's jurisdiction.

At this point, American unwillingness to interrelate the entire question of disarmament, overseas troops and bases, and atomic energy simply rebuffed Russia's feelers. To concentrate on one isolated phase of what both Moscow and Washington saw as an interrelated issue of military power was to foredoom progress on arms control. On December 20 Baruch pushed the United States plan to a successful preliminary 10 to 1 vote in the UN Atomic Energy Commission, and now a chorus of disapproval arose, including even the New York *Times,* that American haste and rigidity were sacrificing a last opportunity to attain progress on disarmament, atomic included. Apparently the British, too, decided the unseemly speed was questionable and that they might better table the Baruch Plan to consider first the larger problem of disarmament. But the Americans would not tolerate delay, for they wished to close up the losing charade. The recalcitrant British got back into line. On December 30 the commission finally approved, with Russia and Poland abstaining, an American plan the essential details of which had not been altered in over six months.

Baruch had accomplished his task, and his nine months of continuous haggling and personality clashes, and finally his tight restriction, were more than enough for him. On January 4, 1947, he suddenly submitted his resignation to Truman, who was probably relieved to have it and to terminate the unsuccessful propaganda effort. Not even *Time* or the New York *Times* had praise for Baruch's inept handling of the issue, which obliquely damned an American policy of which Baruch had been but the instrument. If they could not avoid future discussions of disarmament, key Washington leaders decided at the end of January, they could channel them into harmless directions via emphasis on the details of inspection and control, as well as essential political preconditions. The approach had worked, however clumsily, with the atomic bomb, but scorn for disarmament in any form remained the crucial motive of American policy-makers from this time onward. "By the summer of 1948," concluded Bernhard G. Bechhoefer, a senior State Department adviser on the topic, "United States policy on the entire subject of arms control had reached a state of poverty never thereafter duplicated."[30]

The cynical discussion of disarmament was based on a total realism that presented Washington with a number of assets and liabilities of which it was fully aware. The various atomic bomb plans involved a UN structure essentially under Anglo-American domination. There was never the remotest possibility, as everyone knew, that Russia would agree to forgo the power of the bomb under supervision of a control agency quite pliably under United States control. There was no substitute for direct great power agreements on essential questions, as the Russians had often made clear. But the United States wished to persist with the chimera of atomic disarmament, for fear of losing its existing military superiority over the USSR and England. It refused to relinquish its temporary military lead because its diplomatic and political goals required superior force as an indispensable instrument of policy. The consequence, which America's leaders fully anticipated, was the spread of the atomic bomb to Russia and England, technological escalation, and an arms race in which, it was expected, the United States would maintain its lead. Because of that fateful decision, and the American refusal to consider options when they were still possible and the scale of arms problem was relatively minor, civilization remains close to universal destruction till this day. Yet Washington's choice of this path was not a mistaken judgment, but a logical and necessary consequence of the American desire to consolidate power and to reorganize a world in profound disarray. Given the poverty of the ideological appeals of American capitalism, Washington sought to achieve with material power—economic and military—what it lacked in political inspiration for the large masses of the world.

5

The Future of Germany

World War II brought to a head the civil war in Western society that is the dominant theme in twentieth-century history. No major nation of Europe, save England, was immune from it, and at the war's end class conflict and incipient class warfare added the problem of a treacherously unstable politics to the realities of hunger, economic paralysis, and mounting state economic intervention. To all who might care to see, it was plain that the future of Russian power in Europe was connected to these developments, which might also define the United States' relations with the Soviet Union as well as its ability to establish its own essentially economic goals for a reconstructed, cooperative European capitalism. Political and economic events increasingly merged, and by the end of the war there could be little doubt that there would be an intimate relationship between the Western European political forms, whether they be Left, Right, or something more complex, and Europe's economic future. If the United States were to attain its objectives, it would first have to solve the emerging crisis of European politics and its inevitable diplomatic consequences. The tools available to Washington ranged from advice to the application of military and economic power.

The internationalization of internal social crises and conflict in Europe as well as Asia therefore became the defining contextual fact of the postwar era. It alters the process of social innovation and transcends the normal confrontations of classes and power in national states to distort and often modify the outcome everywhere. For now the intimate relationship of all change in Europe to America's peace aims creates the problem of United States intervention into the affairs of European states, profoundly coloring the entire historical process in the postwar era.

Historians traditionally regard the question of Germany in postwar Europe as an essentially exclusive problem, and while it has its distinctive character as a result of being the defeated enemy, to isolate it in narrative and context from Italy, France, and the rest of Europe does violence to the more essential manner in which American leaders always perceived Germany in the far greater framework of European recovery, transformation, and security. For the problem of Germany involves relations with Russia in the broadest sense: the questions of Western European economic revival and the form it might take, and the necessity of containing the Left, both in its Communist and socialist wings, everywhere in Europe. Developments in any of these fields impinged on the policy toward the others, as Washington, seeing the question of Western Europe in its multifaceted dimensions, evaluated the implications of its policy toward one nation in its largest context. In the end, it based its decisions on the ultimate goals of United States policy: to transform the character of European capitalism in a manner compatible with the advancement of American interests and to contain Russia and the Left. Despite highlights, after the war Western Europe is one grand image in America's vision.

Germany's distinction was both that it was a defeated enemy, as opposed to Italy's status as a cobelligerent at the end of the war, and that it was potentially the most important power in Central and Western Europe. It became the most significant element in relations, for better or worse, with the USSR. Germany might be either an object of an accord with Russia or an attempt to mobilize German power, alone or in a Western European bloc, against it. Independent of both the two former allies, Germany might revive into a new locus of power in Europe, singly or associated with other European nations; and radicalized and pro-Soviet or neutral, German power might prove the decisive element in transforming all of Europe. Lastly, political and economic events elsewhere on the Continent, but especially France, could not but profoundly color all these fateful options. It was this intricate, multidimensional framework that the end of the war in Europe was to unfold, leading to countless, yet quite predictable, crises.

The Dilemma of Germany

Official Washington's wartime discussion of the future of Germany had been intense and often bitter, but by the end of 1944 it had reached a high degree of political and economic sophistication, so that nearly everyone had anticipated the major consequences of any policy. Before the Yalta Conference, despite inconsistencies American policy was committed to a purified Germany, not excessively decentralized, and its ultimate goal was ". . . the assimilation—on a basis of equality—of a reformed, peaceful and economically non-aggressive Germany into a liberal system of world trade."[1] This meant, too, that reparations could not be so large or sustained as to greatly complicate United States goals for the world economy, which a Germany paying for the reconstruction of the war's devastation and supplying free the world's industrial needs would inevitably do. By May 1945, when JCS 1067, the laboriously prepared policy directive for Germany, was handed Major General Lucius D. Clay, the United States Chief of Military Government, the value of Germany as a barrier to Soviet power was a substantially greater consideration in American planning. At this time, as well, the State Department was more than ever anxious to minimize the reparations burden on Germany and the War Department was striving for maximum autonomy for the American zone, a position that in spirit undermined the agreement for four-power coordination of the various occupation zones for a unified Germany that had been signed at Yalta the preceding February.

Apart from JCS 1067 being so vague as to prove as discretionary as political exigency might demand, it was both unilateral and, until October 1945, secret. The British, Russians, and French were not, at this point, asked to work out an all-German plan for the functional economic and political control of the four zones, and implicit in JCS 1067, which remained the official policy guideline for over two years, was the belief in a maximum zonal autonomy that bordered on partition. While it stated such obvious broad principles as restraining Germany from endangering world peace again, it avoided fixing specific economic standards and responsibilities, save to prevent starvation, disease, and the destruction of existing industrial facilities. Even if prohibited from producing certain basic industrial goods, Germany would have its economic resources frozen until the four powers agreed on an alternative plan. Since four-fifths of Germany's industrial capacity remained intact at the end of the war, and the main problem was to utilize it, Germany was immediately to become a dormant giant.

Clay and his advisers were shocked by the arbitrary and indefinite character of JSC 1067, and in this he was reinforced by his two economic advisers, Lewis H. Douglas, an important financier, and William H. Draper, Jr., formerly of Dillon, Read & Company, a major investment house in prewar Germany's economy. Clay's superior, Henry L. Stimson, secretary of war and one of the key advocates of strengthening Germany as a barrier to

Russia, added his weight by pointing out that Germany had already suffered amply for its adventure, and that further vengeance would only weaken the entire European economy, adding to America's problems and costs. Given the vagueness of their mandate and their political analysis, which Robert Murphy, Clay's and Eisenhower's political adviser, further buttressed, the men in charge of running the United States zone in Germany inclined toward making their area a barrier to Russia, the Left, and socialization, and a region fully oriented toward the larger United States goals for Europe. Even by the end of April, Clay wrote the War Department that the war had already destroyed most of Germany's war potential, that ". . . we must have freedom here to bring industries back into production," and that immediately reparations would conflict with this goal.[2]

Where JCS 1067 was explicit Clay and his advisers loyally implemented it, but where it was not—as with most critical issues—they engaged in tortured bureaucractic debates which tend to give the impression that the occupation government was essentially an organizational dilemma rather than a political and ideological instrument. Notwithstanding the vast literature on the administrative aspects of the military government, which reveals some minor though real difficulties men faced, the seeming air of confusion reflects the way in which profoundly political decisions were being reached about the incorporation of Germany into a United States–led world economic and military structure. In Germany, in effect, the United States was retaining options on the uses to which it could put the former enemy's power. The thrust of United States planning and policy for Germany before the Potsdam Conference was scarcely designed to eliminate that defeated power as a major source of potential future conflict.

The reparations issue became the most exacerbating effect of the strategy the United States was to follow, but it always reflected rather than created policy. In principle, the State Department policy of minimizing reparations, articulated by the fall of 1944, was the one the United States was to follow privately and in practice until the chimera was formally abandoned in 1947. For the United States, high reparations consisted of a potential double loss: a weakened Germany open to the Left internally and reducing United States exports, and a strengthened Soviet Union. While the United States had agreed at Yalta to discuss an abstract $20 billion reparations level, it was not committed explicitly to that amount, and as other priorities moved to the fore it increasingly downgraded shipping German goods to Russia that might further weaken German and Western European social and economic strength. By the summer of 1945, Edwin Pauley, the United States representative in Moscow negotiating the matter with Russia and England, had attached numerous provisos making reparations from the Western-controlled zones increasingly unlikely.

Apart from demanding that reparations would have to be collected from an all-German economic unit, for which there would first have to be an agreement or borders (which only a peace conference could resolve) and internal political and economic systems, the United States was also to insist on the "first charge" principle, permitting it to credit German export income against necessary imports before making any surplus goods available for reparations. Since the Russian zone was agricultural, with the Ruhr and over two-thirds of German industrial capacity in Western hands, initiative on the reparations issue was always to remain with the Anglo-Americans. By the time the allies held their Potsdam Conference the United States was determined to downgrade reparations, which would certainly further weaken a wobbling German society, while not publicly giving up a nominal commitment to it, and to offer the Russians a percentage of an undetermined reparations figure which would be fixed when time and circumstances made the future clearer. Such a strategy was perfectly compatible with suspending German power until the larger trends in diplomatic and economic affairs warranted definitive decisions. Until then, lesser American officials could scurry about in confusion, complaining about vagueness in a policy that in reality was supremely explicit regarding the stakes of world power. This policy might reflect world conditions or, as was to be the case, also help profoundly to define them.

By Potsdam the American definition of Germany's potential key role in postwar Europe, and even firmer dedication to maximum autonomy for the United States zone, meant it was going to smother far-reaching policy decisions in technicalities which would be subjected to future negotiations, thereby creating another source for inflaming United States–Soviet relations. We have already described in detail the bitter debate over reparations that was to occur at Potsdam, where Molotov chopped a billion dollars off Russia's $10 billion claim, and Byrnes deliberately distorted the industrial resources in the Soviet zone and the consequences of the Soviet transfer of the Oder-Neisse region to Poland, implying the Russians had already removed far more reparations than they actually had. Assiduously refusing to mention figures as to what might be available from the Anglo-French-American zones, Churchill, whom Attlee succeeded in the midst of the conference, Truman, and their aides could only offer the Russians an agreement allowing all sides to draw reparations from their own zone, trading a portion of the West's unquantified industrial surplus for food. Reluctantly, Stalin agreed, and haggling over the percentages, they concluded that they could trade 15 percent of the available reparations from the Western zones for Soviet-zone food and coal, with the Russians obtaining another 10 percent of total Western reparations outright. Before Potsdam, State Department officials had predicted that increasing zonal political and economic autonomy would lead to the partition of Germany into different states based on distinct social systems, and British authorities also thought this the logic of the plan that the United States had forced through to avoid a commitment on reparations. Aspects of the Potsdam Agreement on Germany, such as its vague insistence that the allies treat Germany economically as a single unit, gave others reason to hope that unity, too, might be arranged along with zonal reparations. Some found solace that the four powers were also committed to maintaining sufficient resources to permit Germans to ". . . subsist without external assistance."[3] While men such as Clayton were to draw back from the logic of American actions, if only because they did not wish to see the Soviet zone in Europe closed to United States exports and influence, the net effect of the diplomacy of World War II was to create the foundations for Germany's definitive partition and the terms for its restoration to world power. All this was the legacy, and the limitations, within which United States policy moved after August 1945.

Given different economic and political objectives and circumstances, the Potsdam and earlier agreements on Germany were vague enough to suit any strategy, including one of cooperation. But because the United States was never interested in large German reparations to speed Soviet recovery, but nominally supported them in principle without commitments as to their size, it created special organizations to deal with the complexities of reparations, and these groups met with the other three occupying powers until March 1946. Their ultimate failure was a reflection of policy rather than personnel.

While others have treated exhaustively the details of these reparations and economic debates, their general thrust, as well as the policy context in which they floundered, is worth outlining. There was, most importantly, the unchanging conflict between American political and economic goals for the world and high reparations, and the fact that only in its zone in Germany, in all of Western Europe, did the United States have the power to fully control a region's future economic structure. Apart from these considerations, in the period 1945–1946 there was never any chance for an all-

German political and economic entity so long as the French, who explicitly denied any obligations to the Potsdam decisions in which they had not participated, refused to collaborate with the other three occupying authorities. Until 1947, in effect, French policy left the currency and Berlin Kommandatura as the only operating four-power institutions. The issue for the United States was the partition of Germany, not into two regions, one of which was Soviet-oriented and controlled, but into four, and during most of the pre-1947 period the French were far more responsible for this danger than the Russians. So long as these risks existed, Paris reinforced the American preference for zonal autonomy and low reparations. It was in this context of French obstruction and American fears that Washington was to interact with Russia on the German issue during the first months of peace —and to realize its ends.

French impediments, which the United States staff in Berlin regarded as the leading political problem at the end of 1945, prevented any progress on unified four-power economic and political administration. By the end of 1945, indeed, the United States wished to abolish the principle of four-power unanimity in the Control Council in order to overcome the French, who in September and October had vetoed the creation of unified transport and rail authorities. The French made no secret of their goal: security from the threat of yet another war with Germany. If the former allies created a central German authority which led to the extension of its power over the Ruhr, the Rhineland, and Westphalia, Germany would again become a threat to the peace of France and the world. The separation of these regions from Germany was therefore vital, with France reannexing the Saar and permanently occupying the west bank of the Rhine. The Ruhr, Paris hoped, might be placed under permanent international control. French leaders, with infinite detail and care, repeated these goals to top American officials, stressing as well their fear that Russia might communize and incorporate Germany into its orbit, thereby posing a decisive threat to French security. Without the resolution of the overriding fact of French obstructionism, necessity would reinforce the American tendency to avoid an effort to fulfill the nebulous Potsdam clauses. In a critical sense, French reticence became a plausible excuse for preventing an agreement that the United States was disinclined to make in any case.[4]

The vast panorama of chaos, hunger, and confusion which Germany presented in the summer of 1945 transcends the capacity of prose to convey, but Germany was by no means alone in its terrible sufferings, and its purgatory was both less intense and far shorter than that of the nations it had ravaged since 1939. It was the immediate suffering, however, which most impressed the motley array of Americans sent to occupy the nation. To Clay and his key advisers, charged by JCS 1067 to prevent starvation, disease, and unrest, to drain Germany's resources further to aid the recovery of its victims seemed inexplicable. Apart from the already common admonitions of generals such as George S. Patton, who freely informed Stimson that only Communism would profit from additional German suffering, it was administratively less troublesome to attempt to reactivate the German economy than to dismantle and tax it further. No less significant, if the German economy did not revive, the United States treasury would have to subsidize the German people, and since JCS 1067 stipulated that Germany become self-supporting, after Potsdam, Clay concluded that economic revival was the first order of business and a precondition of later reparations to any nation. To help articulate the economic basis of this unmistakable shift in the premises of the United States policy, in August, Truman sent Byron Price, an editor, to Germany to reconsider quickly the future of the occupation government, even as Joseph Dodge, the Detroit banker who was to become a leading policy-maker for many more years, arrived to begin what became a comprehensive redefinition of Germany's economic future.

Into this setting also came lesser Americans—soldiers and civilians eager to enrich themselves in the black market, technicians assigned functions while never perceiving policy, instant experts of every sort ready and willing to transform Germany overnight. The black market, which was to profoundly further dislocate the German economy and result in a currency speculation racket among soldiers which cost the United States as much as $300 million before it stopped it at the end of 1945, only intensified the social disintegration of German society. The net result of these carpetbaggers, and the conditions they found and aggravated, was to undermine the ability of the occupation authorities to administer any coherent policy with reasonable efficiency.[5]

Unless the question of four-power common functions were resolved, the inevitable consequence of United States policy was to move more clearly toward the partition of Germany and its reincorporation into an American-led world—the policy that Washington had essentially spelled out after the fall of 1944. Yet the functional difficulties of economic revival and the presence of Russian and French forces that had their own claims on Germany's future, as well as elements of confusion that existed at high levels of American officialdom and became even more pervasive at lower ranks, make the history of this period appear more like a series of complicated zigzags to a quite predictable set of objectives.

While the first months of the Four Power Allied Control Council sitting in Berlin had been marked by uncommonly good cooperation on such matters as access to Berlin and the like, the function of this body, given the existence of a unanimity rule that automatically gave zonal commanders authority to operate where there was no common policy, quickly fixed on its economic role, especially on reparations. Immediately after Potsdam, Pauley informed Clay that although each side would draw reparations from its own zone, Potsdam also authorized them to treat Germany as a single economic unit for other purposes. Since the United States zone had a food deficit, it was here, most of all, that the United States was to encourage all-German economic cooperation, even though Potsdam entitled the Russians to trade the food surplus of their zone for 15 percent of the industrial reparations generated in West zones. But as long as each power collected reparations from its own zone, it was technically not possible to treat the zones as part of a single economic unit. This could occur only before or after the reparations period, and to ask the Soviets to integrate their zonal economy with the Western zones was tantamount to demanding that it not extract reparations until Germany had reached a minimum subsistence level or trade balance. Apart from French obduracy making this unlikely, German economic unity was also not the intent behind the United States zonal formula the Russians accepted at Potsdam. In the summer of 1945 the United States thought large German reparations both impossible and undesirable, though later it was to define the Potsdam Agreement on Germany's economy as it suited its particular argument. But it was the zonal reparations system and economic autonomy that Pauley publicly strongly emphasized at the end of August, scarcely assigning any economic function to the Control Council other than negotiating the amounts available for reparations, either in the form of plant removals or from current production —a calculation that would first demand the determination of what portion of the existing German economy was unnecessary for a peacetime economy allowing Germans to "subsist" without external aid. This "level-of-industry" calculation would also have to reflect the goal of depriving Germany of its economic means for waging war. "The method of paying reparations, that is the method of Administration, rests equally on the zones because the occupation government is set up by zones and it is this occupation government which must manage the German economy. . . ."[6]

Even before Pauley had outlined the thrust of the Potsdam reparations agreement, the Russians and Americans were locked in a sordid debate over details that revealed both American intent and the probable outcome of the controversy. The Potsdam agreement was entirely explicit on Soviet-Polish removals of their reparations claims from their zone, with no references or allusions to limits, amounts, or restrictions in their region from the other three powers. Negotiations between the four powers would occur only regarding the amounts of industrial equipment available in the Western zones for reparations removals, one-quarter of which would be given to Russia or traded for raw materials. Even so, consistent with the *de facto* partition agreed on at Potsdam, any of the Western zone commanders could veto the amount the reparations commission of the Control Council proposed. The only issue, therefore, was not what went on in the Soviet zone, but the level of industry elsewhere in Germany necessary to pay for subsistence and balance essential trade—and what economic excess was available for reparations. There were, as the Russians pointed out, two systems of reparations collection specified in the agreed American plan at Potsdam.

One minor ambiguity appeared in the Potsdam Agreement: the Control Council's reparations group would determine the amounts available for reparations ". . . under policies fixed by the Allied Commission on Reparations," which the three powers had created at Yalta and was still stationed in Moscow.[7] By mid-August, Pauley and the State Department decided the Moscow Commission should disband and transfer its functions to Berlin, a small point the Russians conceded in mid-September, but also that they would now have to measure the level of reparations from the Western zones against removals from the East, which the Russians correctly pointed out was a major distortion of the Potsdam accord. By early September the State Department was insistent that the Russians permit the other three powers into its zone, and, in effect, that they discard the very terms Pauley had announced one week earlier for an essentially new principle. If they did not agree, Acheson proposed excluding them from the determination of reparations and levels of industry in the West—in obvious violation of Potsdam. The Russians were scarcely inclined to agree to the American disavowal of Potsdam, not the least because French actions must have convinced them an all-German economy and reparations were likely to produce nothing for themselves. But they were anxious to obtain reparations from the West, which had at least two-thirds of Germany's industry, and on September 16 they agreed to permit mixed commissions to enter their zone but still refused to allow the creation of a new four-zone reparations scheme.[8]

The Russian concessions forced Washington to continue with the reparations chimera at a time that it was quite prepared to scuttle the illusion, but from this point onward there was no possibility that Soviet demands would be met. For one thing, as Murphy pointed out at the end of September, given JCS 1067's instructions to prevent starvation and unrest, the United States was going to pay large sums to keep Germany afloat for perhaps two more years. "The second issue relates to the problems of the relationship of the German economy to the rest of Europe. . . . [I]t is becoming clearer that extreme, ill-considered deindustrialization of Germany may well have the effect of creating and extending chaos in Europe."[9] Going one step further toward burying the issue, in early October the War Department instructed Clay to ask the Russians to trade non-German raw materials, presumably from Eastern Europe, for the 15 percent of German reparations that ordinarily was to be traded for East zone commodities. To the State Department, such trade might exploit reparations to economically reintegrate Eastern European economies as well. Clayton did not believe that large German reparations were incompatible with German recovery, but he emphasized the need for Germany's aiding European recovery via coal, iron, and consumer goods exports, an analysis that stressed the reintegration of Germany into an all-European economy without fixing any magnitudes for reparations. At the same time, they could dismantle excessive German steel, machine tool, and chemical capacities built for war production without hurting its normal integration into Europe. But Potsdam required that the occupation produce such data by February 2, 1946, and it was out of the question that they could do this by that time at a level acceptable to the Russians. Given dominant American assumptions, all subsequent negotiations on reparations and levels of industry were anticlimactic and inevitable, certain to prove fruitless and aggravate relations with the Russians. By the fall of 1945 the American reparations experts gathered in Germany concluded that the United States neither had a policy on the question nor was working on one.[10] But this illusion of confusion concealed a real policy that existed at the highest levels for almost a year: not to force Germany to pay substantial reparations.

While a certain amount of confusion existed on other questions, it was almost always on the technical means of best implementing what was a coherent policy. On an administrative level, the War Department and military authorities wanted to unload the problem of running Germany onto a civilian agency, an effort that the civilians thought commendable but premature. For one thing, apart from the issue of economics, French actions had left no significant central control mechanism, and Clay felt that unless the occupiers did something Germany would gradually dismember into four states, a danger Washington thought they might perhaps circumvent by setting up some form of control machinery with the British and Russians. Above all, various experts who had been assigned the task offered new estimates of larger United States policy and made JCS 1067, willy-nilly, more specific.

The first report, by Calvin Hoover, an economist on Clay's staff, argued that industrial dismantling could not go too far if the four powers were to maintain a minimum standard of living for Germany. While Clay had to make it clear the Hoover report was not official policy when its release in early October created a minor storm, it merely documented a prevailing school of thought. More influential was Price's November 9 report to Truman, which was less a positive recommendation than a series of questions implying that the United States was failing in its task in Germany, partially because of French obstruction but also because it was unclear on ". . . how far we are going in destroying the industrial structure of Germany."[11] But the stalemate in reparations shortly before Price handed in his report left no doubt that the Americans would not ruin Germany for the sake of Russia. In effect, by implication it was nonutilization of plant-in-being rather than actual physical destruction that posed a real dilemma for the United States. So long as the United States was determined to stand by the "first charge" principle, which demanded a sufficient industrial capacity to earn foreign exchange for vital imports to maintain living standards far higher than those prevailing at the time, and was willing to define a role for Germany in Europe that led to facile reinterpretations of the Potsdam reparations terms, there was no chance of a vengeful peace being inflicted upon the Germans. For them, there was but one way from the cesspool of misery in which they found themselves along with their victims: upward.

The lack of a completely systematic, comprehensive United States policy statement at this time is less significant than the assumptions and trends in functional policy. If administrators in Germany felt unsure of the desirable response to every situation, it was still unlikely that the allies might inflict a Carthaginian peace on Germany by inadvertence. Because of the confusion in jurisdiction among American authorities, and unexpected problems with France and Russia, the bureaucratic mechanism was less than ideal. So, at the end of October, Clay and his key adviser, Murphy, decided to return to Washington for consultations, and there was more reflection.

Clay and the War Department sought clarification from the State Department, since it now had responsibility for the larger issues of economics and diplomacy that Clay had to administer. They asked what were essentially economic questions, but these had, as well, far-reaching diplomatic consequences to relations with Russia. To our knowledge, Washington did not meet their request for guidance on how to cope with French and Russian policy. How much industrial plant would Germany retain? What would be the standard of living? What aid should they give for economic recovery? And how did all this affect Europe as a whole? The State Department's reply, publicly issued December 12, only further confused the issue, for it was open-ended as to what the United States would do for Germany and it ignored the political context in which they would make such economic decisions: relations with France, which singlehandedly was smashing the Potsdam accord, with Russia, and with developments in Europe, and what kind of social relations were to emerge in Germany itself. So long as these were unmentioned, it made little difference that the United States still claimed to favor reparations. More to the point was the willingness to declare that Germany could expect in time to see its peaceful industry grow without onerous restrictions after a two-year period of reparations, and that sufficient resources, both in balance and in quantity, would be left ". . . to see Germany's economy geared to a world system and not an autarchical system."[12] The Germans themselves after February 1948 would run their economy, subject only to still undetermined limitations, but in the meantime the United States would not allow a volume of reparations that reduced Germany's ability to pay for essential imports with its own export earnings. The clarification, in brief, could mean anything, and a hint of the interpretation came the same day, when Byrnes stated that European economic recovery was dependent on increased coal output, which Germany would be asked to supply to the greatest extent possible. To link European and German recovery, even in quite specific areas, was tacitly to accept a logic that they might later apply to a much broader context. In the name of European recovery the Americans might justify not only German revival but also minimal reparations, indirectly forcing the Russians through abstinence to make a massive contribution to European reconstruction. In the meantime, since no one in Washington wished to eliminate the open-ended freedoms that JCS 1067 permitted by writing a more specific policy, out of the new flurry of words came a continuation of the *de facto* paralysis on the reparations question—a paralysis that left open all possibilities for Germany later, when they could better assess the larger direction of postwar European political and economic affairs.

A better index of America's strategy was its refusal to seriously pressure France on its sabotage of progress on reparations, Washington's contrived redefinition of the Potsdam decision on the role of the four powers in the East zone, and its desire to trade a small number of German plants for Eastern European raw materials. Back in Berlin, the four powers laboriously attempted to come to agreement on the levels of industry and standards of living that were a precondition to the determination of what was available for reparations. Steel was the most critical issue, and during November three weeks were lost when the United States stripped its representative of all power to discuss steel levels and transferred responsibility to Clay's adviser on the matter, a former president of Republic Steel. The Russians, eager to maximize their gains, pushed for a reduction of 60 to 70 percent in German industrial capacity, the Anglo-Americans for 30 to 40 percent. But of this intricate, convoluted topic, more later.[13]

The Future of German Politics

The question of the future of Germany's social system and political and economic life was intimately connected to its future role in world politics, whether as a source of conflict or peace. From the viewpoint of France and Russia, the paramount issue of Germany was not whether it would become a pliant client state or democracy, fulfill a mission in the world revolution, or something else, but essentially whether they would have to engage Germany in war yet another time. To both, it was inconceivable that they could permit Germany again to become a hostile nation on behalf of any abstract ideal. The limitations of this strategy, which guided both nations, is that without a far-reaching internal social transformation the elements that had led to German expansionism since 1870 would remain in a position to reassert themselves. For the problem of Germany was not merely that of politicians or a class that had supported Nazism, but of those who had earlier sustained the Kaiser's imperialism and Weimar republicanism as well. Without a new social system and economy, even as converted "democrats" the leaders of German society might once more choose the road toward expansion and war. In brief, Germany's future was really a question of the future of a German capitalism much older than the Nazi Party.

To develop a short-range theory of individual guilt was deliberately to skirt the meaning of German history in the twentieth century, especially before Nazism, and to divorce the sources of German expansion from its effects in one form only. Yet to permit Germany to transform itself profoundly was to open other dangers that conservative forces elsewhere ultimately deemed even more dangerous. To the United States, far worse than German fascism, which in any event scarcely looked formidable midst the rubble, was socialism—a system that might not only open the door to Russian predominance in Central and Western Europe but isolate the United States from the main stream of European affairs.

For a brief moment, at most, the danger of the radicalization of Germany appeared real, though nothing more formidable than a threat which might feed on chaos. The German workers at the end of the war, liberated not only from Nazism but from the bureaucratic strictures of the Social Democrats and Communists, had quite spontaneously created workers' councils to run the factories and many local towns as well, holding substantial power in the vacuum of devastation. Soon the older Social Democrats and Communists incorporated or eliminated many of the younger, less doctrinaire, and more radical leadership, but mainly the occupation authorities banned or formally co-opted them in impotent roles. By the end of August, in the three Western zones the genuine workers' council movement was moribund, and the danger of extraparliamentarian mass action was never to revive. What the Americans were to call German "politics" therefore became an elitist exercise, significant insofar as it served a useful function in aborting and rechannelizing the danger of a radicalism that under no circumstance would have been allowed to succeed.

The United States military authorities banned the genuine workers' councils in their zone until April 1946, when they permitted them to return on a carefully controlled basis. By that time there were about 600,000 union members in the United States zone, with the older Social Democrats (SPD) largely in their command. The military government required unions to obtain permission to organize, but only on a plant-wide basis until the end of 1946, and they had no rights to negotiate on substantive economic matters. Their employers suffered no equivalent restrictions. The British zone, with about the same union membership, was organized much like the American, save that the British permitted local unions to federate. The French, too, allowed nominal unions, with even fewer rights. While JCS 1067 did ostensibly provide for the " . . . self-organization of employees along democratic lines" and "free collective bargaining," the American governors largely ignored this explicit aspect of an otherwise general statement.[14]

The fate of extraparliamentarian institutions reveals the parameters within which the four powers tolerated German political life to reemerge after its long—much longer than twelve-year—record of docility, bureau-cratism, and failure. It was simply impossible, from the American view-point, that they permit German radicals to define the social framework of their future society. Those decisions were not to be made to satisfy and cultivate German democrats, but rather to attain the overriding, and ulti-mately limiting, American ends in Germany and Europe. After the initial months of liberation, whose contagious euphoria spread to politics, the inhibiting United States, British, and French efforts contained the possibili-ties of change within carefully delineated and circumscribed channels that they might more easily control. Older, more predictable leaders had time to consolidate their power. By early October, Clay could report that the masses were, so far, dormant and not ready for revolt. The " . . . relatively slight political activity . . . is largely led and inspired by holdover leaders of pre-Hitler parties. No cleansing convulsion of political reform has yet gripped the German body politic."[15]

Within this controlled structure German politics became a kind of harm-less game, the outcome of which was known in advance and the object being to win the favor of the occupation authorities. Those who could sway them were to achieve their programs insofar as they were in harmony with the occupying power.

The history of West German politics after World War II is inordinately complex and predictably simple at one and the same time, not only because of the way world politics was to dictate its outcome but also because the German people themselves were once again moving, or compelled, along familiar paths. In any event, their main preoccupation was to survive rather than reform, and after the first days of freedom the workers were once more seemingly quite quiescent. For our purposes, generalities regarding the political environment must suffice.

The critical party to emerge in Western Germany, but especially the United States zone, was the Christian Democratic Union (CDU), a group the State Department described as "middle-class" and "deeply concerned with the preservation of the present social order, tempered somewhat by liberal reform."[16] This description of the Catholic party is superficially correct in the Western zones, where the CDU was to attract not only middle-class groups but clericalist reformers and, above all, big business elements in search of a new political home. In the East zone it was a dramatically different organization, but its western branch increasingly found a politics that was reflected in the career of Konrad Adenauer, former mayor of Cologne in the British zone. Adenauer, after World War I, had been an advocate of Rhineland separatism and the cooperation of French and German heavy industry. By October 1945, though in unpleasant straits because of British hostility, Adenauer was convinced that Germany was irrevocably partitioned and that its future lay with a variation of his earlier separatist theme: an economic integration of Western Europe, perhaps including England, politically bound in a loose, federation system that would evolve into a Union of the States of Western Europe. While already a figure of modest reputation, one of the few on the Right with a cautious but proved anti-Nazi record, his personal connections were such as to attract attention: his half-American wife, a Zinsser, was also the cousin of the wives of Lewis Douglas and John J. McCloy. More important, however, was his ability both as a political infighter and man with a relevant strategy.

The CDU was permitted to form in the United States zone on a district level in August 1945, and throughout the British zone the following month. Some CDU sections favored the socialization of mines and monopolies, but the party suspended a firm decision on the question and immediately endorsed the institution of private property moderated by "ethical" proscriptions that later became even less significant.[17] More important was its passionate dedication to the economic and political reconstruction of Germany. Under the leadership of men such as Adenauer, its overriding, prime objective in the postwar decade was how to eliminate the consequences of having lost the war and to gain reentry into the world community on the basis of real equality. Given the integrative political and economic framework of Adenauer's vision, one compatible with the United States' own design for Germany, it was inevitable that the CDU's policy, in conjunction with its eventual firm opposition to socialization, make that party Washington's favored vehicle for Germany's revival. For the United States needed loyal Germans as much as the Germans wished to recoup their power.

The SPD, by contrast, had little to commend itself to the United States or, despite a certain sentiment in Labour circles, to the British as well. Kurt Schumacher, the party's most influential and charismatic leader during this period, was a mélange of impulses—sectarian, bureaucratic, and radically indignant—none of which the American or British authorities could trust. Moreover, unlike Adenauer he never had a fairly cohesive party behind his program, for the old-line leaders tended to more traditional ways. A Marxist whose rhetorical commitment to the class struggle was as intense as his desire to purge all vestiges of Nazism, his open contempt for the occupation authorities also made him appear as a true nationalist when more compromised men held their tongues. His vision was a socialist third force in

Europe, and he never wavered in demanding far-reaching internal structural changes. His redeeming usefulness to the occupation, which saved him time and again, was his bitter anti-Communism, which, combined with militancy on other issues, thwarted what was initially probably a majority sentiment among SPD rank-and-file members to collaborate politically with the Communist Party (KPD) in a United Front, or even to discuss the organic unification of the two parties. Schumacher, in brief, helped outflank the Communist Party in Western Germany at a time it might have attained a very real success. That, to many in the occupation governments, was a major contribution to the restoration of what was the traditional pre-Nazi party structure.

The other, lesser party, the Liberal Democrats (LDP), apart from the Communists discussed later in this chapter, was secular and appealed to the Protestant equivalents of the CDU followers, and it was essentially conservative. Its main strength was in the Soviet zone, which was predominantly Protestant, and, like the Communists, it was to obtain less than a tenth of the Western electoral support.[18]

It was with these political ingredients that the United States was first to confront the fact that French policy made a unified four-power political policy in Germany improbable, at least in time to confront the administrative chaos that prevailed in the summer of 1945. The Russians had quickly created political mechanisms in their zone. If only to meet administrative imperatives, but also to avoid invidious comparisons, during the early fall Clay proceeded to weld the three Länder (states) in the United States zone into a Council of Minister-Presidents (Länderrat) that was to coordinate a whole variety of governmental functions under close American supervision. As opposed to economic affairs, which reparations and self-interest would require be handled on a zonal basis, the Americans running the occupied zone hoped eventually to eliminate the zones on a political level, but first to develop strong Länd structures. The Länderrat were to fulfill the most important administrative role during 1946, during which time a variety of elections were held which gave the CDU control of two of the three Länder, the SPD the other.[19] In the much more heavily industrial British zone, the SPD was to emerge as coequal to the CDU.

Purge or Restoration?

The nature of Germany's future European role would depend, in the long run, on the type of social-economic system the conquerors permitted to reemerge there. The Anglo-American assumptions on this question were so narrowly focused as to predetermine the outcome. There was no doubt that a kind of sincere mechanistic naïveté led the United States to begin denazification of its zone, a topic which received extensive detail in JCS 1067 and demanded excluding from labor, sanctioning, and trying untold multitudes of Nazis. The assumption that by merely locating and eliminating specific individuals who had been party members, presumably out of personal choice only, one thereby ended the threat of militarism once and for all, entirely ignored the class basis of the Nazi movement and the larger, more permanent economic goals of the United States. Once this fact became clear —and it was understood almost immediately by Clay's key advisers—the decision the United States had to make was whether or not to effect a partial revolution in Germany by destroying the economic basis of German capitalism for its miscalculation in sustaining Hitler.

Under the American scheme, at least twelve million Germans were fair game for denazification, which in itself presented a monumental obstacle. The occupation, of course, immediately detained key Nazis as well as known war criminals and SS officers, but for the rest a vast program of questionnaires—"Fragebogen"—led to the completion of many millions of such documents. By the end of 1945, over 300,000 persons, mainly from the upper and middle classes, were designated unemployable save as common laborers. The immediate economic consequences were far-reaching, the long-range implications even more so. Save for the Communists, the other German parties, especially the CDU, resisted and objected to the denazification injustices in a manner they never dared show against Nazism. But by October the key United States officials in Germany admitted that some military men, such as Patton, not only were ignoring denazification laws but that the laws were counterproductive to other, more important United States goals. Clay was convinced that the only alternative was to transfer the administration of the matter to the Länderrat, where the fate of denazification in the hands of predominantly CDU officials was preordained to failure. Despite continued obeisance to the goal of denazifying Germany, from March 1946 onward, when the change was made, only a tiny portion of the highest Nazi elite had any fears of retribution, a fact that Clay's experts and other official inquirers repeatedly confirmed. The British were yet more lenient; the French scarcely made gestures to eliminate key Nazis; and the Russians delivered the sternest judgment on Nazis even as they left the door open for the incorporation into their zone of cooperative, low-level officials.[20] For to have denazified would have been to prevent the return to power of much of Germany's traditional ruling class, at the political as well as the economic level, and to have embarked on such a course was unthinkable without concomitant changes in Germany equivalent to a form of real socialism. Such a step, as well, would have demanded far-reaching redefinitions in the American vision of Europe's security. As we shall see, to Washington all this was inconceivable.

Other plans for Germany also floundered in a manner that left the German social order essentially intact. In addition to purging schools and culture of all Nazi and militarist legacies, JCS 1067 ordered the occupation merely ". . . to encourage the development of democratic ideas."[21] The occupation imposed no educational reforms of consequence, and it brought no important changes to mass culture. Its control of the press, as in the other zones, was total, and licensed newspapers were simply treated as official organs, and threatened with closure should they move too far from the United States position. Instead of changing more than superficial externals, a variety of American athletic jocularity arose as a justification for inaction. Both high and low, officers decided baseball was an adequate alternative to fascism. As a result of a sergeant's initiative, in early 1946 a mass German youth athletic program became a main thrust in Clay's reeducation work. Brigadier General Frank Howley, who became American commandant of the Berlin Kommandatura, and by 1955 was publicly advocating preventive war against Russia, was a good example of prevailing moods. "I consider the [athletic] program the best thing we ever did in Berlin to sell young Germany on American ideas of democracy and fair play."[22] The Russians strained to find some ulterior political meaning in the games, without much success. In fact, the Americans had unhesitatingly banned unauthorized political discussions and groups among youth, which led key officials such as Howley to confess in mid-1946, "On the other hand, we don't know for sure what we do want ourselves. . . . And so we favor teaching youth fair play, sport, and that sort of thing, letting him flounder a bit in order that later he may make up his own mind on the very tricky subject of politics."[23] Clay's public attitude polls revealed the measure of success in reeducating American-zone Germans, indicating that over the two years after December 1945 an almost unvarying percentage of the public—one-half—thought Nazism a "good idea badly carried out."[24]

The test for all such reforms, which illustrated the ultimate intent behind American purposes, was the issue of the deconcentration of industry, where no illusions caused men to wonder about their goals. Deconcentration, more directly than denazification, was an issue of purging the existing industrial elite and retarding economic recovery. In the end, both programs were not implemented as their consequences became apparent, even though they remained on the books long enough to generate later recriminations.

JCS 1067 included an unequivocal prohibition on all cartels and required the broad dispersion of the ownership of industry. Draper, Clay's director of economic affairs, was reinforced in his emphatic disapproval of the instruction by a bevy of other big business executives he brought to Germany. The British also shared this dominant skepticism toward the program, which lower officials less privy to the grand view of the German problem hoped nevertheless to implement. By the fall of 1946 the American military government recorded no significant progress, and not until February 1947 did it write a systematic decartelization law. The American authorities alternately diluted, tabled, and reinterpreted the law, leaving the structure and ownership of the German economy, after some legalistic juggling that had slight effect, with the men who had always owned it.[25]

Once JCS 1067's more platitudinous objectives threatened further to weaken German power, or to open the door to genuine social transformation, then Washington overrode the obvious conflict between these goals and American interests, wiping away the rhetorical confusions from which men of lesser responsibility in government often suffer. That the Americans would utilize German resources to contain Soviet power and to further their objectives became clearer with the months, until by 1946 the question was simply one of finding appropriate instrumentalities. Even as the war was closing, in July 1945 the United States authorities in Germany had begun to round up the first of over six hundred of Germany's best scientists, predominantly in rocketry. The following month the Russians decided to imitate the American precedent. Germany's resources in this instance were too tempting for the Americans to resist, not the least because they feared that otherwise the Russians would obtain them.[26] From its beginning to its ultimate resolution, this quite small matter tested American leaders and once again revealed how they would treat the remainder of Germany's immense power.

The Soviet Zone and Russian Strategy

Like the other occupying powers, the Soviet Union ultimately defined its policy in its zone to suit its own interests and goals, which were essentially to obtain high reparations for the vast damage Germany had inflicted on Russia and to insure that the defeated nation would never again become an enemy. Within this framework, during the first postwar years the Russians were entirely expedient and undoctrinaire, and they were drastically to alter their relative tolerance of internal events in the East zone only when it became undeniably apparent that the United States' policy in Germany would be to reintegrate Germany into its bloc.

The Soviet policy in Germany in the months after May 1945 was a synthesis of opportunism, spontaneity, chaos, and planning. The Russians explicitly prevented German Communist cadres sent back with their troops from implementing more radical changes and required them to seek out and place non-Communists in leading posts. On June 10, over two months before the Western zones permitted any parties, such Soviet toleration resulted in the legal formation of the SPD, CDU, and LDP. Confronting numerous ANTIFAS and workers' councils, the Russians encouraged them to assume tasks assigned to them, leaving them far stronger than their Western counterparts. The Soviets muzzled the more ideological Communists; the first KPD program did not even mention Marx and recognized a future for private business. Even as the Communists discouraged some elements of the SPD seeking unity on the left, in the largest sense the Russians encouraged a united front political movement in their zone, one they could start and control from above.

Such a strategy was also administratively practical, even to the extent of permitting former low-level Nazis back into positions of responsibility, and it eased the way for the greater Russian goal of taking large reparations from the zone. Incidentally, however, it was much closer to what the German people desired, and the allies had agreed upon, than any program in the Western zones until the end of 1945.[27]

Until the fall of 1946, the SPD was the most important party in the East zone; yet ultimately it was constrained by the occupation in precisely the same manner as the parties in the West. As a result of its comparatively real privileges, many of the SPD leaders, led by Clement Grotewohl, ranked close collaboration and unity with the KPD—and thereby the Russians— as the prime objective, a strategy that Schumacher fought to the extent that the Anglo-Americans might forgive his militant socialism they in any event had no intention of permitting to bear fruit. It was this role, as well, that gained him the support of the more conservative old-time SPD leaders.

While the politicians organized, the ultimate arbiters of power, the Russians, feverishly dismantled German industries and shipped as much material as possible back to the USSR. Special units assigned to do nothing else within several months found that not only was the hasty process wasteful, leading to vast losses, but it paralyzed the East zone economy as well. Soon the Soviet occupation authorities were restraining the experts sent from Moscow, for they had to administer the zone and were caught in many of the same ambivalent situations as their Western counterparts, and thoughtless dismantling, looting, and violence against Germans came to an end.[28] Only in 1946 were the Russians able sufficiently to organize the East zone economy to extract approximately a billion dollars in reparations annually for three years, largely from current production.

The ambiguities in Soviet policy at this time were less compelling than the desire to extract maximum reparations, a program that was scarcely compatible with turning Germany into a Communist state—since heavy reparations also generated political and organizational consequences likely to lead in other directions. Still, the Russians, far more than the other occupiers, wanted some reforms, but never went so far during 1945–1946 as to create irrevocable structural barriers to complete eventual integration between the zones. Quite genuine mass land reform agitation, which the Russians could scarcely control, culminated in legislation in the fall of 1945, and struck Murphy as a successful demagogic way of winning landless peasant and refugee support—which it unquestionably did; but it was merely a redistribution of large estates into initially uneconomical small holdings rather than collectives. While it still permitted a later merger of the agrarian economies of the East and West zones, land reform progress, along with a more extensive and democratic educational system, also led to invidious comparisons with Western zone conservatism.[29]

Industrial reforms were more profound and unavoidable. The businessmen simply abandoned their plants, which workers ran at every level and which the Russians had to regulate in some fashion. Unlike the Western zones, where the capitalists remained and the occupation was ready to force workers out of management posts, the Russians, for lack of a better alternative, permitted the very genuine mass desire to follow its course. From an initial policy of restraining workers' councils, which wished to purge all vestiges of Nazism and unquestionably spoke for the politically active German Left, the Russians shifted to letting them formalize their *de facto* control, later imposing their own over them. The Germans nationalized all phases of the coal industry with Soviet encouragement, but at question was the nearly one-third of industry belonging to the state, Nazi Party, or leading Nazis. During the fall the various Länd governments began to legalize the reality, ranging from workers' council laws to mass votes in favor of expropriation. ". . . [I]t seems clear," Murphy reported to Byrnes in November, "that urban eastern Germany is now experiencing the beginning of social revolution. Perhaps the most important change so far is psychological. Radical workers, supported by Soviet MG . . . are taking possession of the economic instruments of power." This experience, more than any other, caused the middle-class elements in the East zone to desert the regime, and the United States to regard the future relations between the zones as tenuous, at best. "This procedure," Murphy observed in early December, "contrasts with the American MG policy of discouraging revolutionary changes as long as the German people cannot express their desires freely," but he acknowledged that all that was happening was ". . . formalizing many of the social changes initiated by the Communist and trade union leadership. . . ." And he did not preclude that indeed they were the will of the masses: "Whether any or all of these reforms actually do correspond to popular desires is not known."[30] What was vital, to the United States, was that the disparity between the two societies not grow so large as to increase socialism's attractiveness to the West zone. By the end of 1945, the substantially greater freedom the Russians had allowed in their zone, largely due to a combination of ideology, ineptness, and permissiveness, had left in doubt the United States goal of containing German radicalism.

Apart from ideology, the Soviets found that the policy of acceding to genuine mass sentiment, which the SPD enjoyed to its own gains, also speeded recovery more quickly than in the West—and made possible larger reparations. During 1946 East zone coal output was 98 percent of the 1936 level, compared to 53 percent in the Anglo-American zones, with industrial output at 50 and 34 percent, respectively. Ideological affinity did not prevent the Russians from taking for their own use up to one-half the output of all industry, socialized or not. The United States, by contrast, restricted the Left without ever heeding its demands for economic reform, and economic paralysis froze the Western zones. In general, by the turn of the year the Russians had yet to pursue a fixed policy regarding Germany's internal political and economic future, other than draining it economically and preventing its reemergence as a hostile state, while the United States by both decision and default had decided effectively upon its own—one that was compatible with American interests and would lead to the restoration of Germany's traditional social order.

The partial transformation of the East zone economy was possible because the majority of the people endorsed a radical Social Democratic program or, to a lesser extent, the Communists. This was to create political dilemmas for the Russians, which the United States apprehensively watched. Succinctly, the main problem was the future of the SPD in their zone, and its relationship to the Communists. During the fall of 1945, undoubtedly aware that time favored the SPD, the Communists began agitating for the unification of the two parties into a "single labor party." The SPD's leaders in the West, with active United States and British aid, opposed the merger, but in the East many opportunistically moved more circumspectly for fear of losing influence with the Russians, while some strongly favored it. Among the rank and file, in the United States zone in March 1946 fully one-third favored a unity party, but the majority in Germany preferred a united front with the Communists in one form or another, which would have given the Left political predominance in all of Germany. In the end, the average member was ignored as the leaders prevailed in both zones; during early spring 1946, Grotewohl forced through an East zone merger in the form of the Socialist Unity Party (SED), and in the West the SPD became the implacable enemy of the Communists. Though initially able to attract popular support, and despite its quite reformist character and militant social democratic rhetoric, the SED's close association with the Russians later was to cost it much backing. Yet the Russians insisted on keeping alive the other parties in the zone until 1947, permitting them to maintain independent programs without having access to real power.[31] As with the CDU in the United States zone, the SED now became the openly favored party in the East. To a greater or lesser extent, the dominant party in each zone adopted the political coloration their occupations demanded of them, but only in the East did it reflect in some significant measure the desires of the people.

Both the Russians and the Western powers pursued their interests regardless of German mass opinion, which, after twelve years of subjugation to Nazism, could never become the measure of successful policy. Ideally, what was critical was to end Germany's recurrent role as a threat to world peace, and not cater to the priorities of the Germans themselves. Self-interest was the basis of great power policy, and led the United States to freeze and thereby preserve and protect the old social system from radical action. But the fact that the Russians followed their interests in a way more in tune with German opinion during the first months of peace led to invidious comparisons the United States occupation authorities thought damaging to their hegemony in their own zone. After mid-1946, when German moods began to shift and the application of Russian power to protect their interests and needs appeared more naked, the United States was to find it easier to proclaim its support for German desires; at that point, and not before, many

Germans were ready to work for United States goals as well as their own. In every instance, having paid the price in blood, each occupying power did what it thought best for its own welfare.

The United States officials recognized early in the occupation the role they were playing and the dangers involved. "Our policies tend to be negative, which puts us in the position of not approving the Russian plan but very often having no plan to substitute," Howley wrote in his diary. "The Russians also from the start freely recognized the Germans as liberated, whereas we have considered them a conquered people."[32] Until early 1946, such Russian initiative, combined with a significant indigenous reform movement, appeared dangerous over the long run. The advantage of United States policy was that, above all, it kept German power and the social order intact for eventual future reintegration. In the short run, it left leadership and reform in Germany with the Russians. As he watched developments in the East zone, Murphy regarded events there as a travesty, with the Russians holding all the cards and domineering all the parties (including those that were in reality quite independent). Although he could admit that some Socialists, such as Grotewohl, had favored organic unity with the KPD long before that party accepted the idea, Murphy saw the emergence of the SED as just one more aspect of a larger malicious Soviet intent in Germany—one, we must add, which had a mass base on which to grow. As the proposal was being debated, Clay and his British counterparts attempted to gain jurisdiction over all-German political organizations and trade unions, utilizing technicalities to prevent the SED and the East zone unions from entering all areas under Western occupation. Then, early in April the Control Council enacted a workers' councils law that both attempted to restrict their functions to minimal appendages of the orthodox trade unions and laid a firmer basis for inhibiting them. The issue of all-German political parties and trade unions obviously impinged on the future unity of the nation. The Russians, Kennan warned in response to Murphy's analysis during early March 1946, ". . . see in central agencies a possibly indispensable device for entering at an appropriate moment into other three zones and facilitating there accomplishment of Soviet political program."[33] Central control, therefore, was a "two-edged sword," which, to interpolate, would aid the Left so long as the East zone monopolized reform and combated economic and social stagnation. They could then expect the Russians to advocate centralization, as indeed they did via national parties and unions. The historian can see the past no more clearly on this absolutely vital question, so central to the fate of Europe, than key American advisers in early 1946 saw the future. There were two alternatives, Kennan correctly concluded: unity and Soviet predominance, or

... to carry to its logical conclusion the process of partition which was begun in the east and to endeavor to rescue western zones of Germany by walling them off against eastern penetration and integrating them into international pattern of western Europe rather than into a united Germany. I am sure Russians themselves are confident that if rump Germany west of Oder-Neisse were to be united under single administration, there would be no other single political force therein which could stand up against Left Wing bloc with Russian backing.[34]

Political partition was the key to quarantining most of Germany from the economic virus of the Left; then the Western occupation forces could determine the larger part of Germany's political fate and that of the European economy and strategic balance as well.

From Dilemma to Action

It was in the political context of Soviet zone radicalization and a mass impulse toward the left elsewhere that the United States confronted the question of economic stagnation in the Western zones and its larger implications to the German social system as well as to the Western European economy.

Superficially, the reparations question played a role in Germany's history at this time, but the Potsdam decision and economic realities precluded anything more than a polite façade which, in the end, could ultimately only result in the most minimal reparations, thereby aggravating relations with the USSR. Tenacious French resistance and demands for annexation of the Saar and internationalization of the Ruhr economy alone made the laborious levels-of-industry talks that continued during the fall and winter of 1945–1946 quite irrelevant. Here the British, whose zone was the most paralyzed and by far the most expensive to occupy, were the main obstacles in the levels-of-industry conference to agreements on the outputs and industrial capacities, of which steel, metals, chemical, and machinery were the most controversial. As numbers replaced reality, the British argued for minimal reductions of about one-third in the 1938 general level, the Russians for twice that in the hope that the difference would be available for reparations. Ultimately, on March 28, figures equivalent to 50 to 55 percent of the 1938 level were approved. But numerous other technical and vital political questions, from the number of labor shifts that might alter capacity drastically to how the zones would proceed to reduce plants, were left in abeyance. And since industry in the United States zone was producing at about one-fifth of its capacity during April, the plan was not inconsistent with recovery measures. Suffice it to say, nothing came of the convoluted calculations, either in reparations or disarmament of Germany's future military potential.

Germans such as Adenauer and Schumacher, constantly searching for openings that would allow them to recoup control of the fate of their country, thought the reparations plan impossible. They entirely missed the crucial point that the key administrators of the Western zones also thought German recovery and the reduction of occupation costs critical problems to be quickly solved. Clay specifically regarded the level-of-industries plan as dependent on operating Germany as a unified state, on complete French cooperation and abnegation, as well as on other contingencies. This alone explains why he made no significant effort to implement the plan. Since the French during preceding months had resisted American efforts, the fate of reparations was foregone. To project ahead, with the exception of a few plants, which along with all other transfers were to produce around $25 million from the Western zones for the Russians, no effort was made to dismantle Germany's industry to conform to agreed levels.[35]

The real story during the first half of 1946 is the United States' efforts to aid German recovery, thereby strengthening the entire Western European economy, and its confrontation with the diplomatic and ideological offensive from the Left and Russia. During this period of gestation, American leaders understood that prolongation of the paralysis in Germany would intensify multiple dangers potentially of vast consequence: spread the appeal of socialism and a united front internally; deprive Western Europe of German coal and resources essential for its own recovery; drain Britain's scarce foreign exchange by continuing an occupation expense that was to amount to around a quarter-billion dollars in 1946 alone. Clay by March had already decided that "[w]e must either have central machinery and then central government or go it alone. . . ."[36] Yet it was patently clear that this was neither possible nor, given United States opposition to national, East-West German parties, desirable; nor was it consistent with high reparations, an old commitment the Americans were not yet prepared to abandon publicly. At the same time and over subsequent months, both Kennan and his superior in Moscow, General Walter Bedell Smith, were advising the State Department that the Russians were seeking ultimately to dominate Germany and that steps toward partition were imperative. Kennan advocated a total, formal break with Potsdam, including its implied concession of the Oder-Neisse region to Poland.

But quite apart from a rupture with Russia was the problem of France, which the United States worked on via pleas, compromise solutions, and financial baits that were too courteous to produce significant results. So long as the other key questions remained, the United States did not find it necessary to twist the rather vulnerable French into line, and at least their zone was insulated from radicalism. Far more important yet was the British zone, the most critical in the whole of Germany, for it contained almost one-third of Germany's industrial capacity and, above all, much of its coal. Clay banned local governments in the United States zone from initiating socialization measures and effective workers' councils, ostensibly because it prejudged a future united Germany's economic structure but also because ". . . it was our duty under our directive to point out the merits of free enterprise."[37] He was less successful in the British zone, where both the greater strength of the SPD and more toleration from a benign Labour government posed especially great dangers for the future. The loss of the British along with the Soviet zone to varieties of leftism would have meant, in effect, a socialist Germany that would have shattered American goals for both Germany and Europe. But by spring 1946, although the Russians could not be brought into line, Britain's willingness to sell Ruhr coal, electricity, and gas to the United States and France at low prices meant that it was really subsidizing its allies at an intolerable rate. This vast loss to the British treasury was America's opening.

Aside from the threat of socialism in the British zone was the critical problem of its lagging coal production, which in 1946 was to reach only 40 percent of prewar levels and in the spring of that year was but one-third of the essential export levels which American planners had set the preceding summer. By the end of April both Murphy and Byrnes were ready to alter all reparations plans and industrial restrictions to create the incentives and conditions that would maximize coal output. For the Americans fully realized, as Acheson put it in mid-May, that "European coal production now limiting factor on entire European recovery and virtually equal in urgency to food supply. . . . United States economic policy for Europe . . . requires that increasing amounts of German coal be made available to help recovery in France and other Western European countries."[38] From this viewpoint, Germany was the key to Europe and the restoration of stability. To sacrifice it to Russia by producing for reparations rather than European recovery was unthinkable. And even if the Germans were to attain socialism at the polls, the United States could not tolerate the monumental implications of such an event for the future of European—and American—power.

By early April all the destabilizing elements in the German situation, from French intransigence to economic crisis and the challenge of Russia and the Left, led Byrnes to authorize a reconsideration of the basic premises of United States policy toward Germany and JCS 1067. In the meantime, key Americans explored new options and confronted new crises. Clay thought that they might attain French goals for the Ruhr by placing its iron and steel industry under an international corporation that would work for the profits of the German capitalists, who would retain only dividend-bearing stocks, but leave voting rights with the governments. This scheme, which Bevin favored in a more general form as part of a plan to place the Ruhr into all-European international consortia, modified an earlier plan that Thomas Blaisdell, then chief of the United States economic mission in Europe, had circulated in early 1945. The plan's main asset was that it prevented a socialized Ruhr, which, apart from the identities of the owners, the United States strongly opposed in principle. Yet over four-fifths of the Ruhr's top-grade coal industry, which the Hugo Stinnes Corporation owned, actually belonged to a Maryland holding company which the United States Alien Property Custodian controlled. Without changing the structure of ownership of Ruhr coal, which virtually was certain to occur under British, international, or SPD control, the United States could hope partially to manage it in the future.[39]

During May 1946, just as the opening of the Council of Foreign Ministers meeting in Paris on April 25 underlined Washington's concern for the Soviet political danger in Germany and Europe, United States leaders outlined far-reaching policy conclusions. The most significant was Clay's announcement on May 3 that reparations and dismantling operations in the United States zone would cease until the Russians agreed to common economic policies for all of Germany and to pool East zone food and coal with the Western zones. This decision, for which the British share major responsibility, involved far more than reparations and mercurial American interpretations of the nature of the Potsdam Agreement, but really was a decision not to further penalize and weaken Germany, and to partition the country and insulate it from the East zone and Russian bloc. It was also an oblique testimony to the relative success of socialism in rehabilitating the East zone. Apart from France's guarantee that it could veto any move toward economic unity, termination of dismantling in the West hardly affected the Russians, who drew the vast bulk of their reparations from the

East zone. Neither could the Americans justify their demand that the Russians cease drawing reparations from their own zone until all Germany had a balanced trade and minimal consumption on the basis of the Potsdam terms, much less any subsequent agreements.[40]

This basically profound political decision was intended to place the onus of partition on the Russians at a point where the political and economic initiative rested with Russia and the Left, and it must have further convinced them that the Americans were going to administer their zone to suit their own interests. Though the State Department was to outline terms for Russian cooperation in a unified Germany, it was not probable that Moscow would discard its essentially accurate definition of Potsdam, and Acheson saw the offer as ". . . designed to force Soviet Union to show its real attitude toward unification of Germany within European framework and to avoid any danger that Soviets might put on . . . breaking with Potsdam on US." What was critical was that Russia, too, accept the ". . . desirability of treating Germany as an economic unit within framework of European economic system," one, we should add, which in American minds could not be reconciled with socialism in any German zone. The Americans warned the Russians that refusal to collaborate on their terms would lead to the ". . . inevitable alternative of treating Western Germany as economic unit and integrating this unit closely with Western European economy."[41]

Political unity and integration, as the Western nations had shown on the issues of parties and unions, was a danger to their interests; yet something had to be done to mitigate Western Germany's economic paralysis and its effects on Europe. "If Germany ended in economic chaos," Clay later wrote of the events, "it would be even more susceptible to Communist indoctrination."[42] How could German capitalism be made to work once again, deprived of its imperialist atavism? If there was no immediate answer, insulating it from a dynamic Left based on the East zone was at least a vital precondition.

One solution to this question was offered in May in the form of the Dodge Plan, on which Dodge had labored since the preceding August—a fact which made its political assumptions outdated. Yet the Dodge Plan holds interest both for its premises, Dodge's own perception of German realities, and the later acceptance of its harshest parts in 1948. The plan was an extremely detailed outline for a new currency to reduce existing monetary claims and obligations, impose a progressive capital levy, and adjust prices and wages. While it was based on the treatment of Germany as a single economic unit, it also allowed some regional variations, but within a capitalist economy only. It assumed, as well, that reparations would not be drawn from current production and that imports would be the first charge on Germany's export earnings. Essentially, Dodge, like Clay's top advisers, expected to work within the framework of Germany's prewar banking and industrial system, and his plan proposed a 15 to 20 percent price increase while holding wages constant. It was this last clause, which prompted one army expert to observe ". . . it would be unfortunate to impose on the workers an undue share of the burden of war and defeat," that showed how far the plan was from the limits that both Russia and the German workers themselves still might impose. And Dodge's insistence on a common currency, which he thought was the only way to avoid partition, revealed his distance from current American thinking.[43]

That frame of mind was articulated in Clay's now famous May 26 cable to the War Department, which merely systematized many earlier decisions and proposals that were largely not his own. It was, in essence, a summation of the economic events of the preceding year and the impact of Russian and French independence, the latter sharing equal blame for the failure of four-power government. It included his Ruhr control scheme, announced the termination of reparations, prophesied imminent economic chaos if something decisive were not done, and ended with a proposed merger of the British and American zones.

This was the economic setting in which the Council of Foreign Ministers inserted the German question into its first of two meetings scheduled primarily to decide on the peace treaties exclusively with Hitler's satellites. Byrnes had arrived intent on offering the Russians a twenty-five-year four-power treaty to demilitarize Germany, with inspection teams to begin operating *after* the signing of a peace treaty, a scheme he had proposed in a quite different form to both Molotov and Stalin late the preceding year. The project was benign, and scarcely the basis of American policy toward Germany or a substitute for one, especially since the United States had no plans for a German peace treaty. The Teheran, Yalta, and Potsdam agreements already bound Russia, England, and the United States, and since Byrnes left out every other phase of the German question, and entirely ignored the issues of industry and borders so essential to a meaningful treaty, the move was essentially an effort to clear the way later for unilateral and less moralistic American actions on more substantive issues. Molotov, when discussing the arrangement informally with Byrnes, told him Russia favored it but that existing agreements covered the matter and it would be better to get on with implementing them. Rather than iron out details privately, on April 29 Byrnes publicly threw the proposal at the Russians, making it clear that it was world opinion rather than Russian agreement that was at stake. Since propaganda was the function of the suggestion, Molotov upped the ante and called for a forty-year treaty and more comprehensive military and economic provisions, and from this point onward the topic led to current issues on which known past disagreements were merely rephrased. Claims and countercharges of violations of existing demilitarization agreements only muddied the scene. In this background, then, discussion on the unity of the German economy, the future of the Ruhr, and reparations led into a dead end. As soon as the meeting adjourned the Russians went to some pains to explain privately their response to Byrnes's cynical proposal, noting its major loophole in the peace treaty, lack of provisos for mutual assistance against future aggression, and the Western failure to apply existing agreements—all to no avail. The United States was shortly to resubmit the treaty proposal to the Paris Peace Conference.[44]

The Paris Peace Conference's discussion on Germany therefore became an exercise in stagecraft, with Molotov on July 9 now prepared to play America's game and also speak over the heads of state directly to the people. Pointing out that Russia would accept a revision of Byrnes's treaty, he stressed that the key issue was to disarm German industry immediately, to democratize the regime, and to deliver reparations out of current production as well as dismantling. The following day he attempted to score with the Germans as well as the French by stressing Russia's desire to welcome a peaceful industrialized Germany back to Europe, with a unified government, at some future time. Four-power control over German industry and the Ruhr, he vaguely implied, did not necessarily require separating the Ruhr from Germany.

The unconvincing Russian effort to promise something to everyone was not offset when Byrnes recited the now standard American litany on Potsdam's economic terms for Germany, and both sides proposed various investigations not likely to bear fruit. More significant was Byrnes's invitation essentially to France and Britain to join their zonal economies—no reference was made to political bodies—with that of the American zone, an invitation Bevin had already agreed to accept and which freed the United States for further action. This merger was to be on American terms regarding Germany's socioeconomic future. The proposal met a tolerant, even sympathetic, official French response, and at the end of July the Russians pointed out the obvious: by ignoring political unity the United States plans would further divide Germany into autarchic regions. In reality, Germany was being irrevocably partitioned, save if the Russians were willing to abandon all the economic, strategic, and political assets which their control of the East zone provided.

Such a shift in Soviet policy was unlikely unless Moscow received something substantial in return, and the Americans made no effort to reach such an arrangement. Russia's willingness to move toward partition, Dodge correctly perceived at the beginning of July, was quite recent, for ". . . six months ago the Russians were quite literal about the Potsdam Agreement and could have been persuaded to agree to anything based on it. . . ." Their change was undoubtedly due to many factors: tight Western control of a truly free German Left and immobility on altering the class basis of Nazism, Anglo-American abandonment of reparations and their desire to utilize the resources of the more dynamic East zone economy to bail out the West instead, and a refusal to make a concerted effort to remove the French blockade to four-power cooperation on every level. France's role was a cause as well as an effect. The United States had enormous economic leverage to bring to bear on Paris, but it refused to do so until it was ready —which is to say, late in 1946. Dodge saw this clearly and feared it could ". . . very easily encourage the Russians to modify their original intention to follow the terms of the Potsdam Agreement."[45] So long as the United States was uncertain of its policy toward the Soviet zone, it had little to lose from French obstinacy, which became annoying and utilitarian at one and the same time. As Clay later confessed: "French unwillingness to accept central German administrations until the questions of the Saar, the Ruhr, and the future political structure of Germany had been resolved seemed of less importance as the intransigent Soviet position made it appear unlikely that these central agencies could operate successfully."[46] For every French reservation that was articulated, the Americans had just one less doubt to express.

Washington favored cooperation in Germany, but on its own terms and within its larger European strategy. And so long as it sought to stop socialism in Germany, as elsewhere, and eliminate reparations as a means of reconstructing Russian power, or to create a reasonably powerful, yet responsive, Germany as a balance to Russia in Central Europe, cooperation was impossible. The suspension of German economy and power that was to occur after May 1945 was due in part to the failure of German capitalism as well as the fresh memory of Nazi aggression. Above all, it reflected a very real caution that existed during the year after the war regarding Germany's role as a barrier to Communism. By mid-1946 it was clear that additional delays would foreclose future American options, if only because in Germany itself the Left was becoming a growing threat. Yet more critical was the deepening realization that the restoration of the German economy in a Western European context would not only help save German capitalism but greatly strengthen that regional economy as well, thereby making possible the interaction between the American and European economies so carefully planned over preceding years. And once that integration was planned, German partition became inevitable along with the imponderable future that German reconstruction might ultimately entail.

6

The Political Economy of Western Europe, 1945–1946

America's peace aims were based on the fundamental assumption that the postwar structure of world capitalism would emerge in something akin to its prewar form. That system, preeminently in England, Germany, and Western Europe, Washington expected to reform and then integrate into a unified world economy in which the United States would play the critical role. The clarity with which American policy-makers held this vision is a basic keystone in the conduct of their foreign policy after World War II.

The profound economic, political, and social dislocations the war engendered immediately began to undermine Washington's objectives. The general crisis of European society, with Germany as its central but by no means exclusive point, the United States had first to confront and solve. No purely economic response on America's part would suffice, because the risk of rapid changes in French and Italian politics—where no occupation governments acted as the final arbiters of internal social change—showed the insufficiency of a narrowly conceived policy. Broadly applied, however, economic strategy might help to define the political outcomes of French or Italian politics, but at the very least it could create a dam against the seemingly dynamic Left that had emerged, in its various factions, as the dominant European political force. The realization of the Western European Left's economic goals might irrevocably undermine those of the United States, leading to the emergence of something akin to a socialist economic bloc that might also assume political dimensions.

The issue of Western Europe's internal economic and political future in turn impinged on that area's anticipated world role and whether it would act alone, relate to the Soviet sphere, or integrate into an American-led world system. The implications of the answer to this question to the ultimate nature of the world economic and political structure were so obvious that the United States had to relate immediately to the specific determinants that would prejudge the outcome. In Germany the sheer supremacy of its troops and formal rights as an occupying power sufficed. But in Italy and France the United States had to add its weight to the internal class dynamics—to the conservative parties and to the economic policies of Rome and Paris. The internationalization of the crisis in Western society was to become but a necessary aspect of America's imperial role in the world.

Italy and the Restoration

The United States and England hammered out a policy toward Italy during the final months of the war based primarily on the necessity of keeping the Communists and their allies on the Left from taking power. That transition went far more smoothly than they had anticipated, as Partisans transferred the larger part of their arms, handed control of the industrial north over to the Anglo-American armies, and the workers' councils managing a large number of Italy's plants proved cooperative. The Anglo-American decision to protect the existing moderate Italian government from a more dynamic Left, by arms if necessary, found expression in the Allied Commission's retention of jurisdiction of political control of the north until early December 1945, and also in its continued determination to circumscribe an unruly Left's actions in the future.

The Communists had been collaborators with the Anglo-American design, not only because they preferred cabinet politics and political privileges for themselves as a quite docile part of coalition governments but also because Greece had revealed the willingness of the occupying powers to apply great force in retaining their political hegemony over their spheres of influence. Though relieved that all had gone so well in the north, British and American officials in Italy had many other causes for anxiety, ranging from the unstable and perhaps too radical coalition Ferruccio Parri had formed in Rome in June 1945 to a profound economic paralysis that might yet cause the Communist leaders to accept extraparliamentary means or lose their quite tenuous hold over their followers. The overriding fact was that in 1945 Italian food production was two-thirds prewar, and its gross national product was one-half on 1938. Quite apart from their intentions, these structural realities gave the Communists the capability of challenging existing power.[1] In this sense, and given the considerable holdovers of Partisan-created or -controlled organs of power, the Left in Italy still retained the initiative at the end of the war. It was imperative for Italy's traditional ruling class as well as the United States and Britain to alter this reality and threat.

Relying on their own resources, a passive Communist strategy made it possible for the Italian Center and Right to neutralize and eventually isolate the Communists. The main conservative parties, the Christian Democrats (CD) and Liberals, aided behind the scenes in their specific demands by the State Department, sought first to undo the Parri government's reformist program of aiding small and medium business in preference to the concentrated heavy industries, reverse its refusal to crack down more decisively on strikes and workers' demonstrations, and reverse its plan to hold national before local elections and quickly submit the fate of the monarchy to a referendum. The Parri government's main problem was that it aspired to be a government of the entire nation at a moment when, for the forces of traditional conservatism, the dynamics of the situation called for a class-based political structure. At the end of November the Liberals, followed by the Christian Democrats, brought down the government and early the following month replaced it with a CD-led coalition under Alcide De Gasperi, which the Communists also supported, ushering in a long succession of conservative governments. The passivity of the CP before this rather profound change revealed, better than anything else, that the Communists and their Socialist allies would be the first and only force in Italy to voluntarily sacrifice its program and interests to the goal of national unity. From this point onward they became an essential element in creating an integrated society and an essentially unreconstructed capitalism.

The United States specific role was to reinforce the CD behind the scenes and indirectly let it be known that future economic aid, primarily in the form of UNRRA food and clothing and amounting to $418 million in 1946, was contingent on the replacement of the Parri government with one more acceptable. On the whole, however, it was quite passive and attempted to obtain Rome's commitment to America's principles for the reconstructed world economy, which the Italians obligingly endorsed in the hope more tangible help might follow in return. When translated into practice, however, Italian preference for its national oil company, in part the result of its need to conserve scarce hard currencies that foreign-owned oil required, led to United States intervention to open the Italian market to United States–

controlled exports and guarantee the prewar American share of oil imports.[2] By the beginning of 1946 Italy was to require American concern for yet more serious matters.

The De Gasperi government's reliability warranted, in the eyes of the Anglo-Americans, returning political control of the north to Rome's hands. While the term "counterrevolution" is inadequate to the less critical situation, in fact what occurred in the north was a purge of leftists in the governmental structures, a virtual elimination of the latent powers of the approximately five hundred workers' councils in the north, and the restoration of many of the skilled and reliable fascist bureaucrats to power. Assisted by Palmiro Togliatti, who as minister of justice as well as head of the CP was a cooperative linchpin, it was essentially in 1946 that the conservative order reasserted itself in Italy. In return, a small number of wage concessions to the workers, which the Communists celebrated as major innovations, gave big industry an opportunity to consolidate power and head off antimonopoly legislation that might have circumscribed its future growth. During the critical early part of 1946, preceding the June 2 referendum on the future of the monarchy and vote for a constitutional assembly, Italian conservatives accomplished most of these tasks without significant or additional American help.

In February, Rome asked the Export-Import Bank for a $940 million loan to supplement a paltry $25 million cotton loan Clayton had helped through with the prompting of his former business associates. By May the State Department decided that the United States could not fund large new credits to Italy, and the Italian embassy in Washington warned of the ". . . very grave political and social repercussions that are resulting . . .," but the plea failed and not until the following autumn did Washington find even $50 million to assist Italy.[3] At the beginning of May, however, the pending Italian elections and fear of the triumph of the Left required speedier action than searching for funds likely to prove too little and too late. Apart from any positive action to aid Italian conservatism, which was not forthcoming in 1946, during May, in the context of a parallel discussion among the President and key advisers on sending troops into France in the event of a Communist uprising, it now appears Washington also made the decision to lay down a broad doctrine allowing American military intervention in Italy as well. As will be seen later in this chapter, this doctrine was far more explicit for France than for Italy, and the complete documents on the matter are still classified; but the Pentagon readied one parachute infantry regiment and one regimental combat team for reinforcing United

States troops in Europe ". . . in the event of emergency in Italy. . . ."[4] The following month, as the necessary precondition of any future intervention, the State-War-Navy Coordinating Committee submitted a civil affairs draft to Rome that would have granted the United States omnibus base and access rights to Italy virtually at will—a right far more than Italy dared to approve during 1946.

The precise meaning of this authorization did not have to be tested, for the Communists neither revolted nor won at the polls, and in the June elections they received 19 percent of the vote, while the closely allied Socialists obtained another 21 percent. At the same time, the Italians rejected the monarchy.

Relieved of large reparations burdens, the Italians proceeded to solve many of their most pressing needs alone. About one-fifth of Italy's prewar industry was destroyed, and it was the task of reviving the substantial remainder that it confronted. In a setting of fiscal and political instability, with the greatest danger in the form of 1.65 million unemployed, food production, measured in calories, increased to 90 percent of the 1933–1937 average, for a sharp increase over 1945, while the 1946 level of industrial production more than doubled to 61 percent of the 1938 level, rising to 81 percent in 1947. The main problem this recovery created was inflation, and the new De Gasperi government confronted this not with substantial fiscal reform but by continuing to strengthen the police and conservative control over the state apparatus. Since the net effect of the government's economic action permitted wealthier elements to enrich themselves while compelling peasants to deliver cereals at fixed prices, the Communists were privy to the entire undertaking by objecting verbally while taking no action likely to change the government either via Parliament or the streets. But strikes and demonstrations during the summer hinted that the masses themselves were growing impatient. The Communists, in brief, loyally worked within the system. De Gasperi himself was unwilling to risk a general crisis by throwing them out of the cabinet for their criticisms, but during September he reassured a United States official that when the opportune moment arrived he would eliminate the CP from the government. Local elections over the next two months, however, compelled him to wait a while longer, for the Left held its voters while substantial middle-class elements, badly hurt in the inflation, moved to the rightist parties. In a sense, the Left's loyalty was even more essential if the Italians were to avoid exposing the serious rift in their society.[5]

The new crisis of Italian society that began to emerge in the fall of 1946 was one born from conservatism's successes, but structurally it was much stronger, and its internally financed reconstruction loan at the end of the year, which raised over one-half billion dollars, was a measure of its ability to sustain its own recovery. Yet the government could control the social consequences of its policy only so long as the Communists were cooperative. The United States, for its part, had played a major role in relief, but more critical yet was the remarkable recovery of local agriculture—which in 1946 supplied the large majority of Italy's needs. If the Communists could evoke moderation from the people, it was apparent that Italy could reconstruct its traditional order even without external aid. The question was how this could be done. The mechanisms of repression were now firmly in conservative hands, and at the end of 1946 both the United States and Britain began jockeying to staff a military mission and supply additional equipment to Italy's military. To a vital extent, Italy's economic problems were not a consequence of insufficient resources, but a conservative internal social policy, which in turn aggravated a trade deficit via capital flight and imbalanced economic development. Since the conservatives had no intention of abandoning Italy to the Left, they ultimately could solve their trade and payments problems through restrictionist and autarchic methods—such as those being applied to oil imports.

As the divisions in the Center-Right grew in the fall of 1946, and the Communists appeared as if they might gain from De Gasperi's failures, Washington planners finally took up the Italian loan request of the preceding February, assessed the far greater economic and political problems and dangers, and decided to recommend a $100 million raw materials and oil loan that would later, it hoped, convince Congress to give more, creating a yet larger market for United States exports.[6] Italy would recover in an integrated world economy, or alone.

What was certain, however, was that Italy's rulers might expect American sustenance while consolidating their power, and that the United States in turn was actively hoping to define a conservative Italy's relationship to American economic and military power. And if the Communists restored their commitment to their historic, if rhetorical, goals, Washington also calculated America's military presence.

France: Politics and Economy

During World War II the United States regarded France as an interminable frustration, and it never identified comfortably with either De Gaulle or the Communists—the two most important political forces to emerge by the war's end. De Gaulle's traditional nationalism, which immediately led to an autonomous and divisive French policy toward Germany, and his desire for an Anglo-French alliance independent of both Russia and the United States, all undermined Washington's integrative plans for Europe. Having abysmally failed to find an option in the remnants of Vichy, Washington saw the alternative of the powerful Communist Party as even less palatable.

The Communists at war's end were at the peak of their power and prestige as true nationalists who had fought and sacrificed most for France. Given their legitimacy among the workers, farmers, and intellectuals, they could be neither circumvented nor suppressed, and so the Communists were co-opted into a liberalized version of the traditional parliamentary and economic order. Despite their retention of Jacobin rhetoric which grew less and less ferocious, the CP leadership by war's end had repeatedly proved their faithfulness to the ruling coalition of which they were a part. They managed their ministries well, voted military credits, and, above all, disciplined the working class and urged them on to ever greater production and abstinence. Their control of the unions made their role as taskmaster of labor especially critical during French capitalism's vital breathing spell in 1945, for during that unstable year the residue of the resistance's commitment to social transformation, combined with hunger, seemed to make everything possible. The Communists were for reform, eschewed violence and sectarianism, and ultimately permitted technical criteria of efficiency and output to inhibit their action. They were, in brief, a loyal, integral part of the French system; yet their very size and critical responsibility gave them a formidable capability at any time their intent might alter. And it was this capability, as well as suspicion as to ultimate Communist objectives, that American leaders considered first of all.

France therefore presented several troublesome dimensions to United States policy: the Communist threat as well as a more prevalent tendency toward both political and economic independence and autonomy that was ultimately to become the defining characteristic of postwar Franco-American relations. At war's end the Communist quiescence allowed Washington to focus its attention on France's restrictive economic policies in much the same way as it was to do with the English. For France, even more than Italy, had a vital role to play in American plans for a reformed world economy. France's economic problems were far less durable or profound than England's, for while its reconstruction needs were great, it at least had large foreign exchange reserves and a capacity to earn more. To do so, the government controlled all dollar imports in order to reduce them to a level it could afford, while allowing private traders to handle all exports. During August 1945 American officials began a long, ultimately unsuccessful series of efforts to undo such impediments to the realization of their global vision, concentrating first on getting Paris to allow private traders to handle imports under government licenses—the clear threat being that state trading might become permanent unless capitalists were immediately included. By November, as the French sought an Export-Import Bank loan, Washington insisted on their making declarations of support for the American program of trade, payments, and investments. Sensing the need to pay obeisance to the mystical American passion for commitments in principle, but reluctant to promise specific action according to a timetable, French officials stressed that their agreement would be important to eliminating trade blocs and bilateralism, not the least because it would also involve their colonial system. The Americans, by contrast, were determined to win concessions on specifics as well as generalities.[7]

Dilemmas for the United States arose, however, when political complexities were added to the natural French reluctance to give as much as they wished to get. The October 21 election resulted in the Communists' winning 26.4 percent of the vote, while the Socialists obtained another 23.8 percent —leaving nominal Marxists a majority and a political mastery whose larger implications might prove decisive. Thorez now became Minister of State, while the Communists headed four of the twenty-one ministries—three of them dealing with economics. This critical Communist responsibility for reconstruction, and the Left's general commitment to extensive nationalization and its power to act, posed challenges to the United States that exceeded those in Italy, Germany, and England. They did not have to search long for a solution.

The Socialists (SFIO), headed by Léon Blum, agreed with the Communists on nationalization but on little more, and many of their leaders thought a united front exceedingly dangerous. Because of SFIO's ideological and superficial internationalist perspective, American officials quickly realized that the party regarded Russia and Communism as the greatest immediate danger in Europe. Disarmed both by their own conservative impulses and by inability to perceive the self-interested content of American-style internationalism, the thin Socialist idealism made them the most tractable group with which the United States might work. It was not long before American diplomats recognized that the Socialists would be the only

Frenchmen to cooperate on Germany. As conservative nationalists, De Gaulle and his followers in the Mouvement Républicain Populaire (MRP) inclined to rank Germany as France's most pressing international problem, a view that only compounded America's difficulties in both nations. Apart from their reticence about the SFIO internal economic program, which was reformist but might later prove manageable, Washington designated Blum and his party as the means for splitting the Left, avoiding dependence on the unreliable De Gaulle, and orienting France more closely to the United States and its goals. When De Gaulle resigned from the government and politics the following January, ostensibly because of the paralysis in politics and the power of the Communists in the government, MRP and other elements liberated from the general's control offered America additional allies in the Center. Preeminent among these was Jean Monnet, a Europeanist with close personal and financial ties, dating back to 1926 when he joined an American investment bank. To Dulles and his circle, Monnet was a technocrat who was above parties, but his skills and connections made him a critical figure in financial negotiations and later as head of French economic planning and nationalization.[8] More acceptable to the United States, Monnet also sought first to protect French interests.

Because of the presence of such allies in French politics, but also to gain French adherence to United States trade principles and secure an export market, the United States granted France a $550 million tied loan in December; but Monnet and his associates, comprehending fully the American desire to incorporate France and its empire into the United States trade system, stressed the need for additional loans to make future cooperation possible. At the same time, other Frenchmen informed Ambassador Jefferson Caffery in Paris that the real struggle with the Communists was occurring in the arena of managing recovery, with the CP attempting to prove to the other classes that only it could mobilize the workers to produce, especially in the coal industry so vital to general recovery. On both political and the economic levels more American aid was essential, they argued. The failure of the non-Communists to succeed, and the Communist ability to prove that only they could reconstruct France most efficiently, might lead to disaster in the elections that were scheduled the forthcoming June.

While all these considerations were articulated quite explicitly, what they did not state was the fact that the nominal party of revolution was in the meantime sublimating the working class and forces of change, thereby strengthening the existing social system and incorporating itself into it. Yet Thorez repetitively illustrated this reality in his statements from 1944 until

1947. "I think that work is not only a necessity but also a joy," he told a group of miners in March 1946.[9] Coming from any other man, everyone would have considered reactionary his interminable pleas for greater output, harder work, and less time off, especially in the coal industry. At the same time he, too, welcomed aid from the United States and denigrated a "ridiculous pacifism" which would have cut arms outlays even further.[10] On Indochina and colonialism, the Communists at this time advocated a version of progressive colonialism that would have granted greater autonomy only within the French Union. The Communists, in brief, went to extraordinary lengths to prove their reliability within the United Front and stressed their commitment to a distinctively French path to socialism—one that was in reality indistinguishable from that of the SFIO.

This Communist identification with a superior management of France, which lasted until early 1947, was the context of the consideration of a yet larger loan to France before the June 1946 election. In a sense the CP appeared more dangerous as a cooperative party than outside politics. But also dangerous during these early months to postwar French cooperation with America was the sequence of nationalizations that began in March and April with the coal, petroleum, gas, and insurance industries, along with a number of key financial institutions. Despite the fact that technocrats ran such government-owned firms, for practical purposes, just like private companies, but with a greater stress on meeting the government-defined economic plan, it was a development that profoundly undermined American desires for Europe. In the hands of the Communists in the Confédération Générale du Travail (CGT), the participation of union leaders in certain minimal managerial decisions was simply used as but another reason to keep the workers from striking.[11]

With its second loan the United States hoped to win the French to America's general trade aims while considering it, to quote Caffery, ". . . in terms of its political importance. To refuse it or to chop it down to an unimportant sum . . . will pull out one of the last props of substance and of hope from those in France who want to see France remain an independent and democratic country."[12] Though Washington was also to seek renewed French support for United States commercial principles, by April, as Blum prepared to set out to the United States with Thorez's blessings to bring home the good news, the United States saw the matter essentially as a political maneuver to gain the Socialist victory in the June 2 elections. The size of the loan was gauged not to French needs but to its impact on the electorate, for the December loan was still available and recovery was proceeding rapidly. Just as Blum went to great pains to suppress his nominal commitment to socialism while in Washington, the Americans were too nervous over the possibility of a Communist triumph, at the polls or by revolution, to exact as much as they had from the English. France also vaguely agreed to terminate state trading and purchases for private business needs. The French duly pledged in vague terms to refrain from autarchy, to abolish various import controls and government bans, to sustain the ITO charter, and immediately to allow American motion pictures to enter France—in return for which they received a $650 million loan. When the National Advisory Council met on May 6 to approve the transaction, the political justification weighed most heavily, for time was growing short. Blum triumphantly returned to France several days before the election, claiming to have promised nothing political in return.[13]

The loan to France was but one response to the prospect of Communist success. The anxiety reached a fever pitch when on May 2 the United States forces in Europe headquarters received a report from "rightist circles" of a possible Communist uprising should they lose the May 5 referendum on a constitution that they and the Socialists had proposed. Thorez, it was alleged, favored a coup, while Duclos, secretary of the party, was opposed. Caffery, who had dismissed similar rumors in mid-March, did so again. Now the commander of United States forces in Europe, General Joseph T. McNarney, asked permission to send troops into France should the uprising begin, and on May 2 the War Department moved to authorize him to do so if he thought it essential ". . . to protect United States lives and property," citing the previous authorization to intervene in Italy.[14] At 1:00 A.M. May 3, John D. Hickerson of the State Department learned of the discretionary order and froze it until he could consult Acheson. Not only did he feel the rumor was false, but he pointed out that it was tantamount to a thin justification for later intervention in a civil war, if only because United States supply lines ran through Germany and reserves in France were not essential to United States military security. Acheson prepared an alternative order that avoided intervention and advised an evacuation of United States troops in France if necessary. Later that afternoon Truman, urged on by Forrestal and Patterson, authorized the War Department directive. The following morning Acheson vainly attempted to get the decision reversed. On May 5 the referendum barely defeated the constitution, and the infectious concern over a coup now spread to Caffery, who argued the CP was eventually going to resort to insurrection. "Ever since V-E Day," Vandenberg noted from Paris, "the swing to the extreme Left has been encouraged not only by Europe's post-war chaos and confusion but also by the brutal tenacity with which Moscow has driven its neighbors into submission. . . . the Red tide has swept on. . . . France is the supreme test."[15] In this mood of urgency, Blum had easily gained American aid.

Blum's glad tidings did not impress the French, and while the Communist percentage of votes remained constant, Blum's party slipped nearly three points to 21 percent. It was now clear to men such as Bidault that the CP would remain useful if it were contented with co-option, and he much more than Blum thought this possible. Catering to Thorez's personal vanity, he undertook as the new President of the government, with Thorez as his Vice-President, to use the Communists as the straw bosses of the economy for as long as possible. While he added five Communist ministers to his government, his acceptance of their support was entirely on his own terms.

The Americans and French conservatives, and De Gaulle himself publicly after his ominous totalitarian June 16 address, worried that perhaps the Communists would ultimately exploit this uncomfortable marriage of convenience for their own purposes, but French recovery must largely be attributed to their energy in stifling the workers' demands and maintaining output. By mid-1946 (and for all 1946) industrial production was 79 percent of the 1938 level, and it grew to 95 percent the following year. After an excellent start, poor weather cut agricultural production in 1946–1947 to 83 percent of 1934–1938, but it still represented a strong advance over 1945–1946. The general economic trend was unquestionably rapidly upward and toward recovery—but in aggregate terms only. The problem is that given spiraling prices, which by 1947 were well over ten times 1937, everyone shared in the prosperity save the working class. In October 1946 the real income of Parisian workers was 65 percent of 1938 for skilled workers and 71 percent for unskilled—far less than the industrial revival. Yet the recovery was due preeminently to the revival of the coal fields, which by spring 1946 surpassed prewar output by almost one-tenth, and a universal willingness on the part of unions tolerantly to accept the economic and social costs of reconstruction. Only the Communists could evoke such patience and impose such discipline, and for their associates this was their asset. There were no major strikes in France during 1945–1946, but by mid-1946, as the State Department's analysts reported, the CP leaders ". . . could no longer hold back the discontent of the rank and file. . . ."[16] "We have never let ourselves be impressed by partisan criticisms against our campaign for production," Communist CGT leader Benoit Frachon had earlier admitted, "even when these criticisms claimed to be for the protection of the workers."[17] By mid-1946 only "fascists" and "Trotskyites" led strikes, a theme loyal party workers were compelled to repeat and act upon throughout this critical period.

However obvious such facts to the State Department, their real significance was lost on them, and also on the French workers who in the November 10 elections were unexpectedly to increase the Communist vote to 28.6 percent, making it the largest party, while the Socialists yet again lost another three percentage points. It was not sufficient that the Communists had loyally and successfully contained the workers' radical potential, contributing far more to save the French social system than essentially politically motivated American loans or paper plans to send United States troops into France. From the viewpoint of the danger of Communism and the extension of Soviet power, it was capability rather than intentions that counted, and even the successful implementation of a Communist-supported government's exploitive and inequitable economic policy, which American analysts thought commendable if not strong enough, could not wipe away the menace.[18]

Indeed, not even a full American realization that the Russians were bending every effort to inhibit French Communism from a militant line mitigated the danger that it might later change its strategy. At the end of May 1946, a source Caffery deemed reliable reported that Molotov had advised the French CP not to alter their friendly line toward the Socialists for fear it might drive them toward the British Labour Party and form a Franco-British anti-Communist bloc in Western Europe. Such a vision of the Russians inhibiting not merely the French but all European Communist parties emerged again in November in a long report that Walter Bedell Smith strongly urged Byrnes to read as the ". . . most accurate revealing exposé of present Soviet tactics not only in France but throughout the rest of Europe. . . ." Based on information received via members of the political bureau of the French CP, the remarkable account of Thorez's report on his summer trip to Moscow revealed that "because the Soviet Union is in the position of having to avoid during a relatively long period participation in a major war, it follows that the French Communist Party should not advance too rapidly and above all else must not endeavor to seize power by force since to do so would probably precipitate an international conflict from which the Soviet Union could hardly emerge victorious."[19] The French CP knew it could forcibly seize power, which it was unwilling to do, but the analysis stressed that it also feared parliamentary success despite its passivity. The stunning and surprising victory in the November 10 elections prompted Thorez publicly to reassure the Americans and British, in his conciliatory statements, that the CP's political advancement would not endanger the stability of France. Russia, in brief, would sacrifice the French and Italian Communists at this juncture. This would not keep the French party from strengthening itself on the parliamentary or extralegal level, but at the critical point that Russia's interests were at stake it would not assume power.

During November, Thorez's utterances were indeed conciliatory, and his presence at a British embassy reception was widely noted. No less to the point is that during the maneuvering for a new government that occurred over the end of November and early December, the CP failed to exploit the power its position as the leading party of France warranted. Despite the political chaos that dominated the scene—a harbinger of future events—on December 10 *Izvestia* lavished praise on the French Republic despite its ever-deepening involvement with Anglo-American diplomacy and conservative policies at home. A week later, with Communist backing, the bitterly anti-Russian, pro-American Blum formed a new government, granting the Communists only a single ministry.[20]

The United States' policy toward France by the end of 1946 was a mixture of political anxieties over the triumph of Communism, at the polls or in the street, and a desire to integrate France into an American-led world economy. To gain the latter, it had to pay the price in credits to avoid the further radicalization of France, a strategy that was failing even as recovery proceeded along lines Americans thought sensible but only further drove the workers to the Communists. Indeed, the CP's very cooperation posed its own dangers because of its legitimacy, its retention of the radical mystique for the workers despite its conservative practice, and its options on future action. In the streets, however, the CP was doomed to failure, for Washington had made its decision to intervene. In the parliamentary process it might attain new success despite its own restraint, though victory at the ballot box was still a long way off. Disturbing, as well, was the economic pattern that continued in the trade sector despite French pledges. By the end of the year Paris still tightly controlled all imports and remained on the path toward restrictionism. Unless something were done, France might continue its independent way, perhaps even, as *Business Week* predicted, move to further nationalize industry and create an economy that was ultimately neither Communist nor capitalist.[21] Given the larger patterns that were emerging throughout Europe at this time, there was precious little consolation for Washington in such an option. Postwar France was proving no more satisfying than it had been during the earlier years of common trial.

Food and Power

Official United States food policy was drawn between the desires to use surpluses to undermine the Left's appeals and to avoid excess production that might depress American farm income. Such irreconcilable goals were, to be sure, leavened with genuine concern for the hundreds of millions of hungry people throughout the world, but altruism was not to prevail. Sentiment quickly gave way to caution and resulted in recurrent food shortages and crises.

Agricultural surplus, like surpluses of every variety, can be the bane of any capitalist economy, and it was predictable that during the better part of the war American food planners assumed that the postwar problems would be like those of the 1930's. Hence they erred in favor of avoiding oversupplies until early 1945, when it became all too clear that the immediate problem would be too little food and that the consequences might be social and economic upheaval. By then it was too late to recover what had been already consumed or not grown, and United States food exports in 1945 fell below 1944 while hunger radicalized Europe's masses.

Supplementing Washington's benign evaluations of the economic crisis that the war engendered was its growing disenchantment with UNRRA as the basic world organizational structure for distributing food and relief supplies. UNRRA's problem was that it was committed to distributing aid according to need, and although the United States was pledged to give 71 percent of its funds (and actually gave slightly less), it could not use its free relief exports to attain maximum political and economic results in the same way as it had in Central Europe after World War I. In Anglo-American–occupied areas either UNRRA did not operate, as in France and Germany, or it complemented other programs, as in Greece and Italy. But because need was the major criterion, Eastern Europe received a greater share than Western and Southern Europe, though on a global level countries in the Anglo-American orbits were the largest recipients. By the end of the war a growing number of key American leaders, led by Henry Stimson in the War Department, urged that the United States use food, which was simply a form of economic power, as a tool for extracting political and economic cooperation.[22]

American leaders believed that UNRRA offered the Communist-led nations an equally useful means for consolidating their regimes, and such an interpretation, which was far more disturbing than the details of vast corruption that poured out of friendly Greece, grew with each passing month. Herbert Lehman, the American director general of UNRRA, was able to head off congressional efforts at the end of 1945 to attach political conditions to future UNRRA appropriations, if only because it would likely destroy the program in any form, but no later than December the State Department scheduled the termination of UNRRA's work in Europe for the end of 1946.

This diminution in UNRRA's contemplated role was due also to the belief that economic recovery would soon allow the world to solve its food problems normally. Soon deficit nations could buy needed food by earning foreign exchange with their exports or borrowing the funds through usual channels. Though at war's end serious food shortages in Europe were predicted, these were not expected to be catastrophic, and in November the Agriculture Department recommended a lower farm acreage in 1946 than in 1945 to head off depressing surpluses. Its optimism, which was self-serving, continued for another year. The rest of Washington shared it, for after V-J Day rationing was ended and United States food exports in 1945 declined over 1944. But during 1945–1946 European food output, excluding Russian, was four-fifths prewar and far less than the abundant year of 1943.[23]

The logical consequence of these calculations was a food crisis during early 1946, especially profound in the West zone of Germany and Austria, where local agriculture was traditionally minor and import resources nonexistent. By February about 100 million Europeans were receiving 1,500 calories or less a day—about half normal needs—and another 40 million between 1,500 and 2,000 per day. During this period the United States, the British minister of food bitterly observed, was feeding its grain to its livestock; and Secretary of Agriculture Clinton P. Anderson was in April to admit that such feeding was largely responsible for existing shortages. Since the fall harvest in the United States had been lower than expected, during February, Truman introduced a food conservation program and called Herbert Hoover in to supervise a Famine Emergency Committee. Hoover had always opposed reliance on UNRRA and was well known as an advocate of a politically oriented food program based on the assumption that one rewards and wins friends as a matter of policy. This was especially true in nations the Anglo-Americans occupied, for food riots, as Patterson warned, might aid the Left and require sending in more troops.

Despite official predictions of calamity should it not make food available, American efforts were essentially voluntary and fell short of pledges during the first half of 1946 by 15 percent in wheat alone. And what was delivered, in turn, was diverted in many instances to Italy and friendly countries rather than the more hard-pressed Eastern European nations. The unwillingness of American farmers to stop feeding grain to cattle while meat prices were booming, the ever present fear of surplus, and Truman's refusal to reintroduce rationing or decisive action to seize wheat at the elevators all set the stage for what was to follow.[24]

By the summer of 1946, despite Hoover's public fears regarding famine leading to revolution and authoritative predictions of a recurrence of the crisis, the Western European food problem was largely solved. In Western Europe, this was due mainly to domestic agricultural recovery and the area's dependence on its own resources. It was in large part due to this anticipated self-sufficiency in non-Communist areas that the United States finally gave UNRRA the death blow it had planned for the organization the earlier year. There were still vast areas of the world in need of relief, but they were either unfriendly, as in the case of Eastern Europe, or of lesser priority to Washington. Moreover, relief closed off markets the United States could now hope to export to via normal means, and it was critical to further integration of Western Europe through trade and, if necessary, loans. The remarkable industrial recovery that the Americans formally used to justify their abandonment of UNRRA also meant the Western Europeans could solve their relatively small food deficits with their own resources. Clayton, during early August, informed the UNRRA council that it was no longer supply but rather financing that the world had to confront and for this both the IMF and IBRD would suffice. He did not tell potential suppliants what they were to discover later: loans would go only to the politically friendly. UNRRA would not continue into 1947. The United States' food relief ended, therefore, not as a gesture of isolation, but rather of integration, and it was possible mainly because politically uncommitted or friendly nations were on the road to recovery—without the United States' having extracted adequate support for its economic peace aims.[25]

Europe: Integrated or Independent

The decision to terminate UNRRA came at a moment of critical political and economic danger for the United States in Western Europe, for the area's immediate postwar experience revealed that Western Europe's recovery was but a matter of time. Ironically, this rehabilitation, especially in France and the lowlands, was not only largely internally generated but also proceeding in a distinctive, self-contained manner that diminished the United States' role and posed a major danger to America's plans for a reformed world capitalism. The men in charge of UNRRA policy also managed the nation's larger economic strategy, and they continued, as is the wont of all able leaders, to see specifics in the perspective of their grand view. Historians should attempt to do no less.

One can view the European economic picture as a race between the United States' long-term efforts to attain its goals and the immediate measures and regulations that the demands both political and economic necessity imposed on Europe. From Washington's viewpoint, the critical prerequisite to the achievement of its goals was to undo the prewar order of bilateralism, high tariffs, and trade and exchange controls. We have discussed the British and Eastern European dimensions of this effort in other chapters. Stated modestly and simply, to the United States, Europe's recovery without a permanent American participation in it, via exports and investments, was undesirable. The ideal world economy was one open to the United States, not necessarily a prosperous one developing along fairly autonomous regional lines, and this distinction is the difference between abstract ideology and the pursuit of national interest as American export and investment circles defined it. If political dangers from indigenous opposition movements forced the United States temporarily to tailor its strategy, as in France, to head off Communist electoral successes, the loan terms were also written to advance Washington's larger aims. The United States, as we have already noted, therefore defined an abstract standard of economic morality which gave its doctrine of the open door an aura of idealism which scarcely obscured the inconsistencies in its own practices. Ironically, Western Europe was to thwart the United States by resorting to mechanisms which America, too, sanctioned and practiced.

The United States' proposed International Trade Organization for the regulation of the world economy resulted in all member nations' signing an immense series of bilateral treaties with each other, granting one another equality with the most favored nation—a bilateral road to multilateralism. Prewar bilateralism, in large part due to the United States' own actions, had merely excluded America from its predepression trade shares. The attainment, and then enlargement, of this share was Washington's prime objective. In 1946 Britain and France were the two most significant barriers to its realization, and their verbal consent to United States trade principles in return for loans failed to alter the reality of growing and cumulative bilateralism which might later exclude the United States from normal trade and create a European trade bloc.

Necessities defined practice. Dollar and gold reserves were scarce and insufficient for the magnitudes of trade Europe wished to attain. Moreover, the skyrocketing one-third increase in the wholesale prices of United States industrial commodities between 1945 and 1947 forced nations to choose whatever alternative suppliers they might find. Barter agreements were that much better for balancing trade. While more important in Eastern than Western Europe—where we discuss them separately—bilateral trade arrangements of every sort began to cover all Europe immediately after V-E Day. By October 1945 there were thirty-four in force, with many more in the process of negotiation. Sweden at that time had already written over $330 million in loans to assure markets, mainly in Western Europe, for its greatly expanded industry. By May 1946 the number of such agreements had reached sixty, most of them of a short-term character. Worse yet for the United States, more and larger contracts were in the process of negotiation, involving Britain, Canada, France, Argentina, and numerous Western nations. In August the United States formally protested to the Swedes, who were negotiating a five-year billion kroner loan to Russia, pointing out its exclusive bilateral nature and conflict with the projected ITO. The Swedes tartly replied that they, too, welcomed the multilateral world, but that in the meantime they saw nothing wrong with their commercial policy identical to American practice, noting that the United States had yet to ratify the ITO charter—and gave Russia the credit. The following month the British and French opened negotiations for what promised to be the largest bilateral trade pact of them all.[26]

More important than bilateral trade, which was a temporary but effective means of revival, was the persistence of government-controlled private trade in Western Europe and tight regulation of all exchange transactions. During 1946, only the United States abandoned wartime controls, while variations of them remained virtually everywhere else. The net result was that whenever possible the Western European nations with overseas territories forced much of their export-import trade into their colonies. Taken together, all these patterns throughout 1946 threatened to undermine America's goals. Worst of all from the American viewpoint, growing Western European recovery was justifying and reinforcing autarchy. Industrial recovery in every Western European country, save Germany, was rapid.

America's answers to this challenge were both simple and complex. In its German zone the United States banned all barter trade for German exports and imports, demanding gold or dollar payments with which Germany's usual buyers would not willingly part. The policy further paralyzed the Anglo-American zone economically and removed it from the evolving web of European trade, thereby slowing European recovery but also leaving the United States with an immense lever for reorienting the dominant trend. Of this complex strategy, more below. Less involved was American competition with European traders on their own terms. After all, bilateral treaties were often merely tied loans which guaranteed a nation export outlets.

The answer to European bilateralism in 1946 was a yet larger American bilateralism and tied loans. With the exception of the loan to England, the United States tied its other loans, directly or indirectly, to American purchases. During 1946 Western Europe obtained $3.6 billion in new American grants and, primarily, credits, and while this produced otherwise largely nonexistent export outlets for the United States, it was only because that was the condition of aid in most instances. The real question was where and how Europe would spend its money without aid.[27]

By the fall of 1946 the United States had not found a durable means for fulfilling its foreign economic policy. Neither its food policy, vast loans, plans for a spate of international organizations, nor diplomatic strategy brought it success, and the vital issue of how the capitalist world would arrange its postwar relations was still left in suspense. New political as well as economic approaches were imperative if America was to attain its fundamental goals.

The Problem of European Integration

The haphazard, burgeoning pattern of European trade relations to emerge during the first year of peace presented the United States with possibilities as well as dangers, and Washington's groping efforts to find a solution to dissolve the nascent trade bloc set the stage for Europe's development after 1947. In essence, the problem was to find a structure and definition for Europe's necessary interrelationship that was also consistent with United States foreign economic goals.

In addition to the myriad of bilateral trade agreements, Europe was bound by various coal, transport, and economic agencies organized before the war's end, the most important of which was the Emergency Economic

Committee (EEC). Supposed to coordinate the production and distribution of vital scarce commodities, these agencies necessarily discussed larger policy issues without ever transcending their emergency functions. By the summer of 1946, as a UN subcommission on Europe was considering programs for European recovery, thinking in the State Department had moved beyond a simple approach to the attainment of multilateral trade and American goals. Blocs, bilateralism, and barter arrangements of every sort forced a reevaluation. The real question for many boiled down to controlling and structuring these hopefully temporary developments *within* the framework of an ITO and United States principles. When the UN subcommission met in London during August, just as Clayton was closing up UNRRA, the American delegation proposed that it create an Economic Commission for Europe (ECE) which could integrate national economic programs into an all-European recovery plan.

While we discuss the Eastern European and Soviet aspect of the ECE in Chapter 7, suffice it to say here that both the interest of these nations in using the ECE to obtain aid and their commitment to socialism meant that American planners saw ECE as a possible solution to Western Europe's problems—one that had to solve that region's difficulties as well as isolate the Soviet bloc. In particular, Washington conceived ECE as a response to the dilemma—and promise—of Germany's future in Europe and thought the structure might become a means of solving America's immediate problems and attaining its final purposes. America's tactical error was to use the UN framework to advance the notion, automatically condemning ECE to a broader-based membership than was desired, and not until May 1947 did the UN organize the ECE—by which time Washington had abandoned any hope for it. The ECE experience is interesting only because it reveals the contours of the United States' next major policy synthesis which was to bind the German question to Western Europe's economic evolution, hopefully to solve them both. The United States never pinned any large hopes on the ECE, which was quickly discarded for a more manageable entity.[28]

"Autarchy arises not only from nationalistic policies of self-sufficiency but also from the inability to establish patterns of productive international trade," Thomas C. Blaisdell, Jr., warned Clayton. "Thus the current low volume of Germany's external trade is one of the major factors in the revival of autarchic tendencies throughout Europe today."[29] No one in Washington disagreed with Blaisdell's insistence on ". . . the consideration of German problems along [with] other European problems," but American leaders had not yet found the means for employing Germany as a lever for advancing all their objectives in Europe.[30] Neither Clay nor the State Department was moved to operate through any of the existing all-European groups, and the United States' German policy posed other difficulties, as we shall soon see. Yet no one in Washington was willing at this time to see European economic collaboration circumvent and isolate Germany, and thereby the United States as well. German recovery was essential to a certain type of Western European economy—one which was both capitalist and integrated with the United States. "It is general U.S. policy," the State Department concluded during July in a major policy statement, "to favor the re-establishment of economic intercourse between all European countries, and to oppose economic as well as political autarchy either of countries or blocs. . . . As an ultimate objective, the U.S. desires economic integration of Germany and an integration of Germany into the whole European Economy."[31]

Even though they had yet to produce the exact means for attaining this end, it was apparent by the end of 1946 that a form of regionalism was about to emerge, not the least because the French favored this means of control over Germany's raw materials and industry. No later than November, American experts advanced the suggestion of specific all-European industry plans, with emphasis on treating the problem as an integrated whole.[32] To regularize Western Europe's economic relations might not only resolve the German question but also help the region overcome its transition from war to peace in a fashion that would later help solve America's problems.

Germany: Key to Europe

Once the United States had made the decision to merge its German zone with England's, indefinitely postpone reparations, and formalize the *de facto* partition of Germany, its integration with a Western Europe progressing toward recovery, without and despite Germany, was imperative. Such an economic combination would not only solve Western Germany's problems, which economic paralysis made financially expensive and politically dangerous, but overcome the rest of Western Europe's incipient economic heresy and independence. Western Europe needed Germany's resources, for although it was recovering without them, access to the coal and steel in the British zone would accelerate its reconstruction. And the United States by mid-1946 was extending its control over this critical and potentially richest German sector. A *quid pro quo* might solve America's problems in all Western Europe.

Byrnes's invitation to the other occupying powers in July 1946 to merge their zones with the American led to immediate negotiations with the British, who were in the process of losing about $400 million over 1946 in their zone—twice the cost to the United States. By this time the British were so hard pressed financially that they were eager to transfer to the Americans what they now regarded as the dubious privilege of controlling the Ruhr, if they might also shake off the losses. Moreover, their growing fear of Communism was overcoming their nominal commitment to socialism, and in mid-July, much to Adenauer's delight, they merged the conservative state of Westphalia with that of the Ruhr, thereby both diluting the critical Communist position among the workers and creating one more obstacle to French designs for the Ruhr. The Americans, for their part, welcomed the prospective control but not its costs, and while the two powers reached preliminary agreements on organization over the summer, they debated the share of expenses the rest of the year. Publicly the United States and Britain argued that a bizonal merger was not a major step toward partition, and that they could, and should, treat Germany as a single economic unit. Privately, however, Clay admitted at the end of July that a bizonal merger ". . . is forcing the issue and while we hope it will expedite quadripartite action, it may have just the reverse effect."[33]

Such actions constituted a policy, as did the decisions on reparations and solving Germany's problems in a Western European context. There were, however, unresolved questions as well; the vague prescriptions of JCS 1067 did not help the drift in what was a single direction. The four powers had still to act on various reforms, the most important being the Dodge Plan. On July 19 Clay tried his hand at defining a comprehensive new policy, but it clarified none of the major policy decisions and on important points conflicted with Washington's thinking. He was told to table it, and Clay, according to one State Department officer close to him, came to the ". . . discouraging conclusion that we have lost four months of study and effort. . . . If we are truly interested in democracy in Germany and really expect to have free enterprise, then we must face financial reform courageously to be able to create a stable fiscal condition which will be conducive to democracy and free enterprise."[34]

This sense of aimlessness, despite the very real and decisive beginnings to merge the Anglo-American zone, was but one reason for the United States to make a comprehensive statement on Germany. More important was the rankling propaganda success of Molotov's vague catering to German opinion in his July statements in Paris. The carefully calculated speech that Byrnes delivered in Stuttgart on September 6 was aimed at the Russians, then at the French, and, lastly, at the Germans, who were the least troublesome obstacle to America's goals. In addition, it made explicit much that was hitherto only *de facto* policy.

As he expected, the parts of Byrnes's speech that attracted most attention dealt with borders. On the Oder-Neisse line, he argued that Potsdam had agreed only to allow Poland to administer the 40,000-square-mile territory until a final peace treaty, but that ". . . the heads of government did not agree to support at the peace settlement the cession of this particular area." Turning to the French designs, he informed Paris that the German people wished to retain the Ruhr and Rhineland and that the United States would not oppose them, but merely go along with those controls for a unified Germany that security demanded. The United States would, however, endorse French annexation of the Saar. It would reject "outside" "domination or manipulation" of the bizonal area then in the process of passing under United States control.[35] All this was designed to put the Russians on the spot as erstwhile friends of Germany, forcing them to come out in favor of Polish claims.

Disingenuous words on United States economic policy were not so easy to fathom. The occupying powers had to treat Germany as an economic unit, Byrnes argued, even as he praised the bizonal move toward partition. He rejected reparations from current production, and implicitly from dismantling as well, unless Germany were first treated as a single economic unit. More to the point, but scarcely fully candid about American motives, was his declaration that "Germany must be given a chance to export goods in order to import enough to make her economy self-sustaining. Germany is a part of Europe, and recovery in Europe, and particularly in the states adjoining Germany, will be slow indeed if Germany with her great resources of iron and coal is turned into a poorhouse."

As an additional gesture to the Germans, they ". . . should now be given the primary responsibility for the running of their own affairs," though events were soon to reveal what Byrnes really meant. Most important was a statement—which Byrnes was inclined to remove, but which Clay had him reinsert after Truman failed to object—that "we are staying here. As long as there is an occupation army in Germany, American armed forces will be part of that occupation army."[36]

The predictable French reaction was "extremely adverse," as the State Department summarized the French minister's words, and made more difficult than ever the French merger of their zone in the pending bizonal region, even though they left the door open for cooperation.[37] The Russian response was far more complex and, in one vital sense for the United States, dangerous.

In Chapter 7 we discuss the negative Polish reaction to Byrnes's statement on their western borders, a loss the United States could accept because it did not deem Poland a friendly nation. On the border issue the Russians did not equivocate: on September 16 Molotov released an accurate history of the evolution of Big Three policy on the Oder-Neisse boundary since the Yalta Conference, making it plain the borders were neither accidental nor temporary. But on every other issue, the Russians took pause and considered the drift of events in Germany. Apart from the revival of Germany in a Western European bloc, the pending bizonal partition must also have caused them profound anxieties. Moreover, there was still the need to maintain a unified Germany and access to its industrial West, if they were to obtain large and desperately needed reparations from dismantling or current production. During September and October, to head off partition and integration, the Russians offered to negotiate everything save the border issue.

During July and August the various four-power bodies in Berlin considered assorted plans for creating central administration over all of Germany's industry as well as organizing interzonal trade, and the British and French endorsed a general Soviet proposal; but by mid-August the British pulled back for fear of interfering with bizonal merger negotiations. Soon the matter became bogged down on details of a French proposal, but the Russians insisted that they continued to endorse the creation of central economic administrations. Then, at the end of August, General Vassily Sokolovsky, the head of the Soviet occupation, informally approached Clay about freezing all reparations through dismantling for as long as a decade, maintaining the agreed levels of industry, and taking reparations only from current production. The offer, rightly interpreted as a reflection of dire Soviet needs, Byrnes rejected in his Stuttgart speech, but its implications were far-reaching. As a basis of a new start, it would have ended the nominally critical sources of controversy over Germany's economies and reparations and won Soviet support for a high rate of German recovery from which to take reparations; and it was practical. It would have radically lowered the scheduled annual drain on Germany, the Western sectors of which were in any event easily to pay $5.2 billion in reparations, indemnities, and restitutions in 1953–1965. Its political consequences, however, were too dangerous for American acceptance, and by that time the bizone was the heart of America's strategy.[38]

But the Russians were not content to accept one rejection. At the end of September they outlined a solution for the coal problem, which was acute only in the West zones, and suggested that if the other powers accepted all-German planning of coal production they would accept quadripartite allocations—a step from which only the West could gain. By early October, however, the State Department, despite its acknowledgment that the lack of dismantling and the paralysis of Germany's industry were an embarrassment, resolved that neither Russia nor France should obtain any plants that might become available from the Anglo-American zones. The question was how to put the Russians off without revealing this fact, not publicly assuming responsibility for partition, and to get on with the division.

On October 14 the Russians presented an entirely new and more audacious scheme for reparations that was too credible to be rejected out of hand. The Russians and Poles would take half of Germany's reparations, as agreed at Potsdam, but they would supply the defeated nation with raw materials for current reparations production until Germany attained a favorable balance of trade and could supply its own. Zonal economic boundaries "would be entirely removed" save for dismantling reparations plants, and the four powers would agree on a balanced import-export program for an economically unified Germany. They would also establish central German administrative structures, especially to cover reparations, and would renegotiate all existing agreements and claims on reparations and levels of industry. Everything, the Russians seemed to say, was now negotiable.

The proposal was quite breath-taking and was known to every level of the United States government save, possibly, the President. Existing evidence shows the United States rejected it immediately, though Byrnes authorized exploring the matter in case it might come up at the Foreign Ministers Conference scheduled for March 1947. Moreover, there were assets in deferring a rejection while precluding an alteration of existing plans. "The Russian need for commodities out of German production is so urgent and apparent," Murphy cabled on October 14, "that we would be well-advised to use the opportunity to obtain very definite commitments from them on the subject of the introduction into the Soviet Zone of occupation of our form of democratic methods." Murphy spelled out some of these political and economic conditions for a *quid pro quo* two days later, many of which were easily within reach, and warned that "this may be our last opportunity to use such a potent bargaining position in Germany for this purpose."[39] But Elbridge Durbrow, the American chargé in Moscow, warned of inevitable Soviet deceit, and Murphy, who was only slightly less skeptical, could only point to examples of Soviet flexibility and drop the matter to turn to the implementation of existing policy. Dodge and his close associates acknowledged that the Russians had made a major change in approaching Germany as a single economic unit, but they opposed concessions on current reparations and shared the universal American view that "general political relations," and the need for "far-reaching Russian concessions in the political sphere," were the nub of the matter.[40]

Washington did not reconsider the Russian overture when Stalin on October 28 released his answers to questions United Press International (UPI) had submitted to him. In response to the question of merging the four zones Stalin replied, "Not only the economic but also the political unity of Germany should be restored," which he coupled with an increase in Germany's level of industry, reconstruction, and self-sufficiency.[41] Taken alone, such a statement might have been passed off as propaganda, but more likely it was intended to pressure the Americans into taking seriously a detailed proposal already in their hands. If so, it failed.

The German Bizonal Merger

The United States' political and economic terms for a comprehensive German settlement were revealed most clearly in the Anglo-American negotiations over the bizonal merger. In effect, American definitions differed sharply from those of the British as well as the Russians and had far less to do with German self-determination than the simpler and more fundamental issue of capitalism versus socialism. The implications of the outcome of this difference for Western Europe's future was of basic consequence. The Soviet zone was extensively socialized, and France had a Socialist-led and Communist-supported government. A united and free Germany including the Soviet zone would have had an SPD government which, at this time, was seemingly prepared to implement its program. A unified bizone able to structure its own fate would have seen the SPD as the leading party. The SPD twitted and alienated all the occupation governments by its demands for autonomy, which was the prerequisite to its probable political victory. Hence Schumacher's contempt for the Americans and the Russians both, and his insistence that Germany be allowed to define its own future. In 1946, so long as the United States refused to test the Russian offers, Germany's destiny hung in balance in the British zone.

The British wanted, first of all, relief from the immense costs of the economic paralysis in their zone, but they openly favored public ownership of German basic industry and would not have been inclined to stop it. Between ideology and their own budget, however, they unswervingly chose the latter, and so the Americans had to make the bizonal negotiations succeed, placing ideology before cost. By mid-September they had agreed on the essential structure of Bizonia, as it was called, save for the sharing of expenses. The various steps toward full integration stretched into 1948. Immediately, however, the United States' problem was to keep the Social Democrats, growing everywhere and already dominant in the British zone, from implementing their socialist goals. The ability of the various Länd governments to make basic economic decisions was even more circumscribed by the introduction of maximum political autonomy for the six Länder in a manner that consciously prevented essential central economic planning—a strategy that later backfired in the form of continued economic stagnation. Freedom at the lowest level of government, contrary to Byrnes's Stuttgart pledge, was exchanged for the Anglo-American reservation of real power over economic affairs. This meant, in effect, a reduction of one critical aspect of self-government that the Americans had granted before Bizonia was formed, and when the Americans learned that the Germans might not always use their freedom to endorse American interests, they cut it back. It made no difference, for example, when the Hesse electorate at the end of 1946 voted to socialize mines, power, steel, and railroads or passed SPD-sponsored labor legislation. ". . . I made it clear," Clay later wrote about this trend, "that measures in a single state which prejudged future German government could not be implemented."[42] The Russians did no more when they permitted Germans in their zone to have freedom to endorse the occupation's economic preferences, but circumscribed uncontrollable political impulses. By the fall of 1946 such regulation was equally common in all zones, though not yet irrevocably so. For the United States it simply meant that it had to devise parliamentary means for repressing democratic action and economic change unacceptable to itself. Freedom, in this context, meant the right to endorse what was in any case inevitable, giving Germany's traditional ruling class sufficient time and aid to reconsolidate its power after its trial of defeat. The Americans permitted an impotent political democracy totally circumscribed economically, while the Russians merely reversed the pattern.

All of this was at stake for the United States during the last months of 1946 when the British were amenable to pooling ideology, but not costs, on American terms. At first the United States asked the British to share all expenses and income in proportion to zonal population, leaving the British with 56 percent. The British proposed that the Americans pay 60 percent, to which Byrnes would agree only if they traded zones—a proposition which the British erroneously thought was made in jest. By December 2, when the Bizonal fusion agreement was approved, they had settled on 50–50, accepting everything political and economic of substance on American terms. The process of partition was deepening, but at least the richest part of Germany had been saved for the United States goals. As for the Soviet zone, at the end of 1946 Clay outlined the next step to Dodge: "We have set the March [1947] meeting of the Council of Foreign Ministers as the absolute deadline and if it does not bring agreement, we propose to proceed with the establishment of a new currency for the British and American zones."[43] Such a step, as Dodge himself had earlier warned, would lead to the irrevocable partition of Germany.

Unless Germany could be internally integrated on American terms, which was scarcely possible by mid-1946, it could recover only in a Western European context, adding to the region's prosperity in the long run but immediately greatly benefiting itself. To the British, paying half the losses, German recovery would save it perhaps a half-billion dollars a year and ". . . hasten the economic recovery of Europe."[44] The frightful hunger in that nation, which was worse over the winter of 1946 than anywhere else in Western Europe, made recovery doubly imperative, not only for the British but to a Truman administration that after November had a budget-minded Republican Congress to confront. Every American action over the last half of 1946 reinforced Averell Harriman's conclusion that "the rehabilitation of these countries [Germany and Japan] is requisite to world stability. I cannot too greatly stress the importance of their economic recovery. The task is urgent, and time is of the essence."[45] Washington terminated further serious decartelization or denazification measures that upset property relations, and began to chart Germany's reintegration into the Western European economic structure.[46]

This integration of the bulk of Germany into Western Europe assured that Germany, the only major continental power that the United States was able to keep capitalist, might also be reconstructed and contained in its relations with its neighbors. For neither Russia nor Britain would willingly permit Germany again to threaten the peace. And while the United States, with less passion, also shared its former allies' concern, it also believed that a peaceful, reconstructed capitalist Germany might form the keystone for a reformed Western European capitalism.

No less important to the United States was that by so treating Western Europe as a single economic problem it might solve numerous other political and economic challenges: the threat of socialism, bilateralism, Russia, and the United States' long-term relationship to the world economy. By the end of 1946 all the components for a single, comprehensive solution to the numerous difficulties defining the future of United States power in Europe were coming to a head. All that was left was to grasp and unify them—and to act.

7

The Transformation of Eastern Europe, 1945–1947

Time permits myth and ideology to enshroud history, and the postwar history of Eastern Europe perhaps suffers most from the abuses that states impose on truth. And to unravel that fabric of myth we must draw on the critical threads that are tied primarily to the process of reconstruction and development, to the United States' reaction to recovery throughout Europe, to revolution and counterrevolution in the context of an archaic social structure, to the problems of nationalism, and to Soviet security interests. As the events in Eastern Europe mirror Soviet intent and interests, so, too, do they illuminate American policy and aims. And in this overriding context, they also tell us much of the dynamics of political democracy and economic development.

The extent of the devastation that the Nazis wrought in the conquest and occupation of Eastern Europe was unequaled during the holocaust of World War II. And following that orgy of annihilation, the region provided the battlefield as the Red Army rolled back the Nazi forces, and once again the fighting and destruction were savage. This devastation is the crucial backdrop to the subsequent economic and political developments and the international relations of the region. The various statistics of loss and wreckage can only partially reveal the magnitude of the problems that each government in Eastern Europe confronted and which made basic recovery so imperative. Loss of human life under the Nazis totaled at least 6,500,000 persons in Poland; Warsaw alone suffered more casualties than the United States and England combined. Yugoslavia had a toll of 2,000,000, and Czechoslovakia 238,000. In addition to the deaths, the Nazis deported millions to Germany for forced labor, and many never returned. The casualties among the living, both in physical and psychological suffering, were incalculable.

Direct economic devastation again only hints at the total disorganization of the economies. Largely an agricultural region, the losses in livestock represented not only forfeiture of direct food but the inability to plow, sow, or harvest. Through theft or destruction Poland was deprived of 43 percent of its horses, 60 percent of its cattle, and 78 percent of its pigs. Yugoslavia and Hungary retained less than one-half of their livestock, and eastern Slovakia lost 80 percent. The damage to the fertility of the soil and the destruction of the forests seemed overwhelming obstacles, requiring massive imports of fertilizer or generations to recover. Furthermore, during 1945 the peasant, in the midst of the fighting, had been unable to sow, contributing to the world food shortage of 1945–1947 which reached famine proportions in most of Eastern Europe despite UNRRA aid. In Poland, every village, town, and city was damaged to some degree. Twenty-five percent of the farms were totally eliminated during the war. Warsaw was systematically demolished in 1944, with 68 percent of the buildings either destroyed or severely damaged.

The losses in the transportation systems were no less staggering. In Hungary and Yugoslavia nearly all the bridges were destroyed, and the Germans took over three-fourths of the locomotive and freight cars, and all the Danube River barges, when they retreated. In Poland the transportation losses were in the range of $3.5 billion, and industrial damages for the region were of the same proportion. The total material devastation for Poland was estimated at $18.2 billion, in Hungary the equivalent of five years of prewar national income, and in Yugoslavia fifty times the annual prewar national revenue. The other countries of the region experienced comparable damage.

Compounding these problems were the flow of refugees and the forced transfer of minorities, especially affecting Poland, Hungary, and Czechoslovakia. Deportees were repatriated, Germans expelled, borders adjusted, and minorities resettled, all involving the movement and repatriation of millions —eight million in Poland alone.[1] Given the magnitude of the horror of the war and the subsequent famine on the lives of the people of the region, these elements alone led most observers to anticipate a radical transformation of the political and economic social structure. But there were other, perhaps even more decisive, ingredients working for change.

The Soviet Union's security interests precluded a return of the reactionary, anti-Soviet, Western-supported prewar ruling class. More will be said of the Russian role below, but it is clear that the presence of the Red army provided a guarantee against another counterrevolution such as had succeeded in forestalling progress after World War I. Yet in some areas an equally significant new factor compelling social change was the destruction and dispersal of the old ruling class during the war, a class the Nazis either systematically liquidated, as in Poland, or which was in exile or hiding unless willing to cooperate with the new governments.

Despite the lesser threat from the members of the old ruling classes, although their capacity for significant harassment remained, the new coalition governments in Eastern Europe composed of the Socialists, Communists, and liberal antifascist parties inherited the problems of centuries of social stagnation and a colonial-based economy. The prewar Eastern European social structure, especially in Hungary, more nearly resembled pre-1789 Europe than Western Europe in 1945. Political democracy, literacy, land reform, social welfare, and indigenous capitalist enterprise, all accepted parts of the social fabric of the West, had never existed. Vast armies of landless laborers were a perpetual feature of Poland, Hungary, and Rumania. Hungary had what was described as proportionately the largest agricultural proletariat, not just in Europe but in the entire world. Less than 1 percent of the Hungarians owned 48 percent of the land. The Catholic Church of Hungary, the strongest reactionary force, alone owned 17 percent, and in Poland it had only slightly less power. The land, cultivated mainly for export, was characteristically a monoculture system. In Yugoslavia, 82 percent of the land was sown in grain; in Hungary the vast fields grew only grain for export—and both suffered severely during world depressions as well as from United States competition, increasing the mass misery. Bulgaria's agrarian system, involving four-fifths of the population, while as backward as Hungary's, differed totally in that it was characterized by small, uneconomic farms rather than large estates, but it, too, was devoted to the monoculture of corn and wheat. And per capita productivity was, on the average, four and one-half times less than that of Western Europe.

The bureaucracy in each state, except Czechoslovakia, modeled its operation after the Ottoman Empire or Tsarist Russia, including their corruption and cruelty. Known as the illiteracy belt of Europe, the prewar states of the east compiled appalling statistics that revealed indifference and stagnation in education.[2]

Another critical ingredient that dictated change in postwar Eastern Europe was renovated nationalism committed to achieving a self-sufficient national integrity on a broad political and economic level—in effect, a long overdue process of modernization. Prewar nationalism had consisted of warring chauvinisms, a barrier to progress that the economic interests in Western Europe exploited all too frequently in maintaining Eastern Europe in a colonial status and, after 1917, as a *cordon sanitaire* against bolshevism. After World War I the British and French learned that it was impossible to graft capitalist parliamentarianism onto colonial feudalism and still retain the profits and privileges that the latter provided. There could be only revolution or reaction, and there never was any question which they preferred. The regimes the Western powers created for their *cordon sanitaire* in 1918 were uniformly reactionary and clericalist in character (always with the one exception of Czechoslovakia), and they maintained semicolonial ties with Western Europe, especially Germany, and the United States. The native ruling classes held either a feudal landed power or a comprador relationship to foreign economic interests. In fact, nearly all the neocolonial features that we find today in the Third World were present in Eastern Europe before World War II. What little industry existed was largely in the hands of foreign owners. Prewar Eastern Europe, therefore, can best be described as a caldron of reaction, intrigue, anti-Semitism, xenophobic nationalism—all a superficial façade over a panoply of mass misery and ignorance—the *cordon sanitaire* against bolshevism, and a source of raw materials and economic exploitation for Western and, above all, German capitalism.

The war devastation and the inherited decadent and archaic social structure were formidable handicaps with which to commence reconstruction. In this framework, the policies of the various national fronts appeared revolutionary in the milieu of Eastern Europe, but strictly reformist if set in a Western European context. But as elsewhere, in particular where colonial systems exist, even the most moderate aspirations of the people were forced to overcome the forces of reaction that most of Western Europe had eliminated decades or, as in the case of Hungarian institutions, nearly two centuries earlier.

On the other hand, the release of energy and *élan* in those who benefited from the reforms—the vast bulk of the population—and the prospects of constructing a new and better life over the rubble, were an asset that no one can overstate. The remarkable reconstruction, despite these innumerable odds, was material evidence of this new spirit's significance.

Despite a quite similar past, the various national political and economic developments in postwar Eastern Europe differed within the overriding framework of American aims and Soviet security interests. But the international context was initially of little intrinsic concern to the nationalist united fronts bent on relief, reconstruction, and development of their shattered economies. A few states began to develop a parliamentary political life for the first time in their history while still struggling against the remnants of the old order. And their preoccupations, including those of the Communist parties, were ultimately national in focus.

One of the great tragedies of our time is that no nation is permitted the privilege of its own unmolested revolution. Perhaps it has always been so, since the forces of the *status quo* have usually rallied with unexcelled internationalism when threatened with revolution. However, the new dimension of Soviet power was added in the postwar world—for in Eastern Europe the USSR at once fostered and restrained, protected, and ultimately perverted the revolutionary experience of its neighboring states. How and why this occurred is the important lesson of Eastern Europe. But the initial hostility toward the radical restructuring of the prewar *status quo* came from the United States and was to set the context for all subsequent events.

The Imperatives of Reconstruction

As in all of Europe, and especially the former occupied areas, the first demand on the population was national reconstruction. With the economy in ruins, the populace hungry and disorganized, the Eastern European government parties worked in unison to achieve their program of social welfare and an expanded industrial sector and trade as quickly as possible. Resources were frequently limited and certainly undeveloped. The coalition governments looked to their urgent national needs and ignored the international context within which their plans had to proceed. Given their resources, they made optimum plans and anticipated that foreign loans would cover their deficits. Such naïve *élan,* while helpful in sustaining recovery's momentum, helps explain the persistent hopes of the nations of Eastern Europe that the United States would provide the apolitical loans to aid their reconstruction, despite all the evidence to the contrary.

The former enemy states of Hungary, Rumania, and Bulgaria also had reparations to pay, principally to the USSR, which was a significant tax on their internal growth. Beyond reparations and immediate relief, all the states in Eastern Europe had to proceed with the imperatives of internal economic development: land reform, nationalization of the foreign-owned basic industry, certain tariff restrictions to protect new industry, and fiscal reform. These are almost axiomatic needs in recovery from war and a shift from an essentially colonial status to national economic development, whether in a capitalist, socialist, or mixed economy, and any national plan would have had to include them.

The first economic programs in all of Eastern Europe, except Yugoslavia, were modest and aimed only at relief and reconstruction to the prewar level of production and living standard. After 1947 the target of the national plans was economic development. Despite incredible odds, they were able to meet their industrial targets, but were unable to achieve agricultural recovery, primarily because of the disastrous weather conditions between 1945 and 1947.

The Communist parties in each country took the lead in the reconstruction and economic ministries, and they organized recovery in an essentially nonrevolutionary manner, with national, rather than class, objectives. Their invariable purpose was to create order, industrial activity, production, and rapid development out of chaos. Such fundamental reformism and efficiency soon won them the support of large sections of the traditional bourgeois and peasant parties whose basically mediocre leadership contributed disruption when their traditional followers, weary of chaos, sought reconstruction and modernization. "Minc no longer has a single 'ism'!," a Polish Socialist observed of the Communist minister of industry. "All he thinks of is getting the factories running."[3] In Hungary, Ernest Gero, overlooking the severe housing needs of the workers, insisted that Hungary's priorities necessitated constructing bridges. The Communists in Hungary generally regarded time spent on discussion in the workers' councils or trade unions as a waste of time and opposed strikes. After August 1947 strikes were outlawed altogether and deemed sabotage of the national plan. Although the United States frequently claimed that the Communists encouraged chaos as a prelude to power, quite the reverse was true. We discuss details later, but it is sufficient to point out here that wherever the Communists had responsibility for a phase of reconstruction they goaded the workers, traded welfare for production, and demonstrated greater patriotic fervor than ministers from the other parties.

The national plans were not socialist, and the state simply replaced the foreign corporation in the management of industry and allocated the profits to future investment and economic development. Management of industry remained unchanged, for none of the government parties had any interest in changing the role of the working class; on the contrary, the Communist parties, with the aid of the Social Democrats, in Czechoslovakia and Hungary took the lead in emasculating the revolutionary workers' councils and liberation committees that were organized spontaneously at the end of the war. Their functions were made advisory instead of managerial, and they were incorporated into a trade union federation under bureaucratic leadership. In Czechoslovakia, in particular, the struggle to eradicate the workers' councils continued until the end of 1945, leaving profound bitterness among the workers that was to reemerge in subsequent crises.

At the end of 1946, the Hungarian Communist leader Mátyás Rákosi pointed out, according to the American minister, the CP's " . . . resolute handling of labor unrest."[4] In Poland, as the national plan progressed the militants in the ranks of the Communist party " . . . complain that while the proletarians get barely enough to eat, private traders and bankers are making millions. . . ." The State Department official who reported and strongly endorsed these trends in Poland by the beginning of 1947 added that " . . . these left wingers are being pushed into the ranks of the contemporary equivalent of the Trotskyite opposition by the 'Moderates' like [Communist] Jacob Berman who reasons as follows: ' . . . Basic economic life in Poland can best be reactivated by private enterprise in small manufactures and small trade.' "[5]

The Land and Food Problems

Because the landholding system throughout Eastern Europe most directly affected the bulk of the population, sweeping land reforms in the form of distribution of small plots to the landless were the coalition governments' first step toward change. Yet the condition of the ravaged land and transport was inauspicious for an early solution to the agricultural question. After World War I there had been significant land reforms in Czechoslovakia and Yugoslavia; in Rumania, too, more than ten million acres were distributed, but the reform benefited chiefly middle and rich landowners, and in the ensuing world depression the peasants resold their land to the former owners. Bulgaria was a country of comparatively small holdings, and in Poland and Hungary giant estates were the rule.

In Poland there was no opposition to the land reform of September 1944. The government distributed more than a million hectares of the large estates to 379,000 claimants. Most important, however, was the land in former German territories on which the Provisional Government was able to settle 5.5 million people, including the surplus rural population from central

Poland as well as displaced persons from the territory ceded to the USSR in the east. President Boleslaw Bierut stressed to the United States ambassador in 1945 that the chief aim of the land reform was ". . . the elimination of the aristocratic land owning class as a political factor in national life."[6]

In Hungary the land reform came as an early direct order from the Red army in 1945, but only the Catholic Church vocally resisted. The state confiscated 3,222,000 hectares, retained much of the forest and pasture lands, and distributed nearly three-fifths of the remainder to some 663,359 landless peasants and small holders. Rumania redistributed more than a million hectares and Yugoslavia over 542,000, the bulk of which was confiscated from German holdings. The governments encouraged diversification in agriculture and introduced truck gardens, poultry farms, and vineyards in the former exclusively grain-producing regions. Until 1948 all states emphasized individual ownership with state aid. Class divisions among the peasantry were minimal during the first two postwar years, since even the formerly rich peasants had lost all but their land.[7]

Land reform solved the class power problem of centuries in the region, and in Hungary and Poland it was a revolutionary step of the first magnitude. It did not, however, solve the economic problems of development and industrialization. Even after the distribution of land, the number of landless that remained was vast. And like most revolutionary measures, it was enacted at an inauspicious time of disorganized economies, catastrophic weather, minimal national capital, and war-ravaged land. As throughout Europe and Asia, the peasants were unwilling to trade food for inflated currency when no manufactured goods were available. They preferred to eat better themselves and most achieved a normal diet for the first time in their lives. City workers, nevertheless, had to be fed. The method that most of the governments in Eastern Europe used to obtain food was a system that compelled peasants to allocate fixed quotas of their output at low prices and permitted them to sell the remainder on the free market. But adverse weather took its toll in poor harvests, and the governments were forced to depend on UNRRA and imports to prevent starvation. Such diversion of national resources further inhibited development plans. Yet for the first two years the peasants' loyalty, due to the land reform, was firmly committed to the new governments. Despite the reforms, the land remained grossly overpopulated, and the question of transfer of workers to the developing industrial sectors was one of the chief goals facing all the countries in the East. But for the first two postwar years the problems of agricultural production were the most momentous.

Food was the most acute need in Eastern Europe, and indeed of most of the world, during these postwar years. The famine of 1945–1947 was only partially an aftermath of the dislocations of the war. The destruction of livestock and crops and of the transportation system, damaged ports, and shortages of shipping all played their part, but the United States' food policy during and after the war was a most decisive factor in the famine. Had the United States imposed even modest restraints on its domestic consumption it would have substantially minimized the world food shortage and mass suffering.[8]

Truman recalled in his memoirs that "more people faced starvation and even death for want of food during the year following the war than during all the war years combined. America enjoyed a near-record production of food and a record crop of wheat. . . ."[9] The situation was so severe that the traditionally conservative *Economist,* extremely critical of United States greed, proposed Britain cut its consumption, already sparse, to alleviate the shortages elsewhere. Attlee made numerous pleas for greater United States efforts, and Mackenzie King of Canada called for continued rationing. Indeed, all the food surplus nations of the world, with the exception of the United States, continued rationing over the critical year.[10]

UNRRA, whose obligation was to provide relief in the allied nations with the greatest need, distributed goods in Europe primarily in the East; Poland, Yugoslavia, Czechoslovakia, Greece, and Albania received the bulk of the aid. Western Europe had monetary reserves to purchase their needed supplies and had refused UN assistance. Nevertheless, despite the impending famine and a production bounty in the United States, UNRRA experienced extreme difficulties in obtaining the minimum supplies of grain and other foods needed to carry out its tasks. American deliveries fell short of commitments by 10 percent in March 1946. The gap between pledges and deliveries continued to mount in the spring of 1946 as the United States maintained a subsidy on livestock, encouraging this diversion of needed bread grains until June 30, and permitted the diversion of food grains into alcohol production. The State Department in January 1946, in expressing pleasure that the UNRRA had decided to extend aid to Hungary, also indicated that there would be extreme difficulty in obtaining the necessary quantities of wheat to alleviate the shortage. Truman preferred to " . . . put the greatest emphasis on the importance of the personal responsibility of every citizen for food conservation . . . in overcoming the famine situation around the world."[11] And thus began the public relations campaign known as Food-For-Famine-Effort to persuade the American people to cut their consumption voluntarily. Yet throughout 1946 the United States failed to meet its promised UNRRA quotas.

Haunted by the specter of surplus, the Department of Agriculture pursued a program to restrict production during the war and postwar years when it began to come under sharp attack in the United States as well as abroad. As Truman was introducing his quixotic plan of voluntary cutbacks in American consumption, Secretary of Agriculture Clinton Anderson told Congress, "Some people are going to have to starve, . . . We're in a position of a family that owns a litter of puppies: we've got to decide which ones to drown."[12]

Despite the obvious need and the appeals of American UNRRA officials, the State Department did not consider the organization an effective instrument of its policy. The United States was disillusioned with UNRRA in its early stages and decided in August 1945 to wind up its operations at the end of 1946. It reiterated this stand at the UNRRA general council in August 1946, over the pleas of the recipient nations to extend the program to help their staggering food problems. The American move was decisive, for the United States contributed 68 percent of the funds. American UNRRA officials denied the oft-repeated suspicions that UNRRA goods were distributed internally in Eastern Europe on a basis of politics rather than need, but the accusations persisted in undercutting the already disintegrating support. Acheson used them in announcing the new United States policy toward relief on December 8, 1946, and claimed that the relief problems were largely solved and that only three or four countries—Austria, Italy, and Greece—could prove need in 1947.[13]

In reality it was the apolitical nature of UNRRA that determined its end. For the Americans the unfortunate fact remained that the Communist-dominated nations of Poland and Yugoslavia were two of the neediest and therefore two of the largest recipients of UNRRA assistance. Herbert Hoover, who had much experience in using food as a political weapon after World War I, expressed shock after his fact-finding mission for Truman in the spring of 1946 that the bulk of UNRRA aid went to " . . . the Communist puppet states of Poland, Czechoslovakia, and Yugoslavia. . . . The seat of Western civilization is west of the Iron Curtain."[14] The United States ambassadors in Warsaw, Prague, and Belgrade frequently protested on political grounds UNRRA shipments and personnel. Later the United States was to block food relief in other ways as well. While hunger was still acute and UNRRA had ended, at a meeting of the International Wheat Council in 1947 the United States refused the demands of other wheat-producing countries for larger export quotas and lower prices to meet the world food shortage.[15]

After the end of UNRRA the UN sent a mission to Poland to evaluate the remaining need in that country. The members of the mission were all from the West, including the United States, and they remained in Poland one month. The mission concluded in its report of September 1947 " . . . that Polish food supply, agriculture, and forestry are in a state of emergency."[16] At approximately the same time, Secretary of State George C. Marshall also sent a special mission to evaluate Poland's needs. Their report " . . . concludes that the minimum food needs of Poland during . . . 1947 generally can be met without assistance from the United States."[17] The United States ambassador, Stanton Griffis, rather surprised by the brevity of the four-day visit, asked the chairman how he could make a decision based on that length of time. "He answered . . . it was very simple," Griffis recalled. "He simply went to four parts of Poland and looked at the 'behinds' of the citizenry, male and female."[18]

The United States' failure in UNRRA reinforced the fears of many Europeans, both East and West, that the United States, at best, was unreliable. Tightly controlled bilateral trade agreements, increasingly isolating the Americans, was their only viable alternative as United States policy foreclosed the options of cooperation. It was chiefly through these bilateral barter agreements and small intra-European credits that Europe aided itself in the process of recovery over the first two postwar years.

The Loan Problem

When the United States terminated UNRRA at the end of 1946 Acheson asserted, "[t]he . . . United States have made up their minds that the relief problems of the near future are not of a character which would warrant grants . . . under conditions which would leave little or no effective control by the grantor of these funds."[19] Clayton later added that nations seeking aid should apply for loans directly to Washington. The Eastern European governments understood the implications of Clayton's suggestion. Concomitant with their receipt of UNRRA aid, several had tried to negotiate loans directly with the United States and had encountered innumerable complications. Yet confident at the end of the war that it was the sole nation to emerge stronger from that holocaust, the United States believed it could use its economic power to help shape Europe's institutions and, equally important, its loan policy could assist American industry whose wartime growth had exceeded domestic demand.[20]

By the end of World War II the United States had assumed Soviet political preeminence in the nations of Eastern Europe, but over the months following the peace it clung to the hope that it could maintain free access for American investment and trade in the region. Therefore, initially Washington intended to keep its loan negotiations free from direct political considerations. "Dept at present inclined to view that in general, economic rather than political questions should be tied to Eximbank credit negotiations. . . . One of primary purposes advancing credits is to promote economic foreign policy framed to further economic interests this country," Byrnes cabled the ambassador in Warsaw, Arthur Bliss Lane, in November 1945.[21] Despite Lane's pleas that the State Department refuse any credits to the Communist-dominated Polish government, Washington received the Polish request of December 1945 for rolling stock, new materials, and certain industrial supplies favorably and encouraged the Poles to apply for a loan to purchase surplus property as well as an Export-Import Bank loan. Over the first postwar months the State Department consistently reminded its irate and offended ambassadors in Warsaw and Prague of its larger aims. And although the United States loan provisions barred any loans to countries paying reparations or supporting occupation troops, Acheson indicated to the United States representative in Rumania that this policy was subject to modification if they could attain the open door provisions. Only on the question of economic relations in Eastern Europe, an area where it had nothing to lose and much to gain, did Washington consider a quiet accommodation with the Soviet Union.[22] Such an accommodation was unobtainable, however, for inevitably the American aim of securing the open door for its investment and trade collided with the demands of economic development that required first the Czechs and Poles, and ultimately all the Eastern states, to nationalize the foreign interests that controlled their critical industries. Within a short time, political questions and the issue of compensation of nationalized property intruded into loan criteria as the United States was unable to secure its economic interests in the region.

The Czechs nationalized their banks, insurance companies, mines, and two-thirds of their industrial capacity between October 1945 and March 1946, most of it German- or foreign-owned. The Poles introduced their nationalization decree in January 1946 covering all industry with more than fifty workers. In Poland, foreign interests controlled the majority of its vital industries. Washington immediately halted its credit negotiations, and the Poles hastily accepted United States demands regarding compensation and their general theoretical support of United States trade aims, even to the extent of promising to release the text of all future trade agreements with other nations and holding elections within the year.

After extracting these conditions, at the end of April the United States granted the Poles a $40 million Export-Import loan and a $50 million surplus property credit. To Ambassador Lane, who consistently opposed such aid, this decision was "depressing news."[23] Lane had earlier pleaded, "With the greatest earnestness of which I am capable I beg the Department not to approve the extension of any credits facilities at this time."[24] More important than such emotional pleas by the ambassador was the fact that Poland produced coal, an essential commodity of enormous value throughout Europe at the time, and the credit was for coal cars and locomotives " . . . which PolGov has stated in writing will be used ship coal to countries Western Europe," as Byrnes explained in his reply to Lane.[25] Nevertheless, when the Poles had not complied with the conditions of revealing their other trade treaties by May 10, the United States suspended the surplus property credit. As the State Department told Ambassador Lane, "Litauer, in absence of Lange, was told off yesterday by Acting Secretary [Acheson]. He gave him the works."[26] The Poles then relented, and the loan was again released in July.

Despite the United States reluctance to aid in its recovery, and despite the famine and disastrous weather conditions, Poland, the greatest victim of the war, performed the most astonishing feats of reconstruction of any nation in Europe. Their new boundaries aided the Polish people substantially in this task. They lost to Russia 70,000 square miles of rather marginal farmland and 70 percent of their prewar oil capacity, but gained from Germany the vast base of a highly developed industrial and transportation complex—making a balanced industrial economy possible for the first time in Polish history.[27]

Even with these assets, one can hardly overestimate Poland's extraordinary effort and accomplishments, the more remarkable given the near civil war and acts of terrorism of the right-wing underground which harassed the government's endeavors and the food shortages which even the contributions of UNRRA were unable to alleviate fully during the first two postwar years. Its four-year plan, introduced in 1946, anticipated a rise in its per capita production of capital goods by two and one-half times over prewar as well as a substantial increase in consumer goods and agricultural output. The plan for the first year was devoted exclusively to reconstruction, and 1947–1949 to economic development. By April 1948, despite the innumerable odds, an English correspondent noted that Poland had fulfilled its production plan by 103 percent; wages were rising and prices falling. Poland was again exporting some agricultural goods and rationing had been substantially reduced. The Food and Agricultural Organization (FAO) mission commented in September 1947, "The determination and energy shown by the Polish Government . . . have been admired by interested observers throughout the world."[28]

The Dilemmas of Reform: Czechoslovakia

Foreign interests also dominated the prewar Czech industry in an economy which had depended on prosperity in the capitalist states of the West. The Germans alone controlled 60 to 70 percent of the industrial sector, putting emphasis on light industry and consumer goods. The new government intended to stress heavy industry and oriented its reconstruction toward a greater degree of self-sufficiency in the hope of moving into many of Germany's prewar export markets for heavy machinery. The Czechs also consciously planned their postwar trade patterns to prevent the dependence of Czech prosperity on the fluctuations of world capitalism that had proven so disastrous in the 1930's. The steps were successful, and reconstruction of the economy was rapid. In September 1946, Czech food consumption was greater than in any formerly occupied country except Denmark. By the end of 1946 industrial production was 80 percent of the 1937 level and foreign trade yielded a credit balance.[29]

When the coalition government began to nationalize Czech industry in October 1945 there was no internal protest, for before the war both nationalization and land reform—primarily because the property was foreign-owned—had won wide support even among the middle class. But British and American pressures on behalf of foreign owners was immediate. Prague assured both the English and the Americans that it had every intention of paying adequate compensation, but that it would have to await the development of a sufficient trade balance if it were to provide compensation in the demanded foreign currencies. From the end of the war, the compensation issue, involving $30 to $50 million of United States–backed claims, became a problem of intense mutual suspicion and difficulty in United States–Czech relations. Although Ambassador Laurence Steinhardt initially considered nationalization as a " . . . normal development in Europe . . . less of an ideology than a necessity," the major proportion of his time, as well as Washington's insofar as it thought about the Czechs, dealt with claims for compensation, the most important being that of the Socony Vacuum Oil Company.[30] Throughout his tenure as ambassador he maintained a continuous correspondence with John Foster Dulles, professionally representing Socony and other interests in Czechoslovakia, but also a man of formidable political weight.

In September 1945 Steinhardt had advised the State Department that he expected the Czechs to proceed along a moderately socialist economic path, with speedy compensation for United States investments, and that Czechoslovakia would be the first country in Europe to recover sufficiently to aid in the reconstruction of its neighbors. Aware of the difficult economic circumstances, he was reluctant to press the harassed Czechs during 1945, but he assured Dulles that all government officials in Prague fully supported the principle of compensation. But the State Department publicly analyzed the nationalization measures as reflecting the fact that "for many years there has been a strong leftist movement in Czechoslovakia," and in principle it objected to the program.[31]

Over the following months the Czechs, pressed with many demands on their limited resources and committed to the fulfillment of their new two-year plan, insisted that compensation, especially in dollars, would have to wait until their reserves increased. By the summer of 1946, therefore, compensation and a Czech application for an Export-Import Bank loan of $50 million, which they believed would greatly facilitate their accumulation of dollar reserves, were inextricably intertwined with the question of compensation, world economic policies, and Prague's relations with the Soviet Union.

Beginning in mid-1946, or about the time of the Czech elections, Steinhardt continuously pressed the State Department for a policy designed to " . . . cool the Czechs off a bit," since Washington believed that they had failed " . . . to show a proper recognition . . . of United States objectives in Europe."[32] By the first of October 1946 the State Department decided that its loan and diplomatic policy toward Czechoslovakia " . . . need not be governed by what we have done in the case of other countries. . . . The present disposition in the Department is to accord credit to the Czechoslovak Government only after it shows concrete evidences of friendship towards the United States, which would include some reorientation in its general foreign policy as well as an agreement on compensation and commercial policy questions."[33] This shift in emphasis was due not simply to Steinhardt's urgings but also to the general frustration of United States economic aims in Europe, the increasing determination of the United States to establish a reliable bloc in Europe, and, finally, the fact that Byrnes, at the Paris Peace Conference in August 1946, noticed Foreign Minister Jan Masaryk warmly applauding a speech by the Soviet representative, Andrei Vyshinsky, in which, among other things, he attacked United States loan policy as an effort to "enslave" Europe. Byrnes, irate, cabled Washington to suspend the remaining $40 million of the $50 million surplus property credit granted Czechoslovakia in May and cancel all loan negotiations. Later, Byrnes was to make much of Vyshinsky's speech of August 15 which dealt primarily with the question of United States offers of aid to Hungary while refusing to return the Hungarian rolling stock then in the United States zone in Germany. At the end of the speech Vyshinsky also made a statement supporting Czechoslovakia's expulsion of its Hungarian minority. Hence Masaryk's enthusiastic, and costly, applause.[34]

Export-Import Bank negotiators informed the Czechs in September that the conversations were being canceled because of the compensation question. More bluntly, the State Department told them that ". . . we would sell surplus to the Czechoslovak Government only for cash on the barrel head."[35] Byrnes's cable from Paris to the State Department clarified future policy guidelines. "In a word, we must help our friends in every way and refrain from assisting those who either from helplessness or for other reasons are opposing the principles for which we stand."[36] The United States even tried, unsuccessfully, to persuade the British to drop their surplus property credit to the Czechs. But despite the suspension of loan talks, the United States decided to continue the negotiations for compensation and a commercial treaty. Expecting the United States' decision to undermine Czech foreign policy, Washington reported to Steinhardt that hopefully ". . . the news that we are calling a halt on economic assistance . . . wherever possible should considerably encourage those elements desiring some reorientation of Czechoslovak foreign policy."[37] They fully anticipated the cancellation of credits and other economic pressures to accomplish this end. This was not the result, however, for all parties shared the resentment over the heavy-handed pressures. Even the generally pro-West paper of President Beneš's National Socialist Party editorialized on October 4, 1946, "We are afraid that the present policy of the United States is more influenced by an endeavor to force its will upon the world than by the principles of the [UN] Charter."[38] The other party papers voiced even stronger sentiments, and the press for several months aired the Czech anger with the United States. Washington, in turn, regarded such expressions as a hostile act, and demanded that the Czech government control the press, at the very same time, however, that American newspapers were referring to Czechoslovakia as a Russian satellite and attacking their policy of expelling the German minority.[39]

Nevertheless, the Czechs and Poles of all parties, while bitter, still placed a great deal of hope in possible American credits to meet their reconstruction needs. Although both Prague and Warsaw asserted that their economic plans would proceed without the loans, obviously it would be much easier with United States aid. In Czechoslovakia, therefore, the Communist members of the government especially went out of their way to mollify Washington's angry reactions as best they could. Vladimir Clementis, the Communist deputy minister of foreign affairs, called the tense American-Czech relations an ". . . unwelcome episode . . . brought about partly by misunderstandings, partly by certain objective circumstances as they exist in the international situation today."[40]

The Communists in Czechoslovakia were as convinced as the other parties of the need to have good economic relations with the United States, and the American diplomats appreciated this fact. In December 1946, after the United States had canceled the surplus credit and loan discussions, the State Department wrote Steinhardt, "The restraint and good sense apparently shown by some of the Czechs such as Gottwald and Clementis in the present situation have favorably impressed me, and I gather that Bedell Smith and Vandenberg had a similar feeling in Paris. . . . I am inclined to think that Gottwald and Clementis display better judgment than Masaryk. . . ." This "better judgment" consisted of stopping ". . . the press campaign against the United States and to assure us of action in the matter of compensation. . . ."[41]

Nevertheless, despite this background of frustration with United States loan policy, after the termination of UNRRA at the end of 1946 the Poles, Czechs, and Hungarians applied to the World Bank for long-term credits and were refused. Poland's application was considered on strictly political grounds, for Thomas Blaisdell saw no chance for the loan either then or in the future. Despite ". . . the analysis of the significance of coal . . . political considerations are very much in the picture. . . ."[42] But the Poles again requested an Export-Import loan and a cotton credit in November 1946 and were rejected.[43]

The economic concessions in Eastern Europe that they could not achieve with credits the Americans also tried to acquire through other means. A vital ingredient of United States policy in the region was to secure an agreement on the unrestricted use of the Danube as an international waterway. The Danube plan offered Americans an opportunity, at an immense economic advantage, virtually to control the trade of the riparian states. And the traditional offer of economic rights for the Eastern Europeans in the United States equal to those they were demanding for American business in Eastern Europe confused no one. At the Paris Peace Conference, Molotov rhetorically asked, "Is it not clear that such unrestricted application of the principle of 'equal opportunity' in the given conditions would in practice mean the veritable economic enslavement of the small states and their subjugation to the rule and arbitrary will of strong and enriched foreign firms, banks and industrial companies?"[44] The United States diplomats pressed the Danube question at the London Foreign Ministers Conference and again at the Paris Peace Conference. In September 1946 they again submitted a resolution to the UN proposing a conference of "interested states" to decide Danubian commercial policy. At Paris, Vandenberg vigorously attempted to have such a clause inserted in the peace treaties linking it to nondiscriminatory treatment for United States business.[45]

The United States did not rely exclusively on diplomacy to press its points. It held in its zones of Austria and Germany the eight hundred river boats which the Germans took from Hungary, Yugoslavia, and Czechoslovakia when they retreated. Given the nearly total destruction of the transportation systems in these countries, the dire need of the shipping for relief and reconstruction purposes, and the repeated requests for their return, the refusal of the Americans to do so until the end of 1946 underlined their determination to secure their free access to Danube trade.[46]

Another lever of pressure that the United States used against Yugoslavia, Poland, Hungary, and Czechoslovakia during the desperate years of 1945–1946 was their frozen gold assets, retrieved from the Germans and held in vaults in New York or its occupation zone in Germany. As a UN report indicated in September 1946, the return of the frozen gold reserves and other property in American hands would have substantially reduced the Eastern European need for credits.

The United States held the Polish gold until a compensation agreement was reached in December 1946, and it released the Hungarian gold of $32 million in August 1946. For the Yugoslavs, gold amounting to $45 million was held until after their break with the Russians, and then the Americans subtracted compensation on sharp terms. And about $20 million of Czech gold, linked to unsettled compensation claims, still rests in the vaults of New York.[47]

The former Axis states of Hungary, Rumania, and Bulgaria were under economic restrictions imposed by the armistice that required that they pay reparations and support the occupying force of the Red army. Rumania was obliged to pay $300 million and Hungary $200 million to Russia and $100 million to Yugoslavia and Czechoslovakia. Occupation and reparations costs in Hungary amounted to 60 percent of the national budget, and to meet these extraordinary expenses, Budapest operated the printing press, finally making a record in world economic history when in July 1946 the dollar reached the incredible figure of 29,667,000,000,000,000 pengös. Neither the Rumanians nor the Hungarians nationalized foreign property until 1948, but their extraordinary inflation and the controls on industry to extract reparations effectively eliminated any profits from foreign undertakings. Nevertheless, the banks in Hungary were in private hands until mid-1947, effectively holding up economic development, and taxation was nearly nonexistent over the first postwar years.[48]

The victory of the more conservative Smallholders Party in Hungary in the free election of November 1945 led the United States representative, Arthur Schoenfeld, to recommend aid to the Hungarian government to offset the extremely critical economic crisis that he claimed would lead to starvation and civil war by February. Byrnes replied by advising the Hungarians not to nationalize their industry before a peace treaty. Yet Washington's general sympathy with the new government led UNRRA to grant Hungary $4 million of urgently needed foodstuffs in January 1946.

Over the first six months of 1946, the United States offered to help stabilize the Hungarian economy jointly with the Soviets in return for provisions guaranteeing the open door, and it granted a surplus property credit of $10 million in February. But the Russians argued that if the United States were serious in its desire to aid the Hungarians it would return the Hungarian property, including $32 million in gold, held in its German and Austrian occupation zones. Finally, to reinforce the undermined position of the pro-West Smallholders, in August the United States returned gold and other property, and the government introduced a monetary reform which led eventually to currency stabilization and recovery. Yet after the currency reform it was again the Communists who were primarily responsible for the economic recovery that even won the admiration of their conservative rivals. In November even Schoenfeld admitted to Washington, "I am bound to say there is truth in Rákosi's analysis . . ." that the ". . . Communist Party now affords only dynamic constructive leadership . . ." in Hungary.[49]

The Soviet Union repeatedly reduced reparations due to them through 1947 and then sent considerable technical aid and material to the former enemy states. By October 1945 the Soviets returned to Hungary the factories, coal mines, and oil fields which they had been operating, and in lieu of taking industrial equipment the Soviets took 50 percent ownership of key plants and made the same arrangements with Rumania. In the fall of 1945 the USSR also returned Rumanian rolling stock, cut reparations, and granted a loan of 300,000 tons of grain. By February 1946 the Soviets were selling trucks and tractors to Hungary at prices considerably below those prevailing in the United States and, more irritating to Washington, providing all the cotton the region could absorb. Soviet trade with Eastern Europe in 1945 exceeded its average volume of prewar trade with the whole of Europe, and this reorientation of trade was directly influenced by the difficulties of transportation and finance in Western European trade. During 1946, as well, the vast bulk of Eastern Europe's imports and exports were with the USSR. The United States lost no time in protesting to the USSR regarding its economic agreements in Eastern Europe. In October 1945 the State Department told the Russians that they were disturbed by the Rumanian-Soviet five-year "economic collaboration" agreement, which they felt would lead to exclusion of United States investment and trade.[50]

Yugoslavia's situation differed radically from that of its Eastern European neighbors. The revolutionary government made no effort to create a mixed economy or to share power with any element of the old order or the inconsequential bourgeoisie. All important elements of economic and political life were in the hands of the Communist Party from the time of the liberation. Under these circumstances, the United States never considered the August 1945 Yugoslav loan request. The planning commission, under the guidance of Soviet experts, adhered to a gradual policy of economic development, giving heavy weight to handicaps such as lack of trained personnel, lack of credits, wartime destruction, and the like. André Hebrang, a devoted Stalinist, minimized the ambitions of the national Communists around Marshal Tito, who desired to move rapidly toward industrialization. The Soviet experts urged, first and foremost, that the Yugoslavs put all their emphasis on improving their agriculture and extractive industries and, given the poverty and lack of skilled labor, avoid any adventurist effort to industrialize rapidly. But many in Tito's government suspected that the Soviets hoped to maintain Yugoslavia in its essentially colonial role of mining and agricultural exports. Such modest goals were of no interest to Tito, and additional tension over this critical issue exacerbated the already difficult relations with the Russians, becoming a major cause of the break in 1948. Tito's answer was to substitute enthusiasm for technical skills, and to mobilize the population for the task of constructing an advanced industrial state with youth brigades and, so to speak, their bare hands. Tito removed Hebrang, and the party made preparations for the five-year plan that Tito, without once referring to Stalin, introduced in April 1947.[51]

Nationalization, trade agreements, credits, and loans—none of these questions can be viewed in isolation when examining United States–Eastern European relations, nor can they be isolated from the economic and political developments in the Europe of 1946 which jarred the United States into sharp reaction. As we have seen in Chapter 6, nothing in the world economy was proceeding as Washington had planned, for it had not fully anticipated the impact of the war on the economies of Europe. The American goal of a community of capitalist nations engaged in multilateral trade was nowhere in sight, and in fact expanding autarchy and bilateralism were only too apparent. This pattern was not restricted to Eastern Europe, but also penetrated most of Europe's capitalist states. These developments raised the specter of the 1930s and were appalling to the Americans, whose entire wartime planning had sought to avoid such a pattern. Nationalization was only one aspect of the growing state control in Europe which the United States could only regard as actually or potentially exclusionary. It viewed Eastern Europe's trade reorientation toward the USSR as the formation of an isolated trading bloc. As the year progressed the European states tightened their exchange and investment controls and negotiated additional bilateral agreements which indicated a perpetuation of arrangements the United States had hoped were only temporary. The pacts included nearly all European nations, who considered them essential given the financial costs to precious foreign exchange of buying in the United States. Governments were able to protect their currencies by arranging trade with specified items for barter. George McGhee of the State Department, in assessing the problem early in 1947, bluntly noted, "The principal characteristic of state trading as we see it in this country is that it is not the way we do it. . . . [private enterprise] has become so ingrained in our economic thinking that it amounts with us to almost a religion. We believe in it so strongly as a principle that we are perfectly sincere in our conviction that it would be in the best interests of other nations to follow our example."[52] "They are looking for stability in the 'depression proof' controlled economies of eastern Europe," *Business Week* lamented in December 1946.[53] Most European nations were committed to at least ten bilateral agreements. In this troubled context the United States formulated its economic relations with Eastern Europe.

Despite the United States' overwhelming advantages as the sole source of supply for nearly all goods in urgent demand in Europe, by the fall of 1946 it found itself being increasingly excluded from the European markets. It would have been easier to obtain materials from the United States; but for nations in the process of building out of the rubble, Washington foreclosed most options for cooperation, sabotaging UNRRA at the most critical moment of famine and then summarily terminating it, canceling loans already burdened with conditions, refusing to return gold, rolling stock, river barges, and holding political control of the World Bank. Given these factors, there is little wonder, even if they had intended it otherwise, that the European states pursued an independent policy of bilateral trade and barter agreements.

By the fall of 1946 the United States had clearly abandoned any real hope of integrating Eastern Europe into a capitalist trading sphere. Loans were then granted and suspended on a political basis. With prompt action, however, there still remained the possibility of reorienting the Western capitalist states—a policy that eventually evolved into the Marshall Plan. For the Eastern Europeans, without further credits and with an impoverished economic base, recovery and development could be achieved only through austerity for the population. Capital not secured through international loans would be accumulated through the labor of the workers. But the Eastern European governments naturally hoped to avoid reductions in the standard of living and eagerly sought any possibility of foreign credits that would help them realize their plans. Their immediate needs were no less serious. According to a UN estimate, the deficits in Eastern Europe for imports to meet emergency requirements of the essentials for life in 1947, after calculating all their monetary and export resources, would amount to $140 million for Poland, $68 million for Yugoslavia, $40 million for Hungary. Their projected import deficits for reconstruction were much greater. The UN report concluded that only foreign aid could offset the deficits.

By late September 1946 they began to take a greater interest in the work of the UN Emergency Economic Commission for Europe. This was unquestionably the result of the end of UNRRA, their severe needs, and the aspirations their ambitious recovery plans had generated. After the UN subcommittee surveyed the reconstruction needs of Europe and made its August 1946 report calling for concerted government efforts in the problems of reconstruction, the United States member recommended the creation of an Economic Commission for Europe, which again whetted the hopes of the Czechs and Poles. The Soviet delegate argued that there was no need to abolish UNRRA only to replace it with the ECE. The Czechs and Poles, however, urged the Soviets to accept the proposal, for it opened a new possibility for American assistance. In the discussions setting up the ECE, need, as with UNRRA, was the agreed criterion of aid.

In November, disputing the Poles, the Yugoslavs, who had never received United States loans, opposed the ECE ". . . on the grounds that it would be a vehicle for American interference in their domestic affairs."[54] Poland, on the other hand, with Soviet support, told the United States representative that it would endorse the creation of the ECE, and the Poles and Czechs were able to persuade the more skeptical Russians to participate.

The concept of a central organization coordinating the reconstruction plans of the various European states naturally attracted the United States as well. Distressed by the "autarkic" development of bilateralism and state control, it hoped that a central body in which it played a leading part would be the first step in securing for it some direction over reconstruction on a multilateral basis. For this reason the United States proposed the organization of the ECE in August 1946, the very month that it announced the termination of UNRRA. "From the standpoint of American policy that line of approach should be adopted which will have the greatest possibility of preserving a continuing international handling of common European problems," wrote Thomas C. Blaisdell, one of the State Department's leading economic advisers, of the ECE proposal in November 1946.[55] Obviously, given the fact that UNRRA was also an "international" organization and the United States had scuttled it, Blaisdell's definition of internationalism strongly implied American participation in directing what was then independent European recovery. And the American experts also hoped that the Russians would not participate. "Rather than establishing a paper organization," another adviser proposed, "it would be preferable to set up the ECE without Russia and her satellites. . . . I believe that a strong and effectively functioning ECE established without the Eastern Europeans will eventually attract those countries by its achievements alone. . . ."[56]

When the ECE held its first meeting in May 1947, the Soviets sent a large delegation, and it initiated plans for an evaluation of Europe's economic problems and common action. Such an effort, however, while it hoped to secure United States aid, was as nonpolitical as UNRRA had been, and by May 1947 it was evident that such efforts had no place in American planning. Barely one month later Marshall made his offer of aid to a concerted European effort at reconstruction and suggested that the Europeans organize a *new* committee to develop a plan, although it seemed rational to everyone that the ECE was the obvious body to formulate such a response. But the United States attitude toward reconstruction was already determined, and it led in quite different directions.

The Politics of Transformation

There are two interpretations of the nature and evolution of the People's Democracies in Eastern Europe. The first, in retrospect, conjures up an image of a vast Communist plan that plotted in detail the political events in Eastern Europe from 1945 to 1950. Many on both sides of the political spectrum share this view, one to prove conspiracy, the other, omniscience. The interpretation that the events appear to support is that policies were shaped pragmatically with changing circumstances, both internal and international.

At Yalta the great powers had agreed that broadly representative provisional governments would assume power in the liberated and former enemy states in Eastern Europe and that they would arrange elections at the earliest possible date. Denied the opportunity for economic penetration of the region, the United States then laid special emphasis on the political developments there. But politically the environment in Eastern Europe at the end of the war was inauspicious for the successful introduction of parliamentary democracy. Prior to the war only Czechoslovakia had a firmly established middle class oriented toward Western European political forms and a continuity of political attitudes that persisted into the postwar period. In the rest of the area the minute middle class, by and large permeated with anti-Semitism, was a zealous supporter of the fascist rule of the interwar period. Even in Western Europe, the experience of fascist Italy, Nazi Germany, and Vichy France proved how fragile indeed were the parliamentarian forms when crisis threatened the interests of an entrenched ruling class. The number of states where political democracy approaches the ideal type are few, and there it reflects social and economic stability and the traditions of centuries. And even so there has never been any nation where established class interests have permitted themselves to be voted out of power. In Eastern Europe it was equally certain that where elections would undermine Soviet security interests by returning anti-Soviet political parties to power, or threatened to reestablish the old order at the expense of the national fronts, the Provisional Governments would postpone and eventually falsify the elections. Such was the case in Poland, a nation devastated by war, disorganized and famine-stricken, and still torn by open political wounds where opposition was expressed through terror and violence. And the same was true in Rumania, where what were probably the largest political parties were violently anti-Russian and adamantly opposed to cooperation with the Communists. More critical, however, to the Rumanian government's refusal to hold elections until November 1946, then only to falsify the results, was the severe drought causing widespread famine during the critical world food shortage, a condition that guaranteed the defeat of the government parties at the polls. In Bulgaria and Yugoslavia the opposition parties, without pressure, chose to boycott the elections held in the fall of 1945—with the predictable sweeping victory for the government list. By contrast, Czechoslovakia and Hungary, where the more conservative parties in the national fronts determined to maintain friendly relations with the Russians, held elections as free and unfettered as any in Europe, giving a plurality to the Communist Party in Czechoslovakia and an absolute majority to the bourgeois, pro-West Smallholders Party in Hungary.

Neither the United States nor the USSR was sincerely committed to the principles of political democracy. That the United States cared little is amply evidenced by its policy in those areas where it had firm control or overwhelming influence: Korea, the Philippines, Latin America, and elsewhere. The Soviets wished primarily to minimize tensions in the area, both with the West and, as far as possible, among the conservative forces in the Eastern European nations themselves. They also desired a normalization of diplomatic relations in the Balkans and American aid to those impoverished states. In both Poland and Hungary the forces of reaction were strong, and the differing political activity in each country reflected the willingness of the respective bourgeois parties to maintain good relations with the Russians. In Rumania and Bulgaria efforts at parliamentarianism were façades, as only a few members of the opposition parties were willing to play the game under Soviet auspices, and instead hoped for decisive intervention from the West that would circumvent any necessity to compromise.

The great powers then quite cynically used parliamentarianism itself as a tool in their diplomacy. At the Foreign Ministers Conference at London in September 1945, and again at the Moscow Conference in December, Byrnes and Bevin raised the question of elections and political democracy in Bulgaria and Rumania with Molotov. Their insistence on an ideal democratic practice, identical to that in Britain, while ignoring the desperate political situation in Greece, Molotov found ingenuous. At the Moscow Conference the Russian considered the matter of Bulgaria closed, alleging that the Bulgarians had elected a parliament in November on the basis of a free and secret ballot.

Bulgaria's Agrarian Party had participated in the Fatherland Front until the British began their repression of the resistance movement in Greece, which had encouraged its leadership to believe that if they remained adamantly opposed to the Communist-dominated Front they could extract important concessions or provoke Western intervention. While the party boycotted the election in Bulgaria, it also enjoyed unprecedented freedom to publish attacks on the government in the daily press. Politics had always been bloody in Bulgaria, and everyone was surprised by the orderly conduct of both the campaign and an election that was, relative to earlier charades, the freest in Bulgarian history.[57] In Rumania it was a question of the great powers advising the Petru Groza coalition to hold elections and to broaden the Cabinet. The United States and England insisted that they place their choice of members of the opposition parties, including those known to be bitterly anti-Soviet, in the government, particularly in the interior and justice ministries. Molotov agreed to add some further members without portfolio to the cabinet if they would be loyal to the government and the armistice terms, but insisted that the Rumanian government could not accept the West's nominees because they had fought the coalition for nine months. Bevin's argument that he had been fighting Churchill for thirty years did not sway Molotov, who pointed out ". . . that this was a question of a defeated country which had armistice obligations to meet and had only recently emerged from the period of the Antonescu regime and the Iron Guard."[58] Both Byrnes and Bevin were wont to lecture on bipartisanship in the United States, and to make other simple and abstract comparisons between Bulgaria and Rumania with the United States and England. To a man such as Byrnes it did not appear exaggerated to compare Vandenberg's and Truman's bipartisanship with that of the proposed collaboration between a Communist and a right-wing, anti-Soviet in Rumania, any more than he may not have felt it in any way unfair to propose equal economic rights between Americans and Rumanians in both countries. Molotov, however, did not regard Byrnes as naïve and concluded that since the United States did not apply such criteria of democracy in its relations with other states, its reasons for refusing to recognize the coalition of Petru Groza was due to Bucharest's friendship with the USSR.[59]

After the Moscow Conference a representative of both the Liberal and National Peasant parties joined the Rumanian government without portfolio, even though it was generally acknowledged that the purpose of the two historic parties was the overthrow of the coalition government and its replacement by one akin to the prewar regimes. The United States and Britain then recognized the government on the basis of Groza's implied promise to hold elections by May. The conservatives in the coalition pleaded with the United States to ease its persistent hostility. The opportunist, ex-fascist, foreign minister, Gheorghe Tatarescu, attempted to reassure Secretary Byrnes in August 1946 that Rumania was a ". . . capitalist country from the social point of view. . . ." But he reminded Byrnes that Rumania cannot forget ". . . that there are '200,000,000 men across the Prut'. If one is not a friend of the Soviet Union, then one must be an enemy."[60]

The elections that were finally held in November 1946, while the Rumanian people were suffering from extreme economic deprivation, were clearly a disaster for the government, who therefore falsified the returns to gain the victory. The alternative was a victory for an avowedly anti-Soviet government.

In Bulgaria, for several months after the Moscow Conference the Soviets tried to negotiate with the Agrarian Party. The Agrarian Georgi Dimitrov, still under the impression that Western intervention would alter his position, made extravagant demands for new elections and control of the ministry of interior and justice, until finally the Soviets in exasperation advised against continued negotiations. Despite the fact that the coalition governments in Rumania and Bulgaria included a wide range of political and economic views, excepting anti-Soviet, the United States representatives worked persistently to secure representation for the anti-Soviet parties and encouraged active opposition to the governments; and yet Washington remained unwilling to intervene directly, although the hope of such intervention was the basis of the opposition's politics. American verbal support and clandestine contacts with the underground only increased political tensions in the area.[61]

After the election in November 1945 Tito announced the formation of a Federal People's Republic, and Ambassador Richard Patterson advised

Washington to withhold recognition of the new government. But Washington in December, with the qualification that recognition did not imply approval, offered formal ties on the condition that Belgrade would accept all the treaty and financial obligations of the former government-in-exile. The Yugoslavs' reluctance to do so without review led to the delay of recognition until their final agreement in April 1946.

Politically, from that time until the summer of 1949, strong mutual hostility characterized United States-Yugoslav relations. The United States based its attitudes fundamentally on the statist direction of the Yugoslav economy, but the conduct of the American mission also exacerbated tensions. Among their grievances the Yugoslavs accused the United States embassy officials of arming the underground, of conducting spy networks, of extensive black-market operations, and of using the United States information agency to print and circulate articles attacking the government. Patterson admitted frequently to the State Department that the accusations on supplying arms to the underground could "conceivably have some basis."[62] It is certain that the American military attachés maintained contact with the underground, which Patterson judged essential for purposes of information.

These issues reached a crisis point for the United States in the summer of 1946 when, after frequent warnings against the numerous incursions into their airspace, the Yugoslavs shot down an American plane. Byrnes, attending the Paris Peace Conference, cabled Acheson to ". . . do everything that we properly can to stop further shipments of supplies of any sort by UNRRA for Yugoslavia."[63] Acheson advised that action through UNRRA would be futile, and despite Patterson's and Forrestal's urgings, the State Department concluded it was not effective to try to dictate terms to the international organization at that time, especially since ". . . UNRRA is about finished and will shortly be liquidated."[64] Soon the matter was settled by an exchange of notes after Russia pressured Belgrade, and the Yugoslavs paid $150,000 indemnity.

The Partisans, still flushed with a revolutionary *élan,* were sharply critical of the reformist role of the Soviet Union and the other European Communist parties. With an indigenous mass party, and an opposition that removed itself from politics, the Yugoslavs were in a better position to proceed rapidly toward a bolshevization of the country. They did not need the Red Army to keep order or to protect their power. Tito's confidence in his mass support permitted him both to recognize, and ultimately to act on, the economic and political conflict of interests between the Yugoslav and the Russian states.

Politics of Opposition and Consensus

Coalition governments were the rule throughout Eastern Europe, as they were in France and Italy. While there were broad variations between nations, several unifying patterns emerge. In Poland, Hungary, and Czechoslovakia the coalitions were made up of the Communists, Socialists, a liberal party initially representing the urban bourgeoisie or peasantry, and several insignificant parties on the left or right. The political organizations of the old order were dissolved, leaving large sections of the old ruling class without legal political expression, and the energies of this counterrevolutionary force were channeled either into the underground or, inevitably, into the most conservative political parties within the coalitions. As the reactionary elements began first to infiltrate, and then to inundate, the liberal legal parties, they also changed the complexion of those organizations. At the same time, large sections in such parties, unwilling to be isolated in what they viewed as sterile opposition in light of the immense tasks of national reconstruction, eventually split from the old leadership to support united fronts. We may call it opportunism or patriotism, but the reformist role of the Communist parties that aimed at development and modernization, rather than socialist revolution, made the conservatives' adamant opposition appear irrelevant to these modernist bourgeois elements. Given these shared aims of national reconstruction, the real political tension during the period of 1945–1947 stemmed from the United States policy that encouraged unrealistic hopes among the conservative leadership that in any case proved itself to be increasingly isolated and incompetent.

In Poland the prewar Peasant Party, under the leadership of Stanislaw Mikolajczyk, joined the Provisional Government of the Communist-dominated Lublin Committee as part of the Yalta Agreement among the Big Three. As a former member of the bitterly anti-Soviet Polish exile government in London, and as leader of what was generally regarded as the largest political party in Poland, Mikolajczyk's position in Poland was one of ever-growing frustration. Confident of his popularity with the masses, he felt certain of victory in a free election and at first worked seriously with the coalition government to secure UNRRA aid and other forms of reconstruction assistance from Washington. After the victory of the Smallholders in Hungary he even entertained hopes that the Russians might support his election to power. But his well-known pro-West and anti-Soviet sentiments, as well as his deepening connections with the underground, precluded his ever achieving power. Therefore, the context of the counterrevolutionary terror and near civil war in Poland made its political experience radically different from that in Czechoslovakia or Hungary.

The underground in Poland made the most direct effort to overthrow a postwar government in Eastern Europe. During the war, members of the bitterly recalcitrant, anti-Semitic, anti-Soviet WRN and NSZ fought the Red Army with as much vigor as they fought the Nazis. After the war, joined by remnants of the Home Army (AK), they turned their terrorist activities against the Polish Provisional Government. The toll in lives was not inconsequential, but such harassment, at a time when Poland was engaged in the incredible tasks of reconstruction, encouraged suspicion of the open opposition parties and all but excluded parliamentary politics. In this context the Soviet army was an important factor in keeping order and preventing civil war in the early months after liberation.

On several occasions the Polish government accused the United States of harboring and giving aid to the leaders of the NSZ in the American zone in Germany. Its embassy, particularly Ambassador Arthur Bliss Lane, kept in close touch with the Polish underground. On March 11, 1946, Lane reported to the State Department that he had advised his underground connections against a general uprising that would be repressed and give "... the people to the East the excuse of imposing a military dictatorship."[65] In June he forwarded to Washington, with his endorsement, an analysis of Polish politics "... prepared by various persons in the Polish underground. ... '[T]he underground' does not merely refer to the AK ... nor does it necessarily include all members of Mikolajczyk's party. In fact 'the underground,' I was told, is opposed to some of Mikolajczyk's policies and especially to the inclusion in the Polish Peasant Party of leftist elements which are closely identified with the communistic core of the Provisional Polish Government."[66]

Lane's report, and his many others of similar vein, revealed several important facts of the Polish political situation: the sympathetic regard and close ties of the American ambassador with an organization attempting to overthrow the Polish government, the underground's deep penetration of the Peasant Party, and the large segment in that party who opposed it and clearly wanted to get on with the task of rebuilding Poland.

In February 1946 the Polish government postponed the election because of the political and economic conditions; as the Communist leader, Wladyslaw Gomulka, put it, elections would have to wait until the Polish people were no longer starving. Meanwhile the Communists proposed to Mikolajczyk that the coalition government run on a common ticket. Mikolajczyk agreed on the unacceptable condition that the Peasant Party receive 75 percent of the posts, while the Communists offered him one-fifth. In place of the election, the government organized a referendum on June 30 with three noncontroversial questions of approving a unicameral legislature, the new western frontier, and the economic reforms. Mikolajczyk asked his supporters to vote No on the first issue, and the referendum was viewed as a preelectoral test of political strength. The government claimed to have won overwhelmingly, and the underground reacted with increased terror and on July 4 an anti-Semitic pogrom in the town of Kielce. Anti-Semitism, endemic in the Polish Right, was closely linked to anti-government and anti-Soviet propaganda. Ambassador Lane, on the other hand, attributed all acts of anti-Semitism, including two pogroms, to the presence of Jews in the government. And he made little effort to hide his own bias, either in his reports to the State Department or in his memoir, where he continually pointed to the Semitic appearance of certain government figures and differentiated them from the "Poles." He invariably described them as the Soviet "agents."[67] Later Mikolajczyk observed to Lane that the NSZ was murdering Jews and Soviet soldiers in "considerable number," and he was worried that their activities would be linked to him.[68]

In July, Lane reported to the State Department that he had refused to act as intermediary for the underground, but that it kept him closely informed. He expected an outbreak of new violence and anti-Semitism from that quarter if the election scheduled for January 1947 was unfavorable to Mikolajczyk and his party. By and large, Lane reported only the measures taken by the government against the terrorist activities of the underground, and portraying them all as unjustified political persecution, and the American press echoed this theme. As always, Polish issues touched on United States domestic politics, particularly in Michigan, and Senator Vandenberg at the UN meeting in London wanted to accuse the Polish government of "political murders" for which Secretary of State Byrnes insisted there was no evidence.[69]

While the underground had some support among the peasantry in the early months, as it became clear to all Poles that the Provisional Government was seriously attempting to rebuild Poland, the underground increasingly became isolated and lost any base it may have had among the people. It either resorted to more extreme acts of terrorism or sought refuge in Mikolajczyk's Peasant Party. Toward the end of 1946, the problems from the underground diminished, and the government granted a general amnesty in February 1947 to all those who wished again to lead a normal productive life. Nearly a hundred thousand took advantage of the offer.[70]

After the government postponed the elections, and as the Peasant Party became a rallying place for the dispossessed Right seeking a legal home and was ever more identified with the clandestine terrorists, Mikolajczyk's political position was further undermined. Large sections of the old party, recognizing his lack of realism, broke from his leadership and supported the government. Mikolajczyk then had only the United States and Britain to lean on, and they proved to be a shaky prop. By insisting on running on a separate slate and then suggesting that he might boycott the election, Mikolajczyk expected to be expelled from the government and in this way to force the United States and England to intervene. He also hoped to secure intervention by protesting formally to the Big Three that the elections would not be fair or free. While Ambassador Lane offered encouragement to his schemes, the State Department during 1946 forcefully advised against such tactics, which could only "embarrass" the United States. Mikolajczyk was rather slow to realize that what Senator Vandenberg might say for his 500,000 Polish constituents would not necessarily be translated into policy in Washington. This strategy of expecting direct Western intervention on his behalf, and basing his politics on it, led Mikolajczyk, as with his counterparts elsewhere, into an inevitable political cul-de-sac.[71]

Mikolajczyk ran against the government bloc in the elections that the Poles finally held in January 1947. The government disqualified part of his list regionally and permitted the Peasant Party only 28 seats out of 444. There was little pretense that it was a free election. Although most observers speculate that the Peasant Party would have won a truly fair election, much had changed in Poland by 1947. One Communist leader later admitted, "Had we known before the January election by what a large margin we would win, we would not have engaged in those pressures and minor dishonesties which did take place in many localities. The next election, I believe, will be very much closer to what you in America call a democratic election and I am not talking about Jersey City or Alabama."[72]

The Socialists, despite their minimal differences with the Communists, supported the coalition as the alternative to reaction on the one hand and Russian occupation on the other. More critically, especially during the reconstruction years of 1945–1947, they had few differences on either strategy or goals. Nevertheless they had more popular support in Poland, and prior to the election, to assure a unified government list, the Communists concurred in their demand for a larger share of the government list, and Socialist Joseph Cyrankiewicz replaced Osobka-Morawski as Prime Minister. While they were both Socialists, Cyrankiewicz had greater independent stature in the party.[73]

The Czech Gamble

The National Socialist Party in Czechoslovakia took a different course from the Peasant Party in Poland. During the war its President-in-exile, Eduard Beneš, understood that Czech independence would rest on his nation's ability to maintain good relations with both West and East, and he placed his hope in a continuation of the wartime alliance, or at least in a *modus vivendi* between the two blocs. The Munich experience, but primarily the facts of geography, operated to convince all Czechs that while they desired close ties with the West, their ultimate security and independence would depend on strong and friendly relations with the USSR. It was with this in mind that Beneš, against the advice of England and the United States, journeyed to Moscow in December 1943 to sign a treaty of friendship and mutual aid. In Moscow the Soviets convinced him that they had no interest in Czech internal affairs if they could work in harmony on international questions. Beneš obtained Soviet support for the transfer of minorities, restoration of the pre-Munich boundaries, and equipment for the Czech army. Stalin also agreed that the Czechs would operate the civil government of the liberated areas. "I saw at once that we really would agree —our views were fundamentally identical," Beneš recalled of his conversations with Stalin.[74]

While in Moscow, Beneš also arranged with the Czech Communists for a postwar coalition of the four political parties that were not compromised by collaboration. The Czech leaders defined the details of this coalition when they met at Košice in April 1945. Their moderate statement of goals, on which they based their National Front, included land reform, expulsion of the German and Hungarian minorities, punishment of collaborators, and greater autonomy for the Slovaks. The program placed an alliance with the USSR as the cornerstone of its foreign policy. Each party was to share equally the number of ministries, and the National Front chose the Socialist Zdenek Fierlinger as interim Prime Minister until they could hold elections.

The impact of the war on Czechoslovakia, as on all of Europe, had moved the population well to the left in its political sentiments. Collaboration had compromised the parties of the Right, and the propertied class—primarily composed of Germans, Jews extensively murdered by the Germans, other Czechs in permanent exile, or collaborators—had largely disappeared. There was, therefore, slight internal opposition to the National Front's commitment to a program of nationalization of basic industry, agrarian reform, and social welfare measures.

The conduct of its election held in April 1946, unlike others throughout Eastern and Western Europe alike, was irreproachable. The Communists won a plurality of 38 percent and assumed key ministries, but continued in a coalition government. There is little question that the Pan-Slav sentiment, a radicalized population, and the leading Communist role in the distribution of the German lands were important factors in their success. The population was further to the left than the political party leadership and more closely tied to extraparty organizations and personal loyalties. As the war drew to an end local committees of the resistance, recognized by the exile government, at first assumed the functions of administration throughout the liberated country, and workers' councils organized in the factories. These committees and councils were radical in aspiration, and without the restraining influence of both the exile government and the Communist Party would have pressed for a far more extensive and immediate reorganization of Czech society. As it was, they were incorporated into the National Front, but remained as local administrative units under the coalition government until 1948.

The political affiliation of the Czech people continued to rest on such fraternal resistance ties rather than the political parties, and a nominal member of the National Socialist Party might support a Communist if he were of the same resistance group, ex-prisoner association, or factory council. The reverse was true as well. But the workers' councils were emasculated shortly after liberation and integrated into the centralized trade union which made their function in the factories advisory instead of managerial. They remained, however, the core of the most radical sentiment in the nation—dormant, but present.[75]

Coalition government was not new to Czechoslovakia. Ever since the democracy was organized in 1918, each government had been a coalition of several parties. During and for the first two years after World War II the political leaders developed almost a mystique of national unity and devotion to the goals of reconstruction which reduced party rivalries to a minimum. Under the international and political pressures of 1947 this mood dissolved rapidly as the political parties in the National Front moved to sharpen their distinctive characters.

The National Socialist Party of President Beneš, the largest and most important non-Marxist party, was left of center by American standards. Theoretically, it differed in the early postwar years from the Communists and Social Democrats in that it based its moderate socialism on humanitarian social welfare aims rather than class interests and perhaps could be considered analogous in ideology to the British Fabians, although, in fact, the Communists also emphasized national rather than class goals. The party endorsed land reform and nationalization of basic industry, and it fully supported the Czech-Soviet alliance. For these reasons the United States never identified its interests with Beneš' Party, as it was wont to do with the residue of the Right and Center in the other nations of Eastern Europe. Nevertheless, as in other areas of Eastern Europe, conservative elements naturally drifted toward the National Socialists, and over the years the new recruits altered the composition and outlook of the party. It became the exclusively bourgeois party and in 1947 began to oppose any extension of social legislation which both the Social Democrats and the Communists proposed.

The Populist Catholic Party was slightly to the right of the National Socialists and stood for the interests of property and small-scale private enterprise, but it also adhered to the Košice program of the Front. Steinhardt admitted to Washington that the range of views in the government was wide. "There are three or four members of the Cabinet that are just downright reactionary, they are more reactionary than any of my friends up on Wall Street. Then there are three or four others who . . . are very conservative."[76]

In Slovakia the situation was more complex. There had been a substantial indigenous fascist support for the Slovakian nationalism of Monsignor Tiso during the war, and the Democratic Party, although also a part of the Front, absorbed a good part of these elements. Many of its leaders participated in the resistance, but there was no doubt that its avowed conservative character attracted many of the right-wing Slovak nationalists attempting to get back into politics under a respectable aegis.

At the end of the war the Social Democratic leaders were old and weary, and the leadership of the party fell to Zdenek Fierlinger and younger militants. Fierlinger had been the Czech ambassador to the USSR during the war and was, by all acccounts, strongly pro-Soviet—more so, in fact, than many Communists. No one regarded this as a handicap in the early years, since pro-Soviet sentiment in Czechoslovakia was nearly unanimous.

Only in late 1947, as we shall see, did essentially external pressures create a real split in the party. Steinhardt assessed the Social Democrats for Washington as a rather unreliable mélange. ". . . [T]here were some very moderate leaders . . . and there were some very wild ones. The Social Democratic Party, curiously, within itself, has one or two leaders that I consider more dangerous, as far as Communism is concerned than any of the Communist leaders, and it also has two or three leaders who are just as conservative as the members of the Catholic Party. . . ."[77]

Among the Eastern European Communist parties, only the Yugoslavs had a mass base comparable to the Czech party. Committed to nationalist reconstruction and a gradualist, nonrevolutionary approach to socialism, it was one of the staunchest defenders of the National Front. Many factors, therefore, guaranteed substantial mass support for the CP in 1945–1946. The wartime radicalization of the masses, pro-Russian sentiment due to Soviet opposition to Munich, the Red army's principal role in the war against the Germans, Pan-Slav sentiment, and the Czech reliance on the Soviets as a counterbalance to a possibly resurgent Germany all enhanced the Communists' following. USSR-Czech interwar relations, moreover, had been relatively good. Prior to Munich the leaders of the party, due to the relative freedom in Czechoslovakia, were in close touch with the people. After the war they made a concerted effort to enroll a mass membership, and by 1947 it exceeded that of the other three parties combined. The other parties felt rather smothered by the CP and remained unable to find a unique position in electoral campaigns, for the Communists had co-opted both nationalists and moderate social welfare aims.

Steinhardt assessed the Czech Communists quite realistically:

. . . I personally know some of the Czech communist leaders who, in my opinion, are really Socialists. . . . the Communist Party . . . probably consists of 10 percent paid "stooges" I mean the direct representatives of Moscow. . . . Then there is probably another 10 percent who, . . . from the point of view of ideology and their sympathies . . . [are] so close to Moscow . . . as being completely in the hands of Moscow. Then there is probably another 10 percent sort of borderline cases. . . . The other 70 percent are Czechs and Slovaks and they're very patriotic and they're very loyal to their country and that's 70 percent, and I'm being very cautious, some people put it as high as 80 percent. . . . I know most of the leaders personally, and for example I consider the Prime Minister a 100 percent Czech. . . . He has talked back to Moscow . . . and he has flatly refused to do what they have asked him to do several times. . . . [T]here are one or two of the others who are also

Communists who, at times, have gone out of their way to help us because they thought it was good for Czechoslovakia, and who in so doing, . . . have nettled the Russians.[78]

Alarming to the Czech hopes for securing their coveted neutral and independent ground between East and West was the sharpened antagonism between the great powers. Churchill's Fulton speech, and even more his Zurich address of September 19, 1946, calling for a European Federation, frightened the Czechs. Hubert Ripka, one of the more conservative cabinet members, interpreted the speech to mean an anti-Soviet bloc. "To build a union without the participation of the U.S.S.R. would mean to create an anti-Russian union. Not a European Federation, but understanding and co-operation between the big powers and other states in the world can secure a better peace and economic and political reconstruction. Such proposals as Churchill made would mean in reality a new interventionism against the U.S.S.R."[79] Byrnes's Stuttgart oration, implying reconstruction of a strong Germany, intensified the growing anxiety all Czechs felt for their security—especially in an anti-Soviet context, which had been the origin of the Munich Agreement. Such expressions only solidified their Pan-Slav sentiment.

Hungary: The Dilemmas of Power

In Hungary, the Independence Front that assumed power in Budapest as the Red Army liberated the country more openly represented the conservatives than did the other coalitions of Eastern Europe. Nevertheless, in September 1945 the United States representative insisted that the Soviets would not permit free elections in Hungary because they were rapidly removing all the non-Communist voices in the government, leaving it in the hands of the Smallholders Party, the Communists, the Social Democrats, and the small National Peasant Party that was closely aligned with the CP. Reflecting this supposition, Byrnes, at the London Conference, referred to the Hungarian government as totally subservient to the USSR.

Subsequent events proved these assumptions completely erroneous. The Smallholders, despite their name, had little connection with the peasants and represented the small, Protestant urban bourgeoisie. The foreign minister later explained to the State Department in Washington that his party ". . . placed great emphasis on the preservation of the bourgeois mode of living and of pro-Western middle-class Hungary."[80] "In this desire," he went on, "they are opposed by a minority . . . of industrial workers, who are pro-Eastern in their sympathies and are not interested in the continuation of a middle-class Hungary."[81] Yet the leaders of the Smallholders understood that as long as the Soviet troops occupied Hungary, they could maintain power only through a coalition government. Sections of the party, however, opposed any concessions to the Left and were known to intrigue with the wholly discredited reactionaries of the old order against the republic.

Claiming that antirepublic disturbances in the countryside at the time required a show of unity from the coalition, the Soviet representative, Kliment Voroshilov, in October 1945 asked the leaders of the Smallholders Party to accept 47 percent of a common ticket for the November election. Although the Smallholder leadership at first agreed with the CP on 51 percent, the American and British radios attacked the proposal and the party conference rejected it. The Russians acceded to their decision and in the election, by all accounts the first free and unfettered vote in Hungarian history, the Smallholders won an absolute majority of 57 percent and the Communists and Social Democrats, 17 percent each. The Russians, to the surprise and relief of the Smallholders, and, according to Nagy, to the irritation of the Communists, indicated to the new Prime Minister Ferenc Nagy their eagerness to cooperate closely with the party.

The parties in the Independence Front agreed to maintain a coalition government in which the Smallholders took the leading posts. At the last minute, however, CP leader Mátyás Rákosi demanded the interior ministry for the Communists, claiming that bands of Smallholders throughout the country were terrorizing them. The Prime Minister could not deny the fact, and the CP took the critical ministry. The Socialist Michael Karolyi described the election as a vote against socialism and against the Soviet Union.[82]

Given the power of the prewar reactionary, ruling class, it is not surprising that it made real, if unsuccessful, attempts to wrest control from the pro-West-led republican government and sabotage its efforts. The center of Hungarian reaction was the Catholic Church and its Prince-Primate, Cardinal Mindszenty, who advocated the traditional order in its every dimension —the Hapsburg throne, the great estates, the privilege, and the oppression. He opposed not only the Communists but also the liberal Protestants in the Smallholders party who sought at least to bring Hungary into twentieth-century Europe. The government was extremely patient with Mindszenty, although he challenged it on every issue of reform and remained recalcitrant despite the pleas from the Smallholders, for he was confident, as Schoenfeld reported to Washington, that the ". . . Americans will soon use atom bomb to drive Soviets out of Hungary."[83] The Smallholders, primarily Calvinists, described the Cardinal as ". . . stubborn, has small intellect, basically uncultured."[84] But his power and that of the Church was great and the state allowed it to preserve its prerogatives, to the great detriment of the Hungarian people, until 1949—long after the Communist Party had taken full control.

When the government in 1947 introduced secular education, including biology for the first time in Hungarian history, the Church rallied its forces to counteract such modernizing reforms. The Protestants accepted the new policy and merged their elementary schools, still leaving 63 percent of the elementary education and 73 percent of the teachers colleges under Church control. But not until May 1948 did the state move to assume direction of all education, and it was motivated primarily by the need for technically trained cadre. The Church met this threat to their privilege head on when Cardinal Mindszenty threatened to excommunicate all who supported the new education policy, and the Catholic opposition party protested public education as contrary to natural law. Nevertheless, the new law provided that two hours of religious training per week were compulsory for every child, and this provision remained in effect until September 1949, when the subject was made optional.

Despite these incursions on the Church's exclusive power over the social and cultural life of the nation and their adamant opposition to the government on every level, the bishops remained on the state's payroll in the highest category of civil servants, and the state paid the Church a direct subsidy until 1948. The continued strength of the Right was also the outcome of the backwardness of a peasant society, where the symbols of the old order—the Church and the aristocracy—had deep holds based on their control of the limited education. And, remembering the counterrevolution of the 1920's, the peasants were more reticent in giving support to the government, fearing reprisals from their former landlords just over the border in Austria.[85]

Allied with the Church were the dispossessed landlords, aristocrats, and a large assortment of others who had favored the prewar regime of Admiral Nicholas Horthy. These representatives of the old order used every opportunity to attack the Soviet Union as well as the republic. Tensions finally erupted when in July 1946 several Soviet officers and soldiers were shot, and the police uncovered a plot that they alleged involved the Church, a number of important members of the Smallholders Party, and exiles who were providing arms in preparation for a *Putsch* when the Red Army withdrew. The Soviet command subsequently ordered the government to prosecute certain members of Parliament, disband a number of youth organizations, and curb the Catholic Church's anti-Soviet campaign.

In October the Socialists and Communists presented several demands as conditions for maintaining the coalition. The measures were modest, according to Nagy, and readily acceptable to the Smallholder leadership. They included help for workers and peasants, state control of banks and textbook production, and the like. Nagy reported to Schoenfeld that "Leftists are honestly fearful of possible counter revolutionary action by certain elements which do exist and must be guarded against."[86] Schoenfeld nevertheless warned Nagy against further concessions to the "Leftists." Yet Nagy, too, felt in a perilous position as "He recalled that in 1919 Communist regime was installed here by 150 armed sailors. . . ."[87]

In December 1946 the government uncovered another plot to overthrow the republic and arrested some military officers and a few members of the Smallholders Party. The Prime Minister, Ferenc Nagy, without conviction, denied knowledge of the conspiracy and dismissed it as merely "discussions." Later the secretary of the Smallholders, Bela Kovacs, "jokingly" threatened the Communists with bringing out the peasants and "reactionaries" to demonstrate against them. Nagy in his memoirs admits that the fear of counterrevolution among the Communists, who had been tortured and spent years in Horthy's prisions, made Kovacs' "joke" anything but amusing.[88] Public trials for the accused were planned for the spring of 1947, and the Communists advised Nagy that Kovacs should temporarily retire during the trial. He did not do so, and in March 1947 the Soviets arrested Kovacs for conspiracy. Given the background, few seriously questioned the plots. The United States and British notes regarding Kovacs' arrest alarmed Nagy, who feared that it would further prejudice his case with the Russians. Shortly thereafter Nagy went into exile, and the Hungarian cabinet was reshuffled on May 31. The Smallholders retained the majority of the posts, but lesser figures replaced the old leadership, and the United States responded by immediately terminating its credits to Hungary.

The Russians and Eastern European Politics

The Soviets played an essentially opportunistic, nonideological role in Eastern Europe's initial postwar development. They cared little about the previous policies or the ideology of the men in power in the coalition governments so long as they were not anti-Soviet in the postwar period. This is clearest in Rumania, where the government included the King and the ex-fascist foreign minister and chief of police, and in Hungary, where the dominant party represented the bourgeoisie and was basically pro-West. The fact remains that Russia, like the countries in Eastern Europe, was largely preoccupied with its own reconstruction, and all other facts were secondary to that all-consuming aim. The Soviets had definite national security interests in the region through which the Germans had twice invaded their homeland, but these interests did not include revolution. They knew the area was one of tension with the United States, and they wanted to minimize it short of undermining their security interests or their economic demands on the area in the form of reparations and trade. These relations and interests would have differed little if Russia had been a traditional capitalist state. Their efforts to minimize tension took the form of a broad political pluralism and moderate internal economic policies. Through the Communist parties, and often directly, the Soviets castigated and frequently jailed the more militant elements in the population that pressed for rapid revolutionary change. The Russians also used the strictly racial device of Pan-Slav sentiment to mobilize solidarity among all classes against the West. Their call for a Slavic Congress in December 1946 rang with chauvinism on the allegedly superior Slav culture and science of the prebolshevik era.

In foreign affairs the Soviets made it very clear to all the Eastern European governments that while their internal development was their own concern, on international questions they expected them to tailor their policies after the Soviet pattern. This the foreign ministers, most of them non-Communist, tried to impress on the United States in all their diplomatic contacts. Thus Tatarescu, Rumania's foreign minister, insisted to Byrnes that Rumania was a capitalist state and desired ties with the West, but that it would always support the USSR in foreign affairs. And in their relations with the United States and British in the Allied Control Commissions in the former enemy states, the Soviets continued to model their behavior on the precedents set in Italy and Japan, which granted only a minimal advisory role to the United States and Britain.[89]

The political and economic dynamics in Eastern Europe and the world inevitably altered what Steinhardt regarded as the Soviets' "benign" indifference toward the internal political policies and class relations of its neighboring states.[90] Russia was strong enough after World War II to insure that these nations did not suffer the same fate as after World War I. But by 1947, as multiple pressures mounted both in Eastern Europe and from the West, its policy stiffened and became at once defensive and vigilant. For Eastern Europe's interests were *not* the same as those of the USSR, either for the old ruling class bent on counterrevolution, or the bourgeoisie aiming at close ties with the West, or, increasingly, for the national Communists who frequently placed the needs of their own national plans and development above any other consideration. The future held growing and inevitable tension between the objectives of all these forces.

The two years following the war, then, did see revolutionary change in Eastern Europe—but revolutionary only in the context of the region's past. These former semicolonial nations had begun the process of economic development and modernization by breaking the grip of foreign industry and the archaic landholding and comprador class. So long as the questions of reconstruction were their primary concerns, there could be harmonious, cooperative relations in the national fronts between parties of the bourgeoisie and the Communists, since they shared the same aims. The state would assume the functions of economic development, as it alone could fulfill the task in the interests of the nation-state—a policy that led to early conflict with America's goals.

The United States did make a sincere effort to secure the area for its framework of multilateral trade and an open door for American investment, using many means of pressure to secure those ends. When it failed, less because the area was in the Soviet orbit than because the goal was incompatible with national economic development, Washington chose instead a policy of harassment and employed the image of an iron curtain to blur, for strictly political purposes, the variations in an area whose political experiences at the time ranged from pluralist Czechoslovakia to bolshevik Yugoslavia. As 1946 drew to a close such categorizations were useful to magnify the ideological distinctions, both within Eastern Europe and between the region and the West. To impose the myth of the iron curtain at this time was utilitarian to the United States' imperative need to create a capitalist trading bloc. And the multiple pressures that the Americans applied to isolate the East soon became a self-fulfilling prophecy.

8

Greece and the Middle East: Tradition and Turmoil

Greece and the Middle East had known conflicts in previous decades and generations such as were to arise during and after World War II. The border disputes and imperial pretensions of small states dated back centuries, and the struggle of Macedonians to assert national identities over the yet stronger nationalisms of their oppressors was no less old. Repression, corruption, court politics—all these, and yet more venal acts, were by 1946 the expected ways of the old order. And the alliance of the small nations of the region with larger expansive powers, whether Germany or Britain, or now the United States, was also a traditional aspect of the diplomacy of Greece and Turkey. Nor was the desire of the great powers for the economic and strategic wealth of the eastern Mediterranean and Middle East a new episode, and the bloody history of nineteenth- and twentieth-century diplomacy, of England, Russia, and Germany locked in struggle for mastery in the region, testifies to the antiquity of the imbroglios into which the United States was willingly to plunge in the years after 1945.

What was new, and of which the historian should make neither too much nor too little, was the social revolutionary quality and sources of many of the movements the great powers had to confront in Greece and the Middle East, for two bloody world wars had taken their toll of the resilience and durability of the older orders of the region. Within the framework of traditional conflicts, the emerging forces of the Left and revolutionary nationalism sought to strike at the root causes of their malaises.

Nowhere was this more valid than in Greece, where the divided character of the postwar Left, with its ambiguous, undisciplined relationship to Russian objectives, served to complicate the effort on the part of the classic and unregenerate Greek Right, backed initially by Britain, to restore its mastery over a nation that a traumatizing war had sundered. If Greece, unlike any other nation, reveals the tragedy of the European Left in Southern and Western Europe after the war, and the sacrificial strategy of the USSR with its commitment to its own state interests, it also exposes the willingness of the United States to act severely and decisively to make certain that an independent Left willing to act on its own initiative would not survive to challenge larger American objectives in the region.

The question of Greece, and indeed the entire Middle East, is both traditional and distinctive, as the admixture of imperialisms and revolution unfolded and the United States sought eventually to emerge as the guiding, principal power in the region.

Greece After the War

Greece, to a great measure, was ultimately the problem of an unregenerate Right, traditionally expansive and parasitic on a great power behind whose aegis it sought to move, closing all options to the voluntary co-option of a Left which, at least in its Communist wing, was always ambivalent about reliance on arms as the road to power. This Right, predatory as well as opportunistic, managed to raid and further impoverish a war-torn land, and through its repression of all forces on the left it defined for the opposition the relatively limited responses it might afford. The further internationalization of Greek internal affairs was the inevitable consequence of the cost of this self-serving reactionary policy, but foreign direction of Greece's affairs was scarcely a new phenomenon. Only the vast material expense of pursuing such a course made it inevitable that the United States would eventually become the protector of Greek reaction.

The Varkiza Agreement of February 1945 had ended the armed conflict between the ELAS, the main resistance movement, and the British and their insubstantial and, in many cases, compromised local allies. This armed conflict, which raged through the month of December 1944 and into January, was scarcely a civil war, for the forces of repression were overwhelmingly foreign. At Varkiza the ELAS agreed to hand in its arms in return for the promises of amnesty, immunity from rightist reprisals, and political freedom to operate through its political arm, the EAM. The EAM was a coalition of five leftist, republican parties, of which the Communists (KKE) were the dominating but hardly the exclusive element. For no less significant than the genuine pluralism in the EAM was the split within the KKE itself between the militants, who were hardened by their wartime experiences as the leaders of the most important resistance movement, and the parliamentarians, who were sensitive to Russian direction. By June 1945, despite the overwhelming evidence that the Right and the British were using the Varkiza Agreement as a breathing spell during which to consolidate power and repress the Left, the KKE elected to purge its militants and opt for a peaceful role in Greek affairs. The KKE publicly recognized British predominance in the eastern Mediterranean, as the Russians were already pledged to do, and it even advanced some of the traditional nationalist Greek claims to disputed border regions.

Had the Varkiza Agreement been implemented, the Communists would have gladly gone the way of the French and Italian Communist parties. Yet Nikos Zachariades, the party's secretary and moderate leader, never fully controlled his own party, even after many purges, nor could he establish control over the Macedonian nationalist elements both within and without the KKE, much less the other EAM parties quite unresponsive to Moscow's direction. Above all, the Greek Right and the British themselves defined the future options for the Greek Left by deciding to repress it, for the structurally decadent nature of the Greek *status quo,* and especially its moribund economy, made the Left appear potentially more dangerous in democratic politics than they were likely to be in the hills.

By the end of the war it was generally acknowledged that the successive British-backed governments in Athens had embarked on a policy of jailings, terror, economic incompetence and corruption at home, and national aggrandizement in their diplomacy. Even as they filled their National Guard with former collaborationist police officials, and "X" bands roamed unmolested about the country shooting former ELAS and EAM leaders, the Athens regimes advanced exaggerated claims on Albanian, Bulgarian, Italian, and Yugoslav territories—in part to regain via international adventures the nationalist support they were losing through consistent internal failures. By the Potsdam Conference all three of the great wartime allies were plainly disturbed over the course of events in Greece.[1]

The "nonpolitical" government of right-wing elements under Admiral Petros Voulgaras that headed Greece at the end of the war and until October 1945 wasted no time before continuing the post-Varkiza repression and consolidating political power. On the fact of the repression there is slight controversy, and only its extent is questioned; but since only the executioners in history know how many victims they have felled, such figures are always elusive. Suffice it to say, the most conservative source—the British Parliamentary Legal Mission—in January 1946 suggested the Greek regime arrested at least 50,000 persons in the most arbitrary fashion and locked them up in miserable prisons, and that while it released many, new arrests were even more rapid. The Communist estimate of about 80,000 arrests at the end of 1945, and well over 1,000 assassinations, is probably quite close to the mark. Collaboration with the Nazis was considered a far lesser crime than activity in the wartime ELAS, and as former collaborators filled the ranks of the civil service and police at every level, and as the British insisted on the purge of politically doubtful elements, they laid the basis of an even more extensive repression. Under the circumstances, during the winter of 1945–1946 some former ELAS fighters fled to the mountains on their own initiative, rather than face the mounting terror, many to return to their homes before the spring.[2]

The KKE itself tried, as best it could, to function in a parliamentarian environment which was fatally circumscribed so long as Britain aided the police and army in their policy of repression. The harassed Communist offices and newspaper in Athens, which remained there until 1947 as a symbol of the fable of Greek democracy, permitted the KKE to retain its illusions as to the future. During November 1945, when a new, essentially antimonarchial, government was formed under the Liberal Themistocles Sophoulis, the KKE initially supported it until it became painfully clear that it would only continue the repression or be unable to stop it. In a sense the Sophoulis government, which was more liberal than any Greece was to see for nearly two decades, was well intended but impotent, for real power in Greece had moved to the army, police, and armed rightist bands, over whom Britain alone might exercise ultimate control. Even as the government declared an amnesty at the end of December, it had no more effect than the Varkiza pledges on the subject. Yet it is still obvious that the KKE was split on an appropriate strategy and that its conservatives under Zachariades were not fully in control. In June the KKE and two other EAM parties asked for a reversal of the Varkiza Agreement that general elections would follow a future plebiscite on the status of the exiled monarchy. They also asked for four-power supervision of the elections. That the Communists, perhaps because of their proclamations of neutrality in foreign affairs, thought that the British would let the EAM win the power at the polls which they had fought to prevent in the fields was an act either of consummate naïveté or conscious abdication. The Russians, in part because they had assigned Greece to the British sphere of influence, but also because they wanted no parallel schemes in East Europe, declined throughout 1945 to legitimize the rigged elections of a repressive government.[3] To the Russians, Greece was an excellent twit to Anglo-American moralism every time they waxed righteous regarding the political situation in Eastern Europe. Before the end of the year, too, the KKE had serious doubts as to its future in elections of any sort, given the fact many of its supporters and allies were in jail, the British troops effectively dominated power, and repression was growing. Only at the end of 1945 did they pass over to a stance of true opposition to constituted power, for the first time calling for a withdrawal of British troops.

The issue of the elections and plebiscite revealed the true measure of power in Greece by 1946. The decision to reverse the Varkiza voting order came not because the EAM had asked for it, but because the British, after Washington's prompting, during September 1945 had the Regent, Archbishop Damaskinos, come to London to take the new procedure back to Greece. The general election was announced for January 20, 1946, and the switch created a storm, helping Sophoulis and his coalition to come to power. The parties in the Sophoulis cabinet split on the election, in part because the British had prevented them from purging the army and police of royalists, and hence they, too, were doubtful of the outcome; but their antimonarchial heritage also caused them to be suspicious that the British were striving to retain the royal family. Even the British Ambassador, Reginald Leeper, thought a postponement desirable, but Bevin overruled him and urged haste, in large part because England now preferred an even more pliable government. The most they managed to accomplish was to delay the elections until March 31. The Communists, after equivocating and in a step they later condemned as a great error, decided to boycott the election, and the other EAM parties also urged their followers to stay at home. Sophoulis himself publicly had grave doubts as to how honest it would be, and he openly complained about the rising terrorism of the X bands and the fact that only the monarchists and Right could freely campaign. Yet he could not control matters, for power rested with the British and their proroyalist allies.

The British, for their part, by the fall of 1945 had become highly impatient with the Greeks, whose successively unstable governments they thought were concerned too exclusively with additional foreign loans rather than putting their own house in order. By this time, as well, the British admitted their inability to cope alone with the voracious Greeks, and began urging the Americans to share the burdens with them. During November,

Byrnes accepted the principle of leaving the military responsibilities to the British but aiding its economy, though no commitments were made for many months. From Athens, American Ambassador Lincoln MacVeagh correctly but critically warned that the English were far too hostile toward Greek business leadership and prone to sympathize too much with the Left, slighting the larger Balkan context and Communist threat. "Cannot stress too strongly," MacVeagh cabled at the beginning of the new year, ". . . that Greece only Balkan country attempting retain orthodox ideas private property and free enterprise along American lines."[4] What was to appear a costly liability to straitened British Labourites was to seem like an asset to the United States.

The conditions in Greece prior to the election of March 31 still left the initiative as to the outcome of that nation's future with the British and the Right, and Sophoulis vainly attempted to postpone the poll. The so-called "anarchist" bands that appeared in the northern mountains were few in number, and the effect rather than the cause of government policies—and not the result of KKE determination to fight. At the beginning of 1946 the Russians strongly advised the KKE to forget about revolution and to form a united front in the forthcoming elections. Zachariades accepted this moderate line, but left the door open to later urban insurrections—rejecting the rural guerilla strategy—should the repression intensify. The question was therefore less the honesty of the election than whether the new government would pursue a repressive or conciliatory policy after its so-called legitimation. The election itself was all the EAM claimed it would be, and three independent republican parties followed the EAM policy of calling for its boycott. The Anglo-American-French observation teams, some 1,155 men in all, sent in to attest to the democratic character of the event itself, provided the evidence to the contrary, despite their sanguine approval. Indeed, its final official report certifying the ". . . freedom, fairness and validity of the elections" was largely completed a week before the event itself.[5] Nearly all these observers were military men, and they were hardly independent or competent, and few, if any, knew Greek. Suffice it to say, the existing Greek registration lists dated from 1928 to 1935, and in the months preceding the election the authorities revised the lists to an extent the observer report would not reveal, but the mission vouched for only about 70 percent of the 1,850,000 actual registrants, and it could not account for 360,000 additional voters the government claimed on the lists. Yet even this biased mission admitted significant intimidation against the Left, and it placed a cloud of grave doubt over the entire procedure. What was not in doubt is that a mere 1,117,000 votes were cast, or half the number the government said possible, and no one could tell to what extent they were real or falsified ballots. More significant is that the regime under the royalist Tsaldaris now held 231 of the 354 seats in Parliament, and it was free to impose its will.

It was at this point in Greece's history that reaction moved into high gear, and the civil war became inevitable despite the Communist Party's reticence. The condition of Greece until the summer of 1946 was summarized for various Americans when John Sofianopoulos, former foreign minister for several Greek governments, visited America:

> The Varkiza Agreement to end the civil strife of 1944, which I negotiated for the then Greek Government, was not carried out by subsequent administrations; reactionary elements, active during the Metaxas dictatorship and the enemy occupation, have been kept in key positions in the Civil Service, Army, Police and Gendarmerie. Under such pressure the elections of March 31, 1946, were neither free nor genuine.
>
> The Tsaldaris Government issuing from these elections has declared a ruthless war against all democrats, branded as "Communists," and has imposed fascism in the country in a form more ferocious than we ever experienced under Metaxas. The terror exercised by the Government and the vindictive military operations against the outlawed democrats have strengthened the ranks of those who have taken refuge from persecution in the hills. The spreading internal struggle now covers nearly the whole of Greece. Thus free political life has ceased, our relations with our Northern neighbors have been jeopardized, and the economic reconstruction vital to a war-torn people has become impossible.[6]

In a word, it may be suggested, if the Left initially refused to resist destruction, the events of April 1946 onward gave them precious little option. The official KKE's reticence to turn to violence could not prevent a spontaneous resistance motivated, above all else, by self-defense. By this time, as well, the intricate problem of the special repression that had been meted out to the Macedonian minority in Greece, comprising about one-fifth of the nation, brought that age-old question to an explosive point. For the Macedonian Greeks had fought hard and well for the ELAS during the war, though many had done so because of their separatist goals and desire, in many cases, to merge Greek Macedonia with those sections in Bulgaria and mainly Yugoslavia. To Macedonians, Communism had become an almost traditional expression of their separatism and hatred of their persecution. This independence movement, which also had led during the war to a number of bitter, armed jurisdictional conflicts between the

Macedonian SNOF and ELAS, the Greek KKE treated with circumspection in the hope they could promise full equality to Macedonians within a Greek nation—a nebulous formula intended to offend as few as possible. When the various rightist police and military units moved back into the Macedonian regions, however, the terror levied against this group was especially severe, for both political and historic reasons. An estimated 25,000 escaped the terror by fleeing across the borders to Yugoslavia and Bulgaria, and about 23,000 refugees of the Cham minority could be found in Albania. Here, too, was an important source of support for a renewed struggle.

By June 1946, when the Tsaldaris government enacted its repressive Resolution III, the number of leftists just then organizing in the primarily Macedonian mountains it could cite as justification for the step was far less than the 4,000 to 6,000 that were in all Greece by October. Until then most bands were composed of seven to ten men equipped with old firearms. Yet this resistance was in no sense strictly northern-based, despite the Greek government's persistent claim it was actually a war Bulgaria and Yugoslavia were fostering, for over the next six months a quarter of the official complaints of clashes dealt with events in Thessaly, isolated in the center, and about one-tenth in the Peloponnesus in the far south, and major pockets in which the Democratic army existed could be found spread evenly throughout Greece. That Macedonia in the north accounted for half the clashes was a reflection of the location of the terror. What was clear was that Tsaldaris had elected to apply his armed resources in the hope that he might stamp out an essentially spontaneous resistance faster than he made it grow. He was to fail.[7]

As his next step in consolidating power for the Right, Tsaldaris decided to speed up to September 1, 1946, the plebiscite on the question of return of the monarchy, which had originally been scheduled for March 1948. Given the growing repression, the results were even more dishonest than the preceding election. The government claimed that nearly 100 percent of the possible electors voted, despite EAM opposition, and of these 69 percent favored the return of King George II. This measure, which, according to Sophoulis and others (including a confidential Anglo-American report), was the product of generous ballot-box stuffing and other irregularities, only moved the strongly republican elements more firmly into the opposition and intensified the need for further repression.

The structural conditions in Greece precluded the possibility of successful repression, not the least because the condition of the economy and society throughout 1946 made the army and police of approximately 100,000 men increasingly unreliable for the task of maintaining order. There had been a few of the usual cabals among some units, and both Greek and American sources confirm the fact that at the end of 1946 the army, despite its size, was likely to fail: "The strength of the bands," the State Department wrote in a confidential March 1947 analysis, "lies not in their numbers (which total only 13,000 men by latest estimates) but in their organization and leadership, and in the extreme weakness of the Greek armed forces. The latter are poorly armed, poorly trained, and poorly paid. Their low morale leaves them open to the undercover tactics of Communist agitators, who are numerous within the ranks of the army itself. Desertions from the army in recent months have seriously alarmed the Greek authorities."[8]

When the British Parliamentary Delegation in August surveyed Greek conditions as part of a reconsideration that ultimately led to America's taking up England's burden, one of their observations in their understated report was that in certain places the police and army were avoiding confrontations with many of these bands. "It would be a mistake, however," the delegation suggested, "to assume that the activities of these bands are entirely due to foreign inspiration. . . . There is evidence that amongst these bands are many Left-wing supporters who have fled to the mountains to escape terrorism exercised by the extreme Right." Trade unions had been subjected to "exceedingly drastic measures," and the local government was "undemocratic and authoritarian."[9] By October, even MacVeagh thought that certain Greek policies were "tending toward Fascism," and he believed that less repression would eliminate the large majority of "banditry."[10] But, for reasons that ultimately became relevant, the Tsaldaris regime was to treat the entire problem of the uprising as an issue of a foreign-sponsored intervention rather than as a domestic rebellion against oppression and corruption.

Corruption, Ambition, and Sponsorship

In a sense, Greece after World War II was the China of Europe. At the same time as terror and repression were employed against political opponents, the ruling elite exploited every opportunity to enlarge its personal fortunes via peculation and corruption, casually permitting economic paralysis and chaos to mobilize ever greater internal opposition and create a "communist" problem. Yet the analogy with China breaks down insofar as the Athens rulers also insistently engaged in advancing belligerent national claims against neighboring territories, reviving ancient Balkan feuds. Still, in both cases it was an instance of a decadent ruling elite being consciously aware of the need to obtain great power sponsorship if their control was to be maintained and ultimate ambitions realized. Such a courtship of England and then, increasingly, the United States was the basic strategy the Greek rulers were to pursue after World War II.

Regarding the economic condition of Greece there is little doubt: stagnation and corruption were rampant. By 1947 the cost of living was 176 times the 1937 level, while wages had fallen far behind. Prices from November 1944 to September 1946 alone increased about twenty times, and in mid-1946 industrial production was only about 40 percent of the 1938 level. The Greek governments confronted their crisis simply by printing ever larger quantities of drachmas, and from the beginning to the end of 1946 the number in circulation increased about five times, doubling again the following year. By any standard, save one, the Greek economy had collapsed.

That exception was the ". . . small class of wealthy people chiefly residing in and around Athens," which the British Parliamentary Delegation observed during August 1946. "Members of these families live in great luxury."[11] This class enriched itself as speculators and black-marketeers, and for this task their political connections were vital. UNRRA alone contributed $347 million in goods to Greece for "relief" purposes, and most of it the rightist officials channeled into the black market rather than to the hungry. UNRRA officials were unanimous in condemning the Greek government's handling of food, but for the Greeks who made vast tax-free profits on such graft, and shipped immense quantities of gold to safe countries, Greece's condition was beneficial. By the end of 1946 both official British and American sources concluded that the Greek economy's condition was "critical."[12]

If misery breeds suffering for some, for the Greek rulers it offered a potentially rich opportunity to plead with the Anglo-Americans to bail them out of a situation of impending disaster, and for much of 1946 they sedulously cultivated potential saviors. Leeper recalled how, from 1945 onward, each government in Athens ignored the economic problems of reconstruction: "They always excused themselves for doing nothing by saying that nothing could be done without a foreign loan."[13] Both the British and American governments were openly to comment on this dependence on foreign salvation.

The British assumed the greatest financial obligations until the end of

1946, but the Greeks came, hat in hand, to the United States as early as October 1945, asking for a $25 million Export-Import Bank loan and $250 million in credits. As a preelection gesture, the Americans granted the $25 million loan the following January, but implied more might be forthcoming should Athens attempt a serious program of economic stabilization. The sum was merely to whet Athens' omnivorous appetite, for within a few months numerous hints or requests for future aid were advanced, eventually to reach as high as $6 billion. In a sense this was a necessary precaution, for the British were becoming increasingly critical of Greek financial policy, giving advice Athens could hardly accept. By mid-July the British made it plain the end of their expensive toleration was not far off: "We must bring in the Americans," Hugh Dalton, chancellor of the exchequer, told Tsaldaris; "alone we cannot bear this burden, and we should be very glad to bring America into our partnership."[14]

The result was that the Greeks soon sent an economic mission to Washington to plead for $175 million in new loans. When they saw Truman on August 7, the Greeks stressed the strategic role of Greece in the region, but the stories of Greek corruption were too well known in Washington for an immediately favorable reply. To some critical extent this reticence was merely an added burden on Britain, and seen in this light Byrnes shortly thereafter assured the British that the United States would not permit Greece and Turkey to go Communist, and that Washington would now assume primary responsibility for at least economic aid to the Greeks if the British continued military aid for the time being. American diplomats informally told the Greeks that aid in some form would be forthcoming if they expanded their government's membership. By September 25 Byrnes, Forrestal, and Secretary of War Robert Patterson were all agreed on the need to aid Greece and Turkey, but they took no action, and treasury officials still urged that Greece first undertake far-reaching economic reforms.[15]

But that the Americans would soon have to fulfill their commitment, and more, was made clear in the October 10 report of the Parliamentary Delegation, which was too controversial to make public for nearly three months, but whose general contents were probably known. By and large, the delegation held the Athens regimes responsible for most of the political and economic repression and chaos plaguing Greece, and it attached such stern conditions to future British economic aid that it was obvious none would be forthcoming. Most important, it now felt there was a "strong case" for an "early withdrawal" of British troops to avoid involvement in the growing "civil disorder."[16] On the question of British troops there was now essential unanimity in the British government, and no surprises were possible, if only because Bevin had informed the State Department the preceding April he wished to withdraw British troops during the fall. That September the British confirmed that at least partial withdrawals would soon begin, and all American planning was premised on them. During early December, Bevin personally informed Byrnes they would do so as soon as practicable.

The Athens government was aware of Britain's pending disengagement, and during early October, Byrnes conveyed to Prime Minister Tsaldaris the general American policy, leaving the questions of timing and amounts in abeyance. But the Greeks could not wait, for economic disaster moved ever closer with each month. On October 18, MacVeagh assured King George on Truman's behalf that America was prepared to help Greece survive, but that internal economic reforms and a new coalition would greatly smooth the way with the American public. The Greeks did not oblige, but at the beginning of November, Washington confidently informed them that aid would in any event come before Greece capsized to the left. On the sixth, too, the State Department told Forrestal and others that the United States would supply arms to Greece and Turkey via the British should that protector be unable to afford the toll. Under the circumstances the Greeks increased their demands for arms, seeking now to build an army of 180,000 rather than the previous goal of 100,000, and Tsaldaris himself now embarked for the United States in mid-December to advance his cause with Byrnes. Byrnes merely revealed America's willingness to take on the cost of arming Greece should England fail it, but in light of Bevin's warning he alerted both Truman and Acheson that additional aid to Greece was now required.[17] The Greeks estimated they would require nearly $200 million during 1947, a sum the State Department thought poorly substantiated, but it agreed in principle that significant aid would be forthcoming in about three months, the minimum time required for the necessary congressional appropriation. Tsaldaris departed from America with the impression he had won over his rich hosts. Yet the United States still saw no special urgency, and in fact consented only to send an already announced mission under Paul A. Porter to study the economic situation and the manner in which outside assistance might best help. Porter had no sooner set off on the task, which he ultimately fulfilled by sending back scathing denunciations of Athens' corruption, than on January 6 the British government finally released its Parliamentary Delegation's report. It was now merely a question of timing, but it was certain the British would soon hand the expensive responsibility of Greece entirely to the Americans. There could be no surprises in this regard, for the two nations had already negotiated the broad contours of the transfer.[18]

Concomitant with the Greek elite's hunt for new treasuries was its effort to advance its border claims against its northern neighbors and Italy, and it generally made these demands at the same time. To the extent that Athens could internationalize its cause, making it part of an expansionist crusade against the Soviet bloc, the oligarchy might hope to attain its objectives. Those controversies were a legacy of Balkan history. But even before the end of World War II the successive right-wing regimes endlessly agitated for the northern Epirus region bordering Albania, from which the Moslem Chams had recently been expelled, the Dodecanese Islands belonging to Italy, and sections of Bulgarian Thrace—to mention only the most important. Anglo-American diplomats generally agreed that the Greeks were primarily responsible for growing regional tension over these issues.

The significance of Greek expansionism is less in its comic-tragic quality, the fact that some of the claims the EAM also sustained, or the Anglo-American desire to avoid turning a nuisance into a more serious crisis, than that Athens chose pugnaciously to define its relations with the neighbors on this basis, fanning hostility and yet more tension. For the new neighbors quickly realized that the easiest way to settle such belligerence was to aid, to some measure, that section of the Left in the Greek civil strife most likely to establish amicable relations with them. The significance of this situation, for which neither Russia nor the Anglo-Americans shared any great measure of responsibility, was to become most apparent after civil conflict graduated to civil war.

In this sense, Athens mobilized its own opposition, and gave direction to Yugoslavia's paternalistic interest in the fate of the persecuted Macedonians who became perhaps the most serious victims of rightist repression. For the next several years Athens papers and politicians openly called for invasions into disputed territories, hopefully with the aid of British troops. Officials, while more restrained, kept up the din, and at every meeting with Anglo-American diplomats Greek leaders did not neglect to register their desires, even linking it to an expanded Greece's strategic importance in the defense of the eastern Mediterranean. The EAM joined the nationalist chorus by concentrating on the less objectionable issues of Turkish Thrace and British Cyprus, both of which Athens also coveted. At the Paris Peace Conference, to the United States' dismay, the Greeks were especially adamant on obtaining northern Epirus as well as the Dodecanese, plus large reparations from the Axis satellites, the question of the Albanian territory especially irritating the Yugoslavs now that they were moving toward acting as that tiny nation's protector. The outcome at Paris was less than satisfactory: Bulgaria was to pay Greece a mere $45 million in reparations, and the Russians rapped Greek belligerence but also consented in principle to its eventually getting the Dodecanese.[19] The Americans, for their part, politely discouraged the Greeks in this particular folly throughout the period, but in a way designed not to give them offense and without taking a public stand on their substantive demands.

What was most significant about the Greek strategy was its impact on northern policy, and a gesture which no less incensed Bulgaria, Yugoslavia, and Albania was the constant Greek accusations that these three countries were provoking border incidents along their common frontiers, to which they replied in kind. During December 1946, on the United States' initiative, the UN Security Council authorized a commission to establish the facts, and its report placed the burden of responsibility primarily on the Greeks. The Greeks claimed more neighboring territory than any of the four nations, and this ". . . tended to increase the tension. . . ."[20] Most of the Greek evidence was rejected as spurious and false, the alleged frontier violations much more the product of Greek terror against minorities forced to escape over borders than any other cause. The worst that could be said, *The Times* of London's Athens correspondent concluded during early January 1947, was that the three northern nations tolerated movements across their borders, but Greece could not provide direct evidence of their aid to the guerillas, much less blame its neighbors as the cause of domestic chaos and resistance. Indeed, there was even serious question as to the KKE's ability to control the uprising, which was both a response to necessity and also had an independent Macedonian separatist wing seeking to attain its own objectives. What was certain, however, was that Greek belligerence toward virtually every nation in the region created the possibility of responses in kind. For without openly intervening, the Athens government now stimulated Yugoslavia or Albania to unite national interest with ideology to sustain the increasingly massive revolt against injustice in Greece.[21]

At the beginning of 1947 the realities of Greece were well known, and no surprising facts emerged to change the political direction of the region. A corrupt, self-serving, and increasingly repressive Right had so mismanaged the affairs of the nation that now even their British protectors had freely confessed their desire to withdraw from the scene. The resistance was still small and poorly equipped, and nothing suggested significant material aid from the north, much less an immediate threat to the fundamental security of Greece. Yet the ultimate fate of such a Greek elite, left to its own devices, was scarcely in doubt, but its demise would have inevitably come over a time span measured in years rather than months. No one believed Athens' allegations of an external Communist menace, for in fact there was none. But to survive, and to maintain the power which was the prerequisite of exploitation, the rulers of Athens would need foreign aid, and this they set out to obtain from the United States. All these facts were well known to contemporaries. And for their own purposes, the leaders in Washington were to find the Greek regime extraordinarily useful.

United States Policy Toward Greece and the Eastern Mediterranean, 1946

The United States had all of 1946 to consider the facts regarding the condition of Greece, and this it did with thoroughness, fixing its responses according to its definition of American national interests. But ultimately it set its policy in the larger context of the future of American power not merely in Greece, or even in the Eastern Mediterranean and Middle East, but in the world. That the United States would have an active postwar policy in Greece was a foregone conclusion even before the end of the war, when it knew relatively little of local conditions but decided in June 1945 that "to take an active and benevolent interest in Greece at this time offers one of the most practical means of demonstrating this Government's determination to play an international role commensurate with its strength and public commitments."[22]

The most important expression of American concern over Greece was its growing financial support and its preparation toward the end of 1946 to help the British with their economic burden in that small but costly nation. But the other aspect of American policy prior to 1947, which linked the question of Greece to the larger problem of strategic control over the Near East, was the extension of American military power into the Mediterranean.

The idea of stationing a portion of the United States Navy in the Mediterranean, ". . . for reasons of politics and sentiment," as the navy's records phrase it, began with Admiral H. K. Hewitt, whose wartime experiences in the region made him keenly aware of the potential value of the move. During the autumn of 1945 he argued for the step, and the germ of the approach fell on fertile ground when he linked it to the unstable political conditions of Europe. His superior, Secretary of the Navy James Forrestal, on January 11 had already publicly indicated that American naval power —the strongest in the world—might extend to the Mediterranean as well, but this was not meant to imply a continuous presence there. Early the following month he agreed to return the body of the Turkish ambassador to the United States to his native land aboard a man-of-war, and the most prestigious and powerful ship in the United States fleet, the battleship *Missouri,* was selected to maximize the "splendid effect" of the mission on the area. The gesture was designed solely as a carefully calculated "political manifestation," appropriate for the unsettled conditions of the region at the time, and to embellish it Forrestal got Byrnes's approval for plans for an accompanying task force in the region—one that might be made permanent later on.[23]

Although Truman heartily endorsed showing of the flag there, the notion of asserting American power in the eastern Mediterranean was preeminently compatible with Forrestal's concern for expanding American power into that oil-rich area. For geopolitical reasons alone, more than sufficient cause in his case, Forrestal quickly adopted Hewitt's plan as his own. Yet Forrestal's vision was even more grandiose, for he believed American power existed and had to be applied to realize its potential rewards. "Our security is not merely the capacity or ability to repel invasion," he was to argue at the end of 1947; ". . . it is our ability to contribute to the reconstruction of the world, and that is why I say that our military requirements have to be fitted into the pattern. . . ."[24] It was not sufficient to have the largest military establishment in the world; it was, in his view, no less essential to station it everywhere in the world—and to use it. The Mediterranean venture was, in its way, the first important application of a by no means exclusive view of American power. The ". . .U.S. has now established independent policy in Near and Middle East based on defense of its own interests in this region . . . ," America's ambassador in Ankara defined the gesture.[25]

On April 10 the *Missouri* arrived in Athens, and the Greek rightist newspapers celebrated the event. The Greek government understood the significance of the visit, the American chargé, Karl L. Rankin reported home, "nor was it lost on the Greek Communist Party or on the Russian Embassy in Athens." On May 11 the cruiser *Helena* also visited Athens ". . . to reassure the Greeks of quiet watchfulness on the part of the United States over the welfare of their country," and the embassy in Athens hoped

". . . that the precedent now established will be continued."[26] The idea certainly appealed to Forrestal, who took it up with Byrnes, who was no less enthusiastic, and it was agreed that American boats would continue visiting various Mediterranean ports on a casual basis. Over the following weeks, in the context of the Turkish crisis we consider later in this chapter, the State and various military departments defined a general policy, which Truman strongly endorsed and declared ready to apply "to the end," linking United States interests to the entire region. Russia's objective, Washington concluded, was to gain physical mastery over the Dardanelles and Turkey, and if it did so it would eliminate Western influences in the entire Middle East, deprive the non-Communist world of its oil, and ". . . be in a much stronger position to obtain its objectives in India and China."[27] This early geopolitical version of the domino theory naturally defined policy toward the entire Mediterranean basin—a policy that opted for the maintenance of the *status quo* in the region, and prejudged the decision to aid Greece. The application of American naval power was the first logical expression of this strategy.

During August, Washington administered the principle in expanded form. On the second it announced that the aircraft carrier *Roosevelt* would tour the region from Lisbon to Naples, but the intention of also sending it and accompanying destroyers to Athens and Salonika was withheld until a few days before the Greek plebiscite. "In many ways," Ambassador Caffery advised Washington in late July, "it would appear that Communism wears a cloak of nationalism and local autonomy in North Africa and perhaps more especially in Algeria."[28] For this reason, with the approval of both the State Department and the French, on the fifteenth, the navy ordered all of its Twelfth (European) Fleet destroyers into the Mediterranean, and two units decended on Algerian ports, where, according to the official records, ". . . Algerian Nationalists, instigated by Russia, were stirring up sentiments for independence. . . ."[29] At about the same time United States naval air power demonstrated over Greece.

Such a policy was appealing to all in Washington, for the exhibition of military power—and the implication that it might be unleashed if need be —was quite related to the decision at the end of September to aid Greece and Turkey with military aid should that be necessary, thereby adding teeth to a similar policy enunciated the preceding March. The concomitant decision to keep American military forces hovering nearby, should the local elements of order prove inadequate, was now logical and inevitable. On September 25, to help, in Forrestal's words, ". . . carry out American policy and diplomacy . . . ," Washington decided to create a permanent fleet in the Mediterranean, and the decision was made public at the end of the month.[30] Over the next year, Washington considered this fleet, with its ominous implications so familiar to preceding generations of global saber rattling, as a warning to Russia, and it was eventually to mount more than one intervention from it. Both the French and the British welcomed the gestures of solidarity implied in this display of power. With near certainty, such a strategy prejudged the American response to the imbroglios that were to reappear in the region, of which the Greek crisis was to be only one of many.

What was distinctive about the Greek situation, however, was that it did not involve an external invasion, but the disintegration of a social system that was creating a civil war, one whose causes Washington clearly perceived was the primary responsibility of an ineffectual and corrupt regime. For all its reservations, during the autumn of 1946 Washington determined not to allow Greece to fall to the Greek Left, whatever the cause, for Greece and Turkey it now defined as the sole obstacles to Soviet domination of a region which was in turn the link to Asia. Intervention against Russia was now joined in principle, for purposes of United States foreign policy, to American intervention to save decadent capitalist and colonial states, with conflicts between nations and within social systems becoming indistinguishable from the very inception of the postwar era.[31]

The Middle East, Iran, and Turmoil

American interest in the Middle East long predated the Greek crisis, which was actually the last in a chain of United States preoccupations with the region. American decision-makers regarded Greece and the entire Middle East as part of one integrated question, and in a critical sense Greece and the creation of a Mediterranean fleet were the final by-products of the momentum of America's penetration of the area, an involvement that was planned, desired, and by no means an unexpected accident in postwar history.

In only one sense was Greece a surprise: it had slight economic attraction, and was certain to prove a costly strategic overhead charge of economic penetration into the region. That influx was to replace British power to some great measure, essentially economically, but it was not intended to supersede it entirely and create a total vacuum into which United States power would move. To the extent Britain's demise exceeded America's plans, or radical nationalism and possible social revolutionary movements entered the scene, America confronted unanticipated risks.

The supplanting of British imperialism in the Middle East began in earnest during World War II, when the United States started to probe for new oil concessions in Iran and elsewhere, and to plan for much greater postwar control over the region's oil supplies. The extent of this Anglo-American rivalry, which soon assumed bitter proportions, we have described elsewhere, but suffice it to say that by the end of the war the United States had carved out an active role for itself in the region, bringing itself into conflict not only with England but also, somewhat less expectedly, with Russia as well.

As Truman later described it, the significance of the question of Iran was ". . . the control of Iran's oil reserves," the removal of which ". . . would be a serious loss for the economy of the Western world."[32] It was in the context of oil that the first Iranian crisis arose and left a smoldering legacy that was to be rekindled in 1945 and 1946, and again in yet more dangerous form in several years.

During the war the three major allies had agreed to evacuate their troops from Iran—placed there in 1941 because of the government's pro-German position—within six months of the termination of the war, which is to say, March 2, 1946. The British and Russians had also agreed not to upset existing oil concession arrangements, but from 1943 onward both the English and the Americans had begun scrambling for important oil privileges. In the fall of 1944 the Russians, too, joined the scene, demanding concessions in the north of Iran and causing the Iranian Majlis (parliament) to freeze all concession rights until the end of the war. Though the Russians had shown some interest in Iranian concessions between the wars, they had plenty of oil at home, and it is more than likely that strategic factors were the source of Soviet conduct in Iran from 1944 onward. Iran traditionally had aligned itself with great powers hostile to Russia, Germany having been the last, and, as the Russians were to indicate in May 1946, ". . . in the future Iran's relations with her great northern neighbor must be built on a new basis free from hostility and adventurousness. . . ."[33] By the end of the war Iranian leaders were seeking to align themselves with the United States, against the British and Russians alike, for neither of these nations had any great respect for the Teheran governments and Britain feared that the United States would succeed in its energetic moves to replace English control of Iran's oil fields. For this reason the British were to pursue their own strategy in Iran.

Washington, for its part, welcomed Iranian overtures, since the United States hoped its businessmen would penetrate Iran and at war's end feared the nation would sorely test the allies' solidarity. If the Russians extended their influence over Iran, American Ambassador Wallace Murray warned in September 1945, "it would end all possibility of an American oil concession in Iran," as well as create a ". . . potential threat to our immensely rich oil holdings in Saudi Arabia, Bahrein, and Kuwait."[34] More subtle was Britain's role, which key Americans in Iran suspected was to use the United States as a buffer and foil to Russia. It was in this context of suspicion of the intentions of both its former allies, and desire to protect and advance its own economic goals, that the United States was to respond to the Iranian question over the postwar era.

The position of Russia and England was simplified by the existence of separatist movements, and the Russians sponsored the Azerbaijan and Kurdish elements in the north while the British covertly aided the Arab tribes of Khuzistan in the oil-rich west. The Azerbaijans, while they had the support of the Russians and the pro-Communist Tudeh Party, were a traditionally independent people who hated the corrupt, foreign central government of Teheran, but also disliked the Russians. When, in December 1945, a Russian-backed regime was created in the north after several months of agitation, the American embassy reported to Washington that most of the people in the north were not Communists, but nevertheless backed the new administration's demands for autonomy from the central government. They were also attracted to the unprecedented reforms, including a rather mild land reform, that were brought to the poor region's social services and government. The Kurds, ever anxious to collaborate with anyone against the hated Iranians, were led by their traditional religious and tribal leaders rather than leftists.

Local grievances aside, the Americans wanted the Anglo-Soviet troops out of an Iran that everyone knew was voluntarily moving toward the United States orbit, and during late November they urged Moscow to withdraw its troops before the year was out. Then, when the Iranian government moved troops to stop the Azerbaijanian uprising, Soviet forces blocked them. At the Moscow Conference of Foreign Ministers, at the end of December, Bevin stressed to Byrnes the need to foster provincial autonomy and formally submitted a plan to create a commission to structure a decentralized regime almost certain to lead to the division of the country into spheres of influence. Stalin, for his part, made it clear that the basic question was a hostile government to Russia's south, and that Soviet troops would remain on after the March deadline and for as long as the Iranian government necessitated. In principle, however, the Russians were ready to support the British commission scheme. But the Americans would not, and confined their demands to general troop withdrawals. When Byrnes pressed too hard, Molotov simply linked Soviet troop removals in Iran to the question of American withdrawals in China or British from Greece.[35] There was no agreement at Moscow, and Byrnes pointedly warned Stalin that Soviet intransigence was likely to lead to an "embarrassing situation" at the opening meeting of the UN General Assembly the following month.[36]

There the matter rested. The British, with their so-called "Bevin Plan," presented it to the Teheran government, which, with the prompting of United States Ambassador Wallace Murray, rejected it in horror as a partition scheme likely to permit the British, as well as Russian troops, to remain. Iran's Premier Ibrahim Hakimi was assured that should Iran take its dispute with Russia to the UN it could count on United States backing, and on January 15 Murray again suggested submitting the case to the UN, where the United States would make certain the Security Council would debate it. Byrnes's threat to Stalin was now to be realized four days later when, against British advice, Iran placed the matter before the Security Council.[37]

For the Russians, making them a defendant at the very first meeting of the Security Council was the realization of all their fears regarding wartime American threats to transform the UN into a bar of world opinion. They could only respond to the situation realistically, and it must have reinforced their wartime suspicion of a world organization packed with nations amenable to American direction. That Iran was acting on behalf of the United States seemed unquestionable, and the Russians apparently were convinced that Britain was behind the matter too, for on the twenty-first they responded to the Iranian charges by filing complaints on British troops in Greece and Indonesia. What had originally been a desire for a secure southern flank, or oil, now became a question of future Soviet relations with the UN, the character of that body, and prestige. The council therefore, from its inception, became a propaganda forum for the great powers, much to the chagrin of Trygve Lie, its Secretary General, who was convinced, as a Norwegian who had negotiated Russian troop evacuation of his nation, that Iran should have tried direct negotiations a while longer.

The Hakimi government fell on January 20 to the less extreme leadership of Qavam Saltaneh, and Iran was ready to pursue the UN's bidding when it was told at the end of the month to try direct negotiations and to report back. It was at this point that the Iranians entered a tortured state of attempting to exploit the UN strategy as well as direct negotiations, and that the United States was able to capitalize both on vague Iranian decisions, indecisiveness, and disagreement to turn the question to its own use. At the end of January, Byrnes insisted the UN retain jurisdiction over the matter regardless of direct Iranian talks with Russia.

Qavam himself arrived in Moscow on February 19 to negotiate the evacuation of Russian troops, and he was not to leave until March 11. In the meantime, the March 2 deadline for withdrawal came and went, with Russian troops still in the north. The United States knew, of course, that Russian troops would stay on, and the strong note of protest sent to Moscow on March 6 was therefore fully considered. Unquestionably this was a period of hardening United States policy, for the day before Churchill had delivered his famous Fulton speech, but Truman's later inconsistent recollection that he sent the Russians a true ultimatum, with threats of sending in United States troops to drive them out, is incorrect.[38] At the worst, American official public statements at this time were ambiguous but threatening. What was certain was that as the negotiations in Moscow failed, and as it received rumors of a massive Soviet troop build-up and imminent coup, the United States chose to use the UN as a forum for excoriating the Russians.

On March 18 Lie once more urged Hussein Ala, the excitable Iranian ambassador to the United States, to continue with private talks rather than resort to public trials. But Ala unconvincingly claimed he had his instructions to present the matter again to the Security Council, which, even if true, had also been accompanied by a request to take a more moderate tone. Lie was certain, however, that Ala was in close contact with the State Department, which on the fourteenth had declared that it would take the issue to the council if Iran did not, and after visiting Washington, Ala asked that the item be placed on the council agenda the twenty-fifth—with the United States requesting it be inserted at the top of it. Three days later the ambivalent Qavam goverment announced that Ala's action was unauthorized, but the item remained on the agenda nevertheless. Indeed, it was at this time that Murray and Washington began turning against Qavam, who they thought was conceding far too much to the Russians, an opinion Qavam's hints of major oil concessions to the United States failed to mitigate. The United States would happily discuss oil concessions, Byrnes cabled Murray, but after Soviet troop withdrawals lest it appear the Americans had been paid off along with Russia. At about the same time, Byrnes sent Stalin a

general but strong note which Truman believed caused the Soviets to announce on the twenty-fifth that their troops would be out of Iran within six
weeks "if nothing unforeseen occurs."[39] Despite this, and despite the debatable nature of Ala's agenda item—Qavam on the twenty-third publicly
asked that the UN drop the issue—the United States insisted that the
Security Council meeting in New York debate the Soviet-Iranian question.
Byrnes himself arrived to take command, and for the first time kept in full
and close contact with the press, revealing whatever confidential information he had on the question.

The "unforeseen" element to which the Russians referred may have been
the American persistence on trying the USSR before public opinion despite
the better advice of Lie, the English, and probably the Iranians, who tended
to play roles satisfactory to all sides. On the twenty-sixth Gromyko walked
out of the Security Council after it refused to postpone discussion until
April 10, as if to say that if the Americans were going to use the council
as a forum the Russians would not play the desired role of penitents. The
United States had pressed its advantage to the limit, and under circumstances in which the facts warranted delay if a peaceful settlement of a
dispute were the objective of diplomacy. The affair warned the Russians
that in the future the UN would serve as an instrument of advancing
American objectives, not as a tool for solving problems.

The British, for their part, were convinced that the weakness of the
existing Iranian government was never more fully revealed than by the
seemingly open disagreement between Ala in New York and his government, and *The Times* of London complained that legitimate British interests were likely to suffer even if Soviet troops left—implying the need to
return to the Bevin Plan. But the Americans were to define the thrust of
the anti-Russian campaign. Only on March 29 did Byrnes ask Lie to find
out whether there was already an accord between Iran and Russia, and on
April 3 the word came back that indeed there was. The Russians had agreed
to leave by May 6; they created a joint Irano-Soviet oil firm (subject to
ratification of the Majlis); and Teheran was to supervise an autonomous
government in Azerbaijan under terms vague enough to permit the reimposition of its control, and similar to those the Persian constitution had
provided for nearly forty years earlier and Teheran had ignored since then.[40]
The Russians and Lie now wanted the Iran item removed from the council
agenda, but the United States insisted that it be tabled until May 6 to see
where the Russian troops were at the time. Ala supported the American
position, but on April 15 he was compelled to report that Iran, too, wanted

the matter taken off the agenda. But the United States was to insist the item remain there (it stayed until May 22), and shortly thereafter Ala was eliminated as Iran's representative to the council for having disobeyed Teheran's orders.

The intransigence of the American position on a question that was close to resolution via normal diplomacy reflected Washington's belief that its interests could be better served by a UN organization now obviously fully amenable to American control. "This area contains vast natural resources," Truman declared in a public address on April 6 in which the Middle East received critical attention. Its ". . . great economic and strategic importance" might lead to ". . . intense rivalry between outside powers, and . . . such rivalry might suddenly erupt into conflict."[41] When Truman suggested the UN as the forum for the settlement of such disputes, in effect he meant forgoing the give-and-take of conventional diplomacy for an erstwhile "international" instrument that would permit the United States to vanquish its rivals in the name of the world. The Iran crisis was the first application of such a strategy.

The Soviet treaty with Iran meant little, despite occasional American fears that Qavam would prove too weak. The Majlis, with explicit United States backing, never ratified the oil agreement, and so it was void. And at the end of the year, Teheran, after much American pressure to act, sent troops into Azerbaijan easily to disperse (or execute) the pro-Russian Democratic Party leaders and the local dialect presses and schools, and reimpose the corrupt control over the Azerbaijans and Kurds that had been a major source of the upheaval in the first place. The British, in the meantime, attempted to protect their interests in the traditional manner, fanned an uprising of southern tribes during September, and covertly aided Iraqi elements seeking to annex Khuzistan.

It was a traditional scenario, and in it the United States gladly accepted its part. By November it was preparing to give Iran arms. Washington influenced the course of Middle Eastern politics by providing moderate nationalists a balance to Britain; it won oil for American firms; and the UN became an unabashed instrument of American diplomacy which gave no quarter to Soviet interests. And since the first major crisis of the postwar period had been over the Middle East, it is hardly surprising that the United States was, within a matter of months, to assume an even larger role in the region.

That new role was designed, when it was first articulated, to take the Middle East out of the British sphere of influence to the extent of creating "free competition in trade," "complete liberty" on the part of local states to deal with America, and ". . . a friendly vying among the Powers. . . ." Stated simply, it was to win oil for the United States. An Anglo-Russian *détente* in the region was no less dangerous to America's designs. The United States would support Britain only where ". . . such policy was not inimical to our own interests."[42] The Iran crisis, as much as any during 1946, caused the American leaders to broaden and articulate their vision of their nation's future in the area—a vision that was to postulate not only firm resistance to Russia but considerable practical opposition to England as well. The Joint Chiefs of Staff in mid-October decided that the loss of Iran to Russia, even "by means other than war," would gravely affect American power in Saudi Arabia and the entire region, profoundly influencing the material and economic conditions in which a war between the nations might be fought.[43] Defined in these terms, with Saudi Arabia described in an earlier State Department analysis as ". . . a stupendous source of strategic power, and one of the greatest material prizes in world history," that the United States would actively intervene everywhere in the region was a foregone conclusion.[44] For the logic of a domino theory of closely interdependent states is that one must prevent any and all from falling, making interests in one nation contingent on the control or stability of the rest.

Turkey's New Ally

The Turkish government had been ardently anti-Russian during all of World War II and had taken a position of friendly neutrality toward Germany during its first years. It had repeatedly urged the Anglo-Americans to unite against the Soviet menace, even form an alliance with Nazi Germany toward that end, and it had quietly attempted to organize a postwar *cordon sanitaire* with the exile governments. It had stayed out of the war as long as possible in the hope it might form an effective balance of power to Russia in the Balkans. Turkey was a hostile southern neighbor, and this central fact in turn colored Russia's response to that nation's control over the critical Dardanelles Straits entrusted to Turkey by the Montreaux Treaty of 1936. Turkey's hostility long preceded the discussion of the future of the straits at the end of the war, and it defined Soviet policy as well it might that of any state.

In June 1945 the Turkish ambassador had asked Molotov his views on a revision of the 1921 treaty of friendship, and injudiciously inquired if the USSR wished bases on the straits as part of an alteration of control over it. Naturally the Russian thought it desirable, but he offered on his own initiative the need for a settlement of the disputed, largely non-Turkish eastern provinces of Kars and Ardahan that Turkey had acquired from the Soviet Union after World War I. Although the Turks had taken the initiative on a change of the *status quo,* and Russia indicated readiness to let matters rest, but without formal ratification, Turkish diplomats spent the next months conjuring up imminent Russian invasions that even Washington found annoyingly overdrawn. Still, while Washington thought a revision of Montreaux desirable, it decided not to force unacceptable changes on the Turks, and though the Potsdam Conference had endorsed alterations via three-power and Turkish negotiations, it gave no hint of the direction changes might take. What was perhaps most significant in this statement was that although the United States had not signed the Montreaux Treaty it now accepted a major obligation for its change. Privately, however, the United States urged the frequently hysterical Turks to calm themselves.

The eastern border controversy was rather more complex than that implied in later United States official interpretations of the basis of Soviet policy. The disputed regions in Turkish hands had once been a part of Armenia and Georgia, and Armenians everywhere supported their return to Russian control. Even as late as 1942 Turkey imposed a special property tax on its non-Muslim residents, and its Pan-Turkish agitation among the large Turkish minority in the USSR during the war undoubtedly further alienated the Russians. It was, in brief, a traditional prebolshevik dispute having nothing to do with Communism. It is unquestionable, however, that the matter was important only to the Turks, and Russia for nearly a year took no interest in the minor topic. When Bevin asked Stalin about the controversy in December 1945 he was quite flexible about desirable border changes in the east, but when the foreign minister mentioned the issue of a Russian base Stalin naturally said the claim stood, though he did not press it further. "All talk of a war against Turkey was rubbish," Stalin made it plain regarding the overexcited Turks.[45]

By and large, however, the three former allies still regarded Turkey as a minor issue of no special urgency. The British had said as much to a November 1945 American proposal that sustained the Montreaux Treaty save insofar as it opened the straits to the warships of the Black Sea powers during war—which the existing treaty permitted Turkey to close. But even the Turks hedged their response to the American proposal, contenting themselves for the next months with continuing their military mobilization and predicting imminent dark conflicts with Russia.

On August 7, 1946, however, the Russians finally made their proposals for a change in the straits, dropping all references to changes in Turkey's borders. They accepted the earlier American plan, but added that Turkey and the Black Sea powers should establish a regime of the straits and that the two nations should ". . . organize joint means of defense of the Straits."[46] As vague as the Soviet proposals were, they failed to refer to negotiations and imparted a brusque, unilateral quality; moreover, they came at an inopportune time, for the Americans had just announced a new and expanded series of fleet visits to the Mediterranean, and they reacted hotly to the Russian *démarche*. Truman and his cabinet regarded it as a trial balloon warranting the strongest response for fear that the Russians might precipitate armed conflict with Turkey. The sharp American reply in effect made it possible for the Turks to refuse any changes in the *status quo* or concessions to Soviet interests. For now they insisted that both Britain and the United States, even the UN, share in any changes that might be effected. What the Americans once recognized as legitimate Soviet interests they now denied altogether.

By the end of September, Byrnes, Forrestal, and Patterson approved a Pentagon recommendation to sell military equipment to the organized Turkish army of nearly a million men, still the peak wartime strength, with reserves twice that size. Economic aid, too, was endorsed. And several months later, in the context of the Greek crisis, they understood that the two countries would be linked together for purposes of arms exports. During October, Washington designated Turkey as the strategic keystone of the entire region. The Russians, for their part, at the end of 1946 predicted imminent American military aid and missions to Turkey. Still, Turkey was different from Greece in several regards. The Turks faced not guerillas— they had few internal leftists outside jail—but the Red army, and nothing the United States might do, short of sending American man power, would save the Turks in case of a war. Moreover, the Soviet claims were not considered entirely unjustified, for throughout the war both the United States and England had repeatedly endorsed the justice of some major change in the control of the straits. And what was perhaps most complicating, the Turks still had traditional claims and enemies elsewhere, Greece in particular, and Turkish officers were not loath to refer to the fact. Both sides still remembered the wars of 1912 and 1922, and still cherished unresolved grievances. Even in 1946 there existed the possibility that rather than fight a mighty Soviet Union they might again turn their guns toward each other.[47]

It was into this vast and intricate imbroglio that the United States willingly entered during the year and one-half after the end of the war. Conceiving its interest in the Near East in terms broad enough to require the full exertion of its power, it was but a matter of time before it was to supplement and then finally replace traditional British supremacy in the area. Washington's next moves could now be fully anticipated, but what could not be known is how the admixture of nationalism and revolutionary ideologies would confront the Americans with demands and challenges infinitely more elusive and uncontrollable than anything the British had ever faced.

9

China: From Chaos to Revolution

World War II in the Far East left a total power vacuum in the wake of the profound trauma that had begun in 1931. It was not so much that the prewar social structure had disappeared, either in China, Japan, or the entire Far East with its precarious internal balance, but that the prolonged bloodletting had gravely stunned all the old forces and powers, and had made possible the nearly universal emergence of Left and anticolonialist movements that ultimately became the dominating factor in Asia. The history of Asia in the world after 1945 is one of the conflict between self-generating nationalist movements of reconstruction and stability in conflict with the efforts of Western powers to create a new balance of Asian power more compatible with the attainment of their own larger national interests. In this vast epic, ultimately the most significant of the postwar era, the United States played a leading part, and the first act was in China.

The impact of the war on East Asia resulted in no sudden crisis, but rather it accelerated a sustained, ceaselessly intensifying collapse of the old order that thoroughly broke down the conservative resistance to change—indeed, a disintegration so complete that in much of Asia it simply wiped out the political and economic foundations of the traditional ruling class, Western or local. In no country was this truer than in China. Yet, by virtue of this kind of gradualism of upheaval, no dramatic episodes existed for American policy-makers to confront, or for historians to describe. For Washington, this process of inexorable collapse in slow motion was all the more horrifying precisely because it reflected a pervasive decadence and inevitable defeat too widespread, too deep, for anyone to hope confidently to prevent.

The breakup and transformation of China reached its final stage after the war, but the United States had confronted the essential question during the wartime period itself. Without significant exception, all its leaders had become deeply pessimistic as to the future of Chiang Kai-shek's Kuomintang government as a result of the sordid, ceaseless reports of his clique's corruption and venality that all Americans on the scene sent back. Via ill-concealed threats to surrender or collapse before the Japanese or Chinese Communists, Chiang had extorted hundreds of millions of dollars for the personal fortunes of his family and followers. It was essentially this corruption that had made the wartime alliance between the Kuomintang (KMT) and Washington a profoundly uneasy one. It was only the negative American dread of the only existing alternative—Communism—that kept the United States from deserting Chiang altogether; yet it was a relationship without illusion or sentiment, and it always suffused every American action with despair and hopelessness.

For the United States, the ideal goal was a renovated China capable of serving as the anchor of American power in the Pacific and Far East, a China that was stronger but not too strong, independent but also open to the furtherance of American interests. If this vision was partially strategic, it was primarily economic, postulating the integration of China into a liberalized, American-led world capitalism, a China that American capital could eventually penetrate and develop. For this reason, Chiang's incipient, occasionally expressed, theories of economic nationalism and protectionism had caused some consternation in Washington during the war, raising the question as to the Chinese ruler's receptivity to American objectives. In brief, the United States was not so much for the Chiang government as it was for the protection and advancement of American interests in Asia. If the dreaded Communist option resolved the matter, lingering doubts as to Chiang persisted for reasons of ideology as well as efficiency. Yet, by the end of the war, many in Washington's decision-making elite understood that for strategic purposes a reformed and renovated Japan also offered an anchor for the implementation of American security and tactical goals in Asia. If these alternatives were not resolved before the end of the war it was partially because the last act in the drama of China had yet to unfold, or the pervasive pessimism finally justified, but above all because to the United States the greatest stakes in the emerging world crisis were in Europe, and for the next four years it was here that the Americans assigned their overwhelming attention and priorities.

Chiang Kai-shek had the support of the United States, despite its reservations, and he assiduously courted the backing of the Soviet Union against the internal Communist challenge. Both in the Yalta Accords and the Sino-Soviet Treaty of August 14, 1945, the Russians pledged to sustain Chiang's Nationalist government against the Communists, and to transfer land that they had conquered from the Japanese to Chiang's government only. The Soviets based their deference on a desire to see a weak China to its south, one not likely to attempt to recoup the Tsarist patrimony in Outer Mongolia or the Manchurian economic concessions that Chiang reassigned to Russia. As a state rather than an ideological force, the Soviet Union hewed a cautious line in the incipient Chinese civil war, but it pursued this course because it had explicitly acknowledged China as an area of predominant interest to the United States, and it wished to avoid a conflict with the Americans in what was, after all, an area of peripheral interest to it. Like the Americans, the Soviets defined their main interests in terms of the future of Europe.

Chiang, for his part, understood the need to court the Russians and gain their support if possible, or their neutrality at the very least. This he did, and the Russians actively attempted to persuade the Chinese Communists to abandon a resolution of their struggle by force of arms. ". . . [W]hen the war with Japan ended," Djilas recalls Stalin as saying, "we invited the Chinese comrades to reach an agreement as to how a modus vivendi with Chiang Kai-shek might be found. They agreed with us in word, but in deed they did it their own way. . . ."[1] At the end of the war, therefore, Chiang was essentially victorious insofar as international diplomacy was likely to determine the Chinese civil war. His army numbered almost three million men with armaments far superior to that in the hands of the 900,000 Communist troops and their militia of twice that size. Chiang held an estimated five-to-one advantage in combat troops and rifles, a near monopoly of heavy arms, and the only air force in China. The Communists controlled 100 million people in large patches of territory in the poorer regions of North China; yet, abstractly, Chiang's power was far greater in material terms. He had vast holdings of foreign currency and gold for postwar reconstruction, about $1 billion in dollars and gold alone, and the Japanese-occupied regions in the North and Manchuria represented a vast potential increment in industrial and political power—if the KMT were able to exploit them. Perhaps most important of all, in the last two weeks of the war the United States resolved its doubts regarding possible options in China and actively backed Chiang's reconquest of Japanese-dominated China. On August 14, in the General Order Number 1, the Americans with Anglo-Soviet approval ordered the Japanese to surrender only to Chiang's forces. This placed the power of almost two million Japanese troops in China, and their unreliable but large puppet army, squarely on the side of the KMT, where they remained, in declining numbers, for well over a year. No less consequential was the new American willingness to pledge at least two United States divisions to the reconquest of North China, beginning at the end of September 1945.[2] When compelled to make the decision, the United States prepared to use Japanese power to stop the momentum of revolutionary change not only in China but in all of Asia.

The Chinese Communists and Mao Tse-tung reacted essentially cautiously to this vast international alignment against themselves. If they claimed the right to take Japanese surrenders where they could, and actually proceeded to do so, they were nevertheless unwilling wholly to ignore Soviet pressures that they hew a moderate line. Moreover, Mao's great flexibility and pragmatism, which had emphasized national unity of all patriotic, reform-oriented classes throughout the war against Japan, made him fully aware of the need to neutralize Chiang's international backing by negotiating with him. For despite Mao's criticisms during the summer of 1945 of Patrick J. Hurley's efforts as official United States mediator in China, he knew that American backing of Chiang was the largest obstacle to a Communist victory. To neutralize or minimize United States support of the KMT was therefore a prime Communist goal, for which Mao would go to extraordinary lengths even as his troops were being shot at with ever-growing quantities of American guns. For despite Chiang's vast material resources, initial military superiority, and impressive international support, Mao knew that ultimately he would defeat Chiang and the KMT because of their venality and corruption and the ensuing political and economic chaos resulting from it. For in this vast disorganizing process Chiang was losing the support of all classes of the Chinese social structure, including the small but critical middle classes and national bourgeoisie. All the backing and guns of all the great powers together could not overcome this profound, determining reality. Time was not on the side of Chiang Kai-shek.[3]

The United States and the Civil War

The Communists had nothing to lose via negotiations, for their military disadvantage was too great to forgo diplomacy. Above all, given Chiang's aggressive northward movements into the formerly Japanese-occupied areas, as political leaders squabbled they also drew up their armies in preparation for the sustained civil war that was to wrack China for four more years, and these were the overriding defining realities that both Communists and Chiang's allies understood. Mao had publicly warned of the danger of Chiang's initiating the civil war the entire preceding summer, and he thought Hurley's partiality raised serious doubts regarding America's role in China; yet it was the collapse of Japan that made inevitable the clash between the competing Chinese forces seeking to fill the vacuum. Chiang, with American backing, pushed forward and defined the inevitable, bloody crisis.

If, in the last analysis, combat or the economic fortunes of peasants were to determine China's destiny, the diplomacy of the times reveals the policies and strategies of the contestants and crudely mirrors the successes of the various sides in the contest.

Despite grave doubts concerning Hurley, the American role, and Chiang's intentions, Mao in August still hoped to avoid the civil war which increasing armed clashes between Communist and KMT troops presaged. After some reticence, he succumbed to Hurley's urgings that he himself come to Chungking at the end of August to meet with Chiang for the first time since 1927. Instrumental in this decision were the Soviet pressures and the signing of the Sino-Soviet Treaty, for on the day the treaty was made public, Mao announced his planned trip to Chungking. These conversations, however, had no more chance of succeeding than the interminable talks of the preceding years, and in this they set the precedent for the rest of our story. Both sides could agree on a vague formula for a future Chinese army, one which would have given Chiang dominant power by freezing the existing troop ratios, and the Communists even agreed to evacuate many of their southerly regions. But Chiang would give no solid guarantees on the future of the Chinese political structure, nor would he firmly assure the Communists of some important participation in the political administration of regions that they already largely held. To Hurley it was accomplishment enough that both sides were talking to each other, but in fact Chiang was determined to get his troops into the Japanese-occupied regions of North China as quickly as possible—indeed, with growing American aid. To the Communists this offensive was changing the existing balance of power and a modicum of stability which were preconditions of serious talks, and they began to cut railroad lines and communications to the North. As the political leaders quibbled, armies clashed and the actual civil war intensified in scale and seriousness. The Communist goal of stabilizing their position was untenable in light of Chiang's determination to exploit his initiative, and before November everyone acknowledged the continuing *pro forma* negotiations as a failure. The reality was elsewhere, in the fields.[4]

Even as the United States encouraged negotiations and defined political responses to the maze of Chinese affairs, it took decisive military action that ultimately greatly contributed to the demise of the Kuomintang on the field of combat. For without the small, but vital, American military assistance Chiang Kai-shek would have been less willing to risk his future on the successful conclusion of a civil war; indeed, during the first months after the Japanese defeat, only American policy made civil war plausible to him. And, to the Communists, it made all American mediation efforts worthwhile only insofar as the foreigners could be convinced to restrict their already substantial, growing involvement. In the end, the United States gave Chiang sufficient military aid to perpetuate turmoil, but not enough to attain a victory that was probably beyond American man-power capacity. And it also relied on a diplomatic strategy utterly incompatible with its claims to impartiality, an illusion few American decision-makers shared. For quite apart from abstract disputatious questions of diplomacy—which were to cause so many crises over the remainder of 1945—was the reality of American guns supporting the extension of Chiang's power toward the north. It is this reality we must first consider, if only because for the Communists it, too, was the primary fact of American involvement in China.

To extend his control over North China and Manchuria for the first time, Chiang needed the armed assistance not only of the Americans but of the Japanese and Russians as well. During the first weeks after the Japanese surrender the KMT was able, with American support, to take Peking, Shanghai, Tientsin, Nanking, and Hankow, as well as chase the Communists from several other cities, but it could not move up most of the railroads to North China, much less to Manchuria, without aid. The Japanese, as best they could, obeyed American instructions to hold their ground until KMT or American troops arrived. Key United States leaders fully appreciated that their movement of Chiang's forces to the north was an intimate part of the effort to exclude the Communists from those regions. On September 30, the first of 53,000 United States marines began landings at the northern Chinese ports, and American military personnel was to reach 113,000 by the end of the year. With the additional assistance of Japanese and puppet troops, Chiang was soon on the offensive with the aid of United States transport services that ultimately moved about a half-million KMT troops toward the Japanese and Communist-dominated areas, including 110,000 by air lift to North China. Washington had initially planned to station the marines only several months, or about as long as the actual disarmament of the Japanese might take; but Chiang, in line with his consistent efforts to drag American man power as well as matériel into his struggle, on November 5 urged the United States to leave the marines in China. The first American encounter with the Communists involved threats and counter-threats, and despite occasional American restraint to avoid head-on clashes, it was the Communists who did most of the withdrawing or made gestures to cooperate by not taking Japanese surrenders. By the middle of October it was plain, however, that the Americans would not confront more than minor Communist harassment and guerilla attacks, and indeed only fifteen armed clashes of consquence between marine and Communist forces occurred during 1945–1946. Yet the provocative show of marine air power, to ". . . cause the Communists to take heed," also led to Communist sniping and, above all, their widespread sabotage of rail tracks essential for Chiang's northward movements.[5]

The Communists frankly told the Americans that the marines constituted direct intervention in the civil war, and by November the American officials on the scene reported that the marines' nominal functions in repatriating Japanese troops would soon end. Throughout November key American leaders considered, without real dissent in Washington, the full political implications of the marine presence. It was understood that Chiang was being helped to protect the area from the Communists and, indirectly, Russian influence. The military and political leaders—overriding the strenuous advice of Major General Albert C. Wedemeyer, commander of United States forces in China—thought it a logical extension of political policy to keep the marines on indefinitely.

If there could hardly be any illusions concerning American intent in sending in its troops, there could be less for continuing arms shipments to build a Kuomintang army of thirty-nine well-equipped divisions and eight air groups. Publicly, the purpose of the marines was to disarm and repatriate the Japanese troops in China; yet that they would permit only Chiang to fill the vacuum left behind made it quite plain that the action was political. But the marines were to remain in China until mid-1949 ". . . in the untenable position," to quote the official history, ". . . that made them at once neutral and partisan in China's civil strife."[6] And, from the end of the war until the end of 1948, the United States army's approximately 1,000-man-strong Nanking Advisory Group attempted to modernize and train to greater efficiency Chiang's army. Despite a vague obeisance to a desire to avoid provoking "fratricidal war" with further arms aid to Chiang, the official, confidential American policy in October justified its continuation because it was necessary to assist Chiang to impose "internal peace and security" in China and Manchuria, and also because it was ". . . compatible with our basic objectives in the Far East."[7] Besides appreciating the significance of arms and marines in stopping Communism, such aid also assured that Chiang would not turn to the Russians for military help. And military aid might also provide leverage to obtain ". . . certain economic and military rights and concessions in China in return for U.S. support, past and present."[8] Indeed, much desired access to trade and raw materials might be guaranteed only in this manner, given Chiang's erratic nationalist eruptions. All this was obvious, and for these reasons American proclamations of peaceful intent and neutrality scarcely impressed the Communists, who unquestionably shared Forrestal's July 1946 estimate ". . . that the Marines were the balance of order in China during the last six months."[9] Without that balance, and American arms, Chiang faced certain defeat.

The clarity of America's already substantial and growing commitments to oppose the Communists was scarcely in doubt by the end of 1945. When Hurley returned to Washington at the end of September the alternatives were debated; yet the destabilizing element in American planning was, now as always, the incompetence and unreliability of Chiang and his government. This anxiety was compounded when, on November 20, General Wedemeyer warned that Chiang was courting disaster by attempting to take over all China, especially Manchuria, overextending his limited man power and resources. The weaknesses of his administrative organization, and its pervasive corruption, had already alienated important sectors of the newly liberated Chinese population. Rather, Wedemeyer believed, Chiang would do best to consolidate his power south of the Great Wall in North China. Yet this, too, the American argued, would have to be accompanied by the far-reaching internal political and social reforms that he and his predecessor, General Joseph Stilwell, had futilely urged upon Chiang for years. Manchuria, Wedemeyer now suggested, might be made an Anglo-American-Soviet trusteeship. He repeated an earlier recommendation that the United States quickly withdraw the marines, for fear they would be increasingly dragged into the civil war. Over these very days Forrestal, Byrnes, and Patterson debated the question of the future use of the marines, concluding that they should remain. As Forrestal observed: ". . . Such United States support to the National government will definitely involve American forces in fratricidal warfare. There can be no mistake about this. . . . If the unification of China and Manchuria under Chinese National forces is to be a United States policy, involvement in fratricidal warfare and possibly in war with the Soviet Union must be accepted. . . ."[10] The necessity for Chiang's speedy reconquest of North China, and especially Manchuria, was now welcomed in Washington as a significant step toward maintaining American power in the Far East. Then, during early December, Truman authorized a new plan to send six Chinese armies northward. Nor was there any illusion regarding the entirely political function of this act, as intentions and consequences moved in unison.[11]

The more serious problem facing Washington was that once it chose Chiang as the best available instrument for advancing American objectives it had to also confront the well-known weaknesses of the man and the great political difficulties entailed in shipping even more American troops to his aid. Short of a miracle in which a third political force would emerge from the maze of Chinese politics to advance American goals with popular support, the United States had now to buttress Chiang with diplomacy as well as money and arms. It is in this fundamental context that we must set all discussions of various American mediation undertakings from this time onward. For with the clarification of anti-Communism as a primary objective in China at this time came the grand diplomatic undertakings and crises discussed later in this chapter.

Perhaps more than any other region, the United States was interested in the future of Manchuria and economic access to it. Both Communist and KMT troops rushed to fill in the vacuum the Japanese defeat had created there, and now the role of the Soviet Union in China became yet more vital, not merely because it occupied Manchuria, but also because the United States was determined to win anew Soviet support for its aims in China prior to diplomatic efforts with the Communist Chinese. Presumably Russian support would clear the way. The first signs, however, were inauspicious, for the Russians had not actively blocked Communist movements into northern and western Manchuria, including some of the cities, nor did they aid their entrance.[12] The KMT had initially negotiated for Soviet withdrawal from all Manchuria by the end of November, but when American-transported KMT troops arrived at various ports they found the Communists already there or, in the case of Darien, the Russians now unwilling to see them debark. The result was that the Russians finally compelled Chiang to use much slower rail and air transport, thereby opening the danger of Soviet withdrawal before Chiang could effectively occupy the region ahead of the Communists. Chiang then requested the Russians to delay their departure until early January 1946 to allow him more time to get his troops in position. This the Russians granted, and they now relented on sea movements. At the beginning of December the Kuomintang asked for a further Soviet delay in departure until February 1. On December 13 Chiang's troops arrived in the capital city of Mukden. During the month of December, therefore, Chiang won the race for the domination of China's most valuable prize; the Communists shifted their efforts to taking over the countryside as best they could, and the Russians rewarded themselves by systematically stripping much of the region's industrial equipment—an indication that they were expecting Chiang rather than the Communists to dominate the area.

While Chiang's emissaries won concessions from the Soviets, Byrnes hoped to gain no less in December while in Moscow for the Foreign Ministers Conference. Whatever else may be said about Russian policy in China at this time, it is certain that the Kremlin's paramount objective at the end of 1945 was to prevent a new, possibly vast, influx of American troops on its southern borders and, if possible, to see the marines withdrawn. For these reasons alone the Russians were anxious not to run counter to what they still defined as American supremacy in China; hence they were eager to do anything that might restrict American involvement. But since they also understood they could not undo the war and Chiang's corruption, they prepared to play only a passive, cautiously self-serving role.

This was the import of the Moscow talks, and it greatly freed American hands. Molotov quickly made it plain to both Harriman and Byrnes that he knew the marines in North China were not there to disarm Japanese troops. On December 19, Byrnes freely discussed with Molotov the role of the marines in keeping North China and Manchuria from falling to the "revolutionists," as he called them after referring to Stalin's comment at Potsdam that they were not Communists. ". . . It was without question," the American record quotes Molotov, "that we had all agreed to support Chiang Kai-shek and that the Soviet Union had embodied this in writing. . . ."[13] Yet, several days later, the Russians formally proposed a coordinated Soviet-American troop withdrawal from China no later than mid-January 1946, and a policy of noninterference in China's internal political affairs. Byrnes rejected the idea, and Molotov unhappily observed that the continued presence of American troops in North China was an unanticipated development that might color the Soviet interpretation of its agreements with Chiang. Byrnes's insistence that United States troops were there to help unify China hardly mollified obvious Russian anxieties. When the secretary of state talked to Stalin on the evening of the twenty-third he recalled past Soviet comments regarding the inauthenticity of Chinese Communism and Russian pledges of support of Chiang. Stalin glumly acknowledged the binding character of his treaty with Chiang, but added that the man's dependence on foreign troops to unify China would lead to his undoing with the Chinese people. Yet despite the obvious Soviet unhappiness over the presence of American troops in China, the following evening Stalin reassured British Foreign Minister Ernest Bevin that China and Japan were in the American sphere of interest. The Moscow Conference encouraged Byrnes to believe Russia would not deliberately interfere with the American design for China. And, as if words would make it so, in his public statement on the outcome of the meeting several days later Byrnes claimed Anglo-Soviet backing of General George C. Marshall's forthcoming mission to China.[14]

Basic Goals of United States Policy in China

It is now a commonplace belief that American policy in China from the end of World War II until 1950 was ambiguous and indecisive, and on a tactical level this was certainly the case, if only because the United States' goals exceeded the means available for attaining them. But closer inquiry concerning the basic objectives of American actions in China reveals a consistent pattern that imparts logic to the twisting tactics to which the United States resorted after the war. For the essential purpose of American action was to advance a quite sophisticated interpretation of United States national interests that all Americans in charge of their nation's China diplomacy accepted in its basic premises.

Without exception, every American familiar with China regarded the Kuomintang regime as corrupt and incompetent. Washington's desire for peace and mediation was, in every instance for which information is available, based not on favoritism toward the Communists but rather on a dread fear that Chiang's regime was so weak that by embarking on a crusade against Mao's forces it would bring down what remained of the Kuomintang government—and really open the door to Communism. Chiang's liability was not merely that he was foolhardy, and thereby able to bring on a bolshevization that was even more incompatible with American interests. Chiang's occasional capacity to reveal a nationalist, anti-Western independence that had disturbed American officials throughout the war also alarmed Washington. While true that his corruption in practice mitigated whatever nationalist element remained in Kuomintang ideology, Chiang's forays into economic policy—protectionist and statist for the most part—compelled the Americans to delineate their own goals for China in an ideal world community.

In the weeks and months following the end of the war, American officials again articulated a theory of China's economic future and its relationship to the United States. Edwin A. Locke, Jr., Truman's personal representative to China after May 15, and a banker by trade, took the initiative in this reconsideration, but it was logically the outcome of the model of the world economy which was universally accepted in Washington as a desired goal. Locke had an entirely realistic understanding of the Kuomintang's weaknesses, and he wanted it to avert a civil war for fear that it would likely lose. Locke attempted to convince the men around Chiang temporarily to transfer much of the economic administration of the country's industrial and mining sector to American experts and firms. Donald M. Nelson, former economic adviser in China, and others joined this undertaking, and Truman endorsed the contours of this policy before sending Locke back to China in October 1945. During the same weeks, the State Department joined the effort " . . . to get businessmen back into China for their sake and for China's sake," even to the extent of the War Department's providing transport and housing whenever possible.[15] This expansion of " . . . commercial trade on a non-discriminatory and mutually beneficial basis," one that led to ever lower tariff barriers, had no relationship whatsoever to China's basic problems and needs—but it was a precondition to the American realization of its ultimate aims for the region. Yet such a concern at this time was essential, too, because, as during the war, officials in Washington again worried that the "Chinese Government intends to follow a policy of regulation of trade and regulation of, and participation in the industrial and economic development of China."[16]

From the viewpoint of an exclusively anti-Communist policy, such an autarchic economic program, if it worked, made a certain kind of sense, but it would also have represented the defeat of American hopes of someday actively sharing China's potential wealth. In fact, Washington acted to discourage loans to vital Chinese enterprises in competition with existing American firms, and during 1946 the State Department initiated negotiations which were to lead to Chinese approval of the General Agreement on Tariffs and Trade (GATT) multilateral reciprocal trade agreement in 1947 and a nondiscriminatory treaty of commerce in 1948 that pledged Chiang to avoid state monopolies and economic measures objectionable to long-range American goals.

Locke's specific December 1945 recommendations to Truman on future American policy—which Wedemeyer endorsed—are excellent examples of exactly what content the United States wished to give to a reformed Kuomintang regime, and precisely why it could not support independent tendencies in the Communist camp—and ultimately why the irrelevance of American goals superficially imparts the appearance of ambiguity to its policies. Locke also understood very precisely what was wrong with the Chiang regime. Like his predecessors, he wished Chiang to reform China administratively to the core, but ultimately for the interests of the United States rather than of China. Locke's plans, and the State Department's commercial treaty discussions, all postulated political reform to be followed by American-guided "liberal" economic measures—leaving China open to American economic penetration.[17]

Despite a willingness to pay obeisance to such American principles when pressed to do so, the Kuomintang never really shared them—or a true nationalist program either. For, as a clique devoted to enlarging its own fortunes, it was beyond ideology, and given this fact American anxieties reveal only American purposes rather than actual facts. But these purposes required also a thoroughgoing anti-Communism as a preliminary tactical priority, for the triumph of bolshevism, even if it eliminated all the internal chaos and misery so well portrayed in American reports to Washington, nevertheless entailed the inevitable exclusion of American economic and political power in China—in the future much more than in the present. And the basis of United States policy was neither reformism, nor even the preservation of Chiang's power, nor altruism, but the protection of the future of American capitalism in the Far East.

This being the case, the Americans before the end of 1945 were prone to help Chiang against Communism, all the while seeing his many faults as obstacles to the attainment of American objectives on other levels. This meant, though, that first China must reform, preferably under Chiang's leadership, if American goals were to be realized; if Chiang could not assume the role, Americans wistfully hoped that a new government would emerge to efficiently identify future Chinese fortunes with United States interests and desires. Given the utter lack of realism of American goals in relation to Chinese conditions, all that was left over the next years was to help Chiang, as best as one might consistent with far greater commitments elsewhere, to defeat Communism, all the while retaining reservations concerning Chiang's abilities to serve American interests. This policy was neither ambiguous nor equivocal, and it was certainly compatible with American national interests as those in power defined them. It was merely irrelevant to the realities of China—realities that exposed the limits of United States power even in a broken world.

Locke's essentially economic mission for Truman also gave the President an alternative source of information and advice. After Mao's public denunciations of Hurley in July 1945 it was clear that the American's usefulness was rapidly coming to an end. At the same time, Washington was rethinking its future course in China, and the value of wartime appointees. At the end of August, Locke recommended to Truman that he send a personal envoy in good standing to China, one who would hopefully be supported by Britain and Russia, who might also join a mediation commission. Implicitly, Hurley was not the proper choice. Hurley himself gave point to this evaluation of his talents when, returning to Washington at the end of September, he freely accused members of the State Department and press corps in China of being pro-Communist. The peppery diplomat immediately made several overtures to resign, which he finally managed to do on November 26 in a curious condemnation of American support for British and French "imperialism" and "Communist imperialism."[18] Yet it now seems clear that his action only speeded a policy reconsideration well under way at the time at higher levels, and the following day Truman and his cabinet decided to send Marshall to China, not merely to take the press spotlight away from Hurley but to implement the main aspects of Locke's proposals. And it was at this time, as well, that Byrnes determined to win Soviet backing for the new American endeavor at the forthcoming Foreign Ministers Conference.[19]

The Marshall Mission

General Marshall went to China in mid-December in the hope of attaining the larger objectives of American national interests, and in this process his actions on behalf of peace or war, dictatorship or democracy, were purely instrumental toward those ends. What was seemingly contradictory about Marshall's mission was the diverse, inconsistent military and diplomatic means it was left to him to employ in his task—means so conflicting that most historians have interpreted them as a reflection of basic confusion in American policy at this time. In fact, however, Marshall's sole goal was to protect and, if possible, advance United States interests in the Far East, and to use all means available to him in an extremely difficult political situation. It was only the irrelevance of these goals to the conditions and possibilities in China that imparts a seeming futility to American diplomacy at this time.

Even as Washington prepared at the end of 1945 to send Marshall on his mission, the decision to keep marines in China indefinitely, and aid Chiang's conquest of the North, presaged one certain objective of United States policy: it would not permit the Communists to replace the expendable Kuomintang government. Given this fact, and its obvious inconsistency with true mediation, Stimson urged Marshall to have Truman define his mission as purely military, but in any event not to forget that the devious Chiang could never favor union with the Communists. The use of American troops themselves, the experienced former secretary of state and war now urged, should be strictly circumscribed, their quick withdrawal being most desirable. "The main principle for which you should fight (if this political problem is forced on you) is for equal commercial rights through the ports and over the Manchurian railways."[20] Even before arriving in China, therefore, Marshall was warned that his ostensible task of restoring an internal political tranquillity, one that had never existed in this century, was impossible.

In the several weeks before Marshall's departure, the only discussion was of the means for implementing United States policy, but not the final objectives. In addition to Stimson's admonitions, top American decision-makers exposed Marshall to their views on the interim use of United States troops, military and financial aid to Chiang, and the relation of these independent programs to mediation efforts. When Marshall left Washington, therefore, he took with him several policy directives of varying degrees of consistency. First, the United States designated Chiang's Nationalist government ". . . the proper instrument to achieve the objective of a unified China." It would assist that government with continuing military supplies and Marines, ". . . so that it can re-establish control over the liberated areas of China, including Manchuria."[21] Marshall was to pressure Chiang into broadening his government, and Byrnes then and at the end of December vaguely suggested withholding economic, and perhaps military, aid should Chiang prove reticent. Yet it is nearly certain that Byrnes meant only partial or temporary withholdings, for under no circumstances, Washington explicitly acknowledged, would Chiang be abandoned to the Communists—even if the Communists accepted all American proposals and Chiang none.

A key measure of Washington's determination to sustain Chiang was its goal of eliminating the autonomous armies and authority of the Communists and war lords. If Chiang were abandoned, however intransigent he might prove, Truman, Byrnes, and Marshall felt that Russia would likely move into Manchuria, China would be divided, and United States goals in the Pacific would be defeated. Marshall insisted on a clear definition of his course under such circumstances, and was told that the United States would still back Chiang. "This would mean," the State Department's account reads, "that this Government would have to swallow its pride and much of its policy in doing so."²² Having decided on the approach, Washington left only its intensity and timing to Marshall's discretion. The policy was predestined to fail.

Despite the secrecy of the details, President Truman's December 15 public statement on the Marshall mission to China revealed enough of the firm American commitment to preservation of Chiang's government to make even the pretense of disinterested mediation a thin one at best. He even announced the possibility of immediate credits and loans. Under these circumstances, as anyone could predict and time was to prove, Chiang had no reason to negotiate in earnest, but rather merely to attempt to gain even more emphatic American support for a military solution to his internal problems. Once the United States claimed that the Nationalist government was the official government for all of China, it merely revealed that America was seeking a useful myth to justify policies determined for much more basic reasons. Since the Revolution of 1911 the Kuomintang had not succeeded in uniting all China, which was now beginning to find its path toward national unity under the leadership of the Communists. In fact, the United States intervened in China's great transformation and conflict in the hope that the party eventually succeeding in this vast, decades-old transformation would be friendly to United States objectives in the Far East. In the end, America was to back the losing side.

By the end of 1945 America sustained the only alternative to the Communists because the key American leaders were firmly convinced that the Communists were true Marxists and pliant tools of Moscow in all their actions. For this reason Byrnes had sought to win the Russians at the Moscow Conference publicly to American diplomacy in the region. Confidential Communist avowals of independence at the end of December notwithstanding, Marshall accepted the official view that he was dealing, via Mao, with Moscow. Marshall later claimed that Chou En-lai had assured him of as much, and his staff in China certainly thought this was the case.

Yet no important group, so far as the presently available records reveal, attempted as during the war to assess the independent origins and distinctive ideology of Maoism. In brief, as American diplomacy moved toward the mobilization of an international economic, military, and political camp against Russia and the Left, the Americans thought that they were both fighting Soviet control in China and advancing their larger traditional interests and goals in the Far East.[23]

Given this American perspective, Chiang had no real desire nor reason to negotiate a true settlement with the Communists, and as soon as Marshall arrived in China, Chiang made it clear that "the key to this question is in the hands of Soviet Russia."[24] In essence, of course, the American view was identical. But it was patently obvious, as during World War II, that Chiang was going to depend on the further internationalization of his problems. From this time onward he sought to drag the Americans into his camp with their arms, manpower, and money. Again and again, as Marshall recalled in 1949, Chiang and his officers reported fictional battles with Russian tanks and soldiers, but such tales, it must be added, aimed at the American propensity to hold Russia heavily responsible for the drama of China.

The inordinately complex negotiations between the Communists and Kuomintang that Marshall oversaw during most of 1946, therefore, were an immense charade, with positions shifting and words barely concealing the fact that the fate of China would be determined on the battlefield and in the real world of its social system. So long as Chiang's troops moved northward with American aid, the ever-changing realities of power made proposals and compromises irrelevant time and time again. The details need not detain us, but suffice it to say that the Communists had every reason to believe that they could not depend on Chiang to fulfill an agreement creating a democratic China in which they might function peaceably, and that their main objective in the discussions was to try to influence Marshall to restrict, even neutralize, the American role in China. The unabated suppression of civil liberties in the Kuomintang-controlled regions, and Chiang's disregard of the cease-fire agreement of January 10 restricting unauthorized troop movements in large areas, must have reinforced Communist unwillingness to trust the wily Chiang. Yet, until Marshall's temporary return to the United States in mid-March, according to Truman ". . . the Communist representatives appeared more tractable to Marshall than the leaders of the Central Government. . . ."[25]

Despite the obvious Communist desire to arrange a political settlement, an attitude stimulated in large part by Chiang's unprecedented military successes, to American leaders the Communists—both Chinese and Russian—posed a special challenge to United States interests during early 1946. No other area exceeded Manchuria in attractiveness for American economic expansion in the Far East. During December 1945, as a result of what was probably a Kuomintang initiative, the Russians agreed to further delay their departure until February 1, 1946, permitting Chiang to take over the area; but during this period the Soviets continued systematically to remove as much movable wealth from the region as they could. Moreover, though they transferred control of many of the cities to Chiang's troops, the Russians did not assume the task of purging the region of advancing Communist forces. Above all, the highly independent Manchurians, who had never been under Chiang's rule and much resented his earlier sluggish resistance to their Japanese oppressors, soon began to take the reins of power into their own hands and to gather a very large part of the discarded Japanese arms. In brief, the Russians served neither Chiang nor the Communists, but only themselves, thereby upsetting American aspirations in the rich region.

The event that triggered American diplomatic action on Manchuria was a secret Soviet probe to Chiang, at the end of December 1945, concerning the creation of joint Sino-Soviet firms to operate most of the heavy industry in the area, and the following month the Russians implied that they would make troop withdrawals contingent on a satisfactory economic agreement. When the withdrawal deadline arrived, the Russians were still in Manchuria. To the Americans it looked as if the cherished open door was about to be closed.

The Americans refused to condone the Soviet removal of allegedly nearly one billion dollars of Japanese-owned industry, and on February 9 the State Department formally denounced the Soviet joint enterprise scheme as a violation of the open door and discrimination against "American commercial interests."[26] Harriman always saw Manchuria in terms of its potential economic value and especially urged a strong stand on the question, and in the end the Russians backed down. They eventually continued their withdrawal from south to north, and on May 3 the last Russian troops left China and Manchuria to their fate.

The Russian policy at this point was hardly enigmatic—it was to advance their own state interests rather than the Chinese revolution—but their means for attaining this goal began to shift somewhat. The Moscow Conference had revealed Soviet anxieties over continued American troop concentrations to their south, as the Russians urged coordinated Soviet-American troop withdrawals, and they no doubt were aware of Chiang's effort to obtain greater American backing and man power. When they gave firm assurances of support to Chiang during the last months of the war the Russians had not counted on his new strategy. Hence they partially backed off from him, cooling toward the dictator but not entirely deserting him.

But the Manchurian episode did reveal that the Russians were now ready to take a more passive, truly neutral stand in China. To the Kuomintang and its later defenders it was criminal enough that the Russians did not suppress the local "Communist" movement and prevent infiltration via the countryside, much less help Chiang impose tight control over the essentially foreign land. Yet without some modicum of Russian cooperation, Chiang would not have been able to undertake his Manchurian adventure in the first place. Indeed, it was only the aid and support of American, Japanese, and Soviet troops in the first place that had made possible Chiang's unusual but artificially successful military advances northward until the spring of 1946. Ironically, Chiang later admitted that by sending his best troops to the area he was to weaken his strength elsewhere in China. But throughout this critical year no one among Washington's decision-makers assumed that the Russians were actively aiding the Communists in Manchuria or North China. At the worst, Henry R. Luce, the influential magazine owner and a Chiang admirer, admitted in November 1946 upon his return from China that the retreating Russians had permitted Japanese arms to fall into Communist hands. In fact, most of these arms first passed into the hands of local elements whom the Kuomintang occupiers excluded from home rule, exposing them to their well-known venality. The Communists gladly accepted these new, well-armed Manchurian allies. "When it came to Soviet assistance," Marshall recalled in late 1949, ". . . I never could get my hands on it. . . . In the opinion of all my advisers and Intelligence, they were not supporting them." Marshall correctly understood that ". . . there is a great difference between actually supporting the thing [treaty to support Chiang] and just remaining quiescent," for "they could accomplish almost all their purposes by negative action."[27] In brief, given Chiang's weakness, mere Soviet withdrawal or passivity meant new chaos in the vacuum, however temporarily Chiang might fill it.

By early 1946 the Russians were ready to give Chiang one last chance before moving toward an essentially neutral stand in China, thereby removing one of the dictator's vital sources of support, as well as a minor element of restraint on the Communists. At the end of December 1945, according to Chiang's memoir, his son, Ching-kuo, on Stalin's invitation, left for Moscow as Chiang's personal representative. Stalin advised Ching that he hoped China might take an independent policy in the world, neither pro-Soviet nor pro-American, and not open Manchuria to American domination. Stalin now asked for a meeting with Chiang himself. Chiang claims that he consulted Marshall concerning the proposed meeting, and that the American raised no objection, but he refused nevertheless. During May 1946 the Russians renewed their request for discussions, and although Chiang again declined, independent evidence reveals that Harriman sounded the tocsin in Washington against a separate Sino-Soviet *détente* that might exclude the United States from Manchuria.

Not content to wait for a personal meeting, according to Chiang the Russians also communicated their neutralist political proposals to him via normal channels. Stalin insisted that the relations between Soviet and Chinese Communism were independent, even that he had refused a formal Communist request to admit their troops into Manchuria. Again Stalin asked for an autonomous Chinese policy in the world and joint action to prevent the reemergence of Japanese power. In return, the Russians would give complete backing to the Kuomintang against the Communists, and aid efforts to reconcile the parties. He implied, too, that excluding "third powers" from Manchuria was the essential condition of this general *démarche*.[28] Chiang rejected the proposal, of course, and it is meaningful that by the late summer of 1946 the Russian press comment on China focused more on the presence of United States troops than on any other theme, often in the context of the establishment of United States bases throughout the globe. The effect of Chiang's refusal to take a neutral stand in the world, and forgo his strategy of attempting to involve the Americans ever more deeply in the civil war, was that the Russians themselves began moving toward genuine neutrality in China's affairs after having supported the Kuomintang for years. Even if some American officials regarded such Soviet "correctness" and nonmeddling as likely to lead to invidious comparisons with United States intervention, they also acknowledged the Russians were playing a neutral, low-keyed role in the Far East.[29] The ultimate significance of this shift was not too great, since the Communists were hewing an independent line well before Soviet renewal of real sympathy for their cause. Yet one cannot find convincing evidence of Soviet material aid to the Communists from this time onward, for during the spring of 1946 and the rest of the year the Communists were to suffer major military defeats, even as the structure of Chinese economy and society continued to disintegrate and the opposition to the Kuomintang spread through all sectors of the nation.

Marshall's Mediation and Chiang's Expansion

Before Marshall had left China in mid-March he had unsuccessfully proposed a drastic reduction in United States troops in China. While he was in Washington the United States pledged substantial new aid to Chiang's government. During the little more than one month that Marshall was away from China the poorly enforced cease-fire agreement of January 10 deteriorated further as Chiang's authorities arrested Communist cease-fire team members and buzzed Mao's headquarters at Yenan, and both sides rushed to fill the vacuum left by the Soviet evacuation of Manchuria. Then Chiang's forces surrounded Communist troops north of Hankow, cut off their food supplies, moved troops into Jehol Province, and initiated numerous violations elsewhere—causing Marshall to shift to Chiang the greater responsibility for the collapse of the cease-fire. That breakdown came on April 15 when Communist troops attacked and finally took the Manchurian city of Changchun and acquired the city of Harbin at the same time without any resistance from the Kuomintang forces. When Marshall returned to China on April 18 the Communists offered to negotiate future military dispositions and political matters for a cease-fire, but Chiang refused to compromise and chose to continue the war. By May, despite Marshall's efforts to arrange a temporary settlement, Chiang's troops mounted a successful offensive in Manchuria. His appetite whetted, Chiang was prepared to maintain his advantage and, despite some significant but still insufficient Communist concessions to Chiang, or a fifteen-day truce in June, the Kuomintang risked a solution via arms. That solution was the inevitable result of the purposes of American policy in China—and American arms.

In mid-1946 Chiang's army consisted of about three million armed men, against whom the Communists could marshall 600,000 regular troops and 400,000 irregulars—a ratio that shifted only slightly to Chiang's disfavor by the end of the year. Yet despite the fact that not all Communist troops had rifles, they were mainly volunteers, well led, and spirited, and Chiang's army still consisted of oppressed, underfed draftees subject to their officers' venality and exploitation. Though the Communists began to acquire substantial stores of Japanese arms, the chiefly American equipment of the Kuomintang troops always remained far superior. From V-J Day through February 1946 the United States gave about $600 million in Lend Lease aid, with less thereafter. Under these circumstances, and with this backing, it is not surprising that Chiang opted for a military solution to his internal problems. "We must not permit another state to exist within a state; nor permit a private army to operate independent of a national army," Chiang announced on August 13, after preceding weeks of renewed hostilities and sending new armies to the north.[30] During those weeks Marshall and the new American ambassador, John Leighton Stuart, had futilely attempted to steer Chiang back to a peaceful course for fear that his further weakening of China would make the triumph of Communism inevitable.

For despite a verbally more stern policy toward Chiang from the middle of 1946 onward, the more realistic Americans reacted mainly against Chiang's shortsightedness, not his desire to eliminate the Communists. That this fear of Communist and Russian predominance in China was also an American obsession is unquestionable. As an instrument for the protection of its interests, the United States had always understood Chiang's weaknesses, and by August 1946 the American cabinet decided that while they could chastise Chiang by withdrawing the marines they could not desert him. Truman scolded Chiang on the tenth, in a note in which the President frankly referred to ". . . extremist elements, both in the Kuomintang and Communist Party, [who] are obstructing the aspirations of the people of China." Yet the burden of the message was with the suppression of civil liberties under the Kuomintang, and above all its militaristic response to Chinese internal affairs. "It cannot be expected that American opinion will continue in its generous attitude towards your nation unless convincing proof is shortly forthcoming that genuine progress is being made toward a peaceful settlement of China's internal problems." The Kuomintang let the note cool for over two weeks before replying that the entire responsibility for peace rested with the Communists, who in turn were part of an international movement engaged in expansion throughout the world.[31] Chiang continued his vast military offensive, and the Communists withdrew from the cities before his advance, content to hold the countryside as best they might.

By August, at the very latest, Marshall and the Americans in China were convinced that neither Chiang nor the Communists had any other desire but ". . . to achieve complete mastery over the other party and complete domination over China." The problem is that only Chiang felt confident enough at this point to win the civil war by force of arms, and that the United States still ranked the Communists ". . . in the camp with the USSR," while Chiang was friendly despite his suicidal course.[32] From the viewpoint of finding some means of giving direction to Chinese events, the Americans—and Marshall in particular—saw the impossibility of the situation and their total lack of instruments of persuasion.

Marshall therefore attempted without hope to mediate, all the while his government aided Chiang with arms. On August 30, despite Truman's still-fresh threat, the United States agreed to transfer to Chiang immense quantities of United States military surplus in the Far East—whose original procurement cost was $900 million—an act that only further exacerbated the declining relations between Marshall and the Communists. During August, as well, shipments of certain arms and ammunition to Chiang were suspended—yet not enough to cause shortages—in the hope of reducing his willingness to fight, an order that Washington alternately relaxed and made more stringent until May 1947, when it abandoned such pressures altogether. But despite its profound pessimism and distrust of both sides, the United States had its representative, Marshall, continue with the nominal motions of establishing a military truce and resuming political discussions, a sham none of the three parties believed had any significance. The Communists would not negotiate while Chiang's offensive persisted, and by October, Marshall refused to maintain discussions until Chiang stopped fighting. On October 5 Marshall considered asking Washington to recall him, but Chiang's entreatments and promises—later proved spurious—caused him to delay. Suffice it to say, only in November did Chiang stop his successful military offensive and order a cease-fire, and by that time it was too late for diplomacy. On November 19 Chou En-lai left Nanking for Yenan, finally to abandon the illusion that the conference room rather than the fields would resolve China's future. At the end of December, Marshall asked to be recalled, and on January 7, 1947, the United States formally terminated its efforts to negotiate peace in China.[33]

America's mediation was foredoomed to failure, a fact most decision-makers understood even before it began, not simply because Chiang was never willing to sacrifice any part of his power to any faction of Chinese society, much less the Communists, but because United States diplomats went to China ready to support Chiang's regime despite all eventualities and Communist reasonableness—unless they could locate a viable pro-American third force. Above all, diplomacy was only a sham glossing over military realities, which in and of itself was never an unacceptable alternative to the United States so long as the military victories could be made permanent. Given the profound economic and social weaknesses of China, the

Americans correctly feared that the military solution, if pressed too far, would ultimately be self-defeating.

Marshall publicly acknowledged these gloomy options in his public statement upon his return to the United States in early January, in which he was most critical of the Communists but even more outspoken in blaming Chiang for the failure of his mission. Yet the basic American policy did not alter, and this fact was made plain the prior December 18, when Truman mildly rebuked Chiang but made it clear the United States would continue to recognize his government. Yet what was also obvious was that the United States was preparing to cut most of its losses in a situation entirely beyond its control. The Americans gradually reduced their troops in China to 12,000 from the peak of 113,000 at the end of 1945, and Truman openly implied that economic and military aid would flow far less bountifully. The United States did not so much abandon Chiang as make a realistic, painful assessment of the conditions and direction of China and permit him now to suffer the full consequences of his own persistent folly. In an important sense, Chiang, by pursuing his foolhardy course, had abandoned the United States, and cut off the possibility of China's becoming the stabilizing anchor of American power in the Pacific and the country open to its commercial penetration. Given the United States' consistent pursuit of its own national interests in the Far East, there was now no option but to disengage from the events there, to wait, and perhaps to hope.[34]

Economic Foundations of the Chinese Revolution

No one can fully weigh the causes of the Chinese Revolution—whether the wartime-induced breakdown, the military factors, or the deeper, corrosive impact of modernism on Chinese society—but surely the unique character of Chiang Kai-shek and his Kuomintang government must be assigned some decisive role in making inevitable the most important of all post-1917 global political changes. For Chiang had failed to harness the deeper, older elements working to transform China since 1911, and by no later than 1940 he had created a distinctive political elite based on gangsterism and the maximization of the private fortunes of a clique rather than the protection of his class. Indeed, it was Chiang's role in the disintegration of Chinese society and the destruction of its urban ruling class that made inevitable the upheaval of Chinese society that led to the success of Communism. It is in this larger structural context alone that all the political and military events of 1943–1949 can be fully comprehended.

The impact of the war on Chinese society was profound, and on the economy no less significant because the Japanese captured most of the regions containing China's small industrial capacity. Yet, save for Manchuria, much of occupied China's industry was returned largely intact to the Kuomintang, and during the wartime period itself China experienced a remarkable growth in industrial capacity in the regions under Chiang's control. The index of industrial production for "Free China," using the prewar output as 100, increased to a peak of 376 in 1943 and hovered somewhat below that point until the end of the war. The output of fuels of various sorts was especially accelerated, but new cotton and certain consumer goods plants were opened in response to the promise of high profits. If much of this development was marginal and temporary, the least that must be said is that Chiang's economic possibilities were far more potentially favorable at the end of the war than is commonly assumed. The Japanese industrial and other holdings Chiang acquired at the end of the war were conservatively valued at $3.6 billion in 1945 dollars. Chiang himself during early 1947 could, with some exaggeration, point to the immense increases since the war in absolute output of coal, yarn, steel, and electricity—increases that reflected the extension of the regions under his control but also the substantial expansion of output elsewhere.[35]

In the far more essential area of food output the picture was mixed, but hardly all black. For rice, between 1937 and 1945 the production in the fifteen provinces that Chiang controlled fell not more than one-quarter below the 1931–1937 output in any year, but generally less than one-fifth for the average year. By 1946–1948, however, in the twenty-two provinces Chiang now controlled output increased remarkably, reaching 96 percent of 1931–1937 during 1948. However, during 1937–1946, output in the fifteen provinces of wheat, rapeseed, oats, corn, and sweet potatoes nearly equaled or exceeded the 1931–1937 output, and by 1948 for the twenty-two provinces agricultural output surpassed 1931–1937 levels for seven of thirteen crops measured, and came within 10 percent for four others. More serious than output were the gravely deranged distribution system and the inflation that encouraged farmers to withhold their produce from the markets. The collapse of China, therefore, can be explained far less by looking at economic productivity patterns, which were remarkably resilient under the circumstances, than by considering the political and economic structure imposed on the farmers and the small industrial sector.

The basic problem of China at this time was the Kuomintang itself—its policies, corruption, and direction of the state power. It was this that the Americans could see most clearly, and it was this decadence that so filled United States officials with pessimism, for it was breeding its own destruction.

For the United States, the largest immediate source of economic rather than military difficulty was in Chiang's handling of the $658 million in UNRRA relief supplies he was to receive after November 1945, over two-thirds of which was paid for by the United States. By June 1946, China was the only recipient in the world with large stock piles of UNRRA goods— some 50,000 tons that month—stored in warehouses while starvation was rampant. Ultimately Chiang's friends obtained control over the distribution of UNRRA supplies and channeled much of it—we will never know the precise extent—into their black-market operations. The Export-Import Bank opened further opportunities for gain when it loaned the Nationalist government $83 million after the war's end, largely early 1946. One example, the raw cotton which comprised 22 percent of UNRRA imports, will suffice. Cotton mill owners received 800 pounds of cotton for each 400 pounds of yarn they returned. But since they could make a fair profit by returning 600 pounds, they pocketed immense profits and built new plants in Hong Kong to prepare for the deluge. The quite open and functionally sanctioned smuggling of foreign goods, especially from the United States, drove numerous small Chinese industries out of business. This pervasive corruption and incompetence among the cronies of Chiang and the Kuomintang was a standard fact of Chinese existence, one familiar to all Americans in China at this time. Commodity speculation, hoarding, corruption —all these corrosive realities were rampant in 1946. Who obtained such favors, or administered the tax system, depended on their relations to the clique around Chiang. The jockeying among rival groups attempting to use political connections for personal profit was described in detail in various reports to Washington, and the result of this larger situation in which corruption flourished is that even as Chiang won military battles he consistently weakened the internal structure of that portion of Chinese society still under his command.[36]

The ultimate result of such economic policies was the longest serious inflation of any nation in the twentieth century. Using July 1937 and 1 as the base, by June 1945 retail prices for all of Nationalist China had increased to 2,167. Postwar data exist only for various cities, but during 1946 wholesale prices increased only by one-half in Shanghai, though a good deal more in Nanking. By the end of 1947, Nanking prices reached 129,384 on the 1937 base of 1, and 8,740,600 on September 20, 1948. Using May 1946 as the base of 1, wholesale prices in Shanghai were 22 in December 1947, 48,300 in December 1948, and 7,476,520 in March 1949.

Given the inherent economic and military situation, the inflation that ripped Chinese society asunder was largely Chiang's fault as the dictator made no effort to offset his deficits, save by running the printing presses, and shifted his energies to throwing onto the market his vast dollar-gold reserves, amounting to at least $858 million in December 1945. Such policies permitted insider speculators to reap vast new windfalls, but reduced Chinese reserves to $414 million in December 1946 and $187 million in December 1947, and what he did not dispose of in this manner Chiang eventually sent to Formosa for his later use. The net result of this policy of profitable chaos for Chiang was that before the Communists captured the major urban regions, or even a majority of China, Kuomintang policies had greatly transformed the Chinese social and economic structure, at least temporarily liquidating the power of whole classes that were the last hope of the United States. The result, too, was the radicalization or demoralization of major elements of the critical classes of traditional order, and it is in this context alone that one can comprehend the remarkable and quick victory of the Communists over a Kuomintang government that by any objective had greater material, as opposed to moral and political, strength.

Speculators made fortunes if they were major entrepreneurs with political connections and able to get raw materials. The critical point is who lost. The soldiers suffered most of all as their superiors funneled off their meager allowances. Even granting a large margin of error and changes over time, the fact that a soldier's cash allowance in Chengtu in June 1944 was about 9 percent of 1937 purchasing power is one approximate indication. In the same city over the same period, farm wages dropped 29 percent, clerical salaries 69 percent, the salary of professors by 89 percent. The real income of farmers stabilized and even increased slightly during 1944–1946, but never reached prewar levels, and farm wages probably continued their decline. But those who suffered most were many of precisely those traditional supporters of the Kuomintang and moderate nationalism. The real income of teachers and government employees after the war fell to something like 6 to 12 percent of the prewar level income, and the soldiers remained in a condition of near starvation and oppression.

In the end the soldiers would not or could not fight, and much of the government bureaucracy was forced into graft and corruption. Translated into social and political terms, Chiang mobilized vital potential support for the Communists and melted the possible resistance to them. The result was student strikes, food riots, hunger, defeatism high and low, decadence. In the vast human drama of China from the end of the war until 1949, the political options polarized between chaos and Communism. By the end of that period more and more men would welcome Communism as a respite from their profound misery; some would remain neutral; and those few who had profited from it all prepared their escape.[37]

In a direct sense, neither civil war nor revolution annihilated the Chinese elite and the Kuomintang. Rather, that society first destroyed itself to some great extent, introducing cataclysmic elements, ultimately no less profound, as a vital, even decisive, cause of the Chinese Revolution. In the end, only a small clique of Chiang's followers rather than a class of urban bourgeoisie had anything more to lose from Communism, which in turn might impose a period of stability and development on the weary, bloodied nation. It is against this larger, more essential backdrop of vast social upheaval below that the remaining political and military aspects of the epic of China may now be told.

The Communist Response

In this context of tactical retreat and military defeat in the sixteen months after the war, but also of quickly ripening possibilities in the economic and political sphere, Mao and the Communists formulated their strategy. In one sense, however, quite apart from their intent, all the Communists had to do was to survive Chiang's attacks, wait for the dictator to push China farther down the abyss of economic chaos, and prevent the United States military intervention which alone could rob them of the inevitable victory. Yet, after all is said and done, the long-conditioned Maoist pragmatism helped the Communists make the very best of a temporarily difficult situation. On the military plane the Communists simply beat tactical retreats from urban areas in the North, permitting Chiang to extend his lines and diffuse his man power while the Communists built yet larger political bases in the countryside, gathering what arms could be found from deserted Japanese and Kuomintang sources.

Mao, whose tactical agility during this period reflected his characteristic nondogmatism, understood the internal realities and made the most of them. He quickly abandoned useless stands in the cities and shifted his army to a type of mobile warfare Chiang was unable to fight. Chiang's overextended battle lines and inadequate reserves were as obvious to Mao as they were to American military observers, who all plainly realized that Chiang had neither adequate man power nor ideology for the task of conquering China. Mao fully perceived, even during the adversity of military defeat of the fall of 1946, that the ". . . domestic political situation is extremely favourable." This meant avoiding excessive haste in land reform, continuing to work with the "middle" and "rich peasants" and "middle and small landlords." Party membership was open to all classes of society, and party rules explicitly indicated there was no dichotomy between the interests of the working class and those of all the people. In the cities, he declared in July 1946, it was essential to unite with the ". . . working class, the petty bourgeoisie and all progressives," a theme he had stressed throughout the war against Japan and continued until the ultimate demise of Chiang.[38] In brief, given the utterly destructive consequences of Chiang's internal policies to national capitalism as well as to the peasantry, Mao had only to unite behind the banner of nationalism and peace all those urban groups that had traditionally sustained the earlier Kuomintang and were now being economically wiped out by its policies. At the very least, however, he had to neutralize the role of those not ready to rally to Communism in the great polarization of causes that was then taking place. But of this, more follows.

Mao's greater immediate problem during the period of Marshall's mission was the restriction of United States involvement in China's struggle. He could not hope for American neutrality, for the wartime experience had shown that to the extent America acted in China it would do so through the Kuomintang. The basic task facing the Communists was simply to minimize, hopefully eliminate, American aid to Chiang, and to prevent massive United States intervention. It was Chiang, in the end, who did most to convince the Americans. In the long diplomatic maneuvers of 1945–1946, what Chiang needed was total, active American support and man power, and the Communists required only true American neutrality. In practice, the Americans displeased both sides, and Chiang's shortcomings were too great to make any serious use of the substantial material aid he did get—at least to retain power, if not enlarge his fortunes. As always, in the meetings over which the Americans presided it was the United States to whom the Communists addressed themselves, and in this task they never had any illusions.

Given this strategy, as well as a temporary military initiative with Chiang, the Communists were extremely tactful in dealing with the Americans in light of the fact that Chiang's aggressive policies would never have been possible without American soldiers and arms. Mao no more believed

Marshall's pretense of being a disinterested neutral part than did anyone in Washington. By agreeing time and time again to the compromises Marshall suggested, most of which would have required uncanny trust on the part of the Communists toward Chiang and his followers, the Communists highlighted Chiang's responsibility for the civil war in China. Chiang's refusal to meet the Communists halfway further disillusioned the Americans, and made it possible for the Communists to convince Washington that Chiang was not a viable, reasonable force in whose behalf it should massively intervene. But they could not persuade the United States to abandon modest aid to the Nationalists, and by mid-1946 the Communists could not avoid the reality that America would back Chiang irrespective of his actions. There then began a period of mounting criticism of the American policy, even as Chou En-lai stayed in Nanking until mid-November.

Public Communist criticism of the United States began in June when Mao announced that Chiang could fight a civil war only because of United States military aid in the form of both guns and support troops. The Communists now called for United States troop withdrawal and cessation of arms shipments. These continued criticisms caused Marshall to warn that further Communist attacks on United States arms aid to Chiang might cut short the mediation role he was then playing. By this time, however, many other Chinese nationalists, including Madame Sun Yat-sen, had begun to denounce the dual American role and its intervention into Chinese affairs. During August, Mao again made plain that the duration of the Chinese civil war depended on the extent and duration of American aid, which had become the critical factor in the crisis. Yet that month the Americans agreed to the nearly $1 billion surplus military goods transfer, which now struck even Marshall as rather inconsistent with his erstwhile neutral role. It was relatively easy for Chou En-lai the following month to document the patent inconsistency in the American role as mediator in a war in which it was supplying arms to the aggressor. This frank but cautious Communist criticism of American policy continued throughout the year, but it did not lead to a rupture, and the United States Army Liaison Group in Yenan continued to receive cordial treatment and was permitted to function freely.[39] In the end it was Chiang who convinced Washington of his basic hostility toward the Marshall mission. Yet despite their restraint, the Communists correctly perceived that the long-term danger to their ultimate success, the nation best able and most likely to snatch victory away from them in a China that Chiang was conditioning for revolution, was the United States. Anything that might keep civil war from becoming an even more substantial international intervention was of paramount importance to the Communists. Ironically, in the end Chiang himself performed that function.

So long as Chiang pursued his strategy the United States had no means for handling the magnitude of the China problem. It could alter the course of the Chinese revolution only by sacrificing its global priorities, for short of doing so the United States had exhausted its political and economic resources. By the end of 1946 America's leaders could merely hope that events in China would eliminate their dilemmas and transcend their impotence.

10

Korea, 1945–1948: The American Way of Liberation

Until the outbreak of war in June 1950, Korea was in the shadows of world politics, but the tortured struggle in that artificially divided nation in the five years after World War II was critical to the nature and origins of the Korean War. But even more, Korea was yet another example of the consistent postwar American policy to counter or, through its direct military occupation, reverse the momentum and accomplishments of revolutionary movements. In the United States' policy in Korea we can examine in microcosm the meaning and consequences of an exclusively American trusteeship over an agrarian nation in the process of making a revolution.

During World War II the formulation of the United States' policy toward an occupied territory reflected its intelligence estimate of the nature of the resistance movements likely to come to power with the defeat of Japan and Germany. If conservative nationalists likely to shift the economic assets of a new state from the old colonial power toward the United States dominated the resistance, as in the Dutch East Indies, Washington was anticolonial and pro-independence. Where, on the other hand, the Left controlled the resistance and had a mass base, the United States recommended trusteeship or a prolonged but "liberalized" continuation of colonialism, as in Indochina and Korea.

Korean historians concur that the nation was for many years astir with revolutionary consciousness and that the resistance to the Japanese was articulate and well organized among the peasants, the fishermen, and the small working class. There was little doubt in American analyses that with the defeat of Japan this already organized underground governmental structure would simply assume formal power.[1] There were also many Korean revolutionaries in exile. After the Russian Revolution thousands of Korean Communists fled from the Japanese repression and settled in Siberia, the majority becoming Soviet citizens. In Yenan, with the Chinese Communists, others organized a Korean Independence Group. And by confiscating the best land for themselves and by their ferocious effort to destroy Korean culture, a policy similar to that of the Nazis in Poland, the Japanese decisively alienated a part of the propertied class which, in exile, organized the Korean Provisional Government around Kim Koo in Chungking. This handful of conservative nationalists had no mass following in Korea, although they were respected as individuals for their anti-Japanese position. They had a close ideological affinity with the Kuomintang (KMT), which subsidized their activities toward the end of the war. This element was represented in the United States by Syngman Rhee, who so assiduously cultivated American political figures that by 1945 he was widely known in Washington as a champion of Korean independence as well as a militant anti-Communist.[2]

Based on its understanding of the political forces in Korea, the State Department formulated a policy of trusteeship for an indefinite duration. At the conference in Cairo, Roosevelt and Churchill in an offhand manner expressed it in the ambiguous terms of ". . . [I]n due course Korea shall become free and independent." At Yalta, Roosevelt suggested a trusteeship period of twenty to thirty years, and Stalin concurred, though adding, "[t]he shorter the period the better."[3] But they did not translate the vague policy into an operational plan. As Russian entry into the war became imminent, General Douglas MacArthur's staff estimated that the Soviets could reach the southern tip of the peninsula before the arrival of United States troops, which made it urgent to secure an agreement with the Russians for a boundary between the two forces. They arbitrarily chose the 38th parallel, north of Seoul, as "the northernmost possible" line for the United States control.[4] Stalin agreed to the demarcation three days after the Red Army entered Korea and the Soviets advanced as far as Seoul and Inchon and then withdrew.

As throughout Asia, it was a matter of great political import as to which forces would take the Japanese surrender at the end of the conflict. In their General Order Number 1 the Americans specifically ordered the Japanese not to surrender to the resistance forces. But while the United States might thus temporarily undercut the power of the Left, it could not so easily control the allegiance of the people. In its assessment of the conditions in Korea at the end of the war, the State Department predicted an ". . . attack by Korean revolutionists and rioters when Japanese authority is relaxed." Referring to the extortionist system of land tenure by both Japanese and Korean landlords, Undersecretary of State Joseph Grew claimed that the Korean peasantry would expect sweeping land reforms at the end of the war and that, in general, "[t]he economic and political situation in Korea would be conducive to the adoption of communist ideology and . . . the policy and activities of a Russian-sponsored socialist regime in Korea might easily receive popular support."[5]

By the time the Japanese surrendered in August 1945, after thirty-five years of ruthless occupation, the resistance was decades old and all the ideological issues had been sharpened and clarified. As with all such resistance movements, it comprised a hard core underground of professional guerillas, skilled in organizational tactics, with close ties to the people, and a periphery of sympathizers among the nationalist, liberal intellectuals and professionals. In early August, with the Japanese defeat imminent, the nationalist groups organized a united front including the underground, the liberal nationalists, and even a good part of the Right. But the right-wing nationalists, committed to preserving existing property relations, broke away after the first organizational meetings, for the Left was clearly in the majority and unwilling to compromise its socialist program. These diverse groups had been able to cooperate against the Japanese, but with the elimination of the unifying opposition their ideological differences emerged. Now the bulk of the nationalist Right, but only a small minority of the resistance, along with the collaborators, decided to await the arrival of the United States forces to let them determine the ultimate outcome.

Although the liberals became the public spokesmen for the Korean People's Republic which the resistance organized on September 6, the republic and the local Liberation Committees were not a spontaneous, disorganized seizure of power but actually an extension of the resistance infrastructure that had existed for years. By August 31 People's Committees functioned in 145 cities and villages throughout the country, maintaining law and order, preventing summary reprisals and violence, and distributing Japanese property. The republic was receptive to the inclusion of members of the Provisional Government in exile in a coalition, and, in fact, Kim Koo and others were elected to posts in the republic. But it would not sacrifice its program for national reconstruction that provided for the confiscation and distribution of the property of all Japanese and collaborators, the nationalization of public utilities and large industry, the guarantee of civil liberties, and advanced social welfare programs.[6]

The Russian army arrived in Korea on August 12 and it accepted the revolutionary People's Committees, placing most administrative functions in their hands by August 25, and encouraged them to proceed with their program of expropriating the property of the Japanese and collaborators. Accompanying the Soviet troops were approximately 30,000 Korean Communist refugees who certainly played a part in the subsequent developments in the Soviet zone, but had little or nothing to do with the People's Republic. The Japanese troops resisted the Russians and then fled south, where, according to George McCune, then chief of the Korean desk at the State Department, they ". . . assumed an attitude of guileless cooperation" with the Americans.[7] The Soviets imprisoned the Japanese they captured and gave short shrift to the collaborators, most of whom fled to the south with the Japanese troops.

Increasingly alarmed by the revolutionary character of the People's Committees, on August 28 the Japanese commander in Korea, General Abe, sent a message to the Supreme Allied Commander, informing him of the general situation and asking for authority to maintain control. "Communist and independence agitators are plotting to take advantage of this situation to disturb peace and order." The reply was immediate: "It is directed that you maintain order and preserve the machinery of government in Korea . . . until my forces assume these responsibilities. . . . You are authorized and directed to retain . . . the minimum forces necessary to preserve order and safeguard property therein." "Am extremely grateful to have received your understanding reply," the Japanese commander responded.[8]

Shortly before landing on September 7 the Americans dropped leaflets over Korea advising the Koreans to obey ". . . orders passed to you through the current [Japanese] Korean Government" and ". . . do not participate in demonstrations against the Japanese or in welcome to American armed forces. Go about your normal pursuits."[9] But the *élan* generated by liberation from an oppressive foreign tyranny, and sparked by nationalism and the hope of a new order, had profoundly moved the population, and on the seventh the Koreans staged an enthusiastic welcome at Inchon as the United States troops disembarked. The greeting had political meaning as well, for it was the formal welcome of a host, the established People's Republic of Korea. In response the Japanese troops fired on the eager crowd, killing two and wounding ten—an action upheld by the American command.[10] This episode, along with the exchange between Generals MacArthur and Abe, revealed the ideological collusion that the two enemy states shared toward a revolutionary independence movement. During the first days of the "liberation" the Japanese maintained full control of the communications system, and their troops, with United States arm bands, guarded Japanese property. Elsewhere in Asia, over the same weeks, Japanese troops were controlling the local leftist movements on behalf of the United States, Britain, and France in much the same manner. After a week of this procedure—one that contrasted so sharply with that of the Soviets —the Joint Chiefs of Staff ordered MacArthur progressively to remove the Japanese from administrative posts. But many were to remain for four months, and a few for much longer still.

The extreme resentment of the Korean people of all opinions over the policy of retaining the Japanese in administrative posts led Truman to restate United States policy toward Korea. "The assumption by the Koreans themselves of the responsibilities and functions of a free and independent nation . . . will of necessity require time and patience."[11] The rationale for the "time and patience" was that the Koreans lacked experience in self-government. Such arrogant speculations were lacking in Grew's assessment earlier which had indicated only that the Korean government might be revolutionary, which, translating the American official diplomatic code, *ipso facto* meant incapable of self-government.

The People's Republic believed, as did all Koreans of every political position, that the American army was there only to accept the surrender of the Japanese and would leave when they were disarmed and returned to Japan, and offered its aid to the United States forces, much as they had done with the Russians. They could hardly anticipate that their erstwhile liberators would use their former oppressors against them. The American military command rebuffed their overtures, informing them that the United States acknowledged no government in the south of Korea but only its own occupation authority. The United States commander, General John Hodge, responded to the official visit of President Lyuh Woon Heung by calling him a "Japanese agent," denied him any authority whatsoever, and then ordered him out of his office.[12] So opened the first chapter of what was to prove a long struggle between the Koreans and the United States.

The American Military Government

While United States diplomatic representatives in the field never formulate the broad contours of policy, their personal qualifications and abilities frequently set the tone of day-to-day conduct, at times precipitating events which inevitably cast their shadow on the evolution of broad strategy as well. This is especially true of areas on the fringes of the United States' principal interests, where the men on the scene are chosen with less care but nevertheless have far greater latitude in the implementation of policy.

General John Hodge was a regular army officer, blunt, conservative, with the breadth of vision characteristic of his milieu, appointed to a position as military commander calling for the maximum of political sensitivity and acumen. Hodge did not receive detailed orders from Washington as to his functions until the end of October. As far as he was concerned, Korea was a part of enemy territory, and he intended to see that the terms of surrender were carried out. It was with the attitude of a conqueror, not a liberator, that he arrived at Inchon. He brought with him a personal message to the Korean people from General MacArthur threatening death to anyone who disobeyed military orders. "Koreans are the same breed of cats as the Japanese" was Hodge's widely quoted assessment on his arrival in Seoul.[13] His staff and political advisers had the limited experience and views of routine American career officers.

For the crucial first five weeks the United States armed forces assumed civil responsibility, and the behavior of the United States troops, characterized by arrogance, assault, and looting, plus retention of Japanese personnel, won the immediate antipathy of the Korean people. The civil affairs officers sent from Japan to relieve the regular soldiers were equally poor choices. Most were trained for duty in Japan and shifted at the last minute to Korea. They certainly did not comprehend the internal political forces.

One week after the United States landing in Korea, H. M. Benninghoff, the State Department's political adviser in Korea, reported to Byrnes that "Southern Korea can best be described as a powder keg ready to explode at the application of a spark." For this situation he in large part blamed the Russians. "There is little doubt that Soviet agents are spreading their political thought throughout southern Korea. . . . Communists advocate the seizure *now* of Japanese property and may be a threat to law and order. . . . The most encouraging single factor in the political situation is the presence in Seoul of several hundred conservatives among the older and better educated Koreans. Although many of them have served with the Japanese, that stigma ought eventually to disappear. Such persons favor the return of the 'Provisional Government.' . . ."[14] He did not even mention the People's Republic. At the end of September, Benninghoff amplified his initial impressions, again contrasting the "democratic or conservative" group with the ". . . radical or communist group . . . which proposes to set up a government known as the Korean Peoples Republic."[15] But it hardly mattered that his reports were neither serious nor knowledgeable analyses of the strength and position of the People's Republic, for the policy remained the same. The entire strategy of military occupation and trusteeship was based on the assumption that the Left had power and that the United States forces were to prevent it from organizing a government in the south.

Language assumed a special significance, for there were few Koreans who spoke English, and they were exclusively among the wealthy landholding class. Those rare Americans who spoke Korean were the sons of missionaries, such as George Z. Williams, Hodge's aide. Assigned the task of recruiting Koreans for administrative posts, he restricted his choice to Christians who were also members of the extreme Right factions or former collaborators. Little care was given to the appointment of suitable men to posts of civil responsibility. According to one official, . . . "an Army lieutenant who has never finished high school is assigned the post of education advisor for a whole province . . . ," another ". . . manager of an . . . important silk mill. . . ."[16] But given the ignorance of the language, such American actions were less critical than decisions made by the right-wing, English-speaking Koreans that the military government recruited. Extending the façade of democratic participation even as the People's Republic was being dissolved, on October 5 the AMG established an Advisory Council of conservative professionals and businessmen, chaired by Kim Sung Soo, a notorious Japanese collaborator. Benninghoff admitted to Byrnes that the Koreans did not respond with much enthusiasm, ". . . perhaps because . . . a similar council under Japanese auspices . . . was regarded as a gathering of collaborationists."[17]

One month after their arrival, MacArthur's aides briefed the chief American personnel in Korea that the primary mission of the occupation was ". . . to form a bulwark against communism."[18] But such reinforcement of the overwhelming anti-Soviet and anti-Left bias of the American officers was superfluous, for they believed that war with the Russians was imminent and that they would be on the first line of defense. Such anxieties proved misplaced, though they did affect policy. More certain, however, was that the occupation was committed to crushing the indigenous Left and immediately building a "bulwark against communism" within Korea itself.

Although opposed by American forces, the People's Republic in most areas continued to function as a government and began to implement its program of distributing Japanese property which brought it into direct conflict with the United States forces. In Seoul, the republic's power was rather quickly circumvented by the Military Government with the assistance of the English-speaking right-wing Koreans and collaborators, who were largely concentrated there. But in the rural areas the republic's power was at first uncontested by the United States forces, who had been unable to provide an alternative. The American officers knew this was only a temporary expedient and refused to consider the republic and its organs as anything more than "[v]arious societies [which] set themselves up as governments. . . ."[19] "When we came here, we found the Korean People's Republic in control," one officer observed. "This was in violation of orders to let the Jap officials stay on in their jobs. So we broke it up."[20] By the end of September, as the Americans began blocking and reversing the decrees of the republic, the Koreans realized that far from being liberated, one conqueror had simply replaced another.

The AMG insisted that all political parties register their platform and officers and ordered the People's Republic to register as a political party. Nevertheless, on October 5 an important member of the republic promised national elections on March 1, 1946. The infuriated American command responded with an order that it alone represented the only government south of the 38th parallel and indicated that it would use force to crush any future claims of governing power.[21]

Not in any way a placid or docile people, the Koreans, who had struggled against the Japanese for thirty-five years only to be subjugated by their "liberators" after less than one month of freedom, launched an attack on the AMG via posters, leaflets, public meetings, and other peaceful protests. The contrast between the two zones was too apparent, and the People's Republic underlined the differences in their attacks on the AMG. As the talk of the return of Syngman Rhee and the Provisional Government in Chungking continued, the members of the People's Republic indicated a willingness to organize a coalition, but mentioned including members of the Korean Independence Group in Yenan as well. These organized efforts further persuaded Hodge and his staff of the necessity to use force in dealing with these "ruffians" and "communists."[22] The power and influence of the People's Republic and its components, based as it was on the mass support of a politically sophisticated people, continued to make itself felt. On November 2, with considerable irritation, Hodge reported to MacArthur that "Communistic activities are reaching point where they may gain control unless positive action is taken. Am sure most radical elements are Russian instigated but cannot get positive proof."[23] He advised MacArthur that he would shortly use force against the Left. At its conference in mid-November the People's Republic continued to use the word "republic," which according to Hodge ". . . gained them many followers among the uneducated and laboring classes, and has fostered radical actions in the provinces under the guise of orders from the Korean People's Republic."[24] Now he advocated a formal denunciation rather than the current effort of trying to treat the republic as a political party. "This will constitute in effect a 'declaration of war' upon the Communistic elements in Korea, and may result in temporary disorders. It will also bring charges of political discrimination in a 'free' country, both by local pinko and by pinko press."[25]

In Washington there was some discussion as to how far to proceed in taking explicit political sides in Korea as distinct from barring the Left from power. John Carter Vincent in the State Department asked Hodge to restrain his overt support for Kim Koo and the Right and at the same time to indicate what steps he was taking against the Left. This caution reflected some uncertainty as to the final resolution of the Korean question vis-à-vis the Russians, since four-power trusteeship was still official policy. John J. McCloy intercepted this line of analysis by proposing, in effect, that they give Hodge a carte blanche, and he strongly advocated the use of the exiled right-wing Koreans as the basis for a Korean administration.[26]

Behind these exchanges between Seoul, Washington, and Tokyo was the fact that the local commanders were already moving against the People's Republic in the rural areas on the administrative levels. The Military Government arrested and tried members of the republic on trumped-up charges and replaced them with right-wing appointees. Trials of members of the People's Republic were in military courts, where the United States local commander issued the conviction and the sentence to the judge before the trial began.[27] While it took some time to crush the committees on a local level, it was a far more difficult task to crush their popular base, and the Americans were no more successful than the Japanese. In January the United States press was still reporting that all factions of the Right had fallen far behind the Left in popular support. A *Christian Science Monitor* dispatch indicated that ". . . the so-called People's Republic, composed of Socialist and Communist elements, enjoys far more popular support than any other single political grouping."[28] Such facts only strengthened the AMG determination to crush the Left. By November 26 MacArthur had forwarded a request to build and arm a central police force of 25,000 to combat the activities of the People's Republic, and Washington approved it by the end of the year.[29]

After persistent appeals from the AMG in Seoul, on October 20 the United States flew Syngman Rhee to Korea. Throughout the war Rhee had exchanged a long correspondence with the leading men in the State Department, and they knew his position. On Rhee's arrival in Seoul, Hodge enthusiastically introduced him to an audience of fifty thousand, where Rhee made a characteristically violent speech attacking the Left and the Soviets, and accused the United States of appeasement. Rhee's extreme right-wing opinions soon found sympathetic ears in the United States headquarters, which encouraged him and sought his advice on political matters, even using Rhee to negotiate with the Left. The State Department, however, was annoyed at the excitable Korean's lack of finesse and tried to induce Hodge to temper Rhee's utterances and not to identify the command exclusively with his faction. But all was not always harmonious even between Rhee and Hodge, despite their shared sympathies, for Rhee's personal ambitions and disruptive tactics, even among the Right, increased rather than ameliorated Hodge's problems.[30]

Despite growing repression, the People's Republic sought to transcend the polarization that the United States was artificially imposing on Korea. In November 1945, when the rightist Kim Koo and his aides returned from Chungking, the People's Republic attempted to set up a coalition with him supported by Pak Hanyong, the leader of the Communist Party. The effort was, of course, fruitless, for the Right had no incentive to compromise as long as it had American support. The AMG admitted in a report to Washington in December that there was no enthusiasm among the Koreans for either Rhee or Kim Koo. Nevertheless, in February 1946 Hodge appointed a Representative Democratic Council to advise the military government and to begin to assume many of the administrative functions of government, particularly in the police and judicial system. The individuals on the council were all rightists and Rhee was the chairman. By April the State Department felt compelled to deny that it was making unilateral moves to establish a separate state, but the facts were to prove otherwise.[31]

The Strategy of Restoration

It was the administration of economic policy that most clearly demonstrated the effect of the American occupation on South Korean society. Within the overriding framework of containing the Left and the Soviets there remained a number of economic options. The measures that the AMG introduced early in the occupation reflected the dogmatism of conservative men, essentially ignorant of economic affairs, in imposing their concepts of a laissez faire capitalist state on an underdeveloped agrarian economy.

Their policies created indescribable chaos in the South Korean economy, vastly magnifying already serious political problems.

Within a month of its arrival the AMG removed all controls on the production, collection, and distribution of rice and imposed a free market on prices and distribution. South Korea was normally a rice export region, and the 1945 harvest produced a 60 percent increase in yield over 1944. But profiteers, most of them close to the AMG, cornered the food and hoarded it. Rationing was reintroduced shortly thereafter, but, as one officer in charge of rice collection pointed out, ". . . it was already too late. The rice had vanished and there was hunger. We collected only a fifth of what we should have."[32] As a result of such imposed dislocations, during the entire occupation and for many years following, the United States had to export food, including rice, to South Korea. And without its surplus, South Korea was unable to barter rice for Soviet zone coal, compounding its economic paralysis.

Under the Japanese the standard of living of the Korean workers and peasants had been extremely low, but their conditions under the AMG were worsened drastically. A chart published by the AMG in November 1946 revealed the situation in real wages between July 1945 and March 1946. Using June 1937 as a base of 100, in July 1945 both wages and prices had reached 200, but in November wages were 2,000 while prices had soared to 8,000. In January 1946 the AMG passed an anti-inflationary law freezing wages but not prices, and the situation grew increasingly desperate for the Korean masses. By March, while wages were still at the January figure of 3,200, prices had reached the incredible index of 19,000.[33]

The AMG declared that all transactions of the People's Republic involving the distribution of Japanese property were illegal. The resistance had quickly taken over Japanese property while liberating the country in August and September 1945. The tenants simply took the land, and the workers began to manage the Japanese businesses. The AMG speedily dispossessed the peasants and workers, using the old Japanese registration records of ownership. First the occupation intended to sell the land and then in December 1945 a regulation vested all property temporarily with the AMG, retroactive to one week before the Americans landed in Korea.[34]

Economic and social reforms that were deemed necessary in conquered Japan the military command rejected in liberated Korea. Indeed, occupation authorities in Korea soon developed a hostility toward personnel from Tokyo in the nominally superior Japanese occupation. As Governor General A. L. Lerch, in charge of military government under Hodge, publicly referred to a SCAP representative: "He comes here from Tokyo, and tells me there are too many little children working in factories, and we must change this and change that. I told him, 'As long as I am Military Governor, we change nothing.' "[35]

The AMG consistently opposed land reform of any kind and shelved even modest reform proposals for the Japanese-owned land, the best available, which the occupation had confiscated. And since the People's Republic had already distributed the land to the peasants without charge, the occupation's essential function was to reimpose the prewar land system under its own control. Washington, too, endorsed this policy when the Department of State's economic mission in 1947 sanguinely concluded, ". . . on the basis of several opinion polls, the Koreans preferred to wait for the establishment of a Provisional Government before proceeding with land reform."[36]

The one innovation that the AMG did impose on the Japanese rental system only further handicapped the peasant. The Japanese took a fixed portion of only rice, but the AMG demanded an equal portion of all grain. Finally, in October 1946 the State Department directed the AMG to sell the land. There were approximately 1,000,000 acres of Japanese-owned land in Korea, over four-fifths of it in the south. The Koreans in the north distributed it to needy peasants, and the AMG sold the land in the south to anyone able to pay the price. The land therefore passed into the hands of landlords, businessmen, and war- and black-market profiteers. While legally the sale was limited to around 30 acres per buyer, exceptions were common.[37]

The continued strength and popularity of the People's Committees in the provinces led to the occupation's determination to centralize and strengthen the police system, leaving no vestige of responsibility to a local authority. Beginning in early 1946, the Americans quickly greatly exceeded the Japanese police centralization. Supervising the process was an American, Colonel William Maglin, a professional policeman who at the time candidly outlined the program: "What we did after sending the Japs home, was to push the Koreans up, and . . . incorporating all the young men who had been helping the policy. . . . Many people question . . . keeping men trained by the Japanese. But many men are born policemen. We felt if they did a good job for the Japanese, they would do a good job for us."[38] Another AMG officer, however, characterized the police chiefs as men whom the Japanese had decorated ". . . for their cruelty and efficacy in suppressing Korean nationalism."[39] An American police adviser was sent to each province, in addition to a group in Seoul. These advisers, John Caldwell, an information officer who was strongly anti-Communist and pro-Rhee, later wrote, ". . . were themselves convinced through race prejudice, ignorance, . . . that the 'gooks' only understood force."[40] Soon, Caldwell recalled, such functionaries were providing American direction to wanton physical torture of the population.

By the summer of 1946 the police force had grown from a few despised men in hiding at the time of Japan's defeat to a belligerent force of 25,000 enthusiastic to aid the United States occupation and the political ambitions of the Right. Thus began a significant, intimate link between the police and the AMG until the end of the occupation in 1948. And, as a senior Korean official pointed out to a UN representative in 1948, in reality ". . . the inside power of the Department of Police . . . is more or less controlled by the occupation forces."[41]

Soviet-American Negotiations

General Hodge understood almost immediately after landing that negotiations with the Russians on unifying the two zones in order to fulfill the joint policy of a four-power trusteeship would fail because of the "insurmountable obstacle" of continued ". . . separation of the country into two parts under opposed ideologies."[42] But during September he was ready to reestablish some contact, if only in terms of trade between the two zones. This remained particularly true of coal and electric power, since the north traditonally had supplied both to the agricultural south. But his conviction that the Soviet consul in Seoul was "assisting the Korean Communist movement" tempered his desire for economic exchange.[43] Until December, therefore, the two occupation zones made no plans or agreements on the question of moving from military occupation to four-power trusteeship.

At the Moscow Foreign Ministers Conference in December 1945, Byrnes and Molotov agreed to instruct the two commands in Korea to establish a joint commission to prepare for Korean unity and independence. The new commission's first order of business was to consult with representative Korean leaders on establishing a provisional, all-Korean government and to reorganize economic exchange between the two zones. Delegates of the two military governments met between March and May 1946 in an atmosphere of intense animosity, and, as could have been anticipated, adjourned *sine die* on May 6.

The principal problems during the negotiations were disputes over which

Koreans to consult and the extreme anti-Soviet attitude of the American command. The Soviets insisted that the commission could not consult with Koreans who opposed the Moscow Agreement providing for five years of trusteeship, thereby excluding the rightist groups. While all Koreans were disappointed, only the Right staged violent protests against the agreement. The Americans demanded that they consult each Korean organization and assume each to be of equal importance, regardless of their relative membership. The Right was fragmented into hundreds of "parties," some comprising no more than a family. The Left organizations, on the other hand, were mass-based, each representing thousands of members. The two commands prepared a list of the organizations in their zone, and the United States submitted seventeen rightist parties and only three from the Left, excluding the largest organizations. At the very same time, the AMG was arresting and intimidating the leaders of the Left, creating an atmosphere of fear and hostility.

The other complicating factor was the attitude of the United States command. General Albert Brown, the United States representative, was outspoken in his belief in the imminence of war with the USSR, and his behavior on the commission reflected this conviction. General Hodge's political adviser publicly commented while the meetings were under way that "I believe in the inevitability and necessity of conflict with Russia. . . ."[44] Preston Goodfellow, the political adviser to Military Governor Lerch, urged an unyielding position during the talks, for he believed that the United States could force the Russians out of Korea as it had pressured them out of Iran.[45]

The Emergence of Resistance

By the spring of 1946 an AMG opinion poll in Seoul revealed that 49 percent of the people preferred the Japanese occupation to the compounded miseries of their "liberation" by the United States. This unflattering fact stimulated Washington to insist that the AMG make an effort to organize a moderate Korean administration and play down its support of the extreme Right. As a result, Leonard Bertch, Hodge's political adviser, unsuccessfully attempted to create a conservative-center coalition with the moderate rightist Kim Kieu Sic and the former head of the People's Republic, the liberal Lyuh Woon Heung. But nothing came of the effort, for Rhee and his followers were retained in the crucial administrative posts, especially in the police and judicial systems.

These new gestures on the part of a few AMG officers, working with several moderate political leaders, did nothing to change the desperate economic misery to which the wage controls, pressures on the peasants, spiraling inflation, and police terrorism had driven the Korean masses. Inevitably, the caldron exploded. In September the Korean Federation of Labor petitioned the AMG for higher wages and rice allotments to alleviate the workers' conditions and received no reply. On September 23 the railway workers in Pusan went on strike; again the federation appealed to the AMG, again with no answer. The federation then called a general strike—and over 300,000 workers left their jobs. In Taegu, the south's third largest city, police brutally smashed a picket line and subsequent fighting resulted in forty-one dead. On October 4 the AMG declared martial law and United States troops began to arrest strikers. At this stage, the national pride of even antilabor Koreans was outraged. Over 100,000 students walked out in solidarity with the workers. In the reign of terror that followed, United States troops arrested large numbers, killing many in the process. Ultimately, 16 of the 1,342 arrested were condemned to death by the military courts, and 557 others were sentenced to prison for "crimes against the occupation." In the thirty-five years of Japanese tyranny there was no precedent for such repression. Even the conservatives blamed the United States for the conditions leading to the revolt. During October the AMG continued to arrest leading intellectuals and labor leaders for circulating literature "disrespectful" to the occupation.[46]

The revolt soon spread to the countryside, primarily against the sadistic Korean police, but in many cases the peasants also rose against their landlords. In the months that followed, the Communist and non-Communist Left and the Federation of Labor were effectively driven underground by the terror of the AMG and the police. The jails were filled, and hundreds of the dissidents fled to the hills—opening a new phase in Korea's history.

It was against this background of the mass revolts, a general strike, and police terror that the Americans offered their first lesson in democracy. As early as February 1946 the AMG had decided to prepare for an election for a provisional legislature in its zone. There were problems, however. At that time Hodge's intelligence had informed him that the Left was certain to win a fair election. The dilemma, therefore, was how to conduct an election that would guarantee a rightist victory. After careful planning, the AMG arranged to predetermine the results in an indirect four-stage election. To make doubly certain that all went well, according to AMG officer George Meade, the American provincial information officers were instructed in

Seoul by the High Command ". . . that while the State Department expected Military Government to continue operating behind a façade of neutrality, the Americans were expected to make every effort to secure a rightist victory."[47] The majority of the administrative posts were in the hands of Korean rightist appointees who handled the election details. They, in turn, applied the Japanese franchise laws, which gave the vote only to landlords, taxpayers, and village headmen. October was also an opportune time for the Right, for the elections immediately followed the revolts and most of the Left was in prison or in hiding. Not surprisingly, it was a sweeping victory for the Right. As one cynical AMG official commented, "This is quite an election. . . . First, they let Syngman Rhee's boys decide the procedure. Second, to make sure nothing slips up, they hold the election in a series of four levels, so that the undesirables might be eliminated. Third, they let only family heads, or heads of ten families, vote. . . . They put all possible opposition in jail, or drive it into the hills. Then they leave us nine days to announce and explain the election to the illiterate farmers."[48] According to McCune, "[i]n most areas there was literally no election at all. . . ."[49] This American lesson in democracy, however, provided a useful precedent for Syngman Rhee.

After the strikes and revolts of September and October, the AMG decided to supplement the police with an additional force. Throughout 1946 the rightist political parties had maintained private squads of young toughs, and the AMG had tended to ignore their atrocities while severely punishing instances of Left terrorism. In the fall, however, the Americans sought to establish an organized and permanent youth corps that could handle internal political insurrection and form the nucleus of a Korean army when the United States withdrew its occupying forces. As its leader and organizer, the AMG chose a former OSS agent, Lee Bum Suk, provided him with $333,000, plus equipment worth much more, to set up his "School for Leaders," and assigned an American colonel to advise the organization. According to Lee, the curriculum of the school included ". . . methods of combatting strikes. And history of the *Hitler Jugend*."[50] The director of the school, who had been an enthusiastic member of Hitler's youth in Germany for three years, explained, "We base our instruction on the German youth movement because the Germans are the only people who really know how to organize young men." The American adviser called them his "boy scouts."[51] By the end of 1946, therefore, the United States had fostered in its zone in Korea the development of a regime as ruthless and oppressive as any to emerge in the postwar period.

North Korea

In the north the Soviets encouraged the People's Committees to become the governing units and usually passed any directive to the Korean people through them. In January 1946, Kim Il Sung, a Communist and national hero of the guerilla war, became the head of the North Korean administration. Since it in no way interfered with Soviet interests, the People's Committees in the north began to implement the program of the republic. In March 1946 they introduced a basic land reform granting farms based on family size to 725,000 landless or land-short peasants, distributing nearly 2.5 million acres formerly belonging to the Japanese, collaborators, or those who deserted the land and fled south when the Soviets liberated North Korea. But there was no effort at collectivization.

The People's Committees nationalized the basic industries, but in October 1946 laid down limitations on nationalization that provided for the sale to Koreans of small, Japanese-owned consumer goods industries and ordered "The Departments of Justice and Industry, for the purpose of encouraging the development of private business enterprises, are to draft laws and plan procedures for the development of commercial activity. . . ."[52] To accomplish their plan for doubling production in 1947, the Koreans in the north introduced a massive education program for technical experts and skilled laborers. In one month alone, January 1947, 1,500 experts and 20,000 skilled workers completed training. They also passed extensive worker welfare decrees in 1946 regulating working hours, vacations, and social insurance.

The American command had frequently reported that the Russians were stripping the northern zone of industrial equipment as they had Manchuria. At the end of May 1946, however, Edwin Pauley was able to visit and observe the Soviet zone and reported to Truman that, on the contrary, the Soviets ". . . are devoting considerable effort to rejuvenate economic activity in Northern Korea."[53]

All these factors contrasted sharply with the conditions in the south.

Toward a Separate State

As early as 1947 Washington had determined to establish an independent state in the southern zone of Korea. During March, Hodge returned to the United States for consultations, and Rhee also met in Washington with

General John H. Hilldring, assistant secretary of state for occupied territories, and secured American support for his program for an independent state in the south. At the Moscow Foreign Ministers Conference that very month, however, the Russians surprised the American delegation by agreeing to consultations with the rightist organizations. The result was that the United States and Soviets decided to resume negotiations of their deadlocked talks on unity in May.[54]

If there had ever been a possibility of fruitful negotiations in Korea, they had been buried by the intervening events. After the United States and Soviets had resumed their talks in Seoul, Rhee incited his followers to violent street demonstrations to oppose the negotiations. The irritated Russians again proposed that they exclude the rightists entirely, at which point the AMG, in effect, encouraged them to openly attack the USSR. The situation deteriorated rapidly; on July 19, People's Republic leader Lyuh Woon Heung was assassinated, and a week later Rhee's toughs molested members of the Soviet delegation in Seoul. The Soviets complained that the United States continued to insist on consulting businessmen and hostile rightists as representative of the Koreans in the south while banning Left groups and jailing their leaders, though American officials admitted that these Left organizations represented tens of thousands of members.[55]

In the midst of the summer negotiations, a prominent Korean in the United States, Kim Yong-jeung, toured the United States zone and on his return wrote his impressions to Edwin Locke, Jr., then vice-president of Chase National Bank and a contact with President Truman on Asian affairs. "In South Korea there is no law and order. Gangsterism rules through intimidation, threats, extortion, violence and murder. . . . The situation grows from bad to worse. A civil war is brewing in South Korea and may break out at any time. . . . the American Command seems to be frozen by its communist-phobia." Kim included many grim details which Locke found impressive enough to send to the President, and Truman answered on August 15. "Korea, of course, is in a bad way," he acknowledged, "and we all feel sorry about it but nearly every place where the Russians have a thing to do with affairs, political or otherwise, there is a mess. I don't know of anything we can do about it at the present time."[56] On the contrary, on that very day the State Department publicly declared that it ". . . wishes to state categorically that there is but one American policy toward Korea and that General Hodge has faithfully and consistently acted in conformance therewith. . . ."[57]

The Role of the UN

As the unification negotiations reached an impasse, Robert Lovett proposed turning the entire question over to the UN for a solution. The Russians responded that instead each occupying power should withdraw its troops by January 2, 1948. Lovett had the UN Commission in Greece as the precedent for his proposal, and the Soviets were convinced that with the withdrawal of foreign troops the Left would easily take control of the entire Korean peninsula. Lovett's proposal also called for each occupying power to arrange its own election in its own way, followed by a merger of the two zones with representation weighted according to the distribution of population. With the majority in the south, the plan would have guaranteed a unified legislature overwhelmingly controlled by the southern rightists. The UN, in Washington's view, was to provide international sanction to a policy already well under way in Washington and Seoul—a unified Korea under United States domination or a separate state in the south.

In October 1947 the United States introduced a resolution in the UN General Assembly calling for a temporary commission to observe national assembly elections throughout Korea to be held before March 31, 1948.[58] The Soviets argued that the resolution had no place under the Moscow Agreement; that the UN should consult with representatives of the north and south before setting up a commission; and that foreign troops should withdraw before elections. Not surprisingly, the General Assembly ignored the Russian objections and passed the American resolution. No less surprising, the Soviets boycotted the vote and indicated that they would not accept any Assembly decision on the issue.

Despite the obvious impossibility of observing all-Korean elections, given the Soviet opposition, the UN set up an interim committee to oversee the resolution that in turn appointed a commission of lesser diplomats and journalists from Canada, France, Australia, China, El Salvador, India, the Philippines, and Syria to proceed to Korea as observers. On arriving, the commission found itself totally compromised by its complete dependence on the AMG. The Soviets would not permit it to cross the 38th parallel, and in the south it was unable to consult with any Korean other than the representatives of the Right. As it pointed out in its second report to the UN, the commission ". . . experienced considerable difficulty in making contact with the left-wing organizations, certain of whose representatives were found to be either in prison, under order of arrest or some form of police surveillance."[59] Clearly, under the circumstances, the commission was unable to carry out its mandate. Yet the United States and the involved governments mounted pressures to observe elections south of the 38th parallel only later that spring. The commission members vainly resisted, but ultimately succumbed and finally sanctioned the south's venture in democracy.

But while the Rhee rightists and the United States command were jubilant, all other groups in South Korea strongly opposed the decision to hold exclusively southern elections. To even the rightist opposition, elections were tantamount to a decision to divide the country permanently and place power in the hands of the Rhee clique. Rhee, for his part, celebrated the decision with a large rally in honor of the UN commission. There, as UN representatives watched in horror, Rhee's toughs mutilated several leftists and vividly illustrated the conditions under which elections would occur.[60]

The election preparations led to protest riots and a new wave of arrests in the spring of 1948, yielding over eight thousand new prisoners. When the increasingly uncomfortable UN commission suggested an amnesty, Hodge denied there were political prisoners in the United States zone. The dissension within the UN commission itself began when the UN Interim Committee forced them to proceed to observe elections about which they now had grave doubts. The Australian and Canadian delegates insisted that the commission was not obliged to accept the advice of the committee, while the Chinese and Philippine members released a statement that they were going to observe an election in the south. The Australian delegate suggested that they reject the advice of the committee and withdraw from Korea by mid-April, basing his stand on the fact that all parties except Rhee's had boycotted the election and that of the fifteen members on the Military Government's appointed election committee, twelve belonged to Rhee's party. The Canadian representative opposed the advice of the Interim Committee because it was ". . . completely contrary to the judgment of the Commission, shared almost unanimously by its members and conveyed to the Interim Committee by Mr. Menon [of India]. . . . If the argument of unity failed, the basis for United Nations participation in the election vanishes. . . ."[61] The Indian and French representatives insisted that the role of the commission was neither one of legality nor objectivity, but that it was strictly political, and it must accept the strictly political advice of the Interim Committee: "We have had a political decision by a political body based on political considerations."[62] After some pressure from the governments of the recalcitrant members, the commission then, quite cynically, decided to observe an election in the south as an instrument of international politics, which, after all, it was designed to serve.

On March 25, 1948, the North Korean leaders invited the opposition leaders in the south to a conference on April 14 to form an alternative plan to that of the UN Interim Committee. They called for a boycott of the election in the south and the organization of a unified election by secret ballot. Some rightists, such as Kim Koo and Kim Kieu Sic, accepted the invitation to the conference in the interest of Korean unity, trusting the nationalist instincts of the north above the reactionary, personal interests of Rhee. But nothing came of the meeting, and Kim Koo returned to attack the Communists—but also to boycott the elections.[63]

The May 1948 Election and the New Republic

The election was set for May 10, and as the State Department's account reported, "The responsibility for preparing for the elections and conducting them fell upon the United States Army Military Government in Korea, which had the task of planning and preparing the mechanical details involved in a democratic election, with which the Korean people are unfamiliar. . . ."[64] The entire question of UN observation was patently farcical, for there were thirty UN representatives available to observe a population of 20 million. Yet despite the superficiality, details of terror increasingly colored the commission's reports. The implications alarmed the French delegate, who tried to keep the records confidential, but the Syrian refused in any way to modify the factual data and insisted that they be made public.

Police excesses and the wanton violence of Rhee's bands of youth were the most obvious characteristics of the electoral campaign and the actual balloting. In addition, the AMG authorized the police, in the interest of "law and order" during the campaign, ". . . to deputize large bands of 'loyal citizens,' called Community Protective Associations."[65] These associations continued to patrol the countryside even after the election until their terrorist acts became so repugnant that the AMG dissolved them on May 22. Individuals with police records were barred from voting, which, of course, included most of the Left and moderate liberals in Korea. Since the Left and the nationalist Right boycotted the election, the election committee chose the slate of candidates from Rhee's party and placed them on the ballot either as independents or under the party name. In the ten days preceding the election, 323 persons were killed in riots or police raids and more than 10,000 arrested. The State Department's history reports that ". . . almost 80 percent of the eligible voters registered, and [on May 10] . . . an estimated 92.5 percent of these cast their ballots in an election characterized by . . . public approval and enthusiasm."[66] These seemingly impressive figures ignored the fact that large blocs of the population were either barred from participating or boycotted the election, and that many of those who voted did so under coercion.

While the diplomats debated the propriety of the election, Rhee grasped the opportunity to strengthen his control over the south, becoming scarcely more than a Korean Chiang—a reactionary who based his power on corrupt personal nepotism and cliques rather than representing the interests of any national class in the modern economic sense. Ultimately, however, his power was based on America's presence and endorsement over three years of occupation, and he proceeded to intensify the terror and torture that were already commonplace under United States military rule.

On August 15, 1948, the American occupation of Korea formally came to an end, concluding, as Paul Hoffman recalled a year later, ". . . a very bright spot in American history. . . . I was very proud of what the Army had done there, not only in its own field, but also in the economic field. . . . I considered it a very good job and it is a pleasure to say so."[67] The official responsibility was over, but the defining American influence remained.

Against the express wishes of all political groups save an extreme contingent of the right-wing, an independent government was established in the southern half of Korea. The National Assembly met on May 31 and elected Rhee President. Rhee then appointed Lee Bum Suk, head of the youth bands, as Prime Minister and defense minister, and the chief of the Korean police as foreign minister. The United States did not recognize the new regime immediately, dutifully waiting for the UN to certify that the election had been representative. These events in the south made inevitable a new, yet more profound crisis in all of Korea.

The North Koreans responded predictably to these developments by holding elections on August 25 for a Supreme Peoples Council, with clandestine balloting in the south. On September 9 they formally organized the Democratic Peoples Republic and claimed jurisdiction over the whole of Korea. The southern regime responded by arresting over 1,300 persons on suspicion of having participated in the Pyongyang underground election.

While the developments in the United States occupation of Korea were virtually unknown to the American people before June 1950, Washington was fully aware of events there and the Military Government's political decisions conformed to official policy. The early discussions on the extent of United States support for specific rightist factions were conducted with a view toward excluding the Left from power. Within that fundamental assumption, and confronted by the massive popular support for the leftist People's Republic, the subsequent events might have varied in detail, but they were essentially inevitable in their larger contours. As the United States discovered again and again, in every area of the Third World where it sought to impose its influence, its real options for internal control were limited to revolution or reaction. There was, in fact, no reliable alternative. Yet the evidence of its direct administration of the southern half of Korea revealed that the United States exceeded the Japanese in the repression and terror that it fostered in suppressing a popular revolution and eventually establishing a rightist police state.

The United States has always preferred docile comprador regimes to direct administration in its colonial role, and in Korea its only alternative was to vest power in the landholding class. But the right-wing landholders were not sufficiently trustworthy, for the commitment of many of the right-wing leaders to national aspirations and eventual unity with the north was in conflict with America's aims for the area. So the United States opted for Rhee, the comprador, whose dedication was less to Korea or its landholding class than to the power of his own small clique. Little did Washington realize the eventual costs, in blood and money, its commitment would demand, or the profound impact it would have on America's role and power in the world.

11

The Dilemma of Japan

Japan emerged from World War II crushed as a military power but completely intact as an organized state. This fact, which created a very different situation from that existing in Germany, had been anticipated, even planned for, by the United States. And as the military threat of the imperialist nation receded, and as civil war swept China and the expanding resistance movements throughout the Far East challenged not only Japanese conquest but the prewar *status quo* as well, Japan inevitably became a vital element in thwarting what Washington perceived as the greater immediate danger of the Left in Asia. After the surrender, the United States command ordered the Japanese troops to maintain control in China and the colonial areas until representatives acceptable to the United States could impose their hegemony. In Japan itself government circles explicitly understood that military defeat would not lead to the destruction of the ruling class. On the contrary, many key leaders expected that American forces would provide a shield against an anticipated internal revolution. "Defeat may lower our national prestige, but British and American opinion has not gone to the length of contemplating making changes in the structure of Japanese State," Prince Konoye advised the Emperor in February 1945. "What we should fear most is the possibility of a Communist revolution following defeat."[1]

The question of retaining the Emperor was a critical index to the future of Japan's ruling class. And Washington formally resolved this issue in the affirmative no later than May 1945, although Stimson insisted ". . . for certain military reasons, not divulged, . . . that the matter should remain temporarily in abeyance."[2] Implicitly, this decision acknowledged the nature of the war itself as a struggle between imperial powers that in the end might unite against the common enemy of a potential revolutionary movement among the masses, a force that their rivalry and conflict had immeasurably helped to create and then release.

Of paramount consideration to the men in Washington as they surveyed Japan in defeat was its future role as the only industrial power in Asia—excluding the USSR—and, given the chaos on the mainland of China, it was likely to remain so for many years. This brought all the considerations of United States economic war aims to bear on the policy debates. Japan's future role would be shaped by those who directed the occupation in the postwar years. During the war the United States had decided that, unlike Germany, Japan would undergo no zonal division and the United States alone would exercise complete authority as the major occupying force. Although sheer military and economic power determined American predominance, Britain, China, and the Commonwealth countries, even more than the USSR, were convinced that they had real interests at stake and deserved a major voice in the reorganization of Japan. The outcome of this conflict, while predestined, added a significant strain to the increasingly frayed relations between the United States and its wartime allies. Washington was united on the minimal role its former allies were to play, but its own internal differences on American occupation policy were still intense when the war ended.

Planning Japan's Future

Although those responsible for planning for Japan had formulated and resolved the most crucial debates much earlier, the specific directive for the occupation was only rather belatedly approved on August 12. As the product of debate and compromise, the initial postdefeat policy document, which remained the basic directive for the occupation's first two years, was an amalgam of a number of essentially contradictory policies and impulses, including vengeance and punishment, preservation of the old order and an intent to undermine it radically, and the curious, ethnocentric American assumption, to be found in the policy toward both Germany and Japan, that American institutions and ideology are *ipso facto* virtuous and universal and can be transferred virtually intact to any nation. In Japan the presence of General Douglas MacArthur as the Supreme Commander underlined this cultural egoism.[3]

The most conspicuous hand in formulating the policy toward postwar Japan during the war was that of Joseph Grew, ambassador in Tokyo for the ten years preceding the war and a conservative who had observed with some sympathy Japan's imperial expansion during the 1930's. Grew believed that American interests rested with the conservative, capitalist ruling circles, who had indeed profited from Japanese expansion but could profit as well by peaceful trade in cooperation with American economic aims. He opposed any plans to introduce democracy in Japan, and until the spring of 1945, planning for the peace, primarily under his direction as chief of the Far East division, contemplated little change in Japanese society beyond demilitarization. Grew retired at the end of the war, but the most critical mark that he left on the final policy was that the United States would retain the Emperor and operate through the existing Japanese government, both the symbols and instruments of the old ruling class.

Others in the military and the State Department, especially those who were China experts, resisted this course and advocated a fundamental change in Japan, a more punitive peace, and reparations to substantially weaken the Asian power vis-à-vis its neighbors and to purge it of "militarism." Byrnes reinforced this viewpoint when he became secretary of state, as did pressure from the allies. Their claim, as with Germany, that Japanese cultural institutions were martial, or that the military spirit was endemic in the Japanese character, was both an absurd internalization of wartime propaganda and a convenient, quite ideological avoidance of the root causes of war and conflict. The origins of the war with Japan, which need not overly detain us here, were akin to the conflict of interests that drove the capitalist powers of Europe to fight World War I, and can eventually be traced to rival imperial interests for markets and raw materials in Southeast Asia and China. While Japan internally was a police state, its drive to expansion had in it the same forces that stirred the British to expand from island to empire a century or more earlier. In any case, given the general mood at the end of the war the policy planners could scarcely concede, either to themselves, to the public, or to their allies, that the United States had fought the war merely to rebuild the prewar Japan with all its repugnant features of a fascist police state.[4]

The final American policy, therefore, specified a democratization of Japan, providing for civil liberties, trade union rights, destruction of monopolies, land reform, and an extensive purge of individuals who participated in Japanese wartime policies, but all within the framework of the old order, using the instruments of the Emperor and the Japanese government to implement these basic changes in Japanese society and to purge the leading members of their own class. Reflecting the ambiguous and contradictory debates in Washington, occupation policy concluded that the Japanese people also had the right of revolution without interference from the occupying forces; but given Washington's prolonged consideration of the value of the Emperor and the threat of the Left in Asia, that right proved as abstract as the Americans' right to revolution in their own Declaration of Independence. At the time, however, such liberal reforms seemed a small price. And except for Grew, few suspected that the formal civil liberties, which had never threatened the capitalist social order in the United States, could, in Japan, undermine the foundations of conservative control. Grew understood, but he retired from the State Department at the end of the war. To those who assumed responsibility for Japan immediately after the war, it seemed reasonable that a conservative Japan, albeit reformed in the manner of America, could assume a crucial role of stability in Asia and in world trade.[5]

Armed with such an ambivalent directive, the American forces entered Japan without resistance in September 1945 to begin an occupation that was to last seven years, with a policy that would pass from equivocation to purpose as its latent meanings, and America's real interests, came into sharper focus.

The Allies and the Occupation

The American decision to monopolize decision-making powers in the occupation created early and lasting animosity among the other nations who had fought the war against Japan. The British and Australians, in particular, believed their most basic interests to be at stake in the questions of reparations, demilitarization, and the economic reforms which they expected to undercut Japan's competitive advantage in the world markets.

In August 1945 Ernest Bevin suggested that the Big Four powers, plus Australia, establish a Control Council in Tokyo to deal with all questions, other than military, relating to Japan. Australia and New Zealand in turn called for a hard peace and the arrest of the Emperor as a war criminal. Faced with these demands, the United States announced the organization of a Far East Advisory Commission of eleven nations to consult with and to advise, but in no sense control, the occupation. Reluctantly the British eventually accepted the invitation, intending to alter the organization's scope and powers at the first meeting. The Russians, however, resented this arbitrary definition of their status and on September 7 Harriman notified Byrnes that the Soviets intended to discuss the control of Japan as a primary

subject at the London Foreign Ministers Conference in September. When
Molotov raised the question with Byrnes in London, the secretary, though
fully forewarned, insisted that he was not prepared to discuss the matter. Molotov responded by indicating reticence to consider anything else.
The conference ended after twenty-one days with no progress on any question.[6]

While Byrnes insisted that the question was only a minor issue, the
Russians could hardly agree. The affront to the dignity of the USSR as a
great power, being relegated with eight minor states to an advisory commission, seriously irritated Stalin. He had already had an acrimonious exchange
with Truman over the Kuriles in August, and in his exceptional conversations with Harriman in October 1945, Japan was the only topic he wished
to discuss. After angrily complaining that his representative in Tokyo was
being treated ". . . like a piece of extra furniture," Stalin outlined the
treatment befitting a great nation, and then turned to the substantive question and suggested a Control Commission similar to those in Hungary,
Rumania, and Bulgaria.[7] The proposition revealed that the Russian was
interested in form rather than substance, since the Control Commissions in
Eastern Europe were powerless. Stalin concurred that MacArthur should
have full authority in Japan, and even suggested that it might be preferable
for the USSR to become "isolationist" and withdraw completely, as Japan
was clearly in the United States' sphere of influence. Harriman demurred,
unwilling to set a precedent of this nature or to carry the Eastern European
analogy too far, since the Americans were then actively pressing for full
tripartite control in that area.

Harriman advised the State Department to accept an arrangement based
on the European precedent, for it would relieve real tension without sacrificing any authority. But Washington resisted the mere word "control," in
part because of the British and Australian demands for a greater share but
also because of MacArthur's adamant opposition. A compromise was
finally reached after lengthy negotiations, and the foreign ministers accepted it at their Moscow Conference in December. The agreement provided for an Allied Council in Tokyo of the four powers to consult and
advise MacArthur and a Far Eastern Commission (FEC) of eleven nations
in Washington which would formulate broad policy and approve all fundamental changes in Japan. Each of the four powers had a veto, a concession
to the Soviets, but in practice, since the British, Chinese, and Soviets were
usually in agreement, the veto later reinforced the United States' *de facto*
control. By the time the FEC and Allied Council held their first meetings,

much had transpired in Japan that greatly circumvented their limited position of authority.[8]

The Occupation Government

One of MacArthur's key aides had early announced that there would be no military government in Japan, and those trained for the function would be sent to Korea, where a military government was required—and where the United States confronted a Left republic of the resistance movement rather than a reactionary cabinet such as it faced in Japan.[9] The United States nevertheless installed an immense bureaucracy in Tokyo to carry out the demilitarization and the reformation of Japanese society.

In choosing General Douglas MacArthur as Supreme Commander of the occupation, Washington added a dimension of personal conflict that was completely absent in the administration of Germany. For although it would be an error to view MacArthur as an innovator of policy in Japan, the entire occupation was under his egocentric shadow. His overwhelming personal vanity demanded fealty from his staff and a public image of himself as the personal creator of Japan's "spiritual revolution." For this reason he tolerated neither the Allied Council nor the State Department representatives—who all implied that he shared his authority with other powers. From the beginning he overstepped his authority by casually issuing pronouncements to the press that were in conflict with policy in Washington, causing general consternation and anger in the White House.

Within Japan, MacArthur intentionally cast an image of unapproachable authority. He refused to meet any Japanese socially, and during his entire presence in Japan he never spoke to any Japanese other than the Emperor and the top government officials—numbering no more than a dozen individuals. Very few members of his staff, for that matter, ever discussed with him the nature of the problems they faced. It was critical to MacArthur's ego that Japan achieve its "spiritual rebirth" in appearance if not in fact, and the phalanx of sycophants who shielded him presented their reports in the most optimistic light.

MacArthur's penchant for flattery and obsequiousness soon convinced him that the Emperor and Japanese government's cooperation revealed their genuine—and sufficient—reformation. But it is vital to understand that all the reforms of the first two years, whose basic outlines were formulated in Washington, meshed well with MacArthur's schoolbook view of Americanism, and he continued to back them vigorously even after they were no longer functional to Washington's larger strategy. Yet to his military mind the liberties of trade union organization, political activity, and the like were merely decorative attachments to a tranquil and orderly society. When the use of the new liberties led to inevitable conflict, MacArthur instinctively reacted against those audacious enough to employ them.[10]

Below MacArthur, however, on a more bureaucratic level that at times passed by him, the Supreme Command of the Allied Powers (SCAP) was, from the beginning, torn by internal tensions on the best way to proceed in Japan. The two major divisions worked at cross purposes on the basis of both ideology and personal rivalries. One division dealt with the questions of civil administration, and it operated directly through the Japanese government to implement all reforms. Under the conservative but literal-minded General Courtney Whitney, the division was staffed by younger officers and civilian specialists in such areas as civil liberties, labor, and antitrust, some of whom were sincerely dedicated to implementing democratic changes in Japanese society. The Public Safety Division, responsible for the occupying forces, demilitarization, intelligence, repatriation, and supplies, under General Charles Willoughby, opposed the liberal reforms and reformers. As the months passed, General Willoughby used the Counter Intelligence Corps, ostensibly established to watch Japanese ultranationalists, to keep the Japanese Left and the liberal Americans under surveillance. When United States policy shifted and the reforms were increasingly frustrated, the "idealists" resigned and more conservative men replaced them. It is important to note, however, that the occupation did not reflect a civil-military dispute. William Sebald, the representative of the State Department after September 1946, was generally more opposed to the reforms and more concerned with a Communist threat in Japan than was MacArthur. Nevertheless, the warring factions in the SCAP bureaucracy added significant confusion to the entire occupation.[11]

SCAP's Relations with the Allied Council

MacArthur had vigorously opposed the formation of the Allied Council, and after it was organized he ignored it and his staff made its work as difficult as possible. Orders in headquarters were to ". . . talk the Council to death," and the council's first two meetings set the tone for its subsequent history.[12] At the inaugural session MacArthur made his only appearance and reminded the members that they were only advisory and would have no authority whatsoever in Japan. At the second meeting, in answer to a question from the Soviet member on the progress of the purge program, General Whitney gave an angry three-hour speech for an answer which, according to W. Macmahon Ball, the Australian representative of the British Commonwealth, ". . . could have been given in five or ten minutes."[13]

In response to a legitimate question by one of the members, Whitney angrily informed the council that it ". . . is not set up for the purpose of prying into SCAP affairs, attempting to find a weak point in SCAP armor. . . ."[14] During the entire history of the council any attempt to secure information as a basis for well-informed advice was regarded as a personal affront to General MacArthur. After the April 1946 elections, scarcely a month after the organization of the council, SCAP no longer controlled the Japanese government through public directives but via informal private contacts. SCAP insisted that all fundamental directives which the Allied Council was qualified to examine had been issued between September 1945 and January 1946; yet all the basic laws and institutional changes involving the Constitution, land reform, or *zaibatsu* were considered after April 1946. Only twice did SCAP ask the council to offer any substantive advice: on land reform and a desperate SCAP attempt to halt inflation in 1947.

SCAP particularly resented Commonwealth representative Ball's criticisms. They felt that he in particular should support the United States on every position. To the Russian, K. N. Derevyanko, SCAP expressed extreme hostility, though Ball felt that he ". . . behaved consistently in a friendly and dignified way."[15] It was not long, as Ball recalled, that, for the council, "[t]here were no problems of Japan: every problem of Japan came to be considered for its effects on Russian-American relations."[16] But this did not prevent the United States from generally being outvoted three to one in the council, a fact which in August 1946 led the State Department unsuccessfully to propose that the seven additional members of the Far Eastern Commission be added to the Allied Council.

Dilemmas of Reform and Reconstruction

The political and economic context in which the occupation operated provided the backdrop for all decisions, since Japan at the end of the war was devastated economically, and the task of reconstruction would have remained formidable even if there had been the most dedicated efforts. For in addition to the horrors of Hiroshima and Nagasaki, 30 to 60 percent of Japan's sixty largest cities had been destroyed in fire-bomb raids, leaving many thousands of the survivors homeless. Compounding the problems of this destruction, soldiers being repatriated were without work, farmers withheld their crops, factories were idle. There remained innumerable questions of the resolution of reparations and the disposal or conversion of military plants. Added to the miseries of the war-devastated nation was the critical world food shortage in the winter of 1945–1946, and the Japanese also suffered acutely from hunger. SCAP was forced to import food from the United States to prevent actual starvation.

The war created the most extreme miseries, but compounding them was the fact that between the surrender and the occupation the Japanese government had distributed billions of yen worth of food and raw materials to leading industrialists and politicians. Given the extreme shortages in Japan, these goods were hoarded and sifted into the black market for several years, vastly enlarging the profits of the ruling class during a period when its future was still ambiguous. Inflation was the natural outcome of a shortage of goods, the black market, and the reactionary regime, and it continued to mount during the first three years of the occupation. The victims of the war, and of the economic conditions that followed, were, as always, the masses.

A notable aspect of the occupation was the American determination to reform the political and economic institutions with very little regard for the immediate, urgent economic needs of the Japanese people. The basic policy directive granted political rights to the Japanese people, including labor organization, but specified that responsibility for the reconstruction of the economy rested solely with the Japanese government.

In October 1945 SCAP issued a general directive to the government that it alone was responsible for the equitable distribution of food, the control of prices and the black market, and the full employment of labor. SCAP then turned its attention to the "basic reforms," occasionally to be rudely reminded of Japan's economic plight by the activities of the newly organized labor movement or the Communist or Socialist demonstrations on behalf of the working class.

The ultraconservative government had no more incentive to be solicitous of the welfare of the Japanese masses after the war than it had been in the prewar period, and it did nothing to alleviate a situation in which members of its own class were reaping profits. The necessity for the occupation to provide essential imports, to keep order, and to cover the Japanese deficit, without in any way controlling the operation of the economy, implicitly encouraged the government to pursue a socially irresponsible, inflationary economic policy while engaged in a rear-guard action to protect its political privileges as best it could. In November, State Department representative

George Atcheson reported to Washington that the Japanese government had failed to take the first steps toward essential reconstruction and was attempting to sabotage all the political changes as well.[17]

In issuing the first major political reform on October 4, 1945—the so-called Japanese Bill of Rights—MacArthur inadvertently added the spark to the tinderbox of the postwar economic chaos. The directive abolished all laws infringing on civil liberties and trade union rights, freed all political prisoners, and dissolved the secret police. It proved too much for the government of Prince Higasho Kuni, which resigned and was replaced by the Shidehara cabinet, including many of the same individuals and again representing only the old ruling circle in Japan.

Much to the shock of MacArthur and many on his staff, the Japanese masses immediately began to use their new rights in unanticipated ways. The reforms of free speech, assembly, political activity, trade unions, and press were modeled on United States laws and the Americans implicitly expected them to be used—or not used—as in the United States, although the setting in Japan was one of potential revolutionary upheaval.

On October 16, barely a week after the occupation proclaimed the new freedoms, the Japanese Left organized a hunger march to MacArthur's headquarters calling for the distribution of the food known to be hoarded by the government and demanding the resignation of the cabinet and the Emperor. MacArthur, unaccustomed to masses of people out of uniform, carrying red flags, and shouting revolutionary slogans, was thoroughly alarmed. He complained several days later to Truman's special representative, Edwin Locke, Jr., then in Tokyo, that "[m]any of the so-called liberal elements in Japan are Communistic," and at this time he was concerned about "underground communist agitation."[18] Such events reinforced MacArthur's new commitment to preserving the Emperor as a force for stability and further strengthened his support to the ingratiating government. Atcheson, for his part, also reported to the State Department that among the new political organizations, "[u]nfortunately, the most vocal and agressive is the communist group."[19]

As the economic situation deteriorated, the demonstrations and demands for the resignation of the government or for food and wage increases continued, along with strikes and attacks on the old order by the newspaper unions who had taken control of the leading newspapers. SCAP's response to the agitation quickly began to shift from lectures on "the American Way" to repression.

Although in his October 4 directive MacArthur had dismissed all the police chiefs and abolished altogether the elaborate system of secret and "thought control" police, the occupation continued to rely on the regular police system. The new orders to democratize, according to Roger Baldwin of the American Civil Liberties Union, all too often meant ". . . revising the uniform . . . to provide sleeve stripes rather than the existing shoulder boards. . . . the average Japanese lives today in just as great a fear of the police as he did before the occupation. He knows that the police are supported by the occupation troops."[20] The police were cooperative and all too efficient in aiding the occupation in keeping order, which soon meant curtailing popular demonstrations and strikes. And the United States Counter Intelligence Corps soon discovered that their most valuable assistants were former officials in the outlawed Japanese secret police.

To successfully implement the reforms that were radically to alter the Japanese social system would have required either a determined military government or a coalition representing different political views in Japan and, above all, those groups most likely to benefit from the reforms and therefore most zealous to carry them out. Coalition governments were set up in Italy, Hungary, Bulgaria, and Rumania after their surrender, and the Socialists and Communists called for such a government in Japan. To use the old regime, of course, was tacitly to set the limits on social changes, and to introduce new groups at that stage would have been to set Japan on an unacceptable leftward course. Later SCAP could make overtures at a coalition with a few Socialists, but only after it had consolidated the power base for conservative rule.

Instead of organizing a coalition government, SCAP scheduled elections for April 1946, despite the doubts of Atcheson, and later the FEC, that the elections at such an early date could produce a democratic Diet. "We seriously fear," Atcheson wrote to MacArthur on November 9, "that such possibility is very slight indeed, especially as the new political parties lack experience and will not have time to develop their organizations to the point of being in a position to exert sufficient influence on the elections. The number and diversity of the new parties alone constitute strong obstacles against successful competition with well-intrenched and reactionary politicians."[21] Ignoring these cautions, MacArthur proceeded with the election plans.

Although military defeat had seriously undermined the entire ruling class, and it had good cause to fear a revolution without the protection of the occupation, within the context of early electoral politics the established order clearly had the advantage. There was little background in Japanese history for mass participation in politics and even elite parliamentary activity had existed for only a brief period. During the 1920's the developing capitalist interests dominated the ruling class, but still operated through parties that were in reality no more than elite clubs in the literal sense. The electorate, as well, amounted to less than 450,000 out of a population of over 30 million. Several Socialist groupings emerged in the mid-1920's, but were founded on intellectuals and segments of the professions and never had a mass base. Parliamentarianism aside, there was a growing militancy and extralegal political organization among both the workers and agricultural tenants. The Communist Party, organized in 1922, was illegal from the beginning and its leaders were generally in prison or exile.

During the world economic activity of the 1920's Japanese industry expanded peacefully. After the depression, as trade constricted and competition intensified, military revival, imperial expansion, and a fascist internal organization, rather than parliamentarianism, were more appropriate to the needs of all sectors of the ruling class. When the political parties were dissolved in 1940 there was no sense of lost democracy, but only a different form of political expression for the small elite.

With the reintroduction of the parliamentary system in 1945 the traditional conservatives reorganized themselves under new names. The differences between them were minimal, resting primarily on personalities rather than interest. Many of the leaders were later purged for wartime activity, but enough had opposed the war or advocated an early peace to supply the key government posts. The Progressive Party included most of the wartime Diet and was later extensively purged. Perhaps the strongest business interests made up the Liberal Party under the leadership of Ichiro Hatoyama, whom SCAP later purged for the duration of the occupation. The party saw no need to develop a public program beyond anti-Communism and preservation of the throne.[22]

After October 1945 new parties mushroomed, some being no larger than a family, many serving in alliance with the larger conservative parties. The bulk of the population lived in rural areas, where the Left parties, with limited time and even more limited resources, never reached. The countryside tended to vote for familiar figures, and so the conservatives could prepare for the election with some confidence. The Left parties, by contrast, were seriously handicapped in electoral activity. Previously outlawed, and with its leaders released from prison in October, the Communist Party had only six hundred members. Although it made a vigorous start and quickly moved to play a leading role in labor organization and protest demonstrations, it could hardly compete on an electoral basis after only five months of existence. As the party organized in the last months of 1945 it stressed abolition of the Emperor system, a new government committed to the distribution of food, land, and the revival of industry, and a united front of all classes to give enthusiastic support to the occupation. In fact, to SCAP's embarrassment, the program of the CP was closest to the occupation's formal policy.

After January 1946, with the return of Sanzo Nosaka from exile in Yenan, the Communists stressed their universal goal of peaceful revolution through class collaboration, a united front, and patriotism. Such a policy for the party proved awkward as the economic and political conditions deteriorated and many schisms emerged on the question of the class base of the party and its reformist politics. Yet Communist options were distinctly limited under the occupation if it wished to maintain its legal status. The dilemma remained and grew more serious as the years passed—for a continued support of a moderate line midst hunger and economic paralysis threatened to undermine their class base, but in the end it was the occupation that finally determined the Communist course. Their greatest strength continued to be in the trade unions, and one Communist leader claimed by mid-1946 that SCAP often asked them to use their power to prevent strikes. The Communists remained the smallest of the major parties over the first year of the occupation, but they were well financed and more tightly organized. SCAP listed the CP membership as 8,700 in December 1946, and the number nearly doubled by July 1947 to over 16,000.[23]

The Socialist Party was a divided mélange. Many of its right-wing leaders were later purged by the occupation, and its left wing advocated a united front with the CP and a party based exclusively on the working class. The party was continuously on the verge of splitting as one faction or the other gained the ascendency, but it persisted loosely united on a program of nationalization and land reform. Both Left parties had their greatest strength in the trade unions, but lacked the vital rural base essential for electoral victory.

At its first meeting in the spring of 1946 the FEC also issued a warning that the April elections were premature, but MacArthur righteously dismissed their fears as being unwarranted and undemocratic. Their concerns were realized, however, when 363 "parties" took part in the election. The election rules, while mildly reformed in December 1945, still included a limited plural-ballot system which was designed to reinforce the Right.

Almost one-third of the new Diet consisted of "independents," nearly all of whom were profoundly conservative, and the two major conservative parties polled 43 percent of the vote. The Socialists, despite their disadvantages, polled 18 percent of the vote, and the Communists, 3.8 percent. The Liberal Party, with the largest bloc of seats, organized a new government under Shigeru Yoshida, a member of the two preceding cabinets, to continue the policies of its predecessor.[24]

This experiment in parliamentarianism did nothing to change the stark realities for the workers. While the new cabinet was being organized, the Socialists, Communists, and unions held a May Day rally, again demanding the equitable distribution of food, price controls, and wage increases. Then, on May 19, about 250,000 held another food rally, and when a group tried to gain entry into the Imperial Palace to demand the distribution of hoarded food, the police fired on the crowd. "Japan had been submerged under a sea of red flags," Yoshida recalled the anxiety of the time, but it was momentary only.[25] The following day MacArthur publicly warned the hungry demonstrators, "If minor elements of Japanese society are unable to exercise such self-restraint . . . I shall be forced to take the necessary steps to control and remedy such a deplorable situation."[26] In addition to "minor elements," SCAP now saw the hand of Russia in the background. At the May meeting of the Allied Council, Atcheson told the members that he believed, though informed to the contrary by his translation service, the grievances the rally had presented to MacArthur had been written in a foreign language and translated into Japanese, and that it ". . . contains unmistakable earmarks of Communist propaganda."[27] The idea that the Communists, and the Russians in particular, rather than economic and political conditions were behind the unrest in Japan grew stronger as the occupation wore on and as the economic situation deteriorated further.

The Workers' Conditions

During its first few months SCAP actively encouraged the labor unions and introduced labor laws based on the United States' Wagner Act, yet labor's early militancy, political activity, and Marxist orientation soon caused SCAP to become increasingly hostile to the unions. But the struggle for wage increases was patently meaningless without political control of the economy. By June 1946 money wages were nine times those of 1937, while real wages were only 24 percent of that year. Such trends were of little concern to the higher echelons in SCAP, who were intent on structuring an orderly carbon copy of the United States in Asia. By October the police and the American Counter Intelligence Corps were violently breaking up labor demonstrations, and within SCAP this policy was known as ". . . housebreaking the labor movement."[28]

The labor movement itself was divided over tactics, in part reflecting the division in the Socialist Party over the issue of a united front with the Communists. The leader of the Sodomei (General Federation of Labor) was a right-wing Socialist, and the leadership's intransigence on the question of tactics led to a leftist split in August 1946 and the formation of the Sanbetsu representing 1.5 million workers, predominantly in the government-owned industries and services. In direct relation to the economic situation, the more militant Sanbetsu, largely under CP leadership, became the dominant organization of labor by the end of 1946. Despite the split in its ranks and the growing hostility of the occupation, the strength and scope of the new organized labor movement was a real force in Japanese society after only one year. And, as the United States failed to orient it in the American style, it became increasingly obvious that as a political force, in the existing system, its activity would further increase the costs of the occupation, and perhaps even radically undermine the political order of the new "reformed" conservative Japan.[29]

The Occupation Reforms

Although there was a growing identification between SCAP and the conservative Japanese governments of Shidehara and then Yoshida, and many in the SCAP bureaucracy began to regard criticism of that government as criticism of itself, others were increasingly frustrated by the government's effort, even while maintaining a cooperative veneer, to sabotage any change that would undermine its power. As we have discussed earlier, at the end of the war the nonmilitary ruling circles advocated a surrender in the anticipation that a United States occupation would protect them from the far greater threat of an internal revolution. Given their understanding of Joseph Grew's position in postwar planning, they did not anticipate that the United States would try to introduce its own institutions and ideology in Japan. Yoshida, in fact, later confessed to a sense of betrayal that the occupation had released the Communists from prison, undermined the police, and given nominal rights to the labor movement. "It is in a way ironical that, after we had surrendered to the United States Forces in order to avoid such a disaster [of a Communist revolution], one of the first acts of the occupation . . . was . . . to adopt an exceptionally lenient attitude towards Japan's Communists."[30]

George Atcheson was keenly aware of the guile in the cooperative demeanor of the Japanese government and big business, and reported early in the occupation that they had merely "repainted their signs," making a few gestures at the revision of the Constitution.[31] He personally opposed the emperor system as inhibiting parliamentary democracy. MacArthur, on the other hand, was captivated by the orderly deference and instructed Atcheson in October 1945 to let the government proceed with its own preparations for a new constitution, economic reforms, the purges, and land reform.

Instead of a new constitution the Japanese introduced some slight modifications of the old. The evasion was widely reported in the press, and MacArthur, in part prompted by a desire to protect the throne by making it symbolic, ordered the Government Section of SCAP to translate in essence the American Constitution and instruct the government to adopt it. This he hoped would undercut the probable demands from the FEC that they abolish the institution of the throne or that they try the Emperor as a war criminal. The new Constitution was prepared in only six days and translated into Japanese just before the first meeting of the FEC.

The provision in his basic directive from Washington instructing him to take no action in case of a revolution deeply shocked MacArthur. He firmly believed that a new constitution and early elections would eliminate any justification for violent change by the people themselves. MacArthur reminded the cabinet that by quickly instituting minimal constitutional and civil libertarian reforms they could forestall more far-reaching changes which the Commonwealth and Soviet members of the FEC would insist upon.

The Japanese conservatives who opposed most of the reforms were forced in the early years to capitulate to the letter if not the spirit of the directives. Perhaps the most decisive factor in the ultimate compliance was their assessment of the world conflict and their knowledge that, with an American occupation force to control the Left, time was on their side.

Although the Japanese government adamantly opposed the labor, political, and police reforms, those directives dealing with the questions of demilitarization and land reform were less alarming to an administration overwhelmingly representing the Japanese industrialists. For in Japanese society there was an added dynamic of a significant rivalry in the ruling class. The background of this tension in part explains why certain reforms succeeded and others were emasculated.

The extension of a premodern, agrarian social structure into the twentieth century, and the late development of a small, family-dominated capitalist class, as Barrington Moore, Jr., has shown, created in Japan many of the preconditions of a fascist industrial society. As a capitalist sector emerged out of the feudal social structure at the end of the nineteenth century and acquired increasing strength vis-à-vis the other elements of the ruling class, especially after World War I, the agrarian landlords and the military, drawn from an increasingly archaic agrarian landholding class with conflicting economic interests, resisted the industrial encroachments on their prestige and privilege and formulated a reactionary, anticapitalist ideology that posed a latent threat to the development of a modern capitalist state.[32] The military-agrarian-capitalist tensions were only in part suppressed during the 1930s and most of the war as each group relied on the other for the success of its respective aims. The military needed the industrialists for their conquests, and the preparation for war and imperial expansion for markets and raw materials generated tremendous profits for Japanese capitalism, and was, in fact, essential to its survival during the world depression and imperial rivalries in Asia. And both groups were logically united against the emerging consciousness of the increasingly militant working class and agricultural tenants. Yet the hostility of the military to a modern capitalism went so far as an attempt by a group of officers to set up an independent ". . . base of operations in Manchuria, where it could be free, it hoped, from the influence of the Japanese industrial combines."[33] But their conflict grew stronger as the war continued. The Left was not the only potential threat that the capitalists in Japan feared at the end of the war. Prince Konoye's call upon the Emperor for a negotiated surrender to the United States reflected this tension. "It is immaterial whether we call this revolution-minded group right-wing or left-wing. . . . It is a well-known fact that at the time of the trouble in Manchuria the military declared the purpose of the Incident to be internal reform here in Japan."[34]

In a critical sense the occupation period resulted in a final victory for Japanese industrialism over the landed aristocracy and their military allies. Whether or not the landlords were absorbed into the industrial class is unimportant here. What is conclusive is that there was no longer a struggle of rival elements in the ruling class and that capitalism was firmly entrenched in Japan.

The Japanese capitalist interests expected and actively desired the purge of the military. But they did not anticipate that the occupation would so broadly interpret the purge as to exclude all who advocated what it termed "militant nationalism" from political activity. Such a ruling penetrated so deeply that it touched nearly everyone but the Left. But the scope of conducting such a purge was too vast for SCAP personnel, so they asked the government to purge itself and the very class it represented. The purge was introduced in January 1946 and applied to the national bureaucracy, the military, and the police. In December 1946 SCAP extended the purge to the local and provisional governments and to the leading industrial firms, some 250, excluding from management all officials from president to director to accompany the process of deconcentration. The total number excluded from public office reached approximately 200,000, although by the end of the occupation, all but 8710 were reinstated on appeal. Most "permanently purged" submitted only to temporary retirement, and at the end of the occupation the purge became their badge of merit. By and large only the unimportant disappeared.

With the vital exception of the military and their allies in the bureaucracy, whose demise was sought by their industrialist opponents, the other purges of the elite were a façade and quite ineffectual. As countless observers have noted, in Japan, as to a great extent everywhere, real decisions are made in private circles. A director of an industry did not have to go to his office to run the company, and a political leader need not hold office to direct the party. Many of the older leaders continued to wield power, but that was less critical than that the interests they represented would continue to rule Japan even if new individuals began to replace them. Injecting a degree of social mobility changed nothing, except, as some have noted in retrospect, insofar as it introduced a certain degree of rationalization and managerial abilities began to rival family ties as a criterion of position. However meaningless on one level, the purge of the military altered the balance of forces in the traditional ruling class.[35]

Although there was an early division in Washington on the agrarian problem as well, reform of the Japanese landlord-tenant relationship emerged as one of the goals of allied policy in Japan, and in the first months SCAP instructed the government to prepare a land reform law. It was not the first time the Japanese had confronted the problem, but due to the power of the landlords all previous efforts at change had been unsubstantial, as indeed this effort proved to be when in March 1946 the cabinet submitted a program that failed to meet American requirements. After some hesitancy, SCAP presented the problem to the Allied Council, and the Commonwealth representative W. Macmahon Ball prepared a model land reform program. In one of the few instances of accepting the council's advice, SCAP ordered the government to prepare the Farm Land Reform Law based on Ball's proposals.

The new law abolished absentee landlordism, and provided compulsory means for three-quarters of the tenants, around two million people, to acquire the land they worked. The government was to purchase the land from the landlords and resell it to the tenants over thirty years at 3.2 percent interest. The remaining tenants were further protected by providing that all rentals would be in cash and would never exceed the value of one-quarter of a year's crop. By the end of the 1950s approximately five million acres had been resold to tenants and only 12 percent of the land remained leased. The land reform still left the Japanese peasant with many grievances, but tenancy was no longer the primary one. It was the only major reform that the Japanese government reinforced after the occupation ended. The land reform also inadvertently proved to be a critical safety valve for the industrialists. It in no way encroached on their privileges, but by eliminating the chief grievance in the countryside the conservatives attained a vital political asset that has provided their electoral victories to this day. The agricultural associations have been intimately linked to the Liberal Party, providing the bulk of votes that have assured their control of Japan since the war. If this were not the case there probably would not be a parliamentary system in Japan today. Yamaguchi Takehide, leader of the farmers union, responded to the land reform with hostility. "When I heard the news I thought 'damn,' if they had not done that we should have had a revolutionary government in Tokyo in a couple of years."[36]

The United States was not devoted to land reform as a principle, and in practice has generally opposed it elsewhere. In other nations that it controlled, and where the need was far more urgent, such as the Philippines and Korea, it either made no attempt to introduce a similar program or actively prevented such efforts. The success of the Japanese program can *only* be understood in the context of the rivalry within the Japanese ruling class and, for the Americans, because there was an alternative conservative capitalist class in Japan. In the other nations, to eliminate the landlord class would have created a power vacuum that only the Left could fill.

The Dilemmas of Economic Reform

Land reform succeeded because the dominant section of the postwar ruling class in Japan did not oppose it to any significant extent. But the occupation's directives also ordered a fundamental restructuring of the mechanisms of industrial concentration and control.

The American policy toward Japanese industry that emerged in the attempts to reconcile the rival factions and interests operating in Washington during and after the war was particularly ambivalent, especially regarding the family-controlled monopolies known as the *zaibatsu,* of which Mitsui, Mitsubishi, Yasuda, and Somitomo were the most prominent. Although very powerful families are common in capitalist states, as the Fords, DuPonts, and Rockefellers testify, in Japan the ten largest *zaibatsu* controlled directly over 70 percent of Japanese industry, and indirectly over 90 percent. In Japan there was no development from small corporations to large mergers, and no concept of competition; a sector of the feudal ruling class had simply industrialized the nation in a short span of years, and these families controlled the process from the beginning. There was no class or group to support a decentralized capitalism. And this dominating fact left only two possible policies: maintenance of the *status quo* or socialism. For if the traditional families were eliminated from industrial control, their legacy of concentrated industry, even in the hands of new managers, would still leave powerful economic forces with a small elite.

Grew had strongly favored the industrialists as the element most likely to cooperate with the United States after the war, but he, too, was willing to entertain a plan to break up the ten chief *zaibatsu* families' control as a symbolic gesture of reform. This distinction between specific, identifiable leaders and a highly concentrated economy ruled by new men was important, for Washington later used it as a semantic rationale for a shift, or a reinterpretation, of policy. Was the United States position to be merely anti-*zaibatsu* or for the redistribution of concentrated economic power? To Grew, both the industrialists and the Emperor represented the nonmilitarist, conservative order in Japan, a future partner in an anti-Left alliance and an important factor in America's economic war aims. United States investors in Japan, such as GE, Westinghouse, and a number of oil companies and banking firms, also supported this conception.

Opposed to this position and in favor of deconcentrating Japanese industry were the "old China hands" who were interested in reducing Japanese industrial predominance in the Far East, some military men who sought vengeance through a stern peace, representatives of United States traders and manufacturers with bitter memories of prewar Japanese competiton, and the laissez faire academic economists that the State Department hired to formulate the specifics of the rather amorphous policy. According to T. A. Bisson, one of the framers of the SCAP deconcentration program, both of the competing United States economic ". . . pressure groups were active in occupied Japan, with the traders, certain American banking firms, and petroleum companies most prominent."[37] In the SCAP organization itself there were also a number of genuine reformers who sincerely desired to break the power of Japanese business, intending to redistribute economic power in the process of democratization. It has always been respectable in the United States to genuflect toward competition and small business, and this ambiguity has confused much of American economic history, so that an antimonopoly, anticartel approach to the reconstruction of Japan was not surprising—nor was the subsequent abandonment of this policy.

The other members of the Allied Council had several views on economic policy toward Japan, but for either strategic, ideological, or competitive reasons they shared a consensus on the desirability of a fundamental structural change in the Japanese economy. The Russians, suspicious of American designs from the beginning, pressed hard in the FEC and Allied Council for any economic reforms that would undercut the power of the intensely anti-Soviet economic elite. For ideological reasons, and as the trading position of Britain deteriorated over the early postwar years, London became actively committed to the economic reforms, especially those dealing with labor and deconcentration. Yet if there was any advocate of a "Morgenthau Plan" for Japan, it was Nationalist China, which consistently supported a punitive peace with a low level of industry and heavy reparations.

By the end of 1945 criticism mounted in the American press over the slow pace in instituting the economic reforms outlined in the policy directive. Of paramount interest were the features that dealt with deconcentration and reparations. Wishing to show some evidence of action on these questions, yet hopelessly ignorant of the intricacies of the Japanese system of ownership and control of the economy, SCAP hastily looked to the cooperative and enigmatic directors of Japanese industry themselves to prepare a plan for their own dissolution. The Yasuda Holding Company, in consultation with SCAP and the government, in October presented a scheme for the dissolution of all the holding companies, the apex of the economic pyramid, requiring that the top four families, the leading *zaibatsu*—who controlled the vast bulk of industry—sell their stock. Despite SCAP's awareness that only the *zaibatsu* had the funds to repurchase the stock, and similar loopholes, MacArthur urged Washington to approve what he regarded as an admirable voluntarism in the Japanese approach to reform. As a temporary measure only, Washington authorized him to assent to the plan. But Clayton questioned the superficiality of accepting a document that the *zaibatsu* themselves had quickly presented, and he asked the Justice Department to send a mission of antitrust experts to Japan as soon as possible to study the situation closely and to recommend a specific policy.[38]

The mission of antitrust experts arrived in Tokyo on January 6, 1946, with Corwin Edwards, an economist at Northwestern University and consultant to the State Department on cartels, as its chairman. After ten weeks of studying the corporate structure of Japan, the group presented many recommendations to SCAP on dissolution, taxes, control laws, and new owners for the *zaibatsu* corporations. Clearly emphasizing not the *zaibatsu*, but the monopolies and the producers of ". . . a large proportion of total supply of a major industry," the mission's goal was a competitive capitalism of small- and medium-sized businesses with a wide dispersal of ownership and control.[39]

The Edwards mission made a report to the State-War-Navy Coordinating Committee (SWNCC), which formulated a policy paper and sent it to SCAP for comments. In October 1946, after several months of discussion back and forth settling the differences between the various divisions within SCAP and between Tokyo and Washington, SWNCC drew up the final United States policy on the deconcentration of industry, known as FEC–230, and submitted it to the FEC for consideration. Meanwhile, Washington sent it to SCAP as an interim directive, and until the FEC approved or altered it, SCAP was immediately to carry out the policy. In Tokyo, those committed to the program, including MacArthur, began to press the Japanese government to enact laws to implement its provisions. The first step was taken in November 1946 when SCAP directed all *zaibatsu* assets converted into nonnegotiable government bonds, and the following January SCAP extended the purge to business leaders.

The directive was so exceptional that one may wonder how it got as far as it did before its recall, and it deserves to be examined in some detail. It provided for the dissolution of ". . . excessive concentration of economic power," broadly defined as: "Any private enterprise or combination operated for profit is an excessive combination . . . if its asset value is very large; or if its working force is very large; or if, though somewhat smaller . . . it is engaged in business in various unrelated fields." The directive also provided for a purge of the executives and forbade them to purchase stock for ten years. Disposal of the holdings was to be carried out as rapidly as possible, even if at a ". . . fraction of their real value. . . . A decided purchase preference should be furnished to such persons as small or medium entrepreneurs and investors, and to such groups as agricultural and consumer cooperatives and trade unions. . . . All possible technical and financial assistance should be furnished the trade unions concerned."[40] Furthermore, FEC–230 applied to all United States property in Japan as well as Japanese interests.

The SCAP program of dissolution of the industrial combines into a competitive economic structure was quixotic at best. There was no tradition or political backing for such an economic system in Japan, since the conservative political parties represented the *zaibatsu* interests. The only economically realistic alternative was the socialization advocated by the Socialists and Communists. Political support for the SCAP program did not exist in Japan.

United States reparations policy in Japan followed a course similar to that in Germany, with the critical difference that the United States had exclusive control of Japan. Initially committed to a program of substantial reparations, Washington sent Edwin Pauley and a delegation to Tokyo in November–December 1945 to make recommendations for removals and a level-of-industry criterion. The commission presented a series of proposals based on the maintenance of a standard of living and industrial capacity equivalent to that prevailing in 1930. While there was no intention to deindustrialize, but simply to remove what the commission considered surplus to a peacetime economy, the proposals were severe. Pauley, as in Germany, recommended removals rather than reparations from current production since the aim was also to weaken Japan's economic base for the future and prevent Japan from dominating the markets of the region through reparation payments. SCAP saw immediately that the implementation of the Pauley recommendations would add to the costs and problems of the occupation and applied steady pressure on Washington for their modification, and the United States had barely submitted Pauley's proposals to the FEC before it had radically revised its policy on the question.

To the other members of the FEC, however, reparations appeared a critical issue. Under American pressure they scaled down many of the Pauley proposals, but then could not agree on the allocation of removals. Soon the discussions were caught in the mire of invective as the United States accused the Russians of having stripped Manchuria, depriving the commission of that inventory of Japanese property outside of Japan. Frustrated in the commission, but not yet ready to take unilateral action, the Americans proposed a special conference to deal only with the question of reparations. The other members refused, recognizing a diversionary tactic and convinced that the problem should be settled in the FEC. The United States then took another approach and in June 1946 suggested a treaty of international control to enforce disarmament and peace as an alternative to stripping Japan of its industrial capacity. Such an abstract and utopian proposition, a procedure similar to the one on Germany that the Americans were introducing in Paris at the same time, held no attraction for the FEC, and the negotiations on reparations remained deadlocked through 1947.[41]

The Limits and Context of Reform

In November 1946, we must recall, the American public elected the Eightieth Congress, and the new conservative mood of fiscal frugality, against the background of the domestic inflation, was quickly felt in Washington. The administration realized that it was necessary to reexamine its specific policies in order to justify the large expenditures so essential to the implementation of its fundamental aims. Occupation costs were certain to receive congressional scrutiny, and it was obvious to all that the United States would not incidentally subsidize reparations from the defeated enemy states. More critical yet to their calculations was the need to make both Germany and Japan self-supporting industrial powers, able once again to play their own role in the world economy. And in Japan, as was increasingly the case in the Western zones of Germany, the United States had unilateral powers to shape events. By the end of 1946 it was clear not only that the occupation of Japan was costly, a condition that the Americans could no longer overlook, but that the economy itself was following an aimless, inflationary course, disastrously dangerous to its other goals. Furthermore, reports were filtering into Washington that many of the reforms being introduced in Japan would perpetuate the costs; for although Japan was required to pay for the occupation expenses, the United States, in turn, had to subsidize the economic policies of the Japanese government.

In December 1946, Secretary of Commerce Averell Harriman sent a letter to all members of the Business Advisory Council requesting the names of ". . . five top-flight executives to assist the Commanding Generals in Germany and Japan in the administration of those countries. . . . The rehabilitation of these countries is requisite to world stability. I cannot too greatly stress the importance of their economic recovery. The task is urgent, and time is of the essence."[42] Even if they could not recommend the ideal executives for permanent posts, many American businessmen began to share Washington's sense of urgency.

In Tokyo, however, the consciousness of the cost of the undertaking, and other global priorities, was only beginning to penetrate the bureaucracy of SCAP by the end of 1946. For while the Japanese elite hoarded or channeled resources into nonproductive but profitable areas, the inflation mounted and wages lagged, MacArthur continued to ignore the desperate economic circumstances. On the first anniversary of the surrender, he announced in his characteristic flamboyant manner that the basic transformation of Japan had been largely completed. With the defeat, "their whole world crumbled. . . . And into this vacuum flowed the democratic way of life. The American combat soldier came. . . . They saw and felt his spiritual quality . . . which truly reflected the highest training of the American home. . . . A spiritual revolution ensued almost overnight. . . . This revolution of the spirit of the Japanese people represents . . . an unparalleled convulsion in the social history of the world." The only danger to this "spiritual revolution" was that the Japanese ". . . might prove easy prey to . . . the philosophy of an extreme radical Left."[43] Given economic failure in the context of political instability and change, this danger was increasing every month.

Others in SCAP did not share MacArthur's glowing optimism. By the end of 1946, officials in the Government Section had begun to reassess the will and capacity of the Yoshida cabinet to stem the economic disintegration, and they raised the possibility of a coalition cabinet with a few right-wing members of the Socialist Party in order to redirect and liberalize some of Yoshida's policies. Yoshida himself agreed, but the discussions failed in part because of Yoshida's insistence on maintaining the finance minister, Tanzan Ishibashi, whose reactionary policies were the source of much of the malaise. The discussions also collapsed because the left wing of the Socialist Party was at that time working on plans for a general strike and found it incongruous that members of their party should also be negotiating for a coalition with the government. Coalition politics, perhaps appropriate a year earlier, could only lead to capitulation as long as the conservatives held the levers of power.

By 1947, therefore, SCAP was implementing a series of reforms in Japan in an attempt to fashion a liberal capitalist state. It had replaced the Meiji Constitution by what was in essence a carbon copy of the American document, changing the role of the Emperor, granting power to the Diet, introducing a bill of rights, and in theory granting full liberty to trade unions and political organizations. The occupation proceeded to reform the police system and distribute the land; it purged hundreds of thousands of military and bureaucratic functionaries; and in January 1947 it extended the purge to industry to accompany a rigorous program for the deconcentration of ownership of the Japanese economy. Yet ambivalence remained the hallmark of American policy. In Tokyo SCAP continued to fulfill the initial occupation policy orders even though the objectives and global premises in Washington had begun to shift. But all the evidence of the internal conditions in Japan—reactionary economic policies, mounting activity on the Left, inflation—pointed to growing political instability, with only the presence of the occupation to maintain order. That presence, however, grew increasingly costly. The worst of all possible worlds was emerging for everyone, for no class in Japan was playing its assigned role insofar as the Americans were concerned. The reforms were a threat to the ruling class, the reactionary economic policies of the government were compounding the miseries of the masses and increasing the costs to the United States, and the labor movement was growing in strength and was Marxist in orientation. The imperative need for new choices in policy was becoming increasingly obvious in Washington by the end of 1946 as the question of the future of both Japan and Germany began to assume the most critical role in the evolving American plans for world reconstruction. It was that global perspective that was to serve as the catalyst of a new American policy in Japan.

BOOK II

From the Truman Doctrine
to the Korean War

12

The 1947 Crisis: The Truman Doctrine and American Globalism

The sixteen months following the conclusion of World War II had been both frustrating and dangerous for the United States' global objectives, and by the end of 1946 unmistakable signs threatened to turn frustration into failures damaging to Washington's basic definition of its national interest. The stakes were monumental, impinging on the very mastery of the direction of world power, and America's means for coping with them by 1947 appeared far too inadequate.

Success for the United States was elusive throughout 1946, for the world had proved too complex and too large for Washington's guidance. America's desire for a unified world economy remained both an ideological conviction and an economic imperative, with England's and Western Europe's cooperation being essential for success. But those nations treated the United States' concept of internationalism with profound suspicion, and England —the key link on the American vision—resisted as best it could. For the British focused on the dual standard in the United States' theory and practice, and its deep-rooted economic weaknesses, which America's loan did little to alleviate, left it precious little recourse but to regulate its own economy. And in Britain and Western Europe the United States was to recognize that there were far more serious political preconditions for the attainment of its economic goals than it had anticipated, a fact that forced it immediately to relate directly to the internal political trends in France, Italy, and elsewhere, seeking both to contain the political threat from the Communists and Left and to reverse the much more prevalent economic policy of trade restrictionism, autarchy, and European sufficiency.

In this context, in which the United States ultimately had most to lose in the long run should Europe and its sphere of influence in the Third World constrict America's role, realities quickly proved the existing instruments for the postwar attainment of America's world economic goals to be sorely inadequate. Ironically, the European recovery which occurred everywhere save West Germany during 1946 involved far less American guidance and participation than that nation could afford. The United States had to find means of both containing and redirecting nationally or regionally based capitalisms and preventing them from falling under the political control of Communist and Left governments rhetorically committed to profound social transformation. For while the Western European Communist parties might, with Russian encouragement, persist in their moderate strategies, and even regulate the working classes on behalf of the propertied, there was no assurance that such passivity might endure forever. Hence the continuing American need to define the outcome of social dynamics wherever it was able to do so, or where its interests demanded that it interfere. And the logic of this imperative was to internationalize social crises, of which there were to be a seemingly endless number, setting the stage for an American interventionism in its many forms which became the hallmark of postwar world politics.

In this sense, even by 1946 Russia was becoming an excuse for policies and goals that had been articulated much earlier and would in any event have shaped the course of America's role in the world. Confident of its military power supremacy, which it would not sacrifice, by the end of 1946 America's vast military lead offered little help in meeting the political and economic challenges in Europe. But Russia had no significant place in the United States' ideal world order, nor could Washington accept Czech neutralism and economic independence as part of an Eastern Europe—still quite mixed in its internal social and political forms during 1946—in which the Russians had primary influence. The Soviet Union and local Communist parties became Washington's enemies during 1946–1947 both out of necessity—for however conservative, they retained the capacity for militancy—and out of choice.

The designation of Communist parties and Russia as America's enemy, with the differences between them being deliberately obscured until they became meaningless, was based on Truman's unsuccessful postwar political experiences with Congress, which the Republicans dominated after the 1946 elections. It had been extremely difficult to persuade Congress to approve the loan to England for the true reasons, and the administration's trade and economic program was in grave danger of being smashed in a manner that could only force Western Europe to move further away from collaboration with America. Crusades in the name of anti-Communism offered an approach which, however cynical, at least promised to obtain results. It was also one that would define Washington's political style for decades.

Such a strategy was utilitarian. The United States had articulated its main goals and its global role before the end of the war, and all that was left was to apply its power to attain its ends in an uncertain domestic and highly unstable, if not hostile, world political environment. Negotiations with Russia were never seen as an essential part of this undertaking. Basically, Washington had both military and economic power and planned to use it to contain and control the forces of change in the world.

In Europe this appeared possible in 1946, if only because the United States did not expect the Russians to embark on military adventures. Moreover, Germany offered a handle by which it might neutralize both Soviet hegemony and Western European autonomy. In West Germany there was no real chance that the United States would lose its total control over the parameters of economic and political change. Germany's economic and political revival was therefore a lever that the United States might utilize to recreate a barrier to Russian power in the East and a means for redefining, to some vital extent, Western Europe's economic course. During 1946 the first steps in this direction were taken.

In the immediate postwar period Europe was the center of Washington's world strategy. Ranked in order of priority, it stood above all the rest, but the rim lands could not be minimized, for there, too, the stakes were vast. In the Near East, especially, traditional national rivalries embroiled the United States in conflicts with both Russia and England, as the conservative leaders of small nations sought new protectors and benefactors, and as Britain's impatience with the costs of its imperial presence forced it to desert the less lucrative field in Greece to the United States. The United States, beginning during the war, generously defined its interest in the entire region, and by establishing its fleet in the Mediterranean, and moving to buttress the conservative forces in Greece and Iran, it began to replace England's traditional supremacy in the area.

In the more remote and uncontrollable Far East, the United States had done the best it could within its resources. In China it had encountered only failure and frustration, but in Korea the American occupation mounted its first postwar intervention in an agrarian revolutionary situation and sustained the forces of reaction. In Japan, where the United States' absolute hegemony had caused the Russians to cite it as justification for their own autonomy in Eastern Europe, the occupation maintained the conservative order against leftist pressures and economic crisis. Yet at the same time the United States sponsored moderate political and economic reforms, all the while seeking to define a consistent policy that overcame ambiguities and advanced America's goals in Asia.

In brief, by the end of 1946 the United States was beginning to systematize and fulfill its unwavering goals by finding new instrumentalities which took into account domestic inhibitions as well as far more formidable foreign resistance to America's objectives than had been anticipated when its aims were articulated during World War II. In this process, the stated purpose of American foreign policy was to become rather more lofty and much more sharply anti-Communist and anti-Russian, but the ends remained as they had always been, however obscured by moral rhetoric, and no less self-serving. But if the new trappings of Washington's policy made it more salable at home, it did not alter the global political and economic prerequisites for its success. Here was the incubating ground for new frustrations, dilemmas, and crises.

The Executive's Freedom to Act

The crisis surrounding the Truman Doctrine's formulation in the spring of 1947 was less a matter of the future of American power in the eastern Mediterranean than a general articulation and expansion of the scope of American foreign policy, its freedom to act in light of domestic constraints, and its ultimate objectives. As such, it involved not just the Middle East but the future of Europe, the prospects for attaining American goals in the world economy, the best means for containing Russia and the Left, and the very efficacy of American diplomatic strategy since the end of World War II. Greece was a reflection more than a cause of this larger fundamental consideration, and a temporary but necessary instrument for attaining Washington's goals in every part of the world. It represented not a departure from the preceding thrust of American policy, but rather its logical conclusion.

Washington saw all these global problems as interrelated, and the necessity for the historian to compartmentalize written history does violence to the unified view that existed in Washington at the beginning of 1947. Several dimensions—the condition of public opinion and the relationship of Congress to the administration—had an especially important role in the so-called crisis.

The question of public opinion impinges centrally on the nature of decision-making and power in the United States, and never was the true significance of this factor better revealed than at the end of 1946. Dominant political theory assigns special significance to public opinion as the origins of a democratic state's conduct, but this proposition only reinforces a positive theory of legitimacy that avoids the more durable reality that it is elite opinion and power that is the source of policy. Conventional political theory ignores the nature of interest in a class society, and the manner in which the overwhelming weight of elite opinions, desires, and needs shapes the applications of national power. The public at the end of 1946 was full of its own private concerns; only one-quarter considered foreign policy the most important problem facing the nation, and it shared a degree of equanimity that reflected world political realities by default—in the sense that the contrived, sudden crises of early 1947 did not so much mirror the global facts as tend to transform and create them. The logical expression of the public's lack of hysteria was apathy, and it was not the poll-taker's extracted opinion that was meaningful, but rather the more significant reality that at this time over three-quarters of the nation simply paid no attention to foreign affairs and was apathetic or ignorant toward it. Even in those periods after March 1947 public attitudes were to remain fickle and tend to relax to a less concerned view of the world scene. For this reason more rigid and totalitarian means of handling mass opposition to ruling policy were uncalled for and liberal rhetoric was possible in a situation where a society neither endorsed nor opposed the actions of leaders.[1] In a society without serious opposition, manipulation replaces the knout.

Suffice it to say, it was not the public but its rulers that defined the purposes and scope of American diplomacy, and the formal existence of democratic theory and structures alleged to reflect open power had nothing to do with its operation. In a stratified society of economic factions and classes, in which ruling-class interests have historically required positive governmental action, it was out of the question that American foreign policy could have reflected domestically oriented mass priorities if American capitalism were to survive in a depressed or hostile world economic and political order. To the United States' leaders, the question was essentially how they might translate their goals into policies of state over the indifference or opposition of the majority of the people, to make plausible and socially sanctioned policies that served class interests in the name of a broader social welfare and erstwhile consensus. The question for controllers of modern American power is not how to reflect the desires of the masses, but to manipulate them so that they endorse the needs and goals of men who might otherwise have to resort to sterner forms of repression to attain their ends.

Traditionally, one way to handle the matter of the erratic and unreliable public is to use the press to give it direction and values, but by the end of 1946 this long-standing method was not proving adequate in neutralizing a clearly growing isolationist mood among the American people and Congress. Via briefings and special information, cabinet officers and American decision-makers have routinely provided direction to the news that publishers and journalists print. Those who cooperated with the government were favored with even more inside data, often indispensable to their personal reputations and success.[2] At the end of 1946 the question before the Truman administration was not how to reflect public opinion, or even to change it, but how to overcome its potentially negative consequences. And for this, ultimately, nothing was superior to a world crisis, real or fancied, and conjuring up the menace of Russia and Communism. It is this mood of crisis and emergency that tends to color Washington's response to each diplomatic question, whether serious or often even quite modest in significance, in the postwar era. For even if it resolved no international questions, it usually removed domestic inhibitions, particularly budgetary.

The immediate political outcome of public apathy and opposition to American globalism was the Eightieth Congress elected November 5. That election gave the Republicans a majority of 6 in the Senate and 127 in the House as of January 3, 1947, and this new political reality posed serious new possibilities for an administration that could no longer evoke wartime necessities to neutralize dormant opposition. Yet the fact that the Republican Party had its own profound internal disagreements, and politically was as diverse as the Democrats, meant that its disruptive potential could be overcome with tact and expertise.

Eastern Republicans, for the most part, were hardly distinguishable from Democrats on questions of the budget and foreign policy, and the confusions of Midwestern Republicans disarmed them as a party of true opposition. To some great extent, what is called "conservatism" in American politics has often been a matter of intelligence and emotion rather than a clear and reasoned comprehension of the interests of propertied classes. The emphasis on the budget in the speeches of Senator Robert A. Taft of Ohio, who emerged as the leader of this faction, should not obscure the essential agreement on diplomatic tactics that he and his caucus shared with the administration. Briefly, Taft wanted largely the same policies—or sterner ones—at less cost, but when confronted with the option of isolationism or an unbalanced budget he and his followers invariably opted for globalism. And they never proposed clear alternatives. Even John Taber, the chairman of the House Committee on Appropriations in the Eightieth Congress, was willing to cut only fringe items in the budget but loath to attack fundamental policies, and personally he was quite amenable to administration flattery and pressures. Above all, however, was the critical role of Senator Arthur Vandenberg, whose belief in a paramount national interest—which he phrased "bi-partisanship"—meant that foreign policy was removed from politics. With occasional exceptions, the Democrats in the Executive branch had also followed this unifying strategy, and although Vandenberg at times reflected on the implications of such monolithic cohesion for democratic politics, he was never to break with it.[3]

For this reason, it is important not to exaggerate the significance of the Republican victory in 1946, especially in contrast to the more profound apathy of the public and, above all else, the growing realization in Washington by the end of 1946 that the administration's own wartime grand designs were either failing or required a far vaster outlay of funds to implement them successfully. The fact that, in the last analysis, the conservative Republicans and liberal Democrats shared a much more fundamental set of diplomatic premises than either cared to acknowledge meant that it was unlikely that the new Congress would repudiate the existing global commitments or prevent their expansion.

The administration chose to take no chances, however, and this profoundly colored its approach to the revamping of American diplomatic tactics, of which the Greek crisis was to be only the first. Truman was concerned about the spread of isolationist theories of "Fortress America" after the war, but throughout the summer and fall of 1946 he refused to enlarge the military budget, and actually cut it in ways that raised doubts regarding its adequacy for growing American overseas obligations. In principle, however, even hard-liners such as Forrestal favored efforts to balance the budget, in part because of the rampant postwar inflation. For this reason, the most vital change that occurred in Washington at the end of 1946 was the administration's new foreign policy tactics rather than in the membership of Congress, for the shift was to cost more—far more—at a time when the Republicans were inclined to continue in the traditional framework.

The general reassessment of American policy then taking place on Germany and Japan, foreign economic policy, as well as on the Middle East would have occurred in any event, and it also would have been "bi-partisan" for all the traditional reasons, not the least of which was the essential ideological integration of the two parties. That many Republicans were absorbed into the higher levels of government was based more on the fact that the key foreign policy decision-making elite was beyond parties than on tactical considerations. Still, when the Republicans took over Congress they promised large budget cuts, and these eventually were fixed on February 14 at $6 billion less than Truman's budget request of $37.5 billion. Since, at this very period, the administration began considering the need for more money not merely for Greece but for its entire foreign economic policy, events defined the context into which the administration placed the entire Middle Eastern issue. At this point, however, Truman himself was still interested in gradually reducing the budget even below the figure the Republican Congress had advanced (but in his own time and manner), and had not yet assimilated the price tag on the new global strategy that his key advisers were just then defining as more appropriate to the attainment of American goals in the world. During January, in fact, no hint of an imminent foreign policy crisis or vast new appropriations could be found in Truman's own modest declarations on the budget.

For a well-placed, sudden "crisis" in the name of anti-Communism, the administration discovered for the first but scarcely the last time, unlocked long-desired funds and overwhelmed what scant opposition remained in the debate over American foreign policy—and the political process.[4]

The Costs of Globalism

Washington's basic problems at the beginning of 1947 were essentially a matter of money and an unresponsive Congress, but especially the failure of its earlier designs for advancing America's global interests. There was no threatened imminent Communist takeover in some nation deemed essential to United States interests, no ominous new Russian military development, or sudden shift in power in some vital region. Basically, the United States' goal was to find more appropriate instrumentalities for advancing its constant objectives in the world.

No one of importance in Washington doubted the premises of America's self-appointed world role, but by the beginning of 1947 key leaders were debating the new means required as part of its mission. They dismissed, publicly and privately, Soviet military power and the threat of war, thinking, to quote John Foster Dulles, that "economically the nation is still weak. . . . the Soviet military establishment is completely outmatched. . . ."[5] Such a vision of America's mastery of the key factors of world power precluded, in Washington's mind, negotiations. One met Soviet intransigence, in this view, by resisting and ultimately enveloping it—a doctrine that long had been conventional wisdom in Washington and one which Kennan later articulated into a systematic theory.[6] Such a strategy did not require the United States to forgo any of its goals or assets, and it demanded confrontation rather than diplomacy as the rule in United States–Soviet relations.

By 1947, however, Washington's main concern was Western Europe's course and its implications for United States interests. The economic institutions created during the war had proved almost entirely irrelevant, and private foreign lending was stagnant, and never again was to attain its prewar peak. There was a dollar shortage but also a sharp general industrial recovery in all of Europe save West Germany, and even in December 1946 Acheson admitted that only three or four European countries now qualified for free relief. Indeed, British and Western European foreign trade in 1947 within the region and Europe exceeded 1946 by a wide margin and surpassed 1938 levels, even without Germany. Britain's trade with its dependent colonial nations showed the same gains. This remarkable increase was attained within a framework of national economic restrictions and bilateral trade and payments treaties which had tripled in a year's time to over two hundred in 1947 and which minimized Europe's dependence on dollar imports. Stated in terms of the export market's ability to absorb the United States' surplus, in 1919–1920 the United States exported 9.1 percent of its gross national product, but in 1946 and 1947 only 5.8 percent.[7] Washington correctly perceived that recovery without United States participation was a basic threat to America's interests. Economic nationalism, Truman warned in his economic report of January, ". . . would tend to break the world into trading blocs and could have profound effects upon world politics and the prospects for creating an enduring peace."[8] More to the point, his economic advisers wrote at the same time, pent-up wartime demands would soon be satisfied, and without the creation of new markets at home and abroad, a business slump, perhaps even a depression, was likely. By this time the only question was which instrumentalities would suffice to meet the problem. The real issue at stake was less the condition of Western European capitalism than its form, and whether it would be cooperative or competitive.

Key American advisers worried about the world-wide trend toward statism and nationalization and their failure to abort it. To some, such as Dodge, their opinions were scarcely more than definite, articulated attitudes. "If the American program for world trade were to fail," Clair Wilcox, Clayton's key aide, told a businessmen's meeting on February 17, "its failure would hasten the spread of nationalization among the other countries of the world. . . . We cannot insulate ourselves against the movements that sweep around the globe. If every other major nation were to go Socialist, it would be extremely difficult, if not impossible, to preserve real private enterprise in the United States." And this in turn would imperil national security, for "Our military strength requires ready access to scarce supplies of strategic materials" as well as markets large enough to sustain heavy industry.[9] Such sophistication, embracing all factors of world power, nevertheless understated Washington's equally grave concern over another challenge to American prosperity: autonomous Western European captialism.

Events in Greece during mid-February were no more alarming to the administration than they had been the prior fall, and it had yet to make the linkage between the Greek question and the larger drift of American diplomacy and internal affairs. On February 14, Secretary of State Marshall at a press conference was asked about the new government and trends in Greece, and he reacted in mild, unworried terms, urging a program of amnesty along with the repression of "illegal bands," stressing internal political and economic reform above all else: ". . . no amount of assistance can prove effective or of lasting benefit unless the Greek people themselves are prepared to work together resolutely for their own salvation."[10] For the "crisis" that was emerging in American leadership's consciousness that month was primarily an economic one, and Washington considered Greece no more significant than many other countries.

Affairs in Greece after the New Year followed those of the preceding months, and the Americans expected imminently to assume the main British responsibilities in the area. Another cabinet and economic crisis was under way when the United States' Porter mission arrived in Athens in mid-January to assess the Greek economy, and for good reason American officials still saw the problem of Greece as a question of necessary internal reforms. On February 3 MacVeagh passed along to Washington information that was long known to be simply a question of timing: the British would soon withdraw half their troops. And, of course, a reduction of British economic aid to Greece was fully anticipated too. Ten days later

MacVeagh urged Washington to plan to supply aid to Greece, a principle it had also accepted the prior year. Porter now joined the chorus, and on the twentieth the embassy in London notified the State Department that the British treasury was opposed to further aid to Greece, and so on the morning of February 21 Marshall told Acheson to get to work on an aid measure that was to be primarily economic in emphasis. Marshall, Acheson, and many other cabinet-level officers were at this time concerned with Congress' budget-cutting gestures, but even more troublesome to them was whether American global strategy now exceeded the Truman administration's own modest budget and original assumptions. On February 22 Marshall delivered a carefully edited and toned down speech at Princeton that stressed the cost and importance of America's role in world economic and political reconstruction and condemned public apathy toward shouldering these burdens. During these same days Truman's March 6 Baylor speech, which spun out this theme, was already in preparation. When, late on February 21, the British embassy in Washington delivered a note that England would discontinue financial aid to Greece and Turkey, there was nothing unexpected about it. The British were ready to drop their Greek subsidy because they had been assured the United States would assume it. What was open to debate was whether the United States would take a narrow or broad approach to the problem, link it to a major shift in global diplomacy then being considered, and treat Greece not so much as a challenge but as an opportunity.[11]

It was almost inevitable that the Greek matter become the basis not simply for consolidating American power in the Middle East, which would have occurred in any event, but for mobilizing Congress and the public for a new departure in foreign policy which expanded the magnitude of America's postwar strategy in degree if not in kind. The internal problems of Greece were such that a modest economic and political program would have solved them had Athens been willing, but, since it was not, a relatively modest military aid program was necessary as well. What was new about Greece, in brief, was that it became a useful excuse for the much more ambitious international line then in gestation, the most dramatic but certainly not the first postwar American intervention to sustain the Right and expand American power everywhere. For the world, Greece was an example of America's determination to resist radical social and political transformations in regions deemed vital to United States interests, whether or not those upheavals were the result of purely internal forces. Washington again made explicit that it preferred the continuation of pro-Western *status quo's,* however corrupt and repressive, to far-reaching internal social and economic changes—changes which might aid Russia even if Washington could not directly blame it for sustaining the opposition forces, but which in any event would threaten American interests. Turkey, however, was to pose the question to Russia of the creation of a new *cordon sanitaire* and encirclement, a new reality that might indeed force it to abandon its conservatism and indifference and stake its own security on the consolidation of power in its own bloc.

Marshall's first response to the British note was to protest to London, but his staff set to work on designing appropriate aid legislation intended to use Greece as a first step toward a major revamping of American foreign policy. Key American leaders understood that Britain's abandonment of Greece was significant mainly as a symptom of the collapse of the British Empire ostensibly far beyond the point that the United States had always desired —thereby opening a power vacuum in large parts of the globe—or, as one State Department official phrased it, as just one aspect of ". . . an economic crisis centered in Britain and Empire, France, Greece, and China."[12] ". . . [I]t was," as Forrestal recorded Marshall's first response, "tantamount to British abdication from the Middle East with obvious implications as to their successor."[13] The immediate problem, therefore, was the shift of power in the non-Communist world and the need to prevent its sliding leftward, but in the larger context it was the crisis in the world economy and the ability of United States policy to cope with it. Russia, it is worth emphasizing, was scarcely the origin of either of these conditions.

No matter what the final tactics, or problem, State Department officials, and especially Acheson, were profoundly impressed ". . . that Congress and the people of this country are not sufficiently aware of the character and dimensions of the crisis that impends," and ". . . a powerlessness on the part of the Government to act because of Congressional or public unawareness. . . ." What was suggested was ". . . bold action at the top," an ". . . information program necessary to inform the people and convince Congress," and the best way to attain this was "a grave, frank statesmanlike appeal," one ". . . with tremendous advance build-up."[14]

Marshall initiated such a strategy on the twenty-seventh by calling together a group of key congressional leaders and painting the broadest possible picture of what might happen "If Greece should dissolve into civil war. . . ." Turkey might then fall, and "Soviet domination might thus extend over the entire Middle East and Asia."[15] Since Marshall emphasized the collapse of British power as the immediate source of the crisis, an event many Americans were not loath to see, the message went over poorly. It was Acheson, at this meeting, who attributed the source of the crisis less to the British and Greeks than to the Soviet Union and its Communist agents allegedly seeking to encircle Western Europe and penetrate the entire globe. Either via a domino theory or dramatic crusade against Communism, it was plain that Congress was capable of going along with the administration's larger program if it couched the policy in suitably anti-Communist terms and a sense of dramatic crisis. The lesson was not lost.

What was really on the mind of the President and his advisers was stated less in the Truman Doctrine speech than in private memos and in Truman's March 6 address at Baylor University. Dealing with the world economic structure, the President attacked state-regulated trade, tariffs, and exchange controls—". . . the direction in which much of the world is headed at the present time." "If this trend is not reversed," he warned, ". . . the United States will be under pressure, sooner or later, to use these same devices in the fight for markets and for raw materials. . . . It is not the American way. It is not the way to peace."[16] Having stated the dilemma, which involved Western European capitalist nations rather than Russia, Truman did not prescribe more than the existing remedies, which he and his advisers had already acknowledged as wanting. Greece, Clayton believed, would go "part of the way" in conditioning Congress for what would have to be done, but many more billions, he estimated on March 5, would have to be spent.[17]

The question of how best to sell the new crusade perplexed the administration, not the least because Greece was a paltry excuse for a vast undertaking of which it "was only a beginning," and in the end it formulated diverse reasons as the need required.[18] The many drafts that were drawn up before the final Truman Doctrine speech was delivered to Congress on March 12 are interesting in that they reveal more accurately than the speech itself the true concerns of Washington. Members of the cabinet and other top officials who considered the matter before the twelfth understood very clearly that the United States was now defining a strategy and budget appropriate to its new global commitments—interests that the collapse of British power had made even more exclusively American—and that far greater involvement in other countries was now pending at least on the economic level.

Quite apart from the belligerent tone of the drafts were the references to ". . . a world-wide trend away from the system of free enterprise toward state-controlled economies" which the State Department's speech writers thought "gravely threatened" American interests. No less significant was the mention of the "great natural resources" of the Middle East at stake.

Loy Henderson, director of the department's Near Eastern office, offered a speech that stuck to Greece alone and avoided the larger world issues, but this was rejected outright on behalf of what was to be the most belligerent and global response possible to a quite limited, not overly pressing situation. Excised were most references to Greece's internal democracy in the drafts which Joseph M. Jones drew up, but which mainly Acheson formulated on a policy level. So were vague references to reintegrating German and Japanese power into the anti-Russian bloc. But yet other drafts dwelt inordinately on "free enterprise" and foreign economic policy, and this was obviously intended to be the burden of the message.[19] Still, the tone of the speech worried even Kennan, who vainly objected, and Marshall wired from Europe, to quote from Charles Bohlen's memoir, that ". . . he thought that Truman was overstating the case a bit. The reply came back that from all his contacts with the Senate, it was clear that this was the only way in which the measure could be passed."[20]

When Truman saw these early drafts he thought they ". . . made the whole thing sound like an investment prospectus," and he much preferred emphasizing general policy, mobilizing Congress and the public, and returning to the substance of the undertaking later.[21] Whether or not Acheson concluded the same on his own initiative is unimportant, for it was universally understood that Greece was only a part of a much larger shift in policy. Truman's speech to Congress is much more interesting, therefore, for what it implied than what it stated explicitly.

At its face value, however, it was a plea for aid to a Greek government he admitted was "not perfect" but argued was also democratic. He stressed, however, that the main emphasis of the $300 million for Greece and $100 million for Turkey would be economic, largely to stop the armed minority in Greece from pushing over the dominoes that might precipitate "disorder" in the "entire Middle East." Though Russia was not mentioned once, it was alluded to continuously, and now Truman indicated he would support "free peoples" everywhere ". . . who are resisting attempted subjugation by armed minorities or by outside pressures," and that he would not hesitate to ask Congress in the future for new funds for other countries and situations that would come under America's protective reach in the ". . . serious course upon which we embark."[22]

Since Truman had already given his important policy speech on foreign economic policy at Baylor, he could afford to organize his message to Congress to stress dramatic format and retain the freedom for greater action implicit in its vagueness. Both the press and Congress understood its general import. *Business Week* several days before its delivery saw the question mainly as one of replacing Britain's ". . . responsibility for policing much of the world," and as stopping short of ". . . replacing Britain as the dominant force supporting western capitalism in the 'middle world' between the U.S. and Russia."[23] The non-Communist European reaction was immediately negative and regarded the speech as much too aggressive, virtually another Monroe Doctrine for the rest of the globe. The advance press build-up, the *Economist* of London concluded in surveying the already deep American involvement in the Middle East, was one that ". . . could only be accorded to a declaration of war."[24] Several days later James Reston in the New York *Times* described the larger global perspective in which Truman had intended his speech, the imminent and vastly more expensive programs Congress would soon receive, the need for America to replace British power, and the administration's desire to generate a crisis atmosphere to discipline Congress. The Republicans, indeed, were much distressed at the contrived manner in which Truman had outflanked their budget plans, and Taft likened the new Truman Doctrine to a Russian intervention in Cuba, unnecessarily polarizing the world into two camps. Few doubted that the GOP would eventually go along with Truman; for the time, at least, the party was split on how best to proceed.

One of the immediate consequences of the Truman Doctrine and the contrived crisis was to undermine the Foreign Ministers Conference due to open in Moscow March 10. Marshall had authorized the department to formulate the doctrine without regard to its negative impact on the conference, for with the doctrine came the abandonment of traditional diplomacy and an emphasis on reliance on power, pure and simple, in confining Russia and Communism. Even before leaving for Moscow, Marshall had issued an extremely gloomy prognostication that only made more credible the imminent new policy. In Moscow itself the American delegation considered the larger question of ". . . sweep[ing] back local political forces which are determinedly on the march"—forces that might be genuinely indigenous but also advanced Soviet foreign policy at the same time and, irrespective of Russian interests, would decisively undermine America's aims in the world.[25] This dilemma, which necessarily pitted the United States against genuine change throughout the world in all its forms, was one with which Washington intended the Truman Doctrine to deal via global American interventionism. That the Moscow Conference was a failure was less consequential than that the Truman Doctrine irrevocably closed off conventional diplomacy for years.

The other consequence of the Truman Doctrine was to reveal once more America's willingness to abandon the UN as a serious forum for the resolution of international conflict, largely, of course, because the specific problem of Greece that would have gone to that body was only a mask for a much more fundamental shift in American policy that the doctrine nominally reflected. Given a measure of Republican discomfort over the doctrine, they were to elect to make much of the fact the administration had explicitly rejected in the strategy any role that the UN might play. At America's behest, the UN already had an investigating commission in Greece, and neither the UN secretariat nor even Warren Austin, the United States representative to the UN, was informed in advance or consulted on the impending policy. Nearly all references to the UN in the original drafts of Truman's speech had been cut, and even before the delivery of the speech some Republicans, growing impatient with the obviously contrived crisis atmosphere, wanted the administration to give the Greek issue to the UN first. Vandenberg did not believe the organization was equipped to handle the matter, but he soon backed off and led the effort to obtain some petty concessions on this matter for his party.

In a sense, the effort of the neoisolationists to lean on the UN only revealed the paucity of Republican alternatives to the Truman policy, for the party was really no less committed to a tough anti-Soviet stand. Vandenberg freely acknowledged that the organization would accomplish little, and felt this would obliquely prove it. In any event, the administration saw nothing to be lost by adding a contingent amendment of a future role for the UN in Greece that in no way altered the essential measure, though Austin did not address the Security Council regarding American policy until March 28. By that time Republican opposition had virtually melted before a clever administration policy to withhold no facts regarding Greece nor the larger strategic importance of the Middle East and oil, but also to minimize the vaguely implied powers in other areas to which Truman alluded. The State Department honestly confronted the most delicate questions, even the internal repression in Greece, or the existence of 13,000 poorly armed, mainly non-Communist guerillas split among Macedonian and Greek nationalists. It publicly answered a list of 111 congressional questions and confidentially circulated a large and authoritative "Black Book." "The loud talk was all of Greece and Turkey," *Time* reported as it found special meaning in Standard of New Jersey's timely denunciation of the Red Line agreement, ". . . but the whispers behind the talk were of the ocean of oil to the south."[26] Forrestal was entirely explicit in revealing the importance of controlling oil and raw materials when discussing the doctrine with acquaintances. But any careful reading of the testimony before the Senate and House reveals precisely how fully informed Congress was on the facts of both Greece and Turkey, and the problems of the region (oil included), with critical assessments as well as Acheson's more polite euphemisms regarding Greek and Turkish freedom. The evasive replies administration spokesmen gave to queries about rumors of vast American commitments to the rest of Europe convinced no one. The fact is that Congress was ready to go along with those imminent ventures, even if in its own way and in its own good time, and all this meant that the administration would continue with "crisis diplomacy," if only because the failure of past policies to meet global realities did indeed create repeated crises for American interests.

Truman had hoped Congress would pass the requested legislation before the end of March, and the carefully planned sense of surprise, the contrived sudden emergency, were all intended to minimize opposition and attain speed. But the Senate was not convinced speed was urgent, and passed the legislation on April 22 by 67 to 23, and the House followed on May 9 with an overwhelming 287 to 107 vote. Truman himself signed the bill two weeks later, but the American aid mission did not reach Greece until mid-July, and the first arms arrived at the end of August.[27] The "crisis" of February was now calmly behind the administration, for by summer it had already turned to those far more significant issues which were the more fundamental reasons for the Truman Doctrine.

Even before Congress had passed the Greek-Turkish aid bills, Forrestal warned the cabinet on April 18 ". . . that in view of the feeling that our support for Greece and Turkey might be the forerunner of many other and very much larger economic political actions in other parts of the world, we should make a study of what may confront us in the next eighteen months."[28] Those far more vital actions, which we discuss later in this chapter, were the real goals of the Truman Doctrine in the first instance, for neither the situation in Greece itself, nor the petty size of aid America rendered, nor the lethargy with which it was administered is compatible with any other view. The United States was replacing British economic and strategic power in the Middle East; it was preparing for a radically more costly approach to foreign economic policy; it was moving toward the resurrection and final reintegration of German and Japanese power in an anti-Soviet alliance, as well as an American-led world economy; it was transforming its intervention against Left revolutions into a standard policy and response; it was disciplining its own nation for a long and increasingly expensive, ostensibly anti-Communist, crusade; and it was once and for all abandoning conventional diplomacy and the UN as a means for resolving conflicts between nations. In brief, using Greece as an excuse, expanding American power was further transforming the nature of the global crisis.

France and Italy: The Politics of Conservatism

Nothing revealed so vividly the nature of Soviet goals, or the quality of Western Communism, as the debacle of the French and Italian Communist parties during the first half of 1947. And the limp character of the "Communist menace" in these key European nations proved once again that it was the reformation and integration of Western European capitalism, not a revolutionary threat, that was the most urgent problem facing Washington.

The French Communist Party leadership, by both temperament and Russian advice, docilely sought to become a loyal fixture in the government coalition, one that could prove its reliability by seeking ever higher production from the working class during the reconstruction of what was still a capitalist economy. By the beginning of 1947, however, France's united front government, with its five Communist ministers, was in economic trouble with its deflationary strategy for combating the postwar inflation. Inflation and the impact of the harsh winter on harvests caused food distribution to worsen, and the workers were the first to pay for the aggravated economic conditions with lower real wages. Yet their output in key industries, such as coal, far surpassed prewar levels. And for the one-fifth increase in that industry, the Communists took exclusive credit for their role as the taskmaster of the working class.[29]

The Communists were in an untenable position, one which anti-Communist politicians acknowledged as a likely source of future political crisis. Their union, the CGT, was being outflanked by the more militant Christian federation, and in February the newspaper and government workers went on strike as the party counseled moderation and dissociated itself from the events. France's effort to defeat the Vietminh in Indochina also greatly embarrassed the Communists. Publicly, the party favored independence for the Vietnamese within the French Union, and in mid-March it denounced the war by refusing, for the first time, to vote for credits to pursue the war. Clearly anguished, Thorez shortly thereafter stressed the need to maintain a united republican government.

But the party leadership was profoundly split, with Thorez counseling a very cautious line which the other government leaders gratefully recognized. It was Thorez's social democratic strategy that offset the rumors of armed plots that might otherwise have alarmed the government. And it was his pleas to the party's political bureau that it work for the restoration of industrial production, even at the sacrifice of workers' demands, that convinced the government that the Communists could still be useful notwithstanding their halfhearted independence on Indochina. Yet the pressure on the Communist leaders from within their own ranks was far greater than that from their political associates, much less the United States. American diplomats had for some time criticized the Communist presence in the government, and after the Truman Doctrine address exerted stronger pressures, but these, too, were ineffective. The government itself, even at the beginning of May, did not consider it needed American aid, at any price, if only because mining and manufacturing output in 1947 was to surpass the preceding year by one-fifth, and Washington had no decisive leverage over Communist membership in the government.[30] More important was the fact that the Communists were ultimately forced to acknowledge that the game of politics involved issues more significant than posts for themselves, but also impinged on economic and foreign affairs.

The French workers imposed the message on the Communists, thereby encouraging the substantial faction opposed to Thorez's penchant to collaborate. By March, inflation forced workers spontaneously to strike throughout France. And in union elections the following month the Communist-controlled CGT lost substantial percentages of votes. Then, on April 26, the workers at the government-owned Renault plants chose to strike despite Communist attacks on strikes as the tools of the trusts or Hitlerite-Gaullist-Trotskyite machinations. Worse yet, both the Socialists and the Trotskyites enthusiastically sustained the workers, raising the specter to the Communists of being outflanked on the left. At the end of the month the Communists and CGT finally demanded that the intractable government meet the workers' demands without raising prices.

The elimination of the Communist ministers from the government on May 5 was a quite friendly affair, with regrets on both sides, and more dangerous to Prime Minister Paul Ramadier was the Socialist threat also to resign. Thorez and Duclos immediately denounced mass demonstrations or a general strike as endangering the party's position, and while Thorez now strongly endorsed higher wages he also hewed to the themes of greater production, a united front of all classes, and parliamentarianism.[31] Quite clearly, the workers had forced the erstwhile revolutionary party of France to embark on an essentially unfamiliar and uncomfortable course.

In Italy the role of the Communist Party was not greatly different from that in France, but there it had to contend with a De Gasperi government more obviously intent on purging the key sectors of the state apparatus prior to a confrontation with the Left. Economically, however, Italy continued to recover at a rapid pace even as inflation deeply cut the living standards of important sectors of the working and white-collar classes. At the beginning of 1947, with the Christian Democrats losing political strength, United States officials thought the political situation improved when Nenni's Socialists, with covert American aid, split. The step was critical in isolating the Communists for the eventuality that the far more conservative government was obviously planning for them.

In January 1947 De Gasperi visited the United States, returning with a $100 million loan and advice to eliminate the Communist-Nenni coalition from the Rome government. The timely split in the Nenni party offered the conservatives important, though small, increments to their coalition. The Communists, aware of the way the ax was about to fall, responded ingratiatingly by becoming the only party on the left to vote during March for "Article Seven," a measure which for practical purposes reaffirmed Mussolini's Lateran Treaty granting the Catholic Church a privileged legal and economic status. The gesture could not save the Communists, who had finally to respond to De Gasperi's obvious desire to introduce classic deflationary policies by reducing credits, expenditures, and, ultimately, workers' incomes. But in Italy the Communists would not take the hints, even after De Gasperi publicly denounced them at the end of April. Unlike their confreres in France, they could not conjure up the will to resign, and on May 12 they were thrown out of the government when De Gasperi dissolved it.[32] In its own fashion, Italian conservatism had found the formula for its own salvation, and given the docility of the Communists it was one predestined to work with or without the Marshall Plan.

The Russian response to the French and Italian events is a measure of their larger European strategy and intentions. For the two enormous Communist parties had hewed a consistently conservative, antirevolutionary line, and it was one Moscow completely endorsed. And the parties were to remain tractable in or out of government.

The Russians immediately publicly attacked the exclusion of the two parties, erroneously assigning the United States main responsibility for the actions. But they also endorsed the French Communists' drive for greater productivity and pointed to its major role in France's recovery. Privately, as well, the Russians the following September were to endorse the French party's reformism, chiding them on marginal points but making it unequivocally clear that Moscow did not want to see an insurrectionary effort. If both the Italians and the French admitted to the Russians that they had been quite opportunist, there is no evidence the Russians said anything to alter that course. Indeed, the Italians excused themselves to the Yugoslavs by stating they were merely fulfilling Russian orders.[33]

The Russians undoubtedly advised a strategy on the Communists consistent with their assumption that Western Europe would develop autonomously or as an American satellite, for it was an obvious fact that they had no chance of extending their influence into the area over the opposition of local conservative forces and the United States. Indeed, they must have acknowledged that any Communist effort to do so could only endanger much more profound Soviet interests along its borders and, above all, in Germany.

Germany: Key to Europe's Future

The fate of Germany impinged on every aspect of Europe's destiny. Independent and reconstructed, its military potential was too awesome for any of its former enemies, including the United States, to favor. Integrated into one bloc or another, it might tip the balance of military power on the entire Continent. For all the European nations, Germany's future in any form was decisive to their national security.

Economically, Germany could move with the dominant European impulse toward the left, as a majority of its voters wished, or the United States could use the Western zones as a weapon to dissolve the currents of socialism and nationalism prevalent everywhere in Europe. For Germany was the only nation over whose economic future the United States had mastery, and by the end of 1946 many American leaders were beginning to acknowledge its potential value as a pawn of decisive significance. For however stagnant at the time, Germany was a dormant economic colossus whose presence no one would be able to ignore.

Internally, the American occupation had managed by the end of 1946 to extend its hegemony over the British-occupied zone and to neutralize the Social Democratic threat there. And by insulating Bizonia from the Soviet-controlled region, the Anglo-Americans had begun to quarantine the rest of Germany from the impressive redistribution of power taking place in the East, also preventing a dominant national coalition of the Left. If stagnation and the *status quo* were the two essential outcomes of American policy through 1946, at least the United States retained its option for a future more compatible with its own interests.

By 1947 the British were ready to sacrifice many of their own desires for Germany in order further to reduce their immense expenditures to support their zone of Bremen, a key to West Germany's frozen economy. During the same period Clay and his advisers acted to muzzle elected Social Democrats—who in January 1947 managed to take over the critical bizonal Executive Committee for Economics and pledge it to socialization—raising insurmountable new obstacles to democratic socialization of West Germany's economy.[34]

Even if such steps did not promote industrial recovery, American leaders saw them as crucial to advancing their ends. It was common, and correct, knowledge that at the beginning of 1947 Clay and his advisers were determined to take decisive action to revive West Germany's economy as soon as the forthcoming Moscow Foreign Ministers Conference in March produced the failure that was anticipated. All that remained for them to decide was the form, and here no great surprises were in store. Dulles articulated the proposition in mid-January: Germany was the central question in Europe, and a potential threat to peace that America could not permit to rise alone. Yet recover it must, but in the context of Western European economic integration and federation that would exploit Germany's resources while preventing it from achieving, ". . . by economic pressures, a mastery of western Europe which they could not achieve by arms."[35] Such a formula implied that West Germany would for practical purposes exist in a region essentially divorced from the Russian orbit, and also that Washington might redefine other Western European economic currents, both nationalist and socialist, in a manner compatible with American goals. Behind Dulles' German solution was a program for a new system of integrated capitalism in Western Europe.

The details of such desires were not worked out at the time, but Dulles' proposal was known to other key decision-makers, who approved the concept, for what was more attractive about it was that it sanctioned German economic reconstruction. Truman at the end of January made it inevitable that the United States would attempt it in one form or another when he asked Herbert Hoover to prepare a special report on the German economy.

For practical purposes, Hoover's recommendations, which were made available to the President during March, called for the elimination of all but the most nominal restrictions on German industry, the effective end of allusions to reparations, decartelization, and denazification, and the mobilization of Germany's resources on behalf of "Western civilization."[36]

In this context, they could not expect much from the Moscow Foreign Ministers Conference which was to open March 10. All that remained was for the United States to add the details to a firm policy. As Marshall departed for Moscow he publicly announced that ". . . the negotiations in Moscow will be extremely difficult," a pessimism that Dulles, his key adviser, shared.[37] He proceeded first to Berlin, where together with Clay and Murphy they reiterated Dulles' belief that Germany had to be both protected from Soviet political penetration and prevented from becoming ". . . independent of both East and West."[38] The only option was that it become America's ally and linchpin in Europe.

Progress at Moscow was therefore impossible. The Russians still demanded reparations from the Western zones, including from current production, but even before the conference they, too, had publicly expressed a realistic pessimism about obvious American plans for integrating Germany into a Western bloc. Yet even Clay, upon seeing the immense damage Germany had inflicted upon the USSR, privately observed that ". . . one only has to visit Russia to realize how much its policy is affected by dire need."[39] To this he might have added Soviet fear of a resurgent German militarism. But the reparations question remained the key to the issues of internal political control, economic forms, and democracy, on which at least a few Americans at the conference felt the Russians might compromise all else.

As it was, there was no opportunity for such trading. Truman, Murphy later recalled, ". . . was in no mood to concede anything," and there is no evidence that any of his key advisers urged him to do so.[40] Given his proclamation of an anti-Communist crusade on the twelfth, there was not much point to the effort. The Russians duly proposed centralizing Germany into one economic unit, raising the levels of industry, and creating a single political structure with all-German parties and unions. They freely attacked American policy as an effort to absorb Germany into an American-led Western bloc as well as circumscribe its radical labor movement, and their proposals, while general, were in principle democratic in form. Marshall, for his part, talked in abstractions about democratic political forms, but resisted the organizational principles the Russians proposed. Centralized unions would lead to "communist domination," his advisers warned, and there was little question that the broader "socialist revolutionary movement" in Germany was very much on their minds.[41] "What is required . . ." for the larger economic and security questions the Russians raised, Marshall informed them, "is a European solution in a Europe which includes Germany."[42] Marshall did not offer such a formula to the Russians, for what he was grasping for was a Europe that could isolate both Russia and the Left.

While in Moscow the American delegates sought especially to win French collaboration for a consolidated Western Germany able to resist Russia in the context that America defined. Ambassador Smith and Dulles both thought the Soviet position served to strengthen three-power unity on the German question. The French came to Moscow mainly to obtain more coal from Bizonia, and acquiring coal became an obsession that overshadowed their desire to internationalize the Ruhr. Here they attained some success, and won support as well for French economic integration of the Saar. But they did not ask the United States for financial credits. The Ruhr question, the Americans informed them, would be resolved as part of a comprehensive Western European economy involving Germany.[43]

Before leaving Moscow, Marshall saw Stalin, who attempted to brush aside the significance of the conference's failure, suggesting that in six months they might all reach agreement. Marshall read ominous meanings into Stalin's unconcerned, confident attitude, but more significant was that perhaps it caused him to move on a program that had been extensively discussed and planned even before March. On his way back from Moscow, Marshall stopped in Berlin and instructed Clay to accelerate the bizonal merger and economic recovery. Then, upon returning to Washington, he ordered his staff to prepare a European assistance plan that quite obviously they were to design preeminently to meet the German problem in a broader, less autarchic Western European context that American officials had been discussing for many months.

On April 28 Marshall made a public report on the conference which spelled out in greater detail what was later to be called his "Plan." But now he set a more accurate context, one which made Germany the heart of American strategy in Europe. Germany, first of all, had to become self-supporting, which meant no reparations from current production and enough economic recovery within three years to terminate United States assistance. Moreover, while ignoring the critical details, Marshall suggested that the German problem had to be considered along with ". . . the character of the economic system and its relation to all of Europe." "The recovery of Europe," he vaguely ended, "has been far slower than had been expected. Disintegrating forces are becoming evident. The patient is sinking while the doctors deliberate. So I believe that action cannot await compromise through exhaustion. . . . Whatever action is possible to meet these pressing problems must be taken without delay."[44] "The challenge we face is not a military one," Dulles added shortly thereafter. "I am confident that Soviet leaders do not want war."[45] The question was purely economic, and now largely German, for recovery in Western Europe hardly warranted such funereal predictions. For by solving the German problem the United States would also seek to control Western Europe's incipient economic independence.

Marshall directed his staff to give form and substance to the policy judgments he and his peers endorsed, and so it is of no import which of his underlings was responsible for drafting his subsequent declarations. Throughout May, with no illusions about democracy by consulting those to be ruled, the British and American occupation governments hammered out a new bizonal administration to implement Washington's new will. On the economic level, the reformed structure was gerrymandered in a manner which circumvented the Länder, five of eight of which had Social Democratic minister-presidents. Since the explicit purpose of this still further reduction of democracy was to prevent socialism—if only because the "radical trend" among the masses continued unabated—the military governors retained yet more of the key control over the bizonal economy.[46]

Back in the United States, the administration found its desires to scuttle JCS 1067 for something more utilitarian being reinforced. Key businessmen called upon to tour Germany for the War Department publicly urged implementation of the Hoover recommendations and scrapping the ineffectual regulations on decartelization and denazification. Informally, American decision-makers heard similar advice. For Washington, the steps that had to be taken were the logic of the situation and its own goals, and on July 11, while Clay was scotching British proposals for socializing German coal, it issued JCS 1779.

The new document, while shorter than its predecessor, eliminated some of the obstacles that allegedly JCS 1067 had created. Its main goal was ". . . the establishment of stable political and economic conditions in Germany . . . which will enable Germany to make a maximum contribution to European recovery." This meant disarmament but also that they could not permanently limit Germany's industrial capacity nor could it pay reparations at the expense of a self-sustaining economy. For practical purposes, the new document indefinitely postponed the question of public ownership, and in the meantime ". . . it is your duty to give the German people an opportunity to learn the principles and advantages of free enterprise. . . ."[47] This required, as well, maximum organizational decentralization of trade unions. In brief, Germany would rebuild its economic power; it would be a capitalist state; and in that role it would be oriented toward the Western European economy.

Toward a Grand Economic Strategy

There had been no doubt in any American leader's mind that the Truman Doctrine was but the beginning of a much more ambitious and comprehensive plan for the entire European situation, and on March 11 a cabinet committee was designated to study emergency aid and long-range policy. It was a major assignment, the objectives of which were virtually conventional wisdom, and they had only to devise the means to attain them.

During March the details involved in the Truman Doctrine and the Moscow Conference preoccupied American policy-makers. But they always assumed that the existing international economic mechanisms were failing to attain those United States goals they privately and publicly made explicit with familiar reasoning. Marshall's thoughts on the condition of Germany quickened the pace of activity, as we have seen in the broader European context, and were certainly the most important influence on policy. The themes of the United States' need for an open world economy in which it could find both markets and raw materials the State Department repeated as part of the ideological litany. The existence of trade barriers very much troubled officials, who frankly reiterated the fact that "[p]rivate capitalism survives in many places, but it is on the defensive and is much less influential than it was before the war."[48] The role contemplated for an American-regulated Germany was hopefully to counteract this shift in the balance of European social systems.

The question, therefore, was really an issue of the form of Western capitalism, which was continuing along regulated nationalist lines or, what was worse, slipping into socialism of one variety or another. Explicitly, the issue was how to use economic power to dissolve this combined and growing threat to America's global aims. The Russians openly and quite accurately discussed this situation, and regarded it essentially as a dimension of the rivalry between the capitalisms of the United States, Western Europe, and, primarily, Britain.[49]

During April, however, the State Department and White House were to suffer momentary embarrassment in their strategy for reform of world capitalism. For while Washington urged the rest of the world to undo its restrictions on trade, the United States still had many of its own that served to exclude imports. The contemplated International Trade Organization, which Congress had yet to approve, was supposed to go a long way toward dissolving such barriers, but the Europeans were skeptical. The heart of the ITO scheme was the general negotiations on tariff reductions, and on April 11 a world tariff and trade conference in Geneva was to begin reductions even before the formal trade structure was created. And the United States' first objective at Geneva was to reduce British imperial preferences by as much as possible. If the GATT meeting at Geneva succeeded, the Americans could realize the most vital part of their trade program.

Clayton represented the United States at Geneva, where the British were in no mood to risk new experiments with the clever Americans. The State Department, however, had postponed the GATT talks until after the elections in order to avoid pressures from domestic agricultural interests protected to the hilt, but also had already added escape clauses designed to protect United States producers in any future trade agreements. This fresh inconsistency, plus United States preferences with the Philippines and Cuba, only strengthened British resolve to resist United States pressure. The logic of this convenient and traditional dual standard hit the world again just as Clayton arrived in Europe, for the United States wool industry had managed to mobilize Congress to introduce a bill imposing a 50 percent fee on the value of imported wool, and then began going through the motions of passing it.[50] Britain, Australia, and their key sterling bloc associates stood firm on any concessions, and Geneva seemed doomed to failure.

Meanwhile, as the doleful news came to Washington from Moscow and Geneva, the special cabinet committee charged with formulating policy quickened its efforts, focusing them during April on a policy statement Acheson was to deliver on May 8 to the Delta Council in Mississippi. When Marshall returned from Moscow and charged Kennan and the State Department policy-planning staff with the task of drawing up a European assistance scheme with emphasis on Germany, Kennan relied heavily on the special committee's work. To Kennan, it was understood that ". . . the revival of productive capacity in the west of Germany be made the primary object of our policy in that area . . .," a thought the special committee shared in a broader economic context.[51] Acheson's famous May 8 speech reflected this broader emphasis, and was intended more as a description and preparatory alarm than an exact plan, but despite careful briefings the press still described it largely as a plea to reconstruct Germany and Japan within a Western bloc. For Marshall had said as much shortly before, and this was in reality a prime objective.

Acheson began and ended his speech with the German and Japanese dilemma and the need to reconstruct those two nations, and in between he hinted that the United States would have to provide credits of about five to eight billion dollars a year, for several more years, to sustain necessary United States exports to Europe. And although he suggested that European ". . . freedom and democracy and the independence of nations could not long survive" without such aid, the crucial specific socioeconomic import of the message was to be filled in later.[52] For the British, Italian, and French leaders did not think they were facing such a final crisis, and indeed they were not in so precarious a condition as to be without means for continued reconstruction. It was simply that those techniques would seriously restrict America's economic role in Europe. From their staunch resistance to the Americans at Geneva it was apparent that the precise form of the salvation Washington offered was quite unappealing to them. And as for the German people, they saw their solution in one or another brand of socialism. In effect, Acheson was presenting an argument preeminently designed to save a type of world capitalism in which America's long-term interests would best be served.

By April and May the consensus on proposed policies and goals was so great in Washington that colorful incidents, or a text's precise authorship, are of no import. Marshall, reflecting the consensus on priorities that had existed among top officials since early in the year, at the end of April planned to give yet another policy formulation designed to prepare the way for a new burst of funds and pressures to attain traditional ends. His April 28 speech and Acheson's Delta address were considerably more explicit than the famous Marshall speech of June 5, but one must also read them between the lines.

One has only to add that to Clayton and the rest of Washington it was apparent that the GATT-ITO approach toward restructuring the world economy was moving toward failure, and in May this was made more obvious when Congress began to pass the wool protection bill and reassert its troublesome independence at a critical moment. The administration had to find new means, and Clayton was aware of the economic conditions that

Congress would add to future massive aid just as it had to the earlier British and French loans. If America could not negotiate its ideal world economy, perhaps it could impose it. Taking the integration of a capitalist Germany into Europe as its core, suffocating internal radicalism there and creating both a balance and barrier to Russian power, the United States was ready to meet its needs in that convenient, unilateral merger of its own national interests and that of other states which was the traditional basis of its expansionism.[53]

The policy of reconstructing Western Germany in a Western European context was tantamount to a decision to divide Europe and isolate the Soviet Union and its allies. America's policy formulators comprehended the import of the departure, which soon they called "containment." By applying its power to political and economic realities the United States hoped eventually to transform or neutralize them, an assumption that precluded negotiations and also, it was thought, would not require military confrontation so long as the United States retained its decisive military superiority.

Later the United States' leaders embraced more unreservedly the view that the Russians were responsible for initiating crises everywhere in the globe—a premise not yet fully rooted in mid-1947—but in the spring of 1947 Washington was still aware of the fact that the primary, immediate threat to America's interests was the emergence of assorted brands of socialism and capitalist nationalism in Europe. What the United States opposed, therefore, was the social and economic consequences of World War II and the civil war in the world that had raged with various degrees of intensity since 1914. However preferable it thought the conservative *status quo* to bolshevism, Washington was also engaged in an effort to transform, and thereby better penetrate, the structure of the old order in Europe, becoming the rival of both nationalism and socialism. It wished to buttress capitalism, but *also* to reshape it in a form satisfactory to the United States, and America never ceased to make that equation.

For domestic political reasons as well as an only partially sincere perception of political realities, anti-Communism and anti-Soviet rhetoric now became an integral part of Washington's political lexicon—so much so that in time it even mystified sophisticated men. Eventually, paranoid visions enveloped many of them. American foreign policy became one that was justified because of dramatic threats, more and more personified by Russia and its leaders. Indeed, it made slight difference that the Russians, aware of the connections Washington was making between local dissidence and the Kremlin, were energetically counseling a most conservative line for the Communist parties of Western Europe, China, and elsewhere as well. That the Russians were still providing capitalism in many nations with a critical respite, allowing conservative social classes to reimpose their hegemony, is of more interest to historians and revolutionaries than it was to Washington. For America's leaders, with understandable justification, saw Communism as the expression of a larger and deeper radical impulse, and it was that source of discontent they sought to quash. In 1947 they thought that the judicious application of essentially economic power would suffice both to contain the Left and to transform recalcitrant forms of national capitalism.

Greece revealed that economic power and also military firepower were America's handmaidens, and that the crusade against Communism was capable of resorting to both. And the decision to reconstruct and integrate Germany as perhaps the most reliable of America's continental allies showed how peripheral the political questions of World War II had become. For Washington's immediate postwar impulse to remove Germany as a threat to the peace was now eclipsed, reopening again the traditional question of the extent and form of Germany's role and power in Europe.

13

The Marshall Plan, I:
Foundations of Policy

Since 1947 the public, as well as subsequent scholars, has regarded the Marshall Plan as an expression of the unprecedented generosity of a powerful nation rebuilding its potential economic competitors from the ruins of the war and spreading the bounty of American production to the ravaged people of Europe. Even otherwise critical historians have discussed the program in terms of enlightened self-interest and as an effort to forestall Communist penetration by raising the living standards of the masses in Europe and to reestablish normal trading patterns through which the entire world would realize prosperity and peace.

The plan itself was actually the outcome of the real alarm with which Washington viewed the direction of the world economy. It was formulated in discussions over many months before June 1947, and its implementation, as we shall see, while based on certain unwavering assumptions, was in continual flux as it responded to the changing economic and political environment. A close examination of both Washington's constant premises and vacillating practice exposes not only the bedrock of American foreign policy but also the workings of contemporary capitalism.

The United States' desire to reestablish the multilateral trade relations that existed before and immediately after World War I was an old policy. In 1926 John Foster Dulles explained that ". . . our foreign loans primarily operate to provide payments in dollars here to our farmers and manufacturers for goods which they sell abroad, and to pay debts previously contracted for such purposes. . . . Actually the dollar proceeds of foreign loans stay in the United States and are used here either to pay principal or interest maturing on dollar loans previously contracted or to pay for American goods or services."[1] In the two years after World War II the United States sought to achieve its aims through much the same approach, again using loans to attain its foreign economic goals. But by 1947 the failure of such an approach was obvious to all. The error that the United States did not wish to repeat was the unbroken circle of loans to repay loans. With a system of grants, the administration now came to believe, it could restructure an ideal world capitalist trading structure within a limited time span, and then allow it to operate in a self-generating system of triangular trade able to purchase America's vast surplus with the earnings of its own products, either in the United States or in the raw materials producing Third World. The primary focus on the repayment of new loans would only perpetuate Europe's dollar shortage and inhibit the continued and growing trade that was the main objective of the United States. Meanwhile, the American interests would have the widest possible markets and free access to essential raw materials. If this description sounds deceptively facile, it is due to the fact that the attempt to implement or impose this truly simple policy on a vastly complex world economy made for a much more complicated story.

Immediately after the war, as we have described in Chapter 6, there were not enough dollars in Europe to purchase American goods, and capitalist and Communist Europe alike was forced, willy-nilly, into state bilateral barter and regulated trade for its essential needs. The obvious danger to the United States was that these arrangements would soon become permanent and similar to the detested sterling bloc, further isolating the United States with its vast unsalable surplus. As a capitalist nation unable to expand its internal market by redistributing its national income to absorb the surplus, the United States would soon plunge again into the depression that only World War II brought to an end. The alternative was to export dollars, primarily through grants rather than loans. This time, however, Washington had no intention of operating within an organization such as UNRRA. By June 1947 what Washington desired was the opportunity not only to subsidize United States exports but to permanently influence and shape Western Europe's internal economic policies.[2]

Secretary of State Marshall's celebrated address at Harvard University on June 5 called upon the governments of Europe to take the initiative in formulating a program for a coordinated reconstruction, promising that the United States would provide "support" and "friendly aid" for their effort. Given the political background of the preceding months, the entire speech was exceptionally vague in its wording, raising more questions than it answered. Marshall declared that his proposal was ". . . directed not against any country or doctrine," implying that the offer included the USSR and Eastern Europe.[3] Yet he was clearly by-passing the new UN Economic Commission for Europe, just organized in May, and calling for a new organizational effort with different goals. Marshall's ambiguous statement was, in reality, more an exercise in public relations, primarily for the European audience, than the substance of the new policy. It emphasized European initiative, and the omission of any reference to United States commercial policy or European concessions was to make the proposal more palatable to the Europeans, many of whom had shown a hostile reaction to the Truman Doctrine.

Within a week Bevin and Bidault welcomed Marshall's proposal and agreed to meet in Paris to discuss a joint response. Bevin could scarcely believe that Marshall had intended including the Russians and dreaded that their participation would imperil the entire offer. Beset with urgent economic concerns, for several days he resisted Bidault's demand that they invite the Russians to join them. Both governments were reluctant at the time to ask Washington any pointed questions concerning the program, and, eager for aid, they hoped that the future would illuminate to their benefit the vast obscurities of Marshall's proposal.

Soviet Reaction

The first Soviet reaction to Marshall's speech was delayed until June 16 when *Pravda* wrote that the proposal was yet another version of the Truman Doctrine ". . . of political pressure by means [of] dollars" in the internal affairs of other states.[4] It compared the timing of the speech with the cutting off of previously granted credits to Hungary because of political shifts in Budapest. Bevin and Bidault's prompt consultation in Paris, with only a belated invitation to the Russians, increased the Soviet suspicions. On June 19 Radio Moscow reported that ". . . these negotiations are nothing less than an attempt to make a deal behind the back of the Soviet Union. . . . [The] invitation . . . coming . . . as an afterthought, could hardly be considered seemly treatment of a great power. . . ."[5] On that same day, however, William Clayton called on the Russians to participate in the reconstruction of Europe, and that invitation, coupled with the great hopes among the Eastern European states for further assistance, as well as the heavy burdens of their own reconstruction, led the Soviets to believe that there was a possibility of aid without interference, based on a strictly economic rationale, and some form of mutually beneficial cooperation with Western capitalism. Three days later the Soviets accepted a British-French invitation to discuss the proposal, and suggested that the foreign ministers meet in Paris on June 27. The Russians rested their decision on the assumption that the nature of the United States economy forced the Americans to expand their market to avoid internal crisis. The premise was correct, but the Soviets' error—and this was colored by their own needs—was to believe that the United States needed the Eastern bloc as well as the Western. "The elimination of the devastating consequences of the second world war is a very far from easy task . . . ," Moscow's *New Times* wrote at the end of the month. "The rehabilitation of the economies of the European countries would be greatly facilitated and expedited if they received aid from the United States in the form of loans, credits and goods."[6] With the hope that the United States would regard the program as a "business transaction" and ". . . serious economic measures . . . contemplated to develop and strengthen the economies [of Europe] and stabilize international trade," on June 27 Molotov went to Paris, taking eighty-nine technicians and advisers to discuss a joint proposal for American aid.[7] Given the political background of the events, only the most severe economic pressures in the USSR could have led it to accept the invitation in good faith, for Molotov's subsequent behavior and his armada of experts soon revealed his sincerity.

In Paris Molotov proposed that each nation prepare a list of its needs, and then that they coordinate their lists and present a joint request to the United States. To this Bevin, whom Clayton had just briefed in London, insisted that Marshall intended the Europeans first to prove that they were helping themselves in their recovery efforts—which only confirmed the Russian's suspicions. How could anyone doubt that after the devastation of the war, and no subsequent aid, the USSR was reconstructing itself to the full extent of its capacities? When Bidault proposed that the conference draw up an integrated economic plan for the whole of Europe, Molotov rejected the proposal as one of unprecedented interference in the internal affairs of sovereign states and suggested instead that the conference restrict itself to, "1. Establishment of the requirements of European countries for American economic aid. 2. Methods for the consideration of . . . countries in respect of American . . . aid. (*a*) Creation of *ad hoc* committees. (*b*) Relations with [ECE]. 3. Ascertainment of the possibilities, nature and conditions of American economic aid to Europe."[8] But Bevin and Bidault were already familiar with those conditions, as, indeed, Molotov should have been. Clayton had already impressed upon Bevin the fact that United States aid was contingent on an over-all European plan to which all the varied European states would agree, and that the system of economic "cooperation" should continue after the end of Marshall aid.[9] In his speech before leaving Paris on July 2, Molotov put the onus for dividing Europe and sabotaging the unknown quantity of United States aid squarely on the French and British. ". . . [I]t is now proposed to make the possibility of any country's obtaining American credits dependent on its obedience to the above-mentioned organization and its 'Steering Committee.' . . . Where may this lead? . . . Today pressure may be exerted on Poland to produce more coal, even at the cost of restricting other Polish industries. . . . Norway will be forced to refrain from developing her steel industry, because this would better suit certain foreign steel corporations, and so on. What will remain of the economic independence and sovereignty of such European countries?" And, touching on an expecially sensitive issue, Molotov added, "Particularly noteworthy is the fact the Franco-British proposals raise the question of Germany and her resources . . . although everyone knows that the just reparations claims of Allied . . . countries still go unsatisfied." Finally, Molotov concluded that ". . . the Soviet Government deems it necessary to warn the Governments of Britain and France against the consequences of such actions, which aim not at uniting the efforts of the European countries for their postwar economic recovery, but at entirely different purposes that have nothing in common with the true interests of the peoples of Europe."[10] With this warning Molotov left Paris and Bevin and Bidault then issued invitations to the twenty-two other European nations to plan an integrated European request for American aid.

There is no question that the United States knew that the Russians would not, in the end, participate in the program. However, if they had it would be only by abandoning bolshevism and state trading, and integrating the USSR and those nations within its bloc into a capitalist trading sphere—largely placing its economy under the guidance of the United States and Western Europe. The Americans could scarcely fear such a possibility.

The British and the French, however, in their desperate desire for further United States aid, did fear the remote chance that the inclusion of the USSR would foreclose congressional support for the European Recovery Program (ERP), and it was with some reluctance, especially on the part of Bevin, that they sent the invitation to Moscow. Bidault was under more internal political pressure against dividing Europe, not to mention reviving German power, and even after Molotov left Paris he insisted that the door would remain open to Russia's possible future reconsideration. When Molotov left Paris, French President Auriol commented that his allegations regarding Germany were "absurd," that the question of reparations was outside the scope of the Marshall Plan, and that Germany, lacking a government, would not participate. Yet Auriol was keenly aware that the question of Germany would be the most vulnerable area in which to attack the entire plan. But no later than July 15 it became vividly clear that the United States intended to increase German power vis-à-vis its neighbors. Auriol then advised the French ambassador in Washington to stress the political folly of this program. Bidault confessed his alarm over British subservience on the German question, but Bevin indicated that on any divergence on the question of Germany, he would side with the Americans.[11]

Sixteen Western European nations accepted the invitation to participate in the talks. The six Eastern European nations, after some pressure (discussed in Chapter 14) followed the Soviet lead and declined. The sixteen organized a general committee, the Committee of European Economic Cooperation (CEEC), and four subcommittees for specialized problems, and began to prepare a recovery plan. At their side were a number of American advisers and consultants, including Clayton, Charles Bonesteel, Henry Labouisse, and the ambassadors to England and France, Lewis Douglas and Jefferson Caffery.[12] But despite close American direction, the CEEC initially proposed $29 billion and the shocked Americans demanded a sharp reduction of the figure. When the CEEC completed its draft on September 11 and showed it to Clayton the following day, he insisted that $21 billion was still too high and that the CEEC revise its report by scaling down the requests for aid and providing greater guarantees of policies for fiscal stability, action on reducing trade barriers, and a pledge to establish an ongoing coordinating organization after all aid had ended. It was this last point that the Europeans found especially repugnant, stating that they were unaccustomed to ". . . looking over the back fence of their neighbors. . . ."[13] The CEEC again renewed its close haggling with Clayton, who threatened to call off the entire plan, and the Europeans finally conceded to the United States demands. They submitted their report on September 22, calling for $19.3 billion in United States aid over four years. The guidance of Clayton and his associates was precise to the extent that the final CEEC report followed in minute detail and vocabulary the basic policy statements that the State Department had prepared months earlier.[14]

The plan listed the goals that the participating nations hoped to achieve by the end of the four-year program as a substantial increase in the level of production over 1938, creation of internal financial stability, establishment of a permanent agency of mutual economic cooperation among the European states (a clause on which Clayton had been adamant), and closing the dollar deficit through an expansion of exports. The assumptions behind these goals were that the standard of living would not increase substantially, that they could reduce their deficit by restricting imports, that they would expand their exports to the United States, that economic growth and demand would be steady, and that there would be no significant political crises. Europe's needs were chiefly for food and fertilizer, industrial equipment, oil and coal, and iron and steel. The plan's projected cost was soon rendered meaningless when the announcement of the program in June accelerated the already escalating United States inflation.[15]

The best-laid paper plans, however, had to be carried out in the dynamic environment of the world economy where events did not wait on the debates of a group of men. As the representatives of the sixteen prepared their report, the economic and political realities in Europe worsened over the summer and fall of 1947.

Great Britain

Britain, having emerged from the extraordinary winter of 1946–1947, was in a truly critical plight. The 1946 loan was disappearing much faster than expected, due in part to the worst winter in memory but primarily due to the American inflation which had reduced the real value of the loan by 25 percent. Then, on July 15, the British implemented the much-criticized convertibility clause in the loan agreement of 1946. As many had predicted when the loan was made, financial disaster accompanied the premature convertibility, for there was a rush on Britain's reserves from all dollar-starved quarters, drawing off $700 million in July alone and plainly indicating the certainty of complete exhaustion of its remaining reserves.

On August 20 Britain again suspended convertibility after persuading Washington that they had to spend what remained of the loan outside the dollar bloc. These new negotiations were onerous, involving many concessions that the United States extracted under pressure, and the level of British resentment against United States policy reached a peak that was hardly mitigated by the prospect of an ERP which they then feared might be more of the same. The embassy in London warned Washington that the general mood was reflected in the outraged commentary from the prestigious *Economist:*

American opinion should be warned that over here . . . one has the feeling of being driven into a corner by a complex of American actions and inconsistencies which, in combination, are quite intolerable. Not many people in this country believe the Communist thesis that it is the deliberate and conscious aim of American policy to ruin Britain and everything Britain stands for in the world. But the evidence can certainly be read that way. And if every time that aid is extended, conditions are attached which make it impossible for Britain ever to escape the necessity of going back for still more aid, obtained with still more self-abasement and on still more crippling terms, then the result will certainly be what the Communists predict. . . .[16]

Most frightening to the British was Washington's concerted pressure against Britain's most vital economic defenses—its links with the Commonwealth. During the summer of 1947 the United States pressed its long-standing policy to completely destroy the imperial preference system simultaneously at the CEEC in Paris, the ITO discussions in Geneva, and, finally, the meetings on the convertibility question in Washington.

ITO negotiator Clair Wilcox outlined the American intent to destroy the sterling bloc in a memorandum on August 6 to Clayton:

We now have in our hands bargaining weapons we may never possess again: . . . [t]he possibility of easing the British financial crisis through relaxation of discrimination in the short run; and . . . [t]he prospect of aid under the Marshall Plan. If we cannot now obtain the liquidation of the Ottawa system [sterling bloc], we shall never do so. What we must have is a front-page headline that says "Empire Preference System Broken at Geneva." With this, the success of this whole series of negotiations is assured. Without it, there is grave danger that the whole trade program will end in defeat.[17]

The United States, with these advantages, pressured the British quite baldly, but, on this near life-or-death issue for their economy, the British negotiator, Stafford Cripps, remained adamant. At that point, it is important to note, the United States yielded. It did not break off negotiations as threatened, nor implement any of its other warnings. In the last analysis, the European states had, despite their desperate economic position, more bargaining power than they generally dared to exercise. The Americans needed Europe and could not afford to let it "go it alone." Nondiscrimination in trade would have been impossible at this time for the British economy even if it had been interpreted in its ideal form, but the United States had carefully outlined its aid program to retain its own discriminations, such as tied loans, shipping subsidies, and the like. As one British source pointed out, the Americans could insist that all their loans be spent in the United States, but strongly objected if ". . . Britain puts Argentina in possession of pounds by purchase of goods and stipulates that these pounds shall be spent in Britain."[18] And since trade policies are directly related to total economic policy, especially in a nation like Great Britain, free multilateral trade that makes an economy completely vulnerable to the slightest fluctuation in the world economy is incompatible with internal economic stability and planning for full employment. Yet such planning was another source of irritation for Washington. Any shift on the part of the Labour Party in economic policy that hinted at socialism or a welfare economy aroused profound distrust as American policy-makers resolved to use their future aid to undermine these efforts. As Forrestal recorded, "Harriman . . . gave it as his view that they [the British] would have small hope of getting additional help from the United States unless they faced up squarely to their problem, which is essentially that of inducing their people to go back to hard work. He thought the spectacle of Britain endeavoring to carry out the drastic program of nationalization and socialization of industry could not be underwritten by Americans."[19]

Meanwhile, the general European situation worsened. On August 27 the British introduced wartime controls, and France and Italy followed, drastically curtailing dollar purchases except for coal and cereals. By September, despite the fact that the sixteen nations were methodically preparing their proposals in Paris, economic necessity was again forcing the European states to turn to bilateral pacts and restrictions, the antithesis of United States economic aims. This tendency, the acting secretary of state told the cabinet, ". . . would finally communicate itself to the Western Hemisphere and would defeat the American efforts for international free trade."[20] The crisis of European capitalism, which hinged more on the form it might take than on its continuity, was no less a profound challenge to the future of American capitalism in the world.

France

In June 1947, France's economic situation remained serious, with prosperity still distant, and the studiously vague terminology of Marshall's speech received a broad welcome in France, including the Communist Party as long as the USSR expressed interest in the program.

The French economy reflected not only the dislocations of the war but the economic policies pursued since its end. The monetary situation at the time of liberation was not disastrous. However, in the best traditions of "liberalism," the government allowed wages and prices to find their own level and expected price rises to encourage production and investment. Nationalization was a nationalist measure of vengeance against Vichy collaborators, never concerned with social relations. The bureaucracy, until May 1947 often in the hands of Communist ministers, was interested in running the industry profitably by keeping prices high and wages low. The workers were exhorted to produce and make demands later as Communist ministers and labor leaders implemented the capitalist economic rationale that labor's standard of living would rise with the increase of production.[21]

The chronic food shortage, as in many parts of Europe, East and West, was due in part to the reluctance of the peasants to deliver food to the city except via the black market. The peasants as a class were eating better than before the war, since they could not buy manufactured goods in exchange for their food. The shortages pushed food costs ever higher. There were no further welfare measures after 1946, and the bookkeeping-conscious bureaucrats and the private industrialists, eager for profit and faced with rising costs in raw materials, all resisted growing wage demands. The wage control law of 1946, which prohibited collective bargaining, remained unaltered until February 1950. By May 1947 the working class was threatening to desert Communist leadership for more radical alternatives and the party left the government barely in time to retain its mass support.

The economic situation continued to deteriorate over the summer of 1947. The French followed the British in cutting all but essential dollar purchases and the government warned that if aid were not forthcoming production would fall by 50 percent for lack of essential raw materials. The circumstances imperiled the whole fabric of society, but the plight of the working class was, inevitably, the most serious. While the workers' living standard was far below the already depressed 1938 level, real wages continued to drop.

There was a series of short strikes over the summer in one industry after the other which did not change the workers' position, but was enough to alarm the government, especially since the American press portrayed them as politically directed from Moscow and the French government was nervously anxious for temporary United States aid before the ERP. But the workers, having been asked to boost their production efforts in light of steadily declining living standards, grew increasingly restive. Faced with a reduced bread ration, and relieved of the inhibiting, conservative pressures of the Communist Party since May, they had no interest in moderating their demands to satisfy American political needs, and by the fall the Communists were also anxious to defeat the entire Marshall Plan.[22]

The miners in the north, in particular, were ready to revolt. Some 200,000 militant workers lived and worked in the fall of 1947 in misery that had remained unchanged since the occupation. They were bitterly disappointed by the nationalization of 1946, which they had believed would mean workers' control but was instead a nationalist measure that made no difference in their lives or working conditions. As was to be revealed again and again, nationalization in a capitalist state puts the workers at even a greater disadvantage than private industry. In November 1947 the Communists, out of power, yielded to the pressure for a strike. The CGT made plans to consult all workers on the question of a general strike, but as with all such events, matters moved entirely out of its hands. Even at the meeting of their central committee as late as October 29–30, the leadership of the Communist Party did not discuss strikes, general or otherwise. Though fully informed of the internal party discussions, the French government proceeded to act as if the social conflict in France was the outcome of the machinations of the Cominform.[23] The CGT never called a general strike, for it spread spontaneously in November through most of the leading industries of France—metallurgy, railroads, mines, and docks. By the end of November more than three million workers were on strike, many occupying factories across France. Marches on city halls and police stations, with a number of occupations, sabotage of the mines, and widespread demonstrations, accompanied the strikes.

The events led to the resignation of the government during November 1947 and a cabinet crisis from which Robert Schuman eventually emerged as Premier and the Socialists Jules Moch and Robert Lacoste as ministers of interior and of industry. The government agreed to a small increase in wages, but refused to consider a sliding scale of quarterly adjustments to price rises, the only wage reform the workers considered meaningful in an inflationary economy. Only the preceding May, ironically, the Socialists had narrowly defeated a motion within the party to leave the government with the Communists, so deep was the concern even in their ranks for the plight of the working class. Over the summer, however, the ideological lines hardened amid the heightened anti-Communist mood. The Socialists continued to participate in the government with assumptions that in reality differed little from those the Communist ministers held when they shared in the ministries.[24]

Since the workers had not revolted earlier, and since their action complicated his problems of management, Moch convinced himself that the strikes were political rather than economic in origin, and he mounted a violent suppression of the workers. With an eye on the congressional discussions of emergency aid in Washington, and in close collaboration with the United States military attaché, Moch implemented a military "Plan Y" to guard the roads of France and even to prevent the influx of Italian Communists and the Communist International Brigades supposedly mobilized in Italy. The Americans and British assured him of cooperation in case of need to recall French troops from Germany. Moch asked the Assembly to call up 80,000 reservists, introduced stiff penalties for interfering with the "right to work," and sent a total of 200,000 troops to the mines to aid 120,000 police ostensibly protecting those who wished to work. On December 9 the CGT called off the strike ". . . to regroup and reassemble our forces for future combats, which will be hard."[25] The unyielding position of the state, the hunger of the workers, and finally a split in the union ranks and leadership forced what appeared to be a bitter end, but was to prove only a temporary respite.

The government parties also knew that they had to prove to the United States that they could "handle" their own Left and provide a stable environment to absorb massive American aid. John Foster Dulles, attending the Foreign Ministers Conference in London, hurried to Paris to confer with French officials and also De Gaulle about the crisis. Publicly he remarked that ". . . what was happening in France was far more important than what was happening in London."[26]

It was in this strike-torn context that the French, in their early enthusiasm for the Marshall aid, abandoned, even more than the British, the bargaining power which they unquestionably had. The French bourgeoisie, until now on the defensive because of its wartime aid to Vichy, fully recognized the support for its class in America's policies. The old "collabo" spirit was revived.[27]

Italy

The Italian bourgeoisie, which had also been on the defensive for the first two postwar years, reasserted its dominant position in the state in 1947 when in May, De Gasperi with United States urging reshuffled his cabinet and excluded the Socialist and Communist parties from the government. On June 21, the new cabinet won a narrow vote of confidence and became dependent on the Right and neofascists. The move was part of a general conservative shift in continental politics which further facilitated the reconstruction of a United States–oriented capitalism.[28]

Premier De Gasperi named an orthodox banker-economist, Luigi Einaudi, as minister of finance, and his policies set the course of the Italian economy over the next decade. His aim was to achieve equilibrium in the Italian balance of payments and to make the lira a strong currency. Einaudi blamed the inflation which had characterized the economy since the end of the war on the government policy of granting wheat subsidies and increasing the pay of civil servants and industrial workers, as well as on the cost of all social services.[29] The new finance minister lost no time in pursuing a single-minded effort to reverse these trends. He increased indirect taxation, especially on food, limited credit, and restricted supplies, thereby paralyzing the revival of Italian industry. Unemployment and business failures followed. Further compounding unemployment, the government, under Einaudi's direction, chose to force rationalization and reorganization of industry to eliminate excess manpower. By November 1947, as in France, the Italian workers reacted to these policies with a general strike. In Italy, however, the state responded with violent repression, resulting in many deaths among the workers, quickly crushing the strike and leaving only a wider and more bitter breach between the state and the working class.

Although the United States granted emergency aid to Italy in December 1947 to support the shaking economy until ERP could begin the following spring, due to the deflationary policies the Italian economy was unable to absorb the moderate amounts of new fuel and industrial material. Industrial production dropped 12 percent between the third quarter of 1947 and the first quarter of 1948. As usual, the workers were asked to pay the price of both the earlier inflationary economy and the new deflationary policies. The inflation had been caused in part by the fact that no one had blocked the wartime bank balances and the rich, with their hoarded savings, were able to push the prices of limited goods upward, while the subsequent deflation increased unemployment and relied on regressive indirect taxation. This advance warning as to what reconstruction would mean in the lexicon of conservative capitalism met full approval in Washington.[30]

Germany

The administration's emphasis on Germany was evident from the inception of the ERP. The three committees that Truman appointed to evaluate the Marshall Plan's significance to the American economy were unanimous with Congress in concluding that the success of the program depended on German recovery and the integration of its economy, and especially the Ruhr, into the ERP. As Britain's withdrawal from Greece strengthened the American position in the Middle East, so did its economic plight in 1947 give the United States the opportunity to move into the dominant role in Germany. In the crucial August 1947 discussion on the convertibility question and the use of what remained of the British loan, Washington pressed for ultimate control of the Ruhr and secured British agreement that the decisions in Bizonia would reflect the proportions of financial support, which now shifted from 50–50 to 80–20 percent.

United States plans for Germany, especially linked to the power leverage of the ERP, had the gravest consequences for the economic plans of the other European states, especially France and England. Aside from the anxiety for their political security with which they regarded the prospect of a resurgent and potentially dominant German state, London and especially Paris feared the effects on their own economic recovery and future markets. Both the Western and Eastern European states had based their earlier national recovery plans on the assumption that to a large extent they would replace German prewar exports to the former German markets. In fact, the first CEEC proposal presupposed a radical reduction in German steel output and placing Germany's coke at the disposal of its neighbors. The Europeans felt, at the very least, that the United States should emphasize the rehabilitation of the British and French mines and French industry before those of the former enemy state. At the Paris meetings in the summer of 1947, when the sixteen states formulated their coordinated plan, only the Dutch, whose own recovery was linked so closely to the revival of German trade, sustained the United States position to include Germany in the report. And not until the meeting in London in February 1948, under definitive United States pressure, did they finally agree to do so. Representing the Western zones of Germany in the Organization for European Economic Cooperation (OEEC) was the United States military command. By making Bizonia a dollar area the United States seriously restricted German trade with its dollar-poor neighbors, thereby having to provide Europe with dollars to maintain the German, as well as the American, economy.[31]

Politically, the ERP guaranteed that Germany would remain divided. The December 1947 Foreign Ministers Conference on the German question could only be *pro forma,* for once the United States had made the decision to include the Western zones in the ERP, and the Soviets aimed at defeating the entire program, the conversations on economic unity were utterly futile. The diplomats indulged in the exercise as a propaganda gesture without once mentioning the Marshall Plan, and the Foreign Ministers Conference put a formal end to the four-power-negotiated phase of the German question. As Harriman told a congressional committee, "Until that [the conference] is finished, it is impossible for anyone to consider what should be done in Germany about many of the problems that are now faced."[32] In fact, Washington had already made its plans, and the gesture of negotiations was merely public relations. The Marshall Plan would reconstruct and integrate a conservative, capitalist German state into the new capitalist trading bloc that the United States was organizing in Western Europe.

After the Russians left the Paris Marshall Plan meeting it was in this general context that they began to consolidate their international position and to offer aid and trade agreements to neighboring states that had, largely due to Soviet pressure, rejected the Marshall offer. By August 3 nearly all the Eastern European states had strengthened their mutual trade ties in what was soon referred to as the Molotov Plan.

At the end of September the Soviets convened a meeting in Poland of representatives of the Communist parties of nine European states to organize the Communist Information Bureau (Cominform), with headquarters in Belgrade to coordinate further activities. One of the chief reasons for the organization, according to Zhdanov, was to combat the ERP, underlined by the exclusion of the non-European Communist parties. "The exposure of the American plan for the economic enslavement of the European countries is an indisputable service rendered by the foreign policy of the USSR and the new democracies. . . . As to the USSR, it will bend every effort in order that this plan be doomed to failure."[33]

Washington Confronts Europe's Crisis

Despite the pressing nature of the crisis of capitalism in Europe, one that could not wait for Congress to deliberate the pros and cons of the ERP, until late October Washington was unhurried in meeting the emergency. Truman then ordered the Export-Import Bank to advance $93 million in emergency aid to France, but Congress still did not sense the urgency. On October 24 Truman was forced to call it into special session during mid-November to deal with the questions of emergency aid and inflation in the United States, which rose 23 percent over the preceding year. Rising American prices, in turn, considerably worsened the balance-of-payments problems of the Europeans dependent on the United States for supplies. Truman insisted that the entire ERP would be in peril if Congress hesitated on the emergency aid, but the administration spokesmen resisted the efforts of Congress to frame the aid program as defense expenditures or economic sanctions against the USSR. On November 10 Secretary of State Marshall addressed Congress, outlining the requirements and justifications for the program. He concluded with a request for $597 million emergency aid for Austria and, primarily, France and Italy, both witnessing significant strikes and class struggles, to support their economies until the ERP aid could commence on April 1, 1948. By that time, Marshall predicted, "Additional countries will . . . have exhausted their dollar resources."[34] Unquestionably influenced by the vigor used in repressing the strikes in France and Italy, Congress voted the aid bill of $580 million on December 1.

Although Congress voted the emergency aid for France, Italy, and Austria, it had yet to be convinced of the viability of a proposal as ambitious as the European Recovery Program that would commit the United States to four years of economic aid. After the end of the war the domestic and foreign demand for both industrial and consumer goods had been sufficient, especially after the removal of price controls in June 1947, to create a major inflation in the United States, especially for food and steel products. This fact alone bred opposition in Congress among legislators who feared further inflationary pressures and shortages as a consequence of expanded American aid.

Preparing America for Crisis

As the Europeans were organizing in Paris, the administration in Washington concluded on the basis of past experience that there was a need to cultivate a more receptive attitude toward the program on the part of the critical sector of the public and, especially, Congress. One effective method was the appointment of prestigious "citizens committees" to delineate the program's basic aims and assess the economic resources available and the effects on the domestic economy preparatory to the actual authorizing legislation of Congress in 1948. Truman appointed three such committees during June: the Committee on Foreign Aid under W. Averell Harriman, which sought to establish the basic aims; Secretary of the Interior Julius A. Krug led a committee to ascertain United States capacity to give aid; and the Council of Economic Advisers under Edwin Nourse examined the impact of foreign aid on the domestic economy. As important, and serving to mobilize business support and as a vital lobby in Congress, was the Committee for the Marshall Plan made up of leading export-oriented businessmen, bankers, and other well-placed "citizens."

By early November the President's committees were proclaiming the Marshall Plan in the national interest to the extent that continued prosperity and full employment in the United States were directly dependent on the program. Although the Harriman committee tried to underplay this aspect of the policy as too self-serving, and regarded ". . . as nonsense the idea which prevails to a considerable degree in this country and abroad that we need to export our goods and services as free gifts, to insure our own prosperity," the Council of Economic Advisers reached a more realistic conclusion.[35] Its report pointed out that the American export surplus rose from $5.5 billion in the third quarter of 1945 to $10.3 billion in the third quarter of 1947 and that United States government aid financed one-third of all exports and two-thirds of the export surplus. Without a new aid program, the council expected American exports to decrease in one year from $21 billion to $13 billion. Such a shift would cause a withering of America's non-European trade as well, and a "drastic adjustment" in the domestic economy.[36] Harriman later gave a similar assessment before the Senate hearings: "The decline of Europe would require far-reaching readjustments of agricultural and industrial production and distribution in this country and in other areas. It might well affect our ability to obtain needed imports and, particularly, essential raw materials. . . . Such readjustments would be costly in terms of employment and standards of living to our people."[37]

The Krug committee on United States resources and European recovery dealt with the question of shortages and consequent inflation and reinforced the contention that the domestic economy was dependent on expanded trade, if only to secure its essential raw materials.[38] The Harriman committee report was the most general and political of the three, summing up the principles of American foreign economic policy. It discussed the necessity of lowering the requests of the OEEC and anticipated an ECA expenditure of from $12 billion to $17 billion for the four-year period. The recovery of

Germany was repeatedly the keynote of the report, in part justified by the continued expense of the occupation, and in this sense it paralleled the revision of the policy toward Japan. The committee now stressed the inter-relationship of general European recovery and German industrial revival that Washington finally publicly acknowledged as a major objective of American foreign policy.[39]

During the year between Marshall's speech and the passage of the Foreign Assistance Act, State Department officials in speech after speech to primarily business audiences reiterated the themes that the United States had grossly underestimated the problems of European recovery, the dollar shortage, the threats of bilateralism, state trading, and other trade restrictions that all necessitated the recovery program. They stressed the same analysis before Congress, expecting it would find an equally sympathetic response. In underlining the point, Secretary of State Marshall publicly admonished, "It is idle to think that a Europe left to its own efforts . . . would remain open to American business in the same way that we have known it in the past."[40]

The State Department took pains in a brief memo to Marshall before his famous speech to point out that it did ". . . not see communist activities as the root of the present difficulties in western Europe. . . . American effort in aid to Europe should be directed not to the combatting of communism as such but to the restoration of the economic health and vigor of European society."[41] No less significant is the absence of references to Communism in the internal position papers, memos, and policy statements that circulated within the administration until the end of 1947. Press interpretations or speeches to Congress and the general public, on the other hand, conjured up the bolshevik threat. One cannot minimize this fact, for the administration, as with the Truman Doctrine, used a Red Scare and crisis atmosphere in a distinctly Machiavellian way to secure its economic aims, not because it feared a danger of the Soviet Union in Europe, but because it feared the danger of a budget-conscious Congress more or less responsive to an indifferent American public.

United States Policy Disputes

The liberal, free trade, export-oriented interests in the American economy which had dominated the State Department at least since Woodrow Wilson's administration, and which had almost single-mindedly formulated the policies culminating in the Marshall Plan, did not represent the full spectrum of interests in the American ruling class. And even among those who accepted multilateralism as the primary goal there was a wide range of attitudes and interests which created disputes over the formulation and implementation of the general policy. These views were eventually reconciled, but in the process the disputes rather sharply modified the original plan and introduced extraneous issues.

The Hullian position was most vividly represented by William Clayton, undersecretary of state for Economic Affairs, who found an uncompromising commitment to free trade harmonious with his cotton export interests. But the situation in Congress was far more complex. More interested in preventing competition to constituents' industries, the legislators worried not at all over the contradictions in United States economic policy, and would never permit general principles to interfere with specific interests. When, to Vandenberg, John Foster Dulles reported a conversation in which Clayton had declared that the United States was ". . . morally committed . . . to a reciprocal tariff reduction, as we could not impose upon the European nations what we were not willing to do for ourselves," Vandenberg replied that ". . . this is an excellent demonstration why Mr. Clayton would not be acceptable to Congress as the ERP administrator."[42]

The role of Congress in the shaping of foreign affairs has always reflected the psychological makeup of the congressmen in general policy, and on specific programs, the interests of their most powerful constituents. By and large, congressmen are not disposed to comprehensive policies of any nature. They are conservative and parochial in outlook, sluggish to react until questions of patriotism or their constituents are involved. Unless the program of aid to Europe were framed in such a way as to link it to a fight against a Communist menace, and made to appear less costly than rearmament in both political and monetary terms, Congress would not vote the necessary appropriation for the economic aid that it liked to refer to as "operation rathole."

The alarm among the real decision-makers of United States policy in light of this potential threat from Congress to their most fundamental economic aims, painstakingly developed over decades, was close to panic. They could ignore the Soviet Union at this period, as in the 1920s. Once having recognized its inability to dominate the Eastern European states, as it had by 1947, Washington concluded that if it could establish Western Europe as a capitalist trading bloc, how the Soviets managed their sphere was of lesser interest. It was Congress during the end of 1947 and early 1948 that again posed a more immediate threat. And to secure the essential funding from

Congress the administration fell back on its most reliable weapon: the specter of war or revolution.

In March 1948 the administration used the Czech crisis and encouraged leaks from the Pentagon on the possibility of a Soviet military threat. Clay cabled from Germany at the beginning of the month that war ". . . may come with dramatic suddenness." This statement was allowed to simmer in the minds of congressmen for ten days before the Central Intelligence Agency (CIA) assured Truman that war was unlikely "within sixty days."[43]

Senator Vandenberg, fully committed to the general program provided "businessmen" administered it, guided the ERP bill through the Senate and with the help of the crisis atmosphere was able to secure a favorable vote on March 13. In the House, on the other hand, the bill had not even left the committees. On March 17 Truman, scheduled to deliver a speech in New York, decided instead to address a special joint session of Congress, and the similarity of this speech with the one he delivered just a year earlier was widely noted. But to stress the urgency, Truman also called for Universal Military Training (UMT), an increase in the draft, and the immediate passage of the ERP.

The government was fully aware of what had taken place in Czechoslovakia; yet Marshall followed Truman on March 19 in comparing the Soviets to the Nazis and called for "urgent and resolute action," and Truman again on March 29 reminded the nation of the crisis that the United States faced in 1940–1941: "We are faced with almost exactly the same situation today."[44] Finally, the approaching Italian election on April 18 caused real alarm in all circles. There were growing predictions of a victory for the People's Bloc, and Congress was convinced that approval of the ERP would indeed affect that crucial election.

Even so, at the last minute, as if to underline their real sentiments, the House amended the bill to include Spain, which Vandenberg later persuaded them to omit—since Spain was not in the CEEC. Put in the context of a Communist threat and a crisis atmosphere, ERP seemed politically less objectionable than the possibility of UMT or an increase in the draft during an election year. The bill was finally passed on April 3, but it amounted only to an *authorization* of $5.3 billion for twelve months. The actual *appropriation* of the funds was to prove much more difficult.

The mercurial mood of Congress, kept high on a diet of crises in March and April, again reached a low point in May and early June when Congress finally voted on the appropriation of funds. The previous month the Soviets had made one of their dreaded peace gestures, a perpetual source of anxiety for the administration, especially when appropriations were pending in Congress. On April 23, after the ERP bill had passed, Truman held a press conference with the editors of the business press and commented that if Stalin came to Washington to say ". . . that he wants peace . . . the first thing you know that would happen, the Congress would adjourn without doing a damn thing. . . . That is exactly what would happen."[45] During mid-May Forrestal expressed to his colleagues and Truman ". . . a feeling of frustration at the success of the Russian propaganda. . . . Lovett deplored the ability of the Russians to capitalize on the ignorance of the American public." All feared the effect on pending appropriations as a result of what Marshall called the ". . . unscrupulousness of Russian diplomatic methods."[46] Forrestal confessed that the ". . . changing tempo of the Congress and . . . the relaxation of tension" threatened policy. "I gave it as my view that the country needed a constant restatement of our objectives and of the magnitude of our task, that we must not approach our international responsibilities in swiftly changing moods. . . . We must have a resolute and firm attitude behind which we can advance on a solid front and not on a jagged and spasmodic line."[47]

The reason Washington did not consider the Soviet overtures as opportunities to achieve a *détente* was that it did not really believe the Soviets were the major problem. The ERP policy would have been the same had the USSR not existed. The basic problem was to reconstruct a capitalist Europe, thereby creating a capitalist trading structure for the export of goods and capital and the import of raw materials, which was a direct response to the imperatives of the American economic system. For this aim the administration needed to extract funds from a reluctant Congress. The danger, of course, in nursing anti-Communism as a means to achieve other ends was that it would build up its own momentum and soon become an important ingredient in policy formulation.

Congressman John Taber's Appropriation Committee reduced the bill by extending it from twelve to fifteen months and including the Japanese occupation costs. By June, however, the Taber wing was able to garner the support of those congressmen whom the mood of March and April had whipped into line. Again the State Department's program was in jeopardy. Again Vandenberg, who had linked his reputation to the success of the bill, fought strenuously on its behalf in the Senate and won the reluctant support of Taft, who tipped the balance; and Congress appropriated $4 billon on June 20.

As important as any question in getting the appropriation through Congress was the role that Germany would assume in the program. From the inception, the State Department had foreseen the Germans playing a major part in the ERP and had forced the CEEC to upgrade allocations of aid to their former enemy. To Congress, and especially to the House Appropriations Committee, referred to as a "pro-German stronghold," Germany provided the essential ingredient that eventually won its support. Congress had played a vital role, in this regard, in halting further plant dismantlement in Germany.[48] But the question of Germany was an area of full agreement, not one of tension, between the administration and Congress.

Although the Americans insisted that the European states organize a permanent multilateral structure to allocate aid and coordinate national plans, they were equally adamant that each nation sign a bilateral pact with the United States specifying the conditions of the aid. Washington also tried to include a number of provisions which infringed rather too grossly on the sovereignty of the individual states or were contrary to their national interest. For example, the Europeans unanimously refused to accept a clause which would make it mandatory to consult the International Monetary Fund regarding devaluation if the United States thought it desirable, or a clause binding them to the charter of the ITO. Britain and France also objected to giving Germany and Japan most-favored-nation treatment. After considerable negotiation the Americans agreed to change the exchange rate clause to a general statement of intent. Nevertheless, Washington was well aware of the unique power it held vis-à-vis the economic policies of the participating countries. "Never before in history . . . has any nation undertaken by solemn international agreement . . . 'to stabilize its currency, establish or maintain a valid rate of exchange, balance its governmental budget . . . create or maintain internal financial stability,' " gloated a State Department official after the United States had signed the bilateral agreements with the OEEC nations.[49] And Congress added another important tool to the Marshall Plan—the counterpart provisions—enabling the United States to influence directly the domestic economic policies of the participating nations.

Paul Hoffman wrote in 1951 of the counterpart clause that "I can say flatly that it made the difference between success and failure for the Marshall Plan in every nation that had a shaky government, and it helped mightily with those that had strong ones. It was, I believe, the indispensable idea—the essential catalyst."[50] An important tool in influencing the economic policies of the European states during the period of the ERP, counterpart thereafter became a provision of all American aid, assuming vast proportions in countries like India. Counterpart required the recipients of United States aid to establish a fund in their own currency equivalent to the sums received in dollars. The United States would own 5 percent of this fund and could use it for various purposes, but primarily to purchase strategic material for its own stock pile. The recipient government could use the remaining 95 percent for projects America sanctioned. Hence the United States had the right not only to control how the dollars were spent but also to approve the expenditure of an equivalent amount of the local currency. This gave Washington substantial power to exercise over the internal economic plans and programs of the European states and attained one of the most fundamental aims of American policy. As Harlan Cleveland emphasized later, "One of Bissell's [ECA's chief economic planner] great contributions was the concept that the important thing is not the volume of our aid, but the effects in Europe and our influence in Europe upon national economic and financial policies."[51] In Britain the total counterpart came to $1.7 billion, of which the United States approved only $3 million for production and other purposes. The rest it required to be used for external debt retirement, despite British desires to allocate funds for welfare. In France the total amounted to $2.3 billion, with $2.1 billion approved for production and other purposes. When the Europeans made early objections to the clauses of the Foreign Assistance Act they were ". . . advised . . . that, if they had any idea, as participants, that they could tell the Congress what they would or would not accept as conditions, they had better give up the idea of ERP."[52]

ECA Organization and Personnel

Although Congress tried to stress the "business" nature of the ERP in its organizational proposals, the issue was hardly a basis for disagreement with the administration. Part of the mythology of Congress was that there was a difference between the interests of government "bureaucrats" and "businessmen" despite their traditional interchangeable character in American history. Congressman Christian Herter initially introduced a bill in the House to create a corporation to administer Marshall aid, and the opposition to vesting the program's administration with the State Department was great enough for Vandenberg to ask the Brookings Institute to develop a compromise plan that made the Economic Cooperation Administration (ECA) a separate government agency whose head would rank with the secretary of state.

Vandenberg intended that the head of ECA be a Republican and manu-facturer with little previous government experience. After vetoing Tru-man's first choices of Clayton and Acheson, Vandenberg complained that ". . . the Senate and the country was assured that the Administrator would be a big industrialist."[53] He then persuaded his constituent, Paul Hoffman, the president of Studebaker, to accept the post. Under Hoffman, in the crucial policy-making staff, were the businessmen-bureaucrats who had worked on these plans for many years: Harriman, Bissell, Lovett, Clayton, Blaisdell, Foster, Cleveland. On the next administrative level Hoffman gathered businessmen to head the sections of direct interest to the compa-nies concerned.

Averell Harriman was director of the operations in Europe and also represented the interests of Bizonia in negotiations within the OEEC. Among his staff in Europe ranged the interested business executives. Wil-liam Foster, Harriman's chief assistant, was president of Pressed and Welded Steel Products until 1946, when he became undersecretary of com-merce, then moving over to ECA. Calvin Hoover, economics professor at Duke University and frequent administrator in government posts, was charged with screening the OEEC country economic plans and being alert to United States investment opportunities. The vice president of Merck & Co., George Perkins, was assigned the job of approving industrial projects in Europe and making certain that the United States received raw materials allocations for its stock pile. To advise on intra-European trade and cur-rency problems Hoffman chose a banker, Thomas McKittrick, who took a leave from the Chase National Bank. Another business school professor scrutinized trade with Eastern Europe before it was cut off entirely in 1951. Hoffman chose four hundred administrators in all, primarily businessmen —a policy that was in perfect harmony with the intent of both the adminis-tration and Congress.[54]

The ECA also mobilized American trade unions to aid in neutralizing opposition among their counterparts in Europe. Although Philip Murray sent a telegram to Truman asking that the program protect the rights of the European workers, the gesture was for the record only. Worker rights were interpreted by the American and European capitalist planners who re-garded the working class as a commodity in the production process, and despite the early rhetoric regarding increasing living standards, the econo-mies of Europe were *intentionally* manipulated to *lower* living standards, create new unemployment, and sharpen inequality—a time-tested capitalist cure for an inflationary economy and an essential aspect of their concept of "recovery."

By June 1948 the United States had embarked on its ambitious program to reconstruct European capitalism in a manner that could sustain American trade, so vital in the postwar world to the very survival of American capitalism as it had emerged from the holocaust of World War II, immensely enriched but yet more vulnerable and dependent because of its very size and wealth. Unable to alter its internal economic priorities, American capitalism could only turn outward, not with disinterested aid but with new designs to save itself. The dilemmas, contradictions, and frustrations in implementing the Marshall Plan were already apparent before the ECA had sent one dollar abroad. The economic policies of the conservative European states under United States guidance, and the antagonistic American private interests bent on securing their own immediate gains—that vital motor force of capitalism—determined the outcome.

14

Czechoslovakia and the Consolidation of Soviet Power

To serve as a bridge between East and West was the facile, idealistic Czech objective during the early postwar years. They based their aspiration on the facts that the Slavic nation's class structure and political institutions were akin to those in Western Europe, but that its geographic position and recent history also linked it irrevocably to the Soviet Union. But despite its democratic and parliamentarian system, Czechoslovakia's relationship to the Russians and the direction of its economy were enough for the United States to regard the developments in Prague with deep suspicion. Hoover in April 1946 placed the country behind the "Iron Curtain" and, in fact, outside of "Western civilization," and Joseph Dodge in July 1947 described the Czechs as among the Soviet "stooges."[1] Daily United States–Czech relations reflected this attitude, and Washington gave no berth to that unfortunate nation in its delicate and tenuous international undertaking. Relations between the two countries grew increasingly strained over the months, and then years, following the war.

Lingering Czech hopes for sympathetic American aid were objectively naïve. For in the context of American policy and aims, what did Czechoslovakia offer the United States in the postwar period? If not a part of the Soviet camp, Czechoslovakia was "leftist." In the free election of May 1946 the Communists won 38 percent of the vote, and the other parties to their right were equally committed to a program of nationalization and controlled trade. On international issues, for whatever the reason, the Czechs were more likely to support the Soviets than the United States. None of these facts were attractive to Washington. But the United States, and especially Ambassador Steinhardt, soon found that Czechoslovakia's delicate position as a parliamentary democracy made it all the more susceptible to the economic and political pressures that America could not apply so easily to the rest of Eastern Europe. As United States leaders increasingly demanded full political support in return for conditional aid, the Czech hope of maintaining friendly diplomatic ties with both West and East became ever more illusory, until Czechoslovakia was forced, for lack of options, to choose sides in the division of Europe.

If we can point to any critical turning point for the political life of Czechoslovakia, or indeed for all of Eastern Europe, it would be the inauguration of the European Recovery Program. And the myth-enveloped experience of democratic Czechoslovakia between June 1947 and February 1948 perhaps most vividly illustrates the connection between international and internal dynamics that decisively altered the politics in that ill-starred country.

The American decision in 1946 to terminate its support of UNRRA, despite Europe's obvious need for continued aid, should have caused every European government to abandon its hopes of receiving nonpolitical assistance. But dire need, or desire for economic growth, had the power of blinding those needing aid from the realities of American economic policy. The lesson of the canceled Polish loan of May 1946, or the termination of Czech credits in October of the same year for political reasons, did not appear to make the Czechs or Poles any wiser. For they needed dollars to facilitate the completion of their reconstruction goals and they were receptive to any possible aid that would not entail a political and economic split in Europe.

The Soviet decision to explore the possibilities of economic cooperation in the Marshall Plan invitation with the British and French encouraged the Czechs in their hopes. Hilary Minc, the Polish minister of industry, was in Prague in early July 1947 when the Czechs and Poles learned that the Russians had left the Paris Conference and had refused to participate in the new American effort. The Poles and Czechs felt, however, that Moscow would not object to their involvement, and the Poles decided to send a delegation led by a cabinet minister, but Czech Foreign Minister Jan Masaryk urged a more cautious attitude. On July 4 he suggested to the Czech cabinet that they accept the American plan, and the ministers agreed to the proposal "without debate and unanimously."[2] Yet they decided also to instruct their representatives in Paris to maintain reserve until the United States clarified the conditions attached to its aid.

Two days later the Czechs sent a long-planned delegation to Moscow to negotiate a trade treaty. At this time, they casually asked Stalin for his views on their participation in the Marshall Plan. To their chagrin, Stalin replied, according to Masaryk's account, that

... the credits which are involved in the Marshall Plan are very uncertain and it became established that through the bondage of these credits, the Great Powers were seeking to form a Western bloc and to isolate the Soviet Union. . . . For us this question puts our alliance at stake. . . . We look upon this matter as a question of principle, on which our friendship with Czechoslovakia depends. . . . All the Slavic States have refused. . . . That is why, in our opinion, you ought to reverse your decision.

Masaryk noted that Stalin spoke with "benevolence" and "calm," but his meaning was no less clear.[3] When Masaryk proposed a graceful departure from Paris at the earliest possible moment, Stalin demurred, for "Switzerland and Sweden are still hesitating. By accepting you will certainly influence their decision. . . ." He then went on to warn, "If you take part in the conference you will prove by that act that you allow yourselves to be used as a tool against the Soviet Union."[4] When the Communist Prime Minister, Clement Gottwald, rather desperately pointed to their need for foreign exchange, Stalin turned to Molotov, laughing: "They thought they could lay their hands on some dollars, and they didn't want to miss the chance."[5]

The warning was decisive, for with the threat of a rupture in the Czech-Soviet alliance even the National Socialist minister of trade, Hubert Ripka, admitted, "I knew that we could not win over the majority of the people for such a policy."[6] Responding to Masaryk's account of the urgent economic situation in the country and his requests for aid, Stalin agreed to increase Soviet purchases of industrial goods and to send enough wheat to Czechoslovakia to alleviate the food shortage.

After the organization of the OEEC, with its implications of a divided European economy, the Czechs made greater efforts to integrate their economy with the resources and needs of Eastern Europe. In late July 1947 they signed a massive trade agreement with the Poles that went far to integrate the economies of the two countries. By merging Polish coal resources and Czech steel capacity, they essentially created an eastern Ruhr complex.

Washington's response to the withdrawal of the Czechs from the Paris Conference was prompt and predictable. The State Department's Division of Investment and Economic Development ". . . seemed to attach as much importance to this as to Munich. . . . The first reaction here to the Czech submission to Moscow," the State Department wrote Steinhardt in August, ". . . was that no credit of any kind should be considered until the Czech situation resulting from this development was clarified."[7] Given the United States aims for the Marshall Plan, it naturally excluded aid to those not binding themselves to its provisions. Washington concluded that the Czechs, by not attending the Paris Conference, also had written off a chance for a World Bank loan and even for an Export-Import $20 million cotton credit. Joseph Dodge, a more sophisticated tactician, was puzzled by the Soviet behavior. "We wonder why they did not let at least one or maybe more of their stooges sit in, if for no other reason than to scramble the deal and make it harder for Congress to swallow—namely, appropriate money to any of them. For the same reason, had Russia played along to fool the boys, just being a part of the deal would give them a chance to sabotage it or create resistance to it in the United States."[8]

Until the summer of 1947, the coalition government in Prague, led by the Communists, had operated compatibly in the unifying task of national reconstruction. In 1947, however, a combination of circumstances, both internal and external, worked to undermine, and eventually destroy, this accord. The State Department clearly recognized the new external pressures on the Czechs, but believed that they would work in a direction beneficial to United States policy. Steinhardt, in a speech to the National War College in December 1947, asserted,

It is no coincidence that the rather benign attitude of Moscow toward the Czech government suddenly hardened after the acceptance [of the Marshall offer]. By benign I mean that up to that time the Russians had not exercised much pressure on them. They had made a few suggestions here and there in connection with their political and commercial decisions, but not much more than other governments make to one another, and they had not, so far as we could see, directly interfered or given orders.[9]

Internal factors also led to political instability. In 1947 Czechoslovakia suffered severely, along with the rest of Europe, from a disastrous drought which significantly reduced its food supply. The Czechs, in order to import their minimum food requirements, were forced to export all their consumer goods originally planned for internal sale. The standard of living was certain to decline, and everyone assumed that the people would direct their displeasure in the elections scheduled for early 1948 against the leading government party—the Communists. Masaryk tried to obtain aid from the

United States outside the ERP and was firmly rebuffed; the Soviet offer of wheat then became vitally important to the Czechs as well as to the CP; and in December 1947 the Soviets promised 50,000 tons more than the Czechs had requested, totaling 600,000 tons of wheat and forage, or 40 percent of Czech needs. Yet the Soviets were also increasing their demands for Czech goods. As Steinhardt pointed out to the State Department, "To all intents and purposes, they are now asking for 100% of the country's production. . . . There is evidence . . . that even some of the Communist leaders . . . are becoming frightened at the Soviet demands and seem at a loss as to what to do."[10] Washington and the embassy in Prague hoped that the Soviets would be unable to meet their promises, and that the Czechs by January or February might be forced onto short rations. And Steinhardt concluded to Washington that the Czech misfortunes were

. . . very much to the good. . . . I think the time to put all the cards on the table will be in about three or four months from now when the real pinch is on and when conditions should approach a point at which we may be able to dictate some terms . . . [when] the Government . . . comes to realize that Santa Claus expects the children to behave a little longer than Christmas Eve. . . . As I do not fear actual starvation, I think we would be well advised to let nature take its course . . . and then to review the situation in the light of the effect worsened conditions have had on the public . . . it seems to me we have everything to gain and nothing to lose by standing back at this time and shutting our ears to the pleas for help. . . . Some of the people around this town have been playing a double game long enough. . . . [They] believe that they can continue to do so even under existing political and economic conditions. To my mind the sooner they wake up the better.[11]

Eventually such policies forced the Czechs to "wake up" from the dream of Beneš and others that they could somehow maintain their democratic society, independent of the global power struggle and free to develop their own political and economic institutions as they desired. The awakening was a rude one, and the United States' role in assisting to bring it on was vital.

To Jan Masaryk, the United States had clearly abandoned the Czechs. "Washington and London have failed completely to understand my position [in not attending the Paris Conference], and they are making a serious mistake in not granting my request for funds and assistance. . . . Now, UNRRA is at an end, and the 1947 harvest has been catastrophic. . . . Czechoslovakia has become completely dependent upon the . . . grain which the Soviet Union has promised to Gottwald."[12] Steinhardt during the fall of 1947 did advocate that Washington and the World Bank maintain the

Czech hope of a loan as a means of sustaining United States influence in Czechoslovakia. Masaryk, however, had ceased to hope.

Steinhardt's recommendations were, of course, unknown to the Czechs, but they watched closely the American discussions of the Marshall Plan, which only reinforced their worst fears. The United States emphasis on Germany, in particular, seemed to prove Soviet allegations, and the fear of Germany was one of the most common sentiments among all Czechs. Equally alarming, the discussions in Washington soon revealed the ERP as the most decisive step to organize a bloc of Western European states to reconstruct in unison—a policy that did not allow for both socialized and captialist economies, and which sought to halt the drift toward economic autarchy, bilateral trade agreements, state trading, exclusionary blocs, nationalization, and all such measures that were designed to serve European economic interests rather than American. The hope for all-European cooperation with American aid, never a real possibility, was laid to rest when the Americans revealed the conditions of their proposal.

The countries of Western Europe were economically desperate enough to ignore temporarily the fine print in the contract that the United States was offering to them, and the possible outcome of the new American plan. The British, in particular, did not want the Eastern European states to participate in the Marshall Plan for fear that dollars would not be forthcoming from the consistently anti-Communist American Congress. No less disquieting to the Czech government was the evidence that the Russians had been at least partially correct in regarding the ERP as an attempt to isolate the Soviets, and the Czechs understood that the USSR would be more vigilant regarding breaks in its own alliance. The Soviets organized the Communist Information Bureau (Cominform) in September 1947 as a direct response to the developments in Western Europe. An Eastern bloc was being consolidated in response to that in the West, further increasing the delicacy of the Czech position.

At the Comiform's first meeting in September 1947, the Yugoslavs vigorously criticized the Czech Communists for playing a nonmilitant, essentially bourgeois role in the moderate National Front. This criticism may have influenced their subsequent advocacy of more militant measures, but it is more likely that the economic conditions in the country and the approaching elections were the decisive factors. In any event, in the fall of 1947 events rapidly superseded one another, radically altering relations in the National Front—and ultimately Czechoslovakia itself.

Beneš told Soviet Ambassador Valerin Zorin in November 1947 that nearly everyone expected the Communists to lose votes in the forthcoming elections. A year earlier the Soviets probably would not have cared overly much since the center parties were equally loyal to the Czech-Soviet alliance, but, with the intervening events and the possibility of the CP's being excluded from the government and the other parties leaning toward participation in the Western economic bloc, this potential internal political shift took on greater importance to Soviet interests. Hence international events, as well as internal economic pressures, sharpened partisan activity in the National Front during the summer and fall of 1947. In this setting of growing political and economic tension and frustration, real plots of subversion were uncovered, vastly increasing the suspicions of external and internal dangers from reaction.

Subversion in Slovakia

In September and October 1947 the police uncovered a conspiracy in Slovakia which they were able to trace all the way to the office of Jan Ursiny, Czech Vice-Premier and leader of the Slovak Democratic Party, the most conservative party in the National Front. Ursiny had as his private secretary a former assistant to the propaganda chief of the wartime Tiso Slovak puppet state. This man was in close contact with extreme reactionary exiles and had passed official documents to them. The police arrested him, and Ursiny resigned. The disclosure led to the discovery of a well-financed espionage ring including two of the three secretaries-general of the Democratic Party.

Much of the trouble in Slovakia originated when groups of White Russian, Ukrainian, and Polish fascists attempted to pass through Slovakia on their way to the American zone of Austria. It was compounded by the nationalist sentiments for autonomy that had characterized Slovakia historically. The Czech army and police arrested followers of the White Russian General Vlasov, and Slovak civil servants—eighty in all—charging them with a plot to assassinate Beneš and overthrow the republic. Arrests continued, totaling over four hundred Slovaks, in the month of October.

The Communists called on the other parties to solidarize against the threat to the republic, presumably by a united front that would minimize party rivalries. The National Socialists refused, but on September 15 the Social Democrats agreed, and the two avowedly Marxist parties organized a united front within the coalition. Then the Cominform leveled a severe attack against the European Socialists for betraying the working class that renewed the animosity between the two parties in Czechoslovakia.

In fact, the Socialists were in the most ambiguous position as the lines between East and West hardened. In Western Europe—especially Britain, France, Belgium, and Germany—they were rather too eagerly joining the ranks of an anti-Communist Western bloc. In Eastern Europe their position was more equivocal, and they were torn between their ties to the old Second International and their working alliance with the Communists. Until the United States imposed the necessity to choose sides, the latent split was submerged in the reconstruction of the nation. Until 1947 the Social Democrats worked rather closely with the Communists in the government and trade unions. Toward the end of 1947 they became restive and began to act more independently and to oppose the CP on various issues. After the Cominform attack on the European socialists, however, the irate right and center wings were able to wrest control from Fierlinger at their November conference and to reinforce further the party's independent status. This trend also reflected a majority of the Social Democrats' desire to sharpen their unique character for the coming national elections and to avoid the stigma of responsibility for the worsening economic conditions in the country.

In 1947 Bohumil Lausman, the minister of industry—certainly not a right-wing member but more independent of the CP—replaced Fierlinger as party leader. The shift represented a break in the Marxist united front that controlled a majority in the Czech coalition government. The Social Democrats began to support the National Socialists or abstained from voting on many issues, and the CP increased its attacks against the "reactionaries" in all the other parties. Rudolph Slansky, party secretary, told the Cominform that the Social Democrats were the weakest party in the government and that it had attributed the cause of its weakness to the party's alliance with the CP. The center and right wing of the party he suspected of making common cause with Bevin. The National Socialists, he believed, had become the refuge for all the malcontents.

The discovery of the Slovak subversion case led to new instances of alleged espionage. The police under the Communist minister of interior arrested thirty-six persons in November 1947, primarily National Socialists. The National Socialist minister of justice arrested several Communists for sending three bombs through the mail to two National Socialist ministers and Masaryk, and an arms cache was found in the home of a CP deputy. The Communists, deeply embarrassed, disowned the deputy. At the end of the year the two ministries were almost in competition, arresting and releasing each other's prisoners.[13] The political parties that had worked smoothly together for the first two years now suspected each other of being either the agents for international and internal reaction, or at the service of Bevin, or, on the other hand, of planning to arrange a *coup d'état* in the manner of Hungary. And as the unhappy events for Czech democracy succeeded each other there appeared to be good reasons for all these suspicions.

As a matter of fact, the leaders of the National Socialist Party were fully committed to the Czech-Soviet alliance, but there were also many who, once the international lines were drawn, would have preferred an alliance with the West. Many of the Social Democrats, too, if forced to choose, found themselves predisposed toward their comrades abroad. In addition, expecting a Communist loss in the next election, all the other parties, for strictly political reasons, desired to emphasize their distinctive character and reap the electoral harvest.

The Events of February

Historians have interpreted the story of a Communist *"coup d'état"* in Czechoslovakia in February 1948 as one of the decisive events in the postwar era. The Truman administration used its account of it to galvanize a reluctant Congress into final approval of the Marshall Plan, much as it had used a Greek crisis the year before to mobilize Congress for the fight against the Left everywhere and to achieve its long-delayed economic aims. The interpretations of the events of February range from the thesis that the Communists had plotted the affair in detail in 1945 to allegations of an Anglo-American plot to overthrow the republic through a *putsch* by the non-Communist parties. The evidence, however, points to a rather different history.

Political events after June 1947 certainly gave rise to internecine fears and suspicions on the part of all parties as partisan activity became sharper. Their expectation that they would lose votes in the next election undoubtedly stimulated the Communists' desire to increase their popularity by proposing measures in the cabinet attractive to the masses.

After the disastrous drought in the late summer, the CP introduced a procedure to tax the very rich for relief to the peasants. The center parties opposed such a discriminatory tax and proposed instead a special flat levy on all Czechs. The Social Democrats were divided on the issues, but the left wing eventually won the party over to support the CP measure. Naturally, in a country where the rich were few and peasants many, Gottwald's proposal enhanced the popularity of the CP. A succession of such issues arose in the winter of 1947–1948. The Communists advocated an extension of nationalization to all plants with over fifty workers, and also an extension of the agrarian reform which had originally affected only German-owned land. The National Socialists and Populists rather bitterly opposed these proposals, which nevertheless were likely to be popular with the bulk of the Czechs. On February 10, 1948, the cabinet strongly disagreed on the question of pay raises for the civil servants. All parties agreed an increase was in order, and the minister of food, a right-wing Social Democrat, proposed a salary increase of 300 koruny for the lowest-paid to 800 for the highest-paid workers. All supported the idea save the Communists, who insisted on a more equalitarian flat wage increase for all. On this dispute the Trade Union Council, still the most militant force on the scene, naturally gave full support to the CP. Within the cabinet, however, the Communists were in the minority on this issue. At this time, as well, the workers' council congress decided to discuss the civil servant salary question at a conference they scheduled in Prague for February 22.[14] Another event highlighting the break in the National Front on economic issues was the justice ministry's denationalization of the Orion chocolate factory and its return to its former owners at the end of January 1948. However, a strike of the factory workers and a protest from the powerful trade unions prevented the transfer. The conservative parties were well aware of the popularity of the issues the Communists proposed, and while they might oppose them in the cabinet they could not exploit them in an election campaign or to provoke a crisis.

International events unquestionably also played their part in the decisions of February. The execution of Nicolas Petkov, the Agrarian leader, in Bulgaria in September 1947, and the CP's assumption of power in Hungary on May 31, 1947, caused the National Socialists to be hypersensitive about their own situation, one that the bomb incidents naturally accentuated. On the other hand, the discovery of the plot in Slovakia, and the May 1947 expulsion of the large Communist parties in Italy and France, undoubtedly convinced the Communists that they would be prudent to appoint a number of loyal police chiefs in the ministry of interior. This act, in turn, fanned the fears of the center parties, and it was on this question of the new police chiefs that they decided to create a government crisis. It was a difficult issue—for it was the constitutional right of the Communist minister of interior to make appointments in his own ministry—denying the Centrists a parliamentary infringement on which to rest their case. And since Czechoslovakia was not a police state, and full civil liberties existed throughout the country, it was also rather difficult to carry this question to the people. Nevertheless, the National Socialist and Populist ministers insisted at the February 17 cabinet meeting that Minister of Interior Nosek was packing the police department and that he recall his appointments. Gottwald, annoyed, declared that they had convened to discuss the national insurance bill, that Nosek was ill, and that the cabinet could not discuss the question of the police in his absence. Thereupon the center ministers refused to discuss any other business until Nosek acted on their demands. Gottwald was forced to adjourn the meeting for three days.

The national congress of workers' councils that was to convene in Prague on February 22 was composed of militant workers in the past considerably to the left of the CP. Eight thousand delegates from all over Czechoslovakia were expected to attend the meeting, and their attitude toward the economic questions dividing the National Front was quite predictable. Nevertheless, the twelve conservative ministers chose to resign on February 20 over the police issue, and they explicitly considered whether or not to resign before or after the workers' councils meeting, and for some inexplicable reason chose to quit before.

The ministers' expectations were simple: they would resign, and they hoped, but never troubled to find out for certain, that the Social Democrats would resign with them. They also anticipated that Beneš would refuse to accept their resignations.[15] They presumed that their own parties and the people would support them, although they never bothered to verify this or to inform their followers of the significance of their act until after they resigned. They believed that by resigning they could force Gottwald to follow suit and dissolve the government, and that Beneš would appoint a caretaker government of technicians until the elections—and, with the expectations of a Communist defeat, they would gain full control of the government. Their ineptness was nothing short of incredible—or suicidal. They created a government crisis, and not one of their expectations materialized. The Social Democrats, Masaryk, and Svoboda refused to resign, and hence the conservatives were a minority of twelve, with fourteen ministers remaining in the cabinet. The delegates of the three non-Marxist parties in Parliament, uninformed of their leaders' plans, were confused and divided, giving Gottwald an even greater majority there. Therefore, there was no constitutional necessity to dissolve the government. It was a minority resignation, and Gottwald, informed of their plans, decided to persuade Beneš to accept the resignations and replace the ministers with new appointments.

All of this was strictly within the bounds of acceptable, if formal, parliamentary procedure. What followed gave the illusion of a *coup*. In fact, there was none.

Beneš, while probably surprised by their action, initially supported the conservative ministers; ". . . he was resolved not to accept the resignation; he wanted to compel Gottwald to reach an agreement with them," his assistant Smutny recalled.[16] The real struggle in Prague was to persuade Beneš to accept the resignations and approve a new cabinet.

The ministers resigned on Friday, February 20, and on Sunday they left Prague for the countryside in a belated attempt to convince the Czech people of the importance of their move. It was obviously futile; the Communists, of course, opposed them and the others were not convinced that a confrontation was a wise course. Meanwhile, Gottwald warned the workers in Prague that the ministers were trying to set back the economic and social gains of the Front. And he also accused them of acting without consulting with their own parties and implied a liaison with foreign powers. The background of the Slovak conspiracy, the ministers' policy on the economic issues of the moment, and, as the English diplomat, Robert Bruce Lockhart pointed out, "Communist propaganda against Munich, against the Marshall Plan and against the alleged attempt of the Anglo-Americans to build up a strong Germany . . . ," all gave credence to Gottwald's assertions, regardless of their precise accuracy.[17] Gottwald appealed to the members of the National Socialist and Populist parties to reject their leaders and solidarize behind the Front. His effort yielded considerably greater support than the belated efforts of the instigators of the crisis could obtain. The problem then was to convince Beneš.

The Communists armed the workers' councils representatives, who organized demonstrations, held mass rallies, and sent messages to Beneš urging him to accept the resignations. Beneš hesitated for five days and then on February 25, fearful of civil war—though there was no evidence of anyone prepared to fight on the conservative side—and convinced by Gottwald's argument that he had a parliamentary majority, accepted the resignations and approved a new government that Gottwald organized. The Communists told Beneš that the new cabinet would be composed of members of all parties and would present itself to the National Assembly with its program and ask for its approval. In reality, for Beneš to have taken any other course at this time would have conflicted with the principles of formal parliamentary democracy. Gottwald's new cabinet included members of all the parties of the National Front, though more susceptible to Communist direction, and Masaryk and Svoboda continued in their old posts.[18] The government crisis came to an end—and, not long after, so did Czech democracy.

Shortly after February the workers took the new slogans on their power seriously and, as in 1945, again set up committees to run the factories. The government reversed their move soon thereafter and the workers were once more left sadder and wiser. Needless to add, workers' control played no part whatsoever in the CP plans. One conservative American journalist traveling freely through Eastern Europe in 1949 was impressed by how little life had changed over the year. Superficially he found the lot of the industrial and agricultural worker substantially improved between 1948 and 1949. The peasants were "better off" and even the managerial class was undisturbed, for they were still managing industry and living well in the suburbs.[19]

Jan Masaryk decided to "go with the people" in the February crisis.[20] Several months earlier he had discussed with Trygve Lie the possibility of the Communists' taking complete control of the government, though he had not anticipated a crisis such as occurred. When asked what he would do, he replied: "I'm not the kind of guy who could be happy to go to the United States and write five articles for the *Saturday Evening Post* for $15,000. No, sir, I'm staying put."[21] He did so during the crisis of February, but on March 11 he apparently ended his life by leaping from the window of his apartment in the Czernin Palace. The Western press cried foul play and hinted at murder. Those who knew Masaryk well, in particular his close friend Robert Bruce Lockhart, believed that he committed suicide. The diplomatic world knew Masaryk as a gay, delightful companion, but his friends understood that this was only one aspect of his personality and that Masaryk had suffered the symptoms of severe melancholia and manic-depressive cycles for many years.[22] There is no question that his hopes and desperate efforts during the last years of his life to maintain a Czechoslovakia free from the global power struggle, on good relations with the East and West, had failed. His bitterness toward the unyielding pressures of the United States was profound. His heart was unquestionably oriented toward the West, but not toward its leaders.

The Americans regarded Masaryk as an unreliable turncoat. James Riddleberger, chief of the Central Europe desk in the State Department, wrote Steinhardt:

I share your feelings of disappointment in this man, who might well have used his background and name to stand up to the Communist extremists in behalf of the pro-western elements. . . . I judge that he has been weak or blind both in his conduct of foreign policy and in cabinet politics when it was a time for firmness and discernment. Many "Westernizers" in Czechoslovakia must attribute to his deficiencies a considerable measure of the responsibility for the present unsettlement in the relations between their country and the United States.[23]

Earlier, when cutting off the surplus credit and canceling the loan negotiations, Riddleberger wrote,

A question also arises concerning the effect of our present policy on Jan Masaryk's position. . . . [T]he news that we are calling a halt on economic assistance . . . should considerably encourage those elements desiring some reorientation of Czechoslovak foreign policy.[24]

Although the official Communist version of the events of February suggests that the Western embassies played a major role in guiding the conservative ministers, there is little evidence that this was the case. Probably coincidentally, both the former Soviet ambassador Valerin Zorin and Steinhardt returned to Prague at the time of the crisis.[25] According to the National Socialist Vice-President, Petr Zenkl, he discussed the political situation with Steinhardt in November 1947 after the execution of Petkov in Bulgaria. Steinhardt indicated that there was little to fear, for he believed that Stalin desired a democratic nation and he stated that the United States would take greater interest in Czechoslovakia than it had in Bulgaria. However, according to Beneš' Secretary, Josef Korbel, Steinhardt told Beneš that Czechoslovakia could expect no United States aid in the event of a Communist coup. This, of course, was a fact that Beneš had understood since the war: an independent Czechoslovakia would depend exclusively on good relations with the USSR. The inept policies of the National Socialists precipitated the crisis, but in the international environment of 1948 a crisis was inevitable, and the outcome predetermined.

The relentless American determination to force the world to choose sides, and to aid only those ready to echo its policy, inevitably forced Czechoslovakia to choose the only side it could, given the geopolitical realities of its situation. The result was the end of the Czech parliamentary system. As Trygve Lie observed in his memoir: ". . . [T]here are times when I wonder —in the light of hind sight—whether the West does not now and then suffer pangs of conscience when reviewing the fate of that country."[26]

There is very little evidence that it did. Quite the contrary, Washington used the Czech crisis for all it was worth, distorting every facet of it to heighten the East-West tensions and to extract a prompt vote from Congress on the Marshall Plan. Otherwise it was business as usual. The one major interest the United States had in Czechoslovakia, whether parliamentarian or a one-party state, was to obtain economic concessions and compensation for nationalized industry. On September 13, 1948, Steinhardt happily wrote Dulles that ". . . they [the Czech government] would be prepared to pay $25,000,000. I have intimated that the American Government will be prepared to accept $45,000,000. In my opinion, these two figures can be compromised without too much difficulty at $35,000,000—which would be $10,000,000 more than the $25,000,000 which the State Department has told me informally would be acceptable to the American Government."[27] This theme dominated Steinhardt's correspondence with Washington in the months before and following February 1948. The persistence of this concern was less a reflection of a man than it was of the basic guiding foundations of American policy toward Eastern Europe.

For the Soviet Union, the Czech bourgeois parties conveniently committed political suicide. They were the last independent representatives of that class that may have sustained a friendlier orientation toward the West. The Russian reaction to the ERP indicated that, even before February 1948, the USSR was interested in a closer integration of Eastern Europe. Neocolonial features were present in the Soviet determination to integrate the economies of the Eastern states, but the Russians had security interests as well. Objectively, the Soviets had more to fear from the United States, immeasurably enriched and made more powerful by the war, than the Americans had to fear from them. Yet a repetition of Russian economic isolation of the interwar decades was the probable outcome of the United States tactics. American efforts to reconstruct a viable capitalist trading bloc certainly did not indicate that the United States anticipated a war in Europe that would only devastate the region once more. The Russians surely understood this, and as the United States began to draw the economic boundaries with the Marshall Plan they followed suit, and Molotov introduced his counterpart to the ERP. Subsequently dubbed the Molotov Plan, it was a program for integrating the economies of Eastern Europe by assigning national specializations. There was an economic rationale for the scheme, but clearly the interests of the Soviet Union was the prime consideration. In Czechoslovakia any question of ambivalent commitments or neutrality was resolved in February 1948, but within a month the Soviets faced what, for them, was a far more ominous threat.

The Yugoslav Challenge

The Molotov Plan had aggravated the already strained Yugoslav-Russian relations. Tito promptly rejected the role that the Russians assigned to Yugoslavia, for it left no place for the development of diversified industry or for raising the standard of living—both critical to the Yugoslav development plans. Belgrade instead tried to expand its avenues of trade with the West at the end of 1947, increasing Soviet fear of a reorientation of the trade of the Eastern states—a reorientation that might occur not under bourgeois auspices but rather those of national Communists who were committed to national economic development, albeit in the bolshevik manner, rather than the primary interests of the Soviet state. From the Yugoslav position, however, the Soviets had been taking 50 to 60 percent of their nonferrous metals and giving little in return, and these exports were in demand in the West on much better terms. The Russians also cut back German reparations over the winter of 1947, supplies the Yugoslavs had already programed into their five-year plan. By the end of 1947 the Russians regarded Tito's pursuit of Yugoslavia's own national interest as a direct economic and political threat.

In early 1948 the Russians were apparently still under the impression that Tito represented only a faction of the Yugloslav Communist Party leadership and that with some well-placed pressure they could replace him with elements primarily loyal to the Kremlin. In March 1948 Moscow withdrew all its advisers and technicians and threw its support behind André Hebrang, a man of unquestioned loyalty to the primacy of the Soviet Union. Tito, forewarned, acted swiftly; in April he rallied the nationalist forces in the party and arrested Hebrang and his followers. Tito then assured the Soviets of his loyalty and solidarity on all international questions. It was too late, however. The example of national independent Communism, while perhaps conceivable two years earlier, was now intolerable to the Soviet Union, and in June, after bitter exchanges between Moscow and Belgrade, the Cominform expelled the Yugoslavs as agents of Western imperialism and called on the Yugoslav party to replace its leadership. The blow was serious for Yugoslavia both materially and psychologically. But despite the escalation in verbal attacks and the subsequent total economic boycott, Tito continued to claim his devotion to the Soviets and to support them in international conferences for another year. In addition, in response to accusations of coddling the peasantry, the Yugoslavs outdid themselves in mili-

tant collectivization measures and bolshevizing the internal party structure.[28]

Inevitably, the strangle hold of the economic boycott forced the Yugoslavs to choose between abandoning their development plans altogether or
making agreements with the West. In July 1949 they reluctantly signed a
trade agreement with the United States and paid the political price of
closing their border with Greece, thereby denying political aid and refuge
to the guerillas. The outcome of this event for Greece we discuss in detail
in Chapter 15.

For the rest of Eastern Europe the Tito break brought the time of reckon-
ing. The Russians had essentially lost in Yugoslavia, in part because Stalin
was too cautious to take the ultimate military steps—which in any event
would have been a costly, and probably losing, drain—and in part because
Tito had an indigenous mass base and never needed the Soviet Union to
sustain his power. It was a different story in the rest of the region, and
preventive action appeared to the Soviet leaders as the best means to keep
the new growth of national Communism from blooming. The roots, in fact,
were already deep in the soil of Poland, Czechoslovakia, and Hungary.
What followed were the more repugnant excesses of Stalinist rule—the
police terror that was directed mainly against the Communist officialdom
and that was fed by local factional rivalries that long predated the Tito split.
Intellectual heresy was hounded and punished, but far more serious in this
essentially colonial relationship was national heresy, and the compradors
who remained in power subordinated even their historic bolshevik function
of economic development, that most fundamental Titoist heresy, to the
interests of the Soviet state. Yet the neocolonial analogy with the West is
only a partial one. In fact, Eastern Europe did rapidly industrialize, even
if Soviet, rather than national, priorities defined its goals.

Even while this consolidation of the region was under way, the Eastern
states never drew an iron curtain in the area of trade. Although trade in
Eastern Europe doubled between 1947 and 1948, multilateral trade between
Eastern and Western Europe also developed during 1948. But, and certainly
disconcerting to the United States, the currency of exchange was sterling.
The Soviets increasingly acted as middleman in these transactions, however.[29] And if reconstruction is measured by production figures, Eastern
Europe compares favorably to the West. A UN study, using 1937 as a base,
revealed that in 1948 France had equaled that prewar level, and surpassed
it by one-quarter in 1951; Czech production in 1948 was 9 percent above
1937, but two-thirds higher by 1951. By 1950 Belgium was still below

prewar and Italy a mere 14 percent above it. Hungary, a comparable country in the East, more than doubled its 1937 production by 1950. Yet normal East-West trade would have also substantially minimized the human costs of development in both sectors of Europe. The East was required to rely on its own limited resources, and for the West normal trade would have substantially minimized its profound dollar problem.[30]

As it was, the Communists controlled the states of Eastern Europe in the interests of the USSR, but they also introduced certain qualitative changes in the lives of the masses. The societies were modernized and traditional feudal and clerical control decisively broken. It is probable that in the second half of the twentieth century only the state can or will perform the industrializing process in the interests of the nation. The developed capitalist powers whose interests lie in extraction of materials or profits are too powerful, too all-encompassing to permit indigenous capitalist development on a national basis in a country in a preindustrial condition. And in a nation where a strong indigenous capitalist class does not exist, the small modernizing elements in the bourgeoisie can gain political support only from the old comprador and feudal elements in the population whose real interests ultimately lie in maintaining the prewar *status quo*.

The People's Democracies served Soviet interests, but they also avoided the crises of war, stagnation, and unemployment that inflicted misery on the working class of the capitalist economies of the West. The consistent autocratic bolshevik demands for increased production eventually met resistance from the workers and then fully exposed the exploitive nature of the new managerial class that claimed legitimacy in the workers' name. Production and growth rates had become the social goals par excellence and the state regarded any effort to resist the increasing work norms as sabotage of the national plan, and a crime. One cannot accuse the Communists of betraying the working class, for such policies and priorities were perfectly consistent with bolshevik ideology. Their function since 1917 was to industrialize rapidly the preindustrial states, using the traditional autocratic and exploitive means, but allocating the profits to the state. And after June 1948 even this single-minded focus on development, which was the Yugoslav heresy, was subordinated to the requirement of serving first and foremost the interests of the Soviet Union.

Compounding the Soviet political pressures and the internal political divisions were the very real problems arising directly out of the transformation from agrarian to industrial states, the increasing trade restrictions that the United States imposed, and the shortage of essential materials that forced the Eastern Europeans to rely on their own limited resources. To this was added the growing hostility from the United States as its politicians used Eastern Europe, much as they used China, to score political points at home. Verbal attacks ultimately escalated to demands for the "liberation" and "roll-back" of Communism in 1952 that were in fact cynical fantasies but they also fed paranoia in both areas. And it gave hope to conservative elements in Eastern Europe that there would be American assistance if they resisted—when in fact there never was any possibility of such aid. In the end, hypocrisy shaped the rationales of both systems as each sought to excuse its own abuses by reflecting on the crimes of the other.

15

Heir to Empire: The Near East and Mastery of the World's Oil

The Near East encompassed all the critical challenges to American goals and power after World War II. There was, preeminently, the question of Britain's future in the region, and the unmistakable United States intention to circumscribe it in some fundamental fashion to reallocate Western influences in the area. Here the essence of the matter was oil, a major element in Washington's postwar policy. The stakes involved in that precious keystone of industrial might reflected on the nature of America's ideal world order as well as British imperial power. In this struggle for mastery of the imperial legacy, emerging local nationalism was to play a vital role and to begin to define the politics of the region as we now experience it.

For the United States, the Near East also involved the future of the forces of radical social and political change, and the extent to which they might shift influence in the vast area toward Russia and away from capitalism in either its American or its British form. Greece remained the test of America's resolution to employ its resources to sustain the physical liquidation of the forces of radical transformation in the region, the first major indication that behind policy there was also physical power. Greece, too, was a critical introduction to the means and consequences of America's global designs in the postwar era, the first of its many decisive and successful interventions.

Greece—The Emergence of Civil War

The emergence at the beginning of 1947 of significant American interest in their land much encouraged the hard-pressed Greek rightists in Athens.

At the end of January a new, yet more reactionary government under Dimitrios Maximos was formed, with Napoleon Zervas as a cabinet member who at the end of February was entrusted with the ministry of public order. The choice of Zervas, who had led the small wartime resistance group, the EDES, to an overweening anti-Communism and collaboration with the Nazis, revealed that the new regime would solve its internal problems with even greater repression. This was possible only because, by the end of February, the American cornucopia was opened to the Greek government with a generosity that eventually made Greece the largest per capita recipient of United States aid in the decade after the war. The Greek Right, in its adversity, had also fallen into America's bounty.

The government in Athens was to need all the Americans could provide, and indeed more, and only good fortune ultimately saved it from disaster in the hands of the growing resistance. Internal economic chaos and corruption were moving to yet more sordid depths. The Porter mission was completely critical of the government's corruption, and Porter publicly condemned the total relaxation of its efforts after the Truman Doctrine speech, when the government called a national holiday and shelved its few petty measures for getting the economy under control. Congressional visitors continued during 1947 and 1948 to issue scathing denunciations of the open governmental corruption, the press continued its detailed accounts of how Greek shipping millionaires were enriching themselves with United States aid, and Porter openly implied that the new wave of arrests of all opposition—non-Communist included—was a consequence of American backing. The American mission's economic advisers who began studying the Greek economy reported to Washington that, for all practical purposes, the Greek government had given up economic direction: it failed to adopt a budget, as provided by law, and those actions proposed were "completely inadequate."[1]

It was easier, the Maximos regime decided, to attempt to stamp out internal resistance, but in reality it succeeded in mobilizing it. But the logic of the situation, and American backing, prompted it to take the seemingly simplest way. The desertion rate in the army had reached alarming proportions among inductees, who were paid less than $1.80 a month. By July, as the repression became even more intense, reports coming back to Washington alarmed Truman and his advisers, who were disturbed to learn that the Maximos regime was concentrating on military victory rather than economic and political stabilization, seeking, in Truman's polite terms, ". . . to further partisan political, rather than national, aims."[2] What was initially sold to Congress as primarily an economic program, and intended to be so, now became essentially a military venture, and only 41 percent of the first year's allocation went to economic aid.

The size of the resistance in the mountains reflected, to some measure, the final collapse of the Greek social system under conditions of mounting repression and corruption. "We will answer terrorism with terrorism ten times as strong," Zervas had announced, "and slaughter ten times greater."[3] Rightist papers now clamored for a termination of the restraints the British Labour government had forced on them, and major roundups of all opposition overflowed from the jails onto special islands for the many thousands of exiles. For, unlike the British, the Americans would put up with the unbridled terror—and pay.

There were about 25,000 political prisoners in Greece in February 1947, perhaps far more, and the number quickly mounted. One raid alone, Porter reported in September, took 1,600 persons and imprisoned over two-thirds of them. The formalisms in the Constitution were ignored in the name of self-preservation. The KKE newspapers functioned until mid-October as something of a legitimating myth for the regime's claims to democracy, though by July most of the party's members were in jail or hiding. The trade unions were taken over, and December's sweeping antistrike laws included death penalties for violators. Again, executioners alone know their victims and never inform the world, but as late as June 1952, long after the war was over, even the Greek government admitted that it held 10,569 political prisoners in jail and another 1,500 in island exile, and of these over 5,000 were under sentence of life imprisonment or death. By then, of course, untold numbers had fallen—far more than the 1,200 admitted executions by October 1949. Without United States aid all of this would have been impossible, and by the end of 1947 Washington's earlier qualms were buried in the name of the emergency in which Greek "democracy" now found itself, and its public defenses of Athens increased with the terror.[4]

To survive, then, it was necessary to flee to the mountains and to fight. The 3,000 guerillas of late summer 1946 had grown to 13,000 by March 1947, rose to 16,000 or 18,000 over the summer, and by the fall of 1947 reached a peak of 23,000 to 25,000, at which point they remained during most of 1948 despite heavy casualties. This poorly armed resistance, equipped mainly with rifles and a few mortars throughout 1947, was 90 percent peasant in origin, and half of them during 1947 and 1948 were located in regions remote from land borders. The percentage of Communists among them ranged from one-tenth in some official American estimates to no higher than 30 to 40 percent in State Department public relations documents. As well it had to be for success, the Greek resistance was a popular movement of protest against a corrupt, repressive regime.

In the last analysis, it was the Athens regime that defined the nature of the growing army of opposition in the mountains, for repression mobilizes its own resistance, and where the net is large the enemies of terror are no less numerous. There was, first of all, the wartime EAM coalition of five parties, once again a power after a period of disunity and partial eclipse immediately after the war. The EAM was the party of the opposition democrats as well as the KKE, of republicans, socialists, and the oppressed —all quite willing, even more so than in earlier years, to work with a dedicated KKE that provided leadership and, in certain of its factions, militancy. To the large predominantly non-KKE backing of the EAM, the enemy was in Athens, or Washington, and together with the Communists they hoped to end the tyranny and poverty enslaving Greece. "But whatever the contributing factors—including deep poverty," a rather mild Twentieth Century Fund report concluded in 1948, "Rightist terror has been the primary recruiting agent for the bands of the Left."[5]

As for the Communists, they were split in too many ways to permit a simple explanation. Zachariades unsuccessfully tried to shift the resistance's main focus from the peasantry to the urban masses. But since it was the rightist policies that recruited guerillas most successfully, in a vital sense the old-line sector of the KKE under Zachariades saw its future in the predictable environment of parliamentary politics, and it repeatedly tried to get back to it even after the KKE was outlawed in October 1947. This faction was preeminently Moscow-oriented, and Russia had treated the advent of the Truman Doctrine in amazingly mild terms as essentially an aspect of Anglo-American economic rivalry. By the fall of 1947, indeed, Zachariades began a cautious purge of many of the militant Markos Vafiades' followers that was to prepare the way for imposing the hegemony of the conservative, pro-Soviet element later in our story. A reflection of this durable conservative KKE influence in the Democratic army came in September 1947 when Markos publicly offered a cease-fire if an amnesty were declared and a new government including the EAM formed. There was no response, of course, and the following December, when Markos announced the membership in a new provisional government, neither Russia nor any of the Eastern European nations recognized it. In fact, the relative indifference of Moscow was translated by the conservative KKE into a policy of accommodation—and defeat.

A more complex aspect of the guerilla movement and internal KKE divisions was the role of the Macedonian elements in the north, for these relations impinged on the split in the Eastern European Communist bloc rapidly coming to a head. If the Macedonians were to provide the resistance with initial strength, in the end they were to prove its weakest point, and to expose once more the traditional Balkan quality of postwar politics in the region. When, in August 1947, the United States finally took the Greek question, garbed as an aggression from Albania, Yugoslavia, and Bulgaria, to the UN, Russia vetoed resolutions embodying this assumption and Washington distorted the traditional nationality and border conflicts that had now become integrated with the resistance to internal repression. The UN investigating commission's own facts, if not its conclusions, reveal this most vividly, as do the State Department's own documents.

By January 1948 approximately half of the Democratic army under Markos was in the "Slav-Macedonian" units of the NOF, a coalition of Greek nationals with very different visions of their future relationship to Greece. The KKE at this time was committed only to greater autonomy for the Macedonians within a Greek state, and it was uncomfortable in going even this far; but many of the Macedonians were irredentists who had visions of a Macedonian state, and these in turn were divided among those willing to accept the KKE's plan, a probably larger group actively oriented to a greater Macedonia as part of Yugoslavia (which had its own Macedonian republic), a small dormant section in the northeast interested in making the new Macedonia a part of Bulgaria, and, finally, some who wished an entirely independent Macedonia carved from Yugoslavia, Greece, and Bulgaria. Officially, however, the NOF endorsed the KKE position on autonomy, and there is little reason to doubt that had the Democratic army won, the majority of Macedonians, who were Greek-speaking, would have accepted the Communist program.[6]

Despite its diversity, this united front of Greeks under Markos' military leadership carried on the war with quite remarkable successes. For the better part of 1947 the Democratic army units operated as small, nearly autonomous, self-supporting bands of less than a hundred, whereas the Greek army engaged on vast search-and-hold operations which, while superficially victorious, spread out and bogged down man power. This government army was to continue growing to 132,000 well-armed regular troops in 1948, plus 50,000 National Guards, increasingly led at the highest levels by over 200 American officers attached to the military mission in charge of operations, with the British in charge of training. Heavy Democratic army losses were made up by new recruits, as the poorly armed force of about 25,000 held its own throughout Greece during 1948 in what is now generally regarded as a military stalemate. Despite Zachariades' urging that the guerillas concentrate to hold fixed regions and fight more conventional warfare, Markos' classic guerilla strategy compensated for weaknesses in arms and numbers. The Americans had hoped to terminate much of the war during 1948, fearing otherwise the need to develop a 15-to-1 man-power superiority to achieve victory. For the guerilla movement, the only significant source of aid was its ability to escape into Yugoslavia and Albania for rest, succor, and some training, but the Eastern European nations provided relatively petty quantities of arms, and these were hardly sufficient to explain the durability of the Democratic army through 1948, not the least because about half of it was not in border regions.

Far more consequential to the outcome of the civil war was the split between Yugoslavia and Russia, of which Greece was a major cause just as the end of the war was its major effect. Tito's interest in Macedonia and Greece, while undoubtedly prompted by the hostility and irredentism of successive Athens regimes, was also rooted in his wartime ambitions for a South Balkan federation. The key to Tito's strategy was the leadership of the Bulgarian Communist Party, which from Georgi Dimitrov down was largely of Macedonian extraction and strongly drawn to a union of the three nations holding parts of historic Macedonia.[7] The British had encouraged Tito's project in the hope of creating a possible balance to Russian power in the region—and the plan even during the war had sorely strained Stalin's patience, perhaps even encouraging a Soviet desire to see a more conservative but less ambitious regime emerge in Yugoslavia. The Russians by 1947 were unquestionably hypersensitive to Tito's goals, and this was one more reason why they did not publicly or covertly encourage the militants in the EAM or KKE to challenge Anglo-American hegemony in Greece. By mid-1947, Tito was ready to return to his wartime dream of a South Balkan federation, and now the major acquisitions were to be Bulgaria and Albania, with Macedonia—perhaps including that portion in Greece—to become a smaller part of it. Meeting at Bled, Yugoslavia, during August 1947, Tito and Dimitrov discussed Macedonian Greece as well as the much larger questions of a South Slav federation. And the following November they partially included their plan in a treaty of friendship. The substance of the Bled Agreement has been the source of great conjecture, but it undoubtedly involved major compromises on ancient Balkan claims to Thrace and Macedonia, perhaps even commitments to the Greek resistance; but the matter still rests in the realm of speculation into which commentators have inserted more political bias than provable facts. What is certain is that the origins of the civil war long preceded the conference, and that whatever aid Yugoslavia gave to the Democratic army was petty and insufficient in comparison to that the United States gave to the Right. And what is more consequential in the Bled Agreement was the Soviet response and the decisive importance this was to have for Greece.

The Russians still harbored many of their wartime suspicions of Tito, and it is clear his South Slav federation would have posed a threat to their hegemony in Eastern Europe. But during the fall of 1947 Yugoslav Communists also had consistently taunted the Russians and Western Communists on their parliamentarian conservatism and opportunism, forming a kind of pre-Maoist Left in the world Communist movement. Moreover, Tito's intransigent wartime behavior, which continued after the peace in a unyielding position on the partition of Trieste and the Julian March, and even in the shooting down of an American plane over Yugoslav airspace during August 1946, probably struck Stalin as dangerous adventurism that might drag Russia into a war with the West. Apparently the Russians had not been consulted regarding the desirability of forming a South Slav federation, nor even informed of its details. They certainly did not approve it, for the principle of autonomy implied in the means and ends were profoundly dangerous to them. Both Dimitrov and Tito were summarily ordered to Moscow, but the Yugoslav pleaded ill and sent Kardelj and Djilas in his place. Dimitrov, who had exuberantly begun to expand the federation to include all of Eastern Europe save for Russia, was the villain of the affair at the violent, insulting conferences held in the Kremlin during mid-February 1948. Stalin summarily rejected the federation and customs union plan, and this aspect of the meeting need not detain us. "The uprising in Greece has to fold up," Stalin admonished. "No, they have no prospect of success at all. What do you think, that Great Britain and the United States—the United States, the most powerful state in the world—will permit you to break their line of communication in the Mediterranean Sea! Nonsense. And we have no navy. The uprising in Greece must be stopped, and as quickly as possible."[8] Then, in June the Cominform expelled the uncontrite Yugoslavs.

From this point onward, the nationalisms and loyalties of the various groups sustaining the Democratic army became the source of a fatal internecine struggle that was to be the most significant cause of the army's defeat. If the pro-Yugoslav Macedonian elements and independent Greek nationalists sided with Tito they would lose aid from Albania and Bulgaria, as well as from the pro-Moscow KKE. Tito, in the meantime, had to redefine his relations not merely to his neighbors but to the United States, and conserve his military resources for a possible conflict with the USSR. The KKE moved secretly to endorse the Moscow decision on Tito and cautiously to purge Macedonians oriented toward Yugoslavia, while now the pro-Bulgarian Macedonians, probably with Soviet encouragement, tried to snatch away the mantle of leadership from them. But since the NOF was so vital to the Democratic army, the KKE in January cautiously and vaguely endorsed the creation of something akin to an independent Macedonia, should that nationality choose it via self-determination, hoping, perhaps, that they might win the loyalties of pro-Yugoslav Macedonians. Markos, during August, was sent into exile, and Zachariades and the KKE abandoned his relatively successful guerilla tactics for conventional combat that led to a series of devastating defeats. Finally, at the end of January 1949 the KKE central committee was purged of elements not loyal to Moscow. Then the Bulgarian-controlled Macedonian nationalists alluded to the creation of a new, independent Macedonian state which would have involved annexing a large part of Yugoslavia by one means or another, a position the Cominform endorsed in February. By this time the internal jockeying and purging meant certain political defeat, the debilitation of a mass following among Greeks and Greek-Macedonians alike, and inevitable military collapse in its wake. For once a guerilla movement abandons rational politics that respond to mass needs, military failure is inevitable.

Still, the Democratic army during the spring and summer of 1949 retained sufficient military capacity to continue the war for a very long time, perhaps enough to relate again to politics and rebuild its political following —an easy enough task given the character of the Athens government. It had approximately 15,000 men under arms, but these were now overwhelmingly concentrated on the northern borders; therefore the position of the northern border states was crucial. In August 1948, shortly after Tito's expulsion, Albania announced willingness to resume diplomatic relations with Athens if it would renounce its claim to Northern Epirus. The Greeks, of course, would not do so. On April 26 the following year, the Russians revealed that they were largely behind the effort to end the war when Gromyko informally endorsed what they alleged to be the revolutionary Democratic government's proposal for a cease-fire, a general amnesty, and free elections. To this the Russian added that his country would be willing to join international supervision of the elections and a border commission to seal off illegal movements across the northern frontier, but that Moscow would want to see Anglo-American military aid and personnel withdrawn. Despite the fact that the implementation of such a package would have led to a Left victory, on May 7 the guerilla radio revealed its independence and disassociated itself from it. But it was all pointless, for both Athens and the United States smelled victory, and Washington formally denounced the compromise. Before the Russians could renew their offer the following October, however, the three northern neighbors and the KKE moved to abandon the Democratic army.

The Yugoslavs had maintained an uncompromising principled position toward the Greek question since their expulsion from the Cominform, continuing some aid and permitting soldiers to use the border as a sanctuary. At the end of May 1949, they even publicly renewed pledges of support to the guerillas and denounced the imminent Soviet desertion of the Greek cause. But the Yugoslavs were hard pressed, and the victory of a Zachariades-dominated KKE would have been unwelcome, and so on July 23 they closed their borders. The next month, Hoxha, Albania's ruler, began disarming all Greeks in his country. At this point the still formidable resistance began to decline to no more than 5,000 men when, on October 16, it declared a cease-fire. The following day Acheson triumphantly announced that there were a mere 2,000 guerillas left in Greece and that the war was over.[9]

Well might Acheson and Washington have felt content with the outcome in Greece, for it was largely a windfall for the United States, and it appears almost certain that, without the split in the Communist world, Greece's destiny would eventually have passed into the hands of its own people—had the United States not intervened with its own troops. Quite apart from the durability of the Democratic army in the face of massive American aid and equipment, which was to total over $2.5 billion from the end of World War II through 1952, poverty and economic stagnation remained the rule. Per capita national income in 1952 was still $155, inequitably spread at that, and the reconstruction of prewar levels of output was slower than in any other part of Europe. In this context, stagnation, corruption, and official scandal were universal, and the most important business of Greece until well into the 1950's was United States aid. About this larger, structural situation no one had any doubts, and for this reason United States Ambassador John E. Peurifoy conceded in 1951, "If the Cominform completely controlled Yugoslavia, there would still be a very nasty situation in Greece."[10]

If both the economy and army failed, and if the internal forces of order, despite full prisons, were rich but not secure, the least that may be concluded is that, in terms of its larger policies and commitments, the United States effectively dominated and ruled Greece. For even the Greek centrist parties, including men who had long collaborated with the British and Americans in the suppression and terror, were quick to learn that the United States worked only to preserve an obedient and docile Right. At the beginning of 1952 the moderate Center parties sought to reestablish a proportional representation system in Greece, a step the Right opposed for fear it would have damaged its political hegemony. On March 14, Peurifoy, whose talents were to later be employed in Guatemala during the 1953 coup, publicly announced that proportional representation would lead to ". . . the continuation of governmental instability. . . ."[11] Not for the first or last time were Greek conservatives and nationalists to discover the ultimate significance of the American penetration of their nation. For when the "freedom and independence" in whose name American intervention was justified began to flicker through the long night of repression that had descended, the Americans repeatedly helped to snuff it out.

Turkey

Nominally, the inclusion of Turkey under the Truman Doctrine was justified for mainly economic reasons, ostensibly because full-scale military mobilization was weighing down that nation's moribund economy. The Turks had emerged from the war, however, with well over a quarter-billion dollars in hard gold and dollar reserves, plus $65 million in other currencies, and Turkey's problems were in reality rooted in the antiquated nationalist vision, corrupted by time, of its rulers. The decrepit army was no match for the Russians, but since the State Department in the spring of 1947 admitted that ". . . the Turks do not consider armed attack to be imminent," the perpetuation of its incompetence scarcely was bothersome.[12] The Turks realized that should they ever go to war with Russia, only full-scale American intervention could save them—indeed, a simple American pledge to do so would have sufficed—and they hoped to win that guarantee. Still, Washington was not so solicitous of Turkey's interest to ignore its own, especially after the Turks during 1948 attempted to gain back the German markets —which had absorbed 40 percent of their prewar trade—and found that American controls and the Marshall Plan had replaced Turkish with Virginia tobacco.

Yet the United States was willing to pay, and included the Turks in the Marshall Plan as well, and by the end of fiscal 1950 the Turks had received $150 million in economic aid, plus over $200 million in military aid that greatly understated its true worth.

The Turks were realists, however, and pressed for admission to NATO in order to gain from its protective shield. For the same realistic reasons, the Turks were prepared to welcome over 1,200 United States military advisers by 1950 but not to allow United States air bases on their territory —which the American military had coveted since 1948—which might truly evoke Soviet hostility and drag Turkey into a third world war. During 1951 they relented after the United States in September 1950 had agreed to Turkey's admission to NATO. But despite the fact that the Turks bowed to American insistence that they abandon their rusty statist theories of economic development and open the door to American investment, the country languished. By 1960, at which time it had received well over $3 billion in postwar United States economic and military aid, there was no doubt that the existing political leadership could only perpetuate the nation's mass poverty and serve itself. The United States had no illusions regarding the *quid pro quo* that they had reached with the ruling elites. "We are, after all," a Council on Foreign Relations report admitted in 1960, "giving the Turks what amounts to a continuing subsidy, not because their international payments are out of balance or because their agriculture is in need of tractors, but because they are steadfast allies and are standing up to Soviet threats and pressures."[13]

Oil: The Rewards of Power

The basic United States objective in the Middle East was that British power emerge neither too weak nor too strong from the monumental struggles under way in that region. In a precarious and intricate diplomatic context, the United States sought to manipulate and control moderate Arab nationalism to serve the attainment of this delicate but utilitarian balance of power in the region. But Washington understood that excessive British weakness would open a power vacuum into which Soviet influence or radical nationalism might rush, and the United States intended the Truman Doctrine to be an effort to balance and restructure the emergent forces of change in the larger area. Yet a Britain that was too strong could deny the United States what it coveted most in the Middle East: oil.

Even as the United States acted to strengthen the conservative forces that

England had abandoned, it moved to reap the rewards of its rising power and role in the region, thereby further removing the British incentive to dissipate their strength by holding all their existing commitments. The English regarded the American intervention in Greece and Turkey as nothing new, and motivated mainly by self-interest. "The truth is that the United States has been involved up to the hilt in the Middle East," the *Economist* of London could bitterly comment immediately after Truman's speech.[14] Officially, the State Department denied that the Truman Doctrine impinged on United States oil policy; yet its own domino theory belied the assertion, and in reality most congressmen treated the oil matter as an integral part of the picture. That the major American oil firms chose this time in the shifting regional balance of political power to pursue aggressively the smashing of the traditional Red Line division of Middle East oil made full sense, and by November 1948, they arranged a laborious, complex new agreement after innumerable Anglo-American court battles. Now the way was clear for American firms to establish their mastery over the Middle East oil that had been one of the major rewards of British imperialism.

Given the *de facto* opening of the Middle East's oil resources to United States interests, there was scarcely any need after mid-1947 for the painfully negotiated and still unratified Anglo-American petroleum agreement that had been submitted to the Senate in the fall of 1945. Moreover, the Texas-based opposition to the treaty was vigorous and pointed, and included key Republican fund raisers who detailed their past services to the party while insisting that "[t]he oil men want this proposed treaty killed. . . ."[15] These domestic producers lived with the fear that someday a treaty might open the American oil market to true world competition of the sort Washington advocated for other nations, at which point Bahrein oil, costing 25 cents a barrel in 1947 including royalties—or a small fraction of the American cost —might squeeze them out of business. Despite the nominal support for the treaty from the national petroleum organizations, the presence of Tom Connally of Texas in the Senate Foreign Relations Committee, and flagging interest from a State Department that saw it would successfully break into the Middle East with or without a treaty, were sufficient to freeze the proposal. The British hope that they might appease and contain the Americans, who had strenuously insisted on the treaty in the first place, proved vain.

During the months that the United States was moving into the Middle East via Greece and Turkey, an interdepartmental committee from the State, Interior, Commerce, Army, and Navy departments hammered out a confidential recommendation which reached advanced form by November 1947 and was effectively to guide "United States Petroleum Policy" globally. In essence it updated and expanded the ambitious oil policy that had been formulated at the end of 1944.

As Washington still saw it, its basic purpose was to ". . . seek the removal or modification of existent barriers (legal, contractual or otherwise) to the expansion of American foreign oil operations and facilitate the entry or reentry of private foreign capital into countries where the absence of such capital inhibits oil development." Such "capital" meant American capital, and this explicitly required diplomatic undertakings to open the way for United States firms: "That the policies and techniques of diplomatic and other support heretofore employed by the United States Government be continued, and be strengthened where appropriate and possible," and that Washington ". . . should promote, by advice and assistance . . . the entry of additional American firms into all phases of foreign oil operations." This would require closer coordination with United States firms, but also with foreign governments, which would be encouraged to adopt laws ". . . properly safeguarding the legitimate interests of all parties concerned." And that, in turn, meant "[t]he Committee agreed that although a country has a sovereign right to nationalize its industries, it does not follow that a country should exercise this right and was of the opinion that all feasible methods of persuasion should be used to induce a country considering nationalization of its petroleum industry to refrain from such nationalization. . . ."[16] Tangibly, the policy spelled out, the United States would loan no public funds to help develop nationalized oil industries, and would continue diplomatic interventions as a matter of course.

This policy reflected the perpetuation rather than a growth of the geopolitical and profit-oriented sophistication of the leading American decision-makers, and it explained much of America's future interventionist responses to not only Middle Eastern crises but Latin American as well. Forrestal, who was always ready to stress the vast stakes involved in the control of the world's oil supply, was scarcely alone at this time. Indeed, the November 1947 statement was global in its scope, but focused specifically on the reentry of United States firms into the Mexican and Bolivian oil fields, both of which had been nationalized for a decade. As in 1944, it was still American policy to obtain a larger share of Middle East output, but to retain the hemisphere as a monopoly against all possible competitors and internal changes.

The United States decided at the end of 1947, therefore, to even more energetically ". . . seek the reentry of private foreign capital" into Mexico and Bolivia, as it would more aggressively several years later in Iran.[17] In Mexico, only several months after the war's end, the State Department had already begun to seek openings for new United States penetration on terms that would neutralize nationalization, and over the following year its enthusiasm far exceeded that of the oil companies. Washington informed the Mexicans not only that nationalization violated the spirit of the Act of Chapultepec but also that they could expect no aid to the nationalized industry until United States firms were readmitted. By January 1948 the matter was before the cabinet, where Forrestal argued for ". . . the appointment of ambassadors with some business experience and background . . . who would vigorously and continuously push the interests of American business," and Mexico was his best justification of the need for such men.[18] Not only had Mexico nationalized its oil industry, but it was inefficient and useless in providing the United States with the precious fluid. A month later, Willard L. Thorp, assistant secretary of state, publicly outlined America's opposition to all nationalization as being confiscatory, along with its intention of continuing to win more concessions for American firms in the Middle East and to get back into Mexico.

The Mexicans wanted United States technical help for their petroleum industry, and they also wished loans. To complicate the matter, as well as sharpen the screws, there was still pending, among others, an outstanding claim of at least $200 million against Mexico for the oil of a nationalized American firm, the Sabalo Transportation Company, which wisely had engaged the law firm of Sullivan & Cromwell. There Allen Dulles had worked on the matter until handing it over to an associate, Edward G. Miller, Jr., who in May 1949 was designated assistant secretary of state for inter-American affairs. At the beginning of July the Mexicans received an *aide-mémoire* suggesting that a United States loan was contingent on Mexico's indication of a favorable attitude toward the reentry of private American firms in oil exploration, development, and production, as well as the settlement of various claims. At that point the United States would be ready to assist Mexico on the refining, transportation, and technical end of the industry. The Mexicans rejected the proposal categorically.

In Bolivia, however, the United States reentry appeared to go better for a time. On December 28, 1950, Ambassador Irving Florman could triumphantly report to Washington, "Since my arrival here, I have worked diligently on the project of throwing Bolivia's petroleum industry wide open to American private enterprise. . . . the whole land is now wide open for free American enterprise. Boliva is, therefore, the world's first country to de-nationalize. . . ."[19] Yet before the agreeable Bolivian President could perform his end of the bargain he was out of office, and the prospect of American success lasted only as long as the frail personalities on whom it was based. Ultimately the prize was gained—only to be lost again later— when a bankrupt and dependent Bolivia was compelled to revert to private foreign penetration or lose the United States' entangling aid.

Meanwhile, the new division of the Middle East finally worked out by the British, their allies, and the American firms did not last long. Upsetting matters was the desire of oil-producing nations to obtain a larger share of the profits on the oil foreign firms were removing from their soil, and in 1948 Venezuela passed a 50–50 law that soon had global repercussions. The Iranian government, still unhappy with British predominance over its wealth, also began pressuring for a greater share from the Anglo-Iranian Oil Company, which had no intention of voluntarily conceding on its immense profits by altering miserable working conditions and discrimination in its fields. Despite eventual financial concessions, in part the result of pressures from the American government, Anglo-Iranian moved too reluctantly, and in December 1950, when the United States–owned Aramco firm agreed to 50–50 for Saudi Arabia, the Iran crisis reemerged in full bloom. The American firm was aware of the intense dispute in Iran between the nationalists in the Majlis, led by Mohammed Mossadegh, and Anglo-Iranian—and the Iranian threat of nationalization if they could not reach a satisfactory arrangement. It was well known that the new American offer, which exceeded the more favorable terms Anglo-Iranian was already giving Iran, would have ramifications throughout the Middle East, and that it was a kind of bidding for the favor of the Arab nations. Whether intended or not, the act accelerated the dispute between Britain and Iran, as did the intimation from the American ambassador in Iran that the United States would be a probable source of economic aid for the advancement of Iran's general economic plans. What is certain, however, is that American public and private actions egged the Iranians on, as American diplomats on the scene openly proclaimed their neutrality, and in May 1951, Iran, under Mossadegh's leadership, nationalized the oil industry and threw the English out.

Iran owned its oil industry and refineries, but the United States and England now collaborated to cut off all its markets and drive it back into the Western-controlled oil economy. To the United States, which initially refused to support the British even on nationalization—thereby filling the British with the reasonable suspicion that the Americans were encouraging Mossadegh—the question, now that the British were out, was for the United States to carve out a share of the oil of a nation whose wealth it had unsuccessfully coveted since 1944. In principle, Mossadegh, who was now Premier, favored compensation to Anglo-Iranian, but the Americans saw the need to prevent genuine nationalization, however temporarily useful it was to be. Truman was unsympathetic to the British cause, but also feared that Iran's total success would set a dangerous precedent for Venezuela and nations where American oil interests were more direct. Mossadegh, whom Acheson regarded as a reactionary nationalist, was still less dangerous than a decisive British victory that might also bring on a Communist coup. "Perhaps the Iranians and the British will agree to have an international management group run the oil industry," Henry F. Grady, the recently retired United States ambassador to Teheran, suggested at the end of 1951.[20]

The British themselves, it soon became clear, had less power in the situation than the much more cautious Americans, who were the only ones able to supply them with desperately needed oil, and they permitted the United States to take the initiative as mediators, quite convinced the Americans had concocted the crisis in the first place to attain their long-standing goal of penetrating Iran. The British, in any event, abandoned their contemplated invasion of Iran. During November, Mossadegh visited Washington and received royal treatment, and for a brief period it appeared possible that America would aid him and exclude the British. But on November 7, Sir Anthony Eden formally assured Acheson and Harriman that London would welcome American participation in a reorganized oil consortium— an offer Harriman berated him for being long overdue, its delay having been a major source of the trouble. Under the new circumstances, the Americans would find a new way to handle Mossadegh. Washington now moved toward closer cooperation with the British, cutting off all military and most economic aid to Teheran at the same time. By mid-1952, however, British patience was running thin, and the presence of American oilmen in Teheran aroused their suspicions, despite State Department disavowals of approval. During the fall, Washington feared once more that British intransigence on the Iranian share of oil might open the door to a Tudeh Party coup, and in November the United States secretly decided to buy Iranian oil to buoy up the bankrupt Iranian economy, publicly authorizing United States firms to do so the following month. But the British wanted Mossadegh out of office, and United States efforts to drag them along on a new compromise—one that would have allocated American firms half of Iran's oil output—failed.[21]

To look ahead, soon after Eisenhower came to office Dulles reevaluated the tacit Anglo-American united front and toyed with the possibility of making Mossadegh the United States' anti-British and anti-Russian ploy. But Washington rejected the alternative and instead warned Mossadegh that he would not receive any further American aid; the United States would continue to boycott his oil, and compensation would have to go well beyond Anglo-Iranian's loss of physical assets—and presumably include compensation for the immense fortune of oil still in the ground for which it was patently obvious Iran could never pay. Otherwise, Eisenhower threatened at the end of June, " . . . the present dangerous situation" would only be aggravated.[22] In effect, Iran could solve its problems only by denationalizing, but since Mossadegh would not, the following August a CIA-directed coup overthrew the government and replaced it with one under General Fazollah Zahedi, a former Nazi collaborator. And having engineered the victory, the United States would now help divide the spoils. For a time the State Department considered a total American takeover of Iranian oil, but strong British protests and perhaps some reluctance on the part of United States oil firms caused Washington to lower its sights.

Three years without oil income had further impoverished Iran to the point, as Zahedi put it, that " . . . there is hardly anything for anyone to steal nowadays. . . ."[23] The State Department assigned the responsibility of working out a new formula for the Iran oil industry to Herbert Hoover, Jr., who had often served as consultant to major American oil firms. To help it protect national interests, the Zahedi regime took Torkild Rieber as its special adviser. Rieber, who had been chairman of the board of the Texas Company until forced to resign in 1940 for alleged pro-German sympathies, was an American citizen. For political reasons it was decided not to denationalize what was once Anglo-Iranian, but rather to give a new western company exclusive management and full rights to the output on commercial terms until 1994. The final contract involved one critical new dimension: a 40 percent interest in the new firm went to the five American majors, among which Texas was one. No longer could the American firms be excluded, for Washington had egged them on and by this time they had also taken over many of Anglo-American's traditional markets. Anglo-Iranian ultimately received $510 million in compensation, mainly from the American participants who were now buying into the once-European firm. The British did not resist the scheme, and perhaps were grateful to be left even

40 percent of the new company for Anglo-Iranian and another 14 percent for Royal Dutch Shell. Ten years of unsuccessful struggle with the Americans had unquestionably chastised them into recognizing that the British Empire in the Middle East had given way to the American.[24]

Palestine: Global versus Domestic Politics

The Soviet Union, despite its anxieties regarding encircling American bases, throughout this period regarded America's expanded role in Greece and the Middle East as just one more aspect of oil diplomacy and Anglo-American rivalries. Turkey's inclusion in the Truman Doctrine, to the Russians, made sense only in the context of United States exploitation of the new balance in world capitalist power since the war. Varga, still a leading Soviet spokesman, took the events as the opportunity to apply the then official Soviet theory of the world crisis to the Middle East, where "[i]t is beyond doubt that the USA is taking advantage of England's great financial difficulties and her need for future credits, in order to exert pressures upon her and to decide in its own interest the numerous questions at issue in the sphere of oil politics in the Near East. . . ."[25] Through 1947 and 1948 the Iranian question also was treated as a struggle over oil concessions, though Turkey was seen primarily as a question of strategic bases and power, relevant as much to Russia as the area to the south and east.

It was largely in this context that Moscow related to the Palestine crisis, which was the only important controversy in the region in the years immediately after the termination of the 1946 Iran dispute in which the USSR and its satellites were to play some significant role. For during much of the 1920's the Soviets had been friendly to left-socialist Zionism, and, after a decade of strong hostility, the Russians had once again adopted a tolerant attitude toward the Zionist movement. Until the Tito expulsion, indeed, the Zionists freely operated in Eastern Europe to remove a large part of the remaining Jewish population.

For the United States, the question of Zionism and Palestine was infinitely more complex. The United States' record toward the Jewish refugee problem during the war was one of casual indifference, and Franklin Roosevelt and the majority of the cabinet refused to take any stand on Jewish emigration to Palestine likely to offend Ibn Saud. Oil, traditionally and until the present time, was the guiding principle and motive of American policy toward the Middle East. The Palestine crisis of 1947–1948 was to prove only a partial exception; yet it must still be placed in the context of the elimination of British hegemony over the region's oil industry. The erratic policy the United States assumed during the controversy was largely the outcome of Truman's desire to win the Presidency in 1948—that is, reasons of domestic politics. The result was an American vacillation that permitted the USSR to play an extraordinarily significant, perhaps decisive, role in bringing into existence the State of Israel.

Roosevelt had a genuine liking for King Ibn Saud, and a week before his death reassured the feudal lord that he would take no action on Palestine " . . . which might prove hostile to the Arab people" and "without full consultation with both Arabs and Jews."[26] It was universally understood, at this time and thereafter, that there was no political solution imaginable to which both the Arabs and Zionists would agree, and such a formula was always a decision to maintain a *status quo* that the Zionists were determined to destroy.

While continuing his support for Roosevelt's essentially oil-oriented political policy, shortly after the war Truman also effectively endorsed the position that the British would do well to permit 100,000 Jews to enter Palestine. Yet he applied no serious pressure, and during October he agreed to release Roosevelt's letter to Ibn Saud of the prior April, with the implication it was still American policy. The British, in response, proposed the creation of an Anglo-American Committee of Inquiry to consider the Jewish refugee problem and possible alternatives to Palestine, believing the refugees to be the crux of the problem—or at least the committee to be an excellent way of postponing matters. The State Department, which was strongly anti-Zionist, urged the American members of the committee to consider the Palestine question in the inextricable context of great power rivalry, and along with Forrestal and most of the wartime cabinet members it consistently regarded oil and good relations with the Arabs as the prime goal of United States policy in the region. Despite initial British anxieties concerning Truman's objectives, the committee's final report was a political disaster for the Zionists. Its only succor was to favor the admission of 100,000 Jews into Palestine " . . . as rapidly as conditions will permit," but it categorically rejected partition into Jewish and Arab states, and called for maintenance of the British mandate until the UN could arrange a trusteeship.[27] The British government then scuttled the report by linking the admission of 100,000 Jews to the disarmament of the illegal Jewish armies in Palestine.

Truman then cautiously sounded out advisers, including the Joint Chiefs of Staff, who strongly urged that American access to oil and preserving the good will of the Arabs remain the basic policy objectives. In effect, by raising the ogre of expanded Soviet influence in the oil states the military added its full weight to the State Department's anti-Zionist position. Then, during the late spring, the President appointed a cabinet committee, consisting of Byrnes, Snyder, and Patterson, to come up with an alternative proposal; this it did, after visiting England, at the end of July with a complex federal scheme involving a semiautonomous Jewish state, on one-third the disputed land, and an Arab state, both under a central government that would control immigration and all federal affairs. The plan, which in fact had been concocted by the British Colonial Office as a contingency measure during the war, had strong official British support as well. But Washington ultimately refused to endorse it, and Jewish and Arab opposition led to its demise.

During the next months Truman showed considerable personal hostility to Zionist pressures in the United States, which were shrill, emotional, immense, and ineffective. But the election of November 1946 was approaching, and Truman was warned that the party would lose New York unless he abandoned the federation scheme and made some more tangible gesture. On October 4, the Jewish holiday Yom Kippur, Truman ignored Attlee's opposition and made a most ambiguous statement on Palestine: he dropped the unworkable partition plan formally, and while referring favorably to the Committee of Inquiry's recommendation that 100,000 Jews be admitted to Palestine, he merely added that "substantial immigration" should begin at once.[28] Thomas Dewey, the opposition candidate, not to be outbid, and confused by Zionist claims that Truman had actually endorsed immigration of 100,000, doubled the figure several days later. Truman was indignant when, before the Commons, Bevin then publicly accused him of bidding for the favor of the New York Jewish vote.[29]

The main import of the October statement revealed that on the levels of both policy and personal inclination the President and his cabinet essentially preferred the maintenance of a political *status quo* compatible with American oil diplomacy in the region, but Truman himself was reluctantly vulnerable to political pressures. Moreover, after the Republicans won the 1946 election in New York, Truman must have had very real doubts concerning his ability to win sufficient Jewish votes to guarantee political victories, and so by the summer of 1947 he was content to avoid further commitments on Palestine and to permit the British to solve their dilemmas midst rising Jewish terrorist attacks. But party leaders, such as Postmaster General Robert E. Hannegan, warned him that not merely Jewish votes but

Jewish donations to the party were at stake in the Palestine question. In the United Nations this cautious American line expressed itself by supporting various partition plans then under consideration, but with the United States provisos that the Arabs and Jews would have to negotiate a mutually acceptable plan, that Britain maintain its troops until independence, and that a volunteer UN force would then have to preserve order. The British, Russians, and Zionists opposed such contingencies, for all wanted to see English troops out and knew that linking partition to peace would doom a division—for the Arabs had repeatedly expressed their determination to fight to prevent a Jewish state in any form. But there was never any doubt that all the major powers would support a partition plan in some form and interpret it to their convenience. The Zionists, for their part, embarked on a pressure campaign in the United Nations " . . . unlike anything that had been seen there before," as Truman recalled, and it spilled over on Washington, creating intense resentment against the Zionist cause among many key, often already hostile, American decision-makers.[30] Yet what was most significant in the American vote for partition on November 29 was Truman's firm belief that the United States had no material obligation to help implement the partition plan. The argument of Forrestal, the State Department, and the Joint Chiefs that Middle Eastern oil was vital to future American economic and military power reinforced this conviction.

Largely as a result of the desire to play down temporary domestic political compromises and return to the basic goals of United States policy in the Middle East, the State Department decided no later than mid-January that partition was "not workable" and should be abandoned as a solution to the Palestine question.[31] Some State Department officials thought America had been outflanked in control over UN policy, and that organization's existence was getting in the way now that it was no longer so tractable. Since the British had declared that they would give up their mandate and be out of the country by May 15, the Arabs pledged that they would fight, and Trygve Lie's efforts to mobilize a peace-keeping force were failing, by the end of January 1948 Washington quietly began to withdraw its support for partition on the assumption that it was no longer feasible.

This redefinition of America's policy toward partition was not so much a reversal as a shift toward yet more explicit strategies intended to maximize a long-standing Middle Eastern policy. It was, obviously, pro-Arab on the question of Palestine, for the British avowed that they would not implement partition with their troops, and to make peace Washington's precondition was to abandon the UN decision. At the end of February the Americans expressed this shift by proposing to the UN that the Security Council attempt to devise means of conciliation to end the threat to international peace, and at the same time they began to prepare a scheme to abandon partition for an Anglo-American-French trusteeship and return to the earlier British cantonal plan. Trygve Lie was apprehensive concerning the new American line, which informally consisted of arguing that the council could take action to maintain peace but not to implement partition, since he now regarded the central issue as the ability of the UN to make and fulfill its decisions. The Zionists, watching American policy unfold over the same months, embarked on such an intensive pressure campaign that Truman refused to see any of their spokesmen, including the most conservative Chaim Weizmann. To Lie, who participated in the American-sponsored Security Council discussions, "Only the Soviet Union seemed to be seriously intent upon implementing partition; the United States clearly was not."[32] His judgment was correct, for the oil-oriented element in Washington now asserted its decisive influence.

On March 19, Warren Austin publicly addressed the Security Council regarding the failure of the partition resolution, which he called "integral," requiring full implementation peacefully or nothing at all.[33] He now asked instead for an abandonment of the partition resolution and a UN trusteeship over Palestine. ". . . United Nations depression, Arab jubilation, Zionist despair, and British self-righteousness," Lie later described the mood that night. The next day Lie went to Austin and pointed out " . . . the danger in which the whole structure of the United Nations has been placed" as a result of the American switch, and proposed that they both resign in protest.[34] The Russians urged Lie to stay on, however, and the American proposal fell on deaf ears in the UN. Then, at the end of the month, Austin urged a truce scheme that only the Arabs were willing to support in its original form. Meanwhile, the future of Palestine was being settled in the fields. As the British withdrew, some 6,000 to 8,000 Arab troops entered Palestine to fight alongside local Arab irregulars, but an Anglo-American arms embargo left the Jews relatively unprepared. At the end of March a load of Czech arms arrived to help offset the Jewish handicap, an event that the State Department feared was part of a Russian effort to use the Jewish state as a wedge for penetrating the region. The frightened association of Zionism with Communism, which grew substantially over the next months, existed along with oil diplomacy to guide American strategy. But all the trusteeship variations and postponements the United States might propose came to nought by May. For the British were determined to withdraw, the

Arabs would not concede, and the Zionists demanded implementation of the partition.

By no later than early May 1948, Truman was coming to the gradual realization that no nation was likely to endorse the American strategy the State Department had formulated with the backing of the military. The policy was a failure, and some of Truman's advisers attempted to convince him that he would gain nothing by unsuccessfully aiding the Arabs and alienating the Jews in the United States. Truman himself, as he later records, suspected that some of the State Department people " . . . were also inclined to be anti-Semitic," and he began to assume a larger measure of control over policy.[35] This was reflected, for the first time, in the question of recognizing the Jewish state.

The State Department, and Marshall in particular, did not favor the recognition of Israel, but in any event thought it certainly should not be sooner than a few days after May 15, when the Zionists were to declare a new state midst the battles raging throughout Palestine. But Clark Clifford, Ed Flynn, the Bronx Democratic boss, and others argued domestic politics and waved about Jewish votes and campaign contributions, and finally convinced the President, over stout resistance. Moreover, they were anxious that Russia might recognize Israel first, further identifying its interests with a Soviet bloc that had been its only ally during its time of greatest need. Truman acted without consulting the State Department again, and recognized Israel just a few minutes after its declaration. Several days later the Russians followed suit, and the Eastern European nations scrambled close behind.

Although American policy was to zigzag over subsequent months in a way that infuriated all and showed a lack of a clear strategy, most American leaders shared Leahy's belief that "Russia is looking for the opportunity to get into the Middle East," perhaps using " . . . the Communist element of Israel," and that "[a]ny further aid on our part to Israel would be detrimental to our tactical and strategical interest and will endanger the lives and property of US citizens. . . ."[36] The fear of Russian power in the region via Israel was fanned by the critical Czech arms, so vital to the new state in light of the American and English arms ban. Moreover, *Pravda* was full of defenses of Israel against Arab attacks and what it called a double-faced American policy that was essentially pro-oil. And so long as the reactionary Arab League and Turkey were the only regional forces hostile to Israel, the Russians gladly defended its right to exist. Bevin, for his part, saw the Russians attempting to incite fighting in the Middle East in order to sustain the pressures they were also applying at the same time via the Berlin blockade. Such alleged Soviet omnipotence therefore filled most of official Washington with very real hostility toward Israel, but at the same time practical politics, and the election of 1948, forced Truman to claim that the United States had cordially supported Zionist demands and the founding of Israel—when, in fact, quite the opposite was closer to the reality.[37]

The End of Empire

With the elimination or drastic reduction of British power and influence in Greece, Palestine, Iran, and Egypt after July 1952 came also the partial replacement of its historical role in the region by the United States. Yet it was this very partiality, and the dissolving impact of the transition on established internal orders, that was to lead to undesired and uncontrollable new changes for America that were to leave the region in constant ferment. The United States, since the war, had sought an orderly replacement of British power with its own, but it conceived of that transformation in essentially economic rather than political terms, and the delicate shift was too elusive to be attainable.

Washington attempted to sustain the British politically on numerous occasions, and no later than 1952 the United States Sixth Fleet was seen as the strategic expression of this desire, for its " . . . suitable visits and displays might be helpful with respect to the British position without involving permanent commitments by the United States." In the case of the Egyptian political crisis of 1952, which led to King Farouk's abdication, the Navy hoped " . . . that the Egyptians surmise that the Sixth Fleet would be behind the British in the event of any holocaust."[38] Still, this did not prevent the United States from aiding mild nationalist changes likely to help America at the expense at the British, and United States support to General Naguib during 1952–1953, including covert CIA assistance, further weakened the British in Suez. But at many junctures, and in many countries, Washington saw political cooperation between the two economic rivals as a desirable goal. The problems arose when the inevitable mixture of politics and economics occurred—the Suez crisis of 1956 was the ultimate example —and the British saw no advantage in remaining to preserve order in a region while the Americans took its wealth. For the Americans could not, as in Iran and Bahrein, resist the temptation to gain oil concessions when British weakness opened new possibilities to do so. Moreover, the United States could not restrain itself during these and subsequent years from using the first manifestations of Arab nationalism to extirpate undesired British influence and domination which it could only partially replace, losing control over the destabilizing and radicalizing tides that followed in the wake of the nationalist movements. Wavering on support for Arab nationalism and British presence was fully consistent with maximizing American interests, which became supreme in the oil sector after 1951. That, in the last analysis, was all America had sought, and it confined its diplomatic and military strategy to preserving the advantageous new *status quo* by one means or another, from military aid and alliances to giving alternating and even simultaneous support to the Arabs and Israel—and occasional interventions.[39]

Thus the United States emerged as the dominant power in the Middle East as the inevitable consequence of its wartime determination to win for itself the major share of the riches of the region.

16

The Marshall Plan, II:
The Economics of
European Restoration

By the time the Marshall Plan began its operations in mid-1948, most of Western Europe's early illusions and extravagant hopes had given way to a realistic appraisal that United States aid would involve much more than acquiring the needed credits and supplies to complete reconstruction. How far the new program would erode national sovereignty in establishing economic priorities remained to be tested. But if Europe were to sacrifice sovereignty on critical economic issues, would it also lose a measure of its freedom of choice on political questions where its interests diverged from those of the United States? Such questions took on new urgency in the capitals of Western Europe as the specifics of the plan unfolded.

America's intention to shape Western Europe's economic policies was the critical fact of the plan from the beginning. Washington did not propose merely to fill Europe's shopping list, and the initial thrust of United States policy was in manipulating European fiscal affairs. Yet the first year of the Marshall Plan after June 1948 illustrated the fundamental dilemmas in efforts at capitalist "planning" and the contradictions inherent in such programs. The dilemma which the Economic Cooperation Administration (ECA) either could not or refused to confront was that, even in a capitalist framework, the requirements of industrial reconstruction and of monetary conservatism, or balanced budgets, were totally incompatible. Yet even before the ink had dried on the statements proclaiming the Marshall Plan a program to rebuild the strength of the Western European economies and a bastion against the Left, both implying a program for increased production and full employment, the ECA planners concluded that they should place the highest priority on deflationary economic policies that would inevitably lead to a very different outcome.

The Economics of Conservatism

The provisions of the Foreign Assistance Act were specific on the financial policies that the United States wished to see the Europeans pursue. To a very real extent, the ECA went beyond the needs of the American economy for stable markets, and pressed orthodox policies on governments of quite varied economic and political complexions. The first result was to strengthen those conservative political forces in Europe that desired a similar program. The ECA, in its general financial policy, introduced strict banker's criteria of balanced budgets, stable currencies, high profits to entice investment, and low wages to discourage consumption. Public pronouncements aside, the American administrators believed that it was essential to keep internal mass living standards at a low level in order to have a surplus for export and to limit imports so as not to upset further the balance of payments. The European governments were now required to restrict their expenditure in social welfare and subsidies in order to balance the budget, and the American advisers always maintained that "excess egalitarianism" in taxation policy suppressed incentive. The ECA used these economic guidelines in the reconstruction of Western Europe. Such solutions are simple and well understood by economists everywhere—but the fog of American ideology, made thicker by liberal commentaries portraying the Marshall Plan as an aspect of unparalleled humanitarianism, has obscured these accepted capitalist principles. At the time, these economic policies meshed well with the interests of the most conservative elements in the Western European ruling class, and they naturally were enthusiastic over American aid which consolidated and then enlarged their power. In Italy, Germany, France, and the Benelux, profits over the first year rose far out of proportion to any other index of reconstruction, and the contours of the old order gradually reemerged in their solid, traditional form after a frightening, though brief, period during which their future seemed in doubt.

A Western Europe united both economically and politically, and including England, was a major aim of the ambitious American program. That unity demanded homogeneous economic policies which, in turn, required conservative political control. But despite their intent and power, to impose these abstract policies on the nations of Western Europe was a far more complicated task than formulating them.

As the first order of business in the summer of 1948, the ECA and the Europeans' Organization for European Economic Cooperation (OEEC) asked the participating governments to submit national plans showing how they expected to operate their economies *after* American aid ended in 1952. Much to American irritation, all the Marshall Plan countries planned substantial increases in heavy industry, and each nation intended to increase its exports over prewar by approximately one-third, but also to stabilize imports at prewar levels. The United States was their chief contemplated market for the expansion of exports, but they also included new areas that were traditional American markets, such as Latin America. The OEEC found such plans unrealistic, especially in their hopes for massive exports to United States markets.[1] This tendency of the member nations to continue to press their national aims, rather than to emphasize a united Europe with regional specialization, was disconcerting to the American policy-makers from the beginning of the program; but Washington hoped that it would be able to redirect this trend as it shared in the economic decision-making in Europe to an ever greater degree over the coming years. Not only the end use but the distribution of resources in the participating states was of great interest to the United States, and in this regard the ECA stipulations barred any American assistance for any internal welfare objectives.[2]

A yet more sensitive question for the European nations was the question of the allocation of aid by country. Although the OEEC's function was supposedly to determine country grants, the United States, over sharp objections, insisted on giving the largest aid to Germany, and in 1948, 28 percent of the total went to the former enemy state. The Bizone, represented by the American occupation, refused to accept the OEEC allocation of $367 million when it had asked for $450 million, and it also refused to grant the $90 million in credits to the other members that the OEEC assigned to it. Harriman finally, and predictably, intervened on behalf of Clay and Bizonia and forced the chagrined OEEC to raise the German share to $414 million and to waive the credit assignment. No other action revealed more graphically that when Washington referred to the use of Europe's own resources to full capacity, it meant the reintegration of German industry into a new European system.[3]

The German Restoration

It was in West Germany, where the United States could most freely impose its will on the broad contours of the economy, that the intended purposes of the Marshall Plan were expressed in their purest form, uninhibited by the more complicating political environment that existed in the other nations of Europe. Well before 1947 the United States recognized that its role as the preeminent occupying force in both Germany and Japan, potentially two of the strongest industrial nations in the world, gave it exceptional power in directing their postwar development. American influence on other states was great, but indirect. It never fully trusted the British, especially the Labour Party, and France, with its strong Left, frequent strikes, and mercurial politics, Washington considered important but unreliable. Once the United States had precisely defined its means and ends in Europe, only in Germany did it have a completely free hand to carry them out.

In order to lay the foundation for the policies that were to reconstruct the German economy, the Americans simultaneously introduced a currency reform in June 1948 that split definitively the Western zones from the Soviet zone and accentuated the class structure in the West. We examine the dramatic political consequences of the currency reform with the Russians over Berlin in Chapter 18, but they were in fact incidental to the imperative need to restore capitalist incentives in the West German economy in order to implement the policies that were the core of the Marshall Plan. And the results of the entire effort vividly reveal the fallacy behind the plan's fundamental assumption that economic reconstruction was possible with deflationary policies, and only subsequent world political crises redeemed the undertaking from total disaster.

To reform a national currency is not a neutral economic function, but, on the contrary, it is a measure permeated with the most profound ideological assumptions concerning the over-all social and economic system. No one doubted that some sort of currency reform was called for and that four-power agreement should have implemented a policy in 1945, although the variation in economic perspectives in each zone, plus initial United States ambivalence regarding Germany, precluded agreement. In the West, both the United States and British occupations refused to block personal bank accounts at the end of the war, and those who had been or became rich under the Nazis retained their savings as well as their nonmonetary wealth. Given the price controls on critical products and the shortages in a vast array of consumer goods, these savings were channeled into the black market or held in abeyance and constituted the "suppressed inflation" that so concerned the American administrators in Germany. The perpetual discussion of an impending currency reform, especially after December 1947, naturally further undermined the mark, and those who had goods, industrial or agricultural, hoarded them in what was to prove a well-rewarded anticipation of a stronger currency.

While some form of monetary reform would have greatly facilitated the lives of the German people, in comparison with what followed the American reform of June 1948, the economic conditions of the year preceding it and the subsequent economic growth have both been grossly exaggerated. Between the end of the war and June 1948, 90 percent of the goods were legally exchanged and the price controls on them functioned relatively well. While the Germans conducted a great proportion of internal trade by means of barter, they based even those transactions on legal prices. The black market, on the other hand, absorbed much of the money, and the bulk of nonessential goods were hoarded. Yet economists at the time were surprised at the black market's limited scope. Although most Germans had dealt with it at one time or another, they looked upon it with opprobrium and some shame before June 1948. It operated chiefly in luxury goods, and there is no evidence that it became more extensive over the three years of controls. In other words, its operation affected primarily the bourgeoisie, and necessities were far better distributed before the currency reform than after. And while the postwar deprivations in Germany, as elsewhere, were great, the cost of living rose at one-half the rate of inflation in the United States in the two and one-half years after October 1945.[4]

To the occupation authorities and the decision-makers in Washington what was clearly absent was an incentive system for saving, investment, and work, so essential to the profitable operation of a capitalist society. In order to attract investment and begin reconstruction, currency had to have "real value." The Americans designed their reform to lay the basis for orthodox capitalist economic policies—policies based less, however, on the needs of reconstruction, whether capitalist or otherwise, than on monetary control for a "sound" financial structure. This means of controlling inflation necessitated a highly inequitable distribution of income that was intended to increase savings through high profits and tax concessions for the upper class while low wages, the most regressive taxation system in Europe, and mass unemployment were to reduce the "propensity to spend" on the part of the working class.[5]

The Germans involved in formulating the early plans for a currency reform in 1946 had stressed the importance of simultaneous equalization-of-burdens provisions. For political reasons, equity had been the most important consideration in earlier reforms implemented elsewhere in Europe, where capital levies and war-profits taxes were the rule. Even Washington had reluctantly approved the equalization provisions in the original Colm-Dodge-Goldsmith plan because it was essential for Soviet acceptance. Once it made the decision to proceed with the reform in the West alone, however, Washington insisted on dropping the equity provisions since they resembled capital levies—which the United States opposed in principle, no matter what the purpose. Clay himself expressed regret at this shift in policy, for he believed it would undermine the confidence of the Germans in the American economic aims.[6]

In April 1948, shortly before the monetary reform, the Christian Democrat laissez faire economist Ludwig Erhard replaced the Social Democrat Viktor Agartz as chairman of the Bizonal Economic Council and the SPD withdrew from participation in the administration of economic policy. With the council safely in conservative hands, the occupation greatly expanded its powers when it introduced the new currency, making it an incipient finance ministry. Under American guidance Erhard established for the subsequent decades the economic policy known as the "social market economy." The currency reform, as it was planned and implemented, decisively laid the foundation for this course, but it in no way accounted for West Germany's subsequent economic growth.

Once having chosen a currency reform predicated on the need for a grossly inequitable income distribution, the occupation introduced the draconian plan piecemeal. The first decree in June 1948, which reduced the money supply by a ratio of 10 to 1, virtually wiped out the small savers and rewarded the hoarder, the black marketeer, and those who possessed real property. Erhard removed price controls on all items except basic food and fuel, and these "controls" were ignored and for practical purposes ceased to exist. Goods reappeared from the hoards, and as a result of pent-up demand a wild spending spree followed. Hoarders made gigantic profits within several months—conservatively estimated at 3 billion new DM—and in the process transferred the bulk of the new money to the most antisocial and reactionary elements of the population. The Germans conducted a poll shortly after the reform and naturally found that low-income groups had suffered most and were alarmed about the future, while business elements were enthusiastic.[7] The stock market enjoyed a brief boom, reflecting the new confidence, and while prices and profits skyrocketed, real wages fell sharply and unemployment nearly doubled by December 1948. Official production figures that indicated a rise of 53 percent between June and December so distort reality as to be nearly useless. During the six months prior to currency reform, unreported production that factory owners had channeled illegally into hoarding or the black market was understood to be about one-half in some industries, and 15 to 20 percent in general. The actual rise that did occur over the last half of 1948 can be more easily attributed to the vast influx of United States aid via the Marshall Plan, the exceptional harvest, and the mild winter that permitted the greater use of coal for industrial purposes. Finally, merely accepting general production figures is misleading in the assessment of reconstruction, for it is critical to know in what sector the rise took place; and in the case of West Germany between June 1948 and June 1950 this distinction was of prime importance. According to a UN study, the growth was in fields of ". . . low priority from the point of view of the economy as a whole."[8]

In October 1948 the Military Government, Washington, and the particular Germans to whom they had given power and responsibility reacted to the unexpected and undesired spending with new determination to institute further drastic deflationary measures by curtailing credit. Again the consequences were serious. The tax reform, reducing taxes on high incomes and corporations and raising those on the workers, and tightened credit, led not to the expected savings, but to heavy capital flight (which Clay in 1950 estimated at $100–$200 million annually) and to conspicuous consumption. Aside from the gross moral image such lavish indulgence of a small group conveyed in a setting of mass destitution, such developments profoundly redirected reconstruction. Purchasing power was concentrated in the hands of a tiny minority that consumed luxury goods on a grand scale, so distorting the income distribution that investment and imports were channeled to meet only their demand. Further facilitating this capricious direction of the economy, the Military Government decreed that the central bank was not subject to "any political body," but responsible to the market economy, which meant, in effect, banking and business interests. The Basic Law, or constitution, made government deficit financing illegal except under the most extreme circumstances. But since the commercial banks refused to make the long-term credits so essential for reconstruction, and instead concentrated on short-term credits for quick profits, the disastrous consequences were quick to follow. Credit went to luxury restaurants, hotels, and shops, which all prospered, and the importation of nonessential luxury goods and food consumed a good part of the foreign exchange while unemployment continued to grow and the bulk of the population suffered great deprivation. Labor unrest throughout the fall of 1948 erupted into several clashes with the occupation troops, and during November the trade unions called a successful Bizonal work stoppage to protest the economic policies, demanding reinstatement of price controls and rationing. It was a reminder of the potential opposition from the working class, but an opposition that the Americans had much earlier anticipated and for which they had already calculated their response.

As with Italy, the extreme deflationary policies soon prevented the German economy from even utilizing the available ERP aid or the drawing rights of the OEEC, and the Military Government continued to block the counterpart funds sorely needed for basic construction. The German economic policies also played a critical role in the rate of reconstruction of the other members of the OEEC. Europe's hopes for increased exports to Germany did not materialize because of the fact that trade was conducted in scarce dollars that the occupation spent in the United States, despite Germany's export surplus with the rest of Western Europe. The shortage of credit prevented German importers from increasing their stocks of anything but the most frivolous goods.[9]

It is important to note that the cause of this economic malaise was not the war, the reparations, nor the refugee problem, and not even the division of Germany. The crisis in the German economy, that critical sector of Europe that the United States was supposedly so intent on reconstructing, rested solely on the socioeconomic policies of the United States and the class it had maintained in power in the Western zones. The evidence fully underlines the fact that the economic outcome was not the reconstruction of German industrial power, but rather the full restoration of the propertied class.

The question of the control of the Ruhr impinged on the future of Germany as a possible military power, on its potential to make reparations available to the nations it had destroyed, and also on the social-economic forms the West German economy might adopt. To say simply that it was central to the concerns of all is to understate its immense significance. And the proposals of the former allies, and Germans, for its future control all reflected their own fears, desires, and ultimate goals. The German Socialists and the British Labour Party advocated nationalization of these critical industries, while the Soviets and French proposed that the entire complex be subject to a four-power international authority. While at the time no one proposed returning the industry to its former owners, the evolving United States and German conservative position of international control by a private structure of international capitalists strongly implied the restoration of the essence of the old order.

At first fearing that nationalization would be the result of any decisive action, the United States sought to postpone the issue until it was better able to control the outcome and channel it along acceptable lines. The British had meanwhile taken steps to reorganize the iron and steel industries in a manner that could only lead to nationalization, and they pursued their policy even after the United States assumed the dominant role in the administration of Bizonia. They broke up the old companies and organized them on strictly functional lines—all steel, coal, and iron in separate companies—and appointed a management board divided equally between labor and businessmen. The Americans violently opposed these plans, and between June and November 1948 were able to wrest the final authority from the British on the control of the Ruhr. In issuing Law 75 on November 10, the United States reversed the British program and placed the entire industry of the Ruhr in the hands of twelve German business "trustees," instructing them to reorganize the industries and vesting them with all the rights of ownership, excepting the distribution of profits, until the German people could "choose" between public and private ownership. If they chose private, as the United States intended to see that they did, the trustees could hope to become true owners as well. To head the trustees, the Military Government appointed Heinrich Dinkelbach, who had played a leading role in the Ruhr under Hitler, as had nine of the twelve trustees. The trade unions in the Ruhr objected to the appointment of these former Nazis, but were disregarded, for the United States had already decided that the Communists dominated the trade unions in the region.

Law 75 also outraged the French by definitively returning ownership to German hands and excluding direct allied control. But although Premier Schuman protested the edict, he told the French public that some form of "European" control could yet be developed. Even the State Department and the ECA disagreed on the question. Thomas Blaisdell asserted that Law 75 would ". . . destroy much of the good which has been accomplished by the Marshall Plan. . . . Such a policy may destroy the middle-of-the-road

Government in France. . . . It will be received with enthusiasm in Moscow, and the propaganda will make clear to Western Europe the intention of the American Government to strike an alliance with the discredited German management of the Ruhr."[10] It was, of course, more than propaganda. By July 1949, *U.S. News and World Report,* after listing the names of the top industrialists under Hitler and under the United States, concluded, "Control of the Ruhr now rests in the hands of a few hundred men, as it did during and before the war. Most of the Ruhr's present bosses are men who reached their peak of power during the Hitler period. . . . German recovery, under U.S. guidance, is to be in the hands of such men. Top power is being taken over directly and indirectly by the same men who held it during the war."[11] Despite the fears of the British, French, and others in Europe, it could hardly be otherwise. These men were the backbone of German capitalism before, during, and after Hitler. The American aim was to rebuild a strong capitalist Germany, and the United States could not avoid the fact that all the major capitalists had been good Nazis, just as they had sustained Weimar and, later, Adenauer.

The other European capitalists, however, distrusted these same men. As the London *Economist* cautioned on August 7, 1948, "The [Nuremberg] trial of Krupp and his fellow directors has given evidence of a mentality in prewar German industrial leadership which forfeits once and for all any right to future power. . . . Willingness to exploit the Continent for the further expansion of German big business is a charge which virtually none can escape."[12] Their self-righteousness was clearly misplaced. What businessman, after all, would shirk to make a profit at the expense, or even the lives, of others? The sin of the Germans was that for decades they had seen Europe rather than Asia, Africa, or Latin America as the primary region to exploit.

Italy: The Road to Stagnation

The governments of Belgium and Italy introduced economic policies similar to those in Germany, with much the same results. The Italian government successfully reduced its balance of payments and budget deficits and renewed confidence in the value of the lira. The economy continued its deflationary trend, and the only important price rises were in pasta and bread after the government terminated its subsidy for those staples of the masses in the summer of 1948. The Italians won praise from the ECA for their monetary stability, but Italy also illustrates the basic contradiction in the ERP that made its deflationary policies utterly incompatible with recovery. During the first year of the Marshall Plan, for instance, Italy was again unable to use its coal allocations because its industry did not have, or was unwilling to use, lire to purchase the coal from the Italian government, which in turn had received it as a grant. But this was only one indication of the stagnation that paralyzed the Italian economy as a result of the ECA-encouraged "recovery" program. During 1948, the UN reported, there were ". . . general symptoms of depression throughout the economic system."[13] As vast unemployment persisted, the United States advised emigration and free labor mobility throughout Europe as the solution to the problem. The British, in particular, resented this pressure, since opening their doors to Italian labor would have required them, in essence, to subsidize the conservative Italian economic policies.

The year 1948 saw a consolidation of the Right politically as well. The Italian bourgeoisie's initial passivity and defensiveness before the working class, in large part due to its fear of reprisals for having supported fascism, now gave way to a much more aggressive stance. The national election of April 1948 was the critical turning point for Italian politics and also indicated the outer boundaries of parliamentarianism in postwar Europe.

The United States' role in the election did much to consolidate the victory of the conservative forces under the Christian Democrats. Washington seriously feared a decisive plurality or perhaps even a majority for the People's Bloc, a coalition of the Socialist and Communist parties. In early March 1948 the bloc was widely expected to poll 45 percent of the votes. The damage such a turn might inflict on the American economic and political plans for reconstructing Europe through the ERP were all too obvious, and it determined to prevent such an event, even to the extent of direct military intervention if intimidation and more subtle pressures proved insufficient.[14] With a good deal of fanfare and some urgency, Washington joined with the Vatican and the conservatives of Italy to gain a "democratic" victory. On the diplomatic front it gave support to the Italian Trieste claims, returned the gold taken from Italy by the Nazis, readmitted Italy to the administration of Tangier, and, with Britain, renounced claims on Italian ship reparations. The State Department announced it would deny visas to any Italian known to have voted Communist, and the Italo-Americans conducted a campaign with form letters urging relatives in Italy to vote against the bloc, and even mobilized Hollywood stars to record messages supporting the Christian Democrats. On a more direct level, the United States warned that Italy would receive no further aid if the People's Bloc won, strengthened its naval contingent in the Mediterranean, anchored warships off the Italian ports during the campaign, and held a military parade of its troops in Trieste. Finally, the United States gave massive financial aid to the Christian Democrats.

The Soviets, aware that the United States intended to use all means to prevent a Communist victory, and fearing the outcome of a new crisis, characteristically did their part to influence the election. Despite their bad terms with the Yugoslavs, with whom they were to break only two months later, they declared their support of Yugoslavia on the Trieste dispute just before the election and demanded that the Italians speed up their reparation payments. All these efforts bore fruit as the Christian Democrats won 48.4 percent and the People's Bloc 31 percent, with the rest distributed among a number of minor parties. Perhaps the most decisive factor in the election, however, was the total solidarity of all elements of the bourgeoisie as it sacrificed factional purity for power.[15] After the general election, the bourgeoisie fully regained its confidence and became aggressive and unyielding on social policy. While the fascists again reorganized publicly, the bulk of the propertied class supported the Christian Democrats as the party which could best protect their interests. The confusion in the ranks of the Socialists, Republicans, and also the Communists, in part inspired by the question of the ERP, strengthened the consolidation of the Right in Italy.

In July 1948 a would-be assassin shot and wounded Communist Party leader Togliatti. The event touched off protest strikes that in some cities were regarded as of "insurrectionary" dimensions. The demonstrations lasted only a day and one-half as the government suppressed them with the threat of military action. The wave of strikes in the fall of 1948, in response to the reactionary economic policies, was again broken by repression, with long-lasting effects. There were no illusions in Italy as to a pluralist democratic society. At least 35 percent of the population was in total opposition to the state, and the reality of their lives knew only exploitation, unemployment, and occasional resistance.[16]

The Marshall Plan in France

The broad economic policies of the ECA were already in operation in France before Congress voted a dollar for the program. Following the defeat of the workers in the general strikes at the end of 1947 and a massive import of food and fuel under the United States Emergency Interim Aid, the French government proceeded with its conservative policies with new confidence. Prices stabilized somewhat over the first two months of 1948, and then rose sharply as the government removed all controls on food and clothing at the same time that it strictly enforced wage controls. The devaluation of the franc in January 1948 eventually increased the cost of living and also general production costs by 20 percent.

Yet by the fall of 1948 the bourgeoisie was already feeling somewhat complacent as *their* economic indicators showed signs of a return to "normality." Industrial production grew each month, the harvest was good, and the budget was closer to equilibrium. The output of capital goods was one-third above the 1938 level, and the volume of net investment in 1947–1948 exceeded 1938 by three and a half times. Compounding their satisfaction, dividends from all investments averaged 6 percent, as opposed to 1 percent in 1947. Furthermore, France's foreign trade deficit, so important to ECA planning, was declining, and for the future the French government planned on a national production in 1952 40 percent over that of 1948, requiring an increase in output per man-hour of one-third during the same period. Concomitant with the consolidation of the capitalist economy, France's political alignment also moved to the right. Vichy elements that shortly after the war had narrowly escaped with their lives were then fully rehabilitated.[17]

For the working class "normality" meant defeat. Although the French workers in 1947 paid 70 percent of all personal income taxes in what *Le Monde* called a tax system ". . . more iniquitous than that which provoked the French Revolution," and though they were chiefly responsible for the rise in production, their standard of living continued to decline precipitously.[18] The average wage for all workers barely covered essential food. Food consumption in 1948 was 18 percent below the already depressed 1938 standard; yet according to the ECA, the per capita aggregate figures were misleading since ". . . the distribution of real income . . . has been considerably less equitable than before the war . . . ," with the shift in shares going primarily to profits but also to the peasantry.[19] And throughout 1948 the French workers' standard of living continued to decline. For the future, according to the ERP plan, the French government expected the food consumption of the urban workers to remain below that of 1938 for the following year.[20]

The French workers had suffered a real blow, both from within their movement and from external forces, during the general strikes of 1947. The trade unions were split to the satisfaction, and on the instigation of, the United States as well as the Socialists and the French employers. This division would have served its sponsors' purposes better, however, had the workers been rewarded with some improvement in their conditions. The new Force Ouvrière (FO), reflecting government considerations, at first fought for price cuts and resisted the workers' demands for higher wages, a policy that even Irving Brown of the AFL, who had done so much to split the labor movement, admitted would completely eliminate the FO if it could not secure some relief for the workers. As it was, the rank and file who had followed the FO either deserted the new federation or forced it to take a more militant position than its original sponsors had intended. Nevertheless, the sharp factionalism in the labor movement continued to weaken the working class in the face of a common enemy.[21] And ultimately the workers, as in 1947, simply ignored the unions of both types and acted on their own initiative in response to their insupportable economic conditions and the conservative policies of the state.

This extreme disparity between wages and prices, and the conservative financial policy of the government, especially during the brief tenure of the laissez faire finance minister, Paul Reynaud, finally led to a new government crisis that forced the Socialists to resign at the end of August. But the resolution of this domestic turmoil no longer rested with the French alone. With a bluntness that outraged even the conservatives, the United States intervened and refused to release the crucial counterpart funds in the French treasury until given assurance that the government would continue policies leading toward a balanced budget, even demanding that the French submit their budget to an American examining commission—the ultimate incursion on their sovereignty. While the horrified French government refused to accede, it was forced to reassure the ECA of its continued conservative policies. In September the United States released the counterpart funds, thereby, according to President Vincent Auriol, "saving" the treasury, but also further limiting the French government in its options in dealing with the critical condition of the working class.[22] The government's subsequent behavior, however, fully revealed its full acceptance of force as the final arbiter of social crises, once more reassuring the Americans that the European conservative interests, even if nominally Socialist, could deal with the hostile working class.

Although there were short sporadic strikes over the summer, by October 1948 the workers, once more, were ready to revolt. The spark came when Robert Lacoste, the Socialist minister of industry, under pressure from ECA and a budget-conscious cabinet, announced on September 18 that in order to save money in the nationalized industries the government would cut the work force by 10 percent. Two-thirds of the first group to go were Communist organizers and labor militants. The CGT called for a general strike in the mine region, which partially spread to the ports and other industries. This time Jules Moch anticipated the workers' action and indeed had prepared for it over many weeks, not by any attempt to alleviate the workers' conditions, but by improving his telecommunications and briefing his prefects.

When the strike broke out Moch intervened massively with the dreaded CRS and 40,000 soldiers recalled from Germany. The strike was qualitively very different from that in 1947. This time the workers and troops fought pitched battles, especially in the mines of the north and the Saint-Étienne region near Lyon. Finally the state drafted the young miners of the region. The massive force crushed the strike completely by the end of November. All told, the government killed three strikers and seriously wounded hundreds, imprisoned approximately 2,000, and finally dismissed another 6,000. For two months the police and troops occupied the area, for Moch intended to make an example of the recalcitrant miners, and the effects were long-lasting. In 1963 one director of the nationalized industry could state, "We have held the basin for 14 years without the least contact with the leaders of the CGT."[23]

It was ultimately cheaper to crush a strike, split the unions, and repress the workers than to pay the price of a higher standard of living which the French government and the ECA saw as an unacceptable inflationary thrust that would shatter their plans for a balanced budget, trade surplus, high profit, and "reconstruction" conforming to their capitalist model.

The Reintegration of Britain

The American attitude toward Britain continued to be ambivalent, although by 1948 Washington had lost its consuming preoccupation of the war and early postwar years to destroy the British economic power and imperial system, coming to recognize that England was no longer the formidable economic threat it had feared. The patent facts of its weakened condition were all too vivid, and as American power replaced British presence in Greece and Germany, Washington placed less emphasis on curbing Britain and more on redirecting it toward ends more compatible with its own. On the one hand, Washington hoped to have a strong junior partner for its economic and strategic aims in the world; but on the other hand, the United States was still determined, if with lesser fervor, to undermine the

British trading system and force England into a minor role in a united, capitalist Europe which the United States intended to dominate. The moderate welfare policies of the Labour Party continued to annoy Washington, which believed they were extravagances the British could not afford while receiving United States aid, and grumbles as to subsidizing socialism were heard in Congress. The fact that Britain was making the most impressive advances in recovery in no way lessened the complaints.

In contrast to the Continent, England had already begun to improve its economic position before the ERP was under way. By the second quarter of 1948 British manufacturing output was 24 percent higher than in 1938 and 15 percent above 1947, and by the last half of 1948 Britain had a small current account surplus with the world as a whole. Exports continued to increase, and London anticipated a progressive end to its dollar deficit by 1951 and full freedom from all United States aid by 1952. Indeed, the British felt confident enough to cut their request for aid allocation with the OEEC by one-quarter for the second year, though they won no praise for their gesture. On the contrary, they were under attack by the other OEEC countries for their new five-year plan made public in the fall of 1948. The plan projected a substantial shift in Britain's pattern of trade with Europe from a debtor to a creditor position. The Marshall Plan nations, having based their own plans on prewar trade patterns, felt betrayed. The British, however, believed that they had made the greatest gains in over-all recovery through severe austerity measures and could not afford the luxury imports from Europe. The gains in their balance of payments had already been achieved at high cost to the welfare goals the Labour Party had originally set. As they cut imports and greatly increased exports, the British by 1948 had reduced their dollar trade deficit by over one-half compared to 1947. This significant recovery, in comparison to that on the Continent, irked Washington because it depended on extensive government controls. Before the end of 1948 the Americans had begun to conclude that the pound was overvalued, and pressure for devaluation grew over the first months of 1949, although there was no objective justification for it whatever within the British economy. But to the Americans, the deflationary developments in the rest of the world necessitated a change in British policies.[24]

Washington intended from the beginning of the Marshall Plan to force a revaluation of the European currencies and to make them freely convertible. "They will need . . . some pretty firm insistence on our part . . . to give value to their money," William Clayton predicted in 1947.[25] The underlying objectives for this policy were, of course, to attain market expansion, break down national discriminations, and achieve freer trade and more profitable investments. The United States inserted provisions in the British loan reflecting its initial eagerness to achieve convertibility, but after the disaster associated with that experiment in 1947, American officials realized that some restraint was necessary.

During the first year of the Marshall Plan, the British were forced to confront the question of whether they could pursue an economic program that diverged from those introduced on the Continent. Identical economic outlooks in the OEEC nations would immeasurably aid the United States concept of reconstruction and world trade based on the deflationary policies of a balanced budget, trade surplus, stagnant economy, unemployment, and minimal internal consumption. And the integration of the European economies would have inevitably forced a shift in the British aim to increase the standard of living and maintain full employment, goals that required strict trade controls. The issue ultimately impinged on whether even modest variations in social aims were possible in an integrated capitalist system of international trade dominated by American power.

Standardization in every sphere of economic and political policy was a critical American goal in Western Europe, and the internationalism and supranational institutions that emerged with the ERP under the United States' aegis were those of a conservative capitalism that reflected the American economic and political calculations. The aim remained paramount, however, and grew in importance as the passing months opened a Pandora's box of new problems and new threats to the United States' original purposes in Europe.

American Business Interests and the Marshall Plan

While Washington had to implement the Marshall Plan in the context of Europe's economic and political problems, it also had to heed the special demands of the American business and agricultural community that expected direct and early profit from the program—and who were well represented in Congress. Their power to shape immediate policy to their own advantage frequently undermined the administration's original intent as well as the long-range interests of the capitalist system in which they, too, operated.

Congress wrote contradictory positions into the ECA authorizing legislation that became a source of considerable dispute in the administration, and the issues were never fully reconciled, although it made an effort to satisfy all the competing interests simultaneously. Congress was, of course, the spokesman and watchdog for the innumerable specific industries that wanted a share of sales, or protection from European imports, and the Department of Agriculture and the majority of Congress were uncompromising in their protection of American agriculture. The general goals of multilateral trade were certainly in the interests of all these constituencies; yet they, unlike the State Department, were willing to undermine the achievement of the general aim for even the smallest immediate gain. Such self-serving use of ERP funds to protect American interests soon created new crises with the Europeans.

The Europeans, during the long summer meetings of the CEEC in 1947, formulated their requests on the basis of their most urgent needs and without regard for America's surpluses, knowing that Washington would cut even their minimal requests. By the time Congress allocated the money in June 1948, there had already been substantial cuts—first Clayton and his advisers in Paris insisted that the CEEC carve $10 billion off the original request of $29 billion, then the State Department and the Harriman committee reduced it by another $2 billion, and finally Congress slashed the total to $13 billion over a four-year period. Beyond the over-all cuts, however, the Americans made changes in the allocations in order to give advantages to specific United States industries, frequently adding large items which no European country, with their urgent needs and austere restrictions, had requested. During the first year the ECA cut certain food requests sharply and made their allocations on the basis of United States agricultural surpluses. To limit future competition, Secretary of Agriculture Clinton Anderson reduced the CEEC request for 65,000 tractors by half with the contrived excuse that European farms were too small for tractors and that Europeans lacked American "know-how."[26] The Western European economies were generally based on extensive railroad transport systems, and the bottleneck in distribution, and shortages in petroleum, led the CEEC to request 47,000 freight cars for the first fifteen months. The Americans reduced this figure to 20,000, all of which they earmarked for Germany. Given other pressing needs, the world oil shortage, and the rather primitive condition of the roads, the CEEC did not request any trucks. The Harriman committee, despite this fact, insisted on allocating 65,000 trucks to the ERP during the first fifteen months.

The CEEC did not request any tobacco, but the United States allocated 40,000 tons for the first year to France and Switzerland as "incentive" products. The Europeans asked for wheat, and Congress stipulated that in the first year, one-quarter of it had to be shipped as flour—a provision that cost an additional $8 million in 1948. The United States even shipped 177 million pounds of expensive and inferior spaghetti to Italy during 1948.

Over administration objections, Congress insisted that the Europeans had to ship at least 50 percent of all aid in United States boats and insure them with American insurance companies. The ECA estimated that this provision alone absorbed a superfluous $10 million between April and December 1948 and that in 1949 it would be about $25 million on bulk cargo alone. Until mid-October 1948, shipping charges were consuming 12 percent of all aid to Europe—and around 20 percent of the aid to France and Italy. In 1949 Congress even required the Europeans to reimburse ECA for the use of non-American ships. Despite the administration's pressure to drop the restriction, in 1950 Congress extended the 50 percent rule to cover all United States imports of strategic goods as well as ECA exports.[27]

The ECA Act of 1948 authorized the Department of Agriculture to transfer United States surplus goods to the ECA administrator at prices as low as half of the going American market price. Participating nations could purchase only United States surplus with their Marshall Plan funds, even if the commodities elsewhere cost less than the subsidized American prices. The United States, in turn, with considerable vigor, combated any effort by another state to regulate its own trade in the same manner. The heaviest impact of these dumping subsidies fell, of course, on Third World commodity producers, but it also hurt the European states that naturally preferred to use soft currencies, and conserve scarce dollars, on goods they could acquire at a lower price elsewhere. Foreign policy planners understood the conflict between the general foreign economic goals and such an agricultural policy, and they impotently despaired over Congress' shortsightedness. In 1949 the ECA purchased 78 percent of its agricultural goods for Europe in the United States. Canada was the major offshore source, and Latin America, chiefly for American–owned oil and sugar, ranked next. For the two decades prior to World War II, what were to become the ERP countries took up to three-quarters of the United States' agricultural exports. In 1948 the American farms were producing one-third more than before the war, and to the agricultural sector the Marshall Plan was obviously critical.[28]

The ERP program began during a world oil shortage that had caused Congress early in 1948 to express its concern over an adequate supply for domestic needs, let alone supplies for Europe. Harriman had reassured the

House, however, that ERP would permit European oil producers to expand their production to meet their own needs. The OEEC nations, spurred by the early shortage as well as the fact that oil was such a basic commodity for recovery, sought to use ERP aid to construct additional refineries in order to save dollars by importing crude instead of the more expensive refined oil. Eventually, as well, they hoped to attain some self-sufficiency in so vital an industrial material. The conflict between European desires and the American industry's demands placed the ECA in an awkward position. It had to acknowledge that some refining capacity in Europe was essential for real recovery; yet the pressure from the United States oil companies was decisive. By the end of 1949 ECA approved no European crude oil production project and greatly pruned requests for refinery aid to $24 million, of which American companies constructed and owned one-third.[29]

The implications of this policy were serious for the Europeans. Eleven percent of the total ECA shipments to Europe by mid-1950 consisted of grossly overpriced oil. The ECA purchased Middle East oil from American firms for the United States gulf price of $2.65 a barrel; but according to Eugene Holman, president of Standard Oil, Middle East oil per barrel, including depreciation, cost fifty cents. "Without ECA the American oil business in Europe would already have been shot to pieces," Walter Levy repeatedly told the National Petroleum Council during 1949.[30] Levy resigned from Socony-Vacuum Oil Company in July 1948 to head the oil division of the ECA, and one of his chief functions was to set the price for all ECA oil purchases. "Without ECA aid Europe would not have been able to afford during the last year, and could not afford during the next three years, to import large quantities of American oil—from either domestic or foreign sources controlled by American companies." As over the past year, "ECA has maintained outlets for American oil in Europe . . . which otherwise would have been lost," and "ECA does not believe that Europe should save dollars or earn foreign exchange by driving American oil from the European market," Levy reassured the American industry.[31] The oil companies fully understood the importance of the Marshall Plan to their industry, and they did not intend to lose even a dollar of that trade without a struggle.

Raw Materials

The Harriman Committee on Foreign Aid, in its justification for ERP in the summer of 1947, placed heavy emphasis on American acquisition of scarce and strategic raw materials via the program of aid to Europe. Under the 1946 Stockpiling Act, Congress allocated $275 million to acquire essential raw materials in short supply or nonexistent in the United States. The Harriman committee pointed out, however, that without the Marshall Plan the United States could expect to obtain only 20 percent of its minimum needs by 1948. The crucial factor was the expansion of production in the colonial dependencies of the European states. The committee foresaw an immense increase in production in return for only a small input of capital. Securing these raw materials, essential to the operation of its industrial system, became one of the chief aims of United States policy in the ERP and one of its prime justifications to Congress.

The European-controlled materials were critical: the African colonies of Belgium, England, and France were the world's major source of cobalt; chromite production in Rhodesia was limited by transportation problems easily solved with ERP funds; the ECA expected aid funds to increase manganese production in the Gold Coast by one-quarter and made similar projections for many other materials that United States industry required. To achieve its stockpiling goal, the ECA wrote into each of its country treaties special provisions to assure American acquisition of these materials —provisions which in essence secured the surplus beyond ". . . the reasonable requirements of the participating country for its domestic use and commercial export of such materials . . . to be agreed to between the two governments. . . ." In addition, there were open door ". . . subsidiary agreements . . . to the right of access of any citizen of the United States . . . to the development of raw materials within participating countries on terms of treatment equivalent to those afforded to the nationals of the participating country concerned."[32] Washington also intended that the development of raw materials would be a major use for the counterpart funds, 5 percent of which Congress specified must purchase raw materials for the United States. In order to prod the Europeans, preoccupied with their own recovery, toward the high-priority task of filling American stockpile orders, the ECA set up a Strategic Materials Division. It pushed the Europeans for surveys, expansion of output in the colonies, and American options to purchase surpluses.

As it considered the extension of ERP, Congress in February 1949 expressed its concern over the slow rate of raw materials acquisition during the first ten months of the program. In the eyes of many, this form of reverse Lend Lease was one of the chief justifications for an otherwise extravagant "giveaway." The ECA officials, with a different perspective, pointed out that recovery in the countries concerned had absorbed much of the existing raw materials supply. To the demand of a number of senators that the Europeans barter rather than sell a large supply of the materials, the administration spokesmen, with some exasperation, reiterated that the United States' aim in the ERP was to eliminate the dollar gap, and the dollars the Europeans did not earn through sale of their raw materials Congress would have to give to them in future grants. Even so, the 5 percent counterpart provision by 1949 automatically provided the United States with $40 million worth of strategic materials for its stockpile.[33]

To the ECA, the most desirable means of obtaining needed raw materials was to encourage appropriate private United States investments. But beyond the stockpile needs, Averell Harriman emphasized in his testimony to the Senate Foreign Relations Committee in February 1949, "There is an increasing need to assure future sources of supply for the growing requirements of American industry. . . . As . . . [it] continues to expand and its productivity continues to increase, the volume of raw materials needed from foreign sources will grow larger." Harriman saw an additional benefit in the investment of United States dollars as ". . . one of the most promising ways to assist [Europe] in reaching a balance of payments."[34]

ERP-subsidized trade was essential to every part of the American economy, and the United States policy-makers, failing to reconcile the simultaneous demands for export and for protection, were unable to devise another method for achieving that ever more elusive goal of a self-sustaining world multilateral trade. Paul Hoffman, in pointing to the dilemma, wrote,

Under such circumstances other nations could not afford to continue buying from us unless we gave them money. And that is, of course, exactly what we have had to do through a dozen loan and grant schemes, starting from after World War I right down to our present ECA. American aid to Western Europe during the last thirty-five years has amounted to some $22,000,000,000 exclusive of direct war outlays. This was . . . a way of subsidizing our exports, for practically all the American money that went abroad . . . always returned to buy American goods.[35]

The importance of the unwanted concessions to special interests for the Europeans can best be seen in the counterpart provisions which specified that for every dollar received from the ECA, the Europeans must set aside an equivalent in local currency. These vast sums in the national budgets were subject to United States direction, and unrequested tobacco, overpriced oil, and inflated shipping charges all created additional American leverage in the internal economic policies of the European states.

The Labor and Social Democratic Role

The American trade unions served as a spearhead to neutralize or destroy the role that European labor might play in hindering the reconstruction of European capitalism. The AFL's representative, Irving Brown, serving both the unions and American intelligence, was in Europe as early as 1946 with ample funds from Washington, attempting to wrest control of Europe's trade unions from the Communists. Active primarily in Germany, France, and Italy, he was able to create a nucleus of social democratic and Christian unionists. Like all those who worked with the CIA, Brown cannot claim full credit for all his activities. As early as 1952, however, he admitted to a leading role in breaking the general strikes in France and Italy in 1947 and 1948, as well as providing the funds to split their union federations.[36]

The implementation of the Marshall Plan divided the World Federation of Trade Unions (WFTU) and caused the split in the French and Italian unions. When the WFTU refused to call a meeting to discuss the ERP in the spring of 1948, the British Trade Union Congress announced a separate meeting of the unions of the states participating in the Marshall Plan, to which both the AFL and the CIO sent representatives. The chief cement at the London conference in March 1948 was anti-Communism rather than a common ideology, although the unions were linked either to ruling parties, as in Britain, or to the socialist parties that were giving their support to ERP's aims. This meeting formed the nucleus of the International Confederation of Free Trade Unions (ICFTU), organized formally in December 1949. The split in the trade unions was not confined to Europe, but played a significant role in American strategy in Asia, Latin America, and Africa as well. A vehicle of United States foreign policy, the ICFTU's ideology followed its source of funds. Beyond its anti-Communism, it ceased to pay even rhetorical homage to the concepts of the class struggle and the replacement of capitalism and stressed exclusively the American trade union precepts of raising worker living standards within the existing capitalist system.

In Europe the chief rationale and activity of the ICFTU was to mobilize the workers for ERP and rearmament, an objective it never attained. For the effort was to compel it to enter into direct conflict with the workers' objective economic interests. The vast majority of the workers, of course, saw this clearly and either protested against their economic conditions under Communist leadership, as in France and Italy, and were defeated, or simply endured in sullen bitterness as it appeared that they had been check-mated once again.

In France and Italy the rival non-Communist labor unions were unable to achieve more than a small minority support, for their ties to the state's repressive wage policies were in direct conflict with the immediate needs of the working class. In Germany the trade unions were far to the right of the leadership of the SPD, especially Kurt Schumacher. Whether for purely opportunist reasons or for ideological affinity, they acted to undermine what militancy existed in that party, collaborated with American plans, and in the end firmly set the course for the future of the Social Democratic Party, especially after the death of Schumacher.[37]

It is redundant at this point in our story to add that the Soviet-oriented Communist unions were no more committed to changing the social rela-tions and the position of the working class than the American-oriented social democratic unions. The working class was a pawn, and would con-tinue to be until objective circumstances moved it to reject its leaders, or forced it to move, if only temporarily, in its own interest.

The question of Communism, while paramount perhaps to the union leaders of the British Trades Union Congress (TUC) or social democratic unions, was secondary to the capitalist managers of the ERP. Their overrid-ing critical need was to emasculate the labor movement by co-opting its leaders or splitting its ranks in order to prevent the working class from pressing its expensive, inflationary demands, let alone threaten the existing order. There is little evidence that the United States feared that the orga-nized Left in Western Europe could assume political power. It certainly had no intention, where it had the most influence, of trying to co-opt the working class, as opposed to some of its leaders, through expensive eco-nomic concessions. A strong army and police, plus a well-nurtured anti-Communist propaganda campaign, were by far the cheapest methods of handling unrest, and key American leaders fully comprehended this fact.

Richard Bissell, one of the chief administrators of the ECA, evaluated the effect of the Marshall Plan on the working classes of Europe at the close of the recovery program in terms that reflected such realism. ". . . [I]n France, labor's relative position is less favorable than before the war. And in both Italy and Germany wages hardly above the subsistence standards prevail alongside of severe unemployment."[38] Only in England and Scan-dinavia did labor's relative position improve.

Despite their rhetoric, the role of the "Left" parties in a capitalist govern-ment has consistently been to restrain their constituencies in order that those wielding real economic power could realize their objectives. Their abdication in face of the massive reconstruction of capitalism at the expense of the workers has deep historical roots, and they developed other rationales as well. As part of the government, the Socialists, and the Communists until expelled, were as concerned with the questions of restoring and managing the social system as were the members of the other parties. And they had other, more political, questions to consider. In France the Socialists rationalized their role as saving the republic against the threat of totalitarianism from both the Right and the Left. In Italy a splinter group clung to the illusion that its participation in the government could modify its inevitable antisocial policies. In West Germany, as we discuss below, the Socialists under Schumacher persisted in a more militant stance, but the opportunist rivals in the party leadership and in the trade unions proved easy prey to the approaches of the Americans and the Christian Democrats.[39]

But for the working class of Europe the ERP experience of capitalist reconstruction was an unequivocal calamity. This class was required to increase its effort in the production process, to abstain from asserting demands, and to reap a falling standard of living and unemployment. A full appreciation of this fact as a crucial dimension of the ERP is essential to understanding the real meaning of the Marshall Plan.

Within less than one year after the beginning of the much-heralded American reconstruction program it was evident to all that the economic policies of the ECA, whatever else they might attain, were not leading to industrial reconstruction by any criterion. On the contrary, within a few short months, the deflationary policies of Germany, Belgium, France, and Italy, coupled with the saturation of effective demand in the United States, were bringing the entire program to a grinding halt. Those countries that did make strides in recovery followed different policies from those the ECA advocated, but they were soon to feel the repercussions from the economic direction in the rest of Europe, as well as from the United States. As the situation on both sides of the Atlantic worsened over the early months of 1949, the policy-makers in Washington were forced to reassess the viability of the Marshall Plan in achieving their economic goals in Europe.

17

The Failure of the Marshall Plan, 1949–1950

The task of reorienting the structure of Western European capitalism was far more formidable than the United States had initially anticipated. It took no more than a few months before the contradictions in the orthodox capitalist planning that characterized the Marshall Plan had shifted the focus of the undertaking. Less than one year after Congress, with much fanfare and grandiose phrases, had voted the appropriation for the ambitious four-year program the entire operation was coming to a standstill. And repercussions from instability in the American economy added the decisive blow to the staggering European policies. The experience, once more, set in motion Washington's troubled search for yet new means to achieve its elusive goals.

As early as November 1948 the United States economy entered a recession, one in part stimulated by the very deflationary plans that the Americans encouraged in Europe, but which mainly reflected the recurrence of the crisis of overproduction and maldistribution of income which periodically stimulates cyclical retrenchment and recession. These developments in the United States only further aggravated the European situation where the ECA, particularly in Germany, doggedly persisted in its restrictive deflationary policies.

Between November 1948 and June 1949 United States production dropped by 15 percent and unemployment in the third quarter rose to the postwar high of 6.6 percent. More serious for future trends, net profits fell by almost one-third and orders for durable goods. especially in iron and steel, declined by more than 30 percent over 1948. On July 13, 1949,

President Truman addressed the nation on the crisis in the economy, pointing to the fall in production and the fact that unemployment had doubled over the year, reaching nearly 4 million (it was to rise further to 7.9 percent of the wage and salary workers by the first quarter of 1950). This trend in the United States, so alarming to policy-makers on both sides of the Atlantic, showed every sign of worsening.

As government administrators might have anticipated, under the circumstances American business was not going to tolerate competitive European imports. Even before the recession, United States imports were only 5 percent more in real terms than in 1929, while 1948 American production exceeded 1929 by 70 percent. Now conditions ruled out any increase in United States imports, despite the European need to earn dollars in order to continue buying United States goods without aid. The Department of Agriculture put a total embargo on the import of agricultural supplies, and the manufacturing and agricultural interests lobbied simultaneously for greater exports to fill the slack in their domestic orders as well as higher tariff protection. The European dollar gap continued to mount, and with it grew the fears of the State Department planners for the future of United States trade. Over administration objections, Congress had inserted a "peril point" clause in the Reciprocal Trade Agreements Act of 1948 and renewed it in 1949. This clause prevented tariff reductions on any product as soon as an American industry felt the pinch of foreign competition. The provision weakened the administration's discretion on tariffs while it strengthened the supervisory powers of Congress. Tariff protection remained the traditional thorn in the side of those who formulated the basic ideology and thrust of United States foreign policy and were oriented toward export trade and the control of raw materials. They continued to distrust, even dread, the parochial Congress which persistently refused to consider the larger effect on the United States economy if a shortage of dollars halted trade and Europe reverted to its bilateral and exclusionary trading habits. The outcome of these various factors was that during the first half of 1949 the United States cut its imports from Europe by one-third of the last quarter of 1948.[1]

As the recession soon became the decisive factor in curtailing further progress in the European balance of payments, to United States policy-makers in 1949–1950 the dollar gap seemed impossible to bridge within the limited time span of the ERP. And the persistent cycle of providing more and more aid to create a market for United States industry and agriculture would soon hit the insurmountable barrier in Congress, which was ever more reluctant to appropriate funds for the purpose of European reconstruction and economic assistance. The administration knew that securing the funds for ERP in 1949 would be even more difficult than in the preceding year. Senator Vandenberg, its most important ally during the first struggle, had let it be known ". . . that I view the *second* year of the ECA quite differently from my view of the first year."[2]

The administration's many bruised encounters had shown that the only palatable rationale for Congress to continue to send funds abroad was a rearmament and an anti-Communist program. This remained one option open to the administration. Indeed, the historian will search in vain to discover why the United States decided to press for North Atlantic Treaty Organization (NATO) and arms aid to Europe in mid-1949 unless he looks at these economic problems in conjunction with the congressional mood. The Soviet military dangers were far less critical than during the previous year. The Russians lifted the blockade on Berlin in May and had embarked on one of their most extensive peace campaigns. There was, in short, no overt military or security crisis in the spring and summer of 1949 when the administration presented the NATO bill to Congress and asked for $1 billion in military aid to Europe. But there was a serious crisis in the domestic economy. Such an approach, from the inception, made the United States military policy on the questions of NATO and European rearmament intimately linked to the policy of European recovery.

During the NATO hearings of spring 1949, administration spokesmen put United States participation and military aid on a long-term basis without a sense of military urgency. None of the administration witnesses considered a Soviet attack at all likely. Both in the congressional hearings and in its public statements, the State Department placed its emphasis on internal military security. Internal order was a dominant concern because most of Western Europe's conservative economic policies precluded welfare measures or a rise in the standard of living. The increasingly reactionary nature of continental politics and the worsening economic conditions encouraged repression in controlling internal disorder, as the events in France during the strikes of the previous winter had revealed. But touching on the vital nerve of the entire program of arms aid, the State Department pointed out that Congress had to make provisions ". . . to cover dollar costs *involved in or incident to* this production" for defense, rearmament, and the struggle against Communism.[3] This was the first introduction of the "defense support" clause that soon came to justify all the export of dollars hitherto granted under the umbrella of the Marshall Plan for the reconstruction of

Europe. In Truman's message to Congress on aid for European rearmament he stressed that the new aid was critical to ". . . support our international economic programs, and in particular the Economic Recovery Program."[4]

Nevertheless, the military rationale to coax funds from Congress was not sufficiently alarming to resolve the crisis in time. Although Congress voted $1 billion, the administration had to turn once more to Europe in the hope of securing a permanent solution to the increasingly dreaded dollar gap. Its only other option was to try once again to manipulate the economies of Europe through such measures as devaluation and to increase the pressure toward creating a single market in a united Europe in order to compensate for the administration's failure to resist the pressures from Congress and private American interests.

In Europe, faced with the reality of a deepening recession, the American policy gyrated from one alternative to another as each met successive failure. First of all the Americans blamed the British for their full-employment policies and for an "overvalued" pound sterling. *Theoretically*, devaluation of the pound and then of the other currencies could make European exports cheaper and investment in Europe more attractive to United States business, and in both cases Europe would earn more dollars with which to buy more United States goods. Then there was the question of European union and the general standardization of their economic policies, which, again *theoretically*, would eliminate the inefficient protected industry in Europe, permitting the surviving rationalized industry to lower costs and compete in the American market and earn dollars. In *theory*, also, low internal mass consumption would provide more goods for export, and by lowering internal demand the OEEC nations could strengthen their currencies and improve their balance of payments. It was with these questionable rationales that the United States continued to press ahead with its deflationary policies in Europe—with predictable and catastrophic results to the goals of reconstruction.

Great Britain: From Crisis to Crisis

Britain was again Washington's most vulnerable and principal target. While hardly socialist, the Labour Party's full-employment policies were clearly out of step with the conservative and reactionary economic policies on the Continent. Washington obsessively blamed the Labour Party's economic program of social security, high taxes, and nationalization for keeping British goods from being competitive, thereby presumably creating the dollar gap and Western Europe's economic crisis. British "stubbornness" on European unity also contributed to America's frustrations. But from Labour's perspective, in an integrated international capitalist system reactionary economic policies would bring down progressive ones. Without strict controls, the deflationary economies of Italy, Germany, Belgium, and France would lead to unemployment, greater inequality, and a sharp reduction in the standard of living in England as well.

The organization of the sterling bloc itself in 1931 was the outcome of an attempt to restore stability and trade and to insulate Britain from the economic crises in the United States, the most unstable capitalist country in the world. By 1949 this prewar pattern was being reestablished in certain significant dimensions. The United States was pushing deflationary policies on the Continent and domestically succumbing in 1949, as in 1929 and 1938, to a recession which, according even to the ECA, was ". . . more severe than in most other industrialized countries."[5] Consequent serious disruptions in America's trade definitively undermined world confidence.

While in 1948 the British had reduced their deficit and increased their exports substantially, in 1949 their exports suffered from the impact of the recession in Europe and particularly in the United States. By the second quarter of 1949 the British dollar deficit again rose to 157 million pounds, or nearly as high as during the 1947 convertibility crisis. The loss in its gold reserves over the same period mounted to 66 million pounds, and its dollar deficit was twice the amount of ECA aid. It was at this very time that Harriman began to apply new pressures on the Europeans to loosen their trade and currency controls. Continental response was favorable, but the British emphasized their need to maintain essential imports rather than their volume of trade, arguing that a relaxation of currency controls would exhaust their dwindling reserves. What the British were increasingly to realize was that so long as their economy was dependent on the United States, all their internal efforts would amount to little. The quick disappearance of their hard-won gains in balance of payments and productivity, purchased at the cost of prolonged austerity, unmistakably dramatized their renewed plight.

Thus, through no fault of their own, the British slid into a deficit because of a fall in their exports to the United States due to that nation's business slump. Contrary to American assertions, there was no uncontrolled British inflation to blame for Britain's deficits. Washington, unwilling or unable to solve its own problems internally, forcefully began to pressure London to devalue the pound—even though a UN study indicated that the pound was not overvalued—and to cut its expenditures on health, public housing, food subsidies, and welfare. Rumors of possible devaluation, encouraged by United States sources, also played their part in reducing British exports and hastening the pound's demise, for so long as importers anticipated lower prices they naturally delayed in placing their orders. To a certain degree, much trade had already been financed with a devalued pound for most of 1949. Other states also in desperate need of dollars, and frequently with large sterling balances in London, were willing to sell their sterling to American traders at large discounts off the official rate—frequently at over one-fifth off the official rate of $4.03 per pound.

Another element aggravating Britain's worsening trade position was the blocked sterling accounts of its Commonwealth creditors. When British exporters sent goods to these creditor nations, such as India and Egypt, these nations would simply write off the cost against the debt and the Bank of London would pay the exporter from the blocked balances. In this way much of Britain's exports were paying for the immense war debt instead of earning dollars. Although the British resisted as best they could, American pressure was decisive, and by the end of August 1949 they agreed to a forthcoming devaluation and additional cuts in domestic spending. In return for devaluation, the United States in September agreed to some additional British offshore purchases in Canada, Britain's right to discriminate selectively against United States goods, and also to increase American imports of natural rubber. The IMF approved the British use of its drawing rights, once it devalued the pound. The United States recession also made foreign investment for United States capital more attractive, especially where foreign currencies were devalued. The terms of the Foreign Assistance Act guaranteed for over fourteen years the right of American investors to take their profits out in dollars. Considerations such as these played a part in the increasing pressure.

On September 18, 1949, the British devalued the pound from $4.03 to $2.80, considerably more than had been expected. This disparity drew angry reaction from the Continent; the French finance minister called it a "trade-war rate." Nevertheless, only Switzerland, among the Western European nations, refused to follow the British in a revaluation of some kind. The countries maintaining full-employment policies devalued the most, the others very little; and the renewed competition from Britain tended to intensify and extend the recession, while the movement toward freer trade threatened to homogenize economic policies and spread unemployment to Britain as well. According to the UN study of Europe in 1949, if the deflationary policies were not reversed ". . . the tendencies toward the disintegration of the European economy may well be accentuated because countries where demand is being kept at a high level will be forced to erect trade barriers in order to defend themselves against the spread of depression from abroad."[6] For the United States, devaluation put the entire burden on the Europeans to compensate for the problems in the American economy and Congress' refusal to reduce tariffs, forcing them to lower their standard of living as all essential imports became proportionately more expensive. Britain, dependent on imports for one-half of its food and four-fifths of its raw materials, was especially affected. Devaluation in theory was supposed to make their goods more competitive in the world markets, which, of course, overlooked the fact that the United States subsidized part of its export prices, tied its loans, maintained high tariffs, and engaged in many forms of trade discrimination that partially neutralized Britain's new competitive position. With devaluation the British had to increase the volume of their exports by 30 percent in order to earn the same amount of dollars, as did the other European nations in proportion to their devaluation. In 1948, when general demand in the dollar markets was still high, devaluation may have conceivably worked, but with a recession and a tariff-prone Congress the devaluation was no substitute for substantially lower United States tariffs.

In the short run the devaluation did renew the dollar and gold reserves of the British treasury to approximately the early 1949 level. But this upsurge was due mainly to speculators returning to take their profit and foreign buyers now placing postponed orders. Devaluation's effect on income distribution increased profits and eventually compelled the government to introduce some new subsidies to prevent the workers from bearing the full brunt of the policy. The real increase in dollar supply came from increased United States purchases of raw materials, especially rubber.

Well before the sterling-dollar oil crisis broke in mid-1949, the ECA had been applying pressure on the Marshall Plan nations to prevent their oil expansion programs in both refinery capacity and output of crude oil. As Walter Levy explained, "ECA has also tried to establish . . . a long-term policy on European petroleum development projects that are designed to maintain for American oil a . . . competitive position in the world markets."[7] Oil was by far the most sensitive industry, but the ECA also discouraged capital development projects in other basic industries, especially steel. ECA, in restricting further aid for expansion programs, underlined its concern that "if such expansion greatly exceeds the absorptive capacity of the markets of the companies of the participating countries, it will lead to a displacement of dollar oil, especially in soft currency markets. . . ."[8] In Europe itself, the United States oil companies had real cause for concern, since the ECA financed nearly 100 percent of their oil sales. The Marshall Plan subsidized the American oil companies perhaps more than any other industry, and they had reason to be anxious over their future markets and pricing structure. For the British, by this time in their dollar deficit crisis, decided in July 1949 to curtail the dollar outlays of the sterling bloc by 25 percent, and the most obvious target was American-owned oil, especially since the British companies themselves were amassing oil surpluses. The American companies, discovering their own surpluses for the first time with the general business decline, sniffed "discrimination" in the British move and precipitated a new crisis.

The United States, England, and Canada during their financial talks in September 1949 appointed a committee to study further this delicate question. The British announced that they would reduce the dollar share of their oil imports, and with the new restrictions they expected to save up to $60 million a year without curtailing consumption. Under pressure from Washington and the United States oil companies, London postponed the reductions in dollar purchases until February 15. The British devaluation made dollar oil much more expensive, and they estimated that oil would comprise one-half of their dollar deficit in 1950. After extending its implementation date for the new dollar-saving restrictions, London once again modified them to reduce the total dollar oil imports only approximately 25 percent. In addition it offered not to impose any additional restrictions so long as ERP continued. The United States companies nevertheless found the new proposals unsatisfactory.

While the ECA's administrators intended to defend American oil interests, they also conceded that they would have to make some compromises: ". . . the American oil industry . . . cannot . . . succeed in selling oil to markets that cannot afford to pay for it. One cannot get water from stone or dollars from non-existing dollar accounts. . . ."[9] The alternative they proposed was to sell oil in nonsterling areas for sterling and increase the United States companies' nondollar costs. But the oil companies continued to insist on the right to convert their profit and investment into dollars through the British treasury. To the British, this was an intolerable drain on their dollar reserves.

The United States companies regarded the developing exclusion from the sterling bloc trade, accounting for 9 percent of their markets, with the utmost alarm. The British-Dutch companies, due to the world-wide shortage of dollars and the readiness of most nations to buy with sterling, were making inroads in markets the American firms assumed to be their own. The plans of the British-Dutch firms for expanding production would more than meet any anticipated growth in demand over the following years. The United States industry's own expansion plans, if they remained unwilling to sell for sterling, would yield only surplus; yet the American companies were not willing to concede on their demand to convert their profits.

By January 1950 the American oil companies were actively mobilizing their political constituencies. In a memorandum circulated in Congress and the administration, John Suman, vice-president of Standard Oil (New Jersey), attacked the British government for

assisting British and British-Dutch oil companies to take business from the American oil companies. It is impossible for the American oil companies effectively to fight such governmental action [as trade restrictions]. . . . Unless some means are developed which will prevent the British Government from marketing the so-called "surplus oil" of British and British-Dutch oil companies, the foreign business of American oil companies might well be liquidated in a relatively short period of time. The effects of such an unfortunate result upon the United States national security . . . are obvious.[10]

Its implications for the profits of America's oil companies were more obvious yet. The National Petroleum Council followed with a report asserting that rather than protecting their reserves, the British were actually obtaining ". . . long-term commercial advantages for the British . . . oil companies at the expense of the American industry."[11] Members of Congress responded by introducing amendments to the ERP legislation prohibiting discrimination against United States oil companies. The administration, knowing that some discrimination was essential to prevent disastrous consequences to the British dollar reserves, persuaded Congress to leave such restrictions to the discretion of the ECA director. In April, however, Washington presented a note to the British government insisting on the right of United States companies to trade anywhere in the sterling area. By June 1950 Standard Oil of New Jersey had persuaded the British to abolish rationing of gasoline in return for Standard's willingness to accept sterling as payment for its share of the expanded British market. It was at that point, the complex negotiations continuing, that the whole problem came to an abrupt end with the beginning of the Korean War. For the war absorbed the world oil surplus and temporarily removed the crisis over markets.[12]

Europe: Orthodoxy and Stagnation

In Germany, Belgium, Italy, and France, the ruling parties largely shared Washington's perspectives, and hence there was little resistance to the fluctuating American schemes and the pursuit of orthodox economic policies that further accentuated the contradictions in the Marshall Plan.

The West German economy in 1949 was sinking ever deeper into an economic stagnation that continued to underline the discrepancy between the ECA's rhetoric and implementation of actual policy. The currency reform had strictly limited the amount of money in circulation, and after the initial buying spree of approximately six months, effective demand dried up, as even many firms were unable to buy the surplus steel from the mills of the Ruhr or other goods available under the Marshall Plan. This pressure of abundance, despite West Germany's critical need for steel, led the occupation to raise the export quota. Yet given the steel surplus in the rest of Europe and the United States as well, the Ruhr's dilemma remained unsolved. Despite the evidence of serious stagnation, the ECA used its substantial counterpart funds with extreme caution and released no funds before April 1949, and then only for the modernization and rationalization of industry rather than sorely needed—and labor-absorbing—building construction.

The malaise was soon reflected in a rapid increase in unemployment. By May 1949 there were one million unemployed in West Germany. The situation continued to worsen until, in a report one year later, the UN dedicated part of its survey of the European economy in 1949 to the question of unemployment in Western Europe, with Germany, Italy, and Belgium being the most glaring examples. In February 1950, according to the report, the Western zones of Germany had an unemployment of 14 percent of its wage and salary earners, plus 300,000, or 30 percent of the labor force, in West Berlin. One conservative paper, quoting official Bonn sources, claimed that 100,000 skilled workers, scientists, and artists went to the Soviet zone in 1949. In early 1950 the mayor and city councilors from all the parties in Stuttgart visited Dresden in the Soviet zone. "I am quite convinced," a Social Democratic councilor observed, ". . . that in the East zone they are doing everything they can, first and foremost, to improve the lot of the working people. . . . The social conditions there are basically different from ours. These social changes in the East cannot simply be denied existence by closing our eyes to them."[13] At the same time the West

German government calculated that unemployment would rise by another million before the end of the Marshall Plan. In the view of the ECA, "[t]he situation is potentially explosive."[14]

Official United States and German economists were inclined at first to dismiss the unemployment as due to the influx of refugees from the East rather than the occupation's economic policies. The economic statistics, on the other hand, revealed that the unemployment was cyclical in nature and a direct result of Bonn's and Washington's economic policies and the social organization. For the refugees were concentrated in the rural areas, and the sharp growth in unemployment between the currency reform and the Korean War occurred in the industrial centers. In July 1949 officials in the United States Military Government were forced to conclude that ". . . unemployment centers around a lack of purchasing power on the part of individual consumers. . . . It expressed itself in the falling off or cancellation of orders, stoppage of production for stock, inability to collect bills, exhausted financial resources. . . ."[15] The UN's Economic Commission for Europe pointed out that along with Italy and Belgium, the unemployment was ". . . at least partly due to deflationary policies."[16] Yet unemployment, like low living standards, had a certain functional value in the United States' narrow perspectives of closing the dollar gap, for it kept wages and internal demand low and supposedly made European goods more competitive.

After the British devaluation, the German government terminated many import controls, and as the imports of luxuries increased, the trade deficit climbed sharply by the end of 1949, despite rising unemployment. So extreme were the economic developments that one leading British economist concluded after a detailed study of the years 1948–1950 in West Germany, "A more reactionary development in the distribution of the national income has hardly ever happened in a highly industrialized country."[17] After $1 billion a year in United States aid, by the beginning of 1950 West Germany still ranked second to the lowest in Western Europe's recovery.

As in Germany, the ECA held the orthodox economic policies of Belgium in the highest regard through 1949–1950 and pressed them on the other nations of Europe as the prime example of acceptable recovery. Yet Belgian unemployment grew from 2 percent in 1947, to 8 percent in 1949, and rose to 11 percent at the beginning of 1950. The deflationary policies introduced in 1946–1947 ultimately led to a sharp depression by 1950, as low productivity, low living standards, and obsolescent plant characterized the economy. Exports that had provided a trade surplus earlier dropped sharply in the fall of 1949 and internal demand was too depressed to make up the difference. Such empirical evidence of stagnation and decline did not daunt Washington's enthusiasm through the spring of 1950.[18]

In its report of the spring of 1949 the ECA expressed its concern that Italy's deflationary policies had gone too far and advocated government action to expand economic activity. But the ECA's expectations that there would be some revival in the Italian economy in 1949 did not materialize, and instead the rest of capitalist Europe and the United States slid into a recession. The economic policies pursued in Italy, as in Belgium and West Germany, contributed greatly to these developments. In August 1949 United States Ambassador James Dunn expressed hope that NATO could possibly employ some of Italy's unused resources in man-power and plant facilities. Yet monetary policy continued to discourage investment, and with it any growth in the economy, as the Italian government persisted in its fear that a dynamic economy requiring imports of raw materials would lead to an adverse effect on the balance of payments. By the spring of 1950 Italy's unemployment mirrored the economic policies, and the UN claimed four million to be a conservative estimate of the true total unemployed— approximately one-fifth of the Italian workers. The ECA continued to advise the government to encourage emigration as a potential solution, even though it was patently clear that it could remove only a small part of the natural increase in the labor force.[19]

Although the deflationary policies in France were not as severe as those in Italy, Belgium, and Germany, a conservative economic program proceeded at the expense of the French people. After crushing the miners' strikes of November 1948, the government continued its reduction of government workers by dismissing some 138,000 by March 1949. General unemployment doubled between 1948 and 1949. As for the production goals, a UN survey later concluded, "So far off were accomplishments in most industries that in 1949 new goals were set for attainment in 1952–53. . . . In other words the first plan was extended by two years." By the end of 1950, "In spite of all the increases in savings and investments, in spite of American aid, . . . only one of the original targets of the [Monnet] Plan had been hit . . . that for petroleum refining—and most had been missed by wide margins."[20] And by the fall of 1949, contributing to the American anxiety over the dollar gap, France was able to cover only a tenth of its dollar imports with its own exports.

ECA's meddling in strictly French concerns, such as the national budget, continued apace. In March 1950 the American agency reported that it had secured a ceiling on the French budget and a ". . . commitment to cover all Treasury expenditures by non-inflationary revenues. . . ."[21] This new habit of the French government of tailoring its policies to American direction, despite the divergence in national interests, did not end with internal economic policy. Politically, the French increasingly found themselves denied independent action on issues that had no direct relationship with the ERP. President Vincent Auriol, for example, concerned over the implications for French sovereignty of blindly following the United States' China policy in the UN, raised the question with the French representative. "Because they pay" was his prompt, and candid, reply.[22] Inevitably, this was increasingly to become the pattern of French affairs at home and abroad.

Not all Frenchmen were unhappy, however. In 1950 government economists unofficially confirmed the CGT statistics that revealed that profits of French industry were 50 percent of its gross income and wages 34 percent, as opposed to the prewar ratio of 29 percent for profits and 45 percent for wages. When wages were decontrolled in February 1950 the workers were at a severe disadvantage and collective bargaining proved to be a wholly unsuccessful strategy. This remarkable gross inequality in French society was noted even by Averell Harriman in a testimony before a Senate committee: "Now, France is one of the countries where there has been criticism that under the Marshall plan certain classes of French society improved their conditions more than the workmen did. That, in my opinion, is a fact."[23]

Toward Economic Unity

To a certain extent the deflationary policies on the Continent succeeded, insofar as budgets were balanced and the balance of payments improved substantially. But effective demand from the masses, and even the industrialists, declined, and instead stagnation and a further reduction in production characterized Europe's economy. Washington, however, did not interpret the signs to mean a failure of its deflationary policies. Instead by October 1949, after the devaluations, and overwhelmed with the problem of the dollar gap, it made another desperate effort to create European unity. On October 31 Paul Hoffman told the OEEC that integration was not merely an ideal but a practical necessity. "The substance of such integration would be the formation of a single large market within which quantitative restrictions, . . . monetary barriers to the flow of payments and, eventually, all tariffs are permanently swept away."[24] Hoffman stressed his earnestness by threatening to cut off all aid if unity efforts were not forthcoming.

Meanwhile, however, the OEEC was coming to the opposite conclusion. In response to Hoffman it pointed out that Europe's real need was to expand its trade with the rest of the world rather than rush into an essentially artificial unity. Historically, the markets and supplies of Britain, Holland, and France were with their former empires, and for Germany and Italy they were in Eastern Europe. And the wide variation in national social planning was another impediment to rapid integration. American experts in the IMF also expressed some concern over Washington's eagerness to press a new financial institution on the European states. They foresaw a time when the Europeans might act without regard to either the desires of the United States or the advice of the Fund. They also pointed out that Europe's problems were world-wide and it could not solve, or even minimize, them in isolation. But Washington had other, more pressing, considerations justifying action. For underlying all its efforts to create the institutions of European unity, such as the European Payments Union (EPU) and the Schuman Plan, during the fall of 1949 was the notion that it could somehow close the dollar gap and forestall bilateralism and trade controls by rationalizing European industry and making it more competitive. And American planners believed that, along with devaluation, a unified Western Europe would attract American private investment and decisively merge the internal economic policies of its member states. With these aims in mind, they formulated the European Payments Union.

The EPU, in simplest terms, eliminated all bilateral relationships in trade between the OEEC countries and provided that each state settle its trade accounts with the Union. It would balance intra-European trade credits and debts, and a state became a net debtor or net creditor to the EPU only, which settled accounts ultimately in gold and dollar credits. Discrimination between hard and soft currencies was no longer possible. In its original proposals the United States had strongly advocated that the EPU function as a central bank for all of Europe, with the obvious powers to direct internal economic policy of the member countries. The British successfully resisted this dimension, and the United States was unable to secure any more concessions on trade and financial unity in 1950.[25]

A payments union was only one aspect of this problem. Along with the EPU, the ECA began to consider the idea of an intra-European capitalist private authority that would direct the basic industries of coal and steel of the participating states as another mechanism for coordinating national economic policies after the termination of American aid. In October 1949 McCloy proposed an international, private authority to control the Ruhr, but indicated that it should manage not only the German industries but also the heavy industries of all of Western Europe, including Britain. This rather premature and ambitious plan was not developed at the time, for it elicited a rather hostile reaction, especially from England, where the coal companies were nationalized and similar plans were under way for steel. But with United States encouragement the European capitalist planners, particularly Jean Monnet of France, continued to develop the concept until it emerged on May 9, 1950 as the Schuman Plan for a European Coal and Steel Authority. The American business press in early April speculated that the OEEC would introduce a "producer-consumer steel cartel" in the spring of 1950 to control the vast surplus productive capacity which threatened to lead to a trade war.[26] The plan was based on France and Germany, but it was also an open invitation to the other European states, provided they accepted its general principles, and it soon included the Benelux and Italy. These general principles were about all that the French had developed as they hastily introduced the plan just before the London Western Foreign Ministers Conference. Acheson recalled in his memoirs that Schuman and Monnet disclosed the whole scheme to him before even discussing it with the French cabinet.

The proposal was very much in line with American thinking on the future of the European economy. In fact, United States experts had urged Monnet in 1949 to pursue the matter and, for political reasons, to wrap it in the rhetoric of European internationalism and Franco-German amity. As it turned out, despite American desires, it evolved into a proposal for a giant private cartel with the power to make binding decisions for the basic industries of the participating states. The Americans had not suggested its cartel features, but rather had sought yet another way to break down trade barriers and to eliminate much of the less productive and noncompetitive French industry. What later happened *in practice,* however, was that the authority approved of most of the concentrations and mergers in the industry submitted to it. It was also to authorize production and prices, standardize wages, allocate distribution, and plan export policies for the combined industries. For France, the anticipated costs were to be that competition would force approximately 20 to 30 percent of its steel capacity to close. The French, in turn, would have a greater control over the Ruhr as well as increased access to German coal. But much of French industry regarded the plan as a German-American scheme rumored to have been forced on Paris in exchange for more aid in Indochina. German business was enthusiastic. Such an arrangement would increase their influence, and it eliminated their fears of nationalization. The British steel industry also saw the plan as a safeguard against nationalization. The British government, on the other hand, reacted coldly, despite the internationalist rhetoric attached to the scheme. Attlee told the House of Commons that his government could not ". . . accept the principle that the most vital economic forces of this country should be handed over to an authority that is utterly undemocratic and is responsible to nobody."[27] To pacify the Americans, London endorsed the desirability of Franco-German amity, but at the same time the Labour Party published a pamphlet strongly criticizing the current antisocialist concepts of the European unity movement, a trend which would clearly undermine its own economic goals. Since Truman had just hailed the plan as an "act of constructive statesmanship," adding, "We are also gratified to note . . . it does leave the industry open to receive . . . the full benefits of the competitive process," England's sour note heightened United States irritation at a time when innumerable other crises were threatening.[28] Protests from Washington to London met lame British government assertions that the Labour Party and the government were not synonymous. Eager to maintain the illusion that the United States was not involved in the plan, Acheson asked that no American officials make public statements on the issue during the negotiations, but ". . . occasion might call for discreet aid to Schuman to avoid watering down his proposal or to retain 'favorable economic elements. . . .' "[29] Such occasions proved frequent over the summer of 1950.

When the Schuman Plan was first introduced there were real prospects of a trade war in coal and steel as inventories mounted. The Korean War immediately reversed that danger and also cooled the enthusiasm of some German industrialists, requiring added pressure from McCloy and others to sustain the project. Naturally enough, Jean Monnet, as the great "European," became president of the authority when it was officially created on April 18, 1951, and in an "informal" meeting with a United States Senate committee two years later he explained some of the operations of the authority. Monnet pointed to their success in incorporating the trade union leadership, particularly in Germany, in the authority's decision-making. This had the utilitarian effect of preventing strikes in France, since they could simply step up production in Germany. Monnet had also convinced the participating governments to drop subsidies to segments of the population in the purchase of coal. However, as with all the other schemes of

European unity, devaluation, and the like, the Schuman Plan failed to achieve Washington's desired aim. Its objective was to rationalize production, and the outcome was cartels and new restrictions.

The net result of all the complicated, laborious American schemes to create intra-European institutions to rationalize and make more competitive European industry was that by March 1950, in nearly every continental country, private consortia made price and market agreements on many products. The following November the President's Committee on Foreign Economic Policy acknowledged that all American efforts had been ". . . frustrated by agreements among business firms to refrain from entering each other's home market."[30] Yet the United States continued to regard European unity as a long-term basic solution to the dollar problem ". . . through the development of supra-national institutions and a harmonization of economic policies."[31]

The administration had always believed that United States private investment was the most desirable means of exporting dollars, and the bilateral ERP treaties had all included guarantees of nondiscrimination against American capitalists. But until 1949 the interest among American investors, save in oil, was inconsequential. All postwar investment in Europe had been in existing subsidiaries of United States firms, and even that was minor. With the decline in domestic demand, however, some American companies showed greater interest in exporting capital, although it could hardly be more than negligible—given the economic condition of Europe. But Washington was determined to make European investment prospects irresistible by forcing changes in Europe. But as Winthrop Aldrich, chairman of the board of Chase National Bank, told a group of British businessmen in the summer of 1949, before massive capital could be attracted to European industry Europe must balance its internal economies and agree on realistic exchange rates. And no less vital was that ". . . the attitude of mind which exists between the people of the country where such investment is to be made is ready to welcome such an investment . . . [and has achieved] political stability. That is to say, the threat of Communism must have been eliminated."[32] But despite Washington's efforts, American business was in no mood to cooperate on anything like the scale required. On the contrary, the ECA had to respond to the growing domestic pressures of specific industrialists who, while the ultimate beneficiaries of the broad aims of United States foreign policy, also operated in response to immediate economic fluctuations in the fortunes of their individual business. These American capitalists used their influence and opportunities for immediate profit or to avoid possible loss, and in 1949 they wanted either tariff protection or the expansion of their exports. Both goals were in direct conflict with the aims of Europe either to earn or to conserve dollars.

The Search for a New Policy

Throughout the fall of 1949 high-level staff reports to the key decision-makers in Washington warned of the dilemmas inherent in the dollar gap. "Any substantial drop in our exports will seriously affect our domestic market, forcing a sharp contraction in production and domestic consumption."[33] As in 1947, one leading government economist recommended, it was again necessary to prepare Congress and the American people for another extraordinary aid program to follow the ERP. But at this time there was still confusion as to the precise nature of the new policy that was required. Washington continued to prod the Europeans in the hope that new institutional arrangements there could somehow save the situation.

By the fall of 1949, OEEC directors Robert Marjolin and Baron Snoy had decided that there was, in fact, no solution to the dollar gap problem. And the economic evidence to sustain that conclusion was decisive. In theory, there were only a few ways to close the gap, and all of them were either not feasible or unacceptable to Washington. In the context of economic aid and European recovery, a continued program of grants would be impossible to sell to Congress. Increased imports were out of the question in a recession, and manufactured imports played only a small role in America's foreign trade at any time. The OEEC could foresee an increase in European exports to the United States by 1951–1952 of only $300 million, while the ECA insisted that it must increase by $1 billion. As a UN report noted, such a figure must be ". . . more in the nature of a goal than a forecast of what is likely to happen."[34] Yet despite the calamitous results of the deflationary policies that were leading much of Europe toward a depression, Truman's Council of Economic Advisers still advocated similar measures in April 1950. The possibility of reducing internal effective demand for United States exports through such deflationary steps as introduced in Italy, Belgium, and Germany was one method, of course, but dimly they perceived that it might be as self-defeating as the dollar gap itself to continued United States exports. Another American proposal was to create a larger triangular trade relationship with the Third World, allowing Europe to earn dollars in those markets that in turn sold raw materials to the United States. In order to earn sufficient dollars in the Third World, however, Europe would have to displace United States exports there by 40 to 50 percent. But this was an unattainable goal, given the fact that United States exports to the Third World had increased four times since 1938 and United States exporters were not about to retreat gracefully. Other considerations pointed to an aggravation of Europe's dollar problem in the future. Payments on loan servicing and the repatriation of profits to America amounted to $3.5 billion per year from 1947 to 1949, and the figure would increase as the postwar loans became due. Moreover, during late 1949 and early 1950, the United States was planning to terminate strategic stockpiling in 1953, causing a further reduction of several hundred million dollars available to the world for United States trade. Calculating the maximum dollars available to the *entire world,* and assuming economic and political stability and no world capital flight, only $9 billion could be secured without massive United States grants. United States exports, on the other hand, amounted to $13.4 billion in 1948. The gap was much greater, of course, than such figures implied, for the ideal circumstances did not exist and not all the available dollars would return to the United States in the form of trade. Europe, from all sources, would have available only $2 billion to purchase goods from the United States after the end of the Marshall Plan.[35] In the first months of 1950 these facts created a nightmare for those responsible in Washington for both the foreign and domestic policies of the United States. For these dry economic statistics pointed to a most fundamental crisis in the entire system, the resolution of which was to lead down a twisting road of further misery and terror for millions.

There was no longer any doubt in early 1950 about the direction of both the American and European economies, nor about the failure of the ERP to achieve the original goals that Washington desired. A crisis more serious than that of 1947 threatened and, if anything, Congress was taking an even more resistant line. The economic outlook had reached a critical point in February 1950, when Acheson sent a detailed memo to the President:

The time is rapidly approaching when the Government and the people of the United States must make critical and far-reaching decisions of policy affecting our economic relationships with the rest of the world. . . . It is expected that unless vigorous steps are taken, the reduction and eventual termination of extraordinary foreign assistance in accordance with present plans will create economic problems at home and abroad of increasing severity. If this is allowed to happen, United States exports, including the key commodities on which our most efficient agricultural and manufacturing industries are heavily dependent, will be sharply reduced, with serious repercussions on our domestic economy. . . . as ERP is reduced, and after its termination in 1952, how can Europe and other areas of the world obtain the dollars necessary to pay for a high level of United States exports, which is essential both to their own basic needs and to the well-being of the United States economy? This is the problem of the "dollar gap" in world trade. . . . the Administration needs soon to affirm that the importance to the United States of a successful economic system among the free nations is so great that the United States is determined to do its full part to achieve it—even if this involves adjustments and sacrifices by particular economic groups . . . in the interest of the nation as a whole . . . and even if it requires more time than was originally contemplated by the [ERP]. . . . It is of such importance . . . that I believe the whole machinery of government must be brought into play if we are to achieve success.[36]

Acheson proposed that Truman appoint a special committee to outline the imperative needs of the United States economy during the twilight of the ERP and after, and to present a report to the public. On March 31 the President appointed Gordon Gray, former secretary of the army, to head the undertaking.

The committee was assigned to prepare ". . . the basis for a reformulation of U.S. foreign economic policies . . . with particular reference to the balance of payments aspects. This involves a clear exposition of the relationship of foreign economic policy to overall security objectives. . . . An . . . equally important part of the project is to lay the groundwork for subsequent public understanding and acceptance of the necessary actions." The administration asked the committee to assess such problems as that "certain U.S. domestic policies, primarily in agriculture, are beginning to have a serious impact on our foreign relationships," and to give serious consideration to such "structural" problems as ". . . the possible secular decrease in U.S. demand for imports of goods. Another is the exaggerated effect, on certain major commodity imports, of short-run instability in U.S. economic activity." Finally, pointing to the only area that contained the seeds of a solution, the policy-makers asked the committee to consider ". . . the revised and expanded military plans for the defense of Western Europe and for the provision of equipment [that] . . . requires a reorientation of economic programs."[37] "The problem now faced," Joseph Dodge advised the committee, "is to assess the prospective requirements of other countries for U.S. goods, if our foreign policy objectives are to be achieved; to assess their ability to pay for these requirements by normal means of financing; and to determine *the best method of providing the part which they will be unable to finance.*"[38]

There was, however, no time to wait for the prestigious Gray committee to make its recommendations on these momentous issues. For the administration had already reached its conclusions and the committee was merely appointed to prepare Congress and the American public for the new policy, as in 1947 when the Harriman committee examined the problems of the Marshall Plan. As early as October 1949 presidential assistant Stephen J. Spingarn cynically proposed, "[t]he problem, of course, is first to develop a policy and then to sell it to the country. Perhaps at some later stage, a commission of one sort or another would be useful as a platform from which to propound a new policy to the country."[39] The commission's time had come, but the policy choices had already been made, and the broad contours of those decisions had begun to leak to the press.

Business Week on April 1 predicted a sharp rise in defense spending. "Doubt about future unemployment favors the military. . . . A defense ceiling was set two years ago, when the economic danger was inflation. . . . Now it's deflation that is the economic worry. . . ."[40] The direction was now clear. Other means having failed, the only acceptable continuous government expenditure for an orthodox capitalist economist—and politically for Congress—was for armaments. Western European rearmament on a massive scale was to supplement and follow ECA. Washington would merge the OEEC with NATO and push Western European unity under a great economic and military umbrella. This was to be Dean Acheson's message to the British and French foreign ministers whom he met in London in May 1950.

The administration felt again required to generate a new sense of urgency, even though Acheson himself said not war but rather Soviet political penetration threatened the alliance. Congress, never the leader in major foreign policy departures, did not see the emergency. This led observers in the business press to expect ". . . phony war crises to get its [the administration's] way in Congress. . . . Scare talk may first be drummed up over Indo-China."[41] They sensed an atmosphere ". . . much like the months just before Marshall set out his plan."[42] Truman made a "nonpolitical" tour of the nation and attacked the isolationist, parochial congressmen. And the State Department followed with public addresses on expanding the United States role in the world and the needs of security. The effort, despite the martial vocabulary, came none too soon, as Congress passed the administration's Point Four program by only one vote. Point Four, which we discuss in detail in Chapter 23, was yet another attempt to spread dollars abroad and secure raw materials by encouraging United States investment in the Third World. And only a tied vote prevented Congress from slashing one-half billion dollars from the ECA request.

In Europe, during this same time, the OEEC director and others were beginning to reach what to them were rather painful conclusions regarding the Marshall Plan's capitalist assumptions and, beyond the ERP, on the very potential of capitalist economies to survive without external stimulus. Marjolin wrote shortly thereafter that

there was in the European economic situation another factor which is worth considering, namely a tendency toward stagnation. . . . I cannot help being struck by the fact that in the spring of 1950 in Europe, not to mention the United States, the rise in production was not very rapid and we seemed to be approaching a ceiling imposed not by lack of capacity or lack of real needs but by inadequacy of demand. Is it really necessary that we remain more or less where we are unless external circumstances such as those of 1950 [Korean War] take control? I have no theory about this and I would not wish to say that it is inherent in our economic system, but there is certainly a disturbing factor here which merits our attention and deep consideration.[43]

During the spring of 1950 the ECA headquarters in Paris sent anxious reports expressing considerable fear that the Western Europeans would again shift their trade eastward if the existing crises could not be resolved quickly under United States auspices. A grand new proposal was essential to instill new confidence in the viability of prolonged economic ties with the United States. And a new American plan for the full coordination of NATO and the OEEC might sound even more enticing if it first came from the mouth of a European.

In April 1950 President Auriol of France was "stupefied" to read a major speech of Premier Georges Bidault that called for the creation of an Atlantic Council, including the United States, to coordinate all European defense and economic activities. Auriol, appalled, insisted that Bidault had never raised this shift from European to Atlantic unity with either himself or the French cabinet. It was the first time any French government leader had publicly recommended a major departure in foreign affairs without mentioning it to any of his peers. Whether or not Bidault consulted the rest of his government, it is likely that he consulted Washington, for his speech fitted perfectly with the preparations for the London conference where Acheson made the very same proposal. But at the time Bidault's trial balloon did not rise, for it was met with a hostile reaction from all sides in

Europe. Acheson later admitted that Bidault's specific proposal turned out to be "stillborn." While willing to forgo such a grandiose structure as Bidault's Atlantic Council for Peace, the United States nevertheless intended rearmament to be the keystone of the future American foreign economic policy.[44]

In London in May, Acheson pressed the Europeans on the need for greater economic and military unity and promised, without congressional authorization, that the Americans would pay for their efforts toward this end. NATO would have a new economic planning staff that would calculate the alliance's needs after the ERP came to an end. Washington anticipated that the report of NATO's new economic section, plus the Gray committee's report, would form the basis for the "new" American policy, military in emphasis but aiming at the ERP's economic goals. In their communiqué, the diplomats at the London Conference reported, "They further realize that the development and strengthening of this community of nations [the OEEC, United States, and Canada] may in the future require formal organizational expression. . . ," but meanwhile they would coordinate into the indefinite future the less grandiose military and economic planning already under way in Washington and in the OEEC.[45]

When Acheson returned to Washington it was not at all certain that Congress would recognize such a nebulous crisis warranting the billion dollars that Truman requested in June to supplement the allocation for the ECA. So indifferent or hostile was Congress that it refused to permit Acheson to make his report to a joint session; instead he was forced on May 31 to address any interested members in a small hall in the Library of Congress. There Acheson linked his overriding concern for the economy with the question of security: "It was also plain that provision of the necessary defense would require a very large economic and financial effort. Therefore, the continued development of production and productivity was essential to underpin the defense effort. . . . In the face of these . . . equally compelling needs for increased defense and strengthened economies, the free nations have come, therefore, to another time of decision. . . . [We] risk not only all the progress we have made but total failure."[46] And he announced that plans were under way to merge the United States and Canada into the OEEC on a permanent basis. The congressmen failed to show any serious concern over the problem.

Although by June 1950 the administration had made its decision to press for expanded rearmament and the accompanying "defense support" economic aid as the most feasible means to continue to export dollars to

Europe, it had not, by any means, abandoned its plans for the restructuring of European economic institutions. These efforts were to proceed apace in the hope that such manipulations would provide an ultimate solution to the recurrent problem.

The administration had not, however, found the device by which to mold Congress into that phalanx of purposeful resolution that it believed the domestic and international situation required. By June, therefore, all elements in America's political and economic predicament were evolving into a now familiar scenario. Fundamental issues were at stake for the United States economic system, and the solution to the essential continuation of the flow of dollars to Europe called for renewed crisis. But a crisis of considerably greater proportion than it anticipated awaited Washington, and it would indeed resolve certain critical aspects of the dilemmas of the two years after June 1948. But those years highlighted the dangers of peace to world capitalism, and the failure of strictly economic means, within the framework of capitalist alternatives, to keep the vast productive capacity of the United States and Western Europe from sinking into the mire of stagnation, if not depression. The artificial stimulus of rearmament needed as its rationale a crisis somewhere in the world if Washington was to resolve its new dilemma, one that was the result of the Marshall Plan's failure to achieve its original goals through purely economic means.

18

Military Power and Diplomatic Policy, 1947–1949: Definitions and Confrontations

One of the major themes in postwar history is Washington's search for a military doctrine sufficient to translate the United States' immense technological and economic power into mastery over elusive and ever-changing political realities. The almost continuous American strategy crisis after World War II, with its tortured, unresolved effort to substitute the power of machines for the appeals of revolutionary ideology, ultimately ended in disaster.

If the disarmament debate revealed nothing else, it was that the United States had become fully wedded to its arms to protect and advance its immense global interests. Ironically, as we shall see, American leaders prepared for a war they never expected to fight, only to find their strength insufficient when it was tested under circumstances virtually no significant American leader anticipated. For no nation in this century has had the capacity to control the destiny of more than a very small fraction of the earth's surface, and in its failure to learn this lesson from its defeated predecessors the United States was ultimately to pave the way for its own profound internal crisis.

Political definitions and military capabilities became mutually reinforcing after World War II, and economic necessities defined limits in a manner that at one period might impose restrictions on spending while at another increase it. Suffice it to say here, after the war the major challenge to the United States in the world was economic rather than military, and until

1950 the export of goods and reforming world capitalism dominated Washington's budget and strategy. Moreover, given backlogged internal savings and demand until 1949, still larger arms expenditures were impossible without intensifying inflationary pressures and unbalancing the national budget. Until 1950, therefore, the basic financial context of American military planning was stringency, one Washington deemed sufficient for the perceived military threats but which also plagued the period with conflicting service demands for shares of a finite budget.

We have outlined the earlier contours of this struggle between the army, air force, and navy in Chapter 4. Such intramural debates need not detain us, for focusing on America's traditionally quite prosaic military leaders will scarcely help us comprehend its foreign policy. By 1947, as Truman and his advisers planned further military reductions and strove for a balanced federal budget, American leaders felt confident that they possessed a decisive air and naval superiority over the USSR and, given their far superior productive capacity, they were not likely to lose their military lead. Universal military training, which Marshall and Truman favored for the army's sake, had only nominal navy and air force support, and even Marshall argued for it mainly as a gesture that would convey American determination not ". . . to abdicate our responsibilities" rather than as essential to its military power.[1] Ultimately, by April 1948 the congressional proponents of air power, some of whom were convinced that reliance on the atomic bomb was consistent with low military expenditures, defeated UMT when they allocated nearly a billion dollars more for air force procurement.

The pork-barreling aspects of military appropriations are always colorful, but they are invariably the effect of command policy decisions rather than their cause. It is true that the government seeks to maintain a technological infrastructure and economic base for the military establishment, and this may guide which company obtains a contract. And it is certain that congressmen lobby to obtain contracts for their constituents, and often succeed at somewhat greater expense to the government and even to the extent of building weapons of dubious utility. There can be little doubt, for example, that air power advocates lobbied energetically and effectively for greater contracts and that Thomas K. Finletter's influential President's Air Policy Commission, which made public its demand for a 70-group air force the first day of 1948, frankly regarded the profitability and maintenance of aircraft industrial capacity as vital to national security. But even granting the influence of specific interests and their blueprint weapons systems in determining general strategy, in the end the level of military expenditures and their larger allocation between sophisticated technology and "conventional" land war reflected more impersonal economic priorities and political perceptions as to the nature of America's enemy. Nor can it be ignored that the large majority of businessmen and their journals and organizations at this time were either indifferent or hostile toward massive arms expenditures, and they in turn reinforced budget-cutters in Congress and the Budget Bureau. For the United States spent about what it could afford on the military establishment, given the Marshall Plan and domestic inflation, and as much as it thought the real, as opposed to publicized, threat of Soviet power and policies warranted to maintain its decisive military supremacy. In fiscal 1947, beginning the year in July 1946, the United States spent $14.4 billion on national security, then fell to $11.8 billion in 1948, and only rose another billion and a quarter in each of the next two years. At no time until late 1949 was this force level, which was probably almost twice Soviet expenditures, deemed inadequate to the real military challenge confronting the United States.[2]

Occasional boondoggling aside, the men who ran American military and foreign policy after World War II had a rather functional and quite disinterested definition of the American system's needs and imperatives. Drawn from the world of big law, finance, and business, generally they conceded to specific company interests only out of political necessity rather than preference. The traditional military leaders' inability to cope with advanced technology and organizational needs meant that increasingly civilians and expert technicians assumed the key military responsibilities for modern warfare. These men, in turn, often chose military responses to political challenges, but never to the extent of making military solutions dysfunctional to the United States' very largest economic and political goals and needs. The civilian-military dichotomy is both false and misleading, for what was most crucial was the consensus on means and objectives that all such men shared. It was this consensus that made the United States' only partial reliance on arms to achieve its goals the effect and application rather than the cause of political policy. Summarizing this perspective, which extended far beyond the military but subsumed America's relationship to world social systems, at the end of 1947 Secretary of Defense Forrestal told the Finletter commission that "[o]ur security is not merely the capacity or ability to repel invasion, it is our ability to contribute to the reconstruction of the world, and that is why I say that our military requirements have to be fitted into the pattern of what we do toward the other larger result, in other words, the reconstruction of society."[3] And for this reason the

United States was to rely first on its economic rather than its military-weapons.

The Definition of Soviet Power

The question of how much arms the United States needed depended not merely on its economic capacities but also on its definition of the extent of the USSR's military power and intentions. However useful the communist bogey in obtaining congressional support for legislation that was desired for quite different reasons—a mobilizing technique Truman's administration employed with increasing frequency—Washington had to premise its internal planning assumptions on greater realism. And here it had a rather consistent vision of Russia's military plans and potential that it based purely on hard facts.

Stated simply, after World War II the United States was strong and the Soviet Union was far weaker militarily and economically. No other assessment was possible, and from it followed inevitable conclusions. Throughout 1946 the American military establishment explicitly assumed that the Russians would take no actions that might risk war. Nothing that occurred during the spring of 1947 shook this premise, and Eisenhower thought it would be at least five years before Russia could deliberately initiate a war. Even Acheson fully accepted the estimate that Russia dared not fight, though he and Forrestal shared the same anxiety regarding Moscow's purported endorsement of civil wars that was to anguish French politicians later that year during the strike wave. After his return from the Moscow Conference, Dulles publicly announced that he was certain that the Kremlin did not wish to fight another war, and shortly thereafter Ambassador Smith privately gave similar comforting assurances, basing them on an evaluation less of ideology than of material facts. During November, indeed, Marshall again pointed to Russia's concern for its internal problems, and other than their encouragement of possible *coups* in France or Italy he thought the Russians were on the defensive. The Americans based their confidence not on its European ground forces, which they acknowledged as weak, but on the decisive role they assigned to the atomic bomb. "I do not think any power is in a position to attack us with any prospect of success in the immediate future," Admiral Chester Nimitz, chief of Naval Operations, told the Finletter commission in December 1947. "We are relatively safe . . . for the next four or five years."[4] The commission itself the following month gave the United States at least five years of immunity from Soviet attack with atomic weapons in any significant quantities, while another executive commission thought three and one-half years reasonable.

Such estimates did not prevent sporadic individual hunches or even tension verging on breakdowns, as when Clay wired to Washington during March 1948 that he expected imminent war, though he had only "a feeling" which "I cannot support . . . with any data or outward evidence."[5] Truman himself, a month earlier, had dismissed the Soviet leaders as men who " . . . have fixed ideas and those ideas were set out by Peter the Great in his will. . . ."[6] What is significant in such comments is not the spice they add to popular histories, but the fact that serious and influential men showed contempt for presidential reliance on well-known forgeries, and in no instance were rash estimates made into the basis of official action. For just as the presidency is an institution surrounded by a committee government which is quite efficient within its premises, so, too, do calculating men circumscribe overwrought diplomats and generals. Haste and new departures thereby become too difficult, adventurism as well as more pacific policies less likely.

The best proof of this relative stability in the political system, however unattainable or dangerous its ultimate goals, is that neither Peter's will nor Clay's impulses were allowed to muddy the official, quite private American estimate of the risk of war with Russia. For public purposes, especially to conjure up congressional votes for Marshall Plan or military expenditures, Truman and other officials successfully trotted out references to amorphous, imminent dangers. Some of his advisers had only contempt and concern for such necessary practices, and in the end the Truman administration was to whip up enough anti-Communist hysteria and paranoia to make McCarthyism its logical internal outcome. But during April and May 1948 even Vandenberg was skeptical about the likelihood of Soviet military activity, various senior State Department officials thought the Russians were in great fear of America's embarking on preventive war, and Marshall himself during May informed Truman and other key leaders that, as Forrestal recorded it, " . . . the policy of this country was based upon the assumption that there would not be war. . . ." Whatever was said to the press, privately Truman's major advisers felt militarily secure within essentially the existing budget, give or take several billions, and they thought it no less essential, to cite Forrestal, that America remain " . . . socially sound and financially solvent."[7]

Soviet Definitions and Capabilities

Publicly, Russia's leaders studiously hewed to a coexistence policy designed to maintain morale at home, lower the international temperature, and work within the unfavorable balance of economic and military power which imposed definite limits on them. Whether or not such a cautious line was rooted in ideology is irrelevant to the limited policy alternatives open to the Kremlin. Whatever the cause, the Russians pursued a very conservative course, given the options in a world in upheaval and revolution, a strategy that gave them time in which to rebuild and consolidate as well as to attempt to balance the military equations.

Any survey of the Soviet press and speeches during 1947 and the first half of 1948 merely reinforces Stalin's April 9, 1947, statement that capitalism and Communism could live peacefully and cooperatively together indefinitely, but also that the United States was actively attempting to encircle Russia with its bases. Quite oblivious to the United States' rhetoric, but highly critical of its growing intervention into the affairs of all nations, even after the failure of the Moscow Conference the Russians reiterated their article of faith that pessimism was unwarranted and cooperation between the great powers was possible, even probable. Zhdanov's official pronouncement of this coexistence doctrine at the founding meeting of the Cominform the following September was also the working doctrine he transmitted privately to the Western European Communist leaders. The Russians continued to excoriate the creation and growth of American military bases, and they did not hesitate to criticize strongly specific American policies, but they never abandoned the coexistence theme and in their newspapers they stressed domestic problems, mainly economic, far more than foreign affairs. Not only were the Soviet people asked to think mainly about reconstruction and peace rather than war, but the Cominform journal, *For a Lasting Peace, For a People's Democracy!*, throughout 1948 stressed a purely reformist, parliamentarian line for Western Europe that focused mainly on the need for higher pay for workers rather than revolution.[8] Informally, French leaders learned (and probably passed the word to Washington) that the Western European Communists had been told that the Soviet Union was preoccupied with its economic problems and certainly wished to avoid war. To forgo militancy that might draw the Americans into Europe was the order of the day.

Apart from its ideological pragmatism, the Kremlin fully perceived its material weakness. In this sense, peaceful coexistence was the only strategy it could afford to pursue. Despite an enormous upsurge in 1947 agricultural output after the preceding drought year, the Russian living standards were still abysmally low. Industrial output in 1947 was 92 percent of the 1940 level, and in 1948 increased to 118 percent of 1940, but even with this remarkable recovery Russia's national income was less than 30 percent that of the United States'—and American material advantage was universally conceded to be decisive. Given its economic base and grossly inferior sea and air power, Russia could not hope successfully to fight a ground war in Europe, and this fact was so self-evident that, intentions aside, it adjusted its foreign policies accordingly. The USSR acted from a position of weakness, limited by external pressures which interacted with a flexible ideology and a strong sense of national interest. The United States, on the other hand, could afford to pursue its diplomacy from a position of strength largely disregarding Russia, but exploiting its existence as a rationale for policies whose origins and objectives had precious little to do with it.[9]

Indeed, to American leaders the value of the Soviet Union was precisely in the carefully contrived appearance of bolshevik ferociousness which they might employ to mobilize Congress and the public to sustain expensive policies for other areas of the world where Russia or its allied parties were docile or irrelevant. Russia's real threat was scarcely military, but its ability to communicate its desire for peace and thereby take the momentum out of Washington's policies. From passage of the 1946 loan to Britain through the Marshall Plan in April 1948, Truman and his aides had with increasing frequency and cynicism inflated the Russian menace to gargantuan proportions in total conflict with Soviet capabilities and intentions. By February 1948 public rumors began to circulate that the Russians were soon to attempt a *rapprochement,* but Marshall's and Truman's alarmist speeches of mid-March were adequate to mobilize a restive Congress and public inclined to take a more indifferent view of the world. During April, as we noted earlier, Truman frankly and publicly linked future congressional cooperation to a sustained image of a bellicose Russia, with Stalin's peace overtures presenting a greater menace than his tanks. Indeed, during early May, as Forrestal and the Pentagon sought an increase in military funds over the ultimately successful Budget Bureau demand to impose a $15 billion ceiling through fiscal 1950, the Russians opened their untimely peace offensive. At the beginning of May, Ambassador Smith visited Molotov to complain about the thrust of Soviet policy and press comments in a manner that placed blame for the entire world crisis on Russia without offering any concrete steps toward an accommodation. Indeed, Smith's main point was that Russia should ignore election year debates on foreign policy and assume it confronted only unity on basic policy. On May 9 Molotov replied in kind, but also added a statement of peaceful intent and hinted that some stabilizing agreements and negotiations would be timely. Curiously, when Molotov then made the exchange public, thereby fanning a peace scare, Marshall quickly denounced the alleged breach of confidentiality and dismissed the usefulness of new or bilateral talks outside already existing forums that were also, it should be added, proven failures. The press saw new openings in the Soviet gesture, but Forrestal warned Marshall that the optimistic mood was producing " . . . a dangerous complacency on the part of certain elements in the country." What was essential, Marshall told a White House meeting of May 21, was " . . . continuity of policy and of the need for sufficient residual force to back up policy."[10] Negotiations and a settlement endangered all this as well as the basic thrust of American foreign policy that was entirely incompatible with coexistence not just with Communism but with socialism and national capitalisms as well. And, as America's leaders explicitly acknowledged at this time, a relaxation of tensions would reduce congressional and public enthusiasm for the financial costs of the vast undertaking. Russia, from this viewpoint, was safer and more useful if it could be made to appear hostile, expansive, and strong. That formula had by now become a keystone of American postwar foreign policy.

Western European Power: Competition or Integration

The United States perceived a powerful Western European political and military bloc in essentially the same light as an autonomous economy in that region. Its main objective was to integrate tendencies toward independence in a way that would complement and reinforce American power and larger global objectives rather than compete with them.

Washington had already confronted all these issues during World War II in the form of British initiatives on behalf of a Western European bloc that would create an Anglo-French alliance that might operate independently of the Soviet and American blocs. But European sentiments for a regional alliance did not die with peace or American reticence. They remained alive, but also more confused—a fact that ultimately was to allow the United States to determine its form.

European Socialists, such as Vincent Auriol and Paul Henri Spaak, vaguely conceived of a Western European bloc as a kind of socialist third force standing independently of Russia and the United States, mediating between them and also performing vague and unspecified economic functions. A sentimental socialist desire for such a coalition was slow in dying, but eventually did so with regrets. Right-wing reinforcement for the concept of a bloc came from British Conservatives, such as Churchill and Macmillan, and later from various European Catholics associated both with various forms of Christian Democracy and with big business. By mid-1947, after having earlier proposed various modes of economic integration without Germany, Jean Monnet, a modern conservative friendly with Dulles and the United States but ultimately deeply dedicated to French big business interests, came up with a scheme for integrating German industrial power into a Europe that France might better control. Indeed, since the Marshall Plan required some form of common European planning, Monnet argued one might more easily muzzle a resurgent Germany by welcoming it into a coalition that was vaguely political and economic at one and the same time.

The economic and political potentials of all these themes were so varied that both the Russians and the Americans watched them with mixed feelings. The Russians regarded the entire undertaking as having a "two-edged character," one that was potentially anti-Soviet, but another that was intended to save Western European power from American domination.[11] And they also saw Western Europeans as being the nervous inheritors of colonialism anxious to protect their empires from American incursions. Apprehensive but not hostile toward the undertaking in early 1947, the Russians were also aware of the ambiguous United States attitude toward the notion. At the end of the war Washington's posture had been one of neutrality toward a purely political bloc and opposition toward an economic alliance —distinctions the Europeans themselves left dangerously vague. A nationalist-led bloc of men such as De Gaulle was bad enough, of socialists worse yet; and in its animosity toward European economic autarchy the United States quite early revealed what it thought of the movement. For the Americans always understood that an independent Europe, with or without Germany, would be critical in the world power balance and inevitably limit America's role not only in Europe but in the entire Third World. By the summer of 1947, however, the Marshall Plan offered the United States a vital means for defining the future content of European impulses to integrate, and meant that such efforts were likely to be benign. At that time, as well, the connections between transnational economic structures and

Europe's desire for military security redirected the bloc movement's main impulses into channels the United States could control and the Russians fear.[12]

The French and British had already signed a treaty in March 1947 which was directed mainly against Germany, and in January 1948 the British initiated discussions with the Dutch, French, Belgian, and Luxemburg governments. Bidault, the nationalist, sustained the effort for its anti-German aspects, and Spaak because it also had vague economic implications. The Treaty of Brussels the five nations signed on March 17 was specifically aimed at Germany and vaguely at other nations, and only promised that each would provide " . . . all the military and other aid and assistance in their power" in the event of an attack.[13] Its references to economic collaboration were broad enough to mean anything. Suffice it to say, the various European factions who endorsed the pact had quite conflicting notions of where they were now heading and what were their ultimate goals. Socialists and capitalists alike found it an advance toward utopia.

Even before it was signed, Bevin had intimated that the five-nation pact was but the first of a number of military agreements England would seek, and on March 12 he asked Washington for meetings to consider Atlantic and Mediterranean security systems. Forrestal immediately warmed up to the idea of encouraging Western European rearmament, but Truman held off despite mounting British and then Canadian pressures. Now the State Department recommended that the United States should enlarge and support the pact, even with force in case of war, without joining it. But the military value of the undertaking against Russia failed to impress the army, which concluded that " . . . it will eventually be to our best interests to assist in the establishment of foreign armed forces at least capable of controlling internal uprisings and maintaining the security of their own borders. . . ."[14] Apart from the fact that some advisers warned Truman the entire step might be viewed as provocative of the Russians, a point Molotov was to make the following month, the national and global politics of the gesture were too delicate. On April 23 Bevin warned Washington that a formal treaty organization might panic Moscow into a military offensive, while too few assurances would force France, out of fear of Germany, to insist that nation not be rebuilt. This hint of need for a nondirected, ambiguous American position, as useful against the Germans as the Russians, simply reinforced the United States' inclination to remain noncommittal. Domestically, the National Security Council decided, the whole undertaking would be far easier if the administration could induce a Republican to propose the measure.

It selected Vandenberg. Robert Lovett was assigned to tailor a Senate resolution to fulfill the vague mission, and he consulted Dulles and Marshall from time to time. Marshall found the formula and undertaking "somewhat artificial," to quote Dulles' notes, and Dulles himself thought that " . . . any firm commitment, either military or economic, would be used by the governments of Western Europe as an excuse to continue their own particular social and economic experiments, which required insulation from others. . . ."[15] But since the Europeans were appealing for the gesture in the name of anti-Communism they could scarcely be refused. Lovett believed the "Vandenberg Resolution," which the Senate passed with little debate and almost unanimously on June 11, made no tangible commitments of United States support, and this explains the Senate's indifference to its homilies. Presenting it as a strengthening of both the UN and Congress' authority, Vandenberg relied on apathy rather than anti-Communism to persuade his colleagues. For the resolution was so vague as to become meaningless, consisting as it did of a reaffirmation of the UN Charter's Article 51 on the right of collective self-defense. At most it declared that there would be a United States "association . . . by constitutional process, with such regional and other collective arrangements as are based on continuous and effective self-help and mutual aid, and as affect its national security."[16] The words "Treaty of Brussels," "Russia," and "Europe" never appeared in what was theoretically to become the Senate's mandate for America's later profound military involvement in Europe. All that was certain was that the interested governments would discuss what to do next.

This compounding of two vague declarations of obligation, nonspecific as to whether the enemy was Russia, Germany, or local revolutionaries, reflected the fantasies and anxieties the postwar world crisis was inflicting on its practitioners. No binding promises were made, and that looseness in turn later made possible a far deeper commitment than was contemplated originally. The Europeans were motivated by their fears and their dreams, and the variations of a Western European system passed into unrecognizable forms. The United States perceived no serious military threat, and its budget constrained it from helping Europe rearm. Indeed, despite its contrived public allusions to the menace of Soviet expansion, the need to rearm Europe was an afterthought, only later to emerge for essentially nonmilitary reasons. Thus were born NATO and the Atlantic Alliance!

Germany and the Berlin Crisis

The American occupation government's problems in Germany were rarely organizational, but rather issues of political and economic policy that involved, in the last analysis, the future of Germany in the world. By the summer of 1947 the United States had made the basic decision to rebuild a capitalist Germany, but leftist resistance in Germany, and, to a lesser extent, its own desire to prevent a resurgent threat to American interests in Europe, hampered the precarious undertaking. The United States intended to reintegrate Western Germany into a region that, in turn, collaborated fully with American designs for the world economy. Unfortunately for Washington, many of the critical preconditions for this ambiguous synthesis were absent during the last half of 1947.

The French, after having easily blocked steps toward zonal collaboration since 1945, were now far more ready to compromise on all their positions —not the least because the Marshall Plan gave the Americans leverage hitherto lacking—and for several years were to prove sufficiently docile on questions the United States thought critical. The British, who had willingly gone into the Bizonal merger, by the fall of 1947 were so deeply in a financial crisis that most American officials saw their weakness as the opportunity to consolidate the United States' political and economic control over Bizonia and, if the French were willing, Trizonia as well. Clay, by September, thought he had Washington's mandate to create a provisional government out of the Western zones—in effect, to partition Germany. That such a step necessarily involved partition with the Eastern zone was inherent in the fact that the East was now largely socialist in its economic organization.

However, to sustain a capitalist West Germany remained a major objective of American policy. Washington therefore insisted more strenuously than ever that the occupation definitively rebuff the SPD efforts to socialize economic sectors in North Rhine–Westphalia, Hesse, and elsewhere. No less significant were the final steps to restore the confidence of the still intact traditional ruling class by ending formally America's at best tepid desire for decartelization, denazification, and dismantling of industry. The essential policy fixed, all that remained was to implement it.

The Russians saw all this and publicly commented on it even before the Council of Foreign Ministers meeting that was to open its periodic ritual of frustration in London on November 25. Molotov therefore came to the meeting without illusions or hope, obviously communicating only to the world outside and repeating the traditional Soviet demands for reparations from current production and all-German political and economic unity. He also attacked the obvious movement toward partition, and in return Marshall denied all substantive Soviet requests while suggesting a number of vague counterproposals, the most significant of which was a currency reform. The meeting, which lasted three frustrating weeks for Marshall, ended by his terminating indefinitely all further council meetings. "We must do the best we can," he reported to the nation, "in the area where our influence can be felt."[17]

The future held few surprises for anyone. Shortly after the conference Marshall and Bevin met with their key advisers, including Clay and Murphy, and agreed on the strategy of introducing a new currency soon, with Russian agreement if possible, but without it if necessary. At the same time, they authorized the creation of a new political structure in Germany, which they outlined in some detail, to be approved at a forthcoming conference hopefully including the French. Currency reform and political partition went hand in hand.

For the United States, separate currency reform had an overriding economic justification, which we consider in Chapter 16; but the West had also considered its political consequences for over a year and, until late 1947, found them too costly. Joseph Dodge had advanced the basic currency reform plan early in 1946, but with the admonition that it not be introduced without Soviet approval lest it irrevocably divide Germany. Now, at the beginning of 1948, Clay recalled that " . . . we knew that the end of Control Council government was in sight."[18] He barely concealed what was in store for the West German leaders with whom he met, or that the United States would maintain control over the future political forms. After January, the Russians proposed currency reforms designed to meet the United States' purely economic goals while avoiding political and economic partition. The Americans ignored them, and attached no significance to Moscow's sudden initiation of small reparations to the West. At the end of February all this was cut short when the three Western powers and Benelux nations met in London mainly to win French support for the break. There, the French concluded, the United States would let nothing keep it from dividing Germany—and Europe—in two. Two strong Soviet protests did not deter the three nations from their goal. Indeed, Moscow's March 6 note made it clear that the end of four-power collaboration not only endangered the future of the Control Council but also undermined the very wartime agreements that were the basis of the West's right to be in Berlin. Then, on March 20, the

Four Power Control Council met, and the Russians asked for the details of the London Conference's decisions. When the other members told him nothing more than what was already in its vague communiqué, Marshal V. D. Sokolovsky rudely adjourned the meeting, walked out, and failed to schedule the next session. Later Clay wrote about this episode, "The Allied Control Council was dead," but none of its four members later asked that it be reconvened.[19] But the Soviets did ask to continue with the promising committee discussions on a new currency. The Americans, however, insisted on abandoning them on behalf of their own currency reform, which they immediately determined to introduce in Bizonia on June 1. Presumably secret, probably only the date was unknown to the Russians. In every meaningful sense, it was the United States that destroyed the Control Council.

While the Americans were drawing up the final plans for a partition, but before the Russians walked out of the Control Council, Clay sent his famous cable to Washington on the new "tenseness" he sensed in his relations with the Russians.[20] It was during this period, as well, that Truman was encountering growing congressional resistance to his budgetary requests, and on March 17 he made his emotional appeal to Congress on the intangible Russian menace. And during these same weeks, we must recall, the Soviet peace scare accompanied the German events, causing consternation in the Executive. "But the next steps," *Business Week* in mid-May commented about Truman's larger program, " . . . can't get through without the aid of another crisis. . . ." Before the Russians released the Smith-Molotov exchange, it added, " . . . you could sort of smell a crisis being shaped up."[21] Whatever else was happening in Germany, the Russians were also on a peace offensive that Washington ultimately feared as much as, if not more than, the events around Berlin itself. The United States elected for the certain, predictable crisis, confident that its decisive military and material advantage would eliminate the threat of war.

On March 30 the Russians refused to allow American, British, and French troop trains to go to Berlin without Soviet inspection, beginning a graduated process of closing off various means of ground transportation that was to reach its climax in June. There was nothing surprising about the action, for which American officers had prepared shortly before the event itself. Months before, Clay himself had anticipated a Berlin crisis of some sort growing out of the United States' contemplated measures. The Soviets immediately made it clear that their restrictions would keep pace with the Anglo-American plans for a final partition. After April 20, when the Western powers convened in London for a month and one-half to reach a final accord, they gave those plans form. "The Russians certainly gave us plenty of warning about the Berlin blockade," Murphy later recalled.[22] He and Clay advised Washington to smash through temporary road blockades —a proposition that only caused Washington to consider the issues more carefully. Clay and his superiors were certain that the Russians were prepared, if necessary, to isolate Berlin's civilian population as well. Indeed, the army feared the Soviets might also cut off Vienna. In April they were fairly confident that they could supply Berlin by air. It was not that the Russians were unjustified, for as Secretary of the Army Kenneth Royall put it, the collapse of four-power control gave the Soviets " . . . some basis for their argument." The point was that the ERP's imperatives " . . . cannot permit continued stagnation in [Germany]. . . ."[23] A manageable crisis that did not lead to war also had useful domestic consequences in spurring on Congress.

Most German leaders disapproved of this strategy, before and immediately after the full-scale Berlin crisis. America's highly publicized favorites, such as the Socialist mayor of Berlin, Ernst Reuter, were really exceptions to this rule. Throughout the spring and summer of 1948 both the CDU and the SPD strongly and openly attacked the new political reforms that the Anglo-Americans proposed as both inadequate and perpetuating indefinitely the division of Germany. At the same time, the strong federalist basis the United States imposed on political reorganization was so obviously intended to curb state-wide socialist legislation that the Germans rightfully felt manipulated. The Germans could see currency reform coming, and the German anti-Soviet press largely opposed it as permanently truncating Germany. When the London Conference on June 2 released its recommendations, they were clearly premised on German economic division which only a currency reform could implement. The reform itself, nominally secret, was postponed to June 20 to incorporate the French zone, but rumors of the impending act were widespread. The Berlin City Assembly on June 16 severely attacked the London proposals. That same day, as well, the Russians withdrew from the Four Power Berlin Kommandatura, allegedly over the behavior of the American representative who was relieved they had not exploited the impending currency reform—" . . . a very good excuse for a walkout."[24] Two days later, the Western authorities announced a currency reform.

The Russian response to the currency reform was fully expected. On June 19 they banned the use of the new Western marks in their zone or the

Western-controlled sectors of Berlin, and over the next week they imposed a nearly total embargo on ground traffic in and out of Berlin. Clay and the British then imposed a yet more stringent counterblockade on all of East Germany. Although the Americans had not originally planned to introduce their new currency into Berlin, on June 23 the Russians introduced a new mark in their own zone and the following day the United States extended their new currency to West Berlin. The next day, as well, the Russians and their Eastern allies vainly called for a general settlement on all German questions. No one ever doubted that Berlin itself was a side issue and that the nub of the controversy was the future of Germany.

Discomfort over the crisis was especially acute in Paris, where the French, most reluctantly, had gone along with the reform and then developed a deep fear of the American tactics in Germany. From this time onward the French were inclined toward a graceful withdrawal from Berlin, while the British counseled a middle course. Among Germans, the unhappiness was ever deeper. The Berlin City Assembly, including the three largest anti-Communist parties, during the first several weeks strongly condemned the currency reform for permanently splitting Germany, and the SPD attacked both its economic and its political consequences. Concern for local feelings, however, played no part in American or Soviet policy, and both sides intensified their practice of eliminating Germans who opposed their will—ultimately to support only those who would condone everything they did.[25]

Clay did not expect armed conflict and was confident of his ability to air-lift necessary supplies, at least for the time. But Washington was less certain of its ultimate course and goals, and over the following weeks it had to define a strategy for the occasion. The Soviets' elimination on June 29 of the travel ban on Germans, and their indifference for months toward the significant traffic in goods surreptitiously pouring into Berlin from the surrounding countryside, probably lowered excitability in Washington. On July 6 Washington sent the Kremlin a note justifying three-power presence in Berlin on the joint victory over Germany as well as "implied" treaty rights. The United States would discuss the problems of Berlin in conference only after the Russians lifted the blockade. The Russians retorted that the Berlin question was inseparable from the problem of Germany, that all agreements on which the United States based its rights were premised on a four-power control which currency reform had destroyed, and that Russia would be glad to negotiate the larger German problem without Western preconditions. But the American leaders chose their course quite independently of diplomatic notes, in which they never had much faith.[26]

Truman immediately decided that the United States would keep its forces in Berlin, but he was less certain of the ultimate price that he was willing to pay. The next critical weeks presented options to him. The men in Berlin, Clay and Murphy, returned to Washington and urged the President to give prior warning and send an armed convoy through the blockade to open ground access, and that the United States fight if it met resistance. Forrestal also supported this position, and later was rumored to have favored using atomic bombs if necessary. In the State Department, only Dean Rusk favored such stern action. But the general mood was against additional adventures that might risk world war. Truman consulted the Joint Chiefs, Marshall, the British, and the French, all of whom opposed forcing open the ground routes out of uncertainty as to the Soviet response. Senators Connally and Vandenberg threw their weight behind exclusive reliance on an air lift. Dulles believed the " . . . Soviet leaders did not want war," but also that they might not retreat unless the United States provided them a reasonable path.[27] The State Department was also convinced the Russians did not want war. It was Dulles who suggested testing Soviet intentions via a controlled crisis. To prevent a Russian miscalculation, he added, they should informally tell them what to expect.

Ultimately, the administration applied something like a synthesis of these views. It decided not to leave Berlin voluntarily, to rely on the air lift, but to avoid a military confrontation on the ground. At the same time, Washington dispatched two additional B-29 groups to England capable of striking Russia with atomic bombs. They intended to attempt diplomacy as well, but to make no substantive concessions. These tactics prevailed over the summer, although Clay remained convinced that the issue was worth the risk of armed conflict, and later a preventive war group emerged around Air Force General Curtis LeMay and lesser officers.[28]

In the fruitless negotiations that took place during the following months the United States sought to concentrate on the immediate issue of the Berlin blockade, while the Russians attempted futilely to discuss the entire German problem. An irritating round of talks between Ambassador Smith and various Kremlin leaders quickly brought this out at the end of July. Then, on August 2, Smith saw Stalin and found him more genial and compromising than his subordinates. The Russian asked again to discuss the larger issue of Germany, but on this the United States representatives could concede nothing. The American version of the meeting, however, alleges that Stalin then said that if the United States permitted the introduction of the new East German mark into West Berlin he would remove the blockade. He added, no longer as a condition but as an "insistent wish," that the West defer implementation of the London decisions.[29] The news reinforced the belief of many in Washington that Soviet difficulties in Europe were forcing them to back down before America's intransigent stance. But when Smith and Molotov sat down to work out details, Smith was bound not to allow the unconditional introduction of the East German mark into Berlin, but first to extend four-power control over its supply. From the Soviet viewpoint, this gave the Western powers a handle to control currency in all of East Germany, but from the American it prevented the way to Soviet domination of West Berlin's economy. The Russians agreed to four-power control in principle, but insisted that they would remove only those controls on traffic imposed after June 18, leaving earlier restrictions until the West suspended the London decisions. And they also asked for a Council of Foreign Ministers meeting on Germany. Basically, of course, for the United States there was nothing to negotiate, for it had embarked on the partition of Germany and conceding to the Russian demands to discuss Berlin in that larger context was never acceptable to Washington. The negotiations, with recriminations back and forth, failed; the controversy's focus returned to Berlin's air lanes; and the crisis—whose outcome Washington thought reasonably predictable and acceptable—continued.

During August the Russians persisted in linking the blockade to the London decisions. American officials at the time claimed that Stalin made concessions which his officials withdrew; but apart from the Russian leader's statements' being vague enough for conflicting interpretations, the Soviet definitions of them were fully consistent with their long-standing position on Germany. Close reading of the State Department's account belies its claims that the Russians retracted on an agreed communiqué, or that they reached an understanding independent of agreement on the future of the London recommendations—on which the United States would concede nothing. Over the coming weeks, despite a deepening tension in Washington, neither side budged from its position, while the United States made explicit its hitherto implied stand that Western marks be accepted in all of Berlin at parity with East German currency. To the United States' leaders their diplomatic failure, which was predictable given new American demands, was more than offset by their growing confidence that the immediate crisis would be overcome by continuing for as long as necessary what proved to be an adequate air lift with which the Russians had not materially interfered in any significant manner. The Russians, with justification, could now claim that they had made the most concessions, and even the British and French governments urged the United States to soften both its language and its position. Their reticence, however, did not prevent their going along with Washington's rupture of the talks on September 22 and referral of the matter to the Security Council.[30]

Truman's handling of the Berlin crisis had not gone well, considering the impending presidential election. There had been far too much talk of use of the atomic bomb, even though no one seriously expected a war. Henry Wallace's Progressive campaign centering on the issue of United States belligerence so frightened the President at the beginning of October that he considered sending Chief Justice Fred Vinson to have a long conference with Stalin. The proposal was so patently political that Vinson himself was most reluctant, while Marshall strongly objected. Then when the plan leaked to the press, bringing a storm of accusations, Truman backed off. The alternative, which he also eventually rejected, was to have a personal telephone conference with Stalin. Truman's aborted gesture was a reflection of America's failure to convince both public opinion and its allies that it could justify its Berlin position. Although the Russians at first insisted that the Security Council had no jurisdiction over the Berlin issue, which properly belonged with the Council of Foreign Ministers, the neutral states in the conflict soon began to advance compromises increasingly close to the Soviet position and irritating to the United States. It was not long before Stalin and the Russians could claim that only they stood for the accords reached with the United States the preceding August, and were ready to agree to UN-sponsored concessions. In fact the United States now was forced into discouraging UN mediation in which the Russians, British, and French found increasing hope. At the end of November the State Department instructed Philip Jessup, its representative in the UN, that the termination of the blockade was a precondition of negotiations—closing off the UN as an avenue of settlement. During November, as well, key American diplomats concluded that the Russians would now accept a face-saving formula, and Soviet approval of the substance and most of the details of the final UN mediation plan at the end of 1948 and beginning of 1949 proved it. But since the compromise was based on four-power operation of the currency mechanism, a position the United States now openly rejected, it was necessary for the United States to suffer the embarrassment of rejecting the UN plan.[31]

By the end of 1948 the Berlin blockade was proving a political blessing in disguise to the administration, for Washington had no fears of real danger arising from it. The blockade had provided an always available but manageable crisis for recalcitrant domestic and foreign politicians alike; it conjured up a sufficiently ominous Soviet presence to afford a justification for its other expansive policies hitherto lacking; the counterblockade probably damaged East Germany's economic program far more than the West's; and it disarmed the German non-Communist parties in a manner that brought to the fore latent Social Democratic animosity toward the Communists. *Business Week* was entirely correct in December 1948 when it reported, "U.S. policy-makers aren't anxious to see the United Nations Security Council come up just yet with a 'face-saving' formula for the Berlin dispute," and when they did the United States rejected it, even though it embodied principles America had earlier advanced.[32] By the end of 1948 Germany had been divided spiritually and economically, the Russians no longer could do anything more to reverse that fact, and they probably perceived the futility of a strategy intended to attain a now impossible goal. A solution to the Berlin question, as *Pravda* freely admitted several times during February with a reasoning Russia's leaders must have carefully pondered, would deprive the United States of its main justification for belligerence. In this context, and given the steps already taken to merge the West German zones politically, Russia had everything to gain by a quick settlement—in any form—of the Berlin blockade.

The nominal reason was an alleged hint Stalin is supposed to have given Kingsbury Smith, an American journalist, at the end of January when he failed to mention reversing the currency reform as a specific precondition for the end of the blockade. Stalin's statement was ambiguous on "trade" questions, however, and Philip Jessup asked the Russians secretly on February 15 whether specific omission of the currency question from the interview had significance. By that time, however, Acheson had made it clear that nothing Moscow might say would halt America's plans for Germany. The Soviets, for their part, took one whole month to convey the message that Stalin's declaration was indeed a hint and that they would like to convene a Council of Foreign Ministers meeting to consider Germany, and then took another week to let the Americans know that they would lift the blockade in return for a council meeting as well as postponement of the formation of a West German government. At first the United States told the Russians that the West would continue but not complete the preparations for a new government, but it soon withdrew from this concession as well, and revealed there was no urgency at all to the removal of the blockade. Indeed, the blockade had so well served to mobilize reticent elements that Bevin in April suggested that its prolongation for a time might help NATO's ratification everywhere. But the Russians retreated again, sensing full well that the wily Americans were in no hurry. On May 4 the two nations announced that the Soviets would unconditionally lift the blockade on the twelfth and that the Council of Foreign Ministers would convene in Paris on May 23. Though the council was to make significant progress toward an Austrian peace treaty, it made none whatsoever on Germany. The Russians had suffered an ignominious diplomatic defeat.[33]

Indeed, as we shall see, the Berlin episode served the administration's policy well on NATO and numerous other issues. This same fear of premature peace in Germany permeated the speed with which the United States rammed through West Germany's political reorganization. The Germans had been considering a Basic Law, as they called the surrogate for a constitution, which in February 1949 Clay and his aides thought placed too much power in the hands of a central government, thereby opening the door to socialism. Federalism, however, became a device whereby the local and central governments were both denied economic functions indispensable to socialist planning. During March, with increasing urgency, the draft law was rewritten to reduce controls on industry, and it gave to a future Three Power High Commission on omnibus authority over foreign and military affairs, or ". . . internal actions which would increase external financial assistance," which made the new West Germany barely more than a client state.[34] At the end of April, Washington told Clay to hasten the formation of a consolidated West Germany, and as he acted to neutralize and divide SPD opposition he would not let them water down the decentralized organizational principles in the Basic Law standing as a durable barrier to socialism. Unceremoniously pushed along, on May 8 the Parliamentary Council, headed by Konrad Adenauer, passed the Basic Law.

By this time, the SPD had been so deeply traumatized by the Berlin events so as to be ready to accept some illusory concessions and make one of those fundamental compromises with existing authority which are recurrent features of that party's history. In the various state Länder over the following weeks it joined with the CDU to ratify the Basic Law. When the Russians met their adversaries in Paris, the Americans had violated their informal pledge not to create a new state. In August there followed elections in which the CDU obtained 31 percent of the vote, while the SPD won 29.2 percent and emerged the largest party in four of the eleven states. "We naturally welcome the results of this election insofar as they indicate a decision by the Germans to seek a solution of their economic difficulties through a system of free enterprise," Acheson immediately commented.[35] Had Germany been reunited, and the traditional SPD stronghold in the east been part of the election, he would not have been able to claim the victory. But the division of Germany was now complete.

The Formation of NATO

The Brussels Pact had been the product of confusion as to its enemy's identity and the strategy with which it was to be fought. Was it a resurgent Germany, Russian aggression, or internal revolution that the new alliance most feared? For the United States, whose strategic concept blithely assumed the superiority of an air and naval power which Western Europe could neither afford nor require, the Brussels Pact's virtue as a balance to Russian military power was the least weighty of its assets. Nor was it clear how the pact, or the subsequent Vandenberg Resolution, obligated those pledged to it. All these profound political and military ambiguities, which struck to the core of the Brussels Pact and its NATO successor, became intrinsic parts of the United States–Western European alliance down to this day.

By mid-1948 all Washington was certain of was only that it had pledged to enter into further talks with the Brussels Pact nations, and it immediately suggested that they include the Scandinavian countries, Italy, Portugal, Canada—and later Germany and Spain—in the discussion. These meetings took place during the Berlin crisis at a time when Washington assumed that Russia was not ready to embark on war and also when it considered ERP to have the far greater priority for all concerned. Budgetary constraints, as well, forbade anything more than modest military assistance to Western Europe, a step that was planned independently and well before the formation of NATO. By September, Canada and the Brussels Pact nations were pushing the United States to sign a North Atlantic pact along the lines of the vague Brussels treaty, adding that the magnitude of aid given in case of an attack would be determined by each nation's usual constitutional procedure. It was not merely nominal military aid the Europeans wanted, but a pledge, in effect, to enter a war on their side should Congress approve.[36]

Against whom was the pact directed? It was perfectly clear by the summer of 1948 that the United States was quite willing to fight Russia in Europe should it initiate the explicitly unanticipated, and it was the United

States that had dragged England and France along on the Berlin adventure. NATO's formation, therefore, was much more the outcome of Europe's desire to prevent a resurgent Germany from yet again disturbing the peace, to which the United States added its desire to strengthen Western Europe's ability to cope with internal revolt as well as to sustain a psychological mood of anti-Soviet tension that the administration thought functional. Moreover, the Europeans were now subjecting the United States to a polite degree of blackmail by exploiting its fear of losing allies.

Since, as America's leaders assumed, Russia was clearly not going to start a war, it was plain to all that the real Communist danger in Western Europe was internal—through either rebellion or a victory at the polls. Kennan argued this to Marshall in November 1948, and Vandenberg—who was a prime mover of the NATO legislation—surely also believed it. It was not, Vandenberg admitted, that NATO could mount an existing force capable of discouraging Russia; to bring its existing army to a state of maximum efficiency was ". . . chiefly for the *practical* purpose of assuring adequate defense against internal subversion."[37] NATO had only the potential some-day to become militarily significant. Western Europe's arms had to be ". . . adequate to control disorders and to convince an aggressor that he would pay dearly," the State Department publicly observed during May.[38] But *coups* aided by outside nations, Acheson admitted, they would consider aggression. That NATO without United States intervention would scarcely have military value against a Soviet advance was made patently clear when senators pressed the generals in the April and May hearings.

Dulles barely concealed his belief that Russia was the least of NATO's concerns; "I do not know of any responsible high official, military or civilian," he told the Senate hearings in early May, ". . . in this Government or any other government, who believes that the Soviet now plans conquest by open military aggression."[39] Indeed, months before, it had been reported that Dulles was for the exclusion of Denmark and Norway from NATO for fear their proximity to Soviet borders would be too provocative. The major problem, as he privately defined it, was Germany. Western Europe had to be strengthened militarily in order to prevent its fear of Germany rather than Russia from becoming the motivating force of its foreign policy. Otherwise, France surely would turn the German menace into the central issue of its national politics. To Dulles, therefore, Germany's permanent division and continued foreign military occupation of its soil were essential. An Atlantic Pact including the United States could integrate a truncated Germany into the West without its overpowering its neighbors. A Germany that was rebuilt and not muzzled in some manner or other, Dulles was always anxiously to fear, would be in a position to form a temporary alliance with Russia and divide Europe with it.

Beyond NATO's value in containing Germany and internal disorder, it had another vital rationale. America's participation in what was essentially an offshoot of the Western European bloc impulse could prevent Germany from becoming a political or economic rival. The Atlantic Union Committee, of which Clayton was vice-chairman and which had powerful export-oriented big business backing, argued that NATO was a logical successor of ECA that would, in turn, open the way for a kind of federal union of white, democratic, and capitalist nations that would lower trade barriers and promote economic expansion. So important and well placed was this group, including as it did former Secretary of War Patterson and former Chief Justice Owen J. Roberts, that its arguments to Congress weighed heavily. Yet Senate ratification was never in doubt, despite the profound legal and constitutional arguments Senator Taft and his school advanced, and despite their minute dissection of its contradictions and ambiguities. Taft thought that NATO was a provocation of Russia, that the inclusion of Portugal made a sham of its pretense to defend democracy, and that it would become a constricting millstone for decades. Only twelve other senators were to support his opposition when the vote was taken the following July.[40]

The NATO bill carried no appropriations with it, promised neither troops nor military aid, contained no hint of integrated military forces, and transferred no Constitutional authority to the Executive or foreign states. Yet it was, as predicted at the time, one of the most far-reaching commitments the United States had ever made, and its ambiguities opened the door to later adventures that probably not even Acheson foresaw at the time. Insofar as it was the product of Western European cajolement it was a reflection of America's fear of losing its allies. But ultimately the United States in turn wished to see NATO emerge, even to the extent of threatening to cut off arms sales to the reluctant Danes and Norwegians should they not join, also to sustain the psychological momentum against Russia it was building up in Congress and in Britain and France—a mood that would free the administration from the inhibitions those reticent constituencies had often imposed in the past. "This is the time of all times," Vandenberg reflected, "to keep up our peace momentum in Western Europe and not let down for a single instant—which means ECA, Atlantic Pact and arms implementation. . . ."[41] It was at this point that Bevin thought a prolongation of the Berlin blockade might sustain the mood advantageously. By this time, Acheson admitted to a closed group of senators prior to embarking for the Paris Conference of Foreign Ministers, "It is not our intention, no matter how much we may desire agreement, to accept anything which would tend to undo what has been accomplished."[42] The secretary, Vandenberg observed, ". . . is so *totally* anti-Soviet and is going to be so *completely* tough that I really doubt whether there is any chance *at all* for a Paris agreement."[43] So tough, indeed, was Acheson to the defensive Vyshinsky that America's terms on Germany irrevocably closed the doors to a German reunification that it no longer desired.

From the viewpoint of its strategic assumptions on external combat, NATO was a hodgepodge of conflicting theories which have yet to be reconciled and at the time contradicted the United States' primary reliance on air and sea power. It was rational, in the peculiar eyes of its proponents, only for Germany, revolution, and, ultimately, colonial wars and conflicts among small powers. The Portuguese could suppress the Angolans, the Greeks and Turks could threaten each other, and, above all, French colonialism could survive a while longer in Algeria and Indochina. NATO, Acheson made clear, treated Algeria as ". . . a part of metropolitan France."[44] Washington had favored moderate arms aid to Western Europe since mid-1948, and the imperative economic reasons for actually initiating and sustaining it a year later we discuss in Chapter 17. But arms aid was conceived as something entirely independent of NATO, performing economic as well as martial functions, and even before the treaty was ratified it was public information that a large arms aid bill would be required in any event. The French were very frank that a pact without arms was useless and that they would need abundant equipment. Truman asked for $1.4 billion worth as soon as NATO was ratified.

The hearings on arms aid revealed much of America's larger strategic and political thinking by the summer of 1949. ". . . [T]here can be no question about a race to catch up with the Russians," Acheson admitted, "for that can never be done. . . . Europe cannot support large forces." Indeed, since Acheson saw no imminent Soviet threat at all, he was trapped by contradictions in the purely military rationale for arms aid. What was essential, at that point, was to communicate a sense ". . . that the state of the world at the present time is a very sorry one. It is certainly not a condition which allows anybody to relax or think that all is well. . . . I do not think that the peacetime world has ever been in a more troubled state than it is now, or a more hazardous one."[45] But the hazard was not from Russia, it must be observed, but from the economic and social condition of the world and the desire in the United States to have an end to the frightful postwar tensions associated with its imperial aspirations.

For a fleeting moment in their long struggle for mastery, America's leaders now saw success in the contest with Russia even as they found little solace in their more ambitious aims for the world's social and economic system. Berlin had been an American victory, and the anxiety it produced was critical for the much larger global program for which Russia had increasingly served as a convenient excuse. The end of the Berlin blockade and new Soviet peace offensives posed a political danger to programs that required money. If belligerence produced tension, it also overcame resistance at home. "There is a natural and understandable temptation, as the advantage moves to us, to relax from relief, to economize, and to turn to other problems," General Omar Bradley told the Senate during early August. "But seizure of the initiative is then most important, and the momentum there gained has meant victory. . . . This is that moment for us in our position of leadership in world affairs."[46]

The Russian Problem, 1949

By the end of 1948, as the USSR again and again retreated from earlier positions to facilitate a Berlin settlement, it was undoubtedly apparent to the Russians that Washington was exploiting their alleged bellicosity to advance its own expansive military and economic plans. To many key American leaders it was no less clear that Russia posed a quite manageable military problem and that it was far more dangerous, at least in the short run, anxiously seeking peace rather than firmly defending its national interests, much less its ideological commitments, in a manner which conflicted with American goals. The Russians drew the only rational conclusions from this, and at the beginning of 1949 they not only ignominiously withdrew all their immediate demands on Germany but also embarked on an overwhelming world peace propaganda campaign.

At home, the Kremlin refused to panic the population with predictions of war, but also made it plain that it believed the United States and its allies had embarked on an aggressive, though fruitless, policy of threatening war. For despite American preparations for conflict, the Russians and the Communist parties now saturated the world with the belief that coexistence between the great powers was attainable, even inevitable, if the peoples of the world struggled for peace. The World Peace Congress in April 1949 was the beginning of a vast and sustained crescendo of peace agitation that implied that by wishing hard enough one could make it so.

In fact, Stalin's January 1949 interview on Berlin also made much of his willingness to enter into a nonaggression pact with the United States, have a personal conference with Truman, and reach a disarmament agreement. One must add, as well, that the Russians also often referred to their formidable, if purely defensive, military capacity. There can be little doubt that the peace campaign had some impact on Washington, if only the irritating one of forcing it to conjure up new alleged Soviet threats. Allusions to military capabilities undoubtedly were taken far more seriously, for Washington was quite confident of Soviet intentions—which the peace campaigns further clarified in a reassuring manner.[47]

By early 1949 Washington assumed that the Russians and their bloc were encountering major economic difficulties and seeking a respite from international tensions to solve domestic problems. Even though official American speeches marshaled anti-Communism as an article of faith and attached formidable, even mystical, powers to Russia, it is clear that Washington thought it had gained the initiative in world affairs and that sustaining its momentum, even by falsely asserting the presence of spurious dangers, was vital. Informal overtures from the Russians during April regarding their desire to reach a *détente,* with the aim of suspending key NATO clauses, probably strengthened Acheson's resolve to get on with his mobilization. At the Paris Foreign Ministers Conference, Dulles reported to Vandenberg, Vyshinsky gave the impression of being "really a pathetic figure," and "They evidently know they have lost the cold war in Western Europe."[48] Russia's goals in Europe, Dulles even made public the next month, were essentially dependent on nonmilitary means for their attainment. Ironically, the more the Russians agitated for peace, the weaker American leaders thought them to be in material terms and the more disingenuous and dangerous as a political threat. But the appearance of Soviet strength also offered short-term advantages for America's programs that might otherwise flounder.

At the end of August, when Russia looked the weakest and most defensive to the United States, it exploded its first atomic bomb, and on September 23 Truman announced the event. The Russians immediately admitted the fact and, probably falsely, claimed to have possessed the weapon since 1947. Truman's timing of the announcement, Connally later recalled, was successfully designed to spur the House into restoring several hundred million dollars cut off the arms-aid-for-Europe bill. It was not the first or last occasion that Washington exploited a convenient crisis to dissolve resistance to implementing its policy.

For the Russians, the acquisition of the bomb was an important fact which they never minimized, as their immediate intimation that they had a stockpile revealed. Basically, however, the Soviet peace offensive continued unabated, with the themes of atomic disarmament and coexistence saturating Russian and European Communist statements. Its official position was that war in Europe was virtually impossible, but that national liberation movements in the Third World, including the national bourgeoisie, were certain to continue and succeed in coming years. Moscow did not say, however, that it would materially contribute to that ultimate triumph, and it did not believe that weapons altered the far more critical underlying economic and social forces of change in the world. As Kennan argued at the time, the Soviets believed that capitalism would inevitably destroy itself and that there was no need for the Red army to intervene in this process at the risk of world war. The Russians were politically expansionist, according to this view, but that was all. It was this political faith underlying Soviet foreign policy that assured that its professions of noninterference reflected genuine ideological commitments which in the end might be more constraining on Russian conduct than external material forces.[49]

The Arms Race

Politically unencumbered as never before, during late 1949 the Truman administration confronted that improbable congruence of economic and military circumstances which forced it to consider a qualitative new increase in its arms budget. For the Russian acquisition of the atomic bomb threatened to become the great equalizer of global military power—the balance of terror.

Every strategy has a price tag, and the United States could control its arms spending for purely military reasons so long as it had limited and attainable foreign policy objectives. At the same time, the military budget had an economic function, which also defined in a very critical manner the level of expenditures. Until 1949 the Pentagon, for the most part, had a confident sense of military adequacy within the framework of a military budget the administration imposed on it. For fiscal 1950, which began in mid-1949, that budget was $14.4 billion, and although the three branches of the military also calculated a maximum "ideal" budget of about $9 billion more, they obediently worked within the given limits. There was nothing inherently militarily rational or adequate about this budget. It was merely what was most utilitarian to the country's economic needs and political possibilities at the time. Forrestal himself, who strongly favored an additional $3 billion for the military, even more emphatically admired the conservative economic reasoning that led to his requests' being rejected: ". . . we can't afford to wreck our economy in the process of trying to fight the 'cold war. . . .' "[50]

The only alternative for the three military services was to turn on each other in an attempt to carve out a greater share of the limited budget for themselves. This process of bickering, which guaranteed unchallenged civilian supremacy over the military, was a constant factor in the postwar era that in late 1948 and 1949 became a public scandal in the form of the so-called "B-36" controversy. Nominally a continuation of the debate over the relative merits of long-range bombers and the navy's projected supercarriers, which had been officially resolved to the air force's favor in September 1948, the main significance of the affair was why civilians fix ceilings which force military men into bitter rivalries. In fact, the B-36 debate, despite the navy's disingenuous reliance on arguments more appropriate for pacifists than admirals, merely showed that both services were offering different methods for delivery of the atomic bomb and that their mutual ultimate strategic dependence on it was total. Apart from the fact that the B-36 was a mediocre bomber that even the air force regarded as inadequate, the hearings revealed the intimate personal and business relations between each service and its contractors and the willingness of the administration to let contracts for even inferior weapons to maintain an industrial mobilization potential for later developments. The army's defensive justification for its own future in war, especially in its early stages, was perhaps one measure of how dependent on the bomb the Pentagon had become in both its psychology and its planning.[51] Ironically, the Americans and their allies were at that very time organizing NATO around a strategic doctrine that had precious little credence in Washington for a war against Russia—a fact which only reinforced the then prevailing belief that NATO would serve very different functions than the one it was later wholly reputed to have been organized to perform.

Ultimately, what was most significant about the B-36 controversy was that it revealed a near unanimity among military and civilians alike that, to quote General Omar Bradley, chairman of the Joint Chiefs of Staff, ". . . a nation's economy is its ultimate strength," and that appropriations entirely controlled military policy.[52] But by the end of 1949 economic necessities and military realities were outstripping the embarrassing public search for a coherent doctrine on which to base American military power. Yet the moral that economics defined strategy was not to alter.

The Soviet atomic bomb explosion also shattered the supreme sense of military and political self-confidence that had prevailed in Washington during much of 1949. American political and military policy's basic assumptions and premises were scrutinized during a long and anxious reappraisal of the balance of power in the world.

The shock of the event penetrated very deeply, and the loss of China and the realization it had shifted the balance of power in Asia only compounded the depression that was quite general in Washington at the end of 1949. Acheson took the revelation of America's limits especially hard, and he authorized his Policy Planning Staff under Kennan to begin a grand reappraisal of the United States' position in the world. But Kennan was clearly out of tune with the dominant mood as he argued that he did not expect the Russians to embark on military adventures and that so long as the United States retained control of Germany, Japan, and the NATO countries, it would also retain mastery over the key elements of world power. For allegedly personal reasons, Paul Nitze replaced him at the end of the year, and since his inclinations were closer to Acheson's, they were able to pursue their great reformulation in agreement.

There could not be many surprises in that search. The B-36 controversy had revealed how totally American military planning depended on strategic atomic bombing, and its foreign policy had shown that it was ready to confront Russia only with superior power. Now the only question was how quickly the administration would embark on the construction of the hydrogen bomb. Since economics was still the great inhibitor, the American generals thought it was too costly for the United States to match Russia's ground forces, and only the thermonuclear bomb was consistent with a qualitative increase in military power at relatively modest cost. Hesitancy over making the decision to build the H-bomb was due largely to the debate whether it could be technically accomplished or whether its cost might be better applied to other weapons, and every precedent prejudged the outcome once the scientific question was decided affirmatively. For at the end of November the Joint Chiefs of Staff decided that they wanted the H-bomb if it could be built.

The argument of a small minority of key decision-makers such as David

Lilienthal that reliance on total destruction would unbalance America's military power presumed only a limited budget. Militarily, however, it was persuasive insofar as it suggested that something less than total apocalypse was possible. For all that this argument suggested to men such as Acheson was that the United States should construct other forms of military power in addition to the H-bomb. By December, when Acheson decided that he would recommend work on the H-bomb, he was convinced that much else would also be required. From this point onward he far surpassed the military in eagerness for greater military preparations. For while the Pentagon planned mainly for a total war, Acheson was beginning also to calculate on the less grandiose—and more expensive.[53]

The large majority of Truman's advisers had made the decision to proceed with the H-bomb even before the Klaus Fuchs espionage case in England at the very end of January revealed that the Russians knew of the American debate over the technical problems of building the H-bomb. It was thought not only that Russia would be far less able to afford the arms race, and take considerably longer to match the weapon, but that it was essential to restore the weapons mastery over Soviet land power in Europe. Technically, Truman on January 31 approved his advisers' unanimous recommendation the he authorize a study to determine whether the scientists could build the H-bomb, but there was little question that a solution of the technical problems would then lead to the bomb's becoming the mainstay of America's strategic policy. Indeed, since he made the decision public at the time there would be no doubt what would happen when, as the following March, the eager scientists predicted they could test the first H-bomb by late 1952. They were told also to begin plans for quantity H-bomb production. At the same time, Truman authorized Acheson to cooperate with the Pentagon in expanding his policy inquiry into a full-scale review of America's global military and political objectives that they were eventually to title the still-classified "NSC–68."[54]

The State Department turned NSC–68 into its own forum, and assigned Nitze chairmanship of the inquiry. The paper unquestionably reflected Acheson's world view and his publicly stated belief that there was nothing worth negotiating with Russia until it withdrew from Eastern Europe, foreswore "indirect aggression," and ceased expounding a Marxist view of capitalist motives.[55] Enough has been leaked on the contents of NSC–68 to reveal that it simply discarded all alternatives save relating to Moscow from a position of overwhelming and defining power, and assumed that Russia had embarked on a campaign of world domination. But the document was not merely a pedestrian ideological tract. It made specific weapons proposals which would have given the United States a greater limited war capability without abandoning its main reliance on an expanded capacity for strategic bombing, urged a build-up in the ground forces of both the United States and Western Europe, and probably assigned priorities to America's global interests—with Europe at the top of the list. The paper went to Truman at the beginning of April 1950 without any cost estimates attached to it, and although the President approved it he also asked for figures.

The Joint Chiefs of Staff and Defense Secretary Louis Johnson mulled over the price and decided that they could defend America's national security, within NSC–68's premises, by adding another four to five billion dollars to the existing military expenditures—or a maximum of $18 billion. But the State Department, far more keenly aware of the world economic trends and armament's role in advancing United States economic goals in Europe, offered a budget of up to $50 billion a year along with the novel principle that the United States ought effectively to scrap budget ceilings. Truman again approved the paper, but without deciding on the optional figures. Truman himself was still inclined to lower the budget, and probably made no commitment other than those of principle when he signed NSC–68. No significant decision was made on implementing the policy until Korea moved it from the abstract to the feasible.

If politics is the art of the possible, Acheson's main dilemma in implementing what was surely his program—even since 1946—was how to pay for it all. That challenge was freely discussed at the time. The lost momentum and confidence in the success of America's course of mid-1949 had somehow to be restored and geared to far more ambitious and costly undertakings, even as its failures in the economic sphere made such expenditures especially timely. Given deepening public apathy and congressional reticence, the goal appeared unattainable in the spring of 1950.[56] But fixed budget planning is possible only when there are a stable economic, political, and military environment and limited goals. Without these, there was theoretically no end to what the United States might pay to contain the forces of change and revolution continuing to spread throughout the world. In the spring of 1950, NSC–68 revealed that the civilians were far more martial than the generals when containment doctrine was failing to turn the political tide in Asia and sustain military mastery in Europe. The desire also to spend money as a tool of foreign economic policy as well was scarcely comprehensible to the docile military men. But now, galvanized by its own fears and needs, frustrations and ambitions, seeking tools for politically and economically managing Europe and the world, Washington had only to find the excuse to embark on that tortured, endless, and infinitely costly and dangerous arms race which terrorizes our civilization.

19

The Restoration of Japan

The year 1947 was as pivotal in American policy toward Japan as it was toward the rest of the world. Basically, the reorientation was a response to the paradoxes of the first two years of occupation, and Washington eventually resolved these contradictions through changes that paralleled the policies of the Marshall Plan, especially in regard to Germany. Although many have attributed the shift in policy to the events in China, few in Washington, even by 1945, believed that China offered much hope for American plans, and by 1947 such realistic pessimism was more than ever warranted. United States relations with Russia were also unrelated to the reappraisal of occupation policy which began to take place in Washington in 1947. While a strategic component will always, at some time and in varying degrees, enter the policy deliberations on nearly every critical question, Washington's considerations in Japan were first and foremost economic.

The paramount motivation in the United States' global policy in early 1947 was its urgent desire to restore a world capitalist trading structure that would operate independently of direct United States aid. Because it was engrossed in formulating the policy and organization that would prod and guide the economies and politics of the European states, Washington paid scant attention to the exceptional developments in Japan. Although the United States never doubted that the industrial potential of that Asian state would be critical in its over-all plans, the European crises had held America's primary focus. In 1947 a combination of pressures from the FEC and SCAP on the reparations question, the increasing costs of the occupation to the United States treasury, and from American businessmen with direct interests in Japan who were outraged by the implications of the deconcentration program and labor reforms—all thrust the Japanese problem to the forefront in the policy deliberations in Washington.

In Japan itself, American officials also had to reconsider the essential vulnerability of the old ruling class vis-à-vis the rest of the population as a result of the occupation-sponsored labor, police, industrial, and political reforms. There could be no peace treaty, and hence no relief from the costs, until the United States had fully restored political stability and, as in Europe, set the economy on a financially conservative foundation. The political and economic reforms, which the United States hastily inserted into occupation policy at the end of a protracted war, it now reappraised as expendable if they undermined the basis for social control of the essentially pro-American, capitalist ruling class. The policy was then said in Washington to have shifted its emphasis from reform to recovery. But, as in Europe, in the lexicon of the American men of power the concept of recovery held singular connotations, and we cannot use the word without bearing in mind their definition and how they formulated policies to achieve it. And being conservative, even within the context of capitalist economics, they persistently outlined recovery in terms of financial stability. But there were still other factors necessitating a reassessment.

In mid-January, Assistant Secretary of War William Draper sent a representative to Tokyo ". . . to observe the implications of existing policy (quantitatively and qualitatively), . . ." with the assumption that the United States must make new decisions unilaterally and that "[t]he present economy program of the Congress evidences the need for haste in reaching decision. . . . The Congress will not permit the present heavy cost of the occupation to continue very long and failure on the part of the War and State Departments to present a workable program to reduce expense can result in a sudden decision to withdraw from Japan, thereby losing all previous investment and endangering the future."[1] For economic and security reasons, and to keep Japan linked to a "capitalistic democracy," Draper's representative recommended that the United States halt reparations and that a new staff of economists replace those in Tokyo in order to develop an entirely new economic policy.[2]

Yet in the early months of 1947 these modifications of policy were only beginning to crystallize. In response to the pressures from SCAP on the reparations question, as well as the deadlock in the FEC, Washington also hired and dispatched a special commission of executives from the top eleven industrial engineering firms, headed by Clifford Strike, to survey the Japanese economy and the reparations issue. A number of the other members were old hands at reparations problems; Strike himself had been deputy chief of the German reparations section and R. J. Wysor was a former president of Republic Steel who had been head of the metals branch in the occupation of Germany. After a study lasting several months, the commission issued a report in April, for which the army paid them $750,000, that rejected all but a minor $79 million in reparations payments. It called for the complete rehabilitation of the very industries that the Pauley Commission had recommended be totally dismantled. And, most critically for future policy, the commission criticized all the democratic reforms as adding ". . . additional difficulties in the process of quickly achieving self-sufficiency."[3] The United States thereupon informed the irate members of the FEC that it insisted on reintegrating the economies of the enemy states into the international economy as the most promising method of reconstructing the world—as well as reducing the expense to the United States of indefinitely subsidizing Germany and Japan.

Economic Crisis and American Policy

By January 1947 the serious consequences of the Japanese government's economic policies were becoming ever more apparent. The food situation was again acute, for despite the excellent harvest in 1946 all the rice had been channeled into the black market. Reconstruction was impaired as resources were directed into nonessentials; the government increased its note issue to pay for its expenditures, which consisted chiefly of subsidies to nonproductive businesses; and the masses were hungry and increasingly restive as wages lagged far behind prices. While some in SCAP were acutely aware of Yoshida's lack of interest in altering his economic policy, it took the threat of a general strike to shake the confidence of MacArthur in the good faith of the government.

Living conditions were especially serious for the government workers in the railroads, postal, salt, and tobacco monopolies. These workers were well organized and militant, and they comprised over one-quarter of Japan's organized work force. Achieving nothing through collective bargaining, the government unions decided to call a general strike February 1, 1947, and it was widely anticipated that nearly four million workers, including sympathizers, would participate. Such a threat was too much for SCAP; on January 31, with approximately six hours' notice, MacArthur ordered the trade union leaders to cancel the strike.[4] Given the dangers of defying the occupation, the unions had no choice but to comply.

Coming at a time when Washington was reconsidering the basis and costs of its policies in Japan, the threat of a general strike caused some consternation, George Atcheson reported to the Allied Council after a trip to Washington. "I heard considerable surprise expressed that, in the midst of severe economic crisis, unions of Government employees should contemplate a strike which would be ruinous to Japanese economy. . . . The strike threat was generally regarded . . . as purely political in purpose. . . . The union members were regarded as dupes and tools of the aggressive minority which . . . has been manipulating unions in this country for selfish and ulterior political purposes."[5]

Although MacArthur canceled the strike, proving once again that he would act to curtail the unrest the economic activities of the government had generated, he expressed his disapproval of Yoshida's policies by calling for new elections in April, and on March 22 he reminded the Prime Minister of the Japanese obligations to stabilize the economy. SCAP then formally purged the reactionary finance minister, Tanzan Ishibashi. But with the occupation interceding to prevent strikes, and in other ways subsidizing the economy (such as providing two exchange rates for the yen for export and import trade), the Japanese government continued to have no incentive to change its policies. The United States was faced with the predicament of supporting a regime which, while politically desirable, was recklessly running up the costs of occupation.

While Washington was pursuing its own investigations of Tokyo's economic policies, MacArthur made what was apparently a unilateral and desperate move, given his hostility toward the Allied Council, and sent his economists to ask the council's advice on how to stabilize the economy. The Commonwealth representative, W. Macmahon Ball, believed this to be a SCAP acknowledgment of the failure of the policies of private enterprise, and he prepared a set of recommendations which emphasized strict controls on prices, restriction on profits, and the equitable distribution of goods as the only just means of controlling inflation.[6]

The economic philosophy on which Ball based his program, although not necessarily socialist, adhered to principles of equity which in Japan could receive support only from the Socialists and Communists and would certainly entail state control of all basic industries, with an emphasis on welfare and equality. It conflicted with Washington's aim of rebuilding a capitalist economy in Japan and Germany and highlighted the fact that the SCAP reforms were indeed quixotic—that the options in Japan were extremely narrow and had to rest on the power of one class or the other. Faced with this option, the United States made the only choice credible to it.

The elections in April 1947 gave SCAP what it thought to be another opportunity to reorient the economic and political trends in Japan. The voters returned a plurality for the Socialists, although the two conservative parties continued to hold a substantial majority in the Diet, and while the election indicated the unpopularity of the Liberal Party, it was hardly a shift to the left. One-half of the population lived in the country, and satisfied with the land reform and well fed, the peasantry gave their votes to the conservative "independents." Nevertheless, SCAP was anxious to change the economic policies of Yoshida and, confident that the balance in the Diet precluded a move toward socialism, it encouraged the Socialist Party to set up a coalition government with the conservative Democratic and People's Cooperative parties.

The irresolute Socialists, as anxious as their counterparts in Europe to grasp the illusion of power, so compromised their principles and program to retain the support of their conservative partners that they were unable to alter the course of an economy which only worsened considerably over the year. By June 1947, official food prices were three times higher than June 1946, and the black-market rate twenty times. Three-fourths of an average family's income went to essential food alone, and in June SCAP reduced the daily ration to 997 calories for two months. During the transitional year in the American approach to the problems in Japan, the Socialists either led the government in Tokyo or participated in it. And this fact proved to be of utterly no consequence for the course of events, except to disillusion those Japanese who had supported the party at the polls in the hope of achieving some relief from their serious economic plight.[7]

As both Washington and SCAP were reassessing the malaise in Japan, American business interests began to organize forceful pressure to halt and reverse the economic reform policies that the bureaucrats in SCAP were obliviously implementing in Tokyo. James Lee Kauffman, an American lawyer who represented United States investment interests in Japan, made the first public outcry against the reforms. He visited Tokyo in the summer of 1947 and submitted a report to the State and War departments. Ignoring the question of reparations, he vigorously attacked the new labor laws, the purges, and particularly the deconcentration of industry program—FEC–230—with its most startling provision providing for the sale of *zaibatsu* property to the trade unions (a good percentage of which were Communist-controlled). "Were economic conditions otherwise," Kauffman concluded, "I am convinced Japan would be a most attractive prospect for American industry. . . . Whether Japan can be made such a place depends . . . upon the willingness of our government to do two things: First, put an end to the economic experiment being conducted in Japan. Second, replace the theorists now there with men of ability and experience who can restore Japan's economy."[8] Such views only reinforced the prevailing concerns in Washington, especially in the context of extracting ever greater sums from an increasingly reluctant Congress.

In the months that followed, Tokyo was host to a whole series of visiting policy-makers, special commissions, and powerful business interests. After a trip to Tokyo in September, William Draper determined to reverse the deconcentration program in much the same way as he had in Germany. The Diet introduced SCAP's deconcentration bill on September 28, but following Draper's visit to Tokyo a request from Washington held it up pending a reevaluation of policy. The top men of power in Washington had been aware of the general policy of deconcentration, but not of its specifics. Once they learned, they were uniformly appalled. Forrestal reflected this exaggerated but real alarm when in October 1947 he wrote that ". . . the most vicious feature of the de–Zaibatsuing process in Japan was the regulation [in FEC–230] . . . that all plants, businesses, over a certain size were to be sold to small buyers, not on the basis of their worth but on the basis of what the buyer could afford to pay, with the result that a fifteen-thousand–dollar plant might be sold for seven-fifty. Another equally vicious feature is a provision by which labor unions are to elect the boards of directors and control management."[9] George Kennan and others in Washington raised the cry of socialism, which baffled the Japanese as much as it infuriated MacArthur.

There was a note of absurdity in referring to an effort to fashion a competitive, small business capitalism as socialism, but in a sense the alarmists were correct in assuming that it could only undermine Japanese conservatism. And the Communists and Socialists did support the antitrust measures as second best to nationalization and as a means of weakening the power of the ruling class while the occupation was still in control. By the fall of 1947, moreover, MacArthur himself had become committed to deconcentration as a step toward constructing an ideal free enterprise economic system based on his own view of Americanism. He cabled his strong feelings to the Department of the Army on October 24:

Involved in the failure or success of this program is the choice between a system of free private competitive enterprise . . . and a Socialism of one kind or another. . . . State socialism, openly avowed, at least retains lip service to the good of the common man, for the instruments of production are owned by the state ostensibly for the benefit of all the people, but even this fiction was not observed in Japan . . . for here the economy was in the grip of a system of private socialism largely owned and operated by and for the benefit of only 10 family clans.

He urged that there be no revision of the program, and added that although the Russians had wished to introduce the principle of confiscation, he had ". . . [i]nsisted on strict observance of the American principle of just compensation."[10] Such arguments only reinforced Washington's conviction that there was a dire need for far greater economic sophistication in Tokyo. For, socialist or not, FEC-230, if implemented, would have undermined the newly formulated policy of transforming Japan into a strong capitalist nation, an ally against the Left, and a profitable area for United States investments. While Washington now intended to reverse the deconcentration program, the truly surprising fact is that it lasted as long as it did.

No later than the end of 1947, Washington had articulated its general policy on the future of the Japanese economy. "The U.S. Government . . . considers that the Japanese Government must devise and develop plans under SCAP supervision for the economic recovery of Japan to the end that the Japanese economy will be balanced at the earliest possible time. . . . Not only is a self-sustaining . . . economy necessary to the early achievement of political stability in Japan, but the U.S. people cannot be expected indefinitely to subsidize the economy of Japan. . . ."[11] This was unquestionably the policy, but stabilizing the economy in their terms of reference was a far more difficult task than reversing the reform program, and, as in Europe, they hardly foresaw the outcome at the time.

Washington withdrew FEC-230 from the FEC, ostensibly for redrafting, and never resubmitted it. The State and War departments told SCAP to instruct the Diet to pass the deconcentration bill with the proviso that they would also submit new standards for evaluating economic concentration to Washington for Draper's scrutiny. Finally, the United States set up a review board of interested United States businessmen to pass on the deconcentration decisions. In this way the number of industries scheduled for dissolution dropped from the original 1,200 to 325, then to 19, and finally to 9. Once SCAP had dissolved those nine, it announced in December 1948 to the increasingly cynical Japanese that deconcentration had been successfully accomplished.[12]

Coupled with the outcry against the deconcentration program, Washington began to reexamine the economic purge. United States businessmen in Japan protested that it was undermining Japanese capitalism, and they were echoed in Washington by George Kennan, who noted that by 1948, 700,000 persons had been processed for purge, though closer to 7,000 were actually purged, and he found "Particularly strange and unfortunate was the regularity with which the purge had seemed to hit persons known in the days before the war for their friendly attitude toward the United States. It was as though pro-Americanism, especially among upper-class Japanese, was particularly suspect. . . . Important elements of Japanese society essential to its constructive development were being driven underground."[13]

MacArthur, angered by the criticism, quoted his directives and issued a stunned response. "It is fantastic that this action should be interpreted or opposed as antagonistic to the American ideal of capitalistic economy. . . . But . . . even if such [economic] revival is wholly impossible without the guidance of those several thousands of persons involved [in the purge] . . . Japan must bear and sustain the consequences, even at the expense of a new economy geared down to the capabilities remaining."[14] The antimonopoly vocabulary associated with the economic purge, as well as the *zaibatsu* dissolution orders, appealed to his concepts of an ideal competitive capitalism. But alarm that such a literal interpretation could only lead to the destruction of the entire ruling class was now widespread in Washington.

George Kennan's visit to Tokyo in March 1948 was apparently an important factor in convincing MacArthur of the necessity of reversing the policies. By assuring the general that the occupation had already fulfilled the essential requirements of the surrender and that the FEC was no longer in a position to advise or direct, Kennan persuaded MacArthur that, in coordination with Washington, he must proceed entirely on a unilateral basis. MacArthur, beginning at this time to feel some discomfort over the nature of the criticism from the United States, welcomed this redefinition of his preeminence and ". . . slapped his thigh in approval."[15] Kennan also stressed that the purges were being carried too far and would leave the United States at the end of the occupation bereft of allies in Japan. Once again Kennan's fortunes in politics reflected his ability to articulate with style the ruder thoughts of men of power. And MacArthur, satisfied with flattery, fell into line—at least on the direction of the Japanese economy.

Japan's Road to Stability

By early 1948 Washington had altered the direction of its economic reform policy in Japan, but had not been able to stem the inflationary course of the economy itself, fundamentally because the reforms had nothing to do with Japan's economic crisis. At the end of 1947 industrial production had reached only 45 percent, exports 10 percent, and imports 30 percent of the 1930–1934 average. The United States was supporting the trade deficit of $300 million to keep the economy from total collapse.[16]

In February, Washington dispatched yet another commission to assess the situation in both Japan and Korea and to make a definitive recommendation on reparations and economic stabilization. Percy H. Johnson chaired a committee that included Paul Hoffman and was assisted by Herbert Feis, although the dominant influence was that of William Draper. On April 26, the committee recommended that the United States settle the reparations issue quickly, since the uncertainties were impeding Japanese industrial recovery. Specifically, it proposed that the United States allot all Japanese property found in allied countries, estimated to have a total value of about $3 billion, to those countries and that the United States unilaterally, and without reference to the FEC, assign percentages of the very minor equipment in Japanese government-owned arsenals as reparations, thereby closing the question. Yet members of the FEC were still demanding further reparations.[17]

The major recommendations of the Johnson committee included a guarantee of raw materials for Japan, a shift of exports from dollar to sterling and Far East markets, and the reestablishment of Japanese shipping to cut down on the foreign exchange drain. The objective of the occupation was henceforth to be industrial recovery, and the Americans intended to accomplish it through the same policies that they were simultaneously preparing to introduce in Europe via the Marshall Plan: deflationary measures to curb inflation, increased production for export, lower imports and living standards, and establishment of a stable foreign exchange. The committee emphasized the role of cotton in Japanese recovery and the development of United States–Far East triangular trade: American cotton sold to Japan for production of textiles exported to the East Indies, which in turn would sell tin and other raw materials to the United States. Yet the world cotton textile industry was highly competitive, and the committee suggested Japan would have to ". . . adjust its marketing practices to this reality." Naturally, it was of ". . . great interest to American cotton growers that this problem be solved realistically so that the large potential Japanese market not be lost."[18]

In order to achieve a balanced budget, in their opinion the *sine qua non* of a stable economy, the committee concluded that the Japanese government must substantially reduce the number of its employees, eliminate subsidies to industry (which would, incidentally, also increase unemployment), raise the prices of its services, and make a greater effort to collect its taxes. Finally it recommended that the occupation return foreign trade to private hands and that Washington apply diplomatic pressure on nations that were discriminating against Japan in trade. American policy-makers then formulated a rationale that the Japanese simply could not "afford" the luxury of the political freedoms for the masses. They had to export to live, and to get off the American dole. To export, Japanese industry had to compete, which meant that ". . . the Japanese workers should . . . labor hard and well . . . ," consume little, and be disciplined and quiescent.[19] Meanwhile Japan had to accumulate capital in the traditional manner of paying low wages to the workers, and not through the government printing press backed by American funds. This economic policy had immediate and obvious political implications. To implement it, as in Europe, required that the United States emasculate the organizational expressions of the working class and strengthen the military and police to keep order. And since there appeared little hope for class collaboration, the policy also meant that the United States must reinforce the propertied class vis-à-vis the rest of the population before a peace treaty, and before the Americans could contemplate a withdrawal. The new policy clarification that evolved represented Washington's belated realization that the reforms were indeed illusory and that the options were limited, in essence, to revolution or reaction.

These proposals, welcomed in Washington, impinged directly on the economic plans and hopes of the British. Coupled with the emphasis that the United States was at the same time placing on Germany in the ERP, Japanese developments increased British alarm and opposition to United States occupation policies. England had strongly endorsed the industrial and labor reforms in Japan, which it believed would reduce the Japanese competitive advantage in foreign markets. Yet England was absorbed in its own recovery and forced to withstand the United States' pressure on many fronts. The shift in American policy also elicited bitterness and anxiety in China, the Philippines, and Australia.

The political developments in China, while not the cause of the shift, only accentuated the urgency of Japanese industrial recovery. But more crucial was the determination that the cost to the United States in subsidizing the inflationary economy had become insupportable. The $400 million in aid that was required to prevent collapse in 1947 only underscored that basic fact.[20]

When Draper returned to Washington, he asked Joseph Dodge to go to Japan to introduce specific policies of economic "recovery" and guide and direct the economy along the lines of the Johnson committee's recommendations. But Dodge had just completed his program of currency reform for the Western zones of Germany and in April declined, pleading his preoccupation with banking affairs in the United States, but also indicating that he would be willing to go at the end of the year. In the interim, Washington sent a commission of fiscal experts, under a Federal Reserve Board member, Ralph Young, to examine the economy from a banker's viewpoint and to make further policy recommendations. The commission arrived in Tokyo in May 1948 and proposed sometime later a nine-point stabilization program.

Meanwhile, in Japan, Tetsu Katayama's Socialist government was paralyzed and indistinguishable from that of the conservatives, and it soon lost all support of the wage earners, who had expected some benefits. Ultimately the left wing of the party forced the government's resignation in February 1948 by refusing to support its economic policies. But SCAP, unwilling to call for new elections at that time, instead merely reshuffled the cabinet, and a leader of the Democratic Party, Hitoshi Ashida, became Prime Minister, while the Socialists continued to participate in the coalition.

The coalition government of Ashida eventually broke apart on the shoals of political scandal involving subsidies and political payoffs, ultimately leading Ashida to prison; and Shigeru Yoshida again organized a Liberal cabinet in October 1948 as a caretaker government until the next elections, scheduled for January 1949. Under United States aegis, in Japan no less than in Europe, 1948 was a year in which the Right consolidated power, dropped its initial postwar defensive posture, and asserted itself in an anti-Communist and antiworking class campaign.[21]

This was the natural political correlate to the economic policy of attempting to stabilize capitalist, self-sustaining economies in Japan and in Europe. The men in Washington believed that it would be too expensive to yield to any of the demands of a strong working class movement and that such a labor movement, in frustration and in reaction to the calculated worsening of their conditions, could only be a dangerous political force on the left.

There was no question but that before the United States could proceed on its stabilization program it would have to break this potential threat.

The Workers' Response

As the living and working conditions of the Japanese masses continued to deteriorate, and the strength of the trade unions mounted, an increase in labor struggles was predictable. By the end of 1947 the real per capita income of the Japanese was roughly one-half the 1934–1936 level. The conditions among the government railway and communications workers were particularly difficult, and the unions of government workers, some 2.5 million by early 1948, and chiefly Communist-led, were militant. The canceled general strike of February 1947 had left only a residue of bitterness and frustration. In March 1948 the unions threatened another nationwide strike, and again SCAP ordered them to cancel it. But the steady worsening of their lot left no recourse, and they called another strike for August 7 that brought an immediate and definitive response from MacArthur. This time on July 22 he ordered the Ashida government to amend the National Public Service Law to deny government employees the right to strike or to bargain collectively. The government followed with an order invalidating all existing contracts with its workers. SCAP made it clear that violators would have to answer to the occupation, and the unions, with considerable bitterness, once again canceled the strike. Nevertheless, in August there were nearly 2,000 cases of job "desertion," and SCAP responded by arresting over 900 workers. SCAP's unofficial pressures also repressed strikes in private industry. American policy, shorn of ambivalence, was laying the essential groundwork for the future, yet more draconian measures, included in the nine-point stabilization program that SCAP issued in December calling for longer hours, fixed wages, and mass layoffs, termed euphemistically "personnel retrenchment" policy. The retrenchment naturally and openly chose as its first victims the union leaders and activists, and a new regulation banned all dismissed government employees from future union activity. The policy was quickly adopted by private industry as well.[22]

The Dodge Plan

During the six months after Draper had asked him to go to Japan, Dodge studied the conditions of the country and in October 1948 sent Draper a memorandum on a Japanese recovery program which reinforced the Johnson and Young committee's concerns. In December, Dodge felt free to accept the post as director of the Japanese economy.

Washington now viewed the direction of the Japanese economy as a matter of great urgency. Truman met with Dodge on December 11 before the banker left for Japan. The President pointed out that the developments in China had compounded Japan's importance, and that the National Security Council considered the Japanese economy as one of the most important international issues it had to face at the time. It had decided unanimously that Dodge should take charge of the matter.[23]

It is significant that the leading men of power in Washington chose Dodge, "without qualification or dissent," to deal with the most urgent economic problems for which the United States had direct responsibility— Germany and Japan.[24] Dodge turned down as many jobs as he accepted, for he was asked to direct the economies of Korea and the Philippines as well, and his views colored the policies of the European Recovery Program. There was no old school tie in his relationships to Washington. The son of a poster painter, Dodge was a car salesman in 1917, and in the 1920's he entered banking at a very modest level to rise to president of the Detroit Bank in the next decade. But the positions that he held during and after World War II were so critical that it is worth examining his views in some detail, for they were shared by the most important men in Washington of both the Democratic and the Republican parties.[25]

A conservative, orthodox banker—"antediluvian" as some have said— Dodge held policies that inevitably led not to reconstruction of a complex industrial economy, supposedly essential to America's political, economic, and strategic goals, but to a balanced budget accompanied by severe economic depression. His random jottings on controlling inflation capture the essence of his approach. Dodge noted that an ". . . increase in unemployment will in turn lead to increased efficiency of labor and a greater production. . . . A disinflation policy intends to bring the aggregate demands . . . to slightly below the aggregate of supply. . . . There should be no fear of mass unemployment. . . . What is the combined cost of health, welfare and education? . . . Get the country into hard condition for the struggle in the export market. . . . Radicals . . . can't make it in a free society. . . . Remedial actions are always unpleasant. . . ."[26]

Virtually simultaneous with his arrival in Tokyo, SCAP introduced Dodge's program for economic stabilization which embodied these views and came to be known as the Dodge Plan. But even the Liberal Party of

Premier Yoshida, whose corrupt and reactionary policies had created the economic morass, found the negative social implications of Dodge's program to be politically unpalatable.[27] Yoshida, however, overestimated his power and misjudged once more Washington's intentions regarding Japan. Convinced that United States interests were primarily strategic, he assumed that he held a trump card in securing continued subsidies for his economic policies by offering the United States a conservative, anti-Communist bastion in Asia. When Washington ordered SCAP to introduce the nine-point stabilization program he sought to ignore the features which were politically unattractive. It therefore became necessary for Secretary of the Army Kenneth Royall to go to Tokyo in February 1949 to further reinforce the position of Dodge and his virtually dictatorial power over the Japanese economy. Royall sought to remedy the fact that too many in SCAP and the Japanese government had overemphasized Japan's strategic importance to the United States and now had to confront the fact that the primary American policy was to establish a conservative, capitalist, but self-supporting economy by 1953. Paramount in these considerations was the need to make Japanese goods more competitive in the world markets and to put greater emphasis on the production of hard capital goods for export, primarily to Southeast Asia. This policy continued until the Korean War, for as Dodge pointed out to the top administrators of the ECA, ". . . if Japan is stabilized financially, she is not likely to be outpriced. . . ."[28] Yet until December 1949, despite extreme diplomatic pressure, no nation other than the United States accepted Japanese traders. In October 1949 SCAP removed the price floors on exports, allowing the Japanese to lower prices as far as they wished—in other words, to resume the "dumping" practices of the prewar period to meet competition. Coming as it did in the midst of a severe world recession and following the British devaluation, the measure heightened international tension and increased British demands that the Japanese be given access to their natural market in China.

The nine-point program, while establishing the direction of policy, still left specifics open to interpretation. It was not until several months later that Dodge released more precise directives on the implementation of the program. They elicited an immediate protest from the labor division of SCAP for having ". . . disregarded dangerous social, political, and economic consequences inherent in them."[29] But it was the labor division that was completely out of tune with the current American aims. The reduction of government subsidies in certain high-cost industries, encumbered with scarce raw materials, guaranteed immediate layoffs and wage reductions, and the restrictions of credit were expected to have the same effect. The Dodge program proposed an increase in the price of essential services, such as commuter trains and staple foods, coupled with tight wage controls and other policies increasing unemployment. Anticipating trouble from the workers, it proposed a ban on strikes for all workers in private as well as public industries. The labor division predicted there would be 1 to 1.5 million unemployed government workers as a result, and mass unemployment in private industry as well. Dodge, in principle, disapproved of unemployment compensation, for ". . . there would be no incentive to the individual to answer his own problem by seeking other employment," and public works were "inflationary."[30] The burden of the entire program was placed squarely on the back of the working class, as in Germany and the Marshall Plan in general.

When again a member of SCAP raised the matter of the political implications of forcefully lowering the already minimal standard of living of the Japanese worker, Dodge responded, ". . . the standard of living has probably been permitted to go too high—cannot increase further—we cannot give them everything they want."[31] At the same time, SCAP estimated with equanimity that removal of subsidies would result in a 13 percent increase in staple food prices. The program also met strong objections from the Japanese conservatives, although they were perhaps more vocal than sincere. Nevertheless, even in private meetings with Dodge they pleaded for the abolition of the sales tax, one of their party's important slogans in the last election, as well as for the continuation of public works and, in particular, the new nine-year compulsory education program. Dodge adamently rejected all pleas. Rather than expansion, he noted, "A completely realistic approach would suggest that public works should be eliminated entirely. . . ."[32] In every instance where there was a choice between concessions to business and to workers, Dodge insisted on the former, despite even the arguments of Japan's conservative politicians.

By June 1949 Dodge had succeeded in his aim of a balanced budget for 1949–1950 and a single exchange rate for imports and exports, resulting by September in one of the most drastic shifts in economic history. And the Japanese economy, along with the rest of the capitalist world, was sliding into a depression. That the outcome was not even more serious was due only to the fact that the Japanese conservative government was able to forestall or sabotage some of the most damaging consequences. Ultimately Japanese recovery depended on war in Asia.

The Left in Reconstructed Japan

As the men in Washington modified their policy in Japan, events in China only added urgency to a strategy that was the only one conceivable for the United States. And fear of a Soviet threat was never an influence on policy. Specific political measures evolved from the steps required to insure a *self-supporting* capitalist Japan. All the so-called orthodox economic policies had immediate political implications to the new strength and activity of the working class. Clearly, there were only limited means to meet their demands: either concessions that the men in Washington saw as expensive and defeating the imperatives of "recovery," or police repression, a ban on strikes, and an anti-Communist campaign.

The draconian measures that SCAP introduced under Dodge's direction met expected opposition from the Japanese people. In anticipation, Washington had taken steps to revise the process of police reform. SCAP bureaucracy, operating on its own timetable on many issues, had forced the government to pass the Police Reorganization Law in December 1947, decentralizing the police along American lines, a law that Yoshida considered to be the occupation's worst mistake. He complained that the new arrangement prevented effective action against ". . . Communists in small towns and villages [who] took possession of police stations and occupied municipal offices. . . . Strikers occupied factories in the same way and began operating them for their own profit. The police had, in truth, ceased to mean much. . . ."[33]

The fear that the police reforms left Japan vulnerable to pressure from the Left was prevalent in Washington's discussions of Japan in early 1948, and such considerations led George Kennan and others to speculate that American Communists had infiltrated the higher bureaucracy of SCAP. MacArthur was much less concerned, knowing that the origin of these reforms was a literal attempt to copy American institutions. However, in November 1948, the National Security Council, in the context of its over-all policies for Japan, made the decision to establish a formidable national police force. The discussions of enlarging and strengthening the Japanese military police, including adding a marine unit, always reflected anticipated internal disorder. Some United States military officers in Japan foresaw the possibility of using these police as the nucleus of an armed force that they might employ against the Chinese or the Soviets. But this was not a consideration of the men of power in Washington, who simply had real anxieties over their plans for the Japanese working class and the adequacy of the "reformed" police. Their strengthening of the police was to prove most timely.[34]

With the introduction of the Dodge Plan in 1949 the unequal struggle between the occupation and the labor movement reached its peak. The unions, now handicapped by the mass layoffs and the consequent fears of many still employed, nevertheless mobilized for further combat. The climax was reached in June 1949, one year after their last futile attempt to strike, with widespread agitation against the United States' retrenchment policy which only led SCAP to mobilize further its countermeasures. During June workers seized the police station in the town of Taira and held it for most of the day; in Hiroshima the workers occupied the Japan Steel Company for forty-eight hours until driven out; and demonstrations, sabotage, and wildcat strikes finally culminated, as far as the occupation was concerned, in the assassination of the president of the national railways. In many cases, United States troops aided Japanese police in the clashes with the workers.

The United States responded to this show of resistance in a variety of ways and never deviated from its purpose. It added further pressure on the quite agreeable Yoshida government to purge, without appeals, several thousand teachers as Communists. More indirectly, and paralleling the European experience, SCAP sponsored "Democratization Leagues," which in reality were well-financed anti-Communist cells working within the Communist-dominated labor federation. The leagues were first organized in early 1948, but they played their principal role in 1949. The significance of these groups, which split the unions at this critical juncture, lies in their decision to support the Dodge Plan, despite its draconian antilabor implications, in the same way that the socialist unions in Europe supported the ERP. In July 1949 they set up a new federation, which later naturally affiliated with the pro-American International Confederation of Free Trade Unions. Coupled with the selective dismissals of key militants and unemployment, the total number of union members dropped from a peak of nearly 7 million at the end of 1948 to 3.3 million by 1950. The deflationary policies of the Dodge Plan created lower wages, unemployment, and massive underemployment that further eroded union strength. But the collaborationist unions could risk going only so far before they would become exclusively paper organizations, as the Force Ouvrière realized in France. By offering no economic concessions to the workers, the occupation forced the new federation in Japan finally to act in the interests of the workers. In

February 1950 it joined the Communist unions in a nationwide wave of strikes over the continued antilabor economic policy. At the same time, the volatile issues of a separate peace and rearmament further agitated the mass protests.[35]

Despite the growing ferocity of the anti-Communist measures during 1949 from both SCAP and the Yoshida government, the Communist Party pursued its efforts at parliamentary politics. It had temporarily improved its position at the expense of the Socialists in the election of January 1949, gaining 9.7 percent of the national vote, and the party membership had grown from 1,180 in December 1945 to an official count of nearly 109,000 by April 1950. The party continued to hew to the nonrevolutionary position of the possibility of democratically acquired power even under the aegis of the occupation. In January 1950 the Cominform, reflecting Soviet alarm at the developments in Japan, leveled a surprise attack on party leader Sanzo Nosaka for this position, which, at that particular moment, the Russians found deviated from Marxist-Leninism. It certainly deviated from reality.

The Socialist election defeat in 1949, and the debacle of the coalition experience, sharpened the perennial tensions within that party, and during 1949 its left wing secured control. The times were propitious for the Left, which sought to identify the party exclusively with the working class and the class struggle. The conflict with the right wing, which was paralleled in the labor unions, finally ended in the walkout of the Right at the party's January 1950 convention. A substantial body of centrists were able to reunite the factions a few months later, but the serious internal dispute continued.

A more militant Communist stance after the Cominform attack, and the fact that the policies of the government and occupation after the February 1950 strikes were again cementing a united front of opposition, convinced SCAP that it must purge the leading members of the Communist Party. Using the purge directive of January 1946, MacArthur during June 1950 ordered twenty-three members of the CP excluded from all political activity, and he followed it by a similar ban on the seventeen editors of the party paper. Known as the "Red Purge," unlike its predecessor it was permanent for some 20,997 Communists and other leftists.[36]

The Communist Party had prepared for the SCAP purges over the preceding months, and most of the leaders wanted by the police went into exile in Peking. The party also conducted its own internal purge in June and split into two factions. While Nosaka only slightly modified his position on the role of peaceful revolution after the Cominform attack, Kyuichi Tokuda in May presented a document, allegedly drafted by Stalin himself and imposed upon the Japanese. The new course reversed the 1946 Nosaka position of peaceful revolution, attacked the United States, and called for a period of armed struggle modeled in part on the Chinese experience of the 1930's and in part on the political conditions in Japan at the time. The party, forced underground by the occupation, developed an ideological basis for its position. But the new tactics were not successful in rallying the masses and instead led the party militants to exile or prison. In 1953 the tactics changed once more as the Tokuda thesis was referred to as ". . . ultra-left-wing adventurist tactics of the Korean war."[37]

Given Washington's complete confidence in Dodge and his dictatorial powers in Tokyo, it is possible to perceive most clearly the type of society it sought to create in Japan. Despite the plethora of political rhetoric on stopping the spread of Communisn by raising the standard of living in a reconstructed world economy, when forced to decide on tangible options the United States committed itself to socially retrograde policies that even sectors of Japan's paternal ruling class thought too conservative. In reality, then, the real contours of America's reorientation of Japan from the inception took on an unmistakably reactionary shape.

By June 1950 the full impact of the Dodge "recovery" was apparent to all. Production at barely one-third the 1931 level, investment at one-half the 1949 level, and a nearly exhausted capital market all revealed what was in fact a critical depression. It is academic to speculate on the outcome of a continuation of America's recovery program, for the outbreak of the Korean War, as in Europe and the United States, reversed the process of economic stagnation. Paralleling the German experience, that bloody conflict provided the essential economic stimulus and actuated the Japanese economic "miracle" that has endured, despite periodic lapses, until this day.[38]

The Peace Treaty

On March 17, 1947, MacArthur irritated Washington once again by announcing that the Japanese were ready for a peace treaty. Given the growing concern over the chaos in the economy, the unstable political circumstances, the allied pressures for a "hard" peace, and the possibility of the Left's assuming control in the absence of the occupation forces, the State Department was in no hurry to press for an early treaty. Pressure for a treaty also mounted in the FEC during the spring of 1947, in part out of irritation over its negligible role in the occupation policy and also because of its conviction that it would be easier to deal directly with the Japanese than with the Americans in SCAP. Given all the circumstances, the United States perferred delay to hasty action, and Washington reminded MacArthur that he lacked authority to speak on the question. Next, the efforts of the Australians to initiate unilateral discussions on this question with the other Commonwealth powers in the summer of 1947 brought a precipitous call from Washington for an eleven-nation conference to discuss the formulation of a treaty. The Soviets, British, and Chinese buried this gesture by insisting that the United States had overstepped its many agreements from Yalta to Moscow and that only the four-power Council of Foreign Ministers could arrange procedures for peace treaties.

Joseph Dodge questioned the reluctance to discuss a peace treaty in a memo to Draper in October 1948, and he indicated a potential solution. ". . . Plans for an early peace treaty [should] not be shelved on the theory that Russian acquiescence to holding a peace conference would stem only from a plan to 'get the Occupation Forces out.' What is necessary here is not to avoid a peace treaty in order to ensure continuance of the Occupation, but to draft a peace treaty which will ensure Japan protection comparable to that afforded by the Occupation."[39] However, it seemed easier to ignore the problem for as long as possible.

The Russians next raised the question with the Council of Foreign Ministers in June 1949, asking that the council prepare a peace treaty with Japan at its next meeting. Acheson again insisted that only a special conference of the eleven FEC states was competent to deal with the question. Privately, he maintained that the Council of Foreign Ministers was ". . . the most impossible institution ever invented by man. . . . a body which is unable to function and which has no right to exist."[40] The situation remained deadlocked, with the veto power in the council nominally remaining the core of the dispute.

As the Americans reoriented the economic and political conditions in Japan they began to discuss a unilateral preparation of a treaty that they could then present to all belligerent states who wished to sign it. MacArthur announced the approach in early November 1949, this time after clearance with the State Department. The department asserted several days later that the peace treaty would include arrangements for the stationing of United States military forces in Japan for its external and internal defense for an indefinite number of years following the conclusion of a treaty. While this unilateral decision resolved the dilemmas of the preceding years for the United States, the proposals fell into the world diplomatic arena with an explosive impact. The Australians strongly opposed both a separate peace and the continued presence of American troops and were able momentarily to convince the British. With this development of a split in the Western camp, in November the Soviets also retreated on their position, this time declaring that they had no objection to the FEC nations' attending a peace conference. The United States, however, was unwilling to retract. Its new, frankly unilateral, position had the asset of achieving the exact arrangements it desired without compromise. Since the Americans were fairly confident that the USSR and China would probably reject a treaty presented to them on a take-it-or-leave-it basis, they could then definitively tie Japan to their economic and political sphere. Essential to the success of this policy, however, was the enthusiastic support of the Japanese. And to the Americans' surprise, at the end of 1949 the United States did not have even passive Japanese support. On the contrary, the policy elicited intense opposition, for the majority of the Japanese of all classes were hostile to a separate peace, especially one that would exclude China. This hostility was strong enough in early 1950 for the United States once more to postpone the consideration of a treaty. In Washington there was unanimous agreement that there could be no treaty without the provision of military base rights that would insure continued, although reduced, American military presence in the northern Pacific, or before they had corrected the reformist excesses of the occupation. And since the United States controlled Japan, it could afford to avoid compromises with the other members of the wartime alliance.[41]

Despite the hostile reception in Japan to the notion of a separate peace, in April 1950 Truman appointed John Foster Dulles as Acheson's assistant charged with preparing a peace treaty with Japan. And by June 1, Yoshida, also ignoring public sentiment on both the left and right, and representing only a tiny minority, declared that he was willing to sign a treaty with any power ready to recognize the independence of Japan. Dulles was in Tokyo to consult with SCAP and the Japanese government on treaty questions when the Korean War began, but that conflict had really surprisingly little effect on the subsequent negotiations. The United States outlined its unilateral policy in a draft in October 1950, and the Soviet representative at the UN, Jacob Malik, indicated his readiness to discuss the matter informally. The draft provided for United States–Japanese security arrangements, no restrictions on rearmament, and American control of the Bonin and Ryukyu islands, and it raised again the question of the future disposition of Formosa and the Kuriles which had already been settled at Yalta. It elicited an immediate denunciation from the Soviets, and in December the Chinese demanded the right to participate in all future negotiations of a treaty with Japan. The United States ignored this demand as Dulles began his second trip to Tokyo, the Commonwealth nations, and Paris to persuade them to accept the American terms. The Japanese government found the proposals to be ". . . of a far more generous nature than we had been led to expect . . ." and were "greatly heartened," especially when the Americans agreed they would be relieved of all economic restrictions and occupation-imposed reforms.[42] But all the other governments consulted rejected, with varying degrees of vehemence, all or part of the American proposals.

The British responded to the American draft by preparing an alternative one of their own. In tense discussions both with Dulles and with other United States representatives, they insisted that China be a part of all negotiations and that they permit Japan to normalize relations with the Peking government, which two-thirds of the FEC members recognized. The British interests were primarily economic, for if Japan were barred from trade with China it would inevitably penetrate the British markets in South Asia and elsewhere, a process that was beginning even during the discussions of the peace treaty. While they were willing to concede on other points, the British were adamant on this issue during the first months of 1951. Dulles finally advised Washington to proceed without them. This was too extreme, however, and the United States determined to secure British agreement. In May the Anglo-American drafts were merged by making a few inconsequential concessions to the British position, and Dulles in June convinced Foreign Secretary Herbert Morrison to accept a compromise on the issue of China by allowing the Japanese government, after the peace treaty was signed, to recognize the Chinese government of its choice. The outcome of that agreement was predictable, but the British were no longer in a position to resist the American pressure. Their economic condition during 1951 had worsened drastically, and they were faced with their most serious economic crisis since World War II—which we discuss in Chapter 23. The Americans made doubly sure about the outcome when in December 1951, in violation of the Dulles-Morrison agreement, two senators accompanied Dulles to Tokyo to apply pressure on the Japanese government to maintain ties with Chiang lest the Senate refuse to ratify the peace treaty. And the Japanese were also reminded that existing American legislation barred future aid to any nation trading with China.[43]

Despite their eagerness to conclude a peace treaty and return full authority on economic policy to Japan's conservatives, the United States was anxious to see the Japanese government continue Dodge's orthodox, anti-inflationary program that had proven so disastrous to recovery prior to the Korean War. In June 1951, General Matthew Ridgway, MacArthur's successor as supreme commander, asked the Pentagon to send Dodge to Tokyo once more to advise the Japanese on financial stabilization. Secretary of the Army Frank Pace stressed that "[i]t is considered especially important . . . when the peace treaty is imminent to prevent the development of any thought on the part of the Japanese Government that there is any lessening of United States interest in the economic welfare of Japan or that continuing stabilization measures are any less essential."[44] Dodge agreed to go to Japan in September, the month the peace conference was to open, but he was also aware that it was too late for him to assume anything like the dictatorial power he had in 1949. His function could only be advisory. The State and Defense departments believed that the Japanese would realize that cooperation on budgetary matters, as all else, ". . . will be very much in Japan's self-interest. . . ."[45] Dodge then sent a very specific memorandum to Finance Minister Ikeda pressing for measures that he implemented in 1949, with the reminder that ". . . if these are not done, there may be little case for additional United States aid."[46] The United States dropped the provision to maintain United States troops in Japan from the draft of the treaty itself and instead persuaded the Japanese to request future occupation and military aid. The two nations agreed that, after the peace conference, they would conclude a defense treaty under the cryptic title of an administrative agreement.

After the final accord with the harassed British, the Americans called a peace conference for September 1951, where they were easily to attain their goal of a unilaterally prepared peace settlement. Washington sent a routine invitation to the Soviets, but no one expected them to attend, given the fact that the conference procedures excluded debate. The Soviets did accept, however, indicating that they would submit their own proposals for a treaty. Gromyko attended and used his allotted time for his counterproposal, but Acheson as chairman immediately ruled him out of order. The conference, with a distinct lack of enthusiasm, proceeded to vote for a formal peace with Japan, one tailored to America's needs and interests.[47]

In February 1952, subsequent to the formal conclusion of the peace, the United States and Japanese governments exchanged notes on their future economic relationship. Summarizing its responsibilities, the Japanese government privately assured the United States that "Japan will contribute to the rearmament plan of the United States, supplying military goods and strategic materials by repairing and establishing defense industries with the technical and financial assistance from the United States, and thereby assure and increase a stable dollar receipt. . . . Japan will cooperate more actively with the development of South East Asia along the lines of the economic assistance programs of the United States. . . ."[48] It went on to specify the type of economic activity that would be geared to United States needs in the area and would also guarantee Japan a predictable demand for its continued industrial growth as well as a supply of dollars to make Japan one of the chief American markets. In the post-treaty relationship, Dodge concluded, the United States would rely on Japan for: "(1) Production of goods and services important to the United States and the economic stability of non-Communist Asia; (2) Production of low cost military material in volume for use in Japan and non-Communist Asia; (3) Development of its own appropriate military forces as a defensive shield and to permit the redeployment of United States forces."[49]

Superficially, the United States had in large part achieved its goals in Japan when the occupation ended in 1952. There was nothing to prevent it from doing so, given the relative power of the nations of the world which might have opposed Washington's policies at the time. Politically the conservative ruling class was firmly entrenched in power, and the working class, for the time, was effectively subjugated. And, above all, the Japanese economy had been reintegrated into the American economic orbit.

20

China: The Triumphant Revolution, 1947–1950

In China the United States confronted a situation that had entirely escaped its control, and which a far greater investment of American men and funds also might not redeem. The termination of the Marshall mission in January 1947 acknowledged not only the collapse of any hope for a political rather than a military solution to China's profound internal divisions but also the abandonment of any American thin pretense to neutrality. All that was left now was for Washington to support Chiang's government materially at the very same time as a profound pessimism colored its assessment of a tortured China's future.

By early 1947, as American military observers in China wrote at the time, Chiang's party ". . . was as hide-bound and as dictatorial as it had been any time during its existence."[1] Yet the United States was now backing this side with the full realization of all its weaknesses—its venality, insincerity in negotiations with other parties, and quickly declining urban support. "I have tortured my brain," Marshall confided in June 1947, "and I can't now see the answer."[2] He was never to find it.

The Balance of Forces

By the beginning of 1947, Chiang's successful military offensives had left him with a seeming military superiority over the Communists. His army was still about two and one-half times larger than that of the Communists, and he retained a three- or four-to-one superiority in rifles, despite the Communist acquisition of some Japanese arms, and an even greater superiority in other, heavier arms. The Communists had large pockets of strength north of the Yellow River and on the coast directly to the south, and they controlled at least one-half of the Manchurian countryside. Chiang thought he had the advantage and made the fatal decision to expand his military campaign. During mid-March he struck at the Communist capital in Yenan and quickly captured it.

There was never any hope for a negotiated political settlement after January 1947, if only because Chiang was willing only to discuss the future political control of the Communist regions, and for the other, minor parties he asked only that they enter a reorganized government prior to any firm guarantees as to their rights. These gestures need not detain the historian very long, for the basic Kuomintang strategy, as American Ambassador John Leighton Stuart correctly reported it to Washington in early March, was ". . . to embark on an all-out military campaign to free as much of China proper from Communist control as possible. . . . The Generalissimo . . . does not envisage any improvement promising permanency in Soviet-American relations and therefore is not without hope that the United States will in due course come in some fashion and to some degree to the Government's assistance."[3]

In fact, after the withdrawal of the Marshall mission, the reduced marine force regrouped gradually in smaller numbers at Tsingtao, the port city in the Shantung Peninsula, where it remained over two more years. Some, such as Senator Arthur H. Vandenberg, regarded this partial withdrawal as an abandonment of American efforts to create a coalition between Chiang and the Communists and a welcome endorsement of Chiang's military effort to "clean out" the Communists.[4] But Washington considered the continued presence of American forces at Tsingtao, which historians have hardly analyzed, as the prerequisite of two options it wished to retain: Chiang's use of the region to invade the north again, cutting the Communist territory in half, or, less probable, the employment of American troops for the same purpose. Only in 1949 were the options foreclosed.

The 2,600 marines in the north were an indication that, despite realism and unavoidable pessimism, the United States would continue to aid Chiang's military strategy without eventually being dragged into his trap of sending American man power to do for the Kuomintang what it eventually could not accomplish for itself. Despite the Kuomintang's organization at this time of the so-called China Lobby for the purpose of advancing its strategy in American government circles, there is no evidence whatsoever that the extensive operation ever influenced United States policy in any significant manner. On the contrary, the crudeness of the undertaking managed to alienate not a few important American decision-makers. Given the priorities of American global objectives, and the restricted options in China, United States policy reflected national interests and the limits of an uncontrollable reality.

It was for Chiang himself to take the initiative, and the Americans to respond. Drunk with his military successes of 1946, Chiang could not attain mass political support or stop the rampant inflation in the areas under his control. The result quickly proved disastrous. Mao's troops had carefully shepherded their strength by deserting the northern cities to Chiang's forces and continuing to extend and consolidate their rural bases, and now that the KMT army was exposed and overextended they could aim for victories. By the spring of 1947 the well-coordinated Communist armies moved increasingly to the offensive and confirmed one vital fact that made the crucial difference: the KMT army—poorly led, underfed, and exploited—was near total demoralization. This one reality determined the military events of the next two years, for ultimately Chiang's army would not fight. Worse yet, from his viewpoint, important sectors of it, officers as well as draftees, defected to the other side or sold arms to the Communists, changing the balance of power as measured in armament.[5]

In Manchuria, where the KMT's representatives held only the cities, they managed completely to alienate the local population by mid-1947, when the American consul general reported, "Nationalist southern military forces and civil administrators conduct themselves in Manchuria as conquerors, not as fellow countrymen, and have imposed a 'carpet-bag' regime of unbridled exploitation on the areas under their control."[6] In this context, and given the economic paralysis, the Communists could move through Manchuria with little opposition and with a warm welcome from many. And there, as elsewhere in North China, Chiang's military commanders increased their autonomy in a manner that progressively undercut the dictator's authority. Chiang's rule was being fractured more from within than from Communist attacks, and the Communists then realized that victory in the field was possible, indeed inevitable. Cities surrendered almost without a struggle, as Chiang's men failed to destroy their superior weapons and increasingly switched sides to become spirited Communist fighters after a brief time.

Throughout the months of 1947 the American leaders watched the events of China with growing despair as the highly accurate reports of the great drama piled up. Stuart's efforts to convince Chiang to adopt internal reforms, and seriously negotiate with the Communists, failed. By June, as the Communist victories in Manchuria continued unabated, and Chiang's representatives in Washington began intensive lobbying for aid of every kind, the American government lifted its last minor restrictions on arms exports to Chiang and searched anew for a more relevant policy. Realism and interest in preventing Communism could not help but lead to pessimism. Nothing more was decided than to continue existing aid to Chiang and to urge him to reform, an exercise Marshall fulfilled on July 6 with little hope of success. The only new gesture was Lieutenant General Albert C. Wedemeyer's return to China on a "fact-finding mission."[7]

In a sense, the Wedemeyer mission could hardly discover facts not already well known to the United States government, much less come up with new and practical policies. What is most significant is that Wedemeyer's mission also went to Korea, and that the entire undertaking was set in the greater context of the future of United States policy in the larger Far Eastern situation. While in China during August, Wedemeyer in personal meetings openly criticized the Kuomintang leaders in the strongest possible terms regarding their corruption and nepotism, their suppression of civil liberties, and their residue of belief in state ownership as opposed to "free enterprise."[8] It was the sort of statement one gives to dependent satellites, and hardly graceful, and it alienated Chiang's circle. Upon his return to Washington the undiplomatic general drafted a memo for Truman that embodied largely the same analysis of China, one excoriating the utter reaction and corruption of the Chiang government, and pointed to the great danger of "disintegration" in China.[9] Without giving desired magnitudes, Wedemeyer now urged a program of economic and military aid to the National government under the supervision of American advisers, but linked it to the unattainable condition that Chiang make imperative internal reforms in all fields. Manchuria, he added for good measure, should be taken from Chiang and placed under a five-power guardianship or UN trusteeship. In a sense, Wedemeyer again merely reflected the desire widely shared at the time that America could best realize its interests in China via the emergence of a new third force of pro-laissez faire democrats who might create an alternative to both Communism and the Kuomintang. It was, for all practical purposes, merely a restatement of what was already well known and desired, but also irrelevant. Since Wedemeyer was neither a radical nor a reactionary, there was no reason to suppress the report, as Marshall proceeded to do, save for fear its contents would only further alienate Chiang. But Wedemeyer's ego was assaulted, and from this time onward he became a strong, if confused, critic of United States policy in China.

Still, Wedemeyer probably buttressed the growing despair in Washington regarding China and reinforced the government's next basic policy decision. On November 7 the cabinet met to consider the global picture and to fix a firmer course. According to Forrestal, Marshall described Chiang as being in a condition of "critical instability." Looking at the world, "Marshall stated that the objective of our policy from this point on would be the restoration of balance of power in both Europe and Asia and that all actions would be viewed in the light of this objective." In brief, to interpolate, key American leaders now rearticulated the wartime consideration of Japan as the possible anchor to American power in the Far East, should China prove beyond redemption. Its meaning was very clear to Forrestal and all others: "At this juncture I repeated my inquiry about the review of the levels of industry in both Japan and Germany; I said that the policy of restoration of balance of power must necessarily be related to the elements of balance of power and those elements must include obviously the two nations which we have just destroyed."[10] Given the objective of protecting only American national interests in the Far East, the reconstruction and eventual rearmament of the former Axis powers was now imperative.

In this sense, America's ultimate solution to the problem of China and the Far East at the end of 1947 was Japan. So long as the major premise of Washington's policy was that a large American presence was required in the region, no other policy option was possible. China fully understood that the developments in Japan from this time onward, which we discuss in Chapter 19, directly affected the future of China, and by mid-1948, in response to the open restoration of Japanese economic power as a firm American goal, growing anti-American sentiment among all Chinese political factions was just one more problem to plague the American leaders.

Despite this shifting basic policy, which was the more fundamental response to the China debacle, America accelerated military aid to Chiang from the spring of 1947 onward, encouraging the dictator to embark on campaigns that only further weakened his tenuous hold on China and debilitated his army while strengthening the Communists via defections and captured arms. As the marines began to withdraw toward Tsingtao after April they transferred 6,500 tons of ammunition to Chiang's army, and in May, Washington agreed to sell 130 million rounds of rifle ammunition to Chiang at one-tenth the procurement cost. Later that year Chiang purchased 150 C–46 airplanes at 2 percent of original cost, along with numerous other military supplies.

Notwithstanding this immense assistance in materiel to Chiang, during October, Mao Tse-tung could report, "Wherever our troops go, the enemy flees pell-mell before us and the people give thunderous cheers. The whole situation between the enemy and ourselves has fundamentally changed as compared with a year ago." Capitalizing on the infectious demoralization in Chiang's army, Mao now urged Chiang's officers and men to switch sides or go home in peace. His own men he admonished to "speak politely," "Don't take a single needle or piece of thread from the masses," "Don't damage crops," and the like.[11] This iron discipline, which had a revolutionary quality as well as an immediate organizational function, won the support of growing masses of Chinese anxious to end the chaos of the period, turning Chiang's deserters under Communist leadership into effective soldiers. The Communists dealt strictly with, and even shot, offenders. Such discipline was the beginning of the end of China's chaos, a critical foundation of a new society as well as military victory.

At the end of 1947 Mao could report the capture of over one million of Chiang's troops, and the killing or wounding of 640,000 over the seventeen preceding months. More reliable data reveal that by January 1948 the Communist regular forces numbered 700,000 men, mostly volunteers, with an increasingly large proportion of excellent American arms, while Chiang had a regular force of one and one-quarter million of his typically dispirited, poorly led troops. The Communists controlled most of Manchuria, much of the territory of China north of the Yellow River, and important new pockets in central China. By this time there was no question as to the ultimate outcome of the contest, and only the timing was in doubt.[12]

1948: China and American Politics

By the beginning of 1948 the Truman administration regarded its actions in China as a mere holding operation, but one in which it would continue to aid Chiang to a limited degree, knowing full well that a far greater commitment would produce precious little results. And while it naturally hoped the Communists would lose, Washington realistically assumed there was less and less it could do about China's inexorable destiny. It may also be fairly said that despite occasional reservations intended primarily to score political points, the Republican Party—if not all its representatives—endorsed the larger contours of Truman's policy. Too much may be made of the exceptions, but 1948 was an election year, and during such periods the two parties attempt to define artificial differences between themselves.

Vandenberg was the chief architect of Republican Party strategy on China, and the admixture of political considerations and realism is best personified in the Michigan senator. Well before 1948 Vandenberg had halfheartedly condemned Truman's alleged policy of encouraging unity in China between Chiang and the Communists—an interpretation which ignored the administration's consistent refusal to impose unity on Chiang on terms unacceptable to him. Yet even as he criticized the Truman policy, in part because he claimed China was the one issue on which he was rarely consulted, Vandenberg throughout the period 1947–1949 never ceased to believe in the necessity that ". . . we insist that the Chinese nationalist government shall put its own house in better order."[13] This impossible condition mitigated any Republican tendency to press too far on the China issue.

In this context the Republicans reacted to the Truman administration's proposed China Aid Bill in February 1948. The measure, which included $570 million administered by the director of the ERP, Marshall described, in Forrestal's memory, as a compromise in a "practically unsolvable" situation: ". . . we cannot afford to withdraw entirely from our support of the Chiang Kai-shek government and that neither can we afford to be drawn in on an unending drain upon our resources."[14] Throughout 1947 Chiang's representatives had dunned Washington for vast grants, some requests reaching $1.5 billion. By the end of the year Marshall was quite ready to accept the demand in principle, if only to cultivate the illusion of activity while in fact he knew nothing could be accomplished. By February 1948 Marshall wanted the aid to be purely economic, but he also admitted that such a policy would free China's own funds for additional military purchases. Vandenberg, too, felt that the aid ". . . must be completely clear of any implication that we are underwriting the military campaign of the Nationalist Government."[15] Since detailed reports of Chiang's military defeats in North China were then freely available, Marshall for one publicly asked for aid to China with the explicit assumption that, given the chaos on the Nationalist side, the Communists might win. The Republicans, no less aware of this fact, but also anxious somehow to adopt a tougher line at less cost, cut Truman's request in the Senate to $363 million plus $100 million as an open grant that might be used for military procurement. The House changed the figures somewhat, but wished to see military advisers sent to direct the military aid. In the end, the House proposal was rejected in the Senate, and the final aid act came to only $275 million in economic and $125 million in military aid—or less than Truman had requested. Moreover, $70 million of the economic aid was earmarked for reconstruction projects extremely difficult to approve, but designed to end up in the hands of American firms. Hardly anyone in Washington believed the money would save Chiang, and 61 Republicans and only 11 Democrats in the House opposed the passage of the bill and further loss of taxpayers' funds. It was this ambivalence that was a better measure of the dominant Republican position on China. No less an indication of larger United States policy were the clauses it added to the aid treaty in the subsequent informal talks with the Chinese concerning the implementation of the program in the context of Chinese internal economic reform. "Clarification . . . of fields open to private enterprise without government intrusion" and "Elimination of special privilege in foreign trade and domestic enterprise" still retained a cherished place in the fading American desire to create the China of its dreams.[16]

In the larger sense, the quandary of China confused both parties during the first half of 1948. The Democrats showed this most clearly when, on March 10, Marshall indicated before a press conference that it was United States policy to encourage a coalition, including the Communists, as part of a political settlement of the war and China's internal problems. The next day the State Department demurred. Without retracting its oft-stated desire for political reform in China—which really implied a third force—Marshall now said that the Communist "rebellion" precluded their inclusion in a broadened government unless Chiang himself desired it.[17] On March 15 Truman was more resolute on the matter in a press conference of his own. He was categorical in opposing Communist inclusion in a broadened government. "We don't want a Communist government in China, or anywhere else, if we can help it." It was the ". . . great many liberals in China" in which he now placed his faith. "We would like to see them included in the broadening of the base of the Chinese Government."[18] The third force to save China for America did not emerge, despite American behind-the-scenes maneuvering and lobbying throughout 1948.

Chiang himself during this period was content to remain immobile on internal economic chaos, manipulate the creation of a new "constitutional Assembly" that immediately acclaimed him the new President of China, accept his military losses, and hope that the impending Republican victory would eventually save him from disaster. By mid-1948 the irresistible Communist military advances, which swept into much of the territory between the Yellow and Yangtze rivers, with numerous pockets of new guerilla activity throughout South China, left Chiang no option but to hope for massive American military intervention. By June the Communists had a parity with Chiang in rifles, a slight superiority in artillery, and a larger army. At least half of the United States armament was now thought to be in Communist hands.[19]

A Republican electoral triumph was imperative to Chiang because his reverses throughout 1948 had not led to increased American support after February. During August, Marshall attempted once more to give greater coherence to United States policy in China after Stuart on the tenth recommended that the United States oppose any coalition with the Communists, attempt to partition China into non-Communist and Communist regions after arranging a cease-fire, and support non-Communist regional governments likely to replace Chiang in non-Communist China—which were already reappearing in the form of aggravated warlordism. Marshall could endorse the opposition to any form of coalition with the Communists, but he decided not to make such a policy public for fear that the United States be accused of prolonging the civil war, and he insisted that the United States never again mediate the Chinese civil war. This policy did not change, for Marshall knew that American intervention on any scale could not alter Chiang's fundamental military and economic problems. Save for Leahy, most of the leaders in Washington regarded the basic stakes of world power at that time as being in Europe, and Marshall frankly acknowledged that it would be impossible to save China at the neglect of America's other global commitments—not the least, it should be added, because Japan offered another option to the future of American power in the Far East.

Such weighting of American global responsibilities was too well known for Chiang not to base his planning on them, and so over the summer of 1948, as paralysis marked his domestic and military policies, and whole divisions of his well-supplied troops surrendered without firing a shot, Chiang anxiously sustained himself on Governor Thomas Dewey's carping complaints regarding Truman's China policy and the candidate's not-altogether-clear statement that he would provide "far greater assistance" to Chiang. ". . . There is surprisingly frank admission in official circles," Stuart could report to Marshall at the end of August, "that the Government's eyes are glued to a sympathetic Republican Congress in January. . . ."[20]

Chiang's assumption was just one more measure of his utter lack of realism, for nothing the Republicans had actually done prior to the election warranted optimism on his part, much less taking campaign oratory at its face value. Indeed, as the November election approached, the key Republican leaders confronted the seeming certainty of managing the country, and this led to private caution and growing Republican endorsement of essentially Truman's policy on China. They had established their own means of gathering information from American officials in China, but these reports were no less critical of Chiang and differed only with marginal aspects of the official policy. Indeed, Vandenberg worried that Truman might commit the United States to some more ambitious course in China that Dewey would be forced to implement. ". . . [I]f we are to give military aid to China on a comparable basis with Greece," he warned Senator William F. Knowland, one of the China Lobby's important allies, "it would involve an *enormous* obligation. . . . [T]his burden (of unpredictable size) would be superimposed upon what appears to be the unavoidable necessity of military aid to Western Europe." If the China issue ". . . must be one of the first *major* decisions of the new Administration," it would be in a situation in which "things are going from bad to worse," and in which many Republicans realized that ". . . there are limits to our resources and boundaries to our miracles."[21]

The election on November 2 shattered even Chiang's misplaced hopes for the Republicans. The next day the National Security Council met in Washington and failed to come to a conclusion on the question of holding up further American shipments to China, exports that were falling into the hands of either triumphant Communist troops or utterly corrupt Kuomintang officials who were exploiting their final weeks of power only to enrich themselves. Then, only four days after the election, the Chinese delegate to the United Nations meeting in Paris informally approached Marshall as to whether the Americans would be willing to send officers to China to take over the actual command of the rapidly disintegrating KMT army, plus expedited munitions shipments. Truman received a similar message from Chiang himself on the ninth, this time couched more in terms of the global struggle against anti-Communism and Russia. Neither Truman nor any of his advisers were willing to sustain Chiang's schemes, and the President only reassured him that the United States would continue the already authorized programs. Chiang was now at the end of his resources, as interminable reports of defeat poured in, most of them involving the defection of well-armed troops—as in the case of 320,000 men in Manchuria during the fall, with nearly a quarter-million intact rifles. Try though he might to convince the Americans that he was their ally in a struggle against Russia in China, Chiang's profound cynicism hardly altered the United States' course, not the least because on December 17, Sun Fo, the newly designated Prime Minister, asked Stuart to explore the possibility of joint Soviet-American mediation of the war.[22]

The Communists: Chinese and Russian

The Kuomintang's desperate effort to rely on Soviet help was possible only because of the ambiguous, semidetached Soviet posture that made such chimerical illusions possible in the first place. Only the future revelation of new facts will expose the full dimension of the relationship between the Russians and the Chinese Communists after 1946, but certain generalizations are now possible.

The basic aim of Soviet policy at this time was military security, and the continued presence of American troops in North China presented an obvious threat that the Russians acknowledged publicly. This was the critical theme in the Soviet press throughout 1946, and at the spring 1947 Foreign Ministers Conference in Moscow, Molotov again urged American troop evacuations. Yet despite numerous criticisms of the Kuomintang, the basic Soviet complaint was much like that of the United States: Chiang refused to negotiate and accept a mediated settlement to the civil war. Such comments were often made without mentioning the Communists, whose claim for the right to govern all of China was never advanced in the increasingly friendly articles on them that appeared in the Soviet press throughout 1947. It was perfectly clear that the thrust of the Soviet strategy was against war to its south—a war that Russia saw involved the Americans as well as the Kuomintang acting as their agents, and might escalate into a threat to Russian security. Such an interpretation led to a search for peace. Unlike the Americans, the Russians proclaimed that they were not supplying arms to either side in China—arms that alone made the war possible. The Russians understood that United States policy was veering toward the reconstruction of Japan as the solution to Far Eastern instability, and this, in conjunction with the growing American domination of the Kuomintang, meant the further encirclement of the USSR. Perhaps for the first time, the victory of Communism in China held out the welcome possibility of securing Russian borders in much of Asia, but also the danger of further dragging the Americans yet more deeply into the civil war.[23]

The Russians therefore walked a tightrope between increasingly open verbal support for the Communists and the desire to attain peace before the Americans shipped more troops into China. When the Cominform was created in September 1947, it did not include any Asian Communist party in its membership, as if to suggest that the Russians, like the Americans, also felt that the basic future of Communism and world power was in Europe or that they regarded Asia as being in the Anglo-American sphere of influence. So, despite glowing press comment, the cautious Soviet policy resulted in the Russians' playing both sides. Hopefully, they may have thought, the Kuomintang might be convinced to take a position more independent of the United States.

At the end of December 1947, one of Chiang's important generals, Chang Chih-chung, asked the Soviet embassy in Nanking for aid in mediating the conflict in China, and the Russians eventually consented before Chiang vetoed the project. In part, at least, the refusal was due to an American belief that what the Russians had in mind was the partition of China, which, at the time, had the approval of neither Chiang nor the United States. By March 1948, however, the American embassy interpreted the Russian position as actually being pro-mediation. During the same period, even as they publicly praised the Communists, the Russians also renewed the Sino-Soviet Non-Aggression Treaty of 1937. That the Russians should have taken such a position, at a point when *Pravda* predicted further Communist military victories, reflects an innate Soviet refusal to press a favorable situation too far for fear of evoking a strong American response.

During July 1948, when victory was clearly in sight, the Soviets expressed caution in their advice to the Communists to avoid a new offensive, and to restrict their continued warfare to guerilla action on the edges of the Kuomintang-controlled regions. To the Kuomintang the Russian ambassador urged measures to stop the war, and left everyone aware of Soviet anxieties over Mao's "Titoist" role in the future. But the Chinese Communists would not cooperate, for total victory was now plainly within their grasp. This disagreement over strategy, which must be integrated with the question of Titoism in China considered below, may have reflected a Soviet belief in the Communists' inability to capture South China, a fear of American intervention, a desire to keep a divided and weak neighbor—or even a suspicion of what a Communist China might portend in the future. Whatever the cause, in the subsequent events of the civil war the Russians failed either to aid openly the Communists or to desert the Kuomintang. By the end of 1948, when Stuart discouraged Sun Fo from attempting Soviet-American mediation of the war, the Kuomintang's leaders not in the inner Chiang clique began to explore the possibility of a primary reliance on Russia to end the war. As Chiang prepared to desert China for Formosa, these men began playing increasingly vital roles in a disintegrating Nationalist government.

Acting President Li Tsung-jen now negotiated with the Soviet embassy a comprehensive agreement involving future Chinese neutrality in Soviet-American disputes, the elimination of American influence in China, and the establishment of cooperative relations with Russia. As Soviet Ambassador Roschin hurried to Moscow for approval, Li presented the matter to the United States, which was horrified that it should be asked to consent to ". . . elimination of American influence from China."[24] This final act only intensified American desire to disengage from the fantastic Kuomintang demise. Yet what is most significant, even as the Kuomintang acted to betray the United States, the Russians took steps to betray the Communists as they stood on the edge of victory. When, during February 1949, the Kuomintang moved its capital to Canton to escape the advancing Communist armies, only the Russians, of all the major states, sent their ambassador to accompany it.

The Russian hesitation before the imminent victory of the Communists must be placed in the context of the profoundly significant dispute with Mao that had begun toward the end of World War II and was to culminate several decades later in a total rupture. Mao's distinctive claim to have formulated a doctrine reflecting the practice, experience, and theory of Chinese history, lore, and Marxism-Leninism all combined was, by the end of World War II, a central aspect of Chinese Communist theory. What was unquestionably less palatable to the USSR was the Chinese Communist claim, as expounded by Mao himself and Liu Shao-ch'i, that Maoist doctrine had a vital role to play in creating a unique theory and practice for the Far East and peasantry throughout the Third World. If this assumption is less pretentious in its strategy than classic Stalinism, or even if Chinese Communist references to its special quality are much less frequent in Mao's writings from 1946 through 1950, the fact that it encouraged flexible localism represented a significant threat to Soviet spiritual domination over the world Communist movement. What made this pluralism especially dangerous was Yugoslavia's defection from the Russian orbit after June 1948.

Mao's close associates were unquestionably aware of the extent to which they had embarked on an independent course vis-à-vis the Kuomintang, one far exceeding Russian pleas of caution, and they must have been conscious of the manner in which the Soviet press underplayed their triumphs as Russian diplomats advanced their state's interests in China. It is of some consequence, therefore, that using the American journalist Anna Louise Strong, Liu and others helped her to prepare articles and documents on Chinese Communism that advanced the notion, in Liu's words, that "Mao

Tse-tung's great accomplishment has been to change Marxism from a European to an Asiatic form. . . . There are similar [to China's] conditions in other lands of south-east Asia. The courses chosen by China will influence them all."[25] Strong especially criticized those Chinese who had spent too much time in Moscow and were responsive to Soviet directions, for quite apart from questions of abstract theory, Maoism was, above all, a justification of an autonomous political line for local parties. Though Miss Strong's propagandistic activities on behalf of Maoism were spread throughout the world, they had their greatest impact on the Indian Communist Party, which assimilated the Maoist heresy partially through her writings and quickly adopted a Maoist theory by June 1948.

After Tito's defection Moscow could hardly tolerate the dangers of this drift. Even *Business Week,* in December 1948, could predict that ". . . the chances are that Stalin won't want a centralized state under Mao Tse-tung. The danger that Mao might become a Chinese Tito is too great."[26] Pro-Moscow elements reorganized the Indian Communist Party during 1949. "It is impermissible," the new leadership wrote publicly, "for communists to talk lightly about new discoveries, enrichment, because such claims have proved too often to be a thin cloak for revisionism. . . . It must be admitted that some of Mao's formulations are such that no communist party can accept them. . . ."[27] As for Strong, in February 1949, while she was stopping in Moscow, the Russians accused her of being a spy and deported her immediately, only to rehabilitate her six years later.

One can only conjecture the full condition of Chinese Communist–Soviet relations at this time. However, Mao thirteen years later admitted that in 1949 Moscow suspected that he would become an Asiatic Tito. It is likely, too, that the Russians, realizing that the Communists would establish power in China irrespective of their advice, finally relented and took a pragmatic, nonideological stance toward their new neighbor to the south. Mao, for his part, while not dropping his distinctive reliance on ancient Chinese parables and wisdom, went out of his way after mid-1949 to pay homage to the inspiration and primacy of the USSR—not the least, as we shall see, because he now saw Russia as the only source of external aid for reconstruction. The Indian Communists publicly apologized to Mao in mid-1950 for their previous offensive remarks, and for the time, at least, the Russians laid to rest their concern over Mao's threat to their hegemony.[28]

Theory and doctrine aside, China's realities and possibilities dictated the practice of Chinese Communism. Had it not been so, Mao, too, would have followed Chiang to defeat. For in the immense drama that was Kuomintang

China from 1947 onward—the corruption, inflation, and suffering—the central reality the Communists had to confront was the utter chaos and power vacuum. Unless they could organize and discipline China, what had been perhaps the most important asset in making possible the Chinese Revolution would also be the cause of its eventual destruction. What was far more important than Communist military victories over a starving, moribund army—an army that lost with scarcely significant resistance— was the organizational success of the Communists in preventing China from being sucked further down the whirlpool of chaos that Chiang had left behind. For if Chiang made possible the Communist conquest of power, only the Communists themselves could act to retain it.

The ease and speed of the Communist victory amazed the Communists themselves, who logically regarded their own strength and Chiang's still significant material power as at least some important determinant of their future. The utter collapse of Chiang's venal administration, which also swept aside many of the traditional institutions of resistance that revolutionaries must usually confront, was as much a surprise to the Communists as anyone, and this made even more imperative an internal strategy that successfully and quickly consolidated power and provided time for reconstruction. To this extent, history temporarily defined tactics and functional ideology.

As late as October 10, 1948, Mao discussed future Communist strategy in terms of the probability of continued fighting until July 1951, and then he refused to advance the notion of a total victory over Chiang. The following month, however, he admitted ". . . the war will be much shorter than we originally estimated," but even by the end of the year he anticipated at least a full year of combat during 1949. Surprised again by events, on February 15 Mao confessed, "The reactionary Kuomintang rule is collapsing more rapidly than was expected."[29] Several weeks later Mao expected victory soon to come, when, in the military sense, it was already in hand.

Mao understood that the problem of China was, in the first instance, organizational, and that anything that ended chaos, reestablished order, and made reconstruction possible was the essential precondition to socialism. The question of the army and its discipline was perhaps the easiest of his problems, for the army remained a coherent structure for both military and internal political purposes, and with it the Communists could fix a check on the natural tendency toward anarchy as well as create a work force and school for cadres. Indeed, the *élan* and dedication of the army and its political commissars, as well as younger party organizers, was essential in advancing successfully Communist rule and goals from theory to practice.

The Communists were increasingly critical of United States policy after 1947, for they correctly regarded American backing of Chiang as the major cause of the prolonged civil war. Yet this was a realistic assessment of fact, not a reflection of ideology, and it is a measure of Communist pragmatism that no later than the fall of 1948 they informally encouraged Western traders to stay on after the war and help supply goods required for reconstruction. Much the same was true of Communist relations to the internal bourgeoisie and intellectuals, for it was impossible for them to remove such elements from positions of power without furthering internal chaos and confronting its concomitant political dangers. The urban middle classes, despite grave reservations, had lost both the will and the capacity to resist the Communists, and the Kuomintang repulsed many of them even more. Mao hoped these administrators, technicians, and various experts would help in the process of reconstruction during a most critical period in the Communist consolidation of power, when they could ill afford sectarianism. Throughout 1947 he reiterated that the Communists were a mass united front of almost all social strata—". . . urban petty bourgeoisie, national bourgeoisie, enlightened gentry" all combined—and he especially courted the students on behalf of a new nationalism that proved irresistible. This insistence on avoiding "adventurist policies" toward industrialists and merchants was a hallmark of Communist policy through 1949, and a largely successful effort to mobilize China's internal resources, in the name of nationalism as well as social progress, to end chaos.[30] Only pro-Kuomintang capitalists were castigated, but by April 1948 Mao advocated a temporarily lenient policy toward even these men, as he quietly took a significant number of Chiang's former officers and allies into the organizational apparatus of the new China. Mao defined the restoration of production, under any auspices, as an imperative objective, and even if he was slightly less charitable during early 1949 toward the foreign investors and Chiang's important allies, who had largely deserted China despite extraordinary Communist tolerance, he did not cease to press the point, as in June 1949, that "to counter imperialist oppression and to raise her backward economy to a higher level, China must utilize all the factors of urban and rural capitalism that are beneficial and not harmful to the national economy and the people's livelihood; and we must unite with the national bourgeoisie in common struggle."[31] Whatever else may be said about this approach, no later than 1952 the Communists had managed to reconstruct prewar industry and probably to exceed it, and even if it was not the 26 percent increase in industrial production claimed, it is certain that the strategy helped to make possible China's emergence as a great power.

Much more disturbing to the Communists, and potentially immensely disruptive organizationally, was the unpredictable and sudden movement toward land reform which momentarily escaped Communist control during 1947–1949. This problem caused Mao much concern and compelled him to make many critical references to the spontaneous movement. Prior to 1946 the basic Communist land program was designed to maximize production and at the same time to introduce a new but limited element of equity into the landownership system. The result was a moderate land reform intended more to co-opt medium peasants than to dispossess them. The cooperative land system that emerged behind Communist lines before 1946 often left the more prosperous farmers in control of the system, while the poorer peasants were also given greater responsibility for production. The civil war, however, brought about the militarization of many villages and, in effect, placed the guns in the hands of younger men from the masses of poorer peasants who found the traditional control of power undesirable. Communist literature is still vague on the nature of the precise class position of the "rich peasant," or the "middle peasant," but it is clear that such elements often had contacts with the traditional gentry and landlords, frequently advancing into that class themselves, and that Communist conservatism prior to 1946 had deliberately left the "middle peasants" with critical power in the villages. Given the electric atmosphere that the civil war generated among the younger and poorer peasants, who were overwhelmingly Communist by 1947, it is not surprising that they began to use their rifles not merely against the Kuomintang troops but also against the wealthier peasants, thereby entering into conflict with the official Maoist line. Given the tendency toward decentralization of political authority even in the vast Communist regions, an organizational danger fraught with immense risks to the party, that such critical initiative from below was possible posed dual risks to Mao. For him the problem was not to stimulate agrarian upheaval, but to contain and channelize it to help the party to attain power. Moreover, as Franz Schurmann points out, the use of land reform to recruit peasants for Communism and the Communist army created a momentum that soon got out of hand and created "left excesses" that threatened not only to create a counterrevolutionary impulse among the well-to-do peasants but to disorganize food production.

During May 1946, and all the following year, the Communists tried to create a new land law that compromised between insufficient and excessive reform, but apparently the party lost at least partial control over the radical-ized peasantry who were willing to fight both against Chiang and for justice at one and the same time. ". . . [W]e must unite firmly with the middle peasants," Mao declared in February 1947, "and it is absolutely impermissi-ble to encroach on the interests of the middle peasants (including the well-to-do middle peasants); if cases occur where the interests of the middle peasants are encroached upon, there must be compensation and apology." Variations of this theme stud Mao's statements for the next year, and by early 1948 he was strongly denouncing "impetuous" party newspapers and cadres who were endorsing the ". . . poor peasant–farm labourer line."[32] Mao correctly predicted that too much disruption would create a food problem, and the one-fifth of the farm population that he characterized as "middle peasant" were potentially capable of offering stout resistance. Moreover, by April 1948 he was certainly anxious to discourage costly peasant and urban working-class social demands. The party's leadership spent much time and effort stopping this leftward movement, if only be-cause, most fundamentally of all, it challenged the traditional party's au-thority. From 1948 onward Mao and his associates made continued efforts to impose tighter centralization over the party cadres. In large part the poor peasants' need to act was due to the many years of Communist conservatism on the land question in regions under their control, a caution that had become ingrained and had led to a rupture between the party leadership's perception and the desire of the masses. By spring 1949 the party was ready to stress its urban organizational basis much more emphatically in the hope that it could impose control over the chaos the Left as well as the Kuomin-tang demise was creating. The party dealt with revolutionary terror and direct action in the villages as best it could, and from the end of 1949 through mid-1950 the party attempted to introduce a new land reform program that gave representation to the rich peasants and tried, in as moderate a fashion as possible, to channelize the dynamism of China into the hands of the party's leadership to win the battle for production before confronting socialization of land. Such organizational control was both economic and political in purpose, but Mao thought it imperative to avoid the risk of chaos and to consolidate power.[33]

To some important degree, the Chinese Revolution was the reaction of the Chinese masses, often acting alone, to the chaos and social disintegra-tion that the Kuomintang imposed on a war-torn nation. In this sense, we must regard the events of the vast epic less as deliberative actions on the part of the Communist Party than as a series of responses to conditions and events that larger objective forces and factors indigenous in the realities of China created. The flexibility and pragmatism of Chinese Communism after World War II were circumscribed to this extent by an impersonal dynamism over which Mao frequently had slight control. In this context, the Communists after 1950 related to the necessities of a world which, like China from 1946–1949, they could hardly control but to which they could only react from the viewpoint of retaining power. It was for the United States, therefore, to determine the limits and possibilities of the pragmatic Communists' interaction with the world.

The United States Confronts the China Dilemma

Whether the Chinese Revolution was a nationalist, agrarian upheaval from below, only partially under the control of the Communists, or even the fantasized Moscow creation, the United States government saw the revolution challenging its vital interests in Asia. More frustrating, however, was that there was no longer any way to relate to the momentous tides of change sweeping through China. Now, toward the end of 1948, the United States had to confront the immense irony that everything it had done in China since the end of the war had been self-defeating, perhaps even the decisive factor in destroying the Kuomintang. Haphazardly, the feeling in Washington began to be that the United States had allocated Chiang too much rather than not enough.

From the end of World War II until mid-1949 the United States gave the Kuomintang regime over $2.8 billion in economic and military assistance, and other nations added almost a quarter of a billion dollars. It was this aid and the support of United States troops that had made it possible for Chiang to embark on his Manchurian and North China adventure in 1946 when only internal stabilization in the areas under his control made his regime's survival possible. The economically destabilizing consequences of aid to Chiang only helped to rip apart a moribund economy even as it enriched Chiang's circle. Then, finally, long after Japanese arms could have been a factor in the war, the Communist capture of American arms eased their military victory immeasurably. During the last months of 1948, the Communists took at least 60 percent of the American arms in the hands of 320,000 defeated KMT troops in Manchuria. Statistics of this nature profoundly disturbed American decision-makers, who at the end of 1948 had to relate to the events of China as best they could.

Vandenberg carped about Washington's China policy, but he agreed that

Chiang had to clean house before the United States could do anything more —and so he precluded major Republican innovations. During December various Kuomintang officials embarked on their campaign to remove Chiang and attained an elusive success when Li Tsung-jen became Acting President at the end of January, leaving Chiang with sufficient power, however, to hamper military defense, control the secret police, and ship China's remaining $138 million in gold and dollar reserves off to his new Formosan empire. Washington knew fully of the wild intrigues of the time —Li's offer of an alliance with Russia, Chiang's effort to corral Rhee of Korea and Quirino of the Philippines into an anti-Communist alliance— and discouraged them all. The only way in which the United States could relate to the final disintegration of the KMT was to decide on its existing aid policies. By mid-January 1949 Vandenberg shared the common feeling that new appropriations for China would probably ". . . fall into the hands of the Communist armies" and that ". . . it is now probable that the Nationalist Government will fall before we could ever sustain it with a new program of aid."[34] Indeed, over those very days Tientsin and Peking fell, and KMT armies continued to melt away before the Communist advance. Then the National Security Council recommended freezing the remaining arms appropriations and cutting off the KMT to keep the arms out of Communist hands. It is a measure of Vandenberg's and Truman's ambivalence that, on February 5, a White House meeting to consider the recommendation resulted in its rejection after Vandenberg made an impassioned plea that the United States not symbolically desert China at this point. As the Michigan senator freely admitted, he could not recommend alternative policies, and virtually everyone was agreed that additional help to China would actually be aid to the Communists.[35]

For the skeleton of the Kuomintang government, busy with its cabinet crises and intrigues, the end of decades of growing inefficiency and misrule was approaching. The Communists saw no reason to negotiate on anything less than a total reformation of China, and this Li could not accept even as the Communists crossed the highly defensible Yangtze River and took the undefended Nationalist capital of Nanking amidst the cheers of the population on April 24. In reality, Chiang's refusal to loosen his *de facto* control of many vital agencies of government meant, in effect, that the internal political paralysis behind the KMT lines reached its logical culmination. Hankow and Shanghai fell at the end of May; Tsingtao on June 2; and over the remaining months the other cities and southerly regions of China collapsed before the Communist advance—the last Nationalist authorities deserting the mainland in early December. For the first time in centuries, China was truly reunited.

The Communist triumph in China forced the United States to reassess its larger policy in the Far East and, in turn, the Far East's relationship to the global political and military scene. Yet it did so with much of the same emphasis on European affairs that had inhibited more far-reaching and ambitious action in China in the years after the war. China, of course, had never been the exclusive option by which the United States might exert its influence in the Far East, a presence that it nevertheless emphatically wished to maintain in the region's affairs. Had the United States regarded China as the central arena of the world crisis, or even as the first major postwar revolution to succeed by force of arms and likely to spread, it might have been more deeply disturbed. But the fact remains that during the summer of 1949 there was no such view, if only because it appeared as if the nation's insoluble problems would stymie the Communists as well and that the ancient culture's pervasiveness would either replace or transform Communism.

Washington's response to its China debacle, therefore, was regional, but also weighed against its global priorities, and relatively restrained as to the magnitude of the stakes involved for the United States. With this clearly in mind, Acheson authorized Ambassador-at-Large Philip C. Jessup in July 1949 to head a committee to reconsider future United States policy in the Far East. But Acheson left Jessup's committee with remarkably slight leeway for policy initiatives: "You will please take as your assumption that it is a fundamental decision of American policy that the United States does not intend to permit further extension of Communist domination on the continent of Asia or in the southeast Asia area."[36] Indeed, the practical implications of this monumental premise, which meant opposing guerilla and anticolonial movements everywhere in the region, left the Jessup committee with little more to do than formulate appropriate means for administering a predetermined policy. Consequently, Acheson was able to respond to the ongoing events of Asia even before the Jessup committee completed its task.

During the spring of 1949 there was no one of importance in Washington who believed that the elimination of the Communists in China was possible immediately, or worth the required effort—if only because there was no one to replace them. Truman was still extremely bitter about the "grafters and crooks" in the Kuomintang, and he was skeptical of the Communist ability to create a truly bolshevik society in China. "Well, nothing can be done about China until things kind of settle down," was his hesitant philosophy.[37] Along with many of his advisers, Truman thought Chinese nationalism would eventually drive out Soviet influence, not as an aspect of the Communist Party's transformation, but rather as a result of new parties and forces emerging. In one sense, such an estimate was correct, but it erred in believing that the United States might again reassert its influence in China, for it did not comprehend that independent nationalism was no less dangerous to the neocolonial West as to a neosocialist Russia. Publicly, however, Acheson and the State Department had embarked on a campaign of attacking the Communists as early as January 1949, when John M. Cabot, a senior American official, gave a well-publicized speech in Shanghai condemning the Communists as complete tools of the USSR. The Communists, for their part, rather naïvely took the initiative during April to explore informally with Stuart the possibility of United States recognition, but there was not much chance for the Communists' overture to succeed. Acheson and Truman had decided, in effect, truly to wash their hands of the conundrum at least for the time, and they prepared the way with the publication of the 1,054-page so-called White Paper on China on August 15.

If the White Paper was an impressive record of the failure of United States policy in China over the preceding six years, it was also cast in such a way as to perpetuate that policy, not the least because on August 14 the State Department announced that it would continue to recognize the Nationalist regime as the government of China. More provocative to the new China was Acheson's letter of transmittal in the book, and his press statement to accompany it. While confessing the failure of past American policy, Acheson insisted on labeling the Communists as having ". . . publicly announced their subservience to a foreign power, Russia. . . ." Indeed, the erstwhile anti-imperialist rhetoric of both statements was unusually sharp and undiplomatic, and it was to prove provocative as well as self-fulfilling to the extent that it unquestionably informed the Chinese Communists that they could expect only bitter hostility from the United States and would do well to make friends where they could. The only glimmer of optimism in Acheson's statements was that the "individualism" of the Chinese people, which was to say the chaos of a society in total disarray, might reassert itself to defeat the plans of the Communists as well.[38] And for the next year Acheson persisted with his theme of the Communists as puppets of a Russian imperialism bent on "taking" the four northern provinces of China into the USSR.[39] The purpose of the accusations was unclear, for Angus Ward, the American consul in Mukden throughout 1949, reported that there was no evidence that the Russians were bent on political integration of the border provinces into the USSR—though special Soviet economic rights were another matter. Mao, for his part, took the calumnies as they were intended, and in five public statements during August and September bitterly exposed the immense inconsistencies between the functional role and noble declarations of the American government. As the seemingly last chapter of the history of old China was being enacted, the United States prejudged its future policy by cultivating the enmity of the new civilization that was groping to emerge out of the misery of the old.

American hostility came at an inopportune time for the Communists. Like their internal policy, their external policy was quite pragmatic, for they had forborne the United States' aid to Chiang far longer than even the most cautious discretion dictated. They needed friends where they might find them, for the Communists had no desire to see China continue to stagnate. Western hostility simply made China dependent on the USSR, eventually creating a self-fulfilling prophecy that won for the United States the hatred of a nation that was potentially one of the most powerful on the globe. When Mao arrived in Moscow on December 16 as head of the Chinese delegation to negotiate a treaty of alliance and friendship, Russia was his only possible source of external economic aid.

Mao's problems with Russia were very real. The Kremlin still feared him as an incipient Tito, the Soviet press had given the monumental events of China relatively scant space during 1949, and in fact the Russians allocated only routine coverage to Mao's visit. More serious yet for Mao, the Russians had already made significant gestures toward making it possible for an autonomous Manchuria to survive within a loosely centralized Chinese state which Mao and the nationalist elements of the Communist Party were determined to reintegrate at all costs. During July 1949 the Russians had signed a one-year trade agreement with the People's Government in Manchuria under Kao Kang, a kind of traditional war lord who five years later was stripped of all power and committed suicide. Most of the Manchurian Communist leaders, indeed, were Moscow-trained and oriented, with relatively cool relations with the majority of the Communists. The Russians at this time were most likely interested in using Manchuria as a source of food and raw materials, which, while rather different from Acheson's interpretation of the matter, still posed a grave challenge to the emergence of the kind of China that Mao hoped to organize.

Mao's negotiations with the Russians went poorly. He had publicly announced that he would conclude the negotiations by mid-January, but in fact he left Moscow on February 17. Representatives of the Manchurian and Sinkiang Communist parties were also present and given ample publicity, even to the extent of the protocol-conscious Russians' assigning the Manchurian vice-chairman of regional administration precedence over the Chinese ambassador at the signing of the Sino-Soviet Treaty on February 14. And earlier there were many sharp exchanges. As Premier Khrushchev himself admitted in June 1956, Soviet demand for control over Chinese affairs embittered Mao, and he refused to concede. Stalin, as Mao later revealed, did not wish to sign on Chinese terms, and thereby caused the prolonged delay in the talks. Later, during the anti-Stalin campaign in Russia, the treaty terms were condemned as excessively harsh on China, but Mao probably held out long enough to make it much closer to a real compromise. As in the photo *Pravda* showed of the signing, neither side had a smile for the occasion, but it was likely that Mao got the better of the bargain. Russia abandoned nearly all the Manchurian privileges it had obtained from China in the Sino-Soviet Treaty of 1945. But China acknowledged future Russian control over Outer Mongolia, which the Tsars had first acquired and Chinese nationalists had always regarded as an unacceptable injustice. In turn, the Russians agreed to $300 million worth of credits over five years, or the equivalent of a paltry fifty complete industrial units. We do not know the finer details of the treaty dealing with commercial matters, but suffice it to say that the massive shift in China's trade toward the Communist bloc at this time was inevitable, given United States hostility. After all, the Chinese would have to trade somewhere and take the best terms the penurious Russians might offer, for as Khrushchev later asserted, America's belligerence prevented China from becoming independent of the USSR during these first critical years.[40]

The hard United States line welded the Chinese and Russians together, for the Americans contemptuously responded to a poor, disorganized China as they had always known it rather than as what it might someday become. When the Chinese went to Moscow they could be quite certain that American recognition was a long way off, for as early as May 1949 Washington had acted to discourage its allies from taking the diplomatic step. Even earlier, the American press had reported that Washington would prevent all trade between Japan and Communist China—a prediction that proved true. There was no surprise, therefore, when on October 19, Truman declared to the press that the United States would not only avoid recognizing the new China but also urge its Western European allies to follow the American lead.

The behind-the-scenes deliberations of the Jessup committee would not have given the Communists any more confidence, and what is interesting about it was not how they influenced policy, which was already being independently determined and implemented, but how key American leaders articulated the scope of their perception of the problem of China in the setting of Asia and the world.

Both Kennan, who was not overly important, and Marshall, who was, argued before the Jessup committee that the major stakes in future world power were hardly to be found in China, which impressed Kennan as having slight long-term economic or offensive military potential, but rather in Europe. In absolute terms, the greatest danger to American power was a Soviet combination with Germany and Central Europe. In the Far East itself Japan was a much more critical economic element and a more likely ally for the United States. It was here that the first reassertion of American power in the region was logically and likely to occur.

Yet two dilemmas emerged in the Jessup committee's deliberations. One was roughly articulated but not acknowledged. Kennan, for one, did not consider war with Russia as likely, but "[e]vents are proving the Marxist analysis of what was going to happen to capitalism and people's reactions to capitalism to be correct almost everywhere where capitalism is not very far developed and not correct in the countries where it is." And this implied that revolution, upheaval, and war would continue on the rim lands of the great centers of world industrial states, either changing the balance of power in those regions or involving the United States and its allies in guerilla and counterrevolutionary wars for seemingly marginal stakes. And the direct relevance of this likely preoccupation to the second dilemma was not fully confronted at this time. For, stated simply, it was that the absorption of the NATO allies in colonial ventures was weakening the anti-Communist bloc in the arena of central importance—Europe. " . . . [W]hen we reached the problem of increasing the security of western Europe," Marshall reported, "I found all the French troops of any quality were all out in Indo-China and I found the Dutch troops of any quality were out in Indonesia, and the one place they were not was in Western Europe. So it left us in an extraordinarily weak position there. . . ."[41] And the inevitable logic of this position for the Americans was to be that one does not abandon anticolonial wars but helps to win them, if possible, quickly and definitively. In this sense, the key to military security in Europe ultimately became to some critical degree the triumph over the Left in Asia.

The obverse of this position, which they never even considered, was that China could become a great power and that wars in Asia might be lost, thereby further weakening the United States alliance and American power in Europe. Given Washington's intention to stop the Left along China's rimland, the hidden dilemmas and traps awaiting the United States in Asia could be anticipated quite independently of the immediate legacy of problems that the China debacle left in its wake. As for these, the more important consultants to the Jessup committee were not in favor of recognition of China in the near future, even though they equivocated on the possibility that an independent nationalist regime might emerge. Yet pessimism suffused their other specific predictions. "The excesses of the Nationalist administration in Taiwan since V-J Day have earned the Chiang Kai-shek regime the earnest hatred of the Taiwanese," the CIA's representative informed the committee. The danger of a Communist takeover was more from internal uprisings than from an invasion from the mainland. Moreover, the policy-makers the Jessup committee consulted were not so much unconcerned about China as ready to postpone any sort of new action there in order to meet head on the probability, as one State Department aide put it, that "in respect to Southeast Asia we are on the fringes of crisis."[42] They anticipated this crisis not in China or Formosa, areas over which the United States could exert precious little control, but in Indochina. Here, too, France was indirectly weakening Europe. Despite the fact that the United States in March 1949 had publicly welcomed the puppet emperor Bao Dai's adherence of Indochina to the French Union, privately both the State Department and the CIA thought the war there was passing from bad to worse and that the Vietminh under Ho Chi Minh would win in perhaps two years unless the anti-Communist cause took decisive action.

It was therefore essentially with eyes on holding the rest of Asia that the United States formulated its policy toward the future of China and Formosa. At the end of December 1949 the State Department circulated an ambivalent confidential policy information paper on Formosa in which it stressed all of Chiang's weaknesses and the fact that the United States had no present intention of meddling in the fate of the island. However, it also added that the loss of Formosa would be a blow to American prestige and damage the morale of other anti-Communist nations in the Far East. The policy so contradicted MacArthur's desires that his headquarters leaked it to the press in the futile hope of reversing the trend toward disengagement in Asia he so feared, illustrating once again his ingrained habit of attempting to define United States policy rather than obeying it. On January 5, 1950, therefore, both Truman and Acheson publicly declared America would not intervene in any way to save the dispirited Formosan regime, or establish military bases there "at this time." When reporters asked Acheson about the meaning of the reservation, he added, "It is a recognition of the fact that, in the unlikely and unhappy event that our forces might be attacked in the Far East, the United States must be completely free to take whatever action in whatever area is necessary for its own security."[43] This lopsided, contingent policy implied, in effect, that America would permit Chiang to go under unless it were to its national interests to save Formosa for its own purposes. Much the same pursuit of self-interest had been the basis of United States policy in China for years.

It is in this context that one must read Acheson's widely debated, yet deliberately vague, January 15 speech on the Far East. Its significance for Korea and Japan we discuss elsewhere, but on China it damned the Communists there "as puppets of Moscow," and while it mentioned a Pacific defense perimeter that ran from Japan to the Ryukyus to the Philippines, thereby excluding Formosa, he was still committed to the vital earlier "at this time" contingency.[44] In fact, the speech said almost nothing about United States policy in Southeast Asia—where Washington anticipated the next real crisis—save to congratulate the British, Dutch, and French on their alleged reforms.

Lest it be thought that the United States was in the process of withdrawing from the affairs of the Far East after its sad failure in China, a more realistic view is that it left open all options in the areas in which it did not expect serious, imminent crises—such as Korea—and it attempted to disengage from China with a policy that might be described as neither peace nor war.

Despite bitter Republican complaints, which Senator Joseph McCarthy's cynical fabrications regarding the loyalty and intentions of the State Department aggravated, it was apparent that Washington had no intention whatsoever of recognizing the Communist regime in China, or encouraging its allies to do so, or endorsing a UN seat for it. Allegations, especially in politics, should not be mistaken for facts. The administration and the important senators of both parties were opposed to recognition of China, and prior to British recognition of China on December 16, 1949, the State Department had strongly urged it not to take the step. In confidential discussions Acheson was no less emphatic that recognition was impossible in the foreseeable future.

The consequence was the beginning of the United States' long, sustained effort to keep the Chinese out of the UN. The United States voted against admission in the Security Council on January 13, 1950, and the Russians walked out of the UN on that day, not to return until July 29. The UN Secretary-General, Trygve Lie, then unsuccessfully attempted to neutralize American opposition over the following months, only to receive Washington's active resistance.

It was in Indochina that the United States attempted during the first five months of 1950 to respond to the larger implications that the collapse of Chiang's China augured for the future of all of Asia. China was lost, and even as the United States was withdrawing from that disaster it was beginning to become engaged in yet another—Vietnam. On February 7, as the controversies over recognition of China and defense of Formosa raged and McCarthy and his followers were accusing the State Department of being "soft on communism," the United States extended *de jure* recognition to the French puppet regimes in Vietnam, Laos, and Cambodia. And during that month the French submitted a formal request for military and economic aid to help them to fight their war.

Washington's belief that Vietnam was an affair involving European as much as Asian security colored its probable response to that request. A French victory in Vietnam could accelerate European rearmament. Charles E. Bohlen, an important State Department adviser at that time, explained it to a key Pentagon group in essentially these terms:

As to Indo-China, if the current war there continues for two or three years, we will get very little of sound military development in France. On the other hand, if we can help France to get out of the existing stalemate in Indo-China, France can do something effective in Western Europe. The need in Indo-China is to develop a local force which can maintain order in the areas theoretically pacified. . . .

It is important, in order to maintain the French effort in Indo-China, that any assistance we give be presented as defense of the French Union, as the French soldiers there would have little enthusiasm for sacrificing themselves to fight for a completely free Indo-China in which France would have no part.[45]

Indochina's fate impinged, as well, on Japan's future in Southeast Asia, which men such as Dodge believed would form a complementary economy. "The Japanese are the natural workshop of the East," he argued in April 1950, "and to get them off our shoulders, we must build up their trade." As " . . . a bulwark against Communist expansion in the Far East," Japan might regulate the area on America's behalf.[46] Cut off from the region, this position also implied, Japan might compete for the West's export markets, again becoming a rival rather than a client state, or undergoing internal crisis and radicalization itself.

Given this vision, on May 8, the United States agreed to extend military and economic aid to fight a war in Vietnam, but one should never confuse its motives. The virtue of this policy was that it could satisfy those who felt Europe was still the center of the world conflict, or the majority of the Truman administration, and men such as John Foster Dulles, who was convinced that the loss of China threatened the balance of power in the world and that it was an error to rely wholly on NATO and the Western Hemisphere. A " . . . series of disasters can be prevented," Dulles wrote in a memo in mid-May, "if at some doubtful point we quickly take a dramatic and strong stand that shows our confidence and resolution. Probably this series of disasters cannot be prevented in any other way." It would be necessary, he believed, even to "risk war."[47]

There was no conflict in United States planning in the spring of 1950, for action in Asia was seen as complementary to the defense of Europe, and so American interests were to be served in both places. Whether Indochina, which the administration preferred, or Formosa, which had more appeal to Republicans, or the uninhibited reconstruction of Japan, the United States was determined prior to June 1950 to continue giving direction to the affairs of Asia. It was this commitment that prejudged the response when the first crisis rather surprisingly arose in Korea, but it was ultimately to be no less vital in the area for which it was first designed—Indochina.

BOOK III

The Korean War and the Limits of American Power

21

Korea: From Civil War to Global Crisis

By the spring of 1950 United States foreign policy had reached an impasse—in Europe, in Asia, in military and economic policy—and Washington regarded the events in any one nation or area in the context of its global perspective. The crisis that arose in Korea in June 1950 therefore was but one aspect of America's international vision, interacting with that world view, reflecting it but also helping to shape it. Indeed, to understand any specific aspect of the conduct of American foreign policy one must understand every important part of it, and Korea was no exception. In a vital sense, therefore, the United States confronted the crises in Asia with its head turned backward to the consequences of action in Asia on European problems, as well as to domestic economic needs and broad military planning. Leading American decision-makers did not, and could not, slight the interrelated nature of foreign policy.

Washington fully understood the immense implications of the Russian atomic bomb explosion in August 1949. Its first response was the January 1950 decision to proceed with the hydrogen bomb, hopefully to recoup the offensive capacity that the Soviet A-bomb was about to neutralize. During the spring came National Security Council policy guideline NSC–68, with its proposed tripling of defense and military spending. Later Washington was to decide on increased United States troops in Europe and massive military aid to the NATO countries in the hope that this new infusion of dollars could sustain United States exports in the wake of the Marshall Plan. "I knew," Truman recalled years after Korea, "that in our age, Europe, with its millions of skilled workmen, with its factories and transportation network, is still the key to world peace."[1] This remained an essential American premise for three more years, but it was an expensive one, and by May 1950 there was very serious doubt whether both Congress and the Europeans themselves would sustain it financially. Indeed, one may fairly suggest that the mood of May 1950 was not unlike that of January 1947 preceding the Truman Doctrine crisis, with the administration's aspirations far outstripping the political means for their implementation.

In Asia, however, the United States anticipated a crisis, and its general strategy appeared irrelevant and, partially at least, unformulated on vital specifics. The China debacle did not prevent Washington from energetically blocking Communist China's admission to the UN or launching attacks on it as allegedly being a Moscow puppet. The Jessup committee, after touring the region, found no support for a Pacific military pact to oppose "Communism's" expansion, and the United States determined now to consolidate Japan's role as an ally and balance to Asia's Left by signing a peace treaty with it. The Americans also resolved to aid the French struggle against the Vietminh. What was most significant about American policy at this time was not that it was vague, but that it was open-ended. Acheson made his January 1950 reference to a "defensive perimeter" from the Aleutians to Japan to the Philippines at a time the United States was determined to help the French prevail in a nation to the south and as the administration was forcing through a continuation of economic and military aid to South Korea. In intent and implication, the speech was in no sense an American withdrawal from the affairs of Asia; the reverse was true. The United States anticipated a crisis in Asia, and it was prepared to react to that challenge in the larger context of its European and global strategy. But it expected that crisis to appear first in Indochina, and the United States fully intended not to avoid it when it came. Indochina primed Washington for Korea.

The question of Asia was far more an affair of Europe and the Third World in the largest sense. As a constant premise, the key formulators of United States diplomatic and military strategy always comprehended the economic interdependence between the United States and the Third World. "It is hard to see how both the U.S. and Europe can fully utilize their industrial capacity unless they can obtain expanding markets in 'third areas,' " one group of top-level economic advisers and big businessmen concluded in early June 1950. To preserve these areas as a source of sales and raw materials was a responsibility that fell, according to such men, essentially on the United States, which would have to provide the capital to develop the "rich resources" of these nations and to help them channel their nationalist impulses in directions compatible with American interests. "There is not other country that can do the job."[2] This universal vision helped to define the American response to all Asian crises, to Africa ("a prime source of strategic raw materials"), to the Middle East, and to Latin America, on which " . . . the industry and agriculture of the United States depends . . . for raw materials and markets."[3]

The Korean Enigma

To say that the United States entertained grave reservations toward the Rhee dictatorship, or that it did not regard Korean affairs as the central problem of global diplomacy, is not to conclude that it was ready to abandon the corrupt regime; quite the contrary was the case. But Rhee was a small-scale Chiang, no more viable, and much more outspoken and militant in his desire to end the artificial partition of his nation and stamp out internal opposition of every political hue. For the fact was that South Korea was beginning to disintegrate internally, and Washington harbored profound doubts regarding it.

Washington knew more than enough to realize fully that Rhee was running a police state, and Truman in his memoir reveals his dismay over the terrible repression as well as his belief that "[y]et we had no choice but to support Rhee."[4] The scale of repression, which reached a new peak in October 1948 when Rhee closed all opposition papers, jailed editors, and put even his right-wing critics under more intense surveillance, begot its inevitable resistance. On October 20 over 12,000 South Koreans, led by mutineers from Rhee's army, revolted in Chulnam. The same month, the people of Cheju Island also took to arms and fought until the spring of 1949. And despite Rhee's claims that he had crushed the Chulnam rebels, his army was still pursuing them in the mountains the following June. For the scale and frequency of the peasant-based guerilla activity grew in 1949 with Rhee's repression, and by the end of the year, the North Koreans claimed, there were 90,000 guerillas fighting in the south. Seoul, for its part, claimed killing 19,000 enemies in the South's border regions. Certain it was, as *Time* reported in June, that Rhee had arrested twenty-two conservative National Assembly opponents, brutally tortured them, and then quickly released them. As for the Left, as Senator Tom Connally later recounted, "One of Rhee's cabinet members said, 'The torturing of communists by police is not to be criticized.' "[5] By September, according to official data, there were 36,000 political prisoners in South Korea.

More important yet was the continuous and rising tension on the 38th parallel, often leading to armed clashes of considerable proportions. And above all were Rhee's and his associates' incessant public demands for a march north to reunify the nation by force of arms. During October and November 1949 they reiterated their usual threats to reunify the country by force, and at the end of the year Rhee again called for reunification, peacefully if possible, but "[i]f, unfortunately, we cannot gain unity this year, we shall be compelled to unify our territory by ourselves."[6]

The sole key to the political objectives of both Seoul and Pyongyang was reunification, even by civil war, and indeed such a war was already under way between the two sectors on a small scale and within South Korea itself in the form of agrarian resistance and uprisings. Rhee, who continuously appealed to the Americans for offensive military equipment, only succeeded in frightening Washington, which was ready to sustain his corrupt regime but not to endorse his adventures. "Because of Rhee's constant belligerency," the State Department representative in Japan, William J. Sebald, recalled, "United States advisers refused to give this [South Korean] force tanks, medium or heavy artillery, or military aircraft. It was feared that, properly armed for offense, Rhee promptly would punch northward across the 38th parallel."[7]

Rhee did not confine himself to Korean affairs, however, but in May 1949 had attempted to organize a Pacific equivalent to NATO that the State Department was compelled to discourage. There can be little doubt that in the politically charged atmosphere existing after the fall of China, Rhee reinforced the Asia-first wing of the Republican Party and embarrassed the administration at that delicate moment when it sought to emphasize its far greater priority in Europe. Rhee, in brief, by 1950 was both a nuisance and an impending liability to the United States.

Rhee's adventures on the political level were accompanied by economic chaos and corruption that only massive American aid prevented from turning into total collapse. By mid-1949, Congress was beginning to show resistance to further aid, a situation that compelled a cynical administration ready to support him to hold out South Korea as " . . . a symbol to those people who we believe want the democratic way of life." In any event, Acheson also argued more pragmatically, without $150 million aid " . . . the whole situation in Korea will collapse and Korea will fall into the Communist area."[8]

Washington would not abandon Rhee, and when the Republicans voted in mid-January 1950 to defeat the requested $150 million aid for the Korean "rathole," as one Ohio congressman called it, Truman rammed it back through.[9] The Republicans, aptly enough, argued that an imminent northern takeover, by one means or another, would simply mean the Communists would inherit the American goods. Congress, indeed, had not shown such independence for some years, and it was as troublesome to the administration as Rhee. Publicly, the administration alternated between describing South Korea as a test case for "democracy" in the Far East, a nation in which internal affairs were improving " . . . and the threat of Communist overthrow appears at least temporarily to have been contained," and confronting actual facts.[10] For South Korea during the first months of 1950 was in a stage of internal economic and political decay unprecedented in Rhee's years of misrule. The price of rice tripled in the five months after December 1949, taxes were still collected on a voluntary basis, the national budget was in chaos and being raided as United States foreign aid was channeled into private rackets—in brief, South Korea was a miniature of China three years earlier. Even much of the traditional Right was largely horrified by the course of events, or was divided over patronage or personality clashes, and it moved into the opposition and demanded new elections for the National Assembly. During the first months of 1950, midst occasional fist fights among legislators, Rhee finally tried thirteen of them arrested in mid-1949 for allegedly being or supporting Communists, sentencing them to up to ten years in prison on the basis of confessions some insisted were extorted by torture. At the same time he beat down efforts to extend the assembly's control over government ministries. He postponed national elections scheduled for May until November, and during the interval Rhee was to rule by decree. At the end of March, ECA head Paul Hoffman warned Rhee officials that unless the economic chaos were controlled he might cut off economic aid, and on April 3 Acheson added the holding of elections to the list of American demands. It is unlikely that the threat was serious, but Rhee consented to hold elections May 30, and in the meantime he sternly resisted the National Assembly's efforts to control his ministerial appointments. In brief, despite the extensive police harassment and intimidation that he exerted, Rhee was willing to tolerate an election of a new National Assembly solely because he intended to leave it no significant powers and most candidates were too intimidated or too conservative to warrant much anxiety on his part.[11]

The May 30 elections represented a major but not decisive defeat for Rhee and opened what was certain to become a long period of internal political chaos. Eighty-six percent of the eligible voters gave Rhee's party and its fronts only 67 of 210 seats—enough to block critical constitutional amendments—and while the mélange of independents elected reflected all sorts of ideologies and interests, chiefly on the Right, they were united in their hostility to Rhee, and probably a majority desired cautiously to open unification negotiations with the North Koreans.

During these same months of internal political and economic disorder Rhee continued to beat the drums for increased armaments that, alternately, he justified as equipment to attack the North or to defend his government from an invasion. The defensive theme increased even as reported North Korean raids across the 38th parallel dropped radically by April. On May 10 South Korean Defense Minister Shin Sung Mo announced an imminent invasion from the north, and this allegation was linked to pleas for heavier armament. Washington regarded such charges with some skepticism, despite CIA reports throughout the spring that the North Koreans might indeed mount a full-scale attack. The head of the 500-man United States Military Aid team in Korea, Brigadier General William L. Roberts, on May 28 denied that such a build-up was taking place and expressed supreme confidence in the superior fighting abilities of Rhee's army. In any event, large-scale border fighting was a standard aspect of the Korean civil war, and Washington, for the most part, shared Roberts' belief that the South Korean army was good enough for defense, and that better equipped it would itself move northward to ignite a yet larger conflict. And warnings of imminent North Korean invasions, as well as attacks northward, were so common after mid-1949 that they evoked indifference. As an operational assumption, officials in Washington understood that the Korean civil war was already under way. At the beginning of June 1950, as in previous years, the United States was willing to sustain the Rhee regime, but it was no more ready than before to underwrite his adventures on behalf of unity—at least not willingly.[12]

But Rhee and his associates were too determined to confine their pleadings to a skeptical Europe-oriented Washington, and they knew that American power in the Far East was to some, as yet undetermined, measure controlled by the Supreme Commander in Tokyo, General Douglas MacArthur. It was to this demigod that Rhee was to turn. Although the exceedingly stringent restriction on MacArthur's papers make the extent of the communion between Rhee and MacArthur a matter of conjecture, perhaps even to Washington, we know enough now to suggest that it was very important—perhaps, even, the essence of the story of Korea during 1950.

MacArthur was an American general, but during World War II he had abandoned himself to destiny and to history for lack of much land combat with which to preoccupy his attention. Vain to a degree that alienated all but his adoring sycophants, his ability to equate his own desires with that of the unarticulated wishes of the American public made him prone to a megalomania rare in the decade. He spent the war posturing for photographers, distributing pictures of himself, and calculating the political effectiveness of his every move, and he remained profoundly indignant over Washington's choice to fight World War II in Europe and deprive him of the historic role of the great liberator. In his frustration MacArthur fixed upon De Gaulle in the role of a man of history ("He is, as I am myself, upheld by public opinion. . . .") he was also determined to play.[13] MacArthur, in brief, aspired to become America's De Gaulle, to transcend the petty banalities of ordinary men of affairs and, if need be, to treat their powers as subservient. To steel himself, he refused to return to the United States after the war, even for a momentary visit, and in Japan he waited for destiny's call.

MacArthur detested the official American emphasis on European affairs and never ceased to regard the Orient as America's "new frontier," as he phrased it. It was the place to engage the communists, with whom, as he told one reporter, "There can be no compromise. . . . We must help anyone who will fight communism." This meant an alliance with the Asian forces of reaction, Chiang being the foremost of them all, for "I would help the devil, if he would come to this earth and offer to help fight the Communists."[14] Since such a strategy was in accord with that of the vocal, if inconsistent, Asia-first wing of the Republican Party, MacArthur became its idol. Hence he was the sole American general—save Eisenhower—with significant political support, an insulation that only reinforced his independence.

MacArthur's vision of his personal role in fulfilling America's destiny in Asia was both political and military. His deep interest in the political factions in the Republican Party, and the possible presidential nominee, was evidenced no later than the summer of 1949, probably much earlier. As for his military vision, that part of the story follows, but this interlocked political and military perspective, and MacArthur's awareness of the implication of his actions in one field for desired success in the other, cannot be forgotten.

There was scarcely any secret regarding the Supreme Commander's views and inclinations. No later than October 1949 Rhee began assiduously cultivating MacArthur, pleading for greater armament—arms Rhee vowed he would use to reconquer the North. On October 31 Defense Minister Shin Sung Mo called on MacArthur, unquestionably to seek arms, and told a press conference that he would gladly march on Pyongyang. At the end of December he attempted to embarrass Washington's inclination to minimize Formosa by releasing its confidential guideline. The following mid-February Rhee himself saw MacArthur in Tokyo, calling, as the New York *Times* summed it up, for " . . . an anti-Communist alliance under the leadership of General Douglas MacArthur" to stop Communist expansion in Asia.[15] It is probable that Rhee also outlined his own critical situation in Korea and his ambitions, and that MacArthur listened with tolerant sympathy. What went on in the general's mind over the subsequent months we shall probably never know, but it is fully certain that by May he was more openly complaining about the various strictures and confusions of Washington. "One of the greatest difficulties I have to overcome, and a growing one, is the basic difference in the policies we are imposing here and the policies being followed in the United States."[16] Such an attitude, applied to numerous questions, reflected MacArthur's traditional deep longing to act, to fulfill his destiny by overcoming the equivocations and doubts of his nominal superiors.

Whether, even before June, MacArthur was more than thinking, and actually preparing to act, is still an open question. The existing evidence permits no definitive judgment, including the traditional one that there was no American culpability in bringing on the Korean War. For while we can be fairly certain regarding Washington's policies before June, MacArthur's conduct remains an enigma.

The military balances of power in Korea prior to the outbreak of fighting on June 25 were in the process of transition, and in this regard MacArthur's role is obscure. In the larger context, however, the vital fact is that both North and South Korea since mid-1949 were engaged in an arms race. Given the open political declarations of both sides to reunify the country by force if necessary, that arms race deserves closer analysis.

The North Koreans had one critical asset: control of a rudimentary industrial sector inherited from the Japanese. Around this, and with Soviet aid, they began with an army of 30,000 in early 1948, and until the end of 1949 a "defensive-type army," to quote an official American description, of four divisions and one armored regiment was its main strength.[17] The South Korean army was formed out of the constabulary and right-wing elements in August 1948 and was composed of 60,000 men at the end of the year.

By March 1949, midst active recruiting, the South Korean army had grown to 65,000, the coast guard to 4,000, the police to 45,000—for a total of 114,000. While this military force was equipped with standard infantry weapons and nothing heavier than 81-mm mortars, its rate of growth and Rhee's energetic search for arms—especially for a 99-plane air force—must certainly have caused anxiety in Pyongyang. When the last United States occupation forces evacuated Korea in June 1949 they left behind $110 million in arms, including 100,000 small arms with an immense quantity of ammunition, 2,000 rocket launchers with ammunition, a large number of 105-mm howitzers, 20 training airplanes, 79 light naval craft, and the like —a quantity of arms that permitted a large expansion of South Korean military power, and a less defensive capacity. Also, 482 United States officers and men remained to teach them how to use this equipment. Rhee filled in his ranks even as he made yet greater plans, and from 114,000 men in March 1949 his armed forces jumped to 151,000 by May 1950 and an additional 3,000 before June 25. In light of Rhee's repeated intention to march north, the Communists unquestionably must have worried about this impending superiority, and even more by Rhee's other, yet unfulfilled military plans. Official American accounts indicate that the North Koreans began expanding their defensive army *after* January 1950. Twelve thousand Korean veterans from the Chinese army were transferred home; the Russians gave them 150 T34 medium tanks along with a large amount of artillery that gave the North Korean army a three-to-one lead with longer-range weapons, and a small tactical air force. In March more North Korean divisions were slowly activated, but this process must have accelerated in April when Rhee made the decision to create twenty-one combat police battalions to relieve the army of its task of putting down the rebellious population. These battalions, each composed of about 1,200 men, would have given Rhee a significant offensive potential, but he was able to organize only one before June 25. The question arises, however, where did Rhee intend to get arms for them, and what did the Communists think of this development?

On April 16 *Pravda* asserted that Rhee and MacArthur had reached a secret agreement to have the Japanese build war materials for Rhee's army. Propaganda or not, the allegation came at the time when Rhee had created a structure predicated on new arms supplies from some place, and it was certainly not from the United States. And it was not until April and May that the Soviets began to ship large arms deliveries and more modern equipment, matériel that the North Koreans hardly had time to master. Pyongyang believed in Japan's complicity, as well they might, and by June

25 their total military force had been increased to 135,000 men, including 78,000 in seven infantry divisions, for a total military force somewhat smaller than that of South Korea.[18]

Although the North Korean military build-up prior to June has always been interpreted as proof of aggressive intent, in fact it was more a response to the military imbalance of power that Rhee and the United States had created during 1949 and 1950, the aggressive declarations of Seoul, and the possibility of further military growth in the south. Objectively, the internal political and economic chaos in South Korea, and the massive indigenous guerilla movement, merely required the North to wait for the Korean Right's ultimate demise, and never was that likelihood greater than during the spring of 1950. Until April, it can be argued, the North Korean military build-up was designed mainly to restore military equilibrium in the region, and probably only later did Pyongyang decide that Rhee's military and political ambitions were too pressing and dangerous for it to wait for the corrosive disintegration in the South to eliminate him.

Although the North Korean army in June was better equipped than Rhee's, and certainly in far better morale, the American officials who evaluated the situation rationally concluded that Rhee's forces had more than an adequate defensive capacity, and they probably suspected that his numerous warnings of an impending North Korean invasion were attempts to eke out the equipment to fulfill his own aggressive designs. The unusual confidence that his American military advisers expressed in Rhee's army was based on its selective conservative ideological composition, which made it appear highly capable and committed. Given their awareness of the border tensions, the Americans logically assumed that the element of surprise would not give an attacker a critical edge over the equally large ROK (Republic of Korea) army.

Such rationality failed to take into account Rhee's intense determination to make any sacrifice to conquer the North and reunite Korea. The United States after mid-1949 had attempted to control Rhee's capacity for offense by restricting arms, but it scarcely suspected that Rhee's control over the way his army might employ its sufficient power of defense would open the door to new adventures beyond Washington's imagination.

The Preliminaries to a Crisis

Members of the new South Korean National Assembly, composed heavily of anti-Rhee elements, immediately embarked on a denunciation of

Rhee and their own enforced impotence, and despite its condemnation of the election as fraudulent, Pyongyang attempted to reach an accord with Rhee's new opponents. Events now moved into high gear, probably stimulated by North Korea's fear that unless peaceful unification could quickly be attained the arms race would turn against it and Rhee might fulfill his pledge to march north. For at the beginning of May, Rhee broadcast an appeal to the people in North Korea to support the unification of the nation, not by compromise, but by absorption into his regime. He urged them to wait for ". . . unification through a joint struggle with us in the South. . . . The longed-for day will come soon."[19] On June 3 the Pyongyang radio called for a new, intensive national campaign for peaceful unification, and midst rising propaganda for a merger it offered four days later a specific plan for unity. First there would be a meeting of all democratic parties, on either side of the parallel, within ten days to organize a general election for a single legislature in all of Korea early in August. This legislature would then meet in Seoul and presumably run the unified nation. By "democratic," Pyongyang made clear, it meant everyone but Rhee, his followers, and their small parties, but it indicated that the new National Assembly would supervise the August election in both sections. On the eleventh Pyongyang sent three representatives across the parallel to deliver the unity proposal to all the southern parties save Rhee's, and they were immediately arrested and forced to broadcast falsified recantations to the North—an act that aroused the North to furious rage. Rhee, in turn, proposed elections under UN supervision in the North only, the elected legislators to have a minor position in the Seoul Assembly.

While it is true the Communist plan was negotiable for many in the South, it is improbable that the North Koreans thought Rhee would relinquish power so easily. Still, everything Pyongyang did from this point onward showed unmistakable signs of haste. No official American account claims that North Korea moved its hurriedly assembled, partially trained army toward the 38th parallel before June 15, and this at a time when the monsoon season had just begun and offensive operations were more difficult. Pyongyang gave reconnaissance orders only on the eighteenth, and the following day it repeated its unification position in a somewhat more flexible form and called for immediate negotiations between the assemblies of the two nations. Over the next week North Korea had fully mobilized only seven of the thirteen to fifteen divisions it was to have in the field over one month later, and it did not issue operations orders, according to American sources, until June 22.[20]

While these precipitate diplomatic and military preparations were taking place under the careful eyes of United States and South Korean intelligence, American leaders in various roles were reconsidering the whole spectrum of issues in the Far East on which the United States had yet to formulate a firm, detailed policy. For MacArthur there was the largest question of American global priorities and its refusal to take its major stand in Asia. For most of Washington there was the perplexing dilemma of the future of Formosa and the possibility of a Communist invasion or internal rebellion. Related to this was the clear possibility that the UN would override United States desires and admit Communist China to membership. There was also the problem of a Japanese peace treaty and a near-universal American desire to maintain bases there after a treaty was signed, not the least because of Yoshida's large losses to the Left during the national elections of early June. Then there was Indochina, where the United States saw a major crisis brewing. In the light of these perplexities, Washington sent several teams of visiting dignitaries to Asia during the first weeks of June, and their experiences did not so much alter American policy as offer the historian the opportunity to understand it.

Defense Secretary Louis Johnson and General Omar Bradley, chairman of the Joint Chiefs of Staff, returned to Washington on June 24 after a two-week tour of the Far East, including Tokyo but not Korea. The two men had decided that under no circumstances should Formosa fall to Communist China, even if the United States had to rule the island itself. MacArthur had encouraged this policy as well, and it meant a more direct confrontation with Communist China. It was a much stronger line than an equivocal Acheson, totally preoccupied with Europe, was ready to define. Their sentiment, as well, was for doctoring a peace treaty with Japan to permit the continuation of United States bases—which is to say, a treaty without Chinese or Russian approval, but also in conflict with dominant Japanese opinion as well. These general recommendations were no sooner made than they somehow became public in the London *Times,* whose enterprising Tokyo correspondent MacArthur's officers then declared *persona non grata.*

John Foster Dulles' trip to Korea and Japan was no less significant. Without losing a global perspective, Dulles was among those who in May felt that a ". . . series of disasters [in Asia] can be prevented if at some doubtful point we quickly take a dramatic and strong stand that shows our confidence and resolution," even, he added, to the extent of being willing to "risk war."[21] He expected this crisis to come in Formosa or Indochina, but he saw the vital importance of Asia to the United States, was certain that Russia was behind a discontent that had to be eradicated, and remained ready for an American response far in excess of the provocation. With this disposition he left for Korea, accompanied by an old friend, William R. Mathews of the *Arizona Daily Star*. There the two men toured the 38th parallel, receiving optimistic reports on the fighting ability of the ROK army and the infallibility of American intelligence. On June 18 Dulles delivered a speech to the opening session of the National Assembly that had been approved and strengthened in Washington by Paul Nitze, head of policy planning in the State Department, and Dean Rusk, the assistant secretary of state. The speech was not merely a denunciation of the North Koreans but a vague declaration that "[n]ever, for a minute, do we concede that Soviet Communists will hold permanently their unwilling captives. . . . You are not alone. You will never be alone so long as you continue to play worthily your part in the great design of human freedom."[22] Too much has been read into these words, but Rhee unquestionably found them comforting, and he followed Dulles publicly to declare, "If we lose this cold war by default, we shall regain our freedom in the end by a hot war, regardless of cost. Of that I am sure." Afterward, Rhee and his defense minister saw Mathews and added details to their plans for reunification at any price, and the Americans thought they were ready to launch an offensive within a year, ". . . even if it brought on a general war."[23] Mathews told Dulles of all this immediately and warned that ". . . within months we are going to have a couple of hot potatoes in our hands."[24]

Dulles reported several weeks later that the purpose of his speech in Korea had been to reassure Rhee that the United States would do "something" if Korea were invaded, without revealing precisely what.[25] In Tokyo in the days preceding the twenty-fifth, Dulles alluded to America's determination to take "positive action," but he referred to any number of sensitive spots in Asia.[26] In fact, Dulles and MacArthur quickly reached a meeting of minds on the need to hold Formosa and maintain United States bases in Japan after the peace treaty. Neither had any intention of abandoning American interests in Asia, Korea included, and Korea was as good as any place to express this aggregate concern for the vast region.

It is certain, however, that Dulles' trip to Seoul greatly encouraged Rhee and reinforced his profound dedication to attain unity at any cost and in any way.[27] And it unquestionably reinforced the North Korean belief that the United States would sustain Rhee's plans and his corrupt regime, and that the decay in the structure of South Korea's economy and society might proceed too slowly to thwart the strike northward that Rhee had vowed to make. The North Koreans had fallen behind in the arms race once before; they would not fail to exploit their momentary advantage.

The Korean Civil War, June 24–30

The North Korean army moved across the 38th parallel about 4:00 A.M. * on June 25, but one must not make too much of this as a causal fact, for the crossing was one of many links in a long civil war that had seen many such attacks from both sides, and the Rhee government was anxious and preparing to embark soon on its own crusade northward. The real questions are not who attacked first, despite the ambiguities in the existing accounts, but are much more serious. More important was the basis of the spectacular northern success, especially given its lack of genuine surprise and the formidable size and advantages of the defending army, and the objectives the northern troops hoped to attain. No less essential was that the excessively easy North Korean advance also served the designs of Rhee. Next we must ask whether the response was proportionate to the provocation and, if it exceeded it, what larger goal did the Americans achieve.

The North Koreans attacked after the opening of the monsoon season. It was raining at the time and almost certain to continue, and their relatively superior air power and tank force were seriously immobilized from the outset. The captured North Korean attack orders reveal that they directed their attack toward Seoul alone, and that the vast bulk of their troops were engaged in that limited campaign without explicit orders to carry the war beyond Seoul. An offensive against all of South Korea, to have been quick and completed before America could land its troops, would have required a total mobilization of all of North Korea's army—about half was thrown into the attack—and equipment. In fact, first reports indicate that they committed only one-quarter of their tanks to the battle. In brief, both the manner in which they deployed their troops, and the expected resistance of the defenders, suggest that the North Koreans had embarked on a limited war to capture the Seoul region and shake loose Rhee's government, possibly to open negotiations with the new assembly on favorable terms.

The facts on precisely what happened during June 25–30 remain obscure, especially regarding the speed of the North Korean advance and the re-

*Korean time, which is fourteen hours later than Washington time. We use the time of the locale where the events occur.

sponse of the South Korean army. We can, however, establish certain essentials. Total and decisive surprise was impossible, given the numerous South Korean warnings of an imminent attack, and *if* there was a quick North Korean advance it was due to either the collapse of the ROK army or its deliberate withdrawal. The first unofficial American report to be sent from Seoul—about four hours later—left the scope of the attack open, but noted that the monsoons had grounded most of North Korea's air power, as it would bog down all heavy equipment, and this left the advantage with the defense. The extent of the advance was also in doubt. But despite the generally admitted vagueness of the facts, which were available only from ROK army officers and Rhee's government, the American ambassador in Seoul, John J. Muccio, first cabled Acheson that the nature of the assault appeared to make it an "all-out offensive."[28] The ROK army high command itself made the same evaluation at about the same time, and at 11:00 A.M. Radio Pyongyang announced that North Korean troops had gone on a counteroffensive after having repulsed a ROK surprise attack. It seems probable that the North Koreans had used their advantage of surprise to cross the parallel with relative ease, advancing the first day ten to fifteen miles along the major routes toward Seoul.

The news of the conflict began to arrive in Tokyo shortly before noon, and John Gunther, the journalist, recalls that a senior American official told him, "A big story has just broken. The South Koreans have attacked North Korea!"[29] Sebald received the news at the same time, but since it sounded like a border clash not much different from many earlier ones, he proceeded with other business. MacArthur, who saw a reporter in the early afternoon, did not mention the war but concentrated on bitterly criticizing ". . . those asses back in Washington" and stressing the need to fight Communism in the entire Far East.[30] MacArthur then met Dulles and Sebald and ". . . did not appear unduly concerned," according to Sebald's recollection, quite confident the ROK army was strong enough to hold the line.[31] He did venture to add, however, that Washington had already asked him to send munitions to South Korea. Mathews saw MacArthur immediately thereafter and his calm and confidence impressed the journalist, who was told in secrecy that two small boats were already on their way to South Korea, sent on the general's own initiative. But he was much more interested in talking about the 1952 election and presidential candidates, volunteering "I am ready to serve at any time in any capacity, anywhere."[32] Even if he had not yet seen the connection between Korea and his ambitions, that MacArthur would eventually link them was inevitable.

Dulles, for his part, was less placid and immediately shot off a cable to Acheson, which MacArthur's communications officers held up for several hours for being the equivalent to a declaration of war. For Dulles was so eager to take a stand in Asia that Korea seemed to him as good as any place to do so. If the South Koreans could stop the attack, Dulles counseled, he preferred it that way. If not, he urged employing "US force," even at the risk of Russian countermoves. The alternative would be a "chain of events" in Asia that probably would lead "to world war."[33] Here was yet another application of the domino theory.

Back in the United States, Truman was in Independence late on the twenty-fourth when Acheson telephoned Muccio's news to him. The following day he returned to Washington, but not before Acheson convened the Security Council (which Russia had boycotted since January because of China's exclusion from the UN) and successfully urged the council to call for a North Korean withdrawal and a cease-fire. The night of June 25, Truman met with his leading State and Defense Department officials and the Joint Chiefs of Staff, and Acheson directed the meeting. From the viewpoint of actual information, Truman in his memoir suggests that ". . . no one could tell what the state of the Korean army really was on that Sunday night."[34] In reality, almost all his reports and advisers expressed optimism regarding the ability of the South Koreans to overcome the attack. But he unquestionably knew that the event had generated a crisis atmosphere throughout America, and Acheson and the State Department appreciated the value of a moderate crisis in getting numerous global projects and appropriations out of an indifferent and hostile Congress, and over the following days Acheson far exceeded the military in advocating stern measures. "No one can say what would have come of these projects if the North Koreans had not marched south on the 25th of June, 1950," a senior official anonymously recollected the following year.[35] But the Secretary of State was unwilling to go as far as MacArthur, who managed to communicate to the meeting his belief that a commitment to defend Formosa was now required—an action that would have immediately involved the United States in strife with China and spread the crisis far more widely. Such adventurism, which struck Acheson as significant a few months later, never prompted him to inquire about MacArthur's possible involvement in causing the June events.

Acheson does claim also to have been concerned about what the United States' failure to intervene might do to its global prestige, on which depended the plausibility of its military "deterrents." European and nuclear armament, a sluggish economy, and the like—a useful crisis might solve all these bottled-up programs, and many others, but it would have to be neither too large nor, it must be added, too small. Washington could elect to respond to the still vague facts and traditional problems of Korea, or attempt something more grandiose. But that it saw Korea's implication for the entire globe is unquestionable. Acheson was, first and foremost, Europe-oriented, as were the Joint Chiefs, and for the next year he concentrated all his efforts on restoring American interests in Europe. But on June 25, Acheson recommended that MacArthur evacuate United States citizens and dependents from Korea and use his air force to help Rhee to hold Kimpo airport outside Seoul as well as the Seoul-Inchon area, thereby engaging in combat south of the 38th parallel. He also favored sending ammunition and supplies to the ROK army and stationing the Seventh Fleet between Formosa and China to prevent its fall. The military leaders did not oppose the recommendations, although they pointed to mechanical difficulties that might arise; but all who gathered there felt they had to draw the line at Korea or else "collective security" would fail, and the Russians might presumably attempt to take over yet another victim.[36]

While the American leaders prepared for a major crisis rather than the specific problem of Korea, military realities proceeded to confound everyone's plans. Desires, facts, allegations, all became hopelessly jumbled as they quickly distorted, even invented, facts to reinforce preconceived desires. The first response of Rhee and his generals was to employ their formidable large army to resist. Less than six hours after the invasion began they authorized a standing counterattack plan for the next morning, retaking the city of Pochon without opposition. By Sunday night, less than a day after the first shots, American military advisers and ROK army spokesmen claimed that the North Korean drive had been stopped. "Our only cause for dissatisfaction," according to one South Korean officer, "is that there has been no order to advance into the North."[37] This assessment was the basis of Washington's first response. Facts, as well as the general optimism in South Korea, appear to have warranted it. In Tokyo on the twenty-sixth, local time, Sebald found that ". . . the reports we received were conflicting and misleading," but that MacArthur, who was presumably better informed, was ". . . still confident that the South Koreans could hold."[38] Logically they could, and apparently they did. Two National Assembly declarations issued on the twenty-sixth refer only to defense against an attack that had been anticipated, and failed to describe the military situation as critical. The reports from the American military in Korea that day were so favorable, indeed, that a dozen quickly marshaled United States air transports in Japan were released for other duties.

Had Rhee's forces sustained this successful defense, the Korean episode would have been essentially like many earlier ones. The useful, mild crisis would have passed, and it is unlikely that a sudden major turn in American foreign policy would have occurred at this time. Premature good news, in brief, also had its pitfalls.

On the twenty-fifth Rhee had unsuccessfully pleaded with Muccio for airplanes and artillery that would have given him a new offensive capability. The following day MacArthur's confidence suddenly turned to a profound pessimism, which he alone among the Americans expressed. On Monday evening, the twenty-sixth, Washington time, and early the twenty-seventh in Korea, MacArthur cabled that ". . . a complete collapse is imminent."[39] The South Koreans had neither tanks nor planes, their will to fight had disappeared, and the loss of Seoul was impending before the speedy North Korean onslaught. Truman immediately authorized MacArthur to use the United States navy and air force in the Far East against all North Korean targets south of the parallel.

At this point Rhee and his associates embarked on a strategy of predicting doom, and whether it was coordinated with MacArthur is a matter of conjecture, but we cannot rule it out in light of the rather different and more complex military facts. Rhee sent his ambassador in Washington on the twenty-sixth to convey the most dire predictions and plead for far more equipment—equipment that greatly exceeded South Korea's more than adequate defensive armaments. South Korean officials began to announce that Russian officers and crews were involved in the fighting, a conscious falsehood that must have alerted Washington to Rhee's unreliability. On the twenty-seventh retreating ROK units began to pour into Seoul, and, according to the official air force history, that morning the "ROK chief of staff told all who would listen that the loss of the capital city meant the collapse of South Korea."[40] Then Rhee's officers claimed, quite falsely, that Seoul and Kimpo airfield had fallen that very morning, without resistance from ROK troops. In fact, Rhee already had decided early the day before to move the government out of Seoul.

To the North Koreans, advancing, retreating, and then advancing toward Seoul, the spectacle must have come as a shock as well as an opportunity on which they had not counted. They had committed not more than half of their military power to taking an admittedly critical but relatively small part of a nation, and against a larger army now sustained with overwhelmingly superior air power. Their first days of combat had gone well, but they also took some heavy losses and they had not done so spectacularly as to warrant total defeat for an army that had to some extent resisted ably and within months was to prove its very substantial military quality. Why this series of quick transformations of the ROK army occurred appears to us as far more important than its precise location each day. For it reveals why and how a modest traditional civil war became a global crisis.

Seoul did not fall on the twenty-seventh, despite contrary reports, even though the government deserted it that day and left the easily defended capital invitingly empty. News emanating from Tokyo, where MacArthur controlled much of it, was highly pessimistic and usually inaccurate, while that coming from other sources was less downcast. On the twenty-eighth UN headquarters reports from New York were highly optimistic about the South Korean military position, and until the thirtieth they assumed that a stable front was emerging. Seoul fell on the twenty-eighth, though some reports suggest it may have, in effect, been deserted and left unoccupied by either side for several days thereafter. On the thirtieth, other reports had it, South Korean troops regained Kimpo airfield. As the London *Times* modestly suggested on June 29, one had to treat accounts of what was happening in Korea with "the greatest reserve."[41]

Truman and his advisers could only depend on whatever data they had, which their desires and calculations leavened. The authoritative Hanson Baldwin of the New York *Times* openly acknowledged this contradictory mass of information on what was going on in Korea during the first week and on the twenty-ninth wrote, "The normal fog of war—greatly accentuated in the Korean campaign by the paucity of communications—has left Washington with insufficient information to determine with precision our future course. Major elements of the South Korean Army still appear to be intact. . . ."[42] Washington's decisions, in brief, were to reflect its acceptance of those facts that reinforced its preconceived desires. Truman and Acheson did not want to see the sudden crisis die, for the key to decisive action on Europe and much else was in Korea, and also because political pressures were beginning to mount. After talking to Republican and congressional leaders the morning of the twenty-seventh, and arranging for Security Council endorsement of any aid required for South Korea, Truman revealed his orders to MacArthur to use air and sea forces south of the 38th parallel, to station the Seventh Fleet off Formosa to stop invasions in either direction, and to speed aid to the French in Indochina. The measures were politically popular and received ten-to-one mail support from the public, and Truman and Acheson assumed that this limited aid would suffice to help Rhee's army to hold the ground; but they did not risk formally consulting Congress on any of these or later key decisions.

Logically this new aid to Rhee should have been decisive, just as Rhee's forces should have continued their successful resistance of the first two days. But Rhee wanted American land forces as well as vast increases of supplies, offensive as well as defensive. Continued retreat confronted the Americans with the alternatives of defeat or a massive commitment, and, for whatever the cause, the South Korean army began its long, ever faster, trek southward. That much is fact. When MacArthur flew to Korea on the twenty-ninth to survey the scene, he reported the retreat of the South Korean army as confused but also in columns, most men still being in posession of their rifles. Other accounts were less doleful: Rhee's soldiers were fully armed with ammunition, often in trucks, and proceeding southward in good physical condition, even singing in some instances. An army in rout, allegedly destroyed or demoralized to the extent of being generally willing to surrender, does not proceed in this fashion, nor is it capable of being reconstituted into an effective offensive army within months.[43]

That MacArthur was ready to take the Korean situation in his own hands at this point is unquestionable, and that Rhee had been doing so for some days is certain. Both men had the independence born of dedication to some higher destiny and authority, and there is no reason to suppose that their consistent penchant for intrigue and insubordination in subsequent days had not already found outlets from June 24 onward. The two men consulted together on the twenty-ninth, and MacArthur immediately urged Washington to commit American ground troops into Korea. Rhee at that time claimed that three-quarters of his army had been lost, which was patently false, and he and his generals made it plain that they had no serious plan to stop the invasion. That same day, at the later Washington time, Chiang offered 33,000 ground troops for Korea, thereby threatening also to bring China into the war. Acheson prevented Washington's acceptance of the dangerous aid, and relying on his "instinct" he kept MacArthur from going to Formosa to explain the rejection.[44]

But MacArthur sought action, with or without authorization, and early on the twenty-ninth he ordered the United States air force to hit targets north of the 38th parallel, in what was probably his second unilateral act of the crisis. Only some hours later, under Acheson's prodding, and despite some military reticence, did Truman authorize MacArthur to initiate air attacks against North Korea. Then, on the thirtieth, Truman, despite the hesitancy of the Defense Department, authorized a naval blockade of all Korea and the use of American ground forces in offensive combat, starting with a regiment and building up to two divisions as quickly as possible. Both MacArthur and Rhee learned from this experience that Washington would sustain their unilateral acts. For Rhee it meant that, with retreat and the vision of defeat, the Americans would seriously commit themselves to fighting for his cause and arming his forces. For MacArthur it opened, at the least, the possibility of victory and, perhaps, attainment of the destiny for America in Asia that was his profound vision. His nation's triumph might also become his own. And for Acheson and the State Department a sustained crisis meant the possibility of cutting through all the tiresome, immobilizing political and economic restraints that had so interfered with the full realization and application of American power everywhere on the globe.[45]

Russia and Korea

Russian foreign policy in 1950 was still oriented toward Europe, and at the moment of the Korean crisis Russia and the European Communist movements were deeply involved in a massive peace and coexistence propaganda campaign—one whose effectiveness Korea was to shatter. While it is true that Moscow's influence in Korea was far greater than that of the Chinese Communists, who at the time were not overly cordial toward Pyongyang, the importance of this relationship should not obscure the low priority that the Kremlin attached to it or the independence of Kim Il Sung and the North Korean Communists. The Russians supplied North Korea with important quantities of arms after April 1950 as a response to the arms race in the divided nation. And since these arms were not sufficient to assure victory over the probable defense from Rhee's larger army, the Russians may have thought their stabilizing arms shipments were actually assuring peace in the region.

From a logical viewpoint, the Russians must have realized that a true crisis in Korea would have mobilized the United States Congress and advanced the many bottlenecked military programs that the Truman administration had on paper, thereby reversing the narrowing gap between Soviet and American military power. Time, in brief, was on Russia's side only with the continuation of peace, and physically Russia was still too weak to risk war over an area as marginal to its interests as Korea. The Russians not only had boycotted the Security Council and UN meetings since January but had refused to return before August to veto and immobilize full UN endorsement of American intervention. The Russians were probably quite as surprised as anyone by the events of June.

The first Soviet press accounts of the Korean events were quite distinctive, and along with dutiful reporting of Pyongyang's version they printed highly impersonal, objective Reuters, France Presse, and Associated Press communiqués; Russian readers were given their choice of what to believe, an approach that was rare indeed. *Pravda* even included the full text of an American diplomatic note along with the official reply, and while Moscow condemned UN action in relatively mild terms, and verbally sustained the North Koreans, Western press analysts understood that the Russians were avoiding statements that engaged their prestige too deeply.[46]

The entire Korean affair conflicted not only with Soviet global political strategy but with their military practice as well. Less than a month after the crisis began the former United States military governor of Seoul province during 1945–1948, Colonel Maurice Lutwack, offered the view that the highly individualistic North Koreans had started the war themselves at the opening of the monsoon season, at precisely the time the Russians would have avoided had they had any responsibility for the affair. With Russian leadership, he observed, the rather slovenly North Koreans would have taken all the South within two weeks. Russian military strategy emphasized avoiding direct attacks on cities, and preferred starting major campaigns during the winter months. The North Koreans, clearly, were doing it their own way, and at the end of 1953 the Russians were successfully to demand the elimination of much of North Korea's independent leadership.

The administration had very profound doubts about the extent of Russia's culpability in the affair and what it would do materially to sustain the North Koreans. The world's press freely discussed Soviet coolness in their reports along with Moscow's failure to return to the UN and block American action. American officials were aware of Moscow's reticence, and they explicitly chose not to go too far in labeling the Russians as fully responsible for the event, at this time or in subsequent weeks, even though the current vision of world Communism as a monolithic entity directed from Moscow should have warranted it. Instead, Truman on the twenty-seventh referred to "communism" as passing from subversion to armed invasion. The same day, apparently after editing out accusations of direct culpability, the State Department gave the Russians an *aide-mémoire* asking them to disavow responsibility for the attack and to use their influence to have the North Koreans withdraw immediately. Two days later the Russians replied that the South Koreans had attacked the "North Korean border regions" and that Russia would advocate a policy of foreign noninterference in Korea.[47] Acheson immediately and correctly defined this reply to mean that although the Russians might help the Chinese do so, they themselves would not intervene in Korea. The interpretation was quite valid, for the Russians were not so deeply involved as to deny the Americans a free hand in the affair. From this point onward, the Soviet Union was neither a danger—nor deterrent—in Korea for the United States.

Retreat to Victory: July–August

The scenario of the first week of the Korean War was repeated in various forms throughout July and August. When Rhee's army stood and fought during the first days, the Americans showed both reticence and confidence. Rhee quickly saw, however, that his defeats led to further United States military interventions. Soon the retreat outstripped the North Korean advance, and the American retaliation was to exceed official explanations, much less the magnitude of the alleged provocation, as MacArthur escalated the American commitment and a somewhat reluctant Washington trailed behind him.

Rhee and his followers deserted Seoul on June 27 for Suwon, twenty miles to the south. Reports conflict on how quickly the Communists managed to cross the Han River to the south, but by June 30, MacArthur's headquarters ordered the evacuation of Suwon without a defense. Although MacArthur claimed three weeks later that Suwon fell July 2, American and South Korean forces merely deserted the city on the thirtieth to continue their southerly retreat. Next they abandoned P'yongt'aek without resistance. The United States air force repeatedly struck defending ROK units on July 2–4, causing major damage and undoubtedly hastening their retreat. One unit was hit five times in one day, and a northbound ROK ammunition train in P'yongt'aek was blown up, inflicting major damage to the friendly town. It repeated many of the same actions during the loss of Chonan, a major city thirty-five miles farther south, as MacArthur claimed superior North Korean might required yet new retreats.[48] On July 8 MacArthur was designated commander of all UN forces in Korea, leaving in his hands formal control over what resistance, or lack of it, the United States was to mount in the field.

While the military aspect of the story was taking place, with Washington rushing 7,350 troops and equipment to Korea, larger political questions kept intruding to create the broader context in which one must place all nominally military events. In effect, policy-makers began reexamining the larger question of China and Asia as a by-product of the Korean affair and the June 27 decision to freeze the *status quo* in Formosa. MacArthur profoundly disagreed with the general drift of affairs, for Truman and his aides were unwilling to move to take the vast risks in Asia he counseled, including reuniting all Korea by arms. Their rejection of Chiang's 33,000 troops revealed their relative caution, but also Washington's preference to strengthen the Anglo-French position in South and Southeast Asia rather than fight China. And Truman was unwilling to sacrifice America's global activities on behalf of yet greater adventure in Korea, but at the same time, in the fatal ambivalence that characterized his policy for the next half-year, he was unprepared to end the war by negotiations. The logic therefore permitted MacArthur unmistakably to lead American policy in Korea.

The option that Truman refused to exercise was a negotiated settlement of the war at the beginning of July, which the North Koreans may have desired from the inception. On July 1 the Indian ambassador to China, K. M. Panikkar, proposed a package compromise on Korea; the Chinese Communists would replace Chiang on the Security Council, Russia would give up its boycott, and the new Security Council would mediate the Korean dispute. The Chinese answered favorably ten days later, then the Russians agreed, and on the eighteenth the United States dismissed the plan. Most significant, it did not offer another for ending the Korean crisis, save unconditional North Korean withdrawal. During the end of June and early July the British and Russians agreed in principle on a return to the *status quo ante* in exchange for American neutrality on Formosa—a position Washington categorically rejected.[49]

While Truman was resisting MacArthur, the British, and the Indians, he moved to solidify his political support at home and to reap the benefits of the crisis atmosphere that a premature negotiated peace would have ended. He easily obtained the practical support of such leading Republican spokesmen as Dulles and Vandenberg, who might criticize marginal aspects of Truman's Asian policy but on whom he could rely. Dulles, at the same time, kept cordial ties with MacArthur and began to entertain doubts about leaving a disunited Korea at the 38th parallel again to plague world peace.

In Korea, itself, however, the position of the ROK army and the ever-growing United States units appeared to go from bad to worse. By July 24, when MacArthur sent his first report on military operations to the UN, the North Koreans had captured well over half of the South, and their advance was not halted as they traveled as much as twenty-four miles a day. Looking back at the report, the historian can only conclude that it was so inaccurate as to be deliberately misleading. It referred to a "well-planned attack," ". . . the size of their force, their logistical support" as the reason for the North Korean advance, and it claimed that the ROK army was "forced to withdraw" until July 2 by ". . . sheer weight of numbers and material."[50] In fact, the United States retained tactical air superiority throughout this period and employed massive strategic air power after July 13. By the beginning of August the North Koreans had suffered 58,000 casualties, and their remaining 70,000 men were not only substantially outnumbered, as was the case at least at the start of the war, but outequipped on the ground. Their logistics, as MacArthur described it much later, were "confused," and clearly they did not have enough equipment or preparation to take all of South Korea.[51] On July 24, however, MacArthur admitted that his casualties had been "relatively light," but he promised that ". . . the issue of battle is now fully joined," though he expected ". . . planned withdrawals as well as local advances."[52] At that point the ROK army had an effective strength of 86,000. What MacArthur would not admit was that Rhee and his own small army had retreated without fighting, virtually deserting most of South Korea to the undersupplied, poorly trained, and probably stunned North Koreans. Rather than testing his existing resources, MacArthur continuously pleaded to Washington for more and more troops, and he continued his retreat. By the end of July, Rhee and the United States appeared to be confronting a major military disaster.

At this point MacArthur preferred to venture into Asian political affairs rather than the battlefield, and he alternated in this course for the remainder of his career—to the extent that his manner of conducting military affairs was directly, probably wholly, related to his political objectives. On July 27 Truman and the National Security Council decided to give extensive military aid to Chiang, to initiate reconnaisance flights along the China coast, and to have MacArthur's headquarters survey Chiang's needs. MacArthur journeyed to Formosa himself four days later, refusing to take Sebald along to represent the State Department, and on August 1 Chiang and MacArthur released a communiqué stating that they had agreed on ". . . joint defense of Formosa and . . . Sino-American military cooperation," predicting the eventual "final victory" against the "menace of Communism." To compound the damage, MacArthur offered his own addition ". . . that all peoples in the Pacific area shall be free—not slave."[53] Truman and his advisers were dumbfounded at the unauthorized visit, for while they were willing to aid Chiang with guns, they had not decided to fight by his side, much less assume the immense obligation of liberating China, Korea, and much else from Communism. The American press and allied opinion were no less shocked, and Truman immediately dispatched Harriman to see the independent general. MacArthur implied to him, as he had to the Joint Chiefs the preceding month, that the political aim of the war was to attain unity in all of Korea around Rhee's government. On the Formosa question, Harriman was not certain they had reached full agreement. He did not have to wait long to discover that MacArthur still felt ". . . uneasiness that the situation in the Far East was little understood and mistakenly downgraded in high circles in Washington."[54] Four days after Harriman's departure MacArthur publicly accused those critical of his agreement with Chiang of being advocates ". . . of defeatism and appeasement in the Pacific." Hoping to exert some control, the Joint Chiefs of Staff sent more specific instructions to MacArthur regarding Formosa and Chiang to make certain ". . . that no action of ours precipitates general war or gives excuse to others to do so." MacArthur merely replied that he understood Truman's policy ". . . to protect the Communist mainland."[55] Then, to give further weight to his profound disagreement with official policy, on August 17 he accepted an invitation to send a long statement to the Veterans of Foreign Wars, for release eleven days later, attacking ". . . those who advocate appeasement and defeatism in the Pacific that if we defend Formosa we alienate continental Asia."[56] Truman took the message as it was intended, and unsuccessfully attempted to suppress it, even considering removing MacArthur from the Far East command. Instead, he sent the general a passive reiteration of public American policy to neutralize military action against or from Formosa.

This dispute between MacArthur and Washington was over Formosa and Asia as well as command authority, but on the question of Korea there were no serious differences. Indeed, Washington pursued a tough political line through all of August, even as ROK and American soldiers consistently retreated. On August 1 Jacob Malik took the Soviet seat on the Security Council, and while publicly denouncing the UN role in Korea, privately he attempted informal negotiations with Philip Jessup, the American member on the council. In effect, he proposed that both the Rhee and Pyongyang governments, as well as representatives of Formosa and Communist China, enter into discussions on an *ad hoc* basis. If Malik also called for an end to hostilities and a withdrawal of all foreign troops, the United States still refused for the entire month to accept any part of the proposal as a basis of negotiations, nor did it offer any alternatives. On August 10 Warren Austin implied that the United States aimed at reuniting Korea, and one week later he made this goal explicit. This policy inevitably meant crossing the 38th parallel and a march northward, the implementation of Rhee's supreme but elusive goal of unification. On a political level, Washington and not MacArthur determined that the war in Korea would become one of liberation rather than containment. This fateful decision was to alter the scope of the entire Korean affair and its implications to the future of American power. It was also to narrow the differences between MacArthur and Washington, making plausible his subsequent gambles with America's fate.

While Truman and MacArthur sparred on questions of grand strategy, the war in Korea during August went from bad to worse. By early August, 65,000 American ground troops were in the constantly diminishing perimeter that was to be created around the far southeasterly port of Pusan. This number of Americans was alone almost as great as all the North Korean forces, who continued their advance until the first week of September. MacArthur's second report on August 16 implied that there were twice the number of North Koreans on the line of contact at the end of July as at the start of the war, but in fact their numbers had declined by at least one-fifth, their equipment by much more. For MacArthur never referred to numbers of men, but only to divisions. These troops were tired or scarcely trained—but victorious. The secret of their startling advance was only implied in MacArthur's report when he revealed that during the last half of July "Army operations were basically planned withdrawals and delaying actions to gain time." In his third report of September 2, covering the first two weeks of August, the terms "withdrawal" and "readjustment" appear repeatedly, but with the explicit premise that his forces were "out-numbered" and retreating under pressure.[57]

Rhee was fully aware of this strategy, and perhaps he was the first to start it several days after the war began, but by August 12 he was profoundly concerned that it was being pursued too long. On that day he wrote MacArthur, "For tactical reasons we have been withdrawing from city to city in the hope that American reinforcements would arrive soon enough to launch an offensive before losing too much ground. This plan has been followed strictly by our military leaders and it has helped the enemy gain ground too easily. There must be some way to stop this southward push by the Communists." "We have inflicted heavy losses on the enemy and captured large quantities of their weapons," he admitted, and the North Koreans had inferior heavy armaments. The Communists, Rhee added, were sending "school children" to the front ". . . while Russian or North Korean officers keep them at gun point."[58] It was essential to counterattack after the long trek south.

MacArthur waited another month, however, before cutting through the ragged, dazed former victors. By that time his generals were ignoring his orders to retreat further, and he possessed an army adequate for much more than a war against North Korea, or so he thought. On September 1 his man power in Korea consisted of 180,000 men, including 79,000 Americans, plus 70,000 nearby United States air force and navy men. Against this force the North Koreans could deploy 98,000 men, about one-third of them fresh recruits, many of whom they could not supply with small arms. Whether consciously or not, MacArthur had transformed a civil war, intensified by what was likely a preemptive attack, into a greatly expanded American involvement in the Far East. While he juggled his strategy to increase the size of his forces, confronting Washington with the threat of defeat unless they met his interminable demands for more troops and arms, he attempted to negotiate an alliance with Chiang which Washington thought risked plunging the United States into war with China over Formosa. Yet no evidence we have seen suggests that Washington perceived that his strategy of consistent retreat and build-up also promised to bring on war with China over Korea. But that MacArthur believed that such a conflict, such a liberation from bolshevism, was part of America's Pacific destiny is undeniable. For his army now appeared sufficient to confront a nation far more formidable than North Korea.

Rhee's motives were clear enough, and he was widely regarded as a man ready to go to any lengths to reunite Korea under his own leadership—even to bring on World War III. To escalate, rather than to resist or negotiate, a serious border incident to attain his ultimate goal was a small price to pay, even if it ravaged his nation in what soon became an orgy of death rare even in this century. ". . . [T]he United Nations should prepare to deal a much heavier blow to remove Soviet influence from Korea," he advised MacArthur on August 12. "In addition, with firm bases of operation established on the eastern side of the Manchurian border, the United Nations will have great advantage over the enemy when the global conflict begins."[59] There were no basic differences between the two men on tactics or immediate goals. From the inception of the conflict, both had already shown repeated willingness to take matters into their own hands to advance their personal ambitions and goals over those of Washington, and they continued to do so again and again during the following months. But that their actions were premeditated in both intent and consequences is now unquestionable.

Still, by the end of August, MacArthur had fully revealed his propensity to push Washington in unwanted directions, but Acheson, Truman, and those of like mind were martial and adventurous enough to make the entire undertaking possible. Their willingness to accept a useful crisis at the moment only complemented MacArthur's strategy. But once Washington decided on its own volition that the transformation of a five-year-old civil conflict into a war of liberation against Communism was desirable, the gap between its own vision and that of MacArthur's was only one of degree.

The War of Liberation

To MacArthur, Korea was but a means to the realization of his dreams for Asia, and he had early attempted to expand his jurisdiction over policy in Formosa and thereby confront China, the key to the future of Asia.

From late 1949 until June 1950 the Chinese Communists had cut their military budget drastically and stationed nearly all of their remaining army in the south or in the area across from Formosa. Demobilization was the order of the day at the time the Korean conflict began, with a slight redeployment to return troops to their home areas. Both in 1950 and later, United States intelligence and official scholars agreed that China had no part in sponsoring the North Korean offensive and that initially it scarcely expected the civil war to involve its forces. Yet China's interests in the new Asian crisis was fundamental, not only because America's Formosa policy represented direct intervention in the last phase of its own civil war but also because the Chinese expected Manchuria to be their new Ruhr, the heart of their industrialization program.

The Chinese began to redeploy significant numbers of troops toward the north and Manchuria after the outbreak of the crisis; yet the larger bulk remained far to the south as China sustained various diplomatic efforts to negotiate an end to the conflict. After June, in any event, the Chinese submerged their discomfort and reticence regarding Russia as Peking saw very clearly its pressing tactical dependence on the USSR. The inevitable Sino-Soviet division was postponed for many more years.

Formosa, more than any other issue, alarmed Peking. Washington was fully conscious that the Chiang regime regarded major United States intervention in Asia, even at the risk of a world war, as its only hope of returning to the mainland. Rhee was no less desperate, and MacArthur after his voyage to Taipei seemed deeply committed to fulfilling this vision. MacArthur clearly perceived that the events in Korea might alarm the Chinese, for at the beginning of July he warned the Joint Chiefs of Staff that should the Chinese enter the war it would be necessary to employ strategic air power to destroy their supply lines. From this time onward the Chinese gave frequent advance warnings of their intentions before escalating their military commitments. Their responses interacted with American policies and the changing military realities in Korea. Until late August, Peking continued to urge a peaceful solution to the Korean crisis via negotiations, but made it plain that the question was of prime concern. They did not threaten intervention, but American journalists publicly discussed the possibility. The United States, therefore, proceeded in Korea fully aware of the possibility of Chinese intervention.[60]

Truman saw all these grave dangers when on September 1 he made a special report to the nation, referring to a desired "united" Korea as well as the need to prevent the conflict from becoming a "general war."[61] In fact, of course, unity under United States auspices and a general war were intertwined issues, and to advocate one was to risk the other. But the entire question had been carefully debated in Washington since July, with the dominant opinion favoring crossing the 38th parallel and uniting the country. And since Rhee had publicly proclaimed his intent to do so, MacArthur could expect endorsement of what was to follow. On September 11 the National Security Council decided to authorize the conquest of North Korea unless Russia or China first entered the war, and what originally was merely a desire for unity became the basis of new and greatly expanded military action.

Since there was no doubt that crossing the 38th parallel would risk war with China, which began to shift more divisions to Manchuria at this point, one must relate the timing of the fateful decision to Truman's and Acheson's larger vision of Korea in the world. The Korean affair had prevented innumerable domestic crises and resistance to European rearmament and economic issues, and even on September 10 Acheson again reiterated America's primary commitment to NATO and Europe.[62] A few days earlier Truman had authorized a major increase in United States troops in Europe, and urged NATO members to follow suit. Administration members over these same weeks sustained demands for continued high levels of military spending, urged UMT, and pressed to consolidate the immense strengthening of American global military and economic power that had begun the prior June. A quick end to the war in Korea at the 38th parallel, which the administration could reasonably anticipate by virtue of the massive offensive then being planned, might immobilize all its economic and military efforts. For their differing reasons, therefore, the administration in Washington and MacArthur disagreed on ends but not on tactics. Truman and Acheson saw Korea as a handle with which to control world affairs essentially outside Asia, while MacArthur still hoped to use the crisis to deepen America's commitment to fulfill its destiny in Asia. During the fateful months of September and October this common agreement led to temporary unanimity on immediate tactics that could only risk an expanded Asian crisis.[63]

On September 15 American amphibious forces landed at Inchon, west of Seoul, and the next day began an offensive from the southern perimeter. Although Americans hailed the campaign as a stroke of MacArthur's genius, in fact North Korean logistics and man power were so thin and weak at the time that almost any offensive strategy would have had the same results. These military successes reveal, more than any other fact, the contrived nature of the American and ROK retreat. On October 1 MacArthur ordered a halt to strategic bombing in North Korea because there were no targets of importance left. Not more than 30,000 North Korean troops managed to retreat beyond the 38th parallel, and behind them were 230,000 UN troops, plus about 100,000 supporting United States navy and air force men. By that time it was clear North Korean military power had been utterly destroyed.

This was the optimistic, tempting military picture when Washington on September 27 again authorized MacArthur to cross the parallel and unite the country unless the Russians or Chinese were in the fight. But the Joint Chiefs insisted on approving his plans for the northern invasion, a restriction MacArthur managed to get removed several days later. By this time Washington was fully aware that Chinese troops were beginning to mass in Manchuria, but American planners were unclear about Chinese intentions. On October 1, Rhee's troops crossed the parallel and MacArthur called upon North Korea to surrender unconditionally. That night the Chinese unequivocally passed the word along via the Indian ambassador in Peking that China would intervene in the war if the Americans crossed the parallel as well.[64] Furthermore, on October 2 the Russians introduced a highly specific resolution to the UN for a general settlement of the Korean crisis, a step that was a measure of their fear of an escalation of the war. The new resolution, which provided for a national election under UN supervision as well as a cease-fire, was immediately voted down under American pressure

—in part, of course, because the Communists would probably emerge victorious in a fair election. Instead, the UN authorized its forces in Korea to attain unity by continuing the armed struggle, passing over the issue of elections very vaguely. The same day, October 7, United States troops crossed the parallel, well after Washington was aware of the likely consequences. Three days later the Peking radio again warned that China would enter the war.

Truman was so conscious of the likelihood of Chinese intervention that on October 10 he modified his earlier directive to permit MacArthur to fight Chinese troops that might enter the war so long as there was ". . . a reasonable chance of success."[65] Now all he demanded was that the general receive official approval before mounting any kind of attack against China itself. And he also arranged to meet the erratic general on Wake Island five days later.

By this time Truman and his advisers were deeply in doubt about the course on which they had embarked, as well as the designs of the man who had been given the power to implement a policy that was still unquestionably their own. It can be said that Washington hoped MacArthur might succeed in conquering Korea without the logical and inevitable consequences that were threatened, but that the general was the aborted outcome of its own adventurism. For MacArthur, however, the mandate and his power opened the door to endless possibilities. It was only this daring that Truman feared, but he himself had embarked the United States on a bloody and disastrous course on behalf of a war of unification.

The Wake Island conference was necessary because of MacArthur's repeated past independence, and the dangers he might create should the Chinese enter the war. While the two men reviewed the past and briefly alluded to other Far Eastern questions in the course of the ninety-six-minute discussions, the main question was whether the Chinese would enter the war. MacArthur tried to convince Truman that they would not do so, but if they did, they could not mount sufficient power to snatch victory from the United States. Truman regarded the general as abrupt and anxious to return to Tokyo before lunch, unwilling to dally with his nominal superior. MacArthur, who had not wanted to go to the meeting, found Truman irresolute.[66]

By mid-October everyone responsible was aware of the mounting Chinese troop concentrations in Manchuria, their warnings of intervention, and the risk of war. Truman did not have to get MacArthur's advice on the matter; Washington was also fully capable of predicting the future. MacArthur knew the Chinese were earnest, but he had contempt for their military capacity and welcomed the opportunity of striking a blow against them. That this risked war against Chinese territory was certain and was the basis of MacArthur's plans since July. He opened his arms to the possibilities.

The Chinese on October 14, and repeatedly in the following weeks, showed their might and then withdrew in the hope that the United States would seek to limit the war. That day Chinese planes twice bombed Kimpo airfield and flew back to Manchuria, from which point China knocked down an American plane the following day. On the eighteenth the Chinese parked more than seventy-five fighter planes near the Yalu, removing them the next day. The United States air force correctly interpreted all this as a warning. Chinese troops crossed into Korea itself on the fourteenth. Three days later MacArthur authorized the movement of all non-ROK troops to within thirty to forty miles of the Manchurian border. The CIA several days later warned that the Chinese would intervene to protect their electric plants on the Yalu, but when the State Department proposed to MacArthur that he consider a public statement disavowing plans to attack these plants, the general successfully discouraged the idea. On the twenty-fourth he unilaterally removed all prohibitions on United States troops going to the Yalu. The Joint Chiefs of Staff immediately protested that MacArthur had violated their directive of September 27, but they did not countermand his new departure. Everyone could see its significance, and MacArthur was probably encouraged to believe he might be free to disobey Washington again. War with China was now inevitable.[67]

By October 20, when MacArthur's intelligence had alerted him that 400,000 Chinese troops were on the Yalu ready to cross, the likelihood of war with China still depended entirely on how far the United States was ready to press its hand. But MacArthur wanted victory over Asian Communism, even at the risk of an enlarged war. Over the next days, UN forces took the first Chinese prisoners and ROK troops suffered their first serious reverses in weeks as MacArthur's command consistently downgraded the danger of Chinese intervention. The general estimated that the war was about over, but it was patently obvious at the time that it might be just beginning.[68]

The question of MacArthur's objectives is clear, but the reasons for Truman's and his advisers' actions are more complex. No one in Washington wished a war with China; yet they were privy to sufficient information to know that its likelihood grew the closer United States troops moved to China. Truman was concerned that MacArthur would provoke an unwanted crisis, and both he, the State Department, and the Joint Chiefs of Staff wished to concentrate American attention and power in Europe. Still, MacArthur could not conceal the basic facts regarding Chinese deployments and intentions, thereby gulling others into a false sense of security and an unwanted crisis—though he may have hoped to do so. The Wake Island meeting was a manifestation of their profound concern with obvious realities. The question therefore remains as to why Washington did not stop MacArthur at this time.

The answers are essentially the same as those of the preceding summer, when a limited response to a limited crisis would have ended an emergency that was politically necessary to Washington's main emphasis on European goals—objectives for which it needed congressional appropriations. But Congress was still not acting quickly enough on administration requests, and during October, Washington was urging the Europeans to rearm to meet a world crisis that it insisted had begun with Korea. Once more, the White House regarded congressional reticence as sufficient cause for contrived crises. On his way back from Wake Island, Truman stopped in San Francisco to urge publicly that the remarkable victory in Korea ". . . not delude us into any false sense of security. We must be better armed and equipped than we are today if we are to be protected from the dangers which still face us." Since, during those same days, the military were planning for the redeployment of troops in Korea to Europe and canceling scheduled troop movements toward Korea, when Truman urged, "We must continue to increase our production for military purposes . . . and less to civilian consumption," he hoped to capitalize on Korea to attain his objectives elsewhere.[69] The arms, and especially the politically more difficult man power the administration was determined to extract from Congress after the November election, were not meant for Korea and were but the prelude to sustained and greatly expanded military expenditures over the coming years. An end to the war before the congressional campaign might make cutbacks an attractive campaign issue. Truman did not want war in Korea, but he did not want peace too quickly either, and this seemingly ambiguous but quite functional tension persisted for another year. In this context, MacArthur was able to remain the master of the situation. On October 24 he ordered his troops to move toward the Yalu as quickly as possible, removing the few inhibitions Washington later claimed to have imposed on him.

While the grand drama of a Sino-American conflict unfolded, and Washington and MacArthur struggled among themselves, Rhee moved to gather the fruits of the war and proceed to fulfill his dream of unification. South of the 38th parallel, Rhee began a widespread purge of his opponents, Communist or otherwise, via military courts which at the beginning of October were sentencing some thirty people a day—most to death—in Seoul alone. Generally, his henchmen used more direct methods until early October, when efforts were made to stop what was too arbitrary a process even for the ROK army. Rhee's reputation as a liquidationist became so great that by the end of September officials in Washington considered pushing him off the scene.

More of a challenge was Rhee's effort to extend his political domination north of the parallel and unify Korea under his own control. While Washington did not muster sufficient concern to remove Rhee from the South, it was resolved that administration of the North be left in UN control and, much more vaguely, supervised elections. Rhee claimed his own legitimacy on the basis of UN supervision of the May 1950 election, which, of course, had thrown his followers out of office, and he cautiously moved to challenge UN rule of the North. During mid-October his government repealed all Communist land reform laws and later announced that it would sell most nationalized industry to individuals. He sent hundreds of Seoul representatives north to take over civil affairs, and although MacArthur on October 30 was forced to bar five of Rhee's governors, over the first two weeks in November, Rhee shipped 4,000 policemen over the parallel, and these had sufficient power to arrest the UN-appointed police chief in Pyongyang. The UN had no civil affairs structure, and it is likely that with time and further purges Rhee would have indeed unified Korea into one police state. Larger events soon cut the trend short.[70]

22

Korea: The War with China

At the beginning of November 1950 it was unequivocally clear that the issue in Korea was now the extent to which the United States was willing to go to war against China, and the steps toward that vast confrontation were no less obvious. If American troops persisted in going all the way to the Yalu, the Chinese would intervene. MacArthur welcomed the prospect: ". . . the greatest political mistake we made in a hundred years in the Pacific," he stated the following May, "was in allowing the Communists to grow in power in China."[1] The Truman administration considered the risk worth taking, but for reasons having only a superficial relationship to the future of Korea itself.

Washington certainly was privy to all the facts in Korea, despite the occasional vagueness and inconsistencies in MacArthur's reports, and it did not have to rely on either his advice or his estimates in light of the universal suspicions of the general's intentions. On November 3 MacArthur reported to Washington that over 800,000 Chinese troops were in Manchuria, and while he did not believe it probable that they would cross the border, neither would he rule it out. But he also made fully explicit his desire to have a confrontation with China as the alleged great expansive military danger in all of Asia and the source of the Korean War. Several days later he publicly downgraded the extent of the Chinese intervention even as American and ROK troops were reeling backward in defeats; yet at the same time he also referred to the "privileged sanctuary" the Chinese retained in Manchuria as if it were now the major source of danger.[2]

This "sanctuary" was the object of MacArthur's strategy at this time. When American troops fell back in certain sectors MacArthur's headquarters demanded justifications from the commanding field general, and on

November 6 MacArthur directed his air force to destroy all the bridges on the Yalu River. The Joint Chiefs of Staff, upon seeing MacArthur's order, instantly countermanded it and instructed the intrepid general not to bomb within five miles of the Yalu. MacArthur immediately protested, claiming that unless given this freedom the movement of Chinese across the bridges ". . . threatens the ultimate destruction of forces under my command."[3] Washington again backed down, but insisted that American planes hit only the Korean side of the bridges.

At this point, while MacArthur toyed with a dramatic resignation as a protest against Washington's restraints upon him, two events coincided to strengthen the general's hand. The congressional elections on November 7 returned large numbers of Taft Republicans who, like their mentor, nominally called for a tougher Korean policy and greater emphasis on Asia. Taft appeared a likely presidential candidate and winner. MacArthur's political base was strengthened at just the critical time. On virtually the same day the largely successful Chinese troops broke contact and withdrew from the war for a period of two weeks.

MacArthur now had the threats of his own resignation or military defeat as well as independent political backing unless Washington yielded to his strategy. This combination was successful, despite the largely correct estimates of Chinese power in Manchuria. The options were now perfectly clear to all: the Chinese would intervene in yet larger force or they would not. They had already intervened in part, and now men such as Dulles warned that if the Americans went to the Yalu ". . . we shall become bogged down in an interminable and costly operation. . . ."[4] The Chinese began on November 7 to admit that they had intervened in the war, and they made scarcely any reservations about the fact they would do so again if necessary. But MacArthur saw his advantage, and he pressed it without delay. On the seventh he cabled Washington twice, arguing now that full-scale Chinese intervention was not likely, that in any event he had to resume the offensive north, if only to test Chinese strength and intentions, and that unless he were promptly given permission to pursue Chinese aircraft into Manchuria and also bomb their bases the restraint could have "decisive" implications for the war.[5]

At first the Joint Chiefs were inclined to explore diplomatic alternatives, but they would not restrict MacArthur's freedom to advance, despite their profound reservations. Even Acheson, who favored creating a demilitarized buffer zone along the border, did not uphold changing MacArthur's existing orders to reunite Korea by arms or his freedom to march to the Yalu. Yet everyone on the National Security Council retained grave doubts regarding this freedom, fearing that the impending war with China would distract from the far more critical European arena. The key decision-makers appeared inclined for a time to allow MacArthur his request to send aircraft across the Yalu, but when the British and other allies were consulted, they unanimously opposed the notion and expressed their mounting alarm over the course of American policy. For two weeks, therefore, Washington did nothing to inhibit MacArthur's plans for a final offensive, even though a *de facto* cease-fire existed, and to the general this inaction was encouragement.

That the war would escalate seemed certain. Dulles now became alarmed, and after consulting with Vandenberg he warned MacArthur on their joint behalf that they were opposed to getting involved in any land war in Asia, a view Dulles made widely known during November. MacArthur himself freely admitted to Sebald on November 14 that should his imminent offensive fail it would be vital to bomb Manchuria, and his officers in Tokyo revealed their impatience to bomb China. The future, in brief, held no surprises.

MacArthur ordered his offensive to begin November 24, seemingly quite aware of the immense number of Chinese troops in Manchuria and possibly that a quarter-million rather than 60,000 to 70,000, as he claimed at the time, were actually in Korea. Publicly he proclaimed victory to be at hand, but privately he also issued retreat instructions to his generals should it become necessary. At the same time, he deployed his troops in an exposed manner that some Pentagon leaders thought risked disaster. The Joint Chiefs of Staff, profoundly disturbed, urged him to be cautious; but MacArthur dismissed their advice, and they still refused to tie his hands in any degree. MacArthur knew again that he was free to act and that in temporary defeat, should it come, he might attain yet another escalation—and ultimate victory and war with China. Three days later the Chinese threw about a quarter-million men at the American and ROK line and shattered it, threatening MacArthur with a major disaster.

MacArthur later with dialectical logic claimed his offensive was really a "reconnaisance in force" to determine Chinese intentions and capabilities rather than a disastrous defeat on the field of battle.[6] In fact there was no military need for the offensive at that juncture, and the reason was entirely political and could only lead to a confrontation with China. MacArthur had successfully escalated the war from its inception on June 25 by timely defeat, retreats, and threats of new defeats if not sustained, and he thought his strategy would work again. On the twenty-ninth he again revealed that his real objective was China when he urged Washington to permit him to blockade China and to incorporate Chiang's troops on Formosa into his command and bring them immediately to Korea. The issue now was not merely the use of American air power against China, which MacArthur demanded, but also the creation of a situation in which Chiang would unquestionably have become a ploy for sending Nationalist man power back into China itself, bringing on the crisis in Asia that MacArthur sought.

Washington, for the first time in a month, balked. MacArthur's plea had warned that the new situation ". . . broadens the potentialities to world embracing consideration[s] . . .," and this ominous fact the National Security Council realized when it considered the new situation. At the same time, MacArthur freely used the press and radio to attack the few inhibitions Washington had imposed on him. By this time his carefully cultivated promises, facts, and illusions, which the administration had also exploited for its own purposes, were too much for men such as Vice-President Alben Barkley, who frankly exclaimed, "[t]his is an incredible hoax."[7] The generals and civilians all agreed on the urgency of avoiding a war with China that would undercut the basic American commitment to Europe: they would give no further authority to MacArthur, but neither would they publicly undercut him. Yet the traditional theme of not exhausting American power against China, or the less vital rim lands, if only because the Soviet Union alone would be strengthened by it, prevailed once more—though not before profoundly alarming America's European allies.

It was Truman himself who on November 30 at a press conference provoked the greatest crisis when a reporter asked him whether the United States might use the atomic bomb in Korea. "There has always been active consideration of its use," the President retorted, and a clarification later that day merely reiterated the thought that he might indeed authorize the use of the bomb.[8] At the beginning of the month, in fact, the State Department had sought to clarify the procedures for obtaining presidential permission to use the bomb—the first thought given to the possibility. It also appears almost certain that MacArthur at about this time proposed dropping thirty to fifty atomic bombs in Manchuria along with using up to a half-million Formosan troops. He probably suggested the creation of a radioactive belt along the northern border to make it impassable—he definitely did so by the following mid-February—but the Pentagon studied the approach and found it impractical. Since Washington failed to concede to MacArthur at this time, on December 1 he released two public statements that only further frightened the English into believing that Truman had lost control of the situation. MacArthur argued that the war in Korea was "critical and serious," but not hopeless if he were sent reinforcements and permitted to pursue Chinese forces across the Yalu and bomb their bases. He freely alluded to war with China and also refused to rule out use of the A-bomb. He then downgraded the relative significance of Europe so critical to Washington's planning.[9] Three days later, still threatening defeat unless his wishes were met, he argued to the Joint Chiefs of Staff that a defensive line was too difficult to maintain unless the full panoply of military measures, including use of atomic bombs, were employed. The alternative, he warned, was total withdrawal. Washington immediately told him to preserve his forces as best he could, dispatched its own general to find out what the real truth was, and on the fifth banned all unauthorized public, political, and military statements. For the moment, at least, MacArthur had been leashed.

Throughout November the British and French had watched the events in Korea with mounting alarm, fearful that the Americans would withdraw their attention from Europe, and Prime Minister Clement Attlee was under strong pressure from both parties, but especially the Bevan faction of Labour, to bring the Americans to their senses. They saw MacArthur, in particular, as an independent menace. When Truman made his statement on the possible use of atomic weapons, Attlee wired for an appointment on December 4, and after obtaining the support of the French proceeded to Washington.

By the time Attlee arrived in Washington, MacArthur was not able to define United States policy, but neither would American leaders consent to serious diplomacy. They exposed to the English leader all the belligerent impulses that had made MacArthur's earlier political successes possible in the first place. They blamed Russia for the entire crisis, discounted China merely as its satellite, and totally dismissed the Titoist impulses Attlee attributed to China. Washington would not recognize any of China's gains in Korea and ruled out negotiations until the military situation improved. It again exploited the domino theory, and the United States made it clear that the UN would be called upon to further sanction American policy. America's leaders simply informed Attlee that they would isolate China diplomatically and keep it out of the UN, build up and sustain militarily the surrounding Asian nations, and protect Chiang on Formosa without permitting him to drag the United States into a mainland adventure. The exchanges were sharp, and Attlee thought Acheson's persistence in Korea and refusal to negotiate highly belligerent. "The Americans found it hard to realise that in the eyes of Asia they had become almost a spearhead of imperialism," Attlee later recalled.[10] But he achieved the goal of his visit: the Americans promised that they would not get into a major war with China and that they would not neglect their commitments in Europe unless the Chinese mounted heavy air attacks from Manchurian bases, at which point the British agreed to support a limited campaign against China itself.

Military defeat, which pushed American and ROK troops back to the 38th parallel by the end of 1950 and led to the loss of Seoul on January 4, generated a mood of defeatism and pessimism not without its beneficial consequences to Washington planners. As during the summer, the UN retreat often outstripped the Chinese advance, again conjuring up the prospect of rout and defeat. The speed of the ordered retreat was so great, and contact with the scantily equipped Chinese so minimal, that in the three weeks after November 24 total UN casualties were 13,000, or a small fraction of comparable World War II campaigns. MacArthur wished to use the propitious situation of imminent disaster to blockade China, bomb its mainland, and employ Chiang's troops in Korea and help them to invade South China, but Washington totally ignored his proposal to this effect during early December. Truman was now convinced that the man was ready, perhaps eager, for a general war. Yet Truman and his major advisers, with the same characteristic ambivalence that had always marked their policies, did not want immediate peace either. Soviet peace overtures and feelers, they concluded, would weaken American efforts to rearm Europe, despite the fact that they did not expect war in Europe. In brief, given the international context, Washington still wished to maintain the crisis atmosphere. At this particular point neither the United States nor China was prepared to consider a return to the *status quo* at the 38th parallel.[11] America's leaders were still trapped both by their global aims and by their persistent need to implement their goals midst a sense of emergency.

MacArthur immediately claimed that his flight southward was not the result of military disaster, but fully planned and with light casualties. His forces in January 1951 consisted of 365,000 ground troops against 486,000 Chinese and North Koreans, but his air and naval power was overwhelmingly superior, as was his equipment. This army was able to stop south of the 38th parallel, eventually to return to it, and successfully to maintain the defensive with essentially the same resources. There is ample reason to accept MacArthur's admission that he ordered his soldiers south as part of the truth, but also their own panic and surprise as another cause of the precipitate retreat.[12] But the fact remains that so long as MacArthur might threaten defeat he could also hope to discipline Washington.

Washington now appeared fully chastised from its past adventures in Korea, determined to avoid a world war, but it was ready to fight a defensive war to avoid being thrown out of Korea. Unprepared to commit new man power to the battle, the administration communicated these policies to MacArthur at the end of December, and he interpreted them as a loss of "will to win" and "defeatism."[13] His own solution had not changed: he asked to blockade and bombard China and use Chiang's troops to invade it. Again Washington rejected the advice, and when it so informed MacArthur he replied on January 12 that the administration's restrictions would probably lead to the "complete destruction" of his forces.[14] The Joint Chiefs of Staff were ready to consider MacArthur's proposals only if defeat appeared likely or if the Chinese also attacked outside Korea, but the net effect of MacArthur's threat of defeat was to intensify the now widespread suspicion of him in Washington. Truman was obviously losing patience with the man, and after consulting the National Security Council he reiterated for MacArthur the essentially secondary importance of Korea in the world and even in Asia. To find out what was really happening in the war, he sent off a top-level fact-finding committee to Korea.

The facts only reinforced Truman's determination, for MacArthur had again grossly distorted them. After January 7 the Chinese broke off their offensive, such as it was, and the United States held its lines, even starting a slow return north that eventually culminated at the 38th parallel—and in over two more years of stalemate. Coincidentally, MacArthur's obedient commander of the Eighth Army in Korea, Lieutenant General Walton Walker, was killed in an accident at the end of December and Washington immediately replaced him with the politically reliable Lieutenant General Matthew B. Ridgway, who was loyal to the Pentagon alone and did not endorse MacArthur's strategy of retreat and escalation. The CIA then also successfully overcame the MacArthur-imposed blackout over their operations in the region. Having organized his alternatives, Truman was now in a position to destroy the American proconsul in Asia.[15]

Truman and his key aides were ready to restrain MacArthur, but they would not assent to a policy of stopping the war via negotiations. During late November and December, the United States would not enter peace negotiations—and Truman as much as told Attlee this during their talks. But many UN members, especially India, were profoundly concerned, and their pressures compelled the United States to respond to their peace initiatives. On December 9 Indian diplomats had revealed that China was ready to negotiate on Korea as part of a larger Far Eastern discussion, and Vyshinsky the same day proposed a withdrawal of all foreign troops from Korea. The initial American response was again to ask the UN to label China an aggressor, and Warren Austin poured forth a stream of invective that Vyshinsky matched. The subsequent byzantine complexities need not detain us, for they proceed only from policy, and the United States was to brand China an aggressor and argue that the Chinese had categorically rejected various UN proposals that China was in fact by mid-January quite ready to discuss. The time was not ripe for diplomacy, and the United States mobilized its power to bring recalcitrant UN members into line. At the beginning of 1951, Washington had embarked on a policy of neither escalation nor peace. The war would go on.[16]

War of Attrition

After mid-January American and Korean forces stopped their hasty retreat, began to reestablish contact with the more slowly advancing Chinese, and cautiously moved back toward the 38th parallel—the beginning of a long war of attrition roughly along that line. On the diplomatic front Washington managed to get the UN General Assembly on February 1 to brand China an aggressor, but for the first half of 1951 the most important events occurred in the ranks of the American decision-making elite as MacArthur sought to exploit the military stabilization for his own advantage.

MacArthur's vision was geopolitical, involving the future of American priorities and power in Asia, but also personal and a reflection of his own inordinate ambitions. Within the context of continued vacillation in Washington, MacArthur had every reason to hope that he might yet win acceptance of the basic thrust of his strategy, and that if so he might then capitalize on victory to advance his own political career. If it did not succeed, he might then blame defeat on his opponents and perhaps still sweep them aside.

In the strictest sense of the term, MacArthur's dispute with Washington was one not between military and civil authority, as is usually suggested, but between one man and all civil and military elements who stood in his way, for the vast bulk of the military establishment's leaders loyally sided with Truman against MacArthur's plans for escalating the war with China. This open conflict of authority had begun the prior summer, had nearly reached a breaking point by October, and was inevitable by the end of November, when MacArthur could no longer even partially swing Washington to his strategy. Even as he was being thwarted and isolated during December, MacArthur had begun quietly to lobby in Washington for his position on using Chiang's troops, and he received some assistance in this task from Formosa itself. By mid-February, as his troops were moving toward the recapture of Seoul, MacArthur pressed Washington for a strategy of total victory in Korea, including the creation of a radioactive wasteland across a strip of North Korea and a whole panoply of his measures to spread the war to China itself. Rhee, for his part, publicly agitated for the reconquest of the North. The decision whether again to cross the parallel, however, remained the key to the immediate issue on how long the war might continue and whether negotiations were possible. On February 15 Truman publicly declared the crossing to be a question for MacArthur to decide, with which he would not interfere. The statement again passed the initiative to the general, revealing Washington's recurrent ambivalence on war and peace which had made the general's strategy possible all along.[17] His freedom to act was not to last long, for Acheson and the Pentagon even then were energetically attempting to rescind the September 27 directive that had removed the limits on ground action north of the 38th parallel. By the end of March, however, they had not yet fully reconciled their differences on precisely how to muzzle the general.

In his February 23 public report on operations, MacArthur complained about restrictions that Washington had imposed on him, implicitly transferring to it responsibility for his defeats. Then, on March 7, the very day his army began a major northward offensive, MacArthur publicly threatened an impending "military stalemate" in the Korean War unless Washington made unspecified "vital decisions" regarding China. This threat of depriving the nation of victory, a variation of his now common threat of defeat unless the administration sustained his plans, struck a popular and responsive chord in the Republican Party. The next day Joseph W. Martin, Jr., the Republican House minority leader, wrote MacArthur as an avowed follower of his global strategy, one of his "legion" of admirers, asking for his confidential or public views on a "second Asiatic front" against China.[18] For MacArthur, whose interest in the Republican presidential nomination was already intense, the opportunity was too great to ignore. Without disobeying formal orders, which remained vague enough for him to continue his land offensive toward, and eventually slightly over, the parallel,

MacArthur now chose to grasp at the 1952 presidential nomination via a public crisis with Washington.

Since he had already been forbidden for some months from making unapproved statements on foreign policy, MacArthur unquestionably knew that his post was at stake—but that the potential rewards were worth it. On March 20 he replied to Martin that the war against China required "maximum counterforce," including unleashing Chiang, and that the main arena in which to combat Communism was Asia. "There is no substitute for victory."[19] Then, the following day, the Joint Chiefs of Staff informed MacArthur that Truman and the State Department wished to freeze major military operations north of the parallel in order to test diplomatic prospects and respect the desires of America's allies. MacArthur immediately retorted, asking that the Joint Chiefs impose no further military restriction on his command. Then, while Washington prepared to offer publicly a cease-fire and negotiations, on March 24 MacArthur astounded the world with a public statement that derided China as militarily impotent and implied that the extension of war against the Chinese mainland was desirable. Truman was shocked, and America's allies even more so; but he contented himself with having the Joint Chiefs remind MacArthur of the December 6 ban on foreign policy statements. Then, on April 5, Martin released his letter from the general, one the aspiring candidate had not told him to keep confidential, and that very day MacArthur sent a response to an inquiry from the right-wing journal, *The Freeman,* tartly implying that Washington was delinquent in not arming more South Korean troops.

The release of the Martin letter was the "clincher," to quote Truman, especially its contention that the major American commitment should be given to Asia rather than to Europe. The British were profoundly disturbed.[20] In a sense, the Truman administration, for its own reasons, had willingly permitted MacArthur to maneuver it into a complex situation in Korea that now threatened to far outstrip the partial utility of a Korean crisis. The main arena of the world crisis, in Washington's nearly unanimous view, was still Europe. As a result of Korea, Washington had made major commitments to Europe and to the field of military technology development, and many more were pending. An expanded war against China threatened to transform the partial instrumentality of Korea into a trap. MacArthur, from the inception, had been the source of this persistent tendency to escalate. On April 6 the President informed General Omar Bradley that he was considering firing MacArthur, and the Joint Chiefs unanimously agreed with the proposed action, for they not only shared the commitment to Europe but feared that a war with China would inevitably drag in Russia. Four days later, having obtained the support of all whom he asked for an opinion, Truman retired MacArthur from all his commands.

Although he immediately took the posture of an innocently wounded hero, MacArthur must have surely been aware of the risk that his obvious play for Republican support could lead to his dismissal. He certainly missed no opportunity to capitalize on the dramatic possibilities to optimize his political chances, and he was visibly impressed at the immense crowds that welcomed his triumphant return in San Francisco and then in Washington on April 19. His dramatic speech to a joint session of Congress was simply a reiteration of his call for military victory in Asia, the need to employ Chiang's troops on the mainland, and a rather patent eulogy to his own accomplishments in administering Japan. Then, to attain maximum political impact, he toured twenty American cities to expose his person to ecstatic, adoring crowds, and finally returned to Washington during May to answer questions before a special Senate inquiry that ultimately smothered the issue of MacArthur and Far Eastern policy under a mountain of undigested words and documents. Returning to New York to confront his 170,000 eulogistic letters and telegrams, it was now time to determine whether MacArthur's gamble would pay him political dividends. For he was obviously seeking the Republican nomination, a success that would have dramatically altered the United States' global priorities. To the traditional foreign policy leaders in both parties, MacArthur's defeat in 1952 became an imperative goal.[21]

In the meantime, the war continued. On April 5 the UN forces began their limited offensive and managed only to drive about ten miles over the parallel in most places, further proving the point that the conflict was stalemated. A defensible line a bit north of the 38th parallel now became Washington's more modest military objective in Korea. But while Washington now reluctantly accepted the military reality and its diplomatic consequences, Rhee moved to perpetuate the policy of adventurism without MacArthur's aid. At the end of May, while the United States considered armistice talks, Rhee announced that he would not ". . . agree to any compromise until we have driven the enemy out of Korea and achieved the unification of the country. . . ."[22] At the same time he unsuccessfully attempted to get arms for ten new divisions, but during June and July he further used his police and military power to intimidate the National Assembly and embarrass Washington with his repressive consolidation of power. In principle the United States did not dispute the desirability of the reimposition of Rhee's control over all of Korea, but it knew that only its own forces might aspire to implement such a policy, and during May the Americans were ready for an armistice they hoped would also lead to the withdrawal of all foreign troops. Trygve Lie and most of America's European allies also openly favored an armistice and negotiated end to the war. When on June 23 Jacob Malik called for a cease-fire and troop withdrawals to the 38th parallel, the American bloc welcomed the initiative. Two days later China endorsed the proposal as well. Washington then instructed General Ridgway to take steps to open talks restricted exclusively to military matters leading to an armistice. After some preliminaries, on July 10 North and South Korean, American and Chinese military delegations met for the first round of talks that were to last for two more years.[23]

From the very opening meeting it was obvious that the Communists wished to see a return to the 38th parallel and the withdrawal of all foreign troops, while the Americans endorsed a cease-fire along the existing battle lines, now mostly to the north of the parallel. At the opening of these interminable verbal wrangles, the North Korean and Chinese forces comprised 450,000 men armed with a motley assortment of American, Russian, Japanese, and local arms. UN forces comprised 555,000 far better-equipped ground troops, almost half of whom were Americans, plus an enormous air and naval armada. The Americans were certain that they could not lose the war, but they were unsure of victory without a general war in the Far East. For the rest of 1951, while the diplomatic negotiations at Kaesong were bogged down—or at the end of August even adjourned for two months—the Americans relied on their air and naval power to inflict massive destruction behind the front lines, striking Pyongyang itself with an immense attack only three weeks after cease-fire talks began. On the ground the Americans probed northward, but made little progress against an enemy whose will and fighting capacity they consistently underrated.

From the very inception of these talks Rhee made it repeatedly clear that his goal was the same as it had been for years: unity, not peace. To some extent, this danger remained abstract so long as the Communists refused to back down on the issue of a satisfactory truce line, and the Americans drew up contingency plans for a greatly escalated war should China seek victory in the field. The British, however, sharply proscribed the conditions under which they would participate in measures so drastic as a naval blockade of China or bombing across the Yalu, but events kept such deep

Anglo-American disagreements academic. Then, during late October, the Communists backed away from the 38th parallel as the possible truce line. While this issue was not resolved during 1951, if only because Ridgway insisted on a yet tougher policy in response to what Washington thought important concessions, the progress toward a solution was marked enough to warrant some optimism. By the following March both sides had agreed on the principle of the armistice itself. It was the repatriation of prisoners of war that proved far more difficult.[24]

The American position on repatriation of prisoners shifted radically after the opening of negotiations, but since the facts of the prisoner situation were constant, the changing way the Americans handled the matter reflected the intensity of their desire to reach an accord. The issue was extremely complicated and far less ideological than the Americans were inclined to suggest. When the North Koreans moved south they recruited or impressed many troops from the region, including former ROK army personnel. Quite apart from politics, these men naturally wished to remain near their homes, and most were tired of war. That they did not wish to be repatriated north was not at all testimony to Rhee's attractions. Others were South Korean civilians and innocent bystanders, including women and children, whom American and ROK troops had indiscriminately picked up and imprisoned in massive antiguerilla operations throughout the war. Some had actually sought to get into the prison camps so as at least to obtain food and escape the sea of misery in the outside world. None of these people wished to be sent to North Korea, and in large part the Americans inflicted this segment of the problem on themselves when they labeled such victims of war as legitimate prisoners rather then victims of American and ROK disregard for the innocent and hungry. For the Chinese prisoners, of which there were about 20,000 by April 1952, the situation was less straightforward. The larger majority of them did not wish to be sent back to their leaders, and while the Americans attributed this choice to ideology, closer to the truth was that many were tired of years of war against Mao, Chiang, or America, and they longed for the civilian life that the American plan for nonrepatriation promised. Indeed, given the terror both anti-Communist and Communist cadres applied in the camps, there was scarcely any accurate method of determining, as the Americans insisted they had to do, whether or not prisoners wished to be repatriated. Fear and force often determined votes. Humanitarian justifications for American policy were hardly more credible, for during the year and one-half of delay in the war, essentially over this issue, the UN forces alone suffered 140,000 casualties, including 9,000

American dead, and it was ending the war quickly that was most consistent with humane impulses—of which there were very few.[25]

From a legal and practical viewpoint, the prisoner issue was a sordid use of men on behalf of politics. The greatest tragedy was the innocents impressed into the camps against their will or there in search of succor and food. To aid actual soldiers to desert the army would be legitimate from a pacifist nation, but not from the United States. Since the Americans regarded United States soldiers who refused repatriation as traitors and shirkers, and drew up plans to try those who returned, there was no reason to expect the Chinese and North Koreans to think differently. And as the Communists often correctly pointed out, the American position totally violated the 1949 Geneva Convention on the repatriation of prisoners of war. The simple solution, which the United States never proposed, was to separate the actual soldiers from the others and send them north, and, as part of a comprehensive settlement, identify the remainder and return them to their original homes and status, perhaps implementing the scheme via a neutral commission. But no real progress was made on this issue during 1952, as Truman and American negotiatiors contented themselves with usefully ideological and humanitarian statements that belied the nature of a bloody conflict that was a far greater menace to humanity than forcing troops back to their officers. In 1952 the UN command claimed it held 130,000 prisoners, and that all but 14,000 would be repatriated—a number ten times that the Communists claimed would return south. Progress appeared likely with this formula until late April, when Ridgway lowered the number of his prisoners willing to be repatriated to 70,000, profoundly exacerbating the armistice negotiations. The issue was only further complicated when during the summer the United States released 27,000 Korean civilian internees, including women and children, who should never have been in prison camps in the first place. With numbers constantly changing, the prisoner issue seemingly remained the insoluble nub of the diplomatic problem.[26]

The military dimension was essentially constant, despite persistent pressures from Ridgway or his successor after May 1952, General Mark W. Clark, and other officers, to expand and intensify the war along most of the lines MacArthur had demanded earlier. Washington resisted such advice on much the same basis as it had during 1950 and 1951: it still identified the United States' major vital interests with Europe, and even the Middle East, rather than Asia. UN ground forces nearly doubled to 933,000 by July 1953, but Chinese man power by early 1952 had brought the Communist forces to 867,000 men, giving the United States only a nominal edge. Yet despite the improved Chinese artillery and aircraft, the overwhelming technological superiority rested with the UN forces. The war remained stalemated.

Hanging over the frustrating negotiations was the profoundly disturbing role of Rhee, who from the end of 1951 had covertly encouraged demonstrations in the area under his control around the theme of "No Armistice Without Unification"—which was to say, continued war.[27] Ridgway and various American officials were deeply disturbed by his avowed and sustained opposition to American policy, and especially by the fact that Rhee had an army capable of smashing a truce. After considering more stringent alternatives, in March 1952 Truman contented himself with a message to Rhee warning him that economic aid after the war would depend on his immediate good behavior. Essentially, however, Washington decided the issue was still abstract, for peace was a long way off. Rhee himself, while he continued to make clear his hostility, by May and June was once again embroiled in a preoccupying conflict with his National Assembly, arresting some as alleged Communists, and declaring martial law in the capital of Pusan. The actual issue—Rhee's effort to alter the Constitution before the summer's national election in order to save his own power—embarrassed the American government's campaign to promise "liberty" to prisoners, and Washington succeeded in pressuring the strong man into only partially revoking his suppressive measures.[28] The capacity of Rhee to take the most extreme unilateral steps to fulfill his goal of unity was now more obvious than ever.

The Korean War was the second most expensive in American history; yet the manner in which it was fought made it without precedent in the annals of warfare. Ranging the most powerful industrial nation of all time against comparatively poorly armed peasants, for the United States the war almost immediately became an assault against the population of an entire nation —some 30 million persons—and the war was scarcely less destructive in its impact on the 20 million Koreans south of the parallel than the 10 million north of it. As such, in proportionate terms it inflicted at least as much death, destruction, and misery on a civilian population as any war against a single nation in modern history. For warfare between a great technological power that relies on indiscriminate mass bombing and shelling and a poor nation leads inexorably toward genocide—a final solution that the United

States avoided only because the war came to an end without a conventional military victory for the Americans.

The United States air force had completely destroyed all usual strategic bombing targets in North Korea within three months' time, and by the end of the first year of combat it had dropped 97,000 tons of bombs and 7.8 million gallons of napalm, destroying 125,000 buildings that might "shelter" the enemy. In mid-1952 it turned to the systematic destruction of mines and cement plants, and in June it hit the Suihu hydroelectric complex on the Yalu.[29] In the South the destruction was almost as great, aggravated by Rhee's own special contributions to the elimination of lives. The most notable and publicized episode was his roundup of well over 400,000 men at the end of 1950—men he hoped to arm and put in his army but in the meantime left in concentration camps under guard. Unable to arm them, he also failed to feed them adequately, and an estimated 50,000 died of disease and starvation over the next half-year, the large majority of the remainder becoming physical wrecks. Tens of thousands escaped, and ultimately Rhee was compelled to release large numbers under pressure from his irate National Assembly. In reality, however, these men were prospective enemies and guerillas as well as potential ROK soldiers, for the Korean people sustained major guerilla operations behind American lines throughout the war, a skill the Koreans had first mastered against the Japanese decades earlier.[30] The Korean War, in effect, became a war against an entire nation, civilians and soldiers, Communists and anti-Communists, alike. Everything—from villages to military targets—the United States considered a legitimate target for attack.

The press fully reported the misery and suffering throughout the war, and when the final accounting was taken the human pain exceeded measurement as each family alone was aware of what it had suffered. UN combatant deaths were over 94,000, 34,000 of whom were Americans. Wounded came to over four times that figure, and American sources estimate Communist military casualties at over a million and one-half. Over a million South Korean civilians died, and probably a substantially larger number of civilians died in the North, for almost a decade after the end of the war the North Korean population was only equal to its 1950 level. Half the South Korean population was homeless or refugees by early 1951, and 2.5 million were refugees and another 5 million were on relief at the end of the war.

This process of utter destruction was virtually complete by the end of the first year of the war, when the head of the Far Eastern Bomber Command,

Major General Emmett O'Donnell, Jr., publicly declared, "I would say that the entire, almost the entire Korean Peninsula is just a terrible mess. Everything is destroyed. There is nothing standing worthy of the name."[31] This fact created very real military problems, and meant that short of escalating the war to China or committing vast new troops to ground combat, the United States quickly lost most of its military levers for making the Communists more responsive at the armistice negotiations. The bombing of the Suihu hydroelectric complex on the Yalu in June 1952 and thereafter, which the British had feared would lead to an end of truce talks, nearly exhausted that threat. The most important remaining targets to attack were the irrigation dams so vital to the rice crop and the civilian population. Only the Nazis in Holland during 1944–1945 had dared to perform so monstrous an act, one the Nuremberg Tribunal later judged a war crime. Air force planners were fully aware of such humanitarian objections, and for the moment restraint prevailed.[32]

By early October 1952, however, the American representatives at the truce negotiations declared they had no further proposals to make, and the military felt additional military pressures were essential. Despite a substantial increase in American offensive efforts over the autumn, Clark and his aides attempted to obtain vast new man-power commitments from Washington and extend the war to China via air and naval power. Washington rejected the proposal. The war was now irrevocably stalemated unless the new President were willing to unleash a fresh wave of massive destruction —or negotiate an end to the war. Even so, the United States had so far failed to impose its will on poor Asian nations with the determination to resist. At the end of 1952, and for well over another decade, virtually all of Washington could not comprehend the historic significance of this monumental event to the limits of American power in the world.

Still, the war in its perverse way had proved utilitarian to the Truman administration's achievement of its larger goals in Europe and the world. It had helped to mobilize a reticent Congress, and it galvanized an apathetic population as well as wandering allies. Certainly throughout 1950 Washington had been unwilling to negotiate an end to the war, or merely stop once its troops had again reached the 38th parallel, because of its desire to exploit the new crisis to attain yet other, quite unrelated, objectives. If the Truman administration also kept the war alive later for reasons of domestic politics or fear of being politically outflanked with accusations of appeasement, the dilemma was one of Acheson's making. And if desire to make more credible the vision of America as the masterful military giant also led to prolonged combat rather than an easily negotiated peace, this consequence was also a reflection of the condition of self-mystification that was increasingly to become a self-defeating element in the conduct of United States foreign policy. Both in its cynicism, destructiveness, and illusion, the Korean War was an introduction to what was later to become the most sustained crisis of the modern American experience—Vietnam.

23

The Dilemmas of World Economic Power, 1950–1953

From the end of World War II until the spring of 1947 the United States' leaders saw the formation of an International Trade Organization as the basis of a comprehensive integration of the global economy compatible with America's interests. That durable goal of a world open to its trade and investment, operating essentially in capitalist economies, was a chimera that realities again and again compelled the United States to adopt new techniques to attain. If the initial means were to prove inadequate, requiring constant improvisations, the ends themselves were never to vary from 1945 —or even 1915—onward. For the ITO was but a means toward that unwavering goal.

The process of improvisation began in earnest with the GATT (General Agreement on Tariffs and Trade) conference that opened in Geneva in May 1947, and the Marshall Plan provided the United States with new, powerful means of extracting the Western European trade and investment concessions we have already discussed. GATT was the heart of the ITO structure, but its exclusive focus on tariff and trade terms could not provide solutions for other anticipated, if still quite abstract, problems. But its commitment to an abbreviated version of the ITO's most essential principles, and its practical effort to negotiate away the trade restrictions that the thirty years of crisis in world capitalism had created, led even Washington's strongest proponents of the ITO to acknowledge during 1947 that the failure to create the ITO would not defeat the United States' foreign economic policy. This recognition was essential, for apart from profound doubts as to whether the Senate would overcome its own protectionist biases to ratify an ITO treaty, it also prompted America's policy-makers to produce new instrumentalities for attaining their larger ends. Indeed, from the high point of domestic support for the ITO toward the end of 1946, each new concession or proviso in the proposed ITO Charter that the State Department's negotiators were to make to other nations at the Geneva GATT conference and the Havana ITO Conference, which ran from November 1947 through March 1948, resulted in declining support for the ITO among crucial domestic business constituencies.

In mid-1947, however, the immediate problem that Washington confronted was England's obstinacy in maintaining the imperial preference system and its threat to refuse to endorse the charter—a warning it later fulfilled. Since the two nations accounted for over two-thirds of world trade, the State Department saw ever-elusive British cooperation as the real test of the entire undertaking—a story we have already recounted. The Western Europeans went along with American demands, at least temporarily, because they wanted ERP aid, but they were fully aware of all the inconsistencies between America's trade practices and the principles it advocated. Many of these were written into the Geneva draft of the ITO Charter, which left the way open to tied United States loans that could be spent only in America and permitted the continuation of the United States' preferential, monopolistic trade relations with Cuba and the Philippines, but also specifically attacked state trading by others and greatly circumscribed future national efforts to correct balance-of-payment difficulties by controlling foreign trade. And while America's delegates managed to insert an amendment in the charter protecting international private investment, at the same time beating down India's desire to use import quotas freely to stimulate and protect Third World industrialization, at Geneva the other nations were in turn able to force through a clause attacking those export subsidies that had become so critical to big American farmers. The State Department withheld its position toward this traditional American violation of multilateral free trade, but the power of the rest of the world to so define the contemplated ITO to damage United States agricultural interests brought to the fore the Agriculture Department's always deep, latent hostility toward the scheme. Politically, this was enough to assure the ITO's failure in Congress.[1]

By the time the Havana Conference opened it was clear that the State Department was operating without solid political backing at home, and that it had defined a position that in one way or another aligned most of the capitalist and Third World nations against its comprehensive program.

High-tariff industries flatly opposed further tariff reductions, and the major United States business organizations bided their time before coming out against all compromises to Third World and European interests—and therefore rejection of the ITO. Even the army, represented by Herbert Feis, thought the charter did not protect the national security in petroleum questions. Foreign opposition was also troublesome, and of the close to five hundred amendments to the Geneva draft charter, mainly from Latin American nations, the United States opposed the large bulk outright. The convoluted compromises forced through at Havana satisfied no one, including most American interests and the British; and the draft charter is mainly curious as an expression of the United States' determination to protect international investment and its access to raw materials and trade on the most favorable terms possible. Its ambiguities on export subsidies pleased few.

After the Havana Conference the ITO scheme became the sole concern of the trade officials in the State Department, and Truman and Acheson decided to postpone any serious ratification effort and concentrate instead on ECA as a means of dissolving Europe's economic restrictions. In principle they favored the ITO, but they surveyed Congress' mood and decided not to press the matter too strongly. The charter went to Congress, but was never reported out of committee, and despite occasional statements of support for the ITO, by early 1950 the President and State Department had effectively abandoned their hopes for its passage. For the remainder of the Truman administration, GATT was exploited to perform whatever useful functions might have been anticipated from the ITO, and the ECA gave the United States its real opportunities to attain its goals. By 1949 it was patently clear that the United States had conceived ITO for a world infinitely less traumatized by the war and its social and economic consequences.[2]

Point Four and the World Economy

The ITO's collapse left the practical problem of developing new instruments for the attainment of world economic integration outside of Europe, for this goal remained unshaken even after the original means for reaching it had failed. In 1949 it was an issue of significant, if not urgent concern to Washington, for only preoccupation with European affairs lessened consideration of the future of the Third World economic structure outside of the oil-producing regions. Long before 1949 the United States had deeply immersed itself in the affairs of the Middle East because American companies had defined the rich stakes there and also because that region's instability opened it to competing Russian or British influences. But the remainder of the Third World was also vital, if less immediately compelling, and when consciousness of the imminence of upheaval and independence there was pressed upon Washington, then, too, did the destiny of Asia, Latin America, and Africa increasingly move toward the center of the world arena.

The ITO was crucial both for what Washington intended to attain and also because of the quite placid means the Americans originally hoped to employ in restructuring the world economy. Nations were to negotiate away economic conflict, thereby allowing the United States to gain its traditional ends without violence and direct intervention. The collapse of this assumption now meant that if the United States was to create its ideal world economic order it would have to find new, more effective means. The political preconditions of economic integration, with all its eventual human consequences, now became a central matter for Washington. The manner in which the United States would define its interests in the Third World, and then seek to attain them, by 1949 began to emerge as one of the fundamental problems confronting the world.

The first response was largely economic. The United States had hoped throughout World War II to open the world's economic channels to a high level of private United States capital export, and it expected that the task would require only a short period of governmental aid to reconstruction. Then, via the ITO, the World Bank, and private capitalist efforts, it would rather quickly establish a reformed world economy. Later, the Marshall Plan and loans to England and others were seen as but temporary expedients. With the failure of the ITO it was crucial to find new means of returning to the original objective of relying on American business to export capital to maintain prosperity at home via markets and profits abroad.

By the end of 1948 it was all too plain that private foreign lending and investments would scarcely suffice to fulfill America's foreign economic goals. In the aggregate, American private capital investment abroad recuperated very slowly, and adjusted for inflation had fallen far below the levels of the late 1920's. As a percentage of real national product, even during 1950–1955 private investment was almost half of 1925–1929. Deducting investment in Canada and Latin American petroleum, United States capital exports during the postwar years held out no hope of replacing the economy's governmentally financed dependence on overseas outlets. Indeed, only 15 percent of the United States' vast capital exports during 1945–1948 came from private sources. By 1949, with declining demand at home and growing industrial dependence on rather small but critical production accretions for export which historically have made entire industries profitable, nearly half of America's exports were in the form of foreign aid shipments. In brief, in the manner integral to the post-1865 American historical development, the national political structure was again doing for capitalists what they could not do to advance their own vital welfare—totally identifying the interests of the state with the profitability and power of American capitalism.

But it also remained Washington's constant intention ultimately that American business and finance should have the main responsibility for overseas capital exports if possible and that Third World countries should welcome them. Such United States assistance in resources development Washington deemed to be in everybody's best interest, but no less critical was to make certain that private capital export begin playing the role United States planners assigned to it. By 1948 the Export-Import Bank, originally created to help ship United States equipment and management into primarily Latin American raw materials sectors, was bogged down in its own rigid criteria for immediate profitability. If American capitalism were eventually to realize its vast potential, virtually all concerned government and business leaders acknowledged before 1949, United States interests would need hard assurances against all the political dangers and economic liabilities they confronted in the Third World: expropriation, exchange controls, the absence of an adequate basic public sector of roads, ports, and services indispensable to investment but too costly for foreign capital to construct. The American government, in brief, would have to bear certain risks and establish essential political preconditions.[3]

It was with this thought that Truman mentioned the Point Four program during his inaugural message of January 1949. It was scarcely more than an outline of an approach, but the State Department planners who were given the main jurisdiction for turning it into a full-bodied scheme were keenly aware of the meaning of the ITO's failure and the need to attain American capitalism's central role in future foreign economic policy. They, in turn, were pushed along by export-oriented businessmen who also agreed on the need ". . . to create a business 'climate' in other countries more attractive to private investment, . . . using government loans to develop basic resources in such a way as to increase the opportunities for *private investment* in the borrowing countries."[4] This program, all the interested sectors felt, had to focus mainly on the production of raw materials for export.

The first detailed expression of this effort to create a "favorable climate" for private investment, as Truman's advisers called it, came in Truman's special Point Four message to Congress on June 24.[5] The statement was entirely explicit as to means and goals, stressing the need to increase private capital outflow by first building a services infrastructure in the Third World capable of welcoming vastly increased American business investments. At the same time, Washington would obtain economic treaties to give American corporations their much-desired assurances against nationalism and radicalism. But Truman asked for only a modest $45 million to begin the program, a figure which left Point Four in the realm of abstractions rather than material fact. Yet it is such abstractions that give coherence to much else that the United States was undertaking at the time and that remind us of its basic objectives in the world.

Practically, Washington's key planners wanted to see United States industry annually invest $2 billion overseas by 1952—or twice the actual amount it was to attain—to lower government loan and grant burdens and sustain a large export market. Point Four, which was always set in the larger world economic context with Europe at its center, was one part of a long-term effort to plan for American prosperity after the ERP ended. This meant procuring future supplies of raw materials as well as allowing Europe indirectly to earn dollars via its predominant control over African and Asian raw materials exports—thereby also sustaining an export market for American goods in Europe. And, no less important, Washington expected that timely United States dollar inflows into the Third World would prevent import and exchange controls by nations unable to balance their foreign trade. In principle, Point Four promised endless windfalls, but it was too petty to produce any in fact. Even in fiscal 1953 its budget was only a paltry $156 million. And in Latin America, as Acheson and the State Department often made plain, no government funds would be employed where private United States money was available, or where there existed obstacles to private investors—local or foreign—for whatever reason. This postulated everything from stable government to freedom to remit enormous profits back to the United States. It also meant that in Latin America, for practical purposes, Washington felt that the region's stability by contrast to the rest of the Third World would allow United States capitalists to assume the greater responsibility there, with minimal government grants.[6]

Despite some quite traditional haggling over its precise structure, Congress, the administration, and key export trade associations shared a fundamental consensus that Point Four was to increase the flow of private invest-ment for all the reasons we have already mentioned. There was no need even to make the dangers of Communism a significant argument. More critical was the fact that scarcely anyone expected Point Four alone to accomplish what it defined as its ends, and even Truman's low-pressured efforts to pass the measure—which bore fruit in June 1950—indicated that Washington had a realistic sense of its limitations. The immediate problem of the dollar gap and the maintenance of United States exports after ECA we have already discussed in the context of European rearmament. But as a long-range strategy the administration retained its profound hope that a dra-matic increase in trade and investments would give it new means of coping with domestic economic needs as well as achieving its basic goals in the world economy.

The patent failure of Point Four even to approach the export sector's needs, despite the negotiation of many investment guarantees and treaties, led also to new reviews of the instruments for attaining a constant objective. But the impact of the Korean War on world raw materials supplies made the need for success more urgent and strengthened what had always been Point Four's major emphasis on assuring a secure and adequate supply of critical raw materials for the United States.[7]

Raw Materials: Sinews of Power

Imported raw materials in American industry have a value and role which superficially appear quite slight, but their value far exceeds either their weight or their cost. Small imported inputs to domestic resources make whole industries, particularly technologically sophisticated ones, pos-sible. Frequently even a rather minor foreign supply allows those modest increases in output from which, after the break-even point is reached, most profit is drawn. And free access to scarce materials eliminates constraints on industrial development and diversification.

There was no mystery regarding the importance of oil and minerals to profits prior to the Korean War, as we have already seen. The United States had been a large net importer of raw materials during the 1920's, and time only increased this dependence. By 1930 the United States was importing 64 percent of its bauxite as a share of its consumption, 65 percent of its copper, 9 percent of its lead. By 1948 it was a net importer of oil, and then iron ore. In 1950 it imported 8 percent of its iron ore as a share of its consumption, 76 percent of its bauxite, 48 percent of its copper, 43 percent of its lead, 40 percent of its zinc, and it was utilizing close to one-half of the world's total output of these commodities alone. In 1956–1960, to project ahead, the United States imported over one-half of its total metal consumption, and over four-fifths of its supply of thirty-nine mineral and crude commodities, one-half to four-fifths of fifteen others, and up to one-half of the supplies of twenty more. Though the Western Hemisphere was the largest supplier, Africa, Europe, and Asia were also vital for certain commodities. Whole industries and, indirectly, entire economic sectors of which they were a part, were dependent on them. Moreover, these supplies were increasingly and largely to be found in the Third World, the politically least predictable regions. Without such access, even before 1950 the American economy would not have been able to operate at anything like its existing level. To conjecture on quantitative magnitudes is both impossible and superfluous, save to note that the trauma of total isolation from the world would have been very profound. America's key decision-makers also believed this to be the case, and it was one of the central thoughts prompting their global policies.[8]

World economic integration was therefore a question not merely of opening channels to private United States overseas investments, thereby lessening the need for government aid in one form or another, but also of using American funds to develop raw materials supplies urgent to the entire domestic economy. For to a vital extent, American firms established in the Third World provided much, often the bulk, of the most essential materials. Third World development therefore necessarily meant development along capitalist lines that left the door open to United States penetration, currency convertibility, and nondiscrimination against foreign corporations. Washington never doubted this durable tenet.

Raw materials shortages and the need to expand Third World supplies were among the major arguments for Point Four, and as we shall show, the materials shortage and price spiral that accompanied the Korean War only added weight to this rationale. And competition with other industrial nations for scarce materials, and the need to guarantee the United States secure supplies, now became a new, vital element in the relations between the world's industrial, capitalist nations. In this sense, success in creating new supplies in the Third World was also essential to maintaining a unity within the NATO bloc that raw materials rivalry was sorely testing long before Korea.[9]

The Korean War brought to the fore a complex, interrelated American policy decision that was profoundly to color its future relations with the

Third World. There was, even more than any American leader had previously acknowledged, a raw materials crisis, but also a desire and need to locate investment outlets essential to America and to the development of these foreign supplies—to which was added, as a kind of afterthought, a commitment to raising local living standards to cope with the revolutionary threats incipient or in motion throughout the Third World. This synthesis, which was a part of Point Four, the presidential commission headed by Gordon Gray articulated in greater detail in November 1950 and also cast the problem in the context of future economic relations with Western Europe. The Gray commission also made clear, however, that ". . . it is vital not to lose the sources of these needed raw materials to the forces of Communist aggression."[10] In the short run, the Gray commission believed, it would be crucial to use greater military aid to hold on to these vital regions—to establish, in effect, the political preconditions of later successful economic integration.

Attitudes and policy both expressed this mood and profoundly further broadened the area of the world the United States was now ready to deem vital to its essential interests—an attitude that was to unfold in countless interventions over subsequent years. And it was also to define yet more precisely America's position on noncapitalist modes of economic development and the Third World's many and diverse anticolonial and revolutionary movements. On a practical level, in India the United States resisted the development of a nationalized economic sector while extracting vitally important manganese supplies in return for foreign aid, while in Brazil a combination of Point Four and Export-Import Bank financing opened vast new manganese deposits there to American steel investments. By 1951, as we have seen in many other contexts as well, this concern for access to Third World raw materials was building to a crescendo everywhere, especially drawing attention to Latin America's vital importance to the United States' future economic power. Both publicly and privately, key American leaders believed that they had to guide foreign policy on the premise, as Harriman put it to a Senate committee early in 1952, that "I do not believe this country can survive if the sources of the raw materials are in the hands of unfriendly people who are determined to destroy us ."[11] ". . . [T]he interest of the United States is now clearly and inextricably linked to the interest of all nations of the Free World," Stacy May, a key government economic adviser also employed by the Rockefeller interests, argued privately at this time. "This interest extends to all fronts—the security, the political and the economic fronts alike. This community of interest does not rest upon rhetoric or sentiment, but upon the hard and unyielding realities of strategic and economic fact; and foreign investment directed particularly to the obvious and compelling need for raw materials, is one of the instruments, and an important one, that must be employed in our overall strategy."[12] By the end of 1951, indeed, it would be difficult to find any exceptions on the part of business or government officials toward this reasoning. Scanning America's interest in the world in a memo to Truman in January 1952, there was virtually no region that Harriman would rule out—with raw materials supply being the only common single justification for the United States' involvement in the entire Third World.

It was in this context and mood that Truman created a Materials Policy Commission at the beginning of 1951 under William S. Paley of Columbia Broadcasting System to formulate a comprehensive national policy on the topic, and its final conclusions reflected this consensus among business and government leaders. Apart from defining the objective needs of the American economy in raw materials, the commission surveyed interested business opinion, but corporate pleas for greater government aid in creating secure foreign investment opportunities could add nothing to Paley's belief that ". . . we have to be more mindful than ever before of the importance of creating either climate or mechanisms of one kind or another which would make it easier for us to get these materials from foreign sources at lowest prices possible under circumstances which are most advantageous to us."[13] With some verbal accommodation to the sensibilities of the Third World nations who were the main subjects of its work, the Paley commission's massive final report in June 1952 reiterated this utilitarian view and called for intensified political efforts via treaties and tax aids, as well as Point Four and governmental bank participation, to develop new supplies of raw materials in the hands of America's business. And in rejecting self-sufficiency and endorsing world economic integration—which it defined as objectively essential to the United States' needs—the commission further solidified the strategy for Third World development that had been a constant assumption in United States foreign economic policy for decades.

The problem, of course, is that the political, psychological, and economic condition of a large and growing section of the Third World made these American objectives utopian, and the attempt to attain them could only lead to endless intervention in the great process of decolonization and development that was becoming the overriding historical fact of the post-World War II epoch. This perceptible shift in American priorities, as much the result of articulating old premises as of becoming aware of new needs inherent in Europe's recovery, was to contribute heavily to the movement of American involvement in the Third World that has become the defining reality of conflict and economic development in the Third World in our time.

Washington saw clearly the political preconditions of economic success in the Third World and the need for temporary monetary losses to make possible later economic gains. Point Four had been designed with this willingness to assist American business interests through a transitional period, during which time planners thought that investment treaties, guarantees, and seed money for an essential development infrastructure would suffice. By 1951, when raw materials shortages dramatized the costs of failure, it was apparent that it was more immediately essential to have local governments willing to accept the United States on its own terms. And this meant aligning itself more fully yet with the forces of stability and comprador leaders wherever possible. For this reason, after 1950 the United States adopted a much more respectful attitude toward the colonial regimes of its NATO allies, for while it wished to open those areas to commerce, it also was anxious to prevent leftist forces from controlling their future.[14]

As had been the case since the war's end, all the right-wing elements of the world were appealing to the United States for sustenance, and the collapse of the colonial systems for maintaining order meant that in many areas only United States backing to local antirevolutionary constituencies protected them from the forces of change. Often the challengers to the neocolonial regimes were but competing elites capable of being co-opted—risks the United States would take only if certain this were possible. But, in a general way, the United States further took on, as it had since 1945, the colonial burden that the decline of Britain and France imposed on it, for fear of opening the entire Third World to endless and unpredictable changes—changes invariably based on mass indignation and action rather than any meaningful Russian involvement beyond rhetorical support. In Latin America, after a period of quite nominal hostility toward local dictators, the United States in 1951 began its long and ultimately futile effort to supply them with the guns and intelligence for finding and rooting out what Acheson described as "subversive elements."[15] In 1952 alone, Washington signed military pacts with the military dictatorships in Cuba, Peru, and Colombia, a precedent Eisenhower was to extend. For the authoritarians who welcomed United States business, ample kind words were their reward. America thereby became the bastion of established orders and, where necessary, counterrevolution. Hopefully, many American leaders thought, later gains would follow from the military and political investments it was to make, with trade following the flag once the suitably conservative social preconditions were created along with a minimal economy to service investment. The long process of working with all the world's compradors, military elites, and private fortune-builders was to continue and become more universally the rule. The cornucopia of arms and prison locks for all the world's conservative totalitarians was to grow larger with each passing year. In the name of liberal integration, the United States had become the foundation of conservative order.

The larger structural relationship between the peasant and landownership was a guarantor of an irresistible impulse toward revolution throughout the Third World. America's need to intervene in that upheaval throughout the Third World became the conditioning and limiting factor of the whole process of development, making the necessity and will to resist the United States' direct and indirect role, with its man power or arms and aid to local conservative comprador elements, an important part of change in many nations. And this ever real fact or threat of American intervention, rather than imperatives of the accumulation process or ideological predilections, meant that only fully mobilized, internally disciplined revolutionary societies were likely to survive. In time, sections of the Left developed a structured justification and rationale for their response to America and the Right's artificial and externally imposed obstacles to basic social transformation, a rationale that also impeded deeper pluralist and humanistic impulses which, in another time and world, would have been ultimately more compatible with rapid economic development and freedom in the former colonial areas. The Left's road to power, and the outcome once it was attained, were the defensive effects of the hard struggle for survival, and not a conscious choice that can be divorced from the limited options of the historical process. The United States was now in the process of stymieing and checkmating the easier, more tolerant options most of its radical opponents preferred. The world crisis and national development and independence had become one.

The manner in which the United States defined its future interest in the Third World necessitated its intervention, with thoroughgoing nationalism being at least as dangerous as the nominal and eclectically defined Communism which many of the nationalist leaders also evoked. This process of intervention, while often a small effort by America's standards, usually had vast repercussions for the power balance in smaller nations, upsetting the frequently decisive power of forces of radical change against the colonial elements and their local allies. Such small meddlings, which are almost too numerous to be itemized in a general history, individually were of no critical import to America's interest. Collectively, however, they all impinged on the essential question of the future structure of the world, and very profound damage to America's power in it, should each area embark on development to the exclusion of foreign trade. For if world economic development proceeded to the point where the world's resources were not fully available to the United States, and outlets for investment were greatly circumscribed or closed, the crisis of American society inherent in its existing inequitable distribution of income and consumption, as well as its inadequate resources, would be profoundly, and perhaps even decisively, traumatic.

Abstractly, the United States claimed to favor Third World development, but in the context of an efficient specialization of labor whereby the raw materials producers would increase their exports to meet America's need and eventually generate sufficient funds for diversification. Ultimately, however, American analysts drew satisfaction from the fact that the rate of growth in the Third World remained too slow to compete seriously with the industrialized nations' needs. In fact, as well, after the peak Korean War demand of 1950–1952, the Third World's share of world exports began to decline dramatically, a process that continues to this day. And the terms of trade—the cost of its imports compared to the prices it received for its exports—after 1957 were to shift again dramatically against the Third World. The American argument for efficient export specialization also conveniently ignored that the United States and European firms controlled a large sector of those Third World industries—as Washington deemed proper—leading to a vast continuous flow of repatriated profits back to the United States, capital which was not locally available for development and diversification.[16]

The End of the Marshall Plan

By June 1950 the economy of Western Europe was stagnating, and the Truman administration, frustrated in its attempts to secure congressional approval of long-term aid to Europe, had focused on rearmament as the only palatable way to maintain a supply of dollars to purchase American exports abroad. As in the past, a world crisis was necessary to convince Congress to sustain such an alternative, and the Korean War with astonishing swiftness wiped out the economic dilemmas and political restraints confronting Western capitalism during the preceding year, only eventually to introduce new calamities for Europe and the Third World. For the United States, however, war once again brought renewed prosperity.

The most significant feature of the last half of 1950 was the almost hysterical race throughout Europe and the United States to amass as much raw material, industrial, and consumer goods as possible. By August new domestic orders flowed into an American industry that was quickly losing interest in foreign sales. Steel and coal, which only a few months earlier had been a glut on the market, were in short supply as many United States companies scurried to Europe for what they could obtain, and the oil crisis with the British was forgotten for the moment. European governments, fearing inflation, released their hitherto guarded dollar reserves, since commodities of all kinds were suddenly more precious than dollars. Inventories of every sort were accumulated as a hoarding impulse gripped industrialist and housewife alike. By far and away the most serious aspect of this trend was the accelerated United States stockpiling of strategic raw materials. While America's massive purchases, especially of tin, wool, and rubber, put new dollars in the hands of the British via their colonies and trade allies, other European states were soon faced with aggravated dollar and raw material shortages, and the worsening terms of trade and inflated prices shortly wiped out the temporary British gains as well. During the last half of 1950, for example, the price of rubber rose by three times, the price of tin and wool doubled, and all commodities combined rose about two-thirds. Since the United States was the largest consumer of the world's raw materials in 1950, the fluctuations in its demand had the most immediate impact on prices, but the inflation did not affect all countries equally. Because the United States produced a significant proportion of its own raw materials it was better able to control the price of what it imported, while Europe paid an average of at least one-quarter more for the same commodities. The plight of England highlighted the severe consequences of these rapid changes in the world economy.[17]

The impact of the Korean War and the vast shifting in the prices and supply of raw materials dealt successive blows to the British economy. The flood of new dollars into the colonies, primarily from the United States, at first gave the sterling bloc a surplus of dollars and led to an Anglo-American agreement in the fall of 1950 to terminate all ERP assistance at the end of the year. However, the balance of payments is not the only index to the health of an economy, and by November high prices and shortages of raw materials threatened to close many British factories. Attlee, in his discussion with Truman in December 1950, accused the United States of stockpiling practices which created Britain's shortages, strong inflationary pressures, and growing unemployment. As a result, seemingly as a gesture of cooperation, the United States tempered its stockpiling slightly, and prices dropped over the early months of 1951, although they remained over 50 percent higher than in June 1950. But combined with England's seriously worsening terms of trade and shift toward rearmament, the decline in raw materials prices almost wholly concentrated in tin, rubber, and wool, in turn had an unanticipated, devastating effect on Britain. United States demand for imports of all kinds, saturated by the hoarding of 1950, had sharply contracted by mid-1951, and by October Britain's balance of payments, according to a key ECA official, was once more "little short of disastrous."[18] England was, in fact, struck by its worst economic crisis since World War II. From an increase of gold and dollar reserves to $3.8 billion in mid-1951, its holdings declined drastically to $2.3 billion by the end of the year, and over the first two months of 1952 it lost another half-billion dollars. The British treasury calculated that one-half of the deficit was due to rearmament, the other half to the worsening terms of trade. During these same months the Iranians nationalized British oil property, amounting to an annual dollar loss of over $350 million. Washington confronted an imminently bankrupt Britain, and a France succumbing to a renewed dollar crisis and on the edge of financial collapse complicated the emergency. The United States again had to formulate a new response to resolve persistent economic disasters. In February 1952, the United States granted $300 million to England and $100 million to France as an emergency measure until it could develop a more permanent solution.

The British position as a creditor to the European Payments Union (EPU) was also radically reversed in 1951, and in November the new Conservative government imposed stringent quotas on imports from the Continent. The French quickly followed suit, making a further shambles of the United States policy of intra-European trade for which Congress had specifically earmarked $600 million of its 1951 European aid. Inevitably, as Europe's conservative governments took new deflationary steps, England and a portion of the Continent slid once more into stagnation and recession. British industrial activity declined during 1952, but most severely in the first quarter. Throughout Britain and Western Europe there was constant alarm as to the dangers from the fluctuations in the United States economy. British firms began to cancel orders for consumer goods, bankruptcies increased, there was a sharp fall in the stock market, and the capital goods industry, despite a backlog of orders, worked only part time due to a shortage of raw materials.

But it was rearmament that caused the most serious structural shift in the British economy, dealing the final blow from which it never fully recovered. The industries that the English most relied on for export were those that were diverted to arms. England made a greater effort at rearmament than any other Western European nation and paid a cost not only in terms of current economic austerity but also in the loss of markets, permanently affecting its future trade. As with their eager acceptance of the Marshall Plan in 1947, the British embraced rearmament as a predictable source of dollars and a stable demand that might keep the economy on an even keel, but they failed to give adequate consideration to rearmament's ramifications on other sectors of the economy or future trade.

While the British shifted their capital and consumer capacity to arms production, Germany and Japan, relieved of the arms pressure and denied their traditional markets in Eastern Europe and China, moved into England's markets. While the British production was near full capacity before the Korean War, Germany and Japan, facilitated by the unemployment and plant idleness permitting rapid expansion in the months following the Korean War, successfully penetrated the protected sterling bloc because of England's inability to fill the new orders. Japan could even sell steel and ships to Australia at prices substantially higher than the British. England's greatest fear was that Japan would replace it in the textile industry, formerly comprising the bulk of British exports. Indeed, in the hope of diverting Japan from England's traditional markets, London tried unsuccessfully to persuade the United States to permit Japan to resume trade with China.[19]

Shortly after the Korean War began the Germans began to buy and hoard huge supplies of raw materials, going into debt to the EPU until it refused to grant further credits. With these accumulated supplies, its unused industrial capacity, and unemployment, Germany was in a position to fill the war-generated orders and replace the exports of the other industrial states that were shifting toward rearmament.

As early as November 1950 German industry already produced 17 percent of Europe's industrial output, almost equal to its 1938 share, but its immense post-Korea growth was only for export. Internally, the West German government continued its regressive and conservative policies. Private entrepreneurs continued to funnel investment into luxury industries while steel, coal, and building remained at low level. For the bourgeoisie, profits soared, and its purchasing power rose 25 percent between June and November 1950, while its consumption of luxuries, according to the UN Economic Commission for Europe, ". . . flourishes as in few other countries as a result of high profits and low tax-morality."[20] By the end of the year unemployment remained around 10 percent, and the income distribution continued to worsen until even Gordon Gray's report in November expressed concern over Germany's internal conditions.

Yet as rearmament accelerated elsewhere, West Germany's capital and heavy industry expanded until by 1953 its world exports were nearly four times the value of 1950. Under conditions of new prosperity, German steel corporations began to lose their enthusiasm for the Schuman Plan and accepted it only after heavy pressure from McCloy and the final removal of the occupation's limit on German steel production. To the alarm of the British and French, by January 1952 West Germany was the strongest industrial power on the Continent. And of special concern to the French was the fact that German steel production by the end of 1951 greatly exceeded their own. ECA had encouraged these efforts, and in 1951 allocated more funds to Germany than to the other ERP nations until a financial emergency brought France an additional grant. But by 1953 German competition was keenly felt by the United States industries as well, especially in machine tools and heavy capital goods. West Germany's leaders always explicitly understood the reasons for their great success, despite the tendency of Economics Minister Ludwig Erhard to credit his free market philosophy. With the rearmament efforts of the other capitalist powers, and the spin-off which the Germans enjoyed, German industrialists saw export markets as their greatest opportunity for future growth and profit.[21]

It was not until the end of 1950 that the so-called Korean boom began to pull France and Belgium out of their recession, but even at the end of the year total industrial employment was lower than in 1947. Typically, in France prices and profits rose sharply and the workers' living standard dropped still further. By May 1951, the French economy was again staggering as the increased cost of raw materials had reached the point, according to *Le Monde*, where ". . . ten months of the raw material boom . . . cost [France] the same amount as all the aid she received under the Marshall Plan."[22] And during 1952 and 1953 France's industrial activity failed to exceed the 1951 output. In Italy there was only slight industrial expansion in 1952 as the government clung rigidly to its cautious monetary policy.

Unemployment at the end of 1950 was still 20 percent, and De Gasperi's government expressed hope that rearmament could absorb some of the idle workers.

The Future of European Aid

By November 1950 the Truman administration feared that Congress' growing belief that it should confine all aid to rearmament would lead to renewed attacks on ERP. Concluding that "[i]n presenting to Congress the needs for this year, probably continued economic assistance and additional dollar assistance for military purposes will be launched as one program," the ECA thought that the best means of obtaining support would be to tell Congress that the ERP "had achieved its objective" but that the new global military situation threatened its accumulated gains. Such institutions as the EPU, secured after much toil, they could justify as an instrument to distribute the rearmament burden and ". . . to induce the European governments to harmonize their internal financial policies. . . ."[23]

The Gray committee on foreign economic policies delivered its report to the President and the public on November 10, 1950. The basic purpose of the committee, as we discussed in Chapter 17, had been to prepare Congress and the public to accept the necessity of continuing United States economic aid to Europe after the end of the Marshall Plan and changing American import and agricultural policies. The Korean War made its task both easier and more complex. The final Gray report glossed over the problems of trade that were the original impetus for the committee and cynically claimed that before the Korean crisis Europe had succeeded in its objectives and could have solved its remaining economic problems without United States aid. Referring to the military crisis and rearmament, the committee pointed to "new" needs and threats to progress already achieved. Rearmament and security ". . . forces a postponement of the time when the United States . . . can end economic assistance."[24] Inflation and maldistribution of essential supplies, rather than stagnation and recession, it now designated the major dangers. The Europeans had to find a way to rearm, to produce goods for export, and to meet minimum consumer needs so that after the military crisis they would not find themselves in the same condition economically as in 1945. The report specifically attacked United States agricultural and shipping subsidy policies as detrimental to America's general foreign and security interests. The committee, representing the administration, recommended to Congress three to four more years of continued economic aid in addition to military aid, a separate agency for economic and military assistance (although the White House now used military security as the rationale for all aid), support of GATT and ITO, the reduction of tariffs, and the elimination of agricultural embargoes. It also warned against pressing European rearmament too quickly and advised that Europe not use its counterpart funds for military purposes.

For Congress it was a different story. The nation was at war and the grim mood on Capitol Hill would entertain only requests for military aid; Congress demanded proof that the Europeans were doing their part in the general mobilization. As the military situation in Korea worsened, the arguments of the Gray report fell on deaf ears as the administration strained to make the connection between cotton and tanks and had to classify all nonmilitary aid under the term "defense support." Congress abandoned European recovery as a goal and cut the administration's request for ERP by $700 million, leaving little to meet the emergencies that Europe faced during the coming year. In direct conflict with the administration's aims and requests, Congress required that the Europeans use not less than $500 million of their counterpart for military production or equipment, retained the "peril point" clause in the Reciprocal Trade Act, emphasized that it had *not* endorsed GATT, added *new* quotas for agricultural imports, continued the export subsidies, and in general pursued a protectionist policy throughout 1951. But although penurious on general economic aid, Congress in 1951 granted a loan to Spain and allocated $100 million to organize defectors from Eastern Europe ". . . into elements of the military forces supporting [NATO]. . . ."[25]

In 1951, unable to win its battle against Congress and with Europe's dollar trade gap higher than at any time since 1947, Washington turned to Europe to attempt once more to manipulate economic policies there to compensate for congressional obstacles. This time the effort was even more quixotic than in the past. Starting in June 1951, the United States initiated a program of "productivity teams" with exchanges between representatives of European management and labor and their American counterparts. In effect, the administration now hoped that it could make European industry more competitive and increase exports to the United States and American-dominated dollar markets, as devaluation and the various schemes for European unity were supposed—and failed—to do. The American trade union productivity teams in France in 1952 reported complete failure in their efforts due to ". . . anti-NATO sentiment . . . based on [the] fact that NATO because of its military expenditures contributes to the lowering of the standard of living of the French people."[26] And even the pro-American Force Ouvrière in France, after all the efforts of United States labor teams, came out in opposition to the productivity programs. Experience had shown that they operated against the workers' interests, creating unemployment instead of higher wages. Productivity rose 40 to 50 percent over prewar, but even American experts admitted that most of the gains went into profits. Such marginal gestures were scarcely adequate. To the ECA, however, they seemed essential, for the United States was asking the strained economies of Europe simultaneously to produce for rearmament and export, despite the congressional obstacles, and to tolerate the violent shifts in the American economy that had such devastating repercussions throughout the world. And Washington also expected the Western Europeans to evidence political solidarity with the United States as it embarked on a dangerous and destructive course in Korea.

But the United States' most important mechanism for attaining its economic aims in Europe was now rearmament. By the fall of 1950 the United States was grooming the Western European economies for massive rearmament, more to make them attractive to Congress than because of any Soviet threat. In the immediate post-Korean War atmosphere Truman asked and received from Congress $3 billion in addition to the $1 billion he had requested earlier for European rearmament. Although the Europeans had reluctantly begun a modest arms effort in the summer of 1950, they did not have their heart in the program. The Western European public was generally hostile to the Korean War, and anti-American sentiment reached a new high by the end of the year. By December the Europeans had barely made a dent in the $4 billion American grant, and the administration planned to ask Congress for another $5 billion in the spring—which Congress was unlikely to grant if the original sum remained unspent. But the Europeans understood the costs to their own economies; for rearmament, after the first stimulus to production, was guaranteed ultimately to worsen their situation by increasing the cost of imported raw materials, leaving them much less to export or consume. Such detrimental effects on the Europeans were of lesser consequence to Washington, for rearmament now appeared the quickest and easiest way to solve America's persistent dilemma. To attain this new target the ECA was even willing to modify the EPU and its sacred goal of multilateral trade. The aim of trade liberalization ". . . will not . . . be permitted to interfere with the adoption of controls essential to the arms effort," wrote the ECA policy-makers in a proposal to reinstate the quantitative import controls and other restrictions that they had only a year earlier forced the Europeans to drop. "[W]e can no longer assume that freedom of individual choice . . . will always lead to the optimum direction of resources," they continued, but controls must be "multilaterally agreed" upon—which was to say American-directed.[27]

Washington quickly created mechanisms designed to achieve its integrative ends. At the December 1950 meeting of NATO in Brussels the Americans increased the pressure to rearm, secured agreement to establish a common Defense Production Board, appointed General Eisenhower as NATO head, and committed itself to an American troop increase that meant the bulk of NATO's troops would come from the United States and England. And by March 1951 the United States introduced a new device that was soon to assume vast importance in the economies of Europe and Japan: under the Mutual Defense Aid program it began "offshore procurement"—buying arms in Europe for other Europeans.

During the Senate hearings of July 1951 on the foreign aid program in Europe the administration told the skeptics of its efforts to get the Europeans to rearm despite the political costs. One ECA official explained, "There was a lag of at least 6, 8, or 9 months between our appreciation of what Korea meant and their appreciation of what it meant. . . . During that lag . . . we were in there pushing and they were saying, 'Oh, well, we don't see it; we don't see it; we need more help.' . . . We got started in a situation in which we were shoving them and they were holding back."[28] Such analyses reinforced congressional views that Europe's economic condition was the result of a chronic reluctance to get off the American dole. Yet by the end of the first quarter of 1951 Western Europe's defense expenditures, excluding Germany and adjusted for inflation, were nearly double those of 1938.

Since the Truman administration had failed to secure strictly economic concessions from Congress in 1951, much less its endorsement of the Gray recommendations, the administration essentially abandoned the ERP in 1951 and in its place substituted a Mutual Security Act (MSA) whose martial terms and military priorities conformed to Congress' inclinations and susceptibilities, even though the administration was unable to conjure up any military threat from the Russians. It did obtain approval to send American troops to Europe, whose support amounted to the export of $700 million per year over the first two years. Such steps were imperative, for by mid-1951 Western Europe's dollar crisis was worse than in 1947, and the shift in the terms of trade in the year following Korea had already cost it $1.5 billion. These developments alarmed the decision-makers in Washington no less than those in the European capitals. The United States still had to grant additional emergency aid to Britain and France to stave off a financial collapse, even though it was freely understood that it was the American policy of rearmament and stockpiling that were the root causes of Western Europe's renewed plight.

In early 1952, as an outcome of the events and policies of the previous years, Western Europe and Japan slid once more into a recession, and the administration asked for an additional $4.1 billion in military aid to Europe. Harriman once again predicted that one last huge effort in 1953, for a " . . . large scale capital build up," would then allow aid to Europe to "taper off."[29] The administration also asked for another $1.8 billion for "defense support," a total approaching the peak years of the Marshall Plan. To this it added offshore procurement, which by August 1953 had reached the cumulative sum of $2.3 billion and had become especially important to the French and British. Massive arms and government capital exports rather than multilateral trade had by 1953 become the most reliable means of sustaining overseas markets for United States goods, an immensely costly process that Eisenhower pledged to continue, despite a reticent Congress, shortly after his accession to the presidency.

Again, as with the past economic programs, Western European workers were the victims of the shift to rearmament. ECA economist Richard Bissell concluded that rearmament, and the ERP in general, helped to swell industrial profits, but that the workers fared badly. "[I]n France, labor's relative position is less favorable than before the war. And in both Italy and Germany wages hardly above subsistence standards prevail alongside of severe unemployment."[30] In the Netherlands the standard of living in 1952 was below that of 1948. In Germany, even in 1953, after vast economic expansion the workers were among the lowest-paid in Europe. The artificial stimulation of the stagnant economies, caused by the Korean War and the wasteful production of arms, created inflationary pressures to which the governments of Western Europe, with United States prodding, chose to react by lowering further the living standards of the masses. In January 1952 Churchill publicly estimated that he needed three years to pursue a deflationary policy and cut consumer demand, which is to say, to lower the living standard of the working class. In France, the drain of the Indochina war and the pressures for rearmament led to increased deficits and the government, again with ECA encouragement, compensated by pruning the budget for social services and increasing the workers' taxes.

While at the end of 1952 the United States saw rearmament as the defining feature of its foreign economic policies for the coming years, its shift in focus and vast new efforts had not resolved any of the basic structural problems that confronted the United States in 1947. Measured against its initial goals, the Marshall Plan was both a success and a failure. Probably its most important accomplishment was its aid to the firm consolidation of the conservative class in its control of Western Europe, guaranteeing the continuation of a capitalism Washington hoped would become even more receptive to American direction. This was the *sine qua non* of the entire undertaking. Firmly in control of the leading states on the Continent were center-right Catholic coalitions, frequently ruling with the collaboration of the Social Democrats. These governments were susceptible to pressure and partially adopted Washington's recommendations even when they were in conflict with their own national interests. With American help, and through repression rather than expensive economic concessions, they had effectively defeated any threat from the working class. The United States also temporarily defeated the economic nationalism of the Right, in particular Gaullism in France.

Washington had successfully guided Western Europe's economic policies to enhance profits and investments and prodded the region's governments to pursue orthodox economic policies. The United States also attained its ends in the absolutely vital function of subsidizing its exports and securing significant concessions in Europe and its colonies for American industries, many of which would have suffered critically without the ERP. No less important was Washington's reintegration of West Germany under conservative leadership into Western Europe. The special position of the United States in the German occupation guaranteed that it could accomplish this aim, despite the considerable initial opposition from the other European governments. The Americans also partially achieved their goal of halting bilateral trade, especially between Eastern Europe and the West. Finally, the Marshall Plan had effectively quarantined the Russians once more from full participation in European trade, but it also helped immeasurably to consolidate Soviet political and economic control in the affairs of Eastern Europe.

By its original criteria, however, the American effort to reconstruct Europe also failed. There were too many contradictions in its aims, too many conflicting interests in Europe and, primarily, in the United States, and too many variables existed in the world economy for Washington to be able to impose its almost mystical ideal system of free, nondiscriminatory, multilateral trade upon the world. Granting that they eventually relegated that objective to the sphere of ultimate desires, their more immediate prosaic goals also failed, and their failure led to the constant shifting in American demands on the Europeans—demands basically required to compensate not only for Congress' refusal to cooperate and reduce the tariff but also for the very nature of capitalism itself.

While Congress played a major role in imposing an anti-Communist rationale on the program, we cannot conclude that the Marshall Plan was an essentially good program perverted by a conservative Congress. Nor was the shift to rearmament a qualitative change from a positive to a negative objective. The nature of the original capitalist aims of the plan made inevitable its socially negative results for the European people. As capitalist states have unquestionably always preferred to avoid war among themselves, if possible, so the policy-makers in Washington would have favored attaining their goals without a primary reliance on arms as a rationale for spending. Economic stagnation and a tightfisted Congress, however, necessitated this recourse to a far greater extent than any military threat, real or imagined, from the Russians.

When measured against criteria other than the goals of Washington, we can see the European Recovery Program in yet a different light. We have examined what happened to the working class in the process of the reconstruction of European capitalism out of the rubble and chaos of war. The policies that the ruling classes pursued with United States aid led to inevitable unemployment, inflation, and recessions—with the incumbent miseries for the vast bulk of the population. United States demands for standardization of economic policies, as well as their dependence on world trade, soon forced the British to abandon most of their measures of a mixed economy and adopt virtually the same internal policies as the continental nations. Finally, having achieved the conservative goal of a strong currency and balanced budget, Western European economies began to stagnate and head straight toward depression, only to be revived temporarily by the Korean War and arms production before again confronting renewed crises. The meaning of these violent shifts in the economies of the capitalist states over the four brief years of the Marshall Plan is profound. Although faced with severe problems, Western Europe was recovering from the war before the program began, and it was clear to most contemporary observers that the United States needed Western Europe nearly as much as Europe needed American aid. Western Europe also feared linking its economies too closely to the United States, given past experience and the knowledge that it was the most unstable, as well as the most powerful, capitalist nation. Even from their own conservative point of view it had far greater bargaining power than it chose to exercise. But the chimera of a cornucopia of dollars deterred the conservative rulers of Europe who, in the last analysis, shared the same social goals as their Atlantic partner. Nevertheless, once they accepted the conditions and linked their economies intimately to the United States, the slightest variation in the American economy had profound repercussions in Europe. And in granting the Americans power over fundamental choices of economic policy, Western Europe temporarily abdicated its sovereignty.

Finally, recourse to arms as the basis for economic expansion, policies that lowered the living standards of the vast bulk of the population or that even eventually evolved into a superficial prosperity, was a most dangerous economic foundation that could rest only on war or the preparation for war in some part of the world. By 1953 the evolution of American economic policy had failed to resolve the contradictions implicit in capitalism and had reconciled itself to the perpetual production of arms and the support of the military machine in Western Europe and throughout the world. Expedients born of earlier failures now developed their own logic and dynamism, resulting in social waste and tragedy for the Western world.

Japan: The Path Toward Restoration

America's postwar strategy in Japan had imposed temporary political stability and economic orthodoxy, but failed to attain the economic recovery that was a prerequisite to its complete, permanent reintegration into a world conforming to Washington's desires. But without economic recovery, a conservative Japan would be a precarious society—and unpredictable over the long run. At the outbreak of the Korean War, while Japan's manufacturing output was a mere one-third of the 1931 level, the United States acted decisively to end Japan's protracted stagnation and to define for it the nature of its future. During the last six months of 1950, United States war procurement orders in Japan amounting to $149 million, and the worldwide upsurge in economic activity, created a virtual boom for a Japanese industry whose directors also eagerly anticipated reconstruction orders for Korea following the conflict.

The repercussions of the war in Korea also hastened the American occupation's final reversal of its postwar reforms. On July 8 SCAP called upon the Japanese government to expand the national police to 75,000 men. While internal order remained the primary consideration, the occupation introduced military training into this corps, and it was in fact a nucleus of an armed force. The next month SCAP exonerated those individuals affected by the economic purge of 1947, and then in November it essentially reversed even the limited antimonopoly rulings that were still in force. Finally, in May 1951, commemorating the fourth anniversary of the Constitution, General Ridgway gave the Japanese government permission to revise all ". . . laws framed in accordance with the Potsdam Declaration."[31] Yoshida promptly appointed a committee of leading conservatives to report on repeal of all earlier reform legislation dealing with labor, education, and administration. As the peace conference approached, the occupation had come full circle. While the other nations that had fought Japan during World War II strongly opposed these developments, they lacked the power to thwart successfully the United States designs. And most important, the Japanese people suffered a setback as their rulers reinstated the legal basis for the state's repressive policies.

With the Korean War the United States began to consider the role of Japan as a major industrial supplier of American involvement and aid not only in Korea but in Southeast Asia as well. Washington increasingly viewed that region as the natural Japanese market and source of supply for its food and raw materials, one vital to achieving a self-supporting Japan. Japan's alternative was to trade with China, but for decisive political reasons in the United States an economic link between those two nations was incompatible with a continued American presence in Japan. The British, on the other hand, recognized Japan's threat to their own vital interests in Southeast Asia. England had hoped to have a role in the development of the region and at least keep its resources tied to the Commonwealth, and naturally it resented an influx of Japanese competing for rice and other materials. But in the end the British were too vulnerable, and themselves in need of renewed American assistance, to extract any concessions on the structure and direction of the Japanese economy.

Japan's enthusiasm for its new status and prosperity, generated by the revival of economic activity and profits, was soon partially shaken by a moderate shift in the United States military procurement practices in mid-1951 which forced a number of bankruptcies among newer firms and further concentration of industrial control. Nevertheless, America essentially created Japan's revival and prosperity with its vast inflow of procurement dollars, amounting to $592 million in 1951, $824 million in 1952, and $806 million in 1953—expenditures intolerable to Congress in peacetime, but acceptable for war and arms. And along with Germany, forbidden to arm and therefore able to meet the demands of the rest of the world while Western Europe built its armies, Japanese export trade increased 61 percent during the first year of the Korean War, although almost three-quarters of its industry was geared to United States–procured arms production in January 1951.

While the Japanese capitalists clearly recognized that a link to conservative America was more to their interests than enlarged trade with Communist China, they always held the threat of a shift toward China as their trump card in order to secure the concessions from the United States that they desired. Such a strategy was effective during the negotiations for a peace treaty, but even more so at the end of the Korean War. During the spring of 1952 shifts in American procurement caused severe dislocations in key industries. Sharply affected were cotton textile machinery, iron and steel, shipping, and rubber. The recession continued throughout the year, responding as well to the general economic slowdown throughout the capitalist world. By mid-1953 Japan again had an unfavorable trade balance of $193 million. When the Korean armistice was signed in July of that year, Japanese industry, fearing a severe economic crisis in the United States but also to gain further American concessions, gave lengthy consideration whether it should orient its trade primarily toward the West or toward China. It inevitably decided to link its economy to the United States through the "defense support" clause of the Mutual Security Act, a provision that Japanese business found too enticing to resist. The arrangement provided that "[i]n carrying out the present agreement . . . the United States will give every consideration . . . to the procurement in Japan of supplies and equipment to be made available to Japan, as well as to other countries. . . ."[32] Japan, for its part, pledged to provide a market for America's agricultural surplus. Following the economic impact of the Korean War, this integrative relationship was the decisive factor in sustaining the development and growing strength of the Japanese economy over the subsequent decade and one-half.[33]

The Continuing Dilemma

The Eisenhower administration continued the Democratic regime's foreign economic policy, defining identical goals and largely selecting the same men to implement them. And having inherited the same predicaments and needs, the new government was to experience similar frustrations and failures.

In his inaugural address Eisenhower enunciated his basic commitment to the historical American foreign economic creed—and he was never to vary from it. The United States' need for export markets and raw materials imports required world integration, and on subsequent occasions the President, Dulles, and lesser officials were to detail this vision in entirely familiar terms. There had to be lower tariff barriers to trade and a free flow of United States private investment overseas, and the nation would require yet more of the globe's commodities. The world had not only to welcome United States investors but protect them from the risks of nationalization and inconvertibility, and Washington constantly reiterated capitalism as the desired world economic framework. Such an international welcome for American business would not only greatly develop local economies, Washington was to argue, but also fulfill the United States' vital demands for raw materials.

All this, of course, was easier said than done. But the new administration during its first months rededicated itself to the effort and busily concerned itself with the details of finally mastering the equation of greater investments, markets, and raw materials supplies in the framework of an integrated world capitalism. There were other reasons for intensifying this effort. Some of Eisenhower's appointees were more orthodox in their definition of a desirable domestic budget, and when the President in May 1953 asked Congress for close to $6 billion, mainly for arms and military support, it became more and more evident that the puny private overseas investment that year was a primary cause of the government's need to finance exports. Unless American business began playing the large global role that political leaders desired, a balanced budget and control over inflation at home were going to become increasingly difficult, perhaps ultimately impossible. The failure of these immense postwar outlays to undo the impulse and need of England and Europe to cut themselves off from the dollar area, and their growing inclination to trade with the Soviet bloc, made ever more imperative the success of the United States' larger goals.[34]

It was in this context that the President in late spring created a Commission on Foreign Economic Policy, under Clarence B. Randall, chairman of the board of Inland Steel, to recommend new approaches to traditional objectives. In essence, the Randall commission was precisely like its numerous predecessors in the ends and means it advocated. It assumed that the United States could attain something like a "normal" world political structure and capitalist economy which would identify the interests of Europe and the Third World with massive American private investments. With convertibility, lower tariffs, investment safeguards, tax laws, and the like, as well as greater American consistency in its own practices, the world might yet realize the ideal international order. The Randall commission is curious mainly as a statement of faith and definition of American interests in tangible goods, but it ignored politics and revolution throughout the earth, and Congress' mood as well. And the fact remained that the scale of government expenditures overseas far exceeded those of American business, and such private investment as occurred was to an increasingly vital extent the result of Washington's having created the politically essential prerequisites for its welcome.

Dulles, for his part, realized the central role of politics and power in the future of world capitalism, and even before the Randall commission offered its advice he was arguing that "[t]he financial rules of the game are now made and changed by governments . . . and foreign policies are similarly unrelated to foreign investments. . . ."[35] The goals of those policies might be economic, directly and indirectly, but the world had become too complicated for Washington to wait for Wall Street to attain their common ends. Specific firms could not and would not lose money to sustain the larger interests of the whole system, much less create the structural preconditions in which it might later prosper. Moreover, the exigencies of practical power and politics, both in Congress and in the nation, did not permit the Eisenhower administration, any more than its predecessor, to overcome the specific pressures and constituencies that since 1945 virtually ruled out consistency in American foreign economic policy.

Private business, in any event, neither could nor would fulfill Washington's larger goals, as much as businessmen demanded—and got—increasing legal protection for their overseas operations. As a percentage of gross national product, private direct foreign investments in 1953 were scarcely one-third of the 1928 share, and adjusted for inflation even the net annual private capital outflow during 1952–1955 was far less than in 1928. By contrast to Britain's capital export during its forty years of imperialist supremacy preceding World War I, the United States' performance, including government funds, was trivial. Though reinvested earnings and local borrowing greatly increased the real value of United States overseas investment—which repatriated profits in turn also sharply reduced—this did not eliminate the domestic problems created by industry's and finance's failure to obtain adequate profitable overseas investments. For the Third World, as well, economic stagnation, even in the level of exports to the industrial world, remained the defining characteristic of its material existence.

Upheaval and revolution for many nations became increasingly inevitable —and necessary.[36]

The Randall commission report disappointed European leaders, and the British found in it justification for further postponing sterling convertibility. Washington still deeply hoped to attain Western Europe's economic cooperation on many levels, but Ambassador Winthrop Aldrich in London warned Eisenhower that any delay in implementing even the mild Randall reforms would persuade the British to go their own way irrevocably. But existing political facts and growing fear of foreign competition convinced the White House that it had to be ". . . realistic in terms of the rate at which change can be made," and it continued to practice a dual-standard policy on tariffs and export subsidies to American interests that catered to congressional moods and lobbyists for various constituencies.[37] Apart from the Third World's inability to develop even in America's ideal international economic system, the industrialized capitalist powers could not give it that opportunity, and Europe, too, was now irrevocably forced to defend its economic future against Washington's inconsistencies, deepening the natural conflict of interests between the United States and its allies. The manner in which America would not practice what it preached for others, but concentrated on maximizing its exports by whatever means were possible, is too voluminous to itemize here. But with the restoration of world agricultural output and the growth of European industry, Washington's use of all the mechanisms available to it—from counterpart funds to foreign aid and Export-Import Bank loans—was to sustain the nation's agricultural export market, provide export outlets for manufactures otherwise unable successfully to compete, and fill the holds of United States–owned boats charging almost twice as much as foreign bottoms. Congress' refusal in the spring of 1954 to alter existing legislation, or even to endorse GATT, and its ban on tariff reductions in defense-related industries, only again made clear what Europe had known about the United States' endemic inconsistency since 1945.[38]

To employ foreign aid to service the need of specific American economic sectors, but also to win the world to a structural reorganization incompatible with development as well as America's functional conduct, was a chimera doomed to failure. Like its predecessor, the Eisenhower government could only service the immediate needs of the American economy while reiterating an ideology whose structural objectives were increasingly unrealizable. Arms aid therefore also became its means, as well, for sustaining adequate exports, a response that also had a logical political function where, as in Indochina, guns might help in preventing the triumph of revolutionary anticolonialism. That such repression would create its own resistance, ultimately becoming a decisive factor in mobilizing the populations of numerous Third World nations to successful struggle, was less consequential in the short run—but ultimately was to become one of the significant causes of the Third World's revolutionary transformation. And that its arms, in all its forms, and interventions would define the quality and purpose of American life, and that nation's relations to the industrialized world as well, was thought less consequential than doing for American economic interests and power in the world what specific industries could not accomplish with their own resources. To attain the political preconditions of total world economic integration, exploiting political and military means toward that greater, elusive end, was now the task before the Truman administration's successors. And so the Republican government was to maintain the essential continuity in the postwar American foreign policy that has endured to this day.

24

Europe and the Dilemmas of Military Power, 1950–1952

By the spring of 1950 the Truman administration's military goals had far outstripped its political and financial resources for attaining them. That predicament was already a familiar one, which in the past useful crises had solved. Internal economic and political realities complicated all the dilemmas the United States faced in the world—the declining military superiority over Russia, the need again to regulate economic relations with Europe, the decisive shift in forces in Asia—and posed a grave challenge to the administration's ability to pursue its global course.

Perhaps the best example of this deepening paralysis was Washington's incapacity to translate the ambitious NSC–68 into a formal budget request that had any chance of congressional passage. Yet domestic economic considerations made it increasingly urgent to overcome the restraints lest the economic slowdown and unemployment deepen. Important sectors of the arms industry were working well below capacity by spring 1950, and many decision-makers regarded the administration's initial fear of inflation or a budget deficit as excessively pessimistic and the attainment of America's international objectives as worth the economic costs. Deflation and economic stagnation now seemed the more ominous domestic threat, America's declining power in the world the greater international risk. The issue was how to mobilize Congress to cooperate with the desired immense military expansion.

This struggle took place at a time when the great domestic debate over "McCarthyism" was beginning to emerge. It is, of course, clear that the administration's earlier vision of the "international Communist conspiracy" differed from that of McCarthy and his followers only in its location of the danger. The paranoid vision emerged from precisely the same categories of thought, and McCarthyism was the logic of that system of political perception in many obvious ways. But there was another dimension of this struggle worth noting in the context of the entire postwar struggle between Congress and the administration over the budget and foreign commitments. Time and again the administration had exploited the multifaceted "menace" of Communism to mask America's postwar expansion into Europe and the world for reasons having little, if anything, to do with bolshevism. Now the fiscal conservatives and isolationists, whose patriotism and anti-Communism the administration had continuously impugned, found their defense in the proposition that they could fight the primary Communist menace at home and at very little cost. Cynicism and paranoid visions beget their counterparts, leading both to McCarthyism and to conventional liberal wisdom. In the end, the respectable convoluted official ideological definition of the world was to prevail, ultimately to prove infinitely more dangerous and costly than its domestic variety.

To an important degree, as well, the administration's problems reflected the fact that it had obscured its real goals in Europe behind contrived rationales to make them convincing to Congress. Both privately and publicly, during the spring of 1950 key decision-makers were quite confident that there would be no war with Russia simply because the United States was a much stronger industrial power. Soviet respect for American power was not in its superior number of bombs, but rather its large economic productivity, Charles Bohlen confided to a Pentagon group during April; "The Russians are certainly not held back by anything now on the Continent of Europe in the way of military defense."[1] But the contradictions in military doctrine made for endless confusion and paralysis. Was the United States relying on strategic air power to fight a war, as it generally asserted? If so, how then to justify requests for refurbishing Europe's land armies to a standard that would still be insufficient for a war against the immense Red army? And was Russia the real enemy, or social revolution—calling for another kind of force altogether?

During 1950 Acheson, in particular, keenly saw the need to maintain a sense of danger from Russia and Communism that was the prerequisite for mobilizing protracted American efforts and high allocations. There could be "no moral compromise" with international Communism, he reiterated in a major address during mid-March, for "... subversion, threats, and even military force" were integral to it.[2] Only constancy in building Western power would ultimately lead to a reduction in tensions, and premature negotiations that aroused false hopes were much worse than nothing at all. This refrain, this plea for an unwavering policy in Europe, Asia, and the world based on the expansion of America's economic and military power, was to remain Acheson's article of faith until the end of his years, as his preconditions for an eventual *détente* became more and more remote.

It was in this context that Congress began during the spring of 1950 to undermine Acheson's strategy of again expanding the nation's military and economic efforts even as a critical sector of it defended its ideological integrity by demanding instead a search for Communists at home. During May the Point Four program passed the Senate by one vote and a tie vote kept a half-billion dollars from being cut from ERP. The congressional European military aid hearings, involving a petty sum of $1.2 billion that was far less than the administration wanted for its more ambitious military and economic plans, were bogged down and the outcome was in doubt. The world Communist peace campaign was in full swing, which precluded using the Russians as an easy excuse for greater funds. Truman and his aides publicly spoke against the relaxation taking place nationally, and on June 9 the President attempted to neutralize the pattern and to buttress flagging public and congressional enthusiasm, doggedly stressing that "[w]e must be willing to bear the temporary costs of defensive armaments as well as those of constructive economic development."[3] The Europeans were no less reticent. Washington wanted French man power back from Indochina, though not at the cost of defeat, and for this reason during the first months of 1950 the United States began massive infusions of military aid in the hope that a quick victory would bring the officer corps of the French army home.

Looking back at the mood on the military, economic, and European plans of June 1950, a high Washington source one year later observed, with almost a sense of relief, "No one can say what would have come of these projects if the North Koreans had not marched south on the 25th of June, 1950. Until that day 'economy' was still the official slogan of both the Administration and the political opposition in Washington. . . . Under the impact of that attack the Congress did authorize many, although not yet all, of the projects contemplated in NSC #68. June 25, 1950, converted abstract plans into physical projects."[4] Had the Korean crisis not occurred, it would have been necessary to manufacture an equivalent or to accept a major defeat for the White House's efforts to reassert American interests in a world slipping even further beyond its grasp. Then, on July 19, Truman went before Congress to denounce "appeasement" and conjure up visions of worse crises to come. Since Truman and his advisers were quite uncertain about Soviet responsibility for Korea, the administration's strong desire, dating well before the Korean affair, to proceed with the business of maintaining and expanding American military and economic power in Europe and throughout the globe was the major reason for the speech. For while Truman talked much of Korea, most of the approximately $10 billion for which he asked was to be spent on European rearmament, various economic programs justified in the name of military security, and the enlargement of the American military forces ". . . over and above the increases which are needed in Korea."[5] During August, as well, the United States began a vast expansion of American nuclear bomb production facilities and intensified work on the H-bomb. The useful crisis in Korea unlocked numerous global restraints for the United States. As we have already discussed in Chapter 21, during the fall of 1950 the Truman administration chose to sustain this crisis mood even as the risk of intensified, prolonged war with China mounted, using the new freedom for those ends in Europe we consider below.

Truman's inability to discipline Congress sufficiently throughout 1950, however, led to the administration's decision that a declaration of national emergency would solve innumerable problems that a reticent Congress was creating with a budget that was still inadequate for the United States' goals in Europe and the rest of the world.

On December 11, CIA head General W. Bedell Smith, in common with administration leaders, thought it unlikely that the Russians would initiate a general war; but two days later Truman, in an effort to win backing for a proclamation of national emergency, told a gathering of congressional leaders that war was a distinctly greater possibility than it had been. Though he added that Soviet peace overtures were a more formidable immediate danger to United States plans and NATO's unity, many members of both parties hesitated to recommend declaring the drastic step. The situation in Korea, they may have reflected, was hardly as critical as in the preceding August, when Truman failed to convoke those powers. But six months of war in Korea had not produced the political willingness necessary to pay for NSC–68 and other plans laid down even before Korea. Still, Congress had never been more worried about the war than during early December, when reports of major American retreats were deluging the nation.

On December 15 Truman went on the radio to declare a national emergency and to tell the nation that "[o]ur homes, our Nation, all the things we believe in, are in great danger. This danger has been created by the rulers of the Soviet Union." Specifics dealt not with Russia but with "Communist imperialism," and in the name of Korea, Truman talked about the build-up of United States military man power and equipment intended not for Korea, where he thought forces and equipment were adequate, but rather for Europe. "[W]e will not engage in appeasement"; and the patriotic fervor was enough to succeed at last.[6] Congress finally granted Truman his funds; military spending increased from $13.1 billion in fiscal 1950 to $44.1 billion in 1952 and the armed forces from 1,650 million to 3,594 million men over the same period. Ironically, Truman's relations with Congress were no less disingenuous than MacArthur's threats to Washington or McCarthy's crude accusations, and it was in this contrived atmosphere of danger that they all succeeded.

Germany's Military Power

This intense crisis atmosphere was the setting in which the United States finally resolved its policy as to the future of Germany's military role in Europe. But the reasons for Germany's eventual rearmament were far more complex and can be understood only in the context of Washington's thoughts regarding Europe's future in the world. Suffice it to say, from World War II onward the United States saw Germany as an element in a larger power struggle and balance, and after 1947 had made the decision to employ Germany's economic potential to advance American capitalism's destiny in Europe. The Marshall Plan had been tailored specifically for that purpose, and NATO had in large part been encouraged to prevent Western Europe's fear of an economically reconstructed Germany from recasting the region's political anxieties back into traditional channels. Of all the reasons for Western Europe's rearmament, its military utility in stopping a Russian military advance was the least consequential.

From this viewpoint, controlled German rearmament might serve as an integrative mechanism designed essentially to define the direction and future of Germany's inevitable and desired resurgence, preventing it from becoming the balance of power in Europe or reaching a *détente* with Russia. At the explicit urgings of the army, as early as May 1948 the National Security Council decided to leave the door open to later German and Spanish adherence to the Brussels Pact and NATO. Although they left it in abeyance as a practical issue, men such as Dulles saw Germany's integration into a United States–dominated Western system as essential to circumventing the reemergence of an unresponsive and independent German power, perhaps one even temporarily allied with Russia. Dulles' vision of NATO as a mechanism primarily to reassure Western Europe regarding Germany in part reinforced the proposition that its controlled rearmament was preferable to allowing Germany no participation at all. An occupation-imposed disarmament was possible, but this might also lead to a reconstructed Germany's desire to rebuild its military power despite even the Western powers—possibly even independently of the United States. For these reasons, the State Department was patently vague on Germany's role in NATO during the Senate hearings in the spring of 1949. Acheson talked, on one hand, of Germany's complete disarmament, but only excluded its entry from NATO "at the present time." Lovett, only somewhat less vague, let it be known he thought that ". . . a strong, friendly Germany . . . would naturally be in the interest of European recovery as well as peace."[7]

Adenauer saw America's strategy in Germany as one that reinforced both their national interests, but primarily as an opportunity to dissolve the restraints Germany's defeat had imposed and to attain both a "partnership and equality" with the West. It was this genius in carefully calculating how to attain new freedoms in exchange for Germany's favors, possible only because of the delicate European diplomatic and power structure, that was Adenauer's greatest feat. For Adenauer, Germany's rearmament—which he may have secretly proposed at the end of 1948—was but a means to attain other goals, rather than an end in itself. In that process he was to exploit both the United States' and Western Europe's fears and needs, but he never sacrificed prosperity for the sake of greater armed power that might pose a real military threat to Russia or the West.

From Adenauer's viewpoint, the most important immediate objective during 1949 was to terminate definitively the quite nominal threat of dismantling heavy industry suitable for war purposes and to remove the abstract limits on capital goods output. West Germany's economic integration into Western Europe had sufficiently calmed the French—so that by November a new three-power policy on Western Germany's economy further narrowed the remaining restraints. Cleverly, Adenauer especially played on the United States' desire to invest in Germany by virtually promising foreign exemption from possible future nationalization, thereby giving the conquerors an additional interest in Germany's economic growth. Such policies did not reconstruct Germany, but gave it the option to rebuild, if it could, along lines compatible with essentially American interests.[8]

At the end of 1949, despite French fears that the United States was contemplating Germany's rearmament, persistent American disclaimers that it was under discussion were largely correct. Strategically, West Germany's numbers could scarcely offset its grave political liabilities to the NATO alliance, and American military doctrine allowed no crucial role to the small increment Bonn might add to NATO's existing manpower. Economically, and most important, it was not yet necessary for rearmament to replace the ERP. On December 4, Adenauer released a statement that the defense of West Germany was the occupation's duty and that he opposed the creation of a new Wehrmacht. But, he added significantly, should the occupiers demand a rearmed Germany he would insist on defining the terms of cooperation, and they would be an all-German contingent integrated into a European force. What Adenauer sought was not German rearmament, but another lever for gaining yet more autonomy and freedom from remaining occupation restrictions. For Germany could gain only from peace rather than a war that would surely totally destroy it—regardless of who was the victor.

Adenauer therefore treated the United States' consideration of possible German rearmament as a mechanism for obtaining ". . . complete equality between Germany and the other European nations," and his alternating coyness and belligerence were but means to this end of undoing the restrictions of Germany's defeat.[9] Necessary to his strategy, which Acheson realized was a bargaining ploy that might nevertheless prove utilitarian to the United States' own plans, was a heightened sense of the alleged Soviet military menace by West Germany's prospective allies. During early 1950 Adenauer embarked on the course which was to so endear him to Washington until his political demise: he was to stress Western laxity before the Russian danger, even as Germany did far less than its neighbors to enlarge its military, and he was firmly to oppose any diplomatic moves likely to lessen international tension. His ultimate means of extracting American support for his goal of full equality was to hold aloft the danger that many United States leaders feared most—a West Germany neutral to the Russian presence in Central Europe or, what was even worse, allied with it.

By the spring of 1950 NATO remained an unimpressive military force, and Washington was perfectly aware that Western Europe's own arms offered no significant military deterrent to a Russian attack. No member had fulfilled its troop and rearmament obligations, and military coordination was at best nominal. For the United States, the economic prerequisites for a more substantial effort had not yet been reached, and in Chapter 17 we have outlined the economic circumstances that were to convince Washington that European rearmament was both a utilitarian economic necessity and an integrative mechanism. For practical purposes, before Korea the overwhelming opinion among United States and Western European leaders was that the Russians were not going to embark on a European war and that the United States' only significant military deterrent was its nuclear supremacy and economic base to sustain protracted conflict. The United States saw its main problem as integrating Europe with the American economy; but Truman and his aides were under considerable pressure, given their primary commitment to Europe as the main arena of the world struggle, to escape from domestic criticism, and especially from Asia-oriented elements around McCarthy, by a seeming aggressiveness on military defense as well.[10]

These integrative impulses were far more economic than political, much less military, in origin. They found partial expression in the London Foreign Ministers Conference during May, when Acheson, Bevin, and Schuman made a number of nominal military agreements, embarked on greater rearmament and military coordination, and assured the Germans that they might, for practical purposes, consider themselves behind NATO's protective shield—such as it was. Most of the topics discussed, it must be noted, were economic in nature and implication. But London was a modest beginning, committing neither the Americans nor the British to send new troops to Europe, nor the French to bring theirs back from Indochina. Many French leaders suspected it was but an American overture to further West German involvement in the alliance, but beyond the economic integrative mechanisms, nothing new was added to the evolving alliance structure. From a military viewpoint, all NATO had planned was the orderly retreat of its forces to the west of the Rhine in the case of a Soviet attack.

The London meeting was useful to the United States mainly to continue its sedulous advancement of the notion that a "Western interest," binding together an "Atlantic Alliance," existed to transcend specific national interests. So long as an induced or forced dependence prevailed, of course, such a bloc was a rhetorical fact, but little more. Once mutual coincidence of specific national interests melted in the changing political-economic environment, the classical impulse toward competition could assert itself once again. That point was never far off in many areas of the Third World, where dormant rivalries could always be found beneath the surface verbiage of good feelings.

The French showed their suspicion of Washington's intent almost immediately, suspecting that the Americans were bent on Germany's rearmament following its economic reconstruction. Both for traditional reasons and because two-fifths of their military potential was bogged down in Southeast Asia, they were determined to do everything to prevent Germany's military resurrection. The United States, for its part, was in 1950 never too concerned about the Soviet Union to ignore its own interests in the matter. At the end of May the United States might complain to the Russians that the alleged creation of an East German military force of 50,000 was a violation of existing disarmament agreements, but these shabbily armed, dispirited new police posed no serious military threat to anyone, and making an issue of it after the three nations had already decided to buttress their own military power was to justify a flabby martial impulse by inventing one that in fact was far less formidable. But before Korea, men such as John J. McCloy, the United States high commissioner in Germany, had genuine and profound conflicting impulses about Germany's future role. The mass neutralist sentiments among West Germans, he worried, were being strengthened by an amoral business element that wished to trade with the Communist bloc. On the other hand, NATO was militarily unimpressive, but McCloy feared that the creation of a German army, along with the scarcely chastened big industrialists, might do far more harm than good in Europe. German democracy, he frankly acknowledged, was too fragile to absorb a great military role in Europe.[11]

It was with genuine reticence, even ambivalence, that the United States' decision-makers considered West Germany's future military role after Korea. But Truman, in the weeks after Korea, strongly resisted German rearmament. Eisenhower shared McCloy's views, but the large majority of the military and Pentagon had for many months urged that NATO mobilize German man power rather than American troops as part of a much greater effort. Britain's desire to see Germany rearm to prevent it from filling England's markets while its own industry was preoccupied with arms reinforced the Pentagon's arguments. But Korea reaffirmed Washington's assessment that the conflict was but a "Russian feeler" and that Europe remained the area with the largest stakes for the United States.[12] The argument therefore dissolved opposition to the principle of German rearmament and shifted it toward the deeper issue of its structure. Washington did not deny that the ". . . bulk of the German people have very strong feelings against German rearmament," but the real question was its conviction that West Germany's military resurgency was inevitable. Therefore, the point for many in the State Department was ". . . to get, in the last analysis, the right type of Germany in the future."[13] The form of rearmament would

decide that future. And the organization of rearmament in America's interest rather than that of the German people led to an unenthusiastic, controlled, limited armament. Acheson and McCloy now felt the issue was how
further to integrate West Germany militarily so as to control it politically,
preventing it from later becoming the balance of power in Europe. Merging
it into a European army was their way out. The State Department insisted,
however, that the United States send four to six American divisions to
Europe as part of Germany's rearmament, and formed an indivisible package which linked a United States troop build-up in Europe to greater NATO
commitments and German rearmament. In this context, a strengthened
NATO could more than handle any danger a rearmed West Germany
might pose to its most reticent new allies.

If Korea prodded the preexisting American desire to ship arms to
Europe, it also gave the Germans their greatest opportunity to recoup their
lost sovereignty. West Germany public opinion remained strongly proneu-
trality and antirearmament in 1950 and over the coming half-decade. But
even the Social Democrats, with their increasingly characteristic ambivalence, endorsed the strategy of trading greater autonomy for the possibility
of rearmed German forces integrated into a supranational European body.
Adenauer, for his part, grasped the possibility and exaggerated the number
of divisions he could raise to increase his bargaining power. At the end of
June he proposed that the Western occupation permit West Germany to
create a police force. In mid-August he again renewed the request, also
demanding approval and arms for a 150,000-man army, adding that he
could recruit this force from former Nazi soldiers and officers. Then, on
August 29, he prepared a memo for McCloy, copies of which he also sent
to Allen Dulles. In it Adenauer played on all the West's anxieties: fear of
Russian expansion, the incorporation of Germany into the Soviet bloc, the
reemergence of nationalism. To this he added the bonus that West Germany
". . . is today still free from communist infection," unlike France and Italy,
and might be America's only important continental ally in the future.[14] But
Adenauer's precondition for rearmament was high: NATO would have to
add twelve armored divisions to the four occupation divisions already in
Germany. And, in turn, it would have to integrate German forces into a
European army. To the three foreign ministers about to meet in New York
on September 12 he sent a memo that radically redefined the terms of the
occupation in exchange for German military participation. The three Western powers would terminate the nominal state of war and replace the
remaining occupation statutes by contractual agreements; and the function

of the occupation would be only to protect Germany against Russia and its allies. In effect, the audacious German leader proposed, the occupiers were to give his nation total equality and costly protection on terms that would certainly prevent Germany's military resurgence.

The French arrived at the New York meeting resolved to prevent Germany's rearmament. They had already proposed a plan for total NATO military and even political integration, a daring and quite utopian scheme they were to press unremittingly. And they pointed out that insufficient arms were available for NATO's existing plans, much less Germany as well, and that until they built NATO into something more than a paper organization there would be no real structure into which to integrate German units. French leaders scrutinized every detail, some because they saw technicalities as a means of preventing any form of German rearmament; but they were vulnerable on one point: they were also anxious to obtain American aid for the war in Indochina. Torn, the French conceded on Germany's rearmament in principle only after Acheson threatened Congress' wrath, but the two nations had yet to find a compromise alternative. Other than consenting to study Germany's military integration into a European force and the improvement of West Germany's police, the three allies agreed only to the removal of more economic restrictions and control over Bonn's foreign affairs. Adenauer was quite pleased. And the French did sanction the premise that NATO should fight any war against Russia as far to the east as possible—the "forward strategy" principle that clearly was not going to work without German rearmament or massive NATO man-power transfers which none of its members were yet prepared to authorize.[15]

The French wobbled, argued among themselves, worried that the Anglo-Americans would proceed with German rearmament despite them, weighed their own need for more arms, and finally came up with the inordinately complex Pleven Plan on October 24. Each NATO nation was to merge only part of its army into a small force of 100,000 which was to be highly integrated, employ common arms, and be able to keep West Germany from building its own arms industry or general staff while it contributed all its forces in battalion-size contingents with an obvious second-class role. Managing to offend the nationalist pride of the Social Democrats and Christian Democrats alike, the French also permitted the State Department to break loose from its agreement with the Pentagon to make sending American troops to Europe contingent on German rearmament. Adenauer was less disturbed than many of his colleagues, for he was winning new political gains in his campaign for equal rights regardless of military autonomy. No one, indeed, pressed too hard for that alternative, and the French embarked on a stalling strategy that was eventually to postpone general acceptance of a rearmament formula until October 1954. Their task was made easier at the end of October, when Truman assigned Eisenhower to the post of NATO's supreme commander. For unlike the rest of the Pentagon, Eisenhower was, at best, lukewarm toward West German rearmament.

With the German rearmament question left to diplomacy for a period of years, with French reticence and American ambivalence resulting in an impasse, and with France's political instability constantly threatening to dissolve occasional areas of agreement, suffice it to say that NATO's existence had not significantly altered Europe's military balance by the end of 1950. Nominal paper agreements and organizational steps, such as those its council approved in its mid-December meeting at Brussels, did precious little to alter military facts, but only succeeded in adding to the sovereignty which was, in the final analysis, West Germany's major objective. NATO's total of 10 to 12 divisions in Western Europe, as against 50 Soviet divisions in East Germany and Poland alone and its equivalent of 110 United States–size divisions altogether, was hardly a deterrent, and West Germany's man power and resources were not going to alter that fact. Clearly, the United States was not depending on land armies and limited warfare to fight a war in Europe, and sending five more divisions to Europe by the end of 1951 was not a departure from the basic American reliance on air power. The year 1950 had seen a hodgepodge of improvised actions, for which no one could find a coherent and comprehensive doctrine, even though every action had a pragmatic explanation. European rearmament was, first of all, tailored to solve the crisis in United States foreign economic policy, and German rearmament to allay Washington's fear of traditional German militarism. The American-sponsored integration of the Western bloc, therefore, was an effort to broaden the links that tied the uneasy alliance and not to stop an alleged Soviet military menace—which it never was able to do —but to control in as many ways as possible Western Europe's diplomatic, economic, and political policies. Western military security increasingly rested not with its military superiority, which was rapidly declining, but with actual Soviet intentions.[16]

Yet NATO had other assets for the United States as well. Given strategic air power's total dependence on bases at this time, there was no real dichotomy between NATO's minimal ground forces and the United States' dependence on nuclear bombs. Apart from everything else, the United

States needed bases in Europe and elsewhere, and even the air force admitted that ground forces were crucial to its own protection. "Neutralism," which Acheson so freely condemned, was more a danger because it cut off access to bases than its denial of man power to the American-led bloc. Apart from the utility of a domestic military in containing a Left, which by 1950 was certainly no threat in Western Europe, was the value of the alliance system in integrating all the resources of a region and its colonial dependencies on behalf of a cause and world system over which Washington was attempting to assert its hegemony. This integrative theory of the alliance, with all its intangibles in the area of economic and politics, was an acknowledged and vital justification for NATO as the United States now sought to define it.

The need for bases created oblique, increasingly mixed justifications for NATO's membership. Denmark, for example, had no military value and was considered indefensible, but access to Greenland installations was crucial to the United States' strategic air force. This pressure to allow weapons systems or the desire for economic integration to locate friends had obvious implications for Washington's self-styled claim to be the defender of world freedom, since many of the attractive land and mineral prizes were found in totalitarian and feudal nations. In May 1950, Acheson implicitly extended America's protection to Greece, Turkey, and Iran—the exact nature of the commitment remaining for time to reveal. The intricate and eventually endless web of agreements, alliances, and commitments the United States was in the process of spinning was to know no bounds. The common denominator of that alliance system, as Paul Nitze wrote later in the decade, was not internal freedom or social progress, but the desire ". . . to work out a political future in some other way than subject to Soviet hegemony."[17] After 1950, Washington's ideological pretensions were less shamefacedly discarded for the nasty task of building a coalition under America's direction and, if possible, domination, and this was to include all the forces of social reaction in need of external sustenance against their domestic oppositions of every hue. Bases, some American officials were not loath to admit publicly, helped those internal elements favorable to the United States, permitting aid to local armies should the need arise.

Franco's Spain was the best example of America's deepening alliance with the Right during 1950. The pressure on Truman and Acheson to incorporate that fascist protégé into the American bloc began in 1948, when Forrestal and the navy first advocated the use of Spanish bases to control the Mediterranean lifelines to oil. During 1949 the air force added its weight, for it wanted facilities there as well, and it received powerful congressional backing. During early 1950 Acheson and Truman were still resisting Spain's integration, but they stood alone against overwhelming administration opinion. The Spanish government, for its part, actively lobbied for recognition and aid, letting it be known that its raw materials, and especially precious manganese, awaited the Americans. By the summer, massive United States loans and aid began to go to Spain, and before the end of the year Acheson was fully won over to the new phase in relations with Franco. To foretell the inevitable conclusion, during 1951 the United States sent its first ambassador to Spain since 1946, opened negotiations on bases, and presenting itself as ". . . the champion of private enterprise" it saw to it that ". . . many of the restrictions now applied to American business operations can be ameliorated or removed."[18] Spain was neither the beginning nor the end of this vast coordination of global reaction on which the United States had embarked.

NATO and the Western European alliance, in brief, was far less an end in itself than a pragmatic, highly flexible means by which the United States hoped to attain ends quite incidental to a maximum military posture against Russia. It was, first of all, an integrative economic mechanism that offered practical solutions for the United States' immediate needs and future hopes, and then operated on an ideological and political plane. Its military value was still essential to the autonomous American air and sea forces. It coped with the threat of internal upheaval, which in itself required incorporating more reactionary allies who had still to confront local resistance, and it provided a framework for an integrated West Germany's future role in Europe.

Russia and Rearmament

Just as the United States and its allies feared a neutral Germany capable of defining Europe's balance of power, much less incorporated into a hostile bloc, so, too, did the Soviet Union regard America's goal of West German integration and rearmament. It would be difficult, indeed, to find any postwar issue that had such terrible emotional overtones for the Russians, who understandably saw the power realities in Germany from the vantage point of what that nation had often been rather than its rather modest contemporary position. Russia's desire for security along its western border was one of the Kremlin's deepest impulses, a preoccupation that caused it to cajole, threaten, and even offer extravagant compromises in the European power struggle.

The Germans on both sides of the partition handled themselves with a vituperation that changed nothing. Adenauer propounded the fiction that his government spoke for the entire German people, and he made no secret that he did not recognize the Oder-Neisse boundary and merely sought to regain East Germany for his regime, eliminating the SED in the process. His solution was to embark first on all-German elections which he persisted in wrapping in patently nonnegotiable packages. The East Germans replied in kind, also proposing all-German coalitions even less likely to gain acceptance in the West. In an entirely vague manner, at the beginning of 1950 the United States formally endorsed the ambiguous West German election scheme, not to waver from it as virtually the exclusive basis for a solution to the German issue for the rest of our period.

All-German elections provided Washington with a useful shield against detractors who argued it was abandoning a negotiated settlement of the German question. As a rule in diplomacy, any utopian proposal righteously clears the way for what one really wishes to do. In fact, of course, the question in Germany was never local democracy, which both the United States and Russia had consistently violated when their interests were at stake, but security. The United States knew the Germans did not want rearmament and would likely opt for a form of socialism, just as the Russians must have been aware of the unpopularity of the SED. National interest alone was the basis of their functional German policies, and for the United States its interest was defined not merely in terms of military security but in its ambitious socioeconomic categories as well. In the end, the United States could lose the most from negotiations, and hence its paralyzing preconditions around an issue of self-determination that it cynically contrived.

To make the functional Western policies appear less belligerent, during May 1950 the three Western foreign ministers asked the Russians to negotiate all-German elections preceding discussion of a peace settlement, a proposition that was not likely to end the impasse. After the September NATO meeting, however, the Russians took the diplomatic offensive, asking that the West stop remilitarization and negotiate a peace treaty, and that the East and West German governments not merge but form a council, representation on which the Russians left vague, which would then negotiate an all-German government. Hazy enough to have potential for a neutral, demilitarized Germany, the Soviet proposal rightly assumed that all key issues involving Germany would have to be negotiated as a package. This was, indeed, its major distinction from earlier and later American schemes. Informally and formally, Acheson attacked the "perversion of language" in the Soviet position, inviting it to accept the election scheme first and, in effect, to confess full responsibility for having caused all postwar tensions in Europe.[19] But the Russians would not be put off, and on November 3 asked the three Western Powers for a foreign ministers conference to discuss the German question.

The British and French supported the American position that a conference was useless, and might be turned against the Russians only by broadening the agenda to include alleged Soviet threats to the peace while excluding such issues as NATO and United States bases springing up everywhere in the world. The French, however reticent on Germany's rearmament, had imbibed enough ideology to wish to negotiate such things as alleged Cominform subversion. The West's insistence that it could not consider Germany as a separate problem, but only the entire global role of Russia at any four-power meetings, led to a tiresome exchange of notes and exploratory talks, with interminable quibbling over an agenda, which the three powers finally terminated at the end of June 1951. For the rest of the year both sides merely amplified their position for propaganda. More to the point was the fact that the United States was determined to get on with the question of rearming Germany and NATO, and Acheson was not for a moment ready to consider lowering the tension and momentum he had built, only to see a neutral Germany emerge in a form explicitly in conflict with America's goals.

Truman's state of the union message of January 1951 struck the dominant note of the remainder of his administration, and in it he discussed the ". . . ambitious, more crafty, and more menacing imperialism of the rulers of the Soviet Union," men who foment "subversion and internal revolution," "encourage sabotage," "put out poisonous propaganda."[20] With military mobilization under way and a main thrust of American policy, Washington enlisted words, too, with even less restraint than before as it used an ideological fog to enshroud congressional and mass political perceptions.

Leadership was not so naïve, however, and the historian will look hard to find responsible men who thought the Russians were an immediate military threat to the United States or Western Europe. This fact alone explains NATO's and European rearmament's lackadaisical growth.

Adenauer thought a Russian attack quite improbable, and merely continued to use West Germany's willingness to rearm to get at the substance: West Germany's sovereignty. Truman was still being warned that West Germany's rearmament might prove more provocative of the USSR than was useful, and when Eisenhower and his peers attempted to justify sending five divisions to Europe before the Senate in February 1951, war with Russia was minimized, almost offhandedly dismissed. Since, as we shall see, no coherent strategic doctrine relevant to Soviet power existed to justify more troops to Europe, much less the level of arms NATO contemplated with or without West Germany, the official economic justification for rearmament, including the integration of Europe's and its dependencies' raw materials, must be taken at face value.[21]

The year 1951 therefore remained inconclusive for NATO; its relative weakness compared with Russian power remained approximately the same as before Korea. The Senate during April duly endorsed sending four new American divisions to Europe, and the NATO diplomats and West Germans continued their interminable meetings that gave birth to impressively little agreement or military power. Perhaps the key message of such negotiations was that the Atlantic Alliance was uncoordinated, of many discordant minds, weak militarily without the United States—and largely a mythical entity over which Washington unsuccessfully sought to establish control. Concessions to West German autonomy were, of course, far-reaching and frequent. Basically, endless negotiations could not solve the morass of political problems connected with German rearmament, of which France's hopeless involvement in Indochina and delicate political condition at home were but two examples. McCloy's implied threat in June that the United States might proceed with Germany's rearmament without France's endorsement of its form carried precious little weight.

For the rest of 1951 the Western European powers debated every conceivable approach to West Germany's military integration, only to have the French continuously raise new conditions that left their real intentions in doubt. The Germans, for their part, were loath to accept any second-class status in the European Defense Community (EDC) which was then emerging as an infinitely complex paper scheme. By this time NATO's nominal military plans were a good two years behind schedule, a fact that was of far less military than psychological consequence. Of greater concern by March 1952 was Washington's fear that the Germans in their indignation might indeed pursue remilitarization in their own way—alone.[22]

The Russians were no less agitated at the course of events. In January 1952 the East Germans published an extremely detailed all-German election proposal, modeled after the 1924 Weimar electoral law, which more than met the American prerequisite for democratic all-German elections to precede negotiations on other issues. The United States simply ignored it. During February the Russians announced they would examine the issue, and on March 10 they sent a draft treaty to the three powers which they indicated was flexible and quite negotiable. It proposed German unity, but now the Russians failed to prescribe a mechanism such as that contained in their earlier plan. The scheme guaranteed civil liberties and political democracy, and implicitly the East German election proposal offered the means for attaining unity. All foreign troops would withdraw one year after a peace treaty, and Germany would obligate itself not to join any alliance directed against the Soviet or American blocs—in effect, it would be neutral. And it could maintain a small independent military force, join the UN, and be free of all economic limitations. But, the proposal added, a united Germany must also accept the Oder-Neisse line. Temperate in tone and content, the Russians offered the proposition not as propaganda but as a flexible approach to a grave issue. It was also a measure of the residue of naïveté in Russia's perception of the United States' objectives in the world. "Here again," Acheson later recalled, "was a spoiling operation intended to check and dissipate the momentum toward solutions in the West brought about by three years of colossal effort."[23]

But the proposal was too serious for a cavalier dismissal. Even Adenauer praised its tone, but urged no delay in getting on with building EDC. After two weeks of consultation, the three powers sent the Russians a common rejection which harped again on the precondition of free elections, only now referring the topic to the UN instead of the Germans themselves, and insisted that a post-treaty Germany be free to join any bloc it chose, including, implicitly, EDC. And Germany's boundary, they added, was still undefined. Germany, Acheson insisted, must be part of a European community capable of defending itself. But the Russians pressed, on April 9 accepted the immediate participation of the Germans in working out an all-German government, and suggested that the four powers rather than the UN supervise free elections in all of Germany. Now, Moscow asked, would the United States enter into discussions or offer a counterproposal? Acheson chose to reply to this equally moderate note first in a public speech on the nineteenth, distorting the Russian position on elections and painting their stand and intentions with emotional, factually false terms. After three years of "colossal effort" the United States was not going to be stalled, and only over a month later did it formally reply to the second Russian note, insisting that a UN commission first study voting conditions in East Germany, with a four-power conference to be held to consider its report.[24]

In the meantime, despite a certain ambivalence in the Bonn Bundestag —especially its Social Democratic wing—over what was clearly an important new possibility, EDC was rushed through as the French piled on more and more conditions, to protect themselves against Germany, and left their intentions in doubt till the last moment. On May 27 EDC was signed, but without England, which entered into only separate treaties with the EDC and its various members. It was small consolation to the Russians that they could point out on May 24 that Washington had inordinately delayed dealing with their offer, adding new conditions and ignoring Soviet concessions on fundamental points. But the United States would not waver from its earlier stand, and so the matter died.

Acheson's haste after years of frustration over German rearmament and European security was explicable only in terms of the main objectives and style of American diplomacy at this time, and in that context peace with Russia was a far lesser concern, if not a tangible threat. Negotiations were alien, disarmament in Europe inconceivable, for arms in themselves gave the United States a multitude of economic and political levers over its allies. From the viewpoint of military security, the disengagement scheme the Russians proposed offered far more than the hodgepodge of forces confronting the titanic Red army. Without more arms than were essential for economic needs and limits, much less a coherent strategy, NATO without America's bombs lacked everything for fighting a war against Russia. And, as was suspected and feared, the French eventually refused to ratify EDC, and hence that undertaking, too, was stillborn. But as British Prime Minister Anthony Eden and Acheson publicly admitted shortly after they introduced EDC, Germany's military integration made impossible its aggression and free rein in the future—at least, we must add, against the West. What superficially led to continued conflict between the United States and Russia —much less obvious military weakness for the West—had a larger function and deeper importance to the premises and goals of United States foreign policy. For within that context, however inadequate America's military strategy, it made both economic and political sense—and was the only conduct consistent with its assumptions.[25]

Dilemmas and Assumptions of Power

Strategic theory can be successful only if all the key elements in a military equation are predictable and controllable as a kind of rational problem, in which case generals and those whom they hire may risk reasoning about the unreasonable. Such an approach must necessarily ignore the decisive role of nonmaterial factors of ideology and politics that have dominated the Third World since the war, and must assume no budget limitations on the definition of a comprehensive, pure strategy. But after 1946 budgets dictated strategies, and their size, in turn, was largely a response to economic needs and, to a lesser extent, military perceptions. The historian who seeks to locate a coherent strategy in American military planning after World War II, and especially after 1949, will fail, for the reality was eclectic and improvised save in one regard: all strategy was postulated on the notion that warfare would occur only between industrial powers with concentrated economic and urban targets. Any other premise was incompatible with a notion that a finite military budget was possible and that American material power could somehow give it decisive strength in the world. In fact, the basic thrust of American military planning, with its reliance on aerospace, was geared only to conflict with Russia. Korea only planted the gnawing doubt that the fundamental premise was false and that the United States was weak in certain critical ways. Vietnam was to prove it.

At the least, therefore, the military budget became a mechanism of economic regulation centered mainly around technologically sophisticated industries. "Another upswing in industry and business looms this Presidential election year," the New York *Times* predicted in its annual economic survey in January 1952; "Optimism rests on the scheduled rise of defense expenditures to a new peak. . . ."[26] With military purchases now over 13 percent of the gross national product, the arms race guaranteed a measure of prosperity without solving the basic problems of assuring either military superiority or adequacy for the endless global tasks Washington had assigned itself. Indeed, it was the only means of economic management politically available to the administration which in 1951, not for the first or last time, took the position, as the *Wall Street Journal* described it, that "[h]iking the arms goals would be a new propaganda weapon for use against budget-cutting Congressmen."[27] So long as it defined Russia as the prime enemy, technological escalation and new expenditures that maintained economic prosperity were credible and inevitable. For as Russia's material capacity grew, and along with that its ability to narrow America's absolute strategic bombing and naval superiority, successive administrations never deemed their military arsenal adequate. For the industries that sold exotic hardware, such a spiral was a boon.

The administration's definitions of its basic military doctrine frequently changed to suit the immediate political objective, but essentially the United States was relying on its strategic air power to deter and, if necessary, defeat Russia. But this did not mean Washington anticipated war, for in fact it did not. The larger American assumption, insofar as there was one, was " . . . that time is on our side if we make good use of it," that what was essential was an "effective deterrent force," and only after it was created would there be some ". . . chances of negotiating successfully with the Soviet Union."[28] Succinctly, during what was expected to be a long period of global tension the United States would confront Russia from what were later called "positions of strength."

Hence America's leaders' frustrations, since the Russians possessed the secret of the bomb. In mid-1951 one well-informed commentator suggested the United States possessed between 750 and 1,000 bombs and the Russians might already have as many as 200. If the Russians indeed held 200 bombs, which may have been possible, they, too, possessed a formidable deterrent against any American response should Moscow decide to invade Europe, and in fact the two powers already had attained what we now call the "delicate balance of terror." Acheson virtually admitted this fact in February 1951, and in the hearings on MacArthur's dismissal as much as declared America's decisive respect for Russia's atomic force in being at that time. In reality, however, by mid-1951 the United States estimated it did not have sufficient atomic arms to cripple Russia's industrial base. Whether its superiority over Russia was increasing or growing smaller was probably a mystery to Washington. What was even more consequential was the uselessness of the bomb in nonindustrial, Third World areas of decentralized economies. At the beginning of 1952, General Omar Bradley thought there were no worth-while targets in the Far East against which to use the bomb.

During the last two years of the Truman administration, however, atomic power was America's basic military keystone. Acheson himself admitted this publicly, and never convincingly explained how the quite minor manpower increments in NATO or EDC would change this dependence on the bomb. He never defined the ambiguous notion of "adequacy" or a suitable balance of conventional and nuclear forces. And since America's military planners acknowledged that a Soviet land attack in Europe would lead to a general atomic war that would not prevent Russia from reaching the Channel, Europe's rearmament had, at best, only a marginal military justification.[29]

Ultimately, the United States' greatest protection in Europe was the Soviet Union's intentions and capabilities, which postwar history had repeatedly proved were both quite modest. The Kremlin's preoccupation after 1950 with internal economic growth was nothing new, but it was a fact from which Washington could only draw confidence. Even if their vituperative rhetoric increased to match Washington's verbal escalation, the Russians continued to develop an extensive ideological system which rationalized their profound desires to avoid war. The theory was "coexistence," and it slighted the inevitable upheaval, conflict, and violence between social systems in the world almost as much as did the American pronouncements. Indeed, it ignored the proven significance of the United States' postwar global interventions against the Left and social transformation by either peaceful or violent means. In fact, the Russians also developed an international theory relevant to their needs and, more specifically, their relations to the United States.

Though Varga had been criticized for his specific analysis of Western capitalism, the major core of his theory on the continuation of capitalist rivalries and conflict remained the heart of the Soviet world view. In one way or another, whether it was the internal crisis of colonialism or capitalism, or the ceaseless reiteration that coexistence between different social systems was possible if not inevitable, the Kremlin attempted to calm its population so that it could get on with the economic tasks at hand without fear or demoralization. The Russians continuously attributed quite fantastic powers to the organized world peace movement, whose activities thereby allowed them to offer optimism for their people despite the movement's virtually nonexistent restraining influence in the West. But insofar as such mobilizing myths had material results in the form of higher morale, they made as much sense as Washington's conspiratorial theses did in marshaling its otherwise reticent constituencies. And they made less credible the anti-Communists' apocalyptic visions. Just as Washington attributed an incorrigible ferociousness to the Russians, so Moscow found irresistible—and mythical—restraints staying the imperialists' hands.

In September 1952, Stalin systematized the Soviet theory of international relations, and the following month the nineteenth party congress duly endorsed his thesis. Structurally, he argued, the world capitalist market was shrinking, thereby constricting the capitalist states' opportunities and deepening their natural internal contradictions. Despite a superficial ideological consensus among them, Stalin saw that the British, French, and Americans were already scrambling for scarce resources and that eventually Germany and Japan would again join the race. Wars between capitalist states were therefore still inevitable, the vaunted American hegemony only transitory. The world peace movement, he suggested unconvincingly, would somehow play a role in heading off wars between capitalist and socialist nations—with coexistence remaining the prognosis of probable future relations between Russia and the West.[30] On its face value merely an act of faith, for many other, unstated reasons Stalin was correct when he predicted Russia would avoid war. But, we must interpolate, by 1952 it was clear that avoidance of war with Russia was never to be synonymous with peace. The significance of this enduring reality the Russians refused to consider fully.

For the serious historian the question is never what the United States should have done in the postwar era, but rather why it never pursued a course more likely to avoid conflict with Russia—in brief, America's fundamental motives and needs and their economic and political context. The Truman administration based its foreign policy on the need for tension at home and abroad which permitted both integration and mobilization—of citizens, congressmen, nominal allies, and the entire non-Soviet bloc—into an alliance under America's hegemonic direction. Such tension consciously became integral to the conduct of American diplomacy and the direction of the world system it wished to establish, and it was based on the premise that tension must lead neither to war nor to peace. By necessity, such an approach required a patently exaggerated view of Russian power, and the endless allegedly nefarious ways—ranging from military to conspiratorial —by which the Soviets might apply it.

Truman's instinctive opposition to conventional diplomacy—"From our experience with them they make agreements merely to break them," he wrote in mid-1950—reinforced the approach of Acheson and those who preferred to get on with the task of integrating a world alliance in the necessarily troubled atmosphere.[31] The Russians designed their peace overtures, Acheson argued in 1952, explicitly to produce discord in the American-led camp. Although Acheson acknowledged that Russia was not threatening Western Europe in 1952, and even that there would be no early confrontation with Russia elsewhere, what was more essential to him was to bind further non-Communist Europe and its dependencies into a cohesive bloc such as Americans had sought since World War II. To jeopardize what the United States had accomplished until 1952 in exchange for a neutral, reunited Germany was inconceivable to him.

Such an integrative vision was not at all a reaction to Soviet initiatives; rather it was a means for accomplishing the fundamental goals of American foreign policy defined a decade, even generations, earlier. The alliance system and NATO never provided adequate military security to any of its members, the United States included, but it became Washington's means for attempting to regulate Europe's affairs on other levels. Mobilization, psychological and military, became a prerequisite to the achievement of its goals. Alternatives such as disarmament were inconceivable because they were viable only in a profoundly different political and economic structure, and such insubstantial proposals as the United States made were only an aspect of psychological and ideological warfare against both Russia and more demanding citizens in the West. The architects of United States foreign policy molded the sense of danger to attain finally the profoundly sought-after integrated world political-economic structure, and to construct a new American-dominated international balance and order to replace the collapse of nineteenth and twentieth century empires and spheres. And given the omnibus economic categories by which they defined America's strategic interest in such a world order, especially insofar as Washington acknowledged raw materials as the backbone of economic potential and growth, by 1952 America's leaders explicitly outlined their national stake in every area of the world and prepared the justification for the interminable interventions that have occurred since.[32]

These were the assumptions and aspirations that the Truman administration bequeathed to the new Republican government at the end of 1952. Truman, in his last message to Congress in January 1953, reflected the premises of his postwar foreign policy and summed up its myths, leaving to Eisenhower some crucial advice on his basic course. Paranoid images of Communist chieftains building a vast war potential in their camp, drugging masses of deluded followers throughout the world to insurrection, sabotage, and aggression, of cynical Communist identification with the forces of nationalism and economic change throughout the world merely ". . . to enslave more millions of human souls"—all this Truman conjured up for future politicians to confront. There could be no respite, no peace; and in his final words the departing President reflected the essence of America's postwar policy and the rationalizations under which its more enduring objectives had long since been buried. "Were we to grow discouraged now, were we to weaken and slack off, the whole structure we have built, these past 8 years, would come apart and fall away. Never then, no matter by what stringent means, could our free world regain the ground, the sheer momentum, lost by such a move."[33] The crisis of mankind, the tension and pain by which history had been tormented for so long, could not cease.

25

Eisenhower and the Crisis of American Power

The Truman administration had been in favor of neither peace nor a larger war in Korea. On one hand Truman and his advisers saw the value of the Korean crisis in furthering their previously conceived rearmament plans and their desires for Europe and the world economy. Time and again Truman took no decisive steps toward negotiated peace when it was in his grasp, and it was in this context that much of MacArthur's adventurism was possible. The Taft wing of the Republican Party repeatedly exploited Truman's indecisiveness, which filled the American people with a politically critical war-weariness that made them receptive to any solution that promised to bring the sustained bloodletting to a certain, quick end. The Republicans used MacArthur as a foil to Truman's vague policy, and the general thought that he might control this political movement for his own ends, first to shape American strategy in Asia, perhaps then to win the presidential nomination for himself. Soon Truman and the Democrats were trapped by a dilemma they themselves had created, for they increasingly feared that a decisive peace policy in Korea would also lead to charges of appeasement in Asia and win the Republican nomination for Taft or MacArthur. MacArthur, of course, was unequivocally dedicated to committing all of America's resources to a war in Asia. Taft, on the other hand, mixed an inconsistent hodgepodge of criticism and alternatives that many feared would lead the man to significant global withdrawals, perhaps even isolation, incompatible with the aims of an expansionist America.

What was at stake in this dilemma was the nature of American priorities in the world; in effect, Europe versus Asia. Initially, at least, Asia for the

Truman administration was but an instrumentality by which to solve European and other problems. The commitments of the various leading presidential contenders on this vital issue were far more critical than which party came to power, for the ruling party's global priorities were virtually identical to those of the eastern and big business wing of the Republicans. If the Democrats saw themselves outflanked and increasingly restricted politically, heading toward defeat in the election of 1952, at least Truman was aware of the significance of the future of the Republican nomination to the continuity in American foreign policy. By 1950 Vandenberg was gravely ill, and that pillar of bipartisanship died in April of the following year. Dulles had revealed over many years that the administration could fully trust him to work with his business colleagues who directed the affairs of state as well. The question was whether Dulles and his circle in the party would find a candidate willing to follow their initiatives.

Truman had already made his choice. As early as July 1945 he had offered Eisenhower the presidential nomination in 1948 and may have done so again in 1947; and more liberal Democrats actually briefly advanced the general for that post during the 1948 campaign. But Eisenhower was a Republican and too low-keyed willingly to seek arduous new tasks. As the genial compromiser, prone to take advice and allocate sensitive responsibilities to others, he preferred the obscurity of the presidency of Columbia University. Eisenhower disappeared to that pleasant post until December 18, 1950, when Truman insisted that he take on the job of NATO's supreme commander.

The NATO post returned Eisenhower to the public's view, and the war hero's reinvolvement in European affairs not only strengthened his own devotion to Europe as the main area of American concern but brought another general into the public arena to balance MacArthur's alternate strategy and, by then, obvious political ambitions. Moreover, there was no better way of winning recalcitrant Republican pro-Taft congressmen to the European strategy and increased troop commitments there than to make Eisenhower its proponent. The politically astute Truman unquestionably understood the larger political implications of the Eisenhower appointment, which were quite obvious. By the summer of 1951 Eisenhower was widely considered a leading contender for the GOP nomination, and in September Henry Cabot Lodge, on behalf of the critically important group of eastern Republicans, offered the general their full support and pleaded with him to head off the likely victory of the Taft wing. One account alleges that Truman even offered Eisenhower the Democratic nomination early the following November. More certain is the fact that on December 18 Truman himself wrote Eisenhower concerning the isolationist threat, implying that if Eisenhower would run for President he, Truman, would step aside in 1952. Eisenhower did not decline to run, and by the following February he was in the race.[1]

In this sense, Eisehower had always been the candidate of a critical faction of the Democratic Party in power as well as the virtually inter-changeable eastern wing of the GOP. MacArthur himself quickly discovered that he had no independent political machine with which to capture the nomination, and although he was asked to make the keynote speech to the Republican convention, in effect he became the useful ploy and figure-head for a Taft faction that hoped to give the nomination to the senator. The bitter struggle at Chicago must have only further alienated Eisenhower from the Taft wing.

No sooner had Eisenhower won by the largest popular vote in American history than MacArthur tested the President-elect's commitment to the bipartisan strategy. On December 17 Eisenhower and Dulles met MacArthur, and the retired general offered the new President a comprehensive and ambitious plan that consisted of two parts: a mixture of utopian naïveté and dangerous atomic escalation. In brief, MacArthur proposed that Eisenhower and Stalin meet to agree to a democratically reunited Germany and Korea, making these two nations plus Japan and Austria neutral areas from which both sides would withdraw all their troops. Both great powers were then to adopt constitutional amendments outlawing war as an instrument of national policy. Should Russia reject this improbable package, MacArthur suggested the United States use atomic weapons against North Korea as part of its reconquest, against China's airfields and industrial bases as well, and aid Chiang's recapture of China. In effect, the scheme was a mere repetition of MacArthur's by now well-known strategy, and Dulles and the President-elect politely dismissed it.

Truman's alternative provided for the smooth transition of power, and permitted Eisenhower to capitalize on his victory and good will to cut through numerous difficulties the Democrats had confronted. Eisenhower reassured Truman of his dedication to bipartisan foreign policy, and conti-nuity and stability were the watchwords. There should be no doubt, save when transitory political circumstances required them to draw false distinc-tions between the two parties, that Eisenhower and Dulles, both before and after 1953, believed ". . . that the national interest dictates that it [foreign policy] be conducted in a *bipartisan,* entirely objective manner."[2] Eisenhower's somewhat heavier utilization of businessmen in his administrations should not obscure the fact that many of them had already gained their experience under Truman, but especially that they shared the same goals, and represented the same power constituencies, as those that preceded and followed Eisenhower's government. As Truman and his key aides had hoped, the new administration grasped the basic consensus on the necessity of American expansion and power in the world. Eisenhower's intimate dependence on the Democratic Party–eastern Republican coalition colored his legislative record the entire first year of power, and fifty-eight times in 1953 Democrats provided the margin of victory in Congress essential to save his proposals from Republican opposition. "It seems to me," Truman jibed in September 1954, "that President Eisenhower should be secretly wishing for a Democratic Congress . . . and hope that we can save him from the misdeeds of his own party."[3] In reality, however, the Democrats had reason to be just as grateful to Eisenhower and his faction of the Republicans for saving their policy from being gravely undermined. The relationship was usefully reinforcing in creating the monolithic ideology and coalition that guided American foreign policy and served American interests after the World War.

This literal continuity also left the Eisenhower administration with all the predicaments and failings that had so troubled the Truman administration. Korea, Europe, the world economy, military alternatives—everything remained unresolved to plague the men in Washington. Eisenhower, of course, was a predictable factor by 1953, and for this reason Truman had favored his accession to power. It is scarcely sufficient, as some of his own aides were later to do, to accuse Eisenhower of being devoid of clarity or incapable of giving precision or direction to American policy. Harsher yet, and largely irrelevant, is speech writer Emmet John Hughes's characterization of him as being inconsistent, perhaps even oafish and stupid, on occasions. Eisenhower was familiar to all, and he was aware of his own limits as well, and hence he virtually transferred all real responsibility for the conduct of foreign policy to Dulles, his secretary of state. He was—and this explained his effortless success—the spokesman for those who knew both how to administer and define policy, whether it was in the military or the civilian branches of government. His addiction to platitudes, which he showed again in his inaugural address and first message to Congress, were really helpful to those who sought time and patience from Congress and the people for less attractive and potentially more testing policies. He could offer to negotiate and preserve all alliances and stress the futility of "appeasement" at one and the same time, identifying the United States with the forces of "lightness against the dark" even while insisting as well that the French cause in Indochina, or the United States' access to the world raw materials, were part of the same global struggle.[4]

But such visions were essentially not those of Eisenhower. Dulles, for the most part, communicated them to him. The new secretary of state's complete acceptance of Truman's foreign policy was in large measure his endorsement of a global strategy that he himself had participated in formulating since 1945. But his continuity with the perspectives of past American foreign policy was far older, and much more profound than perhaps that of any other man in American history. Grandson and nephew of two secretaries of state, deep admirer of Woodrow Wilson's grand visions of America in the world since their days together at Princeton as student and sometimes teacher, the head of the most important Wall Street law firm in American history specializing in the diplomatic prerequisites of corporate expansion—Dulles was part of the very marrow of the twentieth-century American power structure. His conduct as secretary of state was the least doubtful aspect of what the new administration might undertake. Here the continuity was not merely with the Truman administration but with American history itself.

Dulles' detractors regarded him as legalistic, given to excessive moralism, and somehow under the delusion that Christian doctrine specially guided him. Doubtlessly, his public allusions to ". . . justice as revealed to us" or ". . . our sense of mission in the world" reinforced this image.[5] One should not make too much of this interpretation, for, however much Dulles was attracted to Christian theology and talked about it, his conduct of diplomacy was of a radically different, much less ethereal order. Dulles was pragmatic and politically astute, and when forced to make a choice between obvious evils he did not delude himself about their meaning. His concern for congressional approval was far greater than his contemplation of the righteous theological course, and his deference to Congress inhibited his action time and again under circumstances that Acheson would never have tolerated. From the first day he addressed Congress in his new role in January 1953, he initiated the process of promising everything to everyone in Congress, from the "liberation" of Eastern Europe to peace, so that he might continue the main contours of America's historic expansion in the world with as much tranquillity from that quarter as potentially troublesome Congressmen might provide.[6]

1953: Korea and the Dilemma of Asia

Other than pledging to visit Korea if elected, and increasing the numbers of South Korean troops, Eisenhower promised very little on the topic during the campaign. While Dulles was more disposed than his predecessor to rate Asia as having greater significance to Soviet policy, his contemplated policies meant that a continuation of Truman's emphasis was probable. Not only was he concerned that too much emphasis on Asia would tax the European allies and NATO, but he had consistently opposed MacArthur's plans for escalation and, indeed, anything that threatened to embroil further American man power in an Asian war. When Eisenhower voyaged to Korea during early December he made it explicit that he would rely on the truce talks rather than arms to bring the war to an end.

But Eisenhower had to reconcile a number of conflicting impulses and dilemmas: he had to make peace in Korea while avoiding charges of appeasement; he had to end the war in order to begin a reduction of the military costs he had promised during the campaign as a first step toward a balanced budget; he had to end the Korean War so as to devote a larger share of America's anticipated constricted military resources to Europe and a strategic warfare capacity, all of which he expected would cost less; and he had to reduce greatly one commitment in Asia at a moment when crises that he could not avoid were appearing in Indochina. The delicate juggling act between specific issues, crises, costs, and strategy was to trigger the unsuccessful search for an American global strategy that was relevant to all needs and conditions.

The economy and armaments dimension of Eisenhower's dilemma, and the other aspects of the Asia crisis, we discuss later in this chapter. The Korean dilemma was soluble. On February 2, 1953, as the administration was planning new concessions at the Korean truce talks, which had been reduced to a simple liaison contact since October, Eisenhower announced that the Seventh Fleet would no longer prevent Chiang from invading the mainland of China. He insisted, "This order implies no aggressive intent on our part," and since Chiang had no resources for an invasion, in fact he intended the gesture to salve the more bellicose and pave the way for what was to follow.[7]

By the end of the Truman administration most of America's European allies and the neutral nations were thoroughly out of sympathy with the American negotiating position on the repatriation of Korean war prisoners.

Acheson had gravely warned the NATO powers on their compromise proposals, hinting ominously that the United States might even pull out of NATO and Europe. Eisenhower and his advisers had already rejected the vast costs of a military victory, and so on February 22 the first major alteration in the United States position came when Clark offered to repatriate immediately all sick and wounded prisoners should the Communists reciprocate. No one consulted these soldiers, ultimately numbering 6,670, as to their wishes, and Washington justified this departure in the name of the 1949 Geneva Convention it had hitherto studiously ignored. On March 5, however, Stalin died, and the Communists delayed their response as the Kremlin's new leaders probably thought again about their own strategy in Korea—and how their control of arms allowed them to influence China and North Korea. On the twenty-eighth the Communists proposed the resumption of full-scale truce talks, and two days later Chou En-lai publicly endorsed a plan to hand all prisoners opposed to repatriation over to a neutral state that would objectively explain their rights to return home to them without intimidation. At the beginning of April the Communists announced their readiness to exchange sick and wounded prisoners and settle this last troublesome phase of the armistice talks. Progress from this time onward was, by comparison to earlier years, speedy—too fast, indeed, for Rhee.

Although Rhee had always opposed an armistice, until March 1953 he had slight cause for concern. Rhee had ruthlessly prosecuted a war of unity for almost three years, and that goal was his life's ambition. He did not intend to abandon his well-known propensity to take matters into his own hands. On April 5 he publicly denounced negotiations and called for a march to the Yalu, and several days later he expressed these thoughts directly to Eisenhower. Both publicly and privately over the next weeks, Rhee's government made it altogether plain that it would sabotage the imminent truce by refusing to repatriate all Koreans and perhaps even by attacking northward alone. By the end of April, Rhee indicated that he was ready to withdraw his troops from the UN command, should Chinese troops stay on in North Korea after the armistice. The United States prepared for a major crisis.[8]

Rhee's threats, which had much sympathy from both Clark and other key American officers, caused the American truce negotiators to move more cautiously and to refuse compromise, and the talks slowed down over the composition of the neutral supervisory nations and procedures by which they were to screen and release voluntary nonrepatriates. At this point the

United States decided to mollify Rhee and indulge its own impulses via the application of military pressures intended to gain Communist concessions.

With the exception of a few remaining power installations that the air force attacked on May 10 and 11, to quote an official account, "The production of food in North Korea was the only major element of North Korea's economy still functioning efficiently after three years of war." Twenty-odd irrigation dams contained three-quarters of the controlled water supply for North Korea's rice production, and the air force fully realized the potentially genocidal human consequences of the destruction of the dams. "The Westerner can little conceive the awesome meaning which the loss of this staple food commodity has for the Asian—starvation and slow death."[9] The grotesque nature of such an act of destruction had stayed the American hand until May, for it violated all international codes intended to prevent war crimes. To attack the dams would make clear to the Communists America's willingness to destroy their nation if necessary. Starting May 13, planes attacked five dams, and the first flash flood scooped clean twenty-seven miles of valley.[10] On June 8 the Communists signed a prisoner-of-war agreement that satisfied the American objections, and the way was open for an armistice and an end to the three-year war.

South Korea's representative boycotted the armistice talks from May 25 onward. Rhee and his associates threatened every conceivable measure designed to undermine the impending armistice, but the old tyrant knew the limits of his own power and the advantages of retaining some American sympathy and much economic and military aid after the war. To risk all was to court inevitable defeat if the Americans, in their frustration, withdrew their troops.

On May 12, after talking to Rhee, Clark advised Washington to permit Rhee simply to release the Korean nonrepatriates, and then ask the Communists to approve the step as part of the armistice. According to his memoir, Clark also proposed that the release take place whether or not the Communists consented, which, naturally, they did not. But Washington hoped to stay Rhee's hand and promised military and economic aid if he went along with the armistice. Rhee, for his part, exploited the occasion to ask for yet more aid as well as a mutual defense pact. To all this Washington soothingly agreed, but Rhee and his associates only intensified their threats. Given American toleration, and the fact they had earlier proposed such a plan themselves, on the night of June 18 Rhee's guards released about 27,000 allegedly North Korean prisoners of war who had refused repatriation, thereby shattering the basis of the laboriously arranged agreement with the Communists. Clark feigned surprise and strongly chastised Rhee, but the Communists fully blamed the Americans for not taking precautions, considering Rhee's repeated threats, to prevent such episodes. The Communists asked whether any agreement to which Rhee was a party had any value —"I must confess, with some right," Eisenhower later admitted.[11]

To discover the answer to this dilemma, and to save the armistice, Washington prepared to use the stick along with the carrot against Rhee. The Korean, having exhausted his most disruptive tactic, now attempted to get as much as possible from the rich Yankees. Washington bluffed Rhee with threats of total troop withdrawals, which it in fact never seriously considered, and pointed out to him the weaknesses of his own forces. Then it sent Walter Robertson, assistant secretary of state, to Korea to intimidate, cajole, and promise a mutual security pact and future economic and military aid if Rhee would cooperate. Rhee threatened and attempted to get more and more commitments, especially to the principle of unification and a renewal of fighting if no progress toward it were made within ninety days, but the United States was reluctant to give more than money, arms, and vague pledges.

But he became more tractable after June 9, when the Communists, probably for the purpose of impressing Rhee on his military fate without the Americans, launched a major offensive against ROK-held lines which sent Rhee's forces reeling back as far as seven miles on a twenty-three mile front. On July 11 Rhee publicly proclaimed support for the armistice.

Eisenhower was deeply pessimistic whether the Communists would now consent to an armistice after such a rank betrayal, and he was even less certain as to how long it would last. But the Communists wanted peace, and on July 27 both sides signed an armistice that actually brought the Korean War to an end. Rhee, despite subsequent American willingness to release nebulous statements favoring unification of the divided nation, had lost his capacity to get the Americans to do for him what he was unable to accomplish himself. The internationalization of the Korean civil war came to an end, save insofar as American economic and military aid alone sustained the South. By April 1960, when a coup threw Rhee out of power, his regime had received over $3 billion in military and economic aid from the United States, and South Korea continued as a replica of Chiang's China. Political repression, poverty, and inflation, inequitable landholdings and debt-ridden farmers, corruption and stagnation—the South Korea that the United States had imposed in 1945 and that had led to peasant rebellion and civil war remained quite intact, waiting for the inevitable revolutionary upheavals that one day will seek to right its accumulated wrongs.[12]

The Indochina Crisis

Stalemate in Korea forced the Eisenhower administration to consider yet more carefully the implications of Indochina for the future of Asia. Ironically, it was here that Washington had anticipated the first Asian crisis after the fall of China, and, as during 1950, the impact of the war in Indochina on France and European rearmament was still a prime consideration. But now the larger context was more complex and more dangerous.

American aid to the French cause in Indochina began in earnest before the Korean War, but immediately after its outbreak Truman pledged greater support to the French and Bao Dai regime. At first the French deeply resented America's pressures to give greater independence to the Bao Dai regime, and they suspected the United States was seeking a government there that would transfer raw materials concessions to American interests, but necessity soon overcame French hesitation.

During mid-October 1950, shortly after serious military reverses, Jules Moch, the French minister of national defense, arrived in Washington to attempt to obtain even greater United States military aid. By this time, despite earlier reticence, the French had come to realize that the key to their colonial war was in Washington, and Moch was already quietly disturbed that the Pentagon was taking orders for military equipment directly from the Associated States themselves and the French high commissioner in Vietnam. In their enthusiasm the Americans had sent quantities of radar to protect the land from Vietminh airplanes that did not exist, but on the whole the French were deeply pleased with the quantities the Americans gave and the remarkable speed with which they delivered it.[13]

The aggregate military aid the United States contributed to the French effort in Vietnam is a difficult matter of bookkeeping, but total direct military aid to France in 1950–1953 was $2,956,000,000, plus $684 million in 1954. Truman's statement in January 1953 that the Americans paid for as much as one-half of the war seems accurate enough, and aid rose every year to 1954. The manner in which they disbursed this aid is more significant.

The Americans paid, but they did not appreciate French political direction, though they put no serious political pressure on the French until 1954. Dulles, for one, was aware of Bao Dai's political unreliability and inability to create an alternative to the Vietminh, and he regretted it. "It seems," he wrote a friend in October 1950, "as is often the case, it is necessary as a practical matter to choose the lesser of two evils because the theoretically ideal solution is not possible for many reasons—the French policy being only one. As a matter of fact, the French policy has considerably changed for the better. . . . However, the future is perplexing and I do not see the future at all clearly."[14] It was Dulles who in the middle of 1951 discovered in Bao Dai's former premier under the Japanese, Ngo Dinh Diem, the political solution for Indochina. At the end of 1950 he was willing to content himself with the belief that the expansion of Communism in Asia must be stopped. The French might serve that role, at least for a time.

Throughout 1951 and 1952 the French and their puppet troops fought a war that the United States financed to an ever-growing extent. In developing a rationale for this sustained aid, Washington advanced three major arguments, only one of which was later to disappear as a major source of the conduct of American policy in Vietnam. There was, first of all, the desire to bring France back to Europe via victory in Vietnam: "The sooner they bring it to a successful conclusion," Henry Cabot Lodge explained in early 1951, "the better it would be for NATO because they could move their forces here and increase their building of their army in Europe. . . ." The French insistence until 1954 on blocking German rearmament and the European Defense Community until they could exist on the Continent with military superiority over the Germans, a condition that was impossible until the war in Vietnam ended, gave this even more persuasive consideration special urgency. From this viewpoint, Vietnam was the indirect key to Germany. In the meantime, as the ambassador to France, David Bruce, explained it, "I think it would be a disaster if the French did not continue their effort in Indo-China."[15] Only an intensification of the war and victory made sense to the Americans.

Victory was necessary because of the two other basic and more permanent factors in guiding American policy. The Americans were always convinced that the domino theory would operate, should Vietnam remain with the Vietnamese people. "There is no question," Bruce told a Senate committee, "that if Indo-China went, the fall of Burma and the fall of Thailand would be absolutely inevitable. No one can convince me, for what it is worth, that Malay wouldn't follow shortly thereafter, and India . . . would . . . also find the Communists making infiltrations. . . ." From this viewpoint, the political character of the regime in Vietnam was less consequential than the larger American design for the area, and the seeds of future American policy were already forecast when Bruce suggested that ". . . the Indo-Chinese—and I am speaking now of the . . . anti-Communist group—will have to show a far greater ability to live up to the obligations of nationhood before it will be safe to withdraw, whether it be French Union forces or any other foreign forces, from that country."[16] If the French left, someone would have to replace them. The United States continued to oppose complete independence not merely in Vietnam but anywhere the Left dominated the nationalist opposition, and preferred the inhibiting integration of colonial states into the French Union or British Commonwealth where conservative local elites were not in control of the anticolonial movements. ". . . [W]here we exercise restraint," Dulles defensively argued in November 1953, "it is because of a reasoned conviction that precipitate action would in fact not produce independence but only transition to a captivity far worse than present dependence."[17]

Should Vietnam, and through it Asia, fall to the Vietminh, the Americans would realize their last major fear. ". . . [Of] all the prizes Russia could bite off in the east," Bruce also suggested, "the possession of Indo-China would be the most valuable and in the long run would be the most crucial one from the standpoint of the west in the east. That would be true not because of the flow of rice, rubber, and so forth, . . . but because it is the only place where any war is now being conducted to try to suppress the overtaking of the whole area of southeast Asia by the Communists."[18] "The strategic geographical position of the area," Secretary of Defense Robert A. Lovett told the Senate in the spring of 1952, "as well as the vitally important raw materials such as tin and rubber which it supplies, makes it important for us to maintain an effective support of the gallant [French] effort. . . ."[19] Eisenhower, Dulles, and Nixon also put much greater emphasis on the value of raw materials, and it is the constant basis of American policy in Vietnam since 1951. "Why is the United States spending hundreds of millions of dollars supporting the forces of the French Union in the fight against communism?" Vice-President Richard Nixon asked in December 1953. "If Indo-China falls, Thailand is put in an almost impossible position. The same is true of Malaya with its rubber and tin. The same is true of Indonesia. If this whole part of Southeast Asia goes under Communist domination or Communist influence, Japan, who trades and must trade with this area in order to exist, must inevitably by oriented towards the Communist regime."[20] Eisenhower wrote in his memoir:

The loss of all Vietnam, together with Laos on the west and Cambodia on the southwest, would have meant the surrender to Communist enslavement of millions. On the material side, it would have spelled the loss of valuable deposits of tin and prodigious supplies of rubber and rice. It would have meant that Thailand, enjoying buffer territory between itself and Red China, would be exposed on its entire eastern border to infiltration or attack. And if Indo-China fell, not only Thailand but Burma and Malaya would be threatened, with added risks to East Pakistan and South Asia as well as to all Indonesia.[21]

The Japanese, of course, had advanced similar arguments prior to World War II. From the American viewpoint, a strong Japan would serve as a major stabilizing factor in the Far East, but an impoverished Japan might turn toward the left. Eisenhower made the "falling domino" analogy explicit at a April 7, 1954, press conference, at which time he also worried about the loss of Southeast Asia's tin, tungsten, and rubber, as well as Japan's being forced into dependence on Communist nations.[22]

Because of this domino theory and raw materials, aid to the French continued and the statements of support poured from the Departments of Defense and State in 1951–1953, with NATO in December 1952 expressing ". . . its wholehearted admiration for the valiant and long continued struggle by the French forces and the armies of the Associated States against Communist aggression. . . ."[23] Given this larger American conception of the importance of the Vietnam war to its self-interest, which impelled the United States to make it financially possible, the future of the war largely no longer depended on whether the French would fight or meet the demands of the Vietnamese for independence. Already in early 1952 Secretary of State Dean Acheson told Foreign Minister Anthony Eden, as recorded in the latter's memoir, ". . . of the United States' determination to do everything possible to strengthen the French hand in Indo-China. On the wider question of the possibility of a Chinese invasion, the United States Government considered that it would be disastrous to the position of the Western powers if South-East Asia were lost without a struggle."[24] If Acheson promised prudence by merely greatly increasing arms aid to the French, he also talked of blockading China and air strikes against its communications with Indochina. Eden could only express opposition. For the moment they would help the French to solve the problem in the field. The war, even by 1952, was being internationalized, with America assuming ever greater initiative for its control. When Eisenhower came to the presidency he was told of military plans to attack China that had been drawn up should it intervene in Vietnam. Acheson presented Vietnam to him as ". . . an urgent matter on which the new administration must be prepared to act."[25] Given Dulles' experience and views on the question, Acheson did not waste his words.

By spring 1953 the American government was fully aware of the largely tangential role of the French in the greater American global strategy, and it was widely believed in Congress that if the French pulled out the Americans would not permit Vietnam to fall. In June the American government sent Lieutenant General John W. O'Daniel to Saigon to offer direction to the local French military authorities. The United States was increasingly irritated with the French management of affairs. The economic aid sent to Vietnam resulted merely in the creation of a complex speculative market for piastres and dollars which helped the local compradors enrich themselves while debilitating the economy. "Failure of important elements of the local population to give a full measure of support to the war effort remained one of the chief negative factors," the State Department confided to Eisenhower. ". . . [It] was almost impossible," Eisenhower later wrote, "to make the average Vietnamese peasant realize that the French, under whose rule his people had lived for some eighty years, were really fighting in the cause of freedom, while the Vietminh, people of their own ethnic origins, were fighting on the side of slavery." Bao Dai, whom the Americans had always mistrusted, now disturbed the Americans because, as Eisenhower recalls, he ". . . chose to spend the bulk of his time in the spas of Europe. . . ."[26]

The French, for their part, were now divided on the proper response the massive American intervention into the war demanded. Some in the Laniel government wished the war to remain French so that the political fate of that nation might be decided according to French interests; but if they were to win the war it would have to be with more military power, and during the summer Bidault and Pleven, foreign and defense ministers, decided the war must now be "internationalized" with proportionate increases in American financial responsibility. During July, Bidault and Dulles conferred and Dulles promised all the French desired, also admonishing them not to seek a negotiated end to the war. In September it was agreed to give the French a special grant of $385 million to implement the Navarre Plan, a scheme to build French and puppet troops to a level permitting them to destroy the regular Vietminh forces by the end of 1955. By this time the essential strategy of the war increasingly supplanted a strict concern for bringing France back to NATO, and the Americans determined to make Vietnam a testing ground for a larger global strategy of which the French would be the instrument. Critical to that strategy was a military victory that had proved unattainable in Korea—a victory that was deemed possible only if the joint estimate of the American and French military authorities were correct and the Chinese did not send troop reinforcements over the border to prevent the Vietminh from being crushed. To the Vietnamese themselves there was no longer any doubt as to whom they were fighting: ". . . American imperialism," Ho stated in November 1953, "drives the French colonialists to continue and extend the war of reconquest in Viet-Nam with the object of making France weaker and weaker and overtaking her place in Viet-nam."[27]

Yet the now essentially American undertaking still confronted the difficulty that, as General LeClerc had suggested several years earlier, there was ". . . no military solution for Vietnam."[28] One could obliterate it, but never reconquer it.

The Threat of Peace

A mobilizing sense of danger and crisis that could overcome the reticence of the American people and Western European states alike had become the necessary precondition for the implementation of American foreign policy long before the Eisenhower administration. Given the many and seemingly insoluble predicaments confronting Eisenhower, that organizational weapon was one he and his aides were determined not to forgo. Indeed, the increased intensity and difficulty of American foreign policy in the world then evolving made a greater American effort abroad more likely. The growing understanding that Asia was more central to the world crisis than Truman or Acheson had ever imagined, the gnawing doubt as to the efficacy of existing military power to the political realities of the era, the virtual neutralization of America's strategic power against Soviet capabilities, the troubled divisions in the American-led bloc—all these enigmas the United Stated could never solve save if Congress and the nation sustained yet greater efforts, dangers, and costs. The entire new administration understood this central political reality.

In the last days of 1952, Stalin gave one of his rare interviews and welcomed a meeting with Eisenhower to discuss easing world tensions, a gesture the significance of which the new President understood but preferred to let pass unnoticed. Stalin, Eisenhower thought at the time, was a conservative prone to avoiding risks. During the following months, however, various NATO leaders were still aware that the Russians were standing by their plan for German unity and neutrality, a fact that evoked less interest than even the preceding year. Then, on March 5, Stalin died.

Eisenhower's first inclination was to offer Russia's new leaders some scheme toward peace, but when he turned to his advisers they disparaged the notion. Still, the President's knowledge of the leadership struggle that was beginning to take place in Moscow, as well, perhaps, as his own sense of the limits of America's arms in the event of war, forced some gesture. While Paul Nitze and Dulles took a hand in controlling the text, which soon became a laborious, slow effort, the diplomatic focus shifted toward the Kremlin. It is still impossible to know everything that occurred in the Soviet power structure during the first months after Stalin's death, but from the viewpoint of foreign policy there were no qualitative changes, for Stalin, too, had pressed for negotiations. Psychologically, however, the need and perhaps the possibility to test the new leaders now forced many to look more carefully at what the Russians had already been proposing for some time. Georgi M. Malenkov, who now became chairman of the Council of Ministers, sounded the theme again in immediately stating that all questions were negotiable and that coexistence remained the Soviet policy. By the end of the month, however, as the Kremlin issued an amnesty for a vast number of political and labor prisoners, lowered food prices, and then admitted the first group of American editors to visit Russia since the war, Soviet declarations that they desired four-power talks on Germany embellished the dynamism behind the peace campaign. On April 2 reporters asked Eisenhower what he thought of the Russian peace offers, and he replied he took them at face value until proven otherwise. The following day Dulles intervened brusquely to get the President back into step: "Nothing that has happened, or which seems to me likely to happen, has changed the basic situation of danger in which we stand." From their use of "violence," to a lack of belief in "moral law," the "heavily armed totalitarian state" posed a "grave danger" to the West.[29] It was in this context that Adenauer arrived in the United States on April 6, at a time, he later recalled, when ". . . a large part of American public opinion was only too ready to succumb to the blandishments of a détente which for the time being was nothing but a pipe-dream."[30]

In Dulles the German chancellor had a friend whose desire to integrate Germany into the West could help his struggle to remove the last legal vestiges of Germany's wartime defeat. Even as Dulles sought to maintain a fear of Russia in the West, so Adenauer could play on Dulles' grand design for Europe. They therefore complemented each other perfectly at this critical juncture. Adenauer admonished the Senate not to bend before a Russian Trojan horse strategy, and assured it that he would never trade reunification for neutrality, unity, and a disengagement of all troops from Germany. ". . . We must be prepared for the worst," he warned in a theme he repeated often and widely over these days.[31] Three days later, Eisenhower committed himself to a joint communiqué in which they insisted that ". . . the free nations of the West must not relax their vigilance" and must continue to press for the ratification of EDC.[32] If the Russians wished peace, they added, Moscow first could allow East Germany free elections—in return for which they offered no concessions.

By the time that Eisenhower gave his major April 16 address on the chances for peace, therefore, the general American posture remained frozen. His vague platitudes about disarmament could not conceal his preconditions for progress on this front: Germany's accession to EDC and free elections in the East in return for no guarantees against its future expansion, an end to "direct and indirect" warfare in Indochina and Malaya, and "full independence" in Eastern Europe.[33] Yet even this platitudinous statement was too much for Dulles, and nothing more was said of it. For it was the secretary of state who defined the United States' main course publicly and privately—a fact the Russians immediately noted in their polite critique of Eisenhower's speech—and here Dulles made it clear that ". . . the West must not be sucked [in] by any phony peace campaign, and that it *must (a)* go on building its strength; (*b*) move toward greater European unity."[34]

Such a response left the initiative for peace entirely with Moscow, and Churchill, for one, was deeply disturbed by American indifference to Russia's gestures. More significantly, his concern for the general dangers of the arms race were overcoming his instinctive hatred of bolshevism. Relations between Washington and London had already been sinking over Korea when on May 11 the Prime Minister rose in the Commons to reflect critically on mankind's dangerous course and the need to make a serious effort to find a way out. If his own proposals consisted of nothing more than a suggestion that perhaps the West guarantee Russia against a German attack and that the great powers convene a summit meeting, its tone was fully sympathetic to serious negotiations and won the backing of Labour and, indeed, struck responsive chords throughout the tension-ridden world. Washington immediately issued a chilling, curt notice, while privately American diplomats were livid, and relations with England fell to a new low as the press freely discussed the profound rift. "It looks as if Europe was breaking up under Malenkov's sunshine," Harold Macmillan, then a British cabinet member, jotted in his diary.[35]

The Russians, however, warmly welcomed the tone and purpose, if not the substance, of Churchill's speech, and at the end of May the Russians endorsed Churchill's call for a four-power conference to deal with the questions the leaders had speculated on in their speeches. It was also at this time that they initiated a series of far-reaching organizational and economic steps in East Germany preparatory to a merger of the two sections of Germany, including a transfer of control of their zone from military to civilian direction. In effect, Moscow insisted that the East Germans abolish socialism in the Eastern zone, remove the "dogmatists" from the SED leadership, and dissolve the institutional barriers to zonal unity. The desperate efforts of Walter Ulbricht and his followers to sabotage the undertaking was made possible because internal divisions in the Soviet leadership left Ulbricht's faction room in which to manuever. Previously the advocate of ever higher production norms that had been especially taxing to the workers, he adroitly coupled the abolition of socialist and welfare institutions, which the workers hoped to reform but also to keep, to more work, which the masses had grown to detest. Like Dulles and Adenauer, he also had too great a stake in the *status quo* to risk a united Germany the Social Democrats were almost certain to lead. Concessions were made to most classes in East Germany save the workers, who saw change and turmoil in the state —but also the prospect of more work and less socialism.[36]

The United States and West German governments chose to ignore the profound significance of these developments for fear of being pushed to the negotiating table. The Russians, however, introduced their changes in fits and starts, leaving East Germany in upheaval by mid-June. On June 15 the Berlin building workers threatened to call a general strike unless work norms were revoked, and the following day a spontaneous movement among Berlin workers led to the formation of workers' councils as strike sentiment electrified the city. Until this point, the entire phenomenon was a radical workers' action like hundreds that had caused Europe's *status quo* to quiver time and again during preceding decades.

Though the United States had an important intelligence network throughout East Germany at this time, no evidence exists for its involvement in these first causal events. On June 16, however, the United States broadcasting services began playing a crucial role by supplying the entire East German population with information that only caused the uprising to spread and intensify—a decision that was carefully thought out beforehand. At this point, as well, agents from West Berlin joined the crowds—but they did not create them or seriously deflect from the essentially radical workers' demands. Confronting the uncontrollable pandemonium, the Russians did not hesitate to use their full military power to bloodily put down the June

17 uprising. It is also certain that the various factions in the Kremlin used the failure of East Germany to turn on Lavrenti Beria, the major architect of the new strategy, for he was arrested early in July—and later executed for ". . . criminal anti-Party, anti-state actions. . . ."[37] Yet the events in East Germany itself, and the way the various Soviet factions exploited them for their ulterior purposes, did not diminish Russia's commitment to a fundamentally new course for all of Germany. The episode allowed Washington to evoke its usual moral rhetoric, but that fact did not obviate its larger responsibility for being one of the gravediggers of the East German workers' objectives and dreams.

The pressure for negotiations on Germany continued unabated. Nor did Churchill's stroke on June 23 lessen the demand, for he insisted the three-power foreign ministers consider it in Washington during their mid-July conference. But his absence greatly weakened the force of his position, for now the Americans compelled the group to retreat to the earlier United States stand that free elections precede a discussion of a peace treaty or security issues. It was only those points that the three nations offered to discuss with Moscow. Then, one week later, cynically evoking all the emotionalism associated with the moving events in Berlin, even to the extent of praising working-class militancy and urging more of it in Eastern Europe in the future, Eisenhower publicly assured Adenauer that under no circumstances would the United States bend from its position that a unified Germany have the option to be an integral part of EDC and the Western European bloc. This condition, which precluded negotiations with the Russians, was a guarantee to Adenauer that the wartime alliance would not again emerge to prevent Germany from attaining total freedom and equality in the world. Conversely, as Churchill freely acknowledged at this time, "The only thing the Russians fear is a re-armed Germany."[38]

The Soviets indeed feared a rearmed Germany, and for this reason they urged during August that a four-power meeting consider the entire German question and other international questions as well—and they included a synthesis of their most appealing past plans on Germany as a start, including a workable free election procedure. But they also asked, in line with a sedulous recognition of Peking's special status on which the new Kremlin leaders had embarked, that China be invited to such a conference—implicitly to deal only with discussion involving Asian questions. Malenkov, in his famous August 8 address, also made it clear the Russians strongly wished to shift to greatly expanded food and consumer goods production and normalize diplomatic relations with nations as diverse as Yugoslavia and fascist Greece. Coexistence remained the Soviet goal in its relations with the world.

Pressed to its disadvantage, Washington now agreed to a summit conference, and on September 2 insisted that the meeting deal only with the German and Austrian question without any formal agenda. At the end of September the Russians responded that they could exclude China from discussions of Germany, but the Soviets wanted assurance that proposals they might introduce on Germany would at least be considered. The United States held back, and on October 18 merely reiterated its proposal for an ambiguously defined "discussion" on Germany and Austria. Plaintively commenting on the failure of his peacemaking efforts during the Conservative Party conference on October 10, Churchill reiterated his loyalty to the alliance and EDC but regretted that he had ". . . raised a considerable stir all over the place. . . . I still think that the leading men of the various nations ought to be able to meet together without trying to cut attitudes before excitable publics or using regiments or experts to marshal all the difficulties and objections, and let us try to see whether there is not something better for us all than tearing and blasting each other to pieces, which we can certainly do."[39] But he could not convince the United States to budge on the terms of a conference, and so the Russians, aware of certain defeat otherwise, abandoned all their earlier positions at the end of November. They would exclude China, but raise the question of a later five-power conference at the meeting they suggested for Berlin in early January 1954. The discussion would deal with Germany and not be bound by any preconditions. Within this framework, surely preordained to failure, the three powers were compelled to accept the Berlin Conference that eventually opened on January 25. Almost one year after Stalin's death, the United States condescended, under strong pressures from its closest friends, to talk to Russia.

The Emerging Strategy Dilemma

Whatever else its utility, the United States' vast military expenditures had not provided it with either defense or security. Its 3.5 million men in uniform were inferior to Russia's 4-million-man armed forces only in that America's global ambitions had scattered its forces to the far corners of the earth while Russia's military power remained concentrated in Europe. When America exploded its first hydrogen bomb on November 1, 1952, it did not qualitatively alter the frustrating strategic balance. Essentially, the

United States' main security came from a passive Russia—a fact that Washington understood at the time.

America's leaders insisted that their defenses in Europe were inadequate, and hence the dire need for ratification of EDC and accelerated rearmament. Eisenhower later recalled that his plan was to launch a nuclear attack against Russia in the event of an attack on the West, but political and military realities made the assumption both superfluous and debatable, especially after Moscow on August 20, 1953, announced its explosion of an H-bomb and further equalized the balance of terror. But war in Europe was unlikely, and hence the nuclear arsenal was irrelevant there, and the absence of targets in the Far East made strategic air power insufficient to determine the outcome of war in that tumultuous region. By 1953, as well, Russia's fleet surpassed England's. No place was American superiority decisive. It was in the midst of this very real stalemate that the new administration undertook the impossible effort to attain more military power at less cost.

By the spring of 1953 NATO had not yet achieved the force levels it had set out for 1950, and Washington never ceased asking its allies to persevere in rearmament. The American desire to save money, however, reduced the credibility of the demand, and the Soviet peace campaign even more deeply mitigated the impact of Dulles' calls to action. Above all, the internal economic and political situations in the NATO countries led to further delays in reaching ambitious arms goals. With war in Europe unlikely, the outcome for rearmament schedules was certain. More critical for the United States was how far the alliance might crumble, if not dissolve.

The budget-cutting effort was due to the fact that the function of arms expenditures is economic, so that the United States historically spent only what it could afford and needed, but it also reflected a Republican frame of mind rather than something as serious as a distinctive ideology of American power and purpose. When forced to choose between the costly pretensions of being the world's policeman, with its economic assets as well as high costs, and true isolation, Taft and his followers only nibbled on the margins of the overhead charges of the imperial role. During the presidential campaign Eisenhower had promised to reduce military spending without weakening military power, a proposition about which he was somewhat ambiguous. As was his wont, he reflected the strains and disagreements among his advisers, though from experience he also knew how the military budget was padded with superfluous expenditures. Treasury Secretary George Humphrey and the Budget Bureau consistently exerted pressure to reduce funds; yet the political ideology of the world struggle which some of his other advisers argued kept the reductions from going too far. Traditional expensive pork-barreling also prevented decisive reductions. Even Dulles had earlier expressed profound doubts about building area defenses, preferring to develop a capacity to counterattack ". . . which would be only partly military and largely political and psychological, picking what is the Achilles heel of this vast, overgrown, despotic society. I am sure there is such an Achilles heel if we are smart enough to find it. . . ."[40] Such vague gropings only reflected profound doubts and confusions, not easily translated into original policy. In the end, however, the defense budget fell from $44 billion in fiscal 1952 and $50.4 billion the following year to $46.9 billion in fiscal 1954—but $40.6 billion the next year.

So the search for a cheaper defense accompanied Washington's effort to bolster NATO and to prevent a diplomatic round that could only debilitate the American hegemony in NATO and the fear of Russia on which that alliance was based. The end result of these conflicting strains and efforts was a further profound weakening of the United States' alliance.

Dulles' forced public optimism notwithstanding, the Eisenhower administration ran into frustrations from the inception. Apart from alleged military dangers, NATO's actual and potential economic power aligned with the United States was worth any military ties, however useless the latter might be. ". . . [T]o hope that the members of NATO will move forward consistently toward a closer and more profitable relationship," as Dulles phrased it later the next year, justified all other failures.[41] "The United States needs allies in the existing struggle," the Defense Department argued early in 1954. "Such allies should be as strong, economically and militarily, as possible. But, strong or weak, they must be tied as closely as possible to the United States."[42] Mobilized against the United States, Europe's economic power could ultimately tip the military balance as well.

As this vision was articulated and acted on, the new administration immediately proceeded to reorganize and rationalize the Defense Department to extend civilian control and bring in officers more amenable to a new reevaluation of the United States' military power. By June 1953 the President was ready to initiate in earnest that larger reappraisal, later euphemized as the "New Look," which we consider below. More immediately pressing, however, was Dulles' need to maintain an alliance that the renewed Russian peace offensive threatened to rend asunder. Superficially, Dulles succeeded in that undertaking, but only on the level of arid communiqués such as those forthcoming from the three-power talks in Washington during mid-July. French Foreign Minister Georges Bidault had made it perfectly clear that France would not attempt to ratify EDC—which it was never to do in any event—until another effort was made to negotiate a European settlement with Russia. "Nothing could put us or our policy back into the pre-May stagnation," Harold Macmillan flatly informed the American ambassador in London.[43] Adenauer alone, without popular backing in Germany itself, sustained the United States' efforts to block the settlement on Germany that was enticingly close at hand. Churchill was reasonably polite with the Americans, but desperate to reach a European settlement. The unity and integration which the United States could temporarily impose on the Western Europeans it had never based on more than economic pressures and fear, and now that Europe was escaping from necessity and anxiety, and into a less troubled era, the weak bonds of unity were breaking. In mid-October, Dulles met with Bidault and Eden, who once again insisted on a conference with the Russians. To Dulles, the Soviets were merely attempting to frustrate NATO and EDC, and he strongly opposed any meeting. But the Anglo-French persisted, and Dulles responded by "brutally," to quote Eden, talking of a reappraisal of the United States' fundamental relationship toward Europe.[44] The "agonizing reappraisal" had in fact already been well under way for some time. And it was not merely in response to the six-months-old Soviet peace overture or equally long Anglo-French insistence that the West explored it, but a reflection of the profound and confused reassessment of American military power in the world that was to begin in earnest in the fall of 1953.

The Limits of Power

The military lesson of the Korean War was unequivocally clear to American leaders: they had failed to win the war in the field against two impoverished nations. Both the North Koreans and the Chinese had entered the conflict poorly equipped and prepared, with primitive logistics and only sufficient food for two meals a day for their troops. By the end of the war the Communist forces were eating three meals a day, deploying abundant artillery, and well supplied and equipped—a million strong. Indeed, while the Americans by the end of 1952 relied on artillery to fight the enemy, Chinese and Korean troops soon developed the art of fortifications and tunnel defense to a state of perfection that more than compensated for American barrages, and their casualties at the end of the war were reduced to twice those of their opponents. The Chinese and North Korean soldiers became a first-class, ably led army, ". . . a formidable foe who bore little resemblance to the feeble nation of World War II," to quote the official United States history.[45] Politically, the troops were often dedicated in the highest degree. Their leaders, according to Clark, ". . . breathed communism into their spirit."[46] It was this resourceful infantry, more than any other factor, that neutralized the colossal American military machine and fought it to a draw.

The implications of this outcome were far-reaching to the United States. Washington had failed to find the means to translate its immense military and technological material superiority into victory, or compensate for the political liabilities of its allies and the American cause. American power was based on its industrial might, and its ideological appeals in Asia provided no assistance in sustaining the compradors, oligarchs, and forces of order. When the Korean War came to an end the clear question for the United States was whether it could snatch inevitable, long-term defeat from Asia's political chaos and economic misery, or whether it might find some new means of making its military and physical power relevant to Asia and the world. For in the answer to the dilemma lay the political future of the Third World in modern times.

The tortured American strategic reconsideration which began in earnest at the end of 1953 and beginning of 1954 reflected the desire to find an economical but superior military posture as well as America's failure to win the war in Korea by conventional means, the inability of the costly Navarre Plan to stem the tide of French defeat in the Indochinese jungles and fields, and the growing reticence of the Anglo-French to follow Washington's lead in European affairs. The problem, in brief, was how to relate immense American military and economic power to the political realities of highly decentralized agrarian societies in revolt, chastise the United States' allies, and avoid debilitating land wars that seemingly led only to disaster—and all at less expense.

Despite a panoply of conflicting and unattainable motives behind the New Look at the Pentagon's role in foreign affairs, it was but one more chapter in the long and futile postwar American effort to find a strategic doctrine that would employ technological mastery to compensate for what was now clearly a more or less consistent decline in American political and economic power to control the world. If, in its desperation, America appeared to be becoming more dangerous, with emphasis on its ability to destroy rather than build societies, the very real risks to the world should not obscure the fact that America's loss of mastery over the fate of friends and foes alike was nonetheless the main cause of the new crisis in priorities and goals that began in earnest at the end of 1953.

Because of its fear of economic dangers and inflation at home, Eisenhower's own experience with the feast-and-famine cycle in military budgeting, as well as the decisive change in the Soviet-American military balance from superiority to deterrence and the balance of terror, Washington's effort to define a new strategic balance within the context of its inflexible political and economic goals for the world was alone sufficient cause for the new appraisal. It was now essential to demote the idea of eventual war with Russia and prepare for the long haul in a manner that made the military budget more clearly the tool of national goals—economic as well as military—than it had been since Korea. The planning for the shift, which began much earlier than Dulles' famous "agonizing reappraisal" speech of December 1953, was inevitable regardless of NATO's unhappy course for the United States.[47] For despite American urgings to the Europeans that they rearm with greater dispatch, including West Germany in the undertaking, the lopping of $5 billion off the Pentagon's budget between fiscal 1954 and 1955, or the reduction of its man power by 600,000 over the next year and one-half, made it clear that the Americans would define their own military policy in quite different ways. Only the objectives and tone of American foreign policy would remain unvaried.

The manner in which the United States reduced its military budget to more rational economic proportions, while quite unprepared to acknowledge the limits of American power and anxious to sustain the mobilizing sense of global crisis and danger, reflected its response to the growing Indochina war, the condition of Asia, and, above all, the Korean experience. The sheer number of greater crises in Asia was forcing the United States, willy-nilly, to confront the fact that Asia and the Third World were becoming the decisive arena of the world struggle, thereby downgrading its commitment to Europe and dragging it yet more deeply into the Asian maelstrom. As early as April 1953 Eisenhower had warned that a peace in Korea that led to the expansion of warfare in Southeast Asia, even by releasing Chinese armies to move to that region, would be no peace at all. This view, which the United States did not abandon, made China the key to the future of Asia and largely responsible for the area's difficulties. And once Washington accepted this, and it absolved poverty, oligarchies, and colonialism as the source of upheaval, it was logical that the United States' larger military view reinforced a decision, in part made independently, to stress nuclear power. Such a decision made sense, from the American viewpoint, only if China were indeed the source rather than the effect of the great revolution sweeping Asia since the war, or if a nuclear blitz could indeed break China's military back. In any event, to Washington such a strategy appeared to be the one it could best afford.

The public shift in American policy came at a politically irrelevant time for the Indochina crisis, for on November 29 Ho Chi Minh offered to enter into negotiations leading to a diplomatic settlement, a solution Washington eventually opposed unequivocally. In September, Dulles had already placed primary blame for the Indochina crisis on China and warned that should it send troops to that quarter the United States might attack China itself. Given the repeated reiteration of this theme over subsequent months, while France and the Vietminh moved toward the peace table, the United States intensified military tensions over the area.[48]

Dulles' major January 12, 1954, speech in New York, perhaps the most important of his career, reflected all these moods and impulses. The prohibitive cost of maintaining conventional armies was the initial premise of the statement; yet implicit in it was that, at any cost, such armies could not guarantee victory. America's allies would require local military forces; yet the United States would shift its policy toward greater reliance on "massive retaliatory power" as the ". . . modern way of getting maximum protection at a bearable cost." This meant that it had now made "[t]he basic decision . . . to depend primarily upon a great capacity to retaliate, instantly, by means and at places of our choosing."[49] Still, if read closely the statement did not necessarily threaten nuclear war and referred to optional means of warfare, not the least because the army was uncertain of the efficacy of strategic nuclear warfare. And since, as Eden pointed out, the Vietminh were doing well enough on their own and Chinese intervention was unlikely, the threat was irrelevant to the probabilities of the region. By late March, when Dulles repeated this theme, and reiterated his threat of the prior September that Chinese intervention in Vietnam ". . . would result in grave consequences which might not be confined to Indochina," French and British insistence on convening the Geneva Conference of May, hopefully to settle the fate of the area, outflanked America's diplomatic strategy.[50] Essentially, the United States was to engage in obstructionist opposition to the establishment of peace in the region—eventually to wreck the Geneva Accords of the following July and to lay the basis of its own assumption of France's colonial burden.

Quite apart from the fact that massive nuclear attacks were primarily relevant to industrial and urban nations such as Russia, who had their own atomic arsenal and whom the Americans could not strike with impunity, was the assumption that China was indeed the offensive power in Asia—something only Washington fully believed. Dulles and American military leaders tried energetically over the early months of 1954 to give more precision to the massive retaliation doctrine, pointing again to the need to prepare for a long-range strategy consistent with America's economic resources, and the secretary especially stressed that retaliation meant many forms of military intervention far below that of nuclear war. This definition was also cast specifically in the context of the deepening Indochina crisis, in which Dulles implied that Chinese intervention in that war would lead to nuclear attacks against the Chinese mainland. In later months and years Dulles was to add confusing and inconsistent dimensions to the doctrine, which he believed would act mainly as a deterrent to local war if accompanied by regional pacts; then he embellished it with his theory of "brinkmanship" and the willingness to move to the verge of war to avoid it, ultimately to tack on the theory of small tactical nuclear weapons as a kind of special device to avoid the global holocaust.[51]

The outcome of this effort to find the adequate strategic mixture was not so much irrelevance to realities as the need for the United States to pose itself as the opponent to the stormy and inevitable changes sweeping all of Asia, Latin America, and the Middle East. Frustrating it in the task of relating to this monumental upheaval was the irrelevance of its ideology to the aspirations of mankind in revolution, as well as the apparent weakness of its armaments, as revealed first of all in North Korea and later in Vietnam, to transform fire, barbarism, and an industrial goliath into victory over resourceful peasants in revolt.

Yet the United States, despite its ultimate inability to control the flow of world social change, was able even during 1953 and 1954 to interfere profoundly with that development and to necessitate far more martial and violent preconditions for the Left's success in the Third World, compelling it to struggle mainly against indirect or direct American intervention as well as the generally weak and declining local conservative forces. Even as key American decision-makers debated the problems of grand strategy, they acted in Guatemala to stop social change there in a manner that presaged the larger contours of America's interventionism over the next decade and one-half. What men such as Dulles did not do, however, was reflect on the significance of the Guatemala events and incorporate them into a central place in their vision of American power in the world and the manner by which they would largely apply it in the future.

We need not more than outline the events that were to lead to the CIA-sponsored coup in Guatemala at the end of June 1954. In February 1953 the Arbenz government, which had been in power almost three years, initiated an agrarian reform law which resulted in the seizure of 225,000 acres of unused United Fruit Company property. Jacabo Arbenz Guzman was a rather mild reformer who had outlawed the Communist Party until the end of 1952, but his insistence on paying for the confiscated American land at the price United Fruit itself had fixed for tax assessment purposes infuriated the State Department. At the end of 1953, sharing Ambassador to Guatemala John E. Peurifoy's contention that Arbenz ". . . thought like a Communist and talked like a Communist, and if not actually one, would do until one came along," Washington set the wheels for his overthrow in motion.[52] Anti-communism would now become the justification for preserving the United States' informal empire in the Western Hemisphere.

Throughout the first half of 1954 the State Department, in increasingly strong terms, denounced the Arbenz government as Communist-dominated. In March it had the conference of the Organization of American States meeting in Caracas endorse the proposition that the existence of a "Communist" state anywhere in the hemisphere was a threat to its peace. Covertly, the CIA worked with exiled Guatemalan officers to prepare for the final event, aiding them with arms and critical airplanes.[53] The Americans had defined the vital precedent and alternative to Armageddon, and found new means to stay the ultimately irresistible dynamics of change in the world.

The Berlin Conference

While America acted to preserve its power in the field, it had resisted its Anglo-French allies' efforts to impose diplomacy into the conduct of Washington's foreign policy. If only to prove to London and Paris that talk with Russia was futile and disarming to the sense of urgency the United States thought so vital, and to prevent a serious split in the NATO alliance, Dulles finally consented to a four-power conference in Berlin to consider the German question.

Dulles' fears were misplaced, for there never was any chance that England or France would offer the Russians terms at Berlin likely to lead to a German settlement and a relaxation of international tensions, but it was also no less plain by the end of 1953 that the French were never going to ratify EDC and, thereby, welcome Germany's rearmament. Essentially,

Anglo-French strategy was not coherent, and it was quite unable to sustain a genuine *détente* effort based on new principles or willing to engage in the massive rearmament which gave it military strength where it lacked diplomatic skill. With this policy of too little, too slowly in every area, all that Western Europe could do was to interfere with both Russian and American plans while failing to offer any original alternative. But the lessening sense of danger from the alleged Soviet menace was to permeate Western European thinking despite all this.

The British, for one, were hopelessly paralyzed by contradictory impulses as to what to do about European security. Churchill alone, in his deepening concern for the face of mankind in a nuclear age, impelled onward the effort to meet the Russians, but the ailing Prime Minister was also talking of retiring and so his influence had diminished. Eden, Macmillan, and others were much less interested in a negotiated end to the German question. Macmillan thought the Russians would treacherously attempt to split the alliance and scuttle EDC, and Eden was determined to press for all-German elections that would then permit Germany to align itself with the West and EDC. They were to persist in this position for some years, convinced that a Germany integrated into the West would ultimately be safer than one independent and able again to disturb the peace of Europe. The French were more divided, but all that was clear in January 1954 was that EDC was nearly certain to fail in their hands.[54]

Dulles left for Berlin supremely confident that the discussion of Germany would fail, thereby helping to reunite the sagging NATO alliance, but also aware that there might be progress in reaching an Austrian peace treaty after years of fruitless negotiation. He based his opposition to negotiations on his fear of the ensuing relaxation of international tensions—and military efforts—and the possibility of the Russians' obtaining moral sanction from the Western agreement to meet with them. By 1954, however, it was apparent that the basis of the United States' policy toward Germany remained its own deep desire to integrate Germany in order to control it in future years, with its military value in an anti-Soviet bloc remaining quite minimal. To protect the West against Germany rather than Russia was the ultimate basis of this calculus, which Dulles retained until his death. Adenauer's existence, and his seeming preference for Western rather than German unity, provided perhaps the last opportunity to realize such a goal. With or without French approval, therefore, the United States would proceed to integrate West Germany militarily and economically into the West, and the irritating Soviet efforts to seek a *détente* were the greatest threat to America's attainment of its aim. To satisfy Dulles, the Berlin Conference had to fail in a certain manner, and in this respect all precedent favored his strategy.

The Russians based their position on Germany on their deep fears understandably colored by history rather than a rational calculus of existing German potential. Because of this strong emotional sensitivity, they were ready to trade a great deal for guarantees against a resurgent German militarism, even to the extent of risking the future of socialism in their zone of occupation. Even when Eden candidly explained the real basis of Western strategy to them, and negotiations appeared patently futile, the Russians were not persuaded to abandon them for more realistic alternatives. Molotov, as soon as the conference opened on January 25, struck a very moderate and reasonable tone which failed to stymie the three allies. They were to consolidate behind a British plan for free all-Germany elections which in no way would bind the united Germany's foreign and military policy thereafter. The Soviets' proposal was identical, word for word, to their no less democratic March 1952 plan, save that it dissolved both East and West Germany's existing military alliances along with guaranteeing neutrality in the future, abolished all future reparations payments, and circumscribed the size of a future Germany's armed forces. From these positions neither side was to budge. When it became clear that the West would not discuss German neutrality, the Soviets proposed an all-European security treaty pledging nonaggression and mutual aid in the event of a German attack against any member. The Russians followed up this suggestion at the end of March by asking to join NATO, gaining and losing nothing by such utopian suggestions.[55]

The Russians won nothing on the German question, though they did add a small contribution to France's already overwhelming desire to reject the EDC. But they did leave at least two more traps for the United States to confront in the future. For the conference, at the United States' insistence, had met without an agenda, and so each delegation could propose anything. The first challenge, which was also a measure of Russia's intense desire to reach agreement on Germany, was the proposal to conclude an Austrian peace treaty. The treaty would include the withdrawal of Soviet troops, if the West agreed to add the future neutralization of Austria in the world conflict to already existing accords. It was this Soviet proposal that bore fruit in an actual treaty the following year—proving that a withdrawal of

Soviet troops from Central Europe in return for security guarantees was certainly something the West could hope to obtain if only it were compatible with its other, more fundamental, interests.

The second danger to Dulles' policy of neither war nor peace, a strategy far too difficult for him to implement, was the Russian insistence, with Anglo-French help, on convening a later conference at Geneva, including China, to attempt to resolve the Indochina war. But at Berlin, Dulles did not feel he could successfully block the attempt at negotiated settlement.

Dulles feared that the French might exploit American opposition to the Geneva Conference, which eventually opened May 8, to extract yet more aid and even direct American military participation in a war that they could not win. At the same time, Washington worried that the French would abandon the military effort for a negotiated settlement such as the United States opposed everywhere else in the world. Never before had American policy been entangled in such a web of contradictions or become so impossible to implement. Opposed to a peace conference, politically the administration was unable even to hope for Republican approval to send significant forces to Indochina. To compound its confusions, the administration itself was extremely cautious about any form of direct intervention and had lost its means for relating to the drift of events—save to create obstacles for those who sought a peaceful resolution to the Indochina crisis.[56]

Yet the ambivalence could hardly be otherwise, for the United States perceived its larger interests in the world at stake in the Indochina conflict, a struggle it was now ready to define in several complementary ways at the same time. First there was the "falling domino" principle Eisenhower outlined on April 7, with its danger ". . . of a disintegration that would have the most profound influences" for the entire region. From this threat followed a second: the loss of the area's "tin and tungsten . . . rubber plantations and so on." Should they lose this vast expanse, and since ". . . Japan must have . . . a trading area," Japan would be impelled to turn ". . . toward the Communist areas in order to live."[57] Such explanations made sense to the United States' interests, but the cost of maintaining Asia's integration appeared too formidable—at least for the moment. Here were planted the seeds for perhaps the greatest crisis in modern America's history, one that would prove no more successful to it than the numerous many smaller confrontations in which it was to engage after World War II. But the conditioning of such earlier actions was but the preface to those that were to follow in seemingly a never-ending, increasingly dangerous succession.

The Strategy of Fear

A mobilizing sense of danger had cut through innumerable political obstacles during the postwar era, increasingly binding Congress, the public, and European allies into a cult of fear dedicated to the policies and goals that the Truman administration had set for itself for a whole spectrum of reasons, most of which had all too little to do with Russia. The Soviet Union and the alleged menace it posed became the handle whereby it could act on all other problems, and in the period that the United States retained a clear military mastery the tension and seeming threat of conflict such truculence also risked seemed a quite manageable cost. After 1950, however, with the increasing equalization of the military balance, and with the eventual success of the Soviet peace offensive in convincing a few Western leaders that diplomacy has a place, after all, in the scheme of things, the alliance based on fear and terror was challenged at its very core. For practical purposes, the continuing, gradual erosion of Washington's tenuous mastery over its bloc was to become a defining trend of postwar history.

The Eisenhower administration confronted this development in several ways, ultimately never to develop a coherent response. It never abandoned an ideological, mystifying view of the nature of the world crisis, which read history as a conspiracy of cynical and almost magical elites of agitators fanning the flames of discontent, nationalism, and secularism in a manner that entirely ignored the structural roots of the postwar world crisis. The historian cannot casually dismiss this elitist explanation merely as pure cynicism or as one more aspect of Dulles' legalism or too close reading of bolshevik theory. Essentially, it was a utilitarian proposition which men such as Dulles and Eisenhower quite genuinely believed, but not to the extent of permitting it to overcome a clear perception of facts and the need to sustain a sense of danger even when they knew none existed.

Privately and publicly, Dulles showed he accepted Eisenhower's gingerly defined fear of ". . . an atheistic materialism bent upon domination of the world."[58] Leavening this definition, however, was the entirely explicit awareness that "for eight years," as Dulles wrote about the American-led alliance in the summer of 1955, "they have been held together largely by a cement compounded of fear and a sense of moral superiority."[59] ". . . [T]hey cannot do what is necessary and maintain defensive power unless there is a feeling of need in the face of danger," he argued with America's erstwhile allies until his death.[60] From this viewpoint, as such leaders as

Admiral Arthur Radford, chairman of the Joint Chiefs, told Congress in 1956, "In a period of general relaxation and reduction of . . . tensions, the Soviet threat to the free world by alternative means is perhaps even more dangerous and insidious than military action."[61] Such a vision, therefore, also required the cynical attribution of aggressive designs to Russia that exceeded even the ability of ideological deductions to explain the facts. During the first years of the Eisenhower administration, Dulles publicly greatly exaggerated the danger of war, which in reality he privately admitted was much less likely. The cultivation of fear and anxiety became a conscious organizational weapon.

Against the American public, which Dulles explicitly saw as an amorphous, uninformed obstacle to discipline rather than a force to obey, fear of Communism was a familiar chord worth plucking. The public, and more particularly Congress, was not yet so tired of the contrived dangers as to be incredulous. For the Western European allies, especially at NATO conferences, denying the significance of changes in the Soviet leadership structure, or the sincerity of their diplomatic overtures, became pro forma. "Stalinism lives, though Stalin died," ran this theme.[62] The dilemma for America was that war with Russia would prove suicidal to each, and no later than the end of 1956, Dulles concluded, "[b]oth morality and expediency now reject deliberate resort to war as an instrument of national policy.[63] Such an acknowledgment did not, however, lead to the conclusion that the arms race and global crisis must be terminated via diplomacy, for the impression of agreement and peace with Russia would end in something yet more ominous: "The Free World's efforts would rapidly decline. . . . There would be what seems to be a great danger—a tendency to fall apart."[64] Hence the policy of neither peace nor war continued, with somewhat less tension and fear than before but sufficient maintenance of anxiety to mobilize the recalcitrant as well as sustain American leadership's own, if lesser, fear of the consequences of war with the USSR. Russia, from this viewpoint, was more useful isolated and allegedly hostile than integrated. The Soviet bloc would change internally over future generations, thereby laying the structural basis of a durable peace, Dulles was to argue, but, "[u]ntil that day comes, we shall need to remain on our guard."[65]

Maintenance of a tough posture was crucial to his belief, as well, that the United States could not retreat from challenges, especially in Asia, without having its allies lose confidence in Washington's hegemony in the world. Not to interfere where America's interest was very minimal, even nonexistent, was to thereby open the door to the relaxation that might later endanger the future of American power where its interests were primary. And it might also lead to the dissolution of the critical mobilization of the American people which was the prerequisite of vast arms expenditures and the role of global policeman. For this reason, such issues as disarmament or disengagement in Central Europe were preordained to failure, however technically feasible Soviet proposals on these issues might be. And, because Washington often saw its response to a specific area as intimately related to a much larger global context, in its willingness to act where specific interests were not immediately at stake rested a psychological rationale for interventionism everywhere. Ultimately, America's leaders could justify their acts because of a larger universal definition of the nature of the world crises that was essential to direct involvement and risks where they could find and control most of the stakes of world power without fear of Soviet response. In this sense, the will to act everywhere became the prerequisite and *raison d'être* for the control of the American bloc of nations, including its often indirect ramifications in Asia.

Such a vision, which men like Acheson and Nitze held with a greater rigor than even Dulles, was in its first phases both ideological and strategic, making the taking of uncanny and dangerous risks an integral aspect of American foreign policy. But one should not make too much of this American ideological definition of its global role, for when asked to provide a coherent, explicit overview of the basic purposes of American foreign policy —and this was attempted at least several times—men such as Dulles retreated to banalities, clichés, and vague polemics. Acheson was better able to articulate a vision of a "world system" under the United States' leadership, but ultimately he, too, like Dulles, could give a precise definition of America's interest and role in that world order only in economic terms.[66]

Yet, in the end the Eisenhower administration by 1954 was even more firmly locked in that fatal predicament of American foreign policy since the end of World War II, for which it ultimately failed to produce a satisfactory answer. The danger to America's interests in the world was not Russia, but profound social change and the seemingly irresistible movement of major portions of the globe toward economic independence and even, in sections of the Third World, social transformation. The world was too large, the number of local crises too numerous, for the United States to be able to regulate the affairs and fate of every nation. American military technology might solve domestic economic problems, but it could not cope with the currents of autonomy in Europe and Asia, and it could not produce military victory in every agrarian society. Russia, too, by 1953 was being challenged in its bloc by nationalist impulses, for the world was irretrievably moving beyond any one nation's domination. America's attempt to reverse the main current in modern history was to generate misery for numerous nations of the world without eliminating their ultimate ability to define their own destinies. And, in the following decades, the inevitable consquences of its role abroad was to impose growing chaos, alienation, and economic crises on the American social system itself.

Conclusion:

The Limits of Integration

The central theme in postwar American foreign policy is that of an expansive capitalist nation constantly seeking new means by which to attain its increasingly elusive goals. The issue at stake in the resolution of its profound dilemma is scarcely one of fulfilling disinterested ideology, much less idealism, but of the future of United States power in the world and the inextricably linked health of capitalism and its social system at home as well as internationally.

The hopeless inadequacy of its wartime plans for global economic and political integration, and Washington's gross underestimation of the social, economic, and political trauma of the war on the world, left the United States with the almost immediate need to devise new mechanisms by which to attain its clearly defined economic ends. These articulated economic objectives carried with them the need to preserve world capitalism and traditional societies in some manner, if only to later bring them closer to America's model of a reformed, integrated international economy which postulated the United States as the heart of that system.

That search never ended because ultimate success for America's leaders remained forever elusive. So, too, did its frustrations prejudge the nation's response to the political options and increasingly essential political preconditions it had to attain throughout the world in order eventually to achieve its goals. If Washington's wartime thoughts regarding the postwar global political structure were far less explicit than its economic planning, it nevertheless predicated the perpetuation of the world's prewar classes and capitalism and colonialism in their conventional framework, hopefully to be renovated to conform to America's ideals and needs. The fact that the prewar social elites and their societies had been profoundly weakened, compromised, or fundamentally challenged from below compelled the United States to align itself, at increasing expense and energy, with established conservatives. Conservatism's fragility and revolution thereby became interrelated with the United States' economic program, evolving into a complex matrix of costly interventions to preserve traditional societies and efforts to attain a profitable world economic integration at one and the same time. This parallel development was not contradictory, but simply different dimensions of America's basic expansion and its increasing need to address itself to the more immediate, unavoidable obligation to maintain or create the political prerequisites for its eventual success.

This succession of new efforts and programs during the first postwar decade is evidence that despite some generally short-lived accomplishments the United States' effort was, on the whole, increasingly a failure. The triumph that America needed and desired was ever more remote, and the disparity between its objectives and its means for reaching them grew until the irrelevance of its selected tools to its ends made failures virtually the rule. Even though it established priorities, Washington never had a realization of its endemic weakness and insufficiency in a world in which the limits of the possible increasingly circumscribed ideology and goals. By 1947 it was plain even to the United States' leaders that its means and goals could not cope with reality, and they had to formulate more ambitious mechanisms, only to realize by 1950 that these had also largely not succeeded on their own terms. The ITO, Marshall Plan, NATO, EDC, A-bomb—to mention a few of the alphabetized instruments of America's ambition—did not attain for it the overt, or even the covert, purposes for which they were intended.

Just as we insist on making an expansive American capitalism the central theme of postwar history, so, too, must we place a distinct emphasis on its relative failures—defeats the outcome and consequences of which have led to an escalation of the American attempts to master its ever more elusive self-assigned destiny. But we must also place the significance of its mounting efforts in the context of whether the multiplying undertakings were ever sufficient for the American economy's needs and for the fulfillment of its ambitious global objectives. For despite the fact that the magnitude of America's postwar program satisfied specific agricultural and industrial interests, in the largest sense it was inadequate to attain its maximum objectives. The British loan of 1946 was followed by the Marshall Plan, which in turn required massive arms aid, Point Four, and the like. By the time the intensifying transformation of the Third World, and evolution in

Europe itself, could be gauged, it was evident to all in Washington that the role of capital exporter initially assigned to American business in the postwar world was woefully utopian. The state therefore undertook that key role during the first postwar decade, and wholly assumed the obligation of furnishing the political and military protection it knew an integrated world capitalism demanded. This merger of public and private power and goals, so traditional in American history, despite its vastly greater extent also fell short of the goal's monumental requirements. There were tactical successes and benefits, but the United States never attained the ideal world order it confidently anticipated during World War II.

America's leaders never fully realized the limits of American power in the world, and the use of foreign policy to express and solve the specific needs of American capitalism continued during the first postwar decade and thereafter, circumscribing the nature of American society and the process of social change throughout the globe. This interaction between a nation with universal objectives but finite power and the remainder of mankind is critical in modern history and the essence of the American experience.

The United States' goal of world integration subsumed, but also transcended, the question of the Left and Soviet power in the world. It first articulated its ends on the assumption that there would be a capitalist world which America could bind together under a universalist doctrine and relationship. Had the Left and revolution not become the most significant outcomes of the war, or had they not even existed, the postwar experience would have been profoundly troubled nonetheless. The nonsocialist nations of the world saw America's brand of universalism merely as a mask for its expansion and advancement of its specifically national interest—a profound skepticism that temporary need kept them from articulating more brusquely. In the end, just as the United States never abandoned its self-interest, neither would Western Europe forgo its own.

The Western alliance, with NATO at its core, was the United States' effort to utilize internationalism as a mode of integration, and its marginal success was due largely to Western Europe's transitory weaknesses rather than a genuine overlapping of interest. Given the profound inconsistencies between the United States' trade and financial practices and what it advocated for others, which appeared to the world merely to be a doctrine of convenience, Europe's irresistible desire and need to pursue its own course was a constant American anxiety. It was Western Europe's first postwar impulse toward autarchic economic relations, rather than fear of a quite passive and conservative Communist movement, that made the threat of an independent, nationally oriented capitalism Washington's first perceived great postwar challenge. Not the threat of revolution or the collapse of capitalism, but the failure of integration was the initial and most basic issue at stake in Western Europe—and it was never to disappear. From this viewpoint, the various expressions of the alliance, from ERP to NATO and an integrated German army, were but means of heading off future crises that independent blocs—capitalist and socialist alike—might create for the United States' hegemony.

Although the establishment of military bases and military integration had a certain political value, it brought neither military security nor genuine integration. The arms were used in colonial wars, or turned against nominal allies, and Western Europe's economy kept almost irresistibly moving beyond Washington's grasp and toward becoming a competitive trade bloc. Its continuation within the framework of capitalism was due more to the lack of a Communist will and ability to assume power, and Western Europe's short-range utility as an outlet for American exports and investments was far less than the United States' needs and aspirations. American power and interests replaced those of the British in the Middle East, but with this change came risks and instabilities for which the United States had neither planned nor found a solution. On the whole, America's most cherished structural plans for Europe proved a chimera as it moved from frustration to failure, with an integrated world capitalism centered around the United States remaining an illusive aspiration.

Despite the United States' desire for self-serving world economic reorganization, World War II left it with a spectrum of more pressing difficulties arising from the war-inflicted internal crises and civil war in societies everywhere. The restoration of traditional ruling classes and forces of stability therefore became a paramount preoccupation, especially in Germany and Japan. The entirely valid assumption that the *status quo* had to be structurally preserved in order to later integrate or reform it placed the United States squarely on the side of counterrevolution in the world, in many nations virtually becoming the old order's sole bastion.

This alliance with global reaction did not occur at one time, but rather remained in gestation until the United States was forced to choose sides during local crises. In China and Korea its decisions were virtually immediate, but elsewhere it took longer. The choice was often as pragmatic as it was ideological, though in due course Washington acknowledged a certain affinity of ultimate values with reactionaries from Athens to Saigon. In Europe the choice was much easier, for despite a fear of eventual conflicting interests, American policy leaders clearly saw the options. In Germany, above all, the United States categorically vetoed the electoral path to socialism, and this in turn required partition and, finally, various instruments of Western European integration also designed to contain the potential re-emergence of expansive German power. In rejecting the desires of the German people themselves, the United States proved once again how utterly expedient it would be regarding national self-determination when democracy opened the way to a conflict with capitalism and the attainment of its own needs and goals. Parliamentarianism and democratic forms thereby became a rhetorical, cynical weapon of ideology in a larger struggle, never an inconveniencing literalism and genuine commitment. American interventions—whether military or political—were to abort the emergence of genuine democracy in countless instances.

The relative stability in Western Europe was due to the Communist leadership's innate cautiousness, the inhibiting Russian advice to them to work along strictly parliamentarian lines, and the readiness of the various regimes and the United States to intervene on every level—from election-law revisions to force—to preserve the existing structures. So long as Washington thought Europe the primary arena in which to make its commitments of men and material, it could succeed in its efforts to control the Left even as it increasingly lost its ability to define European capitalism's course. Given the docile Communist and Soviet strategy, its power was adequate. This symbiotic relationship between capitalism and the Communists was to endure and remained sufficient to preserve order in Western Europe—but not elsewhere.

Outside of Europe, however, neither the United States nor the Soviet Union could master or direct the monumental upheavals and transformation unfolding on the face of the globe. From the elitist nationalist revolutions to the mass armed peasant uprisings, from the military coup and *Putsch* to the urban guerillas, the spontaneous, decentralized nature of change defied America's control. So long as there is oppression, and exploitation exists, there will be resistance, violence, and conflict. The Third World was as remote from Moscow's leadership as it was from Washington's, and what was truly decisive in the shifting international balance exceeded their mutual authority. For this elementary reason the *status quo*'s stability was never negotiable, for just as Moscow had not initiated the endless revolutions, it could not discontinue them in return for American concessions. At best, it could reluctantly endorse the undiminished world movement toward the left which is the hallmark of this century.

Given its ideology, needs, and goals, the United States attempted to intervene in this enormous historical process and to repress it. It was powerful enough to threaten local revolutions, or to determine the conditions of their success or failure in many areas, but ultimately America was too weak to achieve its own goals and to stop the irresistible course toward social transformation. It could turn civil wars into international interventions, and attain temporary, generally short-lived successes, but the realities of the situation outstripped Washington's ambitions. In the end it was able only to generate vast quantities of violence, in the form of repression that it sponsored either directly with its own man power or indirectly through its satellite regimes. And the United States' intervention also made repeatedly clear that to be victorious, movements of social transformation on the left had to be able and willing to confront internal opposition, and even external armies, reinforced with American arms. Hence the survival of the old order was prolonged as a result of the internationalization of social change, but it endured only in a long night of terror, repression, and violence that also unavoidably marks and distorts the character of modern revolution.

Ironically, instead of accepting the lesson of its failures when its goals exceeded its resources, as in China, the United States' inability to control the Asian revolution led to yet new escalations, temporary successes along with final defeats, and to the ultimate *cul de sac*—Vietnam. Ironic, as well, was the fact that it was this very process of violence, repression, and support to traditional regimes—as in Greece, China, and Vietnam—that made them more self-confidently corrupt and violent, mobilizing and generating their own resistance, polarizing each society yet more deeply, and telescoping the development of national revolutionary movements everywhere.

Because the basic source of the world crisis was an expansive American foreign policy's interaction with revolution and national autonomy, capitalist as well as socialist, there was precious little satisfaction the Russians might provide the United States outside Europe. The Soviet Union, in brief, could not deliver the stability the United States sought out of a sustained world crisis of which the USSR itself was but a manifestation rather than a cause. Indeed, even if the Soviet Union had not existed, the condition of the Third World and America's response toward it after 1945 would scarcely have been different—for Washington's goals predated the war and even 1917 itself. It would be extremely difficult to identify areas in which greater Soviet collaboration would have altered the outcome of America's fundamental programs. The greatest danger in Western Europe in the postwar years might have been independent national Left movements unwilling to inhibit their actions at Moscow's behest. And the Chinese Revolution was wholly autonomous of Russia's conservative advice, which failed to change its outcome. In brief, diplomacy's bankruptcy was due to the impossibility of satisfying America's needs with formal treaties. On the contrary, any Soviet offer to negotiate assumed the nature of a threat rather than an opportunity to Washington after 1946, for it diminished the artificial, increasingly contrived sense of national crisis which was far more essential to containing Congress and the American people than bolshevism. This heightened consciousness of danger, as Washington's only reliable mechanism for administering foreign policy, alone precluded a *détente* with Moscow.

As it was, the Russians were extremely defensive in their approach to Europe's destiny. Other than their initial insistence that Eastern Europe not be returned to those elements that had been instrumental in the creation of the *cordon sanitaire,* their laxity until 1947 in consolidating power along their borders revealed a fundamental desire to avoid unnecessarily offending the West. Their later willingness to negotiate a reunified Germany also postulated that it be neutral and taken out of the European power struggle, but the United States had to reject this course because it not only undermined the crisis diplomacy Acheson and Dulles had assiduously cultivated but also meant that a social democratic nation would emerge to alter the character of the Western European economy. Essentially, the Russians applied themselves to the tasks of reconstruction and growth, assuming that incipient conflict among the capitalist nations would exempt the USSR from the probable maelstrom. This Soviet reading of history misgauged the role of the Third World and world revolution as well, and reveals why the Russians energetically attempted to dampen the willingness of the Left to act decisively everywhere. If this policy can be justified as the constraint that reality imposes on the weak, it cannot explain the conservativism in Soviet policy in Europe after 1952, when its atomic power equalized American military strength and gave it far greater latitude for both declarations and actions. In reality, the Russians had long since abandoned revolution elsewhere in Europe on behalf of national security, and had embarked on a policy of minimizing political risks.

The perception of the Soviet danger that successive administrations fostered was therefore based largely on the crisis of domestic legitimacy and the need to maintain a sustaining tension to enact extremely costly legislation generally desired for reasons initially having little, if anything, to do with Russia. To some extent the postwar choice of military procurement reflected the influence of industrial constituencies, but the size of available economic resources was far more significant, and the decision to obtain maximum explosive power for minimal arms allocations compatible with a total economic strategy led the United States to the first of its series of monumental policy miscalculations. The designation of Russia as the likely primary enemy of the postwar era caused the United States to prepare for a war it was never to fight, and later could not—save at the cost of suicide. Yet the nuclear bomb was largely irrelevant to counterrevolutionary wars against peasants and land armies. Western Europe's rearmament was economically motivated and scarcely altered the balance of military power. The inconsistent, futile American search for a coherent strategy and weaponry capable of compensating for the ideological appeals of guerillas, of translating material power into political triumph, was never found. Given its unlimited political and economic objectives throughout the world, no military doctrine or weapon was to produce the coveted success where economics and ideology failed. In the end, the military budget's only reliable function was to serve as a guarantor of domestic economic demand. By 1954 the United States' seemingly decisive military supremacy of the 1940's was lost, and with it occurs the containment and equalization of American power in a manner that effectively, irrevocably recasts the future of warfare among industrial nations: between them there will be peace or cataclysm. Now, in part because it could not afford doomsday, but mainly because of a shifting perception of the source of danger to its hegemony, war with the Third World became the only conflict the United States dared to accept.

And so ended the tortured first decade of what was to become a perpetual international crisis and America's constant, increasingly violent effort to control and redirect a world moving ever further beyond any nation's mastery. In that monumental undertaking to contain and reconstruct the world according to its own needs. the United States was prepared to destroy itself—morally, socially, and economically—in a deepening trauma whose effects began to weaken American capitalism far more than the attainment of its expansive, unattainable goals might ever have strengthened it. America's power having reached and then exceeded its limits, the result is inevitably a profound crisis in the social system.

Our history has no actual end, for today we still live with the consequences and aspirations of the first postwar decade—and the world suffers from its violence and terror. On the ultimate outcome of this continuing experience depend the future of civilization itself and the nature of man's destiny.

Notes

The following code abbreviations are used in the notes:

AAG Mss—U.S. Army Advisory Group, Nanking, Records 92, AGI–0.1, Modern Military Records Division, National Archives, Washington, D.C.

AGO Mss—U.S. Adjutant General's Office (RG 94), Peiping Headquarters Group Records, Modern Military Records Division, National Archives, Washington, D.C.

SA Mss—Stanley Andrews Papers, Truman Library, Independence, Mo.

BB Mss—Bernard Baruch Papers, Princeton University Library.

TCB Mss—Thomas C. Blaisdell, Jr., Papers, Truman Library.

WLC Mss—William L. Clayton Papers, Truman Library.

TC Mss—Tom Connally Papers, Library of Congress, Washington, D.C.

CDSP — *Current Digest of the Soviet Press.*

DC Mss—U.S. Department of Commerce Records (RG 40), National Archives, Washington, D.C.

DS —U.S. Department of State.

DSB —U.S. *Department of State Bulletin.*

FR —U.S. Department of State, *Foreign Relations of the United States* (Washington, 1861—). The year covered and the volume are also cited in the reference note.

JMD Mss—Joseph M. Dodge Papers, Detroit Public Library.

JFD Mss—John Foster Dulles Papers, Princeton University Library.

DDE Mss—Dwight D. Eisenhower Papers, Eisenhower Library, Abilene, Kansas.

JF Mss—James Forrestal Papers, Princeton University Library.

WG Mss—William Gomberg Papers, Library of the London School of Economics and Political Science.

JCG Mss—Joseph C. Grew Papers, Houghton Library, Harvard College.

KWH Mss—Kenneth W. Hechler Files in Harry S. Truman Papers (RG 3), Truman Library.

FLH   Mss—Frank L. Howley Papers, New York University Library.

JMJ   Mss—Joseph M. Jones Papers, Truman Library.

FK   Mss—Fred Kent Papers, Princeton University Library.

JAK   Mss—Julius A. Krug Papers, Library of Congress.

ABL   Mss—Arthur Bliss Lane Papers, Yale University Library.

WDL   Mss—William D. Leahy Papers, Library of Congress.

EL   Mss—Edwin A. Locke, Jr., Files in Harry S. Truman Papers (RG 3), Truman Library.

EAL   Mss—Edwin A. Locke, Jr., Papers (RG 48), Truman Library.

DM   Mss—Douglas MacArthur Papers, MacArthur Memorial Library, Norfolk, Virginia.

WM   Mss—William Mathews Papers, University of Pennsylvania Library.

GSM   Mss—George S. Messersmith Papers, University of Delaware Library, Newark.

ONH   Mss—U.S. Office of Naval History, Washington, D.C.

RP   Mss—Robert Patterson Papers, Library of Congress.

PAP   Mss—President's Air Policy Commission Records, Truman Library.

PMP   Mss—President's Materials Policy Commission Records, Truman Library.

JWS   Mss—John W. Snyder Papers, Truman Library.

SJS   Mss—Stephen J. Spingarn Papers, Truman Library.

LAS   Mss—Laurence A. Steinhardt Papers, Library of Congress.

HLS   Mss—Henry L. Stimson Papers, Yale University Library.

JT   Mss—John Taber Papers, Cornell University Library.

HST   Mss—Harry S. Truman Papers, Truman Library.

AHV   Mss—Arthur H. Vandenberg Papers, University of Michigan Library, Ann Arbor.

JEW   Mss—James E. Webb Papers, Truman Library.

HDW   Mss—Harry Dexter White Papers, Princeton University Library.

CW   Mss—Clair Wilcox Papers, University of Pennsylvania Library.

We have deposited reproductions of a substantial proportion of the manuscripts cited here in the Library of the London School of Economics and Political Science and the York University Library, Toronto.

A note indicates the origin of each preceding quotation or series of quotations from the same source. Such citations frequently include references for nonquoted information following the prior note. Where there are no quotations, notes at the end of several or more paragraphs document the information preceding the note number. Box numbers or manuscript record categories given are those applicable at the time we used particular collections. Since we utilized the bulk of them during 1964–1966, they may now be superseded by other cataloguing designations.

NOTES

Chapter 1: The Reconstruction of the World Economy

1. DSB, December 9, 1945, 914.

2. U.S. Senate, Committee on Banking and Currency, *Hearings: Bretton Woods Agreement Act,* 79:1, June 1945 (Washington, 1945), 7–8. See also Gabriel Kolko, *The Politics of War: The World and United States Foreign Policy, 1943–1945* (New York, 1968), chaps. XI, XIX.

3. U.S. Senate, Committee on Labor and Public Welfare, *History of Employment and Manpower Policy in the United States,* 88:2 (Washington, 1965), VI, 2400.

4. DSB, November 25, 1945, 829.

5. DSB, November 24, 1946, 950. See also William Adams Brown, Jr., *The United States and the Restoration of World Trade* (Washington, 1950), 1.

6. DSB, November 24, 1946, 952–53.

7. DSB, September 22, 1946, 540. See also U.S. House, Committee on Armed Services, *Hearings: Petroleum for National Defense,* 80:2, January–March 1948 (Washington, 1948), 9.

8. Harry S. Truman, *Public Papers of the Presidents of the United States: 1946* (Washington, 1962), 313.

9. House Committee on Armed Services, *Petroleum for National Defense,* 315. See also Joseph M. Dodge, "The General Economic and Political Problem and Its Relationship to Banking," n.d. [1947], JMD Mss, Germany Assignment, box 6.

10. Hal B. Lary, *Problems of the United States as World Trader and Banker* (New York, 1963), 88; Robert E. Lipsey, *Price and Quantity Trends in the Foreign Trade of the United States* (Princeton, 1963), 145, 155; Edward S. Mason, *Controlling World Trade: Cartels and Commodity Agreement* (New York, 1946), 243–44; U.S. Congress, Joint Committee on the Economic Report, *Hearings: Foreign Economic Policy,* 84:1, November 9–17, 1955 (Washington, 1955), 517–18; Raymond S. Mikesell, *United States Economic Policy and International Relations* (New York, 1952), 47; Kolko, *Politics of War,* 245–48.

11. Senate Committee on Banking and Currency, *Bretton Woods Agreement,* 6. See also Brown, *United States and the Restoration of World Trade,* 52–73; International Bank for Reconstruction and Development, *The International Bank for Reconstruction and Development, 1946–1953* (Baltimore, 1954), 6; International Bank for Reconstruction and Development, *The World Bank: Policies and Operations* (Washington, June, 1960), 2–3; Kolko, *Politics of War,* 249ff.

12. Clair Wilcox, *A Charter for World Trade* (New York, 1949), 34.

13. Jack N. Behrman, "Political Factors in United States International Financial Cooperation," *American Political Science Review,* 47 (1953), 435. See also FR (1945), II, 1338–39; FR (1945), VI, 56–60, 84, 118; DS, *Proposals for Expansion of World Trade and Employment,* November 1945 (Washington, 1945), *passim;* Kolko, *Politics of War,* 485–87.

14. Kolko, *Politics of War,* 264.

15. DSB, August 26, 1945, 279. See also U.S. Senate, Committee on Labor and Public Welfare, *History of Employment and Manpower Policy in the United States,* 88:2–89:2 (Washington, 1965–1966), VI, 2391, 2443–504; VII, 1ff.; U.S. House, Committee on Banking and Currency, *Hearings: Anglo-American Financial Agreement,* 79:2, May–June 1946 (Washington, 1946), 3; U.S. Senate, Special Committee to Study Problems of American Small Business, *Report: Economic Concentration and World War II,* 79:2 (Washington, 1946), 38–45; U.S. Department of Agriculture, *What Peace Can Mean to American Farmers: Expansion of Foreign Trade,* October 1945 (Washington, 1945), *passim;* Keith Hutchison, *Rival Partners: America and Britain in the Post-War World* (New York, 1946), 33; DSB, March 10, 1946, 382; Kolko, *Politics of War,* 252–54.

16. U.S. Senate, Committee on Banking and Currency, *Hearings: Export-Import Bank Act of 1945,* 79:1, July 17–18, 1945 (Washington, 1945), 4. See also Lipsey, *Price and Quantity Trends,* 155; Kolko, *Politics of War,* 252–53; Hal B. Lary, "Memo in Response to an Enquiry from Sen. Sheridan Downey of August 21, 1945," n.d. [November, 1945], DC Mss, file 82220–1; Arthur Paul, memo of January 11, 1946, DC Mss, file 93126–64; DSB, November 25, 1945, 830; Howard S. Ellis, "Bilateralism in the Future of International Trade," *Essays in International Finance,* No. 5 (Princeton, 1945), 17; Senate Committee on Labor and Public Welfare, *History of Employment and Manpower Policy,* VII, 18–19.

17. DSB, November 24, 1946, 950.

18. DSB, November 18, 1945, 785.

19. *Ibid.*

20. DSB, November 24, 1946, 953. See also Harry Dexter White speech, October 18, 1945, HDW Mss, file 27; Kolko, *Politics of War,* 254; Mason, *Controlling World Trade,* 137–42; U.S. Commission on Foreign Economic Policy, *Staff Papers* (Washington, 1954), 224–29; Gabriel Kolko, *The Roots of American Foreign Policy* (Boston, 1969), chap. III.

21. DSB, March 10, 1946, 383–84.

22. Wallace to William L. Clayton, February 7, 1946, DC Mss, file 82220–1. See also Raymond A. Bauer *et al., American Business and Foreign Policy: The Politics of Foreign Trade* (New York, 1963), 82–85.

23. DSB, August 26, 1945, 279.

24. Wilcox, *Charter for World Trade,* 34.

25. DSB, September 22, 1946, 539.

26. House Committee on Banking and Currency, *Anglo-American Financial Agreement,* 197. See also DSB, November 25, 1945, 829–32; September 22, 1946, 539–41.

27. House Committee on Banking and Currency, *Anglo-American Financial Agreement,* 330. See also National Foreign Trade Council, *Report of the Thirty-Third National Foreign Trade Convention* [November 11–13, 1946] (New York, 1947), 136–37, for similar business opinions.

28. Dodge, "The General Economic and Political Problem . . ., [1947], JMD Mss, Germany Assignment, box 6.

29. Senate Committee on Banking and Currency, *Export-Import Bank Act of*

1945, 4; Behrman, "Political Factors in U.S. International Financial Cooperation," 434.

30. DSB, November 18, 1945, 785.

31. Truman, *Public Papers: 1946,* 313. See also DSB, July 21, 1946, 111–12; Arthur Paul to Emilio G. Collado, July 22, 1946, JWS Mss, box 10.

32. DSB, November 25, 1945, 829–32; United Nations, Department of Economic Affairs, *The International Flow of Private Capital, 1946–52* (New York, 1954), 8; Robert E. Asher, *Grants, Loans and Local Currencies* (Washington, 1961), table II; *Business Week,* October 12, 1946, 107; La Documentation Française, *La Politique Économique Américaine et l'Aide à la France* [Notes Doc. et Études No. 726], 18 Septembre 1947 (Paris, 1947), 11, *passim.*

Chapter 2: American Diplomacy and Russia, 1945–1946

1. Harry S. Truman, *Year of Decisions* (New York, 1955), 552. See also FR (1945), V, 888–90, 921–25; Walter Millis, ed., *The Forrestal Diaries* (New York, 1951), 107, 254.

2. *Forrestal Diaries,* 135; William D. Leahy Diary, February 21, 1946, WDL Mss; Walter Bedell Smith, *My Three Years in Moscow* (Philadelphia, 1950), 29–31; Arthur H. Vandenberg, ed., *The Private Papers of Senator Vandenberg* (Boston, 1952), chap. XIII.

3. Thomas B. Inglis, Memo, "Soviet Capabilities and Intentions . . . ," January 12, 1946, JF Mss, box 24.

4. John Foster Dulles, "Europe Must Federate or Perish," *Vital Speeches,* February 1, 1947, 234. See also FR (1945), V, 933–36; FR (1946), V, 472–75.

5. Edward S. Mason, "Reflections on the Moscow Conference," *International Organization,* 1 (1947), 482. See also *Forrestal Diaries,* 106, 143–44, 158–59, 171–73, 181–82, 191–92, 195, 210; FR (1946), IV, 881–82; FR (1946), VII, 732–36, 758.

6. Dodge, "The General Economic and Political Problem and Its Relationship to Banking," n.d. [1947], JMD Mss, Germany Assignment, box 6. See also *Forrestal Diaries,* 157–58; FR (1946), V, 436.

7. John Foster Dulles, "Soviet Foreign Policy," *Life,* 20 (June 3, 1946), 116–17. See also DS, *The United States and the Non-Self-Governing Territories,* April 5, 1947 (Washington, 1947), 15, 26, 73; Robert C. Good, "The United States and the Colonial Debate," *Alliance Policy in the Cold War,* Arnold Wolfers, ed. (Baltimore, 1959), 233–44.

8. FR (1945) II, 516. See also *ibid.,* 114–15, 164–72, 180–81, 323–34; FR (Conference of Berlin, 1945), II, 1500.

9. Harry S. Truman, *Public Papers of the Presidents of the United States: 1945* (Washington, 1961), 433. See also FR (1945), II, 515–19, 531–33, 544–46, 554, 560–74; U.S. Senate, Committee on Foreign Relations, *A Decade of American Foreign Policy: Basic Documents, 1941–49* (Washington, 1950), 51–58.

10. FR (1945), V, 1049. See also Truman, *Public Papers: 1945,* 433–34; FR (1945), II, 578–83, 589–93; FR (1945), V, 881, 898–99, 935–36, 1031–52; FR (1945), VI, 820–22.

11. FR (1945), V, 839–43; FR (1946), VI, 794, 820–30, 833–45, 853–61; Arthur Krock, *Memoirs: Sixty Years on the Firing Line* (New York, 1968), 481. There is no truth whatever, as discussed in William H. McNeill, *America, Britain, and Russia: Their Cooperation and Conflict, 1941–1946* (London, 1953), 691, that the loan failed because it was misfiled or forgotten.

12. Truman, *Year of Decisions*, 546, 549. See also FR (1945), II, 605ff., 629, 776; George Curry, *James F. Byrnes* (New York, 1965), 361; Arthur H. Vandenberg to C. E. Hutchinson, December 29, 1945, AHV Mss; Leahy Diary, December 28, 1945, WDL Mss; Henry L. Stimson to Truman, December 28, 1945, HLS Mss.

13. Truman, *Year of Decisions*, 551–52. See also Senate Committee on Foreign Relations, *Decade of American Foreign Policy*, 66–72.

14. Robert Murphy, *Diplomat among Warriors* (New York, 1964), 301; Truman, *Year of Decisions*, 552; John J. McCloy to Henry L. Stimson, November 22, 1946; James F. Byrnes to Stimson, January 17, 1947, HLS Mss; for a different version see Curry, *Byrnes*, 187–86; Murphy, *Diplomat among Warriors*, 301.

15. Harry S. Truman, *Years of Trial and Hope* (New York, 1956), 171, 214. See also *Forrestal Diaries*, 254.

16. *Forrestal Diaries*, 106.

17. Curry, *Byrnes*, 200. See also *ibid.*, 201; *Private Papers of Senator Vandenberg*, 246–49.

18. DSB, March 10, 1946, 357.

19. George F. Kennan, *Memoirs, 1925–1950* (Boston, 1967), 293, 295. See also *Private Papers of Senator Vandenberg*, 251; FR (1946), VI, 696–709; Curry, *Byrnes*, 202.

20. K. Tolley memo to Captain Smedberg, February 26, 1946, JF Mss, box 24. See also Kennan, *Memoirs*, 295; *Forrestal Diaries*, 140; FR (1946), VI, 721–23, 730–31.

21. Kennan, *Memoirs*, 301.

22. Barton J. Bernstein and Allen J. Matusow, eds., *The Truman Administration: A Documentary History* (New York, 1966), 217–19. See also Curry, *Byrnes*, 202–03; Earl Attlee, *A Prime Minister Remembers* (London, 1961), 162–63.

23. Attlee, *A Prime Minister Remembers*, 36–37, 162–63; Joseph V. Stalin and V. M. Molotov, *The Soviet Union and World Peace* (New York, 1946), 21, *passim;* Smith, *My Three Years*, 52; FR (1946), VI, 712, 716–17, 734.

24. Allen Dulles memo, May 14, 1946; James F. Byrnes to Dulles, June 8, 1946, JFD Mss; Dulles, "Soviet Foreign Policy," June 3, June 10, 1946, 112–26, 119–30; Krock, *Memoirs*, 476–77.

25. Curry, *Byrnes*, 129–31; V. M. Molotov, *Problems of Foreign Policy: Speeches and Statements, April 1945—November 1948* (Moscow, 1949), 39, 44; Amelia C. Leiss, ed., *European Peace Treaties after World War II* (Boston, 1954), 18–46; Vandenberg Diary, Paris Peace Conference, May 10, 11, June 18, 20, 1946, AHV Mss; *Private Papers of Senator Vandenberg*, 264–78; Yugoslav Embassy Information Office, *Trieste and the Julian March* (London, 1946), *passim;* FR (1946), II, 141–52, 228–51, *passim;* FR (1946), III, 15–16; FR (1946), IV, 824–25.

26. Vandenberg Diary, Paris Peace Conference, May 11, 1946; Vandenberg to Luce, May 28, 1946, AHV Mss. See also *Private Papers of Senator Vandenberg*, 285,

which do not contain many of his original notes on Soviet compromises; FR (1946), II, 453.

27. *Private Papers of Senator Vandenberg,* 289, 292.

28. Leahy Diary, June 20, 1946, WDL Mss; Leiss, *European Peace Treaties,* 14–15, 24–25; James F. Byrnes, *Speaking Frankly* (New York, 1947), 143–45; Curry, *Byrnes,* 242–43; Senate Committee on Foreign Relations, *Decade of American Foreign Policy,* 80; FR (1946), II, *passim;* FR (1946), VI, 910–15, 920–51; Molotov, *Problems of Foreign Policy,* 221–34.

29. Leahy Diary, September 18, 1946, WDL Mss. See also Truman, *Year of Decisions,* 555–60; Byrnes, *Speaking Frankly,* 239–43; *Private Papers of Senator Vandenberg,* 300–02; *Forrestal Diaries,* 206–09; Curry, *Byrnes,* 252–74; Bernstein and Matusow, *Truman Administration,* 239–45; Dean Acheson, *Present at the Creation: My Years in the State Department* (New York, 1969), 191.

30. Senate Committee on Foreign Relations, *Decade of American Foreign Policy,* 88–90.

31. Curry, *Byrnes,* 287–91; Leiss, *European Peace Treaties,* 15; FR (1946), VI, 796–97.

32. Trygve Lie, *In the Cause of Peace: Seven Years with the United Nations* (New York, 1954), *passim;* DSB, October 28, 1945, 654–55; Molotov, *Problems of Foreign Policy,* 50–51, 187–88, 255; Stalin and Molotov, *Soviet Union and World Peace,* 27; Andrei Y. Vyshinsky, *The U.S.S.R. and World Peace,* Jessica Smith, ed. (New York, 1949), 69, 75; *Soviet Press Translations,* December 31, 1946, 8–21; *New Times,* September 10, 1947, 1–3.

33. Senate Committee on Foreign Relations *Decade of American Foreign Policy,* 1061.

34. Nikolai A. Voznesensky, *The Economy of the U.S.S.R. during World War II* (Washington, 1948), 94–97; *The Economist,* December 11, 1948, 974–75; December 18, 1948, 1022–23; December 25, 1948, 1068–69; January 29, 1949, 197–98; Merton J. Peck and Frederic M. Scherer, *The Weapons Acquisition Process: An Economic Analysis* (Boston, 1962), 100; *Business Week,* June 5, 1948, 109–12; February 12, 1949, 101–02; FR (1946), V, 472–75.

35. See the tabulation of space in *Soviet Press Translations,* October 1, 1947, 145, devoted to various topics. This index remains fairly constant for the rest of the year. See also Stalin and Molotov, *Soviet Union and World Peace, passim;* Voznesensky, *The Economy of the U.S.S.R.,* 114–15; *The Economist,* February 14, 1948, 268; March 20, 1948, 458–59; Isaac Deutscher, *Stalin: A Political Biography* (New York, 1949), 551–64. Reports of such liberalization naturally found their way to Washington. See, for example, Michael Forrestal to James Forrestal, April 6, May 22, 1947, JF Mss, box 12.

36. *Soviet Press Translations,* December 14, 1946, 1.

37. *Forrestal Diaries,* 134. See also *ibid.,* 135, 155; Stalin and Molotov, *Soviet Union and World Peace,* 17–19; FR (1946), VI, 695–96; Krock, *Memoirs,* 430–31; Acheson, *Present at the Creation,* 150–51.

38. Deutscher, *Stalin,* 554. See also *Soviet Press Translations,* February 28, 1947, 1–3.

39. Deutscher, *Stalin,* 564; FR (1946), IV, 881–82; Barrington Moore, Jr., *Soviet*

Politics—The Dilemma of Power (Cambridge, 1950), 351, *passim;* J. V. Stalin, *Post-War International Relations* (London: Soviet News, 1947), 16–17; P. M. S. Blackett, *Fear, War, and the Bomb* (New York, 1949), 75–81, 196–210.

40. Frederick C. Barghoorn, "The Varga Discussion and Its Significance," *American Slavic and East European Review,* 7 (1948), 214–36; *New Times,* May 16, 1947, 4–9; E. Varga, "Anglo-American Rivalry and Partnership: A Marxist View," *Foreign Affairs,* 25 (1947), 583–95; Evsey D. Domar, "The Varga Controversy," *American Economic Review,* 40 (1950), 132–51; CDSP, February 1, 1949, 35; Molotov, *Problems of Foreign Policy,* 213–14; A. Zhdanov, *The International Situation* (Moscow, 1947), 13–14; FR (1946), VI, 684, 697, 759, 774, 786.

41. Zhdanov, *International Situation,* 22. See also Stalin, *Post-War International Relations,* 12–13, 21–22; Stalin and Molotov, *Soviet Union and World Peace,* 5–6; *New Times,* May 16, 1947, 1–3.

42. Zhdanov, *International Situation,* 40, 46; Stalin, *Post-War International Relations,* 12–22; Vyshinsky, *U.S.S.R. and World Peace,* 23; Marshall D. Shulman, *Stalin's Foreign Policy Reappraised* (Cambridge, 1963), *passim;* Molotov, *Problems of Foreign Policy,* 49, 287, 326–30; *Soviet Press Translations,* December 14, 1946, 7–12; December 31, 1946, 4–7; *New Times,* February 14, 1947, 10–15.

Chapter 3: Great Britain and the New World Economy

1. Harold Macmillan, *Tides of Fortune, 1945–55* (London, 1969), xv. See also Michael Barratt-Brown, *After Imperialism* (London, 1963), 136–38; *The Economist,* December 15, 1945, 850; Fred M. Vinson and Dean Acheson, *The British Loan— What It Means to Us,* January 12, 1946 [DS Commercial Policy Series 81] (Washington, 1946), 7; Gabriel Kolko, *The Politics of War* (New York, 1968), chaps. XII, XIX.

2. Seymour E. Harris, ed., *Foreign Economic Policy for the United States* (Cambridge, 1948), 82; Brookings Institution, International Studies Group, *Anglo-American Economic Relations: A Problem Paper* (Washington, 1950), 11–12; H. Bradford Westerfield, *The Instruments of America's Foreign Policy* (New York, 1963), 276; Kolko, *Politics of War,* 490–91; Keith Hutchison, *Rival Partners: America and Britain in the Post-War World* (New York, 1946), 145; *Business Week,* October 20, 1945, 114.

3. FR (1945), VI, 54.

4. *Ibid.,* 56, 75. See also *ibid.,* 55; Kolko, *Politics of War,* 491.

5. Macmillan, *Tides of Fortune,* 76. See also FR (1945), VI, 55–60, 79–105; Ross J. Pritchard, "Will Clayton: A Study of Business Statesmanship in the Formulation of the United States Foreign Economic Policy" (unpublished Ph.D. thesis, Fletcher School of Law and Diplomacy, 1955), 212; Kolko, *Politics of War,* 492.

6. Earl Attlee, *A Prime Minister Remembers* (London, 1961), 129–30.

7. FR (1945), VI, 121. See also *ibid.,* 110–21.

8. DS, *Anglo-American Financial and Commercial Agreements,* December 1945 (Washington, 1945), 3. See also FR (1945) VI, 123–94, 207–24; Richard N. Gardner, *Sterling-Dollar Diplomacy: Anglo-American Collaboration in the Reconstruction of Multilateral Trade* (Oxford, 1956), chaps. X, XI: R. F. Harrod, *The Life of John*

Maynard Keynes (New York, 1951), 496ff.; E. F. Penrose, *Economic Planning for the Peace* (Princeton, 1953), chap. XVIII; Harry S. Truman, *Year of Decisions* (New York, 1955), 477–80; Hugh Dalton, *High Tide and After: Memoirs 1945–1960* (London, 1962), 74–87.

9. *Economist,* December 15, 1945, 850. See also Harrod, *Life of Keynes,* 594ff.

10. L. S. Amery, *The Washington Loan Agreement: A Critical Study of American Economic Foreign Policy* (London, 1946), xi.

11. FR (1945), VI, 201–02. See also Macmillan, *Tides of Fortune,* 77–78; Penrose, *Economic Planning for the Peace,* 315; Leon D. Epstein, *Britain—Uneasy Ally* (Chicago, 1954), 37–44; Dalton, *Memoirs,* 87; *New Statesman and Nation,* December 15, 1945, 397–98.

12. Harry S. Truman, *Public Papers of the Presidents of the United States: 1946* (Washington, 1962), 98–99. See also John Foster Dulles to Arthur H. Vandenberg, December 17, 1945; Vandenberg to Dulles, December 19, 1945, AHV Mss.

13. Vinson and Acheson, *The British Loan,* 7.

14. Truman, *Public Papers: 1946,* 168. See also Dean Acheson, *The Credit to Britain: The Key to Expanded Trade,* February 1, 1946 [DS Commercial Policy Series 83] (Washington, 1946), *passim;* DSB, March 10, 1946, 381–84; DS, *International Trade and the British Loan* (Washington, 1946), *passim.*

15. *Business Week,* March 30, 1946, 47. See also James K. Vardaman, Jr., memo for the President, February 13, 1946, HST Mss, OF 212–A; Harry D. White speech of April 4, 1946, HDW Mss, file 26; Pritchard, "Will Clayton," 235–36; Clair Wilcox, speech of May 7, 1946, CW Mss.

16. Vandenberg to "Mr. President," April 17, 1946, 4, 6, AHV Mss. See also Bernard Baruch memo to William Clayton, April 17, 1946; Baruch to Pat McCarran, May 1, 1946, BB Mss; Margaret L. Coit, *Mr. Baruch* (Boston, 1957), 611.

17. *Business Week,* May 11, 1946, 103.

18. John Taber to Allen W. Dulles, July 13, 1946, JT Mss, box 77. See also William H. McNeill, *America, Britain, and Russia* (London, 1953), 686; memo of conversation, October 25, 1945, WLC Mss; U.S. House, Committee on Banking and Currency, *Hearings: Anglo-American Financial Agreement,* 79:2, May–June 1946 (Washington, 1946), *passim; Business Week,* July 6, 1946, 103; Gardner, *Sterling-Dollar Diplomacy,* 236, 248–52.

19. Gardner, *Sterling-Dollar Diplomacy,* 246.

20. FR (1945), VIII, 37, 51. See also *ibid.,* 34–53; Kolko, *Politics of War,* chaps. XII, XIX; George S. Messersmith to James F. Byrnes, December 5, 1945, GSM Mss; memo of conversation, May 29, 1945, JCG Mss; Leonard M. Fanning, *Foreign Oil and the Free World* (New York, 1954), 354; DSB, June 15, 1947, 1169–73; DSB, August 5, 1945, 173–75; *Business Week,* October 6, 1945, 26ff.

21. FR (1945), VIII, 45.

22. *Ibid.,* 955, 1214. See also *ibid.,* 895–993.

23. FR (1946), VII, 68.

24. DSB, June 15, 1947, 1171–73; *Business Week,* October 6, 1945, 26: FR (1945), VIII, 57–63; DSB, December 2, 1945, 894–95; FR (1946), VII, 31–45; U.S. Federal Trade Commission, *The International Petroleum Cartel,* August 22, 1952 (Washington, 1952), 101–05; Fanning, *Foreign Oil and the Free World,* 354.

25. Harry S. Truman, *Years of Trial and Hope* (New York, 1956), 95.

26. Leahy Diary, May 20, 1946, WDL Mss. See also *New Times,* January 1, 1947, 3–9; and for a comprehensive outline of United States policy see John A. Loftus, "Oil in United States Foreign Policy," DSB, August 11, 1946, 276–81.

27. For America in the larger regional strategy, see John Marlowe, *Arab Nationalism and British Imperialism: Study in Power Politics* (New York, 1961), 62; Joseph M. Jones, *The Fifteen Weeks: February 21–June 5, 1947* (New York, 1955), 43–47.

28. FR (1945), VIII, 95–96; DSB, November 11, 1945, 769; June 2, 1946, 932–35; June 30, 1946, 1119–20; December 15, 1946, 1078; December 29, 1946, 1163–64.

29. FR (1945), VI, 1291, 1304. See also *ibid.,* 1281ff.; "Statement made by Mr. Clair Wilcox to Representatives of the British Commonwealth of September 15, 1947," 5, CW Mss.

30. FR (1945), VI, 1404. See also *ibid.,* 1281–1415.

31. Report of Westmore Wilcox, August 16, 1945—May 19, 1946, in JF Mss, box 101.

32. FR (1945), IX, 384–431; FR (1946), XI, 191–219, 236, 256, 300; Messersmith to Byrnes, December 5, 1945; Messersmith to Spruille Braden, March 16, 1946, box 6; Messersmith to Byrnes, May 29, 1946, GSM Mss, box 4; Raul Sosa-Rodriguez, *Les Problèmes Structurels des Relations Économiques Internationales de l'Amérique Latine* (Geneva, 1963), 88, 118–19, 210; Kolko, *Politics of War,* 291–92; *Business Week,* June 1, 1946, 111; October 12, 1946, 14–15; January 11, 1947, 96; February 1, 1947, 100.

33. Messersmith to Byrnes, June 15, 1946, GSM Mss, box 4.

34. Messersmith to Dean Acheson, October 2, 1946, GSM Mss, box 4. See also FR (1946), XI, 257–58, 270, 273, 300; Harold F. Peterson, *Argentina and the United States, 1810–1960* (n.p.: State University of New York, 1964), 455–56; Messersmith to Byrnes, May 29, 1946; Messersmith to William B. Pawley, August 6, 1946; Messersmith to Dean Acheson, October 30, 1946; memo of December 10, 1946; Messersmith to Sumner Welles, March 12, 1947; Messersmith to George C. Marshall, March 31, 1947, GSM Mss, box 4; Messersmith memoir, vol. 3, GSM Mss, box 8.

35. U.S. House, Committee on Foreign Affairs, *Hearings: Inter-American Military Cooperation Act,* 79:2, May 28–29, 1946 (Washington, 1946), 17.

36. Robert Patterson to Dean Acheson, April 17, 1947, RP Mss, box 8. See also *Business Week,* February 1, 1947, 100; Peterson, *Argentina and the United States,* 446–58; Alberto A. Conil Paz and Gustavo E. Ferrari, *Argentina's Foreign Policy, 1930–1962* (Notre Dame, 1966), 134–43.

37. George Curry, *James S. Byrnes* (New York, 1965), 219; U.S. Congress, Joint Committee on the Economic Report, *Hearings: Foreign Economic Policy,* 84:1, November 9–17, 1955 (Washington, 1955), 175, 188–89, 215–17, 519; Gabriel Kolko, *The Roots of American Foreign Policy* (Boston, 1969), 74–75; DSB, September 22, 1946, 539–41; Hutchison, *Rival Partners,* 150.

38. FR (1945), VI, 1199, 1218. See also *ibid.,* 1199ff.; Kolko, *Politics of War,* 604–06.

39. Truman, *Public Papers: 1946,* 217.

40. Gardner, *Sterling-Dollar Diplomacy,* 353; Westerfield, *Instruments of America's Foreign Policy,* chap. XX; Kolko, *Politics of War,* 261; U.S. Commission on

Foreign Economic Policy, *Staff Papers* (Washington, 1954), 160, 168–70, 208; D. Gale Johnston, *Trade and Agriculture: A Study of Inconsistent Policies* (New York, 1950), 1–21; DSB, March 30, 1945, 509–10; June 30, 1945, 1119–20; FR (1945), VI, 128.

41. DS, *Proposals for Expansion of World Trade and Employment,* November 1945 (Washington, 1945), 11. See also Clair Wilcox, *A Charter for World Trade* (New York, 1949), 23; Gardner, *Sterling-Dollar Diplomacy,* 196–97.

42. DS, *Proposals for Expansion of World Trade,* 17. See also FR (1945), II, 1340–47.

43. FR (1945), II, 1355–56. See also *ibid.,* 1338–51.

44. DS, *Proposals for Expansion of World Trade,* 25.

45. DS, *Anglo-American Financial and Commercial Agreements,* 3. See also FR (1945), II, 1347–48; Wilcox, *Charter for World Trade,* 40; Gardner, *Sterling-Dollar Diplomacy,* 152.

46. Wilcox, *Charter for World Trade,* 34; Gardner, *Sterling-Dollar Diplomacy,* 136, 258–68; Harrod, *Life of Keynes,* 622–36.

47. International Bank for Reconstruction and Development, *The World Bank: Policies and Operations* (Washington, June 1960), 2–4, 14, 47, 67, 71–89; FR (1945), II, 1353–54; Harris, *Foreign Economic Policy,* 446–80; *Business Week,* September 7, 1946, 95.

48. DS, Office of Public Affairs, "Informal Commentary to Accompany Full Text Suggested Charter for an International Trade Organization of the United Nations," September 1946 (multilithed), 31, 47, CW Mss.

49. Clair Wilcox, ". . . Report to the Secretary of State . . . First Meeting of the Preparatory Committee for an International Conference on Trade and Employment," October 15—November 26, 1946, 1–4, CW Mss. See also DS, "Informal Commentary . . . for an International Trade Organization . . .," September 1946, 30–31, CW Mss; Gardner, *Sterling-Dollar Diplomacy,* chap. XIV; Wilcox, *Charter for World Trade,* 40–42.

50. Truman, *Public Papers: 1946,* 475. See also FR (1945), II, 1347; Pritchard, "Will Clayton," 325–27.

51. *Business Week,* January 25, 1947, 5. See also Truman to Edward A. O'Neil, December 9, 1946, HST Mss, OF 85; Vandenberg to Sinclair Weeks, January 3, 1947, AHV Mss; Pritchard, "Will Clayton," 329–30.

Chapter 4: Military Power and Foreign Policy, 1945–1946

1. Walter Millis, ed., *The Forrestal Diaries* (New York, 1951), 97; Gabriel Kolko, *The Politics of War* (New York, 1968), 480–81; memo on "Premises of Post-War Navy," n.d., JF Mss, box 23; Vincent Davis, *Post-War Defense Policy and the U.S. Navy, 1945–1946* (Chapel Hill, 1966), 18, 24–37, 101, 178.

2. DSB, March 10, 1946, 357. See also Samuel P. Huntington, *The Common Defense: Strategic Programs in National Politics* (New York, 1961), 35–36; Harry S. Truman, *Public Papers of the Presidents of the United States: 1945* (Washington, 1961), 431–33; U.S. House, Select Committee on Post-War Military Policy, *Hear-*

ings: *Universal Military Training,* 79:1, June 1945 (Washington, 1945), *passim;* Major John C. Sparrow, *History of Personnel De-mobilization in the United States Army* (Office of the Chief of Military History, Department of the Army, 1951), 376ff.

3. Harry S. Truman, *Years of Trial and Hope* (New York, 1956), 46–51; Davis, *Post-War Defense Policy,* 25, 222–30.

4. *Forrestal Diaries,* 160, 167–68, *passim;* Truman, *Years of Trial and Hope,* 37; James Powers Mallan, "Conservative Attitudes toward American Foreign Policy: With Special Reference to American Business, 1945–1952" (unpublished Ph.D. thesis, Harvard University, 1964), 80ff., chaps. VI, VII.

5. Arthur Smithies, Bureau of the Budget memo of 1946, "The Economic Situation in 1946, 1947 and Beyond," 7, in JF Mss, box 25.

6. *Forrestal Diaries,* 162, 236–39, 245–46; Merton J. Peck and Frederic M. Scherer, *The Weapons Acquisition Process* (Boston, 1962), 100; Robert Patterson to Julius O. Adler, November 2, 1946, RP Mss; DSB, March 2, 1947, 390–91.

7. Huntington, *The Common Defense,* 44–45, 369–78; Truman, *Years of Trial and Hope,* 53–55; Robert Patterson to Herbert Bayard Swope, February 9, 1947, RP Mss, box 8; Truman to Henry Stimson, September 6, 1950, HLS Mss; Clarence G. Lasby, "Project Paper Clip: German Scientists Come to America," *Virginia Quarterly Review,* 42 (1966), 366–77; Edward L. Bowles, "National Security and the Mechanism for Its Achievement," ca. April 1946, in HLS Mss.

8. Eisenhower, memorandum: "Scientific and Technological Resources as Military Assets," April 27, 1946, in HLS Mss. See also Edward L. Bowles to Stimson, May 3, 1946, HLS Mss.

9. DS, *The International Control of Atomic Energy: Growth of a Policy* (Washington, 1947), 11. See also Kolko, *Politics of War,* 542–43, 560–61; FR (1945), II, 36–40.

10. Memo of June 6, 1945, HLS Mss; FR (1945), II, 40–44; Earl Attlee, *A Prime Minister Remembers* (London, 1961), 97–101; Harry S. Truman, *Year of Decisions* (New York, 1955), 526–27; Stimson Diary, September 12, 13, 1945, HLS Mss.

11. FR (1945), II, 48–60; FR (1945), V, 884–86; Kolko, *Politics of War,* 538; memo to the President, "Atomic Bomb," October 1, 1945, JF Mss, box 2; DS, *Control of Atomic Energy,* 112; Richard G. Hewlett and Oscar E. Anderson, *The New World, 1939–1946* (University Park, Pa., 1962), 456–57; Truman, *Year of Decisions,* 534; Attlee, *A Prime Minister Remembers,* 102ff.; Hugh Dalton, *High Tide and After* (London, 1962), 58.

12. FR (1945), II, 71. See also *ibid.,* 69–70; Attlee, *A Prime Minister Remembers,* 110–13; Hewlett and Anderson, *The New World,* 480–81; Leslie R. Groves, *Now It Can Be Told* (New York, 1962), 401–06; David E. Lilienthal, *The Atomic Energy Years, 1945–1950* (New York, 1964), 26; Dean Acheson, *Present at the Creation* (New York, 1969), 164–68.

13. FR (1945), II, 73. See also Hewlett and Anderson, *The New World,* 460–63; V. Bush to Stimson, November 13, 1945, HLS Mss.

14. DS, *Control of Atomic Energy,* 4–5, 18, 27–30, 118–20; FR (1945), II, 85–89, 96, 663–64, 740–47, 756, 760–63, 823–24; FR (1945), V, 923, 928, 934; Hewlett and Anderson, *The New World,* 472–73; *Forrestal Diaries,* 124; Forrestal to Byrnes,

December 11, 1945, JF Mss, box 2; Vandenberg to C. E. Hutchinson, December 29, 1945, AHV Mss.

15. Hewlett and Anderson, *The New World,* 532–34, 548; Lilienthal, *Atomic Energy Years,* 10–12; DS, *A Report on the International Control of Atomic Energy,* March 16, 1946 (Washington, 1946), 4, 26, *passim.*

16. Baruch to Ickes, March 26, 1946, BB Mss. See also Lilienthal, *Atomic Energy Years,* 30–31; Bernhard B. Bechhoefer, *Postwar Negotiations for Arms Control* (Washington, 1961), 37–40. And especially see the criticisms of P. M. S. Blackett, *Fear, War, and the Bomb* (New York, 1949), chap. IX.

17. F. Eberstadt to Baruch, May 23, 1946, BB Mss. See also DS, *Control of Atomic Energy,* 48–49; Hewlett and Anderson, *The New World,* 556–58; Margaret L. Coit, *Mr. Baruch* (Boston, 1957), 575–76; Robert G. Gard, Jr., "Arms Control Policy Formulation and Negotiation: 1945–1946" (unpublished Ph.D. thesis, Harvard University, 1961), 350–60; Eberstadt to Baruch, March 28, 1946; "JMH Notes of Meeting of May 8, 1946"; John M. Hancock to Byrnes, June 1, 1946, all in BB Mss.

18. Truman, *Years of Trial and Hope,* 10. See also Baruch to Lilienthal. May 27, 1946, BB Mss; Hewlett and Anderson, *The New World,* 472–74; Coit, *Baruch,* 578–81; Gard, "Arms Control Policy Formulation," 370–73; Truman to Baruch, June 7, 1946, and accompanying memo of June 7, BB Mss; Baruch to Stimson, June 3, 1946, HLS Mss; Lilienthal, *Atomic Energy Years,* 42–44, 49–51, 58–59; Acheson, *Present at the Creation,* 154–56.

19. Spaatz to Baruch, [June, 1946], BB Mss.

20. DS, *Documents on Disarmament, 1945–1959* (Washington, 1960), I, 13. See also *ibid.,* 6–16; Hewlett and Anderson, *The New World,* 575–76; Admiral Ernest J. King to Baruch, June 5, 1946; Admiral Carl Spaatz to Baruch, [June, 1946]; Admiral C. W. Nimitz to Baruch, June 11, 1946; William D. Leahy to Baruch, June 11, 1946; General Dwight D. Eisenhower to Baruch, June 14, 1946, all in BB Mss.

21. Baruch to W. M. Jeffers, June 25, 1946, BB Mss. See also Acheson to Baruch, July 15, 1946, BB Mss; DS, *Documents on Disarmament,* I, 17–24; Truman, *Years of Trial and Hope,* 11.

22. Truman to Baruch, July 10, 1946, BB Mss. See also Baruch to Robert Patterson, July 1, 1946; cable from Walter B. Smith to Byrnes, June 26, 1946; Acheson to Baruch, July 1, 1946; Baruch to John M. Vorys, August 2, 1946, all in BB Mss; Gard, "Arms Control Policy Formulation," 394; FR (1946), VI, 764–66.

23. Minutes of U.S. Delegation Staff Meeting, September 10, 1946, BB Mss. See also Barton J. Bernstein and Allen J. Matusow, eds., *The Truman Administration: A Documentary History* (New York, 1966), 238–43; DS, *Control of Atomic Energy,* 55–73; Coit, *Baruch,* 593–94.

24. Coit, *Baruch,* 596. See also Bechhoefer, *Postwar Negotiations for Arms Control,* 47–48; Blackett, *Fear, War, and the Bomb,* 173–74.

25. Minutes of Staff Meeting, September 10, 1946, BB Mss.

26. Baruch to Acheson, November 2, 1946, BB Mss. See also Arthur Krock, *Memoirs: Sixty Years on the Firing Line* (New York, 1968), 470; Franklin A. Lindsay to Baruch, October 21, 1946; Baruch to Byrnes, November 4, 1946, in BB Mss; V. M. Molotov, *Problems of Foreign Policy* (Moscow, 1949), 258–67.

27. Baruch to Byrnes, November 4, 1946, BB Mss.

28. Molotov, *Problems of Foreign Policy,* 314–15. See also *ibid.,* 272–339.

29. Coit, *Baruch,* 603. See also *Forrestal Diaries,* 217, 220–21; Walter Lippmann to James Forrestal, November 11, 1946; memo of telephone conversation between Forrestal and Lippmann, November 29, 1946, JF Mss, box 68; transcript of telephone conversation between Baruch and Acheson, November 26, 1946; Baruch to Byrnes, December 8, 1946; Baruch to William H. Chamberlain, December 11, 1946, BB Mss; FR (1946), VI, 807.

30. Bechhoefer, *Postwar Negotiations for Arms Control,* 99. See also *ibid.,* 52–101; Coit, *Baruch,* 605–07; Lilienthal, *Atomic Energy Years,* 130; *Forrestal Diaries,* 241; Allen W. Dulles, "Disarmament in the Atomic Age," *Foreign Affairs,* 25 (1947), 204–16; Frederic R. Coudert to Stimson, January 6, 1947; Baruch to Stimson, February 10, 1947; George Roberts to Stimson, June 10, 1947; Warren R. Austin to Stimson, January 25, 1947, all in HLS Mss; Baruch to George C. Marshall, August 12, 1948, BB Mss; Leahy Diary, July 18, 1947, WDL Mss.

Chapter 5: The Future of Germany

1. FR (The Conferences at Malta and Yalta, 1945), 191. See also Gabriel Kolko, *The Politics of War* (New York, 1968), chap. XIII.

2. Quoted in John Gimbel, *The American Occupation of Germany: Politics and the Military, 1945–1949* (Stanford, 1968), 6. See also Kolko, *Politics of War,* 512–14; Harold Zink, *The United States in Germany, 1944–1955* (Princeton, 1957), 253; Memo of July 3, 1945, HLS Mss.

3. FR (The Conference of Berlin, 1945), II, 1485. See also Kolko, *Politics of War,* 514–21.

4. Manuel Gottlieb, *The German Peace Settlement and the Berlin Crisis* (New York, 1960), *passim;* Kolko, *Politics of War,* 569–75; Robert Murphy, *Diplomat among Warriors* (New York, 1964), 286–87; Lucius D. Clay, *Decision in Germany* (New York, 1950), 42–43; F. Roy Willis, *The French in Germany, 1945–1949* (Stanford, 1962), 26–29; FR (1945), III, 844, 871, 886, 890, *passim.*

5. General G. S. Patton, Jr., to Henry L. Stimson, September 1, 1945, HLS Mss; Clay, *Decision in Germany,* 41, 62–63; Gimbel, *American Occupation of Germany,* 11, 21–22; D. U. Ratchford and William B. Ross, *Berlin Reparations Assignment* (Chapel Hill, 1947), 9ff.; W. Friedmann, *The Allied Military Government of Germany* (London, 1947), 43; Murphy, *Diplomat among Warriors,* 288; Walter Rundell, Jr., *Black Market Money* (Baton Rouge, 1964), 48–49. The details of Dodge's role are to be found in JMD Mss, Germany Assignment, boxes 1–7.

6. DSB, September 2, 1945, 309. See also Frank L. Howley Diary, July 1, 1945 —July 1, 1946, 42–92, FLH Mss; FR (1945), III, 1251.

7. FR (Conference of Berlin), II, 1506. See also FR (1945), III, 1295.

8. FR (1945), III, 1254, 1284, 1295; Gimbel, *American Occupation of Germany,* 27.

9. FR (1945), III, 1320–21.

10. *Ibid.,* 1320–21, 1331, 1337, 1342–43; Ratchford and Ross, *Berlin Reparations Assignment,* 37.

11. Byron Price, memo to the President, November 11, 1945, HST Mss, OF 198. See also FR (1945), III, 879, 886, 989, 1019; General Dwight D. Eisenhower to Forrestal, January 19, 1946, JF Mss, box 19; Byrnes to Truman, November 12, 1945; Eisenhower to Truman, October 26, 1945, HST Mss, OF 198; Gimbel, *American Occupation of Germany*, 20–22.

12. DSB, December 16, 1945, 962. See also FR (1945), III, 1350–52; Ratchford and Ross, *Berlin Reparations Assignment*, 78ff.; Gimbel, *American Occupation of Germany*, 27; Paul Y. Hammond, "Directives for the Occupation of Germany: The Washington Controversy," *American Civil-Military Decisions* (Montgomery, 1963), 439–40.

13. DSB, December 16, 1945, 964–65; Hammond, "Directives for the Occupation of Germany," 438–41; Gimbel, *American Occupation of Germany*, 31–34; FR (1945), III, 1369, 1485–86, 1499–1502; Ratchford and Ross, *Berlin Reparations Assignment*, 109–15; DS, Office of Research and Intelligence, Division of Research for Europe, "The German Standard of Living and Industrial Capacity Available for Reparations," December 6, 1945, R. and A. 3383 (mimeo), iv, *passim*.

14. DS, *Germany, 1947–1949: The Story in Documents* (Washington, 1950), 28. See also Kolko, *Politics of War*, 507–11; DS, Office of Research and Intelligence, "Status and Prospects of German Trade-Unions and Works Councils," May 27, 1946, R. and A. 3381 (mimeo), 15–26; Gottlieb, *German Peace Settlement*, 71; Lewis J. Edinger, *Kurt Schumacher: A Study in Political Behavior* (Stanford, 1965), 95–96; Friedmann, *Allied Military Government*, 156–58; Franz L. Neumann, "German Democracy 1950," *International Conciliation*, No. 461 (May 1950), 269–70.

15. FR (1945), III, 982.

16. DS, *Occupation of Germany: Policy and Progress, 1945–46* (Washington, 1947), 54.

17. Konrad Adenauer, *Memoirs, 1945–53* (Chicago, 1966), 35–36, 42, 49–51; Charles Wighton, *Adenauer—Democratic Dictator* (London, 1963), 35–40, 49, 84–85.

18. Edinger, *Schumacher, passim;* Raymond Ebsworth, *Restoring Democracy in Germany* (London, 1960), 25–27; DS, *Occupation of Germany*, 53–56.

19. FR (1945), III, 1008–09; Gimbel, *American Occupation of Germany*, 36–37, 44–45; DS, *Occupation of Germany*, 55.

20. Gimbel, *American Occupation of Germany*, 101–10; Friedmann, *Allied Military Government*, 113–22; Clay, *Decision in Germany*, 69–70; FR (1945), III, 971–94; John D. Montgomery, *Forced to Be Free* (Chicago, 1957), 18, 62, 80; Murphy, *Diplomat among Warriors*, 284–85; Gottlieb, *German Peace Settlement*, 72–74; Neumann, "German Democracy 1950," 264.

21. DS, *Germany, 1947–1949*, 26.

22. Frank Howley, *Berlin Command* (New York, 1950), 116. See also *ibid.*, 155–56; New York *Times*, April 29, 1955; Clay, *Decision in Germany*, 64–65.

23. Howley Diary, 1945–1946, 263, FLH Mss.

24. Office of the U.S. High Commissioner for Germany, Office of Public Affairs, *Trends in German Public Opinion, 1946 thru 1949* (n.p., 1950?), 5.

25. The key source on decartelization is U.S. Army, Special Committee to Study

Decartelization and Deconcentration in Germany, "Report to the Honorable Secretary of the Army, April 15, 1949" (n.p., mimeo), 63–73, 80–100; see also James Stewart Martin, *All Honorable Men* (Boston, 1950), *passim;* Documentation Française, *La Récartellisation dans la République Fédérale Allemande* [série economique] (Paris, 1959), *passim;* Documentation Française, *Allemagne: Ententes et Monopoles dans le Monde* [série economique] (Paris, 1952), *passim;* U.S. House, Committee on the Judiciary, *Hearings: Study of Monopoly Power,* 81:1 (Washington, 1950), part 2–A, 430; Clay, *Decision in Germany,* 327–29.

26. FR (1946), V, 683–89; Clarence G. Lasby, "Project Paper Clip: German Scientists Come to America," *Virginia Quarterly Review,* 42 (1966), 366–77.

27. Kolko, *Politics of War,* 508–09; Edinger, *Schumacher,* 95ff.; Friedmann, *Allied Military Government,* 128–29; Gottlieb, *German Peace Settlement,* 43–46; Wolfgang Leonhard, *Child of the Revolution* (Chicago, 1958), 299ff.; J. P. Nettl, *The Eastern Zone and Soviet Policy in Germany, 1945–50* (London, 1951), 55–85; Beate Ruhm von Oppen, ed., *Documents on Germany under Occupation, 1945–1954* (London, 1955), 37–38; Hermann Weber, ed., *Der deutsche Kommunismus: Dokumente* (Köln, 1963), 431ff., 453, 553–55.

28. Robert Slusser, ed., *Soviet Economic Policy in Post-War Germany* (New York, 1953), 1–41; Gottlieb, *German Peace Settlement,* 47–49, 222; Friedmann, *Allied Military Government,* 25–26, 40ff.; Leonhard, *Child of the Revolution,* 345.

29. Gottlieb, *German Peace Settlement,* 54–57; Nettl, *Eastern Zone and Soviet Policy,* 85–86, 172–73, 181; Ruhm von Oppen, *Documents on Germany,* 59–64; Friedmann, *Allied Military Government,* 138, 182–84; FR (1945), III, 1049; Weber, *Der deutsche Kommunismus,* 609–11.

30. FR (1945), III, 1072, 1078. See also *ibid.,* 1065–66; Friedmann, *Allied Military Government,* 138–39; Gottlieb, *German Peace Settlement,* 58–65; DS, "Status and Prospects of German Trade-Unions," 28–43.

31. Gottlieb, *German Peace Settlement,* 80; U.S. Office of Military Government, Berlin District, "Historical Report: Berlin Press Review," Annex F, November 13, 1945 and *passim,* FLH Mss; FR (1945), III, 1056; Edinger, *Schumacher,* 100, 176–77; Albrecht Kaden, *Einheit oder Freiheit: Die Widergründung der SPD, 1945–46* (Hannover, 1964), 256, *passim;* Philip Windsor, *City of Leave: A History of Berlin, 1945–1962* (New York, 1963), 70; Leonhard, *Child of the Revolution,* 350–59; Friedmann, *Allied Military Government,* 77–79, 130; Ruhm von Oppen, *Documents on Germany,* 121–25; Weber, *Der deutsche Kommunismus,* 459, 514; Nettl, *Eastern Zone and Soviet Policy,* 100–03.

32. Howley Diary, July 1945—July 1946, 11–12, FLH Mss. See also Kolko, *Politics of War,* 510–11.

33. FR (1946), V, 517. See also *ibid.,* 505–07, 528, 703–26; FR (1945), III, 1038–56; Michael Balfour and John Mair, *Four-Power Control in Germany and Austria, 1945–1946* (London, 1956), 207, 245; Ruhm von Oppen, *Documents on Germany,* 118–20.

34. FR (1946), V, 517–19. For a similar interpretation, see Edward S. Mason, "Reflections on the Moscow Conference," *International Organization,* 1 (1947), 483.

35. Gimbel, *American Occupation of Germany,* 58; FR(1945), III, 1485, 1499;

FR (1946), V, 42–86, 490–98, 500–48; Ratchford and Ross, *Berlin Reparations Assignment,* 115, 127, 144–45, 172–78; Ruhm von Oppen, *Documents on Germany,* 113–18; Adenauer, *Memoirs,* 55–57; Martin, *All Honorable Men,* 193–94; Gottlieb, *German Peace Settlement,* 138, 241.

36. Quoted in Gimbel, *American Occupation of Germany,* 75.

37. Clay, *Decision in Germany,* 293. See also FR (1946), V, 535, 555–56; Friedmann, *Allied Military Government,* 196.

38. FR (1946), V, 779. See also *ibid.,* 775–77; Friedmann, *Allied Military Government,* 142–45; John Gimbel, "American Military Government and the Education of a New German Leadership," *Political Science Quarterly,* 83 (1968), 253; Gottlieb, *German Peace Settlement,* 78–79.

39. FR (1946), V, 539–44; Thomas C. Blaisdell, Jr., "Re-establishing Economic Life on the European Continent," February 22, 1945; Blaisdell, "Proposal for the Ruhr," July 1946, TCB Mss, box 7; *Business Week,* August 9, 1947, 89.

40. FR (1946), V, 545–48; Gimbel, *American Occupation of Germany,* 57–61; Gottlieb, *German Peace Settlement,* 123–28; Clay, *Decision in Germany,* 120–24. For the definitive study of the reparations issue, see the forthcoming book by Bruce Kuklick, Cornell University Press.

41. FR (1946), V, 551, 554.

42. Clay, *Decision in Germany,* 123.

43. Brigadier General Frank J. McSherry, memo to Colm and Goldsmith, May 17, 1946, JMD Mss, Germany Assignment, box 3. See also FR (1946), V, 557–58; S. L. Klepper to Dodge, April 16, 1946, JMD Mss, Germany Assignment, box 5; Second Draft of "A Plan for the Liquidation of War Finance and the Financial Rehabilitation of Germany," JMD Mss, Germany Assignment, box 3; Raymond Goldsmith to Dodge, October 29, 1946, JMD Mss, Germany Assignment, box 1; Dodge to Clay, May 16, 1946, JMD Mss, Germany Assignment, box 5.

44. Clay, *Decision in Germany,* 73–78; James F. Byrnes, *Speaking Frankly* (New York, 1947), 171–76; Arthur H. Vandenberg, ed., *The Private Papers of Senator Vandenberg* (Boston, 1952), 263ff., 281–84; FR (1946), II, 146–47, 166–73, 431–32; FR (1946), V, 561; V. M. Molotov, *Problems of Foreign Policy* (Moscow, 1949), 45–47.

45. Dodge to Robert D. Murphy, July 2, 1946, JMD Mss, Germany Assignment, box 2. See also Molotov, *Problems of Foreign Policy,* 55–68; *Private Papers of Senator Vandenberg,* 297; Vandenberg Diary, Paris Peace Conference, July 10, 1946, AHV Mss; FR (1946), V, 576–80, 585; George Curry, *James F. Byrnes* (New York, 1965), 74–78; Clay, *Decision in Germany,* 165–68.

46. Clay, *Decision in Germany,* 124. See also *ibid.,* 131.

Chapter 6: The Political Economy of Western Europe, 1945–1946

1. Gabriel Kolko, *The Politics of War* (New York, 1968), 436–39; U.S. Department of Agriculture, Office of Foreign Agricultural Relations, *World Food Situation, 1946–47,* November 4, 1946 (Washington, 1946), 5; George H. Hildebrand, *Growth and Structure in the Economy of Modern Italy* (Cambridge, 1965), 17;

Harold Macmillan, *Tides of Fortune, 1945–55* (London, 1969), 3–4; Harry L. Coles and Albert K. Weinberg, *Civil Affairs: Soldiers Become Governors* (Washington, 1964), chap. XIX; FR (1945), IV, 984–85.

2. Giuseppe Mammarella, *Italy after Fascism: A Political History, 1943–1965* (Notre Dame, 1966), 90–107; FR (1945), IV, 987–91, 1283–84, 1309–19; DSB, December 9, 1945, 936.

3. FR (1946), V, 916. See also *ibid.*, 891–92, 899, 904, 907, 937; Mammarella, *Italy after Fascism*, 121–30; Norman Kogan, *A Political History of Postwar Italy* (New York, 1966), 35–36; Lamar Fleming, Jr., to Clayton, May 18, 1945; Clayton to Fleming, May 22, 1945, WLC Mss.

4. FR(1946), V, 436.

5. FR (1946), V, 849–50, 865–67, 931, 934–35; Mammarella, *Italy after Fascism*, 116, 122, 134–39; Vandenberg Diary, Paris Peace Conference, June 18, 1946, AHV Mss; "Memorandum of Proposal to Make Non-Troop Pay Dollars Available to Italy," July 25, 1945, JWS Mss; United Nations, Department of Economic Affairs, *Economic Survey of Europe in 1948* (Geneva, 1949), 4, 17; Department of Agriculture, *World Food Situation, 1946–47,* 5; Hildebrand, *Economy of Modern Italy,* 157; Tarchini memo to John Taber October 28, 1947, JT Mss, box 128.

6. Tarchini to Taber, October 28, 1947, JT Mss, box 128; Mammarella, *Italy after Fascism,* 130; Bruno Foa, *Monetary Reconstruction in Italy* (New York, 1949), 41–42; FR (1946), V, 942–50.

7. Kolko, *Politics of War,* 439–45; FR (1945), IV, 765–73; La Documentation Française, *La Politique Économique Américaine et l'Aide à la France* [Notes Doc. et Études No. 726], 18 Septembre 1947 (Paris, 1947), 16.

8. Branko Lazitch, *Les Partis Communistes d'Europe, 1919–1955* (Paris, 1956), 194; Georgette Elgey, *La République des Illusions: 1945–1951* (Paris, 1965), 71–72; FR (1946), V, 509–10; Shepard B. Clough, "Economic Planning in a Capitalist Society: France from Monnet to Hirsh," *Political Science Quarterly,* 71 (1956), 542.

9. Maurice Thorez, *Oeuvres* (Paris, 1963), XXI, 243. See also La Documentation Française, *La Politique Économique Américaine,* 16; FR (1946), V, 399–400, 407.

10. Thorez, *Oeuvres,* XXI, 247. See also *ibid.*, 231–46; Thorez, *Oeuvres* (Paris, 1964), XXII, 16–20, 37–39, 83–89, 213; Thorez, *Oeuvres* (Paris, 1965), XXIII, 12, 27, 39–40.

11. Thorez, *Oeuvres,* XXII, 24, 80–81, 224; XXIII, 14–15, 20, 33, 52–54; André Marty, *L'Affaire Marty* (Paris, 1955), 171–73; Jacques Fauvet, *Histoire du Parti Communiste Français* (Paris, 1965), 175–86; Jean Planchais, *Une Histoire Politique de l'Armée: 1940–1967* (Paris, 1967), 115–20; Jacques Duclos, *Batailles pour la République* (Paris, 1947), *passim;* Clough, "Economic Planning in a Capitalist Society," 542–47; Val R. Lorwin, *The French Labor Movement* (Cambridge, 1954), 103–07.

12. FR (1946), V, 413. See also *ibid.*, 411.

13. *Ibid.*, 421–22, 425, 432–34, 440–46, 461–62; Elgey, *La République des Illusions,* 137; Alexander Werth, *France, 1940–1955* (New York, 1956), 314–15; La Documentation Française, *La Politique Économique Américaine,* 19–22.

14. FR (1946), V, 434, 436.

15. Vandenberg Diary, May 7, 1946, AHV Mss. See also FR (1946), V, 436–39, 447; Walter Millis, ed., *The Forrestal Diaries* (New York, 1951), 157–58.

16. DS, Intelligence Research Report, "European Reconstruction Survey: France. Preliminary Draft," OCL 3793.1, August 19, 1946 (n.p., 1946), 25. See also Elgey, *La République des Illusions,* 210–12; United Nations, *Economic Survey of Europe in 1948,* 4, 17; Department of Agriculture, *World Food Situation, 1946–47,* 5; United Nations, Department of Economic Affairs, *Recent Developments in the World Economic Situation* (New York, 1949), 24; Lorwin, *French Labor Movement,* 113; Thorez, *Oeuvres,* XXII, 83.

17. Quoted in Lorwin, *French Labor Movement,* 107.

18. *Ibid.;* Thorez, *Oeuvres,* XXII, 213; XXIII, 27; Lazitch, *Les Partis Communistes,* 194; DS, "European Reconstruction Survey," 17–18; DS, Office of Intelligence Research, "The Monnet Four-Year Plan for the French Economy," OIR Report No. 4287, February 28, 1947 (n.p., 1947), *passim.*

19. FR (1946), V, 472–73, 479. See also *ibid.,* 459.

20. *Ibid.,* 473–76; Elgey, *La République des Illusions,* 231–35; Thorez, *Oeuvres,* XXIII, 9–18; *Soviet Press Translations,* February 15, 1947, 4–5.

21. *Business Week,* November 23, 1946, 113.

22. Kolko, *Politics of War,* 496–99; George Woodbridge, *UNRRA: The History of the United Nations Relief and Rehabilitation Administration* (New York, 1950), I, 47, III, 428–29; Herbert Hoover, *An American Epic* (Chicago, 1964), IV, 116.

23. FR (1945), II, 1026–57; Mark W. Clark, *Calculated Risk* (New York, 1950), 474–75; E. F. Penrose, *Economic Planning for the Peace* (Princeton, 1953), 322; Robert Patterson to Dean Acheson, August 29, 1946, RP Mss, box 7; Bela Gold, *Wartime Economic Planning in Agriculture: A Study in the Allocation of Resources* (New York, 1949), 446–54; Department of Agriculture, *World Food Situation, 1946–47,* 4–5; *Fortune,* May 1946, 89–95.

24. Gold, *Planning in Agriculture,* 455, 463–78; Lewis P. Lochner, *Herbert Hoover and Germany* (New York, 1960), chap. X; Hoover, *American Epic,* 105–17; Allen J. Matusow, *Farm Policies and Politics in the Truman Years* (Cambridge, 1967), chaps. I–III; and relevant correspondence in HST Mss, OF 426.

25. Hoover, *American Epic,* IV, 197; Gold, *Planning in Agriculture,* 460–61; *Fortune,* May 1946, 95; Hoover to Robert T. Patterson, February 9, 1948, HLS Mss; Woodbridge, *UNRRA,* I, 46; Ross J. Pritchard, "Will Clayton: A Study of Business Statesmanship in the Formulation of the United States Foreign Economic Policy" (unpublished Ph.D. thesis, Fletcher School of Law and Diplomacy, 1955), 256; Penrose, *Economic Planning for the Peace,* 335–38; David Wightman, *Economic Co-operation in Europe: A Study of the United Nations Mission for Europe* (London, 1956), 12–15; FR (1946), V, 366; DSB, December 15, 1946, 1107–08.

26. *Business Week,* October 20, 1945, 113–16; May 25, 1946, 109; June 8, 1946, 107–108; September 7, 1946, 95; September 21, 1946, 109; December 14, 1946, 113–14; Henry Chalmers, *World Trade Policies* (Berkeley, 1953), 366–70; *Newsweek,* May 26, 1947, 82; DSB, September 15, 1946, 506–07.

27. Chalmers, *World Trade Policies,* 368–69; Thomas Balogh, *The Dollar Crisis: Causes and Cures* (Oxford, 1950), 46; United Nations, Department of Economic

Affairs, *A Survey of the Economic Situation and Prospects of Europe* (Geneva, 1948), 40–41; United Nations, *Economic Survey of Europe in 1948*, 4; Manuel Gottlieb, *The German Peace Settlement and the Berlin Crisis* (New York, 1960), 83–84; Robert E. Asher, *Grants, Loans and Local Currencies* (Washington, 1961), 72; Miroslav A. Kriz, "Postwar International Lending," *Essays in International Finance*, No. 8 (Spring 1947), 24–25; *Business Week*, July 20, 1946, 109–10.

28. FR (1945), II, 1411–54; Thomas C. Blaisdell, Jr., "The European Recovery Program—Phase Two," *International Organization*, September 1948, 444–45; F. T. Williamson to Laurence A. Steinhardt, August 1, 1946, LAS Mss, box 51; Wightman, *Economic Co-operation in Europe*, 4–5; draft notes of October 18, 1946; Ted Geiger to N. Van D. Cleveland, November 27, 1946, TCB Mss, box 7.

29. Blaisdell to Clayton, October 1, 1946, TCB Mss, box 7.

30. Blaisdell to Paul Porter, December 20, 1946, TCB Mss, box 7. See also Blaisdell to Clayton, October 1, 1946, TCB Mss, box 7.

31. Blaisdell to Clayton, October 1, 1946, TCB Mss, box 7.

32. Wightman, *Economic Co-operation in Europe*, 20–21; Ted Geiger to H. Van D. Cleveland, November 22, 1946, TCB Mss, box 7.

33. Clay to Joseph M. Dodge, July 31, 1946, JMD Mss, Germany Assignment, box 1. See also United Kingdom, Secretary of State for Foreign Affairs, *Selected Documents on Germany and the Question of Berlin, 1944–1961* (London, 1961), 66; Konrad Adenauer, *Memoirs, 1945–53* (Chicago, 1966), 81–82; FR (1946), V, 585–89, 606.

34. John C. deWilde to Dodge, August 8, 1946, JMD Mss, Germany Assignment, box 1. See also John Gimbel, *The American Occupation of Germany* (Stanford, 1968), 76–79; Thomas C. Blaisdell, Jr., "Proposal for the Ruhr," July 1946, TCB Mss, box 7.

35. DS, *Germany, 1947–49* (Washington, 1950), 8. See also James F. Byrnes, *Speaking Frankly* (New York, 1947), 187–92; Robert Murphy, *Diplomat among Warriors* (New York, 1964), 302–03; Lucius D. Clay, *Decision in Germany* (New York, 1950), 78–79.

36. DS, *Germany, 1947–1949*, 5—7. See also *ibid.*, 4–5; Clay, *Decision in Germany*, 79.

37. FR (1946), V, 603–04. See also Byrnes, *Speaking Frankly*, 193.

38. FR (1946), V, 587–95, 602–03; Beate Ruhm von Oppen, ed., *Documents on Germany under Occupation, 1945–1954* (London, 1955), 161–63; Benjamin J. Cohen, "Reparations in the Postwar Period: A Survey," *Banca Nazionale del Lavoro Quarterly Review*, September 1967, 282.

39. FR (1946), V, 622—23, 625. See also *ibid.*, 611–12, 622, 792–93.

40. Gerhard Colm to Joseph M. Dodge, September 9, 1946; Raymond Goldsmith to Dodge, October 29, 1946, JMD Mss, Germany Assignment, box 1. See also FR (1946), V, 628–32.

41. Joseph V. Stalin, *Post-War International Relations* (London: Soviet News, 1947), 15–16.

42. Clay, *Decision in Germany*, 293. See also *ibid.*, 168–69; Ruhm von Oppen, *Documents on Germany*, 184, 191; FR (1946), V, 606, 619; W. Friedmann, *The Allied Military Government of Germany* (London, 1947), 81–89, 199; Gimbel,

American Occupation of Germany, 84–85, 93, 99–100; DS, *Occupation of Germany: Policy and Progress, 1945–46* (Washington, 1947), 57.

43. Clay to Dodge, December 23, 1946, JMD Mss, Germany Assignment, box 1. See also Gottlieb, *German Peace Settlement,* 173; A. N. Overby memo, August 28, 1946, JWS Mss; Byrnes, *Speaking Frankly,* 196; Clay, *Decision in Germany,* 172; FR (1946), V, 636–44; DS, *Germany, 1947–49,* 450–53.

44. Ruhm von Oppen, *Documents on Germany,* 201.

45. W. A. Harriman to W. L. Batt, December 20, 1946, DC Mss, file 104894.

46. Lochner, *Herbert Hoover and Germany,* 177–78; Gimbel, *American Occupation of Germany,* 103–10; Howley Diary, July 1946—July 1947, July 23, 1946, FLH Mss; Dodge to Lucius Clay, August 2, 1946; Clay to Dodge, August 11, 1946, JMD Mss, Germany Assignment, box 1; James Stewart Martin, *All Honorable Men* (Boston, 1950), 176; U.S. Army, Special Committee to Study Decartelization and Deconcentration in Germany, "Report to the Honorable Secretary of the Army, April 15, 1949" (n.p., mimeo), *passim;* Thomas Blaisdell to William Clayton, October 1, 1946, TCB Mss, box 7.

Chapter 7: The Transformation of Eastern Europe, 1945–1947

1. Joseph C. Harsch, *The Curtain Isn't Iron* (New York, 1950), 136–37; United Nations Food and Agricultural Organization, *Report of the FAO Mission for Poland* (Washington, 1948), 5, 12; François Fejtö, *Histoire des Démocraties Populaires: L'Ère de Staline* (Paris, 1969), 130–38; Hugh Seton-Watson, *The East European Revolution* (New York, 1956), 232–33; United Nations, Economic and Social Council (ECOSOC), *Preliminary Report of the Temporary Sub-Commission on Economic Reconstruction of Devastated Areas* (London, 1946), 34, 137–51.

2. Vernon Bartlett, *East of the Iron Curtain* (New York, 1950), 85; R. R. Betts, ed., *Central and South East Europe, 1945–1948* (London, 1950), 197; Emil Lengyel and Joseph C. Harsch, *East Europe Today* (New York, 1949), 28–29, 53–54; Fejtö, *Histoire des Démocraties Populaires,* 139.

3. Quoted in Irving Brant, *The New Poland* (New York, 1946), 62.

4. FR (1946), VI, 347. See also Sheila G. Duff *et al, Czechoslovakia: Six Studies in Reconstruction* (London, ca. 1947), 48–51.

5. John Scott, "Report on Poland," June 1, 1947, 10, LAS Mss, box 55.

6. FR (1945), V, 377. See also Fejtö, *Histoire des Démocraties Populaires,* 141; Seton-Watson, *East European Revolution,* 266.

7. Seton-Watson, *East European Revolution,* 265, 273.

8. *Fortune,* May, 1946, 89–95.

9. Harry S. Truman, *Year of Decisions* (New York, 1955), 467.

10. *The Economist,* January 26, 1946, 124–25; *Fortune,* May 1946, 94; FR (1945), II, 1112.

11. Truman, *Year of Decisions,* 473. See also John C. Campbell, *The United States in World Affairs, 1945–1947* (New York, 1947), 332; Bela Gold, *Wartime Economic Planning in Agriculture* (New York, 1949), 468.

12. *Fortune,* May 1946, 94. See also FR (1945), II, 1089–90.

13. *The Economist,* July 12, 1947, 57; Arnold and Veronica M. Toynbee, eds., *The Realignment of Europe* (London, 1955), 106; FR (1945), II, 1020; DSB, December 15, 1946, 1107–08.

14. Herbert Hoover, *An American Epic* (Chicago, 1964), IV, 116.

15. FR (1945), II, 1030, 1036, 1056; Arthur Bliss Lane to Elbridge Durbrow, December 20, 1945, ABL Mss; FR (1945), V, 421; *The Economist,* July 12, 1947, 57.

16. FAO, *Mission for Poland,* 5.

17. DSB, August 3, 1947, 223.

18. Stanton Griffis, *Lying in State* (New York, 1952), 202.

19. DSB, December 15, 1946, 1108.

20. George Woodbridge, *UNRRA* (New York, 1950), I, 46.

21. FR (1945), V, 411. See also *ibid.,* 374–75.

22. FR (1946), VI, 607–10.

23. Arthur Bliss Lane, *I Saw Poland Betrayed* (New York, 1948), 236. See also Fejtö, *Histoire des Démocraties Populaires,* 152–53; *Business Week,* April 13, 1946, 109–10; Francis Willis memo to Dean Acheson, January 11, 1946, ABL Mss.

24. FR (1946), VI, 432.

25 *Ibid.*

26. Memorandum of conference with Burke Elbrick, May 9, 1946, ABL Mss. See also DSB, July 7, 1946, 33.

27. It was estimated that the new territory provided for an increased industrial capacity of 30 percent in cotton, 70 percent in wool, 30 percent in cement, 60 percent in sugar, 250 percent in flax, 40 percent in iron, and 100 percent in steel. UNRRA, of course, played a critical role in Poland's reconstruction efforts, providing $477,-927,000 by the end of 1946, or one-fifth of UNRRA's total allocations for Europe. *Business Week,* October 20, 1945, 113; April 13, 1946, 109–10; Samuel L. Sharp, *Poland: White Eagle on a Red Field* (Cambridge, 1953), 231–34; Doreen Warriner, *Revolution in Eastern Europe* (London, 1950), 87–88.

28. FAO, *Mission for Poland,* 15. See also *Business Week,* October 12, 1946, 109; *New Statesman and Nation,* April 24, 1948, 331.

29. William Diamond, *Czechoslovakia between East and West* (London, 1947), 61.

30. Steinhardt to William Diamond, May 27, 1947, LAS Mss, box 84. See also Steinhardt to James W. Riddleberger, September 1, 1945, LAS Mss, box 83; Diamond, *Czechoslovakia between East and West,* 132; Andrew Gyorgy, *Governments of Danubian Europe* (New York, 1949), 76.

31. DSB, December 8, 1946, 1027.

32. James Riddleberger to Laurence Steinhardt, October 3, 1946, LAS Mss, box 51.

33. *Ibid.*

34. *Ibid.;* Diamond, *Czechoslovakia between East and West,* 147; James F. Byrnes, *Speaking Frankly* (New York, 1947), 143–44; Andrei Vyshinsky, *Selected Speeches at the Paris Peace Conference* (London: Soviet News, n.d.), 13.

35. James Riddleberger to Steinhardt, October 3, 1946, LAS Mss, box 51.

36. Quoted in *ibid.*

37. *Ibid.* See also Diamond, *Czechoslovakia between East and West,* 223.

38. Quoted in Diamond, *Czechoslovakia between East and West,* 226.

39. James Riddleberger to Steinhardt, December 2, 1946, LAS Mss, box 51.

40. Quoted in Campbell, *United States in World Affairs,* 157.

41. James Riddleberger to Steinhardt, December 2, 1946, LAS Mss, box 51.

42. Thomas C. Blaisdell to Paul Porter, December 20, 1946, TCB Mss, box 7. See also Warriner, *Revolution in Eastern Europe,* 64.

43. Ministry for Foreign Affairs of the Polish Peoples Republic, *Documents on the Hostile Policy of the United States Government toward Peoples Poland* (Warsaw, 1953), 88–89; FR (1946), VI, 519.

44. V. M. Molotov, *Problems of Foreign Policy* (Moscow, 1949), 214.

45. Amelia C. Leiss, ed., *European Peace Treaties after World War II* (Boston, 1954), 82; DSB, October 13, 1946, 658; Byrnes, *Speaking Frankly,* 148–49.

46. Francis P. Williamson to Steinhardt, July 1, 1946, LAS Mss, box 51; FR (1946), VI, 315; *Soviet Press Translations,* January 15, 1947, 9; DSB, October 20, 1946, 712–13.

47. UN, ECOSOC, *Economic Reconstruction of Devasted Areas,* 197; FR (1946), VI, 548–49; UN, Department of Economic Affairs, *Financial Needs of the Devastated Countries: Interim Report* (Lake Success, 1947), 14–15; New York *Times,* April 14, 1968.

48. Stephen D. Kertesz, ed., *The Fate of East Central Europe: Hopes and Failures of American Foreign Policy* (Notre Dame, 1956), 226; Fejtö, *Histoire des Démocraties Populaires,* 137; Seton-Watson, *East European Revolution,* 235–40; Warriner, *Revolution in Eastern Europe,* 28–33.

49. FR (1946), VI, 347. See also Michael Karolyi, *Memoirs* (London, 1956), 334.

50. *Business Week,* October 20, 1945, 114–16; November 3, 1945, 7; February 2, 1946, 101–02; May 25, 1946, 109; *The Economist,* July 19, 1947, 91–93.

51. FR (1945), V, 1266; Warriner, *Revolution in Eastern Europe,* 53–54; Fejtö, *Histoire des Démocraties Populaires,* 165–70.

52. DSB, March 2, 1947, 371. See also *Business Week,* May 25, 1946, 109; September 21, 1946, 110.

53. *Business Week,* December 14, 1946, 113.

54. Memorandum of conversation between R. Aglion and H. van B. Cleveland, December 2, 1946, TCB Mss, box 7. See also United Nations, Department of Economic Affairs, *Financial Needs of the Devastated Countries,* 13–16, 35; David Wightman, *Economic Co-operation in Europe: A Study of the United Nations Mission for Europe* (London, 1956), 7.

55. Blaisdell memo, November 15, 1946, TCB Mss, box 7. See also Aglion and Cleveland, memo of conversation, December 2, 1946, TCB Mss, box 7.

56. Ted Geiger to H. Van B. Cleveland, November 27, 1946, TCB Mss, box 7.

57. FR (1945), II, 731–32.

58. *Ibid.,* 783.

59. *Ibid.,* 291–92, 784–85.

60. FR (1946), VI, 627–28. See also Toynbee, *Realignment of Europe,* 297; Henry L. Roberts, *Rumania: Political Problems of an Agrarian State* (New Haven, 1951), 301.

61. FR (1946), VI, 668–69; Roberts, *Rumania*, 306–08.

62. FR (1946), VI, 945. See also *ibid.*, 960; FR (1945), V, 1262–92.

63. FR (1946), VI, 930.

64. *Ibid.*, 947. See also *ibid.*, 966.

65. Lane to Elbridge Durbrow, March 11, 1946, ABL Mss.

66. Lane to C. Burke Elbrick, June 17, 1946, ABL Mss.

67. Lane, *I Saw Poland Betrayed*, 141, 154, 165. See also *ibid.*, 246–51; FR (1945), V, 408; FR (1946), VI, 400, 479; Betts, *Central and South East Europe*, 36.

68. FR (1946), VI, 418.

69. *Ibid.*, 390. See also Lane to Burke Elbrick, July 30, 1946. ABL Mss.

70. Brant, *The New Poland*, 86–88, 97; Warriner, *Revolution in Eastern Europe*, 26.

71. Andrzej Korbonski, *Politics of Socialist Agriculture in Poland: 1944–1960* (New York, 1965), 129–33; FR (1946), VI, 407, 516.

72. John Scott, "Report on Poland," 10, LAS Mss, box 55.

73. Toynbee, *Realignment of Europe*, 236–40.

74. Eduard Beneš, *Memoirs: From Munich to New War and New Victory* (Boston, 1953), 260. See also *ibid.*, chap. XII, *passim*.

75. Diamond, *Czechoslovakia between East and West*, 118–19; Paul E. Zinner, *Communist Strategy and Tactics in Czechoslovakia, 1918–1948* (New York, 1963), 102–03, 159, 164–65; Betts, *Central and South East Europe*, 168–69.

76. Steinhardt typescript speech, n.d., 4 [ca. December 1947], LAS Mss, box 55.

77. *Ibid.* See also Diamond, *Czechoslovakia between East and West*, 22–23; Zinner, *Communist Strategy and Tactics*, 114.

78. Steinhardt typescript speech, n.d., 7, 15–16, LAS Mss, box 55. See also Diamond, *Czechoslovakia between East and West*, 206; Zinner, *Communist Strategy and Tactics*, 124, 180–81.

79. Quoted in Diamond, *Czechoslovakia between East and West*, 225.

80. FR (1946), VI, 310. See also FR (1945), IV, 871–72; Karolyi, *Memoirs*, 311; Byrnes, *Speaking Frankly*, 100.

81. FR (1946), VI, 308.

82. Betts, *Central and South East Europe*, 106; FR (1945), IV, 891–92; Ferenc Nagy, *The Struggle behind the Iron Curtain* (New York, 1948), 154, 163; Karolyi, *Memoirs*, 311.

83. FR (1946), VI, 274.

84. *Ibid.* See also Karolyi, *Memoirs*, 339.

85. Betts, *Central and South East Europe*, 120–23; Bartlett, *East of the Iron Curtain*, 80.

86. FR (1946), VI, 338. See also *ibid.*, 320–25; Nagy, *The Struggle behind the Iron Curtain*, 240.

87. FR (1946), VI, 338.

88. Nagy, *The Struggle behind the Iron Curtain*, 344. See also *ibid.*, 326–28, 345–49, 374–75.

89. *Soviet Press Translations*, February 28, 1947, 8–10; FR (1946), VI, 627–32; FR (1945), IV, 911–12.

90. Steinhardt, speech presented at the National War College, December 15, 1947, 10, LAS Mss, box 55.

Chapter 8: Greece and the Middle East: Tradition and Turmoil

1. Gabriel Kolko, *The Politics of War* (New York, 1968), 484–85; Dominique Eudes, *Les Kapetanios: la guerre civile grecque de 1943 à 1949* (Paris, 1970), 316ff.

2. Great Britain, Parliament, *Report of the British Legal Mission to Greece, 17th January 1946* (London, 1946), 10–24; *Recherches Internationales*, No. 44–45 (Juillet–Décembre, 1964), 275–76; Eudes, *Les Kapetanios*, 336, 343–44; U.S. Senate, Committee on Foreign Relations, *Hearings: Assistance to Greece and Turkey*, 80:1, March 24–31, 1947 (Washington, 1947), 180–81; C. M. Woodhouse, *Apple of Discord: A Survey of Recent Greek Politics in Their International Setting* (London, n.d.), 241–43; Reginald Leeper, *When Greek Meets Greek* (London, 1950), 181–82.

3. Leeper, *When Greek Meets Greek*, 193–97; FR (1945), II, 150, 197, 729–31; FR (1945), VIII, 150–55.

4. FR (1945), VIII, 298. See also *ibid.,* 169–92, 252–88; Bickham Sweet-Escott, *Greece: A Political and Economic Survey, 1939–1953* (London, 1954), 45–51; Senate Committee on Foreign Relations, *Assistance to Greece and Turkey*, 207; Leeper, *When Greek Meets Greek*, 200–04; *Recherches Internationales*, 273.

5. FR (1946), VII, 127. See also *ibid.,* 115–21; Stephen G. Xydis, *Greece and the Great Powers, 1944–1947: Prelude to the "Truman Doctrine"* (Thessaloniki, 1963), 138; Eudes, *Les Kapetanios*, 342–44, 350–52; Senate Committee on Foreign Relations, *Assistance to Greece and Turkey*, 207.

6. John Sofianopoulos statement (ca. August 1946), TC Mss, box 178. See also interview with Sofianopoulos, September 15, 1946, TC Mss, box 179; FR (1946), VII, 186–87; DS, *Report of the Allied Mission to Observe the Elections*, Publ. 2522 (Washington, 1946), *passim;* L. S. Stavrianos, *Greece: American Dilemma and Opportunity* (Chicago, 1952), 169.

7. Sweet-Escott, *Greece*, 174–78; R. V. Burks, *The Dynamics of Communism in Eastern Europe* (Princeton, 1961), 79; Eudes, *Les Kapetanios*, 355–61; Evangelos Kofos, *Nationalism and Communism in Macedonia* (Thessaloniki, 1964), 146–48, 164–66; DS, "Briefing Book" [March 1947], *passim,* in TC Mss, box 178; DS, *The United Nations and the Problem of Greece* (Washington, 1947), 69–71; Edgar O'Ballance, *The Greek Civil War, 1944–1949* (New York, 1966), 127, 131; Xydis, *Greece and the Great Powers*, 229; *The Times* (London), January 7, 1947; T. George Kousoulas, *Revolution and Defeat: The Story of the Greek Communist Party* (London, 1965), 240.

8. DS, "Briefing Book," 9. See also Frank Smothers *et al., Report on the Greeks: Findings of a 20th Century Fund Team Which Surveyed Conditions in Greece in 1947* (New York, 1948), 29–30; Xydis, *Greece and the Great Powers*, 300, 370, 407, 530; Stavrianos, *Greece*, 171–75; Great Britain, Foreign Office, *Report of the British Parliamentary Delegation to Greece. August, 1946.* (London, 1947), 7; FR (1946), VII, 98, 204–05, 914–15; Eudes, *Les Kapetanios*, 340; *The Economist*, July 5, 1947, 3–4.

9. Foreign Office, *Report of the British Parliamentary Delegation*, 4, 6, 9.

10. FR (1946), VII, 234.

11. Foreign Office, *Report of the British Parliamentary Delegation*, 13. See also

ibid., 12; DS, "Briefing Book," *passim;* Xydis, *Greece and the Great Powers,* 364–65; DS, *Second Report to Congress on Assistance to Greece and Turkey, December 31, 1947* (Washington, 1948), 13; United Nations, Department of Economic Affairs, *Recent Developments in the World Economic Situation* (New York, 1949), 24.

12. Foreign Office, *Report of the British Parliamentary Delegation,* 13. See also George Woodbridge, *UNRRA* (New York, 1950), II, 104–15, III, 428–29; U.S. House, Select Committee on Foreign Aid, *Report on Greece,* 80:2, March 4, 1948 (Washington, 1948), 9; Senate Committee on Foreign Relations, *Assistance to Greece and Turkey,* 135; U.S. House, Committee on Foreign Affairs, *Hearings: Emergency Foreign Aid,* 80:1, November 1947 (Washington, 1947), 214; Howard K. Smith, *The State of Europe* (New York, 1949), 227; P. W. Sheppard, *An Australian Officer in Greece* (Melbourne, 1947), 16; DSB, May 4, 1947, 899; Paul A. Porter, "Wanted: A Miracle in Greece," *Collier's,* September 20, 1947, 14; DS, "Briefing Book," *passim;* FR (1946), VII, 283, *passim.*

13. Leeper, *When Greek Meets Greek,* 156. See also *ibid.,* 180, 206–07; DSB, May 4, 1947, 899; Foreign Office, *Report of the British Parliamentary Delegation,* 14.

14. Xydis, *Greece and the Great Powers,* 243. See also *ibid.,* 146–53, 232, 256ff.; Harry S. Truman, *Years of Trial and Hope* (New York, 1956), 99; DSB, January 20, 1946, 78–79; FR (1946), VII, 95–96, 176, 184; Royal Greek Embassy to Truman, April 23, 1946, HST Mss, OF 206.

15. FR (1946), VII, 182–91; Joseph M. Jones, *The Fifteen Weeks* (New York, 1955), 5; Xydis, *Greece and the Great Powers,* 317–18, 378; Walter Millis, ed., *The Forrestal Diaries* (New York, 1951), 210; Memo from William H. Taylor and Edward H. Foley, October 1, 1946, JWS Mss.

16. Foreign Office, *Report of the British Parliamentary Delegation,* 8ff.

17. FR (1946), VII, 148–49, 208–09, 243, 250–57, 916–17; Byrnes, *Speaking Frankly,* 300; Xydis, *Greece and the Great Powers,* 400–07, 433; *Forrestal Diaries,* 216; George Curry, *James F. Byrnes* (New York, 1965), 290.

18. FR (1946), VII, 285–87; Xydis, *Greece and the Great Powers,* 444–48; DS, "Briefing Book," *passim;* DSB, January 5, 1947, 29; *The Times* (London), January 6, 1947; Porter, "Wanted: A Miracle in Greece," 14.

19. Kolko, *Politics of War,* 433–34, 484–85; Woodhouse, *Apple of Discord,* 246; Xydis, *Greece and the Great Powers,* 197–98, 219–20, 237, 277–81; Amelia C. Leiss, ed., *European Peace Treaties after World War II* (Boston, 1954), 61, 92; FR (1946), IV, 814–15, 854–56; V. M. Molotov, *Problems of Foreign Policy* (Moscow, 1949), 128; Dean Acheson, *Present at the Creation* (New York, 1969), 199.

20. DS, *United Nations and the Problem of Greece,* 56. See also Xydis, *Greece and the Great Powers,* 270–74, 373, 384, 413; DS, "Briefing Book," *passim;* Acheson, *Present at the Creation,* 199; FR (1946), VII, 135–36, 140–42, 197–98, *passim.*

21. DS, *United Nations and the Problem of Greece,* 54, 68; *The Times* (London), January 7, 1947; DS, "Briefing Book," *passim;* for the general nationality issue, see Kofos, *Nationalism and Communism,* 146–75; Burks, *Dynamics of Communism,* 142–43; Sweet-Escott, *Greece,* 54, 172–76.

22. Kolko, *Politics of War,* 435.

23. Commander, U.S. Naval Forces in Europe, "Narrative of U.S. Naval Forces, Europe, 1 September 1945 to 1 October 1946" (December 30, 1946), 80–82, ONH

Mss, A 12–1/00317. See also Xydis, *Greece and the Great Powers,* 158–68; *Forrestal Diaries,* 141.

24. Forrestal Testimony, December 3, 1947, 2784–85, PAP Mss, box 17.

25. FR (1946), VII, 822.

26. U.S. Naval Forces in Europe, "Narrative of U.S. Naval Forces, 1945–1946," 84, 86, ONH Mss. See also Xydis, *Greece and the Great Powers,* 186–87.

27. FR (1946), VII, 840–41. See also *Forrestal Diaries,* 171, 191–92.

28. FR (1946), VII, 56.

29. U.S. Naval Forces in Europe, "Narrative of U.S. Naval Forces, 1945–1946," 90–91, ONH Mss. See also FR (1946), VII, 51–60; Xydis, *Greece and the Great Powers,* 267.

30. *Forrestal Diaries,* 211. See also FR (1946), VII, 209–12.

31. *Forrestal Diaries,* 258, 302; FR (1946), VII, 235–44, 256–63, 282–87.

32. Truman, *Years of Trial and Hope,* 95.

33. Quoted in George Lenczowski, *Russia and the West in Iran, 1918–1948* (Ithaca, 1949), 293. For a similar expression of this view, see John C. Campbell, *Defense of the Middle East* (New York, 1960), 25.

34. FR (1945), VIII, 419. See also *ibid.,* 397–98.

35. Nasrollah Saifpour Fatemi, *Oil Diplomacy: Powder Keg in Iran* (New York, 1954), 267–90; FR (1945), II, 616, 630–31, 708–09, 771–72, 796; FR (1945), VIII, 436ff., 475–500; Richard W. Cottam, *Nationalism in Iran* (Pittsburgh, 1964), 72–73, 115, 126–29; Truman, *Years of Trial and Hope,* 93.

36. FR (1945), II, 752.

37. Byrnes does not deny the United States advised Iran to place the matter before the council, but claims that he told the Iranians that the council should hear only "the most urgent matters," and that they then acted before he made a more explicit recommendation. Byrnes, *Speaking Frankly,* 123. See also FR (1946), VII, 2–3, 6–7, 289, 297, 300–01, 312; Fatemi, *Oil Diplomacy,* 283–84, 290; Lenczowski, *Russia and the West in Iran,* 294–95.

38. Trygve Lie, *In the Cause of Peace* (New York, 1954), 29–31; FR (1946), VII, 316–27, 340–49; Fatemi, *Oil Diplomacy,* 305–07; Truman, *Years of Trial and Hope,* 94–95; Jones, *Fifteen Weeks,* 53–55.

39. Fatemi, *Oil Diplomacy,* 307. See also FR (1946), VII, 354, 361–62, 371–81; George Kirk, *The Middle East, 1945–1950* (London, 1954), 68; Lie, *In the Cause of Peace,* 75–76.

40. Byrnes, *Speaking Frankly,* 126, 250–51; Lie, *In the Cause of Peace,* 76–77; FR (1946), VI, 381–95; Fatemi, *Oil Diplomacy,* 309; Lenczowski, *Russia and the West in Iran,* 299–300; Kirk, *The Middle East,* 58.

41. DS, *The Problem of the Turkish Straits* (Washington, 1947), 38. See also FR (1946), VII, 400–91; Andrew W. Cordier and Wilder Foote, eds., *Public Papers of the Secretaries-General of the United Nations: Trygve Lie 1946–1953* (New York, 1969), 40–42.

42. FR (1946), VII, 7, 568. See also *ibid.,* 34–35, 316, 373, 413, 514–15, 552–64; John Marlowe, *The Persian Gulf in the Twentieth Century* (London, 1962), 149–51; Kirk, *The Middle East,* 82–83; Jones, *Fifteen Weeks,* 57–58; *Forrestal Diaries,* 216; FR (1946), V, 955–56.

43. FR (1946), VII, 530. See also *ibid.,* 524, 529–32.

44. FR (1945), VIII, 45.

45. FR (1945), II, 690. See also Kolko, *Politics of War,* 586–588; FR (1945), VIII, 1228–35; Kirk, *The Middle East,* 23; Donald F. Herr, "The Truman Doctrine" (honors thesis, Harvard College, 1961), 37–38.

46. DS, *Problem of the Turkish Straits,* 49. See also *ibid.,* 37–38; FR (1945), VIII, 1240–92.

47. *Forrestal Diaries,* 191–92, 210, 216; FR (1946), VII, 211–14, 223–25, 829–41, 847–48, 857–58, 895; Truman, *Years of Trial and Hope,* 97; DS, *Problem of the Turkish Straits, 49ff.; New Times,* January 1, 1947, 15; S. J. Rundt, "The Army of the Crescent and the Star," *Infantry Journal,* 60 (February, 1947), 18–19.

Chapter 9: China: From Chaos to Revolution

1. Milovan Djilas, *Conversations with Stalin* (New York, 1962), 182. See also Mao's recollection in New York *Times,* March 1, 1970; FR (1945), VII, 526.

2. DS, *United States Relations with China, with special reference to the period 1944–1949* (Washington, 1949), 129, 311 [hereafter *White Paper*]; U.S. Office of Naval History [Henry I. Shaw], "United States Marine Corps in North China, 1945–1949" (Ms dated October 1961), 34–36, 58, in ONH Mss; Lionel Max Chassin, *The Communist Conquest of China: A History of the Civil War, 1945–1949* (Cambridge, 1965), 22–25; John F. Melby, *The Mandate of Heaven: Record of a Civil War: China, 1945–49* (Toronto, 1968), 27, 56, 183; FR (1945), VII, 675, 1195.

3. Gabriel Kolko, *The Politics of War* (New York, 1968), chaps. IX, X, XXI, XXIV.

4. Don Lohbeck, *Patrick J. Hurley* (Chicago, 1956), 404–05; Mao Tse-tung, *Selected Works* (Peking, 1965), III, 335–36; *Selected Works* (Peking, 1961), IV, 13, 15, 20, 43, 53–54, 60–63; *White Paper,* 105–09, 579–81; Chassin, *Communist Conquest of China,* 54–55; FR (1945), VII, 467ff.

5. Shaw, "Marine Corps in North China," 115. See also *ibid.,* 77–184; FR (1945), VII, 532, 580, 600; Chassin, *Communist Conquest of China,* 60; *White Paper,* 312; Herbert Feis, *The China Tangle: The American Effort in China from Pearl Harbor to the Marshall Mission* (Princeton, 1963), 374, 378, 396; U.S. Marine Corps, Historical Branch, *The United States Marines in North China, 1945–1949,* Marine Corps Historical Reference Series No. 23 (Washington, 1962), appendices A and B.

6. Shaw, "Marine Corps in North China," 145. See also FR (1945), VII, 481, 600, 606–11, 636, 644–45; DSB, October 21, 1945, 647; November 18, 1945, 812.

7. Feis, *China Tangle,* 375. See also *ibid.,* 370–71; *White Paper,* 346–50; John Leighton Stuart, *Fifty Years in China* (New York, 1954), 206; U.S. Army Advisory Group, Nanking, "Unit History 1946," 10–14, AAG Mss.

8. FR (1945), VII, 596. See also *ibid.,* 587–88.

9. Walter Millis, ed., *The Forrestal Diaries* (New York, 1951), 179. See also FR (1945), VII, 598, 1251–52, 1362–63.

10. *Forrestal Diaries,* 111. See also *White Paper,* 132–33; Albert C. Wedemeyer,

Wedemeyer Reports! (New York, 1958), 447–58; Feis, *China Tangle,* 398; FR (1945), VII, 604, 659–60.

11. *Forrestal Diaries,* 112, 190; FR (1945), VII, 646–47, 664–65, 672–73; Feis, *China Tangle,* 397–402, 417.

12. In Inner Mongolia, the Russians disarmed Chinese Communist troops for a time. Elsewhere, the United States had no evidence of significant Soviet aid for the Communists in Manchuria but much proof of Soviet political support for the Nationalists. See FR (1945), VII, 669, 673–74, 695, 700; Melby, *Mandate of Heaven,* 31.

13. FR (1945), II, 666–68. See also *ibid.,* 605, 608, 616; FR (1945), VII, 634, 694–95, 844–49; Chassin, *Communist Conquest of China,* 66–67; Feis, *China Tangle,* 384–88; Melby, *Mandate of Heaven,* 197–98.

14. FR (1945), II, 720, 757, 776; Feis, *China Tangle,* 427; DSB, December 30, 1945, 1036; FR (1946), VI, 680–81.

15. DSB, October 28, 1945, 699. See also Edwin A. Locke memo to Truman, August 20, 1945, EAL Mss, box 2; FR (1945), VII, 1247ff.

16. DSB, October 21, 1945, 647; "Government Control of Trade and Industry in China," [November 1945], DC Mss, file 82220–1. See also Edwin A. Locke to T. V. Soong, August 29, 1945, EAL Mss, box 2; Harry Truman to Locke, October 3, 1945, EAL Mss, box 1; Donald M. Nelson to T. V. Soong, September 11, 1945, EL Mss, box 8; DSB, November 24, 1945, 961–62; FR (1945), VII, 448–53, 1197.

17. *White Paper,* 224; DSB, November 24, 1945, 961–62; Emilio G. Collado to P. W. Parker, December 11, 1945, EL Mss, box 7; Locke memo to Truman, December 18, 1945, 24, *passim;* A. C. Wedemeyer to Locke, December 29, 1945, EAL Mss, box 2; S. J. Janow memo, March 28, 1946, EL Mss, box 7; FR (1945), VII, 1363ff.

18. *White Paper,* 581–83. See also Locke memo to Truman, August 20, 1945, 9–10, EAL Mss, box 2; *Forrestal Diaries,* 98–99; FR (1945), VII, 556ff.; Feis, *China Tangle,* chap. XXXVI.

19. *Forrestal Diaries,* 113, 123.

20. Stimson to Marshall, November 29, 1945, HLS Mss.

21. Harry S. Truman, *Years of Trial and Hope* (New York, 1956), 69.

22. FR (1945), VII, 768. See also *ibid.,* 770; Dean Acheson, *Present at the Creation* (New York, 1969), 142–43; Truman, *Years of Trial and Hope,* 68–72; Feis, *China Tangle,* 413–22; FR (1945), II, 812.

23. *White Paper,* 607–09; U.S. Senate, Committee on the Judiciary, *Hearings: Institute of Pacific Relations,* 82:1, 2, July 1951—June 1952 (Washington, 1951–1953), 2305, 2310; DS, "Conference on Problems of United States Policy in China. October 6–8, 1949" [multilithed transcript of proceedings], 398–99; U.S. Senate, Committee on Armed Services and Committee on Foreign Relations, *Hearings: Military Situation in the Far East,* 82:1, May 1951 (Washington, 1951), 377–78; U.S. Army, Peiping Headquarters Group, "History, Peiping Headquarters," fourth quarter, 1946, section XIII, part A, 9–10, AGO Mss, box 76; Henry L. Stimson notes of talk with Henry R. Luce, November 20, 1946, HLS Mss; FR (1945), VII, 633, 659, 708–09.

24. Chiang Kai-shek, *Soviet Russia in China: A Summing-Up at Seventy* (New York, 1957), 155.

25. Truman, *Years of Trial and Hope*, 74. See also DS, "United States Policy in China," 397–98.

26. *White Paper*, 597. See also *ibid.*, 596–604; FR (1945), VII, 652–53, 694–95, 700, 710, 797–99, 837; Owen Lattimore, *The Situation in Asia* (Boston, 1949), 143.

27. DS, "United States Policy in China," 399–400. See also Leahy Diary, February 21, 1946, WDL Mss; Tang Tsou, *America's Failure in China, 1941–50* (Chicago, 1963), 336–39; Melby, *Mandate of Heaven*, 94, 197–98; FR (1945), VII, 695, 700; FR (1946), VI, 761–62; Chiang, *Soviet Russia in China*, 232–33; Stimson notes of talk with Luce, November 20, 1946, HLS Mss; Lattimore, *Situation in Asia*, 143–45; *Forrestal Diaries*, 175; Wedemeyer, *Wedemeyer Reports!*, 449.

28. Chiang, *Soviet Russia in China*, 150–51. See also *ibid.*, 147–49; Leahy Diary, May 20, 1946, WDL Mss; FR (1946), VI, 680–81.

29. FR (1946), VI, 761–62. See also *Soviet Press Translations*, November 15, 1946, 7–9; December 14, 1946, 7–10; Melby, *Mandate of Heaven*, 94.

30. *White Paper*, 650. See also *ibid.*, 146–51, 313–14, 691; Truman, *Years of Trial and Hope*, 79; Chassin, *Communist Conquest of China*, 94–112.

31. *White Paper*, 652. See also *ibid.*, 176, 653; *Forrestal Diaries*, 175–76, 189–90.

32. "History, Peiping Headquarters," fourth quarter, 1946, section XIII, part A, 9–10, AGO Mss, box 76. See also Stimson notes of talk with Luce, November 20, 1946, HLS Mss; George C. Marshall to Bernard Baruch, August 21, 1946, BB Mss, part XI,

33. Stimson notes of talk with Luce, November 20, 1946, HLS Mss; Truman *Years of Trial and Hope*, 83–89; *White Paper*, 180–220, 227, 652–95; Tang Tsou, *America's Failure in China*, 453.

34. *White Paper*, 686–94.

35. *White Paper*, 382, 705–06; FR (1945), VII, 811; Arthur N. Young, *China and the Helping Hand, 1937–1945* (Cambridge, 1963), 354–55; Shun-hsin Chou, *The Chinese Inflation, 1937–1949* (New York, 1963), 94, 102. John K. Chang suggests that industrial production declined during the war but rose dramatically between 1945 and 1947, and even in 1948 exceeded the 1933 level of output; see his "Industrial Development of Mainland China, 1912–1949," *Journal of Economic History*, 27 (1967), 66.

36. Shun-hsin Chou, *The Chinese Inflation*, 92–93, 175–78; *White Book*, 222, 225–26, 243, 735–36, 796; UNRRA, Aide Mémoire, June 12, 1946, JT Mss, box 77; Charles Wertenbaker, "The China Lobby," *The Reporter*, April 15, 1952, 9–10; "History, Peiping Headquarters," third quarter 1946, section XI, part C, 2–5, AGO Mss, box 73; "History, Peiping Headquarters," fourth quarter, 1946, section XIV, part A, 4, AGO Mss, box 76.

37. Arthur N. Young, *China's Wartime Finance and Inflation, 1937–1945* (Cambridge, 1965), 317–21, 358; Shun-hsin Chou, *The Chinese Inflation*, 11, 15, 34–35, 170–71, 239–44; Derk Bodde, *Peking Diary—1948–1949* (Greenwich, Conn., 1967), 42–45, 278; *White Paper*, 209–10, 238, 278, 729–30, 877–81, 886; Tang Tsou, *America's Failure in China*, 394; K. M. Panikkar, *In Two Chinas: Memoirs of a Diplomat* (London, 1955), 35–36.

38. Mao, *Selected Works*, IV, 89–90, 117. See also *ibid.*, 113–16, 121, 175, 182–85, 235–36; Franz Schurmann, *Ideology and Organization in Communist China* (Berkeley, 1966), 120–21.

39. "History, Peiping Headquarters," second quarter, 1946, section IX, 3–6, AGO Mss, box 70; "History, Peiping Headquarters," third quarter, 1946, section XII, "Chinese Communist Party Views," 1, AGO Mss, box 73; "History, Peiping Headquarters," fourth quarter, 1946, section III, "Yenan Liaison Group," *passim*, AGO Mss, box 74; *White Paper*, 159, 171, 183–84, 654–56; Soong Ching Ling, *The Struggle for New China* (Peking, 1952), 180; Mao, *Selected Works*, IV, 97.

Chapter 10: Korea, 1945–1948: The American Way of Liberation

1. E. Grant Meade, *American Military Government in Korea* (New York, 1951), 34ff.; FR (1945), VI, 561–63.

2. O.S.S., R. and A. Branch, "Korean Independence Movement," R. & A. 3302S, July 20, 1945 (n.p. 1945), 2–3; FR (1945), VI, 1022–24, 1028–41.

3. FR (Conference of Berlin), I, 309; FR (Conference at Yalta, 1945), 770.

4. U.S. House, Committee on Foreign Affairs, *Hearings: Korean Aid*, 81:1, June 1949 (Washington, 1949), 141. Truman later noted that the State Department had pressed for an effort to take all of Korea before the Russians, but that it was not militarily feasible. The United States, for its part, did not intend to respect the Soviet zone if it could get up the peninsula in time. Harry S. Truman, *Year of Decisions* (New York, 1955), 434, 455; Truman, *Years of Trial and Hope* (New York, 1956), 317.

5. FR (1945), VI, 561, 563.

6. Meade, *American Military Government*, 71; Richard E. Lauterbach, *Danger from the East* (New York, 1947), 197–98; FR (1945), VI, 1045.

7. George M. McCune, *Korea Today* (Cambridge, 1950), 45. See also Lauterbach, *Danger from the East*, 212.

8. Harold Isaacs, *No Peace for Asia* (New York, 1947), 94.

9. *Ibid.*

10. New York *Times*, September 9, 1945; Lauterbach, *Danger from the East*, 184.

11. FR (1945), VI, 1048. See also *ibid.*, 1045; House Committee on Foreign Affairs, *Hearings: Korean Aid*, 36.

12. John Gunther, *The Riddle of MacArthur: Japan, Korea and the Far East* (New York, 1951), 181.

13. *Ibid.*, 180. See also Mark Gayn, *Japan Diary* (New York, 1948), 428; Meade, *American Military Government*, 103.

14. FR (1945), VI, 1049–51. See also Meade, *American Military Government*, 47–51, 83.

15. FR (1945), VI, 1061, 1063.

16. John C. Caldwell, *The Korea Story* (Chicago, 1952), 9–10. See also Lauterbach, *Danger from the East*, 202–03.

17. FR (1945), VI, 1069. See also Lauterbach, *Danger from the East*, 202–03;

Richard E. Lauterbach, "Hodge's Korea," *Virginia Quarterly Review,* 23 (1947), 353; Hagwon Sunoo, "Need for a Democratic Program," *Far Eastern Survey,* 15 (1946), 228.

18. Meade, *American Military Government,* 52.

19. William M. Angus, "Aim of Military Government," *Far Eastern Survey,* 15 (1946), 228.

20. Gayn, *Japan Diary,* 401.

21. Meade, *American Military Government,* 60; FR (1945), VI, 1069; McCune, *Korea Today,* 48.

22. FR (1945), VI, 1070.

23. *Ibid.,* 1106.

24. *Ibid.,* 1134.

25. *Ibid.*

26. *Ibid.,* 1123–24.

27. Meade, *American Military Government,* 134–36.

28. Quoted in George M. McCune, "Occupation Politics in Korea," *Far Eastern Survey,* 15 (1946), 36.

29. FR (1945), VI, 1156–57.

30. McCune, "Occupation Politics in Korea," 36; FR (1945), VI, 1104, 1115, *passim.*

31. FR (1945), VI, 1142; Meade, *American Military Government,* 8.

32. Quoted in Gayn, *Japan Diary,* 401.

33. FR (1945), VI, 1151; McCune, *Korea Today,* 165.

34. Meade, *American Military Government,* 66, 206–07; Angus, "Aim of Military Government," 231.

35. Quoted in Gayn, *Japan Diary,* 374.

36. Quoted in McCune, *Korea Today,* 130. See also Gayn, *Japan Diary,* 433.

37. Meade, *American Military Government,* 66; Sunoo, "Need for a Democratic Program," 229.

38. Quoted in Gayn, *Japan Diary,* 391. See also Meade, *American Military Government,* 130; FR (1945), VI, 1076.

39. Quoted in Gayn, *Japan Diary,* 353.

40. Caldwell, *The Korea Story,* 8.

41. *Voice of Korea,* May 15, 1948, 284.

42. FR (1945), VI, 1055.

43. *Ibid.,* 1072.

44. Quoted in Gayn, *Japan Diary,* 393.

45. Lauterbach, *Danger from the East,* 244.

46. *Ibid.,* 237–39, 247; Meade, *American Military Government,* 186–89; Gayn, *Japan Diary,* 352–54.

47. Quoted in Meade, *American Military Government,* 165. See also *ibid.,* 186.

48. Quoted in Gayn, *Japan Diary,* 398.

49. McCune, *Korea Today,* 79.

50. Quoted in Gayn, *Japan Diary,* 437.

51. *Time,* June 30, 1947, 25.

52. Quoted in McCune, *Korea Today,* 187. See also *ibid.,* 52, 172–81, 202–03; Lauterbach, *Danger from the East,* 213–14; Shannon McCune, "Land Distribution in Korea," *Far Eastern Survey,* 17 (1948), 16; House Committee on Foreign Affairs, *Hearings: Korean Aid,* 47.

53. Truman, *Years of Trial and Hope,* 322. See also McCune, *Korea Today,* 184, 209–12; FR (1945), VI, 1118.

54. Robert T. Oliver, *Syngman Rhee: The Man behind the Myth* (New York, 1955), 233; DSB, March 23, 1947, 547.

55. McCune, *Korea Today,* 65–67.

56. Kim to Locke, August 11, 1947; Truman to Locke, August 15, 1947, HST Mss, OF 471.

57. DSB, August 24, 1947, 399.

58. Leon Gordenker, *The United Nations and the Peaceful Unification of Korea: The Politics of Field Operations, 1947–1950* (The Hague, 1959), 18–19; DS, *Korea, 1945 to 1948: A Report on Political Developments and Economic Resources with Selected Documents* (Washington, 1948), 9.

59. *Voice of Korea,* March 20, 1948, 267. See also McCune, *Korea Today,* 70; Gordenker, *The United Nations,* 19.

60. Gayn, *Japan Diary,* 507.

61. Quoted in Gordenker, *The United Nations,* 81. See also *ibid.,* 80.

62. Quoted in *ibid.,* 82.

63. *Voice of Korea,* April 16, 1948, 276; May 1, 1948, 279–80.

64. DS, *Korea, 1945 to 1948,* 14.

65. McCune, *Korea Today,* 228.

66. DS, *Korea, 1945 to 1948,* 15. See also McCune, *Korea Today,* 228–30; Gordenker, *The United Nations,* 94–106; *Voice of Korea,* June 1, 1948, 287–88.

67. House Committee on Foreign Affairs, *Hearings: Korean Aid,* 19.

Chapter 11: The Dilemma of Japan

1. Shigeru Yoshida, *The Yoshida Memoirs: The Story of Japan in Crisis* (Boston, 1962), 25.

2. FR (1945), VI, 548–49.

3. *Ibid.,* 549–56, 584–90.

4. For a more extensive discussion of wartime planning in Japan see Gabriel Kolko, *The Politics of War* (New York, 1968), 543–48; FR (1945), VI, 545–47.

5. FR (1945), VI, 609–12.

6. *Ibid.,* 712–20.

7. *Ibid.,* 791. See also *ibid.,* 782–95.

8. *Ibid.,* 770–73, 886–90; DS, *Occupation of Japan: Policy and Progress* (Washington, n.d.), 9; George H. Blakeslee, "Negotiating to Establish the Far Eastern Commission, 1945," *Negotiating with the Russians,* Raymond Dennett and Joseph E. Johnson, eds. (Boston, 1951), 136–37.

9. Quoted in Arthur D. Bonetree, Philip H. Taylor, and Arthur A. Maass,

"American Military Government Experience in Japan," *American Experiences in Military Government in World War II*, Carl Friedrich *et al.*, eds. (New York, 1948), 336.

10. W. Macmahon Ball, *Japan: Enemy or Ally?* (New York, 1949), 11; FR (1945), VI, 717; John Gunther, *The Riddle of MacArthur* (New York, 1951), 7, 52–79.

11. Charles A. Willoughby and John Chamberlin, *MacArthur: 1941–1951* (New York, 1954), 323; Gunther, *Riddle of MacArthur*, 74–75; Mark Gayn, *Japan Diary* (New York, 1948), 237; Robert B. Textor, *Failure in Japan: With Keystones for a Positive Policy* (New York, 1951), 233; William J. Sebald, *With MacArthur in Japan: A Personal History of the Occupation* (New York, 1965), 43.

12. Quoted in Gayn, *Japan Diary*, 180.

13. Ball, *Japan*, 34.

14. *Ibid.*, 28.

15. *Ibid.*, 43. See also *ibid., passim;* Courtney Whitney, *MacArthur: His Rendezvous with History* (New York, 1956), 298–99; Sebald, *With MacArthur in Japan*, 150; Herbert Feis, *Contest over Japan* (New York, 1967), 129–32.

16. Ball, *Japan*, 45.

17. E. J. Lewe van Aduard, *Japan: From Surrender to Peace* (The Hague, 1953), 89; Textor, *Failure in Japan*, 48; FR (1945), VI, 731–33, 825–27.

18. Harry S. Truman, *Year of Decisions* (New York, 1955), 519. See also Kazuo Kawai, *Japan's American Interlude* (Chicago, 1960), 164; Gayn, *Japan Diary*, 235–39; Ball, *Japan*, 158.

19. FR (1945), VI, 826.

20. Quoted in Bontree *et al.*, "American Military Government Experience in Japan," 352–53.

21. FR (1945), VI, 844–45. See also Textor, *Failure in Japan*, 121.

22. R. P. Dore, *Land Reform in Japan* (London, 1959), 56–116; George Totten, "Collective Bargaining and Work Councils as Innovations in Industrial Relations in Japan during the 1920's," *Aspects of Social Change in Modern Japan*, R. P. Dore, ed. (Princeton, 1967), 203–43; Robert A. Scalapino, *The Japanese Communist Movement, 1920–1966* (Berkeley, 1967), 23–47; Robert Scalapino and Junnosuke Masumi, *Parties and Politics in Contemporary Japan* (Berkeley, 1962), 10, 20; Yoshida, *Memoirs*, 72–73.

23. Gayn, *Japan Diary*, 468; Supreme Commander for the Allied Powers (SCAP), *Political Reorientation of Japan, September 1945 to September 1948* (Washington, 1959), 355.

24. Scalapino and Masumi, *Parties and Politics*, 33–39.

25. Yoshida, *Memoirs*, 75.

26. SCAP, *Political Reorientation of Japan*, 356.

27. Quoted in Gayn, *Japan Diary*, 218.

28. Quoted in *ibid.*, 332. See also Helen Mears, *Mirror for Americans* (Boston, 1948), 260; Kawai, *Japan's American Interlude*, 162–64.

29. Evelyn S. Colbert, *The Left Wing in Japanese Politics* (New York, 1952), 133–36; Yoshida, *Memoirs*, 212; Scalapino, *Japanese Communist Movement*, 68–69.

30. Yoshida, *Memoirs*, 225.

31. FR (1945), VI, 826.

32. Barrington Moore, Jr., *Social Origins of Dictatorship and Democracy* (Boston, 1966), 287–91, *passim*.

33. *Ibid.*, 303. See also Yoshida, *Memoirs,* 150.

34. Quoted in Robert J. C. Butow, *Japan's Decision to Surrender* (Stanford, 1954), 48–49.

35. Yoshida, *Memoirs,* 149–61; Ball, *Japan,* 70, 162–65; Kawai, *Japan's American Interlude,* 96; Hans H. Baerwald, *The Purge of Japanese Leaders Under the Occupation* (Berkeley, 1959), 78–79.

36. Quoted in Dore, *Land Reform in Japan,* 468. See also Ball, *Japan,* 114–21; Kawai, *Japan's American Interlude,* 172–73; Scalapino and Masumi, *Parties and Politics,* 90–92.

37. T. A. Bisson, *Zaibatsu Dissolution in Japan* (Berkeley, 1954), 42–43.

38. FR (1945), VI, 811–12.

39. SCAP, "History of the Non-Military Activities of the Occupation of Japan: Reform of Business, Elimination of Zaibatsu Control (1945 thru June 1950)" (typescript, November 30, 1951), vol. X, part A, 12–13, DM Mss.

40. *Newsweek,* December 1, 1947, 38.

41. Walter Millis, ed., *The Forrestal Diaries* (New York, 1951), 177–79; FR (1945), VI, 999–1011; Ball, *Japan,* 98–99; Robert W. Barnett, "Occupied Japan: The Economic Aspect," *Foreign Economic Policy for the United States,* Seymour E. Harris, ed. (Cambridge, 1948), 110–11.

42. Harriman to W. L. Batt, December 20, 1946, DC Mss, file 104894.

43. Quoted in Ball, *Japan,* 10–11.

Chapter 12: The 1947 Crisis: The Truman Doctrine and American Globalism

1. Paul A. Smith, "Opinions, Publics, and World Affairs in the United States," *Western Political Quarterly,* 14 (1961), 701; Gabriel A. Almond, *The American People and Foreign Policy* (New York, 1950), 73, 91; Martin Kriesberg, "Dark Areas of Ignorance," *Public Opinion and Foreign Relations,* Lester Markel, ed. (New York, 1949), 49–64.

2. Walter Millis, ed., *The Forrestal Diaries* (New York, 1951), 192–93, 425, 487–88; Bernard C. Cohen, *The Press and Foreign Policy* (Princeton, 1963), chaps. V, VI; Robert P. Patterson to Julius O. Adler, November 2, 1946, RP Mss, for one of many examples of official intervention with the press.

3. Robert A. Taft, *A Foreign Policy for Americans* (New York, 1951), 62ff.; John P. Armstrong, "The Enigma of Senator Taft and American Foreign Policy," *Review of Politics,* 17 (1955), 206–31; H. Bradford Westerfield, *Foreign Policy and Party Politics* (New Haven, 1955), 33–34; John Taber to Mrs. George B. Williams, February 16, 1946; Taber to B. W. Kearney, April 8, 1946, JT Mss, box 77; Arthur H. Vandenberg to Robert E. Hannegan, October 28, 1946; Vandenberg to Dean Acheson, March 29, 1950, AHV Mss.

4. Harry S. Truman, *Years of Trial and Hope* (New York, 1956), 102; *Forrestal Diaries,* 197–99, 236–39, 246; Harry S. Truman, *Public Papers of the Presidents of*

the United States: 1947 (Washington, 1963), 1–12, 40–57, 66–68; Joseph M. Jones, *The Fifteen Weeks* (New York, 1955), 89–99; Warren L. Hickman, *Genesis of the European Recovery Program: A Study on the Trend of American Economic Policies* (Geneva, 1949), 237–40.

5. John Foster Dulles, "Europe Must Federate or Perish," *Vital Speeches,* 13 (February 1, 1947), 234.

6. George F. Kennan, *Memoirs, 1925–1950* (Boston, 1967), 302–03, chap. XV.

7. GATT, *Trends in International Trade: A Report by a Panel of Experts* (Geneva, October 1958), 32; Richard N. Gardner, *Sterling-Dollar Diplomacy* (Oxford, 1956), 287; DSB, December 15, 1946, 1108; UN, Department of Economic Affairs, *A Survey of the Economic Situation and Prospects of Europe* (Geneva, 1948), 40–41, 61, 97; Henry Chalmers, *World Trade Policies* (Berkeley, 1953), 384–87; United Nations, Department of Economic Affairs, *World Economic Report, 1948* (Lake Success, 1949), 10, 48; for an example of official unhappiness, see W. A. Harriman to Dean Acheson, April 10, 1947; Acheson to Harriman, April 22, 1947, DC Mss, file 93126–64.

8. DSB, January 19, 1947, 127.

9. Clair Wilcox, *The American Trade Program: What Do We have at Stake* [DS, Commercial Policy Series 100] (Washington, 1947), 12. See also U.S. Senate, Committee on Labor and Public Welfare, *History of Employment and Manpower Policy in the United States,* 89:2 (Washington, 1966), vol. VII, part 1, 43–45; Joseph M. Dodge, "The General Economic and Political Problem . . ." [1947]; "Title for Speeches and Articles," [1947], JMD Mss, Germany Assignment, box 6.

10. DSB, February 23, 1947, 341.

11. Stephen G. Xydis, *Greece and the Great Powers, 1944–1947* (Thessaloniki, 1963), 463, 469–70; Truman, *Years of Trial and Hope,* 99; Jones, *Fifteen Weeks,* 131; DSB, March 2, 1947, 390–91; Arthur Krock in New York *Times,* March 23, 1947.

12. Joseph Jones to Mr. Benton, February 26, 1947, JMJ Mss, box 1.

13. *Forrestal Diaries,* 245.

14. Jones to Benton, February 26, 1947, JMJ Mss, box 1. See also Dean Acheson, *Present at the Creation* (New York, 1969), 222.

15. "Marshall's First Statement to Congressional Leaders at White House," February 27, 1947, AHV Mss.

16. DSB, March 16, 1947, 484. See also Acheson, *Present at the Creation,* 219; Jones, *Fifteen Weeks,* 139–42.

17. Ellen Clayton Garwood, *Will Clayton: A Short Biography* (Austin, 1958), 115–18. See also DSB, March 2, 1947, 371ff.

18. Acheson, *Present at the Creation,* 221.

19. Draft of March 10, 1947, JMJ Mss, box 1. See also *Forrestal Diaries,* 249–52; Leahy Diary, March 7, 1947, WDL Mss; draft of March 4, 1947, JMJ Mss, box 1; and other drafts in JMJ Mss, box 1; Jones, *Fifteen Weeks,* 154–58.

20. Charles E. Bohlen, *The Transformation of American Foreign Policy* (New York, 1969), 87. See also Kennan, *Memoirs,* 315.

21. Truman, *Years of Trial and Hope,* 105.

22. DSB, March 23, 1947, 534–37. See also Jones, *Fifteen Weeks,* 157–58.

23. *Business Week,* March 8, 1947, 103. See also *ibid.,* 5.

24. *The Economist,* March 15, 1947, 377–78.

25. Edward S. Mason, "Reflections on the Moscow Conference," *International Organization,* 1 (1947), 482. See also New York *Times,* March 16, 23, 25, 1947; Jones, *Fifteen Weeks,* 146, 174–76; *The Economist,* March 29, 1947, 457; DSB, March 16, 1947, 497; Vincent Auriol, *Journal du Septennat: 1947* (Paris, 1970), 148.

26. *Time,* March 24, 1947, 83. See also Trygve Lie, *In the Cause of Peace* (New York, 1954), 104; Arthur H. Vandenberg, ed., *The Private Papers of Senator Vandenberg* (Boston, 1952), 340; John B. Bennett to Vandenberg, March 3, 1947; Vandenberg to Bennett, March 5, 1947, AHV Mss; *Forrestal Diaries,* 257; Jones, *Fifteen Weeks,* 180–85; DSB, May 4, 1947, supplement, *passim;* DS, "Briefing Book," March 1947, TC Mss, box 178; James Forrestal to Paul C. Smith, March 19, 1947; telephone conversation, Forrestal and Paul Shields, March 20, 1947, JF Mss, box 91.

27. U.S. Senate, Committee on Foreign Relations, *Hearings: Assistance to Greece and Turkey,* 80:1, March 24–31, 1947 (Washington, 1947), 5–43; Truman, *Years of Trial and Hope,* 108; Donald F. Herr, "The Truman Doctrine" (honors thesis, Harvard College, 1961), 65, 83.

28. *Forrestal Diaries,* 263.

29. Maurice Thorez, *Oeuvres* (Paris, 1965), XXIII, 65; Auriol, *Journal,* 174, 727; UN, *World Economic Report, 1948,* 34.

30. Thorez, *Oeuvres,* 78–79, 87; Jacques Fauvet, *Histoire du Parti Communiste Français* (Paris, 1965), 193–94; Georgette Elgey, *La République des Illusions: 1945–1951* (Paris, 1965), 248–49, 259–60, 278–79; Auriol, *Journal,* 37, 54, 64–65, 82–84, 95–96, 139–40, 162, 206–07, 248–49, 278–79; UN, *World Economic Report, 1948,* 10.

31. Elgey, *La République des Illusions,* 280–85; Auriol, *Journal,* 99, 204–13, 758–59; Val R. Lorwin, *The French Labor Movement* (Cambridge, 1954), 107; Fauvet, *Histoire du Parti Communiste,* 196–99; Thorez, *Oeuvres,* 108–33.

32. Auriol, *Journal,* 74, 742; Henry J. Tasca to Andrew N. Overby, January 16, 1947, JWS Mss; Norman Kogan, *A Political History of Postwar Italy* (New York, 1966), 44–45; Giuseppe Mammarella, *Italy after Fascism: A Political History, 1943–1965* (Notre Dame, 1966), 135–45.

33. *New Times,* May 23, 1947, 9–13, 18–19; May 30, 1947, 12–15; Eugenio Reale, *Avec Jacques Duclos* (Paris, 1958), 176, *passim;* Vladamir Dedijer, *Tito* (New York, 1953), 296.

34. Hugh Dalton, *High Tide and After* (London, 1962), 221–22; DS, *Germany 1947–49: The Story in Documents* (Washington, 1950), 152; John Gimbel, *The American Occupation of Germany* (Stanford, 1968), 117–20.

35. Dulles, "Europe Must Federate or Perish," 236. See also Lucius Clay to Joseph M. Dodge, December 23, 1946, JMD Mss, Germany Assignment, box 1; *Business Week,* January 1, 1947, 129.

36. Lewis P. Lochner, *Herbert Hoover and Germany* (New York, 1960), 185. See also Allen W. Dulles, "Alternatives for Germany," *Foreign Affairs,* 25 (1947), 421–32; John Foster Dulles to George C. Marshall, February 9, 1947; Dulles to Vandenberg, February 9, 1947, AHV Mss; Kenneth C. Royall to John Taber,

August 8, 1947, JT Mss, box 142; Herbert Hoover, *The President's Economic Mission to Germany and Austria. Report No. 3* . . . (March 24, 1947), 14–16, in JT Mss, box 142; Herbert Hoover, *An American Epic* (Chicago, 1964), IV, 255.

37. DSB, March 16, 1947, 497. See also John Foster Dulles, "Report on Moscow Meeting of Council of Foreign Ministers," *International Conciliation,* No. 432 (1947), 449.

38. John Foster Dulles, *War or Peace* (New York, 1950), 102.

39. Lucius B. Clay to Joseph M. Dodge, March 24, 1947, JMD Mss, Germany Assignment, box 1. See also *New Times,* March 7, 1947, 1–2.

40. Robert Murphy, *Diplomat among Warriors* (New York, 1964), 306. See also Mason, "Reflections on the Moscow Conference," 483.

41. Mason, "Reflections on the Moscow Conference," 482–83. See also V. M. Molotov, *Problems of Foreign Policy* (Moscow, 1949), 359–98; *New Times,* April 18, 1947, 8–11; *Soviet Press Translations,* April 30, 1947, 11–15; May 31, 1947, 9–10; DS, *Germany, 1947–1949,* 152–55, 188–90, 441–45.

42. DS, *Germany, 1947–1949,* 330.

43. Dulles, *War or Peace,* 104; Auriol, *Journal,* 17, 21, 28, 45, 167–68, 180, 184–85, 222–23, 673–74.

44. DS, *Germany, 1947–1949,* 58, 63. See also *ibid.,* 60, 63, for a more sanguine description; Bohlen, *American Foreign Policy,* 87–88; Lucius D. Clay, *Decision in Germany* (New York, 1950), 174.

45. Dulles, "Report on Moscow Meeting of Council of Foreign Ministers," 457.

46. U.S. Army, Office of Military Government—Berlin Sector, "Weekly Intelligence Reports," May 15–21, 1947, No. 23, 7, FLH Mss. See also Kennan, *Memoirs,* 335; Bohlen, *American Foreign Policy,* 89; Clay, *Decision in Germany,* 174; Gimbel, *American Occupation of Germany,* 123–29; *Forrestal Diaries,* 273.

47. DS, *Germany, 1947–1949,* 34, 40. See also James Stewart Martin, *All Honorable Men* (Boston, 1950), 232; George C. Marshall to Henry L. Stimson, April 28, 1947, May 30, 1947; Acheson to Marshall, May 28, 1947, HLS Mss; M. S. Szymczak memo to Truman, May 14, 1947, HST Mss, OF 198–B; Robert Patterson to Allen W. Dulles, April 21, 1947, RP Mss, box 8; memo of telephone conversation, Stimson and John J. McCloy, May 5, 1947, HLS Mss; John Steelman memo of telephone call from Alvin Browning, ca. August 20, 1947, HST Mss, OF 275–A; Gimbel, *American Occupation of Germany,* 152–58.

48. Willard L. Thorp, *Problems of United States Foreign Economic Policy* [DS Commercial Policy Series 104] (Washington, 1948), 16–17. See also Acheson, *Present at the Creation,* 226; *Forrestal Diaries,* 263; Gardner, *Sterling-Dollar Diplomacy,* 298–99; Joseph Jones memo to Acheson, May 1, 1947, JMJ Mss, box 1.

49. Acheson speech of April 18, 1947, in JMJ Mss, box 1; *New Times,* February 21, 1947, 10–11; May 16, 1947, 5; *Soviet Press Translations,* July 15, 1947, 34; October 1, 1947, 136–38.

50. Gardner, *Sterling-Dollar Diplomacy,* 349–59; Ross J. Pritchard, "Will Clayton: A Study of Business Statesmanship in the Formulation of United States Foreign Economic Policy" (unpublished Ph.D. thesis, Fletcher School of Law and Diplomacy, 1955), 325–31; Allen J. Matusow, *Farm Policies and Politics in the Truman Years* (Cambridge, 1967), 92–99.

51. Kennan, *Memoirs,* 334. See also Jones, *Fifteen Weeks,* 203, 241–43.

52. Jones, *Fifteen Weeks,* 276. See also *ibid.,* 212, 274–81; Acheson, *Present at the Creation,* 226–29.

53. Joseph Jones memo of May 20, 1947, JMJ Mss, box 2; Pritchard, "Will Clayton," 281, 292–95; Kennan, *Memoirs,* 341–43; Acheson, *Present at the Creation,* 232; Jones, *Fifteen Weeks,* 251–54; William L. Clayton, "GATT, The Marshall Plan, and OECD," *Political Science Quarterly,* 78 (1963), 493–503.

Chapter 13: The Marshall Plan, I: Foundations of Policy

1. John Foster Dulles, "Our Foreign Loan Policy," *Foreign Affairs,* 5 (1926), 37.

2. Gardiner Patterson and Judd Polk, "The Emerging Pattern of Bilateralism," *Quarterly Journal of Economics,* 62 (1947), 118–42.

3. U.S. Senate, Committee on Foreign Relations, *A Decade of American Foreign Policy: Basic Documents, 1941–49,* 81:1 (Washington, 1950), 1269.

4. Moscow Embassy to George C. Marshall, June 17, 1947, JMJ Mss, box 2. See also Vincent Auriol, *Journal du Septennat: 1947* (Paris, 1970), 284, 311–12.

5. Quoted in Paul Eric Koefod, *New Concept in the Quest for Peace: Marshall Plan, Aspect of Power Politics* (Geneva, 1950), 120.

6. *New Times,* June 27, 1947, 1. See also Royal Institute of International Affairs, *Documents on International Affairs, 1947–1948* (London, 1952), 32, 36, 43.

7. *New Times,* June 27, 1947, 3. See also James P. Warburg, *Germany: Key to Peace* (Cambridge, 1953), 45.

8. V. M. Molotov, *Problems of Foreign Policy* (Moscow, 1949), 464. See also RIIA, *Documents on International Affairs, 1947–1948,* 36–38, 53.

9. William L. Clayton, "GATT, The Marshall Plan, and OECD," *Political Science Quarterly,* 78 (1963), 500; *The Economist,* July 12, 1947, 51–52.

10. Molotov, *Problems of Foreign Policy,* 466–70.

11. Auriol, *Journal,* 324, 348, 354.

12. *Ibid.,* 352; Harry Bayard Price, *The Marshall Plan and Its Meaning* (Ithaca, 1955), 27; Clayton, "GATT, The Marshall Plan, and OECD," 501–02.

13. Clayton, "GATT, The Marshall Plan, and OECD," 502. See also New York *Times,* September 14, 23, 1947.

14. *Ibid.; The Economist,* December 4, 1948, 925–26; Koefod, *New Concept in the Quest for Peace,* 150–51; Warren L. Hickman, *Genesis of the European Recovery Program: A Study on the Trend of American Economic Policies* (Geneva, 1949), 260–61.

15. *The Economist,* September 20, 1947, 482; September 27, 1947, 505–06; Price, *Marshall Plan and Its Meaning,* 37–38.

16. U.S.I.S. (London), "British Press Summary," August 23, 1947, CW Mss.

17. Wilcox to Clayton, August 6, 1947, CW Mss. See also Auriol, *Journal,* 359–60.

18. *The Economist,* August 9, 1947, 229.

19. Walter Millis, ed:, *The Forrestal Diaries* (New York, 1951), 302.

20. *Ibid.,* 304.

21. George Elgey, *La République des Illusions: 1945–1951* (Paris, 1965), 336; Pierre-Lucien Simon, "Bilan sans gloire de l'économie française," *Esprit,* 16 (1948), 524–40.

22. Alexander Werth, *France, 1940–1955* (New York, 1956), 359; Elgey, *La République des Illusions,* 329.

23. Auriol, *Journal,* 504–05.

24. Elgey, *La République des Illusions,* 339–65; Val R. Lorwin, *The French Labor Movement* (Cambridge, 1954), 121.

25. Quoted in Lorwin, *French Labor Movement,* 125. See also Auriol, *Journal,* 521–22; Elgey, *La République des Illusions,* 357; André Géraud, "Insurrection Fades in France," *Foreign Affairs,* 28 (1949), 30–42.

26. Quoted in Werth, *France,* 384. See also Auriol, *Journal,* 617–18.

27. Paul Fraisse, "Les français face à leurs responsabilités," *Esprit,* 16 (1948), 623–31; Werth, *France,* 400.

28. Giuseppe Mammarella, *Italy after Fascism: A Political History, 1943–1965* (Notre Dame, 1966), 149, 274–81.

29. Bruno Foa, *Monetary Reconstruction in Italy* (New York, 1949), 70, 86.

30. *Ibid.*, 116, 126; Mammarella, *Italy after Fascism,* 154–55; Economic Cooperation Administration, *Italy Country Study* (Washington, 1949), 2, 20–21; UN, Department of Economic Affairs, *Economic Survey of Europe in 1948* (Geneva, 1949), 4.

31. *The Economist,* July 12, 1947, 51–52; May 1, 1948, 716–17; October 2, 1948, 589–90; Auriol, *Journal,* 354, 360, 382–83.

32. U.S. Senate, Committee on Foreign Relations, *Hearings: Interim Aid for Europe,* 80:1, November 1947 (Washington, 1948), 126.

33. Quoted in U.S. Senate on Foreign Relations, *Hearings: European Recovery Program,* 80:2, January–February 1948. (Washington, 1948), 47. See also *ibid.*, 15; Eugenio Reale, *Avec Jacques Duclos* (Paris, 1958), 143–50.

34. James Warburg, *Put Yourself in Marshall's Place* (New York, 1948), 76. See also U.S. House, Committee on Foreign Affairs, *Hearings: Emergency Foreign Aid,* 80:1, November 1947, (Washington, 1947), 67, 122.

35. President's Committee on Foreign Aid, *European Recovery and American Aid: A Report* (Washington, 1947), 3.

36. Council of Economic Advisers, *The Impact of Foreign Aid upon the Domestic Economy: A Report to the President* (Washington, 1947), 30–31. See also *ibid.*, passim.

37. Senate Committee on Foreign Relations, *European Recovery Program,* 249.

38. Reprinted in Warburg, *Put Yourself in Marshall's Place,* 62.

39. President's Committee on Foreign Aid, *European Recovery,* 18, 34, 117–22.

40. DSB, January 25, 1948, 111. See also *ibid.*, June 22, 1947, 1237–38; July 27, 1947, 185; November 16, 1947, 992; December 21, 1947, 1213; House Committee on Foreign Affairs, *Emergency Foreign Aid, passim;* Senate Committee on Foreign Relations, *Interim Aid, passim.*

41. Quoted in Price, *Marshall Plan and Its Meaning,* 22. See also George S. Kennan, *Memoirs: 1925–1950* (Boston, 1967), 341; Joseph M. Jones, *The Fifteen Weeks* (New York, 1955), 249.

42. Dulles to Vandenberg, March 4, 1948; Vandenberg to Dulles, March 6, 1948, AHV Mss.

43. *Forrestal Diaries,* 387, 395.

44. New York *Times,* March 30, 1948. See also John C. Campbell, *The United States in World Affairs 1947–1948* (New York, 1948), 507.

45. Harry S. Truman, *Public Papers of the Presidents of the United States: 1948* (Washington, 1964), 233.

46. *Forrestal Diaries,* 442–43.

47. *Ibid.,* 443–44.

48. H. Bradford Westerfield, *Foreign Policy and Party Politics: Pearl Harbor to Korea* (New Haven, 1955), 287; William Adams Brown, Jr., and Redvers Opie, *American Foreign Assistance* (Washington, 1953), 152.

49. DSB, July 11, 1948, 36. See also Brown and Opie, *American Foreign Assistance,* 158.

50. Paul Hoffman, *Peace Can Be Won* (New York, 1951), 91.

51. Price, *Marshall Plan and Its Meaning,* 114.

52. Robert A. Lovett to Arthur Vandenberg, January 19, 1948, AHV Mss. See also Brown and Opie, *American Foreign Assistance,* 244.

53. David E. Lilienthal, *The Atomic Energy Years, 1945–1950* (New York, 1964), 329.

54. *Business Week,* September 4, 1948, 105–07; Price, *Marshall Plan and Its Meaning,* 77.

Chapter 14: Czechoslovakia and the Consolidation of Soviet Power

1. Herbert Hoover, *An American Epic* (Chicago, 1964), IV, 116; Joseph Dodge, "Notes about Hungary, Czechoslovakia and Russia," July 1947, JMD Mss, Germany Assignment, box 7.

2. Hubert Ripka, *Czechoslovakia Enslaved: The Story of the Communist Coup d'État* (London, 1950), 54.

3. *Ibid.,* 67.

4. *Ibid.,* 68.

5. *Ibid.,* 69.

6. *Ibid.,* 59.

7. Harold C. Vedeler to Laurence Steinhardt, August 12, 1947, LAS Mss, box 55.

8. Dodge, "Notes about Hungary, Czechoslovakia and Russia."

9. Laurence A. Steinhardt, speech presented to National War College, December 15, 1947, 10–11, LAS Mss.

10. Steinhardt to Francis P. Williamson, October 29, 1947, LAS Mss, box 85. See also Howard K. Smith, *The State of Europe* (New York, 1949), 341–42; Ripka, *Czechoslovakia Enslaved,* 128.

11. Steinhardt to Williamson, October 29, 1947, LAS Mss, box 85.

12. Quoted in Trygve Lie, *In the Cause of Peace* (New York, 1954), 233.

13. Paul E. Zinner, *Communist Strategy and Tactics in Czechoslovakia, 1918–*

1948 (New York, 1963), 192–93; R. R. Betts, ed., *Central and South East Europe, 1945–1948* (London, 1950), 185; Steinhardt to William Diamond, May 27, 1947, LAS Mss, box 84; *The Economist,* January 10, 1948, 61–62; Eugenio Reale, *Avec Jacques Duclos* (Paris, 1958), 105; Morton A. Kaplan, *The Communist Coup in Czechoslovakia* (Princeton, 1960), 19.

14. Betts, *Central and South East Europe,* 188; Jindrich Vesely, *Prague 1948* (Paris, 1958), 63–64, 68–69.

15. There is some dispute on this point. Ripka and Vesely, the CP official, claim Beneš knew of their plans and encouraged them; Smutny, Beneš' aide and a Social Democrat, insists he was surprised by their acts. Josef Korbel, *The Communist Subversion of Czechoslovakia, 1938–1949* (Princeton, 1959), 211–12; Vesely, *Prague 1948,* 87–93; Ripka, *Czechoslovakia Enslaved,* 221.

16. Quoted in Korbel, *Subversion of Czechoslovakia,* 212.

17. Robert Bruce Lockhart, "The Czechoslovak Revolution," *Foreign Affairs,* 26 (1948), 641.

18. Zinner, *Communist Strategy and Tactics,* 216; Betts, *Central and South East Europe,* 191; Lockhart, "The Czechoslovak Revolution," 641–44; Korbel, *Subversion of Czechoslovakia,* 206–09.

19. Zinner, *Communist Strategy and Tactics,* 222; Joseph C. Harsch, *The Curtain Isn't Iron* (New York, 1950), 89–91.

20. Quoted in Doreen Warriner, *Revolution in Eastern Europe* (London, 1950), 37.

21. Quoted in Lie, *In the Cause of Peace,* 232–33.

22. Robert Bruce Lockhart, *Jan Masaryk, A Personal Memoir* (London, 1956), 42, 55; *Le Monde,* Sélection Hebdomadaire, September 5–11, 1968; Michael Karolyi, *Memoirs* (London, 1956), 346.

23. Riddleberger to Steinhardt, December 2, 1946, LAS Mss, box 51.

24. Riddleberger to Steinhardt, October 3, 1946, LAS Mss, box 51.

25. Kaplan, *Communist Coup in Czechoslovakia,* 18–19; Zinner, *Communist Strategy and Tactics,* 217; Korbel, *Subversion of Czechoslovakia,* 212–13.

26. Lie, *In the Cause of Peace,* 236.

27. Steinhardt to Dulles, September 13, 1948, LAS Mss, box 54. The compensation issue was never resolved to American satisfaction, however, and Washington regards it as the outstanding question with the Czech government to this day, although it has grossly inflated compensation claims to $110 million. In addition, the United States still holds in its vaults some $22 million of Czech gold that the Americans captured from the Nazis. Washington has always regarded this gold as the trump card in its negotiations with the Czechs. New York *Times,* April 14, 1968, April 20, 1968.

28. See what is unquestionably the best study of the politics of Eastern Europe from 1945 to 1952, François Fejtö, *Histoire des Démocraties Populaires: L'Ère de Staline* (Paris, 1969), 226–49; *Business Week,* July 24, 1948, 108–11; Vladamir Dedijer, *Tito* (New York, 1953), 278ff.; Dedijer, *The Battle Stalin Lost* (New York, 1971) chap. 3; for a pro-Soviet account, see Warriner, *Revolution in Eastern Europe,* 53–54.

29. United Nations, Department of Economic Affairs, *Economic Survey of Europe in 1948* (Geneva, 1949), 146–47, 160.

30. United Nations, Department of Economic Affairs, *Recent Changes in Production* (New York, 1952), 4.

Chapter 15: Heir to Empire: The Near East and Mastery of the World's Oil

1. Report of the Economic Adviser, The American Mission for Aid to Greece, September 26, 1947, JT Mss, box 144. See also Stephen G. Xydis, *Greece and the Great Powers, 1944–1947* (Thessaloniki, 1963), 464, 478–81, 533; Paul A. Porter, "Wanted: A Miracle in Greece," *Collier's,* September 20, 1947, 106; U.S. Senate, Committee on Foreign Relations, *Hearings: Assistance to Greece and Turkey,* 80:1, March 24–31, 1947 (Washington, 1947), 180–81; Frank Smothers *et al., Report on the Greeks* (New York, 1948), 30–31; U.S. House, Committee on Foreign Affairs, *Hearings: Emergency Foreign Aid,* 80:1, November 1947 (Washington, 1947), 213–14; U.S. House, Select Committee on Foreign Aid, *Report on Greece,* 80:2, March 4, 1948 (Washington, 1948), 9–11; *Business Week,* April 30, 1949, 117–18; DSB, May 4, 1947, supplement, 899.

2. Harry S. Truman, *Years of Trial and Hope* (New York, 1956), 109. See also F. A. Voigt, *The Greek Sedition* (London, 1949), 21; "Comments made by General Livesay before Congressional Group, . . . 25 September, 1947," JT Mss, box 144.

3. Smothers, *Report on the Greeks,* 32. See also DS, *Second Report to Congress on Assistance to Greece and Turkey, December 31, 1947* (Washington, 1948), 8.

4. Smothers, *Report on the Greeks,* 32–33; House Select Committee on Foreign Aid, *Report on Greece,* 4; Porter, "Wanted: A Miracle in Greece," 106; R. V. Burks, *The Dynamics of Communism in Eastern Europe* (Princeton, 1961), 22–23; *The Times* (London), May 7, 1948; Bickham Sweet-Escott, *Greece: A Political and Economic Survey, 1939–1953* (London, 1954), 73; DSB, October 19, 1947, 776; October 26, 1947, 831; March 7, 1948, 315; U.S. Senate, Committee on Foreign Relations, *Hearings: Military Assistance Program,* 81:1, August 8–19, 1949 (Washington, 1949), 141–42.

5. Smothers, *Report on the Greeks,* 153. See also *ibid.,* 38–40; "Comments made by General Livesay . . .," September 25, 1947, JT Mss, box 144; Edgar O'Ballance, *The Greek Civil War, 1944–1949* (New York, 1966), 142; DS, *Second Report to Congress on Assistance to Greece,* 4; House Select Committee on Foreign Aid, *Report on Greece,* 3–4; *The Economist,* July 5, 1947, 3–4; August 7, 1948, 233; DSB, October 19, 1947, 777; Burks, *Dynamics of Communism,* 47.

6. *New Times,* March 21, 1947, 1–3; Sweet-Escott, *Greece,* 65; Dominique Eudes, *Les Kapetanios: la guerre civile grecque de 1943 à 1949* (Paris, 1970), 399–403; DS, *The United Nations and the Problem of Greece* (Washington, 1947), *passim;* Burks, *Dynamics of Communism,* 102; Evangelos Kofos, *Nationalism and Communism in Macedonia* (Thessaloniki, 1964), 167–73; DSB, May 4, 1947, supplement, 894; Hugh Seton-Watson, *The East European Revolution* (New York, 1956), 354–58.

7. "Comments made by General Livesay . . .," September 25, 1947, JT Mss, box

144; Sweet-Escott, *Greece,* 63–64; Eudes, *Les Kapetanios,* 422–23, 435; O'Ballance, *Greek Civil War,* 167–77; DSB, February 29, 1948, 276; *The Economist,* August 7, 1948, 233; February 11, 1950, 324–25; FR (1946), VI, 104–05.

8. Milovan Djilas, *Conversations with Stalin* (New York, 1962), 181–82. See also Burks, *Dynamics of Communism,* 100–01; Kofos, *Nationalism and Communism,* 161–64; Eugenio Reale, *Avec Jacques Duclos* (Paris, 1958), 109–18, 129–38, 143–50; Vladimir Dedijer, *Tito* (New York, 1953), 316–22; Dedijer, *The Battle that Stalin Lost* (New York, 1971), 193; Vincent Auriol, *Mon Septennat, 1947–1954* (Paris, 1970), 117–19; *The Economist,* February 11, 1950, 324–25.

9. Kofos, *Nationalism and Communism,* 175–84; Eudes, *Les Kapetanios,* 429ff.; Sweet-Escott, *Greece,* 65, 69; Harry N. Howard, *Greece and the United Nations, 1946–49* [DS International Organization and Conference Series III, 40] (Washington, 1949), *passim;* Harry N. Howard, *The Greek Question in the Fourth General Assembly of the United Nations* [DS International Organization and Conference Series III, 47] (Washington, 1950), *passim;* O'Ballance, *Greek Civil War,* 196–201; *The Economist,* May 7, 1949, 829; CDSP, June 21, 1949, 37; DSB, May 29, 1949, 696–97; September 19, 1949, 416; October 31, 1949, 658.

10. U.S. Senate, Committee on Foreign Relations, *Hearings: United States Foreign Aid Programs in Europe,* 82:1, July 1951 (Washington, 1951), 140. See also *ibid.,* 138–43; C. A. Munkman, *American Aid to Greece* (New York, 1958), 70, 97–98, 148ff., 219ff; L. S. Stavrianos, *Greece: American Dilemma and Opportunity* (Chicago, 1952), 213ff.; Sweet-Escott, *Greece,* chaps. V, IX; New York *Times,* January 6, 1953; United Nations, Department of Economic and Social Affairs, *The Growth of World Industry, 1938–1961: National Tables* (New York, 1963), 341.

11. Quoted in Theodore A. Couloumbis, *Greek Political Reaction to American and NATO Influences* (New Haven, 1966), 54.

12. DS, "Briefing Book," March 1947, TC Mss, box 178. See also George Kirk, *The Middle East, 1945–1950* (London, 1954), 40.

13. John C. Campbell, *Defense of the Middle East* (New York, 1960), 284. See also Kirk, *The Middle East,* 40–42; *Soviet Press Translations,* October 15, 1947, 155–57; *Business Week,* November 6, 1948, 120; DS, *American Foreign Policy, 1950–1955* (Washington, 1957), II, 2187–88; Senate Committee on Foreign Relations, *United States Foreign Aid Programs,* 160; Walter Millis, ed., *The Forrestal Diaries* (New York, 1951), 357.

14. *The Economist,* March 15, 1947, 377–78.

15. Marrs McLean to Arthur H. Vandenberg, June 21, 1947, AHV Mss. See also DSB, May 4, 1947, supplement, 894; *Time,* March 24, 1947, 83–84; *Congressional Record,* vol. 93, 4632; Federal Trade Commission, *The International Petroleum Cartel,* August 22, 1952 (Washington, 1952), 104–05; *Business Week,* November 20, 1948, 124; Beauford H. Jester to Tom Connally, June 2, 1947, TC Mss, box 101.

16. DS, Technical Committee on Petroleum, "U.S. Petroleum Policy," November 10, 1947, 2–3, 8, JAK Mss, box 66. See also Benjamin Shwadran, *The Middle East, Oil and the Great Powers* (New York, 1955), 382.

17. DS, "U.S. Petroleum Policy," 8. See also *Forrestal Diaries,* 367; U.S. House, Committee on Armed Services, *Hearings: Petroleum for National Defense,* 80:2, January–March 1948 (Washington, 1948), 9.

18. *Forrestal Diaries,* 358. See also FR (1945), IX, 1161–62; FR (1946), XI, 1006–16.

19. Irving Florman to Donald Dawson, December 28, 1950, HST Mss, OF 56. See also House Committee on Armed Services, *Petroleum for National Defense,* 307–15; U.S. House, Committee on Interstate and Foreign Commerce, *Hearings: Petroleum Study,* 81:2, February-May 1950 (Washington, 1950), 231–43; DSB, August 1, 1949, 153; C. V. Whitney to Lawrence Morris, May 17, 1949, DC Mss, file 71744; for Standard Oil of New Jersey's desire to enter Brazil, see R. T. Haslam to John R. Steelman, July 7, 1949, HST Mss, OF 56–A.

20. Henry F. Grady, "Oil and the Middle East," *Foreign Policy Bulletin,* 31 (December 15, 1951), 2. See also Leonard M. Fanning, *Foreign Oil and the Free World* (New York, 1954), 111–15; Kirk, *The Middle East,* 102–04; Dean Acheson, *Present at the Creation* (New York, 1969), 501–08; Shwadran, *The Middle East,* 110–16, 136ff.; *Business Week,* May 19, 1951, 152; May 26, 1951, 155; July 21, 1951, 119; July 28, 1951, 135; Anthony Eden, *Full Circle* (Boston, 1960), 219; Harold Macmillan, *Tides of Fortune, 1945–55* (London, 1969), 343; Royal Institute of International Affairs, *Documents on International Affairs, 1951* (London, 1954), 498ff.; Arthur Krock, *Memoirs* (New York, 1968), 262.

21. Macmillan, *Tides of Fortune,* 344–46; Acheson, *Present at the Creation,* 506–10, 600, 679–85; Eden, *Full Circle,* 221–24; Shwadran, *The Middle East,* 147–48; Royal Institute of International Affairs, *Documents on International Affairs, 1952* (London, 1955), 337–53.

22. Royal Institute of International Affairs, *Documents on International Affairs, 1953* (London, 1956), 353. See also Dwight D. Eisenhower, *Mandate for Change, 1953–1956* (New York, 1963), 162; Eden, *Full Circle,* 232–37.

23. Quoted in Fanning, *Foreign Oil and the Free World,* 301. See also David Wise and Thomas B. Ross, *The Invisible Government* (New York, 1964), 110–13; Shwadran, *The Middle East,* 59; Eisenhower, *Mandate for Change,* 163–64; Fitzroy Maclean, *Eastern Approaches* (London, 1949), 266–74; Eden, *Full Circle,* 237.

24. Shwadran, *The Middle East,* 179–89; Fanning, *Foreign Oil and the Free World,* chap. XXIV; Macmillan, *Tides of Fortune,* 501–02. Throughout this period, United States and British interests were also locked in conflict for control of the oil-rich protectorate of Buraimi on the Persian Gulf, which spilled over to neighboring Oman. During 1949, Saudi Arabia for the first time claimed jurisdiction over much of the region, and Aramco provided it with its legal case. By mid-1953, Saudi troops had moved into the region, and Aramco blocked arbitration efforts. Since the State Department claimed neutrality in the matter, the British began arming and leading local tribesmen to resist the Saudi invaders, and by the summer of 1957 they were forced to send in their own troops to put down dissident local tribesmen whose connection with Saudi Arabia, and Aramco, is still a mystery. By mid-1956 Dulles regarded British behavior in the region as an "act of aggression," and fully expressed this view. See Eden, *Full Circle,* 373. Also see Bushrod Howard, Jr., "Buraimi: A Study in Diplomacy by Default," *The Reporter,* January 23, 1958, 13–16.

25. *Soviet Press Translations,* July 15, 1947, 34. See also *ibid.,* October 1, 1947, 136–38; *New Times,* March 21, 1947, 1–3.

26. FR (1945), VIII, 698. See also *ibid.,* 681ff.; *Soviet Press Translations,* March

15, 1948, 188; April 15, 1948, 237–39; Gabriel Kolko, *The Politics of War* (New York, 1968), 297, 494.

27. U.S. Senate, Committee on Foreign Relations, *A Decade of American Foreign Policy: Basic Documents, 1941–49* (Washington, 1950), 812–14. See also Truman, *Years of Trial and Hope*, 133–41; Kirk, *The Middle East*, 206, 213–14; Acheson, *Present at the Creation*, 169–71; FR (1945), VIII, 705–819.

28. Senate Committee on Foreign Relations, *Decade of American Foreign Policy*, 817. See also Truman, *Years of Trial and Hope*, 149–52; FR (1946), VII, 585–91, 598, 612–14, 632–33, 644–61, 675–82, 704–05; Kirk, *The Middle East*, 223–28; *Forrestal Diaries*, 346–47.

29. Truman, *Years of Trial and Hope*, 154; Kirk, *The Middle East*, 229; Acheson, *Present at the Creation*, 176–77. Truman's memoir glosses over the obliqueness of his statement. It is true that he claimed that he was in favor of the admission of 100,000 refugees ". . . at the earliest possible moment," but only ". . . substantial immigration . . . should begin at once." Senate Committee on Foreign Relations, *Decade of American Foreign Policy*, 817. The men who prepare notes such as these are aware of distinctions.

30. *Forrestal Diaries*, 305, 309, 344–47; FR (1946), VII, 712, 732–34; Senate Committee on Foreign Relations, *Decade of American Foreign Policy*, 819–20; Kirk, *The Middle East*, 248; Truman, *Years of Trial and Hope*, 158; Robert H. Ferrell, *George C. Marshall* (New York, 1966), 187.

31. *Forrestal Diaries*, 360. See also *ibid.*, 346, 357–58.

32. Trygve Lie, *In the Cause of Peace* (New York, 1954), 169. See also *ibid.*, 166–68; *Forrestal Diaries*, 361–65, 371–72; Kirk, *The Middle East*, 257; Truman, *Years of Trial and Hope*, 159–62; Herbert Feis, *The Birth of Israel* (New York, 1969), 52–53; Ferrell, *George C. Marshall*, 188–89.

33. Senate Committee on Foreign Relations, *Decade of American Foreign Policy*, 840.

34. Lie, *In the Cause of Peace*, 170–71.

35. Truman, *Years of Trial and Hope*, 164. See also Lie, *In the Cause of Peace*, 171–72; Kirk, *The Middle East*, 259–60; Feis, *Birth of Israel*, 56–57, 80; *Forrestal Diaries*, 410; Arnold A. Rogow, *James Forrestal: A Study of Personality, Politics, and Policy* (New York, 1963), 191ff.

36. "Middle East Situation—May 1948," Leahy Diary, WDL Mss. See also *Business Week*, June 5, 1948, 15; June 12, 1948, 16; Ferrell, *George C. Marshall*, 190–91; Kirk, *The Middle East*, 267–70; *Forrestal Diaries*, 440; Truman, *Years of Trial and Hope*, 164.

37. *Soviet Press Translations*, July 1, 1948, 398–402; October 1, 1948, 517–19; *Forrestal Diaries*, 470–71; Truman, *Years of Trial and Hope*, 167–68.

38. Commander-in-Chief, U.S. Naval Forces, Eastern Atlantic and Mediterranean, "Report of Operations and Conditions of Command, 1 July 1951 to 14 June 1952," 3–4, ONH Mss.

39. RIIA, *Documents on International Affairs, 1952*, 322–24; Macmillan, *Tides of Fortune*, 501–02; Acheson, *Present at the Creation*, 563–67; *Forrestal Diaries*, 342; Eden, *Full Circle*, 274–82. Eden reflects on this pattern of behavior to explain the background of American policy on the 1956 Suez crisis. See Eden, *Full Circle*, 373–75.

Chapter 16: The Marshall Plan, II: The Economics of European Restoration

1. Richard M. Bissell, "The Impact of Rearmament on the Free World Economy," *Foreign Affairs,* 29 (1951), 388; UN, Department of Economic Affairs, *World Economic Report—1948* (Lake Success, 1949), 167.

2. William Adams Brown, Jr., and Redvers Opie, *American Foreign Assistance* (Washington, 1953), 188–90.

3. *Business Week,* September 11, 1948, 123; U.S. Senate, Committee on Foreign Relations, *Hearings: European Recovery Program,* 80:2, January–February 1948 (Washington, 1948), 1221; *The Economist,* September 11, 1948, 407; Lucius D. Clay, *Decision in Germany* (New York, 1950), 217–18; Richard H. Heindel to Arthur Vandenberg, August 24, 1948, AHV Mss; N. H. Collisson, Memo to J. A. Krug, August 30, 1948, JAK Mss, box 66.

4. Thomas Balogh, *Germany: An Experiment in "Planning" by the "Free" Price Mechanism* (Oxford, 1950), 16; Horst Mendershausen, "Prices, Money, and the Distribution of Goods in Postwar Germany," *American Economic Review,* 39 (1949), 650–56; Karl W. Roskamp, *Capital Formation in West Germany* (Detroit, 1965), 39; Howard K. Smith, *The State of Europe* (New York, 1949), 108–09.

5. Walter Heller, "The Role of Fiscal-Monetary Policy in German Economic Recovery," *American Economic Review,* 40 (1950), 536–41; William Y. Elliott *et al., The Political Economy of American Foreign Policy: Its Concepts, Strategy and Limits* (New York, 1955), 120; Balogh, *Germany,* 21ff.

6. Fred H. Klopstock, "Monetary Reform in Liberated Europe," *American Economic Review,* 36 (1946), 578; Clay, *Decision in Germany,* 210; Charles P. Kindleberger, "The Marshall Plan and the Cold War," *International Journal,* 23 (1968), 381; Roskamp, *Capital Formation in West Germany,* 42–46; Clay to Joseph Dodge, January 26, 1949, JMD Mss, Japan 1949, box 1.

7. Balogh, *Germany,* 21–22; Mendershausen, "Prices, Money, and the Distribution of Goods," 663–64; United Nations, *World Economic Report—1948,* 154; Roskamp, *Capital Formation in West Germany,* 44–45.

8. United Nations, Department of Economic Affairs, *Economic Survey of Europe in 1948* (Geneva, 1949), 29. See also United Nations, Department of Economic Affairs, *Economic Survey of Europe in 1949* (Geneva, 1950), 65–66; Roskamp, *Capital Formation in West Germany,* 44; Balogh, *Germany,* 11–12, 66–72; Kindleberger, "The Marshall Plan and the Cold War," 381.

9. Mendershausen, "Prices, Money, and the Distribution of Goods," 672; Roskamp, *Capital Formation in West Germany,* 37; DS, *Germany, 1947–1949: The Story in Documents* (Washington, 1950), 300–01, 474; Clay, *Decision in Germany,* 291–97; Balogh, *Germany,* 22–23, 48; UN, *Europe in 1948,* 28–29; UN, *World Economic Report—1948,* 154; *The Economist,* April 9, 1949, 660.

10. Blaisdell memo, "Marshall vs. the Marshall Plan," November 29, 1948, TCB Mss, box 8. See also Harold Zink, *The United States in Germany, 1944–1955* (Princeton, 1957), 201–03; *Business Week,* June 19, 1948, 120–21; November 27, 1948, 109; Alexander Werth, *France, 1940–1955* (New York, 1956), 426.

11. *U.S. News and World Report,* July 29, 1949, 20–21.

12. *The Economist,* August 7, 1948, 218.

13. UN, *Europe in 1948,* 30. See also Giuseppe Mammarella, *Italy after Fascism: A Political History, 1943–1965* (Notre Dame, 1966), 152; Bruno Foa, *Monetary Reconstruction in Italy* (New York, 1949), 121, 126.

14. *Business Week,* April 3, 1948, 115; David Wise and Thomas B. Ross, *The Invisible Government* (New York, 1964), 95.

15. Smith, *State of Europe,* 206; *The Economist,* March 27, 1948, 492–93; Mammarella, *Italy after Fascism,* 192–95.

16. H. Stuart Hughes, *The United States and Italy* (Cambridge, 1953), 157; Mammarella, *Italy after Fascism,* 202ff.

17. Val R. Lorwin, *The French Labor Movement* (Cambridge, 1954), 128–32; *The Economist,* April 10, 1948, 589–90; *Business Week,* June 25, 1949, 53; August 13, 1949, 79; Economic Cooperation Administration, *France: Country Study European Recovery Program* (Washington, 1949), 2–5; Werth, *France,* 420.

18. Quoted in Lorwin, *French Labor Movement,* 137.

19. ECA, *France,* 11. See also *ibid.,* 10; Irving Brown, "Who Will Win in France," *American Federationist,* October 1948, 6; UN, *World Economic Report, 1948,* 33; UN, *Europe in 1949,* 25.

20. ECA, *France,* 11, 34; UN, *World Economic Report—1948,* 34.

21. Brown, "Who Will Win In France," 4–7; Lorwin, *French Labor Movement,* 127–29.

22. Vincent Auriol, *Mon Septennat, 1947–1954* (Paris, 1970), 162. See also *ibid.,* 153.

23. Quoted in Georgette Elgey, *La République des Illusions: 1945–1951* (Paris, 1965), 404. See also *ibid.,* 399; Lorwin, *French Labor Movement,* 129–30; Werth, *France,* 404–05; *Business Week,* October 9, 1948, 115.

24. *Business Week,* October 9, 1948, 117; *The Economist,* November 27, 1948, 865–66; April 9, 1949, 660; Thomas Balogh, *The Dollar Crisis: Causes and Cures* (Oxford, 1950), 114; U.S. Senate, Committee on Foreign Relations, *Hearings: Extension of European Recovery,* 81:1, February 1949 (Washington, 1949), 49; Economic Cooperation Administration, Special Mission to the United Kingdom, *The Sterling Area: An American Analysis* (London, 1951), 71–75; UN, *World Economic Report—1948,* 63.

25. Will Clayton, "Is the Marshall Plan 'Operation Rathole'?," *Saturday Evening Post,* November 29, 1947, 138.

26. U.S. House, Committee on Foreign Affairs, *Hearings: United States Foreign Policy for Postwar Recovery Program,* 80:1, 2, December 1947—February 1948 (Washington, 1948), 519; Senate Committee on Foreign Relations, *European Recovery Program* 348–49.

27. Gardner Patterson, *Survey of United States International Finance—1949* (Princeton, 1950), 13, 23; Fred A. Ossanna memo to Major Arthur R. Wilson, February 6, 1949, HST Mss, OF 233; Senate Committee on Foreign Relations, *Extension of European Recovery,* 57; *The Economist,* December 4, 1948, 925; Gardner Patterson and Jack N. Behrman, *Survey of United States International Finance—1950* (Princeton, 1951), 25.

28. D. Gale Johnson, *Trade and Agriculture: A Study of Inconsistent Policies* (New York, 1950), 14–16; Patterson, *United States International Finance—1949,* 21–22, 157; Senate Committee on Foreign Relations, *European Recovery Program,* 315.

29. U.S. House, Committee on Foreign Affairs, *Hearings: Emergency Foreign Aid,* 80:1, November 1947 (Washington, 1947), 113–14; *The Economist,* April 16, 1949, 714–15; Patterson, *United States International Finance—1949,* 26; Horst Mendershausen, "Dollar Shortage and Oil Surplus in 1949–1950," *Essays in International Finance,* No. 11 (Princeton, 1950), 13.

30. *The Economist,* May 14, 1949, 901. See also Sydney J. Neal, "Oil Profits and ERP," *The Nation,* December 4, 1948, 632.

31. Walter J. Levy, Address to National Petroleum Council, July 28, 1949, TC Mss, box 105. See also Joint Committee on Foreign Economic Cooperation, Report to the Committee—No. 6, July 10–23, 1948 (mimeo), JT Mss, box 115.

32. DSB, July 11, 1948, 36–37. See also President's Committee on Foreign Aid, *European Recovery and American Aid.* November 7, 1947. (Washington, 1947), 273–76.

33. *Business Week,* September 18, 1948, 25–26; Senate Committee on Foreign Relations, *European Recovery Program,* 225–26; Senate Committee on Foreign Relations, *Extension of European Recovery,* 333.

34. Senate Committee on Foreign Relations, *Extension of European Recovery,* 107–08.

35. Paul Hoffman, *Peace Can Be Won* (New York, 1951), 57.

36. *Time,* March 17, 1952, 23; *Le Monde,* May 12, 1967.

37. Arnold L. Steinbach, "Changing Concepts and Practices in the International Labor Movement," *National Labor Movements in the Postwar World,* Everett M. Kassalow, ed. (Chicago, 1963), 34–50; *Business Week,* March 17, 1951, 149; Balogh, *Germany,* 52–53; John P. Windmuller, *American Labor and the International Labor Movement 1940–1953* (Ithaca, 1954), 130–31.

38. Bissell, "The Impact of Rearmament," 391.

39. Kassalow, *National Labor Movements,* 37, *passim.*

Chapter 17: The Failure of the Marshall Plan, 1949–1950

1. *Business Week,* April 2, 1949, 104; June 18, 1949, 26; June 25, 1949, 54; Thomas Balogh, *The Dollar Crisis: Causes and Cures* (Oxford, 1950), 75–77; Harry S. Truman, "Our Economic Situation," *Vital Speeches,* July 15, 1949, 605–08; United Nations, Department of Economic Affairs, *Economic Survey of Europe in 1949* (Geneva, 1950), 126.

2. Vandenberg to B. E. Hutchinson, August 27, 1949, AHV Mss.

3. DSB, May 22, 1949, 647. Italics added.

4. Harry S. Truman, *Public Papers of the Presidents of the United States: 1949* (Washington, 1964), 395–96.

5. Economic Cooperation Administration, Special Mission to the United Kingdom, *The Sterling Area: An American Analysis* (London, 1951), 42.

6. UN, *Europe in 1949,* 71. See also William Adams Brown, Jr., and Redvers Opie, *American Foreign Assistance* (Washington, 1953), 205; Balogh, *The Dollar Crisis,* 84, 115–16; United Nations, Department of Economic Affairs, *Economic Survey of Europe in 1948* (Geneva, 1949), 106; *Business Week,* October 9, 1948, 117; May 21, 1949, 123, 125–26; August 27, 1949, 19–20; September 17, 1949, 19–20; *The Economist,* September 24, 1949, 681–82; Gardner Patterson, *Survey of United States International Finance—1949* (Princeton, 1950), 133–34; *New Statesman and Nation,* October 16, 1948, 320.

7. Walter J. Levy, address to National Petroleum Council, July 28, 1949, TC Mss, box 105. See also Howard K. Smith, *The State of Europe* (New York, 1949), 25–27; *Business Week,* June 25, 1949, 53; UN, *Europe in 1949,* 59; ECA, *The Sterling Area,* 38–39.

8. *The Economist,* July 23, 1949, 203.

9. Levy, address to National Petroleum Council, TC Mss, box 105. See also Horst Mendershausen, "Dollar Shortage and Oil Surplus in 1949–1950," *Essays in International Finance,* No. 11 (Princeton, 1950), 2; *The Times* (London), February 2, 1950; *Business Week,* December 24, 1949, 52; DSB, February 20, 1950, 292.

10. John R. Suman, "Dollar-Sterling Oil Problem," January 26, 1950 (mimeographed memo), TC Mss, box 227.

11. New York *Times,* February 1, 1950.

12. New York *Times,* March 16, 1950; April 5, 1950; *The Economist,* June 3, 1950, 1229–30; *Business Week,* July 29, 1950, 77–78.

13. *New Statesman and Nation,* June 17, 1950, 677. See also *Business Week,* May 14, 1949, 121–22; Economic Cooperation Administration, *Western Germany Country Study* (Washington, 1949), 3; Walter Heller, "The Role of Fiscal-Monetary Policy in German Economic Recovery," *American Economic Review,* 40 (1950), 534; Thomas Balogh, *Germany: An Experiment in "Planning" by the "Free" Price Mechanism* (Oxford, 1950), 38–44; UN, *Europe in 1949,* 63–66; Economic Cooperation Administration, *Country Data Book: Western Germany* (Washington, 1950), 3; *The Economist,* July 30, 1949, 226–27; June 10, 1950, 1284; Lucius D. Clay, *Decision in Germany* (New York, 1950), 200–26.

14. ECA, *Germany (Fed. Rep.) Country Data Book.* (Washington, 1950), 3. See also Balogh, *Germany,* 40.

15. Quoted in Heller, "Role of Fiscal-Monetary Policy," 536. See also *ibid.,* 534–37; Balogh, *Germany,* 38–41.

16. UN, *Europe in 1949,* 71.

17. Balogh, *Germany,* 36. See also *ibid.,* 48–49.

18. Otto Zausner, "Rebuilding German Steel," *Atlantic Monthly,* February 1950, 662; Economic Cooperation Administration, *Belgium and Luxemburg Country Study* (Washington, 1949), 1–6, 23–25; European Cooperation Administration, *Country Data Book: Belgium and Luxemburg* (Washington, 1950), *passim;* Balogh, *The Dollar Crisis,* 69, 138; UN, *Europe in 1949,* 63; *The Economist,* June 10, 1950, 1283–84.

19. Economic Cooperation Administration, *Italy Country Study* (Washington, 1949), 1–6; DSB, August 29, 1949, 297; UN, *Europe in 1949,* 68–69.

20. Shepard B. Clough, "Economic Planning in a Capitalist Society: France from Monnet to Hirsh," *Political Science Quarterly*, 71 (1956), 547. See also *Business Week*, March 19, 1949, 121.

21. Economic Cooperation Administration, *France Country Data Book* (Washington, 1950), 1. See also *The Economist*, October 29, 1949, 933.

22. Vincent Auriol, *Mon Septennat, 1947–1954* (Paris, 1970), 256.

23. U.S. Senate, Committee on Foreign Relations, *Hearings: Mutual Security Act of 1952*, 82:2, March–April 1952 (Washington, 1952), 35. See also *Business Week*, October 21, 1950, 124; Val R. Lorwin, *The French Labor Movement* (Cambridge, 1954), 133.

24. Quoted in Brown and Opie, *American Foreign Assistance*, 271.

25. Irving S. Friedman to A. N. Overbee, memo of November 2, 1949, JWS Mss, box 16; Brookings Institution, *Anglo-American Economic Relations: A Problem Paper* (Washington, 1950), 32–33; *The Economist*, September 11, 1948, 424–25; May 7, 1949, 826–28; *Business Week*, June 25, 1949, 50–51; October 29, 1949, 107; Balogh, *The Dollar Crisis*, 62–63; Brown and Opie, *American Foreign Assistance*, 194–95, 200–01, 208.

26. *Business Week*, April 8, 1950, 112. See also Richard Stebbins, *United States in World Affairs, 1949* (New York, 1950), 206.

27. Quoted in W. O. Henderson, *The Genesis of the Common Market* (Chicago, 1962), 141. See also *ibid.*, 153–54; Dean Acheson, *Present at the Creation* (New York, 1969), 382; *Business Week*, May 20, 1950, 133–34.

28. DSB, May 29, 1950, 828.

29. Acheson, *Present at the Creation*, 388.

30. Gordon Gray *et al.*, *Report to the President on Foreign Economic Policies*, November 10, 1950 (Washington, 1950), 35. See also U.S. Senate, Committee on Foreign Relations, *Hearings: European Coal and Steel Community*, 83:1, June 4–5, 1953 (Washington, 1953), 5–7; UN, *Europe in 1949*, 103–05.

31. Advisory Committee on Fiscal and Monetary Problems, Economic Cooperation Administration, Minutes of meeting of June 27, 1950, 14, JMD Mss, Japan 1950, box 5.

32. Winthrop Aldrich, "Economic Problems of Western Europe," *Vital Speeches*, June 1, 1949, 489–90. See also UN, *Europe in 1949*, 180.

33. Stephen J. Spingarn memo to Clark Clifford, October 3, 1949, SJS Mss, box 17.

34. UN, *Europe in 1949*, 178. See also *The Economist*, October 29, 1949, 932–33.

35. Council of Economic Advisers, draft memo, "Basic Foreign and Domestic Economic Problems . . . ," April 14, 1950, KWH Mss; UN, *Europe in 1949*, 177–84.

36. Dean Acheson, memo for the President, February 16, 1950, JMD Mss, Japan 1950, box 1.

37. Statement of problem for Gray Project staff, n.d., JMD Mss, Budget Bureau, box 10.

38. Dodge, draft memo: "Future Problems for United States Foreign Economic Policy," n.d., JMD Mss, Budget Bureau, box 10.

39. Spingarn memo to Clifford, October 3, 1949, SJS Mss.

40. *Business Week,* April 1, 1950, 15.

41. *Business Week,* April 8, 1950, 111.

42. *Business Week,* April 15, 1950, 21.

43. Robert Marjolin, *Europe and the United States in the World Economy* (Durham, 1953), 23, 30–31.

44. Auriol, *Mon Septennat,* 259–60; Acheson, *Present at the Creation,* 383. See also *Business Week,* April 15, 1950, 21.

45. DS, *American Foreign Policy, 1950–1955* (Washington, 1957), I, 1460.

46. *Ibid.,* 1434. See also *ibid.,* 1436; *Business Week,* May 20, 1950, 20; Brookings Institution, *Anglo-American Economic Relations,* 35; Acheson, *Present at the Creation,* 400–01.

Chapter 18: Military Power and Diplomatic Policy, 1947–1949: Definitions and Confrontations

1. Walter Millis, ed., *The Forrestal Diaries* (New York, 1951), 337. See also *ibid.,* 350–53.

2. *Ibid.,* 369, 401, 426–27; Oliver P. Echols to Thomas Finletter, October 7, 1947, PAP Mss, box 6; Lawrence Bell to John McCone, October 1, 1947, PAP Mss, box 7; and letters from aircraft industry representatives in PAP Mss, boxes 7–12; U.S. President's Air Policy Commission, *Survival in the Air Age,* January 1, 1948 (Washington, 1948), 45–70; James Powers Mallan, "Conservative Attitudes toward American Foreign Policy; With Special Reference to American Business, 1945–1952" (unpublished Ph.D. thesis, Harvard University, 1964), *passim;* Warner R. Schilling, Paul Y. Hammond, and Glenn H. Snyder, *Strategy, Politics, and Defense Budgets* (New York, 1962), 102–03, 138; Merton J. Peck and Frederic M. Scherer, *The Weapons Acquisition Process* (Boston, 1962), 100.

3. Forrestal statement, December 3, 1947, 2784, PAP Mss, box 17. See also Gabriel Kolko, *The Roots of American Foreign Policy* (Boston, 1969), chap. I; *United States News,* May 23, 1947, 20–21; Forrestal conversation with Reese H. Taylor, March 25, 1947, JF Mss, box 73; Samuel P. Huntington, *The Soldier and the State* (Cambridge, 1957), 354–56, 377–79.

4. Nimitz statement, December 3, 1947, 2793, PAP Mss, box 17. See also *Forrestal Diaries,* 171, 195, 265, 281, 340; David E. Lilienthal, *The Atomic Energy Years, 1945–1950* (New York, 1964), 215; Vincent Auriol, *Journal du Septennat: 1947* (Paris, 1970), 521–22, 632; John Foster Dulles, "Report on Moscow Meeting of Council of Foreign Ministers," *International Conciliation,* No. 432 (1947), 458; Leahy Diary, October 17, 1947, November 12, 1947, WDL Mss.

5. *Forrestal Diaries,* 387. See also President's Air Policy Commission, *Survival in the Air Age,* 14.

6. Harry S. Truman to Grenville Clark, February 18, 1948, HLS Mss. See also Clark to Truman, February 16, 1948; Clark to Robert A. Taft, March 26, 1948, HLS Mss.

7. *Forrestal Diaries,* 432, 444. See also *ibid.,* 424; Lilienthal, *Atomic Energy Years,* 350–51; Paul A. Smith, "Opinions, Publics, and World Affairs in the United

States," *Western Political Quarterly,* 14 (1961), 701; Athan Theoharis in *Politics and Policies of the Truman Administration,* Barton J. Bernstein, ed. (Chicago, 1970), 196–268.

8. "Transcript of conference between . . . Stalin and Harold E. Stassen, . . . April 9, 1947," *International Conciliation,* No. 432 (1947), 460–63; *New Times,* February 14, 1947, 10–15; May 16, 1947, 1–3; A. Zhdanov, *The International Situation* (Moscow, 1947), *passim; Soviet Press Translations,* March 15, 1947, 165–67; April 1, 1947, 215; October 1, 1947, 145; November 15, 1947, 223–26, 229–31; February 15, 1948, 99–106, 128; May 1, 1948, 288; May 15, 1948, 320; A. Y. Vyshinsky, *For Peace and Friendship among the People . . .* (Moscow, 1948), 24; *For a Lasting Peace, For a People's Democracy,* January 15, 1948, 2, 4; April 15, 1948, 1, 4; May 1, 1948, 2; June 1, 1948, 1–3; July 1, 1948, 1–2; October 1, 1948, 1ff.; October 15, 1949, 1, 3.

9. Auriol, *Journal,* 630; *Business Week,* June 5, 1948, 109–10; *The Economist,* December 11, 1948, 974–75; January 29, 1949, 197–98.

10. *Forrestal Diaries,* 438, 443. See also *ibid.,* 429–32; *Business Week,* February 7, 1948, 15; Smith, "Opinions, Publics, and World Affairs in the United States," 701; Royal Institute of International Affairs, *Documents on International Affairs, 1947–1948* (London, 1952), 159–60; Walter Bedell Smith, *My Three Years in Moscow* (Philadelphia, 1950), 157–66; *Business Week,* May 15, 1948, 15, 123; May 22, 1948, 15, 115.

11. *New Times,* February 21, 1947, 11. See also Auriol, *Journal,* 49, 57, 79–80, 445, 467–68, 695–99; Vincent Auriol, *Mon Septennat, 1947–1954* (Paris, 1970), 103, 114–17; Harold Macmillan, *Tides of Fortune, 1945–55* (London, 1969), 152–55.

12. *New Times,* January 31, 1947, 15; Gabriel Kolko, *The Politics of War* (New York, 1968), 482–83; Macmillan, *Tides of Fortune,* 157–61, 168–69.

13. RIIA, *Documents on International Affairs, 1947–48,* 227. See also *ibid.,* 211–25.

14. Kenneth Royall to Henry Stimson, April 21, 1948, HLS Mss. See also Macmillan, *Tides of Fortune,* 160–61, 168–69; RIIA, *Documents on International Affairs, 1947–48,* 211, 234–43; *Forrestal Diaries,* 392, 403, 422–23; Thomas Balogh, *The Dollar Crisis* (Oxford, 1950), 54–56; George F. Kennan, *Memoirs, 1925–1950* (Boston, 1967), 404.

15. Dulles memo of April 27, 1948, JFD Mss. See also *Forrestal Diaries,* 423; Harry S. Truman, *Years of Trial and Hope* (New York, 1956), 244–45; DSB, May 23, 1948, 681–82.

16. Arthur H. Vandenberg, ed., *The Private Papers of Senator Vandenberg* (Boston, 1952), 407ff. See also *Forrestal Diaries,* 434.

17. DS, *Germany, 1947–1949* (Washington, 1950), 66. See also F. Roy Willis, *The French in Germany, 1945–1949* (Stanford, 1962), 46–53; Southard memo to Snyder, September 19, 1947, JWS Mss., box 9; John Gimbel, *The American Occupation of Germany* (Stanford, 1968), 194–95; Lewis J. Edinger, *Kurt Schumacher* (Stanford, 1965), 163; translation of General Kotikov statement of August 30, 1947; Lewis Glaser, "Socialization in Berlin," January 27, 1948, FLH Mss; U.S. Army, Special Committee to Study Decartelization and Deconcentration in Germany, "Report to the Honorable Secretary of the Army, April 15, 1949" (n.p., mimeo),

63, *passim;* N. H. Collisson, memo to J. A. Krug, February 19, 1948, JAK Mss, box 20; U.S. House, Committee on the Judiciary, *Hearings: Study of Monopoly Power,* 81:1, November 1949 (Washington, 1950), part 2–A, 430; John Taber to Henry M. Allen, June 10, 1948, JT Mss, box 83; National Foreign Trade Council, *Report of the Thirty-Fourth National Foreign Trade Convention* [October 20–22, 1947] (New York, 1948), 466–68; V. D. Sokolovsky, *On the Question of Germany,* November 21, 1947 (Washington: Embassy of the U.S.S.R., 1947), *passim;* V. M. Molotov, *Problems of Foreign Policy* (Moscow, 1949), 506–28; Robert Murphy, *Diplomat among Warriors* (New York, 1964), 312.

18. Lucius D. Clay, *Decision in Germany* (New York, 1950), 349. See also Murphy, *Diplomat among Warriors,* 312; *Soviet Press Translations,* January 15, 1948, 36–41; Gimbel, *American Occupation of Germany,* 195–96; Dodge memo to Clay, May 16, 1946, JMD Mss, Germany Assignment, box 5.

19. Clay, *Decision in Germany,* 356. See also Gimbel, *American Occupation of Germany,* 197–99; Manuel Gottlieb, *The German Peace Settlement and the Berlin Crisis* (New York, 1960), 186–87; *Soviet Press Translations,* May 1, 1948, 259–66; DS, *Germany, 1947–1949,* (Washington, 1950), 75–76, 85–86; Auriol, *Mon Septennat,* 1002; Great Britain, Secretary of State for Foreign Affairs, *Selected Documents on Germany and the Question of Berlin, 1944–1961* (London, 1961), 99.

20. *Forrestal Diaries,* 387. See also Gottlieb, *German Peace Settlement,* 186–87; Murphy, *Diplomat among Warriors,* 313; DS, *Germany, 1947–49,* 200.

21. *Business Week,* May 15, 1948, 15.

22. Murphy, *Diplomat among Warriors,* 313. See also *ibid.,* 312ff.; *Business Week,* May 15, 1948, 123; May 22, 1948, 15, 115; Clay, *Decision in Germany,* 358–59; Frank Howley, *Berlin Command* (New York, 1950), 201; *The Economist,* July 3, 1948, 1–2.

23. Kenneth Royall to Henry Stimson, April 21, 1948, HLS Mss. See also Clay, *Decision in Germany,* 362; *Forrestal Diaries,* 407–08.

24. Howley, *Berlin Command,* 180. See also Konrad Adenauer, *Memoirs, 1945–53* (Chicago, 1966), 113–14, 119–20; Edinger, *Schumacher,* 167; Gimbel, *American Occupation of Germany,* 207–37; DS, *Germany, 1947–1949,* 76–83; Great Britain, *Documents on Germany,* 114.

25. U.S. Army, Office of Military Government—Berlin Sector, "Berlin Press Review," June 1948; U.S. Army, Office of Military Government—Berlin Sector, "Weekly Intelligence Reports," weeks ending October 6, 1948, 5; October 13, 1948, 4; May 18, 1949, 2; "Political Report," weeks ending June 18, 1948, 1; July 3, 1948, 1, 7–8, all in FLH Mss; Clay, *Decision in Germany,* 363–64, 388–89; Soviet News, *On the Situation in Berlin* (London, 1948), 11–20; USSR Ministry of Foreign Affairs, *The Soviet Union and the Question of the Unity of Germany and of the German Peace Treaty* (Moscow, 1952), 39–49; *The Economist,* November 6, 1948, 734; Auriol, *Mon Septennat,* 129; W. Phillips Davison, *The Berlin Blockade: A Study in Cold War Politics* (Princeton, 1958), 153–54; DS, *Documents and State Papers,* February 1949, 648–50.

26. Clay, *Decision in Germany,* 365–66; Gottlieb, *German Peace Settlement,* 198, 265; DS, *The Berlin Crisis: A Report on the Moscow Discussions, 1948* (Washington, 1948), 5; DS, *Germany, 1947–49,* 205–09.

27. Dulles memo, "Washington conference, July 19, 1948," JFD Mss. See also Murphy, *Diplomat among Warriors*, 316; Clay, *Decision in Germany*, 374; Tom Connally, *My Name Is Tom Connally* (New York, 1954), 329–30; Lilienthal, *Atomic Energy Years*, 406.

28. Dulles memo of July 22, 1948, JFD Mss; Connally, *My Name Is Tom*, 330; Arthur H. Vandenberg to Robert Lovett, [late 1948], AHV Mss; *Forrestal Diaries*, 451–59; Dean Acheson, *Present at the Creation* (New York, 1969), 262; Truman, *Years of Trial and Hope*, 123–26; Murphy, *Diplomat among Warriors*, 316; Clay, *Decision in Germany*, 376; Curtis E. LeMay, *Mission with LeMay: My Story* (New York, 1965), 481–82; Howley Diary, 1948–1949, 72–74, FLH Mss.

29. DS, *The Berlin Crisis*, 20. See also DS, *Germany, 1947–1949*, 210–11.

30. DS, *The Berlin Crisis*, 21–49; Truman, *Years of Trial and Hope*, 126; *Forrestal Diaries*, 469–70, 479–90; Leahy Diary, July 22, 1948, October 1, 1948, WDL Mss; *Business Week*, December 4, 1948, 111; DS, *Germany, 1947–1949*, 218–19.

31. *Forrestal Diaries*, 485–88, 520, 533; Truman, *Years of Trial and Hope*, 113–18, 130; USSR, *Soviet Union and the Berlin Question (Documents)*, second series (Moscow, 1949), *passim;* Davison, *The Berlin Blockade*, 241–49.

32. *Business Week*, December 4, 1948, 111. See also Gottlieb, *German Peace Settlement*, 208–10; Clay, *Decision in Germany*, 388–89.

33. CDSP, March 15, 1949, 22, 33; New York *Times*, January 31, 1949; DSB, February 13, 1949, 192–94; Acheson, *Present at the Creation*, 267–74, 286; DS, *Germany, 1947–1949*, 273–74.

34. Clay, *Decision in Germany*, 428–29. See also *ibid.*, 419ff.; Gimbel, *American Occupation of Germany*, 226ff.

35. DS, *Germany, 1947–1949*, 320. See also *ibid.*, 282, 319; Clay, *Decision in Germany*, 433–36; Edinger, *Schumacher*, 169–70; Charles Wighton, *Adenauer— Democratic Dictator* (London, 1963), 102.

36. Truman, *Years of Trial and Hope*, 246–49; *Forrestal Diaries*, 500–01, 511, 521, 525.

37. Vandenberg to James P. Warburg, August 23, 1949, AHV Mss. See also Arnold Wolfers, ed., *Alliance Policy in the Cold War* (Baltimore, 1959), 71.

38. DSB, May 22, 1949, 647. See also Kennan, *Memoirs*, 409–10; Auriol, *Mon Septennat*, 200.

39. U.S. Senate, Committee on Foreign Relations, *Hearings: North Atlantic Treaty*, 81:1, April–May 1949 (Washington, 1949), 343. See also *ibid.*, 58–59, 314–17.

40. *The Economist*, March 26, 1949, 562–63; Dulles memo of February 11, 1949, JFD Mss; Dulles to William Mathews, February 10, 1948, WM Mss; Senate Committee on Foreign Relations, *North Atlantic Treaty*, 341, 355–56, 376–406, 526–41; Richard J. Barnet and Marcus G. Raskin, *After Twenty Years* (New York, 1965), 18; Robert A. Taft, *A Foreign Policy for Americans* (New York, 1951), 89–96; Barton J. Bernstein and Allen J. Matusow, eds., *The Truman Administration* (New York, 1966), 280–82.

41. *Private Papers of Senator Vandenberg*, 487. See also New York *Times*, May 19, 1949; Walter Lippmann to Vandenberg, July 22, 1949, AHV Mss.

42. Acheson, *Present at the Creation*, 293.

43. *Private Papers of Senator Vandenberg*, 485.

44. Senate Committee on Foreign Relations, *North Atlantic Treaty*, 60. See also Acheson, *Present at the Creation*, 291–92; *Business Week*, April 2, 1949, 15.

45. U.S. Senate, Committee on Foreign Relations, *Hearings: Military Assistance Program*, 81:1, August 8–19, 1949 (Washington, 1949), 27, 33–34. See also DSB, May 22, 1949, 646–47; *Business Week*, April 16, 1949, 15; Walter Lippmann to Vandenberg, July 22, 1949, AHV Mss; RIIA, *Documents on International Affairs, 1948–49* (London, 1953), 265–67.

46. Senate Committee on Foreign Relations, *Military Assistance Program*, 89.

47. CDSP, January 14, 1949, 27; March 22, 1949, 15–17; April 12, 1949, 35–36; April 26, 1949, 24–33; May 3, 1949, *passim;* August 9, 1949, 9–10, 47; August 23, 1949, 15; October 11, 1949, 65–66; November 1, 1949, 40; Andrei Y. Vyshinsky, *The U.S.S.R. and World Peace* (New York, 1949), 23, *passim;* Marshall D. Shulman, *Stalin's Foreign Policy Reappraised* (Cambridge, 1963), chaps. I–IV; DSB, February 13, 1949, 192–94.

48. *Private Papers of Senator Vandenberg*, 487. See also Auriol, *Mon Septennat*, 183, 201–02; *Business Week*, February 12, 1949, 19–20, 101–02; Harry S. Truman, *Public Papers of the Presidents of the United States: 1949* (Washington, 1964), 112–13.

49. *U.S. News and World Report*, July 8, 1949, 30–33; Richard G. Hewlett and Francis Duncan, *Atomic Shield, 1947–1952* (University Park, Pa., 1969), 366–67; CDSP, November 15, 1949, 42–43; November 22, 1949, 6–8; January 3, 1950, 3–7; January 24, 1950, 44–45; March 25, 1950, 3–12; New York *Times*, August 19, 1966; Connally, *My Name Is Tom*, 339; Cominform, *Working Class Unity for Peace* (New York, 1950), 19, *passim;* DS, "Conference on Problems of the United States Policy in China. October 6–8, 1949" [multilithed transcript], 20.

50. *Forrestal Diaries*, 537. See also *ibid.*, 498–510, 535–36.

51. U.S. House, Committee on Armed Services, *Hearings: Investigation of the B-36 Bomber Program*, 81:1, August–October 1949 (Washington, 1949), 53, 63, 67–69, 129–36, 165–69, 210–14, 317, 379, 477–78, 482–92, 525–27; U.S. House, Committee on Armed Services, *Hearings: The National Defense Program—Unification and Strategy*, 81:1, October 1949 (Washington, 1949), 41ff., 207–12, 351, 419, 521–23; V. Bush to James Forrestal, December 20, 1948, JFD Mss.

52. House Committee on Armed Services, *The National Defense Program*, 518. See also *ibid.*, 545, 565; Harry S. Truman to Fred I. Kent, April 14, 1949, FK Mss.

53. Kennan, *Memoirs*, 465–66; Lilienthal, *Atomic Energy Years*, 580–84, 621; DS, "United States Policy in China," 19–21, 40; Hewlett and Duncan, *Atomic Shield*, chap. XII; Acheson, *Present at the Creation*, 345–49; Samuel P. Huntington, *The Common Defense: Strategic Programs in National Politics* (New York, 1961), 48–49; Schilling *et al.*, *Strategy, Politics, and Defense Budgets*, 288ff.

54. Robert Junjk, *Brighter than a Thousand Suns* (New York, 1958), 284–85; Hewlett and Duncan, *Atomic Shield*, 403–05, 408; Warner R. Schilling, "The H-Bomb Decision," *Political Science Quarterly*, 76 (1961), 34–37; Lewis L. Strauss, *Men and Decisions* (New York, 1962), 218; Truman, *Years of Trial and Hope*, 309–10; Acheson, *Present at the Creation*, 751; Lilienthal, *Atomic Energy Years*, 624–66.

55. Dean Acheson, *The Pattern of Responsibility* (Boston, 1952), 36–39; Acheson, *Present at the Creation*, 377–78.

56. Acheson, *Present at the Creation,* 373–77, 397, 753; Schilling *et al., Strategy, Politics, and Defense Budgets,* 306–11, 331, 345ff.; Walter Millis *et al., Arms and the State: Civil-Military Elements in National Policy* (New York, 1958), 321, *passim;* New York *Times,* April 13, 1964; *Business Week,* October 29, 1949, 107–108; Paul A. Smith, "Opinions, Publics, and World Affairs in the United States," 701.

Chapter 19: The Restoration of Japan

1. R. M. Cheseldine, "Report on Policy Matters in Connection with Military Government and Civil Affairs Activities for Japan, February 17, 1947," 1–2, DM Mss.

2. *Ibid.*

3. *Newsweek,* March 15, 1948, 38.

4. Supreme Commander for the Allied Powers (SCAP), *Political Reorientation of Japan, September 1945 to September 1948* (Washington, n.d.), I, 357; W. Macmahon Ball, *Japan: Enemy or Ally?* (New York, 1949), 159; Kazuo Kawai, *Japan's American Interlude* (Chicago, 1960), 164; Evelyn S. Colbert, *The Left Wing in Japanese Politics* (New York, 1952), 185.

5. DSB, March 30, 1947, 597.

6. Ball, *Japan,* 60–63.

7. Russel Brines, *MacArthur's Japan* (Philadelphia, 1948), 203–05; Helen Mears, *Mirror for Americans* (Boston, 1948), 254; Ball, *Japan,* 158–59.

8. *Newsweek,* December 1, 1947, 37.

9. Walter Millis, ed., *The Forrestal Diaries* (New York, 1951), 328–29.

10. MacArthur to Department of Army, October 24, 1947, HLS Mss.

11. "Statement of U.S. Policy Toward Economic Recovery of Japan," November 1947, HLS Mss. See also Gordon Gray, memo: "Japanese Economic Situation," November 14, 1947, HLS Mss.

12. *Newsweek,* December 22, 1947, 37; Kawai, *Japan's American Interlude,* 147.

13. George S. Kennan, *Memoirs, 1925–1950* (Boston, 1967), 389. See also Faubion Bowers, "How Japan Won the War," *New York Times Magazine,* August 30, 1970, 39.

14. Quoted in Edwin M. Martin, *The Allied Occupation of Japan* (New York, 1948), 58.

15. Kennan, *Memoirs,* 386.

16. Royal Institute of International Affairs, *Survey of International Affairs, 1947–1948* (London, 1952), 334.

17. Percy H. Johnson *et al., Report on the Economic Position and Prospects of Japan and Korea and the Measures Required to Improve Them* (Washington, 1948), 26–27; Robert A. Fearey, *The Occupation of Japan: Second Phase: 1948–50* (New York, 1950), 144–45.

18. Johnson *et al., Report on the Economic Position and Prospects of Japan,* 21–22.

19. *Ibid.,* 15, 20, 32–33.

20. Jerome B. Cohen, "Japan: Reform vs. Recovery," *Far Eastern Survey,* June 23, 1948, 137–41.

21. Draper to SCAP, December 11, 1948, JMD Mss, Japan 1949, box 1; SCAP, *Political Reorientation of Japan,* 351; Ball, *Japan,* 76–79.

22. Fearey, *The Occupation of Japan,* 84, 111–12, 119, 127; Kozo Yamamura, *Economic Policy in Postwar Japan* (Berkeley, 1967), 21; Ball, *Japan,* 170–71; E. J. Lewe Van Aduard, *Japan: From Surrender to Peace* (The Hague, 1953), 88; Frederick S. Dunn, *Peace-making and the Settlement with Japan* (Princeton, 1963), 74–75.

23. Dodge to Cleveland Thurber, December 13, 1948, JMD Mss, Japan 1949, box 1.

24. *Ibid.*

25. *Fortune,* June 1948, 120–22.

26. Dodge, notes (handwritten, n.d.), JMD Mss, Japan 1949, box 6.

27. "Summary of Meeting with Finance Minister Ikeda on the Japanese Government Budget held 3 March 1949," March 4, 1949, JMD Mss, Japan 1949, box 1; Shigeru Yoshida, *The Yoshida Memoirs: The Story of Japan in Crisis* (Boston, 1962), 92–93.

28. Economic Cooperation Administration, Advisory Committee on Fiscal and Monetary Problems, Minutes of Meeting of April 28, 1950, JMD Mss, Japan 1950, box 5. See also *Business Week,* February 26, 1949, 124; March 26, 1949, 121.

29. "ESS/LAB Comments on Draft Supplementary Budget Recommendations of the Dodge Mission dated 7 March 1949," JMD Mss, Japan 1949, box 6.

30. Dodge memo of meeting with Ikeda, March 10, 1949, JMD Mss, Japan 1949, box 1.

31. Minutes of budget meeting, March 14, 1949, JMD Mss, Japan 1949, box 2.

32. Dodge, memo on meeting with members of Diet, April 14, 1949, JMD Mss, Japan 1949, box 1.

33. Yoshida, *Memoirs,* 176–77. See also *ibid.,* 44.

34. Kennan, *Memoirs,* 390; Dunn, *Peace-making and the Settlement with Japan,* 77.

35. Fearey, *The Occupation of Japan,* 43, 56–57, 82–83; Yamamura, *Economic Policy,* 33; DSB, July 25, 1949, 107–08.

36. Max Beloff, *Soviet Policy in the Far East, 1944–1951* (London, 1953), 141–42; Colbert, *The Left Wing in Japanese Politics,* 299–301; Hans Baerwald, *The Purge of Japanese Leaders Under the Occupation* (Berkeley, 1959), 78–79.

37. Quoted in Robert A. Scalapino, *The Japanese Communist Movement, 1920–1966* (Berkeley, 1967), 81. See also *ibid.,* 80–87.

38. Yamamura, *Economic Policy,* 31–39; Robert Guillain, "Japanese Uncertainties" *International Affairs* 26 (July 1950), 335; Chitoshi Yanaga, *Big Business and Japanese Politics* (New Haven, 1968), 37.

39. Dodge memo to William Draper, October 18, 1948, JMD Mss, Japan 1949, box 6. See also Dunn, *Peace-making and the Settlement with Japan,* 66; Van Aduard, *Japan,* 67–71; Beloff, *Soviet Policy,* 117; Yoshida, *Memoirs,* 245; RIIA, *Survey of International Affairs, 1947–1948,* 329–30.

40. William J. Sebald, *With MacArthur in Japan: A Personal History of the Occupation* (New York, 1965), 94. See also CDSP, July 19, 1949, 25–27; August 2, 1949, 18.

41. *The Economist,* November 19, 1949, 1107–08; Van Aduard, *Japan,* 121–24, 149–53; Sebald, *With MacArthur in Japan,* 245.

42. Yoshida, *Memoirs,* 250–51. See also Van Aduard, *Japan,* 154; Beloff, *Soviet Policy,* 146–47; Dunn, *Peace-making and the Settlement with Japan,* 105–09.

43. Dulles, memo on Japan's relations with China, March 6, 1952, JFD Mss; U.S. Senate, Committee on Foreign Relations, *Hearings: Japanese Peace Treaty and Other Treaties Relating to Security in the Pacific,* 82:2, January 1952 (Washington, 1952), 10.

44. Frank Pace, Jr., to Dodge, July 16, 1951, JMD Mss, Japan 1951, box 1. See also Ridgway to Pace, June 22, 1951, JMD Mss, Japan 1951, box 1.

45. Earl D. Johnson to Dodge, September 28, 1951, JMD Mss, Japan 1951, box 1.

46. Dodge to Ikeda, September 7, 1951, JMD Mss, Japan 1951, box 1.

47. Senate Committee on Foreign Relations, *Japanese Peace Treaty,* 10; Sebald, *With MacArthur in Japan,* 279ff.

48. Hideo Suto to W. F. Marquat, February 12, 1952, JMD Mss, Japan 1951, box 4.

49. Dodge, "Japan: Post-Treaty Relationship," January 17, 1952, JMD Mss, Japan 1951, box 4.

Chapter 20: China: The Triumphant Revolution, 1947–1950

1. "History, Peiping Headquarters," first quarter (Part), 1947, section XI, part A, 1, AGO Mss, box 78.

2. David E. Lilienthal, *The Atomic Energy Years: 1945–1950* (New York, 1964), 201. See also "History, Peiping Headquarters," first quarter 1947, 3–4, AGO Mss, box 78.

3. DS, *United States Relations with China, with special reference to the period 1944–1949* (Washington, 1949), 235 [hereafter *White Paper*]. See also *ibid.,* 314.

4. Arthur H. Vandenberg, ed., *The Private Papers of Senator Vandenberg* (Boston, 1952), 523.

5. Leahy Diary, October 22, 1948, WDL Mss; U.S. Senate, Committee on Armed Services and Committee on Foreign Relations, *Hearings: Military Situation in the Far East,* 82:1, May 1951 (Washington, 1951), 2742; U.S. Marine Corps, Historical Branch, *The United States Marines in North China, 1945–1949,* Marine Corps Historical Reference Series No. 23 (Washington, 1962), 21; Charles Wertenbaker, "The China Lobby," *The Reporter,* April 15, 1952, 2–24; April 29, 1952, 4–24; Ross Y. Koen, *The China Lobby in American Politics* (New York, 1960), *passim;* Christopher Emmett to Elmer Davis, March 26, 1951, JFD Mss; Derk Bodde, *Peking Diary —1948–1949* (Greenwich, Conn., 1967), 39–117; K. M. Panikkar, *In Two Chinas: Memoirs of a Diplomat* (London, 1955), 33; Lionel Max Chassin, *The Communist Conquest of China* (Cambridge, 1965), 113.

6. *White Paper,* 247–48.

7. Albert C. Wedemeyer, *Wedemeyer Reports!* (New York, 1958), 459. See also

White Paper, 240–52, 733–35, 774; Chassin, *Communist Conquest of China,* 112–13; Walter Millis, ed., *The Forrestal Diaries* (New York, 1951), 285–87.

8. *White Paper,* 758–63.

9. *Ibid.,* 773. See also *ibid.,* 815, 824–26.

10. *Forrestal Diaries,* 341. See also *White Paper,* 773–74, 779; Wedemeyer, *Wedemeyer Reports!,* 396–98; Arthur H. Vandenberg to William Knowland, December 11, 1948, AVH Mss.

11. Mao Tse-tung, *Selected Works* (Peking, 1961), IV, 147, 155. See also *White Paper,* 246, 870–71, 970–75; Panikkar, *In Two Chinas,* 38–39.

12. Bodde, *Peking Diary,* 87; Panikkar, *In Two Chinas,* 49–50; Mao, *Selected Works,* IV, 160; Chassin, *Communist Conquest of China,* 158–61.

13. Vandenberg to J. B. Montgomery, January 27, 1947, AHV Mss. See also *Private Papers of Senator Vandenberg,* 335, 519–22.

14. *Forrestal Diaries,* 372.

15. *Private Papers of Senator Vandenberg,* 524. See also *White Paper,* 364–79; U.S. Senate, *Review of Bipartisan Foreign Policy Consultations since World War II,* Senate Doc. No. 87, 82:1, October 20, 1951 (Washington, 1952), 22.

16. *White Paper,* 396. See also *ibid.,* 267, 270, 380–84; Koen, *The China Lobby,* 105–06; *Business Week,* October 9, 1948, 122.

17. *White Paper,* 271–72.

18. Harry S. Truman, *Public Papers of the Presidents of the United States: 1948* (Washington, 1964), 180–81.

19. *Ibid.,* 181; Chassin, *Communist Conquest of China,* 171–77; *White Paper,* 357; *Business Week,* November 20, 1948, 127.

20. *White Paper,* 876–77. See also *ibid.,* 279–86, 885–87; Leahy Diary, December 13, 1947, WDL Mss.

21. Vandenberg to William F. Knowland, October 21, 1948, AHV Mss. See also Knowland to Vandenberg, September 2, 1948; Robert A. Griffin to Knowland, September 30, 1948; Vandenberg to F. W. Newton, November 22, 1948, AHV mss.

22. *Forrestal Diaries,* 517–18; *White Paper,* 320–21, 357, 887–90, 895–97, 919.

23. *Soviet Press Translations,* January 15, 1947, 1–3; February 15, 1947, 1–3; April 30, 1947, 1–6; May 15, 1947, 5–8; May 31, 1947, 1–3; June 14, 1947, 5–8, 17–18; August 1, 1947, 64–69; November 15, 1947, 226–29, 234–36; Max Beloff, *Soviet Policy in the Far East, 1944–1951* (London, 1953), 56–57; FR (1946), VI, 785; *Business Week,* December 11, 1948, 103.

24. *White Paper,* 293. See also *ibid.,* 265–66, 846; John F. Melby, *The Mandate of Heaven* (Toronto, 1968), 254–55, 275, for a slightly different version; *Soviet Press Translations,* February 15, 1948, 107–09; April 15, 1948, 233–35; May 1, 1948, 273; Beloff, *Soviet Policy,* 60; C. P. Fitzgerald, *Revolution in China* (London, 1952), 103–05; New York *Times,* March 1, 1970.

25. Philip Jaffe, "The Strange Case of Anna Louise Strong," *Survey,* No. 53 (October 1964), 133. See also Beloff, *Soviet Policy,* 63–64.

26. *Business Week,* December 11, 1948, 103.

27. Jaffe, "The Strange Case of Anna Louise Strong," 136. See also *ibid.,* 132ff.;

the first discussion of this episode appeared in Robert C. North, *Moscow and Chinese Communists* (Stanford, 1953), 242–43.

28. Jaffe, "The Strange Case of Anna Louise Strong," 135–38; *Le Monde*, March 11, 1967; New York *Times*, March 1, 1970; Mao, *Selected Works*, IV, 415–17; Franz Schurmann, *Ideology and Organization in Communist China* (Berkeley, 1966), 123.

29. Mao, *Selected Works*, IV 288, 341. See also *ibid.*, 272.

30. *Ibid.*, 121, 183. See also *ibid.*, 135, 150–51, 203, 219, 263, 273; Bodde, *Peking Diary*, 87; Panikkar, *In Two Chinas*, 48–49; Chassin, *Communist Conquest of China*, 163; *The Economist*, June 25, 1949, 1189; *White Paper*, 709–10, 840, 913; *Business Week*, November 20, 1948, 125; Owen Lattimore, *The Situation in Asia* (Boston, 1949), 154–57.

31. Mao, *Selected Works*, IV, 421. See also *ibid.*, 247, 364–67.

32. Mao, *Selected Works*, IV, 124, 197, 201. See also *ibid.*, 165, 182–85, 203, 219; A. Doak Barnett, *Communist China and Asia* (New York, 1960), 40; Schurmann, *Ideology and Organization*, 427–33; Chassin, *Communist Conquest of China*, 162–63.

33. Mao, *Selected Works*, IV, 175, 203, 219, 235–36, 248; Schurmann, *Ideology and Organization*, 433–37.

34. Vandenberg to Eugene F. Zeimet, January 18, 1949, AHV Mss. See also *White Paper*, 293–96, 357, 405–06; *Private Papers of Senator Vandenberg*, 527; Panikkar, *In Two Chinas*, 40–44; *Forrestal Diaries*, 542; *Business Week*, August 27, 1949, 83–84.

35. Vandenberg Diary, February 5, 1949, AHV Mss; *Private Papers of Senator Vandenberg*, 530–40; *White Paper*, 299–300, 407, 1053.

36. U.S. Senate, Committee on Foreign Relations, *Hearings: Nomination of Philip C. Jessup*, 82:1, September–October 1951 (Washington, 1951), 603.

37. Lilienthal, *Atomic Energy Years*, 525.

38. *White Paper*, xvi. See also DSB, February 13, 1949, 179–83; August 15, 1949, 236–37; Tang Tsou, *America's Failure in China, 1941–50* (Chicago, 1963), 513; Dean Acheson, *Present at the Creation* (New York, 1969), 328, 340.

39. DSB, January 23, 1950, 111–18; September 18, 1950, 463.

40. Beloff, *Soviet Policy*, 70–71; Mao, *Selected Works*, IV, 425–58; *Business Week*, December 11, 1948, 103; June 3, 1950, 101; Schurmann, *Ideology and Organization*, 239–40; *The Economist*, March 18, 1950, 598–99; Klaus Mehnert, *Peking and Moscow* (New York, 1963), 251–52, 264–65; Adam D. Ulam, *Expansion and Coexistence: The History of Soviet Foreign Policy, 1917–67* (New York, 1968), 492–95; "On the Question of Stalin," *Peking Review*, September 20, 1963; *Le Monde*, March 11, 1967; New York *Times*, March 1, 1970.

41. DS, "Conference on Problems of United States Policy in China. October 6–8, 1949" [multilithed transcript], 42, 405. See also *ibid.*, 21–26, 35–47; Tsou, *America's Failure in China*, 514; *Business Week*, February 12, 1949, 99; Harry S. Truman, *Public Papers of the Presidents of the United States: 1949* (Washington, 1964), 519–20.

42. DS, "United States Policy in China," 115, 207. See also *ibid.*, 44, 186.

43. DS, *American Foreign Policy, 1950–1955* (Washington, 1957), II, 2449, 2452. See also DS, "United States Policy in China," 222–25; Senate Committee on Armed Services, *Military Situation in the Far East,* 1667–69; Acheson, *Present at the Creation,* 350.

44. DS, *American Foreign Policy,* 2317.

45. Charles E. Bohlen statement, April 3, 1950, JMD Mss, Japan 1950, box 5. See also Senate Committee on Armed Services, *Military Situation in the Far East,* 517; *Private Papers of Senator Vandenberg,* 537–40; *U.S. News and World Report,* May 5, 1950, 28–31; Trygve Lie, *In the Cause of Peace* (New York, 1954), 254–65; Andrew W. Cordier and Wilder Foote, eds., *Public Papers of the Secretaries-General of the United Nations, 1946–1953* (New York, 1969), 259–60; Washington *Post,* July 3, 1971.

46. Minutes of the Advisory Committee on Fiscal and Monetary Problems, Economic Cooperation Administration, April 28, 1950, 9, JMD Mss, Japan 1950, box 5.

47. Dulles memo of May 18, 1950, JFD Mss.

Chapter 21: Korea: From Civil War to Global Crisis

1. Harry S. Truman, *Years of Trial and Hope* (New York, 1956), 360.

2. Advisory Committee on Fiscal and Monetary Problems, Economic Cooperation Administration, Minutes of meeting of June 27, 1950, 9, JMD Mss, Japan 1950, box 5. See also Trygve Lie, *In the Cause of Peace* (New York, 1954), 260–65; DS, *American Foreign Policy, 1950–1955* (Washington, 1957), II, 2317; *Business Week,* April 8, 1950, 113; Washington *Post,* July 3, 1971.

3. W. A. Harriman memo to Truman, January 5, 1952, HST Mss, OF 335–B.

4. Truman, *Years of Trial and Hope,* 329.

5. Tom Connally, *My Name Is Tom Connally* (New York, 1954), 343. See also U.S. House, Committee on Foreign Affairs, *Hearings: Korean Aid,* 81:1, January 8–23, 1949 (Washington, 1949), 157, 165; DSB, October 31, 1948, 562; *Voice of Korea,* October 15, 1948, 325; March 1, 1950, 439; September 23, 1950, 466.

6. United Nations, *Report of the United Nations Commission on Korea . . . 15 December 1949 to 4 September 1950* (New York, 1950), 15. See also *ibid.,* 16; *Voice of Korea,* August 15, 1949, 408; July 14, 1950, 453.

7. William J. Sebald, *With MacArthur in Japan* (New York, 1965), 180–81.

8. House Committee on Foreign Affairs, *Korean Aid,* 27, 191. See also *ibid.,* 19; Robert T. Oliver, *Syngman Rhee: The Man behind the Myth* (New York, 1955), 294–95.

9. *Voice of Korea,* March 1, 1950, 434.

10. DS, *American Foreign Policy,* II, 2536.

11. UN, *Report of the United Nations Commission on Korea,* 22–24, *passim; Voice of Korea,* April 28, 1950, 446. Many candidates were arrested, and all were subjected to treason charges if they criticized the regime too strongly. See UN, *Report of the United Nations Commission on Korea,* 24.

12. A. J. Muste to John Foster Dulles, March 15, 1951, JFD Mss; *Voice of Korea,*

March 1, 1950, 438; DSB, April 24, 1950, 627; UN, *Report of the United Nations Commission on Korea,* 28; Truman, *Years of Trial and Hope,* 331; Sebald, *With MacArthur in Japan,* 182; DSB, June 26, 1950, 1042; Douglas MacArthur, *Reminiscences* (New York, 1964), 324; I. F. Stone, *The Hidden History of the Korean War* (New York, 1952), 58–60, 64.

13. Charles de Gaulle, *The War Memoirs of Charles de Gaulle: Documents* [1942–1944] (New York, 1959), 151. See also John W. Spanier, *The Truman-MacArthur Controversy and the Korean War* (Cambridge, 1959), 67–68.

14. William R. Mathews to John Foster Dulles, June 5, 1950, JFD Mss. See also MacArthur, *Reminiscences,* 324.

15. New York *Times,* February 17, 1950. See also Rhee to MacArthur, October 24, 1949; December 2, 1949; February 20, 1950, DM Mss; William R. Mathews to Dulles, June 5, 1950, JFD Mss; Dean Acheson, *Present at the Creation* (New York, 1969), 350, 422; *Voice of Korea,* July 14, 1950, 453.

16. MacArthur to Joseph M. Dodge, May 22, 1950, JMD Mss, Japan 1950, box 4.

17. Roy E. Appleman, *South to the Naktong, North to the Yalu (June–November, 1950)* (Washington, 1960), 10.

18. *Ibid.,* 8–13; Robert F. Futrell *et al., The United States Air Force in Korea, 1950–1953* (New York, 1961), 17; U.S. Marine Corps, Historical Branch, G–3, *U.S. Marine Operations in Korea, 1950–1953: The Pusan Perimeter* (Washington, 1954), 33; CDSP, June 3, 1950, 24; Allen S. Whiting, *China Crosses the Yalu: The Decision to Enter the Korean War* (New York, 1960), 43; John R. Steelman to Mathew Woll, June 28, 1948, HST Mss, OF 386.

19. UN, *Report of the United Nations Commission on Korea,* 17.

20. CDSP, July 22, 1950, 28; July 29 1950, 37; DS, *The Record on Korean Unification, 1943–1960* (Washington, 1960), 97–98; UN, *Report of the United Nations Commission on Korea,* 18; Democratic People's Republic of Korea, *For Korea's Peaceful Unification* (Pyongyang, 1961), 35–37; Appleman, *South to the Naktong,* 19; General Headquarters, Far Eastern Command, Military Intelligence Section, "Interrogation Reports: Documentary Evidence of North Korean Aggression," October 30, 1950, 1, DM Mss; New York *Times,* July 31, 1950; Marine Corps, *Marine Operations in Korea,* 22; Appleman, *South to the Naktong,* 10, 20.

21. Dulles memo of May 18, 1950, JFD Mss. See also U.S. Senate, Committee on Armed Services and Committee on Foreign Relations, *Hearings: Military Situation in the Far East,* 82:1, May 1951 (Washington, 1951), 2614–15; *The Times* (London), June 14, 1950; June 16, 1950; June 21, 1950; A. J. Muste to John Foster Dulles, March 15, 1951, JFD Mss.

22. DSB, July 3, 1950, 13. See also William R. Mathews, "Diary: Korea with the John Foster Dulles Mission, June 14 to June 29, 1950," 10–12, WM Mss; Glenn D. Paige, *The Korean Decision: June 24–30, 1950* (New York, 1968), 74.

23. Mathews Diary, 15, 17, WM Mss. See also Mathews to John Foster Dulles, June 5, 1950, JFD Mss.

24. Mathews to Dulles, June 5, 1950, JFD Mss.

25. Dulles to Walter Lippmann, July 13, 1950, JFD Mss.

26. Dulles to A. J. Muste, March 24, 1951, JFD Mss. This letter was not sent.

27. Syngman Rhee to Douglas MacArthur, June 20, 1950, DM Mss.

28. DS, *Record on Korean Unification*, 87. See also *ibid.*, 88; Appleman, *South to the Naktong*, 21; *The Times* (London), June 26, 1950; General Headquarters, Far Eastern Command, "Documentary Evidence of North Korean Aggression," *passim;* Paige, *Korean Decision*, 97.

29. John Gunther, *The Riddle of MacArthur* (New York, 1951), 165. See also Appleman, *South to the Naktong*, 21, 28; Paige, *Korean Decision*, 123–24; Ministry of Foreign Affairs, Democratic People's Republic of Korea, *Aggressive Acts of the United States against Korea* (Pyongyang, 1962), 26–32.

30. Mathews Diary, 37, WH Mss. See also Sebald, *With MacArthur in Japan*, 183.

31. Sebald, *With MacArthur in Japan*, 184.

32. Mathews Diary, 32, WM Mss. See also *ibid.*, 29ff.; J. Lawton Collins, *War in Peacetime: The History and Lessons of Korea* (Boston, 1969), 11.

33. Truman, *Years of Trial and Hope*, 336. See also Mathews Diary, 32, WM Mss.

34. Truman, *Years of Trial and Hope*, 335. See also DS, *Record on Korean Unification*, 87–92; Paige, *Korean Decision*, 130.

35. Anonymous, "The Balance of Military Power," *Atlantic Monthly*, June 1951, 22. See also Senate Committee on Armed Services, *Military Situation in the Far East*, 2584–85.

36. Acheson, *Present at the Creation*, 405–06, 422; Truman, *Years of Trial and Hope*, 331–35; Senate Committee on Armed Services, *Military Situation in the Far East*, 1818, 2584–85, 3192; Albert L. Warner, "How the Korea Decision Was Made," *Harper's Magazine*, June 1951, 102.

37. Paige, *Korean Decision*, 105. See also *ibid.*, 87–88; Appleman, *South to the Naktong*, 28–30; Acheson, *Present at the Creation*, 407.

38. Sebald, *With MacArthur in Japan*, 185. See also Paige, *Korean Decision*, 130.

39. Truman, *Years of Trial and Hope*, 337. See also DS, *Record on Korean Unification*, 93–94; Futrell, *Air Force in Korea*, 10–11; Marguerite Higgins, *War in Korea: The Report of a Woman Combat Correspondent* (New York, 1951), 21–22.

40. Futrell, *Air Force in Korea*, 14. See also Paige, *Korean Decision*, 156–58, 171–72; Truman, *Years of Trial and Hope*, 336.

41. *The Times* (London), June 29, 1950. See also *ibid.*, June 28, 1950; June 30, 1950; Paige, *Korean Decision*, 112. I have also benefited from Alan N. Kopke's unpublished "The Beginnings of the Korean War," an excellent survey of the press of the period, unfortunately marred by unwarranted conjecture.

42. Quoted in Paige, *Korean Decision*, 223.

43. DS, *Record on Korean Unification*, 99; Truman, *Years of Trial and Hope*, 338; incoming mail in HST Mss, OF 471–D; Paige, *Korean Decision*, 235–38; MacArthur, *Reminiscences*, 334; Senate Committee on Armed Services, *Military Situation in the Far East*, 3211. David Rees, *Korea: The Limited War* (New York, 1964), 36, claims that over one-half of the ROK army was destroyed by the end of June, whereas Marine Corps, *Marine Operations in Korea*, 45, claims that one-third were simply missing. Appleman, *South to the Naktong*, 35, shows that 55 per cent were accounted for at the beginning of July.

44. Acheson, *Present at the Creation*, 412. See also *ibid.*, 411; Sebald, *With MacArthur in Japan*, 187–88; Paige, *Korean Decision*, 232; MacArthur, *Reminiscences*, 334.

45. Paige, *Korean Decision*, 230–31; Truman, *Years of Trial and Hope*, 341–43; Futrell, *Air Force in Korea*, 34–35; memo of conversation, July 1, 1950, JFD Mss; Collins, *War in Peacetime*, 18–19.

46. Marshall D. Shulman, *Stalin's Foreign Policy Reappraised* (Cambridge, 1963), *passim;* Whiting, *China Crosses the Yalu*, chap. III; Wilbur W. Hitchcock, "North Korea Jumps the Gun," *Current History*, 20 (1951), 136–44; CDSP, July 15, 1950, 12–14; July 22, 1950, 10; *The Times* (London), June 28, 1950.

47. Royal Institute of International Affairs, *Documents on International Affairs, 1949–50* (London, 1953), 634–35. See also New York *Times*, July 21, 1950; Heinz Brandt, *The Search for a Third Way: My Path between East and West* (New York, 1970), 187; Senate Committee on Armed Services, *Military Situation in the Far East*, 99; Truman, *Years of Trial and Hope*, 342, 345; Stone, *History of the Korean War*, 71.

48. Appleman, *South to the Naktong*, 56–63, 81–82; Higgins, *War in Korea*, 47, 77; Kopke, "The Beginnings of the Korean War," 98–109; Senate Committee on Armed Services, *Military Situation in the Far East*, 3385.

49. Senate Committee on Armed Services, *Military Situation in the Far East*, 3382–83; Harry S. Truman to Arthur H. Vandenberg, July 6, 1950, AHV Mss; Collins, *War in Peacetime*, 81–83; *Business Week*, July 1, 1950, 73–74; July 8, 1950, 97–98; Truman, *Years of Trial and Hope*, 345–48; Whiting, *China Crosses the Yalu*, 59–60; RIIA, *Documents on International Affairs, 1949–50*, 705–08; Acheson, *Present at the Creation*, 416–19.

50. DS, *American Foreign Policy, 1950–1955*, II, 2560–64. See also John Foster Dulles to MacArthur, July 10, 1950; MacArthur to Dulles, July 11, 1950; Dulles to Walter Lippmann, July 13, 1950; Dulles to Truman, July 20, 1950; William R. Mathews to Dulles, July 22, 1950; Dulles to Mathews, July 24, 1950, all in JFD Mss; Arthur H. Vandenberg, ed., *The Private Papers of Senator Vandenberg* (Boston, 1952), 543–44.

51. MacArthur, *Reminiscences*, 339. See also Futrell, *Air Force in Korea*, 160–61, 177; Appleman, *South to the Naktong*, 264; Rees, *Korea*, 41–43.

52. DS, *American Foreign Policy, 1950–1955*, II, 2565. See also Appleman, *South to the Naktong*, 191.

53. RIIA, *Documents on International Affairs, 1949–50*, 658; Sebald, *With MacArthur in Japan*, 215. See also Truman, *Years of Trial and Hope*, 348; Collins, *War in Peacetime*, 77–83; Spanier, *Truman-MacArthur Controversy*, 71.

54. MacArthur, *Reminiscences*, 341. See also Truman, *Years of Trial and Hope*, 349–53; Acheson, *Present at the Creation*, 422; Collins, *War in Peacetime*, 82–83.

55. Sebald, *With MacArthur in Japan*, 215–16.

56. Senate Committee on Armed Services, *Military Situation in the Far East*, 3189.

57. *Ibid.*, 3392–98. See also Truman, *Years of Trial and Hope*, 354–58; Acheson, *Present at the Creation*, 423–24; Whiting, *China Crosses the Yalu*, 69–79.

58. Syngman Rhee to Douglas MacArthur, August 12, 1950, DM Mss.

59. *Ibid.* See also Walt Sheldon, *Hell or High Water: MacArthur's Landing at Inchon* (New York, 1968), 30, 62; Appleman, *South to the Naktong,* 382, 393, 395; Collins, *War in Peacetime,* 111.

60. Colonel C. S. Babcock memo to John Foster Dulles, n.d. [ca. December 1950], JFD Mss; Whiting, *China Crosses the Yalu,* chap. II, 64, 79–81; CDSP, July 29, 1950, 34; Appleman, *South to the Naktong,* 757; William R. Mathews to Dulles, August 18, 1950, JFD Mss; RIIA, *Documents on International Affairs, 1949–50,* 658–59; New York *Times,* September 1, 1950.

61. DS, *American Foreign Policy, 1950–55,* II, 2570–71.

62. Acheson, *Present at the Creation,* 445, 450–52; Collins, *War in Peacetime,* 144–49; Truman, *Years of Trial and Hope,* 359; DSB, September 18, 1950, 464.

63. RIIA, *Documents on International Affairs, 1949–50,* 332; Stone, *History of the Korean War,* chap. XV; *Business Week,* September 2, 1950, 84.

64. Appleman, *South to the Naktong,* 493, 500, 545–46, 572, 600, 604–08; Futrell, *Air Force in Korea,* 195; Senate Committee on Armed Services, *Military Situation in the Far East,* 758–59, 1268, 1833; Truman, *Years of Trial and Hope,* 350; Sebald, *With MacArthur in Japan,* 200; K. M. Panikkar, *In Two Chinas* (London, 1955), 110.

65. Truman, *Years of Trial and Hope,* 362. See also *ibid.,* 361; Whiting, *China Crosses the Yalu,* 112–13; DS, *Record on Korean Unification,* 105–07; Stone, *History of the Korean War,* 119–21; Senate Committee on Armed Services, *Military Situation in the Far East,* 1833; Acheson, *Present at the Creation,* 453–55.

66. Truman, *Years of Trial and Hope,* 364–67; MacArthur, *Reminiscences,* 360–64; Sebald, *With MacArthur in Japan,* 217; Appleman, *South to the Naktong,* 760.

67. Futrell, *Air Force in Korea,* 205; Truman, *Years of Trial and Hope,* 372; Appleman, *South to the Naktong,* 670; Collins, *War in Peacetime,* 180.

68. Appleman, *South to the Naktong,* 669, 673, 687–88, 717, 761. Ironically, many of these Chinese were former Chiang troops armed with American weapons.

69. Senate Committee on Armed Services, *Military Situation in the Far East,* 3489. See also Appleman, *South to the Naktong,* 669; *Business Week,* October 7, 1950, 19–20.

70. Acheson, *Present at the Creation,* 462; *Voice of Korea,* November 21, 1950, 476; December 19, 1950, 483–86; telephone message, Dulles to Dean Rusk, September 29, 1950, JFD Mss; Richard C. Allen, *Korea's Syngman Rhee: An Unauthorized Portrait* (Rutland, Vt., 1960), 127–28; Arthur H. Vandenberg to George Maines, October 24, 1950, AVH Mss.

Chapter 22: Korea: The War with China

1. U.S. Senate, Committee on Armed Services and Committee on Foreign Relations, *Hearings: Military Situation in the Far East,* 82:1, May 1951 (Washington, 1951), 32.

2. DS, *American Foreign Policy, 1950–1955* (Washington, 1957), II, 2583. See also Douglas MacArthur, *Reminiscences* (New York, 1964), 366–67; Senate Committee on Armed Services, *Military Situation in the Far East,* 3427; Harry S. Truman, *Years of Trial and Hope* (New York, 1956), 373.

3. Truman, *Years of Trial and Hope*, 375. See also *ibid.*, 373–76; Robert F. Futrell *et al.*, *The United States Air Force in Korea, 1950–1953* (New York, 1961), 210; Roy E. Appleman, *South to the Naktong, North to the Yalu (June–November 1950)* (Washington, 1960), 749–55; Dean Acheson, *Present at the Creation* (New York, 1969), 464–65.

4. Dulles to Ferdinand L. Mayer, November 9, 1950, JFD Mss. See also John W. Spanier, *The Truman-MacArthur Controversy and the Korean War* (Cambridge, 1959), 151–61; Allen S. Whiting, *China Crosses the Yalu: The Decision to Enter the Korean War* (New York, 1960), 131–31; MacArthur, *Reminiscences*, 369–70; Truman, *Years of Trial and Hope*, 376; William J. Sebald, *With MacArthur in Japan* (New York, 1965), 203.

5. Truman, *Years of Trial and Hope*, 377. See also Whiting, *China Crosses the Yalu*, 137–50; Acheson, *Present at the Creation*, 465; J. Lawton Collins, *War in Peacetime* (Boston, 1969), 205–08.

6. Senate Committee on Armed Services, *Military Situation in the Far East*, 21. See also Truman, *Years of Trial and Hope*, 378–82, 386; Acheson, *Present at the Creation*, 466–67; Dulles to MacArthur, November 15, 1950; Dulles memo to Acheson, November 30, 1950, JFD Mss; Sebald, *With MacArthur in Japan*, 203–04; Appleman, *South to the Naktong*, 765–69; MacArthur, *Reminiscences*, 373–74; DS, *The Record on Korean Unification, 1943–1960* (Washington, 1960), 111.

7. Truman, *Years of Trial and Hope*, 384, 387. See also MacArthur, *Reminiscences*, 375; Acheson, *Present at the Creation*, 471ff.

8. Truman, *Years of Trial and Hope*, 395. See also *ibid.*, 384–88; Acheson, *Present at the Creation*, 471–75; DSB, December 11, 1950, 925.

9. Senate Committee on Armed Services, *Military Situation in the Far East*, 3532–35. See also Richard G. Hewlett and Francis Duncan, *Atomic Shield, 1947–1952* (University Park, Pa., 1969), 538; Acheson, *Present at the Creation*, 477, 517; MacArthur, *Reminiscences*, 384; New York *Times*, April 9, 1964; April 10, 1964; Collins, *War in Peacetime*, 228. Published data on the radioactive waste scheme are vague on when it was first advanced, mid-February 1951 being the latest date implied. The New York *Times* version suggests late November as well. But Washington, not MacArthur, gave first thought to the possibility of the bomb's use.

10. Earl Attlee, *A Prime Minister Remembers* (London, 1961), 238. See also Truman, *Years of Trial and Hope*, 383, 391–93; Collins, *War in Peacetime*, 228–32.

11. Attlee, *A Prime Minister Remembers*, 236–39; Truman, *Years of Trial and Hope*, 415–19; *New Statesman and Nation*, November 11, 1950, 413–16; November 18, 1950, 447; Tribune, *One Way Only* (London, 1950), 12; Leon D. Epstein, *Britain —Uneasy Ally* (Chicago, 1954), 227; Acheson, *Present at the Creation*, 478–83; Sebald, *With MacArthur in Japan*, 205–06; I. F. Stone, *The Hidden History of the Korean War* (New York, 1952), chap. XXIX; David Rees, *Korea: The Limited War* (New York, 1964), 176; K. M. Panikkar, *In Two Chinas* (London, 1955), 118.

12. MacArthur, *Reminiscences*, 377; Senate Committee on Armed Services, *Military Situation in the Far East*, 3444–51; Rees, *Korea*, 184–85. All evidence shows that MacArthur's troops broke contact with the Communists and fled south under minimal pressures, at most, and that December was a repetition of the first months of the war. Stone, *History of the Korean War*, chaps. XXIX, XXXII, is an accurate

summary of the military events. Rees, *Korea,* 176, calls the month a "moral collapse" and "bug-out fever," but does not deny the facts that American soldiers retreated and that top officers made no effort to compel them to stand and defend.

13. MacArthur, *Reminiscences,* 378.

14. Rees, *Korea,* 181. See also MacArthur, *Reminiscences,* 377–80; Truman, *Years of Trial and Hope,* 433–34.

15. Truman, *Years of Trial and Hope,* 434–37; Rees, *Korea,* 176–83; Senate Committee on Armed Services, *Military Situation in the Far East,* 324, 334, 3451; Acheson, *Present at the Creation,* 514–15; Collins, *War in Peacetime,* 239, 248–52.

16. For a discussion of the diplomacy of the period see Panikkar, *In Two Chinas,* 118–24; *Voice of Korea,* January 19, 1951, 487–92; Spanier, *Truman-MacArthur Controversy,* 193–94; DS, *United States Policy in the Korean Conflict, July 1950–February 1951* (Washington, 1951), 27–37; DS, *American Foreign Policy,* II, 2593–609; Acheson, *Present at the Creation,* 513. Chou En-lai's January 17 partial acceptance of the UN resolution of January 13, and the immediate United States interpretation of it as "an outright rejection," are especially noteworthy. See DS, *United States Policy,* 35–36.

17. Douglas MacArthur to Frank W. Boykin, December 13, 1950; Madame Chiang Kai-shek to Boykin, February 24, 1951, HST Mss, OF 471–B; MacArthur, *Reminiscences,* 384; Richard C. Allen, *Korea's Syngman Rhee* (Rutland, Vt., 1960), 131; Harry S. Truman, *Public Papers of the Presidents of the United States: 1951* (Washington, 1965), 154–55.

18. Senate Committee on Armed Services, *Military Situation in the Far East,* 3182, 3540. See also *ibid.,* 3449; Collins, *War in Peacetime,* 263–68.

19. Senate Committee on Armed Services, *Military Situation in the Far East,* 3182.

20. Truman, *Years of Trial and Hope,* 446. See also *ibid.,* 440–42; Senate Committee on Armed Services, *Military Situation in the Far East,* 3180–82, 3193, 3544; MacArthur, *Reminiscences,* 387; Harold Macmillan, *Tides of Fortune, 1945–55* (London, 1969), 331; Acheson, *Present at the Creation,* 518–19.

21. Senate Committee on Armed Services, *Military Situation in the Far East,* 421, 594, 730–40, 878–79, 3546–47; Truman, *Years of Trial and Hope,* 445–49; Acheson, *Present at the Creation,* 521–22; MacArthur, *Reminiscences,* 400–06.

22. Royal Institute of International Affairs, *Documents on International Affairs, 1951* (London, 1954), 632.

23. *Ibid.,* 632–33; Truman, *Years of Trial and Hope,* 454–59; Allen, *Syngman Rhee,* 144–54; Walter G. Hermes, *Truce Tent and Fighting Front* (Washington, 1966), 63.

24. Hermes, *Truce Tent and Fighting Front,* 25, 33, 35, 56, 77, 79, 110–11, 115–19, 130–33, 513; RIIA, *Documents on International Affairs, 1951,* 632ff.; Anthony Eden, *Full Circle* (Boston, 1960), 17–20; Truman, *Years of Trial and Hope,* 459–60; DS, *American Foreign Policy, 1950–1955,* II, 2630. Stone, *History of the Korean War,* 284–309, argues that America deliberately attacked the truce zone to obscure Chinese and North Korean concessions and to postpone a settlement before it could sign a Japanese peace treaty. Despite some evidence for this case, the question remains why progress was not made after September, for a whole spectrum

of other issues would have sufficed to end the conference. There is no doubt, however, that the worst incident of which the Communists complained was the work of "... partisans friendly to the ROK," perhaps assigned to the task by Rhee. See Hermes, *Truce Tent and Fighting Front,* 42. Also see *Voice of Korea,* August 30, 1951, 532.

25. Hermes, *Truce Tent and Fighting Front,* 137–38; Mark W. Clark, *From the Danube to the Yalu* (New York, 1954), 62–67, 109; A. Y. Vyshinsky, *Korea: Speeches at the Seventh Session of the U.N. General Assembly . . . 1952* (London: Soviet News, 1952), 49–50; Allen, *Syngman Rhee,* 156; Robert Murphy, *Diplomat among Warriors* (New York, 1964), 358; RIIA, *Documents on International Affairs, 1951,* 661–62.

26. Clark, *Danube to the Yalu,* 72, 250; A. Y. Vyshinsky, *Two Speeches at the Seventh Session of the UNO, October 18 and 29, 1952* (London: Soviet News, 1952), 85; Acheson, *Present at the Creation,* 654; DS, *American Foreign Policy, 1950–1955,* II, 2627ff.; Truman, *Years of Trial and Hope,* 460–61; RIIA, *Documents on International Affairs, 1952* (London, 1955), 429.

27. Hermes, *Truce Tent and Fighting Front,* 215. See also *ibid.,* 199, 205, 513; W. A. Harriman to Truman, January 5, 1952, HST Mss, OF 335–B; Clark, *Danube to the Yalu,* 69–71, 99; Truman, *Years of Trial and Hope,* 462–63; Murphy, *Diplomat among Warriors,* 354–57.

28. Hermes, *Truce Tent and Fighting Front,* 345–47. See also *ibid.,* 215.

29. *Ibid.,* 501; Futrell, *Air Force in Korea,* 195, 344, 452–53, 482–83, 645; Rees, *Korea,* 440–41. There were 698,000 tons of ordnance—bombs and 32,000 tons of napalm being the larger part—dropped on Korea during the entire war.

30. Senate Committee on Armed Services, *Military Situation in the Far East,* 3545–46; *Voice of Korea,* June 25, 1951, 518; Clark, *Danube to the Yalu,* 85.

31. Senate Committee on Armed Services, *Military Situation in the Far East,* 3075. See also Hermes, *Truce Tent and Fighting Front,* 501; *Voice of Korea,* February 21, 1951, 493; Rees, *Korea,* 440–41.

32. Hermes, *Truce Tent and Fighting Front,* 321–24, 461; Gabriel Kolko, "Report on the Destruction of Dikes," *Against the Crime of Silence,* John Duffet, ed. (New York, 1968), 224–26.

Chapter 23: The Dilemmas of World Economic Power, 1950–1953

1. Transcript of Clair Wilcox press conference, "Report on ITO," October 1, 1947, 4–5, 13–17; Wilcox, "Report to the Secretary of State . . . First Meeting of the Preparatory Committee for an International Conference on Trade and Employment," October 15–November 26, 1946; memo of conversation, August 20, 1947; "Statement made by Mr. Clair Wilcox . . . September 15, 1947," all in CW Mss; Richard N. Gardner, *Sterling-Dollar Diplomacy* (Oxford, 1956), 361; Arthur H. Vandenberg to Mrs. H. S. Greenawalt, September 17, 1947, AHV Mss; DS, *The Geneva Charter for an International Trade Organization: A Commentary* (Washington, 1947), *passim;* Karin Kock, *International Trade Policy and the GATT, 1947–1967* (Stockholm, 1969), 48ff.; Clair Wilcox, *A Charter for World Trade* (New York,

1949), 44–45; Allen J. Matusow, *Farm Policies and Politics in the Truman Years* (Cambridge, 1967), 102–05.

2. N. H. Collisson memo to J. A. Krug, December 9, 1947, JAK Mss, box 66; "Analyses of Amendments Submitted to the ITO Conference," December 13, 1947, CW Mss; William Diebold, Jr., "The End of the I.T.O.," *Essays in International Finance,* No. 16 (Princeton, 1952), 15, 28–33; Gardner, *Sterling-Dollar Diplomacy,* 365–77; DS, *Havana Charter for an International Trade Organization and Final Act and Related Documents* (Washington, 1948), *passim;* A. A. Fatouros, *Government Guarantees to Foreign Investors* (New York, 1962), 71–72; Wilcox, *Charter for World Trade, passim;* George M. Elsey memo of June 4, 1948; Dean Acheson memo to Harry S. Truman, April 24, 1949; William L. Batt to Truman, March 22, 1950; Truman to Batt, March 28, 1950, HST Mss, OF 85; DSB, November 9, 1947, 907; May 15, 1949, 623–27; U.S. House, Committee on Foreign Affairs, *Hearings: Membership and Participation by the United States in the International Trade Organization,* 81:2, April–May 1950 (Washington, 1950), 10, *passim;* Kock, *International Trade Policy,* 70–76.

3. United Nations, Department of Economic Affairs, *The International Flow of Private Capital, 1946–1952* (New York, 1954), 8; DS, *Point Four (Cooperative Program for the Aid and Development of Economically Underdeveloped Areas)* (Washington, 1950), 56–58; U.S. Senate, Special Committee to Study the Foreign Aid Program, *The Foreign Aid Programs and the United States Economy* [Study no. 9] 85:1 (Washington, 1957), 844–45; William L. Clayton, "GATT, the Marshall Plan, and OECD," *Political Science Quarterly,* 78 (1963), 493–94; U.S. Department of Commerce, Office of Business Economics, *Balance of Payments: Statistical Supplement, Revised Edition* (Washington, 1963), 1–4, 248–58; U.S. House, Committee on Armed Services, *Hearings: Petroleum for National Defense,* 80:2, January–March 1948 (Washington, 1948), 315; DSB, October 17, 1948, 493; March 27, 1949, 374; *Business Week,* February 19, 1949, 117–18.

4. U.S. Associates of the International Chamber of Commerce, press release of February 17, 1949, in HST Mss, OF 192–A.

5. Staff Report, Industry and Commerce Division, Technical Cooperation Administration, "What Is Required to Create the So-called 'Favorable Climate' to Attract Foreign Private Capital . . .," n.d., SA Mss, box 3.

6. U.S. Senate, Committee on Foreign Relations, *Development of Technical Assistance Programs: Background Information and Documents,* 83:2, November 22, 1954 (Washington, 1954), 54–57; Walter S. Salant, "The Domestic Effects of Capital Export under the Point Four Program," *American Economic Review,* 40 (1950), 499–504; no author, "Point Four: A Re-Examination of Ends and Means," *Yale Law Journal,* 59 (1950), 1279–92; Klaus Knorr, ed., *Strengthening the Free World Economy—A Report . . . of a Conference Held at Princeton, November 16–17, 1952,* Centre of International Studies, memorandum no. 3 (Princeton, 1953), 14–15; Stephen J. Spingarn memo to Clark Clifford, October 3, 1949; Spingarn to Clifford, October 5, 1949, SJS Mss, box 17; Harry S. Truman, *Years of Trial and Hope* (New York, 1956), 236; DSB, June 12, 1949, 762; September 26, 1949, 456; February 13, 1950, 232–34; "Note on Conference with Mr. Ivan B. White, . . . June 4, 1951," PMP Mss, box 127.

7. U.S. House, Committee on Foreign Affairs, *Hearings: International Technical*

Cooperation Act of 1949, 81:1, September–October 1950 (Washington, 1950), *passim;* U.S. House, Committee on Foreign Affairs, *Hearings: Act for International Development,* 81:1, 2, January 1950 (Washington, 1950), 451–58, 473–74, 492–93; R. E. Gifford to Arthur H. Vandenberg, July 19, 1949, AHV Mss; DS, *Point 4, passim;* Sam G. Bagett to Tom Connally, September 8, 1949, TC Mss, box 228; Dean Acheson, memo for the President, February 16, 1950, JMD Mss, Japan 1950, box 1; *Business Week,* November 26, 1949, 105–06; Gordon Gray *et al., Report to the President on Foreign Economic Policies,* November 10, 1950 (Washington, 1950), 51–62; B. E. Matecki, *Establishment of the International Finance Corporation and United States Policy* (New York, 1957), 32–33.

8. Hans H. Landsberg *et al., Resources in America's Future: Patterns of Requirements and Availabilities, 1960–2000* (Baltimore, 1963), 15, 45, 427–28; Percy W. Bidwell, *Raw Materials: A Study of American Policy* (New York, 1958), 2–6; Paul Bairoch, *Diagnostic de l'Évolution Économique du Tiers-Monde, 1900–1966* (Paris, 1967), 76; U.S. President's Materials Policy Commission, *Resources for Freedom,* June 1952 (Washington, 1952), I, 91–101.

9. U.S. Department of Commerce, Office of Business Economics, *U.S. Business Investments in Foreign Countries* (Washington, 1960), 66; Council of Economic Advisers, draft memo, "Basic Foreign and Domestic Economic Problems . . .," April 14, 1950, KWH Mss; House Committee on Foreign Affairs, *International Technical Cooperation Act of 1949,* 298–99; Percy W. Bidwell, "Raw Materials and National Policy," *Foreign Affairs,* 37 (1958), 149–53; *The Economist,* February 25, 1950, 449.

10. Gray, *Report to the President,* 8. See also *ibid.,* 9–10, 51–56, 61–62.

11. U.S. Senate, Committee on Foreign Relations, *Hearings: Mutual Security Act of 1952,* 82:2, March–April 1952 (Washington, 1952), 48. See also memo to Gray Commission, "Statement of Problem," [1950], JMD Mss, Budget Bureau, box 10; M. S. Venkataramani, "Manganese as a Factor in Indo-American Relations," *India Quarterly,* 14 (1958), 138–50; U.S. Senate, Committee on Foreign Relations, *Hearings: Mutual Security Act of 1951,* 82:1, July–August 1951 (Washington, 1951), 403–04, 425; Michael Tanzer, *The Political Economy of International Oil and the Underdeveloped Countries* (Boston, 1969), part 2; *Business Week,* January 27, 1951, 125–26.

12. Stacy May, "Foreign Investment and World Peace," [ca. 1951], SA Mss, box 3.

13. Minutes of President's Materials Policy Commission, December 12, 1951, 130, PMP Mss, box 7. See also resolution of U.S. Council of International Chamber of Commerce, May 1, 1951, HST Mss, OF 386; Senate Committee on Foreign Relations, *Mutual Security Act of 1951,* 27; W. A. Harriman memo to Truman, January 5, 1952, HST Mss, OF 335–D; agenda for meeting of President's Materials Policy Commission, February 27, 1951, PMP Mss, box 9; interviews in PMP Mss, box 67.

14. President's Materials Policy Commission, *Resources for Freedom,* I, 3–13, 68–89, V, 110–25; Senate Committee on Foreign Relations, *Mutual Security Act of 1952,* 99–100.

15. Dean Acheson, *Present at the Creation* (New York, 1969), 498. See also *ibid.,* 496-97.

16. Edgar S. Furniss, Jr., *Some Perspectives on American Military Assistance* (Princeton, 1957), 30; Stacy May, "Foreign Investment and World Peace," SA Mss, box 3; Bidwell, "Raw Materials and National Policy," 152; Eugene R. Black, *The Diplomacy of Economic Development* (Cambridge, 1960), 53; United Nations, Conference on Trade and Development, "Review of International Trade and Development, 1967: Part 1 . . .," November 15, 1967 (mimeo report by the Secretary-General of UNCTAD), 19, and charts. For a fuller discussion of the post-1950 world economy, and especially Latin America, see Gabriel Kolko, *The Roots of American Foreign Policy* (Boston, 1969), chap. III.

17. United Nations, Economic Commission for Europe, *Economic Survey of Europe in 1950* (Geneva, 1951), 134; *Business Week,* October 7, 1950, 133–34; Richard M. Bissell, "The Impact of Rearmament on the Free World Economy," *Foreign Affairs,* 29 (1951), 395; Robert Marjolin, *Europe and the United States in the World Economy* (Durham, 1953), 24; United Nations, Economic Commission for Europe, *Economic Survey of Europe in 1951* (Geneva, 1952), 15.

18. Richard M. Bissell, "European Recovery and the Problems Ahead," *American Economic Review,* 42 (1952), 311–12. See also Gardner Patterson and Jack N. Behrman, *Survey of United States International Finance—1950* (Princeton, 1951), 233.

19. UN, *Europe in 1951,* 6–11, 81; Henry Chalmers, *World Trade Policies* (Berkeley, 1953), 503; *Business Week,* September 22, 1951, 169–70; January 12, 1952, 149–50; United Nations, Department of Economic and Social Affairs, *The Growth of World Industry, 1938–1961: National Tables* (New York, 1963), 781; *U.S. News and World Report,* September 26, 1952, 38–41; Bissell, "The Impact of Rearmament," 385, 398–99; UN, *Europe in 1950,* 155–57.

20. UN, *Europe in 1950,* 151. See also *ibid.,* 36; *U.S. News and World Report,* November 17, 1950, 22–23.

21. Thomas Balogh, *Germany: An Experiment in 'Planning' by the 'Free' Price Mechanism* (Oxford, 1950), 69; Gray, *Report to the President,* 34; *Business Week,* January 19, 1952, 165–66; *Wall Street Journal,* December 15, 1953.

22. Quoted in Gunther Stein, *The World the Dollar Built* (London, 1952), 258. See also UN, *Europe in 1950,* 36, 149–50; UN, *The Growth of World Industry,* 272; *Business Week,* September 23, 1950, 121–22.

23. Economic Cooperation Administration, Minutes of Meeting of Advisory Committee on Fiscal and Monetary Problems, October 31, 1950, JMD Mss, Budget Bureau, box 7.

24. Gray, *Report to the President,* 10. See also *ibid.,* 1–44.

25. Quoted in Gardner Patterson and Jack N. Behrman, *Survey of United States International Finance—1951* (Princeton, 1952), 35. See also *ibid.,* 16, 20–21; Harry Bayard Price, *The Marshall Plan and Its Meaning* (Ithaca, 1955), 167.

26. Henry René, memorandum of October 4, 1951, WG Mss. See also William Gomberg, "Report of Mission to Europe, April 18 to June 4, 1951," WG Mss.

27. ECA, Memo, "The Future of EPU and the European Trade Liberalization Program," December 26, 1950, JMD Mss, Budget Bureau, box 7.

28. U.S. Senate, Committee on Foreign Relations, *Hearings: United States Foreign Aid Programs in Europe,* 82:1, July 1951 (Washington, 1951), 64.

29. Quoted in Gardner Patterson and John M. Gunn, Jr., *Survey of United States International Finance—1952* (Princeton, 1953), 19. See also Economic Cooperation Administration, *13th Report to Congress for Quarter ended June 30, 1951* (Washington, 1951), 9; UN, *Europe in 1951,* 81–87; United Nations, Economic Commission for Europe, *Economic Survey of Europe in 1953* (Geneva, 1954), 20; U.S. Senate, Committee on Foreign Relations, *Hearings: Assignment of Ground Forces of the United States to Duty in the European Area,* 82:1, February 1951 (Washington, 1951), *passim;* Senate Committee on Foreign Relations, *Mutual Security Act of 1951, passim;* Marjolin, *Europe and the United States,* 27–30; *New Statesman and Nation,* November 17, 1951, 552; Price, *Marshall Plan and Its Meaning,* 159–63; *Business Week,* July 1, 1950, 73–75.

30. Bissell, *The Impact of Rearmament,* 391. See also UN, *Europe in 1950,* 20, 39, 53; Gardner Patterson, John M. Dunn, Jr., and Dorothy Swerdlove, *Survey of United States International Finance—1953* (Princeton, 1954), 20; Bissell, "European Recovery and the Problems Ahead," 322; *Wall Street Journal,* December 15, 1953.

31. Shigeru Yoshida, *The Yoshida Memoirs: The Story of Japan in Crisis* (Boston, 1962), 46. See also *ibid.,* 41–42, 192; Kozo Yamamura, *Economic Policy in Postwar Japan* (Berkeley, 1967), 39; Shigeru Yoshida, "Japan and the Crisis in Asia," *Foreign Affairs,* 29 (1951), 180; *Business Week,* December 30, 1950, 73–74.

32. Quoted in Chitoshi Yanaga, *Big Business In Japanese Politics* (New Haven, 1968), 261. See also *ibid.,* 156–57, 256–64; *U.S. News and World Report,* January 25, 1952, 54–58; Yamamura, *Economic Policy in Postwar Japan,* 39, 43; New York *Times* July 5, 1971.

33. George C. Allen, *Japan's Economic Expansion* (London, 1965), 230–49; Yamamura, *Economic Policy in Postwar Japan,* 43; Yanaga, *Big Business in Japanese Politics,* 262–70; Leon Hollerman, *Japan's Dependence on the World Economy: The Approach toward Economic Liberalization* (Princeton, 1967), 101–13, 135.

34. DS, *American Foreign Policy, 1950–1955* (Washington, 1957), I, 58–63; DSB, March 30, 1953, 461–62; John Foster Dulles, speech before the Tenth Inter-American Conference, March 4, 1954, DS press release no. 109, 8–9; U.S. Senate, Committee on Foreign Relations, *United States Foreign Policy: Compilation of Studies,* 87:1, Doc. No. 24 (Washington, 1961), 346; U.S. House, Committee on Foreign Affairs, *Hearings: Foreign Policy and Mutual Security,* 84:2, October–November 1956 (Washington, 1956), 25; U.S. Congress, Joint Committee on the Economic Report, *Hearings: Foreign Economic Policy,* 84:1, November 1955 (Washington, 1955), 5; Sherman Adams to George Humphrey, February 10, 1953; Sinclair Weeks memos to Eisenhower, February 25, 1953; Humphrey to Adams, March 18, 1953, all in DDE Mss, OF 116–P; Lincoln Gordon to Gabriel Hague, June 24, 1953, DDE Mss, OF 116–M; Senate Committee on Foreign Relations, *Development of Technical Assistance Programs,* 58.

35. "Memorandum re NAC Meeting," September 30, 1953, JFD Mss. See also U.S. Commission on Foreign Economic Policy, *Staff Papers* (Washington, 1954), *passim;* Clarence B. Randall, *A Foreign Economic Policy for the United States* (Chicago, 1954), *passim.*

36. U.S. Department of Commerce, Bureau of the Census, *Historical Statistics of*

the United States: Colonial Times to 1957 (Washington, 1960), 139; Department of Commerce, *Balance of Payments*, 3; Joint Committee on the Economic Report, *Foreign Economic Policy*, 463; U.S. International Cooperation Administration, *Effects of Foreign Aid on the United States Economy*, April 10, 1957 (Washington, 1957), 26; U.S. Department of Commerce, Bureau of Foreign Commerce, *Factors Limiting U.S. Investments Abroad* (Washington, 1954), part 2, *passim;* Kolko, *Roots of American Foreign Policy*, chap. III; United Nations, *Monthly Bulletin of Statistics*, November 1965, xxiv.

37. Dwight D. Eisenhower to Winthrop W. Aldrich, February 24, 1954, DDE Mss, OF 116–M. See also Lincoln Gordon to Gabriel Hauge, July 8, 1953, DDE Mss, OF 116–U; John Hulley memo to Gabriel Hauge, August 20, 1953, DDE Mss, OF–249; Winthrop Aldrich to Eisenhower, February 4, 1954, DDE Mss, OF 116–N; Miriam Camps, *Trade Policy and American Leadership* (Princeton: Center of International Studies, 1957), 8–9.

38. DS, *The United States Economy and the Mutual Security Program* (Washington, 1959), 21, 66, 80; Special Committee to Study the Foreign Aid Program, *Foreign Aid Programs*, 844–45; Patterson *et al.*, *United States International Finance —1953*, 107–08; Kolko, *Roots of American Foreign Policy*, 57–58; Camps, *Trade Policy and American Leadership*, 4ff.

Chapter 24: Europe and the Dilemmas of Military Power, 1950–1952

1. Charles E. Bohlen statement of April 3, 1950, JMD Mss, Japan 1950, box 5. See also *Wall Street Journal*, August 3, 1951; *Business Week*, April 1, 1950, 15; April 8, 1950, 21; Athan Theoharis in *Politics and Policies of the Truman Administration*, Barton J. Bernstein, ed. (Chicago, 1970), 196–268; John Foster Dulles speech of June 22, 1950, JFD Mss.

2. DS, *American Foreign Policy, 1950–1955* (Washington, 1957), II, 1930.

3. DSB, June 26, 1950, 1036. See also DS, *American Foreign Policy*, I, 10–12, II, 1935–36; Royal Institute of International Affairs, *Documents on International Affairs, 1949–1950* (London, 1953), 91–93; *Business Week*, May 13, 1950, 119–20.

4. Anonymous, "The Balance of Military Power," *Atlantic Monthly*, June 1951, 22.

5. DS, *American Foreign Policy*, II, 2558.

6. RIIA, *Documents on International Affairs, 1949-50*, 83–84. See also Richard G. Hewlett and Francis Duncan, *Atomic Shield, 1947–1952* (University Park, Pa., 1969), 525–30; Harry S. Truman, *Years of Trial and Hope* (New York, 1956), 419–28; *Business Week*, December 9, 1950, 19.

7. U.S. Senate, Committee on Foreign Relations, *Hearings: North Atlantic Treaty*, 81:1, April–May 1949 (Washington, 1949), 61, 282. See also *ibid.*, 57, 281–83; Truman, *Years of Trial and Hope*, 245–46; John Foster Dulles to William Mathews, February 10, 1948, WM Mss; Dulles memo of February 11, 1949, JFD Mss; *U.S. News and World Report*, July 8, 1949, 30–33.

8. Konrad Adenauer, *Memoirs, 1945–53* (Chicago, 1966), 192–217; Rudolf Augstein, *Konrad Adenauer* (London, 1964), 24; Dean Acheson, *Present at the Creation*

(New York, 1969), 286ff.; *Business Week,* November 12, 1949, 111–12; DSB, October 17, 1949, 575–77; December 5, 1949, 863a–864a.

9. Adenauer, *Memoirs,* 270. See also *ibid.,* 267–68; Vincent Auriol, *Mon Septennat, 1947–1954* (Paris, 1970), 241; Harry S. Truman, *Public Papers of the Presidents of the United States: 1949* (Washington, 1964), 570–71; *U.S. News and World Report,* November 4, 1949, 29; Laurence W. Martin, "The American Decision to Rearm Germany," *American Civil-Military Decisions,* Harold Stein, ed. (Montgomery, Ala., 1963), 647–48; RIIA, *Documents on International Affairs, 1949–50,* 310.

10. Acheson, *Present at the Creation,* 389; Adenauer, *Memoirs,* 246, 273ff.; Auriol, *Mon Septennat,* 242; Charles E. Bohlen statement of April 3, 1950, JMD Mss, Japan 1950, box 5; Robert E. Osgood, *NATO: The Entangling Alliance* (Chicago, 1962), 65; *Business Week,* May 6, 1950, 125–26; May 13, 1950, 119–20; John Foster Dulles memo of conversation with Truman, April 28, 1950, JFD Mss.

11. Acheson, *Present at the Creation,* 394–400; Auriol, *Mon Septennat,* 262, 267–68; *Business Week,* May 13, 1950, 119–20; May 20, 1950, 20; Dirk U. Stikker, *Men of Responsibility: A Memoir* (New York, 1966), 297; Jules Moch, *Histoire du Réarmament allemand depuis 1950* (Paris, 1965), 58; Beate Ruhm von Oppen, ed., *Documents on Germany under Occupation, 1945–1954* (London, 1955), 493–94; John J. McCloy to Henry L. Stimson, June 28, 1950, HSL Mss.

12. Harry S. Truman to Arthur H. Vandenberg, July 6, 1950, AHV Mss. See also Henry L. Stimson to John J. McCloy, July 14, 1950, HLS Mss; Tracy S. Voorhees memo to Gordon Gray, July 17, 1950, JMD Mss, Budget Bureau, box 10; *Business Week,* August 19, 1950, 91; John J. McCloy to Henry L. Stimson, July 26, 1950, HLS Mss; Truman, *Years of Trial and Hope,* 380.

13. DSB, September 11, 1950, 428.

14. Adenauer *aide-mémoire,* received September 6, 1950, JFD Mss. See also Acheson, *Present at the Creation,* 436–38; Dean Acheson, "The Illusion of Disengagement," *Foreign Affairs,* 36 (1958), 376–77; Martin, "The American Decision to Rearm Germany," 645ff.; Samuel P. Huntington, *The Common Defense: Strategic Programs in National Politics* (New York, 1961), 317–21; RIIA, *Documents on International Affairs, 1949–50,* 323; Karl W. Deutsch and Lewis J. Edinger, *Germany Rejoins the Powers* (Stanford, 1959), 23; Adenauer, *Memoirs,* 274–77, 300; Gerald Freund, *Germany between Two Worlds* (New York, 1961), 140; Charles Wighton, *Adenauer—Democratic Dictator* (London, 1963), 145.

15. Adenauer, *Memoirs,* 278–81, 286–89; Augstein, *Adenauer,* 24–25; Acheson, *Present at the Creation,* 436–37, 443–44; Moch, *Réarmament allemand,* 45–63, 84; DS, *American Foreign Policy,* II, 1711–13; Stikker, *Men of Responsibility,* 298–99; Truman, *Years of Trial and Hope,* 254–57.

16. Moch, *Réarmament allemand,* 93ff., chap. XII; Acheson, *Present at the Creation,* 458–59, 485–87; RIIA, *Documents on International Affairs, 1949–50,* 336–45; Auriol, *Mon Septennat,* 293, 298–99; Stikker, *Men of Responsibility,* 300–01; Henry L. Stimson to John J. McCloy, July 14, 1950, HLS Mss; Truman, *Years of Trial and Hope,* 257–58; Ruhm von Oppen, *Documents on Germany,* 538–40; U.S. Senate, Committee on Foreign Relations, *Hearings: Assignment of Ground Forces of the United States to Duty in the European Area,* 82:1, February 1951 (Washington, 1951), 168; *Business Week,* December 30, 1950, 19–20.

17. Arnold Wolfers, ed., *Alliance Policy in the Cold War* (Baltimore, 1959), 23. See also Senate Committee on Foreign Relations, *Assignment of Ground Forces*, 61, 78, 226–27; Anonymous, "The Balance of Military Power," 25–26; U.S. Senate, Committee on Foreign Relations, *Hearings: United States Foreign Aid Programs in Europe*, 82:1, July 1951 (Washington, 1951), 83; RIIA, *Documents on International Affairs, 1949–50*, 76–77.

18. Stanton Griffis, *Lying in State* (New York, 1952), 292–93. See also *ibid.*, chap. XIV; Townsend Hoopes, "Overseas Bases in American Strategy," *Foreign Affairs*, 37 (1958), 73–74; Theodore J. Lowi, "Bases in Spain," in Stein, *American Civil-Military Decisions*, 667–702; Dean Acheson to Arthur H. Vandenberg, January 18, 1950, AHV Mss; memo of April 26, 1950, JFD Mss; Senate Committee on Foreign Relations, *Assignment of Ground Forces*, 87, 212, 390, 535.

19. DS, *American Foreign Policy*, 1784. See also *ibid.*, 1778–86; Bundesministerium für gesamtdeutsche Fragen, *Die Bemühungen der Bundesrepublik um Wiederherstellung . . .: Dokumente und Akten* (Bonn, 1958), I, 7–14; Adenauer, *Memoirs*, 298; Ruhm von Oppen, *Documents on Germany*, 467–69; RIIA, *Documents on International Affairs, 1949–50*, 161–62, 165–70; DSB, June 5, 1950, 884–85; USSR, Ministry of Foreign Affairs, *The Soviet Union and the Question of the Unity of Germany and of the German Peace Treaty* (Moscow, 1952), 70–71.

20. DS, *American Foreign Policy*, I, 19–20. See also *ibid.*, 1784–93; Auriol, *Mon Septennat*, 303–04, 313–14; Moch, *Réarmament allemand*, 229–32, 247, 255; *New Statesman and Nation*, November 11, 1950, 415–16; RIIA, *Documents on International Affairs, 1949–50*, 171–79; RIIA, *Documents on International Affairs, 1951* (London, 1954), 248–87; USSR, *Soviet Union and the Question of the Unity of Germany*, 72–78; Soviet News, *The Soviet Union in the Struggle for Peace* (London, 1951), *passim*.

21. Adenauer, *Memoirs*, 325–26; Kenneth C. Royall to Harry S. Truman, January 12, 1951, HST Mss, OF 198; Senate Committee on Foreign Relations, *Assignment of Ground Forces*, 15, 25, 77; DS, *American Foreign Policy*, I, 1514; U.S. Senate, Committee on Foreign Relations, *Hearings: Mutual Security Act of 1951*, 82:1, July–August 1951 (Washington, 1951), 27.

22. Moch, *Réarmament allemand*, 266–67, 273–74, 280–83; Ruhm von Oppen, *Documents on Germany*, 562ff.; Adenauer, *Memoirs*, 351–64; Senate Committee on Foreign Relations, *United States Foreign Aid Programs*, 207–12; Stikker, *Men of Responsibility*, 301–03; Acheson, *Present at the Creation*, 556–60, 599–600, 608–12; Auriol, *Mon Septennat*, 417.

23. Acheson, *Present at the Creation*, 630. See also RIIA, *Documents on International Affairs, 1952* 68–74; DSB, April 7, 1952, 531–32.

24. DSB, April 28, 1952, 650–51. See also RIIA, *Documents on International Affairs, 1952*, 89–93; DSB, April 7, 1952, 530–31; DS, *American Foreign Policy*, II, 1809–13.

25. Anthony Eden, *Full Circle* (Boston, 1960), 46–52; Adenauer, *Memoirs*, 408–18; RIIA, *Documents on International Affairs, 1952*, 91, 94–95, 100–97; Acheson, *Present at the Creation*, 643–47; Auriol, *Mon Septennat*, 448–51, 461; DS, *American Foreign Policy*, 1813; Moch, *Réarmament allemand*, 292; U.S. Senate, Committee

on Foreign Relations, *Hearings: Convention on Relations with the Federal Republic of Germany and a Protocol to the North Atlantic Treaty,* 82:2, June 1952 (Washington, 1952), 15.

26. New York *Times,* January 2, 1952.

27. *Wall Street Journal,* August 3, 1951.

28. DS, *American Foreign Policy,* I, 25–26. See also *U.S. News and World Report,* May 5, 1950, 31.

29. Senate Committee on Foreign Relations, *Mutual Security Act of 1951,* 65; Anonymous, "The Balance of Military Power," 23; Senate Committee on Foreign Relations, *Assignment of Ground Forces,* 79, 83–84, 106–07, 174, 192, 222; Hewlett and Duncan, *Atomic Shield,* 548, 574; Drew Middleton, "NATO Changes Direction," *Foreign Affairs,* 31 (1953), 436.

30. Soviet News, *The Soviet Union at the Fifth Session of the U.N.O., 1950: October 26—December 12* (London, 1951), 33, 51; CDSP, May 6, 1950, 17–19; May 27, 1950, 32; November 4, 1950, 7–8; January 20, 1951, 3–5; RIIA, *Documents on International Affairs, 1951,* 293–304; Joseph Stalin, *Economic Problems of Socialism in the U.S.S.R.* (New York, 1952), 26–33, *passim.*

31. Truman to Henry L. Stimson, July 7, 1950, HLS Mss.

32. DS, *American Foreign Policy,* 32, 35–39; Dean Acheson, *The Pattern of Responsibility* (Boston, 1952), 34–36; Acheson, *Present at the Creation,* 599; Bernhard B. Bechhoefer, *Postwar Negotiations for Arms Control* (Washington, 1961), 137–88; Acheson, "The Illusion of Disengagement," 372–73; Wolfers, *Alliance Policy in the Cold War,* 16–17; W. A. Harriman to Harry S. Truman, January 5, 1952, HST Mss, OF 335–B; Senate Committee on Foreign Relations, *Mutual Security Act of 1951,* 27.

33. DS, *American Foreign Policy,* I, 45, 55.

Chapter 25: Eisenhower and the Crisis of American Power

1. Dwight D. Eisenhower, *Mandate for Change, 1953–1956* (New York, 1963), 5, 12–21; Harry S. Truman, *Years of Trial and Hope* (New York, 1956), 185–87; Arthur Krock, *Memoirs: Sixty Years on the Firing Line* (New York, 1968), 242–43, 268–69.

2. Eisenhower to Brooks Hays, February 27, 1954, DDE Mss, OF 116. See also Eisenhower, *Mandate for Change,* 40–41, 84–85; Douglas MacArthur, *Reminiscences* (New York, 1964), 410–12; New York *Times,* April 10, April 11, 1964; Truman, *Years of Trial and Hope,* chap. XXXII; John Foster Dulles to Harry S. Truman, July 20, 1950, JFD Mss; *Congressional Record,* vol. 101, 2408–10.

3. Eisenhower, *Mandate for Change,* 431. See also Robert J. Donovan, *Eisenhower: The Inside Story* (New York, 1956), 151.

4. DS, *American Foreign Policy, 1950–1955* (Washington, 1957), I, 58–59. See also *ibid.,* 60–64; Emmet John Hughes, *The Ordeal of Power: A Political Memoir of the Eisenhower Years* (New York, 1963), 29–31, 151–53, 295.

5. Draft of speech, January 29, 1947, in AHV Mss.

6. Dulles to Frank C. Laubach, October 31, 1950, JFD Mss; U.S. Senate, Committee on Foreign Relations, *Hearing: Nomination of John Foster Dulles, Secretary of State-Designate,* 83:1, January 15, 1953 (Washington, 1953), *passim.*

7. DS, *American Foreign Policy,* II, 2475. See also Walter G. Hermes, *Truce Tent and Fighting Front* (Washington, 1966), 367, 408–09; Dulles to Kenneth de Courcy, February 28, 1952, JFD Mss; Dulles memo to Eisenhower, November 20, 1952, DDE Mss, OF 196; Donovan, *Eisenhower,* 28–29.

8. Truman, *Years of Trial and Hope,* 517–18; Eisenhower, *Mandate for Change,* 179–81; Hermes, *Truce Tent and Fighting Front,* 411–13, 419, 441–45; DS, *American Foreign Policy,* II, 2633; Mark W. Clark, *From the Danube to the Yalu* (New York, 1954), 240–46, 261; Anthony Eden, *Full Circle* (Boston, 1960), 29.

9. No author, "The Attack on the Irrigation Dams in North Korea," *Air University Quarterly,* 6 (Winter 1953–1954), 40–41. See also Clark, *Danube to the Yalu,* 264–67; DS, *American Foreign Policy,* II, 2634; Robert Murphy, *Diplomat among Warriors* (New York, 1964), 359.

10. No author, "The Attack on the Irrigation Dams in North Korea," 40; Hermes, *Truce Tent and Fighting Front,* 460–61; Clark, *Danube to the Yalu,* 267, claims that on May 23 Washington authorized him to "break off" talks with the Communists if they refused the final American position, ". . . and to carry on the war in new ways never yet tried in Korea"—ways he does not specify. The destruction of dams and the food supply, and mass starvation, were probably an aspect of this plan; if so, he partially applied it. It is in the light of facts such as these, rather than the Communist documentation, that Communist charges of American germ warfare assume credibility, for the Americans considered modes of even greater destruction and, in part, implemented them.

11. Eisenhower, *Mandate for Change,* 185. See also *ibid.,* 183–84; DS, *American Foreign Policy,* II, 2634–35, 2659–60; David Rees, *Korea: The Limited War* (New York, 1964), 423; Hermes, *Truce Tent and Fighting Front,* 426–27, 447–52; Clark, *Danube to the Yalu,* 265–69; DS, *The Record on Korean Unification, 1943–1960* (Washington, 1960), 128–31; New York *Times,* June 21, 1953.

12. Clark, *Danube to the Yalu,* 283–91; Eisenhower, *Mandate for Change,* 186–87, 190; Richard C. Allen, *Korea's Syngman Rhee: An Unauthorized Portrait* (Rutland, Vt., 1960), 164, 168, chaps. XV–XIX; Hermes, *Truce Tent and Fighting Front,* 453–56; DS, *Record on Korean Unification,* 132ff.; Charles Edmundson, "Don't Make Korea Another China," *The Reporter,* October 31, 1957, 31–34; *Wall Street Journal,* August 12, 1958; October 15, 1959; New York *Times,* July 12, 1953, April 12, 1964.

13. Truman, *Years of Trial and Hope,* 339; Vincent Auriol, *Mon Septennat, 1947–1954* (Paris, 1970), 244–46, 295, 364–70, 408–09, 451, 514–15; Dean Acheson, *Present at the Creation* (New York, 1969), 327, 394, 406–08; Jules Moch, *Histoire du Réarmament allemand depuis 1950* (Paris, 1965), 108–13, 125, 216.

14. Dulles to Frank C. Laubach, October 31, 1950, JFD Mss. See also U.S. Senate, Committee on Foreign Relations, *Background Information Relating to Southeast Asia and Viet Nam,* 89:1, January 14, 1965 (Washington, 1965), 137; Truman, *Years of Trial and Hope,* 519; Acheson, *Present at the Creation,* 552; U.S. Agency for International Development, *U.S. Foreign Assistance . . .; Obligations*

and Loan Authorizations, July 1, 1945—June 30, 1961 (revised) (Washington, 1962), 12.

15. U.S. Senate, Committee on Foreign Relations, *Hearings: United States Foreign Aid Programs in Europe,* 82:1, July 1951 (Washington, 1951), 207.

16. *Ibid.,* 208. See also New York *Times,* July 5, 1971.

17. DS, *American Foreign Policy,* I, 74. See also Acheson, *Present at the Creation,* 671–73.

18. Senate Committee on Foreign Relations, *United States Foreign Aid Programs,* 211.

19. U.S. Senate, Committee on Foreign Relations, *Hearings: Mutual Security Act of 1952,* 82:2, March–April 1952 (Washington, 1952), 24. See also New York *Times,* July 5, 1971.

20. Allan B. Cole, ed., *Conflict in Indo-China and International Repercussions: A Documentary History, 1945–1955* (Ithaca, 1956), 171.

21. Eisenhower, *Mandate for Change,* 333.

22. Dwight D. Eisenhower, *Public Papers of the Presidents of the United States: 1954* (Washington, 1960), 383. "It [southeast Asia] is rich in many raw materials," Dulles declared in March 1954, "such as tin, oil, rubber, and iron ore. It offers industrial Japan potentially important markets and sources of raw materials." Royal Institute of International Affairs, *Documents on International Affairs, 1954* (London, 1957), 144. See also Gordon Gray *et al., Report to the President on Foreign Economic Policies,* November 10, 1950 (Washington, 1950), 47, for the same theme.

23. Senate Committee on Foreign Relations, *Background Information,* 25.

24. Eden, *Full Circle,* 92.

25. Truman, *Years of Trial and Hope,* 519. See also Eden, *Full Circle,* 92; Acheson, *Present at the Creation,* 675–77; New York *Times,* July 5, 1971.

26. Eisenhower, *Mandate for Change,* 168, 337–38. See also Gardner Patterson *et al., Survey of the United States International Finance—1953* (Princeton, 1954), 35; Jacques Despuech, *Le Traffic de Piastres* (Paris, 1953), *passim.*

27. United Kingdom, Secretary of State for Foreign Affairs, *Documents Relating to British Involvement in the Indo-China Conflict, 1945–1965,* Cmnd. 2834 (London, 1965), 64. See also Henri Navarre, *Agonie de l'Indochine, 1953–1954* (Paris, 1956), *passim;* Jean Lacouture and Philippe Devillers, *La Fin d'une Guerre: Indochine 1954* (Paris, 1960), 41–42; Ellen J. Hammer, *The Struggle for Indo-China* (Stanford, 1954), 313–14; Eisenhower, *Mandate for Change,* 169, 338; Alexander Werth, *France, 1940–1955* (New York, 1956), 642–44.

28. *New Statesman and Nation,* April 8, 1950, 397.

29. DS, *American Foreign Policy,* II, 1962. See also Royal Institute of International Affairs, *Documents on International Affairs, 1952* (London, 1955), 240; RIIA, *Documents on International Affairs, 1953* (London, 1956), 10–13; Hughes, *Ordeal of Power,* 62, 100–13; Eisenhower, *Mandate for Change,* 143; Rudolf Augstein, *Konrad Adenauer* (London, 1964), 76; Donovan, *Eisenhower,* 40–42; New York *Times,* April 5, 1953; G. D. Embree, *The Soviet Union between the 19th and 20th Party Congresses, 1952–1956* (The Hague, 1959), 29–49.

30. Konrad Adenauer, *Memoirs, 1945–53* (Chicago, 1966), 438.

31. U.S. Senate, Committee on Foreign Relations, *Hearing: Chancellor Konrad*

Adenauer, 83:1, April 9, 1953 (Washington, 1953), 4, *passim.* See also Augstein, *Adenauer,* 77; Adenauer, *Memoirs,* 442ff.

32. DS, *American Foreign Policy,* II, 1729.

33. RIIA, *Documents on International Affairs, 1953,* 48–49.

34. "Results of Paris NATO Meeting, April 21–27, 1953," JFD Mss. See also Hughes, *Ordeal of Power,* 117–22; RIIA, *Documents on International Affairs, 1953,* 51–57.

35. Harold Macmillan, *Tides of Fortune, 1945–55* (London, 1969), 513. See also *ibid.,* 508–11; Winston Churchill in *Vital Speeches,* June 15, 1953, 524–27; New York *Times,* May 17, May 31, 1953; RIIA, *Documents on International Affairs, 1953,* 65–66.

36. Embree, *Soviet Union between the 19th and 20th Party Congresses,* 13; RIIA, *Documents on International Affairs, 1953,* 66–71; New York *Times,* May 31, 1953; Heinz Brandt, *The Search for a Third Way* (New York, 1970), 179–220.

37. RIIA, *Documents on International Affairs, 1953,* 18. See also Edmund Taylor, "RIAS: The Story of an American Psywar Outpost," *A Psychological Warfare Casebook,* William E. Daugherty and Morris Janowitz, eds. (Baltimore, 1958), 146–47; Andrew Tully, *CIA: The Inside Story* (New York, 1962), 157–67; Boris I. Nicolaevsky, "Khrushchev's Foreign Policy," *New Leader,* May 4, 1959, 3–6; Charles Wighton, *Adenauer—Democratic Dictator* (London, 1963), 184; and especially Brandt, *Search for a Third Way,* 179–220.

38. Macmillan, *Tides of Fortune,* 525. See also *ibid.,* 513–19; DS, *American Foreign Policy,* II, 1744–45; RIIA, *Documents on International Affairs, 1953,* 77–81; Wighton, *Adenauer,* 185.

39. RIIA, *Documents on International Affairs, 1953,* 96. See also *ibid.,* 81–100; G. M. Malenkov, *Speech . . . at the Session of the U.S.S.R. Supreme Soviet, August 8, 1953* (London: Soviet News, 1953), *passim.*

40. Dulles to William Mathews, January 3, 1951, WM Mss. See also U.S. Senate, Committee on Foreign Relations, *Hearing: Testimony of General Alfred M. Gruenther,* 83:1, April 1, 1953 (Washington, 1953), 2; Drew Middleton, "NATO Changes Direction," *Foreign Affairs,* 31 (1953), 429; Eisenhower, *Mandate for Change,* 130–33, 140–41, 453; Hughes, *Ordeal of Power,* 74–75, 138–41, 236–41; Dwight D. Eisenhower to Grenville Clark, June 9, 1953, DDE Mss, OF 137–A; Merton J. Peck and Frederic M. Scherer, *The Weapons Acquisition Process* (Boston, 1962), 100; New York *Times,* April 26, 1953.

41. Dulles to William Clayton, November 17, 1954, DDE Mss, OF 116–H–2. See also DS, *American Foreign Policy,* II, 1445–49.

42. Charles E. Wilson to Gabriel Hauge, February 12, 1954 ["Preliminary Department of Defense Views on the Randall Commission Report"] DDE Mss, OF 116–M.

43. Macmillan, *Tides of Fortune,* 523. See also Burton M. Sapin and Richard C. Snyder, *The Role of the Military in American Foreign Policy* (New York, 1954), 20–30; Eisenhower, *Mandate for Change,* 447–48; RIIA, *Documents on International Affairs, 1953,* 73–77.

44. Eden, *Full Circle,* 62. See also *ibid.,* 59; Karl W. Deutsch and Lewis J. Edinger, *Germany Rejoins the Powers* (Stanford, 1959), 29.

45. Hermes, *Truce Tent and Fighting Front*, 499. See also *ibid.*, 477–78, 509–11.

46. Clark, *Danube to the Yalu*, 86. See also *ibid.*, 84–88.

47. DS, *American Foreign Policy*, I, 1453; Warner R. Schilling, Paul Y. Hammond, and Glenn H. Snyder, *Strategy, Politics, and Defense Budgets* (New York, 1962), 400–72; Eisenhower, *Mandate for Change*, 450–53.

48. Eisenhower, *Mandate for Change*, 452; RIIA, *Documents on International Affairs, 1953*, 48–49, 477–78; DS, *American Foreign Policy*, II, 2371; New York *Times*, July 5, 1971.

49. DS, *American Foreign Policy*, I, 82–83.

50. RIIA, *Documents on International Affairs, 1954*, 144. See also Eden, *Full Circle*, 97.

51. U.S. Senate, Committee on Foreign Relations, *Hearings: Statements of Secretary of State . . . Dulles and Adm. Arthur Radford . . .* , 83:2, March 19, April 14, 1954 (Washington, 1954), 4–6, 17–31, 47–50; John Foster Dulles, "The Goal of Our Foreign Policy," November 29, 1954, DS press release no. 674; John Foster Dulles, "Policy for Security and Peace," *Foreign Affairs*, 32 (1954), 353–64; Dulles draft of July 18, 1956, JFD Mss; James Shepley, "How Dulles Averted War," *Life*, January 16, 1956, 78; Dulles, "Challenge and Response in United States Foreign Policy," *Foreign Affairs*, 36 (1957), 31.

52. Eisenhower, *Mandate for Change*, 422.

53. *Ibid.*, 422–27; New York *Times*, February 7, 1954; DS, *American Foreign Policy*, 1303ff.; RIIA, *Documents on International Affairs, 1954*, 499–504; John Foster Dulles, speech before the Tenth Inter-American Conference, March 4, 1954, DS press release no. 109; David Wise and Thomas B. Ross, *The Invisible Government* (New York, 1964), 166–215.

54. Eisenhower, *Mandate for Change*, 245–46; Macmillan, *Tides of Fortune*, 527–30; Eden, *Full Circle*, 65–67, 84–85; William Hayter, *The Kremlin and the Embassy* (New York, 1966), 116; New York *Times*, January 29, 1954.

55. Eisenhower, *Mandate for Change*, 342; DS, *American Foreign Policy*, I, 76; Roscoe Drummond and Gaston Coblentz, *Duel at the Brink: John Foster Dulles' Command of American Power* (New York, 1960), 89, 102–03; Augstein, *Adenauer*, 77; Wighton, *Adenauer*, 204; Andrew H. Berding, *Dulles on Diplomacy* (Princeton, 1965), 36–37; Eden, *Full Circle*, 73; RIIA, *Documents on International Affairs, 1954*, 37–43, 72–75; V. M. Molotov, *Statements at Berlin Conference of Foreign Ministers . . . (January 25—February 18, 1954)* (Moscow, 1954), 51–53, *passim*.

56. Molotov, *Statements at Berlin Conference of Foreign Ministers*, 105–13; Ghita Ionescu, "The Austrian State Treaty and Neutrality in Eastern Europe," *International Journal*, 23 (1968), 412; Eisenhower, *Mandate for Change*, 343; Eden, *Full Circle*, 97–100; Robert F. Randle, *Geneva 1954: The Settlement of the Indo-Chinese War* (Princeton, 1969), 28–37, chaps. IV–V; Gabriel Kolko, *The Roots of American Foreign Policy* (Boston, 1969), 102–09; New York *Times*, July 5, 1971.

57. Eisenhower, *Public Papers of the Presidents: 1954*, 73. See also John Foster Dulles, "The Threat of a Red Asia," speech of March 29, 1954, DS press release no. 165, 3.

58. Eisenhower to Joseph M. Dodge, May 14, 1960, JMD Mss, Correspondence, box 1. See also Dulles, "The Peace We Seek," speech of January 11, 1955, DS press

release no. 11, 2; Dulles, statement of March 8, 1954, DS press release no. 121; DS, *American Foreign Policy,* I, 73; Dulles, "The Threat of a Red Asia," 2; Berding, *Dulles on Diplomacy,* 30–31.

59. Dulles, "United States Post-Geneva Policy," August 15, 1955, JFD Mss. See also Drummond and Coblentz, *Duel at the Brink,* 156.

60. Transcript of Dulles' remarks to SEATO meeting, March 27, 1958, JFD Mss.

61. U.S. House, Committee on Foreign Affairs, *Hearings: Foreign Policy and Mutual Security,* 84:2, October–November 1956 (Washington, 1956), 204.

62. Dulles, "Estimate of Soviet Policy," December 13, 1955, JFD Mss. See also Hughes, *Ordeal of Power,* 207; Dulles remarks to NATO meeting, December 11, 1956; Dulles notes for NATO meeting, May 2, 1957; Dulles remarks to NATO meeting, May 9, 1958, all in JFD Mss; Macmillan, *Tides of Fortune,* 651.

63. Dulles remarks to NATO meeting, December 11, 1956, JFD Mss.

64. Transcript of Dulles remarks to SEATO meeting, March 27, 1958, JFD Mss.

65. Dulles, "Challenge and Response in United States Foreign Policy," 28.

66. Dulles, "Our Foreign Policies in Asia," speech of February 16, 1955, DS press release no. 86, 8, 10; Sherman Adams to Arthur B. Langlie, August 14, 1954; Dulles to Wilton B. Persons, June 13, 1958, DDE Mss, OF 116; House Committee on Foreign Affairs, *Foreign Policy and Mutual Security,* 222–23; Macmillan, *Tides of Fortune,* 651; Dean Acheson, *Power and Diplomacy* (Cambridge, 1958), 7, *passim;* transcript of Dulles remarks to SEATO meeting, March 27, 1958, JFD Mss; Dulles, "Challenge and Response in United States Foreign Policy," 36–37.

Index

72 73 74 75   10 9 8 7 6 5 4 3 2 1